ROYAL HISTORICAL SOCIETY

GUIDES AND HANDBOOKS
No. 2

HANDBOOK OF BRITISH CHRONOLOGY

ROYAL HISTORICAL SOCIETY

GUIDES AND HANDBOOKS
ISSN 0080-4398

MAIN SERIES

1. *Guide to English commercial statistics 1696–1782.* By G. N. Clark and Barbara M. Franks. 1938.
2. *Handbook of British chronology.* Edited by F. M. Powicke, Charles Johnson and W. J. Harte. 1939. 2nd edition, edited by F. M. Powicke and E. B. Fryde, 1961.
3. *Medieval libraries of Great Britain. A list of surviving books.* Edited by N. R. Ker. 1941. 2nd edition, 1964.
4. *Handbook of dates for students of English history.* Edited by C. R. Cheney. 1945. Reprinted, 1982.
5. *Guide to the national and provincial directories of England and Wales, excluding London, published before 1856.* By Jane E. Norton. 1950.
6. *Handbook of oriental history.* Edited by C. H. Philips. 1951.
7. *Texts and Calendars. An analytical guide to serial publications.* By E. L. C. Mullins. 1958. Reprinted (with corrections), 1978.
8. *Anglo-Saxon Charters. An annotated list and bibliography.* By P. H. Sawyer. 1968.
9. *A Centenary Guide to the publications of the Royal Historical Society 1868–1968 and of the former Camden Society 1838–1897.* By Alexander Taylor Milne. 1968.
10. *Guide to the local administrative units of England.* Volume I. *Southern England.* By Frederic A. Youngs, Jr. 1979. 2nd edition, 1981.
11. *Guide to bishops' registers of England and Wales. A survey from the middle ages to the abolition of episcopacy in 1646.* By David M. Smith. 1981.
12. *Texts and Calendars II. An analytical guide to serial publications 1957–1982.* By E. L. C. Mullins. 1983.
13. *Handbook of Medieval Exchange.* By Peter Spufford, with the assistance of Wendy Wilkinson and Sarah Tolley. 1986.

SUPPLEMENTARY SERIES

1. *A Guide to the papers of British Cabinet Ministers, 1900–1951.* Compiled by Cameron Hazlehurst and Christine Woodland. 1974.
2. *A Guide to the reports of the U.S. Strategic Bombing Survey.* I *Europe.* II *The Pacific.* Edited by Gordon Daniels. 1981.

HANDBOOK OF BRITISH CHRONOLOGY

Edited by
E. B. FRYDE, D. E. GREENWAY,
S. PORTER, and I. ROY

THIRD EDITION

LONDON
OFFICES OF THE ROYAL HISTORICAL SOCIETY
UNIVERSITY COLLEGE, GOWER STREET
LONDON WC1E 6BT
1986

First published 1941
Second edition 1961
Third edition 1986

ISBN 0 86193 106 8

British Library Cataloguing in Publication Data

Handbook of British chronology.—3rd ed.—
(Royal Historical Society guides and handbooks;
no. 2)
1. Great Britain—Biography
I. Powicke, *Sir* Maurice   II. Fryde, E.B.
III. Series
920'.041   DA28

ISBN 0-86193-106-8

Photoset by Galleon Photosetting, Ipswich
Printed in Great Britain by St Edmundsbury Press
Bury St Edmunds, Suffolk

TABLE OF CONTENTS

PREFACE TO THE THIRD EDITION

The opportunity to compile a substantially revised and updated edition of the *Handbook of British Chronology* arose when the existing edition, a standard work of reference for which there was a continuing demand, went out of print in 1984. The motive for this third edition was thus essentially the same as that for the second. The intention was at first for a modest revision, based on the suggestions for corrections and improvements sent in by readers (which earlier editors had invited) to the Literary Directors of the Royal Historical Society, together with a listing of office-holders appointed since 1960. But it became clear, in the course of preparation, that a more substantial revision was desirable, to benefit, where possible, from the transformation of knowledge achieved in the past quarter century of historical research. We were encouraged in this task by the hope expressed in 1939 by the first editor of the *Handbook*, Professor F. M. Powicke, that fifty years thence the current edition would be 'hardly recognizable'; it has certainly become, as he hoped, a standard work, but the production of the entirely error-free and impeccably uniform volume which he looked forward to must remain an ideal to be striven for if scarcely achieved, and an index is still missing. The decision by the present editors to employ computer technology to construct a data-base of the material contained in this edition will, however, facilitate the incorporation of new information and the production of updated and revised editions in the future. As the data will be machine-readable, the compilation of an index—or other aid to the user—will be a possibility.

It is probably the case that the *Handbook* has been of greater use to, and is better known by, medieval than modern historians. Since the appearance of the second edition a number of other works of reference, constructed on different lines (although, in many cases, generously acknowledging their indebtedness to the *Handbook*), have supplied a wide range of information, including lists of government ministers, for historians of the modern period. It is not the intention to supersede these works, but by filling gaps in the existing lists of modern officers of state, and by updating and rearranging the most recent lists to take account of governmental changes (including departmental reorganizations) in the past twenty-five years, to render this edition more useful to such historians.

The editors were responsible for the following sections: the bibliographical guide and independent rulers, Professor Fryde and Dr Roy. Medieval English officers of state, Professor Fryde and Dr Greenway; modern, Dr Roy; since 1960, Dr Porter. English and British Parliaments, and Dukes, Marquesses and Earls for England, Ireland and Scotland, Professor Fryde. Archbishops and bishops of England and Ireland, and bishops of Wales, and provincial and national councils of the Church, Dr Greenway. Ireland, governors and secretaries, and all ecclesiastical appointments in England, Ireland and Wales since 1960, Dr Porter.

It is a pleasure to thank those who have made a major contribution to this edition by revising substantially certain important sections. Dr Simon Keynes has provided completely new lists of the English bishops and church councils before 1066, and Dr David Dumville has revised the list of Anglo-Saxon rulers. Dr G. E. Aylmer supplied lists of English, Scottish and Irish office-holders for the period 1642–1660, largely omitted in the second edition. Dr Athol Murray, Keeper of the Records of Scotland (with the assistance of Professor A. A. M. Duncan, Dr David Stevenson and Mr W. W. Scott), undertook the complete revision of the Scottish officers of state. Professor D. E. R. Watt provided new lists of the bishops of Scotland, based on his own recent work.

Many other scholars were generous in the help provided. In the revision of the rulers of England, Dr Judith A. Green supplied new matter on the early regents. In the revision of the medieval officers of state valuable help was received from Dr Judith A. Green (chief justiciars and treasurers), Dr David Bates (stewards of the household and chancellors), Dr David Carpenter (stewards of the household) and Mrs Susan J. Davies (chancellors). Professor Christopher N. L. Brooke, Mrs Susan J. Davies and Dr Patrick Zutshi sent corrections of the lists of medieval bishops of England, Wales and Ireland, Mr Clyve Jones and Dr Ian Green of the early modern lists. Miss Elizabeth Finn, Mr Peter Chadwick and Mrs Audrey Mills supplied chronological material for recent appointments from the records of the Church Commissioners. The staffs of the Guildhall Library, *Church of England Newspaper*, the Church in Wales, the Church of Ireland and the Catholic Press and Information Office in Dublin were very helpful and a number of diocesan secretaries and registrars in England, Wales and Ireland courteously answered the many queries directed to them. Professor P. J. Marshall corrected the information relating to the Presidents of the Board of Control and Secretaries of State for India and for India and Burma. Sir Robert Somerville aided the revision of the Chancellors of the Duchy of Lancaster. Special thanks are due to the board of editors of *A new history of Ireland*, and Oxford University Press, for permission to make use of material relating to lay and ecclesiastical office-holders contained in volume IX of *A new history*. That the editors of that volume have generously acknowledged their debt to previous editions of the *Handbook* is a pleasant indication of the mutual co-operation between scholars in the field. We owe a debt of gratitude to Dr Richard Barber, who not only guided this edition through the press with great skill and patience, but also made an important scholarly contribution.

As in previous editions the editors again ask readers to send suggestions and corrections of detail to the Literary Directors of the Royal Historical Society.

September 1985   E. B. Fryde, D. E. Greenway,
                                             S. Porter, Ian Roy

PREFACE TO THE SECOND EDITION

The main reason for the publication of a new edition of the *Handbook of British Chronology* is that the first edition has been long out of print. Certain additions and modifications have been made, but the new volume incorporates most of the original work. As in the preface to the first edition, the editors ask the indulgence of readers for the manifold faults of this new version of the Handbook and hope that they will again send suggestions and also corrections of detail to the Literary Director of the Royal Historical Society.

The scope of the Handbook and the original authorship of the various sections are indicated in the preface to the first edition, reprinted above with some slight alterations. It remains to mention the new features of the second edition. It omits the section on the Reckonings of Time which proved such a useful feature of the original Handbook that it was reprinted in an improved form in a separate *Handbook of Dates* (ed. C. R. Cheney, 1945), still available in print. The extra space thus gained has been used to include several new lists. For students of medieval English history there are additional lists of Chief Justiciars (to 1265), Stewards of the King's Household and Keepers of the King's Wardrobe (both to 1485); the new list of admirals and Lord High Admirals starts in 1294. Several additions have been made to the lists of modern English officers of state: Lord Presidents of the Council, Lord High Admirals and First Lords of the Admiralty, Presidents of the Board of Trade, Presidents of the Board of Control, Ministers of Defence, Chancellors of the Duchy of Lancaster. Practical obstacles alone prevented the addition of several other ministers. Lists of the principal Scottish officers of state have been included for the first time. Chancellors, Chamberlains, Treasurers, Comptrollers, Secretaries, Clerks Register, Lord Advocates, Lord Presidents of the Court of Session.

To compensate in some measure for the absence of many more lists we have included a guide to the available lists of English office-holders (to *c*. 1800). This is on a more modest scale than had originally been intended and it can only be hoped that a greatly improved version will appear in the next edition.

The list of dukes, marquesses and earls, which ended in 1603 in the old volume, has been extended to 1714. The list of parliaments and related assemblies now runs from 1242 to 1832 and it has been considerably altered by the addition of references to sources and of much other information. The medieval portion of the list of the Keepers of the Privy Seal has been thoroughly revised.

Most sections of the old edition have undergone some alteration. The only exceptions are the lists of the English bishops to 1066 and of the rulers of the Isle of Man which are reprinted virtually without change, with only a few obvious slips corrected. The conditions which decided the promoters of the first edition to exclude an index still prevail.

It remains to ascribe the sections to their authors and to make other acknowledgments. Professor R. R. Darlington has revised his list of the Old English rulers to 1066. The list of English rulers from 1066 to 1509 has been revised with the help of the following scholars: Professor F. Barlow, Professor H. A. Cronne and Mr R. H. C. Davis (1066–1154); Dr D. G. Walker, Professor F. Cazel, Dr R. F. Walker, Professor R. F. Treharne and Dr C. H. Knowles (1154–1272); Miss R. M. T. Hill, Professor E. L. G. Stones, and Mr A. Bruce Webster (1272–1377); Professor N. B. Lewis, Professor J. S. Roskell, Mr T. B. Pugh and Dr Charles Ross (1377–1509).

Dr E. W. M. Balfour-Melville has revised his list of Scottish rulers and Professor T. Jones Pierce has rearranged and expanded the list of Welsh rulers.

The medieval sections of the lists of English officers of state have been contributed by the following: Stewards of the King's Household by Dr I. J. Sanders; admirals by Mr J. W. Sherborne; other lists down to 1399 were revised by E. B. Fryde. All the lists for the period 1399–1485 are the work of Dr R. L. Storey, and the list of the Lord High Admirals for the Tudor period has been contributed by Mr N. E. Evans, both of the Public Record Office. Special thanks are due to the Keeper of the Public Records and to Mr H. C. Johnson for their valuable help and for their constant willingness to assist in the preparation of the Handbook.

The early section of the list of treasurers owes much to the advice of Mr Charles Johnson, Mr G. H. White and Mr H. G. Richardson. Mrs J. Stones and Professor F. Cazel supplied fresh information about thirteenth-century chancellors and treasurers. The list of chief justiciars has been through many hands, but E. B. Fryde is responsible for its final form and contents. Lady Stenton, Professor C. R. Cheney, Professor J. G. Edwards, Professor R. F. Treharne and Mr R. W. Southern have given valuable advice on this short but difficult section, and much assistance has also been received from Professor F. Barlow, Professor H. A. Cronne, Mr R. H. C. Davis, Mr G. W. S. Barrow, Professor F. Cazel, Dr R. F. Walker and Mr C. A. F. Meekings.

Mr R. B. Pugh and Dr R. W. Greaves have supervised the revision and extension of the modern portions of the English lists (from 1485 onwards). They and the editors wish to thank especially Mr R. Somerville for the list of the Chancellors of the Duchy of Lancaster, and Mr A. D. Gidlow Jackson, Miss Jennifer J. Carter and Mr P. W. J. Riley for assistance with various lists. The editors also wish to thank Mr S. H. F. Johnston for advice in connexion with these modern lists.

The lists of officers of state for Scotland have been compiled by the following: Mr A. A. M. Duncan, Mr J. Imrie, Mr A. L. Murray, Mr G. G. Simpson, Mr C. J. S. Sinclair and Mr A. Bruce Webster. Acknowledgments are due to Professor W. Croft Dickinson and Dr Gordon Donaldson, of the University of Edinburgh, Mr G. W. S. Barrow, Mr P. G. B. McNeill, advocate, the late Mr H. M. Paton and the Scottish Committee on the History of Parliament for advice and assistance at various points. Useful material has been derived from the notebooks of J. Maitland Thomson, preserved in the Scottish Record Office, and from the papers of D. W. Hunter Marshall, preserved in Glasgow University Library.

The editors wish to record their gratitude to the Keeper of the Records of Scotland for his willingness to allow the preparation of these lists in HM General Register House.

The preparation of the lists connected with Wales has been supervised by Professor T. Jones Pierce and the editors are also greatly indebted to Professor J. G. Edwards for his advice. Professor J. H. Le Patourel has brought up to date his note on the Channel Islands.

The Reverend Aubrey Gwynn, SJ, supervised the revision and extension of all the Irish lists. He and the editors wish to thank Dr H. F. Kearney, Captain J. L. Hughes, of the Public Record Office at Dublin, and Professor D. B. Quinn for help in preparing and correcting the lists of Chief Governors and Chief Secretaries for Ireland.

The revision of the lists of the archbishops and bishops of the provinces of Canterbury and York since 1066 has been chiefly done by Professor C. R. Cheney, to whom we are deeply indebted for undertaking this task at a late stage in the preparation of the Handbook. The editors also wish to thank Miss Kathleen Major (Professor Cheney's predecessor) and Professor C. N. L. Brooke for supplying valuable information about the bishops of the eleventh and twelfth centuries. Professor T. Jones Pierce and Mr H. D. Emanuel were responsible for the revision of the list of Welsh, and Dr G. Donaldson for the revision of the list of Scottish archbishops and bishops.

The revision of the lists of Irish archbishops and bishops was supervised by the Reverend Aubrey Gwynn, SJ, who is personally responsible for the medieval section down to 1540 and for the lists of the Catholic bishops since Henry VIII. Dr J. G. Simms has revised the lists of the Irish Protestant bishops.

Mr R. W. Southern has supervised the revision and extension of his list of dukes, marquesses and earls with the help of the following scholars: Mr Edwin Chapman (preliminary revision of the entire list and addition of Stuart creations); Mr G. W. S. Barrow, Dr D. G. Walker, Professor F. Cazel (1135–1232); Dr I. J. Sanders, Dr G. A. Holmes (1232–1377); Mr T. B. Pugh and Dr Charles Ross (1377–1485); Mr J. Hurstfield (1485–1603); Mr A. A. M. Duncan (Scotland); Professor J. Otway-Ruthven (Ireland, medieval) and Dr R. B. McDowell (Ireland, sixteenth and seventeenth centuries).

Professor J. G. Edwards, Professor J. S. Roskell and E. B. Fryde (with the assistance of Dr C. H. Knowles) are responsible for the section on English parliaments. Professor C. R. Cheney revised his list of the provincial and national councils of the Church in England.

The bibliographical guide to the lists of English office-holders has been compiled from information supplied by the following scholars: Dr I. J. Sanders, Professor J. S. Roskell, Mr J. Hurstfield, Dr G. E. Aylmer, Professor D. B. Horn, Professor A. Aspinall and Mr S. H. F. Johnston.

F. M. POWICKE
August 1959   E. B. FRYDE

A note should be added here by the editor of the first edition of the Handbook. Discussions about a new edition began in February 1954 between Mr Philip Grierson, then Literary Director of the Royal Historical Society, the Publication Committee and myself. The plan arranged during the next few weeks was adopted by the Council of the Society on 8 May 1954, when an editorial committee was approved and the appointment of Dr E. B. Fryde as assistant editor was confirmed.

Although Dr Fryde and I have discussed personally or in letters all the major problems which have arisen, my share and the advisory committee's share in the editorial task has steadily decreased. Dr Fryde has done the great bulk of the work, and conducted the correspondence with other contributors. He is the actual editor of this second edition. I wish, however, to join him in thanks for their generous help and advice to those already named and especially to Professor C. R. Cheney, Professor J. G. Edwards, Mr R. W. Southern and the successive Literary Directors of the Royal Historical Society, Mr Philip Grierson, Professor D. Hay and Dr P. Chaplais. Nor should those who use the Handbook forget that this edition was put together by Dr Fryde at Aberystwyth. Its preparation would have been much delayed without the secretarial help provided by the secretariat of the Faculty of Arts of the University College of Wales, Aberystwyth. Dr C. H. Knowles and Mr J. B. Smith provided much assistance in a variety of ways and especially in preparing the manuscript for the press. Miss E. D. Commander has given invaluable help with the proofs.

F. M. POWICKE

6 ORIEL SQUARE
OXFORD
August 1959

PREFACE TO THE FIRST EDITION[1]

The plan of the following work was drafted, in a tentative way, in 1932. At that time the 'Commission des listes chronologiques', which had been created a few years earlier by the International Historical Committee, had worked out a scheme and British participation was required. Although, in order to satisfy the needs of the Commission, the British contribution would comprise no more than lists of independent rulers in the Middle Ages, that is to say, part of the first section of this book, an opportunity was given to enlarge its scope for the use of British students in a British publication. A proposal to this effect, first suggested in the course of a discussion at a meeting of the Royal Historical Society on 8 December 1932,[2] was adopted in principle by the Society in 1934. Between June 1934 and June 1936 an informal committee worked out details and invited contributors to undertake particular sections.

The plan of the book, as first drafted in 1932, was sketched by Mr Charles Johnson. It has been followed throughout, but naturally it has, in the course of time, been modified in many particulars. It began as a modest enterprise and has grown into a substantial volume. If we had adopted all the suggestions made to us from time to time, it would have been larger still and its publication would have been indefinitely delayed. It was intended to be a handy and useful contribution to the needs of historical students, not a logical and rounded treatise. Chronology is a vague, ill-defined and intractable field of inquiry, which defies systematic treatment. At the same time we are well aware that, even within the limits which we have imposed upon our work, this book is anything but logical or complete. Some will ask, for example, why there is no list of Scottish bishops after 1688 or of moderators of the Established Church of Scotland, others why the lists of English officers of state seem so haphazardly chosen. The answer in every case is either considerations of convenience or lack of space. We venture to hope that the book as it stands will be so useful as to call for improvement and enlargement; that, at time goes on, it will grow into a standard work of reference, with its errors and slips removed, its gaps filled, its forms reduced to impeccable uniformity, its usefulness increased by an index.[3] Nothing, in short, would please us better than the knowledge, if only we could possess it, that in fifty years' time the current edition would be hardly recognizable by the editors of this first presentation. Hence we urge readers and critics not to give way to casual exasperation, but, while they recognize such positive merits as the book possesses, to send suggestions and also corrections of detail to the Literary Directors of the Royal Historical Society.

[1] Slightly abridged by the omission of matters not relevant to the new edition.
[2] See *Trans. Roy. Hist. Soc.*, 4th ser., xvi (1933), 49–50.
[3] Apart from considerations of space and expense, we decided that an index would more appropriately accompany the task of thorough revision and standardization.

As the work proceeded, we became increasingly conscious both of the need of such a book as this and of the surprising unevenness of available knowledge which is one of the reasons for the need. A few contributors have had sufficient knowledge of more or less manageable themes to be able to give to their sections the quality of original work. We may instance the sections on Anglo-Saxon rulers, Welsh and Scottish bishops and parliaments, although their authors would be the last to claim finality for what they and their helpers have done. Other contributors, in spite of considerable original investigation, have had perforce to deal in the main with a mass of traditional learning or with compilations which could be made definitive, if at all, only by the sacrifice of years of labour. As this fact has not been generally recognized, and as some of the unexpected 'snags' became apparent only in the course of investigation or even after proofs had begun to come in, we find here an additional reason for publication, for we may now hope that persistent attention will be given to work which has long been overdue. Experts assured us, for example, that, until all the available charter-evidence had been critically sifted, it would be useless to try to revise the available lists of Anglo-Saxon bishops; accordingly, we have made use of the lists in Stubbs's *Registrum Sacrum Anglicanum* and Searle's *Anglo-Saxon Bishops, Kings, and Nobles*. Similarly, we should have liked to give more exact dates in the section on Irish bishops and the dates of the *election*, as well as of consecration or translation, of English bishops, but we found that they would involve minute investigation without satisfactory results. Even in the most trodden paths difficulties and perplexities occasionally occurred, and it is not surprising that the most tiresome section of all turned out to be that on 'Officers of State'.

It remains to ascribe the sections to their authors and to make other acknowledgments. Professor R. R. Darlington is responsible for the list of rulers from the English settlement to 1066. The list of English rulers from 1066 to 1939 is based on work done by Professor R. F. Treharne, Mr H. G. Richardson, Professor W. J. Harte, and Dr M. A. Thomson. Professor Sir J. E. Lloyd contributed the list of Welsh rulers, Mr E. W. M. Balfour-Melville that of Scottish rulers, Mr W. Cubbon and Professor Darlington that of rulers of the Isle of Man. The lists of English officers of state were originally undertaken by the late Deputy Keeper of the Public Records, Mr A. E. Stamp, but he had been able to do little before his death, and most of the existing lists are based upon work done by Dr F. R. Lewis. They have been through many hands, and we desire to acknowledge especially the help of Mr L. G. Wickham Legg, who also provided the list of prime ministers, Mr R. B. Wernham, Mr E. S. de Beer, Dr M. A. Thomson, Mr G. E. Morey, and the present Deputy Keeper and Assistant Keepers of the Public Records. The Deputy Keeper also kindly placed at our service the manuscript list of keepers of the Privy Seal, compiled for the use of the Public Record Office. It is only right, however, to remind our readers that, for reasons already given, these particular lists should still be regarded as provisional, in spite of the labour which has been expended on them. We can only feel some confidence that they are the most reliable lists now available.[1]

[1] One point should be mentioned here. The list of chancellors does not give the names of commissioners, and short periods when the seal was in commission are not generally noted.

Mr Herbert Wood compiled the Irish lists of chief governors, deputies, secretaries of state and keepers of the signet or privy seal; and Dr J. H. Le Patourel the note on the Channel Islands.

The lists of archbishops and bishops of the provinces of Canterbury and York were compiled by Miss Kathleen Major and revised, first by Miss Margaret Deanesly, later by Professor Hamilton Thompson, to whom we are deeply indebted. The introduction was written, to some extent on the basis of material provided by Professor Hamilton Thompson, by the writer of this Preface. Professor Wiliam Rees is responsible for the list of Welsh, and Professor R. K. Hannay, Historiographer Royal, for the list of Scottish bishops. The lists of Irish archbishops and bishops were compiled by the Reverend Chancellor J. B. Leslie, and of Catholic archbishops and bishops since the Reformation by the Reverend Myles V. Ronan.[1] The introduction to the first series was compiled by the writer of this Preface, to some extent from material supplied by Chancellor Leslie and Mr Herbert Wood.

The list of dukes, marquesses, and earls is the work of Mr R. W. Southern.

The section on English parliaments was compiled by Mr H. G. Richardson, and that on provincial and national councils of the Church in England by Mr C. R. Cheney.

In the earlier stages of our work we received much help from Professor W. J. Harte, who acted as secretary to the informal committee and undertook the preliminary correspondence with contributors. In addition to their own contributions, Professor Darlington and Mr H. G. Richardson gave frequent and generous help in revising much of the section on independent rulers. Mr Richardson at our request wrote the long introduction to this section. At various times during the last few years we have also received advice from other scholars, including Mr Charles Johnson, Professor V. H. Galbraith, Mr Herbert Wood (one of the contributors), and the Reverend Aubrey Gwynn, SJ. But perhaps we owe most of all to the constant and generous help of Dr Hubert Hall, the Literary Director of the Royal Historical Society, and to Mr C. R. Cheney, one of his successors in that laborious and most exacting office. They have saved us from many mistakes, and their cheerful encouragement has done much to lighten a task which has often been wearisome and has always been dangerous.

F. M. POWICKE

ORIEL COLLEGE
OXFORD
    August 1939

---

[1] A list, compiled by the Reverend Sir John R. O'Connell, of the archbishops and bishops of the Roman Catholic hierarchy in Great Britain, has been omitted for reasons of space.

LIST OF ABBREVIATIONS

FOR convenience of readers specialized abbreviations have been listed under separate headings, the remainder being grouped into the general section. Certain abbreviations have been listed more than once.

Abbreviations of titles of publications listed in the introductions to particular sections of the Handbook have not been included in the list below.

1.   General

a. = *ante*
abp = archbishop
acc. = accession
a.d. = *anno domini*
aft. = after; afterwards
an. = *anno*
appd = appointed
Apr. = April
Aug. = August
bef. = before
bp = bishop
br., brs = brother, brothers
bt = baronet
Burg. = burgesses present [in list of parliamentary assemblies]
C., c. = count
c. = *circa*
Col. = Colonel
C.-in-C. = Commander-in-Chief
cous. = cousin
cr. = created
d. = died, death
da., das = daughter, daughters
Dec. = December
dep. = deposed
dism. = dismissed
diss. = dissolved
e. = earl
E. = East, Eastern
East. = Easter
exec. = executed
Feb. = February
G.B. = Great Britain
gd da. = grand-daughter
gds. = grandson
gt-gds. = great grandson
H.C. = House of Commons
husb. = husband
illeg. = illegitimate
Jan. = January
K., k. = king

K.B. = King's Bench
kt = knight
Kts = Knights present [in list of parliamentary assemblies]
lic. = licence
Lt-Gen. = Lieutenant General
M.-Gen. = Major General
m. = married, marriage
Mar. = March
Mr Gen. = Master General
Mich. = Michaelmas
N. = North, Northern
Nat. = national
neph. = nephew
no. = number
ob. = died
Oct. = October
p. = post
p. = prince
parl., plt = parliament
prob. = probably
proc. = procurator
Q., q. = queen
q.v. = *quod vide*
R. = river
r.c. = regular canon
res. = resigned
s = son, sons
S. = South, Southern
Sept. = September
sis. = sister
St = saint
surv. = surviving
U.K. = United Kingdom
unm. = unmarried
v.p. = *vita patris*
w. = wife
W. = West, Western
wid. = widow
yr = younger
yst = youngest

2.   Publications and Archives

BIHR = *Bulletin of the Institute of Historical Research*
BL = British Library
Chancery Warr. = Chancery Warrants

Cmd, H.C. = Command Papers, House of Commons
DNB = *Dictionary of National Biography*

xix

EHR = *English Historical Review*
Exch. of Rec. = Exchequer of Receipt
HMC = Historical Manuscripts
  Commission
HMSO = Her Majesty's Stationery
  Office
IHR = Institute of Historical Research
KR Exch. Acc. = King's
  Remembrancer, Exchequer Accounts
PC = Privy Council Records
PRO = Public Record Office
RC = Record Commission
Reg. Ho. = Scottish Record Office,
  General Register House

RS = Rolls Series
RHS = Royal Historical Society
Scot. Hist. Soc. = Scottish Historical
  Society
Scotichr. = *Scotichronicon*
SHR = *Scottish Historical Review*
TCD = Trinity College, Dublin
Tout, *Chapters* = T. F. Tout, *Chapters*
  in the Administrative History of
  Mediaeval England (6 vols,
  Manchester, 1920–33)
TRHS = *Transactions of the Royal*
  Historical Society

3.   English Officers of State

appd = appointed
att. = attainder, attainted
ch. = chancellor
dism. = dismissed
forf. = forfeited
K.G. = Knight of the Garter
kp. = keeper

kp.w. = keeper of the king's wardrobe
L.C. = lord chancellor
pr.s. = keeper of the privy seal[1]
res. = resigned
tr. = treasurer
vac., *vac.* = vacated office

4.   Irish

cust. = *custos*
D. = deputy
D.D. = deputies
G. = governor
G.-Genl = governor general
J., JJ. = justiciar(s)
K.L. = king's lieutenant

L. = lieutenant
LL. = lieutenants
L.C. = lord chancellor
L.D. = lord deputy
L.J., L.JJ. = lord(s) justice(s)
m. = marquess

5.   Scottish

enf. = enfeoffed[1]
S. = Scotland
Scot. = Scottish

serv.
serv.h. } = served heir[1]
S.R.P. = Scottish representative peer

6.   Ecclesiastical Lists

abp = archbishop
bp = bishop
coadj. = coadjutor
conf. = confirmed
cons. = consecrated
dep. = deposed
depr. = deprived
el. = elected
inv. = invested
lib. = liberatio (of temporalities)
l.p. = letters patent
nom. = nominated
P. = province

post. = postulated
prov. = provided
qua. = quashed
r.c. = regular canon
res. = resigned
St = Saint
suffr. = suffragan
susp. = suspended
temp. = temporalities restored
trs. = translated
uncons. = unconsecrated
vic. ap. = vicar apostolic
† = died

[1] These two terms are used in connexion with Scottish earldoms to describe the two stages in succession in that country, *viz.* service *i.e.* the verdict of a jury on the rights of a claimant to the heritage, and infeftment *i.e.* the ceremonial procedure by which the heir was put in possession of his lands. Where the dates of both these events are known, only the second is given.

7. Religious Orders (Irish Episcopal Lists)

C.M. = Vincentian (Congregation of Missions)
C.S.Sp. = Holy Ghost Father (Congr. de Spiritu Sancto)
C.SS.R. = Redemptorist (Congr. SS. Redemptoris)
O. Carm. = Carmelite friar
O. Carth. = Carthusian monk

O.E.S.A. = Augustinian (Austin) friar
O.P. = Dominican friar
O. Praem. = Premonstratensian canon
O.S.A. = Augustinian canon
O.S.B. = Benedectine monk
O.S.F. = Franciscan friar
O. Trin. = Trinitarian canon
S.J. = Jesuit

8. Peerage

acc. = accession, acceded
att. = attainder, attainted
bapt. = baptized
c. = count
coh. = coheir, coheiress
cr. = created
d.s.p. = died without posterity ['sine prole']
d.s.p. leg. = died without legitimate posterity
d.s.p.m. = died without masculine posterity
d.s.p.s. = died without surviving posterity
forf. = forfeited

g. = girded with the sword of the county
h. = heir, heiress
hom. = homage[1]
inv. = invested
liv. = livery[1]
m., marq. = marquess
recog. = recognized
res. = resigned
rest. = restored
st. = styled
succ. = succeeded
summ. = summoned
surv. = surviving
visct = viscount

[1] liv. hom. is used with reference to writs to the royal officers announcing that the heir has done homage and is to have livery of his lands.

BIBLIOGRAPHICAL GUIDE TO THE LISTS OF ENGLISH OFFICE-HOLDERS

Place of publication London, unless otherwise stated.

The Royal Historical Society has, in co-operation with other bodies, published the following bibliographical guides:

E. B. Graves, *A Bibliography of English History to 1485* (Oxford, 1975).

C. Read, *A Bibliography of British History, Tudor period, 1485–1603* (2nd edition, Oxford, 1959)

M. F. Keeler, *A Bibliography of British History, Stuart period, 1603–1714* (Oxford, 1970).

S. M. Pargellis and J. Medley, *Bibliography of British History, 1714–1789* (Oxford, 1951). [A supplement to this volume is being prepared by A. Newman and A. T. Milne.]

L. M. Brown and I. R. Christie, *Bibliography of British History, 1789–1851* (Oxford, 1977).

H. J. Hanham, *Bibliography of British History, 1851–1914* (Oxford, 1976).

K. G. Robbins, *Bibliography of British History, 1914–76* (forthcoming).

Writings on British History, 1901–1933, 5 vols (1968–70), and 1934–45, 8 vols (1937–60), ed. A. T. Milne. Continued by the Institute of Historical Research with 1946–48 (1973) ed. D. J. Munro: latest volume (1969–70) ed. H. J. Creaton (1984).

Annual Bibliography of British and Irish History, ed. G. R. Elton. First volume, for 1975 (1976): latest volume, 1983 (1984). Current editor D. M. Palliser.

1. GENERAL

1.1.   A. Collins, *The Peerage of England* (1709; best edn by S. E. Brydges, 9 vols, 1812).

1.2.   G. E. Cokayne, *Complete Peerage of England, Scotland, Ireland* . . . (rev. edn, 12 vols, by V. Gibbs, H. A. Doubleday, G. H. White and R. S. Lea, 1910–59).

1.3.   G. E. Cokayne, *The Complete Baronetage*, 6 vols (Exeter, 1900–9).

Sixteenth–Eighteenth centuries. Non-official publications.

1.4.   Francis Peck, *Desiderata Curiosa: Or, a collection of divers scarce and curious pieces relating chiefly to matters of English history* . . . , 2 vols (1732–35). [A haphazard collection of material from Queen Elizabeth's reign onwards.]

1.5.   M. C. McClure (ed.), *The Letters of John Chamberlain* (Philadelphia, 1939) [for 1597–1628].

1.6. E. (later J.) Chamberlayne, *Angliae Notitia* (1669–1707), continued as *Magnae Britanniae Notitia* (22nd–38th editions, 17 vols, 1708–1755): lists of officers in the household and central administration [not always reliable].

1.7. For useful analytical indexes to it, *see* M. M. S. Arnett, 'Lists of office-holders in *Angliae Notitia', BIHR*, xv (1937).

1.8. G. Miège, *The Present State of England* (1683–1707), continued as *The Present State of Great Britain* (11 edns, 1707–48). [Miège's lists inferior to Chamberlayne's.]

1.9. *See* M. Jolliffe, 'Lists of office-holders in Miège's "New State of England" ', *BIHR*, xvii (1939–40).

1.10. R. Beatson, *A Political Index to the Histories of Great Britain and Ireland* (1st edn, 1786; 3rd edn, 3 vols, 1806). [Has few lesser officers before 1689 and holders of less important offices are given fully only from 1760. Unreliable in detail for the seventeenth century, even for senior officers.]

1.11. J. T. Haydn, *The Book of Dignities* (1st edn, 1851; 3rd edn, 1894). [Successor to Beatson. Holders of less important offices given only from 1760.]

1.12. *Historical Register, containing an impartial relation of all transactions foreign and domestick . . .* , 23 vols (1717–39). [Contains in vols ii–xxiii a useful 'chronological register of births, marriages, deaths and promotions'.]

1.13. *The Court and City Register* (annual publication, 1742–1813). [Contains full lists of office-holders, governing boards, etc.] *See* A. M. Mathews, 'Editions of the *Court and City Register*, 1742–1813', *BIHR*, xix (1941).

1.14. *The Annual Register; a review of public events at home and abroad . . .* (1758–1819). *See General Index to Dodsley's Annual Register . . . , 1758* to *. . . 1819* (1826).

1.15. *An Index to the Biographical and Obituary Notices in the Gentleman's Magazine 1731–80* (1891).

1.16. Sir William Musgrave, *Obituary prior to 1800 . . .* , 6 vols (1899–1901, Harleian Society, vols 44–49). [Useful for deaths, promotions of individual officials etc.: based largely on contemporary lists published in the *Historical Register* and in the various magazines, *e.g. Gentleman's Magazine* and *Annual Register*.]

Volumes in The Oxford History of England series list (in Appendices) major office-holders, from J. D. Mackie, *The Early Tudors, 1485–1558* (1962), 645–65. They list cabinets after 1782.

Nineteenth century and after.

A number of annual, or periodical, publications, in addition to the *Annual Register*, begin in the nineteenth century, and provide authoritative guides to office-holders: Dod's *Parliamentary Companion* (from 1832), *Who's Who* (from 1847), *Whitaker's Almanac* (from 1869), *The Civil Service Yearbook* (in various forms, since 1809). In addition to the lists of cabinets in The Oxford History of England volumes see also the full and up to date lists of ministries and other political data in D. Butler and A. Sloman, *British Political Facts, 1900–* (latest edn.).

Selected Official Records containing much information about holders of offices (mainly sixteenth–seventeenth centuries)

See also **4.**10; **5.**18; **7.**5; **7.**7.

1.17. *Journals of the House of Lords*, 19 vols for 1510–1714 (1846).

1.18. *Journals of the House of Commons*, 17 vols for 1547–1714 (1803–52).

1.19. *Calendar of Letters and Papers, Foreign and Domestic Henry VIII*, 21 vols (1864–1932).

1.20. *The Acts of the Privy Council of England* (new ser., for 1613–31, 1921–, in progress). [References but not many appointments.]

1.21. 43rd and 48th *Reports of the Deputy Keeper of the Public Records*: grants under the Privy Seal, 1625–35.

1.22. *Foedera* (ed. T. Rymer and R. Sanderson), vols xviii–xx (1704–32): alphabetical lists of *most* officers appointed by patent 1625–42, entered at the end of each year.

1.23. *Calendar of State Papers Domestic* (Complete for 1547–1704). [Gives a great many appointments, when the grants passed through the Secretaries of State's Office.]

1.24. C. H. Firth and R. S. Rait, ed., *The Acts and Ordinances of the Interregnum*, 3 vols (1911). [For 1642–60.]

2. ROYAL HOUSEHOLD

I.   To 1485

See also **2.**15.

2.1. T. F. Tout, *Chapters*, vol. vi (Manchester, 1933): Controllers of the wardrobe, 1224–1399; cofferers of the wardrobe, 1274–1399; keepers of the great wardrobe, 1223–1399; keepers of the privy wardrobe, 1323–99; the king's chamberlains, 1207–1399 (including sub-chamberlains under Edward III and Richard II); receivers of the chamber, 1309–99. [*Chapters*, vols i–v (1920–33), contain a mass of information also about other household officials.]

2.2. *History of Parliament, 1439–1509*, ed. J. C. Wedgwood and others, vol. ii, Register of Assemblies (HMSO, 1938), pp. xli ff.: lists of king's chamberlains, 1432–1508; controllers of the household, 1439–1506; stewards of the household, 1433–1538; chief butlers, 1439–1514 [the information in Wedgwood not always wholly reliable].

2.3. Sir Harris Nicolas (ed.), *Proceedings and Ordinances of the Privy Council of England, 1386–1461*, vol. vi (1837), 222–33: Household Ordinance of 1454 containing a list of several members of the royal household [a less satisfactory edition also in **2.**6].

2.4. J. H. Round, *The King's Serjeants and Officers of State with their Coronation Services* (1911). [No lists but much information about various household services. Valuable especially for twelfth and thirteenth centuries.]

2.5. G. E. Cokayne, *Complete Peerage* (rev. edn, 1910–59), vol. ii, Appendix D, list of marshals of the Household, early twelfth century to 1672, and vol. x, Appendix F (list of king's chamberlains).

2.6. *A Collection of Ordinances and Regulations for the Government of the Royal Household . . . Edward III to . . . William and Mary* (Society of Antiquaries, 1790).

2.7. A. R. Myers, ed., *The Household of Edward IV: the Black Book and the Ordinance of 1478* (Manchester, 1959). [Much information about offices of the household but only a few names of officials.]

II. 1485–1603

See also **1.**4; **2.**2; **2.**5; **2.**6.

2.8. W. C. Richardson, *Tudor Chamber Administration, 1485–1547* (Baton Rouge, La, 1952), 484 ff.: lists of treasurers of the household, 1485–1558; cofferers of the household, 1485–1564; treasurers of the chamber, 1465–1558; keepers of the jewel house, 1485–1545; chief butlers, 1485–1535.

2.9. J. D. Mackie, *The Earlier Tudors, 1485–1558* (Oxford, 1952), 649 ff.: lists of stewards of the household, 1485–1553; chamberlains of the household, 1485–1558; treasurers and comptrollers of the household, 1485–1558.

III and IV. 1603–1789

See also **2.**5; **2.**6.

2.10. G. E. Aylmer, *The King's Servants. The Civil Service of Charles I, 1625–42* (1961).

2.11. G. E. Aylmer, *The State's Servants. The Civil Service of the English Republic, 1649–1660* (1973).

Miscellaneous information [useful but not always reliable] in the following:

2.12. S. Pegge, *Curialia* (1791–1803).

2.13. N. Carlisle, *An Inquiry into . . . the Gentlemen of His Majesty's . . . Privy Chamber* (1829).

2.14. V. Wheeler-Holohan, *The History of the King's Messengers* (1935).

2.15. R. Hennell, *The History . . . of the Yeomen of the Guard* (Westminster, 1904).

2.16. H. Kearney, *His Majesty's Bodyguard of the . . . Gentlemen at Arms* (1937).

3. CHANCERY

I. 1272–1485

See also **10.**

3.1. T. D. Hardy, *A Catalogue of Lords Chancellors, Keepers of the Great Seal, Masters of the Rolls and Principal Officers of the High Court of Chancery* (1843): keepers of the rolls from 1286.

3.2. T. F. Tout, *Edward II* (1936) [*see* **6.**6], 290–95; temporary keepers of the great seal, 1307–27; keepers of the rolls, 1295–1327.

3.3. B. Wilkinson, *The Chancery under Edward III* (Manchester, 1929), 199–208: temporary keepers of the great seal, keepers of the rolls and other greater clerks of the chancery, 1327–77.

3.4. Sir Henry Maxwell Lyte, *Historical Notes on the use of the Great Seal of England* (1926). [Much miscellaneous information on officials.]

II. 1485–1642

See also **3.4.**

3.5. Hardy (quoted **3.**1): masters of the rolls (complete); Six Clerks, 1545– ; registrars and deputy registrars of the court of chancery, 1549– ; examiners of the court of chancery, reign of Edward IV– ; masters in the chancery, 1597– ; Clerks of the Petty Bag, 1598– . [Not always reliable on the less senior officials.]

3.6. E. A. Fry, ed., *Index of Chancery Proceedings* (Index Library, 1903), Introduction: Six Clerks, 1522– .

3.7. W. C. Richardson, *Tudor Chamber Administration, 1485–1547* (1952): keepers of the hanaper, 1485–1547.

4. SECRETARIAL OFFICES
(other than the chancery)

I. To 1485

4.1. L. B. Dibben, 'Secretaries in the thirteenth and fourteenth centuries', *EHR*, xxv (1910). [General discussion.]

4.2. T. F. Tout, *Chapters*, vol. vi (Manchester, 1933), 57–58: list of the king's secretaries, 1377–99. [*See ibid.*, especially vol. v, for a general discussion.]

4.3. J. Otway-Ruthven, *The King's Secretary and the Signet Office in the XV century* (Cambridge, 1939); Appendices: king's secretaries, 1377–1485; French secretaries, 1422–90; clerks of the signet, 1399–1485.

II. 1485–1603

4.4. F. M. G. Evans, *The Principal Secretary of State: a Survey of the Office from 1558 to 1680* (Manchester, 1923): list of principal secretaries, Appendix II (complete, 1500–1680) [references to many subordinate officials].

　Biographies of Tudor secretaries of state contain much information about their subordinates and collaborators. *See especially*:

4.5. G. R. Elton, *The Tudor Revolution in Government* (Cambridge, 1953). [Thomas Cromwell.]

4.6. A. J. Slavin, *Politics and Profit. A Study of Sir Ralph Sadler, 1507–1547* (Cambridge, 1966).

4.7. C. Read, *Mr Secretary Cecil and Queen Elizabeth* (1955). [1558–71.]

4.8. C. Read, *Mr Secretary Walsingham and the policy of Queen Elizabeth*, 3 vols (Oxford, 1925).

III–IV. Secretaries of State: 1603–1789

See also **4.4.**

4.9. M. A. Thomson, *The Secretaries of State 1681–1782* (Oxford, 1932). [Information about subordinate officials.]

4.10. T. Birch, ed., *The Thurloe State Papers* (1742) [for 1653–59].

4.11. J. C. Sainty, *Officials of the Secretaries of State, 1660–1782* (Institute of Historical Research, 1973).

5. EXCHEQUER, TREASURY AND OTHER FINANCIAL DEPARTMENTS AND OFFICIALS

I.   Exchequer: 1272–1485

5.1.   T. F. Tout, *Edward II* (*see* **6**.6), 296–313: chief officers, 1307–27 (barons, chancellors of the exchequer, chamberlains of the receipt, remembrancers).

5.2.   G. L. Harriss, *King, Parliament, and Public Finance in Medieval England, to 1369* (Oxford, 1975).

5.3.   A. Steel, *The Receipt of the Exchequer 1377–1485* (Cambridge, 1954), 422–25: chamberlains of the receipt, 1377–1483.

5.4.   J. L. Kirby, 'The rise of the under-treasurers of the exchequer', *EHR*, lxxii (1957): under-treasurers, 1412–83.

5.5.   *History of Parliament, 1439–1509* (ed. J. C. Wedgwood and others), vol. ii, Register of Assemblies (HMSO, 1938): list of chancellors of the exchequer, 1410–1516 (xliii–iv).

II.   Exchequer and other Revenue Courts: 1485–1603
See also **11**.25.

(a)   Lists
5.6.   W. C. Richardson, *Tudor Chamber Administration, 1485–1547* (1952): chancellors of the exchequer, 1485–1558; principal officials of the following revenue courts: the court of augmentations, 1536–47; the offices of wards and of liveries and the court of wards and liveries, 1503–47; the court of general surveyors, 1511–47; the court of first fruits and tenths, 1540–47.

(b)   Other information on officials
5.7.   W. C. Richardson, 'The Surveyor of the King's Prerogative', *EHR*, lvi (1941).

5.8.   H. E. Bell, *An Introduction to the History and Records of the Court of Wards and Liveries* (Cambridge, 1953).

5.9.   J. Hurstfield, *The Queen's Wards* (1958). [Reign of Elizabeth I.]

5.10.   W. C. Richardson, *History of the Court of Augmentations* (Baton Rouge, La, 1962).

III.   Treasury and Other Financial Departments and Officials: 1603–1714
See also **5**.8.

Satisfactory published lists of the officials of central financial departments are lacking for the period 1603–42, though unpublished lists of various kinds are available among exchequer records, state papers and other royal archives.

5.11.   J. C. Sainty, *Treasury officials, 1660–1870* (IHR, 1972).

5.12.   For the customs' farmers *see* references in A. P. Newton, 'The Establishment of the Great Farm of the English Customs', *TRHS*, 4th ser., i (1918), 129–55; W. P. Harper, 'The Significance of the Farmers of the Customs . . .', *Economica*, 1st ser., ix (1929), 61–70; R. Ashton, 'Revenue Farming under the early Stuarts', *Econ. Hist. Rev.*, 2nd ser., viii (1955–56), 310–22.

5.13.   E. Hughes, *Studies in Administration and Finance, 1558–1825* (Manchester, 1934) does not have complete lists of office-holders, but refers to many of those in the customs and the excise.

5.14. *An Account of the Commissioners of Customs, Excise, Hearthmoney and Inland Revenue* (HMSO, 1913): lists of commissioners of the customs, 1642–1909; for excise, 1643–1848; excise and hearthmoney, 1684–89. (An earlier list of commissioners of the customs, 1671–1895, published by HMSO in 1897.)

5.15. W. R. Ward, 'The Office for Taxes, 1664–1798', *BIHR*, xxv (1952): list of Commissioners for Taxes appointed between 1665 and 1828.

5.16. W. A. Shaw, ed., *Calendar of Treasury Books, 1660–1718*, 23 vols (HMSO, 1904–59), and J. Redington, ed., *Calendar of Treasury Papers, 1557–1728*, 6 vols (HMSO, 1868–89). [Mass of information in introductions and calendars.]

IV. Treasury, Financial Departments and Officials: 1714–1789

See also **5.**13, 14–16.

5.17. D. M. Clark, 'The office of the secretary to the treasury in the eighteenth century', *American Historical Review*, xlii (1936): list of the secretaries, 1695–1801 (44–45).

5.18. W. R. Ward, *The English Land Tax in the Eighteenth Century* (1953): lists of commissioners for the Land Tax.

5.19. W. R. Ward, 'The administration of the Window and Assessed Taxes, 1696–1798', *EHR*, lxvii (1952).

5.20. W. R. Ward, 'Some eighteenth century civil servants: the English revenue commissioners, 1754–98', *EHR*, lxx (1955).

5.21. E. E. Hoon, *The Organization of the English Customs System, 1696–1786* (New York, 1938). [Useful chiefly for the period 1746–86.]

6. MISCELLANEOUS FINANCIAL AND OTHER OFFICIALS

6.1. C. A. F. Meekings, 'Justices of the Jews, 1218–68: a provisional list', *BIHR*, xxviii (1955).

6.2. D. Crook, 'The early remembrancers of the exchequer', *BIHR*, liii (1980). [Later years of the reign of Henry III and the reign of Edward I.]

6.3. G. J. Turner, 'Justices of the forest South of Trent', *EHR*, xviii (1903), 112–16; list, 1217–1821.

6.4. S. T. Gibson, 'The Escheatries, 1327–1341', *EHR*, xxxvi (1921).

6.5. R. L. Baker, *The English Customs Service, 1307–1343: a Study of Medieval Administration* (Philadelphia, 1961): lists of collectors of customs and of other officials associated with them, 1294–1343.

6.6. T. F. Tout, *Place of the Reign of Edward II in English History* (2nd edn, Manchester, 1936), 318–25: lists of justices of the forest, escheators, keepers of the exchanges, under Edward II.

6.7. *The English Government at Work, 1327–36*, 3 vols (Cambridge, Mass.): lists of forest officials (vol. i, 1940, 448–65), mint and exchange officials (vol. iii, 1950, 59). These volumes also contain much information for the decade 1327–36 about the following: the collectors of customs, the collectors of lay and clerical taxes (vol. ii, 1947); royal keepers of the escheats, lands in wardship and vacant temporalities; keepers of the stannaries in Devon and Cornwall (vol. iii, 1950).

6.8. Sir John Craig, *The Mint* (Cambridge, 1953). [No lists of officials but much information about them.]

6.9. *See also* W. C. Richardson, *Tudor Chamber Administration, 1485–1547* (1952): list of controllers of the mint, 1485–1551.

6.10. J. C. Hemmeon, *The History of the British Post Office* (Cambridge,

6.11. Mass., 1912) and H. Robinson, *The British Post Office: A History* (Princeton, 1948) have many references but no complete lists.

6.12–13. C. F. D. Marshall, *The British Post Office* (1926), Appendix I, 143–76, and H. Joyce, *The History of the Post Office* (1893), Appendix, 429–35, have lists but are less scholarly.

6.14. G. Sutherland, ed., *Studies in the growth of nineteenth-century government* (1972).

7. COUNCIL AND CABINET

I. Council: 1377–1485

7.1. J. F. Baldwin, *The King's Council in England during the Middle Ages* (Oxford, 1913). [Various brief lists for short periods, especially 1377–80, 1392–93 and during the minority of Henry VI, 1422–37. Not always complete or wholly reliable.]

7.2. Sir Harris Nicolas, ed., *Proceedings and Ordinances of the Privy Council of England*, 6 vols for 1386–1461 (1834–35). [Contains much material about the composition of the council.]

7.3. N. B. Lewis, 'The "Continual Council" in the early years of Richard II, 1377–80', *EHR*, xli (1926). [Better lists than in **7.**1.]

7.4. *History of Parliament, 1439–1509*, ed. J. C. Wedgwood and others, vol. ii, Register of Assemblies (HMSO, 1938), p. xlix: list of clerks of the council, 1436–1509.

II. Council: 1485–1603

See also **7.**14; **11.**24.

7.5. C. G. Bayne and W. H. Dunham, Jr, ed., *Select Cases in the Council of Henry VII* (Selden Soc., vol. 75, 1958). [Prints surviving lists of councillors under Henry VII. *See also* Introduction, xix ff., with references to lists of the council in the Tudor period.]

7.6. W. H. Dunham, Jr, 'The members of Henry VIII's Whole Council, 1509–27', *EHR*, lix (1944). [Table of known members, 207–10.]

7.7. Sir Harris Nicolas, ed., *Proceedings and Ordinances of the Privy Council of England*, vii (1837). [Discusses the composition of the council under Henry VIII in the preface.]

7.8. A. F. Pollard, 'The Council under the Tudors', *EHR*, xxxvii (1922). [Includes a discussion of successive clerks of the council to 1540.]

7.9. List of privy councillors between 1558 and 1587 (written by Sir Julius Caesar), BL, Lansdowne MS. 160, 281–84.

7.10. P. Williams, *The Tudor Regime* (Oxford, 1979).

7.11. R. R. Reid, *The King's Council of the North* (1921), Appendices (list of presidents, Appendix II).

7.12. C. A. J. Skeel, *The Council in the Marches of Wales* (1904): presidents of this council, 1473–1689 (Appendix II).

7.13. P. Williams, *The Council in the Marches of Wales under Elizabeth I* (Cardiff, 1958): presidents, 1473–1602; justices of Chester, 1542–1600; officers of this council, *c.* 1540–1628; members of this council, 1560–1603.

III–IV. Council and Cabinet: from 1603

See also **7.**11–13.

7.14. J. H. Plumb, 'The Cabinet in the reign of Queen Anne', *TRHS*, 5th ser., vii (1957).

7.15. A. Aspinall, 'The Cabinet Council, 1783–1835'. *Proceedings of British Academy*, xxxviii (1952). [With an appendix of the Cabinets, 1783–1835.]

7.16. J. C. Sainty, *Officials of the Board of Trade, 1660–1870* (IHR, 1974).

7.17. *Journal of the Commissioners for Trade and Plantations from . . . 1704 to . . . 1782, preserved in the Public Record Office*, 14 vols (1920–38). [The official minutes of the Board of Trade and Plantations.]

7.18. J. P. Mackintosh, *The British Cabinet* (3rd edn. 1977).

8. PARLIAMENT (HOUSE OF LORDS)

I. To 1509

See also **1.**1–2.

8.1. *Reports from the Lords Committees touching the Dignity of a Peer of the Realm*, 5 vols (1829). [To 1483.]

8.2. Sir Harris Nicolas, ed., *Proceedings and Ordinances of the Privy Council of England, 1386–1461*, 6 vols (1834–35): summons to the Great Councils.

8.3. *History of Parliament, 1439–1509* [ed. J. C. Wedgwood (HMSO), 2 vols, 1936–38].

8.4. J. S. Roskell, 'The problem of the attendance of the Lords in medieval parliaments', *BIHR*, xxix (1956).

8.5. J. Enoch Powell and K. Wallis, *The House of Lords in the Middle Ages* (1968).

II–IV. From 1509

8.6. *Journals of the House of Lords*, 19 vols for 1509–1714 (1846).

8.7. M. A. R. Graves, *The House of Lords in the Parliaments of Edward VI and Mary I: an institutional study* (Cambridge, 1981).

8.8. E. R. Foster, *The House of Lords, 1603–1649* (Chapel Hill, N.C., 1983).

8.9–10. A. S. Turberville, *The House of Lords in the reign of William III* (Oxford, 1913), and 'The House of Lords in the reign of Charles II', *EHR*, xliv–xlv (1929–30).

8.11. R. Beatson, *A Chronological Register of both Houses of the British Parliament*, 3 vols (1807). [1708–1807.]

8.12. A. S. Turberville, *The House of Lords in the XVIIIth century* (Oxford, 1927).

8.13. A. S. Turberville, *The House of Lords in the Age of Reform, 1784–1837* (1958).

8.14. J. C. Sainty, *Leaders and Whips in the House of Lords, 1783–1964* (1964).

9. PARLIAMENT (HOUSE OF COMMONS)

(a) Membership (general works)

9.1. *Return of the Name of every Member of the Lower House of Parliament, 1213–1874*, H.C. Parliamentary Papers, 69, 69–I, 69–II, 69–III of 1878 (issued in 2 parts, 1878–79, 1888–89, each part consisting of 1 vol. of text and 1 vol. of index)—quoted henceforth as *Official Return*. Additions to lists of members made subsequently discussed in **9**.2.

9.2. *The Interim Report of the Committee on House of Commons Personnel and Politics, 1264–1832*, Cmd 4130 (1932): all the publications available in 1932 about the membership of the House of Commons listed and discussed [most of the works listed there are omitted from the present list, except when they are of special value or importance].

9.3. C. Gross, *A Bibliography of British municipal History including Guilds and Parliamentary Representation* (London, 1897). [Section on 'Parliamentary History', 50 ff.]

9.4. W. D. Pink and A. B. Beaven, *The Parliamentary Representation of Lancashire (1258–1885)* (1889).

9.5. J. C. Wedgwood, 'Staffordshire parliamentary history from the earliest times to the present day' [completed to 1841]. *The William Salt Archaeological Society*, vols 42, 44, 46, 57 (1917–33).

9.6. A. Gooder, 'The parliamentary representation of the county of York, 1258–1832', *Yorkshire Archaeological Society, Record Series*, vols 91 and 96 (1935 and 1938).

9.7. G. W. Bates Harbin, 'Members of parliament for the county of Somerset', *Proceedings of Somerset Archaeological and Natural History Society*, 1939–40.

(b) Speakers

9.8. P. Laundy, *The Office of Speaker* (1964).

9.9. W. I. Dasent, *The Speakers of the House of Commons from the earliest times to the present day* (1911): list of speakers from 1376, 347–414.

9.10. J. S. Roskell, 'The medieval Speakers for the Commons in Parliament', *BIHR*, xxiii (1950).

9.11. J. S. Roskell, *The Commons and their Speakers in English Parliaments, 1376–1523* (Manchester, 1965).

I. To 1509

(a) Membership

9.12. M. McKisack, *The Parliamentary Representation of the English Boroughs during the Middle Ages* (Oxford, 1932): Appendix I lists some members omitted in *Official Return* (**9**.1)—various assemblies, 1296–1497.

9.13. Additions to *Official Return* (**9**.1) for particular parliaments: April 1275—H. Jenkinson, *EHR*, xxv (1910); 1294, 1295, 1307—G. O. Sayles, *BIHR*, iii (1925); 1491—W. Jay, *BIHR*, iii (1926).
See also **9**.2, p. 23 (for 1258 and 1439–40 parliaments).

9.14. *History of Parliament, 1439–1509*, 2 vols (HMSO, 1936–38) issued by a Committee of Both Houses (chairman, J. C. Wedgwood):

vol. i, Biographies of Members of the House of Commons; vol. ii, Register of Assemblies (with lists of members of both houses attending).

9.15. J. S. Roskell, *The Commons in the Parliament of 1422* (Manchester, 1954). [Biographical notes on the knights of the shires and some of the burgesses.]

9.16. M. Basset, 'Knights of the shire for Bedfordshire during the middle ages', *Bedfordshire Historical Record Society*, xxix (1949).

9.17. H. Hornyold-Strickland, 'Biographical sketches of the members of parliament of Lancashire, 1290–1550', and J. S. Roskell 'The knights of the shire for the county palatine of Lancaster', *Chetham Society*, vols 93 and 96 (1935, 1937).

9.18. J. S. Roskell, 'Parliamentary representation of Lincolnshire' *Nottingham Mediaeval Studies*, III (1959).

II. 1509–1603

(a) Membership

9.19. S. T. Bindoff, *The House of Commons, 1509–1558* (The History of Parliament Trust, 1982). 3 vols.

9.20. P. W. Hasler, *The House of Commons, 1558–1603* (The History of Parliament Trust, 1981). 3 vols.

III. 1603–1714

(a) Membership

Most of the Parliaments of the seventeenth century are now the subject of individual studies. See the general bibliographies for these.

9.21. Additions to *Official Return* (**9.1**): W. W. Bean, *Notices of various errors and omissions found in* [**9.1**] *1603–1830* (London, 1883); 1604–11—H. Hulme, *BIHR*, v (1927). *See also* **9.2**, 25–26.

9.22. B. D. Henning, *The House of Commons, 1660–1690* (The History of Parliament Trust, 1983). 3 vols.

9.23. C. S. R. Russell, *Parliaments and English Politics, 1621–1629* (Oxford, 1979).

9.24. M. F. Keeler, *The Long Parliament* (Philadelphia, 1954). [Very full for the members elected in 1640–41 only.]

9.25. D. Underdown, *Pride's Purge, Politics in the Puritan Revolution* (Oxford, 1971).

9.26. A. B. Worden, *The Rump Parliament, 1648–1653* (Cambridge, 1974).

9.27. A. S. Woolrych, *Commonwealth to Protectorate* (Oxford, 1982).

9.28. E. S. de Beer, 'Members of the court party in the House of Commons, 1670–78', *BIHR*, xi (1933).

9.29. A. Browning and D. J. Milne, 'An Exclusion Bill division list', *BIHR*, xiv (1936). [For 1679.]

9.30. A. Browning, *Thomas Osborne, Earl of Danby*, vol. iii (Glasgow, 1951). [Appendices III–V, 33–217 useful for members in the last three decades of the seventeenth century.]

9.31. M. Rex, *University Representation in England, 1603–90* (1954).

9.32. G. L. Cherry, *The Convention Parliament, 1689: a biographical study of its members* (N.Y., 1966).

9.33. G. Holmes, *British Politics in the Age of Anne* (1967).

9.34. W. A. Speck, *Tory & Whig. The Struggle in the Constituencies, 1701–1715* (1970).

IV.   From 1714

See also **9**.1–7.

(a)   Membership

9.35. R. Sedgwick, *The House of Commons, 1715–1754* (The History of Parliament Trust, 1970), 2 vols.

9.36. L. B. Namier and J. Brooke, *The House of Commons, 1754–1790* (The History of Parliament Trust, 1964), 3 vols.

9.37. R. Beatson, *A chronological register of both houses of the British Parliament, from . . . 1708 to . . . 1807*, 3 vols (1807).

9.38. H. S. Smith, *The Parliaments of England from 1st George I, to the present time*, 3 vols (1844–50).

9.39. L. B. Namier, *The Structure of Politics at the Accession of George III* (2nd edn, 1957).

9.40. L. B. Namier, *England in the Age of American Revolution* (1930).

9.41. E. and A. G. Porritt, *The Unreformed House of Commons*, 2 vols (Cambridge, 1903–1909).

9.42–45. F. W. S. Craig, *British Parliamentary Election Results, 1832–1885* (1977), *1885–1918* (1974), *1918–1949* (1969), *1950–1970* (1971).

9.46. *The Times* has published a guide to the general election results, and the composition of the new House of Commons, since 1880 (except for 1906).

10.   PARLIAMENT (OFFICIALS)

I.   To 1509

See also **9**.8–11 (Speakers of the House of Commons).

10.1. H. G. Richardson and G. O. Sayles, 'The king's ministers in parliament': *EHR*, xlvi (1931): 1272–1307; *EHR*, xlvii (1932): 1307–77. [Royal clerks in charge of parliamentary business and receivers of petitions.]

10.2. A. F. Pollard, 'The clerical organization of parliament', *EHR*, lvii (1942). [Edward III–Elizabeth.]

10.3. A. F. Pollard, 'Fifteenth century clerks of parliament', *BIHR*, xv (1938). [Continues **10**.1, 1377–1509.]

10.4. A. F. Pollard, 'The mediaeval under-clerks of parliament 1362–1509', *BIHR*, xvi (1938). [Clerks of the Commons.]

10.5. A. F. Pollard, 'Receivers of petitions and clerks of parliament', *EHR*, lvii (1942). [Valuable chiefly for fourteenth and fifteenth centuries.]

10.6. *History of Parliament, 1439–1509* (ed. J. C. Wedgwood and others), vol. ii, Register of Assemblies (HMSO, 1938), xlix–l: list of clerks of the parliaments, 1437–1523.

II.   1509–1603

See also **9.**8–9; **10.**2; **10.**5.

10.7.   A. F. Pollard, 'The under-clerks and the Commons' Journals, 1509–1558', *BIHR*, xvi (1939).

10.8.   A. F. Pollard, 'Queen Elizabeth's under-clerks and their Commons' Journals', *BIHR*, xvii (1939).

10.9.   A. F. Pollard, 'The Clerk of the Crown', *EHR*, lvii (1942). [Yorkist and early Tudor periods.]

10.10.   M. F. Bond, 'Clerks of the parliaments, 1509–1953. A revised list', *EHR*, lxxiii (1958). [List of the chief clerks.]

III–IV.   From 1603

See also **9.**8–9; **10.**10.

10.11.   O. C. Williams, *The Clerical Organization of the House of Commons, 1661–1854* (Oxford, 1954). [Chapter I deals with earlier seventeenth-century clerks of the Commons. This work contains lists of clerks and biographies of many of them as well as some information about the clerical staff of the Upper House.]

10.12.   D. L. Rydz, *The Parliamentary Agents* (1979).

10.13.   *The House of Commons in the Twentieth Century*, ed. S. A. Walhland (Oxford, 1979).

11.   LEGAL HISTORY
(General Works)

See also **3.**1; **3.**4.

11.1.   E. Foss, *Judges of England, with sketches of their lives and notices connected with the courts at Westminster, 1066–1864*, 9 vols (1848–64). An abridgement published in *Biographia juridica* (1870). [Not always reliable.]

11.2.   E. Foss, *Tabulae curiales: or tables of the superior courts of Westminster Hall* . . . (1865). [Includes names of attorneys-general and solicitors-general to 1864.]

11.3.   J. Campbell, *The Lives of the Chief Justices of England . . . till the death of Lord Mansfield*, 2nd edn, 4 vols (1874). [Inaccurate.]

11.4.   H. W. Woolrych, *Lives of eminent serjeants-at-law of the English bar*, 2 vols (1869).

11.5.   *The Records of the Honourable Society of Lincoln's Inn: admissions 1420–1893* . . . , 2 vols (1896).

11.6.   H. A. C. Sturgess, *Register of admissions to the Honourable Society of the Middle Temple from the fifteenth century to . . . 1944*, 3 vols (1949).

11.7.   For lists of members of the other Inns of Court, *see* H. Raven-Hart, 'Bibliography of the registers (printed) of the Universities, Inns of Court . . .', *BIHR*, ix (1931), 24.

11.8.   C. Coote, *Sketches of the lives and characters of eminent English Civilians with an historical introduction relative to the College of Advocates* (1804). [Information on many officials in ecclesiastical courts and the Court of Admiralty.]

I. To 1485

11.9. F. W. Maitland, *Bracton's Notebook* (London, 1887), vol. i, pp. 139–45: list of the justices who sat at the Bench during the reign of Henry III (1218–72).

11.10. C. A. F. Meekings, *Studies in Thirteenth Century Justice and Administration* (1981).

11.11. F. Pegues, 'The *clericus* in the legal administration of thirteenth century England', *EHR*, lxxi (1956). [Much useful information on officials of the courts.]

11.12. J. R. Maddicott, *Law and Lordship: Royal Justices and Retainers in Thirteenth and Fourteenth Century England. Past and Present Supplement*, no. 4 (Oxford, 1978).

11.13. G. O. Sayles, *Select Cases in the Court of King's Bench* (Selden Society, 5 vols): list of judges of the courts of King's Bench and Common Pleas, 1269–1340, in vols 1 and 4 (Selden Soc., vol. 55 for 1936, cxxix–cxli, and vol. 74 for 1955, lxxxvii–xcv).

11.14. For lists of judges in the reign of Edward II, *see also* T. F. Tout, *The Place of the Reign of Edward II in English History* (2nd edn, Manchester, 1936), 326–32.

11.15. For a list of judges of the court of Common Pleas in 1327–36, *see also* N. Neilson, 'The Court of Common Pleas', in the *English Government at Work, 1327–36*, iii (ed. W. H. Dunham Jr, Cambridge, Mass., 1950), 278–82.

11.16. Sayles (*supra*, **11.**13), vol. 1, cxlviii–cxlix: list of keepers of the rolls of the court of Common Pleas, 1266–1307.

11.17. Sayles, vol. 5 (Selden Soc., vol. 76, 1957): lists of king's attorneys, 1290–1340, and king's serjeants, 1278–1340, cii–cxvi.

11.18. *English Government at Work, 1327–36*, iii (*supra*, **11.**15): lists of subordinate officers of the court of Common Pleas, 1327–36, 282–85.

11.19. *Ibid.*, M. Taylor, 'The Justices of Assize', list of general commissions of assize, 1327–37, 248–52.

11.20. M. Hastings, *The Court of Common Pleas in XV century England* (Ithaca, 1947): lists of keepers of writs, 1246–1509; chirographers 1307–1509; clerks of the court, 1461–85.

11.21. *History of Parliament, 1439–1509* (ed. J. C. Wedgwood and others), vol. ii, Register of Assemblies (HMSO, 1938), xlviii: list of attorneys-general, 1429–1509.

11.22. R. Sillem, 'Commissions of the peace, 1380–1485', *BIHR*, x (1932). [Discussion of changes with a list of successive commissions.]

II. 1485–1642

See also **3.**1 and 5; **3.**7.

11.23. M. Blatcher, *The Court of King's Bench, 1450–1550* (1978).

11.24. R. Somerville, 'Henry VII's "Council learned in the law"', *EHR*, liv (1939).

11.25. I. S. Leadam, *Select Cases in the Court of Requests, 1497–1569* (Selden Soc., vol. 12, 1898). [Information on masters of the court of requests, but no lists.]

11.26. W. J. Jones, *The Elizabethan Court of Chancery* (Oxford, 1967).

11.27. B. H. Putnam, 'Justices of the peace from 1558 to 1688', *BIHR*, iv (1926–27). [Guide to enrolments of commissions and to lists of justices.]

11.28. T. G. Barnes and A. Hassell Smith, 'Justices of the peace from 1558 to 1688—a revised list of sources', *BIHR*, xxxii (1959). [Revises and supplements B. H. Putnam's article above.]

11.29. R. Somerville, 'Lancashire justices of the peace in the fifteenth and sixteenth centuries', *Transactions of the Historical Society of Lancashire and Cheshire*, cii (1952).

11.30. J. H. Gleason, *The Justices of the Peace in England, 1558 to 1640. A Later Eirenarcha* (Oxford, 1969).

11.31. *Calendar of Assize Records, James I*, 5 vols, ed. J. S. Cockburn (1975–82).

III–IV.   1642–1789
Most of the relevant works have been mentioned in the general section *supra. See also* **11.**27–8.

11.32. T. D. Hardy, *A Catalogue of Lords Chancellors, Keepers of the Great Seal, Masters of the Rolls and Principal Officers of the High Court of Chancery* (1843). Besides officials listed in **3.**5 there are also lists of the following: accountants-general of the court of chancery, 1726– ; secretaries to lord chancellors, 1778– ; secretaries to masters of the rolls; vice-chancellors, 1813–

12. DIPLOMATIC AGENTS

I.   To 1485

12.1. G. P. Cuttino, *English Diplomatic Administration, 1259–1339* (Oxford, 1940) and a chapter in *The English Government at Work, 1327–36*, vol. i (Cambridge, Mass., 1940). [Much information but no lists.]

12.2. M. C. L. Salt, 'List of English embassies to France, 1272–1307', *EHR*, xliv (1929).

12.3. L. Mirot and E. Déprez, 'Les ambassades anglaises pendant la guerre de Cent Ans', *Bibliothèque de l'Ecole des Chartes*, 1898–1900. [Lists only the embassies for which accounts exist among Exchequer K.R. Accounts Various (E. 101).]

12.4. For numerous additions and corrections, *see* A. Larson, 'English embassies during the Hundred Years' War', *EHR*, lv (1940).

II–IV.   From 1509

12.5. *Handlist of English Diplomatic Representatives, 1509–1688*, ed. G. Bell (RHS Guides and Handbooks Series, forthcoming).

12.6. *See also* 37th *Report of the Deputy Keeper of the Public Records* (1876), Appendix I: lists of French ambassadors in England, 1509–1714 (by A. Baschet).

12.7. D. B. Horn, *British Diplomatic Representatives, 1689–1789* (Camden 3rd ser., vol. xlvi, 1932).

12.8. S. T. Bindoff, E. F. Malcolm Smith, C. K. Webster, eds, *British Diplomatic Representatives, 1789–1852* (Camden 3rd ser., vol. 1, 1934).

12.9. R. A. Jones, *The British Diplomatic Service, 1815–1914* (Gerrards Cross, 1983).

13. MILITARY HISTORY

From 1642 to 1789

For the Civil War period:

13.1–3. (i) royalist: *A List of Officers claiming to the sixty thousand pounds* (1663); W. H. Black, *Docquets of letters patent . . . passed . . . at Oxford (1642–46)* (unpublished, London, 1838; copy in PRO); P. R. Newman, *Royalist Officers in England and Wales, 1642–1660* (New York and London, 1981).

(ii) parliamentarian and Cromwellian:

13.4–5. H. A. Dillon, 'List of the Officers of the London Trained Bands, 1643', *Archaeologia*, lii (1890), 129–44; C. H. Firth and G. Davies, *The Regimental History of Cromwell's Army*, 2 vols (Oxford, 1940).

13.6. C. Dalton, *English Army lists and Commission Registers 1661–1714*, 6 vols (1892–1904).

13.7. C. Dalton, *George the first's Army, 1714–1727*, 2 vols (1910–12).

13.8. Army Lists of Officers from 1702 in MS, PRO, WO 64; printed from 1754 in WO 65.

13.9. The Army List of 1740 [reprinted by Society for Army Hist. Research, Special No. 3 (1931)].

13.10. *The succession of Colonels to all His Majesties land forces from their rise to 1742* (1742).

13.11. *List of Officers of the Royal Regiment of Artillery* [1716–1869], (1869).

13.12. *Records of Officers and Soldiers who have served in the British Army* (PRO, 1985).

14. NAVAL HISTORY

14.1. M. Oppenheim, *History of the Administration of the Royal Navy* (1896). [Valuable for the period to 1660.]

14.2. G. F. James and J. J. Shaw, 'Admiralty administration and personnel, 1619–1714', *BIHR*, xiv (1936): lists of lords commissioners and committees of the admiralty.

14.3. Sir George Jackson and G. F. Duckett, *Naval commissioners . . . , 1660–1760* (Lewes, 1889).

14.4. J. Charnock, *Biographia navalis; or impartial memoirs of the lives and characters of officers of the navy of Great Britain from . . . 1660*, 6 vols (1794–98).

14.5. *See* for this work G. F. James, 'Collected naval biography', *BIHR*, xv (1937–38).

14.6. J. Campbell, *Lives of the British Admirals and other British Seamen*, 4 vols (1742–44; later edn, 8 vols, 1812–17).

14.7. *List of the Flag Officers of his majesty's fleet . . . captains . . . masters and commanders . . . lieutenants* (1749 onwards).

14.8. National Maritime Museum, *The Commissioned Sea Officers of the Royal Navy 1660–1815* (1955). [This is a duplicated typescript and is not on sale, but copies have been given to some large libraries. It is far superior to anything else.]

14.9. J. C. Sainty, *Admiralty Official, 1660–1870*. (IHR, 1975.)

15. LOCAL OFFICIALS AND SPECIAL REGIONS

15.1. *Lists of Sheriffs of England and Wales from the earliest times to 1831* (HMSO, 1896).

15.2. G. Scott Thomson, *Lords Lieutenants in the Sixteenth Century: a Study in Tudor Local Administration* (1923).

15.3. J. C. Sainty, *Lieutenants of Counties, 1585–1642* (IHR, 1970).

15.4. For Justices of the Peace, *see* the section on Legal History (**11**).

15.5. For Coroners from the seventeenth century, *see* references in S. and B. Webb, *English Local Government*, i, *The Parish and the County* (1906), 292–94.

15.6. H. Pease, *The Lord Wardens of the Marches of England and Scotland* (1913).

15.7. R. L. Storey, 'The wardens of the marches of England towards Scotland 1377–1489', *EHR*, lxxii (1957); list 609–15.

15.8–9. R. Somerville, *History of the Duchy of Lancaster*, i, *1265–1603* (1953): lists of officers of the County Palatine of Lancaster, 1351–1603; central officers of the Duchy of Lancaster, 1399–1603; and *idem*, *Office-holders in the Duchy and County Palatine of Lancaster from 1603* (1972).

15.10. 31st *Report of the Deputy Keeper of the Public Records*: lists of officers of the Palatinate of Chester.

15.11. *See also*, for justices of Chester, J. Tait, *Chartulary of the Abbey of St Werburgh, Chester* (Chetham Soc., 1920).

15.12. W. H. Waters, *The Edwardian Settlement of North Wales in its Administrative and Legal Aspects, 1284–1343* (1935): lists of justices of North Wales; chamberlains and controllers of the exchequer at Caernarvon; sheriffs of Anglesea, Caernarvon and Merioneth.

15.13. W. R. Williams, *The History of the Great Sessions in Wales* (1899): several lists of all the justices and other legal officers.

15.14. T. F. Tout, *The Place of the Reign of Edward II in English History* (2nd edn, Manchester, 1936); 332–40: lists of officers of the principality of Wales and the earldom of Chester, *c.* 1307–27.

RULERS

The Sources

The narrative framework of the politics of the early Anglo-Saxon period is provided (in theory at least) by the Anglo-Saxon Chronicle. The many gaps in that very partial record have to be filled, in so far as they can be filled, from a wide variety of sources. For the later seventh and earlier eighth centuries Bede's *Historia Ecclesiastica Gentis Anglorum* is a primary source, and it provides important evidence also for the preceding century. Bede's annalistic recapitulation (*H.E.* V.24) was continued by Northumbrian annalists whose witness is vital to our appreciation of that kingdom's history from 732 to 806: these Northumbrian annals are now known in varying forms, and exclusively in later derivatives (particularly the E[DF] version of the Anglo-Saxon Chronicle) for the period 767 to 806. Celtic annalistic texts have their own important contribution to make to Anglo-Saxon history. For reign-lengths all these may be supplemented by the surviving regnal lists for Mercia (Penda to Æthelred II), Northumbria (Ida to Æthelred I), and Wessex (Cerdic to Æthelstan, and beyond: ed. D. N. Dumville, *Anglia*, 104, 1986, 1–32). Blood-relationships, whether real or alleged, between kings may be followed in some detail in the surviving pedigrees and genealogical collections: the so-called 'Anglian collection' (ed. D. N. Dumville, *Anglo-Saxon England*, 5, 1976, 23–50), compiled in the later eighth century, has royal pedigrees for seven kingdoms (Bernicia, Deira, East Anglia, Kent, Lindsey, Mercia, and Wessex); a small group of East Saxon royal pedigrees survives (ed. D. N. Dumville, *Anglia*, 104, 1986, 31–2); and the Anglo-Saxon Chronicle and related sources contain a substantial quantity of West Saxon royal genealogy. Precise evidence for the date of commencement of a reign often comes from charters, and especially from royal diplomas (which begin to be available from the 670s); here, all charters have been cited according to their number in P. H. Sawyer, *Anglo-Saxon Charters: an Annotated List and Bibliography*, Royal Historical Society Guides and Handbooks no. 8 (London, 1968), preceded by the formula 'S' (for example, S 349). A good many early Anglo-Saxon kings are known only from their appearing in charters, whether as donor or witness. The same is true of numismatic evidence: there are both English and (Anglo-)Scandinavian kings who are known only from coin-legends; and the reign-lengths of other scantily attested rulers must be estimated from the extent of their coinage. Beyond these most important sources, a wide range of other witnesses—including correspondence, hagiography, and lawcodes—contributes useful information. The evidence of post-Conquest sources has in general been spurned: while an exception has been made for the Northumbrian matter embedded

1

in the twelfth-century *Historia Regum* and in the early thirteenth-century *Flores Historiarum* of Roger Wendover, it nonetheless remains the case that the sources of all twelfth-century and later information about Anglo-Saxon history require much detailed analysis (which they have not yet received) before their testimony can be accepted as anything more than speculation.

Chronological Systems
In those cases where doubt has arisen as to how to express in modern usage mediaeval conventions of time-reckoning, generally the information given in the succeeding lists follows the system and views of Kenneth Harrison, *The Framework of Anglo-Saxon History to A.D. 900* (Cambridge, 1976).

Name-forms
Only nine names have been admitted in modern guise as being still in current use in Modern English name-giving: Alfred (OE Ælfred), Cuthbert (OE Cuthberht), Edmund (OE Eadmund), Edgar (OE Eadgar), Edward (OE Eadweard), Edwin (OE Eadwine), Eric (ON Eiríkr), Harold (ON Haraldr / OE Harald, Harold), and Oswald. Others have normally been given according to the approximate Late West Saxon standard generally in use among students of Anglo-Saxon history. For a simple guide to the relationship between Old English orthography and pronunciation, see Henry Sweet, *An Anglo-Saxon Primer* (9th edn, Oxford, 1953), pp. 1–4.

Principles of Revision
No serious attempt has been made at this stage to revise the substance of the lists presented in the second edition of the *Handbook*. Such lists will be prepared for future publication in David N. Dumville, *The Beginnings of English History, A.D. 400–850*, A New Oxford History of England I (Oxford, 1988), and it is hoped that those results can be incorporated in due course into a fourth edition of the *Handbook*. In the meantime, the information presented by previous editions of the *Handbook* has been reorganised to purge its more egregious errors, to remove citations of clearly disreputable evidence, to update forms of reference, and to present the lists in a more sensible (viz alphabetical) order. Nevertheless, it must be said that the result still presents an inadequate account of a very complex period and should be used only in conjunction with more detailed studies of the evidence. It should also be remembered, of course, that the names, dates and very existence of individual pre-Christian Anglo-Saxon kings are all to be viewed with considerable reserve.

Bibliography of texts cited (including abbreviations employed)

Æthelweard, *Chronicon*, ed. & transl. A. Campbell, *The Chronicle of Æthelweard* (Edinburgh, 1962)

Aldhelm, *Opera Omnia*, ed. R. Ehwald (Berlin, 1913–19); transl. M. Lapidge & M. Herren, *Aldhelm: the Prose Works* (Ipswich, 1979), and M. Lapidge *et al.*, *Aldhelm: the Poetic Works* (Cambridge, 1985)

Anglian collection of royal genealogies and regnal lists, ed. D. N. Dumville, *Anglo-Saxon England* 5 (1976) 23–50

ASC = Anglo-Saxon Chronicle: new edition in progress, gen. edd. D. N. Dumville & S. D. Keynes, *The Anglo-Saxon Chronicle: a Collaborative Edition* (23 vols, Cambridge, 1983–); transl. D. Whitelock, *The Anglo-Saxon Chronicle: a Revised Translation* (London, 1961; rev. imp., 1965)

Ann. St Neots = Annals of St Neots, edited in Dumville & Keynes, *The Anglo-Saxon Chronicle*, XVII (Cambridge, 1984)

Annals of Ulster, ed. & transl. S. Mac Airt & G. Mac Niocaill, *The Annals of Ulster (to A.D. 1131)* (2 parts, Dublin, 1983–)

Asser, Life of King Alfred, ed. W. H. Stevenson (Oxford, 1904; rev. imp., by D. Whitelock, 1959); transl. S. D. Keynes & M. Lapidge, *Alfred the Great: Asser's* Life of King Alfred *and Other Contemporary Sources* (Harmondsworth, 1983)

Bede, *Historia Ecclesiastica Gentis Anglorum*, ed. & transl. B. Colgrave & R. A. B. Mynors, *Bede's Ecclesiastical History of the English People* (Oxford, 1969)

Bede, *Vita Cuthberti*, ed. & transl. B. Colgrave, *Two Lives of Saint Cuthbert: a Life by an Anonymous Monk of Lindisfarne and Bede's Prose Life* (Cambridge, 1940)

Cont. Bed. = *Continuatio Baedae*, ed. & transl. B. Colgrave & R. A. B. Mynors, *Bede's Ecclesiastical History of the English People* (Oxford, 1969), pp. lxvii–lxix and 572–7

Felix, Life of St Guthlac, ed. & transl. B. Colgrave (Cambridge, 1956)

Flodoard, *Chronicon*, ed. P. Lauer, *Les Annales de Flodoard* (Paris, 1905)

Frankish 'Annals of Lindisfarne and Canterbury', ed. G. H. Pertz, *Monumenta Germaniae Historica, Scriptores* [in folio], IV (Hannover, 1841), pp. 1–2; cf. W. Levison & H. Löwe, *Deutschlands Geschichtsquellen im Mittelalter: Vorzeit und Karolinger*, II (Weimar, 1953), pp. 189–90

Gregory of Tours, *Decem Libri Historiarum*, edd. B. Krusch & W. Levison, *Monumenta Germaniae Historica, Scriptores Rerum Merovingicarum*, I.1 (2nd edn, Hannover, 1951); transl. L. Thorpe, *Gregory of Tours: The History of the Franks* (Harmondsworth, 1974)

HB = *Historia Brittonum*, ed. T. Mommsen, *Chronica Minora saec. IV. V. VI. VII* (3 vols, Berlin, 1891–8), III.111–222; new edition in progress, ed. D. N. Dumville (10 vols, Cambridge, 1985–)

Historia de Sancto Cuthberto, ed. T. Arnold, *Symeonis Monachi Opera Omnia* (2 vols, London, 1882/5), I.196–214

Hist. Dun. Eccles. = *Historia Dunelmensis Ecclesiae* attributed to Symeon of Durham, ed. T. Arnold, *Symeonis Monachi Opera Omnia* (2 vols, London, 1882/5), I.1–169; transl. J. Stevenson, *The Church Historians of England* (5 vols in 8, London, 1853–8), III.619–756

Historia Regum, edited in Dumville & Keynes, *The Anglo-Saxon Chronicle*, XVI (Cambridge, 1986); cf. M. Lapidge, 'Byrhtferth of Ramsey and the early sections of the *Historia Regum* attributed to Symeon of Durham', *Anglo-Saxon England* 10 (1982) 97–122

Hrotsvitha, *Gesta Ottonis*, ed. H. Homeyer, *Hrotsvit Opera* (Munich, 1970)

Laws of Hlothhere and Eadric, ed. & transl. F. L. Attenborough, *The Laws of the Earliest English Kings* (Cambridge, 1922)

Letters of K. Alhred to Bishop Lul and Ecgburh to St Boniface, ed. M. Tangl, *Die Briefe des heiligen Bonifatius* (Berlin, 1916)

Moore Memoranda regnal list, ed. P. Hunter Blair, 'The *Moore Memoranda* on Northumbrian history', in *The Early Cultures of North-west Europe (H. M. Chadwick Memorial Studies)*, edd. C. Fox & B. Dickins (Cambridge, 1950), pp. 245–57; cf. P. Hunter Blair & R. A. B. Mynors, *The Moore Bede: Cambridge University Library MS Kk.5.16*, Early English Manuscripts in Facsimile IX (Copenhagen, 1959)

Richer, *Historia*, ed. R. Latouche, *Richer: Histoire de France (888–995)* (2 vols, Paris, 1930/7)

RW = Roger Wendover, *Flores Historiarum*, ed. H. O. Coxe, *Rogeri de Wendover Chronica sive Flores Historiarum* (5 vols, London, 1841–4)

S = a charter calendared by P. H. Sawyer, *Anglo-Saxon Charters: an Annotated List and Bibliography* (London, 1968)

Stephanus, *Vita Wilfridi*, edited by Wilhelm Levison *apud* B. Krusch & W. Levison (edd.), *Monumenta Germaniae Historica, Scriptores Rerum Merovingicarum*, VI.119–263; transl. J. F. Webb & D. H. Farmer, *The Age of Bede* (Harmondsworth, 1983)

Whitby Life of Gregory the Great, ed. & transl. B. Colgrave, *The Earliest Life of Gregory the Great* (Lawrence [Kansas], 1968)

Widukind, *Res Gestae Saxonicae*, edd. P. Hirsch & H.-E. Lohmann, *Die Sachsengeschichte des Widukind von Korvei* (5th edn, Hannover, 1935)

KINGS OF BERNICIA

IDA, s. of Eoppa; **acc.** 547; **d.** 559 (ASC *F*; reigned 12 years according to Northumbrian regnal list) or 560 (ASC *E*).

Issue: Various related lists of his sons survive, the only one of pre-Conquest date being that (already much corrupted) in HB § 57. They divide his offspring between sons of his queen and sons of a concubine. The Anglian collection gives Æthelric, Eadric and Ocg as sons. HB § 57 adds, *inter alios*, Adda and Theodric, but in § 63 describes Æthelric as son of Adda (against the other sources).

GLAPPA; **acc.** 559 (reigned one year: regnal list; but om. HB §§ 62–63).

ADDA, ? s. of Ida; **acc.** 560 (reigned 8 years: regnal list).

ÆTHELRIC, s. of Ida; **acc.** 568 (reigned 4 years: Moore Mem. regnal list and HB § 63; Anglian coll. regnal list gives corrupt figure of 7 years).
Issue: K. Æthelfrith *q.v.*; Theodbald (Bede, *H.E.* I.34).

THEODRIC, ? s. of Ida; **acc.** 572 (reigned 7 years: regnal list).

FRITHUWALD; **acc.** 579 (reigned 6 years: Moore Mem. regnal list and HB § 63; Anglian coll. regnal list gives corrupt figure of 7 years).

HUSSA; **acc.** 585 (reigned 7 years: regnal list).
Issue: Hering (ASC 603 *E*).

ÆTHELFRITH, s. of K. Æthelric (Anglian collection; ASC *E*) *q.v.*; **acc.** 592 or 593 (593 in ASC; Bede, *H.E.* I.34, terms 603 Æthelfrith's 11th year). Gained control of Deira; **d.** 616.
m. (1) Bebba (HB § 63; Bede, *H.E.* III.6 and 16, mentions Northumbrian q. named Bebba without stating whose w. she was); (2) Acha da. of K. Ælle of Deira *q.v.*

4

Issue: K. Eanfrith *q.v.*; by Acha—K. Oswald *q.v.*; K. Oswiu *q.v.*; Oslac; Oswudu; Oslaf; Offa (the foregoing is the order in ASC 617 *E*). St Æbbe, abbess of Coldingham, is described by Bede (Life of St Cuthbert, § 10) as *uterina soror* of K. Oswiu (and *amita* of K. Ecgfrith: *H.E.* IV.19 [17]) which suggests that she was da. of Acha by another husband.

(EDWIN k. of Deira ruled both Bernicia and Deira 616–33.)

EANFRITH, s. of K. Æthelfrith; **acc**. late 633 or early 634; **d**. 634.
  m. ? member of Pictish royal house (*see* M. Miller, *Northern History*, 14, 1978, 47–66)
  Issue: Talorgan k. of Picts, d. 657.

OSWALD (SAINT), s. of K. Æthelfrith and Acha; **b**. 604; **acc**. 634; 6th overlord of S. English in Bede's list (*H.E.* II.5); **d**. 5 Aug. 642.
  m. da. of Cynegils, k. of W. Saxons.
  Issue: K. Oethelwald of Deira *q.v.*

OSWIU, s. of K. Æthelfrith and Acha; **b**. 612 (58 in 670, Bede, *H.E.* IV.5); **acc**. 16 Nov. × 31 Dec. 642 (10 Oct. 644 fell in his 2nd year). United Bernicia and Deira 655?–70. 7th overlord of S. English (in Bede's list, *H.E.* II.5), 655–58, during which period he annexed Mercia to Northumbria; **d**. 15 Feb. 670.
  m. (1) Rhiainfellt da. of Rhwyth, s. of Rhun (HB § 57); (2) Eanflæd da. of K. Edwin and Æthelberg.
  Issue: prob. not by Eanflæd—Alhfrith sub-k. in Deira *c*. 655–64; Alhflæd m. (*c*. 653) Peada s. of Penda, k. of Mercians; by Eanflæd (prob.)—K. Ecgfrith *q.v.* (possibly sub-k. in Deira *c*. 664–70); Ælfwine b. *c*. 661 (prob. sub-k. in Deira from some date aft. 664 to 679, called *rex* by Bede and Stephanus, *Vita Wilfridi*), d. 679; Osthryth m. *c*. 679 Æthelred, k. of Mercians, and d. 697; Ælfflæd b. 654, nun, d. 713 or 714. Illegitimate—K. Aldfrith *q.v.*

For the kings of Bernicia 670–867, *see* under Kings of Northumbria. When York was seized by the Scandinavians in 867 and two Northumbrian kings killed, Bernicia (or part thereof) remained under native rulers.

ECGBERHT I, **acc**. 867 (set up by Danes as puppet-k. and given rule over region N. of Tyne (*Historia Regum*); **d**. 873 (*Historia Regum*). Driven out 872 and **d**. 873 according to RW.

RICSIGE, **acc**. 873 (*Historia Regum* and RW); **d**. 876 (*Historia Regum an*. 876 and *an*. 873 where he is said to have reigned 3 years; so too RW *an*. 873 mentions reign of 3 years).
  Issue: ? Eadred *filius Rixinci* (*Hist. de Sancto Cuthberto*, § 24, records that *Edred filius Rixinci* killed *princeps Eardulfus*, perhaps the Eadwulf mentioned below—identity of this Eadred's father uncertain).

ECGBERHT II, **acc**. 876 (*Historia Regum* and RW); **d**. ? 878. Ecgberht ruled region N. of Tyne (*Historia Regum*).

EADWULF, **acc**. ? 878 or later; **d**. 913 (Annals of Ulster; cf. Æthelweard). *Hist. de Sancto Cuthberto*, § 22, describes him as *dilectus* of K. Alfred of Wessex.
  Issue: K. Aldred *q.v.*; Uhtred (*Hist. de Sancto Cuthberto*, § 22).

ALDRED, acc. 913; **d**. ? Still reigning in 927 (ASC *D, an.* 926) when he submitted to K. Æthelstan of Wessex, *q.v.*, first k. of England. *Hist. de Sancto Cuthberto*, § 22, describes him as *dilectus* of K. Edward of Wessex to whom he submitted in 920 (ASC, *A*). Expelled into Scotland by K. Ragnall II of York (*see* Kings of Deira), 913/14 and 918–20.

KINGS OF DEIRA

The most recent account of the native kings is that of M. Miller, *Anglo-Saxon England*, 8, 1979, 35–61. For the Scandinavian rulers see A. P. Smyth, *Scandinavian York and Dublin*, 2 vols, Dublin, 1975/79.

ÆLLE, s. of Yffi; **acc.** 560 (ASC *A, B, E*); Whitby Life of Gregory the Great proves that Ælle was reigning at least as early as 574 x 578; **d**. 588 (ASC) or 590 (reigned 30 years, ASC).
Issue: K. Edwin *q.v.*; Acha m. K. Æthelfrith of Bernicia *q.v.*; s. or da. who was parent of Hereric, father of Hild, abbess of Whitby.

(Deira ruled by k. of Bernicia *c*. 588 or later to 616.)

EDWIN, s. of K. Ælle; b. 584 (48 in 632, Bede, *H.E.* II.20); **acc.** 616 (617 in ASC, but Bede states—*H.E.* II.14—that 627 was his 11th year and that—*H.E.* II.20—he had reigned 17 years in 633, which indicates accession in summer of 616; he may have reigned for a short time between d. of K. Ælle and his expulsion by k. of Bernicia). Ruler of both Deira and Bernicia and 5th overlord of S. English in Bede's list (*H.E.* II. 5); **d**. 12 Oct. 633.
m. (1) Cwenburh da. of Cearl, k. of Mercians (so Bede, *H.E.* II.14); (2) 625, Æthelberg called Tate da. of Æthelberht I, k. of Kent.
Issue: (1) by Cwenburh—Osfrith b. bef. 616, d. 633; Eadfrith b. bef. 616, d. 634 × 642; (2) by Æthelberg—Eanflæd b. 626, m. K. Oswiu of Bernicia *q.v.*; Æthelhun d. bef. 633; Æthelthryth d. bef. 633; Wuscfrea (taken to Gaul with Yffi s. of Osfrith, *c*. 634).

OSRIC, s. of Ælfric (who was paternal uncle of K. Edwin, viz br. of K. Ælle); **acc.** late 633; **d**. summer 634 (Bede, *H.E.* III.1).
Issue: K. Oswine *q.v.*

(OSWALD united Deira with Bernicia 634–42.)

OSWINE, s. of K. Osric; **acc.** 644 (deduced from Bede *H.E.* III.14; 643 ASC); **d**. 20 Aug. 651.

OETHELWALD, s. of K. Oswald (Bede, *H.E.*, III.14, 23, 24); **acc.** presumably 651; **d**. uncertain; lost kingdom in or aft. Nov. 655 (prob. through failure to support K. Oswiu at battle of the Winwaed).

(K. Oswiu of Bernicia annexed Deira in or aft. 655, and any later *reges* in Deira are junior dynasts of the Bernician rulers of Northumbria.)

In 867 York was seized by a Scandinavian force and two native kings killed in the process. Thereafter Deira becomes the Scandinavian kingdom of York while Bernicia (in part at least) remained under the rule of local kings.

HÁLFDAN I, br. of Ívarr (d. 873); responsible for Scandinavian Northumbrian interests from late 872 (ASC 873); founded kingdom at

York for himself in 875/6; expelled from Northumbria 877 and killed at Strangford Lough in Ireland (according to Irish annals).

GUTHFRITH I, s. of Harthacnut (*Historia Regum*); **acc**. 883; **d**. 24 Aug. 895 (894 according to *Historia Regum*, but Æthelweard gives 24 Aug. 896).

SIGFRID, for whom coins struck at York; **acc**. 895.

KNÚTR, for whom coins struck at York, 'either in conjunction with that of [K. Sigfrid], or in succession to it'.

ÆTHELWALD, s. of Æthelred k. of W. Saxons, driven out of Wessex by his cousin K. Edward the Elder 899/900 and took refuge with the Scandinavians of Northumbria who received him as k.; seems to have left Northumbria for E. Anglia soon aft., and was killed at battle of the Holme (? 903).

HÁLFDAN II. Possibly became k. *c*. 902; killed at Tettenhall 910.

EOWILS. Apparently joint-k. with Hálfdan II; **d**. 910 (battle of Tettenhall).

RAGNALL I, gds. of Ívarr the Boneless. Invaded Northumbria *c*. 911; acknowledged overlordship of K. Edward of Wessex in 920; **d**. 920.

SIGTRYGGR (SIHTRIC) CAECH, gds. of Ívarr the Boneless; **acc**. 921; **d**. 927.
m. (1) name unknown; (2) 30 Jan. 926 sis. of K. Æthelstan of Wessex *q.v.* (ASC 925 *D*).
Issue (by 1): Óláfr Sigtryggsson *q.v.*

GUTHFRITH II, br. of Sigtryggr Caech; **acc**. 927; **d**. 934. Expelled by K. Æthelstan 927 and kingdom of York ruled directly by Æthelstan 927–39.
Issue: Óláfr Guthfrithsson *q.v.*

ÓLÁFR (ANLAF) I GUTHFRITHSSON, s. of K. Guthfrith II; **acc**. late 939 (aft. d. of K. Æthelstan); **d**. 941 (in possession of territory N. of Watling St. ceded by K. Edmund).

ÓLÁFR (ANLAF) II SIGTRYGGSSON (Cuarán), s. of Sigtryggr Caech; **acc**. 941. Early 943 acknowledged overlordship of K. Edmund I who had recovered Five Boroughs from him in 942. Expelled by Danes of York summer 943, baptised at court of Edmund, k. of England; in 944 he and his cousin Ragnall Guthfrithsson were driven from York; returned to Dublin 945 but again established himself at York ? 950; expelled again 952 and returned to Ireland where he ruled as k. of Dublin until 981.

RAGNALL II GUTHFRITHSSON, br. of K. Óláfr Guthfrithsson; **acc**. summer 943; expelled 944 (had acknowledged overlordship of K. Edmund 943, and in 944 Edmund drove out both Ragnall and Óláfr Sigtryggsson. Northumbria under direct rule of K. Edmund 944–46 and of K. Eadred 946–47).

ERIC (EIRÍKR) BLOODAXE, established himself as k. 947; driven out 948 but received back aft. expulsion of Óláfr Sigtryggsson 952; finally expelled 954 and killed in same year at Stainmore. With expulsion of Eric, line of Scandinavian ks at York ended. K. Eadred direct ruler of Northumbria 954–55 and successors likewise.

KINGS OF THE EAST ANGLES

The first E. Anglian k. mentioned by Bede is Rædwald. Bede states that Rædwald was the s. of Tytili and he the s. of Wuffa from whom the members of the E. Anglian royal house were called Wuffingas. RW reckons Tytili and Wuffa as ks, assigning acc. of Wuffa to 571 and that of Tytili to 578, but the origin of these annals is unknown. In the genealogy of K. Ælfwald (Anglian coll.) Tyttla is the s. of Wuffa whose father Wehha and other ancestors are given. In HB § 59 they appear as Tydil s. of Guffa s. of Guecha, and Guecha (viz Wehha) is here described as first E. Anglian k. It is possible that Tytili, Wuffa and Wehha were rulers of E. Anglia.

RÆDWALD, s. of Tyttla s. of Wuffa; **acc.** unknown—late sixth or early seventh century. 4th overlord of S. English in Bede's list (*H.E.* II.5); **d.** between 616 and 627.
Issue: Rægenhere d. 616; K. Earpwald *q.v.*

EARPWALD, s. of K. Rædwald; **acc.** between 616 and 627; **d.** 627 or 628. After his d. E. Anglia relapsed into heathenism for 3 years, during which period there may have been a heathen k. whose name is unrecorded.

SIGEBERHT. Parentage uncertain—he was half-br. of K. Earpwald (same mother); **acc.** 630 or 631; **d.** uncertain. Abdicated and retired to monastery; subsequently taken therefrom to assist K. Ecgric against Penda k. of Mercians and was killed in battle of uncertain date.

ECGRIC. Parentage unknown—kinsman of K. Sigeberht; **acc.** uncertain— joint-k. during part or whole of reign of Sigeberht (Bede, *H.E.* III. 18); **d.** at uncertain date fighting against Penda, k. of Mercians.

ANNA, s. of Eni, br. of K. Rædwald; **acc.** uncertain; **d.** 654.
Issue: Sexburh m. Earconberht k. of Kent; Æthelthryth m. (1) Tondberht ealdorman of the S. Gyrwe, (2) Ecgfrith k. of Northumbria; Æthelburh abbess of Faremoûtier-en-Brie; Wihtburh nun at Ely, d. 743 (ASC *F sub an.* 798—she is not mentioned by Bede). Sæthryth abbess of Faremoûtier-en-Brie was his step-da. His w.'s name is unrecorded.

ÆTHELHERE, s. of Eni br. of K. Rædwald (Æthelhere was br. of K. Anna); **acc.** 654; **d.** 15 Nov. 655 (killed at the Winwaed fighting in Penda's army).
m. Hereswith sis. of Hild abbess of Whitby.
Issue: K. Aldwulf *q.v.*

ÆTHELWALD, s. of Eni br. of K. Rædwald (Æthelwald was br. of K. Anna); **acc.** late 655; **d.** ? 664.

ALDWULF, s. of Hereswith, sis. of Hild abbess of Whitby and ? K. Æthelhere (Bede, *H.E.* IV. 23 [21], states that he was the s. of Hereswith who m. K. Æthelhere but does not say that this k. was his father; the oldest authority apart from Bede, the Anglian collection of genealogies, gives Æthelric s. of Eni as his father—this Æthelric would be br. of Anna and Æthelhere, but Hereswith can hardly have taken a 2nd husband for she retired from the world bef. 650 if not bef. 647, viz bef. her husband's d. Æthelric of the Anglian collection is perhaps therefore an error for Æthelhere); **acc.** 663 or 664 (council of Hatfield Sept. 679 held in his 17th year); **d**. 713 (Continental annals; from *H.E.* II.15 it is clear that he was living in Bede's time and that he was dead bef. the *H.E.* was written).

Issue: Ecgburh, abbess (Felix, *Life of St Guthlac*, §48); K. Ælfwald *q.v.*; Elric in HB § 59 seems to be an error.

ÆLFWALD, s. of K. Aldwulf *q.v.*; **acc**. 713 (prob.); **d**. 749 (*Historia Regum*).

HUN, BEONNA and ALBERHT divided the kingdom between them in 749 (*Historia Regum* only, whose annal erroneously reads 'Hunbeanna and Alberht'). For coin of Beonna *see Catalogue of Coins in B.M.*, i, p. 83.

ÆTHELBERHT (origin unknown); executed at command of Offa k. of Mercians in 794 (ASC, Ann. St Neots).

? ÆTHELSTAN, *c*. 825.

? ÆTHELWEARD, *c*. 850.
Literary sources do not record the name of any k. of E. Angles between Æthelberht and Edmund. Coins supply the names of at least two. Æthelstan's coins suggest that he was the contemporary of the Mercian ks Ceolwulf and Beornwulf; he may be the E. Anglian k. whose revolt against Mercia is recorded in 825 (ASC). Æthelweard seems to have been reigning in the time of Æthelwulf k. of W. Saxons.

EDMUND, b. 840 or 841 (14 at accession and 29 at d.); **acc**. 855 (Ann. St Neots); **d**. 20 Nov. 869.

GUTHRUM (assumed name Æthelstan on baptism, 878), first Scandinavian king of E. Anglia. E. Anglia settled by the Danes under Guthrum in 879/80 following the Treaty of Wedmore, but apparently ruled directly by the Scandinavians since Edmund's death. **d**. 889/90 (ASC, Ann. St Neots and *Historia Regum, an*. 890), buried at Hadleigh, Suffolk (Ann. St Neots).

The succession to Guthrum is not clear. Various Scandinavian rulers are mentioned in events which took place in the E. Midlands in the years 890–920, but none of them can be confidently stated to have succeeded to Guthrum's position. K. Edward of Wessex conquered E. Anglia in 917 (ASC, *A*).

KINGS OF THE EAST SAXONS

The names of the heathen ks of the E. Saxons are unknown. Sæberht is the earliest k. mentioned by Bede and ASC. Sledd father of Sæberht, Æscwine father of Sledd, and Offa father of Æscwine occur in the pedigrees in BL MS. Add. 23211 (in which the ancestry of the E. Saxon ks is traced back to Seaxnet) but this by no means necessarily indicates that they were ks.

SÆBERHT, s. of Sledd and Ricula sis. of Æthelberht I k. of Kent (Bede, *H.E.* II.3); **acc**. unknown (bef. 604); **d**. 616 or 617.

Issue: three s. (Bede, *H.E.* II.5, not mentioning names): Ks Seaxred and Sæweard (pedigrees in BL MS. Add. 23211, fo 1v) *q.v.*; name of 3rd s. unknown.

SEAXRED and SÆWEARD; s. of K. Sæberht. Joint-ks with another brother, **acc**. 616 or 617; **d**. ? *c*. 617 (killed fighting W. Saxons soon aft. accession: Bede, *H.E.* II.5).

Issue: Only recorded s. of Sæweard was K. Sigeberht 'Paruus' *q.v.* K. Sebbi *q.v.* was s. of a Seaxred, but perhaps not this one.

SIGEBERHT I 'PARUUS' (Bede, *H.E.* III.22), s. of K. Sæweard (BL MS. Add. 23211, fo 1v); **acc**. ? 617; **d**. unknown (bef. *c*. 653).

Issue: K. Sigehere *q.v.*

SIGEBERHT II, s. of Sigebald (BL MS. Add. 23211, fo 1v); **acc**. uncertain, *c*. 653; **d**. between 653 and 664. For his career *see* Bede, *H.E.* III.22.

Issue: K. Selered *q.v.*

SWITHHELM, s. of Seaxbald (Bede, *H.E.* III.22); **acc**. between 653 and 664; **d**. between 653 and 664. Baptised at Rendlesham (Suffolk), with Æthelwald, k. of E. Angles, as godfather.

SIGEHERE, s. of K. Sigeberht I; **acc**. *c*. 664 (reigning jointly with Sebbi in 664—Bede, *H.E.* III.30); **d**. unknown (predeceased Sebbi—this seems to be implied by Bede; RW, upon what authority unknown, assigns his d. to 683; both ks were reigning when Earconwald became bp of London, 675).

Issue: K. Offa *q.v.*

SEBBI, s. of Seaxred (BL MS. Add. 23211, fo 1v); **acc**. *c*. 664 (reigning jointly with Sigehere in 664); sole k. from d. of Sigehere; **d**. *c*. 694; resigned between 692 and 694 (reigned 30 years and abdicated aft. d. of Bp Earconwald). His sons, Sigeheard and Swæfred, may have reigned jointly with him (S 1171, dated 685 × 694).

Issue: K. Sigeheard and K. Swæfred (Bede, *H.E.* IV.11) *qq. vv.*; Swæfhard k. of Kent *q.v.* appears to have been his son.

SIGEHEARD, s. of K. Sebbi; **acc**. *c*. 694 joint-k. with Swæfred his br.; **d**. uncertain (bef. 709).

Issue: Sigemund father of K. Swithred (BL MS. Add. 23211, fo 1v) *q.v.*

SWÆFRED, s. of K. Sebbi; **acc**. *c*. 694 joint-k. with Sigeheard his br.; **d**. uncertain (bef. 709).

OFFA, s. of K. Sigehere (Bede, *H.E.* V.19); **acc**. between 694 and 709; **d**. in or aft. 709 when he abdicated and went to Rome (Bede, in 4th year of reign of Osred of Northumbria, viz 708/9; ASC all versions except *C* 709; *C* 708).

m. unknown.

SWÆFBERHT (Swebriht); **acc**. ? *c*. 709; **d**. 738 (*Historia Regum*).

SELERED, s. of K. Sigeberht II (BL MS. Add. 23211, fo 1v).; **acc**. ? 738; **d**. 746 (ASC).

Issue: K. Sigeric *q.v.*

SWITHRED, s. of Sigemund descendant of K. Sebbi (BL MS. Add. 23211, fo 1v); **acc**. *c*. 746; **d**. unknown.

SIGERIC, s. of K. Selered (BL MS. Add. 23211, fo 1v); **acc**. unknown; **d**. unknown; ? abdicated when he went to Rome 798 (ASC *F*).

Issue: K. Sigered *q.v.*

SIGERED, s. of K. Sigeric (BL MS. Add. 23211, fo 1v); **acc.** ? 798; **d**. aft. 823 (styled in some charters *rex*; attests as *subregulus* diploma of Ceolwulf k. of Mercia S 187, dated 823, which is also attested by Sigered *dux* and proves that this personage who attests as late as 825 is not necessarily the E. Saxon k.; may have been ruling in 825 when E. Saxons submitted to Ecgberht, k. of W. Saxons; RW records expulsion by Ecgberht of E. Saxon k. whom he calls Swithred *sub an.* 828—*recte* 827 since death of Ludeca, k. of Mercians, occurs in same annal—perhaps in error for Sigered).

KINGS OF THE HWICCE

EANHERE (and his brother EANFRITH ?): Eanfrith's da. *Eabae* (Eafe) m. Æthelwald, k. of Sussex (? × 674–680 × 685) *q.v.* (Bede, *H.E.* IV.13).

OSRIC, **acc.** by 675/6 (S 51); still k. during the (? closing years of the) episcopate of Bosel (Bede, *H.E.* IV.23 [21]), A.D. 680 × 691.
Issue: according to the spurious Evesham charter S 1174, dated 706, a son Ailric (viz Æthelric). In this period one Æthelmod is found issuing a charter (S 1167, A.D. 681), but nothing further is known of him.

OSHERE, **acc.** by 693 (issued S 52, undated but A.D. 678 × 693, and S 53 dated 693); **d.** before 716 (letter of Ecgburh to St Boniface: ed. Tangl, pp. 18–21).
Issue: K. Æthelric *q.v.*

ÆTHELHEARD and ÆTHELWEARD, ruling in 704 × 709 (S 1177); both attest, without title, S 75 (A.D. 692). Æthelweard is the donor of the spurious Evesham charter S 54 (A.D. 706), and an Æthelweard is found attesting S 102 (A.D. 716/17).

ÆTHELRIC, s. of K. Oshere *q.v.*, ruling in 736 (S 89) and in 723 × 737 (S 94). An Osred 'de . . . prosapia regali gentis Huicciorum' is the beneficiary of S 99, A.D. 737 × 740.

EANBERHT, joint-ruler with K. Uhtred *q.v.* and K. Aldred *q.v.*; **acc.** before 757 (S 55); **d.** after 759 (S 56).

UHTRED, joint-ruler with Ks Eanberht and Aldred in 757 and 759 (S 55–56) and with K. Aldred in 757 × 775 (S 63 where Aldred is named first). Appears alone as donor in five charters (S 57–61, but S 60 and 61 are spurious) dated 767 (S 58), 770 (S 59), and 777 × 779 (S 57). Survived by Aldred.

ALDRED, joint-ruler with Ks Eanberht and Uhtred in 757 and 759 (S 55–56) and with K. Uhtred *q.v.* in 757 × 775 (S 63). Appears alone in varying capacities in five diplomas (S 62, 113, the spurious 126, 141, 147) of which only S 113 (A.D. 778) and the spurious S 126 (A.D. 789/90) are precisely datable. A possible, but by no means necessary, interpretation is that Uhtred excluded Aldred from power at a date between 759 and 767, but that Aldred became king in 777/8, perhaps on the death of Uhtred; however, joint-rule may have continued throughout this period.

In the period 793 × 796 (S 146, 148) – 802 (ASC) we meet one Æthelmund as ealdorman of the Hwicce; his relationship to the royal line is unknown.

We meet his son Æthelric in S 1187 (A.D. 804). The name-forms permit, but do not confirm, a conjecture that they were of that line but deprived of royal status.

KINGS OF THE ISLE OF WIGHT

To the extent that Wight and the opposite portion of the mainland were, according to Bede (*H.E.* I.15), inhabited by a Jutish people (Wihtware and Meanware) distinct from the neighbouring West Saxons, it is no surprise to discover evidence for a separate kingship. But this is only attested (and may have come to an end) in the reign of King Arwald when Cædwalla, k. of the West Saxons 685–688, seized his territory (Bede, *H.E.* IV.16 [14]). This kingdom had previously been under the overlordship of Wulfhere, k. of the Mercians (*q.v.*), who had granted his direct overlordship to another dependant, Æthelwalh, k. of the South Saxons (*q.v.*): for all this see Bede, *H.E.* IV.13.

KINGS OF KENT

The most recent accounts are those of K. P. Witney, *The Kingdom of Kent* (Chichester, 1982), and Nicholas Brooks, *The Early History of the Church of Canterbury* (Leicester, 1984).

HENCGEST, s. of Uictgils (Wihtgils) s. of Uitta (Bede, *H.E.* I.15, but according to the Anglian collection Uitta s. of Uihtgils); **acc.** *c.* 455 (Bede dates coming of Hencgest and Horsa his br. between 449 and 456; ASC records Horsa's d. 455 and states that Hencgest and his s. then 'succeeded to the kingdom'); **d.** ? 488.
Issue: Oeric surnamed Oisc (or Ohta, *see below*).

OERIC SURNAMED OISC (Æsc is later form), s. of Hencgest (so Bede, *H.E.* II.5, but Anglian coll. and HB §§ 38, 56 and 58 make him s. of Ohta/Ocga and gds. of Hencgest); **acc.** 488 (ASC); **d.** ? 512 (reigned 24 years, ASC).
Issue: Ohta (except in authorities where order of those personages is inverted; in these Eormenric is s. of Oisc).

EORMENRIC, s. of Ohta (or Oisc, *see above*); **acc.** ? 512 (or much later, after a lost intervening reign, ? of Ohta); **d.** *c.* 560.
Issue: K. Æthelberht I *q.v.*; Ricula m. Sledda father of Sæberht, k. of E. Saxons.
Eormenric's kingship is vouched for (but only obliquely) by Gregory of Tours, IX.26.

ÆTHELBERHT I, s. of K. Eormenric, b. unknown (522 according to ASC, *F* only, but if so he succeeded at the age of 8 which is very improbable); **acc.** 560 (so Bede, *H.E.* II.5; 565 according to ASC, which must be in error). 3rd overlord of S. English in Bede's list (*H.E.* II.5); **d.** 24 Feb. 616.
m. (1) bef. 597, Bertha da. of Charibert, Merovingian k. at Paris, and Q. Ingoberg (Gregory of Tours, IV.26 and IX.26); (2) ? a 2nd w. who survived him and m. K. Eadbald.
Issue: K. Eadbald *q.v.*; Æthelberg m. 625 Edwin, k. of Northumbria *q.v.*

EADBALD, s. of K. Æthelberht and ? Bertha; **acc.** 616; **d.** 20 Jan. 640.
m. (1) his father's wid. (presumably not Bertha); according to post-Conquest sources, (2) Emma da. of a Frankish k.
Issue: K. Earconberht *q.v.*; ? Eormenred *regulus* m. Oslava (not mentioned by Bede; occurs in ASC *F* and other post-Conquest works).

EARCONBERHT, s. of K. Eadbald (Bede, *H.E.* III.8); **acc.** 640; **d.** 14 July 664.
m. Sexburh da. of Anna, k. of E. Angles *q.v.*
Issue: K. Ecgberht I *q.v.*; K. Hlothhere *q.v.*; Earcongota, a nun at Faremoûtier-en-Brie (Bede, *H.E.* III.8).

ECGBERHT I, s. of K. Earconberht; **acc.** 664; **d.** 4 July 673.
Issue: K. Eadric *q.v.*; K. Wihtred *q.v.*

HLOTHHERE, s. of K. Earconberht; **acc.** July 673; **d.** 6 Feb. 685 (Bede, *H.E.* IV.26[24]; 7 Feb. 685, Frankish 'Annals of Lindisfarne and Canterbury'). K. Eadric his nephew *q.v.* possibly associated with him some time during the reign (Laws), and K. Swæfhard *q.v.* certainly joint-k. with him.

EADRIC, s. of K. Ecgberht I; **acc.** 685; **d.** ? Aug. 686 (Bede, *H.E.* IV.26[24], says he reigned one year and a half; issued diploma S 9 in June 686; **d.** 31 Aug. 687 according to Frankish 'Annals of Lindisfarne and Canterbury').

SWÆFHARD, s. of Sebbi, ? k. of E. Saxons *q.v.*; **acc.** unknown (reigning 1 Mar. 690, S 10, presumably joint-k. with Hlothhere); **d.** unknown (reigning jointly with Wihtred in July 692: Bede, *H.E.* V.8).

OSWINE. Known only from charters. Reigning 689 and 690 (S 12 dated 689, S 14 undated but probably *c.* 690, S 13 prob. belonging not to 675 but to 690). He was no doubt one of the *reges dubii uel externi* who (Bede says, *H.E.* IV.26[24]) held the kingdom aft. Hlothhere's d. **Acc.** prob. 688 since S 13, which seems to belong to 17 Jan. 690, was issued in his 2nd year.

WIHTRED, s. of K. Ecgberht I; **acc.** autumn 690 (since Bede, *H.E.* V.23, stated that he reigned 34½ years) but not sole k. until 692 at earliest (Swæfhard *q.v.* reigning jointly with him in this year). ASC dates accession 694 and states that he reigned 33 years; earliest diploma, S 15, is dated 17 July 694 in 3rd year of his reign; **d.** 23 Apr. 725 (Bede, *H.E.* V.23).
m. (1) Cynegyth occurs in S 15; (2) Æthelburh occurs in S 16 (Mar. 696), S 18 (Apr. 697), S 19 (July 697), S 21 (700 or 715); (3) Werburh, S 22, issued 696 × 716.
Issue: K. Æthelberht II, K. Eadberht and K. Alric (Bede, *H.E.* V.23), *qq.vv.* S 22 may suggest that Alric only was s. of Werburh.

ÆTHELBERHT II, s. of K. Wihtred; **acc.** 725. Bede's language (*H.E.* V.23) might suggest that Wihtred's 3 s. succeeded him as joint-ks. Æthelberht and Eadberht his br. *q.v.* were probably joint-rulers 725–62, but there were other contemporary ks, Eardwulf *q.v.* and Sigered *q.v.* Æthelberht's earliest diploma is dated 20 Feb. 732 (S 23); Æthelberht and Eadberht were both reigning in Apr. 738 (S 27) and in 741 (Æthelberht's charter S 24 belonging to 741 [for 750?] and Eadberht's, S 1611, of 741). There were at least three ks in Kent 747–48: S 1612 dated 747 is a charter of Eadberht who attested S 91 in May 748; S 30 belonging to 747 (but dated 762) shows that Æthelberht II and a k. named Eardwulf, possibly his nephew, reigned contemporaneously. Æthelberht's last charter, S 25, is dated 762. The eleventh-century Canterbury insertion in ASC *A* stating that Æthelberht s. of Wihtred succeeded Eadberht, alleged to have died in 748, is contrary to the evidence of Bede and charters; **d**. 762 (ASC).

EADBERHT, s. of K. Wihtred (called Eadberht *cognomento Eating* in S 1611, but this is prob. interpolation by an eleventh-century Canterbury scribe familiar with the name of the Northumbrian k., Eadberht s. of Eata, his contemporary); **acc**. 725; reigning contemporaneously with br. Æthelberht until at least 748 (*see above*); **d**. 748 according to ASC but charters suggest that he reigned until 762 (S 32) if not longer. There seems to be little doubt that K. Eadberht grantor of S 28 and S 29 is identical with the k. who was reigning 725–48, for in S 28, and prob. also S 29, 761 is reckoned as his 36th year.
Issue: ? K. Eardwulf *q.v.*

EARDWULF. Not mentioned by chroniclers; reigning contemporaneously with Æthelberht II 747 (*see above*). In S 31 (undated, assigned by Sawyer to *c*. 767), he speaks of his father Eadberht who may be K. Eadberht *q.v.*

SIGERED. Not mentioned by chroniclers among ks of Kent. Grantor of S 32 dated 762 (attested by K. Eadberht) and S 33 (issued in 761 × 765) where he describes himself as *rex dimidiae partis prouinciae Cantuariorum*.

EANMUND. Confirms K. Sigered's grant, S 33.

HEABERHT. Described as *rex Cantiae* in charter of Offa k. of Mercia dated 764 (S 105); confirms charter of Ecgberht II dated 765 (S 34) and witnesses another grant of that k. belonging to 765 × 785 (S 37).

ECGBERHT II. Reigned *c*. 765–*c*. 780 or later. Grantor of S 34 dated 765, S 35 dated 778, S 36 dated 779 and S 37 belonging to 765 × 785; mentioned as having been dependant of Offa k. of Mercia in S 155, dated 799, by which date he was dead.

EALHMUND. Reigning 784 (S 38 which seems to be abbreviation of genuine charter, and ASC *F*, probably dependent on a version of S 38). Identified in ASC *F* with Ealhmund father of Ecgberht, k. of W. Saxons (*q.v.*); if so, his father was Eafa.

EADBERHT (Præn). **Acc**. 796 (ASC), deposed and mutilated by Cenwulf, k. of Mercia, 798. This brief reign represents an unsuccessful attempt of the Kentishmen to end Mercian rule over the kingdom. Most of the Kentish ks reigning after Wihtred were the dependants of Æthelbald and Offa, ks of Mercia. In the *Historia Regum* (*an*. 798) it is stated that Cenwulf himself assumed kingship of Kent and he is found disposing (as Offa had done) of properties in Kent without reference to a local k. Ceolwulf in S 186 (original of 822) uses style *rex Merciorum uel etiam Contwariorum* and in S 187 (original of 823) *rex Merciorum seu etiam Cantwariorum*.

CUTHRED, s. of Cuthbert, member of Mercian royal house. (He is described as br. of Cenwulf, k. of Mercia, in S 157 dated 801 and in S 160 dated 804, both of which appear to be genuine); **acc**. 798 (that Aug. 805 fell in Cuthred's 8th year is stated in S 40 which proves that accession belongs to 798); **d**. 807 (ASC).
Issue: Cenwald (attests S 39, dated 805).

BALDRED, of whom nothing is known save that he was expelled from Kent by Ecgberht, k. of W. Saxons, in 825 x 827 (ASC and RW); coins of his have survived but no charters. After the W. Saxon conquest, Kent together with Essex and Sussex normally formed in the ninth century an appanage for the heir to W. Saxon throne (*see* ks of Wessex).

KINGS OF LINDSEY

Although there is no reference to a line of ks ruling Lindsey in the writings of Bede, the genealogy of the ks of Lindsey who traced their descent from Woden has been preserved in the Anglian collection. It has been shown that Aldfrith with whom the genealogy terminates is prob. identical with *Ealdfrith rex* who between 786 and 796 attested Offa's confirmation of a grant by Aldwulf *dux Suth Saxonum*, S 1183. The ancestors of Aldfrith can be dated roughly but it is not known whether any of them were rulers of Lindsey, which kingdom was normally subject to either Mercia or Northumbria.

KINGS OF THE MAGONSÆTON

This people and its kingdom are scarcely visible in Anglo-Saxon sources. The diocese of Hereford seems to have been established (in 676) to serve the Magonsæton. To Bede (*H.E.* V.23) they are 'eis populis qui ultra amnem Sabrinam ad occidentem habitant'. The only king of this people to appear in an early Anglo-Saxon source is Milfrith, with his queen Cwenburh, who is named as *regulus* in a metrical epitaph composed for a common tomb of six local notables by Cuthbert, bishop of Hereford 736–740: see M. Lapidge, 'Some remnants of Bede's lost Liber Epigrammatum', *English Historical Review* 90 (1975) 798–820 (no. 21). A more elaborate account of the rulers of the Magonsæton, using substantially later sources, has been given by H. P. R. Finberg, *The Early Charters of the West Midlands* (2nd edn, Leicester, 1972), pp. 217–24.

KINGS OF MERCIA

The earliest k. of the Mercians mentioned by Bede (*H.E.* II.14) is Cearl, whose da. Cwenburh m. Edwin, future k. of Northumbria, when he was in exile (bef. 616). Cearl therefore was reigning in the early seventh century. In the genealogies, Penda, whose relationship (if any) to Cearl is unknown, is the s. of Pybba and gds. of Creoda whose ancestry is traced through Offa and Wærmund to Woden. It remains uncertain whether either Pybba or Creoda was ever k. of the Mercians.

PENDA, s. of Pybba; b. ? 575 (stated to have been 50 years of age at accession, assigned to 626 in ASC, but Bede, *H.E.* II.20, uses language which suggests that he was not k. when he assisted K. Cadwallon of Gwynedd in the war against Edwin in 633—*praebente illi Penda uiro strenuissimo de regio genere Merciorum*; if Penda was 50 in 632 his birth would fall in 582); acc. ? 626 (ASC, but *see above*) or more prob. late 632 as suggested by Bede's language. (Penda's br. Eowa, killed 642, is called *rex Merciorum* in HB § 65; he may have been sub-k.); d. 15 Nov. 655.

m. Cynewise (Bede, *H.E.* III.24, if correctly interpreted).

Issue: Peada, made *princeps* of the Middle Angles by Penda, m. Alhflæd da. of Oswiu, k. of Bernicia, converted to Christianity and Middle Angles with him 653, held kingdom of S. Mercians under Oswiu 655/6, murdered Apr. 656; K. Wulfhere *q.v.*; K. Æthelred *q.v.*; Cyneburh m. Alhfrith s. of K. Oswiu.

[For 3 years aft. overthrow of Penda, Oswiu k. of Northumbria ruled Mercian kingdom, viz 655–8.]

WULFHERE, s. of Penda; **acc.** 658; **d.** 675.
Issue: K. Cenred *q.v.*

ÆTHELRED, s. of Penda; **acc.** 675; **d.** 716 ?; abdicated 704 (Bede, *H.E.* V.24).
m. Osthryth (murdered 697) da. of Oswiu, k. of Northumbria (Bede, III.11, IV.21 [19], V.24).
Issue: K. Ceolred *q.v.*

CENRED, s. of K. Wulfhere; **acc.** 704 (accession recorded *sub an.* 704 in all versions of ASC but *D, E* and *F* also state that he succeeded to the kingdom of the Southumbrians in 702—probably a doublet); **d.** *c.* 709; abdicated and went to Rome in 709 (Bede, *H.E.* V.24).

CEOLRED, s. of K. Æthelred and Osthryth; **acc.** 709; **d.** 716 (Bede, *H.E.* V.24).
Issue: Werburh (d. 782 ASC *D, E*; 783, *Historia Regum*, which says that she was an abbess at time of her d.).

ÆTHELBALD, s. of Alwih s. of Penda's br. Eowa (Anglian collection, ASC); **acc.** 716. Overlord of S. English (Bede, *H.E.* V.23); **d.** 757 (Cont. Bed., *Historia Regum*, murdered *a suis tutoribus*; d. wrongly recorded under 755 in ASC and Æthelweard).

BEORNRED, of unknown origin, established himself as k. 757 aft. murder of Æthelbald, but driven out in same year by Offa (Cont. Bed.; ASC *an.* 755; BL MS. Cotton Vesp. B.vi, fo 104r, *an.* 756); **d.** 769 (*Historia Regum*).

OFFA, s. of Thingfrith gt.-gds. of Eowa, Penda's br. (Anglian collection; ASC); **acc.** 757; **d.** July 796 (26 July according to the *Historia Regum*, 29 July according to ASC—the event is entered under 794 in all versions of ASC, the annals of which are here incorrectly dated by 2 years; entered again under 796 in *D* and *E*; assigned correctly to 796 in Ann. St Neots and *Historia Regum*).
m. Cynethryth (charters and coins).
Issue: K. Ecgfrith *q.v.* crowned k. of Mercians 787 (ASC, *an.* 785; styled *rex Merciorum* in charters); Eadburh m. 789 Brihtric k. of Wessex (Ann. St Neots; cf. Asser §§ 14–15); Ælfflæd m. 29 Sept. 792 Æthelred k. of Northumbria (*Historia Regum*, ASC *D* and *E*); Æthelburh, abbess—in Offa's grant to Chertsey, S 127, dated 787 reference is made to his das, namely Ethelburga *abbatissa*, Aethelfleda, Edburga, and Aethelswithe; but this document is of uncertain quality.

ECGFRITH, s. of K. Offa and Cynethryth; **acc.** July 796; **d.** 14 or 17 Dec. 796 (reigned 141 days, Mercian regnal list in BL MS. Cotton Tiberius A.xiii, fo 114v, ASC *an.* 755, Ann. St Neots; exact date of Offa's d. uncertain, *see above*).

CENWULF, s. of Cuthbert descendant of Pybba, Penda's father (Anglian collection); **acc.** Dec. 796; **d.** 821 (ASC *an.* 819, viz 821, in all versions except *F* which records event *sub an.* 822; Æthelweard *sub an.* 819).
   m. Ælfthryth (charters); in a diploma dated 799, S 156, Cenwulf speaks of his w. Queen Cenegitha (Cynegyth) but text is unreliable and this Cenegitha is probably w. of Wihtred, k. of Kent, *q.v.*
   Issue: Cwenthryth (S 165 dated 811) abbess of Southminster (Minster), Kent (S 1434 and 1436); ? Cenelm (witnesses the doubtful S 156, dated July 799).

CEOLWULF I, s. of Cuthbert descendant of Pybba; **acc.** 821; **d.** unknown (expelled 823: ASC *sub an.* 821; Æthelweard).

BEORNWULF (origin unknown); **acc.** 823; **d.** 825 (Ann. St Neots 825, other chronicles 823). Defeated by Ecgberht, k. of Wessex, at Ellendun 825, and killed by E. Angles later in same year.

LUDECA (origin unknown); **acc.** 825; **d.** 827 (Ann. St Neots).

WIGLAF (origin unkown); **acc.** 827; **d.** 840. Expelled when Ecgberht k. of Wessex conquered Mercia 829; recovered kingdom 830 (ASC *sub an.* 828; S 188; Mercian regnal list in BL MS. Cotton Tiberius A.xiii, fo 114 v).
   m. Cynethryth (S 188, 190).
   Issue: Wigmund (S 188).

BERHTWULF (origin unknown); **acc.** 840; **d.** ? 852.
   m. Sæthryth (charters).
   Issue: Berhtric (S 198 and the doubtful S 205).

BURGRED (origin unknown); **acc.** ? 852; **d.** unknown; driven out by Danes in 873/4 in 22nd year of reign and went to Rome where he d. (ASC, Æthelweard, Asser, 874).
   m. 855 Æthelswith da. of Æthelwulf, k. of W. Saxons (ASC 853 *A*, *D* and *E*, 854 *B* and *C*; Asser 853), d. (on way to Rome?) and buried at Pavia 887/8 (ASC 888).

CEOLWULF II (origin unknown, described in ASC as 'foolish thegn' of K. Burgred); **acc.** 873/4 (puppet-k. set up by Danes who in 877 settled parts of Mercia leaving other parts to Ceolwulf); **d.** unknown (ceased to be k. bef. 883 when, on evidence of S 218, Æthelred II was ruler of English Mercia, and perhaps already in the winter of 878/9—the Mercian regnal list in BL MS. Cotton Tiberius A.xiii, fo 114v, gives him a reign of 5 years).

ÆTHELRED II (origin unknown; consistently described as *ealdorman* by West Saxon sources but with a variety of titles and formulae stating or implying royal power by Mercian and Celtic sources); **acc.** ? 879 (*see* under Ceolwulf II); **d.** 911 (ASC); buried at Gloucester.
   m. 886/7 Æthelflæd, da. of K. Alfred of Wessex *q.v.*
   Issue: da. Ælfwynn, Queen of Mercia *q.v.*

Q. ÆTHELFLÆD, da. of K. Alfred of Wessex and the Mercian noblewoman Ealhswith, and wife of K. Æthelred II *q.v.*; **acc.** 911; **d.** 12 June 918; buried at Gloucester. The titles given her by all sources (*hlæfdige, regina*) imply that she wielded royal power and authority.

Q. ÆLFWYNN, da. of K. Æthelred II and Q. Æthelflæd, *qq.vv.*; **acc.** 918; **d.** unknown, 'deprived of all authority in Mercia and taken into Wessex' by K. Edward of Wessex 'three weeks before Christmas' in 918 or 919 (Mercian Register in ASC *B, C,* and *D, sub an.* 919).

Thereafter Mercia was ruled directly by ks of Wessex, but Æthelstan seems to have been separately elected by the Mercians in 924 (Mercian Register) and Edgar (br. of Eadwig, k. of England) was briefly k. of Mercia and Northumbria 957–9 in circumstances of division which remain unclear.

KINGS OF THE MIDDLE ANGLES

A kingship of the Middle Angles appears once and briefly in the pages of Bede (*H.E.* III.21) when Penda, k. of the Mercians (*q.v.*), created his son Peada (who subsequently married Alhflæd, d. of Oswiu, k. of Northumbria, *q.v.*) k. of the Middle Angles; Peada was converted to Christianity in 653 and a bishopric was established which perpetuated the name of Peada's transitory kingdom. After Penda's death in November 655, Peada's father-in-law, Oswiu (now ruler of Mercia), gave him instead kingship of the Mercians living south of the R. Trent (Bede, *H.E.* III.24); Peada was assassinated the following spring. We hear no more of kingships of the Middle Angles and the Southern Mercians: these units seem to have been *ad hoc* creations for Peada alone.

KINGS OF NORTHUMBRIA

The following kings ruled both Bernicia and Deira, the sum of which came to be known as Northumbria.

ÆTHELFRITH, *c.* 592–616 (*see* Bernicia).

EDWIN, 616–33 (*see* Deira).

OSWALD, 634–42 (*see* Bernicia).

OSWIU, 655–70 (*see* Bernicia), in whose reign the last native king of Deira (Oswine, *q.v.*) was killed.

ECGFRITH, s. of K. Oswiu and Eanflæd; b. 645 (40 years old at death: Bede, *H.E.* IV.26 [24]); **acc.** 21 May × 17 Sept. 670; **d.** 20 May 685.
    m. (1) Æthelthryth da. of Anna, k. of East Angles (Bede, *H.E.* IV.19 [17]), separated aft. being Ecgfrith's consort for 12 years, d. 679 (or less prob. 680); (2) (bef. 678) Iurminburg (Eormenburh).

ALDFRITH, s. of K. Oswiu (Bede, Life of St Cuthbert § 24, calls him illegitimate); **acc.** 686 (Bede, *H.E.* V.18, dates his d. 705 *anno regni sui .xx. necdum completo*); **d.** 14 Dec. 705 (the day and month are given in ASC *D* and *E an.* 705).
    m. Cuthburh sis. of Ine, k. of W. Saxons (ASC *an.* 718).
    Issue: K. Osred I *q.v.*; ? K. Osric *q.v.*

EADWULF (origin unknown) reigned (disputed) for 2 months (late in 705–early 706) aft. d. of Aldfrith (Stephanus, *Vita Wilfridi* § 59).

OSRED I, s. of K. Aldfrith; b. 696 or 697 (about 8 when succeeded: Bede, *H.E.* V.18); **acc.** 705/6; **d.** 716.

CENRED, s. of Cuthwine (Annals of Ulster 718.1); **acc.** 716; **d.** 718.

OSRIC, ? s. of K. Aldfrith (*Hist. Dun. Eccles.*); **acc.** 718 (reigned 11 years, Bede, *H.E.* V.23); **d.** 9 May 729.

CEOLWULF, s. of Cuthwine (Bede, *H.E.* V.23; Anglian collection; Annals of Ulster 731.3; Cutha s. of Cuthwine ASC 731 an error); **acc.** 729; **d.** 764 (*Historia Regum*) or 760 (ASC *D* and *E*); deposed and restored 731; resigned 737 (Cont. Bed.; *Historia Regum*; ASC, *D* and *E*).

EADBERHT, s. of Eata; **acc.** 737 (Cont. Bed. 738, ASC); **d.** 20 Aug. (*Historia Regum*, ASC *D*) or 19 Aug. (ASC *E*) 768; resigned 758 (Cont. Bed., *Historia Regum*) or 757 (ASC *D* and *E*).
Issue: K. Oswulf *q.v.*

OSWULF, s. of K. Eadberht; **acc.** 758 (Cont. Bed., *Historia Regum*) or 757 (ASC); **d.** 758 (or less prob. 757), 24 or 25 July.
Issue: K. Ælfwald *q.v.*

ÆTHELWALD MOLL (origin unknown); **acc.** 5 Aug. 758 (Cont. Bed.) or 759 (*Historia Regum*, ASC); date of **d.** unknown (driven out 30 Oct. 765, *Historia Regum*).
m. 1 Nov. 762 Æthelthryth (*Historia Regum*).
Issue: K. Æthelred I *q.v.*

ALHRED, s. of Eanwine (Anglian collection; the *Historia Regum* says of Alhred 'sprung, as some say, from the stock of K. Ida'); **acc.** 765 (ASC, *Historia Regum*); date of **d.** unknown (exiled 774).
m. 768 Osgearn according to *Historia Regum*. Her name is Osgifu in letter of this k. and his w. to Bp Lul.
Issue: K. Osred II *q.v.*; Alhmund *dux* (d. 800, *Historia Regum*).

ÆTHELRED I, s. of K. Æthelwald Moll; **acc.** 774 (ASC, *Historia Regum*); **d.** 18 Apr. 796 (so *Historia Regum*; 19 Apr. 794 [= 796] ASC *D* and *E*); exiled 779 (*Historia Regum*) or 778 (ASC); restored 790 (ASC, *Historia Regum*).
m. (1) name unknown; (2) 29 Sept. 792 Ælfflæd da. of Offa, k. of Mercians (ASC, *Historia Regum*).

ÆLFWALD I, s. of K. Oswulf; **acc.** 779 (or 778; earlier date supported by *Hist. Dun. Eccles.*, II.4, where 780 is termed his 3rd year; reigned 10 years, regnal list); **d.** 23 Sept. 788 (ASC, *D* and *E*, sub an. 789; *Historia Regum*).
Issue: Oelf and Oelfwine murdered 791 (*Historia Regum*).

OSRED II, s. of K. Alhred (he is also described as *nepos* of K. Ælfwald I, *Historia Regum*; cf. ASC); **acc.** 788; **d.** 14 Sept. 792 (expelled 790, *see above* Æthelred I).

OSBALD, **acc.** 796 and was expelled same year aft. reign of 27 days; **d.** 799 (*Historia Regum*).

EARDWULF, s. of Eardwulf; **acc.** 796 (*Historia Regum*) 14 May (ASC *D* and *E sub an.* 795), crowned 26 May 796; date of **d.** unknown. Expelled 806 (ASC) or 808 (RW *sub an.* supported by Frankish annals). ? Restored 808 through intervention of Emperor Charles and Pope Leo III (Frankish annals), but English sources suggest that restoration, if effected, was very brief.
Issue: K. Eanred *q.v.*

ÆLFWALD II, **acc**. 806 or 808; **d**. 808 or 810.

EANRED, s. of K. Eardwulf; **acc**. 808 or 810 (807, *Hist. Dun. Eccles.*, II. 5); **d**. 840 (RW) or 841 (reigned 33 years, *Historia Regum*).
    Issue: K. Æthelred II *q.v.*

ÆTHELRED II, s. of K. Eanred; **acc**. 840 (RW) or 841; date of **d**. uncertain—but ascribed to 848 by RW who says he reigned for 7 years; expelled by Rædwulf 844 and restored in same year (RW).

RÆDWULF, k. in 844 (part of year, RW, whose statement is borne out by existence of coins of *Redwulf rex, see Catalogue of Coins in B.M., A–S series*, i, 184–86).

OSBERHT, **acc**. 848 according to RW, but 854 was his 5th year (*Hist. Dun. Eccles.*, II.5) which suggests that he succeeded 849 or 850; **d**. 21 Mar. 867. Expelled ? 862 or 863. Restored 867 (RW who reckons reign as 18 years, viz 848–67).

ÆLLE, br. of K. Osberht according to *Hist. de Sancto Cuthberto*, § 10, but according to ASC and RW he was not of royal blood; **acc**. 862/3 or possibly 867 (*see above*); **d**. 21 Mar. 867.

KINGS OF THE SOUTH SAXONS

ÆLLE. Founder of the S. Saxon kingdom, said to have landed 477 (ASC) with his s. Cymen, Wlencing and Cissa. Parentage unknown—genealogy of S. Saxon royal house not preserved. 1st overlord of the S. English in Bede's list (*H.E.* II. 5). Still reigning in 491 (ASC).

ÆTHELWALH, **acc**. unknown, bef. 674 (baptised in Mercia in reign and at instance of Wulfhere—Bede, *H.E.* IV.13); **d**. between 680 and 685 (killed by Cædwalla bef. the latter became k. of W. Saxons—Bede, *H.E.*IV. 15—during period when St Wilfrid was living among S. Saxons). Made overlord of Wight and Meanware by Wulfhere.
    m. Eafa da. of Eanfrith br. of Eanhere, joint-k. of the Hwicce.

BERHTHUN and ANDHUN, two *duces regii* who ruled kingdom aft. driving out Cædwalla. Berhthun killed by Cædwalla 685 x 688 and Sussex subject to Wessex during parts of reigns of Cædwalla and Ine (*c.* 685–726)—Bede, *H.E.* IV.15.

NOTHHELM/NUNNA, reigning late seventh and early eighth centuries (grantor of S 45 dated 692, probably genuine; witnesses S 1173 undated, prob. genuine; grantor of S 42 dated 714; grantor of S 43 dated 775 for ? 725; grantor of S 44, undated). Joined Ine k. of W. Saxons in attack on Geraint of Dumnonia in 710 (ASC).

WATT *rex*, contemporary of Nothhelm (witnesses S 45, dated 692, and S 43, S 1173).

ÆTHELSTAN *rex*, who with w. Æthelthryth *regina* witnesses Nunna's charter dated 714 (S 42).

ÆTHELBERHT *rex* witnesses Nunna's charter S 44 (? 725), and is grantor of S 46 (A.D. 733 x 754 with later confirmation) and S 47 (spurious).

OSMUND *rex*; grantor of S 48 dated 3 Aug. 762 for 765; grantor of S 49 dated 770; ? Osmund *rex* who confirms charter of Nunna S 44, undated; ? Osmund *dux* who witnesses S 108 dated 772 (charter of Offa k. of Mercians).

? OSWALD *dux Suth Saxonum*, who witnesses S 108 dated 772.

OSLAC *dux* witnesses S 108 dated 772 and is grantor of charter confirmed by Offa k. of Mercians (S 1184, original).

EALDWULF, grantor (*rex*) of S 50 undated; grantor (*dux*) of S 1183 undated which belongs to 772 x 787; grantor (*dux*) of S 1178 dated 711 for ? 791.

? AELHWALD *rex*, who attests undated charter (*c.* 765) of Ealdwulf S 50.

KINGS OF SURREY

Two charters from the Chertsey archive (S 69, probably spurious, and S 1165, perhaps authentic—at least in part), attest to the existence in the earlier 670s of one Frithuwold, k. of Surrey, a dependant of Wulfhere, k. of the Mercians, *q.v.*, d. 675. (In S 1165 three other *subreguli* subscribe: Osric, Wigheard, Æthelwold.) No other king of Surrey is known. To the extent that no comparable name is known among Mercian royalty, it seems likely that we have here a native ruler. In as much as Surrey was the southern division (*Suthrige*) of Essex it is to that kingdom and its relationship with Mercia that we must look for further enlightenment as to Frithuwold's position.

KINGS OF THE WEST SAXONS

The dates, reign-lengths, political and genealogical relationships of the West Saxon kings of the sixth, seventh and perhaps even eighth centuries have clearly been subjected to substantial manipulation by the late ninth century: the evidence of West Saxon sources of that date and later is to be treated with considerable reserve. For relevant information about reign-lengths *see* D. N. Dumville, 'The West Saxon Genealogical Regnal List and the chronology of early Wessex', *Peritia: Jnl of the Medieval Acad. of Ireland*, 4, 1985. On the pedigree-texts *see* K. Sisam, 'Anglo-Saxon royal genealogies', *Proc. Brit. Acad.*, 39, 1953, 287–348.

CERDIC, s. of Elesa/Aluca (Anglian collection); **acc.** 519; **d.** 534.
Issue: Creoda (ASC 855, *B*, *C* and *D*, and Anglian collection; Cynric is regarded as s. of Cerdic in W. Saxon regnal list, and ASC *an.* 552, 597, 674, 685, 688 and in *A sub an.* 855, and by Æthelweard)

CYNRIC, s. of Creoda (s. of Cerdic); **acc.** 534 (by some authorities, *e.g.* ASC 519 and Æthelweard, Cynric is said to have ruled jointly with Cerdic 519–34); **d.** ? 560 (assigned a reign of 26 or 27 years).
Issue: K. Ceawlin *q.v.*; Ceolwulf; Cutha; Cuthwulf (? identical with Cutha).

CEAWLIN, s. of K. Cynric; **acc.** 560; **d.** 593 (ceased to reign 591; driven out 592). 2nd overlord of S. English in Bede's list (*H.E.* II.5). Reign given as 7 (or 17) years in copies of the W. Saxon regnal list.
Issue: Cuthwine (also called Cutha?); Cutha (if not the same as Cuthwine).

21

CEOL, s. of Cutha s. of Cynric (ASC 611); **acc.** 591; **d.** ? 597 (assigned a reign of 6 or 7 years).

CEOLWULF, s. of Cutha s. of Cynric (ASC 597 but a Ceolwulf called s. of Cynric, which is improbable if K. Ceolwulf if intended, *sub an.* 674); **acc.** 597; **d.** ? 611 (assigned a reign of 14 or 17 years).
Issue: Cuthgils (ASC 674).

CYNEGILS, s. of Ceola s. of Cutha, Cynric's s. (ASC 611), *or* s. of Cuthwine s. of Ceawlin (ASC 688); **acc.** 611; **d.** ? 642 (assigned a reign of 31 years).
Issue: Cwichelm (ASC 648) apparently joint-k. with Cynegils (described as k. by Bede, *H.E.* II.9, Apr. 626, and in ASC *E* 626, *F* 636; d. 636 leaving s. Cuthred d. 661 who also is described as k. ASC *B, C, F* 639); K. Cenwealh *q.v.*; K. Centwine *q.v.*; da. (unnamed by Bede, *H.E.* III.7) m. Oswald k. of Northumbria.

CENWEALH, s. of K. Cynegils; **acc.** 642 (in exile in E. Anglia 645–48; may have had colleague, Cenberht, described as k. ASC 661); **d.** 672.
m. (1) sis. (unnamed) of Penda k. of Mercians; (2) Seaxburh (reigned aft. him).

Q. SEAXBURH, wid. of K. Cenwealh *q.v.* Apparently reigned 672–74 (her reign is reckoned as 1 year). This reign falls in the period of rule by *subreguli*, according to Bede, *H.E.* IV.12.

ÆSCWINE, s. of Cenfus; **acc.** 674; **d.** 676. This reign falls in the period of rule by *subreguli*, according to Bede, *H.E.* IV.12.

CENTWINE, s. of K. Cynegils; **acc.** 676; **d.** ? 685; abdicated, entered monastery (Aldhelm); overthrown by Cædwalla in 685 (ASC). This reign falls in the period of rule by *subreguli*, according to Bede, *H.E.* IV.12.
m. sis. (unnamed) of Eormenburh w. of Ecgfrith, k. of Northumbria (Stephanus, *Vita Wilfridi*, § 40).
Issue: Bugge (Aldhelm, *Carmina Ecclesiastica*, no. 3).

CÆDWALLA, b. *c.* 659 (epitaph in Bede, *H.E.* V.7); s. of Cenberht (? him described as k. ASC 661) gt.-gds. of K. Ceawlin (ASC 685); **acc.** 685 (ASC; Bede, *H.E.* V.7, states that he had reigned 2 years when he abdicated); **d.** 20 Apr. 689 (abdicated 688 and went to Rome where baptised 10 Apr. 689, Bede, *H.E.* V.7).
m. ? Cynethryth (*Kenedritha* occurs in spurious Canterbury charter dated 687, S 1610).

INE, s. of Cenred (who granted S 1164, of A.D. 670 × 676; attests S 45 of ? A.D. 692 and S 43 of ? A.D. 725 as *rex Westsaxonum*) s. of Ceolwald (gt.-gds. of K. Ceawlin, W. Saxon regnal list); **acc.** 688 (Bede); **d.** in or aft. 726 (Bede, *H.E.* V.7, states that he had reigned 37 years when he abdicated and went to Rome; abdication recorded in ASC 726 *C, D* and *E*, 728 *A*; d. recorded ASC 726 *F* only, possibly error).
m. Æthelburh (S 251; cf. ASC 722).

ÆTHELHEARD; parentage unknown (Cerdic's stock); **acc.** 726; **d.** ? 740 (ASC 740 *C, D, E, F*, 741 *A*; 739 Cont. Bed. and *Historia Regum*).
m. ? Frithugyth (q. in S 253–5, 310–11, 443 and 521, and in ASC 737, but not explicitly stated to be Æthelheard's).

CUTHRED; parentage unknown—kinsman of K. Æthelheard (ASC *D, E; Historia Regum an.* 739 calls him br.); **acc.** 740 (Ann. St Neots); **d.** 756 (reigned 16 years; recorded in ASC *sub an.* 754 for 756).

SIGEBERHT; parentage unknown (Cerdic's stock); called kinsman of K. Cuthred in ASC *D, E*); **acc.** 756; **d.** ? 757 (reigned 1 year, dethroned by Cynewulf 757; language of ASC might suggest that he was killed in year of deposition).

CYNEWULF; parentage unknown (Cerdic's stock); **acc.** 757; **d.** 786 (reigned 29 years, Ann. St Neots) killed by Cyneheard br. of K. Sigeberht (ASC *an.* 755 = 757 and 784 = 786).

BRIHTRIC; parentage unknown (Cerdic's stock); **acc.** 786 (Ann. St Neots); **d.** 802 (Ann. St Neots).
m. 789 (Ann. St Neots; cf. Asser §§ 14–15) Eadburh da. of Offa, k. of Mercians.

ECGBERHT, s. of Ealhmund (gt.-gds. of Ingild br. of K. Ine); father possibly identical with Kentish k. Ealhmund *q.v.*; **acc.** 802; **d.** 839 (reigned 37 years and 7 months, W. Saxon regnal list). K. of Wessex 802–25; acknowledged as king also in Kent, Surrey, Sussex and Essex aft. victory over Mercians at Ellendun 825; conquered Mercia 829 and styled himself k. of Mercians (coins; cf. Mercian regnal list in BL MS. Cotton Tiberius A.xiii, fo 114v); overlord of all English kingdoms 829–30.
Issue: K. Æthelwulf *q.v.*

ÆTHELWULF, s. of K. Ecgberht; **acc.** 839 (sub-k. of Kent, Essex, Sussex and Surrey, now annexed to Wessex, *c.* 825–39 (S 286, 323); ruler of all W. Saxon kingdom 839–56; confined to Kent, Sussex and Essex 856–58—Asser § 12; **d.** 13 Jan. 858; buried at Steyning (Sussex), later at Winchester.
Absence—Rome and Frankish court early 855 to late 856.
m. (1) Osburh da. of ealdorman Oslac (? of Hampshire), K. Æthelwulf's *pincerna*; (2) 1 Oct. 856, Judith da. of Charles the Bald, k. of W. Franks.
Issue: (all children of Osburh) Æthelstan, sub-k. of Kent, Essex, Surrey and Sussex 839–851 x 855; K. Æthelbald *q.v.*; K. Æthelberht *q.v.*; K. Æthelred *q.v.*; K. Alfred *q.v.*; Æthelswith m. 853 Burgred, k. of Mercians, d. 887/8.

ÆTHELBALD, s. of K. Æthelwulf and Osburh; **acc.** 855; **d.** 860; buried at Sherborne.
m. 858 Judith his father's wid.

ÆTHELBERHT, s. of K. Æthelwulf and Osburh; **acc.** 860 (k. in Kent etc. 858–60); **d.** 865; buried at Sherborne.

ÆTHELRED, s. of K. Æthelwulf and Osburh; **acc.** 865; **d.** Apr. 871; buried at Wimborne (Dorset).
Issue: Æthelhelm described by K. Alfred in his will (S 1507) as his br.'s son; Æthelwald (revolted against Edward the Elder and killed at battle of the Holme, ? 903); ? Oswald *filius regis* (S 340, 1201, 1203).

ALFRED, s. of K. Æthelwulf and Osburh; **b.** 849; **acc.** Apr. 871; overlord (from ? 878 × 893) of all Welsh kings (Asser § 79 [80]); **d.** 26 Oct. 899; buried at Winchester.

m. 868 Ealhswith, da. of Æthelred 'Mucill' ealdorman of the 'Gaini' and Eadburh *de regali genere Merciorum regis* (Asser § 29).

Issue: (Asser § 74 [75]) Æthelflæd q. of Mercians *q.v.* m. 886/7 K. Æthelred II of Mercians *q.v.*, d. 12 June 918; K. Edward the Elder *q.v.*; Æthelgifu abbess of Shaftesbury; Ælfthryth m. (893 × 899) Baldwin II, c. of Flanders (for their four children see Æthelweard, prologue); Æthelweard d. ? 16 Oct. 922.

EDWARD THE ELDER, s. of K. Alfred and Ealhswith; **acc**. Oct. 899, crowned 8 June 900. Annexed to Wessex the Southumbrian Danelaw, and overlordship acknowledged by Ragnall I reigning at York (Deira), *q.v.*, by k. of Scots, by k. of Strathclyde Britons, by Aldred 'of Bamburgh' s. of Eadwulf, k. of Bernicia *q.v.*, and by Welsh kings; **d**. 17 July 924, buried at Winchester.

m. (1) ? Ecgwynn (name attested only by post-Conquest writers); (2) by 901 (S 363) Ælfflæd, da. of ealdorman Æthelhelm; (3) Eadgifu, da. of ealdorman Sigehelm (S 1211), d. 966/7.

Issue: as many as 14 children are recorded, but in sources of widely varying merit. They are listed here in two alphabetical series—5 sons, all well attested, and 9 daughters—with following notices of their mothers (for which relationships the evidence is often poor and contradictory).

1. K. Ælfweard *q.v.*—by Ælfflæd (acc. to William of Malmesbury who calls him Æthelweard)
2. K. Æthelstan *q.v.*—by 'Ecgwynn'
3. Edwin, ? sub-king (called *rex* by Folcwin of Saint-Bertin), d. 933, drowned (ASC *E*), according to *Historia Regum* by command of Æthelstan; but Folcwin of Saint-Bertin (where Edwin was buried), while silent as to alleged murder, suggests exile following political rivalry—by Ælfflæd (William of Malmesbury), by Eadgifu (John of Worcester)
4. K. Edmund *q.v.*—by Eadgifu (S 1211)
5. K. Eadred *q.v.*—by Eadgifu (S 1211)
6. da. (unnamed) who married Sigtryggr Caech, k. at York (Deira), *q.v.*, in 926 (ASC 925 *D*)—by 'Ecgwynn' (William of Malmesbury)
7. Ælfgifu (called *Adiua* by Hrotsvitha of Gandersheim; mentioned, but not named, by Æthelweard; called both *Aldgitha* and *Elfgiua* by William of Malmesbury), sent with her elder sister Eadgyth *q.v.* as a possible choice of bride for the German prince Otto (the future Emperor Otto I), but married, according to Æthelweard, 'cuipiam regi iuxta Iupitereos montes de cuius prole nulla nobis notitia extat'—by Ælfflæd (implied by Hrotsvitha?; William of Malmesbury)
8. Æthelhild, a lay recluse, buried at Wilton—by Ælfflæd (William of Malmesbury)
9. Eadburh, *sancta*, a nun at Winchester—by Eadgifu (John of Worcester; William of Malmesbury)
10. Eadflæd, nun, buried at Wilton—by Ælfflæd (William of Malmesbury)
11. Eadgifu (I) who married (916 × 919) Charles the Simple, k. of Franks (Æthelweard; Flodoard; Richer)—by Ælfflæd (William of Malmesbury), by Eadgifu (John of Worcester)
12. Eadgifu (II) who married Louis, *Aquitanorum princeps*—by Eadgifu (William of Malmesbury)
13. Eadgyth who married 929/30 the future Emperor Otto I (Æthelweard,

Hrotsvitha) and d. 26 Jan. 946 (Widukind, II.41)—by Ælfflæd
(implied by Hrotsvitha), by Eadgifu (John of Worcester)
14. Eadhild who married 926 Hugh the Great (*Hugo filius Hrodbyrhti*,
Æthelweard), duke of the Franks—by Ælfflæd (William of
Malmesbury)

Nos 8–10 and 12 are attested only in post-Conquest sources; the mothers
of nos 1–3, 6, 8–12, and 14 are likewise stated only in post-Conquest
sources.

ÆLFWEARD, s. of K. Edward and Ælfflæd; **acc.** on or after 17 July 924;
d. 2 Aug. 924 (ASC *D*) or *c.* 14 Aug. 924 (regnal list in *Textus Roffensis*
gives him a reign of 4 weeks); buried at Winchester.

ÆTHELSTAN, s. of K. Edward the Elder and 'Ecgwynn'; **acc.** summer of
924 (*see above* on d. of Edward the Elder); apparently acknowledged as k.
by W. Saxons and Mercians independently; consecrated 4 Sept. 925 at
Kingston; established direct rule over Scandinavian York from expulsion
of Guthfrith II 927 to end of reign (chronicles and coins); **d.** 27 Oct. 939.
First of Kings of England *q.v.*

KINGS OF ENGLAND
(1) 927–1066

The effective creation of the Kingdom of England may be dated from
A.D. 927 when Æthelstan, king of the West Saxons and Mercians, invaded
and annexed Northumbria (both Danish Deira and such of English
Bernicia as was not in Scottish hands). In the following century or so (until
1037) there are cases of more than one king ruling in England—whether
Scandinavian interlopers seeking to (re)establish themselves in Northumbria (on occasions in 939 × 954) or explicit divisions of the kingdom of
England between two West Saxons (as in 957–9) or one English and one
Scandinavian (as in 1016) or two Anglo-Scandinavians (as in 1035–7).
Nonetheless, it seems clear that Æthelstan's reign marked a significant
point in the history of English royal government, and that from 927 the
presumption (in West Saxon eyes, at the very least) was that a single
kingdom of England now existed, whose kings were of the West Saxon
royal line, however much immediate circumstances might compel a
division of territorial control, and notwithstanding continued references to
'the kingdom of the Mercians' or 'the kingdom of the Northumbrians'
even when they were not under separate rule.

The sources remain of essentially the same types as for the earlier
Anglo-Saxon period—charters, the Anglo-Saxon Chronicle and regnal
lists are the most important, but a wide range of divers sources contributes
useful information. For precise regnal chronology, documentary texts—
royal diplomas, wills, other private charters—become more important in
the last century and a half of Anglo-Saxon England. On the other hand,
numismatic evidence—so vital for the reigns of the various local rulers of
preceding centuries—is now of greater use for administrative and
economic history than for the dates of kings' reigns.

In principle, in this period it becomes possible to speak with confidence of the royal style, to note at what point a king may assume that style and act in accordance with it, to observe (albeit hesitantly) when regency-arrangements were made, and to construct skeletal royal itineraries. But it has to be admitted that work on all these questions is still in its infancy and that the years from 927 to 978 are at present much less well served than those from 978 to 1066. On the latter period the important relevant studies are the following: Simon Keynes, *The Diplomas of King Æthelred 'the Unready' 978–1016. A Study in their Use as Historical Evidence* (Cambridge, 1980); Laurence Marcellus Larson, *Canute the Great, 995 (circ)–1035, and the Rise of Danish Imperialism during the Viking Age* (New York, 1912); Tryggvi J. Oleson, *The Witenagemot in the Reign of Edward the Confessor. A Study in the Constitutional History of Eleventh-century England* (Toronto, 1955); Frank Barlow, *Edward the Confessor* (2nd edn, London, 1979). F. E. Harmer, *Anglo-Saxon Writs* (Manchester, 1952) is also vital.

Three other volumes remain essential for the understanding of royal authority and government in this period, even though parts of them are significantly out of date and some of their main conclusions are now untenable: Laurence Marcellus Larson, *The King's Household in England before the Norman Conquest* (Madison, Wis., 1904); Hector Munro Chadwick, *Studies on Anglo-Saxon Institutions* (Cambridge, 1905); F. Liebermann, *The National Assembly in the Anglo-Saxon Period* (Halle a.S., 1913).

ÆTHELSTAN, s. of K. Edward the Elder and 'Ecgwynn'; for **acc.** to Wessex and Mercia, apparently summer 924, and consecration at Kingston 4 Sept. 925, see under Kings of Wessex. Direct rule over Northumbria was established in 927 and maintained to the end of the reign; **d.** 27 Oct. 939.

Not known to have married or had issue, unless the daughter mentioned in *Liber Eliensis*, III.50, can be credited.

His brother Edwin (drowned 933) was possibly in some way associated in government with Æthelstan (*Edwinus rex* in Folcwin, *Gesta Abbatum Sancti Bertini*).

EDMUND I, s. of K. Edward the Elder and Eadgifu; b. 921; **acc.** Oct. 939; consecration ? 28 Nov. 939; lost Northumbria and the southern Danelaw to Óláfr Guthfrithsson in the winter of 939/40; recovered southern Danelaw 942 and Northumbria 944; **d.** 26 May 946 (killed by one Leofa at Pucklechurch, Glos.); buried at Glastonbury (according to John of Worcester).

m. (1) Ælfgifu *sancta* (ASC 955 D), d. 944; (2) Æthelflæd 'of Damerham', da. of Ealdorman Ælfgar (who seems, after 946, to have taken as her second husband an Ealdorman Æthelstan, probably Æthelstan 'Rota'; her will, S 1494, appears to be later than 975).

Issue: by Ælfgifu—K. Eadwig, *q.v.*; K. Edgar, *q.v.*

EADRED, s. of K. Edward the Elder and Eadgifu; **acc.** May 946; consecration ? 16 Aug. 946 (John of Worcester); the Danish kingdom of York (Deira) independent of him 947–48, 950–54; **d.** 23 Nov. 955 at Frome (Somerset); buried at Old Minster, Winchester (ASC 955 D).

Not known to have married or had issue.

EADWIG, s. of K. Edmund and Ælfgifu; b. before 943 (older than his brother Edgar); **acc.** Nov. 955; consecration ? 25 Jan. 956—at Kingston (John of Worcester); **d.** 1 Oct. 959 (ASC 959 A). His authority was, from 957, confined to England south of the Thames (*Vita I S. Dunstani*), following the withdrawal of allegiance by the Mercians (and Northumbrians).

m. 956 or early 957, Ælfgifu, da. of Æthelgifu (separated 958 on grounds of consanguinity: ASC 958 D).

No known issue.

EDGAR I, s. of K. Edmund and Ælfgifu; b. 943 (ASC 959 BC); **acc.** 957 as k. of Mercians (and Northumbrians; Oct. 959 as k. of all England; consecration ? 960/1; imperial consecration at Bath 11 May 973); **d.** 8 July 975; buried at Glastonbury (ASC 1016 CDE).

m. (1) Æthelflæd, da. of Ealdorman Ordmær; (2) Wulfthryth; (3) 965, Ælfthryth, da. of Ealdorman Ordgar and widow of Ealdorman Æthelwold (eldest son of Ealdorman Æthelstan 'Half-King').

Issue: (1) by Æthelflæd—K. Edward I the Martyr, *q.v.*; (2) by Wulfthryth—Eadgyth, nun at Wilton, d. aged 23 before 988 (William of Malmesbury); (3) by Ælfthryth—Edmund, d. 971, and K. Æthelred the Unready, *q.v.*

EDWARD I THE MARTYR, s. of K. Edgar and Æthelflæd; b. *c.* 962; **acc.** July 975; **d.** 18 Mar. 978 (assassinated at Corfe, Dorset); buried at Wareham (ASC 979 DE), but body soon translated to Shaftesbury by Ealdorman Ælfhere (ASC 980 DE, for ? 979).

Not known to have married or had issue.

ÆTHELRED THE UNREADY, s. of K. Edgar and Ælfthryth; b. ? 968/9 (William of Malmesbury); **acc.** March 978; consecration at Kingston 4 May 979 (ASC 979 C); **d.** 23 Apr. 1016; buried at St Paul's, London (John of Worcester). Dispossessed of kingdom for some months 1013/14 by Swegn Forkbeard, k. of Denmark.

Absence: in exile in Normandy, Jan.–Lent 1014.

m. (1) Ælfgifu, da. of Ealdorman Thored (Ailred of Rievaulx); (2) spring 1002, Emma, da. of Richard I, count of Normandy.

Issue: (1) by Ælfgifu—Æthelstan, d. 1014; Ecgberht, d. *c.* 1005; K. Edmund II Ironside, *q.v.*; Eadred, d. *c.* 1012–15; Eadwig, exiled and killed by command of K. Cnut, 1017 (ASC 1017 CD); Edgar, d. *c.* 1012–15; Eadgyth m. after 1006 Ealdorman Eadric Streona (executed 1017); Ælfgifu m. Ealdorman Uhtred (*De Obsessione Dunelmi*, §2); ? Wulfhild m. Ealdorman Ulfcytel; ? a da. unnamed m. Æthelstan (K. Æthelred's *aðum*) who was killed at Ringmere 1010; ? a da. unnamed, abbess of Wherwell (ASC 1048 E); (2) by Emma—K. Edward II the Confessor, *q.v.*; Alfred, d. 1037; Godgifu m. (1) Drew, c. of Mantes (d. 1035), (2) Eustace, c. of Boulogne.

SWEGN FORKBEARD, k. of Denmark 987–1014; acknowledged as k. of all England from autumn 1013 to his d. 3 Feb. 1014.

Issue: *inter alios*, K. Cnut, *q.v.*

ÆTHELRED THE UNREADY (2nd reign, Lent 1014 to his **d.** 23 Apr. 1016).

EDMUND II IRONSIDE, s. of K. Æthelred and Ælfgifu, b. before 993 (S 876); **acc.** April 1016 (but in 1015 he had gained the submission of the

Five, or Seven, Boroughs, while Cnut gained the submission of Wessex); chosen as k. at London and took Wessex; after defeat by Cnut at battle of *Assandun* (18 Oct.), a royal conference at Alney (Glos.) divided the kingdom, giving Wessex to Edmund; d. 30 Nov. 1016; buried at Glastonbury.

m. 1015 Ealdgyth (name from John of Worcester), wid. of Sigeferth (son of Earngrim), thegn of the Seven Boroughs.

Issue: Edward (d. 1057: father of K. Edgar II the Ætheling *q.v.*), m. Agatha, 'kinswoman' of Emperor Henry II and possibly da. of St Stephen, k. of Hungary; Edmund (probably died young in Hungary).

CNUT, younger s. of K. Swegn Forkbeard, *q.v.*, and Gunhild (of Polish origin, da. of Miseco and sis. of Bolizlav of Poland, according to Thietmar of Merseburg); b. *c.* 995; **acc.**—chosen k. by Danish fleet Feb. 1014 on death of K. Swegn, but failed to establish himself against Æthelred the Unready now recalled by the English; in 1015 he gained a temporary submission of the West Saxons; in 1016 the Northumbrians submitted to Cnut whom the annalist of ASC 1016 CDE now calls 'king'. After battle of *Assandun* (18 Oct.) at which he defeated K. Edmund II (*q.v.*) he secured the succession to Mercia (including London); k. of all England after Edmund's death 30 Nov. 1016 (ASC 1017 CDE); k. of Denmark 1019–35; k. of Norway 1028–35; by his royal style *rex totius Angliae et Denemarchiae et Norreganorum et partis Suanorum* (proclamation of 1027) he also claims authority over Swedes (cf. coins); **d.** 12 Nov. 1035, at Shaftesbury (ASC 1035 CD, 1036 E); buried at the Old Minster, Winchester (ASC 1036 E).

Absences: Denmark 1019–spring 1020 (returned before 17 Apr.); ? Denmark 1022/3; ? Denmark autumn 1025–spring 1026; summer 1026 sailed to Denmark to meet attack of Óláfr of Norway and Ánundr of Sweden (battle of Holy River, Sept. 1026); prob. spent winter 1026/7 in Denmark; in Rome Mar.–Apr. 1027, returned to Denmark, thence to England; later in 1027 led expedition into Scotland; Norway and Denmark 1028/9 (conquest of Norway).

m. (1) Ælfgifu 'of Northampton', da. of Ealdorman Ælfhelm (ASC 1035 CD, 1036 EF); (2) July 1017, Emma (d. 14 Mar. 1052), wid. of K. Æthelred the Unready, *q.v.*

Issue: (1) by Ælfgifu of Northampton—Swegn, appointed (with mother) regent in Norway 1030–5, d. 1036; K. Harold I Harefoot, *q.v.*; (2) by Emma—K. Harthacnut, *q.v.*; Gunhild (called Kunigund aft. marriage) m. 1036 Henry (later Emperor Henry III, d. 1038), s. of Emperor Conrad II.

HAROLD I HAREFOOT, s. of K. Cnut and Ælfgifu of Northampton (but this is doubted or denied in ASC 1035 CD, 1036 EF); b. ? *c.* 1016/17; **acc.**—late 1035 or early 1036 chosen by London, Mercia, and presumably Northumbria as regent of all England 'for himself and for his brother Harthacnut who was then in Denmark' (ASC 1036 EF); Wessex, where this was opposed, was to be held for K. Harthacnut (*q.v.*); in 1037 Harold was recognised universally as king, in view of Harthacnut's continuing absence; **d.** 17 Mar. 1040, at Oxford; buried first at Westminster (ASC 1039 EF), but eventually at London (John of Worcester).

m. Ælfgifu (otherwise unknown).

Issue: ? Ælfwine (Alboynus), founder of monastery of Sainte-Foi at Conques (Aquitaine) *c.* 1060, who, according to the cartulary of that house, was an Englishman born in London—*pater eius Heroldus rex fuit*

Anglorum terrae; mater eius Alueua (see W. H. Stevenson, 'An alleged son of King Harold Harefoot', *EHR*, 28, 1913).

HARTHACNUT, s. of K. Cnut and Emma, b. ? *c.* 1018 (before 1023: ASC 1023 D); **acc.**—seems to have been made heir to all Cnut's dominions by 1035; titular k. of Denmark from 1028; acknowledged as k. of England late 1035 until 1037 with Harold I (*q.v.*) as regent; effective k., after Harold I, from arrival in England June 1040; associated his half-brother, K. Edward II (*q.v.*), with him in kingship 1041 (ASC 1041 CD); **d.** 8 June 1042; buried at the Old Minster, Winchester.
Not known to have married or had issue.

EDWARD II THE CONFESSOR, s. of K. Æthelred the Unready (*q.v.*) and Emma; b. 1002 × 1005; **acc.** 1042, crowned 3 Apr. 1043 (resided from 1041 with household of K. Harthacnut who associated Edward with himself in kingship and seems to have regarded him as his successor); **d.** 5 Jan. 1066; buried at Westminster.
m. 23 Jan. 1045, Eadgyth, da. of Godwine, e. of Wessex.

HAROLD II GODWINESSON, s. of Godwine, e. of Wessex, and Gytha; b. ? *c.* 1020; **acc.** 6 Jan. 1066; **d.** 14 Oct. 1066.
m. (1) (concubine) Eadgyth Swanneshals; (2) 1066, Ealdgyth, da. of Ælfgar, e. of Mercia.
Issue: (1) thought to be children of Eadgyth—Godwine, Edmund, Magnus (all on the evidence of John of Worcester *s.a.* 1068); Ulf (*ibid.*, *s.a.* 1087); ? Gytha m. Waldemar k. of Norgorod; Gunhild, nun at Wilton (William of Malmesbury, *Vita Wulfstani*, II.11); (2) by Ealdgyth—Harold (John of Worcester).

EDGAR II THE ÆTHELING, s. of Edward the Exile (d. 1057) s. of K. Edmund II Ironside (*q.v.*); **acc.**—chosen k. by Archbishop Aldred, the citizens of London, and earls Edwin and Morkere aft. the battle of Hastings, Oct. 1066 (ASC 1066 D; cf. 1066 E); but not apparently crowned; submitted to William the Conqueror bef. Christmas of this year; **d.** uncertain (living *c.* 1125, according to William of Malmesbury).

KINGS OF ENGLAND

(2) 1066–1985

The following list supplies brief particulars of the parentage, birth, accession, death (or removal), marriage and issue of the sovereigns of England, Great Britain and the United Kingdom. Certain additional information is given: the changes in the sovereign's titles, the arrangements for the government of the kingdom made during the minority of a ruler and (up to 1837) the sovereign's absences from England which necessitated the appointment of a regent.

THE ROYAL STYLE

In the Norman period the sovereign's style can be deduced from the legend on his great seal and from the surviving original charters and writs which issued from his chancery. There may, however, be differences between the style upon the seal and the style generally used for documents: whereas the Conqueror's chancery adopted the style *Willelmus rex Anglorum* in the protocol of writs, the legend of his seal read: *Hoc Normannorum Willelmum nosce patronum si* [on the equestrian side] *hoc Anglis regem signo fatearis eundem* [on the majesty side]. With William II begins the use of a terse, straightforward legend which, with some elaboration, has been the model followed by his successors; the legend is *Willelmus Dei gracia rex Anglorum* on both sides of the seal. From 1121 Henry I altered the legend on the reverse of his seal to *Henricus Dei gracia dux Normannorum*, although he rarely styled himself more than *rex Anglorum* even in documents relating to Normandy. The precedent set by Henry I was followed by his nephew Stephen. Henry II naturally expanded the legend on the reverse of his great seal to *dux Normannorum et Aquitanorum et comes Andegavorum*, and incorporated these titles in the style employed in his documents. Richard I's usage followed that of his father. John added to the royal style, on the obverse of his seal and also in his documents, *dominus Hibernie*, a title he had enjoyed before his accession, and substituted *Anglie* for *Anglorum* and so on. The style of later sovereigns reflects political events: for example, the treaty of Paris of 1259, after which Henry III dropped the title of duke of Normandy and count of Anjou; the claim of Edward III to the French throne in 1340 and his temporary disuse of it after the treaty of Brétigny in 1360; the assumption by Henry V in 1420 of the title of heir and regent of the realm of France in accordance with the treaty of Troyes; the addition of *fidei defensor* to the style of Henry VIII in 1521, which has been retained ever since. The words *Dei gracia* were not, as a rule, added to the style of the king in charters and writs until May 1172, when Henry II commenced a practice which has since been consistently followed.

ACCESSION

Until, apparently, the reign of Edward I, no English king assumed the royal style before his coronation. For example, in the interval between his father's death, on 6 July, and 3 September, when he was crowned, Richard I used the style of *dominus Anglorum et dux Normannorum et Aquitanorum et comes Andegavorum*. John, similarly, was called lord of England before his coronation, and, immediately upon Richard's death becoming known in England, John's peace as lord of England and duke of Normandy was proclaimed. Richard and John each dated his regnal years from the day of his coronation, although each had assumed the government as soon as he knew of the death of his predecessor and Richard was certain of the succession. We possess but scanty evidence for previous interregna—using the word in its strict sense—although something may be deduced from the actions of Empress Matilda and her son. Consequent upon a ceremony of election at Winchester in April 1141, the empress called herself *domina Anglorum*, but continued to use a personal seal bearing the legend *Mathildis Dei gracia Romanorum regina*.[1] Both before

[1] J. H. Round believed (*Geoffrey de Mandeville*, 75–95, 299–303) that for a very short time in 1141 Matilda called herself *regina Anglie* in anticipation of coronation. The sole evidence is that of a few transcripts, and it is by no means conclusive. A charter now destroyed, in which she is referred to as *Anglorum domina*, is alleged to have borne a seal with a legend styling her *regina Anglie*: this discrepancy suggests that the legend was misread.

and after this event the empress appears to have exercised royal power so far as she could make her writs run. When, however, her son Henry had been put in possession of the duchy of Normandy late in 1150, he began to address writs to ministers and others in England. It appears certain, therefore, that, from at least 1151 onwards, having replaced his mother as claimant to the throne of England, he was exercising such authority as he was able, although it was not until 1153 that he again visited the country. The treaty of Wallingford of November of that year recognized him as heir to the throne, but the only titles he used were those of his continental dominions, and there seems to be no evidence that he assumed the title of lord of England between Stephen's death and his own coronation. His regnal years date from the latter event. It is reasonable to conclude from these facts that in the twelfth century, and presumably earlier, coronation was essential to full kingship in England, although a claimant to the throne immediately endeavoured to exercise royal authority. Nor was there any change in 1216, for, whatever authority may have been exercised in Henry III's name between his father's death on 19 October and his coronation on 28 October, his regnal years began on the latter date. It is, therefore, correct to equate accession and coronation in the case of all kings from William I to Henry III.

On his father's death, Edward I was far distant and the time of his return uncertain. Special measures were therefore obviously necessary to secure an orderly succession. The conception expressed in the maxim 'le roi est mort, vive le roi' had, however, not yet been reached, for there was an interregnum of four days before the new king's peace was proclaimed and his reign was regarded as having begun. By 1307, quite clearly, political theory had made an advance towards the conception that the king never dies, for Edward II's reign was assumed to begin on the day following his father's death: and this conception, with some exceptions in times of revolution, has been maintained ever since. The reign of Edward V was assumed to begin on the day of his father's death, and this rule has been invariably observed since the accession of Edward VI.

APPOINTMENT OF REGENTS
(during royal absences)

William I and all his successors who ruled territories in France made arrangements for the exercise of royal power during their absences. The way in which this was done has been the subject of much recent discussion (see especially D. Bates, 'The origins of the justiciarship', *Proceedings of the Battle Conference on Anglo-Norman Studies*, iv (1982 for 1981), 1–12). The evidence is too sparse to provide a chronology of office-holders even in the twelfth century when writs and charters become much more numerous, and the terminology is at this period so vague that it is at times uncertain whether a given individual was holding a formal office. No one would now maintain that the justiciarship in its fully defined sense existed before Henry II's reign. Under William I, William fitz Osbern and bishop Odo of Bayeux are known to have acted as vicars in England in 1067. After fitz Osbern's death in 1071, although archbishop Lanfranc, bishop

Geoffrey of Coutances and other great magnates certainly acted on William's behalf, only Odo appears to have exercised full royal authority in William's place. In Normandy Queen Matilda, and perhaps her eldest son Robert, assumed responsibilities equivalent to Odo's in England.

This practice of members of the royal family acting with royal authority in the king's absence was continued in the twelfth century. Queen Matilda acted as regent for Henry I and after her death in 1118 their son William did likewise until he died in 1120. Stephen's queen Matilda also acted on his behalf. From 1087, however, the practice was also becoming established whereby the chief figure in the treasury and, from Henry I's time, the exchequer, could assume control during royal absences. This was true of Ranulf Flambard in William II's reign. Under Henry I bishop Roger of Salisbury was certainly regent in 1123–4 and was always an important presence alongside the nominated regents from the royal family. Nonetheless, Roger's few surviving writs and charters do not indicate that he exercised an authority which was fully that of a king or of a royal relative (*see also* list of justiciars *infra*).

In the early part of Henry II's reign, Queen Eleanor acted as regent in the king's absence, and, during other absences, his mother, Empress Matilda, and the young king Henry acted. It may be stated as a rule that during this reign the justiciar did not act as regent save in the absence of both the king and his crowned associate, whether this was his queen or his son: the position of the empress was clearly exceptional.

Under Richard I the justiciars, or men holding a similar vice-regal position, assumed the regency in the king's absence (*see* the list of justiciars *infra*). When Henry III visited France in 1230, the justiciar, Hubert de Burgh, earl of Kent, accompanied him and Stephen Segrave, a royal justice, acted as regent, being, however, required to act with the advice of the chancellor. On the next absence of the king in 1242–43 the archbishop of York was regent, and in 1253–54 the queen and the king's brother acted. With the temporary revival of the justiciarship in 1258–65, the ancient usage of appointing justiciars as regents was restored, except in 1264, when the justiciar, Hugh Despenser, was in opposition to the king and the king's brother acted as regent for a period of six weeks.

The absence of Edward I on his father's death led to the assumption of the regency by the lieutenants whom he had appointed to manage his affairs while on crusade. On other occasions a member of the royal house acted. Edward II's voluntary absences were few and short, but it is noticeable that no member of the royal house acted as regent. Thenceforward it became the custom to appoint only members of the royal house as keepers of the realm, and the determination so to confine the exercise of royal power is strikingly illustrated by the practice of Edward III in appointing his infant children, although the effective government clearly resided in the council. Edward VI and his successors to James II were never absent from their dominions. From William III onwards the practice has been for the regency to be exercised, according to the circumstances, either by a member of the royal family or by Lords Justices. (The absences of sovereigns are not noticed in the lists that follow after 1837, when the link with Hanover was severed.) The Regency Acts, 1937 and 1943 (statutes 1 Edw. VIII and 1 George VI, c. 16, and 6 and 7 Geo. VI, c. 42), provide for the appointment of Counsellors of State, being members of the royal family.

BIBLIOGRAPHICAL NOTE

For the descent, marriage and issue of English sovereigns, F. Sandford's *Genealogical History of Kings and Queens of Great Britain, 1066–1707* (London, 1707) is still useful as a comprehensive work. The *Dictionary of National Biography* and the *Complete Peerage* between them give the principal facts relating to kings, queens and peers of the blood royal: for the female issue, M. A. E. Green's *Lives of the Princesses of England*, 6 vols (London, 1849–55) supplements them.

The most useful works dealing with the royal style include: T. D. Hardy's Introduction to the *Rotuli Chartarum* (1837), xii–xxiii; reprinted by Sir Harris Nicolas in his *Chronology of History* (2nd edn, London, 1838), 358–79; J. E. W. Wallis, *English Regnal Years and Titles* (Helps for Students of History, no. 40, 1921); A. B. and A. Wyon, *The Great Seals of England* (London, 1887) is a guide to the styles used on the great seal, but must be used with some caution. *See also* P. Chaplais, 'The Making of the Treaty of Paris and the royal style', *EHR*, lxvii (1952), 235–53 and S. T. Bindoff, 'The Stuarts and their Style', *EHR*, lx (1945), 192–216.

NOTE ON ROYAL ITINERARIES

The practice of dating instruments issuing from the royal chancery does not begin before the reign of Richard I, and, consequently, the itineraries of his predecessors must be to a great extent conjectural. Richard's itinerary has been reconstructed from his surviving charters with relative precision, but it is not until the reign of John that the survival of most of the chancery enrolments enables a really full itinerary of the king to be traced, although, even so, there are gaps which must be filled from other evidence, principally from surviving original instruments or copies of them. Already under John we have instances of instruments dated on the same day at places widely separated, and in later reigns such differences become increasingly frequent.[1] For this reason, from the reign of Edward II onwards satisfactory royal itineraries can only be traced from royal household accounts (hitherto unpublished) and no adequate itineraries have been compiled so far for any medieval sovereign after the thirteenth century.

List of available itineraries (to 1399)

WILLIAM I—H. W. C. Davis, *Regesta Regum Anglo-Normannorum*, i, *1066–1100* (Oxford, 1913), xxi–xxii.

WILLIAM II—F. Barlow, *William Rufus* (London, 1983), 449–52.

HENRY I—W. Farrer, 'An outline itinerary of Henry I', *EHR*, xxxiv (1919) and separately, with an index (1919); C. Johnson and H. A. Cronne, *Regesta Regum Anglo-Normannorum*, ii, *1100–1135* (Oxford, 1956), xxix–xxxi; *see also* C. H. Haskins, *Norman Institutions* (Cambridge, Mass., 1925), Appendix G (309–20) for the Norman itinerary of Henry I, 1106–1135.

STEPHEN—H. A. Cronne and R. H. C. Davis, *Regesta Regum Anglo-Normannorum*, iii, *1135–1154* (Oxford, 1968), xxxix–xliv; the itineraries of the Empress, Geoffrey of Anjou and Henry fitz Empress are given *ibid.*, xliv–xlviii.

[1] For illustrations *see* H. C. Maxwell-Lyte's *Historical Notes on the Use of the Great Seal* (H.M.S.O. 1926), 247, 251–53, 405–9.

HENRY II—Z. N. Brooke, 'Henry II, Duke of Normandy and Aquitaine', *EHR*, lxi (1946) for visits to England and other journeys, 1142–53; W. Stubbs, *Gesta Regis Henrici II Benedicti Abbatis* (RS, 1867), ii, cxxix–cxlviii; R. W. Eyton, *Court, Household and Itinerary of King Henry II* (London, 1878), conveniently summarized in L. F. Salzmann, *Henry II* (London, 1917), Appendix, 240–51. For Henry II (in France), *see* L. Delisle, *Recueil des Actes de Henri II, roi d'Angleterre et duc de Normandie, concernant les provinces françaises et les affaires de France* (Paris, 1909), Introduction, 63–81.

RICHARD I—L. Landon, *The Itinerary of King Richard I* (Pipe R Soc, NS, xiii, 1935).

JOHN—T. D. Hardy, *Rotuli Litterarum Patentium . . . 1201–1216* (Rec. Com., 1835); Introduction [also reprinted separately, 1835].

HENRY III—MS. itinerary in PRO, Literary Search Room, press 15, no. 79A [by T. Craib and other PRO officers]; for Henry III 1258–63, *see* R. F. Treharne, *The Baronial Plan of Reform, 1258–63* (Manchester, 1932), 383–87.

EDWARD I—H. Gough, *Itinerary of Edward I* (Paisley, 1900), 2 vols [very imperfect]; MS. itinerary in 3 vols by W. E. Safford (1935), in PRO, Literary Search Room, press 15, nos 79B–D. For Edward I in France—J.-P. Trabut-Cussac, 'Itinéraire d'Edouard Ier en France, 1286–89', *BIHR*, xxv (1952).

EDWARD II—'A rough itinerary of the chancery, and probably of Edward II', during the revolution of 1326 (1 Oct.–10 Nov. 1326), in T. F. Tout, *Chapters in the Administrative History of Mediaeval England*, iii (Manchester, 1928), 2, n. 3.

EDWARD III—*See* references in Maxwell-Lyte, *op. cit.*

RICHARD II—approximate itineraries during certain important periods: (*a*) June–July 1381, *see* W. H. B. Bird, 'The Peasants' Rising in 1381 and the King's Itinerary', *EHR*, xxxi (1916), 124–26 and Tout's *Chapters*, iii, 376, n. 1; (*b*) Feb.–Nov. 1387, Tout, *Chapters*, iii, 418–20; (*c*) July–Aug. 1399, M. V. Clarke, *Fourteenth Century Studies* (Oxford, 1937), 70–73.

LIST OF KINGS, 1066–1985

WILLIAM I, s. of Robert I, duke of Normandy, and Arlette, da. of Fulbert the Tanner of Falaise; b. 1027–28; **acc.** 25 Dec. 1066 (date of coronation. There is no reason to suppose that he assumed title of k. earlier); **d.** 9 Sept. 1087.

Absences: Normandy, c. 21 Feb.–7 Dec. 1067; Normandy, early 1072; Normandy and Maine, early 1073 (at Bonneville 30 March)—between Apr. and Dec. 1075 (Fécamp, Apr. 1075; Westminster, Dec. 1075); Normandy and Brittany, spring 1076–summer or autumn 1080 (Brittany, May 1076; Rouen, July 1077; Caen, July 1080; Berkeley, Christmas 1080); Normandy, summer and autumn 1082; Normandy, Easter 1083; Normandy, summer 1084 (Rouen, 19 June); Normandy, summer 1086 to death.

Regents: William fitz Osbern and Odo, bp of Bayeux, were vicars in 1067 (*see* above p. 31).

m. ? 1050–51[1], Matilda, da. of Baldwin V, c. of Flanders.

[1] Guillaume de Poitiers, *Histoire de Guillaume le Conquerant*, ed. R. Foreville (Paris, 1952), 46–47, 66, n. 1.

Issue: Robert Curthose, duke of Normandy, b. *c*. 1053; d. 10 Feb. 1134. Richard, b. *c*. 1055; d. 1069 × 74. Adelaide, b. *c*. 1057. Cecilia, abbess of Caen, *b*. 1058 × 59; d. 1127. K. William II, *q.v.* Matilda, b. *c*. 1061; d.? *a*. 1086. Constance, b. *c*. 1062; m. 1086, Alan, c. of Brittany; d. 1090. Adela, *b. c*. 1064; m. 1080, Stephen, c. of Blois-Chartres; d. 1137. K. Henry I, *q.v.*

Note on titles—William had succeeded as duke of the Normans in 1035 and in 1063 conquered Maine.

WILLIAM II, s. of William I and Matilda of Flanders; b. 1056–60; **acc.** 26 Sept. 1087; **d.** 2 Aug. 1100.

Absences (in France): 2 Feb.–Aug. 1091; 19 Mar.–29 Dec. 1094; Sept. 1096–4 Apr. 1097; 11 Nov. 1097–*c*. 10 Apr. 1099; June–*c*. 29 Sept. 1099.

Regents: Ranulf Flambard acted on occasion.

Note.—William II succeeded his father only in England; Normandy and Maine passed to his elder br. Robert. From 1096 to 1100 William II held the duchy of Normandy in pledge but was never duke.

HENRY I, s. of William I and Matilda; b. the latter half of 1068; **acc.** 5 Aug. 1100 (date of coronation); **d.** 1 Dec. 1135.

Absences (in Normandy): 4 Aug.–*c*. Dec. 1104; 2/8 Apr.–Aug. 1105; July 1106–Mar./Apr. 1107; July 1108–31 May/2 June 1109; aft. 13 Aug. 1111–July 1113; 21 Sept. 1114–July 1115; Apr. 1116–26 Nov. 1120; 11 June 1123–11 Sept. 1126; 26 Aug. 1127–15 July 1129; Aug./early Sept. 1130–aft. 1 Aug. 1131; 2 Aug. 1133–1 Dec. 1135 (death).

Regents: Q. Matilda appears usually to have acted as regent until her death (1 May 1118); William, s. of Henry I, May 1118 until his death (25 Nov. 1120); Roger, bp of Salisbury, 1123–4, and prob. during absences between 1119 and 1135 (*see also* list of justiciars *infra*).

m. (1) 11 Nov. 1100, Edith or Matilda, da. of Malcolm III (Canmore), k. of Scots, and Margaret; d. 1 May 1118. (2) 29 Jan. 1121, Adela, da. of Godfrey VII, c. of Louvain.

Issue (by 1): child, b. *c*. July 1101, d. in infancy.—Matilda, b. *c*. Feb. 1102; d. 10 Sept. 1167; m. (1) Jan 1114, Emperor Henry V; m. (2) 17 June 1128, Geoffrey, c. of Anjou.—William, b. bef. 5 Aug. 1103; d. 25 Nov. 1120.

Illegitimate issue (9 s., 12 das) included: Robert, b. *c*. 1090; cr. e. of Gloucester, June–Sept. 1122; d. 31 Oct. 1147.—Matilda, d. 25 Nov. 1120; m. Rotrou, c. of Perche.—Reginald, cr. e. of Cornwall *c*. Apr. 1141; d. 1 July 1175. For a full list, *see* Complete Peerage, rev. edn V. Gibbs, xi, app. D.

Regnal years: William II killed, 2 Aug. 1100; Henry elected k., 3 Aug. 1100, and crowned, 5 Aug. 1100.

Note.—Henry annexed the duchy of Normandy aft. the battle of Tinchebray (28 Sept. 1106).

STEPHEN, s. of Stephen, c. of Blois and Chartres, and of Adela, da. of K. William I; b. not later than 1100; **acc.** 22 Dec. 1135; **d.** 25 Oct. 1154.

Absence: Normandy 14/20 Mar.–? 28 Nov. 1137 (regent: Roger, bp of Salisbury).

m. 1125, Matilda, da. and h. of Eustace III, c. of Boulogne.

Issue: Eustace, b. ? 1130–31; cr. c. of Boulogne Christmas 1146, or in 1147; d. 1153.—William, b. ? 1132–37; succ. to c. of Boulogne and

Mortain and was e. of Surrey *iure uxoris*; d. Oct. 1159.—Mary, d. 1182.—Baldwin, d. bef. 1137.—Matilda, b. 1134, d. bef. 1137.

Illegitimate issue: Gervase, abbot of Westminster (1137–57).

Regnal years: Henry I d. 1 Dec. 1135; Stephen at once went to England, was acclaimed k. at London and crowned, 22 Dec. 1135.

Note.—Stephen was captured on 2 Feb. 1141 by adherents of Matilda, da. of Henry I, and kept in captivity (at Bristol 13 Feb.– 1 Nov. 1141). He was superseded 7–10 Apr. 1141, but his wife continued during his captivity to issue charters and writs as q. Matilda assumed the title of *domina Anglorum* on 8 Apr. 1141 (her full style was *M. Imperatrix. Henrici Regis filia et Anglorum domina*), but was never crowned. Stephen was released, 1 Nov. 1141, and recrowned, 25 Dec. 1141.

HENRY II, s. of Geoffrey, c. of Anjou, and Matilda, da. of Henry I; b. 5 Mar. 1133; **acc.** 19 Dec. 1154 (date of coronation); **d.** 6 July 1189.

Absences: France, 10 Jan. 1156–*c.* 8 Apr. 1157, 14 Aug. 1158–25 Jan. 1163, Lent (*c.* Feb.)–*c.* May 1165, *c.* 9 Mar. 1166–3 Mar. 1170, *c.* 24 June 1170–3 Aug. 1171; Ireland, 16 Oct. 1171–17 Apr. 1172; France, *c.* 12 May 1172–8 July 1174 (Northants. Pipe Roll suggests that k. made short visit to England in 1173), 8 Aug. 1174–9 May 1175, 18 Aug. 1177–15 July 1178, *c.* 15 Apr. 1180–26 July 1181, 4 Mar. 1182–10 June 1184, 16 Apr. 1185–27 Apr. 1186, 17 Feb. 1187–30 Jan. 1188, 10 July 1188–6 July 1189 (death).

Regents: Queen Eleanor in early years; Empress Matilda; the young k. Henry (not aft. 1172); the justiciars, Robert, e. of Leicester (d. 1168), Richard de Luci (retired 1178), Ranulf Glanville during absences between 1180 and 1189.

m. 18 May 1152, Eleanor, heiress of William, duke of Aquitaine (she d. 1 Apr. 1204).

Issue: William, b. Aug. 1153; d. 1156.—K. Henry, b. 28 Feb. 1155; crowned 14 June 1170 and used style *rex Anglorum et dux Normannorum et comes Andegavorum*; hence called by contemporaries and certain chroniclers K. Henry III; d. 11 June 1183.—Matilda, b. 1156; d. 1189; m. 1168, Henry the Lion, duke of Saxony.—K. Richard I (duke of Aquitaine), *q.v.*—Geoffrey, duke of Brittany, b. 23 Sept. 1158; d. 19 Aug. 1186.—Eleanor, b. 1161; d. 1214; m. 1176 Alphonso VIII, k. of Castile.—Joan, b. Oct. 1165; d. 1199; m. (1) 1177, William II, k. of Sicily; (2) 1196, Raymond VI, c. of Toulouse.—K. John (c. of Mortain and lord of Ireland), *q.v.*

Illegitimate issue included: Geoffrey, bp-elect of Lincoln (1173–82), abp of York (1191), d. 1212; William Longsword, cr. e. of Salisbury, 1198, d. 1226.

Regnal years: K. Stephen d. 25 Oct. 1154. By treaty of Winchester (ratified at Westminster), 1153, Henry was recognized as Stephen's heir. He reached England 8 Dec. 1154 and was crowned 19 Dec. 1154.

Note on titles.—From his parents Henry inherited Normandy, Maine, Touraine and Anjou, and by marriage acquired Aquitaine.

RICHARD I, s. of Henry II and Eleanor of Aquitaine; b. 8 Sept. 1157; **acc.** 3 Sept. 1189 (date of coronation); **d.** 6 Apr. 1199.

Absences: Richard was in France when Henry II d. on 6 July 1189 and reached England on 13 Aug. 1189; France, crusade and captivity in Germany, 12 Dec. 1189–13 Mar. 1194 [regents (*see under* justiciars): Hugh du Puiset, bp of Durham, and William Longchamp, bp of Ely and chancellor (Dec. 1189–June 1190); bp of Ely alone (June 1190–Oct. 1191); Walter of Coutances, abp of Rouen (1191–93); Hubert Walter, abp of Canterbury (late 1193–Mar. 1194)]; France 12 May 1194–until death, 6 Apr. 1199 [regents (successive justiciars): Hubert Walter (May 1194–11 July 1198); Geoffrey Fitz Peter (from July 1198)].

m. 12 May 1191, Berengaria of Navarre.

Illegitimate issue: Philip, m. Amelie, da. of Hélie, lord of Cognac; d. aft. 1211.

JOHN, s. of Henry II and Eleanor of Aquitaine; b. 24 Dec. 1167; **acc.** 27 May 1199 (date of coronation); **d.** 18–19 Oct. 1216.

Absences: John was in France when Richard I d. on 6 Apr. 1199 and returned to England on 25 May 1199; France, 20 June 1199–25 Feb. 1200, 29 Apr./1 May–1/6 Oct. 1200, *c.* 31 May 1201–6 Dec. 1203, 1 June–12 Dec. 1206; Ireland, 16/20 June–24/26 Aug. 1210; France, *c.* 9 Feb.–13 Oct. 1214.

Regents: the justiciar Geoffrey Fitz Peter during absences between 1199 and 1210; in 1214, the justiciar Peter des Roches and William Briwer, later also Richard Marsh (*Rot. Lit. Pat.*, 108, 139).

m. (1) 29 Aug. 1189, Isabella of Gloucester; (2) 24 Aug. 1200, Isabella of Angoulême.

Issue (by 2): K. Henry III, *q.v.*—Richard, b. 5 Jan. 1209; cr. c. of Poitou bef. 14 Aug. 1225 (renounced *c.* Dec. 1243); cr. e. of Cornwall 30 May 1227; elected k. of the Romans 13 Jan. 1257; d. 2 Apr. 1272.—Joan, b. 22 July 1210; d. 5 Mar. 1238; m. 19 June 1221, Alexander II, k. of Scots.— Isabella, b. 1214; d. *c.* 6 Dec. 1241; m. *c.* 11 June 1235, Emperor Frederick II.—Eleanor, b. 1215; d. 1275; m. (1) 1224, William Marshal, e. of Pembroke; m. (2) Jan. 1238, Simon de Montfort, e. of Leicester.

Illegitimate issue included: Joan, d. 30 Mar. 1237, m. Llywelyn ap Iorwerth, ruler of Gwynedd; Richard de Warenne, lord of Chilham (Kent), d. aft. May 1242.

Regnal years: Richard I d. 6 Apr. 1199; John was accepted at once as successor in England and was crowned Ascension Day, 27 May 1199. So his regnal years, reckoned from Ascension Day to Ascension Day, are of unequal length, as follows:

1. 27 May 1199–17 May 1200.	**10.** 15 May 1208–6 May 1209.
2. 18 May 1200–2 May 1201.	**11.** 7 May 1209–26 May 1210.
3. 3 May 1201–22 May 1202.	**12.** 27 May 1210–11 May 1211.
4. 23 May 1202–14 May 1203.	**13.** 12 May 1211–2 May 1212.
5. 15 May 1203–2 June 1204.	**14.** 3 May 1212–22 May 1213.
6. 3 June 1204–18 May 1205.	**15.** 23 May 1213–7 May 1214.
7. 19 May 1205–10 May 1206.	**16.** 8 May 1214–27 May 1215.
8. 11 May 1206–30 May 1207.	**17.** 28 May 1215–18 May 1216.
9. 31 May 1207–14 May 1208.	**18.** 19 May 1216–19 Oct. 1216.

Note on titles.—John was lord of Ireland bef. he became k. and he added this to his other inherited titles.

Note.—The magnates in rebellion against John offered the English crown late in 1215 to Louis, s. of Philip II of France. Louis came to England May 1216, but abandoned his claim Sept. 1217.

HENRY III, s. of K. John and Isabella of Angoulême; b. 1 Oct. 1207; **acc.** 28 Oct. 1216; **d.** 16 Nov. 1272.

Minority: William Marshal, e. of Pembroke, became regent 29 Oct.

1216 (*rector noster et regni nostri*); he d. 14 May 1219. In Apr. 1223 Pope Honorius III allowed the council to declare Henry of age and this was implemented late in 1223 (prob. Dec.) for certain limited purposes (including the resumption of royal castles). Henry did not assume personal rule until he declared himself to be of full age, Jan. 1227.

Absences (in France): 1 May–27 Oct. 1230 (regent: Stephen Segrave); 8/9 May 1242–24/27 Sept. 1243 (regent: Walter Gray, abp of York); 6 Aug. 1253–27 Dec. 1254 (regents: Q. Eleanor and Richard, e. of Cornwall until 29/30 May 1254, subsequently Richard, e. of Cornwall alone); 14 Nov. 1259–23 Apr. 1260 (regent: Hugh Bigod, justiciar); 14 July–20 Dec. 1262 (regent: Philip Basset, justiciar); 23 Sept.–7 Oct. 1263 (regent: Hugh le Despenser, justiciar); 1/5 Jan.–aft. 18 Feb. 1264 (regent: Richard, e. of Cornwall).

m. 20 Jan. 1236, Eleanor of Provence.

Issue: K. Edward I, *q.v.*; cr. e. of Chester 14 Feb. 1254.—Margaret, b. 29 Sept. 1240; d. 26 Feb. 1275; m. 26 Dec. 1251, Alexander III, k. of Scots.—Beatrice, b. 25 June 1242; d. 24 Mar. 1275; m. 22 Jan. 1260, John de Dreux, later duke of Brittany.—Edmund 'Crouchback', b. 16 Jan. 1245; cr. e. of Leicester 26 Oct. 1265 and e. of Lancaster 30 June 1267; d. 5 June 1296.—Katherine, b. 25 Nov. 1253; d. 3 May 1257.— Also other children (at least 4), who d. in infancy.

Note on titles.—Henry abandoned the titles of duke of Normandy and c. of Anjou in 1259.[1]

EDWARD I, s. of Henry III and Eleanor of Provence; b. 17–18 June 1239; **acc.** 20 Nov. 1272; **d.** 7 July 1307.

Absences: Edward was in the kingdom of Sicily when Henry III d. on 16 Nov. 1272 and stayed in Italy and France until he returned to England 2 Aug. 1274 (regents: Walter Giffard, abp of York, Roger Mortimer and Robert Burnel); France, 11 May–19 June 1279, 13 May 1286–12 Aug. 1289 (regent: Edmund, e. of Cornwall); Flanders, 23 Aug. 1297–14 Mar. 1298 (regent: Edward, k.'s son).

m. (1) Between 13–31 Oct. 1254, Eleanor of Castile; (2) 10 Sept. 1299, Margaret of France.

Issue (by 1): Eleanor, b. *c.* 17 June 1264; d. 12 Oct. 1297; m. 20 Sept. 1293, Henry III, c. of Bar.—John, b. 10 June 1266; d. 3 Aug. 1271.— Henry, b. 13 July 1267; d. 14 Oct. 1274.—Isabel, b. 15 Mar. (year uncertain); d. in infancy.—Joan 'of Acre', b. spring 1272, d. 23 Apr. 1307; m. (1) 30 Apr. 1290, Gilbert, e. of Gloucester; (2) Jan. 1297, Ralph de Monthermer.—Alfonso, b. 24 Nov. 1273; d. Aug. 1284.— Margaret, b. 11 Sept. 1275; d. 1318; m. 8 July 1290, John II, duke of Brabant.—Berengaria, b. 1276; d. in infancy.—Mary, b. 11 Mar. 1278; d. 1332.—Elizabeth, b. Aug. 1282; d. *c.* 5 May 1316; m. (1) 1296, John, c. of Holland; (2) 14 Nov. 1302, Humphrey de Bohun, e. of Hereford and Essex.—Edward 'of Carnarvon' (K. Edward II *q.v.*); created p. of Wales and e. of Chester, 7 Feb. 1301.

(By 2): Thomas 'of Brotherton', e. of Norfolk, b. 1 June 1300; d. Aug.

---

[1] He also renounced claims to counties of Maine, Touraine and Poitou, but these were never included in his style in royal documents or on the Great Seal. For the dates of changes in his style, *see* P. Chaplais, 'The making of the Treaty of Paris and the Royal Style', *EHR*, lxvii (1952), 249–51.

1338.—Edmund 'of Woodstock', e. of Kent, b. 5 Aug. 1301; d. 19 Mar.
1330.—Eleanor, b. 4 May 1306; d. 1311.

Illegitimate issue: John Botetourt (Hailes Abbey chronicle, Ms.
Cotton. Cleopatra D. III, fo. 51); d. 1324.

Regnal years: Henry III d. 16 Nov. 1272; the peace of K. Edward was
proclaimed in London, 17 Nov., and on 20 Nov. 1272 (day of the funeral
of Henry III) the magnates swore fealty to K. Edward. Coronation, 19
Aug. 1274. Regnal years dated from 20 Nov. 1272.

EDWARD II, s. of Edward I and Eleanor of Castile; b. 25 Apr. 1284;
acc. 8 July 1307; **deposed** 20 Jan. 1327; **d.** 21 Sept. 1327.

Absences (in France): 22 Jan.–7 Feb. 1308 (regent: Piers Gaveston, e.
of Cornwall); 23 May–16 July 1313 (regent: John Droxford, bp of Bath
and Wells); 12 Dec.–20 Dec. 1313; 19 June–22 July 1320 (regent: Aymer
de Valence, e. of Pembroke).

Edward, k.'s son, proclaimed keeper of the realm, 26 Oct. 1326, and
acted under this title until 20 Nov. 1326.

m. *c.* 25 Jan. 1308, Isabella, da. of Philip IV of France.

Issue: K. Edward III *q.v.*, cr. e. of Chester, 24 Nov. 1312; c. of
Ponthieu and Montreuil, 2 Sept. 1325; duke of Aquitaine, 10 Sept.
1325.—John (of Eltham), b. *c.* 15 Aug. 1316; cr. e. of Cornwall, 16–31
Oct. 1328; d. 13 Sept. 1336.—Eleanor (of Woodstock), b. 18 June 1318;
d. 22 Apr. 1355; m. May 1332, Reginald II, c. of Guelderland.—Jeanne
(of the Tower), b. 5 July 1321; d. 7 Sept. 1362; m. 17 July 1328, David,
aft. David II, k. of Scotland, *q.v.*

Note.—Edward was a captive from 16 Nov. 1326 until his death.

EDWARD III, s. of Edward II and Isabella of France; b. 13 Nov. 1312;
acc. 25 Jan. 1327; assumed personal rule, 19–20 Oct. 1330; **d.** 21 June
1377.

Absences: France, 26 May–11 June 1329 (regent: John, e. of
Cornwall); France, 4 Apr.–20 Apr. 1331 (regent: John, e. of Cornwall);
Netherlands, Germany and France, 16 July 1338–21 Feb. 1340 (regent:
Edward, duke of Cornwall); Netherlands and France, 22 June–30 Nov.
1340 (regent: Edward, duke of Cornwall); Brittany, 23 Oct. 1342–2 Mar.
1343 (regent: Edward, duke of Cornwall); Flanders, 3–26 July 1345
(regent: Lionel, k.'s son); France, 11 July 1346–12 Oct. 1347 (regent:
Lionel, k.'s son); Calais, *c.* 30 Nov. 1348; Calais, early Jan. 1350; at sea,
c. 29 Aug. 1350; Calais and France, late Oct./early Nov.–*c.* 18/21 Nov.
1355 (regent: Thomas, k.'s son); France, 28 Oct. 1359–18 May 1360
(regent: Thomas, k.'s son); Calais, 9 Oct.–*c.* 1 Nov. 1360 (regent:
Thomas, k.'s son); at sea, shortly aft. 31 Aug.–*c.* 30 Sept. 1372 (regent:
Richard, son of Edward, p. of Aquitaine and Wales).

m. 24 Jan. 1328, Philippa, da. of William I, c. of Hainault.

Issue: Edward (of Woodstock), b. 15 June 1330; cr. e. of Chester, 18
Mar. 1333; duke of Cornwall, 3 Mar. 1377; p. of Wales, 12 May 1343; p.
of Aquitaine, 19 July 1362; d. 8 June 1376.—Isabella (of Woodstock), b.
16 June 1332; d. 1379; m. 27 July 1365, Enguerrand de Coucy, later e. of
Bedford.—Jeanne (of the Tower), b. late 1333; d. 2 Sept. 1348.—
William (of Hatfield), b. 1336; d. in boyhood.—Lionel (of Antwerp), b.
29 Nov. 1338; e. of Ulster by marriage (9 Sept. 1342) with Elizabeth de
Burgh, da. and h. of William de Burgh, e. of Ulster; cr. duke of
Clarence, 13 Nov. 1362; d. 17 Oct. 1368.—John (of Gaunt), b. Mar.

1340; cr. e. of Richmond, 20 Sept. 1342; by marriage (19 May 1359) with Blanche, da. of Henry, duke of Lancaster, succ. to e. of Lancaster (by 14 Aug. 1361); cr. duke of Lancaster, 13 Nov. 1362; duke of Aquitaine, 2 Mar. 1390; aft. marriage (Sept. 1371) to Constance, da. of Pedro, k. of Castile, assumed title of k. of Castile and Leon; d. 3–4 Feb. 1399.— Blanche (of the Tower), b. prob. 1341; d. in infancy.—Edmund (of Langley), b. prob. 1342 (5 June); cr. e. of Cambridge, 13 Nov. 1362; duke of York, 6 Aug. 1385; d. 1 Aug. 1402.—Mary (of Waltham), b. 9–10 Oct. 1344; d. early in 1362; m. summer 1361, John IV, duke of Brittany.—Margaret (of Windsor), b. 20 July 1346; d. late in 1361; m. 19 May 1359, John Hastings, e. of Pembroke.—William (of Windsor), b. 1348 (?), d. in infancy.—Thomas (of Woodstock), b. 7 Jan. 1355; cr. e. of Buckingham, 16 July 1377; duke of Gloucester, 6 Aug. 1385; d. prob. 8 or 9 Sept. 1397.

Note on titles.—In Jan. 1340 Edward formally assumed the title of k. of France, reckoning 25 Jan. 1340–24 Jan. 1341 (his 14th year as k. of England) as his 1st year as k. of France; his 21st year as k. of France runs from 25 Jan. 1360 to 24 Oct. 1360 (treaty of Calais). In consequence of the renewal of the war he resumed the title of k. of France, and 11 June 1369 to 24 Jan. 1370 was reckoned as his 30th year as k. of France.

RICHARD II, s. of Edward, p. of Wales, and Joan, da. of Edmund, e. of Kent; b. 6 Jan. 1367; **acc.** 22 June 1377.

Minority: No regent or chief councillor appointed.

Richard may have been deposed for a few days at the end of Dec. 1387.

Ceased to reign 29 Sept. 1399; **d.** bef. 17 Feb. 1400 (possibly 14 Feb.).

Absences: Ireland, 2 Oct. 1394–7/11 May 1395 [regent (*custos*): Edmund, duke of York]; Calais, 7 Aug.–22 Aug. 1396; France, 28 Sept.–11/16 Nov. 1396; Ireland, 29 May–19/31[1] July 1399 [regent (*custos*): Edmund, duke of York].

m. (1) 20 Jan. 1382, Anne of Bohemia, da. of Emperor Charles IV; d. 7 June 1394. (2) 12 Mar. 1396, Isabelle, da. of K. Charles VI of France; d. 13 Sept. 1409.

Note.—Richard was a captive of Henry, duke of Lancaster (K. Henry IV since 30 Sept. 1399), from 19 Aug. 1399 until death.

HENRY IV, s. of John of Gaunt, duke of Lancaster, and Blanche, da. of Henry of Grosmont, duke of Lancaster; b. prob. Apr. 1366; **acc.** 30 Sept. 1399; **d.** 20 Mar. 1413.

m. (1) July 1380–Mar. 1381, Mary Bohun, da. and coh. of Humphrey, last Bohun e. of Hereford; d. ? 4 June 1394. (2) 7 Feb. 1403, Joan, da. of Charles, k. of Navarre, and widow of John, duke of Brittany; d. 9 July 1437.

Issue (by 1): a son, b. Apr. 1382; d. in infancy.—K. Henry V, *q.v.*; cr. p. of Wales, duke of Cornwall and e. of Chester, 15 Oct. 1399; cr. duke of Aquitaine and duke of Lancaster, 10 Nov. 1399.—Thomas, b. 1388; cr. duke of Clarence and e. of Aumale, 9 July 1412; d. 22 Mar. 1421.—John, b. 20 June 1389; cr. duke of Bedford and e. of Kendal, 16 May 1414; cr. e. of Richmond 24 Nov. 1414; d. 15 Sept. 1435.—Humphrey, b. prob. Aug.–Sept. 1390; cr. duke of Gloucester and e. of Pembroke 16 May 1414;

[1] The most probable date of Richard's departure from Ireland is *c.* 24 July. *See* M. V. Clarke, *Fourteenth Century Studies* (Oxford, 1937), 72, n. 3. For a discussion of the chronology of the last period of Richard's rule *see ibid.*, 70–73.

d. 23 Feb. 1447.—Blanche, b. spring 1392; d. 22 May 1409; m. 6 July 1402 Ludwig, s. of Ruprecht, k. of the Romans, c. palatine of the Rhine.— Philippa, b. 4 July 1394; d. 5 Jan. 1430; m. 26 Oct. 1406, K. Eric IX of Denmark.

HENRY V, s. of Henry IV and Mary Bohun; b. ? 16 Sept. 1387 [see note to e. of Lancaster for a discussion of the evidence]; **acc.** 21 Mar. 1413; **d.** 31 Aug.–1 Sept. 1422.

Absences: France, 11 Aug.–16 Nov. 1415 (regent: John, duke of Bedford); Calais, 4 Sept.–16/17 Oct. 1416 (regent: Thomas, duke of Clarence); France, 23/25 July 1417–1/3 Feb. 1421 (regent: John, duke of Bedford); France, 10 June 1421–1 Sept. 1422 (regent: Humphrey, duke of Gloucester).

m. 2 June 1420, Catherine of Valois, da. of K. Charles VI of France. She d. 1437.

Issue: K. Henry VI. *q.v.*

Note.—By Treaty of Troyes, 21 May 1420, Henry assumed the title of heir and regent of the realm of France.

HENRY VI, s. of Henry V and Catherine of Valois; b. 6 Dec. 1421; **acc.** 1 Sept. 1422.

Minority: On 5 Dec. 1422 John, duke of Bedford, was appointed *regni Anglie et ecclesie Anglicane protector et defensor ac consiliarius principalis domini regis* and during his absence from England, Humphrey, duke of Gloucester, was to exercise the same authority, and have the same title, governing with the k.'s council. The office of protector lapsed on 5 Nov. 1429 (coronation of Henry VI). Henry declared of age, 12 Nov. 1437.

Henry was deposed 4 Mar. 1461, restored 3 Oct. 1470, and deposed again 11 Apr. 1471; **d.** 21 May 1471.

Absence: France, 23 Apr. 1430–9 Feb. 1432 (regent: Humphrey, duke of Gloucester).

m. 23 Apr. 1445, Margaret, da. of Rene, duke of Anjou and c. of Provence; she d. 25 Aug. 1482.

Issue: Edward, b. 13 Oct. 1453; duke of Cornwall at birth; cr. p. of Wales and e. of Chester, 15 Mar. 1454; d. 4 May 1471.

Note.—Henry was prisoner of the Yorkist lords from 10 July 1460 to 17 Feb. 1461; he was prisoner of K. Edward IV from 13 July 1465 to the last days of Sept. 1470 and again from 11 Apr. 1471 until death.

EDWARD IV, s. of Richard, duke of York and Cecily Nevill, da. of Ralph, e. of Westmorland; b. 28 Apr. 1442; **acc.** 4 Mar. 1461; prisoner of Richard Nevill, e. of Warwick, Aug.–end of Sept. 1469; fled to the Netherlands 3 Oct. 1470 and returned to England 14 Mar. 1471; restored to kingship 11 Apr. 1471; **d.** 9 Apr. 1483.

Absence: France, c. 4 July–c. 20 Sept. 1475 (regent: Edward, p. of Wales).

m. 1 May 1464, Elizabeth Woodville, da. of Richard, Lord Rivers; d. 8 June 1492.

Issue: Elizabeth, b. 11 Feb. 1466; d. 11 Feb. 1503; m. 18 Jan. 1486, K. Henry VII.—Mary, b. Aug. 1467; d. 23 May 1482.—Cecily, b. 20 Mar. 1469; d. 24 Aug. 1507; m. (1) late in 1487, John Viscount Welles (d. 9 Feb. 1499); m. (2) bef. Jan. 1504, Thomas Kyme.—Edward V, *q.v.*, cr. p. of Wales and e. of Chester 26 June 1471, duke of Cornwall 17 July 1471, e. of March and e. of Pembroke 8 July 1479.—Margaret, b. 10 Apr. and d. 11

Dec, 1472.—Richard, b. prob. 17 Aug. 1473; cr. duke of York 28 May 1474 and duke of Norfolk 7 Feb. 1477; d. prob. July–Sept. 1483.—Anne, b. 2 Nov. 1475; d. 1510–12; m. 4 Feb. 1475, Thomas Howard, e. of Surrey.—George, b. 1477; d. Mar. 1479.—Catherine, b. 1479; d. 15 Nov. 1527; m. 1495, Sir William Courtenay.—Bridget, b. 10 Nov. 1480; d. *c.* 1513.

Illegitimate issue included Arthur, cr. Viscount Lisle 25 Apr. 1523; d. 1542.

EDWARD V, s. of Edward IV and Elizabeth Woodville; b. 2 Nov. 1470; **acc.** 9 Apr. 1483.

Minority: Richard, duke of Gloucester, was protector of the realm, and exercised effective authority from 30 Apr. 1483 until the deposition of Edward V.

Edward was deposed 25 June 1483; **d.** prob. July–Sept. 1483.

RICHARD III, s. of Richard, duke of York, and Cecily Nevill, da. of Ralph, e. of Westmorland; b. 2 Oct. 1452; **acc.** 26 June 1483; **d.** 22 Aug. 1485.

m. 12 July 1472, Anne Neville, da. of Richard, e. of Warwick; she d. 16 Mar. 1485.

Issue: Edward, b. 1473; cr. e. of Salisbury 15 Feb. 1478, duke of Cornwall 26 June 1483, p. of Wales and e. of Chester 24 Aug. 1483; d. prob. 9 Apr. 1484 (possibly Mar.).

HENRY VII, s. of Edmund Tudor, e. of Richmond and of Margaret Beaufort, gt.-gd.-da. of John of Gaunt, duke of Lancaster (3rd s. of K. Edward III); b. 28 Jan. 1457; **acc.** 22 Aug. 1485; his initial regnal year began on 21 Aug. 1485. **d.** 21 Apr. 1509.

Absences: France, 2/6 Oct.–17 Nov./Dec. 1492 (regent: P. Arthur); Calais, 8 May–16 June 1500.

m. 18 Jan. 1486, Elizabeth, da. of K. Edward IV.

Issue: Arthur, b. 19 Sept. 1486; duke of Cornwall at birth; cr. p. of Wales and e. of Chester 29 Nov. 1489; d. 2 Apr. 1502.—Margaret, b. 29 Nov. 1489; d. 18 Oct. 1541; m. K. James IV of Scotland, *q.v.*—Henry VIII, *q.v.* duke of Cornwall on brother's death, cr. p. of Wales and e. of Chester 18 Feb. 1504.—Mary, b. *c.* Mar. 1496, d. 24 June 1533; m. (1) 1514, K. Louis XII of France; m. (2) Charles Brandon, duke of Suffolk.— Edmund, b. 21–22 Feb. 1499; d. 19 June 1500.—Also other children who d. in infancy.

HENRY VIII, s. of Henry VII and Elizabeth of York; b. 28 June 1491; **acc.** 22 Apr. 1509; **d.** 28 Jan. 1547.

Absences: Calais and France, 30 June–22 Oct. 1513; Calais and Gravelines, 31 May–*c.* 16 July 1520; France, 15/16 July–30 Sept. 1544. Regents: queen (1513); Thomas Howard, duke of Norfolk (1520); queen (1544).

m. (1) 11 June 1509, Catherine of Aragon. Marriage declared null and void 23 May 1533 in Abp's Court, and Mar. 1534 'utterly dissolved', etc., by Act of Parliament (25 Henry VIII c. 22); d. 8 Jan. 1536.—**m.** (2) 25 Jan. 1533, Anne Boleyn. Marriage declared valid 28 May 1533 and invalid 17 May 1536. Anne Boleyn exec. 19 May 1536.—**m.** (3) 30 May 1536, Jane

Seymour; d. 24 Oct. 1537.—**m.** (4) 6 Jan. 1540, Anne of Cleves. Marriage annulled 9 July 1540.—**m.** (5) 28 July 1540, Catherine Howard; exec. 13 Feb. 1542.—**m.** (6) 12 July 1543, Catherine Parr.

Issue (by 1): four children who d. at once and Mary I, *q.v.*—(by 2): Elizabeth I, *q.v.*—(by 3): Edward VI, *q.v.*

Illegitimate issue: Henry Fitzroy, b. ? 1519, cr. 1525 duke of Richmond and Somerset; d. 22 July 1536.

Note.—The title of *fidei defensor* conferred on Henry by Pope Leo X in 1521. From 1525 he styled himself 'Henry VIII' and was the first English sovereign to adopt the custom of formally appending a number to his name. By Irish statute 33 Hen. VIII c. I, he was declared k. (in place of lord) of Ireland. By 35 Hen. VIII c. 3, he assumed the style 'K. of England, France and Ireland, defender of the faith and of the Church of England and also of Ireland on earth the supreme head.'

EDWARD VI, s. of Henry VIII and Jane Seymour; b. 12 Oct. 1537; **acc.** 28 Jan. 1547.

Minority: Edward Seymour, e. of Hertford, the k.'s maternal uncle, designated protector 31 Jan. 1547, cr. duke of Somerset 16 Feb. 1547. Formally appointed *personae regiae gubernator ac regnorum dominiorum et subditorum nostrorum protector* 12 Mar. 1547. Deprived 10 Oct. 1549.— No protector or chief councillor appointed for the rest of the reign. K. Edward **d.** 6 July 1553.

JANE, da. of Henry Grey, marquis of Dorset and duke of Suffolk, and Frances da. of Mary Tudor and gd.-da. of Henry VII; b. Oct. 1537; **acc.** 6 July 1553; deposed 19 July 1553; **exec.** 12 Feb. 1554.

m. 21 May 1553, Guildford Dudley.

MARY I, da. of Henry VIII and Catherine of Aragon, b. 18 Feb. 1516; **acc.** 19 July 1553: **d.** 17 Nov. 1558. **m.** 25 July 1554, Philip, k. of Naples and Jerusalem (k. of Spain on abdication of his father Charles 16 Jan. 1556).

Regnal years: Mary reckoned the 2nd year of her reign from 6 July 1554, thus ignoring the reign of Q. Jane. Philip, though not crowned k. of England, was styled k. and his regnal years begin on 25 July.

Note on titles.—Statute 35 Hen. VIII, c. 3, was repealed by 1 & 2 Ph. & M., c. 8, and the claim to supremacy accordingly dropped. By proclamation of 27 July 1554 the two sovereigns were styled 'Philip and Mary, by the grace of God, king and queen of England, France, Naples, Jerusalem, and Ireland, defenders of the faith, princes of Spain and Sicily, archdukes of Austria, dukes of Milan, Burgundy, and Brabant, counts of Hapsburg, Flanders, and Tyrol'.[1]

ELIZABETH I, da. of Henry VIII and Anne Boleyn; b. 7 Sept. 1533; **acc.** 17 Nov. 1558; **d.** 24 Mar. 1603.

Note.—Q. Elizabeth customarily used the style 'Elizabeth, by the grace of God, queen of England, France and Ireland, defender of the faith, etc.'[2]

---

[1] Style further altered in part after the resignation of Emperor Charles V.

[2] For the suggested explanation of 'etc.' which continued to be added until 1801, *see Selected Historical Essays of F. W. Maitland*, ed. Helen M. Cam (Cambridge, 1957), 211.

JAMES I (of Scotland VI, *q.v.*), s. of Henry Stewart, L. Darnley, and Mary, q. of Scots; b. 19 June 1566; **acc.** 24 Mar. 1603; **d.** 27 Mar. 1625.

m. 20 Aug. 1589, Anne of Denmark.

Issue: Henry Frederick, b. 19 Feb. 1594; d. 6 Nov. 1612; cr. duke of Cornwall 1603, p. of Wales and e. of Chester 1610.—Elizabeth, b. 19 Aug. 1596; d. 13 Feb. 1662; m. Frederic, elector palatine (in 1619 k. of Bohemia).—Margaret, b. 24 Dec. 1598.—Charles I, *q.v.*, duke of Cornwall on br.'s d., created p. of Wales and e. of Chester 1616.—Robert, b. 18 Jan. 1602; d. 27 May 1602.—Mary, b. 8 Apr. 1605; d. 16 Dec. 1607.—Sophia, b. 22 June; d. 23 June 1606.

Note on titles.—k. of Scotland from 24 July 1567. After the union of the crowns 24 Mar. 1603, he used the style 'K. of England, Scotland, France and Ireland, defender of the faith, etc.', although by proclamation of 20 Oct. 1604 he declared his intention of using the style 'King of Great Britain, France and Ireland, defender of the faith, etc.'

CHARLES I, s. of James I and Anne of Denmark; b. 19 Nov. 1600; **acc.** 27 Mar. 1625; **exec.** 30 Jan. 1649.

m. 1 May 1625 (by proxy), Henrietta Maria, da. of Henry IV of France.

Issue: Charles II, *q.v.*, declared p. of Wales and e. of Chester perhaps as early as 1638.—Mary, b. 4 Nov. 1631; d. 24 Dec. 1660; m. 1641, William II, p. of Orange.—James II, *q.v.*—Elizabeth, b. 28 Dec. 1635; d. 8 Sept. 1650.—Henry, b. 8 July 1639; d. 13 Sept. 1660.—Henrietta Maria, b. 16 June 1644; d. 30 June 1670; m. 1661, Philip, duke of Orleans.

Note.—Kingship abolished 16 Mar. 1649. Government by a council of state set up 14 Feb. 1649, dissolved 20 Apr. 1653. Another council of state set up 29 Apr. 1653—Cromwell lord protector 16 Dec. 1653.

OLIVER CROMWELL—LORD PROTECTOR, s. of Robert Cromwell and Elizabeth Steward; b. 25 Apr. 1599; **acc.** 16 Dec. 1653; **d.** 3 Sept. 1658.

m. Elizabeth Bourchier.

Issue: Robert, b. 1621; d. May 1639.—Oliver, b. 1622; d. Mar. 1644.— Richard, lord protector, *q.v.*—Henry, b. 20 Jan. 1628; d. 23 Mar. 1673.— Bridget, m. (1) 1646, Henry Ireton; (2) 1652, Charles Fleetwood.— Elizabeth.—Mary.—Frances.

RICHARD CROMWELL—LORD PROTECTOR, s. of Oliver Cromwell and Elizabeth Bourchier; b. 4 Oct. 1626; **acc.** 3 Sept. 1658; abdicated 24 May 1659; **d.** 12 July 1712.

m. Dorothy Major.

Issue: one s. and three das.

CHARLES II, s. of Charles I and Henrietta Maria; b. 29 May 1630; **acc.** 29 May 1660; **d.** 6 Feb. 1685.

m. 21 May 1662, Catherine of Braganza.

Illegitimate issue included James, b. 9 Apr. 1649; cr. 1663 duke of Monmouth, exec. 15 July 1685 (for other illegitimate issue, *see* G.E.C., *Complete Peerage*, VI, App. F).

Note.—Regnal years date from execution of Charles I, 30 Jan. 1649.

JAMES II, s. of Charles I and Henrietta Maria; b. 14 Oct. 1633; **acc.** 6 Feb. 1685. By legal fiction reign ended 11 Dec. 1688, when he fled from the kingdom; **d.** 6 Sept. 1701.

m. (1) 3 Sept. 1660, Anne Hyde, d. 31 Mar. 1671; (2) 30 Sept. 1673, Mary of Modena.

Issue (by 1): Mary II, *q.v.*—Anne, *q.v.*—(by 2): James 'old Pretender', b. 10 June 1688; d. 1 Jan. 1766, styled 1688 p. of Wales, attainted 1702.—Louisa Maria Theresa, b. 28 June 1692; d. 18 Aug. 1712.

Illegitimate issue included James Fitzjames, b. 1670; created 1687 duke of Berwick; d. 12 June 1734.

Note.—Interregnum 11 Dec. 1688 to 12 Feb. 1689. The peers in London assumed the executive functions 24 Dec., on their invitation William assumed them. A convention parliament offered William and Mary the crown of England and Ireland 13 Feb. 1689. A Scottish convention ordered proclamation of William and Mary, Mar. 1689.

WILLIAM III, s. of William II, p. of Orange, and Mary Stuart, da. of Charles I; b. 4 Nov. 1650; **acc.** 13 Feb. 1689; **d.** 8 Mar. 1702.

Absences: Ireland, 11 June–6 Sept. 1690; United Provinces, 16 Jan.–13 Apr. 1691; United Provinces and Netherlands, 2 May–19 Oct. 1691; 5 Mar.–18 Oct. 1692; 31 Mar.–29 Oct. 1693; 6 May–9 Nov. 1694; 12 May–10 Oct. 1695; United Provinces, Netherlands and Cleves, 6 May–6 Oct. 1696; United Provinces and Netherlands, 26 Apr.–14 Nov. 1697; United Provinces, 20 July–3 Dec. 1698; 2 June–18 Oct. 1699; 5 July–18 Oct. 1700; 4 July–4 Nov. 1701.

Regents: Mary, while she lived, exercised the royal power during William's absences in virtue of statute 2 William and Mary, c. 6. After her death, William appointed lords justices to act during his absences.

m. 4 Nov. 1677, Mary elder da. of James, duke of York, aft. James II of England.

Note.—On 13 Feb. 1689, William and Mary were made k. and q. for their joint and separate lives; William however possessed the sole and full exercise of the regal power.

MARY II, da. of James, duke of York, afterwards James II of England, and Anne Hyde; b. 30 Apr. 1662; **acc.** 13 Feb. 1689; **d.** 28 Dec. 1694.

m. 4 Nov. 1677, William III, p. of Orange.

ANNE, da. of James Stuart, duke of York, aft. James II of England, and Anne Hyde; b. 6 Feb. 1665; **acc.** 8 Mar. 1702; **d.** 1 Aug. 1714.

m. 28 July 1683, P. George of Denmark, s. of Frederick III of Denmark.

Issue: William, b. 24 July 1689; cr. duke of Gloucester 27 July 1689; d. 30 July 1700.—Also several children who were still-born or d. in infancy.

Note on style.—After the Union with Scotland, 1 May 1707, Anne was styled 'Q. of Great Britain, France and Ireland'.[1]

GEORGE I, s. of Ernest Augustus, aft. (1692) elector of Hanover, and Sophia, da. of Frederick, elector palatine; b. 28 May 1660; **acc.** 1 Aug. 1714; **d.** 11 June 1727.

Absences: Hanover, 1 Aug.–18 Sept. 1714; 7 July 1716–18 Jan. 1717; 11 May–14 Nov. 1719; 15 June–10 Nov. 1720; Hanover and Brandenburg, 5 June–28 Dec. 1723; Hanover, 4 June 1725–3 Jan. 1726; 3–11 June 1727. On the latter date the k. d.

Regents: During the k.'s second absence the p. of Wales acted as guardian of the realm. During the k.'s other absences lords justices acted as they had done during the interval between Anne's death and the k.'s arrival.

[1] The phrase 'Great Britain' had been used on the great seal almost continuously since 1625.

m. 21 Nov. 1682, Sophia Dorothea, da. of George William, duke of Lüneburg-Celle.

Issue: George II, *q.v.*, cr. p. of Wales, 27 Sept. 1714.—Sophia Dorothea, b. 16 Mar. 1687; d. 28 June 1757; m. 17 Nov. 1706, Frederick William, p. aft. k. of Prussia.

Illegitimate issue.—By the duchess of Kendal: Petronille Melusine, b. 1693; m. Philip, e. of Chesterfield.—Margaret Gertrude, b. 1703; m. count von Lippe.

Note.—George was elector of Hanover at the time of his accession to the British throne.

GEORGE II, s. of George, elector of Hanover, aft. (1714) k. of Great Britain and Ireland, and Sophia Dorothea, da. of George William, duke of Lüneburg-Celle; b. 30 Oct. 1683; **acc.** 11 June 1727; **d.** 25 Oct. 1760.

Absences: Hanover, 22 May–11 Sept. 1729; 7 June–26 Sept. 1732; 17 May–26 Oct. 1735; 24 May 1736–14 Jan. 1737; 23 May–13 Oct. 1740; 7 May–20 Oct. 1741; Hanover and campaign in Germany, 11 May–15 Nov. 1743; Hanover, 10 May–31 Aug. 1745; 19 May–23 Nov. 1748; 17 Apr.–4 Nov. 1750; 6 Apr.–18 Nov. 1752; 28 Apr.–? 15 Sept. 1755.

Regents: Q. Caroline acted as regent during the k.'s absences in 1729, 1732, 1735 and 1736–37. During his subsequent absences lords justices acted.

m. 22 Aug. 1705, Caroline, da. of John Frederick, margrave of Brandenburg-Anspach.

Issue: Frederick, b. 20 Jan. 1707; cr. p. of Wales 8 Jan. 1729; d. 20 Mar. 1751.—Anne, b. 22 Oct. 1709; d. 12 Jan. 1759; m. 14 Mar. 1734, P. William IV of Orange.—Amelia (Emily), b. 30 May 1711; d. 31 Oct. 1786.—Caroline Elizabeth, b. 30 May 1713; d. 28 Dec. 1757.—George William, b. 2 Nov. 1717; d. in infancy.—William Augustus, b. 15 Apr. 1721; cr. duke of Cumberland, 27 July 1726; d. 31 Oct. 1765.—Mary, b. 22 Feb. 1723; d. 16 Jan. 1772; m. 8 May 1740, Frederick aft. landgrave of Hesse-Cassel.—Louisa, b. 7 Dec. 1724; d. 8 Dec. 1751; m. 27 Oct. 1743, Frederick, p. royal, aft. k. of Denmark.

Illegitimate issue: Madame Walmoden's second son, John Louis, b. 1736, was reputed to be the k.'s, but was not publicly acknowledged.

GEORGE III, s. of Frederick, p. of Wales, and Augusta, da. of Frederick II, duke of Saxe-Gotha; b. 24 May 1738; **acc.** 25 Oct. 1760; **d.** 29 Jan. 1820.

m. 8 Sept. 1761, Charlotte, da. of Charles Louis, heir to duke of Mecklenburg-Strelitz.

Issue: George IV, *q.v.*, cr. p. of Wales, 19 Aug. 1762.—Frederick, b. 16 Aug. 1763; cr. duke of York, 29 Nov. 1784; d. 5 Jan. 1827.—William IV, *q.v.*, cr. duke of Clarence, 20 May 1789.—Charlotte, b. 29 Sept. 1766; d. 5 Oct. 1828; m. 18 May 1797, Frederick Charles, p. aft. k. of Wurtemburg.—Edward, b. 2 Nov. 1767; cr. duke of Kent, 24 Apr. 1799; d. 23 Jan. 1820.—Augusta, b. 8 Nov. 1768; d. 22 Sept. 1840.—Elizabeth, b. 22 May 1770; d. 10 Jan. 1840; m. 7 Apr. 1818, Frederick Joseph, landgrave and p. of Hesse-Homburg.—Ernest Augustus, b. 5 June 1771; cr. duke of Cumberland, 24 Apr. 1799; succeeded as k. of Hanover, 20 June 1837; d. 18 Nov. 1851.—Augustus, b. 27 Jan. 1773; cr. duke of Sussex, 27 Nov. 1801; d. 21 Apr. 1843.—Adolphus, b. 24 Feb. 1774; cr. duke of Cambridge, 27 Nov. 1801; d. 8 July 1850.—Mary, b. 25 Apr. 1776;

d. 30 Apr. 1857; m. 22 July 1816, William, duke of Gloucester.—Sophia, b. 3 Nov. 1777; d. 27 May 1848.—Octavius, b. 23 Feb. 1779; d. 3 May 1783.—Alfred, b. 22 Sept. 1780; d. 26 Aug. 1782.—Amelia, b. 7 Aug. 1783; d. 2 Nov. 1810.

Note.—On 5 Feb. 1811, owing to the insanity of George III, the p. of Wales became regent.

After the Union with Ireland by proclamation of 1 Jan. 1801, in virtue of statute 39 and 40 Geo. III, c. 67, George was henceforth styled 'By the grace of God, of the United Kingdom of Great Britain and Ireland k., defender of the faith'. The title 'K. of France' was thus dropped. Hanover was made a kingdom in 1814.

GEORGE IV, s. of George III and Charlotte; b. 12 Aug. 1762; **acc.** 29 Jan. 1820; **d.** 26 June 1830.

Absence: Hanover, 27 Sept.–8 Nov. 1821. *Regents:* During the k.'s absence lords justices acted.

m. 8 Apr. 1795, Caroline, da. of Charles, duke of Brunswick-Wolfenbüttel.

Issue: Charlotte, b. 7 Jan. 1796; m. 2 May 1816, P. Leopold, 3rd s. of Francis, duke of Saxe-Coburg-Saalfeld; d. without issue 6 Nov. 1817.

WILLIAM IV, s. of George III and Charlotte; b. 21 Aug. 1765; **acc.** 26 June 1830; **d.** 20 June 1837.

m. 11 July 1818, Adelaide, da. of George, duke of Saxe-Meiningen.

Issue: Charlotte, b. and d. 27 Mar. 1819.—Elizabeth, b. 10 Dec. 1820; d. 4 Mar. 1821.

Illegitimate issue: George Augustus Frederick FitzClarence, b. 1794, cr. 1831 e. of Munster; and nine other children by Mrs Jordan.

Note.—On the death of William, the crown of Hanover, where the Salic law obtained, passed to his br. Ernest, *q.v.*

VICTORIA, da. of Edward, duke of Kent, and Mary Louise Victoria, da. of Francis, duke of Saxe-Coburg-Saalfeld; b. 24 May 1819; **acc.** 20 June 1837; **d.** 22 Jan. 1901.

m. 10 Feb. 1840, P. Albert of Saxe-Coburg.

Issue: Victoria, b. 21 Nov. 1840; d. 5 Aug. 1901; m. 25 Jan. 1858, P. Frederick of Prussia.—Edward VII, *q.v.*, cr. p. of Wales, 4 Dec. 1841.—Alice, b. 25 Apr. 1843; d. 14 Dec. 1878; m. 1 July 1862, P. Louis of Hesse-Darmstadt.—Alfred, b. 6 Aug. 1844; cr. duke of Edinburgh, 24 May 1866; succeeded as duke of Saxe-Coburg and Gotha, 22 Aug. 1893; d. 30 July 1900.—Helena, b. 25 May 1846; d. 9 June 1923; m. 5 July 1866, P. Christian of Schleswig-Holstein.—Louise, b. 18 Mar. 1848; d. 3 Dec. 1939; m. 21 Mar. 1871, John, marquis of Lorne, aft. duke of Argyll.—Arthur, b. 1 May 1850; cr. duke of Connaught, 24 May 1874; d. 16 Jan. 1942.—Leopold, b. 7 Apr. 1853; cr. duke of Albany, 24 May 1881; d. 28 Mar. 1884.—Beatrice, b. 14 Apr. 1857; d. 26 Oct. 1944; m. 23 July 1885, P. Henry of Battenberg.

Note.—By proclamation of 1 May 1876, in virtue of statute 21 and 22 Vict., c. 106, Q. Victoria assumed the additional title of 'Empress of India'.

EDWARD VII, s. of Victoria and P. Albert; b. 9 Nov. 1841; **acc.** 22 Jan. 1901; **d.** 6 May 1910.

m. 10 Mar. 1863, Alexandra, da. of Christian IX of Denmark.

Issue: Albert, b. 8 Jan. 1864; d. 14 Jan. 1892; cr. duke of Clarence, 24 May 1890.—George V, *q.v.*; cr. duke of York, 24 May 1892; p. of Wales 9 Nov. 1901.—Louise, b. 20 Feb. 1867; d. 4 Jan. 1931; m. 27 July 1889, Alexander, duke of Fife.—Victoria, b. 6 July 1868; d. 2 Dec. 1935.—Maud, b. 26 Nov. 1869; d. 20 Nov. 1938; m. 22 July 1896, P. Charles of Denmark aft. K. Haakon VII of Norway.—John, b. 6 Apr. 1871; d. 7 Apr. 1871.

Note on style.—By inheritance Edward was 'k. of the United Kingdom of Great Britain and Ireland'. He also assumed on his accession the title 'Emperor of India' in virtue of statute 39 Vict., c. 10. In 1901 Parliament, by the Royal Titles Act, added the phrase 'and of the British Dominions beyond the Seas'. Edward's title then ran 'Edward the Seventh, by the Grace of God, of the United Kingdom of Great Britain and Ireland and of the British Dominions beyond the Seas, K., Defender of the Faith, Emperor of India'.

GEORGE V, s. of Edward VII and Alexandra; b. 3 June 1865; **acc.** 6 May 1910; **d.** 20 Jan. 1936.

m. 6 July 1893, Victoria Mary, da. of Francis, duke of Teck.

Issue: Edward VIII, *q.v.*, cr. p. of Wales, 23 June 1910.—George VI, *q.v.*, cr. duke of York, 4 June 1920.—Mary, b. 25 Apr. 1897; m. 28 Feb. 1922, Henry, Viscount Lascelles, aft. e. of Harewood.—Henry, b. 31 Mar. 1900; cr. duke of Gloucester, 31 Mar. 1928.—George, b. 20 Dec. 1902; cr. duke of Kent, 10 Oct. 1934; d. 25 Aug. 1942.—John, b. 12 July 1905; d. 18 Jan. 1919.

Note on style.—On 12 May 1927 K. George in virtue of statute 17 and 18 George V, c. 4, issued a proclamation declaring that henceforth his title would be 'George V, by the Grace of God of Great Britain, Ireland and the British Dominions beyond the Seas K., Defender of the Faith, Emperor of India'.

EDWARD VIII, s. of George V and Mary; b. 23 June 1894; **acc.** 20 Jan. 1936; abdicated 11 Dec. 1936; d. 28 May 1972.

m. 3 June 1937, Wallis Warfield.

GEORGE VI, s. of George V and Mary; b. 14 Dec. 1895; **acc.** 11 Dec. 1936; **d.** 6 Feb. 1952.

m. 26 Apr. 1923, Lady Elizabeth Bowes-Lyon.

Issue: Elizabeth II, *q.v.*—Margaret, b. 21 Aug. 1930; m. 6 May 1960, Anthony Armstrong-Jones.

Note on titles.—On 22 June 1947 K. George in virtue of, but in anticipation of, his assent to statute 10 and 11 George VI, c. 30, issued a proclamation abandoning the title 'Emperor of India'.

ELIZABETH II, da. of George VI and Elizabeth; b. 21 Apr. 1926; **acc.** 6 Feb. 1952.

m. 20 Nov. 1947, P. Philip, s. of P. Andrew of Greece, cr. duke of Edinburgh, 19 Nov. 1947.

Issue: Charles, p. of Wales, b. 14 Nov. 1948; m. 29 July 1981 Lady Diana Spencer.—Anne, b. 15 Aug. 1950; m. 14 Nov. 1973 Captain Mark Phillips.—Andrew, b. 19 Feb. 1960.—Edward, b. 10 Mar. 1964.

Note on style.—On 29 May 1953 Q. Elizabeth issued proclamations simultaneously in London and other Commonwealth capitals assuming separate titles as queen of the United Kingdom and of other Common-wealth countries. The United Kingdom proclamation was issued in virtue of statute 1 and 2 Eliz. II, c. 9. The style assumed in the United Kingdom was 'Elizabeth II, by the Grace of God of the United Kingdom of Great Britain and Northern Ireland and of Her other Realms and Territories Q., Head of the Commonwealth, Defender of the Faith'. All the styles contain the phrase 'and of her other Realms and Territories Q.' after the name of the particular Commonwealth country and the phrase 'Head of the Commonwealth'.

WALES

Note.—Among the numerous dynasties which emerged in Wales during the sub-Roman period the lines traditionally associated with the names of Maelgwn Gwynedd and Cadell Ddyrnllug—founders respectively of the two major provinces of Gwynedd and Powys—ended in the male line during the ninth century. Rhodri the Great, with whom two of the lists given below begin, succeeded to Gwynedd, it would appear, through his grandmother, and to Powys through his mother, and to Seisyllwg (Ceredigion and Ystrad Tywi) by marriage. Rhodri's grandson, Hywel the Good, added Dyfed to Seisyllwg by marriage to form the leading S. Wales province of Deheubarth. From the division of Rhodri's realm, in accordance with the normal Welsh practice of partible succession, between his sons, Anarawd and Cadell, the subsequent rulers of Gwynedd and Deheubarth traced their rights in almost unbroken succession. Tradition would claim that a third son, Merfyn, carried on the line of Rhodri in Powys. In fact, the dynastic position in Powys remains very obscure (*see Archaeologia Cambrensis*, lxxxv, 1930) until 1063, when Bleddyn ap Cynfyn, with whom, as the real founder of the medieval dynasty of Powys, the list for that province begins, followed his uterine brother, Gruffudd ap Llywelyn, in the governance of Powys.

Most of the minor dynasties mentioned in the earlier pedigrees [*see* Lloyd, *History of Wales* (1912), i, chapter viii, and Phillimore in *Cymmrodor*, ix], came to an end towards the close of the dark ages, or were converted, as in the case of Morgannwg, Gwent and Brycheiniog, and the Dyfed portion of Deheubarth, into marcher lordships, following the first phase of the Norman Conquest of Wales (*see* J. G. Edwards, 'The Normans and the Welsh March', *British Academy Raleigh Lecture*, 1956). Some survived in the hill-country of Glamorgan, in the region between the Wye and the Severn, and in the Arwystli and Cydewain areas of central Wales until the thirteenth century. Members of these dynasties are not included in the lists printed below, but information will be found in the genealogical tables at the end of Lloyd, *History of Wales*, ii. The same applies to those minor dynasties which enjoyed a measure of permanence during the twelfth and thirteenth centuries and which were brought into existence through the operation from time to time of partible succession (*cyfran*) within the three major provinces. Although the lists below do indicate, where possible, the point at which such 'appanages' emerged (the names of their rulers printed in thicker type), fuller details should be sought in Lloyd's tables.

Rules of succession were never clearly defined in medieval Welsh law and practice. Throughout the period covered in the lists the principles of partible and single succession were in conflict, the former triumphing at the end in Deheubarth and N. Powys, the latter in S. Powys, and in Gwynedd where, under the Llywelyns, policy was directed towards translating into reality the concept of the one feudal principality of Wales.

Until the middle of the twelfth century the most common style of Welsh rulers was *brenin, rex*. Thereafter they appear most frequently as lords (*arglwyddi*) of Wales with the exception of the rulers of Gwynedd who appear to have assumed as a distinctive title *tywysog* (prince)—one of several generic terms used in medieval Wales for leader. The variations in the style of the princes of Gwynedd in the thirteenth century are shown in the Gwynedd list.

The authorities on which the lists are based are the chronicles known as *Annales*

Cambriae, Brut y Tywysogyon, Brut y Saeson. For their relations and value, *see* J. E. Lloyd, 'The Welsh Chronicles', in *Proceedings of the British Academy*, xiv (1928). Questions of chronology are discussed, as they arise, in Lloyd's *History of Wales. See also* the pedigrees at the end of that work. English translations of the two best versions of *Brut y Tywysogyon* (The Chronicle of the Princes) are now available—trs. and ed. by Thomas Jones in the *History and Law Series* of the Board of Celtic Studies, nos 11 and 16 (1952 and 1955).

GWYNEDD

RHODRI THE GREAT (RHODRI MAWR), s. of Merfyn Frych (the Freckled) ap Gwriad and Nest, da. of Cadell ap Brochwel of Powys; **acc.** to Gwynedd, 844; to Powys, 855; to Seisyllwg, 872; **d.** 878.

m. Angharad, da. of Meurig ap Dyfnwallon of Ceredigion.

Issue: Anarawd, Cadell, Merfyn and 3 other s. (*See* introductory note.)

ANARAWD, s. of Rhodri the Great and Angharad; **acc.** to Gwynedd, 878; **d.** 916.

Issue: Idwal; Elisedd.

IDWAL THE BALD, s. of Anarawd; **acc.** to Gwynedd, 916; **d.** 942.

Issue: Iago, Idwal (or Ieuaf *i.e.* junior) d. 988.—Meurig, d. 986.— Rhodri, d. 968.

Hywel the Good (see DEHEUBARTH) *ruled Gwynedd from 942 to 950.*

IAGO AP IDWAL THE BALD; **acc.** to Gwynedd, 950; dispossessed 979.

HYWEL AP IEUAF, neph. of Iago; **acc.** to Gwynedd, 979; **d.** 985.

CADWALLON AP IEUAF, br. of Hywel; **acc.** to Gwynedd, 985; **d.** 986.

Maredudd ap Owain ap Hywel the Good (see DHEUBARTH) *ruled Gwynedd from 986 to 999.*

CYNAN AP HYWEL, s. of Hywel ap Ieuaf; **acc.** to Gwynedd, 999; **d.** 1005.

Llywelyn ap Seisyll (see DEHEUBARTH) *ruled Gwynedd until his d. in 1023.*

IAGO AP IDWAL, s. of Idwal ap Meurig ap Idwal the Bald; **acc.** to Gwynedd prob. in 1023; **d.** 1039.

Issue: Cynan.

Gruffudd ap Llywelyn (see DEHEUBARTH) *ruled Gwynedd from 1039 to 1063. Bleddyn ap Cynfyn (see* POWYS), *half-br. to Gruffudd ap Llywelyn, appears to have ruled Gwynedd as well as Powys from 1063 to 1075. Trahaearn ap Caradog, cous. to Bleddyn, and ruler of Arwystli, a minor Welsh Kingdom, ruled Gwynedd from 1075 to 1081.*

GRUFFUDD AP CYNAN, s. of Cynan ab Iago ab Idwal and Ragnhildr, da. of Olaf, s. of Sitric of the Silken Beard; b. *c.* 1055; **acc.** to Gwynedd, 1081; **d.** 1137.

m. Angharad, da. of Owain ab Edwin.

Issue: Owain.—Cadwaladr, d. 1172.—Cadwallon, d. 1132.—Susanna. —Gwenllian.—Marared.—Rannillt.—Annest.

Founder of the medieval realm of Gwynedd and ancestor of all its later rulers.

OWAIN GWYNEDD, s. of Gruffudd ap Cynan and Angharad; **acc.** to Gwynedd, 1137; **d.** 1170.

m. (1) Gwladus, da. of Llywarch ap Trahaern; (2) Christina, da. of Gronw ab Owain ab Edwin.

Issue: Rhun, d. 1146.—Hywel, d. 1170.—Iorwerth Drwyndwn (Flat-nose).—Maelgwn.—David.—Rhodri.—Cynan.—Angharad.—Gwenllian.

DAFYDD AB OWAIN, s. of Owain Gwynedd and Christina; **acc.** (aft. a five-year period of civil war among the s. of Owain) to E. Gwynedd, 1175. Dispossessed in 1194 and **d.** 1203 in exile.

m. 1174, Emma, natural da. of Geoffrey of Anjou.

Issue: Owain.

RHODRI AB OWAIN, s. of Owain Gwynedd and Christina; **acc.** to W. Gwynedd, 1175; **d.** 1195.

m. da. of Rhys ap Gruffudd (*see* DEHEUBARTH).

Issue: Gruffudd.

CYNAN AB OWAIN, s. of Owain Gwynedd by an unknown woman; **acc.** to Gwynedd *c.* 1170; **d.** 1174.

Issue: Gruffudd, d. 1200.—Maredudd, d. 1212. Maredudd's descendants ruled in Merioneth, between the Mawddach and the Dovey, until Llewelyn ap Maredudd (d. 1263) was finally expelled by Llewelyn ap Gruffudd (*see below*) in 1256. [Llewelyn ap Maredudd's s., Madoc ap Llywelyn, led the rising against Edward I in 1294–95.]

LLYWELYN AP IORWERTH, s. of Iorwerth Drwyndwn ab Owain Gwynedd and Marared, da. of Madog ap Maredudd (*see* POWYS); b. 1173; **acc.** to E. Gwynedd, 1195; to W. Gwynedd, 1200; to S. Gwynedd, 1202; to S. Powys, 1208; to the overlordship of Deheubarth, 1216; **d.** 11 Apr. 1240.

m. 1205 Joan, natural da. of K. John.

Issue: Gruffudd, by Tangwystyl, da. of Llywarch Goch of Rhos.—David, by Joan.—Gwenllian, d. 1281; m. William de Lacy.—Helen, d. 1253; m. John the Scot, e. of Chester.—Gwladus Ddu (the Black), d. 1251; m. (1) Reginald de Breose; (2) Ralph Mortimer.—Margaret, m. (1) John de Breose; (2) Walter Clifford.—Susanna.

Known as Llywelyn the Great. From 1230 style changed from 'Prince of Gwynedd' to 'Prince of Aberffraw and lord of Snowdon'.

DAVID AP LLYWELYN, s. of Llywelyn ap Iorwerth and Joan; **acc.** to Gwynedd, 1240; **d.** 25 Feb. 1246.

m. Isabella, da. of William de Breose V.

At the close of his reign assumed the style (in one known document) of 'Prince of Wales'.

LLYWELYN AP GRUFFUDD, s. of Gruffudd ap Llywelyn ap Iorwerth and Senena; **acc.** to Gwynedd (in part) 1246; (the whole) 1256; overlordship of all the lords of Wales, with assumption of title 'Prince of Wales', 1258; official recognition of title and lordship over extensive portions of the March of Wales by Henry III, 1267; **d.** 11 Dec. 1282.

m. 1278, Eleanor, da. of Simon de Montfort, e. of Leicester.

Issue: Gwenllian, a nun of Sempringham; d. 1337.

The last effective native ruler of Gwynedd.

DAVID AP GRUFFUDD, S. of Gruffudd ap Llywelyn ap Iorwerth. Assumed title 'Prince of Wales', 1282. Executed for treason against Edward I, 3 Oct. 1283.[1]

m. Elizabeth Ferrers, da. of Robert, former e. of Derby.

Issue: Llywelyn, d. a prisoner 1288.—Owain, a prisoner alive 1305.—Seven das who became nuns.

DEHEUBARTH

RHODRI THE GREAT (*see* GWYNEDD).

CADELL, S. of Rhodri the Great and Angharad; **acc.** to Deheubarth (Seisyllwg), 878; **d.** 909.
Issue: Clydog, d. 920.—Hywel.

HYWEL THE GOOD (HYWEL DDA), S. of Cadell ap Rhodri; **acc.** Dyfed, *c.* 904; to Seisyllwg, *c.* 920; to Gwynedd, 942 (*see* GWYNEDD); **d.** 949 or 950.
m. Elen, da. of Llywarch ap Hyfaidd of Dyfed.
Issue: Rhodri, d. 953.—Edwin, d. 954.—Owain.
Reintegrated the realm of Rhodri the Great and added Dyfed. The legislative code associated with his name became the foundation of medieval Welsh jurisprudence.

OWAIN AP HYWEL, S. of Hywel the Good and Elen; **acc.** to Deheubarth (*i.e.* Seisyllwg and Dyfed), 954; **d.** 988.
Issue: Cadwallon, d. 966.—Einion, d. 984.—Idwallon, d. 975.—Maredudd.

MAREDUDD AB OWAIN, S. of Owain ap Hywel the Good; **acc.** to Gwynedd (*see* GWYNEDD), 986; to Deheubarth, 987; **d.** 999.
Issue: Cadwallon, d. 992.—Angharad.

LLYWELYN AB SEISYLL, S. of Seisyll and Prawst, da. of Elisedd ab Anarawd ap Rhodri the Great; **acc.** to Gwynedd, *c.* 1005; to Deheubarth, *c.* 1018; **d.** 1023.
m. Angharad, da. of Maredudd ab Owain.
Issue: Gruffudd.

RHYDDERCH AB IESTYN,[1] **acc.** to Deheubarth, 1023; **d.** 1033.
Issue: Gruffudd Rhys, d. 1053.—Caradog, d. 1035. A usurper from S.E. Wales.

HYWEL AB EDWIN, S. of Edwin ab Einion ab Owain ap Hywel the Good; **acc.** to Deheubarth, *c.* 1035; **d.** 1044.

GRUFFUDD AB RHYDDERCH,[1] S. of Rhydderch ab Iestyn; **acc.** to Deheubarth, *c.* 1044; **d.** 1055.

---

[1] Rhodri, a br. of the last princes of Gwynedd, lived on until 1315, as a royal pensioner in England. His grandson, Owain ap Thomas ap Rhodri, better known as Owen of Wales, and in continental chronicles as 'Yevain de Galles', was a soldier of fortune who became a source of embarrassment to the English government because of his claim to the principate of Wales. With his assassination, in 1378, the male line of the house of Gwynedd ended, the succession passing to Roger Mortimer, 4th earl of March, through the distant link of marriage between Ralph Mortimer and Gwladus Ddu, da. of Llywelyn the Great. This Welsh strain was ultimately transmitted through the Mortimers to the Yorkist line.

[2] This dynasty held lands in Gwynllwg, S.E. Wales, to 1270.

GRUFFUDD AP LLYWELYN, s. of Llywelyn ap Seisyll and Angharad; **acc.** to Gwynedd and Powys, 1039; to Deheubarth, 1055; **d.** 1063.
Issue: Maredudd, d. 1070.—Idwal, d. 1070.—Nest, m. Osbern fitz Richard. The only native ruler to exercise power throughout Wales.

MAREDUDD AB OWAIN, s. of Owain ap Edwin ab Einion ab Owain ap Hywel the Good; **acc.** to Deheubarth, c. 1063; **d.** 1072.

RHYS AB OWAIN, s. of Owain ap Edwin ab Einion ab Owain ap Hywel the Good; **acc.** to Deheubarth, 1072; **d.** 1078.

RHYS AP TEWDWR, s. of Tewdwr ap Cadell ab Einion ab Owain ap Hywel the Good; **acc.** to Deheubarth, c. 1078. Consolidated his position there in 1081; **d.** 1093.
m. Gwladus, da. of Rhiwallon ap Cynfyn of Powys.
Issue: Gruffudd.—Hywel.—Nest, m. Gerald of Windsor.
Founder of the medieval dynasty of Deheubarth.

GRUFFUDD AP RHYS, s. of Rhys ap Tewdwr and Gwladus. Exile in Ireland to 1116; **acc.** to Cantref Mawr portion of Deheubarth, 1135; **d.** 1137.
m. Gwenllian, da. of Gruffudd ap Cynan of Gwynedd. (*See* GWYNEDD.)
Issue: Anarawd, d. 1143.—Cadell, d. 1175.—Maredudd, d. 1155.—Rhys.—Gwladus.—Nest.

RHYS AP GRUFFUDD, s. of Gruffudd ap Rhys and Gwenllian; b. c. 1133; **acc.** to Deheubarth: (1) Cantref Mawr on d. of br. Maredudd, 1155; (2) Ceredigion by reconquest from Normans, 1165; **d.** 28 Apr. 1197.
m. Gwenllian, da. of Madog ap Maredudd (*see* POWYS).
Issue: Gruffudd.—Maredudd Ddall (the Blind), d. 1239.—Cynwrig, d. 1237.—Rhys Gryg (the Hoarse).—Maredudd, d. 1201.—Maelgwyn.—Hywel Sais, d. 1204.—Maredudd, archdeacon of Cardigan; d. 1227.—Gwenllian, m. Ednyfed Fychan.[1]

Henceforward Deheubarth was divided under the custom of partible succession among the descendants of the following 3 s. of Rhys ap Gruffudd.

GRUFFUDD AP RHYS, s. of Rhys ap Gruffudd and Gwenllian; **acc.** to Cantref Mawr, 1197; **d.** 25 July 1201.
m. Matilda, da. of William de Breose III.
Issue: Rhys Ieuanc (Junior), d. 1222.—Owain, d. 1235.—from Owain, s. Maredudd, d. 1265.—**Owain ap Maredudd**, d. 1275.—**Llywelyn ap Owain**, d. 1309; lord of S. Ceredigion; aft. 1282, minor marcher lord in S. Cards. commotes of Mabwynion and Gwynionydd to which c. 1355 gd.-das. succeeded, viz:—Helen, m. Gruffudd Fychan (*see* N. Powys), parents of Owain Glyn Dŵr; Margaret, m. (1) William ap Gruffudd of Mawddwy (*see* S. Powys); (2) Tudur ap Gronw of Penmynydd, ancestor of Owen and Henry Tudor.

RHYS GRYG, s. of Rhys ap Gruffudd and Gwenllian; **acc.** to Cantref Mawr, 1204; **d.** 1234.

---

[1] Ednyfed Fychan—ancestor of the Tudors, a principal officer in the court of Llywelyn the Great.

m. Joan da. of Richard de Clare, e. of Hertford.
Issue: Rhys Mechyll, d. 1244.—**Maredudd**, d. 1271.—From Rhys Mechyll, s. **Rhys Fychan**, d. 1271.—**Rhys Wyndod** ap Rhys Fychan; d. aft flight to Gwynedd in 1282.—From Maredudd, d. 1271, s. **Rhys** ap Maredudd, d. 1291 (executed for treason against Edward I).

MAELGWN AP RHYS, s. of Rhys ap Gruffudd and Gwenllian; **acc.** to lands in various parts of Deheubarth, 1216; **d.** 1231.
Issue: Maelgwn Fychan, d. 1257. From Maelgwn Fychan, s. **Rhys ap Maelgwn**, d. 1255; gds. **Rhys Ieuanc**, d. aft. flight to Gwynedd in 1277. Maelgwn ap Rhys Ieuanc, d. a rebel in 1295. His brs, Rhys and Gruffudd, were prisoners in Norwich in 1308.

POWYS

BLEDDYN AP CYNFYN, s. of Cynfyn ap Gwerstan and Angharad, wid. of Llywelyn ap Seisyll (*see* DEHEUBARTH); **acc.** to Powys and Gwynedd, 1063; **d.** 1075.
Issue: Madog, d. 1088.—Rhiryd, d. 1088.—Gadwgan, d. 1111.—Iorwerth, d. 1111.—Maredudd.—Gwenllian, m. Caradog ap Gruffudd ap Rhydderch (*see* DEHEUBARTH).—Hunydd, m. Rhydderch ap Tewdwr (*see* DEHEUBARTH).
Founder of the medieval dynasty of Powys.

MAREDUDD AP BLEDDYN, s. of Bleddyn ap Cynfyn; **acc.** to Powys, *c.* 1116; **d.** 1132.
Issue: Gruffudd, d. 1128 (*see* S. Powys *below*).—Madog.—Hywel, d. 1142.—Iorwerth Goch (the Red).

MADOG AP MAREDUDD, s. of Maredudd ap Bleddyn; **acc.** to Powys, 1132; **d.** 1160.
m. Susanna, da. of Gruffudd ap Cynan (*see* GWYNEDD).
Issue: Gruffudd Maelor (*see* N. POWYS *below*).—Elise.—Owain Fychan,[1] d. 1187.—Llywelyn, d. 1160.—Owain Brogyntyn.[2]—Marared, m. Iorwerth Drwyndwn (*see* GWYNEDD).—Gwenllian, m. Rhys ap Gruffudd (*see* DEHEUBARTH).
Last to rule over whole of Powys.

Southern Powys

OWAIN CYFEILIOG, s. of Gruffudd ap Maredudd ap Bleddyn; **acc.** to S. Powys, 1160; **d.** 1197 (retired 1195).
m. Gwenllian, da. of Owain Gwynedd (*see* GWYNEDD).
Issue: Gwenwynwyn.—Caswallon.

GWENWYNWYN,[3] s. of Owain, Cyfeiliog and Gwenllian; **acc.** to S. Powys, 1195; **d.** 1216 in exile aft. dispossession by Llywelyn the Great.
m. Margaret, da. of Robert Corbet.
Issue: Gruffudd.—Madog.

---

[1] Founder of minor dynasty of Mechain.
[2] Founder of minor dynasty of Edeyrnion.
[3] S. Powys henceforth known as Powys Wenwynwyn.

GRUFFUDD AP GWENWYNWYN, s. of Gwenwynwyn and Margaret Corbet; **acc.** to S. Powys, 1240 (out of possession 1257–63 and 1274–77); **d.** 1286.

m. Hawise, da. of John Lestrange.

Issue: Owain 'de la Pole', d. 1293.[4]—Llywelyn.—John.—William.[5]—David.

Surrendered his rights as native Welsh ruler and became a marcher baron.

Northern Powys

GRUFFUDD MAELOR I, s. of Madog ap Maredudd and Susanna; **acc.** to N. Powys, 1160; **d.** 1191.

m. Angharad, da. of Owain Gwynedd.

Issue: Madog.—Owain, d. 1197.

MADOG[1] AP GRUFFUDD, s. of Gruffudd Maelor and Angharad; **acc.** to N. Powys, 1191; **d.** 1236.

m. Isota.

Issue: Gruffudd Maelor II.—**Gruffudd Iâl**, d. 1238.—**Maredudd**, d. 1256.—**Hywel**, d. *c.* 1268.—**Madog Fychan**, d. 1269.—Angharad.

GRUFFUDD MAELOR II, s. of Madog ap Gruffudd and Isota; **acc.** to N. Powys, 1236; **d.** 1269.

m. Emma, da. of Henry Audley and wid. of Henry Touchet.

Issue: Madog, d. 1277.—**Llywelyn**, d. 1282.—**Owain**, d. 1282.—**Gruffudd**, d. 1289. Madog's s., Llywelyn and Gruffudd, disappeared *c.* 1282, but their uncle, Gruffudd, was in time reinvested with a quarter commote in N. Powys. Gruffudd's s. and successor, Madog, was established as an hereditary lord of the march in this territory of Glyndyfrdwy and in another half commote in Cynllaith. The latter's gds., Gruffudd Fychan, m. one of the last survivors of the line of Deheubarth (*see* DEHEUBARTH), and the heir of the marriage was Owain Glyn Dŵr.

SCOTLAND

Note.—Our knowledge about the early kings of Alba, north of the Forth and Clyde, is not sufficient to satisfy the purpose of this list, which begins with the name of Malcolm II, the first king to reign over approximately the same area as that governed by the later rulers of Scotland.

Style of Scottish kings. The normal style of Scottish kings was 'King of Scots'. The great seal shows *Rex Scottorum* from Alexander I to James II, except Edgar's seal which has *Scottorum Basileus*. From James III onwards the style is *Rex Scotorum*. The great seal of Duncan II is the earliest known (with inscription partly obliterated); that of Alexander I is the first of the double-sided type. From then down to the reign of Alexander III the great seals have *Deo Rectore*, as has that of Robert I. John Balliol introduced *Dei gratia* and this was again used from David II onwards.

While the great seal always has 'King of Scots', the form *Rex Scotie* is used in Duncan II's charter of 1094 to Durham. This style may occasionally have been used in written acts of David I and appears in one surviving original charter of Malcolm IV. It was used by John Balliol and, after his abdication, in charters issued in his name by the guardians William Wallace and John de Soulis.

Mary on her marriage to Francis associated him with her acts of government. Charters were granted from 24 April 1558 by *Franciscus et Maria Dei gratia rex et*

---

[4] Owain's da. and h., Hawise, m. John Charlton who succeeded to the lordship of Powys.

[5] William's gt-gds, John of Mawddwy, was Glyn Dŵr's cous. (*see* DEHEUBARTH).

[6] N. Powys henceforth known as Powys Fadog.

regina Scotorum (sometimes *Scotie*) *delphinus et delphina Viennensis*. From July 1559 this changed to *Franciscus et Maria rex et regina Francie et Scotie*. Again Darnley was associated from 29 July 1565 and charters were in the names of *Henricus et Maria rex et regina Scotorum*. Bothwell was not thus associated. After her deposition in 1567 Mary continued to style herself 'Queen of Scots and dowager of France'.

Regnal years.—The tradition of Scottish historiography is that the regnal year was dated from the day of the last king's death. This was certainly the practice from Robert III onwards, but the dearth of diplomatic evidence renders it impossible to be certain about earlier reigns. There is no genuine Scottish charter extant before that of Duncan II to Durham in 1094, and none of his successors for the next three centuries gives both regnal year and that of the christian era. (David I frequently states the place of granting, but date of granting and the regnal year appear only in 1226.) Analogies from English practice in the use of regnal year are not helpful because of the Celtic origin of the Scottish monarchy with its emphasis on heredity and because of the comparative unimportance of 'coronation' in Scotland. By Celtic custom the tanist was associated with the reigning king and succeeded on his death. Duncan II is styled *constans hereditarie rex Scotie* (Nat. MSS. of Scotland, i). During the lifetime of David I his son Henry was styled *rex designatus* and his grandson Malcolm was recognized and proclaimed as heir to the kingdom (*Scotichr.* v, 44). As late as the coronation of Alexander III *quidam Scotus senex, silvester et montanus* recited in Gaelic the ancestry of the new king, going back to Fergus, first king of Scots in Alba (*Scotichr.* x, 2). In the ceremony of coronation emphasis was laid on enthronement *in cathedra regali* at Scone, often stated with doubtful accuracy to be the privilege of the thanes and earls of Fife. There is no evidence of anything in early Scottish coronations that corresponds to the Anglo-Saxon presentation of the king for acceptance by the people (still in use at the commencement of the English rite). The enthronement may have been regarded as the recognition or proclamation of one who had become king on his predecessor's death rather than as the commencement of his reign. The first Scottish king to receive unction was David II in terms of a bull of Pope John XXII.

Authorities.—The chief authorities used are the *Scotichronicon*, the Exchequer Rolls of Scotland, the Register of the Great Seal, Bain's *Calendar of Documents relating to Scotland*, Rymer's *Foedera, Rotuli Scotiae*, and Sir A. Dunbar's *Scottish Kings* (2nd edn, Edinburgh, 1906). Various manuscripts in H.M. General Register House have also been consulted. For the extensive literature on the history of the coronation in Scotland, see the bibliographical note in P. E. Schramm, *A History of the English Coronation* (Oxford, 1937), 242–43.

MALCOLM II, s. of Kenneth II; mother unknown; b. *c.* 954; **acc.** 25 Mar. 1005; **d.** 25 Nov. 1034.

Absence: Invaded Northumbria as far as Durham, 1006.

Issue: Bethoc.—Muldred.—Donada.

Having succeeded as k. of Alba in 1005, Malcolm II secured Lothian by the battle of Carham *c.* 1016 and about the same time obtained Strathclyde for his gds., Duncan, thus forming the kingdom of Scotland.

DUNCAN I, s. of Crinan, hereditary abbot of Dunkeld, and Bethoc, da. of Malcolm II; **acc.** 25 Nov. 1034; **d.** 14 Aug. 1040.

Absence: besieged Durham in 1040.

m. *c.* 1030 a cous. of Siward, e. of Northumbria.

Issue: Malcolm III, *q.v.*—Donald Bane, *q.v.*—Maelmuire.

MACBETH, s. of Finlaec, mormaer of Moray and ? Donada, da. of Malcolm II; b. *c.* 1005; **acc.** 14 Aug. 1040; **d.** 15 Aug. 1057.

Absence: Rome 1050.

m. *c.* 1032 Gruoch.

LULACH, s. of Gillacomgan, mormaer of Moray, and Gruoch (thus stepson of Macbeth); b. *c.* 1032; **acc.** 15 Aug. 1057; **d.** 17 Mar. 1058.

Issue: Malsnectai, d. 1085.—a da. (name unknown).

MALCOLM III (CANMORE), s. of K. Duncan I; b. *c.* 1031; **acc.** 17 Mar. 1058; **d.** 13 Nov. 1093.

Absences: invaded England, 1061, spring 1070, Aug.–Sept. 1079, and May 1091; at Durham, 11 Aug. 1093; at Gloucester, 24 Aug. 1093; invaded England, Nov. 1093.

m. (1) *c.* 1059 Ingibiorg; (2) *c.* 1069 Margaret, da. of Edward the Etheling.

Issue (by 1): Duncan II, *q.v.*—? Malcolm.—(by 2): Edward, d. 16 Nov. 1093.—Edgar, *q.v.*—Edmund and Aethelred (order uncertain).—Alexander I, *q.v.*—David I, *q.v.*—Matilda, d. 1 May 1118; m. Henry I, k. of England.—Mary, d. 31 May 1115; m. Eustace, c. of Boulogne.

DONALD BANE, s. of K. Duncan I; b. *c.* 1033; **acc.** 13 Nov. 1093. Deposed May 1094, restored 12 Nov. 1094 and finally deposed Oct. 1097.
Issue: Bethoc.
During his 2nd reign he is said to have shared the government with Edmund, s. of Malcolm III and Margaret.

DUNCAN II, s. of Malcolm III and Ingibiorg; b. *c.* 1060; **acc.** May 1094; **d.** 12 Nov. 1094.
m. *c.* 1090 Octreda of Dunbar.
Issue: William.

EDGAR, s. of Malcolm III and Margaret; b. *c.* 1074; **acc.** 1097; **d.** ? 8 Jan. 1107.
Absences: with William Rufus in England, *c.* 1099–1100; with Henry I in England, *c.* 1101–02, perhaps June 1101 [*see* A. A. M. Duncan, *S.H.R.*, xxxvii (1958), 111, 134 n. 1].

ALEXANDER I, s. of Malcolm III and Margaret; b. *c.* 1077; **acc.** ? 8 Jan. 1107; **d.** ? 25 Apr. 1124.
Absence: invaded Wales, summer 1114, in co-operation with Henry I of England.
m. Sybilla, illegitimate da. of Henry I of England, d. 1122.

DAVID I, s. of Malcolm III and Margaret; b. prob. *c.* 1085; **acc.** ? 25 Apr. 1124; **d.** 24 May 1153.
Absences: visited Henry I in England, 1126–27 and 1130; invaded England, 1136–37 and 1138–39; at siege of Winchester, Aug. 1141; at Lancaster, 1149.
m. Matilda (Maud), da. of Waltheof, e. of Northampton and Huntingdon.
Issue: Malcolm.—Claricia.—Hodierna.—Henry, e. of Northumberland and Huntingdon, d. 12 June 1152.

MALCOLM IV (THE MAIDEN), s. of Henry, e. of Northumberland and Huntingdon and Ada, da. of William de Warenne II, e. of Surrey; b. prob. 1041; **acc.** 24 May 1153; **d.** 9 Dec. 1165.
Absences: at Chester, July 1157; at Carlisle, Jan. 1158; in France with Henry II of England, June–Oct. 1159; at Woodstock, July 1163.
Issue: Supposed to have had a s. (illegitimate) on the strength of *Liber de Calchou*, i, 23; but the reference is possibly to the death of the k.'s father, not of this alleged s. (*see* R. L. Graeme Ritchie, *The Normans in Scotland*, App. 9).

WILLIAM I (THE LION), s. of Henry, e. of Northumberland and Huntingdon, and Ada, da. of William II, e. of Surrey; b. prob. 1142; **acc.** 9 Dec. 1165; **d.** 4 Dec. 1214.

Absences: Normandy and Brittany, 1166; England, Apr.–June, 1170; England, Aug. 1173; England and France, Apr. 1174–Feb. 1175; York, Aug. 1175; Northampton, Jan. 1176; England, Oct. 1176; England, June–July 1177; England and Normandy, Apr.–Aug. 1181; London, Mar. 1185; England, May–July and Aug.–Sept. 1186; England, Aug.–Dec. 1189; England, Mar.–May 1194; Lincoln, Nov. 1200; York, 1206; England, 1209.

m. 5 Sept. 1186 Ermengarde de Beaumont.

Issue: Alexander II, *q.v.*—Margaret, m. Hubert de Burgh.—Isabella, m. Roger Bigod, e. of Norfolk.—Marjorie, m. Gilbert, e. of Pembroke.

Illegitimate issue: Robert of London.—Henry.—Isabella, m. (1) Robert de Brus; (2) Robert de Ros.—Ada, m. Patrick, e. of Dunbar.—Margaret, m. Eustace de Vesci.—Aufrica, m. William de Say. The descendants of the last 5 were among the competitors for the crown in 1291.

From the treaty of Falaise, 8 Dec. 1174, to K. Richard's quit-claim of 5 Dec. 1189, William acknowledged the k. of England as overlord of Scotland.

ALEXANDER II, s. of William I and Ermengarde; b. 24 Aug. 1198; **acc.** 4 Dec. 1214; **d.** 8 July 1249.

Absences: invaded England, 1215, 1216, 1217; York, May 1220 and 19 June 1221; Newcastle, 1236; York, 1237.

m. (1) 19 June 1221 Joan, da. of John, k. of England; (2) 15 May 1239 Marie de Coucy.

Issue (by 2): Alexander III, *q.v.*

Illegitimate issue: Marjorie, m. Alan Durward (their gds. was a competitor for the crown in 1291).

ALEXANDER III, s. of Alexander II and Marie de Coucy; b. 4 Sept. 1241; **acc.** 8 July 1249; **d.** 19 Mar. 1286.

Absences: York, Dec. 1251; London, 1261, 1274 and 1278 (Sept.).

m. (1) 26 Dec. 1251 Margaret, da. of Henry III of England; (2) 14 Oct. 1285 Yolande de Dreux.

Issue (by 1): Margaret, b. 28 Feb. 1261; d. 9 Apr. 1283; m. 1281, Eric II, k. of Norway.—Alexander, b. 21 Jan. 1264; d. 28 Jan. 1284.—David, b. 20 Mar. 1273; d. June 1281.

MARGARET, da. of Eric II of Norway and Margaret da. of Alexander III; b. *c.* Apr. 1283; **acc.** 19 Mar. 1286; **d.** *c.* 26 Sept. 1290.

Absences: never in Scotland.

Death of Margaret, known as the 'Maid of Norway', left the throne disputed by 13 competitors.

FIRST INTERREGNUM, 1290–92

JOHN (BALLIOL), s. of John de Balliol and Dervorguilla, gt-gt-gd-da. of David I; b. *c.* 1250; **acc.** 17 Nov. 1292; abdicated 10 July 1296; **d.** Apr. 1313.

Absences: Newcastle, Dec. 1292–Jan. 1293; Westminster (parliament), *c.* 29 Sept. 1293; Westminster (? parliament), mid-Apr. 1294; Westminster (parliament), late June 1294.

m. *c.* Feb. 1281 Isabella de Warenne.

Issue: Edward (*see* under David II).—Henry, d. 16 Dec. 1332.

The crown of Scotland was awarded to Balliol out of 13 competitors by the adjudication of Edward I of England, whose claim to overlordship they admitted. Declaring Balliol to have forfeited his throne for contumacy in 1296, Edward took the government of Scotland into his own hands.

SECOND INTERREGNUM, 1296–1306

ROBERT I, gds. of the competitor of 1291, s. of Robert Bruce, and Marjorie countess (*suo jure*) of Carrick; b. 11 July 1274; **acc.** 25 Mar. 1306; **d.** 7 June 1329.

Absences: Ireland, 1306–07; invaded England, 1311 and 1312; Isle of Man, June 1313; Carlisle, 14 July–3 Aug. 1315; Ireland, autumn 1316–May 1317; Lancashire, July 1322; Yorkshire, Oct. 1322.

m. (1) *c.* 1295 Isabella of Mar; (2) *c.* 1302 Elizabeth de Burgh.

Issue (by 1): Marjorie (ancestress of Stewart ks.); m. Walter the Steward; d. 2 Mar. 1316.—(by 2): Matilda, d. 20 July 1353; m. Thomas Isaac.—Margaret, m. William, e. of Sutherland.—David II, *q.v.*—John.

DAVID II, s. of Robert I and Elizabeth de Burgh; b. 5 Mar. 1324; **acc.** 7 June 1329; **d.** 22 Feb. 1371.

Absences: France, mainly at Château-Gaillard, May 1334–June 1341; invaded England, twice in 1342; prisoner in England, Oct. 1346–Oct. 1357; England, autumn 1358–Feb. 1359; England, Oct.–Dec. 1363; England, July 1369; London, 4 June 1370.

m. (1) 17 July 1328 Joanna of England, d. 14 Aug. 1362; (2) *c.* 13 Feb. 1364 Margaret Drummond, wid. of John Logy.

Edward Balliol, s. of John Balliol, assumed the title of 'K. of Scots' and was crowned 24 Sept. 1332; expelled Dec. 1332, but restored 1333–36, formally acknowledging Edward III of England as his lord Nov. 1333. He surrendered all claim to the Scottish crown to Edward III 20 Jan. 1356 and d. Jan. 1364.

ROBERT II, s. of Walter the Steward and Marjorie Bruce; b. 2 Mar. 1316; **acc.** 22 Feb. 1371; **d.** 19 Apr. 1390 (1st k. of the Stewart dynasty).

m. (1) aft. Nov. 1347 Elizabeth Mure of Rowallan; (2) *c.* May 1355 Euphemia Ross.

Issue (by 1): John (aft. K. Robert III, *q.v.*).—Walter, e. of Fife, d. *c.* 1362.—Robert, duke of Albany, d. 2 Sept. 1420.—Alexander, e. of Buchan, d. 24 July 1394.—Margaret, m. John, lord of the Isles.—Marjorie, m. John Dunbar, e. of March.—Elizabeth, m. Thomas Hay, the Constable.—Isabella, m. (1) James, e. of Douglas and Mar; (2) Sir John Edmonstone.—Jean, m. (1) Sir John Keith; (2) Sir John Lyon; (3) Sir James Sandilands of Calder.—(by 2): David, e. of Strathearn and Caithness, d. bef. 1389.—Walter, e. of Atholl and Caithness, d. 26 Mar. 1437.—Egidia, m. Sir William Douglas of Nithsdale.—Jean, m. David, c. of Crawford.

Robert II's family by Elizabeth Mure was legitimated only *per subsequens matrimonium.*

59

ROBERT III, s. of Robert II and Elizabeth Mure; b. *c.* 1337; **acc.** 19 Apr. 1390; **d.** 4 Apr. 1406.

m. *c.* 1366–67 Annabella Drummond.

Issue: David, duke of Rothesay, b. 24 Oct. 1378, d. 26 Mar. 1402.—Robert.—James I, *q.v.*—Margaret, m. Archibald, e. of Douglas and duke of Touraine, d. *c.* 1451.—Mary, m. (1) George, e. of Angus; (2) Sir James Kennedy; (3) William Graham; (4) Sir William Edmonstone.—Elizabeth, m. Sir James Douglas of Dalkeith.—Egidia.

JAMES I, s. of Robert III and Annabella Drummond; b. July 1394; **acc.** 4 Apr. 1406; **d.** 21 Feb. 1437.

Absences: England and France, Mar. 1406–Apr. 1424 (*see below*).

m. ? 10 Feb. 1424 Joan Beaufort.

Issue: Alexander, b. 16 Oct. 1430; d. 1430.—James II, *q.v.*—Margaret, b. 1424; d. 16 Aug. 1445; m. 1436 the Dauphin, aft. Louis XI, k. of France.—Isabella, m. 1442 Francis I, duke of Brittany.—Joan, m. *c.* 1458 James, e. of Morton.—Eleanor, m. 1449 Archduke Sigismund of Austria.—Mary, m. Wolfart, c. of Grand Pré.—Annabella, m. (1) Louis, c. of Geneva; (2) George Gordon, e. of Huntly.

James was captured at sea by English merchants on 22 Mar. 1406 and kept in captivity in England till the end of Mar. 1424. In his absence the two dukes of Albany ruled successively as 'governors'.

JAMES II, s. of James I and Joan Beaufort; b. 16 Oct. 1430; **acc.** 21 Feb. 1437; **d.** 3 Aug. 1460.

m. 3 July 1449 Mary of Gueldres.

Issue: James III, *q.v.*—Alexander, duke of Albany; b. *c.* 1454; d. 1485.—David, e. of Moray; b. bef. 12 Feb. 1456; d. 1457.—John, e. of Mar; b. ? 1459; d. 1479.—Mary, m. (1) Thomas, Lord Boyd; (2) James, Lord Hamilton.—Margaret.

JAMES III, s. of James II and Mary of Gueldres; b. May 1452; **acc.** 3 Aug. 1460; **d.** 11 June 1488.

m. 13 July 1469 Margaret of Denmark.

Issue: James IV, *q.v.*—James, duke of Ross and abp of St. Andrews; b. Mar. 1476; d. ? 12 Jan. 1503.—John, e. of Mar; b. Dec. 1479; d. 11 Mar. 1503.

JAMES IV, s. of James III and Margaret of Denmark; b. 17 Mar. 1473; **acc.** 11 June 1488; **d.** 9 Sept. 1513.

Absences: invaded England, Sept. 1496 and Aug.–Sept. 1513.

m. 8 Aug. 1503 Margaret Tudor.

Issue: James, b. 21 Feb. 1507; d. 27 Feb. 1508.—da., b. 1508 and d. same year.—Arthur, b. 20 Oct. 1509; d. 14 July 1510.—James V, *q.v.*—da., b. and d. 1512–13.—Alexander, duke of Ross (posthumous), d. 1515.

Illegitimate issue included: Alexander, abp of St. Andrews; b. *c.* 1493; d. 9 Sept. 1513.—James, e. of Moray; b. *c.* 1499; d. 12 June 1544.

JAMES V, s. of James IV and Margaret Tudor; b. 10 Apr. 1512; **acc.** 9 Sept. 1513; **d.** 14 Dec. 1542.

Absence: France, 24 July 1536–19 May 1537.

m. (1) 1 Jan. 1537 Madeleine of France, d. 7 July 1537; (2) June 1538 Mary of Lorraine, d. 10 June 1560.

Issue (by 2): James, b. 22 May 1540; d. 1541.—Arthur, b. and d. Apr.1541.—Q. Mary, *q.v.*

Illegitimate issue included: James *senior*, d. 1557.—James, e. of Moray (regent, 1567–70); b. 1531; d. 23 Jan. 1570.—James *tertius.*—Robert, e. of Orkney; b. 1533; d. 4 Feb. 1593.—John, prior of Coldingham; d. 1563.—Adam, prior of Charterhouse.—Robert, prior of Whithorn; d. 1581.

MARY, da. of James V and Mary of Lorraine; b. 7 or 8 Dec. 1542; **acc.** 14 Dec. 1542; abdicated 24 July 1567; **d.** 8 Feb. 1587.

Absences: France, 7 Aug. 1548–19 Aug. 1561; England, from 19 May 1568.

m. (1) 24 Apr. 1558 Dauphin, aft. Francis II of France; (2) 29 July 1565 Henry Stewart, Lord Darnley; (3) 15 May 1567 James Hepburn, e. of Bothwell.

Issue: James VI, *q.v.*

JAMES VI (*see under* England, James I); b. 19 June 1566; **acc.** 24 July 1567; **d.** 27 Mar. 1625.

Absences: Norway and Denmark, 22 Oct. 1589–1 May 1590; England, aft. 5 Apr. 1603 to the end of reign except 13 May–4 Aug. 1617 when he was in Scotland.

m. and **issue:** *see under* England, James I.

James succeeded to the English throne as James I, 24 Mar. 1603, and so joined the English and Scottish crowns in a personal union only.

THE ISLE OF MAN

[The main authorities for the earlier sections of the following list of rulers are *Chronica Regum Manniae et Insularum*, ed. P. A. Munch (Christiania, 1860), and revised by Goss, 2 vols (Douglas, 1874), (Manx Society, xxii and xxiii); *Annals of Ulster*, ed. W. M. Hennessy and B. MacCarthy, 4 vols (Dublin, 1887–1901); *Annals of the Kingdom of Ireland, by the Four Masters*, ed. J. O'Donovan, 7 vols (Dublin, 1851). A. W. Morre, *History of the Isle of Man*, 2 vols (London, 1900), gives a list of 'kings or lords of Man' (ii, 973–80) beginning with Godred I. He says: 'it is so difficult to identify the rulers of Man before his time that we have not attempted a list of them.'

Abbreviations: M = *Chronica Regum Manniae*; FM = *Annals of the Four Masters*; U = *Annals of Ulster*.]

NORWEGIAN SUZERAINTY

[Of the secular history of the Isle of Man bef. the Scandinavian incursions of the ninth century nothing is known. Man and the other islands between Ireland and Scotland appear aft. the Norwegian settlement 'either to have been subjected to the Norwegian ks of Dublin or to have been ruled by several chieftains or vikings who did not adopt the title of k.' (Goss, *op. cit.*, i, 124, translating Munch's notes). Some of the rulers of Man were clearly subject to the ks of Norway.]

KETIL FLATNEF, a Norwegian noble, is said by some authorities to have ruled Man as the representative of Harold Fairhair, k. of Norway, by others to have established himself as independent ruler against the wishes of that k., and while some statements would indicate that he secured the island late in the 9th century, there is reason to suppose that he may have established himself there about the middle of the century.

TRYGGVI, one of the jarls of K. Harold Fairhair, was entrusted with a region which no doubt included Man aft. that k.'s successful expedition against the Norwegians of these parts *c.* 870 or possibly later.

ASBJÖRN SKERJABLESI succeeded Tryggvi as the jarl of K. Harold and was later killed by the kinsmen of Ketil Flatnef, aft. which event K. Harold does not appear to have appointed another e. In the succeeding period Man was prob. dependent upon the Norwegian ks at Dublin some of whom ruled also the Scandinavian kingdom of York.

RAGNALL (Ragnald) won in 913 (U) a naval battle off Man, of which he was prob. ruler from this date or earlier until his d. in 921 (ruling at York *c.* 919–21). It is uncertain whether Man was dependent upon York or Dublin in the perid 921–27, but between 927 and 939 when K. Athelstan ruled the kingdom of York, Man must presumably have been dependent upon Guthfrith, k. of Dublin, and his s., Anlaf Guthfrithson, who succeeded him in 934.

MAC RAGNALL appears to have been ruler of Man in 940 in which year he d. (FM) and was probably dependent upon Anlaf Guthfrithson (*vide supra*) who reigned at York as well as Dublin from 939 or 940 to 941. Mac Ragnall may have had authority over Man during part or all of the period 921–40. In the period following his death and that of Anlaf Guthfrithson, Man may have been under the rule of Anlaf Sihtricson who was finally expelled from Northumbria and returned to Ireland in 952.

[K. 'Gorree' or 'Orrye', *see* Godred I (Crovan) *below*, is traditionally supposed to have arrived in the obscure period 918–47.]

MAC HAROLD (? Maccus s. of Harold, erroneously called Magnus s. of Harold by later writers, Christian name prob. not preserved) ruler of the Isles, prob. including Man, was reigning in 974 (FM, *sub an.* 972); ? killed 977.

GODRED S. of HAROLD (? br. of 'Mac Harold') prob. ruling 979 when he raided Anglesey; killed by the Dalriadic Scots 989 (Olaf Tryggvason, k. of Norway, appears to have established his suzerainty over Man in 985).

SIGURD, e. OF ORKNEY, may have had some authority over Man from *c.* 989 to 1014 when he was killed at Clontarf, and his s. THORFINN, e. OF ORKNEY, possibly had rights over Man, *c.* 1014–60, but Munch held that from 989 to 1079 'the island of Man must have been an appendage of the Norwegian kingdom of Dublin whereas it would appear that the Isles chiefly belonged to the earls of Orkney'.

[Moore, *op. cit.*, i, 95 refers to the d. of 'Harold, k. of Man', in 1040, citing U, but the k. whose death is recorded in that annal is Harold Harefoot, k. of England.]

MAC RAGNALL (called Godred s. of Ragnall, br. of Eachmarcach, k. of Dublin, by Moore) defeated in 1060 by Murchadh s. of Diarmaid who made Man tributary to Dublin.

GODRED S. of SYTRIC reigning in 1066 (M); d. 1070 (Munch held that Godred prob. belonged to the dynasty at Dublin—possibly identical with Godred 'gds. of Ragnald', ruler of Dublin).

FINGAL, s. of Godred s. of Sytric, succeeded 1070 (M); apparently expelled 1079.

GODRED I (Crovan), 1079–95, ? s. of Harald the Black of Ysland; conjectured by Munch to be gds. of Godred s. of Harold, *q.v.*; ? identical with Godred 'Mananagh', ruler of Dublin; d. 1095 leaving 3 s., Lagman, *q.v.*, Harold (mutilated by Lagman *c.* 1095) and Olaf I, *q.v.* [Godred conquered Man in 1079 (M, *sub an.* 1056); subjugated Dublin and a great part of Leinster (*ibid.*); said to have been deprived of the Isles by Magnus Barefoot, k. of Norway, 1093–94 (M, 147 *seq.*, Munch's notes). He is prob. the k. 'Gorree' or 'Orrye' of Manx traditions.]

LAGMAN, 1095–?96, s. of Godred I. Said to have reigned 7 years (M) and may have ruled Man during part of Godred's reign. Took the cross and d. at Jerusalem 1096 or 1097.

DONALD s. of TEIGE, 1096–?98. Sent by Murchadh O'Brien, k. of Dublin (apparently ally and dependant of Magnus, k. of Norway), as regent for Olaf s. of Godred, but seized the throne; said to have reigned 3 years (M).

MAGNUS, k. of NORWAY, 1098–1103. Magnus himself was in Man 1098–99 and from either 1099 or 1102 until 1103 his s. SIGURD was apparently k. of W. Isles including Man.

OLAF I, 1103–53, s. of Godred I; m. (1) Affrica, da. of Fergus of Galloway (M); (2) Ingibjorg, da. of Hacon, e. of Orkney (Munch). Godred s. of Affrica was apparently Olaf's only legitimate child; other children by concubines—Reginald, Lagman, Harold and many das, one of whom (Ragnhild) m. Sumerled, lord of Argyll, *q.v.* [M places accession of Olaf in 1102 and states that he reigned 40 years. Some modern writers have assumed that Olaf's reign did not begin until 1113, supposing that part of the reigns of Lagman and Donald fall in the period 1103–13, but it is more reasonable to suppose with Munch that Olaf reigned 50 years. Godred, aft. Godred II, went to Norway and did homage on behalf of his father *c.* 1152 (M).]

GODRED II, 1152–58 and 1164–87, s. of Olaf and Affrica. Expelled by Sumerled, lord of Argyll, and took refuge in Norway; recovered Man in 1164 aft. d. of Sumerled and overthrow of Reginald; d. 10 Nov. 1187 leaving 3 s., Reginald (*illegitimate*), *q.v.*, Olaf (nominated successor), *q.v.*, and Ivar.

SUMERLED, lord of Argyll, 1158–64. Usurper; m. da. of Olaf I; expelled Godred 1158; killed 1164.

[REGINALD, 1164. Usurper; s. (*illegitimate*) of Olaf I and br. of Godred II by whom he was overthrown 4 days aft. his seizure of Man on Sumerled's d.]

REGINALD I, 1187–1226, eldest s. (*illegitimate*) of Godred II; expelled by Olaf II 1226; recovered Man for brief period in 1228; murdered Feb. 1229; m. sis. of Lauon of Kentyre (M). Godred Don his s. shared the 'kingdom of Man and the Isles' with Olaf II in 1230 and was killed later in the same year (M).

OLAF II, 1226–37, s. of Godred II. He d. 21 May 1237; m. (1) Lauon of Kentyre (marriage subsequently annulled); (2) Christina, da. of

Ferquhard, e. of Ross, by whom apparently he had 4 s.—Harold I, *q.v.*; Reginald II, *q.v.*; Godred, d. 1237; and Magnus, *q.v.* In 1229 or 1230 Olaf went to Norway and presumably did homage to K. Hacon.

HAROLD I, 1237–48, s. of Olaf II; succeeded at age of 14 years. [Agents of the k. of Norway took possession of the island and revenues 1238 by reason of Harold's refusal to present himself at the Norwegian court. Harold went to Norway 1239 and spent 2 years there with K. Hacon who confirmed to him Man and the Isles. Visited court of Henry III of England Easter 1246 (M and Matthew Paris). Again visited Norway 1247 and m. da. (?Cecilia or Christina) of K. Hacon. Shipwrecked and drowned with w. returning from Norway Oct. or Nov. 1248.]

REGINALD II, 6 May–30 May 1249, br. of Harold II; murdered 30 May (M, but 1 July according to Chronicle of Lanercost) by Ivar, a knight (Harold s. of Godred Don, *q.v.*, apparently his accomplice).

HAROLD II, 1249–50 or 52, s. of Godred Don; usurper (*nomen regis et dignitatem sibi usurpans in Mannia*, M); summoned to Norwegian court 1250 and deprived of Man. Possibly as A. W. Moore conjectures (*op. cit.*, i, 130) the knight Ivar ruled Man, 1250–52.

MAGNUS, 1252–65, s. of Olaf II; m. da. of Eogan of Argyll; in Norway May 1253–54 and made by K. Hacon *regem super omnes insulas quas antecessores ejus jure hereditario possidebant* (M); Easter 1256, visited court of Henry III (M and Matthew Paris); *c.* 1264, became vassal of Alexander III, k. of Scots; d. 24 Nov. 1265.
[His s. Godred was proclaimed k. by the Manx rebelling against the Scots 1275, but rebellion unsuccessful.]

SCOTTISH RULE

ALEXANDER III, k. of Scots, 1266 or 67–?86. [Following the unsuccessful expedition of Hacon, k. of Norway, to the W. Isles, 1263, and his d. in the same year, the treaty of Perth was arranged 2 July 1266 between the Scottish and Norwegian ks, by which K. Magnus IV ceded Man and the Sudreys to K. Alexander III; 'with this treaty Norwegian dominion over Man and the Isles ceased entirely'. Alexander ruled Man through lieutenants or bailiffs, 4 of whom are named in the Chronicle of Lanercost.]

MARGARET, q. of SCOTS (the Maid of Norway), ? 1286–?89 or 90. [Edw. I, k. of England, was in possession of Man bef. Margaret's d. in Sept. 1290.]

ENGLISH SUZERAINTY

RICHARD DE BURGH, e. of Ulster, 1290. [Richard presumably held it of K. Edward who was possessed of Man by Feb. 1290 (*Cal. of Pat. Rolls*, 341); 4 June 1290, Edward appointed Walter de Huntrecumbe custodian of the island (*ibid.*, 359) 'which Richard de Burgo, e. of Ulster, has surrendered into the k.'s hands.']

JOHN BALLIOL, k. of Scots, 1293–96, held Man of Edw. I and on his forfeiture the island was resumed by Edward.

ANTHONY BEK, bp of Durham, received Man from K. Edward bef. 11 Apr. 1298 (*Cal. of Pat. Rolls*, 340) and seems to have held it until his d., 3 Mar. 1311.

HENRY DE BEAUMONT, 1310 (royal grant of 1 May 1310 revoked later in same year and the island committed to Gilbert Makaskyl and Robert de Leiburn).

PETER GAVESTON, 1311.

HENRY DE BEAUMONT restored and again deprived 1312 (Gilbert Makaskyl custodian part of the year).

SCOTTISH SUZERAINTY

THOMAS RANDOLF, e. of Moray, Dec. 1313–?. (Robert Bruce, k. of Scots, seems to have controlled Man, May 1313–17, granting it, Dec. 1313, to Thomas Randolf; the island was in English hands, July 1317, but the Scots appear to have recovered it and by treaty 1328 the English acknowledged the Scottish claim thereto.)

ENGLISH SUZERAINTY

[The rulers of Man styled themselves *Dominus* but in the fourteenth century claimed the right to be crowned (*cf. Annales Ricardi Secundi*, ed. Riley, 157). A. W. Moore, *op. cit.*, ii, 974, thinks that the two e. of Salisbury and the e. of Wiltshire enjoyed 'absolute ownership, there being apparently no suzerain between 1333 and 1399'. This view might appear to be supported by Edw. III's quitclaim of 9 Aug. 1333 (*Cal. of Pat. Rolls*, 464) but is inconsistent with the language of royal letters, etc., of the following period (*see* publications of Manx Soc., vii), in particular the writ authorizing the men of the island to treat with the Scots ('pro commodo et salvatione *populi nostri* in Insula de Man,' 1343) and the reference to a petition 'ex parte hominum communitatis Insulae de Man *ad fidem nostram existencium*' (1343).]

WILLIAM MONTAGUE (1st e. of Salisbury, 1337), 1333–44. [Edw. III having ordered that the island should be seized into his hands gave custody of it to William Montague 8 June and quitclaimed it to the same William 9 Aug. 1333.]

WILLIAM MONTAGUE, 2nd e. of Salisbury, 1344–93. [In 1393 he sold the lordship to William le Scrope of Bolton, aft. e. of Wiltshire (*Ann. Ricardi Secundi*, ed. Riley, 157); but he retained the title *Dominus Manniae* till his death in 1397 (Dugdale *Baronage*, 648).]

WILLIAM LE SCROPE (1st e. of Wiltshire, 1397), 1393–99.

HENRY PERCY, 1st e. of Northumberland, 1399–1405. [Enfeoffed by Henry IV, 19 Oct. 1399, *Cal. of Pat. Rolls*, 27.]

SIR JOHN STANLEY I, 1405–14. [Enfeoffed, 4 Oct. 1405, Rymer's *Fœdera*, viii, 419.]

SIR JOHN STANLEY II, 1414–37.

THOMAS I, LORD STANLEY, 1437–59.

THOMAS II (1st e. of Derby, 1485), 1459–1504.

THOMAS III, 2nd e. of Derby, 1504–21.

EDWARD, 3rd e. of Derby, 1521–72.

HENRY, 4th e. of Derby, 1572–93.

FERNANDO, 5th e. of Derby, 1593–94. [Fernando d. leaving 3 das but no s.; his br. William succeeded to the earldom of Derby, but while the claims of the new e. and his nieces were in dispute Man was resumed by the Crown and administered 1594–1607 by governors appointed by Q. Elizabeth I and James I. Henry, e. of Northampton, and Robert, e. of Leicester, administered Man 1607–10 following the grant of K. James at the request of E. William and his nieces.]

WILLIAM I, 6th e. of Derby, 1610–42. [Lordship of Man confirmed to E. William, 7 July 1609, ratified by Act of Parliament, 1610. The grant was made to the e., Elizabeth his w. and James Stanley, Lord Stanley, his s. and heir; the countess Elizabeth appears to have ruled the island, 1612–27, and James, aft. 7th e. of Derby, from 1627 onwards (*see* 'History and Antiquities of I.O.M.', by James Stanley, e. of Derby and lord of Man, C. xii, Manx Soc., iii, 38).]

JAMES I, 7th e. of Derby, 1642–51. [Actual rule appears to begin 1627, *see above*. Executed 15 Oct. 1651.]

THOMAS, LORD FAIRFAX, 1652–60. [Man granted to Lord Fairfax by Parliament 29 Sept. 1649 (Moore, *op. cit.*, 272). Commonwealth recognized here, Oct. or Nov. 1651; Fairfax formally proclaimed lord of Man 23 Feb. 1652. Charles II proclaimed in the island, 28 May 1660, and restoration of Stanleys followed.]

CHARLES STANLEY, 8th e. of Derby, 1660–72.

WILLIAM II, 9th e. of Derby, 1672–1702.

JAMES II, 10th e. of Derby, 1702–36. ['In 1736 the sovereignty of the isle, on the failure of the heirs male of the sixth e., and on the d. of Lady Harriet Ashburnham, the only da. of Lord Ashburnham, and his w. Henrietta, da. of the ninth e., passed to James Murray, second duke of Atholl, whose maternal grandmother Amelia Sophia Stanley was the third da. of the seventh e. of Derby' (Moore, *op. cit.*, i, 384).]

JAMES III, 2nd duke of Atholl, 1736–64.

JOHN, 3rd duke of Atholl, 1764–65. [John Murray, 3rd duke of Atholl, became lord of Man in the right of his w. Charlotte, da. and only surviving child of James, 2nd duke of Atholl. The evils of smuggling led the British government to buy out certain of the duke's rights; the *Revesting Act* 'became law on 10 May 1765 and by proclamation under the great seal of England dated 21 June the island was taken possession of by the English Crown' (Moore, *op. cit.*, i, 390).]

ENGLISH OFFICERS OF STATE

Note on third edition (1985):

The following lists contain some additions and corrections to those published in the revised second edition. In particular, the sections of the existing lists previous to 1200 (chief justiciars, stewards of the household, chancellors, treasurers) have undergone extensive revision, based as far as possible on research in unpublished sources; new lists have been added of chancellors of the exchequer, 1558–1714, masters of the court of wards, and commanders-in-chief; lists for the years 1642–1660 have been much amplified (as have the corresponding lists for Scotland and Ireland); and the sections of lists subsequent to 1961 have been brought up to date.

General note:

It has not been possible to maintain a uniform system in the records of the dates of appointment, partly because the evidence available is not uniform, partly because consistency has not been observed in previous work of this nature. The best date to take as a basis is that on which the new officer or minister takes the oath of office or receives the seals, and this is the date which the following lists tend to take; but, in the earlier periods, the date of the letters patent of appointment is more accessible and often more reliable. From the later seventeenth century until very recent times the taking of the oath is recorded in *The London Gazette*. The difference in time between the date of the letters patent and the date of taking the oath may vary from a day or two to several weeks.

From an historical point of view consistency is not so important as it might appear to be. Until the later decades of the eighteenth century an officer might enter upon his duties on a day which does not coincide with the day on which he takes the oath. For example, Robert Cecil is generally said to have held office from 5 July 1596; but he seems to have attended the privy council as secretary on 14 May and the letters of appointment are dated 13 June (F. M. G. Evans, *The Principal Secretary of State* (Manchester, 1923), 55, 350). Again, to take an instance at random from the eighteenth century, the e. of Halifax took the oath of office as lord privy seal on 26 February 1770, he received his letters of appointment on 8 March, but his allowances were calculated from 23 February. From about this time the calculation of allowances usually dates from the day on which the oath is taken, and in the following lists this date is given as a rule, though not invariably, from this period. For modern officers of state, the date on which the appointment was announced is usually recorded here. Detailed annotation would encumber the text and would not assist the purposes of ordinary reference.

Note on the arrangement of the lists of officers of state:

I. DATES

1. Main rules

Exact date of assumption of office is given, or, if this is not available, date of appointment to office (for some of the problems and the methods adopted, *see supra* and the introduction to the lists of officers).

Dates of demission of office are not given systematically, except in the cases listed below:

(A) In the list of the stewards of the household and the medieval portions of some of the Scottish lists a separate column for the dates of demission of office is provided for special reasons, explained in the introductions to those lists.

(B) If an office-holder died in office, this is indicated by *ob.* followed by date of death, at the end of the entry.

(C) If an office-holder was dismissed or resigned in circumstances where he had to relinquish office at once, it has sometimes been considered desirable to indicate the date on which he was dismissed (indicated by dism.) or otherwise vacated office (indicated by *res.* or by *vac.*), at the end of the entry. This has also been done, as far as possible, whenever the removal of an official was followed by considerable delay in the appointment of his successor.

2. Italicized dates

When neither the date of assumption of office or appointment to office is available, the date of the first known appearance in office is provided in italics.

Similarly, where the dates of demission of office had to be provided, if the precise time of vacating office is not known, the last known appearance in office is indicated in italics.

II. PROVISIONAL OR TEMPORARY TENURE OF OFFICE

Mention of temporary deputies, or of the provisional acting holders of office, has been avoided, unless they acted for a prolonged period or unless it would be misleading to omit them because of special circumstances. All such appointments are within square brackets.

III. DIGNITIES, TITLES AND OTHER OFFICES OF LISTED OFFICERS OF STATE

1. References to other offices

In the medieval portions (down to 1485) of certain lists (chancellors, keepers of privy seal, treasurers) an attempt has been made to indicate, whenever possible, the last previous royal office held by each person listed there (in round brackets, immediately after the name).

2. Cross-references

If an office-holder held the same office more than once, his full name and titles are given only on the first appearance, and upon a recurrence the phrase *See under* and the date are added in round brackets.

In the medieval portions of some English lists (stewards of the household, chancellors, keepers of privy seal, treasurers, admirals) and in the Scottish lists, similar cross-references are provided between different lists, with the phrase *See under* followed by name of office and the date in round brackets.

3. Ecclesiastical dignities

Bishoprics (or lesser ecclesiastical dignities in the case of non-bishops) held during the tenure of royal office are indicated (bishoprics with dates). The ecclesiastical dignities held after the demission of office are indicated in round brackets at the end of the entry (all bishoprics with dates, or else the highest ecclesiastical preferment attained).

In the case of bishops, the date of initial promotion is given, not of consecration, which might have been considerably delayed.

4. Peerages

To the names of persons who were created peers or who were promoted in the peerage at any time during their tenure of office the successive titles they bore are appended, with the date of each creation or promotion.

To the names of persons who held peerages at the time of their appointment, the most senior title borne by them is appended, without date of acquisition (except sometimes when very recent).

The most senior title acquired after laying down office is added in round brackets with the date of its acquisition. If the year appended to a title is the same as that in which the office-holder laid down his office, it is to be assumed that he was created or promoted before leaving office, unless the title and date are enclosed in round brackets.

Peers are numbered in accordance with their position in the particular creation of which they formed a part. These serial numbers might therefore be different from those in the lists of dukes and earls elsewhere in the present Handbook, where (for the purpose of easier cross-reference) all entries are numbered consecutively, regardless of successive creations.

CHIEF JUSTICIARS

The chief justiciarship does not emerge with any clarity until the reign of Henry II. A succession of holders of this position can be traced from Henry's early years to 1234. The office was revived by the baronial reformers in 1258 and continued to be filled until 1265.

The present list attempts to provide brief chronological information about all chief justiciars from the reign of Henry I onwards. The starting-point chosen here does not reflect any sudden new development c. 1100, but from that time it becomes possible to enumerate these royal deputies with some approach to brevity and to chronological precision (for regents during the absences in France of William I and William II, see the introduction to English kings *supra*). The appearance of any person on the list below does not imply that he necessarily held any definite royal office, unless his *appointment as justiciar* is specifically mentioned in the list.

The title of justiciar was seldom used in the second half of the twelfth century. In no extant justiciar's writ of the twelfth century does he describe himself by this title. At several periods in the reigns of Henry II and Richard I two persons held the office concurrently. All these facts point to the slow institutionalization of the justiciarship.

The title of justiciar had different meanings at different periods and the office had different functions at successive stages of its existence. It had originated in a need to delegate royal power, both in the area of overall supervision of royal finance and justice, and deputizing for the king during the latter's absences abroad. The fragmentary evidence for the Norman period suggests that responsibility for supervision of government and for vice-regency during the king's absences may usually have been committed to different individuals. An exception was Roger, bishop of Salisbury, who not only seems to have had overall supervision of royal administration from *c.* 1120 until his dismissal in 1139 but also acted as vice-regent for Henry I between 1123 and 1126. The emergence of an exchequer board for the auditing of accounts (most probably under Henry I) gave the twelfth-century justiciars, as heads of that board, one of their most important ordinary functions. Growth of the jurisdiction of the king's central court in the reigns of Henry II and his sons gave increasing prominence to the judicial duties of the office: Geoffrey fitz Peter succeeded to the justiciar-ship in 1198 after prolonged service as one of the king's leading justices. Geoffrey's two successors owed their selection to predominantly political and military considerations. In 1258 the office was revived on the coming into power of the baronial opposition to Henry III and was filled by a succession of magnates with considerable experience of royal government, who were well fitted to discharge the judicial functions of former justiciars and to act as authoritative heads of a council ruling in Henry's name, but acting often independently of the king.

F. J. West, *The Justiciarship in England 1066–1232* (Cambridge, 1966) covers the earlier period, but note should also be made of the qualifica-tions expressed by D. Bates, 'The origins of the justiciarship', *Proceedings of the Battle Conference on Anglo-Norman Studies*, iv, 1981 (Woodbridge, 1982), 1–12. See also E. Kealey, *Roger of Salisbury* (Berkeley, Los Angeles, London, 1972), chapter 2. For the revival of the justiciarship in 1258 see C. H. Knowles, 'The Justiciarship in England, 1258–1265', in *British Government and Administration. Studies presented to S. B. Chrimes*, ed. H. Hearder and H. R. Loyn (Cardiff, 1974), 16–26.

HENRY I

Roger, bp of Salisbury 1102–39. Vacated the office of chancellor bef. Sept. 1102. By the second part of the reign had established himself as the king's chief minister, and acted as vice-regent during the king's absences from England between 1123 and 1126. There is no record of his being called justiciar in any official document, but he is styled in a royal writ, issued prob. between Apr. 1123 and Sept. 1126, *sub domino nostro rege Henrico regni Anglie procurator.*[1]

STEPHEN

Roger, bp of Salisbury, continued to exercise the authority of a justiciar,[2] but there is no evidence that he was ever formally appd. by Stephen or that he used the title of justiciar in this reign. In Aug.

---

[1] D. M. Stenton, 'Roger of Salisbury, Regni Angliae Procurator', *EHR*, xxxix (1924), 79–80.
[2] *E.g.* in a charter of *c.* 1137 he commands: *precipio tibi ex parte regis et mea*, ed. J. H. Round, *Ancient Charters, Royal and Private*, Pipe Roll Soc. (1888), 38.

1139, at the council of Winchester, Roger is reported to have asserted that he had never held office under Stephen.[1] He was arrested by Stephen on 24 June 1139 and remained in disgrace until his d. on 11 Dec. 1139.

HENRY II

A distinct office of justiciar existed from an early date in this reign. Its first known holders under Henry II were:

Robert, e. of Leicester, and **Richard de Luci,** kt, acting jointly; e. of Leicester *ob.* 5 Apr. 1168. Richard de Luci continued in office alone until his retirement (between *c.* 29 Sept. 1178 and Easter 1179).

Ranulf de Glanville, kt Appd. justiciar 1179 or 1180.

RICHARD I

Ranulf de Glanville continued in office until his dismissal on 17 Sept. 1189.

William de Mandeville, e. of Essex, and **Hugh du Puiset,** bp of Durham 1153–95, acting jointly as justiciars from 17 Sept. 1189; e. of Essex prob. *ob.* 14 Nov. 1189.

William de Longchamp, bp of Ely 1189–97, chancellor 1189–97. [Never styled himself justiciar and never called justiciar in any official document.]

Acted as one of the k.'s chief representatives in England, late Dec. 1189–Mar. 1190, with Hugh du Puiset.

Longchamp's authority confirmed *c.* 12–14 Mar. 1190 and he acted as the k.'s chief representative in England and as the chief of a council of regency until early Oct. 1191. Hugh du Puiset retained authority N. of the Humber until June 1190. K. Richard's commission to Longchamp of 6 June 1190 ignored Puiset.

Longchamp was declared suspended from his functions by his opponents on 5 Oct. 1191, was compelled to surrender the k.'s seal on 10 Oct. 1191 (but remained chancellor) and was forced to leave England *c.* 29 Oct. 1191.

Walter of Coutances, abp of Rouen 1184–1207 (*see* chancellors, 1181), replaced Longchamp as the chief of a council of regency,[2] assisted by a group of royal justices including William Marshal, Geoffrey fitz Peter, William Briwer and Hugh Bardolf. [Walter of Coutances never styled justiciar in any official document.]

Hubert Walter, bp of Salisbury 1189–93, abp of Canterbury 1193–1205. Appd. justiciar *c.* 25 Dec. 1193. Res. 11 July 1198.

Geoffrey fitz Peter (e. of Essex 1199). Appd. justiciar 11 July 1198.

---

[1] William of Malmesbury, *Historia Novella,* ed. K. R. Potter (1955), 32.
[2] According to *The Chronicle of Richard of Devizes,* ed. J. T. Appleby (1963), 48–9, John, count of Mortain, the k.'s br., was recognized as *summus rector totius regni,* but, if so, he did not retain for long any official authority.

JOHN

Geoffrey fitz Peter remained in office until his d., 14 Oct. 1213.

Peter des Roches, bp of Winchester 1205–38. Appd. justiciar ? on death of Geoffrey; letters patent 1 Feb. 1214. Continued in office until issue of Magna Carta, 15 June 1215.

Hubert de Burgh (e. of Kent 1227). Appd. justiciar 15 June 1215.

HENRY III[1]

Hubert de Burgh remained in office. Appd. justiciar of England for life 27 Apr. 1228. Deprived of justiciarship of England prob. on 21 Sept. 1232 (resigned c. 28 May 1234).

Stephen Segrave, kt Succeeded Hubert de Burgh as justiciar. Dism. c. 25 May 1234.

Thereaft. the office of justiciar was not filled until its revival by the baronial reformers in 1258.

Hugh Bigod, kt Appd. justiciar c. 16 June 1258. Vac. 13–20 Oct. 1260.

Hugh le Despenser, kt Succeeded as justiciar c. 20 Oct. 1260. Dism. c. 12 June 1261 (surrendered office c. 22 June 1261).

Philip Basset, kt Appd. justiciar c. 14 June 1261 (justiciar in *coram rege* plea roll for Trinity term 1261). In office as late as Trinity term 1263 (references in later plea rolls). Dism. by 15–18 July 1263.

Hugh le Despenser, kt Appd. justiciar 15–18 July 1263. He was regent during Henry III's visit to France between 23 Sept. and 7 Oct. 1263, but ceased to act as justiciar about the end of Oct. 1263. He resumed full authority aft. the battle of Lewes (14 May 1264). Remained in office until his d. on 4 Aug. 1265.

STEWARDS OF THE HOUSEHOLD (*to* 1485)

The number of the household stewards holding office at the same time varied. In the reign of Henry I it was possibly normal for four stewards to hold office concurrently, who probably served in turn (C. Johnson and H. A. Cronne, *Regesta Regum Anglo-Normannorum*, ii, p. xi), but at times as many as five may have existed together at this period. In the thirteenth century it was still quite common for two or three stewards to hold office concurrently. From the time of Edward II it would seem that the normal practice was for the office to be filled by only one man.

Under the Norman kings the office of steward tended to be hereditary. The appointments of the working household stewards (as opposed to the hereditary titular stewards) became of a more temporary nature in the reigns of Henry II and his sons. The hereditary stewards have been omitted from the list below after the reign of Henry II.

---

[1] For the regency of William Marshal during Henry's minority, *see under* Henry III in the list of English kings.

The stewards of the household appear to have been created by word of mouth and no letters of appointment have ever been found for the medieval period. Therefore, in the vast majority of cases, the precise dates of assumption and of demission of office are unknown and the surviving evidence about the stewards consists mostly of only incidental references, mainly when they appear as witnesses to royal charters. This has necessitated one departure from the normal layout of the lists of English officers of state: approximate dates of demission of office have been added in a separate column. Most of the dates in the list below represent simply the earliest and the latest occasions on which particular persons are known to have acted as stewards: all the dates of this sort are italicized to distinguish them from the actual dates of appointment and demission.

Previous to the fourteenth century, the name of each holder of the office is listed only once, at the time of his first known appearance as steward. The one exception to this rule has been made in the period 1135–54, in order to indicate the changes of allegiance during the civil war.

The evidence for the stewards in the eleventh and twelfth centuries comes from charters and from the first three volumes of the *Regesta Regum Anglo-Normannorum* (i, *1066–1100*, ed. H. W. C. Davis, Oxford, 1913; ii, *1100–1135*, ed. C. Johnson and H. A. Cronne, Oxford, 1956; iii, *1135–1154*, ed. H. A. Cronne and R. H. C. Davis, Oxford, 1968). The list of household stewards from 1189 to 1399 in T. F. Tout, *Chapters in the Administrative History of Mediaeval England*, vi (Manchester, 1933), 38–45, forms the foundation of the list below and further search among chancery, household and exchequer records has provided only very little supplementary information. The list for the period 1399–1485 is based on the work of R. L. Storey and fuller evidence is published by him in *BIHR*, xxxi (1958), 87–9.

The position and duties of the household stewards under the Norman kings are discussed in the introductions to the *Regesta Regum Anglo-Normannorum* (quoted above) and in G. H. White, 'The household of the Norman kings', *TRHS*, 4th ser., xxx (1948), especially 137–8. References to the office of steward are scattered through Tout's *Chapters* (quoted above, 6 vols., 1920–33). L. W. V. Harcourt in *His Grace the Steward and Trial of Peers* (1907), is concerned predominantly with the hereditary stewardship of the realm.

WILLIAM I

Accession to Office	Stewards of the Household	Demission of Office
a.c. 1040[1]	Gerald	still alive *p.* 1066
a. 1066[1]	Hubert (? de Ryes)	d. ? *a.* 1077
1051[1]	William fitz Osbern	*1070–1*
1061[1]	Stigand	*p.* 1070
1069	Hamo	*1094–99.* d. *a.* 1100
1074	Eudo fitz Hubert	*1115, 28 Dec.* d. Jan. 1120
1078–80	Ralph of Montpinçon	*1103* (?)
1086	Godric	*p.* 1087

[1] Steward of William in Normandy.

73

WILLIAM II

Accession to Office	Stewards of the Household	Demission of Office
1088	William	*1091*
1091	Ivo Taillebois	d. *c.* 1094
1091	Gilbert (? fitz Richard)	
1091	Roger Bigod	*1101, 3 Sept.* Prob. held office until d. 1107

HENRY I

1100, 5 Aug. (?)	Hamo fitz Hamo	*1129.* d. *c.* 1130
1101, 3 Sept.	William de Curci	*1113, Dec.* d. 1114
1101, 3 Sept.	William de Barba	
1115, 28 Dec.	William Bigod	*1120.* d. 25 Nov. 1120
1115, 28 Dec.	William de Pirou	*1126, 28 Feb.–6 Mar.*
1123, 15 Apr. (?)	Hugh Bigod. (*See under* Stephen)	
1131	Robert de la Haie	d. aft. 1135
c. 1129–32	Robert de Curci (*See under* Matilda and Henry II)	
1131, Aug.	Humphrey de Bohun. (*See under* Stephen, Matilda, Henry II)	

STEPHEN

1136	Robert fitz Richard de Clare	d. 1137
1136	Simon de Beauchamp	d. 1137
1136	Robert Malet	deserted to Matilda by 1141
1136	William Martel	dism. 1154
1136	Hugh Bigod reappears as steward	deserted to Matilda by 1141
1136	Humphrey de Bohun reappears as steward	deserted to Matilda by 1139
1137, 22 Mar.– 10 Apr.	? William the Monk	

MATILDA

1141	Robert de Curci	
1142, Apr.–June	Geoffrey de Mandeville, e. of Essex	d. 16 Sept. 1144
1144	Humphrey de Bohun. (*See under* Stephen and Henry II)	
1150–1	Reginald de St Valery	

HENRY [II] AS DUKE OF NORMANDY

1149	Manasser Bisset (*See under* Henry II)	
1150–1	? Alexander de Bohun	
	? *Robert de Neufbourg*	
1151–3	Richard de la Haie	
1153	Robert de Curci	
1153–54	Humphrey de Bohun reappears as steward. (*See under* Matilda and *infra*)	

HENRY II AS KING

	Humphrey de Bohun remained steward	*Feb.–Mar. 1158.* d. 1165
	Manasser Bisset remained steward	*c. Christmas 1170.* d. 1177
1156–59	Geoffrey de Claris	

74

Accession to Office	Stewards of the Household	Demission of Office
1156–65, c. Apr.	William de Curci	*c. 7 July 1175*. d. 1176
1157, c. Feb.	William Malet	1170, c. Mar.
1170, c. Christmas	Gilbert Malet	1177, Apr.
1174, c. 10 Oct.	Alured de St. Martin	*1181*
1175, 24 June	William fitz Aldelin	1190. d. *c.* 1198
1180–83	Hugh de Morewich	*1187, Feb.* d. 1187
1181, Apr.	Hugh Bardulf	*1189*
1182, c. Feb.	William Ruffus	*1189*
1186, Christmas	Roger Bigod[1]	
1189, c. July	Gilbert fitz Reinfrid	

RICHARD I

1189, 16 Sept.	Stephen de Longchamp	*1190, 9 June*
1189, 16 Sept.	Roger des Preaux	*1191, 3 Apr.*
1197	Robert de Turnham	*1201, 27 Jan.*

JOHN

1201	Peter de Stokes	*1205, Sept.*
1204, 25 Aug.	William Cantilupe	*1222, 19 June.* d. Apr. 1239
1213, 3 Oct.	Brian de L'Isle	
1215, 6 Mar.	Fawkes de Breauté	

HENRY III

1217, 19 Sept.	Eustace de Greinville	*1225, 2 Apr.*
1225, 29 Mar.	Osbert Giffard	*1227, 18 July*
1225, 2 July	Ralph fitz Nicholas	d. 1257, *c.* 1 Dec.
1225, 12 Oct.	Godfrey Crowcombe	*1236, 8 July*
1226, 18 Jan.	William Eyneford	*1227, 1 Aug.*
1226	Richard de Argentin	*1228, 20 Nov.*
1227, 11 Mar.	William fitz Warin	
1232, 12 Jan.	John fitz Philip	*1235, 19 Oct.*
1233, 27 Sept.	Amaury de St. Amand	*1240, 15 May*
1239, 4 Apr.	Bertram de Criol	*1255, 6 Mar.*
1239, c. 30 Aug.	William Cantilupe	d. 1251, 22 Feb.
1242	John Lexington	1255, 26 Aug. d. *a.* 10 Jan. 1259
1244	Paul Peyvre	d. 1251, 5 June
1250, 7 July	Robert Walerand	*1270, Sept.* d. 1273
1253, 1 July	John de Grey	*1255, 5 Feb.*
1255, 5 Feb.	Drogo de Barinton	
1255, 5–8 Nov.	William de Grey	1258, 1 Apr.
1256, 12 Nov.	Eubulo de Montibus	*1263, 26 May*
1257, 1 Apr.	Imbert Pugeys	*1262, Sept.* d. *c.* 15 Feb. 1263
1258, 30 Sept.	Giles de Argentin	*1260, 18 Feb.*
1263, 10 Jan.	Alan la Zouche	d. 1270
1263, 15 Aug.	Roger Leyburn	*1265, 28 Dec.* d. *c.* Sept. 1271
1263, 6 Dec.	Robert Aguillon	*1271, 10 Nov.*
1264, 4 July	Adam Newmarket	*1265, 20 Mar.*
1264, 26 Nov.	Walter Creping	*1265, 24 May*
1265, 20 Dec.	William d'Aeth	*1270, Sept.*
1268, 8 Jan.	John de la Lande	*1268, 14 Nov.*
1269, 25 Mar.	William Wintreshull	*1272, 5 Aug.*
1270, 20 Oct.	William Charles	*1270, 20 Nov.* d. *a.* 20 Jan. 1271
1271, 28 Mar.	Stephen Edworth	*1272, 1 Aug.*

[1] Served at table as royal steward, may not have been steward of the household.

EDWARD I[1]

Accession to Office	Stewards of the Household	Demission of Office
1272, ante 11 Apr.	Roger Waltham	
1274, Easter–Mich.	Hugh fitz Otho	*1283, 4 Feb.* d. *c.* 11 Apr. 1283
1278, 17 Mar.	Robert fitz John	*1286, 26 Apr.*
1284, 13 Sept.	John de Montalt	d. *c.* 20 Apr. 1294
1289, 20 Nov.	Walter Beauchamp	*1303, 1 Feb.*
1290, 30 Jan.	Peter Champvent	*c. 1292*
1293, 31 Jan.	Richard de Bosco	
1303, 20 Feb.	Robert de la Warde	*1306, p. 29 Sept.* d. *a.* 25 Jan. 1307
1306, 4 Apr.	Thomas Hide	
1307, 23 May	John Thorpe	1307, 7 Jul.

EDWARD II

1307, *29 Aug.*	Miles Stapleton	*1308, 2 Jan.*
1308, 11 Mar.	Robert fitz Pain	Vac. 1310, 30 Dec.[2]
1310, *c.* 28 Dec.	Edmund Mauley	dism. 4–26 Oct. 1312
[*1312, 27 Oct.*	Hugh Audley, marshal of the household, acting steward]	
1313, 10–12 Feb.	Edmund Mauley	*1314, 23 Apr.* d. 24 June 1314
1314, 17 July	John Cromwell	*1316, 18 Nov.*
1316, *c.* 18 Nov.[3]	William Montague	1318, 3 Nov.
1318, 20 Oct.	Bartholomew Badlesmere	*1321, 14 June,* ? dism. Oct. 1321
1322, 14 Jan.	Gilbert Peche	*1322, 30 Apr.* d. *c.* 26 June 1322
1322, *8* May	Simon Dryby, senr.	d. *c.* 8 Aug. 1322
1322, *11* July	Richard d'Amory	*1325, 5 May*
1325, *14* May	Thomas le Blount	Vac. 1327, 20 Jan.

EDWARD III

1327, *4 Feb.*	John Roos	*1328, 1 Mar*
1328, 3 Mar.	John Maltravers	1328, 12 Apr.
1328, 12 May	John Wysham	*1329, 17 Feb.*
1329, *1 Mar.*	John Maltravers	*1330, 29 July*
1330, *1 Aug.*	Hugh Turplington	*1330, 29 Aug.* d. 19 Oct. 1330
1330, *25* Oct.	Ralph Neville of Raby	*1336, 20 Mar.*
1336, *5* Mar.	Robert Ufford, 1st e. of Suffolk 1337	*1337, 24 Mar.*
1337, *12* Mar.	John Darcy, senr.	Vac. 1340, ? 15 Dec.
1341, 6 Jan.	Ralph Stafford (1st e. of Stafford 1351)	*1345, 29 Mar.*
1345, *4 May*[4]	Richard Talbot	1349, 22 Sept.
1349, *Dec.*[5]	John Grey of Rotherfield	*1359, 15 Aug.* d. 1 Sept. 1359
1359, *29* Aug.	Guy Brian	*1361, 30 May*
1361, *16 Oct.*	John atte Lee	*1368, 27 Jan.*

[1] On 10 and 13 Nov. 1275 Richard Holebrok, Thomas de Normanville and Ralph Sandwich were appointed stewards of royal lands in different counties. They were all called royal stewards, but they probably did not hold this office in the household.

[2] BL, Cotton MS Nero C. viii, fo. 5.

[3] PRO, Placita Aulae Regis, E. 37/2.

[4] PRO, Chancery Warr., C. 81/319, no. 18281.

[5] PRO, Exch. of Rec., Warr. for Issues, E.404/490, no. 319.

Accession to Office	Stewards of the Household	Demission of Office
1368, *16 Feb.*	William Latimer	*1370, 20 Oct.*
1371, 29 Jan.	Henry le Scrope	*1371, 20 Nov.*
1371, 20 Nov.	John Neville of Raby	dism. 1376, 2 June
1376, *2 July*	John of Ypres	*1377, 21 June*

RICHARD II

1377, 4 Aug.	Richard le Scrope, lord Scrope of Bolton	1378, 10 May. (*See* chancellors, 1378)
1378, 19 Mar.	Hugh Segrave	*1381, 18 July.* (*See* treasurers, 1381)
1381, 18 Oct.	John Montague	*1387, Jan.*
1387, 5 Feb.	John Beauchamp of Holt	1387, 31 Dec. exec. 12 May 1388
1388, 1 Jan.	John Devereux	d. 22 Feb. 1393
1393, *c.* 22 Feb.	Thomas Percy, 1st e. of Worcester 1397	*Vac.* 1399, 29 Sept.

HENRY IV

1399, *10 Oct.*	Thomas Rempston	1401, *Feb.*
1401, *1 Mar.*	Thomas Percy, e. of Worcester	1402, *12 Feb.*
1402, *3 June*	William Heron, lord Say	1404, *28 Jan.*
1404, *22 Feb.*	Thomas Erpingham	*1404, 21 Nov.*
1405, 24 Feb.	John Stanley	*1412, 1 Nov.*

HENRY V

1413, 23 Mar.	Thomas Erpingham[1]	*1417, 10 May*
1415, 24 July	Walter Hungerford	*1421, 13 July.* (*See* treasurers, 1426)
1421, *29 Sept.*	Robert Babthorp	1424, 23 Apr.

HENRY VI

1424, 24 Apr.	Walter Hungerford (1st lord Hungerford 1426). (*See* treasurers, 1426)	*1424, 16 July*
1426, 18 Mar.	John Tiptoft, lord Tiptoft. (*See* treasurers, 1408)	*1432, 25 Feb.*
1432, 1 Mar.	Robert Babthorp	
1433 ? 21 Apr.	William de la Pole, 4th e. of Suffolk, 1st marquess of Suffolk 1444 (1st duke of Suffolk 1448)	*1446, 20 Dec.*[2]
1447, 3 Feb.	Ralph Butler, lord Sudeley. (*See* treasurers, 1443)	1457, *20 July*
1457, *7 Dec.*	John Beauchamp, lord Beauchamp of Powick. (*See* treasurers, 1450)	*1460, 30 Dec.*

EDWARD IV

1461, *30 June*	William Neville, lord Fauconberg, 1st e. of Kent 1461	d. 9 Jan. 1463
1463, *24 July*	John Tiptoft, 1st e. of Worcester. (*See* treasurers, 1452)	*1467, 30 July*
1467, *7 May*	Henry Bourchier, 1st e. of Essex. (*See* treasurers, 1455)	1470, *5 Mar.*

[1] The concurrent tenure of office by Thomas Erpingham and Walter Hungerford is considered in *BIHR*, xxxi (1958), 88, n. 2.

[2] Robert Babthorp occurs as steward on 17 Feb. 1434 and John Beauchamp (*see under* 1456) on 13 May 1444, both probably as temporary acting stewards.

HENRY VI (readeption)

Accession to Office	Stewards of the Household	Demission of Office
[1470, 6 Oct.– 19 Nov.	Henry Lewes, 'ruler and governor of the household']	

EDWARD IV (restoration)

1472, 25 Mar.	Thomas Stanley, lord Stanley (1st e. of Derby 1485)[1]	

KEEPERS OF THE WARDROBE

The history of the wardrobe of the king's household can be followed from the reign of Henry II onwards, but no continuous list of its chief officers is possible before the minority of Henry III. At that period the wardrobe was still, to some extent, subordinated to the chamber and down to 1234 a list of the clerical heads of the royal household must include some treasurers of the chamber. Thereafter the keeper (treasurer) of the wardrobe was the chief clerical officer of the household, and, as the head of a household treasury and secretariate, he became by the later thirteenth century one of the most influential royal officials. The records kept by the wardrobe or originating from it are among the most important sources available to the student of the English monarchy between the reign of Henry III and the rule of the Lancastrian kings. Until the reign of Henry IV the offices of the keeper of the wardrobe and of his chief deputy—the controller—were invariably filled by clerks. The appearance, early in the fifteenth century, of lay keepers and controllers, who were henceforth usually men of knightly and even baronial rank, was a reflection of the changing character of these two offices; the effective clerical headship of the household passed to the third officer in the official hierarchy of the wardrobe, the cofferer. Under the Yorkist and Tudor kings the wardrobe itself was eclipsed in importance by the royal chamber. It has seemed, therefore, unnecessary to continue the present list beyond 1485.

The accounts rendered by the wardrobe to the exchequer provide the main evidence for the succession of its keepers. This was the basis of the list, down to 1399, given by T. F. Tout in his *Chapters in the Administrative History of Mediaeval England*, vi (Manchester, 1933), 25–37, from which all the dates of appointment and demission in the present list are derived. Other biographical details listed below are also mainly taken from Tout's *Chapters* (6 vols., 1920–33), which provide the most authoritative account of the royal household down to 1399. The detailed evidence for the period 1399–1485 is set out in R. L. Storey, 'English officers of state, 1399–1485', *BIHR*, xxxi (1958).

The earliest publication of a wardrobe account book in full is: *Liber quotidianus contrarotulatoris garderobe anno regni regis Edwardi primi*

---

[1] Last described as steward on 10 Feb. 1483, in the reign of Edward IV. Thomas Howard (e. of Surrey 1483) appears to have been steward early in the reign of Richard III.

vicesimo octavo, ed. J. Nichols, with an introduction by J. Topham (London, 1787).[1] Modern works, besides Tout's *Chapters*, include C. Johnson, 'The system of account in the wardrobe of Edward I', *TRHS*, 4th ser., vi (1923); J. H. Johnson, 'The system of account in the wardrobe of Edward II', *ibid.*, xii (1929), and the same author's chapter on 'The king's wardrobe and household' in J. F. Willard and W. A. Morris, *English Government at Work, 1327–36*, i (Cambridge, Mass., 1940), 206–49.

HENRY III

1218, 30 Nov.	Peter des Rivaux. (*See* treasurers, 1233)
1222, 6 Dec.	Walter Brackley acting jointly with Peter des Rivaux. Brackley remained in office until 15 June 1232; (bp of Ossory 1232–43). Rivaux *vac.* aft. 12 Dec. 1223
1224, 5 Jan.	Walter Kirkham acting jointly with Walter Brackley. Kirkham, dean of St Martin's-le-Grand 1230; (bp of Durham 1249–60), remained in office until 15 Aug. 1231. Since at least 1225 Kirkham and Brackley were subordinated to Luke, treasurer of the chamber, dean of St Martin's-le-Grand (abp of Dublin 1228–55). Luke *vac.* Dec. 1228
1229, 13 Feb.	Ranulf le Breton, treasurer of the chamber, prob. with Brackley and Kirkham as his subordinates. Ranulf *dism.* 12 Sept. 1231
1231, ? Sept.	Peter des Rivaux (*see under* 1218), treasurer of the chamber and the wardrobe; *dism.* 16 May 1234
1234, 17 May	Walter Kirkham. (*See under* 1224)
1236, 28 Oct.	Geoffrey of the Temple, king's almoner
1240, 4 Feb.	Peter d'Aigueblanche, archdeacon of Shropshire, bp of Hereford 1240–68
1241, 28 Oct.	Peter Chaceporc, archdeacon of Wells and treasurer of Lincoln; *ob.* 24 Dec. 1254
1254, 24 Dec.	[Aubrey de Fécamp, controller, acting kp.]
1255, 10 Jan.	Artaud de St Romain; *ob. c.* 29 Sept. 1257
1257, 29 Sept.	Peter des Rivaux. (*See under* 1218 and 1231)
1258, 8 July	Aubrey de Fécamp jointly with Peter Winchester
1261, 26 July	Henry of Ghent
1265, 1 Jan.	Ralph Sandwich, kt
1265, 7 Aug.	Nicholas Lewknor; *ob. c.* 3 Mar. 1268
1268, 4 Mar.	Peter Winchester (controller 1261–68)

EDWARD I

1272, 4 Nov.	Philip Willoughby (kp. of the wardrobe of Lord Edward 1269–72); (chancellor of the exchequer 1283–1305, dean of Lincoln).
1274, 18 Oct.	Thomas Bek, archdeacon of Dorset, bp of St David's 1280–93
1280, 20 Nov.	William Louth (cofferer 1274–80), dean of St Martin's-le-Grand (bp of Ely 1290–98)
1290, 12 May	[Walter Langton, controller; acting kp. (*See* treasurers, 1295)]
1290, 20 Nov.	Walter Langton, canon of Lichfield
1295, 20 Nov.	John Droxford (controller 1290–95), canon of Lichfield and Wells. (*See* treasurers, 1295)

[1] More recent editions include E. B. Fryde, *The Book of Prests of the King's Wardrobe for 1294–5* (Oxford, 1962); Mary and Bryce Lyon and H. S. Lucas, *The Wardrobe Book of William de Norwell* [1338–40] (Brussels, 1983).

EDWARD II

1307, 8 July	John Benstead (controller 1295–1305); (justice of the common pleas 1308–20)
1308, 8 July	John Droxford. (*See under* 1295)
1309, 8 July	Ingelard Warley, canon of York; *vac.* Dec. 1311
1312, 2 Jan.	Peter Collingbourn (cofferer 1307–08); *vac. aft.* 4 Feb. 1312
1312, 25 Feb.	Ingelard Warley (chief baron of the exchequer 1316–17)
1314, 1 Dec.	William Melton (controller, 1307–14), dean of St Martin's-le-Grand. (*See* treasurers, 1325)
1316, 1 Feb.	Roger Northburgh (pr. s. 1312), archdeacon of Richmond. (*See* treasurers, 1340)
1322, 1 May	Roger Waltham
1323, 20 Oct.	Robert Wodehouse (controller 1323), canon of Lincoln and York. (*See* treasurers, 1329)

EDWARD III

	Robert Wodehouse remained in office until 20 Aug. 1328
1328, 21 Aug.	Richard Bury (cofferer 1327–28). (*See* chancellors, 1334)
1329, 24 Sept.	Thomas Garton (controller 1328–29), (baron of the exchequer 1331–32)
1331, 16 Oct.	Robert Tawton. (*See* kps. of privy seal, 1334)
1334, 31 July	Richard Ferriby (controller 1332–34), canon of Lincoln
1337, 31 Aug.	Edmund de la Beche (controller 1335–37), archdeacon of Berkshire
1338, 12 July	William Norwell (controller 1337–38), (baron of the exchequer 1340), canon of Southwell
1340, 27 May	William Cusance, kp. of the wardrobe of John, duke of Cornwall, the k.'s br., *1332–38*. (*See* treasurers, 1341)
1341, 25 Nov.	William Edington, canon of Salisbury. (*See* chancellors, 1356)
1344, 11 Apr.	Walter Wetwang (controller 1342–44), canon of York; *ob.* 24 Nov. 1347
1347, 24 Nov.	Thomas Clopton, canon of Lichfield; *ob.* ? bef. 17 June 1349
1349, 5 July	William Cusance, dean of St Martin's-le-Grand. (*See under* 1340)
1350, 14 Feb.	William Retford (kp. of the great wardrobe 1349–50), (baron of the exchequer 1354–57), sub-dean of York
1353, 23 Feb.	John Buckingham (controller 1352–53), dean of Lichfield. (*See* kps. of privy seal, 1360)
1357, 26 Feb.	William Retford. (*See under* 1350)
1358, 16 Dec.	Henry Walton (receiver of Henry, e. of Lancaster, 1347–53), archdeacon of Richmond; *ob.* 2–3 Nov. 1359
1359, 3 Nov.	William Farley (controller 1358–59), sole kp. until 26 May 1360, kp. of the wardrobe in France until 7 Nov. 1360, canon of Salisbury
1360, 26 May	William Ferriby, archdeacon of Cleveland, dean of Hereford
1361, 14 Nov.	William Manton (kp. of the wardrobe of Elizabeth of Clare and of Lionel, duke of Clarence, 1340–61), dean of Lichfield
1366, 1 Feb.	William Gunthorpe (baron of the exchequer 1373–87), canon of Southwell
1368, 13 Feb.	Thomas Brantingham (treasurer of Calais 1361–68), canon of St Paul's and Hereford. (*See* treasurers, 1369)
1369, 27 June	Henry Wakefield, canon of St Paul's. (*See* treasurers, 1377)
1375, 14 Oct.	William Moulsoe (chamberlain of the exchequer 1365–75), dean of St Martin's-le-Grand; *ob.* 24 Nov. 1376
1376, 25 Nov.	Richard Beverley (cofferer 1369–76), canon of Lincoln (treasurer of Lichfield)

RICHARD II

	Richard Beverley remained in office, accounting until 26 July 1377
1377, 1 July	William Pakington (receiver of Princess Joan, the k.'s mother, 1376–77), archdeacon of Canterbury, dean of St Martin's-le-Grand; *ob.* 25 July 1390

1390, 27 July	John Carp (cofferer 1376–90), canon of St Paul's and York; dism. 30 Sept. 1399

HENRY IV

1399, 1 Oct.	Thomas Tutbury (treasurer of the household of John of Gaunt, duke of Lancaster, *1389–90*), archdeacon of Wells
1401, 9 Mar.	Thomas More (cofferer of the household of Richard II 1395–98), archdeacon of Colchester
1405, 7 Jan.	Richard Kingston (dean of the chapel in the household *1400–02*), archdeacon of Colchester
1406, 8 Dec.	John Tiptoft, kt. (*See* treasurers, 1408)
1409, 18 July	Thomas Brownfleet, kt (controller *1401*–03)

HENRY V

1413, 23 Mar.	Thomas More. (*See under* 1401)
1413, 31 Oct.	Roger Leche, kt (controller 1403–05)
1416, 1 Jan.	John Rothenall, kt (controller *1413–15*). *Ob.* 13 July 1420
1421, 21 Jan.	Walter Beauchamp, kt
1421, 1 Oct.	William Philip, kt[1]

HENRY VI

1423, 1 Mar.	John Hotoft, esquire (controller of household of Henry V as prince of Wales *1411*)
1431, 25 May	John Tirell, kt *Ob.* 2 Apr. 1437
1437, 17 Apr.	John Popham, kt
1439, 9 Apr.	Roger Fiennes, kt
1446, 15 Nov.	John Stourton, kt, 1st lord Stourton 1448
1453, 27 Mar.	John Sutton, 1st lord Dudley
1454, 3 Dec.	William Fallan (baron of the exchequer 1436–53), archdeacon of London
1456, 11 May	John Brecknock, esquire (clerk of the controlment of the household *1437–54*)
1458, *30 Oct.*	Thomas Tuddenham, kt (kp. of the great wardrobe 1446–50). Dism. aft. 3 Mar. 1460
1460, *13 May*	Gervais Clifton, kt (treasurer of Calais 1451–59). Dism. aft. 21 May
1460, *4 Sept.*	Walter Skull, kt. Dism. aft. 9 Feb. 1461

EDWARD IV

1461, 4 Mar.	John Fogge, kt
1468, 30 Sept. (?)	John Howard, kt, 1st lord Howard 1470 (duke of Norfolk 1483), dism. *c*. 3 Oct. 1470

HENRY VI (readeption)

1470, *26 Oct.*	John Delves, kt. *Ob.* 4 May 1471.

EDWARD IV (restoration)

	John, lord Howard resumed office.
1474, 30 Sept.	John Elrington, kt, cofferer *1471–74*

EDWARD V

1483, *4 June*	Richard Beauchamp, lord Beauchamp of Powick

RICHARD III

1483, 4 July	William Hopton, kt. *Ob.* 7 Feb. 1484
1484, *13 May*	Richard Croft, kt

[1] Remained in office with the army in France after death of Henry V until 8 Nov. 1422.

CHANCELLORS AND KEEPERS OF
THE GREAT SEAL

The title of royal chancellor seems to have been first used in the reign of William I, although a royal secretariat existed earlier (for a recent discussion, *see* F. E. Harmer, *Anglo-Saxon Writs* (Manchester, 1952), 57–61).

T. D. Hardy, *A Catalogue of Lords-Chancellors, Keepers of the Great Seal, Masters of the Rolls and Principal Officers of the High Court of Chancery* 1843), provided the foundation for subsequent lists. There is a valuable list of chancellors and keepers of the seal down to 1399 in T. F. Tout, *Chapters in the Administrative History of Mediaeval England*, vi, 1–17, and this work (6 vols., Manchester, 1920–33) provides the best account of the history of the chancery down to 1399.

For chancery records, *see Guide to the Contents of the Public Record office*, i (1963), 7–48; and the earlier M. S. Giuseppi, *A Guide to the Manuscripts preserved in the Public Record Office*, i (HMSO, 1923), 5–70. V. H. Galbraith, *An Introduction to the Use of the Public Records* (1952) is still useful.

Sir Henry Maxwell-Lyte, *Historical Notes on the Use of the Great Seal of England* (HMSO, 1926), describes the organization of the medieval chancery and contains valuable information and bibliographical references about its practice down to quite modern times.

For the chancery in the Norman period, *see* Introduction, pp. xii–xv, to T. A. M. Bishop and P. Chaplais, *Facsimiles of English Royal Writs to A.D. 1100, presented to Vivian Hunter Galbraith* (Oxford, 1957); *Regesta Regum Anglo-Normannorum*, i, ed. H. W. C. Davis (Oxford, 1913), Introduction, pp. xvi–xxi, and ii, ed. C. Johnson and H. A. Cronne (Oxford, 1956), Introduction, pp. ix–xi, and iii, ed. H. A. Cronne and R. H. C. Davis (Oxford, 1968), Introduction, pp. x–xv, xxix–xxx. For the chancery under Henry I, Stephen and Henry II, *see* T. A. M. Bishop, *Scriptores Regis* (Oxford, 1961). For the chancellors of Henry II before he became king, *see Regesta*, iii, pp. xxxiii–xxxv, and his chancellors after 1154 are discussed in L. Delisle, *Recueil des Actes de Henri II, roi d'Angleterre et duc de Normandie, concernant les provinces françaises et les affaires de France* (Paris, 1909), Introduction, 88–113. For the reign of Richard I the essential information is to be found in L. Landon, *The Itinerary of King Richard I* (Pipe Roll Soc., N.S., xiii, 1935). Some developments in the chancery under Henry II and his sons are discussed by H. G. Richardson in the introduction to *The Memoranda Roll for the Michaelmas term . . . 1 John, 1199–1200* (Pipe Roll Soc., N.S., xxi, 1943). For the Norman and Angevin periods generally, *see also* V. H. Galbraith, *Studies in the Public Records* (1948).

The various series of chancery enrolments start under King John and provide henceforth much more precise information about the custody of the great seal; the appointments of chancellors are often recorded as *memoranda* on the dorse of Close Rolls. Studies of the chancery in the thirteenth and fourteenth centuries can be found in F. M. Powicke, 'The Chancery during the Minority of Henry III', *EHR*, xxiii (1908), 220–35; L. B. Dibben, 'Chancellor and Keeper of the Seal under Henry III', *EHR*, xxvii (1912), 39–51; A. E. Stamp, 'Some notes on the Court and Chancery of Henry III', *Historical Essays in Honour of James Tait* (Manchester,

1933), 305–11; T. F. Tout, 'The Household of the Chancery and its Disintegration', *Essays in History presented to R. L. Poole* (Oxford, 1927), 46–85, and *The Place of the Reign of Edward II in English History*, 2nd revised edn. (Manchester, 1936, ed. H. Johnstone); B. Wilkinson, *Studies in the Constitutional History of the Thirteenth and Fourteenth Centuries* (Manchester, 1937). For the reign of Edward III, *see* B. Wilkinson, *The Chancery under Edward III* (Manchester, 1929) and the chapter on 'The Chancery' in *The English Government at Work, 1327–36*, i, ed. J. F. Willard and W. A. Morris (Cambridge, Mass., 1940), 162–205. For the fifteenth century there is new evidence about the dates of chancellors in R. L. Storey, 'English Officers of State, 1399–1485', *BIHR*, xxxi (1958), 84–6. There have been two important recent publications by P. Chaplais, *English Royal Documents: King John–Henry VI, 1199–1461* (Oxford, 1971) and *English Medieval Diplomatic Practice*, pt I (HMSO, 1982).

For the sixteenth and seventeenth centuries, *see* A. F. Pollard, 'Wolsey and the Great Seal', *BIHR*, vii (1929), 85–97; *Certain observations concerning the office of lord chancellor*, attributed to Sir Thomas Egerton (1657); J. Selden, *A Brief Discourse touching the office of lord chancellor of England*, ed. W. Dugdale (1672); W. Dugdale, *Origines juridicales* (1680). Lord Campbell's vast work, *The lives of the lord chancellors and keepers of the great seal of England . . . till the reign of George IV*, 10 vols (1856–7), is 'useful but inaccurate'. *See also* J. B. Atlay, *The Victorian Chancellors*, 2 vols (1908), and A. B. Wyon, *The Great Seals of England* (1887).

WILLIAM I

1069	Herfast (bp of Elmham 1070–85)
? 1070	Osmund (bp of Salisbury 1078–99)
? 1078[1]	Maurice, archdeacon of Le Mans; (bp of London 1085–1107)
? 1085–86	Gerard, precentor of Rouen; (bp of Hereford 1096–1100, abp of York 1100–08)

WILLIAM II

	Gerard remained in office
by Jan. 1091	Robert Bloet (bp of Lincoln 1093–1123)
a. 19 Mar. 1094	William Giffard, bp of Winchester 1100–29

HENRY I

	William Giffard remained in office until *c.* Apr. 1101
1101, bef. 3 Sept.	Roger (bp of Salisbury 1102–39)
1102, Sept.–Dec.	Waldric (bp of Laon 1107–12)
1107, spring	Ranulf; *ob. c.* 1 Jan. 1123
1123	Geoffrey Rufus (bp of Durham 1133–41)
1133	[Robert de Sigillo (bp of London 1141–50), kp. of the seal]

STEPHEN

1135	Roger le Poer, dism. 24 June 1139 (date of arrest)
1139	Philip de Harcourt, dean of Lincoln; prob. res. Mar. 1140, on being designated bp of Salisbury; (bp of Bayeux 1142–63)
1140, spring	Robert of Ghent, dean of York; still chancellor summer 1154

[1] *Regesta Regum Anglo-Normannorum*, i (1913), no. 147, shows that he was chancellor in 1082.

MATILDA

July 1141   William fitz Gilbert[1]

HENRY [II] AS DUKE OF NORMANDY

In office simultaneously:

1150   Richard de Bohun, dean of Bayeux (bp of Coutances 1151–79); previously chancellor of Geoffrey as duke of Normandy (from *1144*)

1150   William, probably fitz Gilbert; previously chancellor of Matilda

HENRY II AS KING

1155, Jan.   Thomas Becket, archdeacon of Canterbury; (abp of Canterbury 1162–70)

1162   Geoffrey Ridel, archdeacon of Canterbury; (bp of Ely 1173–89)

Prob. not styled chancellor

1173   Ralph de Warneville, treasurer of York; (bp of Lisieux ? 1181–92)

1181–82   Geoffrey, illegitimate son of Henry II, bp elect of Lincoln 1173–82; (abp of York 1189–1212)

[Walter of Coutances, archdeacon of Oxford, bp of Lincoln 1183–84, abp of Rouen 1184–1207, acting kp. of the seal 1173–89. (*See* justiciars, 1191)]

RICHARD I

1189, *Aug.*   William Longchamp, chancellor of Richard I as count of Poitou, bp of Ely 1189–97; *ob.* 31 Jan. 1197

1197, *Sept.*   [Eustace, vice-chancellor 1194–97, dean of Salisbury, bp of Ely 1197–1215, kp. of the seal]

1198, May   Eustace, bp of Ely, chancellor

JOHN

1199, 27 May   Hubert Walter, abp of Canterbury. (*See* justiciars, 1193.) *Ob.* 13 July 1205

1205, 3 Oct.   Walter de Gray, bp of Worcester 1214–15; (abp of York 1215–55)

1214, 29 Oct.   Richard Marsh, clerk of the chamber 1207–14, archdeacon of Northumberland, bp of Durham 1217–26

[Ralph Neville, dean of Lichfield, bp of Chichester 1222–44, temporary kp. of the seal in France Dec. 1213–Oct. 1214]

HENRY III

From 29 Oct. 1216 to 6 Nov. 1218 the seal of William Marshal, e. of Pembroke, *rector regis et regni Anglie*, was used instead of the k.'s seal

---

[1] A grant of the chancellorship to William de Vere was probably not effective (*see Regesta Regum Anglo-Normannorum*, iii, pp. xxix–xxx).

1216, Oct.	Richard Marsh remained chancellor; *ob.* 1 May 1226. [Ralph Neville was probably kp. of the k.'s seal from 6 Nov. 1218]
1226, *17 May*	Ralph Neville. Deprived of the seal 28 Aug. 1238, but remained titular chancellor. [Between Aug. 1238 and Apr. 1240 a succession of kps. held the great seal including William de Cantilupe, kt, steward of the household 1238–51; Geoffrey of the Temple, kp. of the wardrobe 1236–40; Simon the Norman, archdeacon of Norfolk (kp. of the seal *c.* Apr. 1240)]
1240, Apr.	[Richard le Gras, abbot of Evesham, kp. of the seal]
1242, 5 May	Ralph Neville recovered the supervision of the seal; *ob.* 1–4 Feb. 1244. Thereaft. the title of chancellor was apparently not used until 1253
1244, 14 Nov.	Silvester de Everdon (kp. of the seal in England 1242–43), archdeacon of Chester; (bp of Carlisle 1246–54)
1246, Nov.	John Mansel, chancellor of St Paul's, provost of Berverley
1247, Sept.	John Lexington, kt, steward of the household *1242–55* (temporary kp. of the seal in Gascony July–Sept. 1242, Nov. 1242–Aug. 1243)
1248, Aug.	John Mansel. (*See under* 1246)
1249, 15 Oct.	John Lexington. (*See under* 1247)
1250, aft. 28 May	William of Kilkenny, controller of the wardrobe 1249–52, archdeacon of Coventry, bp of Ely 1254–56; styled chancellor Apr. 1253
1255, 5 Jan.	Henry Wingham, dean of St Martin's-le-Grand, bp of London 1259–62. The baronial reformers renewed Wingham's appointment in 1258
1260, 18 Oct.	Nicholas of Ely, archdeacon of Ely (bp of Worcester 1266–68, bp of Winchester 1268–80). (*See* treasurers, 1263)
1261, 12 July	Walter Merton (temporary kp. of the seal 1259–60), archdeacon of Bath; (bp of Rochester 1274–77)
1263, 19 July	Nicholas of Ely. (*See under* 1260)
1263, Nov.	John Chishull, archdeacon of London; (dean of St. Paul's 1268–73, bp of London 1273–80). (*See* treasurers, 1263)
1264, 25 Feb.	Thomas Cantilupe, archdeacon of Stafford; (bp of Hereford 1275–82)
1265, 7 May	[Ralph Sandwich, kp. of the wardrobe, temporary kp. of the seal, dism. 4–6 Aug.]
1265, *8 Aug.*	Walter Giffard, bp of Bath and Wells 1264–66; (abp of York 1266–79)
1267, Mar.	Godfrey Giffard (chancellor of the exchequer May 1266), archdeacon of Wells and York, bp of Worcester 1268–1302
1268, 30 Oct.	John Chishull. (*See under* 1263)
1269, 29 July	Richard Middleton, archdeacon of Northumberland

EDWARD I[1]

1272, by 29 Nov.	Walter Merton. (*See under* 1261)
1274, 21 Sept.	Robert Burnell (chancellor of Prince Edward), archdeacon of York, bp of Bath and Wells 1275–92; *ob.* 25 Oct. 1292
1292, 17 Dec.	John Langton (kp. of the rolls of the chancery *1286*), canon of Lincoln, bp of Chichester 1305–37; *vac.* 12 Aug. 1302
1302, 30 Sept.	William Greenfield, dean of Chichester, abp of York 1304–15
1305, 16 Jan.	William Hamilton (deputy chancellor 1286–89), dean of York; *ob.* 20 Apr. 1307
1307, 21 Apr.	Ralph Baldock, bp of London 1304–13

[1] Temporary kps. of the great seal listed in T. F. Tout, *Chapters in the Administrative History of Mediaeval England*, vi (Manchester, 1933), 6–7.

EDWARD II[1]

	Ralph Baldock remained in office until 2 Aug. 1307
1307, *18* Aug.	John Langton. (*See under* 1292)
1310, 6 July	Walter Reynolds (tr. 1307), bp of Worcester 1307–13, abp of Canterbury 1313–27. From early in 1312 usually called kp. of the great seal[2]
1314, 26 Sept.	John Sandall (tr. 1312), canon of Lincoln and St Paul's, bp of Winchester 1316–19
1318, 11 June	John Hotham (tr. 1317), bp of Ely 1316–37
1320, 26 Jan.	John Salmon, bp of Norwich 1299–1325. *Vac.* 5 June 1323
1323, 20 Aug.	Robert Baldock (pr. s. 1320), archdeacon of Middlesex, imprisoned 16 Nov. 1326
1326, 30 Nov.	[William Airmyn (pr. s. 1324), bp of Norwich 1325–36; acting kp. of the seal; after 17 Dec. 1326 jointly with Henry Cliff, kp. of the rolls of chancery]

EDWARD III[3]

1327, 28 Jan.	John Hotham. (*See under* 1318.) *Vac.* 1 Mar. 1328
1328, 2 July	Henry Burghersh (tr. 1327), bp of Lincoln 1320–40
1330, 28 Nov.	John Stratford (tr. 1326), bp of Winchester 1323–33, abp of Canterbury 1333–48
1334, 28 Sept.	Richard Bury (tr. 1334), bp of Durham 1333–45
1335, 6 June	John Stratford. (*See under* 1330.) *Vac.* 4 Mar. 1337
1337, 24 Mar.	Robert Stratford (chancellor of exchequer 1331–34), bp of Chichester 1337–62
1338, 6 July	Richard Bintworth (pr. s. 1337), bp of London 1338–39; *ob.* 8 Dec. 1339
1340, 28 Apr.	John Stratford. (*See under* 1330.) *Vac.* 20 June
1340, 12 July	Robert Stratford. (*See under* 1337.) Dism. 1 Dec. 1340
1340, 1 Dec.	[William Kilsby, kp. of the privy seal 1338–42, temporary kp. of the great seal]
1340, 14 Dec.	Robert Bourchier, kt
1341, 28 Oct.	Robert Parving, kt (tr. 1341); *ob.* 26 Aug. 1343
1343, 29 Sept.	Robert Sadington, kt (chief baron of the exchequer *1340*–43)
1345, 26 Oct.	John Offord (pr. s. 1342), dean of Lincoln, abp-elect of Canterbury 1348–49; *ob.* 20 May 1349
1349, 16 June	John Thoresby (pr. s. 1345), bp of St David's 1347–49, bp of Worcester 1349–52, abp of York 1352–73
1356, 27 Nov.	William Edington (tr. 1344), bp of Winchester 1345–66
1363, 21 Feb.	Simon Langham (tr. 1360), bp of Ely 1362–66, abp of Canterbury 1366–68 (cardinal 1368); *vac.* aft. 18 July 1367
1367, *10–17 Sept.*	William Wykeham (pr. s. 1363), bp of Winchester 1366–1404; *vac.* 24 Mar. 1371
1371, 26 Mar.	Robert Thorp, kt (chief justice of the common pleas 1356–71); *ob.* 29 June 1372
1372, 5 July	John Knyvet, kt (chief justice of the king's bench 1365–72)
1377, 11 Jan.	Adam Houghton, bp of St David's 1362–89

RICHARD II

	Adam Houghton remained in office until 29 Oct. 1378
1378, 29 Oct.	Richard Scrope, lord Scrope of Bolton (tr. 1371)
1380, 30 Jan.	Simon Sudbury (bp of London 1361–75), abp of Canterbury 1375–81; *ob.* 14 June 1381
1381, 16 June	[Hugh Segrave, steward of the household, temporary kp.]

---

[1] Temporary kps of the great seal are listed in T. F. Tout, *The Place of the Reign of Edward II in English History*, 2nd edn (Manchester, 1936), 290–4.
[2] Tout, *The Place of the Reign of Edward II in English History*, 285–8.
[3] For the reign of Edward III the dates of the actual assumption of office are given in most cases. Temporary kps of the great seal are listed in Tout, *Chapters . . .* vi (Manchester, 1933), 11–16.

1381, 10 Aug.	William Courtenay (bp of Hereford 1369–75), bp of London 1375–81, abp of Canterbury 1381–96; *vac.* 30 Nov. 1381
1381, 4 Dec.	Richard Scrope. (*See under* 1378.) *Vac.* 11 July 1382
1382, 20 Sept.	Robert Braybrook, bp of London 1381–1404; *vac.* 10 Mar. 1383
1383, 13 Mar.	Michael de la Pole, kt, 1st e. of Suffolk 1385; dism. 23 Oct. 1386
1386, 24 Oct.	Thomas Arundel [or Fitzalan], bp of Ely 1373–88, abp of York 1388–96; (abp of Canterbury 1396–97 and 1399–1414)
1389, 4 May	William Wykeham. (*See under* 1367)
1391, 27 Sept.	Thomas Arundel. (*See under* 1386)
1396, 15 Nov.	Edmund Stafford (pr. s. 1389), bp of Exeter 1395–1419; dism. aft. 15 July 1399
1399, *23 Aug.*	Thomas Arundel. (*See under* 1386.) Dism. aft. 3 Sept.
1399, *5 Sept.*	John Scarle (kp. of the rolls of Chancery 1394–97), archdeacon of Lincoln

HENRY IV

	John Scarle remained in office
1401, 9 Mar.	Edmund Stafford. (*See under* 1396)
1403, 28 Feb.	Henry Beaufort, bp of Lincoln 1398–1404, bp of Winchester 1404–47; (cardinal 1426)
1405, 2 Mar.	Thomas Langley (pr. s. 1401), dean of York, bp of Durham 1406–37
1407, 30 Jan.	Thomas Arundel. (*See under* 1386.) Dism. 21 Dec. 1409
1410, 31 Jan.	Thomas Beaufort, kt (1st e. of Dorset 1412, 1st duke of Exeter 1416). Dism. 20 or 21 Dec. 1411
1412, 5 Jan.	Thomas Arundel. (*See under* 1386)

HENRY V

1413, 21 Mar.	Henry Beaufort. (*See under* 1403)
1417, 23 July	Thomas Langley. (*See under* 1405)

HENRY VI

1422, 16 Nov.	Thomas Langley reappd.
1424, 16 July	Henry Beaufort. (*See under* 1403)
1426, 16 Mar.	John Kemp (bp of Rochester 1419–21, bp of Chichester 1421, bp of London 1421–25); abp of York 1425–52; (abp of Canterbury 1452–54, cardinal 1439)
1432, 26 Feb.	John Stafford, bp of Bath and Wells 1424–43, abp of Canterbury 1443–52
1450, 31 Jan.	John Kemp. (*See under* 1426.) *Ob.* 22 Mar. 1454
1454, 2 Apr.	Richard Nevill, e. of Salisbury
1455, 7 Mar.	Thomas Bourchier (bp of Worcester 1433–43, bp of Ely 1443–54), abp of Canterbury 1454–86 (cardinal 1467)
1456, 11 Oct.	William Waynflete, bp of Winchester 1447–86. Dism. 7 July 1460
1460, 25 July	George Nevill, bp of Exeter 1456–65, abp of York 1465–76

EDWARD IV

1461, 10 Mar.	George Nevill reappd. Dism. 8 June 1467
1467, 20 June	Robert Stillington (pr. s. 1460), bp of Bath and Wells 1465–91, dism. Oct. 1470

HENRY VI (readeption)

1470, 29 Sept.	George Nevill. (*See under* 1460.) Ceased aft. 4 Mar. 1471

EDWARD IV (restoration)

	Robert Stillington resumed office. Dism. 18 June 1473
1473, 27 July	Laurence Booth, bp of Durham 1457–76 (abp of York 1476–80)

1474, 27 May	Thomas Rotherham *alias* Scott (pr. s. 1467, bp of Rochester 1468–72), bp of Lincoln 1472–80 (abp of York 1480–1500)
1475, 10 June	John Alcock (kp. of the rolls of Chancery 1471–72), bp of Rochester 1472–76 (bp of Worcester 1476–86, bp of Ely 1486–1500)
1475, 29 Sept.	Thomas Rotherham resumed office[1]

EDWARD V

	Thomas Rotherham remained in office. Dism. aft. 22 Apr. 1483
1483, 10 May	John Russell (pr. s. 1474, bp of Rochester 1476–80), bp of Lincoln 1480–94

RICHARD III

1483, 27 June	John Russell reappd. Dism. 29 July 1485

HENRY VII

1485, 18 Sept.	Thomas Rotherham. (*See under* 1474)
1485, 7 Oct.	John Alcock. (*See under* 1475)
1487, 6 Mar.	John Morton (bp of Ely 1479–86), abp of Canterbury 1486–1500, cardinal 1493. *Ob.* 15 Sept. 1500
1504, 21 Jan.	William Warham (bp of London 1502–03), abp of Canterbury 1503–32. [He had been kp. of the seal since 11 Aug. 1502, succeeding Abp Henry Deane, who had been kp. 13 Oct. 1500 to 27 July 1502]

HENRY VIII

1509	William Warham remained in office
1515, 24 Dec.	Thomas Wolsey, bp of Lincoln 1514, bp of Bath and Wells 1518–24, bp of Durham 1524–29, bp of Winchester 1529–30, abp of York 1514–30, cardinal 1515, legate *a latere* 1518. *Vac.* 18 Oct. 1529
1529, 26 Oct.	Sir Thomas More; *vac.* 16 May 1532
1532, 20 May	Sir Thomas Audley, kp. of the seal. Cr. chancellor, 26 Jan. 1533. 1st lord Audley 1538. *Ob.* 22 Apr. 1544
1544, 3 May	Thomas Wriothesley, 1st lord Wriothesley 1544 [kp. of the seal from 22 Apr. 1544]

EDWARD VI

	Lord Wriothesley remained in office; 1st e. of Southampton, 1547. Dism. 7 May 1547
1547, 7 Mar.	[William Paulet, 1st lord St John, kp. of the seal; (1st marquess of Winchester 1551)]
1547, 23 Oct.	Richard Rich, 1st lord Rich 1547. *Vac.* 21 Dec. 1551
1552, 19 Jan.	Thomas Goodrich, bp of Ely 1534–54 [kp. of the seal from 22 Dec. 1551]

MARY

1553, 23 Aug.	Stephen Gardiner, bp of Winchester 1531–51, 1553–55
1555, 14 Nov.	[Sir Nicholas Hare and others held the seal in commission pending the choice of a successor to Gardiner]
1556, 1 Jan.	Nicholas Heath (bp of Rochester 1540–43, bp of Worcester 1543–51, 1553–55), abp of York 1555–59

---

[1] Alcock had been acting as chancellor in England while Rotherham attended the king in France. *See* Maxwell-Lyte, *The Great Seal*, 68–70.

ELIZABETH I

1558, 18 Nov.	The seal remained with the queen
1558, 22 Dec.	[Nicholas Bacon, lord kp.]
1579, 20 Feb.	The seal remained with the queen
1579, 26 Apr.	Sir Thomas Bromley
1587, 29 Apr.	Sir Christopher Hatton
1591, 22 Nov.	The seal in commission
1592, 28 May	[Sir John Puckering, lord kp.]
1596, 6 May	[Sir Thomas Egerton, lord kp., 1st lord Ellesmere 1603 (1st viscount Brackley 1616)]

JAMES I

1603, 5 Apr.	Sir Thomas Egerton reappd. He was cr. lord chancellor on 24 July 1603
1617, 7 Mar.	Sir Francis Bacon, lord kp., 1st lord Verulam 1618, 1st viscount St Alban 1621. Cr. lord chancellor 7 Jan. 1618
1621, 1 May	Bacon being ill, the seal was put into commission
1621, 16 July	[John Williams, lord kp., bp of Lincoln 1621–41 (abp of York 1641–50)]

CHARLES I

	[John Williams remained in office]
1625, 1 Nov.	[Sir Thomas Coventry, lord kp., 1st lord Coventry 1628]
1640, 17 Jan.	[Sir John Finch, lord kp., 1st lord Finch 1640]
1641, 18 Jan.	[Sir Edward Littleton, 1st lord Lyttleton of Mounslow 1641. He brought the seal to the k. at York, 21 May 1642. *Ob.* 9 Aug. 1645]
1645, 30 Aug.	[Sir Richard Lane, lord kp.]
1653, 6 Apr.	[Sir Edward Herbert]
1658, 13 Jan.	Sir Edward Hyde, 1st lord Hyde 1660, 1st e. of Clarendon 1661

COMMISSIONERS 1643–1660

1643, 10 Nov.	New great seal authorized and commissioners: John Manners, 8th e. of Rutland (excused 28 Nov.), Oliver St John, 2nd e. of Bolingbroke, Oliver St John (Sol.-Gen.), John Wyld (Sergt. at Law), Samuel Browne, Edmund Prideaux MPs
1643, 28 Nov.	Henry Grey, 7th e. of Kent (added)
1646, 19 Mar.	Kent, Bolingbroke, Wyld, Prideaux, St John, Browne
1646, 3 July	William Cecil, 2nd e. of Salisbury (*vice* Bolingbroke, decd.)
1646, 31 Oct.	Edward Montague, 2nd e. of Manchester, William Lenthall MP (as Speakers of the two Houses), replaced the above
1647, 3 Aug.	John Carey, 5th lord Hunsdon, Henry Pelham MP (as acting Speakers of the two Houses)
1647, 10 Aug.	Manchester and Lenthall (restored)
1648, 17 Mar.	Henry Grey, 7th e. of Kent, William, 1st lord Grey of Warke, Sir Thomas Widdrington, Bulstrode Whitelocke MPs (two latter not sworn until 12 Apr. 1648), instead of the two Speakers
1649, Jan.	New Commonwealth seal created
1649, 8 Feb.	Bulstrode Whitelocke, Sergt. at Law, Richard Keeble, Sergt. at Law, John Lysle (or Lisle) MP (*vice* Kent and Grey)
1654, 4 Apr.	Sir Thomas Widdrington (*vice* Keeble), Whitelocke and Lisle (contd.)
1655, 6 June	John Lisle, Nathaniel Fiennes
1659, 14 May	William Lenthall MP, Speaker (alone)
1659, 3 June	John Bradshaw, Sergt. at Law (did not act, due to illness and age, except possibly 22 July–early Oct.), Thomas Terryl, or Tirrell, John Fountaine, Sergt. at Law

1660, 18 Jan.	Terryl, Fountaine, Sir Thomas Widdrington, MP
1660, 5 May	Edward Montague, 2nd e. of Manchester added to Fountaine, Terryl and Widdrington.
1660, 28 May	They ceased to act; the Commonwealth seal was defaced and then broken up.

CHARLES II

1660	Lord Hyde. (*See under* 1658)
1667, 30 Aug.	[Sir Orlando Bridgeman, lord kp.]
1672, 17 Nov.	Anthony Ashley Cooper, 1st e. of Shaftesbury 1672
1673, 9 Nov.	Sir Heneage Finch, lord kp. Cr. chancellor 19 Dec. 1675, 1st lord Finch 1674, 1st e. of Nottingham 1681
1682, 20 Dec.	[Sir Francis North, lord kp., 1st lord Guilford 1683]

JAMES II

	Lord Guilford remained in office. *Ob.* 5 Sept. 1685
1685, 28 Sept.	George Jeffreys, 1st lord Jeffreys 1685, depr. 11 Dec. 1688

WILLIAM III AND MARY

1689–93	The seal in commission
1693, 23 Mar.	Sir John Somers, lord kp. Cr. chancellor 22 Apr. 1697; 1st lord Somers 1697; *vac.* 17 Apr. 1700
1700, 21 May	[Sir Nathan Wright, lord kp.]

ANNE

	[Sir Nathan Wright remained in office]
1705, 11 Oct.	William Cowper, lord kp. Cr. chancellor 4 May 1707 (1st lord chancellor of Great Britain, the Act of Union having come into force on 1 May 1707). 1st lord Cowper 1706 (1st e. Cowper 1718)
1708, 29 Sept.	The seal in commission
1710, 19 Oct.	Sir Simon Harcourt, lord kp. Cr. chancellor 7 Apr. 1713; 1st lord Harcourt 1711 (1st viscount Harcourt 1721)

GEORGE I

	Lord Harcourt remained in office
1714, 21 Sept.	Lord Cowper. (*See under* 1705); *vac.* 15 Apr. 1718
1718, 12 May	Thomas Parker, 1st lord Macclesfield, 1st e. of Macclesfield 1721. *Vac.* 4 Jan. 1725 (impeached 13 Feb. 1725)
1725, Jan.	The seal in commission
1725, 1 June	Peter King, 1st lord King 1725

GEORGE II

	Lord King remained in office
1733, 29 Nov.	Charles Talbot, 1st lord Talbot of Hensol 1733; *ob.* 14 Feb. 1737
1737, 21 Feb.	Philip Yorke, 1st lord Hardwicke, 1st e. of Hardwicke 1754; *vac.* 19 Nov. 1756
1756, 20 Nov.	The seal in commission
1757, 30 June	[Sir Robert Henley, lord kp., 1st lord Henley 1760, 1st e. of Northington 1764]

GEORGE III

	Lord Henley remained in office as lord kp. Cr. chancellor 16 Jan. 1761
1766, 30 July	Charles Pratt, 1st lord Camden 1765 (1st e. Camden 1786)

1770, 17 Jan.	Charles Yorke, *ob.* 20 Jan. 1770[1]
1770, 20 Jan.	The seal in commission
1771, 23 Jan.	Henry Bathurst, 1st lord Apsley 1771, 2nd e. Bathurst 1775
1778, 3 June	Edward Thurlow, 1st lord Thurlow, 1778; *vac.* 7 Apr. 1783
1783, 9 Apr.	The seal in commission
1783, 23 Dec.	Lord Thurlow reappd
1792, June	The seal in commission
1793, 28 Jan.	Alexander Wedderburn, 1st lord Loughborough (1st e. of Rosslyn 1801)
1801, 14 Apr.	John Scott, 1st lord Eldon (1st e. of Eldon 1821)
1806, 7 Feb.	Thomas Erskine, 1st lord Erskine 1806
1807, 1 Apr.	Lord Eldon. (*See under* 1801)

GEORGE IV

	Lord Eldon remained in office
1827, 2 May	John Singleton Copley, 1st lord Lyndhurst 1827

WILLIAM IV

	Lord Lyndhurst remained in office
1830, 22 Nov.	Henry Brougham, 1st lord Brougham and Vaux 1830
1834, 22 Nov.	Lord Lyndhurst. (*See under* 1827)
1835, Apr.	The seal in commission
1836, 16 Jan.	Sir Charles Christopher Pepys, 1st lord Cottenham 1836 (1st e. of Cottenham 1850)

VICTORIA

	Lord Cottenham remained in office
1841, 3 Sept.	Lord Lyndhurst. (*See under* 1827)
1846, 6 July	Lord Cottenham. (*See under* 1836)
1850, 15 July	Sir Thomas Wilde, 1st lord Truro 1850
1852, 27 Feb.	Sir Edward Burtenshaw Sugden, 1st lord St Leonards 1852
1852, 28 Dec.	Robert Monsey Rolfe, 1st lord Cranworth
1858, 26 Feb.	Sir Frederic Thesiger, 1st lord Chelmsford 1858
1859, 18 June	John Campbell, 1st lord Campbell, *ob.* 23 June 1861
1861, 26 June	Sir Richard Bethell, 1st lord Westbury 1861
1865, 7 July	Lord Cranworth. (*See under* 1852)
1866, 6 July	Lord Chelmsford. (*See under* 1858)
1868, 29 Feb.	Hugh McCalmont Cairns, 1st lord Cairns 1867 (1st e. Cairns 1878)
1868, 9 Dec.	Sir William Page Wood, 1st lord Hatherley 1868
1872, 15 Oct.	Roundell Palmer, 1st lord Selborne 1872 (1st e. of Selborne 1882)
1874, 21 Feb.	Lord Cairns. (*See under* 1868)
1880, 28 Apr.	Lord Selborne. (*See under* 1872)
1885, 24 June	Sir Hardinge Stanley Giffard, 1st lord Halsbury 1885 (1st e. of Halsbury 1898)
1886, 6 Feb.	Sir Farrer Herschell, 1st lord Herschell 1886
1886, 3 Aug.	Lord Halsbury. (*See under* 1885)
1892, 18 Aug.	Lord Herschell. (*See under* 1886)
1895, 29 June	Lord Halsbury. (*See under* 1885)

EDWARD VII

	e. of Halsbury remained in office
1905, 11 Dec.	Sir Robert Threshie Reid, 1st lord Loreburn 1906, 1st e. of Loreburn 1911

[1] Died before the patent creating him Lord Morden had passed the great seal.

GEORGE V

	Lord Loreburn remained in office
1912, 10 June	Richard Burdon Haldane, 1st viscount Haldane 1911
1915, 27 May	Sir Stanley Owen Buckmaster, 1st lord Buckmaster 1915 (1st viscount Buckmaster 1932)
1916, 11 Dec.	Sir Robert Bannatyne Finlay, 1st lord Finlay 1916 (1st viscount Finlay 1919)
1919, 14 Jan.	Sir Frederick Edwin Smith, 1st lord Birkenhead 1919 (1st e. of Birkenhead 1922)
1922, 25 Oct.	George Cave, 1st viscount Cave
1924, 23 Jan.	Viscount Haldane. (*See under* 1912)
1924, 7 Nov.	Viscount Cave. (*See under* 1922)
1928, 29 Mar.	Sir Douglas McGarel Hogg, 1st lord Hailsham 1928 (1st viscount Hailsham 1929)
1929, 8 June	Sir John Sankey, 1st lord Sankey 1929, 1st viscount Sankey 1932
1935, 7 June	Viscount Hailsham. (*See under* 1928)

EDWARD VIII

Viscount Hailsham remained in office

GEORGE VI

	Viscount Hailsham remained in office
1938, 9 Mar.	Frederick Herbert Maugham, 1st lord Maugham
1939, 4 Sept.	Thomas Walker Hobart Inskip, 1st viscount Caldecote 1939
1940, 13 May	John Allsebrooke Simon, 1st viscount Simon 1940
1945, 28 July	William Allen Jowitt, 1st lord Jowitt 1945, 1st viscount Jowitt 1947 (1st e. Jowitt 1951)
1951, 30 Oct.	Gavin Turnbull Simonds, 1st lord Simonds 1952 (1st viscount Simonds 1954)

ELIZABETH II

	Lord Simonds remained in office
1954, 19 Oct.	David Patrick Maxwell Fyfe, 1st viscount Kilmuir 1954
1962, 13 July	Reginald Edward Manningham-Buller, 1st viscount Dilhorne
1964, 16 Oct.	Gerald Austin Gardiner, Lord Gardiner
1970, 20 June	Quintin McGarel Hogg, Lord Hailsham of St Marylebone
1974, 5 Mar.	Frederick Elwyn-Jones, Lord Elwyn-Jones
1979, 5 May	Lord Hailsham (*See under* 1970)

KEEPERS OF THE PRIVY SEAL

A privy seal was kept by King John and its use was permanently revived by Henry III (probably in 1230). In the later years of Edward I it was normally kept by the controller of the wardrobe, but the lords ordainers insisted in 1311 upon the appointment of a separate keeper and the two offices seem henceforward to have been regarded as distinct. From the time of John Benstead (controller 1295–1305) to that of William Wykeham (1363–67) the keepers are frequently described as *secretarius regis* (*see* especially L. B. Dibben, 'Secretaries in the Thirteenth and Fourteenth Centuries', *EHR*, xxv (1910), 434–7).

The present list down to 1399 is mainly based on T. F. Tout, *Chapters in the Administrative History of Mediaeval England*, vi (1933), 50–4. New evidence for the fifteenth century is set out in R. L. Storey, 'English Officers of State, 1399–1485', *BIHR*, xxxi (1958), 86–7. Until 1363 keepers of the privy seal were paid by the king's wardrobe and owing to the incomplete survival of the particulars of wardrobe accounts the precise dates of appointment and dismissal are often unknown. Between 1363 and 1470 fairly complete evidence is provided by warrants to the exchequer ordering payment of the keepers' fees (enrolled on Liberate Rolls and also partly preserved among Warrants for Issues of the Exchequer of Receipt). From 1470 keepers usually received letters patent of appointment which can be found in the *Calendars of Patent Rolls*.

The best account of the privy seal and its keepers down to 1399 is by T. F. Tout, *Chapters* (6 vols, Manchester, 1920–33), especially vols i, ii (pp. 282–313) and v (pp. 1–160) and in his *Place of the Reign of Edward II in English History*, 2nd rev. edn (Manchester, 1936, ed. H. Johnstone). *See also* E. Déprez, *Études de diplomatique anglaise, 1272–1485* (Paris, 1908); B. Wilkinson, *Studies in the Constitutional History of the Thirteenth and Fourteenth Centuries* (Manchester, 1937); J. H. Trueman, 'The Privy Seal and the English Ordinances of 1311', *Speculum*, xxxi (1956), 611–25; P. Chaplais, 'Privy Seal drafts, rolls and registers (Edward I–Edward II)', *EHR*, lxxiii (1958), 270–3; *idem*, *English Royal Documents: King John–Henry VI, 1199–1461* (Oxford, 1971) and *English Medieval Diplomatic Practice*, pt 1 (HMSO, 1982).

For the period 1377–1485, *see* J. Otway-Ruthven, *The King's Secretary and the Signet Office in the XV Century* (Cambridge, 1939). Thomas Hoccleve was a clerk of the privy seal, 1387–1424, and in his poems he has set down some valuable information about the privy seal office and the daily life of the clerks—Hoccleve, *The Regement of Princes* (Early English Text Soc., 1897). Richard Fox, 1487–1516, appears to have been the first lord privy seal *eo nomine*. The importance of the office declined after the appointment of two principal secretaries in 1540, but the dignity of the lord privy seal increased. 'In 1798 a single Deputy was doing all the work of the Office' and 'his hours were only from ten o'clock until two'. In 1884 the office was abolished (Stat. 47 and 48 Vict., c. 30), but the lord keeper was retained and is today a member of the cabinet. *See* Sir .Henry Maxwell-Lyte, *Historical Notes on the Use of the Great Seal of England* (1926), especially 21–6, 75–110.

KEEPERS OF THE PRIVY SEAL

EDWARD II

1307, 8 July	William Melton, controller of the wardrobe, dean of St Martin's-le-Grand. (*See* treasurers, 1325)
1312, 18 Sept.[1]	Roger Northburgh, first separate kp., canon of York. (*See* treasurers, 1340.) *Vac.* 1 Feb. 1316
1316, 7 July	Thomas Charlton, jointly with the controllership of the wardrobe until 7 July 1318 and separately thereaft.; archdeacon of Northumberland. (*See* treasurers, 1328)
1320, 27 Jan.	Robert Baldock, controller of the wardrobe. (*See* chancellors, 1323)
1323, 8 July	Robert Wodehouse, controller of the wardrobe, canon of Lincoln. (*See* treasurers, 1329)
1323, *3 Oct.*	Robert Ayleston, canon of Lincoln. (*See* treasurers, 1332.) *Vac. c.* 21 May 1324
1324, *c.* 26 May	William Airmyn, canon of St Paul's, Lincoln and Hereford. (*See* chancellors, 1326). *Vac.* Jan–Feb. 1325

[1] PRO, Exch. K.R., Acc. Various, E. 101/375/8, fo. 6.

1325, *12 Apr.*	Henry Cliff, canon of York (kp. of the rolls of chancery 1325–33). *Vac.* 4 July 1325
1325, *12 Oct.*	William Herlaston, archdeacon of Norfolk. *Vac.* 1 Oct. 1326
1326, 26 Oct.	Robert Wyvill, kp. of the privy seal of Edward, duke of Aquitaine; (bp of Salisbury 1330–75)

EDWARD III

1327, *1 Mar.*	Richard Airmyn (kp. of the rolls of chancery 1324–25); canon of York and Lincoln
1328, Apr.	Adam Lymbergh, canon of St Paul's; (chancellor of Ireland 1331–34)
1329, 24 Sept.	Richard Bury (k.w. 1328), dean of Wells, bp of Durham 1333–45. (*See* chancellors, 1334.) *Vac.* ? Feb. 1334
1334, *Mar.*	Robert Ayleston.[1] (*See under* 1323); *ob.* 21 Mar. 1334
1334, *24 Apr.*	Robert Tawton, until 30 July 1334 jointly with the keepership of the wardrobe,[2] archdeacon of Durham; *ob. c.* 20 Feb. 1335
1335, 20 Feb.[3]	William de la Zouche (controller of the wardrobe 1334–35), dean of York. (*See* treasurers, 1337)
1337, 25 Mar.[3]	Richard Bintworth, canon of St Paul's. (*See* chancellors, 1338)
1338, 6–11 July	William Kilsby (receiver of the chamber 1335–38), canon of York
1342, 4 June	John Offord, dean of Lincoln. (*See* chancellors, 1345.) *Vac.* aft. 29 Sept. 1344[4]
1344, Oct.–Dec.	Thomas Hatfield (receiver of the chamber 1338–44), bp of Durham 1345–81
1345, 3 July	John Thoresby (kp. of the rolls of chancery 1341–45), bp of St David's 1347–49. (*See* chancellors, 1349.) *Vac.* Sept. 1347
1347, *28 Sept.*	Simon Islip, kp. of the seal of Lionel, regent in England, July 1346–Sept. 1347; abp of Canterbury 1349–66. *Vac.* between 21 Feb. and 1 May 1350[5]
1350, *23 Oct.*[6]	Michael Northburgh, archdeacon of Suffolk, bp of London 1354–61. *Vac.* 26 Aug. 1354
1354, *c.* 21 Sept.	Thomas Bramber (receiver of the chamber 1347–49), canon of York. *Vac.* aft. 23 Sept. 1355[7]
1355, *9 Dec.*	John Winwick (previously senior clerk of the privy seal), treasurer of York; *ob.* 12 July 1360
1360, *1 July*[8]	John Buckingham, kp. of the seal of Thomas, regent in England, Mar.–July 1360; dean of Lichfield, bp of Lincoln 1362–98
1363, 10 June	William Wykeham (receiver of the chamber *1361*, and k.'s secretary 1361–63), dean of St Martin's-le-Grand, archdeacon of Lincoln. (*See* chancellors, 1367)
1367, 28 Oct.	Peter Lacy, receiver general of Edward, prince of Wales, 1346–71, canon of Lichfield and Dublin
1371, 26 Mar.[9]	Nicholas Carew, vac. 24 June 1377

RICHARD II

1377, 26 June	John Fordham (kp. of the privy seal of Prince Richard 1376–77), dean of Wells, bp of Durham 1381–88. (*See* treasurers, 1386)
1381, 13 Dec.	William Dighton (previously senior clerk of the privy seal), canon of St Paul's

[1] Exch. of Receipt, Warr. for Issues, E. 404/497, no. 269.
[2] *Ibid.*, E. 404/3/17.
[3] BL. Cotton MS Nero C. viii,fos 219 v, 225v.
[4] E. 404/496, no. 207.
[5] E. 404/5/32 and E. 404/490, no. 282.
[6] Chanc. Warr., C. 81/1334, no. 30.
[7] E. 404/490, no. 255.
[8] Exch. K.R., Acc. Various, E. 101/393/11, p. 64.
[9] Liberate Roll, C 62/143, m. 6.

1382, 9 Aug.	Walter Skirlaw, dean of St Martin's-le-Grand, bp of Coventry and Lichfield 1385–86, bp of Bath and Wells 1386–88; (bp of Durham 1388–1406)
1386, 24 Oct.	John Waltham (kp. of the rolls of chancery *1386*), archdeacon of Richmond, bp of Salisbury 1388–95. (*See* treasurers, 1391)
1389, 4 May	Edmund Stafford, dean of York, bp of Exeter 1395–1419. (*See* chancellors, 1396)
1396, 16 Feb.	Guy Mone (receiver of the chamber 1391–98), bp of St David's 1397–1407. (*See* treasurers, 1398)
1397, 14 Nov.	Richard Clifford (kp. of the great wardrobe 1390–98), dean of York, bp of Worcester 1401–07; (bp of London 1407–21)

HENRY IV

1399, 30 Sept.	Richard Clifford reappd.
1401, 3 Nov.	Thomas Langley (secretary *1399*), dean of York. (*See* chancellors, 1405)
1405, 2 Mar.	Nicholas Bubwith (kp. of the rolls of Chancery 1402–05), archdeacon of Dorset, bp of London 1406–07; (bp of Salisbury 1407, bp of Bath and Wells 1407–24)
1406, 4 Oct.	John Prophet (secretary *1402–05*), dean of York

HENRY V

	John Prophet remained in office
1415, 3 June	John Wakering (kp. of the rolls of Chancery 1405–15), archdeacon of Canterbury, bp of Norwich 1415–25. Dism. 7 July 1416
1416, 11 Sept.	Henry Ware, canon of London, bp of Chichester 1418–20. Dism. 21 Sept. 1418
1418, *3 Oct.*	John Kemp, archdeacon of Durham, bp of Rochester 1419–21. (*See* chancellors, 1426)
1421, 25 Feb.	John Stafford, dean of St Martin's-le-Grand. (*See* chancellors, 1432)

HENRY VI

	John Stafford remained in office
1422, 19 Dec.	William Alnwick (secretary *1421*–22), archdeacon of Salisbury, bp of Norwich 1426–36; (bp of Lincoln 1436–49)
1432, 25 Feb.	William Lyndwood (secondary of privy seal office *1431*), archdeacon of Oxford, bp of St David's 1442–46
1443, 18 July	Thomas Beckington (secretary 1437–43), archdeacon of Buckingham, bp of Bath and Wells 1443–65
1444, 11 Feb.	Adam Moleyns (clerk of the council *1438*–1444), dean of Salisbury, bp of Chichester 1445–50. *Ob.* 9 Jan. 1450.[1]
1450, 31 Jan.	Andrew Holes, archdeacon of York. Dism. 5 Apr. 1452[2]
1452, 12 May	Thomas Lisieux, dean of St Paul's
1456, 24 Sept.	Laurence Booth (chancellor of Queen Margaret *1452*), dean of St Paul's, bp of Durham 1457–76. (*See* chancellors, 1473)
1460, 28 July	Robert Stillington, archdeacon of Wells. (*See* chancellors, 1467)

EDWARD IV

1461, 1 Nov.	Robert Stillington reappd (bp of Bath and Wells 1465–91)
1467, 24 June	Thomas Rotherham, canon of Lincoln, bp of Rochester 1468–72. (*See* chancellors, 1474)

[1] Thomas Kent had temporary charge of the privy seal from 20 Jan. to 1 Feb. 1450.

[2] Kent again held the seal from this day until 13 May following.

HENRY VI (readeption)

1470, 24 Oct.   John Hales, bp of Coventry and Lichfield 1459–90

EDWARD IV (restoration)

Thomas Rotherham resumed office
1474, 28 May   John Russell (secondary of privy seal office 1469–74), archdeacon of Berkshire, bp of Rochester 1476–80, bp of Lincoln. (*See* chancellors, 1483)

EDWARD V

1483, 10 May   John Gunthorp (dean of the chapel in the household *1478*–83), dean of Wells

RICHARD III

1483, 27 June   John Gunthorp reappd.

HENRY VII

1485, 8 Sept.   Peter Courtenay, bp of Exeter 1478–87; (bp of Winchester 1487–92)
1487, 24 Feb.   Richard Fox, bp of Exeter 1487–92, bp of Bath and Wells 1492–94, bp of Durham 1494–1501, bp of Winchester 1501–28

HENRY VIII

Richard Fox remained in office until 1516
1516, 18 May[1]   Thomas Ruthall, bp of Durham 1509–23
1523, 14 Feb.   Sir Henry Marny, 1st lord Marny 1523
1523, 25 May   Cuthbert Tunstall, bp of London 1522–30; (bp of Durham 1530–52, 1553–59)
1530, 24 Jan.   Thomas Boleyn, 1st e. of Wiltshire and Ormond 1529
1536, 29 June   Thomas Cromwell, 1st lord Cromwell 1536, 1st e. of Essex 1540; dism. 10 June 1540 (date of his arrest)
1540, 14 June   William Fitzwilliam, 1st e. of Southampton
1542, 3 Dec.   John Russell, 1st lord Russell (1st e. of Bedford 1550)

EDWARD VI

1547, 21 Aug.   Lord Russell, reappd

MARY

1553, 3 Nov.   e. of Bedford, reappd; *ob.* 14 Mar. 1555
1555   Sir Robert Rochester, controller of the household (temporary; no patent)
1555, 31 Dec.   William Paget, 1st lord Paget

ELIZABETH I

William Cecil, 1st lord Burghley 1571, styled kp. Apr. 1571, June 1572[2]
1572, 15 July   William Howard, 1st lord Howard of Effingham
1573, before May   Sir Thomas Smith, secretary of state 1572–76

---

[1] Date when his salary began.
[2] Sir Nicholas Bacon is said to have acted as kp. at the beginning of the reign (A. F. Pollard, *Political History of England*, vi (1910), 183.)

1576, May–Aug.	Francis Walsingham, principal secretary of state 1573–90
1590, before	
Apr. 1591	Lord Burghley (*see* above)
? 1598, before	
Apr. 1601	Sir Robert Cecil, 1st lord Cecil 1603, 1st e. of Salisbury 1605, principal secretary of state 1596–1612

JAMES I

	Sir Robert Cecil remained in office
1608, 25 Apr.	Henry Howard, 1st e. of Northampton; *ob.* 15 June 1614
1614, before	
30 June	Robert Carr, 1st e. of Somerset 1613
1616, 2 Jan.	Edward Somerset, 9th e. of Worcester

CHARLES I

1628, Mar.	Sir John Coke
1628, May	Sir Robert Naunton
1628, 4 July	Henry Montagu, 1st e. of Manchester; *ob.* 7 Nov. 1642
1643, Apr.	Lucius Carey, 2nd viscount Falkland; *ob.* 20 Sept. 1643
1643, Nov.	Sir Edward Nicholas, secretary of State
1644, 26 Mar.	Henry Bourchier, 6th e. of Bath; *ob.* 16 Aug. 1654

PROTECTORATE

1655, 10 May	Nathaniel Fiennes, sole commissioner
1658, 6 Nov.	Nathaniel Fiennes, keeper of the privy seal. He ceased to act in May 1659 (with the fall of Richard Cromwell's Protectorate)

CHARLES II[1]

1661, 15 May	John Robartes, 2nd lord Robartes; (1st e. of Radnor 1679)
1673, 22 Apr.[2]	Arthur Annesley, 1st e. of Anglesey
1682, 27 Oct.	George Saville, 1st marquess of Halifax 1682

JAMES II

1685, 20 Feb.	Henry Hyde, 2nd e. of Clarendon
1687, 16 Mar.	Henry Arundell, 3rd lord Arundell of Wardour. Res. on the expulsion of James II

WILLIAM AND MARY

1689, 8 Mar.	Marquess of Halifax. (*See under* 1682)
1690, 19 Feb.	[The seal in commission]
1692, 7 Mar.	Thomas Herbert, 8th e. of Pembroke and 5th e. of Montgomery
1699, 22 May	John Lowther, 1st viscount Lonsdale; *ob.* 10 July 1700
1700, 15 Nov.	Ford Grey, 1st e. of Tankerville; *ob.* 24 June 1701
1701, 28 June	[The seal in commission]

ANNE

1702, 27 Apr.	John Sheffield, 1st marquess of Normanby, 1st duke of Buckinghamshire and of Normanby 1703
1705, 21 Mar.	John Holles, 1st duke of Newcastle-upon-Tyne; *ob.* 15 July 1711
1711, 31 Aug.	John Robinson, bp of Bristol 1710–14; (bp of London 1714)
1713, 21 Aug.	William Legge, 1st e. of Dartmouth

[1] The statement, first found in Echard's *History of England* (1720 edn), that lord Saye and Sele was appointed kp. in 1660, seems to be unfounded.

[2] Date when seal handed to him. The date of letters of appointment was 29 May.

GEORGE I

1714, 27 Sept.	Thomas Wharton, 1st e. Wharton, 1st marquess of Wharton Feb. 1715; *ob.* 12 Apr. 1715
1715, 30 Apr.	[The seal in commission]
1715, 2 Sept.	Charles Spencer, 4th e. of Sunderland
1716, 19 Dec.	Evelyn Pierrepont, 1st duke of Kingston-upon-Hull
1719, 14 Feb.	Henry Grey, 1st duke of Kent
1720, 13 June	Duke of Kingston, *ob.* 5 Mar. 1726. (*See under* 1716)
1726, 10 Mar.	Thomas Trevor, 1st lord Trevor of Bromham

GEORGE II

1730, 8 May	Spencer Compton, 1st lord Wilmington, 1st e. of Wilmington 1730
1731, 1 Jan.	[The seal in commission]
1731, 12 June	William Cavendish, 3rd duke of Devonshire
1733, 8 May	Henry Lowther, 3rd viscount Lonsdale
1735, 15 May	Francis Godolphin, 2nd e. of Godolphin
1740, 29 Apr.	John Hervey, 2nd lord Hervey of Ickworth
1742, 13 July	John Leveson-Gower, 2nd lord Gower (1st e. Gower 1746)
1743, 12 Dec.	George Cholmondeley, 3rd e. of Cholmondeley
1744, 26 Dec.	Lord Gower, *ob.* 25 Dec. 1754. (*See under* 1742)
1755, 9 Jan.	Charles Spencer, 3rd duke of Marlborough
1755, 22 Dec.[1]	Granville Leveson-Gower, 2nd e. Gower (1st marquess of Stafford 1786)
1757, 5 July	Richard Grenville-Temple, 2nd e. Temple

GEORGE III[2]

1761, 16 Oct.	[The seal in commission]
1761, 25 Nov.	John Russell, 7th duke of Bedford
1763, 22 Apr.	George Spencer, 4th duke of Marlborough
1765, 15 July	Thomas Pelham-Holles, 1st duke of Newcastle-upon-Tyne 1715
1766, 30 July	William Pitt, 1st e. of Chatham 1766. In Feb. 1768 the office was put in commission for a short time. Chatham took the oath again on 21 Mar. 1768
1768, 2 Nov.	George William Hervey, 5th e. of Bristol
1770, 26 Feb.	George Montague-Dunk, 5th e. of Halifax
1771, 22 Jan.	Henry Howard, 12th e. of Suffolk and 5th e. of Berkshire
1771, 12 June	Augustus Henry FitzRoy, 3rd duke of Grafton
1775, 10 Nov.	William Legge, 2nd e. of Dartmouth
1782, 27 Mar.	Duke of Grafton. (*See under* 1771)
1783, 2 Apr.	Frederick Howard, 8th e. of Carlisle
1783, 23 Dec.	Charles Manners, 4th duke of Rutland
1784, 8 Mar.	[The seal in commission]
1784, 22 Nov.	E. Gower. (*See under* 1755)
1794, 16 July	George John, 2nd e. Spencer
1794, 17 Dec.	John Pitt, 2nd e. of Chatham
1798, 14 Feb.	John Fane, 10th e. of Westmorland
1806, 5 Feb.	Henry Addington, 1st viscount Sidmouth
1806, 15 Oct.	Henry Richard Vassall Fox, 3rd lord Holland
1807, 25 Mar.	E. of Westmorland. (*See under* 1798)

GEORGE IV

	E. of Westmorland remained in office
1827, 30 Apr.	William George Spencer Cavendish-Scott-Bentinck, 6th duke of Devonshire
1827, 16 July	George Howard, 9th e. of Carlisle

[1] Date when oath of office taken. The date of letters of appointment was 13 Jan. 1756.

[2] From this reign the dates given are those on which the kp. of the privy seal took the oath.

1828, 26 Jan.	Edward Law, 2nd lord Ellenborough (1st e. of Ellenborough 1844)
1829, 10 June	James St Clair-Erskine, 2nd e. of Rosslyn

WILLIAM IV

1830, 22 Nov.	John George Lambton, 1st lord Durham, 1st e. of Durham 1833
1833, 3 Apr.	Frederick John Robinson, 1st viscount Goderich, 1st e. of Ripon
1834, 5 June	E. of Carlisle. (*See under* 1827)
1834, 30 July	Constantine Henry Phipps, 6th e. of Mulgrave (1st marquess of Normanby 1838)
1834, 15 Dec.	James Archibald Stuart-Wortley-Mackenzie, 1st lord Wharnecliffe
1835, 23 Apr.	John William Ponsonby, 1st lord Duncannon (4th e. of Bessborough [Irish] 1844)

VICTORIA

	Lord Duncannon remained in office
1840, 15 Jan.	George William Frederick Villiers, 4th e. of Clarendon
1841, 3 Sept.	Richard Plantagenet Temple-Nugent-Brydges-Chandos-Grenville, 2nd duke of Buckingham
1842, 2 Feb.	Walter Francis Montagu-Douglas-Scott, 5th duke of Buccleuch [Scot.], and e. of Doncaster [U.K.]
1846, 21 Jan.	Thomas Hamilton, 1st lord Melros [U.K.], 9th e. of Haddington [Scot.]
1846, 6 July	Gilbert Elliot-Murray-Kynynmound, 2nd e. of Minto
1852, 2 Feb.	James Brownlow William Gascoyne-Cecil, 2nd marquess of Salisbury
1853, 4 Jan.	George Douglas Campbell, 8th duke of Argyll [Scot.], 4th lord Sundridge [U.K.], (1st duke of Argyll [U.K.] 1892)
1855, 7 Dec.	Dudley Ryder, 2nd e. of Harrowby
1858, 3 Feb.	Ulick John de Burgh, 1st marquess of Clanricarde [Irish], 1st lord Somerhill [U.K.]
1858, 26 Feb.	Charles Philip Yorke, 4th e. of Hardwicke
1859, 18 June	Duke of Argyll. (*See under* 1853)
1866, 6 July	James Howard Harris, 3rd e. of Malmesbury
1868, 9 Dec.	John Wodehouse, 1st e. of Kimberley
1870, 6 July	Charles Wood, 1st viscount Halifax
1874, 21 Feb.	e. of Malmesbury. (*See under* 1866)
1876, 12 Aug.	Benjamin Disraeli, 1st e. of Beaconsfield 1876
1878, 4 Feb.	Algernon George Percy, 8th duke of Northumberland
1880, 28 Apr.	Duke of Argyll. (*See under* 1853)
1881, 2 May	Chichester Samuel Parkinson-Fortescue, 1st lord Carlingford
1885, 5 Mar.	Archibald Philip Primrose, 5th e. of Rosebery [Scot.] and 2nd lord Rosebery (1st e. of Midlothian [U.K.] 1911)
1885, 24 June	Dudley Francis Stuart Ryder, 3rd e. of Harrowby
1886, 17 Feb.	William Ewart Gladstone
1886, 3 Aug.	George Henry Cadogan, 6th e. of Cadogan
1892, 20 Aug.	William Ewart Gladstone. (*See under* 1886)
1894, 10 Mar.	Edward Marjoribanks, 2nd lord Tweedmouth 1894
1895, 29 June	Richard Assheton Cross, 1st viscount Cross
1900, 12 Nov.	Robert Arthur Talbot Gascoyne-Cecil, 3rd marquess of Salisbury

EDWARD VII

	Marquess of Salisbury remained in office
1902, 14 July	Arthur James Balfour (1st e. of Balfour 1922)
1903, 19 Oct.	James Edward Hubert Gascoyne-Cecil, 4th marquess of Salisbury 1903
1905, 11 Dec.	George Frederick Samuel Robinson, 1st marquess of Ripon
1908, 19 Oct.	Robert Offley Ashburton Crewe-Milnes, 1st e. of Crewe (1st marquess 1911)

GEORGE V

Marquess of Crewe remained in office

1911, 24 Oct.	Charles Robert Wynn Carrington, 1st e. Carrington, 1st marquess of Lincolnshire 1912
1912, 29 Feb.	Marquess of Crewe. (*See under* 1908)
1915, 27 May	George Nathaniel Curzon, 1st e. Curzon (1st marquess Curzon 1921)
1916, 22 Dec.	David Alexander Edward Lindsay, 27th e. of Crawford, 10th e. of Balcarres [Scot.] and 4th lord Wigan [U.K.]
1919, 10 Feb.	Andrew Bonar Law
1921, 24 Mar.	Joseph Austen Chamberlain (K.G. 1925)
1923, 28 May	Lord Edgar Algernon Robert Gascoyne-Cecil, 1st viscount Cecil of Chelwood 1923
1924, 23 Jan.	John Robert Clynes
1924, 7 Nov.	Marquess of Salisbury. (*See under* 1903)
1929, 8 June	James Henry Thomas
1930, 12 June	Vernon Hartshorn
1931, 27 Mar.	Thomas Johnston
1931, 8 Sept.	William Robert Wellesley Peel, 1st e. Peel
1931, 9 Nov.	Philip Snowden, 1st viscount Snowden 1931
1932, 1 Oct.	Stanley Baldwin (1st e. Baldwin 1937)
1934, 6 Jan.	Robert Anthony Eden (K.G. 1954)
1935, 7 June	Charles Stewart Henry Vane-Tempest-Stewart, 7th marquess of Londonderry [Irish], 5th e. Vane [U.K.]
1935, 27 Nov.	Edward Frederick Lindley Wood, 3rd viscount Halifax (1st e. of Halifax 1944)

EDWARD VIII

Viscount Halifax remained in office

GEORGE VI

Viscount Halifax remained in office

1937, 28 May	Herbrand Edward Dundonald Brassey Sackville, 9th e. de la Warr. *Vac.* 27 Oct. 1938
1938, 31 Oct.	Sir John Anderson (1st viscount Waverley 1952)
1939, 3 Sept.	Sir Samuel John Gurney Hoare (1st viscount Templewood 1944)
1940, 5 Apr.	Sir Howard Kingsley Wood
1940, 12 May	Clement Richard Attlee (1st e. Attlee 1955)
1942, 23 Feb.	Sir Richard Stafford Cripps, *vac.* 18 Nov. 1942
1942, 24 Nov.	Robert Arthur James Gascoyne-Cecil, commonly called viscount Cranborne, summoned to parliament *v.p.* as lord Cecil of Essendon 1941 (5th marquess of Salisbury 1947)
1943, 28 Sept.	William Maxwell Aitken, 1st lord Beaverbrook
1945, 28 July	Arthur Greenwood
1947, 23 Apr.	Philip Albert Inman, 1st lord Inman
1947, 28 Oct.	Christopher Addison (1st viscount Addison)
1951, 12 Mar.	Ernest Bevin
1951, 28 Apr.	Richard Stokes
1951, 27 Oct.	Marquess of Salisbury. (*See under* 1942)

ELIZABETH II

Marquess of Salisbury remained in office

1952, 9 May	Henry Frederick Comfort Crookshank, 1st lord Crookshank 1955
1955, 22 Dec.	Richard Austen Butler
1959, 14 Sept.	Quintin McGarel Hogg, 2nd viscount Hailsham
1960, 27 July	Edward Richard George Heath
1963, 20 Oct.	John Selwyn Brooke Lloyd
1964, 18 Oct.	Francis Aungier Pakenham, 7th e. of Longford
1965, 23 Dec.	Sir Frank Soskice

1966, 6 Apr.	e. of Longford (*See under* 1964)
1968, 16 Jan.	Edward Arthur Alexander Shackleton, The Lord Shackleton
1968, 6 Apr.	Thomas Frederick Peart
1968, 18 Oct.	The Lord Shackleton (*See under* 1968, Jan.)
1970, 20 June	George Patrick John Rushworth Jellicoe, 2nd e. Jellicoe
1973, 5 June	David James George Hennessy, 3rd Lord Windlesham
1974, 7 Apr.	Malcolm Newton Shepherd, 2nd Lord Shepherd
1976, 10 Sept.	Thomas Frederick Peart, Lord Peart
1979, 5 May	Sir Ian Hedworth John Little Gilmour
1981, 14 Sept.	Humphrey Edward Atkins
1982, 5 Apr.	Janet Mary Young, baroness Young
1983, 11 June	William John Biffen

TREASURERS (*to* 1714),
FIRST LORDS OF THE TREASURY (*to* 1742)
AND CHANCELLORS OF THE EXCHEQUER (*from* 1558)

Despite the difficulties presented by the evidence about the origins of the treasurership, it is reasonably certain that the office came into being *c.* 1126, and that earlier references to individuals as treasurers do not denote tenure of this office. During two subsequent periods in the early twelfth century the office seems to have fallen into abeyance: only after the early years of Henry II's reign is it possible to trace its uninterrupted descent. The origins and early history of the office have been reassessed by C. Warren Hollister, 'The Origins of the English Treasury', *EHR*, xciii (1978), 262–75.

The present list from 1217 to 1399 is mainly based on T. F. Tout, *Chapters in the Administrative History of Mediaeval England*, vi (1933), 17–24, supplemented by exchequer records mentioned in notes. Evidence for the fifteenth century is set out in R. L. Storey, 'English Officers of State, 1399–1485', *BIHR*, xxxi (1958), 86.

Information about the treasurers must be sought in works dealing with the development of the exchequer, among which the earliest is T. Madox, *History of the Exchequer* (London, 1712), 'an admirably solid foundation on which many subsequent scholars have built, and [which] still fully retains its value'. On the origins of the exchequer, *see* Tout, *Chapters . . .*, especially i, 74–88, and J. H. Round, *The Commune of London* (Westminster, 1899), chap. iv, 'The Origin of the Exchequer'. The *Dialogus de Scaccario* written by Richard Fitz Neal (best edition by A. Hughes, C. G. Crump and C. Johnson, Oxford, 1902; text reprinted with translation by C. Johnson, London and Edinburgh, 1950; and revised Oxford, 1983) describes the working of the exchequer in the twelfth century. For that period, *see also* R. L. Poole, *The Exchequer in the Twelfth Century* (Oxford, 1912) and works of H. G. Richardson ['Richard Fitz Neal and the Dialogus de Scaccario', *EHR*, xliii (1928); 'William of Ely, the King's treasurer', *TRHS*, 4th ser., xv (1933); Introduction to *The Memoranda Roll for the Michaelmas term . . .* 1 *John, 1199–1200* (Pipe Roll Soc., N.S., xxi, 1943)].

The most useful works on the exchequer in the thirteenth and fourteenth centuries include Tout, *Chapters* [*cit. supra*]; D. Crook, 'The early remembrancers of the exchequer', *BIHR*, liii (1980); R. E. Latham (ed.), *Calendar of Memoranda Rolls, 1326–7* (HMSO, 1968); M. H. Mills,

The Pipe Roll for 1295. Surrey Membrane, Introduction, Surrey Record Society, vii, no. 21 (1924); C. A. F. Meekings, 'The pipe roll order of 12 February 1270', *Studies presented to Sir Hilary Jenkinson* (Oxford, 1957); T. F. Tout, *The Place of the Reign of Edward II in English History* (2nd edn, Manchester, 1936); J. F. Willard, *Parliamentary Taxes on Personal Property, 1290–1334* (Cambridge, Mass., 1934); W. A. Morris and J. R. Strayer, *The English Government at Work, 1327–1336*, ii, *Fiscal Administration* (Cambridge, Mass., 1947). *The Lay Subsidy of 1334*, ed. R. E. Glasscock (Records of Social and Economic History of the British Academy, new ser., II, 1975); E. B. Fryde, *Studies in Medieval Trade and Finance* (1983). There is a useful list of the published tax-assessments of the thirteenth and fourteenth centuries in E. B. Graves, *A Bibliography of English History to 1485* (Oxford, 1975), 483–91.

Older modern works relating to the exchequer include H. Hall, *Antiquities and Curiosities of the Exchequer* (1891; reprinted 1898); F. Palgrave, *The Antient Kalendars and Inventories of the Treasury of His Majesty's Exchequer, together with other Documents illustrating the History of that Repository*, 3 vols (Rec. Comm., 1836).

For the sixteenth century, *see* W. C. Richardson, *Tudor Chamber Administration, 1485–1547*, and *History of the Court of Augmentations, 1536–1554* (Baton Rouge, Louisiana, 1952 and 1962), and the works of F. C. Dietz, now in need of revision: *English Government Finance, 1485–1558* (Urbana, Illinois, 1920); *The Exchequer in Elizabeth's Reign* (Smith College Studies in History, viii, no. 2, Northampton, Mass., 1923), and *English Public Finance, 1558–1641* (1932), which contains a list of treasurers from 1550 to 1641. S. E. Lehmberg, *Sir Walter Mildmay and Tudor Government* (Austin, Texas, 1964), traces the emergence of the chancellor of the exchequer as an important official in Elizabeth's reign.

Two descriptions of the work of the exchequer by contemporaries are important: *The Practice of the Exchequer Court with its Severall Offices and Officers* (1658), attrib. T. Fanshawe but authorship uncertain, and written about 1600; and 'A Book of all the Several Officers of the Court of Exchequer . . . [1642]', by Lawrence Squibb, ed. W. H. Bryson, *Camden Miscellany*, vol. xxvi (Camden 4th ser., vol. 14, 1975), 77–136.

The titles 'lord treasurer' and 'lord high treasurer' came into common use in the sixteenth century (*cf.* 27 Henry VIII, c. 3). They were used continuously from 1612, when the office was first put in commission. Important changes in the nature of the office began with the Restoration, and the commissioners appointed in 1667 controlled a treasury system which was distinct both from the privy council on the one hand and from the exchequer on the other. *See* the major study by C. D. Chandaman, *The English Public Revenue, 1660–1688* (1975); also S. B. Baxter, *The Development of the Treasury, 1660–1702* (1957), which contains lists of officials; and for treasury practice the treatises by W. A. Shaw, prefixed to successive volumes of the *Calendar of Treasury Books and Papers, 1729–45*, and *Calendar of Treasury Books, 1660–1718* (HMSO, 1897–1962, in progress). For the origins and evolution of the modern treasury the most recent authority is H. G. Roseveare, *The Treasury: the Evolution of a British Institution* (1969), and the same author's *The Treasury, 1660–1870. The Foundations of Control* (1973). *See also* J. C. Sainty, *Treasury Officials, 1660–1870* (1972), and *Officers of the Exchequer* (List and Index Soc., special ser., vol. 18, 1983). In the seventeenth century, when the office of lord high treasurer was in commission, the first commissioner was not necessarily the most important member of the board in actual practice. From November 1690 until the formation of the Goderich ministry in September 1827 the first commissioner, if a member of the Commons, was also always chancellor of the exchequer and, in effect, finance minister; if the First Lord was a member of the Upper House, the office of chancellor of the exchequer was always held by a member of the Commons. The relations between the chancellor and the first commissioner during these periods are as yet obscure, but it would seem that the chancellorship did not begin to attain its present importance until after the death of Canning. Two patents of appointment were normally issued to the chancellors of the exchequer, one for that office and one as under-treasurer.[1]

HENRY I

c. 1126   Nigel, nephew of Roger bp of Salisbury; res. when made bp of Ely 1133

STEPHEN

c. 1136   Adelelm, nephew of Roger bp of Salisbury; dism. 1139

HENRY II

c. 1158 or 1159   Richard Fitz Neal, dean of Lincoln, bp of London 1189–98

RICHARD I

     Richard Fitz Neal remained in office until 1196
1196   William of Ely, archdeacon of Cleveland, canon of St Paul's

JOHN

     William of Ely remained in office in the service of K. John until Aug. 1215

HENRY III

1217, *4 Nov.*	Eustace of Fauconberg, canon of St Paul's, bp of London 1221–28; *ob.* late Oct. 1228
1228, 13 Nov.[1]	Walter Mauclerc, bp of Carlisle 1223–46
1233, 14 Jan.[2]	Peter des Rivaux (kp. of the wardrobe and the chamber 1232–34), canon of St Paul's
1234, 1 June	Hugh Pateshull, canon of St Paul's, bp of Coventry and Lichfield 1239–41
1240, Mar.	William Haverhill (controller of the wardrobe 1234–36), canon of Lichfield; *ob.* 23 Aug. 1252
1252, 27 Aug.	Philip Lovel, archdeacon of Coventry. Removed from office by the baronial reformers; Oct. 1258
1258, 2 Nov.	John Crakehall (steward of Robert Grosseteste, bp of Lincoln, *c.* 1235–50), archdeacon of Bedford; *ob.* 8–10 Sept. 1260

[1] Lord Mansfield in 1757 and 1767 received a patent only as chancellor of the exchequer.

[2] K.R. Mem. Roll, 17 Hen. III, E. 159/12, m. 10.

1260, 28 Oct.	John of Caux, abbot of Peterborough; *ob.* Mar. 1263
1263, *6 May*	Nicholas of Ely. (*See* chancellors, 1260.) *Vac.* 19 July 1263
1263, July[1]	Henry, prior of St Radegund, Bradsole, Kent (steward of Boniface, archbp of Canterbury)
1263, Nov.[1]	[John Chishull, chancellor of the exchequer, acting treasurer. (*See* chancellors, 1263)]
1263, 30 Nov.	[Roger de la Leye, chancellor of the exchequer (dean of St Paul's 1283–85), acting treasurer]
1264, 3 Nov.	Henry, prior of St Radegund. (*See under* 1263). In office until summer 1265[2]
1265, *23 Oct.*[3]	Thomas Wymondham (chancellor of the exchequer 1261), precentor of Lichfield
1270, 6 Feb.	John Chishull. (*See* chancellors, 1263.) *Vac.* 9 June 1271
1271, 16 Oct.[4]	Philip of Eye (treasurer of Henry III's brother, Richard, e. of Cornwall), canon of St Paul's

EDWARD I

	Philip of Eye remained in office until 2 Oct. 1273
1273, 2 Oct.	Joseph Chauncy, kt, prior of the Hospital of St John of Jerusalem in England
1280, 18 June[5]	Richard Ware, abbot of Westminster; *ob.* 1283
1284, 6 Jan.	John Kirkby (kp. of the rolls of chancery *1263*–84) archdeacon of Coventry, bp of Ely 1286–90; *ob.* 26 Mar. 1290
1290, 6 Apr.	William March (controller of the wardrobe 1283–90), dean of St Martin's-le-Grand, bp of Bath and Wells 1293–1302; dism. 16 Aug. 1295[6]
1295, 16 Aug.[6]	[John Droxford, controller of the wardrobe; (bp of Bath and Wells 1309–29), acting treasurer]
1295, 28 Sept.	Walter Langton (kp. w. 1290), canon of Lichfield, bp of Coventry and Lichfield 1296–1321

EDWARD II[7]

	Walter Langton remained formally in office until 22 Aug. 1307, but probably ceased to act on 19 July 1307[8]
1307, 22 Aug.	Walter Reynolds (kp. w. of Prince Edward 1301–07), bp of Worcester 1307–13. (*See* chancellors, 1310)
1310, 6 July	John Sandall, provost of Wells. (*See* chancellors, 1314)
1311, 23 Oct.	[Walter Norwich, baron of the exchequer, acting treasurer]
1312, 23 Jan.	Walter Langton. (*See under* 1295)
1312, 17 May	[Walter Norwich, chief baron of the exchequer, acting treasurer. (*See under* 1311)]
1312, 4 Oct.	[John Sandall, acting treasurer. (*See under* 1310)]
1314, 26 Sept.	Walter Norwich. (*See under* 1312)
1317, 27 May	John Hotham, bp of Ely 1316–37. (*See* chancellors, 1314)
1318, 10 June	John Walwayn, canon of St Paul's and Hereford
1318, 16 Nov.	John Sandall, bp of Winchester 1316–19. (*See under* 1310.) *Ob.* 2 Nov. 1319

[1] R. F. Treharne, *The Baronial Plan of Reform, 1258–63*, (Manchester, 1932), 330 and notes.

[2] Liberate Roll, 49 Hen. III, C. 62/41, m. 2 (16 June); L.T.R. Mem. Roll, 49 Hen. III, E. 368/39, m. 11d. (*Communia*, Trinity).

[3] L.T.R. Mem. Roll, 50 Hen. III, E. 368/40, m. 1d. (*Communia*, Michaelmas).

[4] *Annales Monastici*, iv (ed. H. R. Luard, R.S., 1889), 247 (*Chronicon Thome Wykes*).

[5] Receipt Roll, Easter 8 Edw. I, E. 401/95.

[6] Receipt Roll, Easter 23 Edw. I (pt. II), E. 401/137.

[7] For a full list of acting treasurers and lieutenants of the treasurer see T. F. Tout, *The Place of the Reign of Edward II in English History* (2nd edn, Manchester, 1936), 297–8. When they acted during a vacancy their names are given in the present list.

[8] Receipt Roll, Easter 35 Edw. I, E. 401/167.

1319, 29 Sept.	[Walter Norwich, acting treasurer. (*See under* 1312)]
1320, 18 Feb.	Walter Stapeldon, bp of Exeter 1308–26
1321, 25 Aug.	[Walter Norwich, acting treasurer. (*See under* 1312)]
1322, 10 May	Walter Stapeldon. (*See under* 1320)]
1325, 3 July	William Melton (kp. w. 1314); abp of York 1316–40. *Vac.* 14 Nov. 1326
1326, 14 Nov.	John Stratford, bp of Winchester 1323–33. (*See* chancellors, 1330)

EDWARD III[1]

John Stratford remained in office until 28 Jan. 1327

1327, 28 Jan.	Adam Orleton, bp of Hereford 1317–27; (bp of Worcester 1327–33, bp of Winchester 1333–45)
1327, 28 Mar.	Henry Burghersh, bp of Lincoln 1320–40. (*See* chancellors, 1328.) *Vac.* 2 July 1328[2]
1328, 2 July	Thomas Charlton [pr. s. 1316], bp of Hereford 1327–44
1329, 16 Sept.	Robert Wodehouse [kp. w. 1323], archdeacon of Richmond
1330, 1 Dec.	William Melton. (*See under* 1325)
1331, 1 Apr.	William Airmyn, bp of Norwich 1325–36. (*See* chancellors, 1326)
1332, 29 Mar.	Robert Ayleston [pr. s. 1323], archdeacon of Berkshire. *Vac. c.* 9 Mar. 1334[3]
1334, *c.* 9 Mar.	Richard Bury [pr. s. 1329], bp of Durham 1333–45. (*See* chancellors, 1334)
1334, 1 Aug.	Henry Burghersh. (*See under* 1327)
1337, 24 Mar.	William de la Zouche [pr. s. 1335], dean of York; (abp of York 1340–52)
1338, 10 Mar.	Robert Wodehouse. (*See under* 1329)
1338, 31 Dec.[4]	William de la Zouche. (*See under* 1337)
1340, 5 May	Robert Sadington, kt, formerly chief baron of the exchequer
1340, 26 June	Roger Northburgh, bp of Coventry and Lichfield 1322–59. Dism. 1 Dec. 1340
1341, 15 Jan.[5]	Robert Parving, kt, formerly chief justice of the k.'s bench. (*See* chancellors, 1341)
1341, 30 Oct.	William Cusance [kp. w. 1340] (dean of St Martin's-le-Grand 1349–60)
1344, 12 Apr.	William Edington [kp. w. 1341], bp of Winchester 1345–66. (*See* chancellors, 1356)
1356, 29 Nov.	John Sheppey, bp of Rochester 1352–60; *ob.* 19 Oct. 1360
1360, 23 Nov.	Simon Langham, abbot of Westminster, bp of Ely 1362–66. (*See* chancellors, 1363)
1363, 20 Feb.	John Barnet, bp of Worcester 1362–63, bp of Bath and Wells 1363–66, bp of Ely 1366–73. *Vac.* 27 June 1369
1369, 27 June	Thomas Brantingham [kp. w. 1368], bp of Exeter 1370–94
1371, 27 Mar.	Richard Scrope, lord Scrope of Bolton. (*See* chancellors, 1378)
1375, 26 Sept.	Robert Ashton, kt
1377, 14 Jan.	Henry Wakefield [kp. w. 1369], bp of Worcester 1375–95

RICHARD II

Henry Wakefield remained in office until 19 July 1377

1377, 19 July	Thomas Brantingham. (*See under* 1369)
1381, 1 Feb.	Robert Hales, kt prior of the Hospital of St John of Jerusalem in England; *ob.* 14 June 1381

[1] For the reign of Edward III the dates of the actual assumption of office by treasurers are given (not dates of appointment), as listed in Tout, *Chapters* . . . vi, 21–3.
[2] Exch. K.R. Acc. Various, E. 101/332/28.
[3] BL, Add. MS 35181.
[4] *EHR*, lvii (1952), 76–7.
[5] Exch. K.R. Acc. Various, E. 101/333/17.

1381, 10 Aug.	Hugh Segrave, kt, formerly steward of the household. (*See* chancellors, 1381)
1386, 17 Jan.	John Fordham [pr. s. 1377], bp of Durham 1381–88 (bp of Ely 1388–1425)
1386, 24 Oct.	John Gilbert (bp of Bangor 1372–75), bp of Hereford 1375–89; (bp of St David's 1389–97)
1389, 4 May	Thomas Brantingham. (*See under* 1369 and 1377)
1389, 20 Aug.	John Gilbert. (*See under* 1386)
1391, 2 May	John Waltham [pr. s. 1386], bp of Salisbury 1388–95; *ob.* 18 Sept. 1395
1395, 20 Sept.	Roger Walden (k.'s secretary 1393–95); abp of Canterbury 1397–99; (bp of London 1404–06)
1398, 22 Jan.	Guy Mone [pr. s. 1396], bp of St David's 1397–1407
1398, 17 Sept.	William Scrope, 1st e. of Wiltshire; *ob.* 30 July 1399
1399, 3 Sept.	John Norbury, esquire of Henry, duke of Lancaster

HENRY IV

1399, 30 Sept.	John Norbury reappd
1401, 31 May	Laurence Allerthorp (baron of the exchequer 1375–1401), canon of London
1402, 27 Feb.	Henry Bowet, bp of Bath and Wells 1401–07, abp of York 1407–23
1402, 25 Oct.	Guy Mone, bp of St David's. (*See under* 1398)
1403, 9 Sept.	William Roos, lord Roos of Helmsley
1404, 5–9 Dec.	Thomas Nevill, lord Furnival. *Ob.* 14 Mar. 1407
1407, 15 Apr.	Nicholas Bubwith, bp of London. (*See* kps of the privy seal, 1405)
1408, 14 July	John Tiptoft, kt (kp. w. 1406) (1st lord Tiptoft 1426)
1410, 6 Jan.	Henry Scrope, lord Scrope of Masham. Dism. 20 Dec. 1411
1411, 23 Dec.	John Pelham, kt

HENRY V

1413, 21 Mar.	Thomas FitzAlan, e. of Arundel. *Ob.* 13 Oct. 1415
1416, 10 Jan.	Hugh Mortimer, kt (chamberlain of Henry V as prince of Wales). *Ob.* between 13 Apr. and 23 May 1416
1416, 17 Apr.	Roger Leche, kt (kp. w. 1413). Dism. 23 Nov. 1416
1416, 6 Dec.	Henry FitzHugh, lord FitzHugh, k.'s chamberlain 1413–22
1421, 26 Feb.	William Kinwolmarsh (under-treasurer 1417–21), dean of St Martin's le-Grand

HENRY VI

1422, 30 Sept.	William Kinwolmarsh reappd. *Ob.* 18 Dec. 1422
1422, 18 Dec.	John Stafford (pr. s. 1421), dean of Wells, bp of Bath and Wells 1424–43. (*See* chancellors, 1432)
1426, 16 Mar.	Walter Hungerford, 1st lord Hungerford 1426
1432, 26 Feb.	Henry Scrope, lord Scrope of Masham
1433, 11 Aug.	Ralph Cromwell, lord Cromwell, k.'s chamberlain *1432*
1443, 7 July	Ralph Butler, 1st lord Sudley, k.'s chamberlain 1441–46
1446, 18 Dec.	Marmaduke Lumley, bp of Carlisle 1429–50 (bp of Lincoln 1450)
1449, 16 Sept.	James Fiennes, 1st lord Saye and Sele, k.'s chamberlain 1447–50. *Ob.* 4 July 1450
1450, 22 June	John Beauchamp, 1st lord Beauchamp of Powick
1452, 15 Apr.	John Tiptoft, 1st e. of Worcester
1455, 15 Mar.	James Butler, 5th e. of Ormond and 1st earl of Wiltshire
1455, 29 May	Henry Bourchier, 1st viscount Bourchier (1st e. of Essex 1461)

1456, 5 Oct.	John Talbot, e. of Shrewsbury
1458, 30 Oct.	James Butler. (*See under* 1455)
1460, 28 July	Henry Bourchier. (*See under* 1455)

EDWARD IV

1461, 18 Mar.	Henry Bourchier reappointed
1462, 14 Apr.	John Tiptoft. (*See under* 1452)
1463, 24 June	Edmund Grey, lord Grey of Ruthin (1st e. of Kent 1465)
1464, 24 Nov.	Walter Blount (treasurer of Calais 1461–64), 1st lord Mountjoy 1465
1466, 4 Mar.	Richard Woodville, 1st lord Rivers, 1st e. Rivers 1466. *Ob.* 12 Aug. 1469
1469, 16 Aug.	John Langstrother, kt, prior of the Hospital of St John of Jerusalem in England
1469, 25 Oct.	William Grey, bp of Ely 1454–78
1470, 10 July	John Tiptoft. (*See under* 1452.) *Ob.* 18 Oct. 1470

HENRY VI (readeption)

| 1470, 20 Oct. | John Langstrother. (*See under* 1469.) *Ob.* 6 May 1471 |

EDWARD IV (restoration)

| 1471, 22 Apr. | Henry Bourchier. (*See under* 1455.) *Ob.* 4 Apr. 1483 |

EDWARD V

| 1483, 17 May | John Wood, kt (under-treasurer 1480–83) |

RICHARD III

| 1483, 2 July | John Wood reappd. *Ob.* 25 Oct. 1484 |
| 1484, 6 Dec. | John Tuchet, lord Audley |

HENRY VII

| 1486, 14 July | John Dynham, lord Dynham |
| 1501, 16 June | Thomas Howard, e. of Surrey, 1st duke of Norfolk 1514 |

HENRY VIII

| 1509 | e. of Surrey remained in office |
| 1522, 4 Dec. | Thomas Howard e. of Surrey, 1514, 2nd duke of Norfolk 1524. *Vac.* 12 Dec. 1546 (date of arrest) |

EDWARD VI

| 1547, 10 Feb. | Edward Seymour, 1st duke of Somerset 1547, the protector. Deprived 10 Oct. 1549 (date of arrest) |
| 1550, 3 Feb. | William Paulet, 1st e. of Wiltshire 1550, 1st marquess of Winchester 1551 |

MARY

Marquess of Winchester remained in office

ELIZABETH I

Marquess of Winchester remained in office; *ob.* 10 Mar. 1572
| 1572, July | William Cecil, 1st lord Burghley; *ob.* 4 Aug. 1598 |
| 1599, 15 May | Sir Thomas Sackville, 1st lord Buckhurst, 1st e. of Dorset 1604 |

JAMES I

1603, 17 Apr.	Lord Buckhurst reappd for life; *ob.* 19 Apr. 1608
1608, 4 May	Robert Cecil, 1st e. of Salisbury; *ob.* 24 May 1612
1612, 17 June	The office was put in commission for the first time: Henry Howard, e. of Northampton (first lord)
1613, 24 June	Sir Thomas Egerton, 1st lord Ellesmere (first lord)
1614, 11 July	Thomas Howard, 1st e. of Suffolk. Suspended 1618
1618, July	George Abbot, abp of Canterbury 1611–33 (first lord)
1620, 14 Dec.	Sir Henry Montagu, 1st viscount Mandeville 1620 (1st e. of Manchester 1626)
1621, 29 Sept.	Lionel Cranfield, 1st lord Cranfield 1621, 1st e. of Middlesex 1622. Suspended 25 Apr. 1624
1624, 11 Dec.	Sir James Ley, 1st lord Ley 1624, 1st e. of Marlborough 1626

CHARLES I

	Lord Ley remained in office
1628, 15 July	Richard Weston, 1st lord Weston 1628, 1st e. of Portland 1633
1635, 15 Mar.	William Laud, abp of Canterbury 1633–45 (first lord)
1636, 6 Mar.	William Juxon, bp of London 1633–60 (first lord)
1641, 21 May	Sir Edward Littleton, 1st lord Lyttelton (first lord)
1643, 3 Oct.	Francis Cottington, 1st lord Cottington; *ob.* 19 June 1652, at Valladolid

PROTECTORATE

Treasury commissioners, 1654–59: 2 Aug. 1654, lords commissioners (of Great Seal) Whitelocke, Widdrington and Lisle, Henry Rolle (*ob.* 30 July 1656), Oliver St John (did not act in this capacity), Col. Edward Montague (later 1st e. of Sandwich), Col. William Sydenham, William Masham (*ob.* Jan.–Feb. 1655); the survivors (Whitelocke, Widdrington, Lisle, Montague and Sydenham) ceased to act with the fall of the Protectorate, Apr.–May 1659

CHARLES II

1660, 8 Sept.	Thomas Wriothesley, 2nd e. of Southampton; *ob.* 16 May 1667
1667, 1 June	George Monck, 1st duke of Albemarle (first lord); *ob.* 3 Jan. 1670
	[No new commission issued. Anthony Ashley Cooper, 1st lord Ashley, 1st e. of Shaftesbury 1672; was first lord by virtue of seniority]
1672, 28 Nov.	Thomas Clifford, 1st lord Clifford of Chudleigh 1672
1673, 19 June	Sir Thomas Osborne, 1st viscount Oseburne [Scot.] 1673, 1st viscount Latimer 1673, 1st e. of Danby 1674 (1st duke of Leeds 1694)
1679, 6 Mar.	Arthur Capell, e. of Essex (first lord)
1679, 19 Nov.	Laurence Hyde, 1st viscount Hyde of Kenilworth 1681, 1st e. of Rochester 1682 (first lord)
1684, 25 Aug.	Sidney Godolphin, 1st lord Godolphin 1684 (1st e. of Godolphin 1706) (first lord)

JAMES II

1685, 16 Feb.	E. of Rochester. (*See under* 1679.) *Vac.* 10 Dec. 1686
1687, 5 Jan.	John Belasyse, 1st lord Belasyse (first lord)

WILLIAM AND MARY

1689, 8 Apr.	Charles Mordaunt, 2nd viscount Mordaunt, 1st e. of Monmouth 1689 (3rd e. of Peterborough 1697) (first lord)
1690, 19 Mar.	Sir John Lowther (1st viscount Lonsdale 1696) (first lord)
1690, 15 Nov.	Lord Godolphin. (*See under* 1684) (first lord)
1697, 1 May	Charles Montagu (1st lord Halifax 1700, 1st e. of Halifax 1714) (first lord)
1699, 15 Nov.	Lord Grey, 1st e. of Tankerville (first lord)
1700, 12 Dec.	Lord Godolphin. (*See under* 1684) (first lord)
1701, 27 Dec.	Charles Howard, 3rd e. of Carlisle (first lord)

ANNE

1702, 8 May	Lord Godolphin. (*See under* 1684)
1710, 11 Aug.	John Poulett, 1st e. Poulett (first lord)
1711, 29 Mar.	Robert Harley, 1st e. of Oxford and Mortimer 1711
1714, 30 July	Charles Talbot, 1st duke of Shrewsbury; *vac.* Oct. 1714. Since the resignation of the duke of Shrewsbury the office of treasurer has always been in commission. The first lords of treasury until 1742 are listed below

GEORGE I

1714, 11 Oct.	Charles Montagu, lord Halifax. (*See under* 1697); *ob.* 19 May 1715
1715, 23 May	Charles Howard, e. of Carlisle. (*See under* 1701)
1715, 10 Oct.	Robert Walpole (1st e. of Orford 1742)
1717, 12 Apr.	James Stanhope, 1st viscount Stanhope 1717, 1st e. Stanhope 1718
1718, 21 Mar.	Charles Spencer, e. of Sunderland
1721, 4 Apr.	Robert Walpole. (*See under* 1715.) *Vac.* 11 Feb. 1742. From 1730 the list of prime ministers is also the list of first lords of the treasury, except that during the 1st and part of the 2nd and 3rd Salisbury ministries the prime minister was foreign secretary; during the last part of his 3rd ministry Salisbury was lord privy seal. Ramsay MacDonald was both first lord and foreign secretary during his 1st ministry.

CHANCELLORS AND UNDER-TREASURERS OF THE EXCHEQUER[1]

1559, 5 Feb.	Sir Walter Mildmay; *ob.* 31 May 1589
1589, June	John Fortescue
1603, May	Sir George Home, 1st e. of Dunbar [Scot.] 1605
1606, 7 Apr.	Sir Julius Caesar
1614, Oct.	Sir Fulk Greville (1st lord Brooke 1621)
1621, 29 Jan	Sir Richard Weston, 1st lord Weston 1628 (1st e. of Portland 1633)
1628, July	Edward Barrett, 1st lord Barrett of Newburgh [Scot.]
1629, 30 Mar.	Francis Cottington, 1st lord Cottington 1631
1642, 2 Jan.	Sir John Culpepper (1st lord Culpepper 1644)
1643, 3 Mar.	Sir Edward Hyde (1st e. of Clarendon 1661)

For Treasury commissioners under the Protectorate *see under* Treasurers

[1] Until 1806 the dates of appointment of the chancellors of the exchequer are those of the letters patent, from 1806 the dates on which the seals were received.

1661, 13 May	Anthony Ashley Cooper, lord Ashley, 1st e. of Shaftesbury 1672
1672, 17 Nov.	Sir John Duncombe
1676, 28 Apr.	Sir John Ernle
1689, 9 Apr.	Henry Booth, lord Delamer (1st e. of Warrington 1690)
1690, 18 Mar.	Richard Hampden
1694, 27 Apr.	Charles Montagu (1st lord Halifax 1700)
1699, 31 May	John Smith
1701, 26 Mar.	Henry Boyle
1708, 11 Feb.	John Smith. (*See under* 1699)
1710, 10 Aug.	Robert Harley (1st e. of Oxford and Mortimer 1711)
1711, 14 June	Robert Benson, 1st lord Bingley 1713
1713, 1 Nov.	Sir William Wyndham
1714, 13 Oct.	Sir Richard Onslow (1st lord Onslow 1716)
1715, 12 Oct.	Robert Walpole (1st earl of Orford 1742)
1717, 15 Apr.	James Stanhope, 1st viscount Stanhope 1717, 1st e. Stanhope 1718
1718, 20 Mar.	John Aislabie
1721, 21 Feb.	Sir John Pratt
1721, 3 Apr.	Robert Walpole. (*See under* 1715)
1742, 12 Feb.	Samuel Sandys (1st lord Sandys of Ombersley 1743)
1743, 12 Dec.	Henry Pelham
1754, 8 Mar.	Sir William Lee
1754, 6 Apr.	Henry Bilson Legge
1755, 25 Nov.	Sir George Lyttelton (1st lord Lyttelton 1756)
1756, 16 Nov.	Henry Bilson Legge. (*See under* 1754)
1757, 13 Apr.	William Murray, 1st lord Mansfield 1756 (1st e. of Mansfield 1776) (chancellor of the exchequer only)
1757, 2 July	Henry Bilson Legge. (*See under* 1754)
1761, 19 Mar.	William Wildman Barrington-Shute, 2nd viscount Barrington [Irish]
1762, 29 May	Sir Francis Dashwood (11th lord le Despenser 1763)
1763, 16 Apr.	George Grenville
1765, 16 July	William Dowdeswell
1766, 2 Aug.	Charles Townshend
1767, 11 Sept.	Lord Mansfield (chancellor of the exchequer only). (*See under* 1757)
1767, 6 Oct.	Frederick North, commonly called Lord North (4th e. of Guildford 1790)
1782, 1 Apr.	Lord John Cavendish
1782, 13 July	William Pitt
1783, 5 Apr.	Lord John Cavendish. (*See under* 1782)
1783, 27 Dec.	William Pitt. (*See under* 1782)
1801, 20 Mar.	Henry Addington (1st viscount Sidmouth 1805)
1804, 10 May	William Pitt. (*See under* 1782), *ob.* 23 Jan. 1806[1]
1806[2], 5 Feb.	Lord Henry Petty (3rd marquess of Lansdowne 1809)
1807, 26 Mar.	Spencer Perceval, *ob.* 11 May 1812
1812, 9 June	Nicholas Vansittart (1st lord Bexley 1823)
1823, 31 Jan.	Frederick John Robinson (1st viscount Goderich 1827, 1st e. of Ripon 1833)
1827, 20 Apr.	George Canning
1827, 3 Sept.	John Charles Herries
1828, 22 Jan.	Henry Goulburn
1830, 22 Nov.	John Charles Spencer, commonly called viscount Althorp, 3rd e. Spencer 1834
1834, 10 Dec.	Sir Robert Peel, bt
1835, 18 Apr.	Thomas Spring Rice, bt (1st lord Monteagle of Brandon 1839)
1839, 26 Aug.	Sir Francis Thornhill Baring, bt (1st lord Northbrook 1866)
1841, 3 Sept.	Henry Goulburn. (*See under* 1828)
1846, 6 July	Sir Charles Wood, bt (1st viscount Halifax 1866)

[1] Edward Law, 2nd lord Ellenborough, chief justice of the King's Bench, acted from 25 Jan. 1806.

[2] From this year the dates are those on which the seals were received.

1852, 27 Feb.	Benjamin Disraeli (1st e. of Beaconsfield 1876)
1852, 28 Dec.	William Ewart Gladstone
1855, 28 Feb.	Sir George Cornewall Lewis
1858, 26 Feb.	Benjamin Disraeli. (*See under* 1852)
1859, 18 June	William Ewart Gladstone. (*See under* 1852)
1866, 6 July	Benjamin Disraeli. (*See under* 1852)
1868, 29 Feb.	George Ward Hunt
1868, 9 Dec.	Robert Lowe (1st viscount Sherbrooke 1880)
1873, ? 30 Aug.	William Ewart Gladstone. (*See under* 1852)
1874, 21 Feb.	Sir Stafford Henry Northcote (1st e. of Iddesleigh 1885)
1880, 28 Apr.	William Ewart Gladstone. (*See under* 1852)
1882, 16 Dec.	Hugh Culling Eardley Childers
1885, 24 June	Sir Michael Edward Hicks Beach (1st e. St Aldwyn 1915)
1886, 6 Feb.	Sir William George Granville Venables Vernon Harcourt
1886, 3 Aug.	Lord Randolph Henry Spencer Churchill
1887, 14 Jan.	George Joachim Goschen (1st viscount Goschen 1900)
1892, 18 Aug.	Sir William Harcourt. (*See under* 1886)
1895, 29 June	Sir Michael Hicks Beach. (*See under* 1885)
1902, 12 July	Charles Thomson Ritchie (1st lord Ritchie 1905)
1903, 9 Oct.	Joseph Austen Chamberlain
1905, 11 Dec.	Herbert Henry Asquith (1st e. of Oxford and Asquith 1925)
1908, 16 Apr.	David Lloyd George (1st e. Lloyd George of Dwyfor 1945)
1915, 27 May	Reginald McKenna
1916, 11 Dec.	Andrew Bonar Law
1919, 14 Jan.	Joseph Austen Chamberlain
1921, 5 Apr.	Sir Robert Stevenson Horne (1st viscount Horne 1937)
1922, 25 Oct.	Stanley Baldwin (1st e. Baldwin 1937)
1923, 11 Oct.	Arthur Neville Chamberlain
1924, 23 Jan.	Philip Snowden (1st viscount Snowden 1931)
1924, 7 Nov.	Winston Leonard Spencer Churchill (K.G. 1953)
1929, 8 June	Philip Snowden. (*See under* 1924)
1931, 9 Nov.	Arthur Neville Chamberlain. (*See under* 1923)
1937, 28 May	Sir John Allsebrook Simon (1st viscount Simon 1940)
1940, 13 May	Sir Howard Kingsley Wood; *ob.* 21 Sept. 1943
1943, 28 Sept.	Sir John Anderson (1st viscount Waverley 1952)
1945, 28 July	Hugh John Neale Dalton
1947, 17 Nov.	Sir Richard Stafford Cripps
1950, 25 Oct.	Hugh Todd Naylor Gaitskell
1951, 27 Oct.	Richard Austen Butler
1955, 22 Dec.	Maurice Harold Macmillan (1st e. of Stockton 1984)
1957, 14 Jan.	George Edward Peter Thorneycroft
1958, 7 Jan.	Derick Heathcoat Amory
1960, 27 July	John Selwyn Brooke Lloyd
1962, 13 July	Reginald Maudling
1964, 16 Oct.	Leonard James Callaghan
1967, 30 Nov.	Roy Harris Jenkins
1970, 20 June	Iain Norman Macleod; *ob.* 20 July 1970
1970, 25 July	Anthony Perrinott Lysberg Barber
1974, 5 Mar.	Denis Winston Healey
1979, 5 May	Sir Richard Edward Geoffrey Howe
1983, 11 June	Nigel Lawson

MASTERS OF THE COURT OF WARDS

The monarch's interests, as feudal landlord, in the inheritance of estates held of him in chief, were military in origin. By 1500, however, the crown's rights over minor heirs—the wardship of their estates and the disposal of the heir or heiress in marriage—were being exploited for financial profit, and a number of royal officers were involved in their administration. Before the death of Henry VII several office-holders, including a Master of Wards, can be identified, and early in the reign of Henry VIII local officials—feodaries—were appointed. As a department it acquired an increasingly separate identity under Sir William Paulet, joint Master from 1526, and sole Master from 1534. In 1540 it was given a statutory basis as a court of record (32 Henry VIII, c. 46), and in 1542 a surveyor of liveries was added to the offices established (33 Henry VIII, c. 22). Paulet became the first Master of the Court. For a century thereafter the court exercised a full surveillance of the crown's rights, and the profits of fiscal feudalism made a substantial contribution to the royal revenue until the Civil War. Unlike the other prerogative courts it was not immediately abolished by the Long Parliament, and two rival courts (Parliament's being the more effective) operated during the Civil War. The Ordinance of 24 Feb. 1646 ended its existence. See H. E. Bell, *An Introduction to the History and Records of the Court of Wards and Liveries* (Cambridge, 1953), especially chap. 2 on the officers; G. R. Elton, *The Tudor Revolution in Government* (Cambridge, 1953); J. Hurstfield, *The Queen's Wards. Wardship and Marriage under Elizabeth I* (1958); M. Hawkins, *Sale of Wards in Somerset, 1603–41* (Somerset Rec. Soc., vol. 67, 1965).

1540, 26 July	Sir William Paulet, 1st marquess of Winchester 1551
1554, 1 May	Sir Francis Englefield; dism. 26 Dec. 1558
1559, 12 Jan.	Sir Thomas Parry; *ob.* 15 Dec. 1560
1561, 10 Jan.	William Cecil, 1st lord Burghley; *ob.* 4 Aug. 1598
	Post vacant 1598–99
1599, 21 May	Robert Cecil, 1st e. of Salisbury 1605; *ob.* 24 May 1612
1612, June	Sir George Carew; *ob.* 13 Nov. 1612
1612, Nov.	Sir Walter Cope; *ob.* 31 July 1614
1612, 10 Oct.	William Knollys, 1st viscount Wallingford 1616; dism. Dec. 1618
1618, Dec.	Lionel Cranfield, 1st e. of Middlesex 1622; dism. 13 May 1624
1624, 30 Sept.	Sir Robert Naunton; dism. and *ob.* March 1635
1635, March	Francis Cottington, 1st lord Cottington
1641, 17 May	William Fiennes, lord Saye and Sele (for Parliament)
1644, 4 Jan	Lord Cottington (*see under* 1635) (for the King: new seal created at Oxford)

PRIME MINISTERS (*from* 1730)

Long treatises might be written on the origin of the term prime minister and on the question to whom the designation should first be applied. The phrase was in use in the time of Q. Anne, and in the reign of K. George II it was applied to Sir Robert Walpole as a term of reproach by a generation which saw in the prime ministers of France, such as Dubois, Orléans, Bourbon and Fleury, subjects who were exercising in their own person all the royal functions. If such was the meaning of the term in the first half of the eighteenth century, the indignation with which Walpole repudiated the designation is intelligible to a generation which sees in the prime minister only the head of the government, who forms the administration and gives it his name, presides at cabinet meetings, and is the chief link between the sovereign and his other ministers.

It was only spasmodically in the course of the eighteenth century that the present meaning of the term was evolved. Before Sir Robert Walpole's ministry, the most prominent members were often to be found in junior posts, such as the secretaryship of state for the southern department, while less important personages held high office such as first lord of the treasury, and after Sir Robert's fall, ministries drew their names from statesmen who, for one reason or another, like Devonshire, Newcastle, Rockingham, Chatham and Portland, were eclipsed by their more able or more active colleagues. If, therefore, Sir Robert Walpole, as is generally agreed, is the first minister whose functions and policy in any way approximate to those of the modern premier, it seems not unreasonable to begin the list at the retirement of Townshend, which left Walpole free to lay the foundations of that doctrine of homogeneity which is one of the essentials for the easy working of the cabinet system.

As, according to Sir William Anson, 'a man becomes prime minister by kissing the k.'s hands and accepting the commission to form a ministry' the dates given below are those at which the new prime minister kissed hands, but only where ascertainable. It looks as though in the eighteenth and early nineteenth centuries, the dating of a commission or the transfer of seals was the moment of taking office, and that it was not till the middle of the nineteenth century that hands were kissed on the commission being given to form a ministry, as soon as there seemed reasonable prospect of the charge being fulfilled. There is therefore some variation in the policy of determining the dates given below. For the eighteenth century the date given may be taken to be that on which the minister received the seals of office or the commission was made out. In the reigns of George IV and William IV, the date is generally that of an audience, before the formation of the ministry, at which it may be presumed the new premier kissed hands. Under Q. Victoria and later sovereigns it is that at which the prime minister is known to have kissed hands or may be presumed to have done so. Slightly different dates are offered by R. Blake, *The Office of Prime Minister* (Oxford, 1975), chap. iv. Unsuccessful attempts to form ministries, such as that of Lord Granville in 1746, or Sir Robert Peel in 1839, or the summons of the sovereign to ministers who refused to form a ministry, as in the case of Lord Hartington in 1880 or Bonar Law in December 1916, have not been included in this list.

GEORGE II

Sir Robert Walpole	15 May 1730[1]
Earl of Wilmington	16 Feb. 1742[2]
Henry Pelham	27 Aug. 1743[3]
Duke of Newcastle	16 Mar. 1754[4]
Duke of Devonshire	16 Nov. 1756[5]
Duke of Newcastle	2 July 1757[6]

[1] This is the date of Townshend's resignation and may be counted the beginning of Walpole's premiership.
[2] The date of Wilmington's appointment as first lord of the treasury is given thus in the *London Gazette*, no. 8093, 13–16 Feb. 1742, but the most prominent member of the administration was Lord Carteret.
[3] *London Gazette*, no. 8252, 23–7 Aug. 1743. In 1746 Carteret, now earl Granville, made an attempt to form a ministry in conjunction with Lord Bath, but abandoned it in four days' time.
[4] *London Gazette*, no. 9354, 12–16 Mar. 1754.
[5] *Ibid.*, no. 9635, 13–16 Nov. 1756.
[6] *Ibid.*, no. 9700, 28 June–2 July 1757.

GEORGE III

Duke of Newcastle	25 Oct. 1760[1]
Earl of Bute	26 May 1762[2]
George Grenville	16 Apr. 1763[3]
Marquess of Rockingham	13 July 1765[4]
Earl of Chatham	30 July 1766[5]
Duke of Grafton	14 Oct. 1768[6]
Lord North	28 Jan. 1770[7]
Marquess of Rockingham	27 Mar. 1782[8]
Earl of Shelburne	4 July 1782[9]
Duke of Portland	2 Apr. 1783[10]
William Pitt	19 Dec. 1783[11]
Henry Addington	17 Mar. 1801[12]
William Pitt	10 May 1804[13]
Lord Grenville	11 Feb. 1806[14]
Duke of Portland	31 Mar. 1807[15]
Spencer Perceval	4 Oct. 1809[16]
Earl of Liverpool	8 June 1812[17]

GEORGE IV

Earl of Liverpool	29 Jan. 1820[18]
George Canning	10 Apr. 1827[19]
Viscount Goderich	31 Aug. 1827[20]
Duke of Wellington	22 Jan. 1828[21]

WILLIAM IV

Duke of Wellington	26 June 1830[18]
Earl Grey	22 Nov. 1830[22]
Viscount Melbourne	16 July 1834[23]

[1] King's accession: King George II having died at 8 a.m., it is clear that Newcastle resumed the treasury that same day.
[2] *Annual Register*, 1762, 87.
[3] *Ibid.*, 1763, 127.
[4] *Ibid.*, 1765, 166.
[5] This is the date of his appointment as lord privy seal.
[6] The date of the acceptance of Chatham's resignation.
[7] *Annual Register*, 1770, 69.
[8] John W. Fortescue, *Correspondence of King George III*, v, no. 3592.
[9] *Ibid.*, vi, no. 3833.
[10] *Ibid.*, no. 4274.
[11] *Annual Register*, 1783, 223.
[12] *Ibid.*, 1801, 75.
[13] *Ibid.*, 459, says 12 May which seems to be the date of gazetting. *DNB* says 10 May.
[14] *Ibid.*, 1806, 493, again probably the day of gazetting.
[15] *Ibid.*, 1807, 543. Cf. *Morning Chronicle*, 2 Apr., 2, col. 3: 'Yesterday being April Day, his grace the duke of Portland entered on his office as Premier.'
[16] *The Times*, 5 Oct. 1809, 2, col. 3.
[17] *Ibid.*, 9 June 1812, 3, col. 5, which records that Lord Liverpool had an audience the day before, and the next day records that he 'commenced business as first lord of the treasury' on 9 June.
[18] Accession of the new king.
[19] Temperley's *George Canning*; *DNB*.
[20] *Court Circular* in *The Times* of 1 Sept., where the suggestion is that Goderich kissed hands on 31 Aug.
[21] *Ibid.*, 23 Jan. 1828.
[22] *Ibid.*, 23 Nov. 1830.
[23] *Ibid.*, 17 July 1834.

Duke of Wellington	17 Nov. 1834[1]
Sir Robert Peel	10 Dec. 1834[2]
Viscount Melbourne	18 Apr. 1835[3]

VICTORIA

Viscount Melbourne	20 June 1837[4]
Sir Robert Peel	30 Aug. 1841[5]
Lord John Russell	30 June 1846[6]
Earl of Derby	23 Feb. 1852[7]
Earl of Aberdeen	19 Dec. 1852[7]
Viscount Palmerston	6 Feb. 1855[7]
Earl of Derby	20 Feb. 1858[6]
Viscount Palmerston	12 June 1859[6]
Earl Russell	29 Oct. 1865[7]
Earl of Derby	28 June 1866[6]
Benjamin Disraeli	27 Feb. 1868[8]
William Ewart Gladstone	3 Dec. 1868[6]
Benjamin Disraeli (earl of Beaconsfield 1876)	20 Feb. 1874[7]
William Ewart Gladstone	23 Apr. 1880[7]
Marquess of Salisbury	23 June 1885[7]
William Ewart Gladstone	1 Feb. 1886[6]
Marquess of Salisbury	25 July 1886[7]
William Ewart Gladstone	15 Aug. 1892[7]
Earl of Rosebery	5 Mar. 1894[9]
Marquess of Salisbury	25 June 1895[9]

EDWARD VII

Marquess of Salisbury	23 Jan. 1901[10]
Arthur James Balfour	12 July 1902[11]
Sir Henry Campbell Bannerman	5 Dec. 1905[11]
Herbert Henry Asquith	7 Apr. 1908[11]

GEORGE V

Herbert Henry Asquith	8 May 1910[10]
David Lloyd George	7 Dec. 1916[11]
Andrew Bonar Law	23 Oct. 1922[11]
Stanley Baldwin	22 May 1923[11]
James Ramsay MacDonald	22 Jan. 1924[11]
Stanley Baldwin	4 Nov. 1924[12]
James Ramsay MacDonald	5 June 1929
Stanley Baldwin	7 June 1935

[1] *Ibid.*, 18 Nov. 1834.
[2] *Ibid.*, 11 Dec. 1834.
[3] *Ibid.*, 20 Apr. 1835.
[4] Day of accession.
[5] This date can only be presumed from *Queen Victoria's Letters*. The *Court Circular* does not state on which day Peel kissed hands, and it is possible that he did not kiss hands until after the ministry was formed. It is open to question whether in 1839 Peel had kissed hands when, as a result of the Bedchamber dispute, he abandoned the task of forming a ministry.
[6] This is to be presumed from *Queen Victoria's Letters*.
[7] Date of kissing hands given in *Queen Victoria's Letters*.
[8] *Court Circular*, 28 Feb. 1868.
[9] *Queen Victoria's Letters*.
[10] The day aft. the accession of the new sovereign.
[11] *Annual Register*.
[12] This and subsequent entries are taken from the *Court Circular*.

EDWARD VIII

Stanley Baldwin	21 Jan. 1936[1]

GEORGE VI

Stanley Baldwin	12 Dec. 1936[2]
Arthur Neville Chamberlain	28 May 1937
Winston Leonard Spencer Churchill	10 May 1940
Clement Richard Attlee	26 July 1945
Winston Leonard Spencer Churchill	26 Oct. 1951

ELIZABETH II

Sir Winston Leonard Spencer Churchill, K.G. 1953	7 Feb. 1952[2]
Sir Robert Anthony Eden, K.G. 1954	6 Apr. 1955
Maurice Harold Macmillan	10 Jan. 1957
Alexander Frederick Douglas-Home, 14th e. of Home (renounced peerage 23 Oct. 1963)	19 Oct. 1963
James Harold Wilson	16 Oct. 1964
Edward Richard George Heath	19 June 1970
James Harold Wilson	4 Mar. 1974
Leonard James Callaghan	5 Apr. 1976
Margaret Hilda Thatcher	4 May 1979

PRINCIPAL SECRETARIES OF STATE (*from* 1540)

On the early history of the royal secretary, *see* T. F. Tout, *Chapters in the Administrative History of Mediaeval England*, 6 vols (Manchester, 1920–33); there is a list of secretaries, 1377–99, in vol. vi, 57–8. *See also* L. B. Dibben, 'Secretaries in the thirteenth and fourteenth centuries', *EHR*, xxv (1910); F. S. Thomas, *Notes of Materials for a History of the Public Departments* (1846) and J. Otway-Ruthven, *The King's Secretary and the Signet Office in the 15th Century* (Cambridge, 1939), containing lists for the period 1377–1485.

The standard work on the principal secretary is F. M. G. Evans, *The Principal Secretary of State: a Survey of the Office from 1558 to 1680* (Manchester, 1923); it contains lists on pp. 349–51. For the increasing importance of the office of secretary in the reign of Henry VIII, *see also* G. R. Elton, *The Tudor Revolution in Government* (Cambridge, 1953). In 1540 Thomas Wriothesley and Ralph Sadler became the first two principal secretaries and the list below starts with them. Wriothesley compiled a chronicle which was published by the Camden Society (N.S., xi, xx, 1875, 1878); and *see* A. J. Slavin, *Politics and Profit. A Study of Sir Ralph Sadler, 1507–1547* (Cambridge, 1966). Conyers Read's biography, *Mr. Secretary Walsingham and the policy of Queen Elizabeth*, 3 vols (Oxford, 1925), is important; vol. i, appendix, 423–43 prints 'A Treatise of the Office of a councellor and Principall Secretarie to her Majestie', composed in 1592 for Sir Edward Wotton. Between 1662 and 1668 the secretariate was divided, though not officially until 1689, into northern and southern departments. For the history of the secretariate in the eighteenth century, *see* an important work by M. A. Thomson, *The Secretaries of State, 1681–1782* (Oxford, 1932). In 1782 the southern department became the Home Office, and the northern department was converted into the

[1] The day aft. the accession of the new sovereign.
[2] The day aft. the accession of the new sovereign.

116

Foreign Office. *See also* the historical material in the annual *Foreign Office List*, Thomson, *Secretaries of State*, 180–85, and J. C. Sainty, *Officials of the Secretaries of State, 1660–1782* (1973).

1540, Mar.	Sir Thomas Wriothesley (1st e. of Southampton 1547)	Sir Ralph Sadler
1543, 23 Apr.		William Paget (lord Paget 1549) res. 24 June 1547
1544, 21 Jan.	Sir William Petre (secretary alone, 1547–48; res. 29 Mar. 1557)	
1548, 17 Apr.		Sir Thomas Smith
1549, 15 Oct.		Dr Nicholas Wotton
1550, 5 Sept.		Sir William Cecil (1st lord Burghley 1571)
1553, 2 June		Sir John Cheke (additional)
1553, Aug.		Sir John Bourn (to Mar. 1558)
1557, 30 Mar.	John Boxall	
1558, 20 Nov.	Sir William Cecil (*See under* 1550)	(Only one secretary)
1572, 13 July	Sir Thomas Smith (to 1576)	
1573, 21 Dec.		Sir Francis Walsingham, *ob.* 6 Apr. 1590
1577, 12 Nov.	Thomas Wilson, *ob.* 20 May 1581	

Only one secretary 1581–86

1586, 30 Sept.	William Davison (to 1587)[1]	

From 1590 to 1596 Sir Robert Cecil (1st e. of Salisbury 1605) was the acting secretary

1596, 5 July	Sir Robert Cecil, *ob.* 24 May 1612	
1600, 10 May		John Herbert, *ob.* 1617
1612	Robert Carr, 1st viscount Rochester 1611, 1st e. of Somerset 1613	
1614, 29 Mar.	Sir Ralph Winwood (to Oct. 1617)	
1616, 13 Jan.		Sir Thomas Lake
1618, 8 Jan.	Sir Robert Naunton	
1619, 16 Feb.		Sir George Calvert, 1st lord Baltimore [Irish] 1625
1623, 16 Jan.	Sir Edward Conway, 1st lord Conway 1625, 1st viscount Conway 1627	
1625, Feb.		Sir Albertus Morton
1625, Sept.		Sir John Coke
1628, 17 Dec.	Dudley Carleton, 1st lord Carleton 1626, 1st viscount Dorchester 1628	
1632, 15 June	Sir Francis Windebank	
1640, 3 Feb.		Sir Harry Vane, sr
1641, 27 Nov.	Sir Edward Nicholas	
1642, 8 Jan.		Lucius Carey, 2nd viscount Falkland; *ob.* 20 Sept. 1643
1643, 4 Oct.		George Digby, 2nd e. of Bristol 1653. (Res. 1645, reappd 1658)

[1] Davison probably remained secretary in name until 1590. He was paid the secretarial annuity till his death in Dec. 1608. *See* R. B. Wernham, *EHR*, xlvi (1931), 632–6.

Secretaries of State under the Protectorate, 1653–60:

1653, 16 Dec.	John Thurloe, until Apr.–May 1659	
1660, 17 Jan.	Thomas Scott	
1660, 27 Feb.	John Thurloe and John Thompson (jointly) until May 1660	
1660, 1 June ?	Sir Edward Nicholas. (*See under* 1641)	
1660, 27 June		Sir William Morice
1662, 20 Oct.	Sir Henry Bennet, 1st lord Arlington 1665, 1st e. of Arlington 1672 (S.)	
1668, 29 Sept.		Sir John Trevor (N.)
1672, 8 July		Henry Coventry (N. till 1674, then S. till 1680)
1674, 11 Sept.	Sir Joseph Williamson (N.)	
1679, 20 Feb.	Robert Spencer, 2nd e. of Sunderland (N. till Apr. 1680, then S. till 1681)	
1680, 26 Apr.		Sir Leoline Jenkins (N. till Feb. 1681, then S. till 1684)
1681, 2 Feb.	Edward Conway, 1st e. of Conway (N.)	
1683, 28 Jan.	Earl of Sunderland. (*See under* 1679.) (N. till Apr. 1684, then S. till 1688)	
1684, 14 Apr.		Sidney Godolphin, 1st lord Godolphin 1684 (1st e. of Godolphin 1706) (N.)
1684, 24 Aug.		Charles Middleton, 2nd e. of Middleton [Scot.] 1673. (N. till 1688, S. Oct. 1688)
1688, 28 Oct.	Richard Graham, 1st viscount Preston [Scot.] (N.)	

The official division into northern and southern departments begins here

	Northern	*Southern*
1689, 14 Feb.		Charles Talbot, 12th e. of Shrewsbury (duke of Shrewsbury 1694). *Vac.* 2 June 1690
1689, 5 Mar.	Daniel Finch, 2nd e. of Nottingham (7th e. of Winchilsea 1729)	
1690, 2 June	e. of Nottingham sole secretary	
1690, 26 Dec.	Henry Sydney, 1st viscount Sydney of Sheppey (1st e. of Romney 1694). *Vac.* 3 Mar. 1692	e. of Nottingham
1692, 3 Mar.	e. of Nottingham sole secretary	
1693, 23 Mar.	Sir John Trenchard	e. of Nottingham. Dism. Nov. 1693
1693, Nov.	Sir John Trenchard sole secretary	
1694, 2 Mar.	Duke of Shrewsbury. (*See under* 1689)	Sir John Trenchard; *ob.* 27 Apr. 1695
1695, 3 May	Sir William Trumbull. *Vac.* 1–2 Dec. 1697	Duke of Shrewsbury (appd. late Apr.). *Vac.* 12 Dec. 1698
1697, 2 Dec.	James Vernon	

	Northern	*Southern*
1698, 12 Dec.	James Vernon sole secretary	
1699, 14 May	James Vernon	Edward Villiers, 1st e. of Jersey. Dism. 27 June 1700
1700, 27 June	James Vernon sole secretary	
1700, 5 Nov.	Sir Charles Hedges. Dism. 29 Dec. 1701	James Vernon
1702, 4 Jan.	James Vernon. Dism. 1 May 1702	Charles Montagu, 4th e. of Manchester (1st duke of Manchester 1719). Dism. 1 May 1702
1702, 2 May	Sir Charles Hedges. (*See under* 1700)	e. of Nottingham. (*See under* 1689.) *Vac.* on or shortly bef. 22 Apr. 1704
1704, 18 May	Robert Harley (1st e. of Oxford and Mortimer 1711). *Vac.* 13 Feb. 1708	Sir Charles Hedges. Dism. Dec. 1706
1706, 3 Dec.		Charles Spencer, 3rd e. of Sunderland. Dism. 13–14 June 1710
1708, 13 Feb.	Henry Boyle (1st lord Carleton 1714). *Vac.* Sept. 1710	
1710, 15 June		William Legge, 2nd lord Dartmouth, 1st e. of Dartmouth 1711. *Vac.* 6–13 Aug. 1713
1710, 21 Sept.	Henry St John, 1st viscount Bolingbroke 1712	
1713, 17 Aug.	William Bromley. Dism. Sept. 1714	Viscount Bolingbroke. Dism. 31 Aug. 1714
1714, 17 Sept.	Charles Townshend, 2nd viscount Townshend. Dism. early in Dec. 1716	
1714, 27 Sept.		James Stanhope, 1st viscount Stanhope 1717 (e. Stanhope 1718)
1716, 22 June		Paul Methuen. Appd. to act in Stanhope's absence. Remained S. Sec. aft. 12 Dec. 1716
1716, 12 Dec.	James Stanhope. (*See under* 1714)	Paul Methuen. *Vac.* 10 Apr. 1717
1717, 12 Apr.	e. of Sunderland. (*See under* 1706.) *Vac.* 2 Mar. 1718	Joseph Addison. *Vac.* 14 Mar. 1718
1718, 16 Mar.		James Craggs; *ob.* 16 Feb. 1721
1718, 18–21 Mar.	Viscount Stanhope. (*See under* 1714); *ob.* 4 Feb. 1721	
1721, 10 Feb.	Viscount Townshend. (*See under* 1714.) *Vac.* 16 May 1730 [Sir Robert Walpole, appd 29 May 1723, acted in the k.'s absence 5 June–8 Dec. 1723]	
1721, 4 Mar.		John Carteret, 2nd lord Carteret (2nd e. Granville 1744). Dism. at end of Mar. or beginning of Apr. 1724
1724, 6 Apr.		Thomas Pelham-Holles, 1st duke of Newcastle-upon-Tyne 1715. *Vac.* 10 Feb. 1746

	Northern	*Southern*
1730, 19 June	William Stanhope, lord Harrington 1730, e. of Harrington 1742. *Vac.* 12 Feb. 1742	
1742, 12 Feb.	Lord Carteret. (*See under* 1721.) *Vac.* 24 Nov. 1744	
1744, 24 Nov.	e. of Harrington. (*See under* 1730.) *Vac.* 10 Feb. 1746	
1746, 10 Feb.	e. Granville. (*See under* 1721) sole secretary	
1746, 14 Feb.	e. of Harrington. (*See under* 1730.) *Vac.* 28 Oct. 1746	Duke of Newcastle. (*See under* 1724)
1746, 29 Oct.	Philip Dormer Stanhope, 4th e. of Chesterfield. *Vac.* 6 Feb. 1748	
1748, 6–12 Feb.	Duke of Newcastle. *Vac.* Mar. 1754	John Russell, 7th duke of Bedford. *Vac.* 13 June 1751
1751, 18 June		Robert Darcy, 4th e. of Holdernesse
1754, 23 Mar.	e. of Holdernesse. *Vac.* 9 June 1757	Sir Thomas Robinson (1st lord Grantham 1761). *Vac.* Oct. 1755
1755, 14 Nov.		Henry Fox (1st lord Holland of Foxley 1763). *Vac.* 13 Nov. 1756
1756, 4 Dec.		William Pitt (1st e. of Chatham 1766). Dism. 6 Apr. 1757

e. of Holdernesse sole secretary 6 Apr.–9 June 1757

	Northern	*Southern*
1757, 27 June		William Pitt reappd. *Vac.* 5 Oct. 1761
1757, 29 June	e. of Holdernesse reappd. *Vac.* 12 Mar. 1761	
1761, 25 Mar.	John Stuart, 3rd e. of Bute [Scot.], S.R.P. 1761–80. *Vac.* May 1762	
1761, 9 Oct.		Charles Wyndham, 2nd e. of Egremont; *ob.* 21 Aug. 1763
1762, 27 May	George Grenville. *Vac.* on or *c.* 9 Oct. 1762	
1762, 14 Oct.	George Montague-Dunk, 2nd e. of Halifax	
1763, 9 Sept.	John Montagu, 4th e. of Sandwich. Dism. July 1765	e. of Halifax. Dism. 10 July 1765
1765, 10–12 July	Augustus Henry Fitz Roy, 3rd duke of Grafton. *Vac.* 14 May 1766	Henry Seymour Conway
1766, 23 May	Henry Seymour Conway. *Vac.* 20 Jan. 1768	Charles Lennox, 8th duke of Richmond. Dism. 29 July 1766
1766, 30 July		William Fitz-Maurice Petty, 2nd e. of Shelburne [Irish] and 2nd lord Wycombe [G.B.]; (1st marquess of Lansdowne 1784). *Vac.* 19–20 Oct. 1768
1768, 20 Jan.	Thomas Thynne, 3rd viscount Weymouth (1st marquess of Bath 1789)	

	Northern	Southern
1768, 21 Oct.	William Henry Nassau de Zuylestein, 4th e. of Rochford	Viscount Weymouth. *Vac.* 12–17 Dec. 1770
1770, 19 Dec.	e. of Sandwich. (*See under* 1763.) *Vac.* 12 Jan. 1771	e. of Rochford. *Vac.* 9 Nov. 1775
1771, 22 Jan.	e. of Halifax. (*See under* 1762); *ob.* 6 June 1771	
1771, 12 June	Henry Howard, 12th e. of Suffolk and 5th e. of Berkshire; *ob.* 7 Mar. 1777	
1775, 9 Nov.		Viscount Weymouth. (*See under* 1768)
1779, 7 Mar.	Viscount Weymouth, sole secretary until 27 Oct.	
1779, 27 Oct.	David Murray, 7th viscount Stormont [Scot.], S.R.P. 1754–96 (2nd e. Mansfield [G.B.] 1793). *Vac.* Mar. 1782	Viscount Weymouth. *Vac.* 24 Nov. 1779
1779, 24 Nov.		Wills Hill, e. of Hillsborough (1st marquess of Downshire [Irish] 1789). *Vac.* Mar. 1782

In Mar. 1782 the secretariat was reorganized.

FIRST SECRETARIES OF STATE

The post of First Secretary of State was instituted in 1962. Between 1964 and 1967 it was held in conjunction with the post of Minister for Economic Affairs and from 1968 to 1970 with that of Secretary of State for Employment and Productivity. There have been no appointments to the office since 1970.

1962, 13 July	Richard Austen Butler
1964, 16 Oct.	George Alfred Brown
1966, 11 Aug.	Robert Maitland Michael Stewart
1968, 6 Apr.	Barbara Anne Castle

SECRETARIES OF STATE FOR THE HOME DEPARTMENT

In 1782 the Southern Department was converted into the Home Office. The conduct of war was removed from the Home Secretary's hands in 1794 to a separate Secretary for War. Colonies were similarly transferred in 1801 to the Secretary for War and Colonies. For some account of the department, *see* Sir Edward Troup, *The Home Office* (2nd edn, 1926) and Sir Frank Newsam, *The Home Office* (1954), and, more recently, P. R. Nelson, *The Home Office, 1782–1801* (Durham, North Carolina, 1969), J. Pellew, *The Home Office, 1848–1914* (1982), and J. C. Sainty, *Home Office Officials, 1782–1870* (1975).

1782, 27 Mar.	William Petty, 3rd e. of Shelburne [Irish] and 2nd lord Wycombe [G.B.] (1st marquess of Lansdowne 1784)
1782, 10 July	Thomas Townshend, 1st lord Sydney of Chislehurst 1783 (1st viscount Sydney of St Leonards 1789)
1783, 2 Apr.	Frederick North, commonly called lord North (4th e. of Guildford 1790)
1783, 19 Dec.	George Nugent-Temple-Grenville, 3rd e. Temple (1st marquess of Buckingham 1784)

1783, 23 Dec.	Lord Sydney. (*See under* 1782)
1789, 5 June	William Wyndham Grenville, 1st lord Grenville 1790
1791, 8 June	Henry Dundas (1st viscount Melville 1802)
1794, 11 July	William Henry Cavendish Cavendish-Bentinck, 3rd duke of Portland
1801, 30 July	Thomas Pelham, 1st lord Pelham 1801 (2nd e. of Chichester 1805)
1803, 17 Aug.	Charles Philip Yorke
1804, 12 May	Robert Banks Jenkinson, summoned to Parliament *v.p.* as lord Hawkesbury 1803 (2nd e. of Liverpool 1808)
1806, 5 Feb.	George John Spencer, 2nd e. Spencer
1807, 25 Mar.	Lord Hawkesbury. (*See under* 1804)
1809, 1 Nov.	Richard Ryder
1812, 11 June	Henry Addington, 1st viscount Sidmouth
1822, 17 Jan.	Robert Peel
1827, 30 Apr.	William Sturges-Bourne
1827, 16 July	Henry Petty-FitzMaurice, 3rd marquess of Lansdowne
1828, 26 Jan.	Robert Peel. (*See under* 1822)
1830, 22 Nov.	William Lamb, 2nd viscount Melbourne [Irish] and 2nd lord Melbourne [U.K.]
1834, 19 July	John William Ponsonby, 1st lord Duncannon 1834 (4th e. of Bessborough [Irish] 1844)
1834, 15 Dec.	Henry Goulburn
1835, 18 Apr.	John Russell, commonly called lord John Russell (1st e. Russell 1861)
1839, 30 Aug.	Constantine Henry Phipps, 1st marquess of Normanby
1841, 6 Sept.	Sir James Robert George Graham, bt
1846, 6 July	Sir George Grey, bt
1852, 27 Feb.	Spencer Horatio Walpole
1852, 28 Dec.	Henry John Temple, 3rd viscount Palmerston [Irish]
1855, [8?] Feb.	Sir George Grey. (*See under* 1846)
1858, 26 Feb.	Spencer Horatio Walpole. (*See under* 1852)
1859, 3 Mar.	Thomas Henry Sutton Sotheron Estcourt
1859, 18 June	Sir George Cornewall Lewis, bt.
1861, 25 July	Sir George Grey. (*See under* 1846)
1866, 6 July	Spencer Horatio Walpole. (*See under* 1852)
1867, 17 May	Gathorne Hardy (1st e. of Cranbrook 1892)
1868, 9 Dec.	Henry Austin Bruce, 1st lord Aberdare 1873
1873, 9 Aug.	Robert Lowe (1st viscount Sherbrooke 1880)
1874, 21 Feb.	Richard Assheton Cross (1st viscount Cross 1886)
1880, 28 Apr.	Sir William George Granville Venables Vernon Harcourt
1885, 24 June[1]	Sir Richard Assheton Cross. (*See under* 1874)
1886, 6 Feb.	Hugh Culling Eardley Childers
1886, 3 Aug.	Henry Matthews (1st viscount Llandaff 1895)
1892, 18 Aug.[2]	Herbert Henry Asquith (1st e. of Oxford and Asquith 1925)
1895, 29 June	Sir Matthew White Ridley, 1st viscount Ridley 1900
1900, 12 Nov.	Charles Thomson Ritchie (1st lord Ritchie 1905)
1902, 12 July	Aretas Akers-Douglas (1st viscount Chilston 1911)
1905, 11 Dec.	Herbert John Gladstone, 1st viscount Gladstone 1910
1910, 19 Feb.	Winston Leonard Spencer Churchill (K.G. 1953)
1911, 24 Oct.	Reginald McKenna
1915, 27 May	Sir John Allsebrook Simon (1st viscount Simon 1940)
1916, 12 Jan.	Herbert Louis Samuel (1st viscount Samuel 1937)
1916, 11 Dec.	Sir George Cave, 1st viscount Cave 1918
1919, 14 Jan.	Edward Shortt
1922, 25 Oct.	William Clive Bridgeman (1st viscount Bridgeman 1929)
1924, 23 Jan.	Arthur Henderson
1924, 7 Nov.	Sir William Joynson-Hicks, 1st viscount Brentford 1929
1929, 8 June	John Robert Clynes
1931, 26 Aug.	Sir Herbert Samuel. (*See under* 1916)
1932, 1 Oct.	Sir John Gilmour

[1] Date of being sworn at Windsor (*London Gazette*, 1885, p. 2919).
[2] From this year onwards the dates are those on which the oath was taken.

1935, 7 June	Sir John Allsebrook Simon. (*See under* 1915)
1937, 28 May	Sir Samuel John Gurney Hoare, bt (1st viscount Templewood 1944)
1939, 4 Sept.	Sir John Anderson (1st viscount Waverley 1952)
1940, 4 Oct.	Herbert Stanley Morrison
1945, 28 May	Sir Donald Bradley Somervell (lord Somervell of Harrow 1954)
1945, 3 Aug.	James Chuter Ede
1951, 27 Oct.	Sir David Maxwell Fyfe (1st viscount Kilmuir 1954)
1954, 19 Oct.	Gwilym Lloyd-George (1st lord Tenby 1957)
1957, 14 Jan.	Richard Austen Butler (also lord Privy Seal)
1962, 13 July	Henry Brooke
1964, 18 Oct.	Sir Frank Soskice
1965, 23 Dec.	Roy Harris Jenkins
1967, 30 Nov.	Leonard James Callaghan
1970, 20 June	Reginald Maudling
1972, 18 July	Robert Carr
1974, 5 Mar.	Roy Harris Jenkins
1976, 10 Sept.	Merlyn Rees
1979, 5 May	William Stephen Ian Whitelaw (1st viscount Whitelaw 1983)
1983, 11 June	Leon Brittan
1985, 2 Sept.	Douglas Richard Hurd

SECRETARIES OF STATE FOR FOREIGN AFFAIRS

In 1782 the Northern Department (*see* Secretaries of State) was converted into the Foreign Office, and Charles James Fox was appointed first Secretary of State for Foreign Affairs. With the merger of the Foreign Office and the Commonwealth Office on 1 October 1968 the post was redesignated as Secretary of State for Foreign and Commonwealth Affairs. There is an historical account of the Foreign Office by Algernon Cecil in the *Cambridge History of British Foreign Policy*, iii, chap. VIII. *See also* Sir E. Satow, *A Guide to Diplomatic Practice*, 2 vols (2nd edn, 1922); Sir Edward Hertslet, *Recollections of the old Foreign Office* (1901); Sir John Tilley and Stephen Gaselee, *The Foreign Office* (1933); Lord Strang, *The Foreign Office* (1955); R. Jones, *The Nineteenth Century Foreign Office: an administrative history* (1971); J. M. Collinge, *Foreign Office Officials, 1782–1870* (1979).

1782, 27 Mar.	Charles James Fox
1782, 17 July	Thomas Robinson, 2nd lord Grantham
1783, 2 Apr.	Charles James Fox. (*See under* 1782)
1783, 19 Dec.	George Nugent-Temple-Grenville, 3rd e. Temple (1st marquess of Buckingham 1784)
1783, 23 Dec.	Francis Godolphin Osborne, commonly called marquess of Carmarthen, 5th duke of Leeds 1789
1791, 8 June	William Wyndham Grenville, 1st lord Grenville 1790
1801, 20 Feb.	Robert Banks Jenkinson, commonly called lord Hawkesbury (2nd e. of Liverpool 1808)
1804, 14 May	Dudley Ryder, 2nd lord Harrowby (1st e. of Harrowby 1809)
1805, 11 Jan.	Henry Phipps, 2nd lord Mulgrave (1st e. of Mulgrave 1812)
1806, 7 Feb.	Charles James Fox. (*See under* 1782)
1806, 24 Sept.	Charles Grey, commonly called viscount Howick, 2nd e. Grey 1807
1807, 25 Mar.	George Canning
1809, 11 Oct.	Henry Bathurst, 3rd e. Bathurst
1809, 6 Dec.	Richard Wellesley, 1st lord Wellesley [G.B.], 1st marquess Wellesley [Irish]
1812, 4 Mar.	Robert Stewart, commonly called viscount Castlereagh, 2nd marquess of Londonderry [Irish] 1821. *Ob.* 12 Aug. 1822
1822, 16 Sept.	George Canning
1827, 30 Apr.	John William Ward, 4th viscount Dudley and Ward, 1st e. of Dudley 1827

1828, 2 June	George Hamilton-Gordon, 4th e. of Aberdeen [Scot.], 1st viscount Gordon [U.K.]
1830, 22 Nov.	Henry John Temple, 3rd viscount Palmerston [Irish]
1834, 15 Nov.	Arthur Wellesley, 1st duke of Wellington
1835, 18 Apr.	Viscount Palmerston. (*See under* 1830)
1841, 2 Sept.	e. of Aberdeen. (*See under* 1828)
1846, 6 July	Viscount Palmerston. (*See under* 1830)
1851, 26 Dec.	Granville George Leveson-Gower, 2nd e. Granville
1852, 27 Feb.	James Howard Harris, 3rd e. of Malmesbury
1852, 28 Dec.	John Russell, commonly called lord John Russell (1st e. Russell 1861)
1853, 21 Feb.	George William Frederick Villiers, 4th e. of Clarendon
1858, 26 Feb.	e. of Malmesbury. (*See under* 1852)
1859, 18 June	Lord John Russell. (*See under* 1852)
1865, 3 Nov.	e. of Clarendon. (*See under* 1853)
1866, 6 July	Edward Henry Stanley, commonly called lord Stanley (15th e. of Derby 1869)
1868, 9 Dec.	e. of Clarendon. (*See under* 1853). *Ob.* 27 June 1870
1870, 6 July	e. Granville. (*See under* 1851)
1874, 21 Feb.	e. of Derby. (*See under* 1866)
1878, 2 Apr.	Robert Arthur Talbot Gascoyne-Cecil, 3rd marquess of Salisbury
1880, 28 Apr.	e. Granville. (*See under* 1851)
1885, 24 June	Marquess of Salisbury. (*See under* 1878)
1886, 6 Feb.	Archibald Philip Primrose, 5th e. of Rosebery [Scot.], 2nd lord Rosebery [U.K.], (1st e. of Midlothian 1911 [U.K.])
1886, 3 Aug.	Stafford Henry Northcote, 1st e. of Iddesleigh 1885
1887, 14 Jan.	Marquess of Salisbury. (*See under* 1878)
1892, 18 Aug.	e. of Rosebery. (*See under* 1886)
1894, 11 Mar.	John Wodehouse, 1st e. of Kimberley
1895, 29 June	Marquess of Salisbury. (*See under* 1878)
1900, 12 Nov.	Henry Charles Keith Petty-Fitzmaurice, 5th marquess of Lansdowne
1905, 11 Dec.	Sir Edward Grey, 1st viscount Grey of Fallodon 1916
1916, 11 Dec.	Arthur James Balfour (1st e. of Balfour 1922)
1919, 24 Oct.	George Nathaniel Curzon, 1st e. Curzon, 1st marquess Curzon 1921
1924, 23 Jan.	James Ramsay MacDonald
1924, 7 Nov.	Sir Joseph Austen Chamberlain
1929, 8 June	Arthur Henderson
1931, 26 Aug.	Rufus Isaacs, 1st marquess of Reading
1931, 9 Nov.	Sir John Allsebrook Simon (1st viscount Simon 1940)
1935, 7 June	Sir Samuel John Gurney Hoare, bt (1st viscount Templewood 1944)
1935, 22 Dec.	Robert Anthony Eden (K.G. 1954)
1938, 1 Mar.	Edward Frederick Lindley Wood, 3rd viscount Halifax (1st e. of Halifax 1944)
1940, 23 Dec.	Anthony Eden. (*See under* 1935)
1945, 28 July	Ernest Bevin
1951, 12 Mar.	Herbert Stanley Morrison
1951, 27 Oct.	Anthony Eden. (*See under* 1935)
1955, 12 Apr.	Maurice Harold Macmillan
1955, 22 Dec.	John Selwyn Brooke Lloyd
1960, 27 July	Alexander Frederick Douglas-Home, 14th e. of Home
1963, 20 Oct.	Richard Austen Butler
1964, 16 Oct.	Patrick Chrestien Gordon Walker
1965, 22 Jan.	Robert Maitland Michael Stewart
1966, 11 Aug.	George Alfred Brown
1968, 16 Mar.	Robert Maitland Michael Stewart
1970, 20 June	Sir Alexander Frederick Douglas-Home
1974, 5 Mar.	Leonard James Callaghan
1976, 8 Apr.	Charles Anthony Raven Crosland *ob.* 19 Feb. 1977
1977, 21 Feb.	David Anthony Llewellyn Owen
1979, 5 May	Peter Alexander Rupert Carrington, 6th Lord Carrington
1982, 5 Apr.	Francis Leslie Pym
1983, 11 June	Sir Richard Edward Geoffrey Howe

SECRETARIES OF STATE FOR THE COLONIES

In 1768 a 'Secretary of State for the American Colonies' was appointed, but in 1782 this office was abolished by the Establishment Act (22 Geo. III, c. 82). From 1782 to 1801, after the loss of the American colonies, colonial policy was under the control of the Home Secretary, from 1801 to 1854 under the Secretary of State for War and Colonies, and thereafter under the Secretary of State for the Colonies. For these and later developments, *see* A. H. Basye, 'The Secretary of State for the Colonies, 1768–82', *American Historical Review*, xxviii (1923), 13 *seq.*; H. T. Manning, *British Colonial Government after the American Revolution, 1782–1820* (Yale Hist. Publ., Misc. 26, New Haven and London, 1933); J. Beaglehole, 'The Colonial Office, 1782–1854' and E. T. Williams, 'The Colonial Office in the Thirties', *Australian and New Zealand Historical Studies*, i (1941) and ii (1943); W. L. Burn, *Emancipation and Apprenticeship in the West Indies* (1937); Sir Henry Taylor, *Autobiography*, 2 vols (1885); *Letters of Lord Blachford*, ed. G. E. Marindin (1896); Sir George V. Fiddes, *The Dominions and Colonial Offices* (1926); H. L. Hall, *The Colonial Office: A History* (1937); Sir Cosmo Parkinson, *The Colonial Office from Within* (1947); Sir Charles Jeffries, *The Colonial Office* (1956); R. B. Pugh, 'The Colonial Office' in *Cambridge History of the British Empire*, iii (1959); J. C. Sainty, *Colonial Office Officials, 1794–1870* (1976).

SECRETARIES OF STATE FOR THE AMERICAN COLONIES

1768, 20 Jan.	Wills Hill, 1st e. of Hillsborough [Irish], 1st lord Harwich [G.B.], (1st marquess of Downshire [Irish] 1789)
1772, 14 Aug.	William Legge, 2nd e. of Dartmouth
1775, 10 Nov.	Lord George Sackville-Germain, 1st viscount Sackville 1782
1782, 17 Feb.	Welbore Ellis (1st lord Mendip 1794)

SECRETARIES OF STATE FOR WAR AND THE COLONIES

1794, 11 July	Henry Dundas[1]
1801, 17 Mar.	Robert Hobart, 4th lord Hobart (4th e. of Buckinghamshire 1804)
1804, 12 May	John Jeffreys Pratt, 2nd e. Camden (1st marquess Camden 1812)
1805, 10 July	Robert Stewart, commonly called viscount Castlereagh (2nd marquess of Londonderry [Irish] 1821)
1806, 14 Feb.	William Windham
1807, 25 Mar.	Viscount Castlereagh. (*See under* 1805)
1809, 1 Nov.	Robert Banks Jenkinson, 2nd e. of Liverpool
1812, 11 June	Henry Bathurst, 3rd e. Bathurst
1827, 30 Apr.	Frederick John Robinson, 1st viscount Goderich 1827 (1st e. of Ripon 1833)
1827, 3 Sept.	William Huskisson
1828, 30 May	Sir George Murray
1830, 22 Nov.	Viscount Goderich. (*See under* 1827)
1833, 3 Apr.	Edward Geoffrey Smith-Stanley, commonly called lord Stanley (14th e. of Derby 1851)
1834, 5 June	Thomas Spring Rice (1st lord Monteagle of Brandon 1839)
1834, 17 Nov.	George Hamilton-Gordon, 4th e. of Aberdeen [Scot.], 1st viscount Gordon [U.K.]
1835, 18 Apr.	Charles Grant, 1st lord Glenelg 1835

[1] Dundas, though officially only Secretary of State for War, was in practice concerned with an ever-increasing amount of colonial business, chiefly in connection with military operations overseas.

1839, 20 Feb.	Constantine Phipps, 1st marquess of Normanby
1839, 30 Aug.	John Russell, commonly called lord John Russell (1st e. Russell 1861)
1841, 3 Sept.	Lord Stanley. (*See under* 1833)
1845, 23 Dec.	William Ewart Gladstone
1846, 3 July	Henry Grey, 3rd e. Grey
1852, 27 Feb.	Sir John Somerset Pakington (1st lord Hampton 1874)
1852, 8 Dec.	Henry Pelham Pelham-Clinton, 5th duke of Newcastle-under-Lyme

The two departments were separated in 1854

SECRETARIES OF STATE FOR THE COLONIES

1854, 10 June	Sir George Grey
1855, 8 Feb.	Sidney Herbert (1st Lord Herbert of Lea 1861)
1855, 23 Feb.	John Russell, commonly called lord John Russell (1st e. Russell 1861)
1855, 21 July	Sir William Molesworth
1855, 17 Nov.	Henry Labouchere (1st lord Taunton 1859)
1858, 26 Feb.	Edward Henry Stanley, commonly called lord Stanley (15th e. of Derby 1869)
1858, 31 May	Sir Edward George Earle Lytton Bulwer-Lytton (1st lord Lytton 1866)
1859, 18 June	Henry Pelham Pelham-Clinton, 5th duke of Newcastle-under-Lyme
1864, 4 Apr.	Edward Cardwell (1st viscount Cardwell 1874)
1866, 6 July	Henry Howard Molyneux Herbert, 9th e. of Carnarvon
1867, 8 Mar.	Richard Plantagenet Campbell Temple-Nugent-Brydges-Chandos-Grenville, 3rd duke of Buckingham and Chandos
1868, 10 Dec.	Granville George Leveson-Gower, 2nd e. Granville
1870, 6 July	John Wodehouse, 1st e. of Kimberley
1874, 21 Feb.	e. of Carnarvon. (*See under* 1866)
1878, 4 Feb.	Sir Michael Hicks Beach (1st e. St Aldwyn 1915)
1880, 28 Apr.	e. of Kimberley. (*See under* 1870)
1882, 11 Dec.	e. of Derby. (*See under* 1858)
1885, 24 June	Frederick Arthur Stanley (16th e. of Derby 1893)
1886, 6 Feb.	e. Granville. (*See under* 1868)
1886, 3 Aug.	Edward Stanhope
1887, 14 Jan.	Sir Henry Thurston Holland, 1st lord Knutsford 1888 (1st viscount Knutsford 1895)
1892, 17 Aug.	George Frederick Samuel Robinson, 1st marquess of Ripon
1895, 28 June	Joseph Chamberlain
1903, 9 Oct.	Alfred Lyttelton
1905, 11 Dec.	Victor Alexander Bruce, 9th e. of Elgin [Scot.] and 2nd lord Elgin [U.K.]
1908, 16 Apr.	Robert Offley Ashburton Crewe-Milnes, 1st e. of Crewe 1895 (1st marquess of Crewe 1911)
1910, 7 Nov.	Lewis Harcourt (1st viscount Harcourt 1917)
1915, 27 May	Andrew Bonar Law
1916, 11 Dec.	Walter Hume Long (1st viscount Long 1921)
1919, Jan.	Alfred Milner, 1st viscount Milner
1921, 14 Feb.	Winston Leonard Spencer Churchill (K.G. 1953)
1922, 25 Oct.	Victor Christian William Cavendish, 9th duke of Devonshire
1924, 23 Jan.	James Henry Thomas
1924, 7 Nov.	Leopold Charles Maurice Stennett Amery (and for Dominion Affairs)
1929, 8 June	Sydney James Webb, 1st lord Passfield 1929 (and for Dominion Affairs)
1931, 26 Aug.	James Henry Thomas (and for Dominion Affairs)
1931, 9 Nov.	Sir Philip Cunliffe-Lister (1st e. Swinton 1955)
1935, 7 June	Malcolm MacDonald
1935, 27 Nov.	James Henry Thomas. (*See under* 1924)
1936, 29 May	William George Arthur Ormsby Gore, 4th lord Harlech 1938
1938, 16 May	Malcolm MacDonald. (*See under* 1935)

1940, 13 May	George Ambrose Lloyd, 1st lord Lloyd
1941, 8 Feb.	Walter Edward Guinness, 1st lord Moyne
1942, 23 Feb.	Robert Arthur James Gascoyne-Cecil, commonly called viscount Cranborne, summoned to parliament *v.p.* as lord Cecil of Essendon 1941 (5th marquess of Salisbury 1947)
1942, 24 Nov.	Oliver Frederick George Stanley
1945, 3 Aug.	George Henry Hall (1st viscount Hall 1946)
1946, 7 Oct.	Arthur Creech Jones
1950, 2 Mar.	James Griffiths
1951, 27 Oct.	Oliver Lyttelton (1st viscount Chandos 1954)
1954, 30 July	Alan Tindal Lennox-Boyd
1959, 14 Sept.	Iain Norman Macleod
1961, 9 Oct.	Reginald Maudling
1962, 13 July	Duncan Sandys
1964, 18 Oct.	Anthony Greenwood
1965, 23 Dec.	Francis Aungier Pakenham, 7th e. of Longford
1966, 6 Apr.	Frederick Lee

In 1966 the post was discontinued on the creation of the Commonwealth Office.

SECRETARIES OF STATE FOR DOMINION AFFAIRS
(LATER FOR COMMONWEALTH RELATIONS)

On 1 July 1925 the responsibility for 'the autonomous communities within the Empire' [then Canada, Australia, New Zealand, the Union of South Africa, the Irish Free State (later known as Eire), Newfoundland and Southern Rhodesia], was transferred from the Secretary of State for the Colonies to the Secretary of State for Dominion Affairs, whose office was created on that day by executive act. Until 1938 the two secretaryships were often, but not always, held by the same minister. On 3 July 1947 the title of the minister was changed to Secretary of State for Commonwealth Relations and responsibility for United Kingdom relations with the governments of India and Pakistan was conferred upon him. Subsequently his responsibility had been extended to relations with Ceylon (1948), Ghana (1957) and Malaya (1957). In 1966 the Commonwealth Relations Office merged with the Colonial Office, forming the Commonwealth Office, which was itself combined with the Foreign Office on 1 October 1968. *See* J. Garner, *The Commonwealth Office, 1925–68* (1978).

1924, 7 Nov.	Leopold Charles Maurice Stennett Amery (and for Colonies)
1929, 8 June	Sydney James Webb, 1st lord Passfield 1929 (and for Colonies)
1930, 13 June	James Henry Thomas (and for Colonies from 26 Aug. 1931)
1935, 27 Nov.	Malcolm MacDonald
1938, 16 May	Edward Montagu Cavendish Stanley, commonly called lord Stanley
1938, 4 Nov.	Malcolm MacDonald (and for Colonies)
1939, 2 Feb.	Sir Thomas Walker Hobart Inskip, 1st viscount Caldecote 1939
1939, 4 Sept.	Robert Anthony Eden (K.G. 1954)
1940, 15 May	Viscount Caldecote. (*See under* 1939)
1940, 4 Oct.	Robert Arthur James Gascoyne-Cecil, commonly called viscount Cranborne, summoned to parliament *v.p.* as lord Cecil of Essendon 1941 (5th marquess of Salisbury 1947)
1942, 23 Feb.	Clement Richard Attlee (1st e. Attlee 1955); (also Deputy Prime Minister)
1943, 28 Sept.	Viscount Cranborne. (*See under* 1940)
1945, 3 Aug.	Christopher Addison, 1st lord Addison, 1st viscount Addison 1945
1947, 14 Oct.	Philip John Noel-Baker
1950, 2 Mar.	Patrick Chrestien Gordon Walker

1951, 27 Oct.	Hastings Lionel Ismay, 1st lord Ismay
1952, 24 Mar.	Marquess of Salisbury. (*See under* 1940)
1952, 15 Dec.	Philip Lloyd Greame, later Cunliffe-Lister, 1st viscount Swinton, 1st e. Swinton 1955
1955, 12 Apr.	Alexander Frederick Douglas-Home, 14th e. of Home [Scot.], 4th lord Douglas [U.K.]; (also lord President of the Council 1 Apr.–23 Sept. 1957)
1960, 27 July	Duncan Sandys
1964, 18 Oct.	Arthur Bottomley
1966, 11 Aug.	Herbert William Bowden
1967, 17 Oct.	George Morgan Thomson

In 1968 the post was discontinued on the creation of the Foreign and Commonwealth Office.

COMMANDERS-IN-CHIEF, LAND FORCES

The king of England, from earliest times, exercised supreme command over the armed forces of the realm, by land and sea. While he usually delegated his power over the navy to the Lord High Admiral, or commissioners acting in his place (*see* Admirals and First Lords of the Admiralty), he often led his armies in person; George II at the battle of Dettingen, 1743, was the last occasion. At other times, with the existence of a standing army after the Civil War, an officer commanding the nation's land forces was required to deputize for the sovereign. Depending on the willingness of the ruler as supreme commander to exercise nominal or real power this officer had more or less influence. Because of these close links with the crown he was often a prince of the blood; as late as 1895 Queen Victoria demanded, though unsuccessfully, that one of her sons succeed her cousin, the Duke of Cambridge, as Commander-in-Chief. The duties of the commander were mainly related to discipline, promotion and training of the cavalry and infantry; political and financial control was increasingly exercised by civilian ministers, the Secretary at War, originating in the mid-seventeenth century and a significant political figure, as head of the War Office, by the following century, and the Secretary of State for War, who took control in the course of the nineteenth century (*see* Secretaries of State for the Colonies, and Secretaries of State for War). Unless he was also Master General of the Ordnance the C.-in-C. had no control over fortifications, the arming of his troops, or the artillery and engineers: the Office (later Board) of Ordnance, from its inception in the reign of Henry VIII until its abolition in 1855, was an independent department of state. In the list below, where the C.-in-C. was also Master General, the fact has been noted: as also his presence in the Cabinet. The actual title enjoyed by commanders varied widely; in the Civil War they were often styled Lord General, but from the Restoration Captain General became usual, until supplanted by the term C.-in-C. on the resignation of Cumberland. While the Georges preferred to command personally the office was left vacant or given restricted powers, as 'General on staff'. The rank of Field Marshal was introduced from the middle of the eighteenth century, and the Duke of York was commissioned as 'Field Marshal of the Forces' in 1795. He occupied offices in the Horse Guards, Whitehall, which remained thereafter, until the reforms of the 1870s, the headquarters of the British Army. Under York the semi-independent status of the military establishments in Scotland and Ireland disappeared. In the list below the names of commanding officers whose tenure was largely titular, acting or otherwise severely limited have been placed in square brackets. The responsibilities of the post are discussed in C. M. Clode, *The Military Forces of the Crown* (1869), ii. 335–58. The high command and other officers are listed in the annual (later periodical) *Army List*, from 1740. There is a list of Masters General and other Ordnance officers in A. Forbes, *A History of the Army Ordnance Services* (1929), i. App. 1. *See also* works cited under Secretaries of State for War.

THE ROYALIST ARMY, 1642–1646

Charles I was himself C.-in-C., and led his main army in person.

1642, July	Robert Bertie, 1st e. of Lindsey; res. 22 Oct. 1642 (*ob. c.* 24 Oct. 1642)
1642, 22 Oct.	Patrick Ruthven, 1st e. of Forth [Scot.], 1st e. of Brentford, 1644
[1644, 7 Nov.	Prince Charles, Prince of Wales]
1644, 30 Nov.	Prince Rupert, 1st duke of Cumberland, Capt. Gen. under Prince Charles; dism. 14 Sept. 1645

THE PARLIAMENTARY ARMY, 1642–1660

1642, 15 July	Robert Devereux, 3rd e. of Essex
1645, 17 Feb.	Sir Thomas Fairfax; powers successively extended and renewed, 1 Apr. 1645, 18 May 1647, 19 July 1647, 28 Aug. 1647, 30 Mar. 1649. Res. June 1650. (From 14 Mar. 1648, 3rd Lord Fairfax of Cameron)
1650, 26 June	Oliver Cromwell (16 Dec. 1653, also Lord Protector), *ob.* 3 Sept. 1658
1658, 3 Sept.–1659, 25 May (but had ceased to act by early May), Richard Cromwell, as Protector and Capt.-Gen.	
1659, 11 May	Charles Fleetwood, Lt-Gen. and C.-in-C.
1660, 24 or 25 Feb.	George Monck, Capt.-Gen. and C.-in-C. (until reap. by King Charles II), 1st duke of Albemarle 1660

CHARLES II

1660, 3 Aug.	George Monck, 1st duke of Albemarle. *Ob.* 3 Jan. 1670
[1670, Jan.	James Scott, 1st duke of Monmouth. Dism. Sept. 1679]
[1690, 3 June	John Churchill, 1st e. of Marlborough. Dism. Jan. 1692]
1702, 10 Mar.	John Churchill, 1st e. of Marlborough, 1st duke of Marlborough, 1702; Mr Gen. 1702–12. [With Prince George of Denmark as 'Generalissimo']
1712, 26 Feb.	James Butler, 2nd duke of Ormond. Dism. Sept. 1714
[1714, 4 Sept.	1st duke of Marlborough. Mr Gen. 1714–22 (*see under* 1702). *Ob.* 16 June 1722]
1745, 7 Mar.	William Augustus, 1st duke of Cumberland. Res. 15 Oct. 1757
1757, 24 Oct.	John Louis Ligonier, 1st lord Ligonier 1763 (1st e. Ligonier 1766). Mr Gen. 1759–63, and Cabinet
1766, 13 Aug.	John Manners, marquess of Granby. Mr Gen. 1763–72, and Cabinet. Res. 17 Jan. 1770.
1778,	Jeffrey Amherst, 1st lord Amherst. Cabinet
1782, Mar.	Henry Conway. Cabinet
[1783, Apr.	Lord Amherst. Cabinet until 1795 (*see under* 1778)]
1795, 10 Feb.	Frederick Augustus, 1st duke of York. Res. 18 Mar. 1809
1809, 25 Mar.	Sir David Dundas
1811, 26 May	1st duke of York (*see under* 1795). *Ob.* 5 Jan. 1827
1827, 22 Jan.	Arthur Wellesley, 1st duke of Wellington. Mr Gen. 1819–27. Res. May 1827

1827, 17 Aug.	1st duke of Wellington. Res. Jan. 1828
1828, 14 Feb.	Rowland Hill, 1st lord Hill (1st viscount Hill 1842)
1842, 15 Aug.	1st duke of Wellington (*see under* 1827). *Ob*. 14 Sept. 1852
1852, 28 Sept.	Henry Hardinge, 1st viscount Hardinge
1856, 15 July	George William, 2nd duke of Cambridge[1]
1895, 1 Nov.	Sir Garnet Wolseley, 1st viscount Wolseley. Res. 30 Nov. 1900
1901, Jan.	Frederick Roberts, 1st lord Roberts, 1st e. Roberts 1901

The post was abolished, Feb. 1904, on the creation of the Army Council

SECRETARIES OF STATE FOR WAR (*from* 1855)

The office of Secretary at War originated in the reign of Charles II, and in 1801 the first Secretary of State for War and the Colonies was appointed in addition.[2] Before the Crimean War the government of military affairs was 'a medley of conflicting jurisdictions'. In 1855 the Secretary of State for War was relieved of his colonial duties, but acted also as Secretary at War from 1855 to 1863 when the latter office was abolished. (26 and 27 Vict., c. 12.) *See* C. M. Clode, *The Military Forces of the Crown*, 2 vols (1869); J. S. Omond, *Parliament and the Army, 1642–1904* (Cambridge, 1933); Sir W. R. Anson, *The Law and Custom of the Constitution*, vol. ii, pt ii, pp. 222–43 (Oxford, 1935); *The Report on the Civil and Professional Administration of the Naval and Military Departments* (1890); *The Cambridge History of British Foreign Policy*, 3 vols (Cambridge, 1922–3); Sir R. Biddulph, *Lord Cardwell at the War Office* (1904); Hampden Gordon, *The War Office* (1935); J. Sweetman, *War and Administration. The Significance of the Crimean War for the British Army* (Edinburgh, 1984), and W. S. Hamer, *The British Army; Civil-Military Relations, 1885–1905* (1970).

1855, 8 Feb.	Fox Maule-Ramsay, 2nd lord Panmure (11th e. of Dalhousie [Scot.] 1860)
1858, 27 Feb.	Jonathan Peel
1859, 19 June	Sidney Herbert, 1st lord Herbert of Lea 1861
1861, 22 July	Sir George Cornewall Lewis, bt
1863, 28 Apr.	George Frederick Samuel Robinson, 2nd e. of Ripon (1st marquess of Ripon 1871)
1866, 16 Feb.	Spencer Compton Cavendish, commonly called marquess of Hartington (8th duke of Devonshire 1891)
1866, 6 July	Jonathan Peel. (*See under* 1858)
1867, 8 Mar.	Sir John Somerset Pakington (1st lord Hampton 1874)
1868, 9 Dec.	Edward Cardwell (1st viscount Cardwell 1874)
1874, 21 Feb.	Gathorne Hardy, later Gathorne-Hardy, 1st viscount Cranbrook 1878 (1st e. of Cranbrook 1892)
1878, 2 Apr.	Sir Frederick Arthur Stanley (16th e. of Derby 1893)
1880, 28 Apr.	Hugh Culling Eardley Childers
1882, 16 Dec.	Marquess of Hartington. (*See under* 1866)
1885, 24 June	William Henry Smith
1887, 14 Jan.	Edward Stanhope
1892, 18 Aug.	Sir Henry Campbell-Bannerman
1895, 4 July	Henry Charles Keith Petty-FitzMaurice, 5th marquess of Lansdowne
1900, Oct.	William St John Fremantle Brodrick (1st e. of Midleton 1920)
1903, 12 Oct.	Hugh Oakeley Arnold-Forster
1905, 11 Dec.	Richard Burdon Haldane, 1st viscount Haldane 1911
1912, 14 June	John Edward Bernard Seely (1st lord Mottistone 1933)

[1] General commanding, 1856, Field Marshal commanding, 1862, C.-in-C., 1887.
[2] For the position of Dundas, 1794–1801, officially Secretary of State for War only, *see under* War and Colonies.

1914, 31 Mar.	Herbert Henry Asquith (1st e. of Oxford and Asquith 1925)
1914, 6 Aug.	Horatio Herbert Kitchener, 1st e. Kitchener of Khartoum
1916, 7 July	David Lloyd George (1st e. Lloyd George of Dwyfor 1945)
1916, 11 Dec.	Edward George Villiers Stanley, 17th e. of Derby
1918, 20 Apr.	Alfred Milner, 1st viscount Milner
1919, 14 Jan.	Winston Leonard Spencer Churchill (and for Royal Air Force)
1921, 14 Feb.	Sir William Laming Worthington-Evans, bt
1922, 25 Oct.	e. of Derby. (*See under* 1916)
1924, 23 Jan.	Stephen Walsh
1924, 7 Nov.	Sir Laming Worthington-Evans. (*See under* 1921)
1929, 8 June	Thomas Shaw
1931, 30 Aug.	Robert Offley Ashburton Crewe-Milnes, 1st marquess of Crewe
1931, 9 Nov.	Douglas McGarel Hogg, 1st viscount Hailsham
1935, 7 June	Edward Frederick Lindley Wood, 3rd viscount Halifax (1st e. of Halifax 1944)
1935, 27 Nov.	Alfred Duff Cooper (1st viscount Norwich 1941)
1937, 28 May	Leslie Hore-Belisha (1st lord Hore-Belisha 1954)
1940, 16 Jan.	Oliver Frederick George Stanley
1940, 11 May	Robert Anthony Eden (K.G. 1954)
1940, 23 Dec.	Henry David Reginald Margesson (1st viscount Margesson 1942)
1942, 23 Feb.	Sir Percy James Grigg
1945, 3 Aug.	John James Lawson (1st lord Lawson 1950)
1946, 7 Oct.	Frederick John Bellenger
1947, 14 Oct.	Emanuel Shinwell
1950, 2 Mar.	John Strachey
1951, 6 Nov.	Antony Henry Head
1956, 22 Oct.	John Hugh Hare
1958, 7 Jan.	Christopher John Soames
1960, 27 July	John Dennis Profumo
1963, 27 June	Joseph Bradshaw Godber
1963, 21 Oct.	James Edward Ramsden

In 1964 the post was discontinued on the creation of a unified Ministry of Defence.

SECRETARIES OF STATE FOR AIR

In January 1918 Lord Rothermere was appointed President of the Air Council and, very soon afterwards, secretary of state for the Royal Air Force. In 1919 this secretaryship of state was combined with the secretaryship of state for War, and on 29 March of that year it was announced that the title had been changed to secretary of state for Air. In 1921 an independent secretaryship of state was created. *See* C. G. Grey, *A History of the Air Ministry* (1940) and Viscount Templewood, *Empire of the Air* (1957).

1918, 2 Jan.	Harold Sidney Harmsworth, 1st lord Rothermere (1st viscount Rothermere 1919)
1918, 26 Apr.	Sir William Douglas Weir, 1st lord Weir 1918
1919, 14 Jan.	Winston Leonard Spencer Churchill (with War Office) (K.G. 1953)
1921, 5 Apr.	Frederick Edward Guest
1922, 2 Nov.	Sir Samuel John Gurney Hoare, bt (1st viscount Templewood 1944)
1924, 22 Jan.	Christopher Birdwood Thomson, 1st lord Thomson 1924
1924, 7 Nov.	Sir Samuel Hoare. (*See under* 1922)
1929, 8 June	Lord Thomson. (*See under* 1924). *Ob.* 5 Oct. 1930
1930, 18 Oct.	William Warrender Mackenzie, 1st lord Amulree 1929
1931, 9 Nov.	Charles Stewart Henry Vane-Tempest-Stewart, 7th marquess of Londonderry [Irish] and 5th e. Vane [U.K.]
1935, 7 June	Sir Philip Cunliffe-Lister, 1st viscount Swinton 1935 (1st e. Swinton 1955)
1938, 16 May	Sir Howard Kingsley Wood
1940, 5 Apr.	Sir Samuel John Gurney Hoare. (*See under* 1922)

1940, 11 May	Sir Archibald Sinclair, bt (1st viscount Thurso 1952)
1945, 28 May	Maurice Harold Macmillan
1945, 3 Aug.	William Wedgwood Benn, 1st viscount Stansgate
1946, 7 Oct.	Philip John Noel-Baker
1947, 14 Oct.	Arthur Henderson
1951, 1 Nov.	William Philip Sidney, 6th lord De L'Isle and Dudley
1955, 22 Dec.	Evelyn Nigel Chetwode Birch
1957, 19 Jan.	George Reginald Ward
1960, 28 Oct.	Julian Amery
1963, 16 July	Hugh Charles Patrick Joseph Fraser

In 1964 the post was discontinued on the creation of a unified Ministry of Defence.

PRESIDENTS OF THE BOARD OF CONTROL

By Pitt's India Act of 1784 (24 Geo. III, c. 25) the East India Company was placed under the superintendence of six Commissioners for the Affairs of India. At first the Home Secretary was first commissioner, but in 1793 the Board of Control, as the Commissioners were usually called, was given a distinct and salaried President of its own. The office was abolished by the Government of India Act of 1858 (21 and 22 Vict., c. 106) and its functions transferred to the Secretary of State for India (*q.v.*). For some account of the Board of Control *see* C. H. Philips, *The East India Company 1784–1834* (2nd edn, Manchester, 1961); R. J. Moore, *Sir Charles Wood's Indian Policy 1853–66* (Manchester, 1966).

1784, 3 Sept.	Thomas Townshend, 1st lord Sydney 1873, 1st viscount Sydney 1789
1790, 12 Mar.	William Wyndham Grenville, 1st lord Grenville 1790
1793, 28 June	Henry Dundas (1st viscount Melville 1802)
1801, 19 May	George Legge, commonly called viscount Lewisham, 3rd e. of Dartmouth 1801
1802, 12 July	Robert Stewart, commonly called viscount Castlereagh (2nd marquess of Londonderry [Irish] 1821)
1806, 12 Feb.	Gilbert Elliot, later Elliot Murray-Kynynmound, 1st lord Minto (1st e. of Minto 1813)
1806, 16 July	Thomas Grenville
1806, 1 Oct.	George Tierney
1807, 6 Apr.	Robert Dundas, later Saunders-Dundas (2nd viscount Melville 1811)
1809, 17 July	Dudley Ryder, 1st e. of Harrowby 1809
1809, 13 Nov.	Robert Dundas. (*See under* 1807)
1812, 7 Apr.	Robert Hobart, 4th e. of Buckinghamshire
1816, 20 June	George Canning
1821, 16 Jan.	Charles Bathurst
1822, 8 Feb.	Charles Watkin Williams Wynn
1828, 31 July	Viscount Melville. (*See under* 1807)
1828, 24 Sept.	Edward Law, 2nd lord Ellenborough (1st e. of Ellenborough 1844)
1830, 6 Dec.	Charles Grant (1st lord Glenelg 1835)
1834, 20 Dec.	Lord Ellenborough. (*See under* 1828)
1835, 29 Apr.	Sir John Cam Hobhouse, bt (1st lord Broughton 1851)
1841, 9 Sept.	Lord Ellenborough. (*See under* 1828)
1841, 28 Oct.	William Vesey-FitzGerald, 1st lord Fitzgerald 1835
1843, 23 May	Frederick John Robinson, 1st e. of Ripon
1846, 10 July	Sir John Hobhouse. (*See under* 1835)
1852, 5 Feb.	Fox Maule, later Maule Ramsay (2nd lord Passmore 1852, 11th e. of Dalhousie [Scot.] 1860)
1852, 28 Feb.	John Charles Herries
1852, 30 Dec.	Sir Charles Wood, bt (1st viscount Halifax 1866)
1855, 3 Mar.	Robert Vernon Smith (1st lord Lyveden 1859)

1858, 6 Mar.	e. of Ellenborough. (*See under* 1828)
1858, 5 June	Edward Henry Stanley, commonly called lord Stanley (15th e. of Derby 1869)

SECRETARIES OF STATE FOR INDIA AND FOR INDIA AND FOR BURMA

The Government of India Act of 1858 (21 and 22 Vict., c. 106) transferred the control of India from the East India Company to the Crown, and ministerial responsibility for Indian affairs from the President of the Board of Control (*q.v.*) to the Secretary of State for India in Council. By the Government of India Act of 1935 (26 Geo. V, c. 2) the Secretary of State acquired the title of 'Secretary of State for India and for Burma'. So matters remained until 1947, when the Indian Independence Act of that year (10 and 11 Geo. VI, c. 30), transferred power from the United Kingdom Government to the Governments of India and Pakistan. The Burma Independence Act (11 & 12 Geo. VI, c. 3) followed later in the year. Responsibility for United Kingdom relations with the governments of India and Pakistan was then conferred upon the Secretary of State for Commonwealth Relations (*q.v.*) and for its relations with Burma upon the Secretary of State for Foreign Affairs (*q.v.*). For the parliamentary history of the Government of India Act (1858), *see* W. F. Monypenny and G. E. Buckle, *The Life of Benjamin Disraeli*, iv (1916), 83–177. *Cf.* also Sir Courtenay Ilbert, *The Government of India* (Oxford, 1922); Donovan Williams, *The India Office 1858–69* (Hoshiarpur, 1983); S. N. Singh, *The Secretary of State for India and his Council (1858–1919)* (Delhi, 1962); Sir Malcolm C. C. Seton, *The India Office* (1926).

1858, 2 Sept.	Edward Henry Stanley, commonly called lord Stanley (15th e. of Derby 1869)
1859, 18 June	Sir Charles Wood, 1st viscount Halifax 1866
1866, 16 Feb.	George Frederick Samuel Robinson, 2nd e. of Ripon (1st marquess of Ripon 1871)
1866, 6 July	Robert Arthur Talbot Gascoyne-Cecil, commonly called viscount Cranborne (3rd marquess of Salisbury 1868)
1867, 8 Mar.	Sir Stafford Henry Northcote (1st e. of Iddesleigh 1885)
1868, 9 Dec.	George Douglas Campbell, 8th duke of Argyll [Scot.] and 4th lord Sandridge (1st duke of Argyll [U.K.] 1892)
1874, 21 Feb.	Marquess of Salisbury. (*See under* 1866)
1878, 2 Apr.	Gathorne Gathorne-Hardy, 1st viscount Cranbrook 1878 (1st e. of Cranbrook 1892)
1880, 28 Apr.	Spencer Compton Cavendish, commonly called marquess of Hartington (8th duke of Devonshire 1891)
1882, 16 Dec.	John Wodehouse, 1st e. of Kimberley
1885, 24 June	Lord Randolph Churchill
1886, 6 Feb.	e. of Kimberley. (*See under* 1882)
1886, 3 Aug.	Sir Richard Assheton Cross, 1st viscount Cross 1886
1892, 18 Aug.	e. of Kimberley. (*See under* 1882)
1894, 10 Mar.	Henry Hartley Fowler (1st viscount Wolverhampton 1908)
1895, 4 July	Lord George Francis Hamilton
1903, 9 Oct.	William St John Fremantle Brodrick (1st e. of Midleton 1920)
1905, 11 Dec.	John Morley, 1st viscount Morley of Blackburn 1908
1910, 7 Nov.	Robert Offley Ashburton Crewe-Milnes, 1st e. of Crewe, 1st marquess of Crewe 1911
1915, 27 May	Joseph Austen Chamberlain
1917, 20 July	Edwin Samuel Montagu
1922, 21 Mar.	William Robert Wellesley Peel, 2nd viscount Peel (1st e. Peel 1929)

1924, 23 Jan.	Sir Sydney Haldane Olivier, 1st lord Olivier 1924
1924, 7 Nov.	Frederick Edwin Smith, 1st e. of Birkenhead
1928, 1 Nov.	Viscount Peel. (*See under* 1922)
1929, 8 June	William Wedgwood Benn (1st viscount Stansgate 1943)
1931, 26 Aug.	Sir Samuel John Gurney Hoare, bt (1st viscount Templewood 1944)
1935, 7 June	Lawrence John Lumley Dundas, 2nd marquess of Zetland
1940, 15 May	Leopold Charles Maurice Stennett Amery
1945, 3 Aug.	Frederick William Pethick-Lawrence, 1st lord Pethick-Lawrence 1945
1947, 23 Apr.	William Patrick Hare, 5th e. of Listowel, until 15 August 1947 (Secretary for Burma alone 15 Aug. 1947–4 Jan. 1948)

ADMIRALS AND FIRST LORDS OF THE ADMIRALTY

The first admiral appd by an English k. under that title was Barrau de Sescas, who on 1 March 1295 received a commission as admiral of the fleet of Bayonne. Later in the same year the commanders of the English fleet, Sir William Leyburn and Sir John de Botetourt, were described in a royal writ as admirals, as was Gervase Alard in a wardrobe account relating to 1300. The first commission of appointment of an admiral of an English fleet, which has been found, is that of Gervase Alard, who on 4 February 1303 was appd captain and admiral of the fleet of the Cinque Ports, and of all ports as far W. as those of Cornwall. The title of captain is linked with that of admiral until 1344. On occasion, however, the command of a fleet was entrusted to men appointed as captains only, or as captains and commanders. These officers, who have not been included in the following list, are often hard to distinguish from those appointed as captains and admirals. The function of the early admirals was to command fleets in time of war, and they do not emerge as judges of maritime law in courts of admiralty until about 1360. After approximately 1323 the customary practice of the fourteenth century was to divide the coastline of England into two admiralties. The admiral of the N. fleet had under his authority ships of all ports from the mouth of the Thames to the N.; the admiral of the W. fleet commanded those from the mouth of the Thames to the W. Sometimes, and particularly in the reign of Edward II, the ports from which the fleet of an admiral's command were to be drawn are not stated, or they do not conform to the traditional bounds of N. or W. The appointments of the admirals of these fleets are listed under 'Other Fleets'; if the ports of origin of the ships are given, they are stated in square brackets after the name of the admiral. If the purpose of the fleet is given in the patent, this also appears in square brackets.

An admiral of 'all the fleets' was commissioned in 1360; three are named, N., W. and S. References to a S. fleet are rare, and although the W. admiral is occasionally described as admiral of the S. and W., no separate admiral of the S. fleet was ever appd. In 1386 the N. and W. fleets were again brought under single command. This practice was repeated several times until in 1412 the title admiral of England first appears in a patent of appointment. No further change of title occurred until 1540 when John, lord Russell was styled lord admiral (*magnus admirallus*).

In the middle ages the care and maintenance of royal ships was entrusted to the clerks of the k.'s ships, after 1546 to a body that later became the Navy Board. Before 1619 the lord admirals were not charged with the administration of the navy in time of peace. In that year George

Villiers, marquess (later duke) of Buckingham, was appointed *magnus admirallus* and became responsible for the Navy Board;[1] this responsibility he and his successors never lost. On Buckingham's death in 1628 his office was put into commission (for the first time) and is described as the 'office and place of lord high admiral'. After the union with Scotland the title became lord high admiral of Great Britain. After 1628 the admiralty was frequently executed by a commission, and from November 1709 it was never out of commission, except in 1827–28, when the duke of Clarence, advised by a council, was lord high admiral. The office of first lord of the Admiralty succeeds that of the first commissioner of the commissions or boards of Admiralty of the seventeenth century. From 1628 every office-holder is deemed to be a first lord unless the words 'lord high admiral' appear after his name. The dates for the appointment of first lords are those of the letters patent setting up the commission over which they presided, except for the period 1908–35 when they are those of taking the oath. Letters patent which altered the commission without removing the first lord have been ignored.

The office of admiral and the administration of the navy may be studied in Sir N. Harris Nicolas, *A History of the Royal Navy*, 2 vols. (1847); *The English Government at Work, 1327–1336*, ed. J. F. Willard and W. A. Morris, i (Cambridge, Mass., 1940); R. G. Marsden, *Select Pleas in the Court of Admiralty*, 2 vols. (Selden Soc., vi and xi, 1892 and 1897); M. Oppenheim, *The Administration of the Royal Navy, 1506–1660* (1896); Sir Oswyn Murray, 'The Admiralty', in *The Mariners' Mirror*, xxiii–xxv (1937–9); C. S. L. Davies, 'The Administration of the Royal Navy under Henry VIII, and the Origins of the Navy Board', *EHR*, lxxx (1965); G. F. James and J. J. Sutherland Shaw, 'Admiralty Administration and Personnel, 1619–1714', in *BIHR*, xiv (1936–7); N. A. M. Rodger, *The Admiralty* (1979); J. C. Sainty, *Admiralty Officials, 1660–1870* (1975); J. M. Collinge, *Navy Board Officials, 1660–1832* (1978); J. P. W. Ehrman, *The Navy in the War of William III* (1958); ed. R. D. Merriman, *Queen Anne's Navy* (Navy Rec. Soc. ciii, 1961); D. A. Baugh, *British Naval Administration in the Age of Walpole* (1965).

The list to 1422 is based on the catalogues of admirals printed by Nicolas (i, App. v, and ii, App. xiii); these have been revised. The *Complete Peerage*, ii, App. D, and *Haydn's Book of Dignities* contain lists of Admirals and First Lords. The dates for the period 1619–1714 are taken from the article by James and Sutherland Shaw, and those from 1905 from the *London Gazette*.

CAPTAINS AND ADMIRALS
EDWARD I

	NORTHERN FLEET	WESTERN FLEET	OTHER FLEETS
1295, *12 Dec.*			William Leyburn, kt, and John de Botetourt, kt[2]
1297, *8 Mar.*			William Leyburn, kt[3]

[1] In 1832 the Navy Board, and other boards subordinate to the Admiralty Board proper, were abolished.

[2] Described as *amiraux de nostre navie Dengleterre*. On 7 June 1294 Leyburn had been appd captain of the king's sailors.

[3] Described as *amiral de la mer du (dit) Roy Dengleterre*.

	NORTHERN FLEET	WESTERN FLEET	OTHER FLEETS
1300, *25 Sept.*			Gervase Alard [Cinque Ports]
1303, 4 Feb.			Gervase Alard [Cinque Ports and W. to Cornwall; against Scotland]. Re-appd 5 June 1306
1306, 5 June	Edward Charles [against Scotland]		

EDWARD II

	NORTHERN FLEET	WESTERN FLEET	OTHER FLEETS
1310, *2 Aug.*			Simon Montague, kt[1]
1311, 1 June			John Argyll, kt [off W. Scotland]
1314, 12 Mar.			John Sturmy, kt, and Peter Bard [Royal and N. ships; against Scotland]
1314, 25 Mar.			John Argyll, kt [W., Welsh and Irish ships; off W. Scotland]
1315, *15 Mar.*			William Cray, kt, and Thomas de Hewys [off W. Scotland]
1315, 15 Mar.	John de Botetourt, lord Botetourt		
1315, 29 May			William Cray, kt[2] [W., Welsh, Irish and Cinque Ports; against Scotland]
1318, 28 June			John Athy, kt [off W. Scotland]
1319, 23 May			Simon Driby, kt, with William Thewell and Robert Ashman [against Scotland] Driby reappd alone 12 Aug. 1319. (*See* stewards, 1322)
1322, 13 May	John Perbroun		Robert Bataill [Cinque Ports; against Scotland]
1322, 19 May			Robert Leyburn, kt [Fleet on W. sea; against Scotland]
1323, 18 Apr.		Robert Bataill [against Scotland]	

[1] Described as *amirayl de nostre navie*. On 6 Aug. 1310 Montague was appd captain and commander of a fleet against Scotland. He had received a similar appointment on 30 Jan. 1307.
[2] Described as chief admiral on 3 July 1315.

	NORTHERN FLEET	WESTERN FLEET	OTHER FLEETS
1323, 16 May	John Perbroun reappd		
1324, 16 July			John Cromwell, lord Cromwell. (*See* stewards, 1314.) [To Gascony]
1324, *6 Aug.*	John Sturmy, kt	Robert Bendyn, kt [against Scotland]	
1324, 28 Sept.		Stephen Alard	
1325, 8 Dec.		Nicholas Kyriel, kt	
1326, ? 16 Sept.	Robert Leyburn, kt		

EDWARD III

1327, 21 Apr.	John Perbroun	Waresius de Valoignes, kt	
1333, 6 Apr.			John Perbroun and Henry Randolf [against Scotland]
1333, 16 July		William Clinton, lord Clinton (1st e. of Huntingdon 1337)	
1335, 2 Jan.	John Norwich, kt	Roger de Hegham, kt	
1335, 4 Apr.	John Howard, kt		
1335, 6 Apr.			Richard Holand, kt [Welsh and W. ports; to Ireland]
1335, 6 July		John Cobham, kt and Peter Bard	
1336, 10 Feb.	Thomas Ughtred, kt		
1336, 10 Apr.	John Norwich, kt	Geoffrey Say, lord Say	
1336, *Sept.*			John Ufford, kt [Ships of Newcastle and to the N.]
1336, 8 Nov.	John Ros, lord Ros (of Watton)		
1337, 14 Jan.	John, lord Ros, reappd with Robert Ufford, 1st e. of Suffolk Mar. 1337. (*See* stewards, 1336)	William Montague (1st e. of Salisbury Mar. 1337)	
1337, 11 Aug.	Walter Mauny, kt	Bartholomew Burghersh, lord Burghersh	
1338, 28 July	*Thomas Drayton, kt*	*Peter Bard*[1]	
1339, 18 Feb.	Robert Morley, lord Morley	William Trussell, kt	
1340, 20 Feb.			William Clinton, e. of Huntingdon [Thames to Portsmouth] Richard FitzAlan, earl of Arundel [Portsmouth and to the W.]

[1] Drayton and Bard were appd as vice-admirals, but were later described as admirals.

	NORTHERN FLEET	WESTERN FLEET	OTHER FLEETS
1340, 6 Mar.	Robert, lord Morley; reappd 5 Apr. 1341		
1341, 12 June		William Clinton, e. of Huntingdon	
1342, 3 Apr.	Robert, lord Morley reappd	John Montgomery, kt	
1342, 20 Dec.	William Trussell, kt	Robert Beaupel, kt	
1344, 8 May	Robert Ufford, e. of Suffolk	Reginald Cobham kt	

ADMIRALS[1]

	NORTHERN FLEET	WESTERN FLEET	OTHER FLEETS
1345, 23 Feb.		Richard Fitz-Alan, e. of Arundel	
1347, 23 Feb.		John Montgomery, kt	
1347, 8 Mar.	John Howard, kt		
1348, 14 Mar.	Walter Mauny, lord Mauny	Reginald, lord Cobham	
1348, 6 June	Robert, lord Morley; reappd 22 July 1350		
1349, 17 Aug.			John Beauchamp,[2] lord Beauchamp of Warwick [protection of shipping]
1351, 8 Mar.	William Bohun, 1st e. of Northampton	Henry of 'Grosmont', 1st duke of Lancaster	
1353, *15 Oct.*		Thomas Beauchamp, 3rd e. of Warwick	
1354, 6 Mar.			John Gibbon [expedition of duke of Lancaster to France]
1355, 5 Mar.	Robert, lord Morley	John, lord Beauchamp of Warwick	
1356, 1 May		Guy Brian, lord Brian. (*See* stewards, 1359)	
1360, 18 July			John, lord Beauchamp of Warwick [S., N. and W.]
1361, 26 Jan.			Robert Herle, kt [S., N. and W.]
1364, 7 July			Ralph Spigurnell, kt [S., N. and W.]
1369, 28 Apr.		Robert Ashton, kt (*See* treasurers, 1375)	
1369, 12 June	Nicholas Tamworth, kt		

[1] The title captain and admiral is not used again, with the exception of Henry, duke of Lancaster, in 1351.
[2] Described as admiral of the W. fleet on 20 Mar. 1350.

138

	NORTHERN FLEET	WESTERN FLEET	OTHER FLEETS
1370, 6 Feb.			Guy, lord Brian [Southampton and to the W.]
1370, 30 May	John Nevill, lord Nevill. (*See* stewards, 1371)	Guy, lord Brian	
1370, 8 July			Ralph Ferrers, kt [expedition of Sir Robert Knolles to France]
1371, 6 Oct.	Ralph Ferrers, kt	Robert Ashton, kt	
1372, 7 Mar.	William Nevill, kt	Philip Courtenay, kt	
1376, 16 July	William Ufford, 2nd e. of Suffolk	William Montague, 2nd e. of Salisbury	
1376, 24 Nov.	Michael de la Pole, kt (*See* chancellors, 1383)	Robert Hales, kt, prior of the Hospital of St John of Jerusalem in England. (*See* treasurers, 1381)	

RICHARD II

	NORTHERN FLEET	WESTERN FLEET	OTHER FLEETS
1377, 14 Aug.	Michael de la Pole; reappd	Robert Hales; reappd	
1377, 5 Dec.	Thomas Beauchamp, 4th e. of Warwick	Richard FitzAlan, e. of Arundel	
1378, 10 Sept.		Hugh Calveley, kt	
1378, 5 Nov.	Thomas Percy, kt (*See* stewards, 1393)		
1380, 8 Mar.		Philip Courtenay, kt	
1380, 8 Apr.	William Elmham, kt		
1382, 22 May			John de Roches, kt [Southampton and to the W.]
1382, 26 Oct.	Walter FitzWalter, lord FitzWalter	John de Roches, kt	
1383, 13 Nov.		Edward Courtenay, 3rd e. of Devon	
1383, 2 Dec.	Henry Percy, 1st e. of Northumberland		
1385, 29 Jan.	Thomas Percy, kt	John Raddington, kt, prior of the Hospital of St John of Jerusalem in England	
1386, 22 Feb.	Philip Darcy, lord Darcy	Thomas Trivet, kt	
1386, 10 Dec.			Richard FitzAlan, e. of Arundel [W. and N.][1]

[1] By an indenture of 24 Mar. 1388 it was agreed that he should hold office for the next five years (Exchequer K.R., Acc. Various, E.101/41/4). This grant was presumably cancelled on Richard II's assumption of full powers in 1389. Described as admiral of England 16 Nov. 1388.

	NORTHERN FLEET	WESTERN FLEET	OTHER FLEETS
1389, 18 May		John Holand, 1st e. of Hunting-don (1st duke of Exeter 1397)	
1389, 20 May	John Beaumont, lord Beaumont		
1389, 31 May			John de Roches, kt [W. and N.]
1389, 22 June	John, lord Beaumont	e. of Huntingdon	
1391, 22 Mar.	Edward 'of York', e. of Rutland (1st duke of Aumale 1397; 2nd duke of York 1402)		
1391, 29 Nov.			Edward 'of York', e. of Rutland [W. and N.][1]
1398, 9 May			John Beaufort, 1st marquess of Dorset and e. of Somerset [W. and N.; for life]
1399, 16 Jan.			Thomas Percy, 1st e. of Worcester [W. and N.]

HENRY IV

	NORTHERN FLEET	WESTERN FLEET	OTHER FLEETS
			e. of Worcester remained in office
1401, 20 Apr.	Richard, lord Grey of Codnor	Thomas Rempston, kt	
1403, 5 Nov.		Thomas, lord Berkeley	
1403, 28 Nov.	Thomas Beaufort, kt (1st e. of Dorset 1412, duke of Exeter 1416)		
1405, 20 Feb.			Thomas, son of K. Henry IV (1st duke of Clarence 1412). [K.'s admiral]
1406, 28 Apr.	Nicholas Blackburn	Richard Clitheroe[2]	
1406, 23 Dec.[3]			John Beaufort, e. of Somerset [W. and N.]
1407, 8 May			Edmund Holand, e. of Kent. *Ob.* 15 Sept. 1408 [W. and N.]
1408, 21 Sept.			Thomas Beaufort.[4] (*See under* 1403) [W. and N.; for life]

[1] Described as admiral of England and Ireland 12 Aug. 1396.
[2] Blackburn and Clitheroe were nominated by the merchants in Parliament, and were appointed to hold office for one year from 1 May 1406.
[3] Confirmation of grant for life by Richard II on 9 May 1398.
[4] Reappd (for life) as admiral of England, Ireland and Aquitaine on 3 Mar. 1412.

ADMIRALS

HENRY V

ADMIRAL OF ENGLAND	OTHER ADMIRALS
Thomas Beaufort, e. of Dorset; remained in office (duke of Exeter 1416)	

1416, 6 July		Thomas Morley, lord Morley [fleet sailing to Southampton]
1416, 26 July		Walter Hungerford, kt. (*See* stewards, 1415, and treasurers, 1426) [expedition of duke of Bedford]
1421, 2 Mar.		William Bardolf, kt [to guard the sea]

ADMIRALS OF ENGLAND

HENRY VI

Thomas Beaufort, duke of Exeter, remained in office

1426, 26 July[1]	John, 1st duke of Bedford. *Ob.* 15 Sept. 1435
1435, 2 Oct.[2]	John Holand, e. of Huntingdon; cr. duke of Exeter 1444. *Ob.* 5 Aug. 1447
1447, 9 Aug.[3]	William de la Pole, 1st marquess of Suffolk. (*See* stewards, 1435) *Ob.* 2 May 1450
1450, 23 July[4]	Henry Holand, duke of Exeter. Attainted Nov. 1461

EDWARD IV

1462, 30 July	William Nevill, 1st e. of Kent. (*See* stewards, 1461)
1462, 12 Oct.	Richard, 1st duke of Gloucester. Exiled 3 Oct. 1470

HENRY VI (readeption)

1471, 2 Jan.	Richard Nevill, e. of Warwick. *Ob.* 14 Apr. 1471

EDWARD IV (restoration)

1471, Apr.	Richard, duke of Gloucester, resumed office

EDWARD V

Richard, duke of Gloucester, remained in office

RICHARD III

1483, 25 July	John Howard, 1st duke of Norfolk. (*See* kps of the wardrobe, 1468.) *Ob.* 22 Aug. 1485

HENRY VII

1485, 21 Sept.	John de Vere, 13th e. of Oxford

HENRY VIII

John de Vere, e. of Oxford, remained in office. *Ob.* 10 Mar. 1513

1513, 17 Mar.	Edward Howard, kt. *Ob.* 25 Apr. 1513
1513, 4 May	Thomas Howard, lord Howard. Cr. e. of Surrey 1514, 2nd duke of Norfolk, 1524
1525, 16 July	Henry Fitzroy, 1st duke of Richmond 1525. *Ob.* 22 July 1536
1536, 16 Aug.	William Fitzwilliam, 1st e. of Southampton 1537
1540, 28 July	John Russell, lord Russell (1st e. of Bedford 1550)

[1] Appointment for the life of Thomas Beaufort and aft. his d. during pleasure.
[2] Grant renewed for life 14 Feb. 1446, with survivorship to his s. Henry.
[3] During the minority of Henry Holand, duke of Exeter.
[4] Date of livery of his father's lands

1542, Dec.[1]	Edward Seymour, 1st e. of Hertford (1st duke of Somerset 1547)
1543, 26 Jan.	John Dudley, viscount Lisle (1st e. of Warwick 1547, 1st duke of Northumberland 1551

EDWARD VI

1547, 17 Feb.	Thomas Seymour, lord Seymour 1547. Attainted Mar. 1549
1549, 28 Oct.	John Dudley, e. of Warwick. (*See under* 1543)
1550, 14 May	Edward Clinton (otherwise Fiennes), lord Clinton (1st e. of Lincoln 1572)

MARY

1554,[2] 20 Mar.	William Howard, lord Howard of Effingham, 1554
1558, 10 Feb.	Edward Clinton, lord Clinton. (*See under* 1550.) *Ob.* 16 Jan. 1585

ELIZABETH I

1585, 8 July	Charles Howard, lord Howard of Effingham, 1st e. of Nottingham 1597
1619, 28 Jan.	George Villiers, 1st marquess of Buckingham, 1st duke of Buckingham 1623; *ob.* 13 Aug. 1628
1628, 20 Sept.	Richard Weston, 1st lord Weston 1628, 1st e. of Portland 1633, lord high treasurer
1635, 10 Apr.	Robert Bertie, 1st e. of Lindsey, lord great chamberlain
1636, 16 Mar.	William Juxon, bp of London 1633–60, lord high treasurer
1638, 13 Apr.	Algernon Percy, 4th e. of Northumberland (lord high admiral)[3]
1643, Dec.	Francis Cottington, 1st lord Cottington, lord high treasurer (for the king)

COMMANDERS (AND COMMISSIONERS) IN CHARGE OF THE NAVY, 1642–1660

1643, 7 Dec.	Robert Rich 2nd e. of Warwick, lord high admiral (C.-in-C. of the fleet since 1 July 1642)
1645, 19 Apr.	committee of 6 peers and 12 MPs to execute the office of lord high admiral
1645, 4 Oct.	5 more peers and 10 more MPs added to same
1648, 29 May	Warwick again lord high admiral
1649, 23 Feb.	powers of lord high admiral transferred to the Council of State (which had a series of Admiralty committees, 1649–53)
1652, 4 Dec.	Admiralty and Navy Commissioners (a new body): Sir Henry Vane jr, Col. George Thompson, John Carew, Major Richard Salwey (all MPs)
1652, 10 Dec.	James Russell and John Langley (added)
1653, 14 July	Robert Blake, general-at-sea, John Carew, Richard Salwey, George Monck, general-at-sea, John Langley, Denis Hollister, Major William Burton, Col. Nathaniel Rich, Lt-Col. Edward Salmon, Lt-Col. Thomas Kelsey
1653, 26 July	M.-Gen. John Disbrowe (added)
1653, 3 Dec.	Blake, Monck, Disbrowe, Burton, Kelsey, also general-at-sea William Penn, Col. Philip Jones, Col. John Clerke, John Stone, Edward Horseman, Vincent Gookin
1654, 31 Mar.	Col. Anthony Rouse (added)
1654, 2 Sept.	Clerke, Rouse, Kelsey, Penn, Monck, Disbrowe, Blake, Jones
1655, 8 Nov.	Clerke, M.-Gen. John Lambert (dism. 13 June 1657), Kelsey, Col. Edward Montague, Col. William Sydenham, Monck, Disbrowe, Blake (*ob.* 7 Aug., 1657), Jones, Edward Hopkins, Salmon
1656, 4 Sept.	only Clerke, Kelsey, Hopkins, Salmon salaried as such. Major Robert Beake (added)

[1] Appears in the council as lord admiral, 28 Dec.

[2] This appointment was announced by the queen in a letter read in the council 26 Oct. 1553. The patent was not made out until 20 Mar. 1554.

[3] Commission revoked by Charles I, 25 June 1642. He continued to act for Parliament until 19·Oct. 1642, then became first lord.

1659, 26– 31 May	Clerke (continued), Sir Henry Vane MP (restored)[1] Col. Herbert Morley MP, Valentine Wauton MP, George Thompson MP (restored), John Carew MP, Richard Salwey MP, John Langley (all restored), William Say MP, Thomas Boone MP, Edward Salmon, Thomas Kelsey (continued)
1660, 28 Jan.	Robert Reynolds MP, John Lisle MP, Morley, Richard Bradshaw, Wauton, vice-admiral John Lawson, George Thompson, Monck, Edmund West MP, Sir Michael Livesey bt MP, Carew Ralegh MP, Thomas Chaloner MP, John Lenthall MP, John Dormer MP, Boone, Henry Darley MP, John Weaver MP, Col. Thomas Middleton MP, Edward Bushell, Slingsby Bethell, George Cooper (most or all of these continued to act until May 1660)

ADMIRALS OF ENGLAND

CHARLES II

1660, 2 July	James, duke of York and Albany (K. James II 1685) (lord high admiral)[2]
1673, 15 June	K. Charles II (lord high admiral)
1673, 9 July	Prince Rupert, 1st duke of Cumberland
1679, 14 May	Sir Henry Capell (1st lord Capell 1692)
1681, 19 Feb.	Daniel Finch, commonly called lord Finch, 2nd e. of Nottingham 1682 (7th e. of Winchilsea 1729)
1684, 19 May	K. Charles II (lord high admiral)
1685, 6 Feb.	K. James II (lord high admiral)
1689, 12 Feb.	K. William III (lord high admiral)[3]
1689, 28 Feb.	Arthur Herbert, 1st e. of Torrington 1689 (lord high admiral until 8 Mar., then first lord)
1690, 20 Jan.	Thomas Herbert, 8th e. of Pembroke and 5th e. of Montgomery
1692, 10 Mar.	Charles Cornwallis, 3rd lord Cornwallis of Eye
1693, 15 Apr.	Anthony Carey, 5th viscount of Falkland [Scot.]
1694, 2 May	Edward Russell, 1st e. of Orford 1697
1699, 31 May	John Egerton, 3rd e. of Bridgwater
1701, 4 Apr.	e. of Pembroke (lord high admiral from 26 Jan. 1701). (*See under* 1690)
1702, 20 May	Prince George of Denmark[4]
1708, 28 Oct.	Queen Anne (lord high admiral)
1708, 29 Nov.	e. of Pembroke. (*See under* 1690)
1709, 8 Nov.	e. of Orford. (*See under* 1694)
1710, 4 Oct.	Sir John Leake
1712, 30 Sept.	Thomas Wentworth, 1st e. of Strafford (1st duke of Strafford 1722)
1714, 14 Oct.	e. of Orford. (*See under* 1694)
1717, 16 Apr.	James Berkeley, 3rd e. of Berkeley
1727, 29 July	George Byng, 1st viscount Torrington
1733, 25 Jan.	Sir Charles Wager
1742, 19 Mar.	Daniel Finch, 8th e. of Winchilsea and 3rd e. of Nottingham
1744, 27 Dec.	John Russell, 4th duke of Bedford
1748, 20 Feb.	John Montagu, 4th e. of Sandwich
1751, 22 June	George Anson, 1st lord Anson
1756, 19 Nov.	Richard Grenville, later Grenville-Temple, 2nd e. Temple
1757, 6 Apr.	e. of Nottingham. (*See under* 1742)
1757, 2 July	Lord Anson; *ob*. 6 June 1762
1762, 19 June	George Montagu, later Montagu-Dunk, 3rd e. of Halifax
1763, 1 Jan.	George Grenville
1763, 23 Apr.	e. of Sandwich. (*See under* 1748)

[1] Vane and Salwey ceased to act after the end of Dec. 1659 and possibly also Clerke and Kelsey.
[2] This is the date of his letters patent, but he had been nominally lord high admiral from 1649 and effectively so from 2 July 1660.
[3] He was *de facto* lord high admiral from 18 Dec. 1688.
[4] Advised by a council.

1763, 10 Sept.	John Perceval, 2nd e. of Egmont [Irish], 1st lord Lovel and Holland [G.B.]
1766, 10 Sept.	Sir Charles Saunders
1766, 10 Dec.	Sir Edward Hawke (1st lord Hawke 1776)
1771, 12 Jan.	e. of Sandwich. (*See under* 1748)
1782, 30 Mar.	Augustus Keppel, 1st viscount Keppel 1782
1783, 28 Jan.	Richard Howe, 1st viscount Howe (1st e. Howe 1788)
1783, 8 Apr.	Viscount Keppel. (*See under* 1782)
1783, 30 Dec.	Viscount Howe. (*See above*)
1788, 12 July	John Pitt, 2nd e. of Chatham
1794, 20 Dec.	George John Spencer, 2nd e. Spencer
1801, 19 Feb.	John Jervis, 1st e. of St Vincent
1804, 15 May	Henry Dundas, 1st viscount Melville
1805, 30 Apr.	Sir Charles Middleton, bt, 1st lord Barham 1805
1806, 11 Feb.	Charles Grey, 1st e. Grey
1806, 29 Sept.	Thomas Grenville
1807, 4 Apr.	Henry Phipps, 1st lord Mulgrave of Mulgrave (1st e. of Mulgrave 1812)
1810, 1 May	Charles Philip Yorke
1812, 24 Mar.	Robert Dundas, later Saunders-Dundas, 2nd viscount Melville
1827, 17 Apr.	William, 1st duke of Clarence (King William IV 1830) (lord high admiral)[1]
1828, 17 Sept.	Viscount Melville. (*See under* 1812.) *Vac.* Nov. 1830
1830, 25 Nov.	Sir James Robert George Graham, bt
1834, 7 June	George Eden, 2nd lord Auckland (1st e. of Auckland 1839)
1834, 22 Dec.	Thomas Philip Robinson, later Weddell, later de Grey, 2nd e. de Grey
1835, 23 Apr.	Lord Auckland. (*See under* 1834)
1835, 15 Sept.	Gilbert Elliot-Murray-Kynynmound, 2nd e. of Minto
1841, 6 Sept.	Thomas Hamilton, 9th e. of Haddington [Scot.], 1st lord Melros [U.K.]
1846, 8 Jan.	Edward Law, 1st e. of Ellenborough
1846, 7 July	e. of Auckland. (*See under* 1834.) *Ob.* 1 Jan. 1849
1849, 15 Jan.	Sir Francis Thornhill Baring, bt (1st lord Northbrook 1866)
1852, 28 Feb.	Algernon Percy, 4th duke of Northumberland
1852, 30 Dec.	Sir James Graham. (*See under* 1830)
1855, 13 Mar.	Sir Charles Wood, bt (1st viscount Halifax 1866)
1858, 8 Mar.	Sir John Somerset Pakington (1st lord Hampton 1874)
1859, 27 June	Edward Adolphus Seymour, 12th duke of Somerset
1866, 12 July	Sir John Pakington. (*See under* 1858)
1867, 8 Mar.	Henry Thomas Lowry Corry
1868, 21 Dec.	Hugh Culling Eardley Childers
1871, 9 Mar.	George Joachim Goschen (1st viscount Goschen 1900)
1874, 4 Mar.	George Ward Hunt
1877, 14 Aug.	William Henry Smith
1880, 12 May	Thomas George Baring, 1st e. of Northbrook
1885, 1 July	George Francis Hamilton, commonly called lord George Hamilton
1886, 15 Feb.	George Frederick Samuel Robinson, 1st marquess of Ripon
1886, 9 Aug.	Lord George Hamilton. (*See under* 1885)
1892, 25 Aug.	John Poyntz Spencer, 5th e. Spencer
1895, 6 July	George Joachim Goschen. (*See under* 1871)
1900, 12 Nov.	William Waldegrave Palmer, 2nd e. of Selborne
1905, 27 Mar.	Frederick Archibald Vaughan Campbell, 3rd e. Cawdor
1905, 22 Dec.	Edward Marjoribanks, 2nd lord Tweedmouth
1908, 16 Apr.	Reginald McKenna
1911, 24 Oct.	Winston Leonard Spencer Churchill (K.G. 1953)
1915, 27 May	Arthur James Balfour (1st e. of Balfour 1922)
1916, 11 Dec.	Sir Edward Carson (1st lord Carson 1922)
1917, 20 July	Sir Eric Geddes
1919, 14 Jan.	Walter Hume Long (1st viscount Long 1921)
1921, 14 Feb.	Arthur Hamilton Lee, 1st lord Lee of Fareham (1st viscount Lee of Fareham 1922)

---

[1] Advised by a council.

144

1922, 25 Oct.	Leopold Charles Maurice Stennett Amery
1924, 23 Jan.	Frederic John Napier Thesiger, 1st viscount Chelmsford
1924, 7 Nov.	William Clive Bridgeman (1st viscount Bridgeman 1929)
1929, 8 June	Albert Victor Alexander (1st viscount Alexander of Hillsborough 1950)
1931, 26 Aug.	Sir Joseph Austen Chamberlain, K.G.
1931, 9 Nov.	Sir Bolton Meredith Eyres-Monsell, 1st viscount Monsell 1935
1936, 12 June	Sir Samuel John Gurney Hoare (1st viscount Templewood 1944)
1937, 28 May	Alfred Duff-Cooper (1st viscount Norwich 1952); *vac.* 1 Oct. 1938
1938, 27 Oct.	James Richard Stanhope, 7th e. Stanhope
1939, 3 Sept.	Winston Leonard Spencer Churchill (K.G. 1953)
1940, 16 May	Albert Victor Alexander. (*See under* 1929)
1945, 29 May	Brendan Bracken (1st viscount Bracken 1952)
1945, 4 Aug.	Albert Victor Alexander. (*See under* 1929)
1946, 7 Oct.	George Henry Hall, 1st viscount Hall 1946; *res.* 24 May 1951
1951, 30 May	Francis Aungier Pakenham, 1st lord Pakenham (7th e. of Longford 1961)
1951, 5 Nov.	James Purdon Lewes Thomas, 1st viscount Cilcennin 1955
1956, 3 Sept.	Quintin McGarel Hogg, 2nd viscount Hailsham
1957, 17 Jan.	George Nigel Douglas-Hamilton, 10th e. of Selkirk [Scot.], S.R.P. 1945
1959, 16 Oct.	Peter Alexander Rupert Carrington, 6th lord Carrington
1963, 21 Oct.	George Patrick John Rushworth Jellicoe, 2nd e. Jellicoe

In 1964 the post was discontinued on the creation of a unified Ministry of Defence.

LORD PRESIDENTS OF THE COUNCIL

Although Coke,[1] Sir Harris Nicolas,[2] Stubbs and others[3] have claimed an early origin for this office, later authorities have rejected their views. Baldwin dismisses early references to the title 'lord president' as descriptive and personal rather than official;[4] Pollard concludes that the evidence for such an office in the Middle Ages is ambiguous.[5]

A president of the Council of Wales was appointed in 1473, and this precedent appears to have been followed in England by Henry VII. The lord president is first mentioned in 1497, and in 1529 an Act of Parliament (21 Hen. VIII, c. 20) gave him official rank below the chancellor and treasurer and above the keeper of the privy seal. Pollard[6] argues, however, that even in the reign of Henry VII, 'the only conclusive evidence' for the existence of the office 'is an apparently unique reference in the *Calendar of Patent Rolls* to "Edmund Dudeley, esquire, president of the council" '. He suggests, further, that the Act of 1529 was 'merely designed to give high official rank to Suffolk, the king's brother-in-law'. The earliest certain appointment is in fact Suffolk's. During the next one hundred and fifty years the office was not always filled, and the list of lord presidents is continuous only from 1679.

The lord president is appointed by a declaration of the sovereign in council and holds office during pleasure. The Privy Council Register records the declaration and that the president 'took his place at the Board

[1] *Fourth Institute*, cap. II.
[2] *Proceedings and Ordinances of the Privy Council of England* (1834–37), i, p. iv.
[3] J. F. Baldwin, *The King's Council in England during the Middle Ages* (1913), 369.
[4] *Ibid.*
[5] 'Council, Star Chamber and Privy Council under the Tudors', *EHR*, xxxvii (1922), 337–60.
[6] *Ibid.*, 353.

accordingly'. The president's salary was calculated from this date. His appointment was usually announced in the *London Gazette* from the inception of that journal.

The list that follows is based upon that in *The Complete Peerage*[1] and the dates of the first four lord presidents are taken from it. From 1535 the dates are those given in the Privy Council Register (PRO, P.C. 2), from 1841 to 1939 those in the *London Gazette*, and since 1940 those in the *Court Circular*.

1530, Feb.	Charles Brandon, 1st duke of Suffolk.[2] *Ob.* 14 Aug. 1545
1546, Jan.	William Paulet, 1st lord St John, 1st e. of Wiltshire 1550 (1st marquess of Winchester 1551)[3]
1550, Feb.	John Dudley, 1st e. of Warwick, 1st duke of Northumberland 1551.[4] *Vac.* 19 July 1553

[Gap 1553–1621]

1621, Sept.	Henry Montague, 1st viscount Mandeville, 1st e. of Manchester 1626[5]
1628, 15 July	James Ley, 1st e. of Marlborough
1628, 14 Dec.	Edward Conway, 1st viscount Conway.[6] *Ob.* 3 Jan. 1631

[Gap 1631–49]

PRESIDENTS OF THE COUNCIL OF STATE, 1649–59

John Bradshaw, later Sergt-at-Law, 10 Feb. 1649–29 Nov. 1651. For its first week in Feb. 1649 Oliver Cromwell took the chair; from Dec. 1651 to Dec. 1653 the chairmanship rotated monthly. 16 Dec. 1653–17 Dec. 1657, and again 18 Jan.

---

[1] Ed. V. Gibbs, ii, 622.

[2] Suffolk may have been appointed on 6 Feb. 1530 (Pollard, quoting *Letters and Papers of Henry VIII*, iv (3), no. 6199). Suffolk and his immediate successors held the presidency with the office of great master of the household. His predecessor as great master, the earl of Shrewsbury, may possibly have been lord president also (*Complete Peerage*, ii, 622).

[3] Pollard says that though he succeeded Suffolk as great master, Winchester was not made lord president until 21 Mar. 1547. This is the date on which he is first mentioned as lord president in the Privy Council Register (*Acts of the Privy Council, 1547–50*, 70), but he appears as grand master and lord president on 12 March 1547 in the patent rolls Edward VI (*Cal. Patent Rolls, 1547–48*, 97). He is not mentioned as lord president in the Register after 3 Feb. 1550 (*EHR*, xxxvii, 354).

[4] He became grand master on 20 Feb. 1550 (*Cal. Patent Rolls, 1549–51*, 189). In the Privy Council he is first mentioned as lord president on 14 April 1551 (*Acts of the Privy Council, 1550–52*, 259). He is mentioned as lord president in *Lords' Journals*, i (1552), 391. Pollard says 'it was he who, wisely avoiding the title of lord protector, made the office of lord president something very like it'. He held office until July 1553 (*Complete Peerage*, ii, 622). He was succeeded as grand master by earl of Arundel [though that title was soon abandoned in favour of the older one, of lord steward (*Acts of the Privy Council, 1552–54*, xxii)]. According to Pollard, Arundel became president as well as steward at Mary's accession, and continued to be called president until the end of the session 1555. Elizabeth I made him her steward but not president. E. R. Turner (*The Privy Council of England in the 17th and 18th Centuries*, i, 105) quotes a despatch of the Venetian ambassador describing Arundel as 'presidente del consiglio' in 1554. He also says that the lord president was named in an account of proceedings in parliament in 1572.

[5] *Complete Peerage*, ii, 622, adds that the office had been in suspension since the accession of Mary (but *see* note above), and that it was given to Mandeville 'as a solace for being compelled to give up the High Treasurership and . . . no one knew what its duties were'.

[6] Appointed lord president 'upon the voluntary resignation of that place by the earl of Marleborough' (Privy Council Register, vol. 38, fo. 627).

1658–late Apr. or early May 1659, Henry Lawrence. From May 1659 to Apr. 1660 again the chairmanship rotated monthly.

[Gap 1660–79]

1679, 21 Apr.	Anthony Ashley Cooper, 1st e. of Shaftesbury. Struck off the list of the Council 15 Oct. 1679
1679, 24 Oct.	John Robartes, 1st e. of Radnor 1679
1684, 24 Aug.	Laurence Hyde, 1st e. of Rochester
1685, 18 Feb.	George Saville, 1st marquess of Halifax. Struck off the list of the Council 21 Oct. 1685
1685, 4 Dec.	Robert Spencer, 2nd e. of Sunderland (also a Secretary of State from 1683).[1] Struck off the list of the Council 29 Oct. 1688.
1689, 14 Feb.	Thomas Osborne, 1st e. of Danby, 1st marquess of Carmarthen 1689, 1st duke of Leeds 1694[2]
1699, 18 May	Thomas Herbert, 8th e. of Pembroke and 5th e. of Montgomery
1702, 29 Jan.	Charles Seymour, 6th duke of Somerset
1702, 9 July	e. of Pembroke and Montgomery. (*See under* 1699)
1708, 25 Nov.	John Somers, 1st lord Somers
1710, 21 Sept.	e. of Rochester. *Ob.* 21 May 1711. (*See under* 1684)
1711, 14 June	John Sheffield, 1st duke of Buckinghamshire and of Normanby
1714, 22 Sept.	Daniel Finch, 2nd e. of Nottingham (7th e. of Winchilsea 1729).[3] *Vac.* 28 Feb. 1716
1716, 6 July	William Cavendish, 2nd duke of Devonshire. *Vac.* 30 Mar. 1717
1718, 16 Mar.	Charles Spencer, 3rd e. of Sunderland
1719, 6 Feb.	Evelyn Pierrepont, 1st duke of Kingston-upon-Hull
1720, 11 June	Charles Townshend, 2nd viscount Townshend
1721, 25 June	Henry Boyle, 1st lord Carleton
1725, 27 Mar.	Duke of Devonshire. (*See under* 1716.) *Ob.* 4 June 1729
1730, 8 May	Thomas Trevor, 1st lord Trevor of Bromham. *Ob.* 19 June 1730
1730, 31 Dec.	Spencer Compton, 1st lord Wilmington, 1st e. of Wilmington 1730
1742, 13 Feb.	William Stanhope, 1st e. of Harrington 1742
1745, 3 Jan.	Lionel Cranfield Sackville, 1st duke of Dorset (also lord lieutenant of Ireland from 6 Dec. 1750)
1751, 17 June	John Carteret, 2nd e. of Granville. *Ob.* 2 Jan. 1763
1763, 9 Sept.	John Russell, 4th duke of Bedford
1765, 12 July	Daniel Finch, 8th e. of Winchilsea and 3rd e. of Nottingham
1766, 30 July	Robert Henley, 1st e. of Northington
1767, 23 Dec.	Granville Leveson-Gower, 2nd e. Gower (1st marquess of Stafford 1786)
1779, 24 Nov.	Henry Bathurst, 2nd e. Bathurst
1782, 27 Mar.	Charles Pratt, 1st lord Camden (1st e. Camden 1786)
1783, 2 Apr.	David Murray, 7th viscount Stormont [Scot.] (2nd e. of Mansfield [G.B.] 1793)
1783, 19 Dec.	e. of Gower. (*See under* 1767)
1784, 1 Dec.	Lord Camden. (*See under* 1782). *Ob.* 18 Apr. 1794
1794, 11 July	William Fitzwilliam, later Wentworth-Fitzwilliam, 2nd e. Fitzwilliam
1794, 17 Dec.	e. of Mansfield. (*See under* 1783)
1796, 21 Sept.	John Pitt, 2nd e. of Chatham
1801, 30 July	William Henry Cavendish, later Cavendish-Bentinck, 3rd duke of Portland
1805, 14 Jan.	Henry Addington, 1st viscount Sidmouth 1805
1805, 10 July	John Jeffreys, 2nd e. Camden (1st marquess Camden 1812)

[1] The king declared 'that he thought the place agreed well with that of Secretary of State' (Privy Council Register, vol. 71, fo. 167). There is no evidence in the Privy Council Register or the *Gazette* that Viscount Preston, who became Secretary of State for the Northern Department when Sunderland was dism. from the Southern Secretaryship, was 'chosen president of the Council at the end of October 1688', as stated in *DNB*.

[2] Ceased to attend after May 1695.

[3] The Privy Council was dissolved on 29 Sept. 1714 and was re-sworn on 1 Oct. 1714, Nottingham again being declared lord president (Privy Council Register, vol. 85, fos. 86, 88). Haydn is wrong in giving his successor as the earl of Dorset.

1806, 19 Feb.	e. Fitzwilliam. (*See under* 1794)
1806, 8 Oct.	Viscount Sidmouth. (*See under* 1805)
1807, 26 Mar.	e. Camden. (*See under* 1805)
1812, 8 Apr.	Viscount Sidmouth. (*See under* 1805)
1812, 11 June	Dudley Ryder, 1st e. of Harrowby
1827, 17 Aug.	William Henry Cavendish Bentinck, later Scott-Bentinck, later Cavendish-Scott-Bentinck, 4th duke of Portland
1828, 26 Jan.	Henry Bathurst, 3rd e. of Bathurst
1830, 22 Nov.	Henry Petty, later Petty-Fitzmaurice, 3rd marquess of Lansdowne
1834, 15 Dec.	James Erskine, later St Clair-Erskine, 2nd e. of Rosslyn
1835, 18 Apr.	Marquess of Lansdowne. (*See under* 1830)
1841, 3 Sept.	James Archibald Stuart-Wortley-Mackenzie, 1st lord Wharncliffe
1846, 21 Jan.	Walter Francis Montagu-Douglas-Scott, 5th duke of Buccleuch and 7th duke of Queensberry [Scot.] and 5th e. of Doncaster [E.]
1846, 6 July	Marquess of Lansdowne. (*See under* 1830)
1852, 27 Feb.	William Lowther, 2nd e. of Lonsdale
1852, 28 Dec.	Granville George Leveson-Gower, 2nd e. Granville
1854, 12 June	Lord John Russell (1st e. Russell 1861)
1855, 8 Feb.	e. Granville. (*See under* 1852)
1858, 26 Feb.	James Brownlow William Cecil, later Gascoyne-Cecil, 2nd marquess of Salisbury
1859, 18 June	e. Granville. (*See under* 1852)
1866, 6 July	Richard Plantagenet Campbell Temple-Nugent-Brydges-Chandos-Grenville, 3rd duke of Buckingham and Chandos
1867, 8 Mar.	John Winston Spencer Churchill, 7th duke of Marlborough
1868, 9 Dec.	George Frederick Samuel Robinson, 2nd e. of Ripon, 1st marquess of Ripon 1871
1873, 9 Aug.	Henry Austin Bruce, 1st lord Aberdare 1873
1874, 21 Feb.	Charles Henry Gordon-Lennox, 6th duke of Richmond and Lennox, 1st duke of Gordon 1874
1880, 28 Apr.	John Poyntz Spencer, 5th e. Spencer (also lord lieutenant of Ireland from April 1882)
1883, 19 Mar.	Chichester Samuel Parkinson-Fortescue, 1st lord Carlingford
1885, 24 June	Gathorne Hardy, later Gathorne-Hardy, 1st viscount Cranbrook (1st e. of Cranbrook 1892)
1886, 6 Feb.	e. Spencer. (*See under* 1880)
1886, 3 Aug.	Viscount Cranbrook. (*See under* 1885)
1892, 18 Aug.	John Wodehouse, 1st e. of Kimberley
1894, 10 Mar.	Archibald Philip Primrose, 5th e. of Rosebery [Scot.] and 2nd lord Rosebery [U.K.] (1st e. of Midlothian [U.K.] 1911)
1895, 29 June	Spencer Compton Cavendish, 8th duke of Devonshire
1903, 19 Oct.	Charles Stewart Vane-Tempest, later Vane-Tempest-Stewart, 6th marquess of Londonderry [Irish] and 4th e. Vane [U.K.]
1905, 11 Dec.	Robert Offley Ashburton Crewe-Milnes, 1st e. of Crewe (1st marquess of Crewe 1911)
1908, 16 Apr.	Edward Marjoribanks, 2nd lord Tweedmouth
1908, 19 Oct.	Sir Henry Hartley Fowler, 1st viscount Wolverhampton 1908
1910, 21 June	William Lygon, 7th e. Beauchamp
1910, 7 Nov.	John Morley, 1st viscount Morley of Blackburn
1914, 5 Aug.	e. Beauchamp. (*See under* 1910)
1915, 27 May	Marquess of Crewe. (*See under* 1905)
1916, 11 Dec.	George Nathaniel Curzon, 1st e. Curzon (1st marquess Curzon of Kedleston 1921)
1919, 29 Oct.	Arthur James Balfour (1st e. of Balfour 1922)
1922, 25 Oct.	James Edward Hubert Gascoyne-Cecil, 4th marquess of Salisbury
1924, 23 Jan.	Charles Alfred Cripps, 1st lord Parmoor
1924, 7 Nov.	Marquess Curzon. (*See under* 1919)
1925, 2 May	e. Balfour. (*See under* 1919)
1929, 8 June	Lord Parmoor. (*See under* 1924)
1931, 26 Aug.	Stanley Baldwin (1st e. Baldwin of Bewdley 1937)
1935, 7 June	James Ramsay MacDonald
1937, 28 May	Edward Frederick Lindley Wood, 3rd viscount Halifax (1st e. of Halifax 1944)

1938, 15 Mar.	Douglas McGarel Hogg, 1st viscount Hailsham
1938, 4 Nov.	Walter Runciman, 1st viscount Runciman
1939, 4 Sept.	James Richard Stanhope, 7th e. Stanhope
1940, 12 May	Arthur Neville Chamberlain
1940, 4 Oct.	Sir John Anderson (1st viscount Waverley 1952)
1943, 28 Sept.	Clement Richard Attlee (1st e. Attlee 1955)
1945, 28 May	Frederick James Marquis, 1st lord Woolton (1st e. of Woolton 1956)
1945, 28 July	Herbert Stanley Morrison
1951, 12 Mar.	Christopher Addison, 1st viscount Addison
1951, 27 Oct.	Lord Woolton. (*See under* 1945)
1952, 15 Dec.	Robert Arthur James Gascoyne-Cecil, 5th marquess of Salisbury. Resigned 29 March 1957
1957, 1 Apr.	Alexander Frederick Douglas-Home, 14th e. of Home [Scot.], 4th lord Douglas [U.K.] (also Secretary of State for Commonwealth Relations)
1957, 23 Sept.	Quintin McGarel Hogg, 2nd viscount Hailsham
1959, 14 Sept.	e. of Home. (*See under* 1957, Apr.)
1960, 27 July	viscount Hailsham. (*See under* 1957, Sept.)
1964, 16 Oct.	Herbert William Bowden
1966, 11 Aug.	Richard Howard Stafford Crossman
1968, 18 Oct.	Thomas Frederick Peart
1970, 20 June	William Stephen Ian Whitelaw
1972, 7 Apr.	Robert Carr
1972, 5 Nov.	James Michael Leathes Prior
1974, 5 Mar.	Edward Watson Short
1976, 8 Apr.	Michael Mackintosh Foot
1979, 5 May	Arthur Christopher John Soames
1981, 14 Sept.	Francis Leslie Pym
1982, 5 Apr.	William John Biffen
1983, 11 June	William Stephen Ian Whitelaw, 1st viscount Whitelaw

CHANCELLORS OF THE DUCHY OF LANCASTER

The chancellor of the duchy of Lancaster, who is also, by the same letters patent, appointed chancellor of the county palatine of Lancaster, holds two offices which were held separately until the middle of the fifteenth century. Both offices originated a century earlier. In the first half of the fifteenth century the office developed so that the holder became the chief officer of the duchy. He presided, and still presides, over the duchy council, and until the early years of the nineteenth century sat in a judicial capacity in the court of duchy chamber. For the last two hundred years the chancellors have had no heavy 'departmental' duties but they have usually been members of the Government and not infrequently of the Cabinet.

The list is compiled mainly from the enrolments of the letters patent, and the dates are those of the patents, unless otherwise noted.

The chief printed source for the history of the Office is R. Somerville, *History of the Duchy of Lancaster*, i (*1265–1603*) (1953) and ii (*1603–1965*) (1970); *Office-holders in the Duchy and County Palatine of Lancaster from 1603* (1972); and his edition of 'Ordinances for the Duchy of Lancaster', in *Camden Miscellany*, vol. xxvi (Camden 4th ser., vol. 14, 1975), 1–29. *See also Halsbury's Laws of England*, 3rd edn, vii, 546 ff.

1399, [6 Oct.][1]	William Burgoyne
1402, [25 Nov.][2]	John Wakering
1405, 3 Mar.	Thomas Stanley; *ob.* 11 March 1410

[1] Day from which fees were paid.
[2] *Id.*

1410, 30 Mar.	John Springthorpe
1413, [4 Apr.][1]	John Wodehouse; *ob.* 27 Jan. 1431
1431, 16 Feb.	Walter Shiryngton; *ob.* 2 Feb. 1449
1449, 2 Feb.	William Tresham;[2] *ob.* 23 Sept. 1450
1450, 23 Sept.	John Say,[3] kt, 1465
1471, 10 June	Sir Richard Fowler (also chancellor of the exchequer, 1469–71); *ob.* 3 Nov. 1477
1477, 3 Nov.	Sir John Say. (*See under* 1449); *ob. 1478*
1478, 22 Apr.	Thomas Thwaites (also chancellor of the exchequer, 1471–83)
1483, 7 July	Thomas Metcalfe
1485, 13 Sept.	Sir Reynold Bray; *ob.* 5 Aug. 1503
1504, 24 June	Sir John Mordaunt; *ob.* Oct.–Nov. 1504
1505, 3 Oct.	Sir Richard Empson, dism. after 22 Apr. 1509
1509, 14 May	Sir Henry Marny (1st lord Marny 1523)
1523, 6 Apr.	Sir Richard Wingfield; *ob.* 22 July 1525
1525, 30 Sept.	Sir Thomas More
1529, 3 Nov.	Sir William Fitzwilliam; 1st e. of Southampton 1537; *ob.* 15 Oct. 1542
1542, ? Oct.	Sir John Gage[4]
1547, 1 July	Sir William Paget, 1st lord Paget 1549; principal secretary of state 1543–47
1552, 7 July	Sir John Gates
1553, between 19 July and 29 Sept.	Sir Robert Rochester;[5] *ob.* 28 Nov. 1557
1558, 22 Jan.	Sir Edward Waldegrave
1559, 24 Jan.	Sir Ambrose Cave; *ob.* 2 Apr. 1568
1568, 16 May	Sir Ralph Sadler; *ob.* 30 May 1587
1587, 15 June	Sir Francis Walsingham; *ob.* 6 Apr. 1590
1590, *June*	Sir Thomas Heneage; *ob.* 17 Oct. 1595
1595, 23 Oct.	Office in commission
1597, 7 Oct.	Sir Robert Cecil (1st e. of Salisbury 1605)
1599, 18 June	Office in commission
1601, 24 Sept.	Sir John Fortescue
1601, 8 Oct.	Office in commission
1601, 4 Nov.	Sir John Fortescue; *ob.* 23 Dec. 1607. (*See above*)
1607, 23 Dec.	Sir Thomas Parry;[6] *ob.* 24 or 31 May 1616
1616, 5 June	Sir John Dacombe;[7] *ob. Jan.* 1618
1618, 3 Feb.	Office in commission
1618, 23 Mar.	Sir Humphrey May
1629, 16 Apr.	Edward Barrett, 1st lord Barrett of Newburgh [Scot.]; *ob.* Dec. 1644
1644, 10 Dec.	Francis, lord Seymour (for the king)
1645, 10 Feb.	William, 1st lord Grey of Warke, and William Lenthall MP, speaker, to have charge of duchy seal (for Parliament)
1648, 17 Mar.	Sir Gilbert Gerrard, bt, MP
1649, 28 July	John Bradshaw, sergt at law
1653, 17 Sept.	Bradshaw and Thomas Fell, commissioners to keep the seal
1654, 28 Feb.	Fell (alone) as commissioner (county palatine only)
1658, 5 Dec.	John Bradshaw
1660, 27 Feb.	William Lenthall (speaker), commissioner[8]
1660, 14 Mar.	Sir Gilbert Gerrard, bt, MP
1660, 9 July	Francis Seymour, 1st lord Seymour of Trowbridge 1641; *ob.* 12 July 1664

[1] The day on which Springthorpe was ordered to surrender the office.
[2] Granted the office in reversion 3 July 1442.
[3] Granted the office in reversion 10 June 1449; regranted it 22 Jan. 1451.
[4] Granted the office 10 May 1543 with fees from 29 Sept. 1542.
[5] Granted fees from 24 June.
[6] To whom on 23 Oct. 1607 the office had been granted in succession to Fortescue.
[7] To whom on 27 May 1615 the office had been granted in succession to Parry.
[8] Appd chancellor of the county palatine only.

1664, 21 July	Sir Thomas Ingram; *ob.* 13 Feb. 1672
1672, 22 Feb.	Sir Robert Carr, bt; *ob.* 14 Nov. 1682
1682, 21 Nov.	Sir Thomas Chicheley[1] (determined 15 Mar. 1687)
1687, 15 Mar.	Office in commission
1687, 25 May	Robert Phelipps
1689, 21 Mar.	Robert Bertie, summoned to Parliament *v.p.* as lord Willoughby of Eresby (1st duke of Ancaster and Kesteven 1715)
1697, 4 May	Thomas Grey, 2nd e. Stamford
1702, 12 May	Sir John Leveson-Gower, bt, 1st lord Gower of Stittenham 1703
1706, 1 June	James Stanley, 10th e. of Derby
1710, 21 Sept.	William Berkeley, 4th lord Berkeley of Stratton
1714, 4 Nov.	Heneage Finch, 1st e. of Aylesford 1714
1716, 12 Mar.	Richard Lumley, 1st e. of Scarborough
1717, 19 June	Nicholas Lechmere, 1st lord Lechmere 1721; *ob.* 18 June 1727
1727, 24 July	John Manners, 3rd duke of Rutland
1736, 17 May	George Cholmondeley, 3rd e. of Cholmondeley
1743, 22 Dec.	Richard Edgcumbe, 1st lord Edgcumbe of Mount Edgcumbe 1742
1758, 24 Jan.[2]	Thomas Hay, commonly called viscount Dupplin, 9th e. of Kinnoull [Scot.] and 2nd lord Hay [G.B.], 29 July 1758
1762, 13 Dec.	James Stanley, later Smith-Stanley, commonly called lord Strange; *ob.* 1 June 1771
1771, 14 June	Thomas Villiers, 1st lord Hyde of Hindon (1st e. of Clarendon 1776)
1782, 17 Apr.	John Dunning, 1st baron Ashburton 1782
1783, 29 Aug.	Edward Smith-Stanley, 12th e. of Derby
1783, 31 Dec.	e. of Clarendon. (*See under* 1771)
1786, 6 Sept.	Charles Jenkinson, 1st lord Hawkesbury 1786; 1st e. of Liverpool 1796
1803, 11 Nov.	Thomas Pelham, summoned to Parliament *v.p.* as lord Pelham of Stanmer 1801 (2nd e. of Chichester 1805)
1804, 6 June	Henry Phipps, 1st lord Mulgrave of Mulgrave (1st e. of Mulgrave 1812)
1805, 14 Jan.	Robert Hobart, 4th e. of Buckinghamshire
1805, 10 July	Dudley Ryder, 2nd lord Harrowby (1st e. of Harrowby 1809)
1806, 12 Feb.	e. of Derby. (*See under* 1783)
1807, 30 Mar.	Spencer Perceval
1812, 23 Aug.	e. of Buckinghamshire. (*See under* 1805)
1812, 23 June	Charles Bathurst
1823, 13 Feb.	Nicholas Vansittart, 1st baron Bexley 1823
1828, 26 Jan.	George Hamilton-Gordon, 4th e. of Aberdeen [Scot.], 1st viscount Gordon [U.K.]
1828, 2 June	Charles Arbuthnot
1830, 25 Nov.	Henry Richard Fox, later Vassall Fox, 3rd lord Holland
1830, 20 Dec.	Thomas Hamilton, 9th e. of Haddington [Scot.], 1st lord Melros [U.K.]
1834, 26 Dec.	Charles Watkin Williams Wynn
1835, 23 Apr.	Lord Holland. (*See under* 1830)
1840, 31 Oct.	George William Frederick Villiers, 4th e. of Clarendon
1841, 23 June	Sir George Grey, bt
1841, 3 Sept.	Lord Granville Charles Henry Somerset
1846, 6 July	John Campbell, 1st lord Campbell
1850, 6 Mar.	George William Frederick Howard, 7th e. of Carlisle
1852, 1 Mar.	Robert Adam Christopher, later Christopher-Nisbet-Hamilton
1852, 30 Dec.	Edward Strutt (1st lord Belper 1856)
1854, 21 June	Granville George Leveson-Gower, 2nd e. Granville
1855, 31 Mar.	Dudley Ryder, 2nd e. of Harrowby
1855, 7 Dec.	Matthew Talbot Baines
1858, 26 Feb.	James Graham, 4th duke of Montrose [Scot.] and 4th e. Graham [G.B.]
1859, 22 June	Sir George Grey. (*See under* 1841)
1861, 25 July	Edward Cardwell (1st viscount Cardwell 1874)

[1] Patent renewed 9 Feb. 1685.
[2] Patent renewed 27 Feb. 1760.

1864, 7 Apr.	e. of Clarendon. (*See under* 1838)
1866, 26 Jan.	George Joachim Goschen (1st viscount Goschen 1900)
1866, 10 July	William Reginald Courtenay, 21st e. of Devon
1867, 26 June	John Wilson-Patten (1st lord Winmarleigh 1874)
1868, 7 Nov.	Thomas Edward Taylor
1868, 12 Dec.	Frederick Temple Blackwood, later Hamilton-Temple-Blackwood, 5th lord Dufferin [Irish], 1st lord Clandeboye [U.K.], 1st e. of Dufferin 1871 (1st marquess of Dufferin and Ava 1888); (also paymaster general)
1872, 9 Aug.	Hugh Culling Eardley Childers
1873, 30 Sept.	John Bright
1874, 2 Mar.	Thomas Edward Taylor. (*See under* Nov. 1868)
1880, 29 Apr.	John Bright. (*See under* 1873)
1882, 25 July	John Wodehouse, 1st e. of Kimberley
1882, 28 Dec.	John George Dodson (1st lord Monk Bretton 1884)
1884, 29 Oct.	George Otto Trevelyan
1885, 24 June	Henry Chaplin (1st viscount Chaplin 1916)
1886, 6 Feb.	Edward Heneage (1st lord Heneage 1896) (also vice-president of the Board of Agriculture)
1886, 16 Apr.	Sir Ughtred James Kay-Shuttleworth, bt (1st lord Shuttleworth 1902)
1886, 3 Aug.	Gathorne Hardy, 1st viscount Cranbrook (1st e. of Cranbrook 1892)
1886, 16 Aug.	John James Robert Manners, commonly called lord John Manners, 7th duke of Rutland 1888
1892, 18 Aug.	James Bryce (1st viscount Bryce 1914)
1894, 28 May	Edward Marjoribanks, 2nd lord Tweedmouth 1894
1895, 29 June	Richard Assheton Cross, 1st viscount Cross
1895, 4 July	Sir Henry James, 1st lord James of Hereford 1895
1902, 11 Aug.	Sir William Hood Walrond, bt (1st lord Waleran 1905)
1905, 11 Dec.	Sir Henry Hartley Fowler (1st viscount Wolverhampton 1908)
1908, 19 Oct.	Edmond George Petty FitzMaurice, 1st lord FitzMaurice
1909, 28 June	Herbert Louis Samuel (1st viscount Samuel 1937)
1910, 19 Feb.	Joseph Albert Pease (1st lord Gainford 1917)
1911, 24 Oct.	Charles Edward Henry Hobhouse
1914, 12 Feb.	Charles Frederick Gurney Masterman
1915, 10 Feb.	Edwin Samuel Montagu
1915, 27 May	Winston Leonard Spencer Churchill (K.G. 1953)
1915, 30 Nov.	Herbert Louis Samuel. (*See under* 1909)
1916, 12 Jan.	Edwin Samuel Montagu. (*See under* 1915)
1916, 12 July	Thomas M'Kinnon Wood (also financial secretary to the treasury)
1916, 13 Dec.	Sir Frederick Cawley, bt, 1st lord Cawley 1918
1918, 4 Mar.	William Maxwell Aitken, 1st lord Beaverbrook 1917
1918, 8 Nov.	William Hayes Fisher, 1st lord Downham 1918
1919, 10 Feb.	David Alexander Edward Lindsay, 27th e. of Crawford and 10th e. of Balcarres [Scot.] and 4th lord Wigan [U.K.] 1913
1921, 5 Apr.	William Robert Wellesley, 1st viscount Peel (1st e. Peel 1929)
1922, 5 May	Sir William Sutherland
1922, 26 Oct.	James Edward Hubert Gascoyne-Cecil, 4th marquess of Salisbury
1923, 28 May	John Colin Campbell Davidson (1st viscount Davidson 1937)
1924, 23 Jan.	Josiah Clement Wedgwood (1st lord Wedgwood 1942)
1924, 19 Nov.	Edgar Algernon Robert Gascoyne-Cecil, 1st viscount Cecil of Chelwood 1923
1927, 3 Nov.	Ronald John McNeill, 1st lord Cushendun 1927
1929, 8 June	Sir Oswald Ernald Mosley, bt
1930, 24 May	Clement Richard Attlee (1st e. Attlee 1955)
1931, 20 Mar.	Arthur Augustus William Harry, 1st lord Ponsonby of Shulbrede 1930
1931, 26 Aug.	Philip Henry Kerr, 11th marquess of Lothian [Scot.] and 6th lord Kerr [U.K.]
1931, 12 Nov.	John Colin Campbell Davidson. (*See under* 1923)
1937, 28 May	Edward Turnour, 6th e. Winterton [Irish] (1st lord Turnour [U.K.] 1952)

1939, 2 Feb.	William Shepherd Morrison
1940, 5 Apr.	George Clement Tryon, 1st lord Tryon 1940
1940, 15 May	Maurice Pascal Alers Hankey, 1st lord Hankey 1939
1941, 22 July	Alfred Duff Cooper (1st viscount Norwich 1952)
1943, 17 Nov.	Alfred Ernest Brown
1945, 28 May	Sir James Arthur Salter (1st lord Salter 1953)
1945, 14 Aug.	John Burns Hynd
1947, 23 Apr.	Francis Aungier Pakenham, 1st lord Pakenham (7th e. of Longford 1961)
1948, 22 June	Hugh John Neville Dalton
1950, 16 Mar.	Albert Victor, 1st viscount Alexander of Hillsborough 1950
1951, 31 Oct.	Philip Lloyd-Greame, later Cunliffe-Lister, 1st viscount Swinton (1st e. Swinton 1955)
1952, 15 Dec.	Frederick James Marquis, 1st lord Woolton, 1st viscount Woolton 1953 (1st e. of Woolton 1956)
1955, 22 Dec.	George Nigel Douglas-Hamilton, 10th e. of Selkirk [Scot.] 1940
1957, 14 Jan.	Charles Hill
1961, 9 Oct.	Iain Norman Macleod
1963, 20 Oct.	John Hugh Hare, 1st viscount Blakenham
1964, 18 Oct.	Arthur Leslie Noel Douglas Houghton
1966, 6 Apr.	George Morgan Thomson
1967, 7 Jan.	Frederick Lee
1969, 6 Oct.	George Morgan Thomson
1970, 20 June	Anthony Perrinott Lysberg Barber
1970, 28 July	Aubrey Geoffrey Frederick Rippon
1972, 5 Nov.	John Emerson Harding Davies
1974, 5 Mar.	Norman Harold Lever
1979, 5 May	Norman Arthur Francis St John Stevas
1981, 5 Jan.	Francis Leslie Pym
1981, 14 Sept.	Janet Mary Young, baroness Young
1982, 5 Apr.	Cecil Edward Parkinson
1983, 11 June	Francis Arthur Cockfield, lord Cockfield
1984, 10 Sept.	Alexander Patrick Greysteil Ruthven, 2nd e. of Gowrie
1985, 2 Sept.	Norman Beresford Tebbit

PRESIDENTS OF THE BOARD OF TRADE

Commissioners 'for promoting the trade of our kingdom and for inspecting and improving our plantations in America and elsewhere' were appointed by patent of 15 May 1696. The body, often called the first Board of Trade, at first numbered 15 and later 16 persons, seven (later eight) of whom were great officers sitting *ex officio*. The eight unofficial members formed the working core of the board and the senior of these was the President. The board was abolished on 11 July 1782 under the Establishment Act (22 Geo. III, c. 82). On 5 March 1784 the Privy Council set up a new committee for trade and plantations, whose function was mainly commercial. This committee was reconstituted and given a vice-president and a permanent secretariate by Order in Council of 23 August 1786 and its presidents gradually assumed their present position as ministers of commerce for the United Kingdom. From 15 October 1963 until 16 October 1964 the post was held in conjunction with that of Secretary of State for Industry, Trade and Regional Development. From 15 October 1970 it was held in conjunction with the post of Secretary of State for Trade and Industry and from 5 March 1974 with that of Secretary of State for Trade. From 1983 the post was again held jointly with the secretaryship of State for Trade and Industry. For the earlier Board, *see* C. M. Andrews, *Guide to the Materials for American History . . . in the Public Record Office*, i (Washington, 1912), and A. H. Basye, *The Lords Commissioners of Trade and Plantations* (New Haven, 1925) and works referred to therein. For the later Board, *see* Anna L. Lingelbach, 'The Inception of the British Board of Trade', *American Historical Review*, xxx (1925), Sir Hubert Llewellyn Smith, *The Board of Trade* (1928), and R. Prouty, *The Transformation of the Board of Trade, 1830–55* (1957). *See also* J. C. Sainty, *Officials of the Boards of Trade, 1660–1870* (1974).

1696, 15 May	John Egerton, 3rd e. of Bridgwater
1699, 9 June	Thomas Grey, 2nd e. of Stamford
1702, 12 June	Thomas Thynne, 1st viscount Weymouth
1707, 25 Apr.	e. of Stamford. (*See under* 1699)
1711, 12 June	Charles Finch, 4th e. of Winchilsea
1713, 15 Sept.	Francis North, 3rd lord Guildford (1st e. of Guildford 1752)
1714, 13 Dec.	William Berkeley, 4th lord Berkeley of Stratton
1715, 12 May	Henry Howard, 6th e. of Suffolk, 1st e. of Bindon
1718, 31 Jan.	Robert Darcy, 3rd e. of Holdernesse
1719, 11 May	Thomas Fane, 6th e. of Westmorland
1735, 14 May	Benjamin Mildmay, 1st e. Fitzwalter
1737, 27 June	John Monson, 1st lord Monson
1748, 1 Nov.	George Montague, later Montague-Dunk, 2nd e. of Halifax
1761, 21 Mar.	Samuel Sandys, 1st lord Sandys
1763, 1 Mar.	Charles Townshend
1763, 20 Apr.	William Fitz-Maurice, later Petty, 2nd e. of Shelburne [Irish], 2nd lord Wycombe [G.B.], (1st marquess of Lansdowne 1784)
1763, 9 Sept.	Wills Hill, 1st earl of Hillsborough [Irish], (1st marquess of Downshire 1789)
1765, 20 July	William Legge, 2nd e. of Dartmouth
1766, 16 Aug.	e. of Hillsborough. (*See under* 1763)
1766, 18 Dec.	Robert Nugent, 1st viscount Clare 1767 [Irish], (1st e. Nugent [Irish] 1776)
1768, 20 Jan.	e. of Hillsborough. (*See under* 1763)
1772, 31 Aug.	e. of Dartmouth. (*See under* 1765)
1775, 10 Nov.	Lord George Sackville-Germain (1st viscount Sackville 1782)
1779, 6 Nov.	Frederick Howard, 5th e. of Carlisle
1780, 9 Dec.	Thomas Robinson 2nd lord Grantham
1784, 5 Mar.	Thomas Townshend, 1st lord Sydney (1st viscount Sydney 1789)
1786, 23 Aug.	Charles Jenkinson, 1st lord Hawkesbury 1786, 1st e. of Liverpool 1796 (also chancellor of the duchy of Lancaster)
1804, 6 June	James Graham, 3rd duke of Montrose (also joint Postmaster-General)
1806, 5 Feb.	William Eden, 1st lord Auckland
1807, 26 Mar.	Henry Bathurst, 3rd e. Bathurst (also Master of the Mint)
1812, 29 Sept.	Richard le Poer Trench, 2nd e. of Clancarty [Irish], 1st lord Trench [U.K.] 1815 (1st viscount Clancarty [U.K.] 1823) (also Treasurer of the Navy)
1818, 24 Jan.	Frederick John Robinson (1st e. of Ripon 1833) (also Treasurer of the Navy)
1823, 31 Jan.	William Huskisson (also Treasurer of the Navy)
1827, 3 Sept.	Charles Grant (1st lord Glenelg 1835) (also Treasurer of the Navy)
1828, 11 June	William Vesey Fitzgerald (1st lord Fitzgerald 1835) (also Treasurer of the Navy)
1830, 2 Feb.	John Charles Herries (also Master of the Mint)
1830, 22 Nov.	George Eden, 2nd lord Auckland (1st e. of Auckland 1839) (also Master of the Mint)
1834, 5 June	Charles Edward Poulett Thomson (1st lord Sydenham and Toronto 1840) (also Treasurer of the Navy)
1834, 16 Dec.	Alexander Baring, 1st lord Ashburton 1835 (also Master of the Mint)
1835, 18 Apr.	Charles Edward Poulett Thomson. (*See under* 1834)
1839, 27 Aug.	Henry Labouchere (1st lord Taunton 1859) (also Master of the Mint)
1841, 6 Sept.	e. of Ripon. (*See under* 1818)
1843, 16 May	William Ewart Gladstone

1845, 3 Feb.	James Andrew Broun-Ramsay, 10th e. of Dalhousie [Scot.] (1st marquess of Dalhousie [U.K.] 1849)
1846, 6 July	George William Frederick Villiers, 4th e. of Clarendon
1847, 22 July	Henry Labouchere. (*See under* 1839)
1852, 27 Feb.	Joseph Warner Henley
1852, 28 Dec.	Edward Cardwell (1st viscount Cardwell 1874)
1855, 31 Mar.	Edward John Stanley, 2nd lord Stanley of Alderley
1858, 6 Apr.	Joseph Warner Henley
1859, 3 Mar.	Richard John Hely Hutchinson, 4th e. of Donoughmore [Irish], 4th viscount Hutchinson [U.K.]
1859, 1 July	Thomas Milner Gibson
1866, 6 July	Sir Stafford Henry Northcote (1st e. of Iddesleigh 1885)
1867, 8 Mar.	Charles Henry Gordon-Lennox, 6th duke of Richmond (1st duke of Gordon 1876)
1868, 9 Dec.	John Bright
1871, 14 Jan.	Chichester Samuel Parkinson-Fortescue, 1st lord Carlingford 1874
1874, 2 Mar.	Sir Charles Bowyer Adderley (1st lord Norton 1878)
1878, 4 Apr.	Dudley Francis Stuart Ryder, commonly called viscount Sandon (3rd e. of Harrowby 1882)
1880, 29 Apr.	Joseph Chamberlain
1885, 24 June	Duke of Richmond and Gordon. (*See under* 1867)
1885, 19 Aug.	Edward Stanhope
1886, 6 Feb.	Anthony John Mundella
1886, 4 Aug.	Sir Frederick Arthur Stanley, 1st lord Stanley of Preston 1886 (16th e. of Derby 1893)
1888, 21 Feb.	Sir Michael Edward Hicks-Beach (1st e. St Aldwyn 1915)
1892, 18 Aug.	Anthony John Mundella. (*See under* 1886)
1894, 28 May	James Bryce (1st viscount Bryce 1914)
1895, 29 June	Charles Thomson Ritchie (1st lord Ritchie 1905)
1900, 13 Nov.	Gerald William Balfour (2nd e. of Balfour 1930)
1905, 14 Mar.	Robert Arthur Talbot Gascoyne-Cecil, 4th marquess of Salisbury
1905, 11 Dec.	David Lloyd-George (1st e. Lloyd-George of Dwyfor 1945)
1908, 16 Apr.	Winston Leonard Spencer Churchill (K.G. 1953)
1910, 19 Feb.	Sydney Charles Buxton (1st e. Buxton 1920)
1914, 12 Feb.	John Burns
1914, 6 Aug.	Walter Runciman (1st viscount Runciman 1937)
1916, 13 Dec.	Sir Albert Henry Stanley (1st lord Ashfield 1920)
1919, 30 May	Sir Auckland Campbell Geddes (1st lord Geddes 1942)
1920, 25 Mar.	Sir Robert Stevenson Horne (1st viscount Horne 1937)
1921, 5 Apr.	Stanley Baldwin (1st e. Baldwin 1937)
1922, 25 Oct.	Sir Philip Lloyd-Greame, later Cunliffe-Lister (1st e. Swinton 1955)
1924, 23 Jan.	Sidney James Webb (1st lord Passfield 1929)
1924, 7 Nov.	Sir Philip Lloyd-Greame. (*See under* 1922)
1929, 8 June	William Graham
1931, 26 Aug.	Sir Philip Cunliffe-Lister. (*See under* 1922)
1931, 9 Nov.	Walter Runciman, 1st lord Runciman 1932 (1st viscount Runciman 1937)
1937, 28 May	Oliver Frederick George Stanley
1940, 9 Jan.	Sir Andrew Rae Duncan
1940, 4 Oct.	Oliver Lyttelton (1st viscount Chandos 1954)
1941, 1 July	Sir Andrew Rae Duncan. (*See under* 1940)
1942, 4 Feb.	John Jestyn Llewellin (1st lord Llewellin 1945)
1942, 23 Feb.	Hugh John Neale Dalton
1945, 28 May	Oliver Lyttelton. (*See under* 1940.) (Also Minister of Production)
1945, 28 July	Sir Richard Stafford Cripps
1947, 14 Oct.	James Harold Wilson
1951, 28 Apr.	Sir Hartley William Shawcross (lord Shawcross 1959)
1951, 30 Oct.	George Edward Peter Thorneycroft
1957, 14 Jan.	Sir David Eccles
1959, 14 Sept.	Reginald Maudling
1961, 9 Oct.	Frederick James Erroll
1963, 20 Oct.	Edward Richard George Heath

1964, 18 Oct.	Douglas Patrick Thomas Jay
1967, 29 Aug.	Charles Anthony Raven Crosland
1969, 6 Oct.	Roy Mason
1970, 20 June	Michael Anthony Christobal Noble
1970, 15 Oct.	John Emerson Harding Davies
1972, 5 Nov.	Peter Edward Walker
1974, 5 Mar.	Peter David Shore
1976, 8 Apr.	Edmund Emanuel Dell
1978, 11 Nov.	John Smith
1979, 5 May	John William Frederic Nott
1982, 5 Jan.	William John Biffen
1982, 5 Apr.	Francis Arthur Cockfield, lord Cockfield
1983, 11 June	Cecil Edward Parkinson
1983, 16 Oct.	Norman Beresford Tebbit
1985, 2 Sept.	Leon Brittan

MINISTERS OF DEFENCE

On becoming Prime Minister in May 1940 Mr Churchill assumed the ·title of Minister of Defence, and as such presided over the Defence Committee (Operations) of the War Cabinet. No Defence Department was constituted. Mr Attlee also assumed the title on forming his government in 1945. Under the Ministry of Defence Act 1946 (10 and 11 Geo. VI, c. 2), a Minister of Defence was appointed to apportion 'in broad outline' the available resources between the three fighting services according to the strategic policy laid down by the Defence Committee of the Cabinet; to settle questions of general administration on which a common policy for the three fighting services is desirable; and to administer the Imperial Defence College, the Joint Services Staff College and other organizations common to the fighting services. His office was formally constituted on 1 Jan. 1947. *See Central Organization for Defence* [Cmd 6923] H.C. (1945–6), xx. Following the amalgamation of the former Ministry of Defence, the War Office, the Admiralty and the Air Ministry on 1 April 1964, to create a unified Ministry of Defence, the post was redesignated as Secretary of State for Defence.

1940, 10 May	Winston Leonard Spencer Churchill (K.G. 1953)
1945, 26 July	Clement Richard Attlee (1st e. Attlee 1955)
1946, 21 Dec.	Albert Victor Alexander (1st viscount Alexander of Hillsborough 1950)
1950, 2 Mar.	Emanuel Shinwell
1951, 27 Oct.	Winston Leonard Spencer Churchill. (*See under* 1940)
1952, 29 Feb.	Harold Rupert Leofric George Alexander, 1st e. Alexander of Tunis 1952
1954, 18 Oct.	Maurice Harold Macmillan
1955, 12 Apr.	John Selwyn Brooke Lloyd
1955, 22 Dec.	Sir Walter Turner Monckton (1st viscount Monckton of Brenchley 1957)
1956, 22 Oct.	Antony Henry Head
1957, 13 Jan.	Duncan Sandys
1959, 14 Sept.	Harold Arthur Watkinson
1962, 13 July	George Edward Peter Thorneycroft
1964, 16 Oct.	Denis Winston Healey
1970, 20 June	Peter Alexander Rupert Carrington, 6th lord Carrington
1974, 8 Jan.	Sir Ian Hedworth John Little Gilmour
1974, 5 Mar.	Roy Mason
1976, 10 Sept.	Frederick William Mulley
1979, 5 May	Francis Leslie Pym
1981, 5 Jan.	John William Frederic Nott
1983, 6 Jan.	Michael Ray Dibdin Heseltine

SECRETARIES OF STATE FOR INDUSTRY

A Secretaryship of State for Industry, Trade and Regional Development was established in October 1963 and was held in conjunction with the presidency of the Board of Trade. The post was not filled after 16 October 1964. In October 1970 the Ministry of Technology and the Board of Trade were merged to form the Department of Trade and Industry under a secretary of state. From 1970 to 1974, and again from 11 June 1983, the post was designated as Secretary of State for Trade and Industry and held in conjunction with the presidency of the Board of Trade.

1963, 20 Oct.	Edward Richard George Heath
1970, 15 Oct.	John Emerson Harding Davies
1972, 5 Nov.	Peter Edward Walker
1974, 5 Mar.	Anthony Neil Wedgwood Benn
1975, 10 June	Eric Graham Varley
1979, 5 May	Sir Keith Sinjohn Joseph
1981, 14 Sept.	Charles Patrick Fleming Jenkin
1983, 11 June	Cecil Edward Parkinson
1983, 16 Oct.	Norman Beresford Tebbit
1985, 2 Sept.	Leon Brittan

SECRETARIES OF STATE FOR EDUCATION AND SCIENCE

The Ministry of Education was established by the Education Act of 1944 and a Ministry of Science was created in 1959. From 1 April 1964 the two ministries were merged to form the Department of Education and Science under a Secretary of State.

1964, 1 Apr.	Sir Quintin McGarel Hogg
1964, 18 Oct.	Robert Maitland Michael Stewart
1965, 22 Jan.	Charles Anthony Raven Crosland
1967, 29 Aug.	Patrick Chrestien Gordon Walker
1968, 6 Apr.	Edward Watson Short
1970, 20 June	Margaret Hilda Thatcher
1974, 5 Mar.	Reginald Ernest Prentice
1975, 10 June	Frederick William Mulley
1976, 10 Sept.	Shirley Vivien Teresa Brittain Williams
1979, 5 May	Mark Carlisle
1981, 14 Sept.	Sir Keith Sinjohn Joseph

SECRETARIES OF STATE FOR WALES

The post of Minister for Welsh Affairs was created in 1951. It was held in conjunction with the Secretaryship of State for the Home Department until 1957 and subsequently with the Ministry of Housing and Local Government. In 1964 a Secretaryship of State for Wales was created at the head of a separate department.

1964, 18 Oct.	James Griffiths
1966, 6 Apr.	Cledwyn Hughes
1968, 6 Apr.	George Thomas
1970, 20 June	Peter John Mitchell Thomas
1974, 5 Mar.	John Morris
1979, 5 May	Roger Nicholas Edwards

SECRETARIES OF STATE FOR EMPLOYMENT

In 1968 the former Ministry of Labour was reorganised as a new Department of Employment and Productivity. In 1970 this became the Department of Employment and the title of the Secretary of State was changed accordingly.

1968, 6 Apr.	Barbara Anne Castle
1970, 6 June	Robert Carr
1972, 7 Apr.	Maurice Victor Macmillan
1973, 2 Dec.	William Stephen Ian Whitelaw
1974, 5 Mar.	Michael Mackintosh Foot
1976, 8 Apr.	Albert Edward Booth
1979, 5 May	James Michael Leathes Prior
1981, 14 Sept.	Norman Beresford Tebbit
1983, 16 Oct.	Thomas Jeremy King
1985, 2 Sept.	David Ivor Young, lord Young of Graffham

SECRETARIES OF STATE FOR SOCIAL SERVICES

From 1 November 1968 the Ministries of Health and Social Security were merged to form the Department of Health and Social Security under a Secretary of State for Social Services.

1968, 1 Nov.	Richard Howard Stafford Crossman
1970, 20 June	Sir Keith Sinjohn Joseph
1974, 5 Mar.	Barbara Anne Castle
1976, 8 Apr.	David Headley Ennals
1979, 5 May	Charles Patrick Fleming Jenkin
1981, 14 Sept.	Peter Norman Fowler

SECRETARIES OF STATE FOR THE ENVIRONMENT

From 15 October 1970 the Ministries of Housing and Local Government, Transport and Public Building and Works were merged to form a unified Department of the Environment, to be responsible for all of the functions which affect people's living environment.

1970, 15 Oct.	Peter Edward Walker
1972, 5 Nov.	Aubrey Geoffrey Frederick Rippon
1974, 5 Mar.	Charles Anthony Raven Crosland
1976, 8 Apr.	Peter David Shore
1979, 5 May	Michael Ray Dibdin Heseltine
1983, 6 Jan.	Thomas Jeremy King
1983, 11 June	Charles Patrick Fleming Jenkin
1985, 2 Sept.	Kenneth Wilfred Baker

SECRETARIES OF STATE FOR NORTHERN IRELAND

From 31 March 1972 the Stormont parliament was suspended and arrangements were made for the government of Northern Ireland to be exercised through a Secretary of State.

1972, 1 Apr.	William Stephen Ian Whitelaw
1973, 2 Dec.	Francis Leslie Pym
1974, 5 Mar.	Merlyn Rees
1976, 10 Sept.	Roy Mason
1979, 5 May	Humphrey Edward Atkins
1981, 14 Sept.	James Michael Leathes Prior
1984, 10 Sept.	Douglas Richard Hurd
1985, 2 Sept.	Thomas Jeremy King

SECRETARIES OF STATE FOR ENERGY

The Department of Energy was created in January 1974 with responsibility for coal, gas, electricity and oil, atomic energy and nuclear power.

1974, 8 Jan.	Peter Alexander Rupert Carrington, 6th lord Carrington
1974, 5 Mar.	Eric Graham Varley
1975, 10 June	Anthony Neil Wedgwood Benn
1979, 5 May	David Arthur Russell Howell
1981, 14 Sept.	Nigel Lawson
1983, 11 June	Peter Edward Walker

SECRETARIES OF STATE FOR TRANSPORT

The Ministry of Transport was established in 1919. In 1970 it became a part of the new Department of the Environment. In 1976, however, a separate Department of Transport was established with responsibility for inland surface transport.

1976, 10 Sept.	William Thomas Rogers
1981, 5 Jan.	Peter Norman Fowler[1]
1981, 14 Sept.	David Arthur Russell Howell
1983, 11 June	Thomas Jeremy King
1983, 16 Oct.	Nicholas Ridley

[1] From 5 May 1979 until 5 Jan. 1981 the post was held as a ministry outside the cabinet.

IRISH OFFICERS OF STATE

INTRODUCTION

IN the first edition of this *Handbook* the late Mr Herbert Wood published a list of Chief Governors of Ireland, 1172–1939; and also a list of Secretaries of State for Ireland and Keepers of the Signet or Privy Seal, 1560–1829. These lists were based largely on two papers which he had published in the *Proceedings of the Royal Irish Academy*: 'The Office of Chief Governor of Ireland, 1172–1509' (vol. 36, Sect. C, no. 12 (1923), 206–38); and 'The Office of Secretary of State for Ireland and Keeper of the Signet or Privy Seal' (vol. 38, Sect. C, no. 4 (1928), 51–68). For the list of Chief Governors after 1509 Wood followed the list in the *Liber Munerum Publicorum Hiberniæ*, ed. Rowley Lascelles (1852).

For the second edition, the medieval section of Wood's list was revised in the light of research undertaken by Professor A. J. Otway-Ruthven, Mr H. G. Richardson, Professor G. O. Sayles and, for the period 1485–1540, Professor D. B. Quinn. Much of this work has since been published in: H. G. Richardson and G. O. Sayles, *The administration of Ireland, 1172–1377* (Dublin, 1963) and A. J. Otway-Ruthven, 'The chief governors of medieval Ireland', *Journal of the Royal Society of Antiquaries of Ireland*, xcv (1965), 227–36. Further work has also been done for the years 1413–61 by Miss Elizabeth Sykes for her thesis on 'The governing of the Lancastrian lordship of Ireland in the time of James Butler, fourth earl of Ormond, *c.* 1420–52' (University of Durham, Ph.D.) and by Dr Steven Ellis for the period 1485–1534. All of this new material is incorporated in the list published in *A New History of Ireland*, ix, ed. T. W. Moody *et al.* (Oxford, 1984), 469–85, which has been used for the further revision of Wood's list for the medieval period. For the second edition, Dr Hugh F. Kearney revised the lists for the seventeenth century. Mr James L. J. Hughes, of the Public Record Office of Ireland, checked the dates in Wood's lists from the list which John Lodge compiled in the eighteenth century. Lodge's lists of Irish patentee officers (1334–1772) are now preserved in two volumes in the Public Record Office of Ireland; they were used by Rowley Lascelles when he was compiling the *Liber Munerum* (1852). Mr Hughes also checked the dates of swearing into office for the period 1714–1921 with the Oath Rolls, now preserved in the Public Record Office of Ireland. In this edition the lists of chief governors and deputies are presented separately. As the post of deputy was held only intermittently, for the medieval period the last known date of acting in the post is supplied wherever possible. The list of deputies is taken to 1801, after which date no Lord Deputy was appointed and Lords Justices were appointed only very occasionally and briefly.

Wood's list of the Secretaries of State for Ireland and Keepers of the Signet or Privy Seal has been omitted from the second and third editions of the *Handbook* as being of little significance for students of Irish history, although this information is given for periods when Secretaries of State were of unusual importance.[1] It has been replaced by a list of Chief Secretaries in Ireland, 1566–1921.

CHIEF GOVERNORS, 1172–1528

1172, Apr.	Hugh de Lacy, J. and *cust.*
1173, *c.* Apr.	William fitz Audelin, *regis loco et vice*
,, *c.* Aug.	Richard de Clare, e. of Pembroke, *cust.*
1176, *c.* June	Raymond (le Gros) fitz William, *cust.*
1177, *c.* May	Hugh de Lacy, lord of Meath, *proc. gen.* and *cust.* Dublin
1181, *c.* 1 May	John de Lacy, constable of Chester, and Richard de Pec, *custodes*
1181–82, winter	Hugh de Lacy (reinstated)
1184, 1 Sept.	Philip de Braose (of Worcester), *proc.*
1185, 25 Apr.	John, lord of Ireland (25 Apr.–mid. Dec.)
,, Dec.	John de Courci, e. of Ulster, J.
1192	Peter Pipard and William le Petit, JJ.
1194	Peter Pipard, J.
1195	Hamo de Valognes, J.
1198 ?	Meiler fitz Henry, J.
1208	John de Gray, bp of Norwich 1200–1214, J.
1210	John, lord of Ireland (20 June–26 Aug.) (with John de Gray, J.)
,, Aug.	John de Gray, J.
1211	William le Petit (during de Gray's absence)
1213, 23 July	Henry de Londres, abp of Dublin 1213–28, J.
1215, 6 July	Geoffrey de Marisco, J.
1221, 4 Oct.	Henry de Londres, abp of Dublin, J.
1224, 2 May	William Marshall the younger, e. of Pembroke, J.
1226, 25 June	Geoffrey de Marisco, J.
1228, 13 Feb.	Richard de Burgh, J.
1232, 16 June	Hubert de Burgh, e. of Kent, J. (dism. 29 July 1232)[2]
,, 2 Sept.	Maurice fitz Gerald, 2nd baron of Offaly, J.
1245, 4 Nov.	John fitz Geoffrey, J. (arrived in Ireland bef. 8 Aug. 1246)
1254, 16 Mar.	Richard de la Rochelle, L. of Prince Edward, (styled 'justiciar' in Nov. 1254)
1256, bef. 27 June	Alan de la Zouche, J. of Prince Edward
1258, bef. 21 Oct.	Stephen de Lungespeye, J. of Prince Edward, (went to Ireland in Mar. 1259)
1260, bef. Oct.	William de Dene, J. of Prince Edward, (d. *c.* July 1261)
1261, *c.* 28 Oct.	Richard de la Rochelle, J. of Prince Edward, (summoned to England in spring 1265)
1265, 10 June	Hugh de Taghmon, bp of Meath 1252–82, J. (appd by the k.)[3]
1266, Mich.	David de Barry, J.
1268, Mich.	Robert de Ufford, J.
1270, Mich.	James de Audley, J. (d. 23 June 1272)
1272, *c.* 8 Aug.	Maurice fitz Maurice fitz Gerald, J. (last mentioned 1273,
(again) 7 Dec.	mid-Apr.)
1273, bef. 23 Aug.	Geoffrey de Joinville, J.

[1] See notes to p. 164.
[2] Never went to Ireland.
[3] This appointment was made by the k. ostensibly on behalf of Prince Edward, but on 23 Apr. 1266 (*CDI*, ii. 793) the k. addressed a writ to Richard de la Rochelle as justiciar, or to his lieutenant.

1276, 17 June	Robert de Ufford, J.
1281, 21 Nov.	Stephen de Fulburn, bp of Waterford 1274–86 (abp of Tuam 1286–88)
1282, 27 Sept.	Stephen, bp of Waterford and abp of Tuam (1286), *cust.* and J.
1288, 7 July	John de Sandford, abp of Dublin 1284–94, *cust.* and J.
1290, 12 Sept.	William de Vescy, J.
1294, 18 Oct.	William de Oddingseles, J. (d. *c.* 19 Apr. 1295)
1295, 18 Oct.	John Wogan (Oct. 1295–Sept. 1308)
1308, 15 June	Richard, 3rd e. of Ulster, K.L. (did not take office)
,, 16 June	Piers de Gaveston, K.L.
1309, 16 May	John Wogan, J. (left Ireland Aug. 1312)
1313, 30 Apr.	Theobald de Verdun, J. (held office to Apr. 1316)
1315, 4 Jan.	Edmund Butler, J.
1316, 23 Nov.	Roger Mortimer, K.L. and *cust.* (arrived in Ireland 7 Apr. 1317). Edmund Butler was still J.
1318, 6 May	William fitz John, abp of Cashel 1317–26, *cust.* (by council)
,, 11 Aug.	Alexander de Bicknor, abp of Dublin 1317–49, *cust.* and J.
1319, 15 Mar.	Roger Mortimer, J.
1321, 1 Feb.	Ralph de Gorges, J. (never reached Ireland)
,, 23 Apr.	Thomas fitz John Fitzgerald, 2nd e. of Kildare, J.
,, 21 May	John de Bermingham, 1st e. of Louth, J.
1323, 18 Nov.	John Darcy le neveu, J.
1327, 13 Feb.	Thomas fitz John Fitzgerald, 2nd e. of Kildare, J. (d. 5 Apr. 1328)
1328, 6 Apr.	Roger Outlaw, prior of Kilmainham (by council), *cust.* and J.
,, 21 Aug.	John Darcy le neveu, J. (did not take office)
1329, 19 Feb.	John Darcy le cosyn, J.
1331, 3 Mar.	William de Burgh, 4th e. of Ulster, K.L. (recalled Nov. 1331)
,, 27 Feb.	Anthony de Lucy, J. (reached Ireland June 1331; *cust.* Nov. 1331; recalled Nov. 1332)
1332, 30 Sept.	John Darcy le cosyn, J. (held office Sept. 1332–July 1337)
1337, 26 Mar.	Nicholas Welifed, bp of Waterford 1323–37, J. (never took office; d. June 1337)
,, 28 July	John de Charlton of Powys, J.
1340, 3 Mar.	John Darcy le cosyn, J. (appd J. for life 3 Mar. 1340; surrendered his office Feb. 1344)
1344, 10 Feb.	Ralph de Ufford, J. (d. 6 Apr. 1346)
1346, 7 Apr.	John Morice, J.
,, 10 May	Walter de Bermingham, J.
1349, 17 July	Thomas de Rokeby, J.
1355, 8 July	Maurice fitz Thomas Fitzgerald, 1st e. of Desmond, J. (d. 25 Jan. 1356)
1356, 30 Mar.	Maurice fitz Thomas Fitzgerald, 4th e. of Kildare, J. (appd by council 26 Jan. 1356)
,, 24 July	Thomas de Rokeby, J. (d. 23 Apr. 1357)
1357, 14 July	Almeric of St Amand, J.
1359, 16 Feb.	James Butler, 2nd e. of Ormond, J.
1361, 16 Mar.	Maurice fitz Thomas, 4th e. of Kildare, J.
,, 1 July	Lionel, 5th e. of Ulster, (duke of Clarence, 13 Nov. 1362), K.L.
1364, 25 Sept.	Lionel, duke of Clarence, K.L. (*See under* 1361)
1367, 20 Feb.	Gerald fitz Maurice Fitzgerald, 3rd e. of Desmond, J.
1369, 3 Mar.	William of Windsor, K.L.
1372, 28 Apr.	Robert de Assheton, J.
1373, 3 Dec.	William Tany, prior of Kilmainham, J. (by council)
,, 20 Sept.	William of Windsor, G.
1376, 16 Feb.	Maurice fitz Thomas, 4th e. of Kildare, J.
,, 24 July	James Butler, 2nd e. of Ormond, J.
1377, 21 July	James Butler (re-appd as J. by Richard II; and again 20 Aug. 1377)
1379, 22 Sept.	John de Bromych, J.
,, 22 Oct.	Edmund Mortimer, 3rd e. of March and 5th e. of Ulster, K.L. (died *c.* Mich. 1381)
1382, 24 Jan.	Roger Mortimer, 4th e. of March and 6th e. of Ulster, K.L.
1383, 1 July	Philip de Courtenay, K.L.

1384, 26 Nov./ 1 Dec.	James Butler, 3rd e. of Ormond, J.
1385, 1 Mar.	Philip de Courtenay, K.L. (returns to Ireland 6 May 1385)
,, 1 Dec.	Robert de Vere, 9th e. of Oxford, 1st m. of Dublin, cr. 1st duke of Ireland (Oct. 1386)
1387, bef. Nov.	Alexander de Balscot, bp of Meath 1381–1400, J. of the duke of Ireland (continued by the king, ? date)
1389, 5 Mar.	Thomas de Mortimer, J. (did not take office)
,, 1 Aug.	John de Stanley, J. (took office 25 Oct. 1389)
1391, 11 Sept.	Alexander de Balscot, bp of Meath (see under 1387), J.
1392, May	Thomas duke of Gloucester, K.L. (patent cancelled 23 July 1392)[1]
,, 24 July	James Butler, 3rd e. of Ormond, J. (patent renewed 31 May 1393)
1394, 2 Oct.– 15 May 1395	Richard II in Ireland
1395, 28 Apr.	Roger Mortimer, who was J. in 1395, e. of March and Ulster, K.L. in Ulster, Connacht and Meath
1396, 25 Apr.	William le Scrope, J. (patent renewed 25 Sept. 1396)
1397, 23 Jan.	Edmund Mortimer, in 1398 5th e. of March and 7th e. of Ulster, K.L.—William le Scrope, J.
,, 24 Apr.	Roger Mortimer, 4th e. of March and 6th e. of Ulster, K.L. (d. 20 July 1398)
1398, c. 20 July	Reginald, lord Grey of Ruthin, J. (by council)
,, 26 July	Thomas Holland, duke of Surrey, K.L. (sworn 7 Oct. 1398)
1399, 29 May– 27 July[2]	Richard II in Ireland
,, Aug.	Edmund Holland, e. of Kent, cust.—Alexander Balscot, bp. of Meath, J.
1399, 10 Dec.	John de Stanley, K.L.
1401, 18 July	Thomas of Lancaster, K.L. (resident in Ireland 13 Nov. 1401–8 Nov. 1403, renewed 1404, 1405 and 1406; he held office nominally to June 1413)
1404, 3 Mar.	James Butler, 3rd e. of Ormond, J. (by council)
1405, 7 Sept.	Gerald fitz Maurice Fitzgerald, 5th e. of Kildare, J. (by council)
1413, 8 June	John de Stanley, K.L., (sworn 25 Sept. 1413), (d. 6 Jan. 1414)
1414, 18 Jan.	Thomas Cranley, abp of Dublin 1397–1417, J. (by council)
,, 24 Feb.	John Talbot, lord Furnival, K.L. (resident intermittently in Ireland, Nov. 1414–July 1419)
1420, 10 Feb.	James Butler, 4th e. of Ormond, K.L.
1422, c. 10 Apr.	William fitz Thomas, prior of Kilmainham, J. (by council)
1422, 4 Oct.	Richard Talbot, abp of Dublin 1417–49, J.
1423, 9 May	Edmund Mortimer, 5th e. of March and 7th e. of Ulster, K.L. (died 19 Jan. 1425)
1425, Jan.	John Talbot, lord Furnival (see under 1414), J. (? by council)
,, 13 Apr.	James Butler, 4th e. of Ormond, K.L.
1426, 15 Apr.	James Butler, 4th e. of Ormond, J.
1427, 15 Mar.	John de Grey (lord Grey of Codnor), K.L.
1428, 23 Mar.	John Sutton, baron Dudley, K.L.
1430, 8 May	Richard Talbot, abp of Dublin (see under 1422), J.
1431, 29 Jan.	Thomas Stanley, K.L.
1437, 19 Apr.	Richard Talbot, abp of Dublin (see under 1422), J.
1438, 12 Feb.	Leo (Lionel) Welles, lord Welles, K.L.
1442, 27 Feb.	James Butler, 4th e. of Ormond, K.L.
1444	Richard Talbot, abp of Dublin (see under 1422), J.
1445, 12 Mar.	John Talbot, 1st e. of Shrewsbury (see under 1414 and 1425), K.L. (resident in Ireland, 1445–47)
1447, 9 Dec.	Richard, duke of York, K.L. (resident in Ireland, 5 July 1449–Sept. 1450)

[1] Did not go to Ireland.
[2] Most prob. Richard left Ireland c. 24 July.

1453, 12 May	James Butler, 5th e. of Ormond, K.L. (held office for a few weeks against Duke Richard)
1454, *c*. 25 Oct	Thomas, 7th e. of Kildare, J. (by council)
,, 1 Dec.	Richard, duke of York, K.L. (absentee)
1457, 8 Dec.	Richard, duke of York, K.L. (again) (in Ireland Dec. 1459–July 1460)
1461, Jan.	Thomas, 7th e. of Kildare, J. (by council, confirmed 30 Apr., sworn 1 May 1461)
1462, 6 Mar.	George, duke of Clarence, K.L., renewed 10 May 1465[1]
1470, 23 Mar.	John Tiptoft, 1st e. of Worcester, K.L. (d. 18 Oct. 1470)
,, bef. 13 Oct.	Thomas, 7th e. of Kildare (? by council)
,, Mich.	George, duke of Clarence, K.L.
1477	Thomas, 7th e. of Kildare, J. (by council) (d. 25 Mar. 1478)[2]
1478, 10 Mar.	John de la Pole, duke of Suffolk, K.L. (never took office)
,, aft. 25 Mar.	Gerald, 8th e. of Kildare, J. (by council)
,, 6 July	George, son of Edward IV, K.L.
1479, 5 May	Richard, duke of York, K.L.
1483, 19 July	Edward, prince of Wales, K.L.
1484, 21 Aug.	John de la Pole, e. of Lincoln, K.L.
1486, 11 Mar.	Jasper Tudor, duke of Bedford, K.L.
[1487, 24 May–Oct.	Gerald, 8th e. of Kildare, K.L. to the Yorkist pretender 'Edward VI' (Lambert Simnel)][3]
1494, 12 Sept.	Henry, son of Henry VII, K.L.
1509, bef. 1 June	Gerald, 8th e. of Kildare, L.J. (aft. death of Henry VII)
1510, 8 Nov.	Gerald, 8th e. of Kildare, L.D. to the k. (d. 3 Sept. 1513)
1513, 4 Sept.	Gerald, 9th e. of Kildare, L.J. (by council)
1513, 26 Nov.	Gerald, 9th e. of Kildare, L.D. to the k.
1515, 13 Apr.	William Preston, viscount Gormanston, L.J.
,, bef. 28 Sept.	Gerald, 9th e. of Kildare, L.D. (new patent, 24 Mar. 1516)
1519, aft. Sept.	Maurice fitz Gerald of Lackagh, L.J.
1520, 10 Mar.	Thomas Howard, e. of Surrey, L.L. (in Ireland 24 May 1520–Dec. 1521)
1522, 6 Mar.	Piers Butler, pretended 8th e. of Ormond, L.D.
1524, 13 May	Gerald, 9th e. of Kildare, L.D. (appointment kept secret until 4 Aug.)
1526, aft. 20 Dec.	Thomas fitz Gerald of Leixlip, L.J.
1527, aft. 14 Sept.	Richard Nugent, baron of Delvin, L.J.

DEPUTIES, 1176–1528

1176	William fitz Audelin, *proc.*; with John de Courci, Robert fitz Stephen and Miles de Cogan (according to Giraldus Cambrensis)
1211, summer	Richard de Tuit, ? *cust.* or D.
1213, Apr.	Geoffrey de Marisco, ? *cust.* or D. (until July 1213)
1221, 3 July	Henry de Londres, abp of Dublin 1213–28, *cust.*
1224, Nov.	Geoffrey de Marisco, *cust.*
1232, 1 July	Richard de Burgh, D.J.
1232	Ralph fitz Nicholas and others
1245, 18 Nov.	Geoffrey St Leger, bp of Ossory 1260–87, D.J. (until July 1246)

[1] Did not go to Ireland.

[2] The e. died on 25 Mar. 1477 (English style). The contemporary 'Annals of Connacht', followed by the 'Four Masters', give his obit in 1478.

[3] The e. tests letters patent, issued in the name of K. Edward, on 13 Aug. 1487 (*Cal. of Ormond Deeds*, iii. 272).

1258, Oct.	An unnamed D. of Stephen de Lungspeye, acted until Mar. 1259
1265, 13 Feb.	Fulk de Sandford, abp of Dublin 1256–71, *cust.*[1]
1265, 6 May	Roger Waspayl, *cust.*[1]
1270, 6 Mar.	Richard of Exeter, D.J., (until Nov. 1277)
1272, 1 July	John de Muscegros, *cust.* (until Aug. 1272)
1280, Apr.	Stephen de Fulburn, bp of Waterford 1274–86, D.J. (until May 1281, during de Ufford's absence)
1284, *c.* Apr.	William fitz Roger, prior of Kilmainham (until 29 July 1285)
1290, Apr.	William Doddingseles and Walter l'Enfant, LL. of J.
1293, *c.* Dec.	Walter de la Haye, *cust.* and D.J. (until ? 4 June 1294)
1294, 4 June	William fitz Roger, prior of Kilmainham, *cust.* and D.J. (until 19 Oct. 1294)
1294, *c.* Oct.	Thomas fitz Maurice FitzGerald, *cust.* and D.J. (until 2 Dec. 1295)
1295, Nov.	Walter de la Haye, L. of *cust.*
1297, May	Walter de la Haye, *cust.* of office of J.
1299, Mich.	Richard de Burgh, 3rd e. of Ulster, L. of J. (until Hilary 1300)
1301, 23 Aug.	William de Ros, prior of Kilmainham, D.J. (until 31 Mar. 1302)
1302, 30 June	Maurice de Rochfort, D.J. (until 29 Sept. 1302)
1304, 30 Sept.	Edmund Butler, *cust.* and D.J. (until 23 May 1305)
1308, *c.* Apr.	William de Burgh, L. of J. (until 15 May 1309)
1312, 7 Aug.	Edmund Butler, *cust.* and D.J. (until 18 June 1314)
1320, 30 Sept.	Thomas fitz John FitzGerald, 2nd e. of Kildare, L. of J. (until 30 June 1321)
1322, 18 Aug.	William de Bermingham, D.J. (until 18 Feb. 1323)
1324, *c.* July	Roger Outlaw, prior of Kilmainham, D.J. (until Oct. 1324; again 1–13 May 1327 and 31 May 1330–2 June 1331)
1332, 3 Dec.	Thomas de Burgh, D.J. (until 12 Feb. 1333; again 29 June 1333–18 Jan. 1334 and in July 1334)
1335, 15 Mar.	Roger Outlaw, prior of Kilmainham, D.J. (until 26 June 1335; again 28 Aug.–18 Sept. 1335 and 15 Nov. 1336–15 Oct. 1337)
1338, 15 May	Thomas de Charlton, bp of Hereford 1327–44, *cust.* and acting J. (until 7 Apr. 1340)
1340, 8 Apr.	Roger Outlaw, prior of Kilmainham, D.J. (until 5 Feb. 1341)
1341, 22 Feb.	Alexander de Bicknor, abp of Dublin 1317–49, *cust.* and acting J. (by council; until 16 May 1341)
1341, 16 May	John Morice, D.J. (until 14 July 1344)
1346, 10 Apr.	Roger Darcy, acting J. (by council; until 15 May 1346)
1347, 28 Nov.	John Larger, prior of Kilmainham, D.J. (until 26 Apr. 1348)
1349, 3 Oct.	John de Carew, D.J. (until 19 Dec. 1349)
1352, 5 Mar.	Maurice de Rochfort, bp of Limerick 1336–53, D.J. (until 14 June 1352)
1355, 8 Aug.	Maurice fitz Thomas FitzGerald, 4th e. of Kildare, L. of J. (until 20 Aug. 1355)
1357, 24 Apr.	Master John de Bolton (by council), acting J. (until 5 Sept. 1357)
1357, 30 Aug.	Maurice fitz Thomas FitzGerald, 4th e. of Kildare, D.J. (until 26 Nov. 1357; again 9 Oct. 1360–31 Mar. 1361)
1364, 22 Apr.	James Butler, 2nd e. of Ormond, *cust.* (until 25 Jan. 1365)
1366, 7 Nov.	Thomas de la Dale, *cust.* (by council; until 22 Apr. 1367)
1370, 29 Apr.	James de Pickering, D.L.
1372, 22 Mar.	Maurice fitz Thomas FitzGerald, 4th e. of Kildare, *cust.* (until 16 July 1372)
1373, Oct.	Ralph Cheyne, D.J. (until Nov. 1373)
1373, 15 Nov.	John Keppok, G. and keeper (until 31 Oct. 1375)
1379, 13 Oct.	Alexander de Balscot, bp of Ossory 1370–86, acting J. (by council; until Dec. 1379)

[1] This appointment was ineffective.

1382, 10 Jan.	John Colton, abp of Armagh 1383–1404, chancellor, acting J., (until 3 Mar. 1382)
1382, 3 Mar.	Thomas Mortimer, D.J. (until autumn 1383)
1385, 13 July	Alexander de Balscot, bp of Ossory (*see under* 1379), Thomas le Reve, bp of Waterford 1363–94, James Butler, 3rd e. of Ormond, Gerald fitz Gerald, 3rd e. of Desmond, D.D. of K.L.
1386, *c.* Apr.	Richard White, prior of Kilmainham, J. of the m. of Dublin (until 30 Aug. 1386)
1386, 8 June	John de Stanley, L. of the m. of Dublin (until ? Nov. 1387)
1388, 17 July	Thomas Fleming, D.
1389, Aug.	Richard White, prior of Kilmainham, and Robert Preston, D.D. of J.[1]
1390, 31 Jan.	Robert Sutton[2]
1391, 4 Aug.	Richard Northalis, bp of Ossory 1386–95, and Peter de la Freyne, appd as D.D. for co. Kilkenny
1398, Apr.	Edmund Mortimer, D.
1400, 8 May	Gilbert Halsale, D. for Ulster
,, 14 May	Thomas de Burgo, D. for Connacht
1401, May	William Stanley, D. (until Aug. 1401)
,, 19 Dec.	Stephen le Scrope, D. (acting from 23 Aug. 1401–2 Feb. 1404)
1403, 5 Dec.	William de Burgo, D. for Connacht
1404, 18/26 Oct.	Stephen le Scrope, D. (until June 1405)
1405, 25 June	James Butler, 3rd e. of Ormond, D. to le Scrope (d. 7 Sept. 1405)
1406, autumn	Stephen le Scrope, D. (until 8 Dec. 1407)
1407, 8 Dec.	James Butler, 4th e. of Ormond, D. to le Scrope (until 2 Aug. 1408)
1409, 4 Mar.	Thomas Butler, prior of Kilmainham, D. (until 25 Sept. 1413)
1416, 5 Feb.	Thomas Cranley, abp of Dublin 1397–1417, D. (until summer or autumn 1416; he d. 25 May 1417)
1418, bef. Mar.	Thomas Talbot, D. (until mid June 1418)
1419, July	Richard Talbot, abp of Dublin 1417–49, D. (until 6 Mar. 1420)
1423, 4 Aug.	Edward Dantsey, bp of Meath 1412–30, D. (until aft. 3 May 1424)
1424, bef. 11 May	James Butler, 4th e. of Ormond, D. (until aft. 2 Sept. 1424)
1427, bef. 22 Dec.	Edward Dantsey, bp of Meath 1412–30, D. (until aft. 19 July 1428)
1429, bef. 5 Nov.	Thomas Strange, D. (until aft. 26 Apr. 1430)
1432, bef. 10 Dec.	Christopher Plunket, D. (until aft. 9 Apr. 1434)
1435, bef. 22 Nov.	Richard Talbot, abp of Dublin (*see under* 1414), D. (until aft. 11 Apr. 1437)
1439, bef. 13 Apr.	William Welles, D. (until aft. 11 May 1440)
1441, *c.* 15 Mar.	James Butler, 4th e. of Ormond, D. (until late 1441 or early 1442)
1444, 28 Aug.	Richard Nugent, baron of Delvin, D. (until aft. 22 Oct. 1444)
1447, *c.* Nov.	Richard Talbot, abp of Dublin (*see under* 1414), D. (d. 15 Aug. 1449)
1448, bef. 23 Dec.	Richard Nugent, baron of Delvin, D. (until ? 6 July 1449)
1450, 22 Aug.	James Butler (from 23 Aug. 1452 5th e. of Ormond), D. (until 23 Aug. 1452)
1452, aft. 23 Aug.	Edward FitzEustace, D. (until aft. 25 May 1453)
1453, *c.* 25 June	John Mey, abp of Armagh 1443–56, D. (until aft. 8 Mar. 1454)
1454, 23 Apr.	Edward FitzEustace, D. (until 25 Oct. 1454)
1455, bef. 18 Apr.	Thomas fitz Maurice FitzGerald, 7th e. of Kildare, D. (until ? autumn 1459)
1459, 12 Dec.	Thomas Bathe, baron of Louth, D.[3]
1459, 13 Dec.	John Bole, abp of Armagh 1457–71, D.[3]

[1] For other D.D. appointed by bp Balscot at this time, see *Cal. Pat. Rolls* (Ireland).
[2] Appointed to conduct the Parliament at Kilkenny.
[3] This appointment was ineffective.

1460, July	Thomas fitz Maurice FitzGerald, 7th e. of Kildare, D. (until Dec. 1460)
1462, 16 May	Roland FitzEustace, lord Portlester, D. (until Apr. 1463)
1463, 1 Apr.	Thomas fitz James FitzGerald, 8th e. of Desmond, D. (until Oct. 1467)
1464, aft. 24 June	Thomas fitz Maurice FitzGerald, 7th e. of Kildare, D. to e. of Desmond
1465, 11 May	John Tiptoft, 1st e. of Worcester, D.[1]
1467, spring	John Tiptoft, 1st e. of Worcester D. (until ? early 1470)
1470, ? early	Edmund Dudley, D. (until summer 1470)
1471, Feb.	Thomas fitz Maurice FitzGerald, 7th e. of Kildare, D. (until ? Apr. 1471; again 22 × 28 Dec. 1471–? July 1475)
1475, bef. 18 Apr.	William Sherwood, bp of Meath 1460–82, D. (until Feb. 1478)
1477, ? Jan	Robert Preston, lord Gormanston, D. to bp of Meath (until 13 Oct. 1477)
1478, July	Henry Grey, lord Grey, D. (until aft. 15 Dec. 1478)
1479, bef. 14 Jan.	Robert Preston, visct Gormanston,[2] D. to lord Grey (until aft. March 1479)
1479, 7 May	Robert Preston, visct Gormanston, D. (until aft. 18 Oct. 1479)
1479, bef. 5 Oct.	Gerald FitzGerald, 8th e. of Kildare, D. (until 9 Apr. 1483; again 31 Aug. 1483–Mar. 1484; aft. 22 Oct. 1484–? 24 Oct. 1485; ? Mar. 1486–20 May 1492)[3]
1492, 20 May	Walter fitz Simons, abp of Dublin 1484–1511, D. (until aft. 3 Sept. 1493)
1493, 6 Sept.	Robert Preston, visct Gormanston, D. (until Oct. 1494)
1493, 14 Oct.	William Preston, D. to visct Gormanston (until aft. 20 Feb. 1494)
1494, 13 Sept.	Edward Poynings, D. (until aft. 20 Dec. 1495)
1496, 1 Jan.	Henry Deane, bp of Bangor 1494–1500, D. (until aft. 4 July 1496)
1496, 6 Aug.	Gerald FitzGerald, 8th e. of Kildare, D. (until aft. 21 Apr. 1509)
1503, Apr.	Walter fitz Simons, abp of Dublin (*see under* 1492), D. (until Aug. 1503)
1521, bef. 21 Dec.	Piers Butler, pretended 8th e. of Ormond, D. (until bef. 9 Mar. 1522)

CHIEF GOVERNORS, 1528–1922

1528, 15 May	15 May	Thomas fitz Gerald, L.J. (by council)
1528, 4 Aug.		Piers Butler, 1st e. of Ossory, L.D.
1529, 22 June		Henry fitz Roy, duke of Richmond and Somerset, L.L. (d. 22 July 1536)
1534, 30 July	24 Oct.	William Skeffington, L.D. (d. 31 Dec. 1535)
1536, 23 Feb.		Leonard, lord Grey, L.D. (left Ireland Apr. 1540; exec. 28 July 1541)
1540, 1 Apr.	2 May	Sir William Brereton, L.J. (by council)
1540, 7 July	*c.* 12 Aug.	Anthony St Leger, L.D.
1545, 3 July } 1546, 7 Nov. }		Anthony St Leger, L.D., re-appd by new patents
1547, 7 Apr.		Anthony St Leger, L.D. (aft. death of Henry VIII)

[1] This appointment seems to have been ineffective.
[2] Created visct Gormanston, 7 Aug. 1478.
[3] Sided with the Yorkist pretender Lambert Simnel, crowned 'Edward VI' in Dublin on 24 May 1487.

1548, 22 Apr.	21 May	Edward Bellingham, L.D.
1549, 27 Dec.	29 Dec.	Francis Bryan, L.J. (by council)
1550, 2 Feb.		William Brabazon, L.J. (by council)
,, 4 Aug.	10 Sept.	Anthony St Leger, L.D.
1551, 29 Apr.	23 May	James Crofts, L.D.
1552, 6 Dec.	9 Dec.	Thomas Cusack and Gerald Aylmer, L.JJ. (by council)
1553, 1 Sept.	19 Nov.	Anthony St Leger, L.D.
1556, 27 Apr.	26 May	Thomas Radcliff, lord Fitzwalter, (e. of Sussex 1557), L.D.
1558, 9 Mar.	21 May	Thomas Radcliff, 3rd e. of Sussex, L.D. (again 17 Aug. 1558)
,, 12 Dec.	13 Dec.	Henry Sidney, L.J. (by council) (aft. death of Queen Mary)
1559, 3 July	30 Aug.	Thomas, e. of Sussex, L.D.
1560, 6 May	25 June	,, ,, ,, L.L.
1561, 24 May	5 June	,, ,, ,, L.L.
1562, 4 July	29 July	,, ,, ,, L.L.
1565, 13 Oct.	20 Jan. 1566	Henry Sidney, L.D.
1568, 17 Apr.	28 Oct.	,, ,, L.D.
1571, 1 Apr.	1 Apr.	William Fitzwilliams, L.J. (by council)
,, 11 Dec.	13 Jan. 1572	William Fitzwilliams, L.D.
1575, 5 Aug.	18 Sept.	Henry Sidney, L.D.
1578, 27 Apr.	14 Sept.	William Drury, L.J.
1579, 11 Oct.	11 Oct.	William Pelham, L.J. (by council)
1580, 3 Feb.		,, ,, L.J.
,, 15 July	7 Sept.	Arthur, lord Grey, L.D.
1582, 14 July	31 Aug.	Adam Loftus, abp of Dublin 1567–1605, and Henry Wallop, L.JJ.
1584, 7 Jan.	21 June	John Perrott, L.D.
1588, 17 Feb.	30 June	William Fitzwilliams, L.D.
1594, 16 May	11 Aug.	William Russell, L.D.
1597, 5 Mar.	22 May	Thomas, lord Burgh, L.D.
,, 29 Oct.	30 Oct.	Thomas Norreys, L.J. (by council)
,, 15 Nov.	27 Nov.	Adam Loftus, abp of Dublin (see under 1582) and Richard Gardiner, L.JJ.
1599, 12 Mar.	15 Apr.	Robert Devereux, 2nd e. of Essex, L.L.
,, 24 Sept.	25 Sept.	Adam Loftus, abp of Dublin (see under 1582) and George Cary, L.JJ. (by council)
1600, 21 Jan.	28 Feb.	Charles Blount, lord Mountjoy, L.D.
1603, 9 Apr.	9 Apr.	,, ,, L.J. (by council) (aft. death of Elizabeth)
,, 12 Apr.		Charles Blount, L.D.
,, 25 Apr.	26 May	,, ,, L.L.
,, 30 May	1 June	Sir George Cary, L.D.[1]
1604, 15 Oct.	3 Feb.	Sir Arthur Chichester, L.D.[1] (patent renewed 28 Feb. 1607 and 27 July 1614)
1615, 29 Nov.	11 Feb.	Thomas Jones, abp of Dublin 1605–19, and Sir John Denham, C.J., K.B., L.JJ.
,, 2 July	30 Aug.	Sir Oliver St John, L.D. (aft. lord Grandison)
1622, 18 Apr.	4 May	Sir Adam Loftus, L.C., and Richard, viscount Powerscourt, L.JJ.
,, 4 Feb.	8 Sept.	Henry Cary, viscount Falkland, L.D. (patent renewed 29 Mar. 1625)
1629, 8 Aug.	26 Oct.	Adam, viscount Loftus, L.C., and Richard Boyle, 1st e. of Cork, L.JJ.
1633, 3 July	25 July	Thomas Wentworth, viscount Wentworth (e. of Strafford 1640), L.D.
1640, 13 Jan.	18 Mar.	Thomas Wentworth, 1st e. of Strafford, L.L. (exec. 12 May 1641)

[1] Cary and Chichester were appd as D. to assist Mountjoy, who became e. of Devonshire in July 1604 and died on 3 Apr. 1606.

1641, 14 June		Robert Sydney, 2nd e. of Leicester, L.L.[1]
1643, 31 Mar.	12 May	Sir John Borlase and Sir Henry Tichborne, L.JJ. (appd by K. Charles I)
1643, 13 Nov.	21 Jan. 1644	James Butler, 1st m. of Ormond,[2] L.L. (appd by K. Charles I)
1646, 9 Apr.		Philip Sydney, lord Lisle, L.L. (appd by parliament; left for Ireland Feb. 1647; commission expired 15 Apr. 1647)
1647, 19 June	28 July	Arthur Annesley, Sir Robert King, Sir Robert Meredyth, Col. John Moore and Col. Michael Jones, commissioners of parliament
1648, 30 Sept.		James, m. of Ormond,[3] L.L. (returns to Ireland ? 17 Feb. 1649; appd by K. Charles I)
1649, 30 Mar.		Lt-Gen. Oliver Cromwell, C.-in-C.[4]
1649, 22 June		also G.-Gen., commission lapsed June 1652; (by 3 July) referred to as L.L.
1650, 2 July		Com. Gen. Henry Ireton, L.D.; d. 20 Nov. 1651
1650, 2 July		Lt-Gen. Edmund Ludlow, Col. John Jones, MPs, commissioners for civil affairs
1650, 4 Oct.		Miles Corbet, John Weaver, Major Richard Salwey, MPs, added 20 Nov. Salwey excused; 27 Nov. Corbet confirmed
1652, 9 July		Charles Fleetwood, C.-in-C. and a civil commissioner[5]
1652, 13 Aug.		Ludlow, Jones, Corbet, Fleetwood, commissioners
1652, 25 Aug.		Oliver Cromwell, Fleetwood, Ludlow, Jones, Corbet and Weaver, commissioners
1654, 17 Aug.		Fleetwood, L.D. Corbet, William Steele,[6] Col. Robert Hammond (d. almost immediately), Robert Goodwin, Col. Matthew Tomlinson, Richard Pepys, Chief Justice (d. 5 Jan. 1659) councillors
1654, 25 Dec.		Henry Cromwell, councillor (added)
1655, 6 Sept.		Henry Cromwell, acting C.-in-C., as M.Gen. (in Fleetwood's absence)
1657, 17 Nov.		Henry Cromwell, L.D. and C.-in-C.
1658, 6 Oct.		Henry Cromwell, L.L.; res. 15 June 1659
(1656, 4 Aug.		William Bury or Berry, councillor; 1657 Goodwin dropped)
1659, 7 June		Col. John Jones MP, William Steele, Robert Goodwin MP, commissioners
1659, 9 June		Col. Matthew Tomlinson, Miles Corbet MP, added as commissioners
1659, 4 July		Lt-Gen. Edmund Ludlow MP, C.-in-C.
1660, 19 Jan.		John Weaver MP, Robert Goodwin MP, Sir Charles Coote, Sir Hardress Waller, Col. Henry Markham, commissioners
1660 ? June		Lt-Gen. George Monck, duke of Albermarle, L.L.
,, 26 Oct.	31 Dec.	Sir Maurice Eustace, L.C., and Roger, e. of Orrery, L.JJ.

[1] Did not go to Ireland.

[2] Mr, later Sir George Lane, secretary to Ormond, 1644–28 July 1647.

[3] George Lane, secretary to Ormond, Sept. 1648–Dec. 1650; 6 Dec. 1650, Ulick Burke, 1st m. of Clanricarde, L.D. appd by K. Charles II.

[4] 1649 or 1650–52, Col. Thomas Herbert and Col. Vincent Potter, secretaries or attendants on the commissioners in Ireland.

[5] 1652–54, Herbert alone as secretary to the commissioners. Thereafter, until 1659 Herbert acted as clerk to the council in Ireland.

[6] Steele did not arrive until late in 1656, by which time he was also Lord Chancellor of Ireland.

1662, 21 Feb.	27 July	James, duke of Ormond, L.L.
1668, 7 Feb.	25 Apr.	Thomas, e. of Ossory, L.D.
1669, 3 May	18 Sept.	John, baron Robartes, L.L.
1670, 4 Feb.	21 Apr.	John, lord Berkeley, L.L.
1672, 21 May	5 Aug.	Arthur, 1st e. of Essex, L.L.
1677, 24 May	24 Aug.	James, 1st duke of Ormond, L.L.
1685, 24 Feb.	20 Mar.	Michael Boyle, abp of Dublin 1663–79, L.C., and Arthur, 1st e. of Granard, L.JJ.
1685, 1 Oct.	9 Jan. 1686	Henry, 2nd e. of Clarendon, L.L.
1687, 8 Jan.	12 Feb.	Richard, 1st e. of Tyrconnell, L.D.
1689, 12 Mar.		James II in Ireland (left Ireland 4 July 1690)
1690, 14 June		William III in Ireland (left Ireland 5 Sept. 1690)
,, 4 Sept.	15 Sept.	Henry, lord Sydney, and Thomas Coningsby, L.JJ.[1]
,, 4 Dec.	24 Dec.	Henry, viscount Sydney, Sir Charles Porter, L.C., and Thomas Coningsby, L.JJ.
1692, 18 Mar.	4 Sept.	Henry, viscount Sydney, L.L.
1693, 13 June	3 July	Sir Charles Porter, L.C., and Sir Cyril Wyche, L.JJ.
,, 26 June	28 July	Henry, baron Capel, Sir Cyril Wyche and William Dunscombe, L.JJ.
1695, 9 May	27 May	Henry, lord Capel, L.D.
1696, 16 May	18 May	Morrogh, viscount Blessington and Wm Wolseley, L.JJ.
,, 2 June	2 June	Sir Chas Porter, L.C., elected L.J. by council
,, 10 July	29 July	Sir Chas Porter, L.C., Chas e. of Mountrath, and Henry, e. of Drogheda, L.JJ.
1697, 21 Jan.	6 Feb.	Henry de Massue, m. Ruvigny and e. of Galway, L.J.
,, 14 May	31 May	Chas, m. of Winchester, Henry, e. of Galway, and Edwd, viscount Villiers, L.JJ.[2]
1699, 9 Apr.	18 May	Chas, duke of Bolton, Henry, e. of Galway, Edward, e. of Jersey, and Narcissus, abp of Dublin, L.JJ.
,, 29 June	23 Aug.	Chas, duke of Bolton, Chas, e. of Berkeley, and Henry, e. of Galway, L.JJ.
1700, 28 Dec.	18 Sept. 1701	Laurence, e. of Rochester, L.L.[3]
1703, 19 Feb.	4 June	James, duke of Ormond, L.L.
1707, 30 Apr.	24 June	Thomas, e. of Pembroke and Montgomery, L.L.
1708, 4 Dec.	21 Apr. 1709	Thomas, e. of Wharton, L.L.
1710, 26 Oct.	3 July 1711	James, duke of Ormond, L.L.
1713, 22 Sept.	27 Oct.	Charles, duke of Shrewsbury, L.L.
1714, 21 Sept.		Charles, e. of Sunderland, L.L.[4]
1717, 13 Feb.		Charles, viscount Townshend, L.L.[5]
,, 27 Apr.	7 Aug.	Charles, duke of Bolton, L.L.
1720, 18 June	28 Aug. 1721	Charles, duke of Grafton, L.L.
1724, 6 May	22 Oct. }	John, lord Carteret, L.L.
1727, 26 Oct.	19 Nov. }	
1730, 23 June	11 Sept. 1731	Lionel Cranfield, e. of Dorset, L.L.
1737, 9 Apr.	7 Sept.	William, duke of Devonshire, L.L.
1745, 8 Jan.	31 Aug.	Philip Dormer, e. of Chesterfield, L.L.
1746, 15 Nov.	13 Sept. 1747	William, e. of Harrington, L.L.
1750, 15 Dec.	19 Sept. 1751	Lionel Cranfield, duke of Dorset, L.L.

[1] Sir Robert Southwell, Secretary of State, 1690–1702.

[2] The last did not go to Ireland.

[3] Edward Southwell succeeded his father on Sir Robert's surrender of office, just before his death in 1702, and acted as Secretary of State until he died in 1730.

[4] Sunderland did not go to Ireland.

[5] Townshend did not go to Ireland.

1755, 2 Apr.	5 May	William, lord Cavendish, m. of Hartington (aft. duke of Devonshire), L.L.
1757, 3 Jan.	25 Sept.	John, duke of Bedford, L.L.
1761, 3 Apr.	6 Oct.	Geo. Montague-Dunk, e. of Halifax, L.L.
1763, 27 Apr.	22 Sept.	Hugh, e. of Northumberland, L.L.
1765, 5 June		Thomas, viscount Weymouth, L.L.[1]
,, 7 Aug.	18 Oct.	Francis Seymour, e. of Hertford, L.L.
1766, 6 Oct.		George William, e. of Bristol, L.L.[1]
1767, 19 Aug.	14 Oct.	George, viscount Townshend, L.L.
1772, 29 Oct.	30 Nov.	Simon, e. of Harcourt, L.L.
1776, 7 Dec.	25 Jan. 1777	John, e. of Buckinghamshire, L.L.
1780, 29 Nov.	23 Dec.	Frederick, e. of Carlisle, L.L.
1782, 8 Apr.	14 Apr.	William, duke of Portland, L.L.
,, 15 Aug.	15 Sept.	George, e. Temple (aft. m. of Buckingham), L.L.
1783, 3 May	3 June	Robert, e. of Northington, L.L.
1784, 12 Feb.	24 Feb.	Charles, duke of Rutland, L.L.
1787, 27 Oct.	3 Nov.	Richard, baron Rokeby, abp of Armagh } L.JJ. James, viscount Lifford, L.C. }
		John Foster, speaker
,, 6 Nov.	16 Dec.	George, m. of Buckingham, L.L.
1789, 24 Oct.	5 Jan. 1790	John, e. of Westmorland, L.L.
1794, 13 Dec.	4 Jan. 1795	William, e. Fitzwilliam, L.L.
1795, 13 Mar.	31 Mar.	John Jeffries, e. Camden, L.L.
1798, 14 June	20 June	Charles, m. Cornwallis, L.L.
1801, 27 Apr.	25 May	Philip, e. of Hardwicke, L.L.
1805, 21 Nov.		Edward, e. of Powis[2]
1806, 12 Mar.	28 Mar.	John, duke of Bedford, L.L.
1807, 11 Apr.	19 Apr.	Charles, duke of Richmond, L.L.
1813, 23 June	26 Aug.	Charles, viscount (aft. e.) Whitworth, L.L.
1817, 3 Oct.	9 Oct.	Charles, e. Talbot, L.L.[3]
1821, 8 Dec.	29 Dec.	Richard, m. Wellesley, L.L.
1828, 27 Feb.	1 Mar.	Henry William, m. of Anglesey, L.L.
1829, 22 Jan. or 23 Jan.	6 Mar.	Hugh, duke of Northumberland, L.L.
1830, 4 Dec.	23 Dec.	Henry William, m. of Anglesey, L.L.
1833, 12 Sept.	26 Sept.	Richard, m. Wellesley, L.L.
1835, 1 Jan.	6 Jan.	Thomas, e. of Haddington, L.L.
,, 29 Apr. } 1837, 26 Aug. }	11 May 1835	Henry, e. of Mulgrave (aft. m. of Normanby), L.L.
1839, 13 Mar.	3 Apr.	Hugh, viscount Ebrington (aft. e. Fortescue), L.L.
1841, 11 Sept.	15 Sept.	Thomas, e. de Grey, L.L.
1844, 17 July	26 July	William, baron Heytesbury, L.L.
1846, 8 July	11 July	John William, e. of Bessborough, L.L.
1847, 22 May	26 May	George W. Fredk, e. of Clarendon, L.L.
1852, 1 Mar.	10 Mar.	Archibald William, e. of Eglinton, L.L.
1853, 5 Jan.	6 Jan.	Edward Granville, e. of St Germans, L.L.
1855, 7 Mar.	13 Mar.	George William Fredk, e. of Carlisle, L.L.
1858, 8 Mar.	12 Mar.	Archibald William, e. of Eglinton and Winton, L.L.
1859, 24 June	13 July	George William Fredk, e. of Carlisle, L.L.
1864, 1 Nov.	8 Nov.	John, lord Wodehouse (aft. e. of Kimberley), L.L.
1866, 13 July	20 July	James, m. aft. duke, of Abercorn, L.L.
1868, 18 Dec.	23 Dec.	John Poyntz, e. Spencer, L.L.
1874, 2 Mar.	18 Apr.	James, duke of Abercorn, L.L.
1876, 11 Dec.	12 Dec.	John Winston, duke of Marlborough, L.L.
1880, 4 May	5 May	Francis Thomas de Grey, e. Cowper, L.L.

[1] Did not assume office.
[2] Not sworn; did not go to Ireland.
[3] K. Geo. IV, 12 Aug.–5 Sept. 1821.

1882, 4 May	6 May	John Poyntz, e. Spencer, L.L.
1885, 27 June	30 June	Henry H. M., e. of Carnarvon, L.L.
1886, 8 Feb.	20 Feb.	John Campbell, e. of Aberdeen, L.L.
,, 3 Aug.	5 Aug.	Charles Stewart, m. of Londonderry, L.L.
1889, 30 July	5 Oct.	Laurence, e. of Zetland, L.L.
1892, 18 Aug.	22 Aug.	Robert, baron Houghton (aft. e. of Crewe), L.L.
1895, 29 June	8 July	George Henry, e. Cadogan, L.L.
1902, 11 Aug.	16 Aug.	William Humble, e. Dudley, L.L.
1905, 11 Dec.	14 Dec.	John Campbell, e. of Aberdeen, L.L.
1915, 17 Feb.	19 Feb.	Ivor, lord Wimborne, L.L., res. 10 May 1916, reappd 18 Aug. 1916
1918, 9 May	11 May	John, viscount French, L.L.
1921, 27 Apr.	2 May	Edmund, viscount Fitzalan of Derwent, L.L.

DEPUTIES FROM 1530

		From 24 Aug. 1529 to 2 Aug. 1530 the office was exercised by a 'secret council' composed of John Allen, abp of Dublin 1528–34 (chancellor), Patrick Birmingham and John Rawson[1]
1530, 22 June		William Skeffington, D.
1532, 5 July		Gerald, 9th e. of Kildare
1534, Feb.		Thomas, lord Offaly
		Richard Nugent, acting D. (June–Aug. 1534)
1536, 1 Jan.		Leonard, lord Grey, L.J. (by council)
1543, 12 Oct.	10 Feb. 1544	William Brabazon, L.J.
1546, 16 Feb.	1 Apr.	William Brabazon, L.J.; acting to 1 Dec. 1546
1557, 12 Nov.	5 Dec.	Hugh Curwen, abp of Dublin 1555–59, and Henry Sidney, L.JJ.
1558, 18 Jan.	6 Feb. ⎫	
,, 4 Aug.	18 Sept. ⎬	Henry Sidney, L.J.
1560, 18 Jan.	15 Feb. ⎫	
1561, 10 Jan.	2 Feb. ⎬	William Fitzwilliams, L.J.
,, 20 Dec.	22 Jan. 1562 ⎭	
1564, 2 May	25 May	Nicholas Arnold, L.J.
1567, 12 Aug.	14 Oct.	Robert Weston, L.C. and William Fitzwilliams, L.JJ.
1597, 29 Oct.		Thomas, 10th e. of Ormond, appd in charge of military affairs
1614, 15 Oct.	4 Mar. 1615	Thomas Jones, abp of Dublin (1605–19), and Sir Richard Wingfield, L.JJ.
1636, 4 Apr.	3 July	Adam, viscount Loftus, L.C., and Christopher Wandesford, M.R., L.JJ.
1639, 12 Sept.		Sir Robert Dillon, lord Dillon, and Christopher Wandesford, M.R., L.JJ.
1640, 1 Apr.	3 Apr.	Christopher Wandesford, M.R., L.D. (d. 3 Dec. 1640)
1640, 15 Dec.	30 Dec.	Robert, lord Dillon, and Sir William Parsons, L.JJ.
1640, 30 Dec.	10 Feb. 1641	Sir William Parsons and Sir John Borlase, L.JJ.
1660, 25 July		John, lord Robartes, L.D.
1664, 6 May		Thomas, e. of Ossory, L.D. (until 3 Sept. 1665 during absence of Ormond)

[1] See *BIHR*, xii, 175–7.

1668, 10 Apr.		Thomas, e. of Ossory
1671, 11 May	12 June	Michael Boyle, abp of Dublin (1663–79), L.C. and Sir Arthur Forbes, L.JJ. (until May 1676)
1682, 13 Apr.	2 May	Richard, 1st e. of Arran, L.D. (until the return of Ormond in Aug. 1684)
1687, 6 Aug.		Sir Alexander Fitton, L.C., and William, 7th e. of Clanrickarde, L.JJ.
1701, 28 Mar.	4 Apr.	Narcissus Marsh, abp of Dublin (1694–1703), Henry, e. of Drogheda, Hugh, e. of Mount Alexander, L.JJ.
1701, 9 Dec.	4 Jan. 1702	Narcissus Marsh, abp of Dublin, Henry e. of Drogheda, L.JJ.
1702, 30 Mar.	11 Apr.	Hugh, e. of Mount Alexander, Maj.-Gen. Thomas Erle, Thomas Keightley, L.JJ.
1704, 10 Feb.	23 or 24 Mar.	Sir Rich. Cox, L.C., Hugh e. of Mount Alexander, Maj.-Gen. Thomas Erle[1]
1705, 21 May	27 June	Sir Richard Cox, L.C., John, lord Cutts, L.JJ.
1707, 8 Feb.	15 Feb.	Narcissus Marsh, abp of Armagh (1703–13), Sir Richard Cox, L.C., L.JJ.
1707, 30 Apr.	27 Nov.	Narcissus Marsh, abp of Armagh, Richard Freeman, L.C., L.JJ.
1709, 5 Sept.	19 Sept.	Richard Freeman, L.C., Lt-Gen. Richard Ingoldsby, L.JJ.
1710, 15 Aug.	c. 29 Aug.	Richard Freeman, L.C., Lt-Gen. Richard Ingoldsby, L.JJ.
1710, 22 Nov.	28 Nov.	Narcissus Marsh, abp of Armagh, Lt-Gen. Richard Ingoldsby, L.JJ.
1710, 30 Dec. 1711, 29 Oct. 1712, 4 Feb.	22 Jan. 1711 } 3 Dec. } 13 Mar.	Sir Constantine Phipps, L.C., Lt-Gen. Richard Ingoldsby, d. 29 Jan. 1712 Sir Constantine Phipps, L.C., John Vesey, abp of Tuam (1679–1716), L.JJ.
1714, 7 Feb.	7 June	Thomas Lindsay, abp of Armagh (1714–24), Sir Constantine Phipps, L.C., John Vesey, abp of Tuam, L.JJ.
1714, 4 Sept.	21 Sept.	William King, abp of Dublin (1703–29), John Vesey, abp of Tuam, Robert, e. of Kildare, L.JJ.
1715, 6 Sept.	1 Nov.	Charles, duke of Grafton, Henry, e. of Galway, L.JJ.
1717, 22 Feb.	20 Mar.	Alan, lord Brodrick, L.C., William Conolly, speaker, William King, abp of Dublin (sworn 20 July), L.JJ.
1717, 25 Nov.	9 Jan.	Alan, visct Midleton, L.C. (sworn 22 May), William King, abp of Dublin, William Conolly, speaker, L.JJ.
1719, 8 Oct.	20 Nov.	Alan, visct Midleton, L.C., William Conolly, L.JJ.
1722, 31 Jan.	24 Feb.	William King, abp of Dublin, Richard, visct Shannon, William Conolly, speaker, L.JJ.
1722, 30 Dec.	17 May	William King, abp of Dublin, Richard, visct Shannon, William Conolly, speaker, Alan, visct Midleton, L.C. (sworn 13 June), L.JJ.
1724, 7 Apr.	9 May	Alan, visct Midleton, Richard, visct Shannon, William Conolly, speaker, L.JJ.
1726, 9 Mar.	2 Apr.	Hugh Boulter, abp of Armagh (1724–42), Richard West, L.C., William Conolly, speaker, L.JJ.
1726, 15 Dec. 1728, 15 May	23 Dec. } 15 May }	Thomas Wyndham, L.C., Hugh Boulter, abp of Armagh, William Conolly, speaker, L.JJ.

[1] Ormond returned to Ireland 16 Nov. 1704.

1730, 27 Feb. 1732, 16 Mar.	22 Apr. } 24 Apr. }	Hugh Boulter, abp of Armagh, Thomas, lord Wyndham, L.C., Sir Ralph Gore, L.JJ.
1733, 23 May	23 May	Hugh Boulter, abp of Armagh, Thomas, lord Wyndham, L.C., L.JJ.
1734, 23 Mar. 1736, 15 Apr. 1738, 16 Feb.	3 May } 19 May } 28 Mar. }	Hugh Boulter, abp of Armagh, Thomas, lord Wyndham, L.C., Henry Boyle, speaker, L.JJ.
1740, 26 Mar.	18 Apr.	Hugh Boulter, abp of Armagh (sworn 13 May), Robert Jocelyn, L.C., Henry Boyle, speaker, L.JJ.
1742, 17 Jan.	18 Feb.	Hugh Boulter, abp of Armagh, Robert Jocelyn, L.C., Henry Boyle, speaker, L.JJ.
1742, 25 Nov. 1744, 19 Jan. 1746, 26 Mar.	3 Dec. } 12 Apr. } 25 Apr. }	John Hoadley, abp of Armagh (1742–46), Robert Jocelyn (cr. baron Newport 29 Nov. 1743), L.C., Henry Boyle, speaker, L.JJ.
1747, 31 Mar. 1748, 15 Mar.	10 Apr. } 20 Apr. }	George Stone, abp of Armagh (1747–64), Robert, lord Newport, L.C., Henry Boyle, speaker, L.JJ.
1749, 31 Jan.		Robert, lord Newport, L.C., Henry Boyle, speaker, L.JJ.
1749, 31 July 1750, 8 Mar. 1752, 24 Mar.	20 Apr. } 27 May }	George Stone, abp of Armagh, Robert, lord Newport, L.C., Henry Boyle, speaker, L.JJ.
1754, 11 Apr.	11 May	George Stone, abp of Armagh, Robert, lord Newport, L.C., Brabazon, e. of Bessborough L.JJ.
1756, 20 Apr. 1756, 20 Sept.	11 May } }	Robert, visc. Jocelyn, L.C., James, e. of Kildare, Brabazon, e. of Bessborough, L.JJ.
1758, 17 Mar. 1760, 15 Apr. 1761, 15 May 1762, 24 Mar. 1764, 9 Apr.	10 May } 20 May } 27 May } 3 May } 15 May }	George Stone, abp of Armagh, Henry, e. of Shannon, John Ponsonby, speaker, L.JJ.[1]
1765, 8 Feb.	22 Feb.	John, baron Bowes, L.C., John Ponsonby, speaker, L.JJ.
1766, 10 Apr.	11 June	John, baron Bowes, L.C., Charles, e. of Drogheda, John Ponsonby, speaker, L.JJ.
1789, 19 June	30 June	Richard, baron Rokeby, abp of Armagh (1765–94), Lord Fitzgibbon, L.C., John Foster, speaker, L.JJ.
1795, 24 Mar.	25 Mar.	William Newcome, abp of Armagh (1795–1800), John, visc. Fitzgibbon, L.C., L.JJ.

Upon the partition of Ireland, the office of Governor General of the Irish Free State was established by the Irish Free State Constitution Act, 1922 (15 Geo. V, c. 1) and that of Governor of Northern Ireland by letters patent of 9 Dec. 1922 in accordance with the Irish Free State (Consequential Provisions) Act, 1922 (15 Geo. V, c. 2). Under the terms of the 'Constitution of Ireland' Act, which came into force 29 Dec. 1937, the office of President was created, whereby that of Governor General of the Irish Free State ceased to exist. Upon the introduction of direct rule in 1972, the post of Secretary of State for Northern Ireland was created; this is held by a member of the British cabinet, and holders of the office are listed above, p. 152. The office of Governor of Northern Ireland was abolished on 18 July 1973 under the Northern Ireland Constitution Act, 1973.

GOVERNORS GENERAL OF THE IRISH FREE STATE

1922, 6 Dec.	6 Dec.	Timothy Michael Healy
1927, 15 Dec.	1 Feb. 1928	James McNeill
1932, 26 Nov.	26 Nov.	Domhnall Ua Buachalla (Donal Buckley)

[1] Bedford returned to Ireland 7 Oct. 1759.

PRESIDENTS OF IRELAND

1938, 4 May	25 June	Douglas Hyde
1945, 18 June	25 June	Sean Thomas O'Kelly
1959, 19 June	25 June	Eamon de Valera
1973, 31 May	25 June	Erskine Hamilton Childers (d. 17 Nov. 1974)
1974, 3 Dec.	19 Dec.	Cearbhall Ó Dálaigh
1976, 9 Nov.	3 Dec.	Patrick John Hillery

GOVERNORS OF NORTHERN IRELAND

1922, 11 Dec.	12 Dec.	James Albert Edward Hamilton, 3rd Duke of Abercorn
1945, 7 Sept.	7 Sept.	William Spencer Leveson Gower, 4th e. of Granville
1952, 1 Dec.	3 Dec.	John de Vere Loder, 2nd baron Wakehurst
1964, 1 Dec.	3 Dec.	John Maxwell Erskine, 1st baron Erskine of Rerrick
1968, 2 Dec.	3 Dec.	Ralph Francis Alnwick Grey, baron Grey of Naunton

CHIEF SECRETARIES IN IRELAND, 1566–1922

The office of Chief Secretary to the Lord Lieutenant or Lord Deputy of Ireland can be traced from 1566. Until the Union, however, its occupants were rather personal assistants of the Lord Lieutenants than ministers of the Crown, and their term of office began and ended with that of the Lord Lieutenant whom they served. Until 1801 a gap between the final date of a secretary's term of office and the initial date of his successor normally indicates that the Lord Lieutenant was then absent and that Ireland was governed by lords justices.

After 1801 the Lord Lieutenant became increasingly vice-regal and resided more regularly in Ireland. His Chief Secretary assumed a more independent position, defending the government's Irish policy in Parliament and at times in the Cabinet. After 1801 only the date of appointment is therefore given.

For a statement of the sources from which the list below has been compiled, *see Irish Historical Studies*, viii (1952), 59–72. Revisions have been made for the third edition of the *Handbook* in the light of evidence presented in J. C. Sainty, 'The secretariat of the chief governors of Ireland, 1690–1800', *Royal Irish Academy Proceedings*, lxxvii sect. C (1977), 1–33, and the list published in *A New History of Ireland*, ix, ed. T. W. Moody *et al.* (Oxford, 1984), 529–32. After 1801 the dates are those of notifications of the chief secretaries' appointments to the treasury or the Paymaster of the Civil Services. Some comments upon the office in the early nineteenth century will be found in R. B. McDowell, *Public Opinion and Government Policy in Ireland, 1801–46*, chapter 3.

1566, 20 Jan.–1567, 9 Oct. 1568, 28 Oct.–	Sir Edward Waterhouse
1569, 15 July–1571, 31 Mar.	Edmund Tremayne
1571, aft. Mar.–	Philip Williams
1575, 18 Sept.–	Edmund Molyneux
1580, 7 Sept.–1582, 30 Aug.	Edmund Spenser

1584, 21 June–1594, 10 Aug.	Philip Williams
1594, 11 Aug.–1597, 21 May	Sir Richard Cooke
1597, 22 May–1597, 13 Oct.	Philip Williams
1599, 15 Apr.–1599, 4 Sept.	Sir Henry Wotton
1600, 27 Feb.–1600, Mar.	Sir Francis Mitchell
1600, Mar.–1600, 13 Nov.	George Cranmer (died in office)
1600, 14 Nov.–1603, 31 May	Fynes Moryson
1603, 1 June–1605, 2 Feb.	Sir John Bingley
1605, 3 Feb.–1616, 10 Feb.	Sir Henry Piers
1616, 30 Aug.–1622, 3 May	Sir Henry Holcroft
1622, 8 Sept.–1629, 25 Oct.	Sir John Veele
1644, 21 Jan.–1646, Apr.	Sir George Lane (viscount Lanesborough 1676)
1660, June–1660, Dec.	Mathew Lock
1662, 27 July–1669, 17 Sept.	Sir Thomas Page
1669, 18 Sept.–1670, 20 May	Sir Henry Ford
1670, 21 May–1672, 4 Aug.	Sir Ellis Leighton
1672, 5 Aug.–1673, 10 Dec.	Sir Henry Ford
1673, 11 Dec.–1676, 23 Aug.	Sir William Harbord
1676, 24 Aug.–1682, 1 May	Sir Cyril Wyche
1682, 2 May–1685, 19 Mar.	Sir William Ellis
1686, 9 Jan.–1687, 11 Feb.	Sir Paul Rycaut
1687, 12 Feb.–1688, 20 Jan.	Thomas Sheridan
1688, 2 Feb.–1689, 24 Jan.	Patrick Tyrrell
1690, Sept.–1692, Mar.	John Davis
1692, 4 Sept.–1693, 2 July	Sir Cyril Wyche
1695, 27 May–1696, 16 May	Sir Richard Aldworth
1696, 30 July–1697, May	William Palmer
1697, May–1699, Nov.	Matthew Prior
1699, Nov.–1701, April	Humphrey May
1700, 28 Dec.–1703, 18 Feb.	Francis Gwyn
1703, 19 Feb.–1707, 29 Apr.	Edward Southwell
1707, 30 Apr.–1708, 3 Dec.	George Dodington
1708, 4 Dec.–1710, 25 Oct.	Joseph Addison
1710, 26 Oct.–1713, 21 Sept.	Edward Southwell
1713, 22 Sept.–1714, 3 Oct.	Sir John Stanley
1714, 4 Oct.–1715, 23 Aug.	Joseph Addison
1715, Sept.–1717, Apr.	Martin Bladen and Charles Delafaye
1717, 27 Apr.–1720, 7 June	Edward Webster
1720, 8 June–1721, Aug.	Horatio Walpole (lord Walpole 1756)
1721, Aug.–1724, 5 May	Edward Hopkins
1724, 6 May–1730, 22 June	Thomas Clutterbuck
1730, 23 June–1737, 8 Apr.	Walter Cary
1737, 9 Apr.–1739, 11 May	Sir Edward Walpole, K.B.
1739, 12 May–1739, 13 Oct.	Thomas Townshend
1739, 14 Oct.–1741, 7 June	Henry Bilson Legge
1741, 8 June–1745, 7 Jan.	William Ponsonby, viscount Duncannon (e. of Bessborough 1758)
1745, 8 Jan.–1746, 22 June	Richard Liddell (died in office)
1746, 5 July–1746, 14 Nov.	Sewallis Shirley
1746, 15 Nov.–1750, 14 Dec.	Edward Weston
1750, 15 Dec.–1755, 1 Apr.	Lord George Sackville (lord George Germain 1770, viscount Sackville 1782)
1755, 2 Apr.–1757, 2 Jan.	Henry Seymour Conway
1757, 3 Jan.–1761, 2 Apr.	Richard Rigby
1761, 3 Apr.–1764, 2 July	William Gerard Hamilton
1764, 3 July–1765, 4 June	Charles Moore, e. of Drogheda (m. 1791)
1765, 5 June–1765, 6 Aug.	Sir Charles Bunbury, bt
1765, 7 Aug.–1766, 5 Oct.	Francis Seymour Conway, viscount Beauchamp (m. of Hertford 1794)
1766, 6 Oct.–1767, 6 July	Augustus John Hervey (e. of Bristol 1775) (resigned)
1767, 9 July–1767, 18 Aug.	Theophilus Jones
1767, 19 Aug.–1768, 31 Dec.	Lord Frederick Campbell
1769, 1 Jan.–1772, 29 Nov.	Sir George Macartney, K.B. (lord Macartney 1794)

1772, 30 Nov.–1776, 6 Dec.	Sir John Blaquiere (lord de Blaquiere 1800)
1776, 13 Dec.–1780, 28 Nov.	Richard Heron, bt 1778
1780, 29 Nov.–1782, 7 Apr.	William Eden (lord Auckland 1789)
1782, 8 Apr.–1782, 14 Aug.	Richard FitzPatrick
1782, 15 Aug.–1783, 2 May	William Wyndham Grenville (lord Grenville 1790)
1783, 3 May–1783, 26 Aug.	William Windham
1783, 27 Aug.–1784, 11 Feb.	Thomas Pelham (e. of Chichester 1805)
1784, 12 Feb.–1787, 24 Oct.	Thomas Orde (Orde-Powlett 1795, lord Bolton 1797)
1787, 6 Nov.–1789, 5 Apr.	Alleyne FitzHerbert (lord St Helens 1791)
1789, 6 Apr.–1793, 15 Dec.	Robert Hobart (e. of Buckinghamshire 1804)
1793, 16 Dec.–1794, 12 Dec.	Sylvester Douglas (lord Glenbervie 1800)
1794, 13 Dec.–1795, 12 Mar.	George Damer, viscount Milton (e. of Dorchester 1798)
1795, 13 Mar.–1798, 2 Nov.	Thomas Pelham (see under 1783)
1798, 3 Nov.–1801, 26 Apr.	Robert Stewart, viscount Castlereagh (m. of Londonderry 1821)

1801, 25 May	Charles Abbot (1st lord Colchester 1817)
1802, 13 Feb.	William Wickham
1804, 6 Feb.	Sir Evan Nepean, bt
1805, 23 Mar.	Nicholas Vansittart (1st lord Bexley 1823)
1805, 21 Sept.	Charles Long (1st lord Farnborough 1826)
1806, 28 Mar.	William Elliot
1807, 19 Apr.	Sir Arthur Wellesley (1st duke of Wellington 1814)
1809, 13 Apr.	Robert Dundas, later Saunders-Dundas (2nd viscount Melville 1811)
1809, 18 Oct.	William Wellesley Pole (1st lord Maryborough [U.K.] 1821, 3rd e. of Mornington [Irish] 1842)
1812, 4 Aug.	Robert Peel
1818, 3 Aug.	Charles Grant (1st lord Glenelg 1835)
1821, 29 Dec.	Henry Goulburn
1827, 29 Apr.	William Lamb (1st viscount Melbourne [Irish] and 2nd lord Melbourne [U.K.] 1828)
1828, 21 June	Lord Francis Leveson Gower (1st e. of Ellesmere 1846)
1830, 17 July	Sir Henry Hardinge (1st viscount Hardinge 1846)
1830, 29 Nov.	Edward Geoffrey Smith-Stanley, commonly called lord Stanley (14th e. of Derby 1851)
1833, 29 Mar.	Sir John Cam Hobhouse, bt (1st lord Broughton 1851)
1833, 17 May	Edward John Littleton (1st lord Hatherton 1835)
1834, 16 Dec.	Sir Henry Hardinge. (See under 1830)
1835, 22 Apr.	George William Frederick Howard, commonly called viscount Morpeth (7th e. of Carlisle 1848)
1841, 6 Sept.	Edward Granville Eliot, commonly called lord Eliot, 3rd e. of St Germans 1845
1845, 1 Feb.	Sir Thomas Francis Fremantle, bt (1st lord Cottesloe 1874)
1846, 14 Feb.	Henry Pelham Pelham-Clinton, commonly called e. of Lincoln (duke of Newcastle-under-Lyme 1851)
1846, 6 July	Henry Labouchere (1st lord Taunton 1859)
1847, 22 July	Sir William Meredyth Somerville, bt (1st lord Meredyth 1866)
1852, 1 Mar.	Richard Southwell Bourke, commonly called Lord Naas (6th e. of Mayo [Irish] 1867)
1853, 6 Jan.	Sir John Young, bt (1st lord Lisgar 1870)
1855, 1 Mar.	Edward Horsman
1857, 27 May	Henry Arthur Herbert
1858, 4 Mar.	Lord Naas. (See under 1852)
1859, 24 June	Edward Cardwell (1st viscount Cardwell 1874)
1861, 29 July	Sir Robert Peel, bt
1865, 7 Dec.	Chichester Samuel Parkinson-Fortescue (1st lord Carlingford 1874)
1866, 10 July	Lord Naas. (See under 1852)
1868, 29 Sept.	John Wilson-Patten (1st lord Winmarleigh 1874)
1868, 23 Dec.	Chichester Fortescue. (See under 1865)

1871, 12 Jan.	Spencer Compton Cavendish, commonly called m. of Hartington (8th duke of Devonshire 1891)
1874, 27 Feb.	Sir Michael Edward Hicks-Beach (1st e. of St Aldwyn 1915)
1878, 15 Feb.	James Lowther
1880, 30 Apr.	William Edward Forster
1882, 6 May	Lord Frederick Charles Cavendish
1882, 9 May	George Otto Trevelyan
1884, 23 Oct.	Henry Campbell-Bannerman
1885, 25 June	Sir William Hart Dyke, bt
1886, 23 Jan.	William Henry Smith
1886, 6 Feb.	John Morley (1st viscount Morley of Blackburn 1908)
1886, 5 Aug.	Sir Michael Hicks-Beach. (*See under* 1874)
1887, 7 Mar.	Arthur James Balfour (1st e. of Balfour 1922)
1891, 9 Nov.	William Lawies Jackson (1st lord Allerton 1902)
1892, 22 Aug.	John Morley. (*See under* 1886)
1895, 4 July	Gerald William Balfour (2nd e. of Balfour 1930)
1900, 9 Nov.	George Wyndham
1905, 12 Mar.	Walter Hume Long (1st viscount Long 1921)
1905, 14 Dec.	James Bryce (1st viscount Bryce 1914)
1907, 29 Jan.	Augustine Birrell
1916, 3 Aug.	Henry Edward Duke (1st lord Merrivale 1925)
1918, 4 May	Edward Shortt
1919, 13 Jan.	James Ian Macpherson (1st lord Strathcarron 1936)
1920, 12 Apr.	Sir Hamar Greenwood, bt (1st viscount Greenwood 1937)

SCOTTISH OFFICERS OF STATE

INTRODUCTION

The lists of Scottish officers of state published in the 2nd edition of the *Handbook of British Chronology* represented the first comprehensive treatment of the subject based on record sources. The present revision takes account of research in the last 20 years, particularly for the publication of royal acts in the series *Regesta Regum Scottorum*, on other aspects of administration and on Scottish clergy in the later medieval period. It has not been possible to extend the coverage of the lists, and omissions include the constable and marshal (both of which became hereditary at an early date), the admiral and the keeper of the privy seal. The following published lists may also be noted:

Justiciars, *c.* 1165–1306	G. W. S. Barrow, *The Kingdom of Scots* (1978), 137–8
Justice clerks, 1532–1947	*Introduction to Scottish Legal History* (Stair Society 1958), 461–2
Justice clerks, 1651–1972	*Oxford Companion to Law* (1980), 1342–3
Solicitors general, 1647–1979	*Ibid*, 1347–9

The most important offices originated in Scotland at about the same period as in England, but it has not proved possible to trace the Scottish officers of state in the orderly sequence of their English counterparts. The unfortunate gaps in the earlier public records of Scotland can only be partially filled from other sources; and the surviving Scottish medieval records require a good deal of critical sifting before they can make their full contribution to studies of this nature. Recorded appointments to office and demissions of office are, therefore, not to be found consistently before the sixteenth century. In the absence of such precise evidence, the dates given for the earlier period are simply the earliest and latest on which particular persons are known to have been in office. The chief sources of information have necessarily been the financial records, notably the exchequer rolls, and the testing-clauses of royal charters recorded in the extant records of the great seal or preserved among private or other muniments, but experience has shown that the witness lists of recorded charters must be used with great caution. Where actual dates of appointment are available for the later period, these have been given in preference to dates of entry to office.

Layout and conventions conform generally to those in the corresponding English lists. There is, however, one important modification. In order to avoid creating a misleading impression of continuity, approximate dates of demission of office have been placed in a separate column until 1460, when the evidence becomes sufficient to establish a clear succession. Thereafter the standard layout has been adopted. Dates occurring between 1 January and 24 March inclusive in any year before 1600 have been assigned to their historical year according to the modern computation. The following abbreviations have been used for printed sources:

APS	*Acts of the Parliaments of Scotland* (Record edition)
CSP Scot.	*Calendar of State Papers relating to Scotland and Mary Queen of Scots*
ER	*Exchequer Rolls of Scotland*
RMS	*Registrum Magni Sigilli Regum Scottorum*
RPC	*Register of the Privy Council of Scotland*
RRS	*Regesta Regum Scottorum*
RSS	*Registrum Secreti Sigilli Regum Scottorum*
SHR	*Scottish Historical Review*
TA	*Accounts of the [Lord High] Treasurer of Scotland*

CHANCELLORS

G. Crawfurd's *Lives of the Officers of State in Scotland* (1726), 1–249, has yet to be replaced by a modern study of the chancellor, but A. A. M. Duncan, *Scotland: the Making of the Kingdom* (1975) summarizes recent research on the period up to 1286. J. Maitland Thomson gives a brief account of the royal chancery in *The Public Records of Scotland* (1922), 54–76.

ALEXANDER I

c. 1123	Herbert	

DAVID I

	Herbert remained in office	*c. 1131*
c. 1136	William Comyn, archdeacon of Worcester	*c. 1141*
c. 1141	Jordan	
bef. 1144	Edward (bp of Aberdeen *bef.* 1150–71)	*24 Aug., 1147*
bef. 1151	Walter de Bidun	

MALCOLM IV[1]

	Walter de Bidun remained in office	*1161–2*
1161–2	Ingram, archdeacon of Glasgow (bp of Glasgow 1164–74)	*20 Sept., 1164*
1165	Nicholas (*see* chamberlains, 1159)	

WILLIAM I[2]

	Nicholas remained in office	*ob.* 1171
c. 1171	Walter de Bidun (elect of Dunkeld 1178)	*ob.* 1178
1178–87	Office vacant	
c. 1188	Roger (elect of St Andrews 1189–98, bp of St Andrews 1198–1202)	*13 Apr., 1189*
1189	Hugh de Roxburgh (elect of Glasgow 1199)	*ob.* 10 July, 1199
1199, 8 Sept.	William Malvoisin, archdeacon of Lothian, bp of Glasgow 1199–1202 (bp of St Andrews 1202–38)	*20 Sept.,* 1202
1203, 4 Nov.	Florence, elect of Glasgow 1202–7	*ob.* 30 Nov., 1210
1211, 28 June	William del Bois, archdeacon of Lothian	

[1] For Malcolm IV's chancellors, *see RRS*, i. 28–30.
[2] For William I's chancellors, *see RRS*, ii. 29–33.

ALEXANDER II

	William del Bois remained in office	*29 Sept., 1224*
1226, 20 Jan.[1]	Thomas de Stirling, archdeacon of Glasgow	*26 Feb., 1227*
1227, 5 June	Matthew Scot, elect of Dunkeld 1229–30	*30 Apr., 1230*
1231, 30 Mar.	William de Bondington, bp of Glasgow 1233–58	*8 Feb., 1247*

ALEXANDER III

1249	Robert de Keldeleth, abbot of Dunfermline (later abbot of Melrose)	*1251*
1254, 13 Feb.[2]	Gamelin, bp of St Andrews 1255–71	*20 Sept., 1255*
1255, 20 Sept.	Richard de Inverkeithing (*see* chamberlains 1249), bp of Dunkeld 1250–72	*29 Oct., 1257*
1259	William Wishart, archdeacon of St Andrews, bp of St Andrews 1271–9	*1273*
1273	William Fraser, dean of Glasgow, bp of St Andrews 1279–97	*aft. 1279*
bef. 1285	Thomas Charteris (de Carnoto)	

MARGARET

Thomas Charteris remained in office

FIRST INTERREGNUM

	Thomas Charteris remained in office	11 June, 1291
1291, 12 June[3]	Alan de St Edmunds, bp of Caithness 1282–91	*ob.* 5 Nov.–12 Dec., 1291
1292, 23 Feb.	William de Dumfries	*ob.* 22 May, 1292
1292, 12 June	Alan de Dumfries	

JOHN (BALLIOL)

1294, 20 June	Thomas de Hunsinghore	
1295–6	Alexander Kennedy	10 July, 1296

SECOND INTERREGNUM

1301, 31 Jan.	Nicholas Balmyle

ROBERT I

1308, 31 Oct.	Bernard,[4] abbot of Arbroath, bp of Sodor 1328–31	*20 Mar., 1328*
1328, 3 July	Walter Twynham	*28 July, 1329*

DAVID II

1329, *July*[5]	Adam Moray, bp of Brechin 1328–49	*10 Mar., 1332*
1340, 13 Apr.	Sir Thomas Charteris	*ob.* 17 Oct., 1346
1350, 20 Mar.	William Caldwell	*6 Mar., 1352*
1353, 9 Dec.	Patrick Leuchars, bp of Brechin 1351–83	*3 Mar., 1370*
1370, 4 Apr.	John Carrick, canon of Glasgow, elect of Dunkeld 1370	

[1] Though not styled chancellor until 1226, Stirling appears as witness in some royal charters of 1225 in the position of precedence normal for a chancellor.

[2] Appears earlier as king's clerk '*sigillum eius portante*' (D. E. R. Watt, *Biographical Dictionary of Scottish Graduates*, 211).

[3] For associates of the chancellor, appointed by Edward I, *see SHR*, xxv, 38.

[4] G. Crawfurd's identification of the chancellor with Bernard de Linton, parson of Mordington 1296 (*Officers of State*, 17), has been generally accepted but is not confirmed by contemporary sources.

[5] Payment of Twynham's fee ended on 28 July though papal sources call him chancellor up to 30 Nov., 1329. An unnamed chancellor was paid from 24 July and Moray is mentioned by name 28 Aug., 1329 (Watt, *Scottish Graduates*, 406, 550).

ROBERT II

	John Carrick remained in office	*11 Feb.*, 1377
1377, *30 Mar.*	John Peebles, archdeacon of St Andrews, bp of Dunkeld, 1378–90	*18 Mar.*, 1390[1]

ROBERT III

1390, *23 July*	Alexander Cockburn of Langton, kp. of great seal	*2 May*, 1395
1395, *3 July*	Duncan Petit, archdeacon of Glasgow	*14 Jan.*, 1397
1397, *10 May*[2]	Gilbert Greenlaw, bp of Aberdeen 1390–1421	

JAMES I

	Gilbert Greenlaw remained in office	*24 July, 1421*[3]
1422, 4 Jan.	William Lauder, bp of Glasgow 1408–25	*14 Dec.*, 1425[4]
1426, *7 Feb.*	John Cameron, bp of Glasgow 1426–46, kp. of great seal, chancellor *30* May, 1427[5]	

JAMES II

	John Cameron remained in office	1439[6]
1439, *4 May*	Sir William Crichton of that ilk, lord Crichton *c.* 1447, master of household 1433–4	forf. 4 Nov., 1444
1444, *7 Sept.*	James Bruce, bp of Dunkeld 1441–7, bp of Glasgow 1447	*ob. bef.* 4 Oct., 1447
1448, 14 Apr.	William, lord Crichton (*see under* 1439)	*16 Sept., 1453*
1454, 1 July	William Sinclair, e. of Orkney, e. of Orkney and Caithness, 1455	27 Oct., 1456
1456, *20 Nov.*	George Schoriswood, bp of Brechin 1454–62	*4 Apr.*, 1460
1460, *6 July*	Andrew Stewart, 1st lord Avandale	

JAMES III

	Lord Avandale remained in office, vac. *17 June*, 1482
1482, *25 Aug.*	John Laing, bp of Glasgow 1474–83, *ob.* 11 Jan., 1483
1483, *10* Jan.	James Livingston, bp of Dunkeld 1475–83, *ob.* 28 Aug., 1483
1483, *6* Sept.	Colin Campbell, 1st e. of Argyll, vac. *27* Feb., 1488
1488, *21* Feb.	William Elphinstone, bp of Aberdeen 1483–1514, vac. 11 June 1488

JAMES IV

1488, *15* June	Colin, e. of Argyll (*see under* 1483), vac. *24 Oct.*, 1492
1493, 9 Jan.	Archibald Douglas, 5th e. of Angus, vac. *22 Sept.*, 1497
1497, *12 Nov.*	George Gordon, 2nd e. of Huntly, *ob. c.* 8 June, 1501

[1] Alexander Cockburn and others appear as kps of great seal from 12 Aug., 1389 in absence of Peebles, who may have ceased to be chancellor bef. death of Robert II, 19 Apr., 1390.

[2] *See* Watt, *Scottish Graduates*, 238 for misdated ref. to Greenlaw as chancellor 31 Aug., 1394.

[3] *See* Watt, *Scottish Graduates*, 238–9, for date of death and suggestion that John Forrester was kp. of great seal pending appointment of Lauder.

[4] *See* Watt, *Scottish Graduates*, 333, for date of death.

[5] Cameron was keeper of both the great and privy seals before becoming chancellor. The witness lists in the great seal register for 1426–7 (*RMS*, ii. nos. 30–107), which is badly calendared and indexed, have been checked against the original MS entries.

[6] Cameron appears as chancellor in an entry dated 3 May, 1439 in the great seal register (*RMS*, ii. no. 201) but the original charter is dated 1437 (W. Fraser, *The Scotts of Buccleuch*, ii. 30).

1501, 5 July	James Stewart, duke of Ross, abp of St Andrews 1497–1504, *ob.* 13 Jan., 1504
1504–10	Office vacant
1510, 14 June	Alexander Stewart, abp of St Andrews 1504–13, *ob.* 9 Sept., 1513

JAMES V

1513, *29* Sept.	James Beaton, abp of Glasgow 1508–23, abp of St Andrews 1523–39, vac. *24 July*, 1526
1527, 6 Aug.	Archibald Douglas, 6th e. of Angus, vac. *28 May*, 1528
1528, *26* June	Gavin Dunbar, abp of Glasgow, 1524–47

MARY I

	Gavin Dunbar remained in office, vac. *18 Sept.*, 1543
1543, 10 Jan.[1]	David Beaton, cardinal abp of St Andrews 1537–46, *ob.* 29 May, 1546
1546, 5 June	George Gordon, 4th e. of Huntly, *ob.* 28 Oct., 1562
1563, 7 Jan.	James Douglas, 4th e. of Morton
1566, 20 Mar.	George Gordon, 5th e. of Huntly

JAMES VI

	E. of Huntly remained in office
1567, 11 Nov.	James, e. of Morton (*see under* 1563), regent 24 Nov., 1572
1573, 17 Jan.	Archibald Campbell, 5th e. of Argyll, *ob.* 12 Sept., 1573
1573, 8 Oct.	John Lyon, 8th lord Glamis, *ob.* 17 Mar., 1578
1578, 29 Mar.	John Stewart, 4th e. of Atholl, *ob.* 24 Apr., 1579
1579, 17 Aug.	Colin Campbell, 6th e. of Argyll, *ob.* 10 Sept., 1584
1584, 15 May[2]	James Stewart, 5th e. of Arran, dism. 10 Dec., 1585
1585–6	Office vacant
1586, 31 May[3]	Sir John Maitland of Thirlestane, lord Thirlestane 1590, kp. of great seal, chancellor 29 July, 1587, *ob.* 3 Oct. 1595
1595–9	Office vacant
1599, 18 Jan.	John Graham, 3rd e. of Montrose, high commissioner, 13 Dec., 1604
1604, 13 Dec.	Alexander Seton, lord Fyvie, e. of Dunfermline 1605, *ob.* 16 June 1622
1622, 3 July	Sir George Hay of Kinfauns, e. of Kinnoull 1633

CHARLES I–CHARLES II

	Sir George Hay remained in office, *ob.* 16 Dec., 1634
1634, 14 Jan.	John Spottiswood, abp of St Andrews 1615–38, res. bef. 14 Nov., 1638
1638, *13 Nov.*	James Hamilton, 3rd m. of Hamilton (1st duke 1643), kp. of great seal[4]
1641, 30 Sept.	John Campbell, 1st e. of Loudoun; vac. Aug. 1651

INTERREGNUM[5]

| 1652, May | Alexander Jaffray, keeper of the great seal |
| 1656, Feb. | Samuel Disbrowe, keeper of the great seal; vac. *May* 1660 |

---

[1] Imprisoned at end of Jan., 1543, when Dunbar was restored to chancellorship; designated chancellor again 26 Sept. and accepted office formally 13 Dec. 1543 (*APS*, ii. 442).

[2] Appd to act in absence of Argyll (*RSS*, viii. no. 2073).

[3] Office of chancellor left vacant, but Maitland given title of vice-chancellor (*RMS*, vi. no. 997).

[4] Hamilton did not get formal commission as kp. but retained the great seal, by virtue of royal warrant, aft. receiving Spottiswood's resignation until Loudoun was appd.

[5] The keepers of the great seal had more limited powers than the chancellors of S.

CHARLES II

1660, Aug.[1]	William Cunningham, 8th e. of Glencairn, ob. 30 May 1664
1664, 14 Oct.	John Leslie, 7th e. of Rothes, 1st duke of Rothes 1680, kp. of great seal, chancellor 16 Apr., 1667, *ob.* 27 July 1681
1681–2	Office vacant
1682, 1 May	Sir George Gordon of Haddo, 1st e. of Aberdeen 1682
1684, 13 June	James Drummond, 4th e. of Perth

JAMES VII

E. of Perth remained in office until the Revolution

WILLIAM II AND MARY II

1689–92	In commission
1692, 5 Jan.	John Hay, 2nd e. of Tweeddale, 1st m. of Tweeddale, 1694
1696, 2 May	Patrick Hume, 1st lord Polwarth, 1st e. of Marchmont, 1697

ANNE

	E. of Marchmont remained in office
1702, 21 Nov.	James Ogilvy, 1st e. of Seafield
1704, 17 Oct.	John Hay, 2nd m. of Tweeddale
1705, 9 Mar.	James Ogilvy, 1st e. of Seafield, remained in office aft. the Union until appd lord chief baron of exchequer in Scotland 25 May 1708, given title of chancellor again 14 Sept., 1713, *ob.* 15 Aug., 1730

Under the treaty of Union the great seal was replaced by a new seal for Scotland, whose keeper ranked as senior officer of state. Since 1885 the office of keeper has been vested in the secretary for Scotland (secretary of state from 1926).

CHAMBERLAINS

There is no modern study of the office of chamberlain. Information about his financial functions will be found in *Exchequer Rolls of Scotland* vols. i–iv; for list of chamberlains (with references) to 1406 *see ER*, ii, cxviii–cxxv. For his functions in connection with the burghs *see* 'A Chamberlain's Ayre in Aberdeen, 1399 × 1400', *SHR*, xxxiii. 27. G. Crawfurd, *Lives of the Officers of State in Scotland* (1726), 251–354, is still useful for later chamberlains.

DAVID I

| *c. 1124* | Edmund |
| *bef. 1136* | Herbert |

MALCOLM IV[2]

| | Herbert remained in office | *1160* |
| *1159* | Nicholas (*see* chancellors, 1165) | *1164* |

WILLIAM I[3]

c. 1165	Philip de Valognes	*c. 1171*
c. 1171	Walter de Berkeley	*c. 1193*
c. 1193	Philip de Valognes	

[1] Glencairn was one of several officers of state appd by Charles II at Restoration who took office bef. date of commissions under great seal (19 Jan. 1661).
[2] For Malcolm IV's chamberlains, *see RRS*, i. 30–1.
[3] For William I's chamberlains, *see RRS*, ii. 33–4.

ALEXANDER II

	Philip de Valognes remained in office	*ob.* 5 Nov., 1215
c. 1216	William de Valognes	*ob. bef.* 21 June 1219
1223, 18 Mar.	Henry de Balliol	*9 Jan., 1230*
1231, 19 Mar.	John de Maxwell	*9 July, 1233*
1235, 8 Oct.	David de Bernham (bp of St Andrews 1239–53)	*1 Oct., 1239*
1241, 18 July	Henry de Balliol	*ob. bef.* 15 Oct., 1246
1249, 8 Apr.	Richard de Inverkeithing (bp of Dunkeld 1250–72)	

ALEXANDER III

1251, 17 Feb.	Robert de Meyners	*20 Aug., 1251*
1252, 21 Apr.	William, e. of Mar	*20 Sept., 1255*
1255	David de Lindsay	*c. 1257*
1259, 18 Mar.	Aymer de Maxwell	*12 Dec., 1260*
1262, 31 Mar.	William, e. of Mar	*20 May, 1266*
1267	Reginald le Chen	*1269*
1269	Thomas fitz Randolph	*18 Aug., 1277*
1278, 21 May	John de Lindsay	*4 Sept., 1281*
c. 1286	Weland de Stiklaw[1]	

MARGARET–JOHN (BALLIOL)

1287, 7 Dec.	Alexander de Balliol	*6 Dec., 1295*

ROBERT I

1309, 26 Apr.	Stephen Dunnideer, el. of Glasgow 1317	
bef. 1314, June	William Lindsay, parson of Ayr	*10 Sept., 1319*
1319, 10 Dec.	Sir Alexander Fraser	*5 Mar., 1327*
1327, *14 Aug.*	Robert Peebles	

DAVID II

	Robert Peebles remained in office	*ob.* 12 Nov., 1329
1329, *9 Dec.*	Reginald More	*9 Mar., 1333*
1333, 11 Sept.	Robert Lauder	*17 Nov., 1333*
1334, 11 Nov.	Reginald More	*ob. bef. 14 May, 1341*
1341, 22 May	William Bullock	dism. after *11 June*, 1342
1343, 31 Jan.	John Roxburgh	*ob.* 17 Oct., 1346
1350, 15 May[2]	Sir Robert Erskine	
1356, 20 June	Thomas Stewart, e. of Angus	*16 Mar., 1358*
1358	Thomas, e. of Mar	*9 Apr., 1359*
1359, 13 Apr.[3]	Walter Biggar, parson of Errol	*25 Mar., 1363*
1363, 1 Apr.	Sir Robert Erskine	*11 Dec., 1364*
1364, *14* Dec.	Walter Biggar (*see* 1359)	

ROBERT II–ROBERT III

	Walter Biggar remained in office	*ob. Aug.*, 1376
1376–7	Office vacant[4]	
1377, 20 Oct.	Sir John Lyon of Glamis, kp. of privy seal 1370–7	*ob.* 4 Nov., 1382
1382, 16 Nov.	Robert Stewart, e. of Fife and Menteith, duke of Albany 1398, governor of Scotland 1406–20	

[1] Apparently held office towards end of reign (D. E. R. Watt, *Biographical Dictionary of Scottish Graduates*, 516).

[2] Erskine apparently held office for some years round 1350 but precise dates are lacking.

[3] Biggar accounted as chamberlain on this date (*ER*, ii. 4), but for period from 11 Nov. 1358 during which he was only '*locumtenens*' of e. of Mar.

[4] Biggar died aft. 5 Aug. 1376 (*ER*, ii. 523); John Mercer acted as deputy chamberlain until Feb. 1377 and thereafter as receiver during vacancy (*ER*, ii. 581).

JAMES I

	Duke of Albany remained in office	res. 12 Mar., 1407
1407, 12 Mar.	John Stewart, e. of Buchan	ob. 17 Aug., 1424
1425, 8 Jan.	Sir John Forrester of Corstorphine, deputy chamberlain 1406–24	

JAMES II

	Sir John Forrester remained in office	*26 Aug.*, 1448
1448, 6 Sept.[1]	James Livingston, lord Livingston of Callendar *c.* 1455	forf. 19 Jan. 1450
1451, 30 Mar.	Sir James Crichton of Frendraught (2nd lord Crichton 1454)	*26 Apr., 1452*
1454, 1 July	James Livingston (*see* 1448)	

JAMES III

	Lord Livingston remained in office, vac. *26 Apr.*, 1467	
1467, 25 Aug.	Robert Boyd, 1st lord Boyd, forf. 22 Nov. 1469	
1470	James Stewart, 1st e. of Buchan, vac. *16 Dec.* 1482	
1483, 29 Apr.	David Lindsay, 5th e. of Crawford, duke of Montrose 1488, vac. 11 June 1488	

JAMES IV

| 1488, 7 Oct. | Alexander Home, 2nd lord Home, *ob.* 9 Sept. 1506 |
| *1507, 26 Jan.* | Alexander, 3rd lord Home |

JAMES V

	Lord Home remained in office, *ob.* 8 Oct. 1516
1517, 22 Jan.	John Fleming, 2nd lord Fleming, *ob.* 1 Nov. 1524
1527, 20 Nov.[2]	Malcolm, 3rd lord Fleming

MARY I

	Lord Fleming remained in office, *ob.* 10 Sept. 1547
1533, 12 Nov.	James, 4th lord Fleming, *ob.* 15 Dec. 1558
1558–65	Office vacant
1565, 30 June	John, 5th lord Fleming

JAMES VI–ANNE

	Lord Fleming remained in office, forf. 17 Nov. 1569
1569–80	Office vacant
1580, 24 Sept.	Esmé Stewart, 8th e. of Lennox, 1st duke of Lennox 1581, *ob.* 26 May 1583
1583, 23 Sept.	Ludovick Stewart, 2nd duke of Lennox, granted office heritably 21 Feb. 1603, *ob.* 16 Feb. 1624
	Aft. death of 2nd duke, office remained hereditary in his family until death of Charles, 6th duke of Lennox, 12 Dec. 1672, when it reverted to crown.
1673, 1 Feb.	James Scott, duke of Buccleuch and Monmouth, *ob.* 15 July 1685
1680, 20 Aug.	Charles Lennox, duke of Richmond and Lennox, granted officer heritably, under reservation of life grant to Monmouth; does not appear to have acted as chamberlain; res. 2 Feb. 1705.
1705–11	Office vacant
1711, 15 Nov.	In commission[3]

[1] Livingston occurs as chamberlain in a charter dated 29 June 1448, but this only survives in a confirmation of 1458 (*RMS*, ii. no. 618).

[2] G. Crawfurd, *Officers of State*, 326, quotes a charter then (1726) in possession of the e. of Wigtown, showing that Malcolm, lord Fleming, was granted the office on his father's death.

[3] For this attempt to revive the office in 1711 *see* P. W. J. Riley, *The English Ministers and Scotland 1707–27* (1964), ch. 12. The commission terminated with the death of Queen Anne, after which the office was allowed to lapse.

TREASURERS

Between 1424 and 1428 the chamberlain's financial functions were transferred to two new officials, the treasurer and the comptroller. The early history of the treasurership, especially its connection with the royal household,[1] is extremely obscure and only intelligible in relation to the office of comptroller (*q.v.*). For its developed form *see* 'Notes on the Treasury administration' in *Accounts of the Treasurer of Scotland*, xii (1970), xii–xlix. G. Crawfurd, *Lives of the Officers of State in Scotland* (1726), 355–423, is still of some value.

JAMES I

1425, 8 Jan.	Sir Walter Ogilvy of Lintrathen	*1431*[2]
1430, 11 Oct.[3]	Thomas Myrton, dean of Glasgow	*3 June, 1431*
1432, 4 Nov.	Walter Stewart, dean of Moray	*1 Sept., 1433*[4]
1435, July	Thomas Cranston[5]	

JAMES II

1437, 3 May	Sir Walter Haliburton of Dirleton	
1437, 1 June	Sir Walter Ogilvy (*see under* 1425)	
1438, 25 June	Sir Walter Haliburton (*see under* 1437)	*3 Apr., 1440*
1449, 28 Aug.	John Ralston, bp of Dunkeld, *1447–51*	*18 Sept., 1449*
1449, 3 Nov.	Andrew Hunter, abbot of Melrose	*24 Mar., 1452*
1454, July	John Winchester, bp of Moray, *1436–60*	
1456, May	Archibald Crawford, abbot of Holyrood	*15 Oct., 1456*
1457, 11 Nov.	James Stewart, dean of Moray, bp of Moray 1460–2	*25 June, 1459*

JAMES III

1461, *30* July[6]	David Guthrie of Kincaldrum (*see* clerks register, 1468), vac. *21 May* 1468	
1468, *21* June[7]	James Lindsay, provost of Lincluden, *ob.* aft. 19 Nov. 1468	
1469, 24 Jan.	Sir William Knollis, preceptor of Torphichen, lord St John of Jerusalem, vac. *12 July* 1470	
1470, *17* Sept.	John Laing (*see* chancellors, 1482), vac. *3 Feb.* 1476[8]	
1476, 29 May	Archibald Crawford (*see under* 1456), vac. *29 July* 1484[9]	
1484, 9 Dec.	David Lichtoun, abbot of Arbroath, vac. June 1488	

[1] Between 1425 and 1431 the titles 'king's treasurer', 'treasurer of Scotland' and 'treasurer of the king's household' are used, but the distinction between them is not apparent.

[2] Ogilvy appears in the great seal register in 1431 as either [king's] treasurer or master of the household (*TA*, i, xxix).

[3] Myrton was 'alleged treasurer' of James I, 8 Nov. 1429 and treasurer of the household from 1430 (*Cal. of Scottish Supplications to Rome, 1428–1432*, Scot. Hist. Soc., 1970, 50, 142; cf *ER*, iv. 525, where Ogilvy is master of the household); there are also references to him as [king's] treasurer, in the MS great seal register (*TA*, i, xxix).

[4] G. Crawfurd, *Officers of State*, 358.

[5] Cranston was receiver general under an unnamed treasurer in 1434 (*ER*, iv, 597).

[6] Appd aft. Sir Alexander Napier ceased to be comptroller (*ER*, viii. 520, 493). Guthrie was also comptroller 1466–8.

[7] Kp. of privy seal until June 1468 (*ER*, viii. 520, 593).

[8] G. Crawfurd (*Officers of State*, 364), states that Laing ceased to be treasurer when promoted to bp of Glasgow, 1474, but discharges granted by James III indicates that he was still treasurer on 11 Oct. 1475 and probably until early 1476 (*Reg. Episcopatus Glasguensis*, Bannatyne Club, 1843, 426–9).

[9] Lichtoun was treasurer clerk on this date when el. abbot, indicating that Crawford was probably still treasurer, though there are no references to him as such aft. Jan. 1484.

JAMES IV

1488, *15* June	Sir William Knollis (*see under* 1469), vac. *10* Aug. 1492
1492, *12* Aug.	Henry Arnot, abbot of Cambuskenneth, vac. *14* June 1494
1494, 29 June	George Schaw, abbot of Paisley, vac. *22 Sept.* 1497[1]
1497, *26 Oct.*	Sir Robert of Lundy of Balgonie, *ob.* 5 Feb. 1501
1501, 5 Feb.	David Beaton of Creich, *ob.* 24 Jan. 1505
1505, 10 Feb.	James Beaton, abbot of Dunfermline (*see* chancellors, 1513), vac. *31 July* 1509
1509, *18* Aug.	George Hepburn, abbot of Arbroath, bp of the Isles 1510–13, vac. *28 Aug.* 1510
1510, *1 Oct.*	Andrew Stewart, bp of Caithness 1501–17, vac. 29 Oct. 1512
1512, 29 Oct.	Cuthbert Baillie, commendator of Glenluce, vac. *8 Aug.* 1513

JAMES V

1513, 15 Oct.	Andrew Stewart (*see under* 1510), vac. *6 July* 1514
1515, 25 June	James Hepburn, postulate of Dunfermline, bp of Moray 1516–24, vac. 25 Jan. 1516
1516, 25 Jan.	Sir William Ogilvy of Strathearn, vac. 17 Jan. 1517
1517, 22 Jan.	John Campbell of Thornton (later of Lundy), vac. 24 June 1526
1526, 25 June	William Cunningham, master of Glencairn (3rd e. of Glencairn *c.* 1540), vac. *16 Aug.* 1526[2]
1526, 15 Oct.	Archibald Douglas of Kilspindie, vac. 13 July 1528
1528, 19 July	Robert Cairncross, abbot of Holyrood (bp of Ross 1538–45), vac. *8 Feb.* 1529
1529, 6 Mar.	Robert Barton of Over Barnton, vac. 10 Sept. 1530
1530, 2 Oct.	William Stewart, dean of Glasgow, bp of Aberdeen 1532–43, vac. 4 June 1537
1537, 29 May	Robert Cairncross (*see under* 1528), vac. 8 Feb. 1538
1538, 24 Mar.	Sir James Kirkcaldy of Grange

MARY I

	Sir James Kirkcaldy remained in office, vac. 13 Aug. 1543
1543, 13 Aug.	John Hamilton, abbot of Paisley, bp of Dunkeld 1544–7, abp of St Andrews 1547–71, vac. *4 Mar.* 1554
1554, 20 Apr.	Gilbert Kennedy, 3rd e. of Cassillis, *ob. c.* 28 Nov. 1558
1558–61	Office vacant[3]
1561, 5 Mar.	Robert Richardson, commendator of St Mary's Isle

JAMES VI

	Robert Richardson remained in office
1571, 24 June	William Ruthven, 4th Lord Ruthven, e. of Gowrie 1581, *ob.* 4 May 1584
1584, 13 May	John Graham, 3rd e. of Montrose
1585, 2 Dec.	Thomas Lyon of Baldukie, master of Glamis (later Sir Thomas Lyon of Auldbar), vac. *1* Mar. 1596
1596, 6 Mar.	Walter Stewart, prior of Blantyre (lord Blantyre 1606), res. 17 Apr. 1599
1599, 20 Mar.[4]	John Kennedy, 5th e. of Cassillis, vac. 17 Apr. 1599
1599, 19 Apr.	Alexander Elphinstone, master of Elphinstone (4th lord Elphinstone 1602), res. 22 Sept. 1601
1601, 1 Oct.	Sir George Home of Spot, e. of Dunbar 1605, *ob.* 20 Jan. 1611
1611–13	Office vacant[5]
1613, 23 Dec.	Robert Ker, e. of Somerset, vac. 24 May 1616
1616, 9 Dec.	John Erskine, 19th e. of Mar

[1] The evidence of the great seal register is ambiguous; Schaw may have held office until *c.* 12 Nov. 1497.

[2] Campbell appears to have returned to office pending appointment of Douglas (*ER*, xv. 337; HMC 55, *Var. Coll.*, v. 12).

[3] Robert Richardson, treasurer clerk acted as treasurer.

[4] For circumstances of Cassillis's acceptance of office and failure to take up appointment, see *RPC*, v. xc, 547–50; *CSP Scot.*, xii. 434, 444, 450.

[5] It is not clear whether commissioners appd in Apr. 1611 were commissioners of the treasury or assessors to the treasurer depute (*RPC*, ix. 160n, 594–5).

CHARLES I

	E. of Mar remained in office
1630, 3 Apr.	William Douglas, 6th e. of Morton
1636, 21 May	John Stewart, 1st e. of Traquair
1641, 17 Nov.	In commission
1644, 23 July	John Lindsay, e. of Crawford and Lindsay, dism. 13 Feb. 1649

CHARLES II–ANNE

1649, 16 Mar.	In commission,[1] vac. *Aug.* 1651
1661, 19 Jan.	E. of Crawford and Lindsay re-appd (*see under* 1644)
1663, 4 June	John Leslie, 7th e. of Rothes (duke of Rothes 1680), chancellor 16 Apr. 1667
1667, 20 June	In commission[2]
1682, 1 May	William Douglas, m. of Queensberry, duke of Queensberry 1684, dism. 24 Feb. 1686
1686, 24 Feb.	In commission

After the Union new commissioners were appd 23 June 1707, to act under the direction of the lord high treasurer of Great Britain. The separate Scottish treasury was abolished on 1 May 1708.

COMPTROLLERS

For the early history of the office see 'The comptroller 1424–1488', *Scottish Historical Review*, lii (1973), 1–29. From 1466 the comptroller had sole responsibility for financing the royal household to which certain revenues (the property) were appropriated; he was sometimes given the alternative title of receiver general [of the property]. The treasurer was responsible for the remaining revenue (the casualty) and expenditure. The two offices were held by the same person for short periods (as shown in this list) and were finally united from 1610 onwards.

JAMES I

1425, 8 May	David Brown, chancellor of Glasgow[3]	*12 Sept., 1428*
1428, *17 Dec.*	John Spens	*6 May, 1431*
1432	David Brown (*see under* 1425)	bef. *11 July*, 1435
1435, *11 July*	Alexander Nairn	

JAMES II

	Alexander Nairn remained in office	*18 July*, 1438
1439, 26 Apr.	Robert Nory	*May*, 1439
1439	William Cranston	*5 Sept.*, 1441
1442, 5 July	Henry Livingston	27 June, 1444
1444, *1 July*	Alexander Nairn	*18 July*, 1447
1448, 18 Apr.	Robert Livingston	dism. 23 Sept., 1449

[1] Between 1638 and 1651 the treasurer's powers were greatly curtailed by the new financial organization set up by the Covenanters. *See* D. Stevenson, *The Government of Scotland under the Covenanters 1637–1651* (Scot. Hist. Soc. 1982), appendices.

[2] For this and later commissions see 'The Scottish treasury 1667–1708', *SHR*, xlv (1966), 89–104.

[3] '*Contrarotulator*' 1425; '*compotorum rotulator*' aft. 16 Apr. 1426.

1449, 24 Sept.	Alexander Napier of Philde (later Sir Alexander Napier of Merchiston)	27 Aug., 1450
1450, *31* Aug.	John Spalding	8 Sept., 1450
1450, *Oct.*	Alexander Napier (*see under* 1449)	3 Apr., 1451
1451, *5 July*	Alexander Nairn of Sandfurd	15 Jan., 1453
1453, *1 Feb.*	Richard Forbes, archdeacon of Ross	16 Oct., 1453
1453	Alexander Napier (*see under* 1449)	24 July, 1454
1454, *5 Aug.*	William Bonar of Rossie	11 Sept., 1455
1455, *3 Oct.*	Richard Forbes (*see under* 1453)	13 May, 1456
1456, *13 Sept.*	Alexander Napier (*see under* 1449)	1 Oct., 1456
1456, Oct. 15[1]	Ninian Spot, bp of Whithorn 1459–80	19 July, 1459
1459	John Leirmonth	June, 1460
1460, *19 June*	Alexander Napier (*see under* 1449)	

JAMES III

Sir Alexander Napier of Merchiston remained in office, vac. 7 July 1461

1461–4	Office vacant[2]
1464, *19 June*	Sir John Colquhoun of Luss, vac. *18* July 1466
1466, *Aug.*	David Guthrie of that ilk (treasurer 1461–8), vac. *9 Mar.* 1468
1468, *5 May*	Adam Wallace of Crago, vac. *7 Feb.* 1470
1470, *17 Apr.*	David Guthrie, vac. *1* Feb. 1471
1471, *12 Feb.*	James Schaw of Sauchie, vac. bef. 3 Aug. 1472
1472, *3 Sept.*	Thomas Simson of Knockhill, receiver gen. aft. 7 Aug. 1473, vac. 7 July 1475
1475, *15 July*	Alexander Leslie of Warderis, receiver gen., vac. *8 Aug.* 1480
1480[3]	Michael Balfour of Burleigh, receiver gen.
1480	Alexander Leslie (*see under* 1475), receiver gen.,[4] vac. 2 Aug. 1483
1483, *27 Oct.*	Thomas Simson (*see under* 1472), vac. *23 Aug.* 1484
1484, *11 Sept.*	Alexander Leslie (*see under* 1475), vac. *2 Feb.* 1485
1485, *28 Mar.*	Alexander Lumsden, parson of Flisk, ob. 7 Aug. 1485
1485, *17 Aug.*	Adam Wallace (*see under* 1468), vac. 7 Nov. 1485
1485, *16 Dec.*	Thomas Simson (*see under* 1472), vac. 2 May 1486
1486, *May*[5]	David Luthirdale, parson of Arbuthnot
1486, *3 June*	George Robison, vac. 8 Mar. 1488
1488, *20* Mar.	William Bickerton, vac. *20 May* 1488
1488, *June*	Thomas Tod

JAMES IV

1488, *15* June	Alexander Inglis, archdeacon of St Andrews, vac. *16* June 1489
1489, *7 July*	James Douglas of Pitendreich, vac. *15 Apr.* 1490
1490, *7 June*	Thomas Forrest, vac. 31 Oct. 1491
1491, *1* Nov.	Hugh Martin, vac. 4 Aug. 1492
1492, 31 July	Duncan Forrester of Skipinch (later Sir Duncan Forrester of Garden), vac. 10 Nov. 1498
1498, 9 Nov.	Patrick Hume of Powarth, vac. *20* Mar. 1500
1500, *31* Mar.	Sir Robert Lundy (treasurer 1497–1501), *ob.* 5 Feb. 1501
1501, *18 May*[6]	Sir John Stirling of Craigbernard, vac.·*19* Apr. 1503
1505, *1 May*	James Redheuch of Tullichedill, vac. *1* Sept. 1508
1508, *20* Sept.	Sir Duncan Forrester (*see under* 1492), vac. *9* Nov. 1510

[1] Spot rendered an account on this date for his previous office of king's receiver (*ER*, vi. 289).
[2] Duties shared between the treasurer and steward of the household until June 1464.
[3] Balfour appears to have been appd shortly aft. Leslie accounted in [Aug.?] 1480 and to have held office for a short period only (*ER*, ix. 154).
[4] Comptroller *c.* Aug.–Sept. 1482.
[5] All dated references to Luthirdale relate to the period bef. he became comptroller; he probably died in office (*ER*, ix. 360, 373, 439; *cf.* 613).
[6] King's steward until 9 Apr. 1501.

1511, *4 July*	Andrew Stewart, bp of Caithness, receiver gen. (treasurer 1510–12), vac. 3 Nov. 1512
1512, *18 Oct.*[1]	James Redheuch (see under 1505), vac. *23 Sept.* 1513

JAMES V[2]

1513, 15 Oct.	Andrew Stewart (*see under* 1511; treasurer 1513–14) vac. *16 Jan.* 1514
1514, *1 July*	James Redheuch (*see under* 1505) ob. Nov. 1514
1514, *Nov.*	James Kincragy, dean of Aberdeen, receiver gen. (with Hamilton), vac. 1 Nov. 1515
1514, *Nov.*	Sir Patrick Hamilton of Kincavil, receiver gen. (with Kincragy), comptroller aft. 1 Nov. 1515, vac. *11* Feb. 1516
1516, *1 Mar.*	Sir Alexander Jardine of Applegirth, vac. *26 Sept.* 1516
1516, 12 Oct.	Robert Barton of Over Barnton, vac. 16 Aug. 1525
1525, 17 Aug.	James Colville of Ochiltree (later Sir James Colville of East Wemyss), vac. 6 Mar. 1529
1529, 6 Mar.	Robert Barton (*see under* 1516; treasurer 1529–30) vac. 9 Sept. 1530
1530, 9 Sept.	Sir James Colville (*see under* 1525), vac. 13 Sept. 1538
1538, 14 Sept.	David Wood of Craig

MARY

	David Wood remained in office, vac. 18 Mar. 1543
1543, 19 Mar.	Thomas Menzies of Pitfoddels, vac. *12 Dec. 1543*
1544, *24 May*	Matthew Hamilton of Binning,[3] vac. 31 Jan. 1545
1545, 1 Feb.[4]	William Colville, abbot of Culross, vac. *7 Apr.* 1555
1555, 1 May	Bartholomew de Villemore (with Grahame, 1561–2), vac. *25* Feb. 1562
1561, 6 June	Thomas Grahame of Boquhaple (with Villemore), *ob.* 9 Feb. 1562
1562, 16 Feb.	Sir John Wishart of Pittarow,[5] vac. *27 Aug.* 1565
1565, *27* Aug.	Sir William Murray of Tullibardine
1566, 9 June	James Cockburn of Skirling, dism. 5 July 1567[6]

JAMES VI

	Sir William Murray remained in office, vac. *26* Nov. 1582
1582, 29 Nov.	John Fenton, comptroller clerk 1562–82, 1583–1616
1583, *22* Aug.	James Campbell of Ardkinglass, res. 6 July 1585[7]
1585, *21* July	Andrew Wood of Largo
1587, 8 July	Sir John Seton of Barns
1588, 25 Nov.	David Seton of Parbroath, res. 3 Jan. 1596
1596, Jan.	James Elphinstone of Invernochty[8] (*see* secretaries, 1598)
1597, *16* Jan.	Walter Stewart (treasurer 1596–9)

---

[1] *ER*, xiii. 576.

[2] *See* 'Financing the royal household: James V and his comptrollers 1513–1543' in I. B. Cowan and D. Shaw edd. *The Renaissance and Reformation in Scotland* (1983).

[3] Master of Regent Arran's household, described as '*rotulator*' in his accounts between these dates.

[4] '*Rotulator*' in Hamilton's account from this date but may have been in office on 17 Nov. 1544 (*ER*, xviii. 82).

[5] Wishart and Murray (until 1574) were also collectors general of the thirds of benefices.

[6] *RPC*, 1. 526–7. Murray, who had ceased to act bef. 20 May 1567 (*TA*, xii. 55) evidently resumed office without formal reappointment.

[7] Campbell was accountable for receipts and expenditure up to 1 Sept. following (*RPC*, iii. 753–4). The same procedure was followed for Wood in 1587 (*ER*, xxi. 366).

[8] Elphinstone was titular comptroller as one of the 'Octavians', who had collective responsibility for the royal revenues as lords of exchequer (*RPC*, v. xliv). Henry Wardlaw of Kilbaberton acted as their receiver general, Jan. 1596–Jan. 1597.

1597, 29 Dec.	Sir George Home of Wedderburn
1599, 26 Apr.	Sir David Murray of Gospertie, lord Scone 1604 (1st viscount Stormont 1621)
1608, 18 Feb.	Sir James Hay of Fingask, *ob.* Aug. 1608
1610, 23 Aug.	George Home, e. of Dunbar (treasurer 1601–11), *ob.* 20 Jan. 1611

After the death of the e. of Dunbar the offices of treasurer and comptroller remained united until abolished in 1708. Separate accounts were not kept after 1635 and by the 1660s the comptrollery ceased to be treated as a distinct branch of revenue.

SECRETARIES

The king's secretary appears on record in the reign of David II, but a clear and permanent separation of the offices of kp. of the privy seal and secretary does not occur until the middle of the fifteenth century.[1] For the development of the office, *see* R. K. Hannay, 'The Early History of the Scottish Signet', *History of the Society of Writers to His Majesty's Signet* (1936), 1–51 (377–79 for list of secretaries to 1746); M. A. Thomson, *The Secretaries of State, 1681–1782* (1932), 29–37.

DAVID II

1360, 13 Apr.	Robert Dumbarton	*ob. bef. 28 Nov.*, 1362
1363, 14 May	Walter Wardlaw, archdeacon of Lothian (bp of Glasgow 1367–87)	*21 Jan., 1366*
1369, 20 Jan.	John Carrick (*see* chancellors, 1370), kp. of privy seal 1369	*19 Jan., 1370*
1371, 15 Feb.	John Lyon (*see* chamberlains, 1377), kp. of privy seal 1370–77	

ROBERT II

| | John Lyon remained in office | |
| *1380, 29 Feb.* | Duncan Petit (*see* chancellors, 1395), kp. of privy seal 1379–90 | *19 June, 1388* |

ROBERT III

| *1392* | Reginald Crawford, kp. of privy seal 1391–8 | *ob. post 7 Mar., 1401* |
| *1402, 12 June* | Walter Forrester (*see* clerks register, 1403) | *15 Mar., 1406*[2] |

JAMES I

| 1406, June | Andrew Hawick, secretary of Robert duke of Albany, governor of Scotland[3] | *2 Aug., 1420* |
| 1420, *28 Oct.* | Alan Otterburn, secretary of Murdac, duke of Albany, governor of Scotland[4] | *22 Mar., 1424* |

[1] The term 'secretary' is used in papal sources to decribe clerks in the royal service; they are not included in this list unless their status is confirmed by Scottish sources.
[2] Forrester retained title of secretary whilst out of Scotland but John Crawford succeeded him as kp. of privy seal bef. 28 Oct. 1405 (D. E. R. Watt, *Biographical Dictionary of Scottish Graduates*, 198).
[3] Hawick was first secretary; Andrew Lidale (25 Jan. 1413) and Nicholas Hunter (1 Jan. 1418–4 Aug. 1420) also occur as secretaries.
[4] Patrick Houston also occurs as secretary 19 Aug. 1423 (*APS*, i. 423).

1424, *10 July*	John Cameron (*see* chancellors, 1426), kp. of privy seal 1425–7	*16 Apr., 1426*
1426, 6 May[1]	John Benyng, canon of Moray	*ob. 7 Sept.*, 1432
1427, 22 July	William Foulis, provost of Bothwell, kp. of privy seal, 1427–39	
1433, 24 Feb.	John Methven, provost of Lincluden	

JAMES II[2]

	John Methven remained in office	*11 Aug.*, 1440
1441, 22 Apr.	William Turnbull, archdeacon of Lothian (bp of Glasgow 1447–54), kp. of privy seal 1440–8	
1442, 6 Sept.	John Ralston (*see* treasurers, 1449)	*7 May*, 1448
1449, 31 Oct.	Nicholas Otterburn, official of Lothian	*26 Aug.*, 1452
1453, 16 Apr.	George Schoriswood (*see* chancellors, 1456)	*1 July, 1454*
1456, 4 Dec.	Thomas Vaus, dean of Glasgow, elect of Whithorn 1457, kp. of privy seal 1455–6	*21 Oct.*, 1458
1458, 9 Nov.	John Arous, archdeacon of Glasgow, kp. of privy seal 1459–60	*24 July*, 1459
1459, 18 Sept.	George Ledale, parson of Forest	

JAMES III

	George Ledale remained in office, vac. *10 Feb.*, 1462
1462, 27 Aug.	Archibald Whitelaw, archdeacon of Lothian

JAMES IV

	Archibald Whitelaw remained in office, vac. *15 Oct. 1493*[3]
1493, 4 Aug.	Richard Muirhead, dean of Glasgow, *ob. 4 Mar.* 1506
1506, 22 Nov.[4]	Patrick Paniter, abbot of Cambuskenneth 1513

JAMES V

	Patrick Paniter remained in office, *ob.* 18 Nov. 1519
1517, 1 Apr.[5]	Thomas Hay, parson of Rathven, res. 1 Aug. 1524
1525, 8 Mar.	Patrick Hepburn, prior of St Andrews (bp of Moray 1538–73), vac. 15 June 1526
1526, 5 Oct.[6]	Sir Thomas Erskine of Halton (and Brechin), vac. 10 Jan., 1543

MARY I

1543, 20 Jan.	David Paniter, commendator of St Mary's Isle, bp of Ross 1547–58, *ob.* 1 Oct. 1558
1543, 28 Feb.	Henry Balnaves of Halhill, vac. *4 May* 1543
1558, 4 Dec.	William Maitland of Lethington

---

[1] A charter mentioning John Inverkeithing, secretary, 1 Sept. 1426 is misdated and must be 1427 or later (*RMS*, ii. 60).

[2] James II appears to have employed more than one secretary. Ralston (27 Apr. 1446 and 23 Apr. 1448), Otterburn (22 May 1450) and Vaus (21 Oct. 1458) are designated first secretary. Otterburn (25 Aug. 1447) and Arous (30 Apr. 1458) occur earlier than the dates shown here, but presumably in a subordinate capacity.

[3] Whitelaw is also called secretary, 10 Nov. 1495 (*Acta Dominorum Concilii*, ii. 425).

[4] Paniter is described as having recently come to the office from his studies (*Letters of James IV*, No. 59).

[5] Hay acted as secretary in S. while Paniter was in France with the Regent Albany, 1517–19. He appears to have received a new commission, *c.* 1520, after Paniter's death (*RSS*, i. no. 3154).

[6] Warrant for appointment as secretary during king's minority, 6 Mar. 1525 (Spalding Club, *Miscellany*, ii. 177).

JAMES VI

	William Maitland remained in office, forf. 16 May 1571
1571, *28* Aug.	Robert Pitcairn, commendator of Dunfermline, dism. Aug. 1583
1584, 18 May	Sir John Maitland of Thirlestane (*see* chancellors, 1586), res. 17 Apr. 1591
1591, 17 Apr.	Sir Richard Cockburn of Clerkington, kp. of privy seal 28 May 1596
1596, 28 May	John Lindsay of Balcarres (kp. of privy seal 8 Mar–28 May 1596), res. 12 Jan. 1598
1598, 19 Jan.	James Elphinstone of Barnton, 1st lord Balmerino 1603 (with Hay 1608–9), forf. 1 Apr. 1609
1608, May[1]	Sir Alexander Hay of Whitburgh (with lord Balmerino 1608–9), clerk register 24 July 1612
1612, 24 July	Sir Thomas Hamilton of Byres, 1st lord Binning 1613, 1st e. of Melrose 1619, 1st e. of Haddington 1627

CHARLES I

	E. of Melrose remained in office (with Alexander 1626–7), kp. of privy seal 18 Oct. 1627
1626, 8 Mar.	Sir William Alexander of Menstrie, 1st e. of Stirling 1633 (with e. of Melrose 1626–7 and Acheson 1627–34), *ob.* 12 Feb. 1640
1627, 21 Oct.	Sir Archibald Acheson of Glencairnie (with Alexander 1627–34), *ob.* 9 Sept. 1634
1640, 15 Mar.	William Hamilton, e. of Lanark (2nd duke of Hamilton 1649), dism. by k. Jan. 1644 but conf. by parliament 22 July 1644, dism. 13 Feb. 1649
1640, 26 Mar.	Sir James Galloway (lord Dunkeld 1645) (with e. of Lanark 1640–1)[2] not recognized by parliament aft. 1641, vac. *1646*
1644, Jan.	Sir Robert Spottiswoode of New Abbey, appd by k. but not recognized by parliament, vac. Sept. 1645

CHARLES II

1649, 10 Mar.	William Ker, 3rd e. of Lothian, res. 6 Aug. 1660[3]
1660, Aug.	John Maitland, 2nd e. of Lauderdale, 1st duke of Lauderdale 1672, dism. 11 Oct. 1680
1661, 19 Jan.	John Maitland, 2nd e. of Lauderdale, 1st duke of Lauderdale 1672, dism. 11 Oct. 1680
1680, 11 Oct.	Alexander Stewart, 5th e. of Moray (with e. of Middleton 1682–4, and Drummond 1684–8)
1682, 26 Sept.	Charles Middleton, 2nd e. of Middleton (with e. of Moray 1682–4), vac. 24 Aug. 1684
1684, 15 Sept.	John Drummond of Lundin, 1st viscount Melfort 1685, 1st e. of Melfort 1686 (with e. of Moray 1684–8)

JAMES VII

E. of Moray and e. of Melfort remained in office until the Revolution, vac. *7 Dec. 1688*

WILLIAM II AND MARY II

1689, 13 May	George Melville, 1st e. of Melville 1690 (with Dalrymple 1691), kp. of privy seal 29 Dec. 1691
1691, 1 Jan.	John Dalrymple, master of Stair, 1st e. of Stair 1703 (with e. of Melville 1691 and Johnston 1692–5) vac. July 1695
1692, 3 Mar.	James Johnston (with Dalrymple 1692–5), vac. Jan. 1696

[1] Warrant for appointment as secretary at court undated but bef. 20 May 1608; sworn in 5 July 1608 (*RPC*, viii. 122, 519). Re-apptd as sole secretary 15 Apr. 1609.
[2] Master of requests and secretary resident within S., sharing enrolments with Lanark, as principal secretary (HMC, *9th Report*, ii. 250).
[3] Had retained seals, though not acting aft. 1651.

1696, 15 Jan.	John Murray, lord Murray, e. of Tullibardine 1696, 1st duke of Atholl 1703 (with Ogilvy 1696–8), vac. 31 Mar. 1698
1696, 5 Feb.	Sir James Ogilvy, 1st e. of Seafield 1701 (with e. of Tullibardine 1696–8, and e. of Hyndford 1699–1702)
1699, 31 Jan.	John Carmichael, 2nd lord Carmichael, 1st e. of Hyndford 1701, vac. 6 May 1702

ANNE–GEORGE II

E. of Seafield remained in office until 21 Nov. 1702

1702, 6 May	James Douglas, 2nd duke of Queensberry (with e. of Seafield 1702, and e. of Cromarty 1702–4), vac. 16 Oct. 1704
1702, 21 Nov.	George Mackenzie, 1st viscount Tarbat, 1st e. of Cromarty 1703 (with duke of Queensberry 1702–4), vac. 17 Oct. 1704
1704, 16 Oct.	John Ker, 5th e. of Roxburghe (with e. of Seafield 1704–5, and m. of Annandale 1705), vac. 5 June 1705
1704, 17 Oct.	James Ogilvy, 1st e. of Seafield (*see under* 1696) (with e. of Roxburghe 1704–5), vac. 10 Mar., 1705
1705, 10 Mar.	William Johnston, 1st m. of Annandale (with e. of Roxburghe 1705, and e. of Loudoun 1705), president of privy council 29 Sept. 1705
1705, 5 June	Hugh Campbell, 3rd e. of Loudoun (with m. of Annandale 1705, and e. of Mar 1705–8), kp. of great seal of Scotland 25 May, 1708
1705, 29 Sept.	John Erskine, 23rd e. of Mar (with e. of Loudoun 1705–8)

The e. of Loudoun and the e. of Mar were re-appd aft. the Union as secretaries of state within Scotland. Loudoun res. in May 1708, and Mar was dism. in Feb. 1709. Thereafter, the duke of Queensberry was appd to be one of three principal secretaries of state and the specifically Scot. secretaryships were abolished.

1709, 3 Feb.	James Douglas, 2nd duke of Queensberry and 1st duke of Dover, *ob.* 6 July 1711
1713, 30 Sept.	John Erskine, 23rd e. of Mar, dism. Sept. 1714
1714, 24 Sept.	James Graham, 1st duke of Montrose, dism. Aug. 1715
1716, 13 Dec.	John Ker, 1st duke of Roxburghe, dism. Aug. 1725
1742, 16 Feb.	John Hay, 4th m. of Tweeddale, res. 3 Jan. 1746

For the arrangements which followed the resignation of the m. of Tweeddale in 1746, *see* Thomson, *op. cit.*, 37.

SECRETARIES OF STATE FOR SCOTLAND

The office of secretary for Scotland was established in 1885 but did not become a full secretaryship of state until 1926. *See* G. Pottinger, *The Secretaries of State for Scotland 1926–1976* (1979). D. Milne, *The Scottish Office* (1957), 216, lists secretaries for Scotland, 1885–1926.

1926, 26 July	Sir John Gilmour, secretary for S. 1924–6
1929, 8 June	William Adamson
1931, 26 Aug.	Sir Archibald Henry Macdonald Sinclair (1st viscount Thurso 1952)
1932, 1 Oct.	Sir Godfrey Pattison Collins
1936, 3 Nov.	Walter Elliot
1938, 16 May	David John Colville (1st baron Clydesmuir 1948)
1940, 15 May	Ernest Brown
1941, 12 Feb.	Thomas Johnston
1945, 28 May	Albert Edward Harry Mayer Archibald Primrose, 6th e. of Rosebery
1945, 3 Aug.	Joseph Westwood
1947, 14 Oct.	Arthur Woodburn
1950, 2 Mar.	Hector McNeil

1951, 30 Oct.	James Gray Stuart (1st viscount Stuart of Findhorn 1959)
1957, 14 Jan.	John Scott Maclay (1st viscount Muirshiel 1964)
1962, 13 July	Michael Anthony Cristobal Noble (baron Glenkinglas 1974)
1964, 17 Oct.	William Ross (baron Ross of Marnock 1979)
1970, 20 June	Gordon Thomas Calthrop Campbell (baron Campbell of Croy 1974)
1974, 2 Mar.	William Ross (see 1964)
1976, 8 Apr.	Bruce Millan
1979, 5 May	George Kenneth Hotson Younger

CLERKS REGISTER

First appears as clerk of the rolls, then as clerk of the rolls and register from 1373 onwards. For the development of the office see 'The Lord Clerk Register' in *Scottish Historical Review*, liii (1974), 124–56. For a list of clerks register (with references) see *Annual Report of the Keeper of the Records of Scotland* for 1974.

MARGARET–INTERREGNUM

| 1286[1] | William de Dumfries, chancellor, 23 Feb. 1292 | |

ROBERT I–DAVID II

1328	William Irvine	14 Dec., 1331
1342	Robert Dumbarton	1 Aug., 1348
1359, 16 Mar.	John Allincrum	ob. 14 Aug., 1362
1362, 3 July	John Gray[2]	

ROBERT II–ROBERT III

| | John Gray remained in office | ob. Nov., 1402 |
| 1403, 13 June | Walter Forrester, bp of Brechin, 1407–25 | |

JAMES I

	Walter Forrester remained in office	11 May, 1425
1426, 15 Apr.	John Scheves, official of St Andrews	29 May, 1433
1435, 14 Apr.	John Winchester (see treasurers, 1454)	7 Jan., 1436

JAMES II

| 1438, 3 July | John Scheves (see 1426) | 7 Dec., 1452[3] |
| 1454, 1 July | Nicholas Otterburn (see secretaries, 1449) | 8 Mar., 1460 |

JAMES III

1461, 28 Mar.	Archibald Whitelaw (see secretaries, 1462) vac. 6 July 1462
1463, 15 Oct.	Fergus McDowell, vac. 10 June 1468
1468, 9 Aug.	David Guthrie of that ilk, vac. 28 Jan. 1473
1473, 20 June	John Laing (see chancellors, 1482), vac. 22 Oct. 1473
1475, 5 June	Alexander Inglis, vac. 17 June 1482
1482, 25 Aug.	Patrick Leich, vac. 28 Jan. 1483
1483, 5 Feb.	Alexander Scot, vac. 28 May 1488

[1] Although the earliest reference to William de Dumfries is dated 17 Nov. 1288 it shows that he had been paid as clerk of the rolls for the year 1286–7.
[2] Identification with John Gray of Broxmouth appears erroneous (*SHR*, liii. 133).
[3] John Methven appears as clerk register on 15 Nov. 1449 and James Lindsay on 4 Jan. 1452, perhaps in absence of Scheves.

JAMES IV

1488, 12 June	William Hepburn, vac. *3* August, 1488
1488, *19* Aug.	Alexander Inglis, vac. *21* May, 1489
1489, *29* May	Richard Muirhead (*see* secretaries, 1493), vac. *10* Aug. 1492
1492, *12* Aug.	John Fraser (bp of Ross 1497–1507), vac. *11* Sept.[1] 1497
1497, *18* Sept.	Walter Drummond, vac. *4* Oct. 1501
1501, *21* Oct.	Gavin Dunbar bp of Aberdeen 1518–32

JAMES V

	Gavin Dunbar remained in office, *ob.* 10 Mar. 1532
1532, 12 Mar.	James Foulis of Colinton

MARY I

	James Foulis remained in office, *ob. 4 Feb.* 1549
1549, 5 Feb.	Thomas Marjoribanks of Ratho, dism. 31 July 1554[2]
1554, 22 June	James Makgill of Nether Rankeillor, dism. 22 Mar. 1566
1566, 22 Mar.	Sir James Balfour of Pittendreich

JAMES VI

	Sir James Balfour remained in office
1567, 4 Dec.[3]	James Makgill of Nether Rankeillor, *ob.* 16 Oct. 1579
1579, 17 Oct.	Alexander Hay of Easter Kennet, *ob.* 19 Sept. 1594
1594, 19 Sept.[4]	Sir John Skene of Curriehill, vac. Apr. 1612
1604, 14 May	James Skene (with Sir John Skene),[5] vac. Apr. 1612
1612, 21 Apr.	Sir Thomas Hamilton of Byres (*see* secretaries, 1612)
1612, 24 July	Sir Alexander Hay of Whitburgh, *ob. 27 Feb.* 1616
1616, 11 Mar.	Sir George Hay of Nether Liff (*see* chancellors, 1622)
1622, 3 July	John Hamilton of Magdalens

CHARLES I

	John Hamilton remained in office, *ob.* 28 Nov. 1632
1633, 12 Dec.	Sir John Hay of Landis, vac. *8 Sept.*
1641, 15 Nov.	Sir Alexander Gibson of Durie, dism. 13 Feb. 1649

CHARLES II

1649, 10 Mar.	Sir Archibald Johnston of Wariston, reappd by Cromwell 9 July 1657, vac. *May* 1660
1660, 7 Aug.	Sir Archibald Primrose of Carrington (*see* justices general, 1676), vac. 31 July 1676
1677, 1 Nov.	Sir Thomas Murray of Glendoick
1681, 14 Oct.	Sir George Mackenzie of Tarbat, 1st viscount Tarbat 1685 (*see* Secretaries, 1702)

JAMES VII

Viscount Tarbat remained in office, vac. 30 Apr. 1689

WILLIAM II AND MARY II

1689, 7 Dec.	In commission
1692, 3 Mar.	George Mackenzie, 1st viscount Tarbat (*see under* 1681)
1696, 30 Jan.	Charles Douglas, 2nd e. of Selkirk

[1] Later references to Fraser appear to be incorrect.

[2] Marjoribanks continued to sit in the court of session as clerk register until this date; Makgill not admitted until 18 Aug.

[3] Former commission ratified and Balfour's declared null and void.

[4] Commission under privy seal; great seal commission dated 29 Sept. 1594.

[5] James Skene appointed on his father's demission (*RPC*, viii. 458), but latter continued to act until both resigned in 1612.

ANNE

1702, 21 Nov.	Sir James Murray of Philiphaugh
1704, 2 June	James Johnston
1705, 7 Apr.	Sir James Murray of Philiphaugh, *ob.* 1 July, 1708
1708, 16 July	David Boyle, 1st e. of Glasgow

GEORGE I–ELIZABETH II

1714, 4 Oct.	Archibald Campbell, e. of Ilay (*see* justices general 1710)
1716, 6 July	James Graham, 1st duke of Montrose, kp. of the great seal of S. 13 Dec. 1716
1716, 13 Dec.	Alexander Hume, lord Polwarth, 2nd e. of Marchmont 1724
1733, 30 June	Charles Douglas, 2nd e. of Selkirk, *ob.* 13 Mar. 1739
1739, 15 Mar.	William Ker, 3rd m. of Lothian
1756, 12 Feb.	Alexander Hume Campbell, *ob.* 19 July, 1760
1760, 5 Sept.	James Douglas, 14th e. of Morton, *ob.* 12 Oct. 1768
1768, 2 Nov.[1]	Lord Frederick Campbell, *ob.* 8 June, 1816
1816, 25 June	Archibald Campbell Colquhoun, *ob.* 8 Dec. 1820
1821, 8 June	William Dundas, *ob.* 14 Nov. 1845
1845, 12 Dec.	James Andrew Ramsay, 10th e. of Dalhousie, 1st m. of Dalhousie 1849, *ob.* 19 Dec. 1860
1862, 1 July	Sir William Gibson Craig of Riccarton, *ob.* 12 Mar. 1878
1879, 21 Feb.	George Frederick Boyle, 6th e. of Glasgow, *ob.* 23 Apr. 1890
1890, 30 May	Douglas Beresford Malise Ronald Graham, 5th duke of Montrose, *ob.* 10 Dec. 1925
1926, 11 Jan.	John Charles Montagu-Douglas-Scott, 7th duke of Buccleuch and 9th duke of Queensberry, *ob.* 19 Oct. 1935
1935, 27 Dec.	Walter John Francis Erskine, 12th e. of Mar and 14th e. of Kellie
1944, 3 Mar.	Sidney Herbert Elphinstone, 16th baron Elphinstone, *ob.* 28 Nov. 1955
1956, 19 Apr.	Walter John Montagu-Douglas-Scott, 8th duke of Buccleuch and 10th duke of Queensberry, *ob.* 4 Oct. 1973
1974, 28 July	Francis David Charteris, 12th e. of Wemyss and 8th e. of March

LORD PRESIDENTS OF THE COURT OF SESSION

For the institution and development of the Court of Session, see R. K. Hannay, *The College of Justice* (1933); for biographical details of lord presidents from 1532 to 1829, *see* G. Brunton and D. Haig, *Senators of the College of Justice* (1832).

JAMES V

1532, 27 May	Alexander Myln, abbot of Cambuskenneth

MARY I

	Alexander Myln remained in office, *ob.* 19 June 1548
1549, 18 Jan.	Robert Reid, bp of Orkney 1541–58, *ob.* 6 Sept. 1558
1558, *2 Dec.*	Henry Sinclair, dean of Glasgow, bp of Ross 1558–65, *ob.* 2 Jan. 1565
1565, *12 Nov.*	John Sinclair, bp of Brechin 1565–66, *ob.* 9 Apr. 1566
1566, May	William Baillie of Provand (later Sir William Baillie of Provand)[2]

[1] Appd for life 25 Feb. 1777, since when all commissions have been for life.

[2] Baillie was acting president until 11 Nov. 1579 when parliament removed the requirement that the president should be a prelate.

JAMES VI

	William Baillie remained in office, *ob.* 26 May 1593
1567, 6 Dec.	Sir James Balfour of Pittendreich, forf. 30 Aug. 1571[1]
1593, 28 May	Alexander Seton, lord Urquhart, lord Fyvie 1597 (*see* chancellors, 1604)
1605, 1 Mar.	James Elphinstone, 1st lord Balmerino
1609, 6 June	John Preston of Fentonbarns, *ob.* 14 June 1616
1616, 15 June	Thomas Hamilton, 1st lord Binning, 1st e. of Melrose 1619 (*see* secretaries, 1612)

CHARLES I

	E. of Melrose remained in office
1626, 14 Feb.	Sir James Skene of Curriehill, *ob.* 15 Oct. 1633
1633, 17 Oct.	Sir Robert Spottiswoode, e. of New Abbey, vac. *2 Oct. 1641*[2]
1642–50	No permanent president[3]
1652, 27 Apr.	Commission for the administration of justice replaced the court of session (ended Feb. 1650). For membership see Brunton and Haig, 346–7.

CHARLES II

1661, 13 Feb.	Sir John Gilmour of Craigmillar, vac. 22 Dec. 1670
1671, 7 Jan.	Sir James Dalrymple of Stair, 1st viscount Stair 1690
1681, 14 Oct.	Sir George Gordon of Haddo, 1st e. of Aberdeen 1682
1682, 5 June	Sir David Falconer of Newton

JAMES VII

	Sir David Falconer remained in office, *ob.* 15 Dec. 1685
1685, 23 Dec.	Sir George Lockhart of Carnwath, *ob.* 31 Mar. 1689

WILLIAM II AND MARY II

1689, 28 Oct.	Sir James Dalrymple (*see under* 1671), *ob.* 25 Nov. 1695
1698, 17 Mar.	Hugh Dalrymple of North Berwick

ANNE–ELIZABETH II

	Hugh Dalrymple remained in office, *ob.* 1 Feb. 1737
1737, 20 June	Duncan Forbes of Culloden, *ob.* 10 Dec. 1747
1748, 4 June	Robert Dundas of Arniston, *ob.* 26 Aug. 1753
1754, 22 Jan.	Robert Craigie of Glendoick, *ob.* 10 Mar. 1760
1760, 30 Apr.	Robert Dundas of Arniston, *ob.* 13 Dec. 1787
1787, 22 Dec.	Sir Thomas Miller of Glenlee, *ob.* 27 Sept. 1789
1789, 26 Oct.	Sir Ilay Campbell of Succoth
1808, 31 Aug.	Robert Blair of Avonton, *ob.* 20 May 1811
1811, 10 Oct.	Charles Hope of Granton, vac. 20 July 1841
1841, 7 Oct.	David Boyle of Shewalton, vac. 5 May 1852
1852, 14 May	Duncan McNeill, 1st baron Colonsay 1867
1867, 25 Feb.	John Inglis of Glencorse, *ob.* 20 Aug. 1891
1891, 21 Sept.	James Patrick Bannerman Robertson (baron Robertson of Forteviot 1899), lord of appeal 14 Nov. 1899
1899, 21 Nov.	John Blair Balfour, 1st baron Kinross 1902, *ob.* 22 Jan 1905
1905, 4 Feb.	Andrew Graham Murray, 1st baron Dunedin 1905 (1st viscount 1926), lord of appeal 14 Oct. 1913
1913, 14 Oct.	Alexander Ure, 1st baron Strathclyde 1914
1920, 1 Apr.	James Avon Clyde

[1] Baillie had continued to act as president in Balfour's absence. Balfour's forfeiture was reversed but he did not resume the presidency.

[2] The court, which had not sat since 1639, was reconstituted on this date omitting Spottiswood, who had been the first president appd by direct royal nomination.

[3] On 14 Jan. 1642 it was ordained that presidents should be chosen for one session only. For list *see An Introduction to Scottish Legal History* (Stair Soc 1958), 460.

1935, 1 Apr.	Wilfred Guild Normand (baron Normand of Aberdour 1947), lord of appeal 6 Jan. 1947
1947, 6 Jan.	Thomas Mackay Cooper, 1st baron Cooper of Culross 1954
1954, 23 Dec.	James Latham McDiarmid Clyde
1972, 13 Mar.	George Carlyle Emslie

JUSTICES GENERAL

For the early history of the office of justiciar *see* G. W. S. Barrow, *The Kingdom of Scots* (1978) ch. 4 (list of justiciars, *c.* 1165–1306 at pp. 137–8). Separate justiciars for the parts of the kingdom north and south of the Forth were appointed until the reign of James IV when Andrew, 2nd lord Gray combined both offices. In 1514 Colin Campbell, 3rd e. of Argyll, became high justiciar or justice general for the whole of Scotland, this office being re-granted for life to the 4th and 5th earls. Thereafter it became subject to some form of hereditary right until 1628, when Archibald, lord Lorne (afterwards 8th earl) resigned it to the crown, reserving the heritable justiciarship of Argyll and the Western Isles. The justice general became nominal head of the high court of justiciary, established in 1672.

CHARLES I

1628, 11 July	William Graham, 7th e. of Menteith, 1st e. of Airth 1633, vac. 8 Nov. 1633
1635, 23 Dec.	Sir William Elphinstone, dism. 13 Nov. 1641
1641, 18 Nov.	Sir Thomas Hope of Kerse (for the king), *ob.* 23 Aug. 1643
1646, 13 Nov.	William Cunningham, 8th e. of Glencairn, dism. 15 Feb. 1649

CHARLES II

1649, 15 Mar.	John Kennedy, 6th e. of Cassillis, vac. 9 Aug. 1651
1661, 16 Aug.	John Murray, 2nd e. of Atholl (1st m. of Atholl 1676)
1675, 21 May	Alexander Stewart, 5th e. of Moray
1676, 5 May	Sir Archibald Primrose of Carrington
1678, 30 Sept.	Sir George Mackenzie of Tarbat (1st e. of Cromarty 1703)
1680, 1 June	William Douglas, 3rd e. of Queensberry (1st duke of Queensberry 1684)
1682, 1 Mar.	James Drummond, 4th e. of Perth
1684, 13 June	George Livingston, 3rd e. of Linlithgow

JAMES VII

Earl of Linlithgow remained in office until the Revolution

WILLIAM II AND MARY II

1689, 3 Aug.	Robert Ker, 4th e. of Lothian, 1st m. of Lothian 1701, *ob.* 15 Feb. 1703

ANNE–WILLIAM IV

M. of Lothian remained in office, *ob.* 15 Feb. 1703

1704, 17 Oct.	George Mackenzie, 1st e. of Cromarty (*see under* 1678)
1710, 23 Oct.	Archibald Campbell, e. of Ilay, 3rd duke of Argyll 1743, *ob.* 15 Apr. 1761
1761, 27 June	John Hay, 4th m. of Tweeddale, *ob.* 9 Dec. 1762
1763, 15 Apr.	Charles Douglas, 3rd duke of Queensberry, *ob.* 22 Oct. 1778
1778, 23 Oct.	David Murray, 7th viscount Stormont, 2nd e. of Mansfield 1792, vac. 1794
1795, 14 Jan.	James Graham, 3rd duke of Montrose, *ob.* 30 Dec. 1836

By Act of Parliament William IV c.69, the office of justice general was combined with that of lord president on the death of the holder of the office. Charles Hope, lord president, was admitted to the office of justice general, 23 Jan. 1837.

LORD ADVOCATES

The office of king's advocate probably dates from 1478[1] but the surviving evidence for it is so sparse that only from 1494 is it possible to point with confidence to a sole king's advocate as the crown's normal representative in civil litigation and treason trials.[2] His role as public prosecutor in criminal cases dates from 1579–84. For biographies of office holders *see* G. W. T. Omond, *The Lord Advocates of Scotland* (3 vols. 1883–1914).

JAMES III

1478, 8 June	John Ross of Montgrenan, vac. *26 May 1485*[3]

JAMES IV

1491, 23 Mar.	David Balfour of Carraldstoun vac. *25 Feb. 1493*
1494, 25 June	James Henderson of Fordell, justice clerk 1507–13, *ob.* 9 Sept 1513[4]

JAMES V

1513, 25 Oct.	James Wishart of Pitarow, justice clerk 1513–24, remained in office, *ob.* 14–22 Nov. 1524
1524, *4 Dec.*	Adam Otterburn of Auldhame and Reidhall (with Foulis 1527–32), dism. 1538
1527	James Foulis of Colinton (with Otterburn 1527–32), clerk register 12 Mar. 1532
1538, 13 Sept.	Henry Lauder of St Germains

MARY I

	Henry Lauder remained in office (with Spens 1555–59), vac. *bef.* 8 Feb. 1560
1555, 21 Oct.	John Spens of Condie (with Lauder 1555–59, and Crichton 1559–73)
1560, 8 Feb.	Robert Crichton of Eliok (with Spens 1559–73)

JAMES VI

	John Spens remained in office, *ob.* 1573; Robert Crichton remained in office (with Borthwick 1573–81), *ob.* 18–27 June 1582
1573, 15 Oct.	David Borthwick (with Crichton 1573–80), *ob.* Jan. 1581
1582, 27 June	David MacGill of Cranstonriddel (with Skene 1589–94, Hart 1594–96, and Hamilton 1596), *ob.* 13 Feb. 1596
1589, 20 Aug.	Sir John Skene of Curriehill (with MacGill 1589–94), clerk register 19 Sept. 1594
1594, 15 Oct.	William Hart of Livielands (with MacGill 1594–96, and Hamilton 1596–97), vac. 1597
1596, 31 Jan.	Sir Thomas Hamilton of Drumcairnie (*see* secretaries, 1612) (with MacGill 1596, and Hart 1596–97), vac. 15 May 1612
1612, 19 June	Sir William Oliphant of Newton

---

[1] There are references to a king's procurator fiscal in 1457 (*ER*, vi. 343) and a queen's advocate in 1462 (*ER*, vii. 59) but Ross appears successively for the king as commissioner (13 Aug. 1476), procurator (21 June 1477) and advocate 'ut asseruit' (8 June 1478) (SRO, Protocol bk of James Darow).

[2] Between 1478 and 1494 there are references to 'advocates' (usually unnamed) in the plural.

[3] Ross continued in the royal service up to James III's death (11 June 1488) but it is not clear whether he acted as advocate after 1485.

[4] Omond names Richard Lawson (from 1503) and James Wishart (from 1507) as joint advocates with Henderson but there is no authority for this.

. CHARLES I

Sir William Oliphant remained in office (with Hope 1626–28), *ob.* 13 Apr. 1628

1626, 29 May	Sir Thomas Hope of Craighall (with Oliphant 1626–28), *ob.* 1 Oct. 1646
1646, 30 Oct.	Sir Archibald Johnston of Wariston, vac. 10 Mar. 1649

CHARLES II

1649, 10 Mar.	Sir Thomas Nicholson, vac. Aug. 1651

PROTECTORATE

1658, 14 May	Sir George Lockhart of Carnwath, vac. *May* 1660

CHARLES II

1660, Aug.	Sir John Fletcher, vac. 14 Sept. 1664
1664, 14 Oct.	Sir John Nisbet of Dirleton, vac. 20 July 1677
1677, 3 Aug.	Sir George Mackenzie of Rosehaugh

JAMES VII

Sir George Mackenzie remained in office, dism. 17 May 1686

1686–7	Office vacant
1687, 21 Jan.	Sir John Dalrymple, yr, of Stair (e. of Stair 1703), justice clerk 31 Jan. 1688
1688, 31 Jan.	Sir George Mackenzie of Rosehaugh

WILLIAM II AND MARY II

1689, 21 May	Sir John Dalrymple, yr, of Stair (*see under* 1687)
1692, 28 Nov.	Sir James Stewart

ANNE

Sir James Stewart remained in office

1709, 25 May	Sir David Dalrymple of Hailes
1711, 18 Sept.	Sir James Stewart of Goodtrees, *ob.* 1 May 1713
1714, 30 Mar.	Thomas Kennedy of Dunure

GEORGE I–ELIZABETH II

1714, 9 Oct.	Sir David Dalrymple of Hailes
1720, 19 May	Robert Dundas of Arniston (lord president 1748)
1725, 29 May	Duncan Forbes of Culloden, lord president 20 June 1737
1737, 20 June	Charles Erskine of Tinwald, vac. 3 Mar. 1742 (justice clerk 1748–63)
1742, 4 Mar.	Robert Craigie of Glendoick (lord president 1754)
1746, 20 Feb.	William Grant of Prestongrange, vac. July 1754
1754, 16 Aug.	Robert Dundas of Arniston, lord president 30 Apr. 1760
1760, 30 Apr.	Thomas Miller of Glenlee, justice clerk 28 Apr. 1766 (lord president 1787)
1766, 28 Apr.	James Montgomery of Stanhope
1775, 24 May	Henry Dundas (viscount Melville 1802)
1783, 22 Aug.	Henry Erskine of Almondell
1783, 24 Dec.	Ilay Campbell of Succoth, lord president 26 Oct. 1789
1789, 26 Oct.	Robert Dundas of Arniston
1801, 7 May	Charles Hope of Granton, justice clerk 16 Nov. 1804 (lord president 1811)
1804, 16 Nov.	Sir James Montgomery of Stanhope
1806, 5 Mar.	Henry Erskine of Almondell
1807, 28 Mar.	Archibald Campbell of Clathick (later Colquhoun), clerk register 25 June 1816
1816, 9 July	Alexander Maconachie
1819, 24 June	Sir William Rae
1830, 2 Dec.	Francis Jeffrey

1834, 17 May	John Archibald Murray
1834, 19 Dec.	Sir William Rae
1835, 20 Apr.	John Archibald Murray
1839, 19 Apr.	Andrew Rutherfurd, vac. 30 Aug. 1841
1841, 4 Sept.	Sir William Rae, ob. 18 Oct. 1842
1842, 26 Oct.	Duncan McNeill (lord president 1852)
1846, 6 July	Andrew Rutherfurd
1851, 8 Apr.	James Moncreiff (1st baron Moncrieff of Tullibole 1874)
1852, 28 Feb.	Adam Anderson
1852, 18 May	John Inglis
1852, 30 Dec.	James Moncreiff, vac. 19 Feb. 1858
1858, 26 Feb.	John Inglis, justice clerk 9 July 1858 (lord president 1867)
1858, 10 July	Charles Baillie
1859, 15 Apr.	David Mure
1859, 21 June	James Moncreiff
1866, 7 July	George Patton, justice clerk 27 Feb. 1867
1867, 28 Feb.	Edward Strathearn Gordon
1868, 9 Dec.	James Moncreiff, justice clerk 9 Oct. 1869
1869, 9 Oct.	George Young
1874, 26 Feb.	Edward Strathearn Gordon (baron Gordon of Drumearn 1876), lord of appeal 6 Oct. 1876
1876, 12 Oct.	William Watson (baron Watson of Thankerton 1880) lord of appeal 28 Apr. 1880
1880, 1 May	John McLaren
1881, 18 Aug.	John Blair Balfour
1885, 2 July	John Hay Athol Macdonald
1886, 12 Feb.	John Blair Balfour
1886, 5 Aug.	John Hay Athol Macdonald, justice clerk 20 Oct. 1888
1888, 24 Oct.	James Patrick Bannerman Robertson, lord president 21 Sept. 1891
1891, 1 Oct.	Sir Charles John Pearson
1892, 20 Aug.	John Blair Balfour (lord president 1899)
1895, 6 July	Sir Charles John Pearson, vac. 7 May 1896
1896, 12 May	Andrew Graham Murray (lord president 1905)
1903, 17 Oct.	Charles Scott Dickson (justice clerk 1915–22)
1905, 13 Dec.	Thomas Shaw (baron Shaw of Dunfermline 1909, 1st baron Craigmyle 1929), lord of appeal 22 Feb. 1909
1909, 16 Feb.	Alexander Ure, lord president 14 Oct. 1913
1913, 31 Oct.	Robert Munro (1st baron Alness 1934), secretary for Scotland Dec. 1916
1916, 11 Dec.	James Avon Clyde, lord president 1 Apr. 1920
1920, 31 Mar.	Thomas Brash Morrison
1922, 7 Mar.	Charles David Murray
1922, 2 Nov.	William Watson
1924, 11 Feb.	Hugh Pattison Macmillan (baron Macmillan of Aberfeldy 1929)
1924, 13 Nov.	William Watson (baron Thankerton 1929), lord of appeal 1 May 1929
1929, 2 May	Alexander Munro MacRoberts
1929, 18 June	Craigie Mason Aitchison, justice clerk 2 Oct. 1933
1933, 2 Oct.	Wilfred Guild Normand, lord president 1 Apr. 1935
1935, 1 Apr.	Douglas Jamieson
1935, 30 Oct.	Thomas Mackay Cooper, justice clerk 9 June 1941 (lord president 1947)
1941, 9 June	James Scott Cumberland Reid (baron Reid of Drem 1948)
1945, 13 Aug.	George Reid Thomson, justice clerk 13 Oct. 1947
1947, 13 Oct.	John Wheatley (justice clerk 1972– , baron Wheatley of Shettleston 1976)
1951, 3 Nov.	James Latham McDiarmid Clyde, lord president 23 Dec. 1954
1955, 1 Jan.	William Rankine Milligan
1960, 6 Apr.	William Grant, justice clerk 26 Sept. 1962
1962, 15 Oct.	Ian Hamilton Shearer
1964, 21 Oct.	George Gordon Stott
1967, 24 Oct.	Henry Stephen Wilson (The Lord Wilson of Langside 1967)
1970, 25 June	Norman Russell Wylie

1974, 7 Mar.	Ronald King Murray
1979, 11 May	James Peter Hymers Mackay
1984, 15 May	Kenneth John Cameron, baron Cameron of Lochbroom

INTERREGNUM CIVIL AND MILITARY OFFICERS

For a recent account of the government of Scotland during the Interregnum *see* F. D. Dow, *Cromwellian Scotland, 1651–1660* (Edinburgh, 1979).

1650, Aug.	Oliver Cromwell, Lord Gen. Left S. Aug. 1651
1651, Aug.	George Monck, Lt Gen. Later joined by M. Gen. John Lambert and M. Gen. Richard Deane
1653, Jan.	Col. Robert Lilburne
1654, Apr.	George Monck (*see under* 1651)
1655, Sept.	Council in S. appointed, under President, Roger Boyle, lord Broghill
1656, Aug.	George Monck (*see under* 1651). Left S. Dec. 1659
1660, Jan.	(New commission, May 1660); ceased to act 22 Aug.

THE CHANNEL ISLANDS

THE most important general histories of the Channel Islands are the following:

F. de L. Bois, *A Constitutional History of Jersey* (Jersey, 1974).

F. B. Tupper, *The History of Guernsey and its Bailiwick*, 2nd edn (Guernsey, 1876).

J. Havet, *Les Cours royales des Iles Normandes* (Paris 1878)—extrait de la *Bibliothèque de l'École des Chartes*, xxxviii–xxxix (1877–78).

G. Dupont, *Histoire du Cotentin et de ses îles*, 4 vols (Caen, 1870–85).

L. Selosse, *L'Ile de Serk; un état féodal au xxe siècle* (Lille, 1928).

Comte de Gibon, *Les Iles Chausey et leur histoire*, 2nd edn (Évreux, 1935).

Some of these works are considerably out-moded; but they have not yet been replaced. They may be supplemented, for certain periods, by J. H. Le Patourel, *The Medieval Administration of the Channel Islands, 1199–1399* (Oxford, 1937) and A. J. Eagleston, *The Channel Islands under Tudor Government, 1485–1642* (Cambridge, 1949). 'The Political Development of the Channel Islands', by John Le Patourel (Société Guernesiaise, *Report and Transactions*, xiv (1948), 27–34), is a very brief sketch. There is a more solid, though somewhat legalistic, account of political development in Jersey in the Attorney-General's *Memorandum* included in the printed papers prepared in connection with the Jersey Prison Board Case, heard before the Privy Council in 1894. Valuable bibliographical information, particularly on constitutional and legal matters, will be found in R. Besnier, *La Coutume de Normandie: histoire externe* (Paris, 1935), pp. 250–70, and in J. H. Smith, *Appeals to the Privy Council from the American Plantations* (New York, 1950).

The present state of knowledge on the 'prehistory' of the Channel Islands is well set out in T. D. Kendrick and J. Hawkes, *The Archaeology of the Channel Islands*, 2 vols. (London, 1928; Jersey, [1937]), supplemented by reports of more recent investigations to be found, chiefly, in the *Bulletin Annuel* of La Société Jersiaise. No serious attempt has been made, as yet, to piece together the scattered scraps of information relating to their history during the first millennium of our era.

From the middle of the tenth century until 1204 the Islands were an integral part of the duchy of Normandy. The archipelago formed a natural unit of local administration, though it is difficult to say precisely how this local administration was organized. A full discussion of the evidence available, together with the names of such men as are known to have held office in the Islands during this period, will be found in T. W. M. de Guérin, 'Notes on the Early Constitutional History of the Channel Islands', Société Guernesiaise, *Report and Transactions*, viii (1919), 174–91, reprinted in Société Jersiaise, *Bulletin Annuel*, ix (1921), 256–71; G. F. B. de Gruchy, 'The Entries relating to Jersey in the Great Rolls of the Exchequer of Normandy of A.D. 1180', *ibid.*, ix (1919), 18–44; Le Patourel, *Medieval Administration*, 27–8.

In 1204, with the French conquest of continental Normandy, the Islands were thrust into that anomalous position in which they have found themselves almost to the present day—geographically and 'racially', in language, law and custom a part of France, politically and to some extent economically attached to England. From this date a continuous history is possible.

During the later Middle Ages the king governed the Islands either by delegating his seignory to a beneficiary who thereby assumed the title 'Lord of the Islands' (*Dominus Insularum*), or by entrusting the conduct of his affairs there to a responsible official who was usually styled 'warden' (*custos, gardien*). In the fifteenth century the Islands were commonly held in fee by princes of the English royal house who, naturally, performed their duties by deputy (*see* T. W. M. de Guérin, 'Our Hereditary Governors', Société Guernesiaise, *Report and Transactions*, vi (1910), 220–26).

Lists of medieval lords and wardens:

> J. Havet, *Série chronologique des gardiens et seigneurs des Iles Normandes, 1198–1461* (Paris, 1876—extrait de la *Bibliothèque de l'École des Chartes*, xxxvii).
> H. Marett Godfray, "Notes et additions à 'La Série Chronologique des Gardiens et Seigneurs des Iles Normandes, 1198–1461' ", Société Jersiaise, *Bulletin Annuel*, ii (1890), 30–48.

Le Patourel, *Medieval Administration*, Appendix, 121–30.

From the end of the fifteenth century onwards the king has been represented in the Islands by two officials, one in the bailiwick of Jersey, and the other in the bailiwick of Guernsey which includes Alderney and Sark. The two governments have been and still are entirely distinct, and the medieval titles 'lord' and 'warden' were abandoned in favour of 'captain' in the sixteenth century and 'governor' from the seventeenth century onwards. In course of time the governors, in both bailiwicks, came to perform their duties more and more by deputy, until the office of governor became a sinecure. No governors have been appointed to Guernsey since 1835, to Jersey since 1854; and their duties are now performed, as they have been performed for a long time, by a lieutenant-governor in each bailiwick.

Lists of governors and lieutenant-governors from the fifteenth century to the present day:

> (1) Governors and Lieutenant-Governors of Jersey:
> > J. A. Messervy, 'Liste des Gouverneurs, Lieut.-Gouverneurs et Députés-Gouverneurs de l'Ile de Jersey', Société Jersiaise, *Bulletin Annuel*, iv (1901), 373–94; v (1902), 8–26.
> > E. T. Nicolle: 'Liste des Lieut.-Gouverneurs et des Députés-Gouverneurs de 1850 à 1900', *ibid.*, v (1902), 27–32.

La Société Jersiaise has published lists of other Jersey officials in the *Bulletin Annuel* as follows: bailiffs, iv. 92–116, vii. 121–5, xii. 315–18; procureurs-généraux, iii. 293–6, vii. 47–9; vicomtes, iii. 297–302, vii. 49–51; avocats généraux, iii. 303–6, vii. 51–2; receivers-general, v. 101–114, vii. 52; greffiers, viii. 206–17: enregistreurs des contrats, etc., viii.

333–41; dénonciateurs, ix. 301–310; jurats. iv. 213–36, 275–93, viii. 342–53, ix. 8–14; advocates, ix. 141–57, 241–46, xiii. 136; deans, ix. 1–7; rectors, vii. 75–98, 127–46, 265–88, 379–98, viii. 5–29, 81–110, 197–205, x. 263–5; constables, v. 315–35, vi. 11–25, 137–55, 247–65, 393–411, vii. 18–34, xiii. 131–5; deputies, xiii. 335–8, 437–8, xiv. 53–6, 121–5. Useful information on many Jersey officials will be found in G. R. Balleine, *A Biographical Dictionary of Jersey* (1948).

(2) Governors and Lieutenant-governors of Guernsey:

> F. B. Tupper, *The History of Guernsey and its Bailiwick*, 2nd edn (Guernsey, 1876), 570–74.
>
> *'Press' Directory and Almanack* (Guernsey), issues from 1952 onwards (Lieutenant-governors since 1688).

Lists of bailiffs, jurats, procureurs, comptrollers, receivers-general and greffiers of Guernsey were printed in the issues of the *'Press' Directory and Almanack* (Guernsey) for 1937, 1938 and 1939; bailiffs only in issues since 1952. Reference may also be made to E. F. Carey and T. W. M. de Guérin, *List of Bailiffs of Guernsey, 1278–1915* (Guernsey, 1915), though this pamphlet stands in need of considerable correction and amplification.

(3) Governors of Alderney (from 1560):

> L. L. Clarke, *The Island of Alderney* (1851), 76–87 [*cf.* E. F. Carey, 'Peter Le Mesurier, Governor of Alderney, 1793–1803', Société Guernesiaise, *Report and Transactions* (1931), 46–61].

For lists of jurats, judges, greffiers, procureurs, contrôleurs, sergents and priests in Alderney, see A. H. Ewen, 'The Town of St. Anne, Alderney', Société Guernesiaise, *Report and Transactions*, xvi (1959), 347–53.

(4) Seigneurs, Seneschals and other officials in Sark (from 1565):

> J. V. L. Cachelaille (ed. Laura E. Hale), *The Island of Sark* (1928), 294–6; A. R. de Carteret, *The Story of Sark* (1956), 160–62.

In general, it may be said that the above lists, in so far as they concern officials appointed after about 1700, are accurate; but for periods earlier than the eighteenth century none is entirely satisfactory.

ARCHBISHOPS AND BISHOPS
OF ENGLAND

THE lists of bishops which follow include the hierarchy of the Middle Ages and the Anglican episcopate for the period after the breach with Rome in 1534. For the third edition of the *Handbook*, the lists for the period before 1066, newly prepared by Dr Simon Keynes, are printed separately.

EPISCOPAL SUCCESSION IN ANGLO-SAXON ENGLAND

The details of episcopal succession in the Anglo-Saxon period, in the form in which they appeared in the first edition of this *Handbook*, were based on W. Stubbs's *Registrum Sacrum Anglicanum*, 2nd ed. (Oxford, 1897) and W. G. Searle's *Anglo-Saxon Bishops, Kings and Nobles* (Cambridge, 1899). It has long been apparent, however, that the details assembled by Stubbs and Searle hardly provided an adequate basis for the compilation of reliable episcopal lists for the Anglo-Saxon period. The editors of the *Handbook* did not consider it possible to verify the information derived from these works, because they were advised that such an undertaking would be useless until 'all the available charter-evidence had been critically sifted'. Nor was any attempt made to revise the Anglo-Saxon sections of the episcopal lists for the second edition of the *Handbook* (1961), beyond the correction of a few obvious slips. In 1965 R. I. Page wrote that 'our evidence for Anglo-Saxon episcopal succession is often too scanty or confused for us to compile simple lists of names like those of the *Handbook of British Chronology*' ('Episcopal Lists, Parts I & II', p. 92), and he drew attention to the various kinds of errors which the lists published in the *Handbook* contained (*ibid.*, pp. 92–5).

Nevertheless, it is clearly desirable that the attempt should be made to reduce the basic information about Anglo-Saxon episcopal succession to a readily assimilable form; but it is equally obvious that it is impossible within the constraints of the *Handbook* to present anything more than a simplification of the evidence. The lists which follow are the product of a certain amount of revision (explained further below), and should be taken in the spirit in which they are intended: as no more than an interim statement, pending the systematic analysis of all the available evidence.

Our knowledge of episcopal succession in the Anglo-Saxon period depends essentially on four very different types of evidence.

(1) Episcopal lists

Sets of episcopal lists are preserved in several manuscripts, ranging in date from the early ninth century to the first half of the twelfth; but the various sets are by no means entirely independent of each other, and much remains to be done on establishing how the material was first assembled (apparently in the late eighth or early ninth century), and how it was augmented and transmitted thereafter. The surviving lists are printed and discussed (mainly from a textual point of view) by R. I. Page ('Episcopal Lists'); reference should also be made to Dumville, 'Anglian Collection', which is principally concerned with royal genealogies and regnal lists, but which has important implications for our understanding of the episcopal lists as well. The lists have the appearance of being straightforward records of succession to episcopal office, but they should not be taken at face value: they are the products of historical reasoning and reconstruction on the part of their compilers, and they were at the mercy of the scribes responsible for their transmission; it is not surprising to find, therefore, that they are often at variance with other evidence, and in those places where they constitute the only available source it would be hazardous to put absolute trust in their reliability. The manuscripts in which the lists are preserved are as follows:

(A) London, BL Cotton Vespasian B. vi, 108r–109r (ptd Page, 'Episcopal Lists, Part III', pp. 3–7; see also Dumville, 'Anglian Collection', pp. 24–5). The lists were originally written in the early ninth century, and represent a situation at some point between 805 and 814; the majority of the lists were subsequently up-dated, mainly by a second scribe writing c. 833.

(B) Cambridge, Corpus Christi College 183, 61r–64v (ptd Page, 'Episcopal Lists, Part III', pp. 8–12; see also Dumville, 'Anglian Collection', pp. 25–6, and Keynes, 'King Athelstan's Books', pp. 181–3). The lists were written between 934 and 939; but most represent a situation in the middle of the ninth century, and only the lists for Canterbury and the West Saxon sees (Winchester, Ramsbury, Sherborne, Wells and Crediton) are brought down to the 930s.

(C) Cambridge, Corpus Christi College 173, 55r–55v (ptd Page, 'Episcopal Lists, Part III', pp. 22–4, and Bately, MS A, pp. 95–9; see also Flower and Smith, The Parker Chronicle (for a facsimile)). Lists are given for the sees of Canterbury, Rochester, London, Selsey, Winchester, Sherborne, Ramsbury and Crediton, representing the situation at some point between 985 and 988.

(D) London, BL Cotton Tiberius B. v, 21r–22r (ptd Page, 'Episcopal Lists, Part III', pp. 12–17; see also McGurk et al., Illustrated Miscellany (for a facsimile) and Dumville, 'Anglian Collection', pp. 26–8). The lists were written in the second quarter of the eleventh century, but represent situations at different times: those for Canterbury, Winchester, Sherborne, Ramsbury, Wells and Crediton are complete down to the early 990s; those for Rochester, London, Selsey, Lindsey and Elmham are brought down to the first half of the ninth century, and each is then continued with bishops of the later tenth century (but note that the tenth-century bishops in the Lindsey list were in fact bishops of Dorchester); and those for Worcester, Leicester, Lichfield, Hereford, Dunwich, York, Hexham, Lindisfarne and Whithorn are left at different points in the late eighth and first half of the ninth centuries.

(E) London, BL Cotton Otho B. xi (ptd Whelock, Historiae . . . Libri V, pp. 568–70). This manuscript was an early-eleventh-century copy of CCCC 173; it was lost in the Cotton fire of 1731, and its contents can only be reconstructed from early modern sources. The original scribe copied the episcopal lists in CCCC 173 without bringing them up to date; but the lists were subsequently continued by another hand, and brought down to c. 1012. The lists cover the sees of Canterbury, Rochester, London, Selsey and Winchester; a leaf containing lists for Sherborne, Ramsbury and Crediton was lost already before the destruction of the manuscript.

(F) London, BL Stowe 944, 14v–17r (ptd Birch, Liber Vitae, pp. 14–21). The lists were written in the second quarter of the eleventh century. Those for Canterbury, Winchester, Sherborne, Ramsbury, Crediton and Wells are brought down to the time of writing, but the other lists, for London, Rochester and Selsey, are not carried beyond the late tenth century.

(G) Cambridge, Corpus Christi College 140, 115rv (ptd Page, 'Episcopal Lists, Part III', pp. 17–21). The lists were written c. 1100. Those for Canterbury, Winchester, Wells and Worcester are brought down to the time of writing; those for London and Rochester are brought down to the early eleventh century; the rest stop much earlier.

(H) Textus Roffensis, 110v–116r (see Sawyer, Textus Roffensis for a facsimile). The lists were written in the early twelfth century. Those for Canterbury and Rochester are brought down to the time of writing; those for London, Selsey, Winchester, Sherborne, Ramsbury, Wells and Crediton are brought down to the late tenth century; the rest stop in the ninth century.

There are also separate lists for certain bishoprics, for example Sherborne (in Paris, BN lat. 943, 1v) and Winchester (in London, BL Arundel 60, 149v). There are no lists for the dioceses of Cornwall, Chester-le-Street and Durham.

(2) Anglo-Saxon charters

If the episcopal lists provide the essential information on the succession of individuals who held office in a particular see, the charters supply the basis for our knowledge of their absolute dates; for a bibliographical guide to this material, see Sawyer, Anglo-Saxon Charters. Much depends on the detailed analysis of witness-lists: in many cases, the date given below for a bishop's accession is an expression covering the period from the latest known attestation of his predecessor to his own first appearance in a witness-list, and the date given for his death or translation expresses the period from his last appearance to the first of his successor. The complications generated by the charters are endless, and arise from various aspects of the material: above all, from the difficulty of establishing for certain whether a given text is authentic in its received form, but also from the garbling of names and dates in the process of transmission, from the problems of identification, and from contradictions within the surviving evidence. The study of Anglo-Saxon charters has progressed far since the days of Stubbs and Searle, but we are still a long way from being able to claim that all the evidence has been critically sifted; a new multi-volume edition, published under the auspices of the British Academy and the Royal Historical Society, is in progress, and only when it is complete will such a claim be realistic. Even so, much will always be left to individual judgement, and differences of opinion will always remain.

It should be emphasized that not all the bishops who appear in the witness-lists can be assigned to a particular see. In part this must reflect imperfections in the episcopal lists themselves (whether in the omission of names from existing lists, or in the lack of lists for certain dioceses), but some of the 'surplus' bishops are likely to have been men appointed as assistants for those of full diocesan status. The profusion of such unidentified bishops in the witness-lists of the charters of King Athelstan (924–39), in a period for which episcopal lists are likely to be reasonably reliable, is of some significance for our understanding of the organization of the church during his reign; while their apparent absence during, for example, the reign of King Æthelred the Unready (978–1016) may reflect no more than a change in habit on the part of those who compiled the witness-lists in the charters.

More useful information can be gleaned from the professions of obedience to the archbishop of Canterbury, made by bishops at the time of their appointment. The texts of about thirty survive from the Anglo-Saxon period (edited by Richter, *Canterbury Professions*), and all but one date from the period between c. 800 and c. 870; for further discussion, see Brooks, *Church of Canterbury*, pp. 165–7.

(3) 'Literary' sources

The 'literary' (as opposed to 'documentary') sources range from Bede's *Historia Ecclesiastica* (for the period up to 731) and the *Anglo-Saxon Chronicle* (in its various recensions) to the post-Conquest histories compiled by William of Malmesbury, 'Florence' (or John) of Worcester and others. It is all too easy to forget that such sources were compiled by people who, like ourselves, were sometimes concerned to make the best possible sense of the information at their disposal, and who might have manipulated their own sources in order to create a reasonably coherent narrative; it is accordingly difficult always to know how to judge what they say. This applies in particular to the early twelfth-century Anglo-Norman historians: they often supply details not attested elsewhere, but it should not necessarily be assumed that they actually had access to pre-Conquest material which has not otherwise survived.

(4) Obits

The literary sources sometimes specify the precise day of the year on which a bishop died, and in many other cases it is possible to supply this information from entries in calendars and martyrologies. The surviving calendars from the period up to 1100 were assembled and printed by Wormald (*English Kalendars*), but he deliberately omitted any obits that the calendars contained and never produced the projected volume in which these were to be published. The collection and analysis of obits of Anglo-Saxon persons, recorded in pre- and post-Conquest sources of all kinds, thus remain to be achieved. The majority of the episcopal obits given in the lists below are derived from the literary sources (notably the *Anglo-Saxon Chronicle*), or from one or other of the following manuscripts:

Cambridge, Corpus Christi College 57 (s. x/xi martyrology from Abingdon; obits ptd James, *Catalogue of Manuscripts in Corpus Christi College* I, 115–18)
Cambridge, Trinity College 0. 2. 1 (s. xii² calendar from Ely; obits ptd Dickins, 'Day of Byrhtnoth's Death')

London, BL Arundel 68 (s. xv² obituary of Christ Church, Canterbury; copied in London, Lambeth Palace Library 20, and archiepiscopal obits ptd thence by Wharton, *Anglia Sacra* I, 52–64)

London, BL Cotton Nero C. ix (s. xiii martyrology and fragment of s. xii obituary from Christ Church, Canterbury, ptd Dart, *Cathedral Church of Canterbury*, App. pp. xxxii–xli and xli–xlii, and Boutemy, 'Two Obituaries')

London, BL Cotton Titus D. xxvii (s. xi¹ calendar from the New Minster, Winchester; obits ptd Birch, *Liber Vitae*, pp. 269–73)

London, BL Cotton Vitellius C. xii (s. xi/xii martyrology from St Augustine's, Canterbury)

Oxford, Bodleian Library, Bodley 579 (s. x² calendar from Glastonbury; obits ptd Warren, *Leofric Missal*, pp. l–li)

Oxford, Bodleian Library, Hatton 113 (s. xi² calendar from Worcester; obits ptd Atkins, 'Church of Worcester', pp. 29–31)

Further obits of Anglo-Saxon bishops are to be found in the following sources:

William of Malmesbury, *De antiquitate Glastonie ecclesie*, ch. 67 (from a lost Glastonbury calendar): see Scott, *Early History of Glastonbury*, pp. 136–8 and 206–7

Leland, *Collectanea* II, 587–8 (from a lost Ramsey calendar)

PRINCIPLES OF REVISION

It should be clear from the above that the systematic revision of the episcopal lists for Anglo-Saxon England would be a major undertaking; the extent of revision attempted for the purposes of the present edition of the *Handbook* is necessarily limited, and it must be stressed again that the lists which follow represent a provisional statement, pending further research. Ideally, perhaps, one should have employed a system whereby the limits of a bishop's period of office were expressed in such a way as to recognize a distinction between information derived from evidence of uncertain authority and information derived from evidence deemed to be reliable; but such a system would require detailed accompanying apparatus and is accordingly too elaborate for application here. The most obvious aspect of the revision that has been attempted is the change of layout: the information on episcopal succession in Anglo-Saxon England has been gathered together, partly to facilitate reference, but mainly to indicate that this is a period with peculiar difficulties; the special column for the consecration of a bishop has been abandoned, because this kind of precision is rarely attainable. Some attempt has been made to check the details of episcopal succession against the various sets of episcopal lists, and to normalize the spelling of personal names in accordance with common usage; other changes arise from checking details against modern editions of relevant sources (such as the *Anglo-Saxon Chronicle*), in order to respect their chronology as it is currently understood; and use has been made of the various collections of obits mentioned above. The revised lists also incorporate the results of recent work on particular periods (e.g. O'Donovan, 'Episcopal Dates', for the period 850–950, and Keynes, *Diplomas of King Æthelred*, Tables 2 and 3, for the period 978–1016) and on particular sees (e.g. Whitelock, 'Church in East Anglia', for Dunwich and Elmham). No attempt, however, has been made to indicate whether a bishop had previously been an abbot (frequently the case in the tenth and eleventh centuries); for this information one must refer to Knowles *et al.*, *Heads of Religious Houses*.

REFERENCES

I. Atkins, 'The Church of Worcester from the Eighth to the Twelfth Century [pt II]', *Antiquaries Journal* 20 (1940), pp. 1–38

J. Bately, ed., *The Anglo-Saxon Chronicle: a Collaborative Edition*, ed. D. Dumville and S. Keynes, vol. 3: *MS A* (Cambridge, 1986)

W. de G. Birch, ed., *Liber Vitae: Register and Martyrology of New Minster and Hyde Abbey, Winchester* (Hampshire Record Society, 1892)

A. Boutemy, 'Two Obituaries of Christ Church, Canterbury', *English Historical Review* 50 (1935), pp. 292–9

N. Brooks, *The Early History of the Church of Canterbury: Christ Church from 597 to 1066* (Leicester, 1984)

J. Dart, *The History and Antiquities of the Cathedral Church of Canterbury* (London, 1726)

B. Dickins, 'The Day of Byrhtnoth's Death and other Obits from a Twelfth-Century Ely Kalendar', *Leeds Studies in English* 6 (1937), pp. 14–24

D. Dumville, 'The Anglian Collection of Royal Genealogies and Regnal Lists', *Anglo-Saxon England* 5 (1976), pp. 23–50

R. Flower and H. Smith, ed., *The Parker Chronicle and Laws*, Early English Text Society, o.s. 208 (London, 1941)

M. R. James, *A Descriptive Catalogue of the Manuscripts in the Library of Corpus Christi College Cambridge*, 2 vols (Cambridge, 1912)

S. Keynes, *The Diplomas of King Æthelred 'the Unready' 978–1016* (Cambridge, 1980)

S. Keynes, 'King Athelstan's Books', *Learning and Literature in Anglo-Saxon England*, ed. M. Lapidge and H. Gneuss (Cambridge, 1985), pp. 143–201

D. Knowles, *et al.*, *The Heads of Religious Houses, England and Wales, 940–1216* (Cambridge, 1972)

J. Leland, *De Rebus Britannicis Collectanea*, ed. T. Hearne, 6 vols, 2nd ed. (London, 1774)

P. McGurk, *et al.*, ed., *An Eleventh-Century Anglo-Saxon Illustrated Miscellany: British Library Cotton Tiberius B.V Part I*, Early English Manuscripts in Facsimile 21 (Copenhagen, 1983)

M. A. O'Donovan, 'An Interim Revision of Episcopal Dates for the Province of Canterbury, 850–950: part I', *Anglo-Saxon England* 1 (1972), pp. 23–44

M. A. O'Donovan, 'An Interim Revision of Episcopal Dates for the Province of Canterbury, 850–950: part II', *Anglo-Saxon England* 2 (1973), pp. 91–113

R. I. Page, 'Anglo-Saxon Episcopal Lists, Parts I & II', *Nottingham Mediaeval Studies* 9 (1965), pp. 71–95

R. I. Page, 'Anglo-Saxon Episcopal Lists, Part III', *Nottingham Mediaeval Studies* 10 (1966), pp. 2–24

M. Richter, ed., *Canterbury Professions*, Canterbury and York Society 67 (1973)

P. H. Sawyer, *Anglo-Saxon Charters: an Annotated List and Bibliography* (London, 1968)

P. Sawyer, ed., *Textus Roffensis: Rochester Cathedral Library Manuscript A. 3. 5.* I, Early English Manuscripts in Facsimile 7 (Copenhagen, 1957)

J. Scott, *The Early History of Glastonbury: an Edition, Translation and Study of William of Malmesbury's 'De Antiquitate Glastonie Ecclesie'* (Woodbridge, 1981)

F. E. Warren, ed., *The Leofric Missal* (Oxford, 1883)

H. Wharton, *Anglia Sacra*, 2 vols (London, 1691)

A. Whelock, ed., *Historiae Ecclesiasticae Gentis Anglorum Libri V* (Cambridge, 1643)

D. Whitelock, 'The Pre-Viking Age Church in East Anglia', *Anglo-Saxon England* 1 (1972), pp. 1–22

F. Wormald, ed., *English Kalendars before A.D. 1100*, Henry Bradshaw Society 72 (London, 1934)

CANTERBURY

ARCHBISHOPS	ACCESSION	DEATH OR TRS. unless otherwise stated
Augustine	597	26 May, 604 × 609
Laurence	604 × 609	2 Feb. 619
Mellitus	619, trs. from London	24 Apr. 624
Justus	624, trs. from Rochester	10 Nov. 627 × 631
Honorius	627 × 631	30 Sept. 653
Deusdedit	cons. 12 (or 26) Mar. 655	14 July 664
[Wigheard, abp elect	el. 666 or 667	668]
Theodore	cons. 26 Mar. 668, acc. 669	19 Sept. 690
Berhtwald	el. 1 July 692, cons. 29 June 693	13 Jan. 731
Tatwine	cons. 10 June 731	30 July 734

ARCHBISHOPS	ACCESSION	DEATH OR TRS. *unless otherwise stated*
Nothhelm	cons. 735	17 Oct. 739
Cuthbert	740, ?trs. from Hereford	26 Oct. 760
Bregowine	cons. 27 Sept. 761	764
Jænberht	cons. 2 Feb. 765	12 Aug. 792
Æthelheard	el. 792, cons. 21 July 793	12 May 805
Wulfred	el. by 26 July 805, cons. *c.* Oct. 805	24 Mar. 832
?Feologild	el. 25 Apr. 832, cons. 9 June	30 Aug. 832
?Suithred	?rival of Feologild for abp	
Ceolnoth	cons. ?27 July 833	4 Feb. 870
Æthelred	870	30 June 888
Plegmund	890	2 Aug. 923
Æthelhelm, or Athelm	Aug. 923 × Sept. 925, trs. from Wells	8 Jan. 926
Wulfhelm	*c.* 926, trs. from Wells	12 Feb. 941
Oda	941, trs. from Ramsbury	2 June 958
Ælfsige	958, trs. from Winchester	959
Byrhthelm	959, trs. from Wells	dep. 959, bp of Wells, d. 15 May 973
Dunstan	959, trs. from London (? cons. abp. 21 Oct. ? 960)	19 May 988
Æthelgar	988, trs. from Selsey	12 or 13 Feb. 990
Sigeric	990, trs. from Ramsbury	28 Oct. 994
Ælfric	el. 21 Apr. 995, trs. from Ramsbury	16 Nov. 1005
Ælfheah	1006, trs. from Winchester (? cons. abp. 16 Nov. 1006)	19 Apr. 1012
Lyfing (Ælfstan)	1013, trs. from Wells	12 June 1020
Æthelnoth	cons. 13 Nov. 1020	28 or 29 Oct., or 1 Nov., 1038

Between 1035 and 1038, Æthelnoth was assisted by Eadsige, (?)bishop of St Martin's, Canterbury.

Eadsige	1038	29 Oct. 1050

Between 1044 and 1048 archiepiscopal functions were performed by Siweard, abbot of Abingdon and (?)bishop of St Martin's, Canterbury; between 1048 and 1050, Eadsige was assisted by Godwine, bishop of St Martin's.

Robert of Jumièges	ap. March 1051, trs. from London	expelled Sept. 1052
Stigand	1052, trs. from Winchester	dep. 11 Apr. 1070, d. 21 or 22 Feb. 1072

CHESTER-LE-STREET

BISHOPS	ACCESSION	DEATH OR TRS. *unless otherwise stated*
	See transferred from Lindisfarne, 883	
Eardwulf		899
Cuthheard	899	*c.* 915
Tilred	*c.* 915	*c.* 925
Wigred	*c.* 925	? 942
Uhtred	? 942	?
Seaxhelm	?	expelled after six months
Ealdred	? before 946	? 968
Ælfsige	? 968	? 990
Aldhun	990	
	See transferred to Durham, 995	

CORNWALL

Kenstec	823 × 870	before 888 × 893
Asser	888 × 893	909

BISHOPS	ACCESSION	DEATH OR TRS. *unless otherwise stated*
Conan	July 924 × 931	946 or 953 × Nov. 955
Daniel	955 × 956	959 × 963
Wulfsige Comoere	959 × 963	981 × (988 × 990)
Ealdred	981 × (988 × 990)	1002 × 1009
? Æthelsige	1002 × 1009	1011 × 1012
Buruhwold	1011 × 1012	1019 × 1027
Lyfing, bp of Crediton, Cornwall and Worcester	1027	20, 23 or 25 Mar. 1046
Leofric, bp of Crediton and Cornwall	1046 (? cons. 19 Apr.)	

See transferred to Exeter, 1050

CREDITON

Eadwulf	c. 909	934
Æthelgar	934	952 or 953
Ælfwold I	953	972
Sideman	973	30 Apr. or 1 or 2 May 977
Ælfric	977 × 979	986 × 987
Ælfwold II	986 × 987	? × (1011 × 1015)
Ælfwold III	(986 × 987) × ?	1011 × 1015
Eadnoth	1011 × 1015	1019 × 1027
Lyfing, bp of Crediton, Cornwall and Worcester	1027	20, 23 or 25 Mar. 1046
Leofric, bp of Crediton and Cornwall	cons. 19 Apr. 1046	

See transferred to Exeter, 1050

DORCHESTER

As a West Saxon bishopric:

Birinus	634	c. 650
Agilbert	c. 650	resigned c. 660

For later West Saxon bishops, see Winchester and Sherborne

Ætla	? 660	?

As a Mercian bishopric, transferred from Leicester:

Alhheard	869 × 888	893 × 896
Wigmund or Wilferth	893 × 900	903 × 909
Cenwulf	c. 909	909 × 925
Wynsige	909 × 925	934 × 945
Æthelwald	934 × 945	949 × 950
Osketel (abp of York 956)	949 × 950	1 Nov. 971
Leofwine, bp of Lindsey by 953	united Lindsey and Dorchester 971	971 × 975
Ælfnoth	971 × 975	975 × 979
Æscwig	975 × 979	23 Apr. 1002
Ælfhelm	1002	1007 × 1009
Eadnoth I	1007 × 1009	18 Oct. 1016
Æthelric	1016	8 Dec. 1034
Eadnoth II	1034	18 or 19 Sept. 1049
Ulf	1049	expelled 14 Sept. 1052, suspended at Council of Vercelli 1050
Wulfwig	1053	1067

DUNWICH

BISHOPS	ACCESSION	DEATH OR TRS. *unless otherwise stated*

Bishops of the East Angles, established at Dunwich:

Felix	630 × 631	647 × 648
Thomas	647 × 648	652 × 653
Berhtgils (Boniface)	652 × 653	669 × 670
Bisi	669 × 670	res. 672

See divided in two; for later succession, see also Elmham

Æcce	672 × ?	?
Æscwulf	?	?
Eardred	? × 716	716 × ?
Cuthwine	?	?
Aldberht	? × 731	731 × ?
Ecglaf	?	?
Heardwulf	? × 747	747 × ?
Heardred	? × 781	789 × 793
Ælfhun	789 × 793	798
Tidferth	798	816 × 824
Wærmund	816 × 824	824 × 825
Wilred	825	845 × 870
Æthelwold	845 × 870	?

DURHAM

See transferred from Chester-le-Street, 995

Aldhun		1018

See vacant for three years

Edmund	c. 1020	c. 1040
Eadred	c. 1040	c. 1040
Æthelric	cons. 11 Jan. 1041, acc. c. 1041	res. 1056, d. 15 Oct. 1072
Æthelwine	1056	depr. 1071, d. ? 1071

ELMHAM

For bishops of the East Angles before the division of the see, see above under Dunwich.

Beaduwine	672 × ?	693 × ?
Nothberht	? × 706	716 × ?
Heathulac	? × 731	731 × ?
Æthelfrith	736	736 × ?
Eanfrith	? × 758	758 × ?
Æthelwulf	? × 781	781 × ?
Alhheard	? × 785	805 × ?
Sibba	? × 814	816 × ?
Hunferth	816 × 824	816 × 824
Hunberht	? × 824	845 or 856 × ?, or ? d. Nov. 869

Episcopal succession interrupted

Eadwulf (Athulf)	? × 955	966 × ?
Ælfric I	? × 970	970 × ?
Theodred I	? × 974	?
Theodred II	?	995 × 997
Æthelstan	995 × 997	7 Oct. 1001
Ælfgar	1001	res. 1012 × 1016, d. 24 or 25 Dec. 1020
Ælfwine	? × 1019	12 Apr. 1023 × 1038
Ælfric II	1023 × 1038	Dec. 1038
Ælfric III	1039	1042 × 1043

BISHOPS	ACCESSION	DEATH OR TRS. *unless otherwise stated*
Stigand	1043	depr. 1043
Grimketel, bp of Selsey	1043	depr. ? 1043
Stigand (restored)	1044	1047, trs. to Winchester
Æthelmær	1047	dep. 1070

EXETER

See transferred from Crediton, 1050

Leofric		10 Feb. 1072

HEREFORD

Putta	676, trs. from Rochester	676 × 688
Tyrhtel	688	705 × 710
Torhthere	710	727 × 731
Walhstod	727 × 731	731 × 736
Cuthberht	736	740
Podda	741	747 × 758
Acca	747 × 758	758 × 770
Headda	758 × 770	770 × 777
Aldberht	777 or 778	781 × 786
Esne	781 × 786	786 × 788
Ceolmund	786 × 788	793 × 798
Utel	793 × 798	799 × 801
Wulfheard	799 × 801	822 × 824
Beonna	824	825 × 832
Eadwulf	825 × 832	836 × 839
Cuthwulf	836 × 839	857 × 866
Mucel	857 × 866	857 × 866
Deorlaf	857 × 866	884 × 888
Cynemund	el. 888	888 × 890
Edgar	888 × 890	930 × 931
Tidhelm	930 × 931	934 or 937 × 940
Wulfhelm	934 or 937 × 940	934 or 937 × 940
Ælfric	934 or 937 × 940	949 × 958 or 971
Æthelwulf (Athulf)	? × 971	1013 × ?
Æthelstan	1013 × 1016	10 Feb. 1056
Leofgar	Mar. 1056	16 June 1056
Ealdred, bp of Hereford and Worcester	1056	res. 1060, trs. to York
Walter	1060	1079

HEXHAM

Eata	678	681, trs. to Lindisfarne
Tunberht	681	dep. 684
Cuthbert	el. 684	685, trs. to Lindisfarne
Eata (returned)	685	685 or 686
John of Beverley	Aug. 687	706, trs. to York
Wilfrid	706, trs. from Leicester	709
Acca	709	depr. or expelled 731, d. 20 Oct. 737 or 740
Frithoberht	8 Sept. 734	23 Dec. 766
Alhmund	24 Apr. 767	7 Sept. 780 or 781
Tilberht	2 Oct. ? 780 or 781	789
Æthelberht	789, trs. from Whithorn	16 Oct. 797
Heardred	29 Oct. 797	800
Eanberht	800	813
Tidferth	813	821

LEICESTER

For earlier Mercian bishops, see under Lichfield

BISHOPS	ACCESSION	DEATH OR TRS. *unless otherwise stated*
Wilfrid	?	706, trs. to Hexham
Headda, bp of Lichfield and Leicester	?	716 × 727
Aldwine (Uuor), bp of Lichfield and Leicester	716 × 727	737
Torhthelm (Totta)	737	764
Eadberht	764	781 × 785
Unwona	781 × 785	801 × 803
Wernberht	801 × 803	814 × 816
Ræthhun	814 × 816	839 × Dec. 840
Ealdred	839 × Dec. 840	Dec. 840 × 844
Ceolred	Dec. 840 × 844	869 × 888

See Dorchester for later succession

LICHFIELD

For the first bishops of the Mercians (and of Lindsey and the Middle Angles), see below, p. 220. The episcopal seat was established at Lichfield by Chad.

Chad	669	2 Mar. 672
Winfrith	672	depr. 672 × 676
Seaxwulf	? × 676	? × 692

The Mercian province was sub-divided into five bishoprics: Lichfield and Leicester (for Mercia itself); Lindsey; and Worcester and Hereford (for the Middle Angles).

Headda, bp of Lichfield and Leicester	691	716 × 727
Aldwine (Uuor), bp of Lichfield and Leicester	? × 731	737
Hwita	737	749 × 757
Hemele	? × 757	765
Cuthfrith	? 765	c. 769
Berhthun	c. 769	777 × 779
Hygeberht	779	depr. 799 × 801, d. 803 × ?

In 787 Bishop Hygeberht of Lichfield was elevated to archiepiscopal status; but he seems to have retired by 801, and Lichfield reverted to its former status in 803.

Aldwulf	799 × 801	814 × 816
Herewine	814 × 816	817 × 818
Æthelwald	818	830
Hunberht	830	830 × 836
Cyneferth	830 × 836	841 × 845
Tunberht	843 × 845	857 × 862
Wulfsige	857 × 862	866 × 869
Burgheard or Eadberht	866 × 869	869 × 883
	866 × 869	875 × 883
Wulfred	869 or 875 × 883	889 × 900
Wigmund or Wilferth	889 × 900	903 × 915
Ælfwine (Ælle)	903 × 915	935 × 941
Wulfgar	935 × 941	946 × 949
Cynesige	946 × 949	963 × 964
Wynsige	963 × 964	975

BISHOPS	ACCESSION	DEATH OR TRS. *unless otherwise stated*
Ælfheah	975	1002 × 1004
Godwine	1002 × 1004	1017 × ?
Leofgar	1017 × ?	? × (1026 × 1027)
Brihtmær	? × (1026 × 1027)	1039
Wulfsige	1039	1053
Leofwine	1053	1067

LINDISFARNE

Aidan	635	31 Aug. 651
Finan	651	661
Colman	661	res. 664, d. 8 Aug. 676
Tuda	664	664

Complications involving Wilfrid and Chad

Eata	? × 681, trs. from Hexham	685, returned to Hexham
Cuthbert	cons. 26 Mar. 685	res. 687, d. 20 Mar. 687

Vacancy during which Wilfrid administered the see

Eadberht	688	6 May 698
Eadferth	?	?
Oethilwald (or Æthelwald)	? × 731	737 or 740
Cynewulf	737 or 740	res. 779 or 780; d. 782 or 783
Higbald	780 or 781	25 May 803
Ecgberht	11 June 803	821
Heathwred	821	830
Ecgred	830	845
Eanberht	845	854
Eardwulf	854	

See transferred to Chester-le-Street, 883

LINDSEY

For earlier bishops of Lindsey, see under Mercians and Lichfield

Eadhæd	678	expelled *c.* 679; bp of Ripon
Æthelwine	*c.* 680	? 692
Edgar	? 693	716 × 731
Cyneberht	716 × 731	731
Alwig	733	750
Aldwulf	750	765
Ceolwulf	767	796
Eadwulf	796	836 × 839
Beorhtred	836 × 839	862 × 866 or ?
Eadbald	862 × 866	866 × 869
Burgheard or	866 × 869	869 × ?
Eadberht	866 × 869	875 × ?

Episcopal succession apparently interrupted

Leofwine, from 971 bp of Dorchester also	? × 953	971 × 975
Sigeferth	? × 996	1004 × ?
? Ælfstan	? × 1009	1011 × ?

LONDON

Mellitus	604	expelled *c.* 617, d. 24 Apr. 624
Cedd	? *c.* 653	? 26 Oct. 664
Wini	666, trs. from Dorchester	? bef. 672
Eorcenwald	? 675	693
Waldhere	693	705 × 716

BISHOPS	ACCESSION	DEATH OR TRS. *unless otherwise stated*
Ingwald	705 × 716	745
Ecgwulf	745	766 × 772
Wigheah	766 × 772	772 × 781
Eadberht	772 × 782	787 × 789
Eadgar	787 × 789	789 × 793
Coenwalh	789 × 793	793 × 796
Eadbald	793 × 796	796 × 798
Heathoberht	796 × 798	801
Osmund	801 × 803	805 × 811
Æthelnoth	805 × 811	816 × 824
Ceolberht	816 × 824	845 × 860
Deorwulf	845 × 860	867 × 896
Swithwulf	867 × 896	867 × 896
Heahstan	867 × 896	897
Wulfsige	897 × 900	909 × 926
Æthelweard	909 × 926	909 × 926
Leofstan	909 × 926	909 × 926
Theodred	909 × 926	951 × 953
Brihthelm	951 × 953	957 × 959
Dunstan	957 × 959	959, trs. to Canterbury
Ælfstan	959 × 964	995 × 996
Wulfstan	996	1002, trs. to York
Ælfhun	1002 × 1004	1015 × 1018
Ælfwig	cons. 16 Feb. 1014, acc. 1015 × 1018	c. 1035
Ælfweard	1035	25 or 27 July 1044
Robert of Jumièges	1044	1051, trs. to Canterbury
[Spearhafoc	app. 1051	expelled 1051]
William	1051	1075

THE MERCIANS

Diuma, bp of Mercia, Lindsey and Middle Angles	after 655	?
Ceollach	?	res., ?
Trumhere	c. 658	? 662
Jaruman	? 662	? 667

See Lichfield for later succession

RAMSBURY

Æthelstan	c. 909	c. 909 × 927
Oda	c. 909 × 927	941, trs. to Canterbury
Ælfric I	941 × 949	949 × 951
Osulf	949 × 951	970
Ælfstan	970	12 Feb. 981 '
Wulfgar	981	985 × 986
Sigeric	985 × 986	990, trs. to Canterbury
Ælfric II	991 × 993	995, trs. to Canterbury, but retained Ramsbury
Brihtwold	1005	22 Apr. 1045
Hereman	1045	res. 1055; 1058, trs. to Sherborne

See transferred to Sherborne, 1058

RIPON

Wilfrid at Ripon 666–9

Eadhæd	c. 679, trs. from Lindsey	?

ROCHESTER

BISHOPS	ACCESSION	DEATH OR TRS. _unless otherwise stated_
Justus	604	624, trs. to Canterbury
Romanus	624	624 × 625
Paulinus	c. 633, trs. from York	10 Oct. 644
Ithamar	?	655 × 664
Damianus	655 × 664	c. 664
Putta	? 669	res. 676, trs. to Hereford
Cwichhelm	? 676	res. 678
Gebmund	? 678	699 × 716
Tobias	699 × 716	726
Aldwulf	? 727	739
Dunn	? 740	747
Eardwulf	747	765 × 772
Diora	765 × 772	781 × 785
Wærmund	781 × 785	Oct. 803 × 804
Beornmod	804	842 × 844
Tatnoth	el. 844	845 × 868
Badenoth	845 × 868	845 × 868
Wærmund	845 × 868	845 × 868
Cuthwulf	845 × 868	868 × 880
Swithwulf	868 × 880	893 × 896
Ceolmund	893 × 900	909 × 926
Cyneferth	909 × 926	Jan. 933 × May 934
Burgric	Jan. 933 × May 934	946 × 964
? Beorhtsige	946 × 949	955 × 964
Ælfstan	? × 964	994 × 995
Godwine I	994 × 995	? c. 1013 × ?
Godwine II	? c. 1013 × ?	1046 × 1058
Siward	1058	1075

SELSEY

Wilfrid	? 681	? 685, see Leicester
Eadberht	? 706 × 716	716 × 731
Eolla	716 × 731	716 × 731

See vacant for some time following Eolla's death

Sigeferth (Sicgga)	733	747 × 765
Aluberht	747 × 765	772 × 780
Oswald (Osa)	747 × 765	772 × 780
Gislhere	772 × 780	781 × 787
Tota	781 × 786	786 × 789
Wihthun	787 × 789	805 × 811
Æthelwulf	805 × 811	816 × 824
Cynered	816 × 824	839 × 845
Guthheard	839 × 845	(860 × 863) × ?
?Wighelm	? × 900	c. 909, or 909 × 925
Beornheah	c. 909, or 909 × 925	930 × 931
Wulfhun	930 × 931	940 × 943
Alfred	940 × 943	953 × 956
Brihthelm	953 × 956	956 × 963, ? trs. to Winchester
Eadhelm	956 × 963	979 × 980
Æthelgar	cons. 2 May 980	988, trs. to Canterbury
Ordbriht	988 × 990	1007 × 1009
Ælfmær	(1007 × 1009) × 1011	1031 × 1032
Æthelric I	1032	Nov. or Dec. 1038
Grimketel	1039	1047
Heca	1047	1057
Æthelric II	1058	depr. May 1070

SHERBORNE

BISHOPS	ACCESSION	DEATH OR TRS. *unless otherwise stated*
Aldhelm	*c.* 705	709
Forthhere	709	(? res.) 737
Herewald	736	766 × 774
Æthelmod	766 × 774	789 × 794
Denefrith	793	796 × 801
Wigberht	793 × 801	816 × 825
Ealhstan	816 × 825	867
Heahmund	867 × 868	871
Æthelheah	871 × 877	879 × 889
Wulfsige I	879 × 889	(890 × 896) × 900
Asser	(890 × 896) × 900	909

Diocese of Sherborne divided in three: Sherborne, Wells, Crediton

Æthelweard	*c.* 909	*c.* 909
Wærstan	*c.* 909	918, or *c.* 909 × 925
Æthelbald	*c.* 909, or 918 × 925	*c.* 909, or 918 × 925
Sigehelm	*c.* 909, or 918 × 925	932 × 934
Alfred	932 × 934	939 × 943
Wulfsige II	939 × 943	958 × (963 × 964)
Ælfwold I	958 × (963 × 964)	978
Æthelsige I	978 × 979	991 × 993
Wulfsige III	? 993	8 Jan. 1002
Æthelric	1002	1011 × 1012
Æthelsige II	1011 × 1012	1014 × ?
Brihtwine I	1014 × 1017	1014 × 1017
Ælfmær	1017	? 5 Apr. 1023
Brihtwine II	1023	? 2 June 1045
Ælfwold II	1045	1058
Hereman, bp of Ramsbury	1058	20 Feb. 1078

WELLS

Athelm	*c.* 909	923 × Sept. 925, trs. to Canterbury
Wulfhelm	923 × Sept. 925	Jan. 926 × 928, trs. to Canterbury
Ælfheah	Jan. 926 × 928	937 × 938
Wulfhelm	937 × 938	956
Byrhthelm	956	959, trs. to Canterbury, dep. 959, bp of Wells, d. 15 May 973
Cyneweard	973 × 974	28 June 975
Sig(eg)ar	975 × 979	28 June 996
Ælfwine	996 × 997	29 Aug., 998 × 999
Lyfing (Ælfstan)	998 × 999	1013, trs. to Canterbury
Æthelwine	1013 × 1018	(1021 × 1023) × 1024, ejected in favour of Brihtwine, restored, and again rejected in favour of Brihtwine
Brihtwine		? × 1024
Brihtwig (Merehwit)	? × 1024	11 or 12 Apr. 1033
Duduc	11 June 1033	18 Jan. 1060
Gisa	el. p. 18 Jan. 1060, cons. 15 Apr. 1061	1088

WHITHORN (CANDIDA CASA)

Trumwine	681	?
Pehthelm	? × 731	*c.* 735
Frithowald	cons. 15 Aug., *c.* 735	7 May 763 or 764
Pehtwine	cons. 17 July 763 or 764	19 Sept. 776 or 777

BISHOPS	ACCESSION	DEATH OR TRS. *unless otherwise stated*
Æthelberht	cons. 15 June 777	789, trs. to Hexham
Beadwulf	cons. 791	803 × ?
Heathored		

WINCHESTER

For the earliest bishops of the West Saxons, see Dorchester

Wine	660	663, trs. to ? Dorchester
Leuthere	670	? × 676
Hædde	676	? 7 July 705

Bishopric of the West Saxons divided *c.* 705: Winchester and Sherborne

Daniel	*c.* 705	res. 744, d. 745
Hunfrith	744	749 × 756
Cyneheard	756	759 × 778
Æthelheard	759 × 778	759 × 778
Ecgbald	759 × 778	781 × 785
Dudd	781 × 785	781 × 785
Cyneberht	781 × 785	801 × 803
Ealhmund	801 × 803	805 × 814
Wigthegn	805 × 814	836
Herefrith (never attests without Wigthegn)	? × 825	836
Eadhun	833 × 838	838
Helmstan	838 × 839	844 × 852 or 853
Swithhun	Oct. 852 or Oct. 853	2 July 862 × 865
Ealhferth	862 × 867	871 × 877
Tunberht	871 × 877	878 × 879
Denewulf	878 × 879	908

Diocese of Winchester divided in two, *c.* 909: Winchester and Ramsbury

Frithestan	909	932 × 933
Byrnstan	May 931	1 Nov. 934
Ælfheah I	934 or 935	12 Mar. 951
Ælfsige I	951	959, trs. to Canterbury
Brihthelm	? trs. from Selsey	?
Æthelwold I, ab. of Abingdon	cons. 29 Nov. 963	1 Aug. 984
Ælfheah II, ab. of Bath	cons. 19 Oct. 984, inst. 28 Oct. 984	1006, trs. to Canterbury
Cenwulf, ab. of Peterborough	1006	1006
Æthelwold II	1006 × 1007	1012 × 1013
Ælfsige II	1012 × 1013	1032
Ælfwine	1032	29 Aug. 1047
Stigand	1047, trs. from Elmham	1052, trs. to Canterbury, but retained Winchester, depr. 1070
Ælfsige III		

WORCESTER

Bosel	680	res. 691
Oftfor	691	aft. Aug. 693
Ecgwine	693 × ?	30 Dec. 717
Wilfrid	718	743 × 745, ? 29 Apr. 744
Milred	743 × 745	774
Wærmund	775	777
Tilhere	777	780 or 781
Heathured	781	798 or ? 800
Deneberht	? 800	822
Heahberht	822	845 × 848
Alhhun	843 or Dec. 844 × Nov. 845	869 × 872

BISHOPS	ACCESSION	DEATH OR TRS. *unless otherwise stated*
Wærferth	872, or 869 × 872	915, or 907 × 915
Æthelhun	915, or 907 × 915	922, or 915 × 922
Wilferth	922, or 915 × 922	928 × 929
Cenwald	928 × 929	? 28 June, 957 or 958
Dunstan	? 957	959, trs. to London
Oswald	961	971, trs. to York, but retained Worcester, d. 29 Feb. 992
Ealdwulf, ab. of Peterborough	992	995, trs. to York, but retained Worcester, d. 4 June 1002
Wulfstan I	1002, trs. from London, also abp of York	res. Worcester 1016, but retained York
Leofsige	1016	19 Aug. 1033
Brihtheah	1033	20 Dec. 1038
Lyfing, bp of Crediton and Cornwall	1038 or 1039	depr. 1040
Ælfric Puttoc, abp of York	1040	depr. of Worcester 1041
Lyfing (restored)	1041	20, 23 or 25 Mar. 1046
Ealdred, bp of Hereford 1056–60	? cons. by 1044, acc. 1046	1061, trs. to York, but retained Worcester, res. Worcester 1062
Wulfstan II	el. 29 Aug., cons. 8 Sept. 1062	19 or 20 Jan. 1095

YORK

ARCHBISHOPS	ACCESSION	DEATH OR TRS. *unless otherwise stated*
Paulinus	cons. 21 July 625, acc. 626	res. 633, d. 10 Oct. 644

Vacancy 633–64 (see Lindisfarne for Northumbrian bishops during this period)

Cedda	664	res. 669
Wilfrid I	cons. 664, acc. 669	depr. 678, see Selsey

Northumbrian diocese divided: York (Deira) and Hexham/Lindisfarne (Bernicia)

Bosa	678 or 679	706
John of Beverley	706, trs. from Hexham	res. ? 714, d. 7 May 721
Wilfrid II	? 714	res. 732, d. 29 Apr. 744 or 745
Egberht	? 732	19 Nov. 766
Æthelberht	cons. 24 Apr. 766 or 767	8 Nov. 779 or 780
Eanbald I	779 or 780	10 Aug. 796
Eanbald II	cons. 14 Aug. 796	808 × ?
Wulfsige	808 × ?	830 × 837
Wigmund	837	854
Wulfhere	854	892 or 900
Æthelbald	900	904 × 928
Hrothweard	904 × 928	931
Wulfstan I	931	26 Dec. 956
Osketel, bp of Dorchester from 949 × 950	956	1 Nov. 971
Edwald	971	res. 971
Oswald, bp of Worcester from 961	971	29 Feb. 992
Ealdwulf, bp of Worcester from 992	995	4 June 1002
Wulfstan II, bp of Worcester 1002–16	1002, trs. from London	28 May 1023
Ælfric Puttoc, bp of Worcester 1040–1	1023	22 Jan. 1051
Cynesige	1051	22 Dec. 1060
Ealdred, bp of Worcester 1047–62	1061	11 Sept. 1069

FROM 1066 TO THE PRESENT DAY

The most comprehensive episcopal lists for all sees in the world in communion with Rome will be found in Pius Bonifatius Gams' *Series episcoporum ecclesiae catholicae* (Regensburg, 1873), with supplements (Munich, 1879, and Regensburg, 1886) which carry the succession on to 20 Feb. 1885 (the whole work reprinted in 1931 and 1957). An international project to revise Gams is at present in progress, but no volumes have yet been published. Part of the ground covered by Gams is dealt with more thoroughly in a work which makes much use of the Vatican archives: *Hierarchia catholica medii et recentioris aevi*, vols i and ii (1198–1431, 1431–1503), ed. Conrad Eubel, 2nd edn (Münster, 1913–14); vol. iii (1503–92), ed. G. van Gulik and C. Eubel (Münster, 1910); vol. iv (1592–1667), ed. P. Gauchat (Münster, 1935); vols v and vi (1667–1799), ed. R. Ritzler and P. Sefrin (Padua, 1952–58). For the British Isles W. Mazière Brady, *The episcopal succession in England, Scotland and Ireland a.d. 1400 to 1875*, 3 vols (Rome, 1876–77) provides much useful matter. It must be emphasized that all these lists exclude bishops of the reformed churches. On the other hand, the lists of post-Reformation bishops contained in the works which follow only include bishops of the reformed churches. The period between 1066 and 1857 is being covered by the project at the Institute of Historical Research, University of London, to revise John Le Neve's *Fasti Ecclesiae Anglicanae*, in three series, 1066–1300, 1300–1541 and 1541–1857. For 1066–1300 three volumes have been published so far, edited by D. E. Greenway (1968–77); for 1300–1541 the work is complete in twelve volumes, edited by J. M. Horn, B. Jones and H. P. F. King (1962–7); for 1541–1857 five volumes have been published so far, edited by J. M. Horn (1969–79). These volumes, and notes for future volumes, have been used to revise the lists below.

In 1601 Francis Godwin published his *Catalogue of the bishops of England*, of which the Latin translation, *De praesulibus Angliae commentarius* (1616), was edited by William Richardson, 2 vols (Cambridge, 1743). For the purposes of the present work, the fundamental authorities are John Le Neve, *Fasti ecclesiae anglicanae* (1716), ed. T. Duffus Hardy, 3 vols (Oxford, 1854)—of which a new edition is being prepared—and William Stubbs, *Registrum sacrum anglicanum* (Oxford, 1858; 2nd edn, 1897). The latter contains only precise particulars of the consecration of bishops. The transfer of sees after the Norman Conquest is described by F. M. Stenton, *Anglo-Saxon England* (2nd edn, 1947), pp. 658–9. This change included the transference of sees to Chichester, Lincoln, Norwich, and Salisbury. Apart from the creation of the sees of Ely (1108) and Carlisle (1132), and internal arrangements which produced the sees of Bath and Wells, and Coventry and Lichfield, the Norman distribution of dioceses remained until Henry VIII, acting under powers given by statute 31 Henry VIII (1539), c. 9, created the short-lived see of Westminster (1540), and the sees of Bristol, Chester, Gloucester, Peterborough (1541), and Oseney (1542) soon after transferred to Oxford (1545). *See*, for Henry's first plan, the draft *Scheme of bishopricks, with illustrations of the assumption of church property*, etc., ed. H. Cole (1838). At the creation of the see of Chester in 1541 it was assigned to the province of York. A statute of 1542 (33 Henry VIII, c. 31) formally established the English diocese of Sodor and Man alongside the old Scottish diocese of Sodor or The Isles and placed the former in the province of York; but already, during the Great Schism, the original diocese of The Isles was split by a separate English succession in the Isle of Man (which was politically under English lordship), while a Scottish line of bishops continued to administer the northern parts of the diocese. A new period in the history of the Church of England began with the establishment and incorporation of the Ecclesiastical Commissioners for England by the statute 6 & 7 William IV (1836), c. 77. Their extensive powers (*see* F. Makower, *Constit. hist. of the Church of England* (1895), 269–72) did not comprise the creation of new sees, but their general control of the secular administration of the Church has undoubtedly facilitated later parliamentary changes in the distribution of dioceses. In 1836 Bristol and Gloucester were united, and remained united until 1897. The following sees have been created since 1836: in the province of Canterbury, the sees of St Albans (1877), Truro (1877), Southwark (1895), Birmingham (1902), Chelmsford (1914), St Edmundsbury (1914), Coventry (1918), Guildford (1921), Leicester (1924), Derby (1927), Portsmouth (1927); in the province of York, the sees of Ripon (1836), Manchester (1848), Liverpool (1880), Newcastle-upon-Tyne (1882), Southwell (1884), Wakefield (1888), Sheffield (1909), Bradford (1920), Blackburn (1922). For the geography of the English dioceses Geoffry Hill, *The English Dioceses* (London, 1900) may be consulted.

In the post-Conquest lists the dates given by Hardy and Stubbs have been, wherever possible, verified by reference to their sources. These and similar sources (chronicles, bishops' registers, chancery enrolments) have been examined to discover dates which Hardy and Stubbs did not include. For papal records we have usually relied upon the *Calendar of papal letters* (H.M.S.O.) and Eubel's references to *obligationes* of bishops in the papal camera (for which see also H. Hoberg, *Taxae pro communibus servitiis*, Vatican City, 1944). While not all known manuscript sources have been explored afresh, episcopal and capitular archives and the records of Chancery, Home Office, etc., have been examined whenever this was practicable in the time available.

The choice of dates to be included differs as between the medieval bishops and those who were appointed after the act of 25 Henry VIII (153–4), c. 20, ss.3 and 4, had set down in detail a procedure for appointment to sees without reference to Rome. For the Middle Ages we have aimed at including the following dates where they could be exactly, or even only approximately, discovered:

(i) *Capitular election*, or *postulation* (*i.e.* the putting forward by the electors of a person who requires dispensation from some canonical defect or translation from another see), or *royal nomination* (which may in some cases have replaced election in the Norman period).

(ii) *Papal provision*, whether this superseded prior election or was a substitute for it. From the fourteenth century the date of recommendation to the king is identical to that of the act of provision. For the thirteenth century, we give the earliest known date: it is usually that of papal letters notifying the king and/or other persons of the provision; occasionally, when these letters are wanting, the date at which the providee entered into a bond with the apostolic camera (generally not far removed from the date of provision) can be given; all these dates may be a little later than the act of provision: in a few cases this can be proved and the records furnish an earlier date.

(iii) *Consecration*. This was supposed to be celebrated on a Sunday or an important festival (cf. *Decretum*, D. 75, c. 5) and where we have discrepant dates or doubtful dates within the compass of a week, we assume that the rule has been observed. The pontifical year of the bishop was reckoned from this date.

(iv) *Restitution of temporalities* by the Crown. For this is given the date of enrolment of the chancery writ *de intendendo* addressed to the tenants of the see for the first time after the bishop's appointment. The date of restitution is important since upon it hinged the Crown's recognition of the prelate as a spiritual peer as well as the bishop's right to the revenues of his see. Bishops, it may be noted, were sometimes authorized to receive the fruits of the see from a date earlier than the date of the writ; also, they sometimes acted as custodians for the Crown before they were given restitution as bishops.[1]

(v) *Voidance of the see* by resignation, translation (the date of the papal letter), or death. The many minor divergencies in the evidence for the date of death arise not only from errors in our sources but from the uncertainty of dating events which occurred between vespers and midnight and from the habit of shifting obits from the exact anniversary day for liturgical convenience.

For the post-Reformation period the following dates are given where possible:

(i) *Nomination* by the Crown. The procedure was (and is) lengthy, and in any instance the surviving, or most easily accessible, records may be of several kinds. The process is completed by the delivery of a letter of congé d'élire and of a letter missive (which states the name of the nominee, not included in the congé), or of letters patent of appointment in the case of some sees of recent establishment.[2] But often it is possible to come nearer to the real date of official nomination, which may be a week or more earlier than the date of the chancery letter of congé: *e.g.* the dates of warrants for these letters are contained in State Paper and Home Office Entry Books 1688–1868; and nominations are reported in the *London Gazette*

---

[1] For the dating of the account-rolls of episcopal estates *see* W. H. Beveridge, 'The Winchester Rolls and their dating', *Economic History Review*, ii (1929), 93–113.

[2] For the cases of direct appointment in the nineteenth and twentieth centuries *see* Halsbury's *Laws of England* (3rd edn, vol. 13, part 2, sect. 6, 157). In these cases an instrument of investiture replaces the act of confirmation. In Edward VI's reign there was direct appointment by the issue of letters patent pursuant to the statute 1 Edward VI, c. 2.

before the issue of letters.[1] The following lists give in each case the earliest available of these various dates.[2] Where it has not been possible to verify a date of nomination, the date of election is given: election should follow within twelve days of the delivery of the congé and letter missive.

(ii) *Consecration.* This usually follows within a week upon the confirmation of the election by the metropolitan or (in the case of an archbishop-elect) by a commission of bishops. The date is not given in the case of a bishop translated from another see.

(iii) *Confirmation.* This is only included in the case of prelates who, being translated from other diocesan or suffragan sees, did not require consecration. Since the Reformation, the restitution of temporalities usually occurs within a few days of consecration or confirmation. The date is not noted in these lists.

(iv) *Voidance of the see* by resignation, deprivation, translation or death. In cases of translation the date of confirmation in the second see is given as the date of voidance. In cases of resignation occurring since the Bishops Resignation Act 1869 (32 & 33 Vict., c. 111), the date is that on which the vacancy took effect, determined by Order in Council, as reported in the *London Gazette.*

Besides those who achieved the full status of diocesan bishop, consecrated and possessed of the temporalities, we have entered a few of those medieval prelates who were elected or provided and then, for one reason or another, were removed. The entries are set within square brackets.

Under the head of Suffragan Bishops are given lists of bishops consecrated to sees *in partibus infidelium* and Irish and Scottish prelates who are known to have carried out episcopal functions in England before the Reformation. These lists are based on those of Stubbs and Eubel, with additional references to suffragans from English diocesan records. It cannot be hoped that the lists approach completeness, but they may enable students to identify some otherwise elusive persons. A list is also given of bishops of suffragan sees temporarily set up in the sixteenth century; but limits of space have compelled the exclusion of the numerous modern Anglican suffragan bishops, appointed to titular English sees, particulars of which may be found in Crockford's *Clerical Directory.*

Note.—Dates printed in italic are doubtful.

BATH AND WELLS
WELLS

BISHOPS	ACCESSION	DEATH *unless otherwise stated*
Giso	el. *p.* 18 Jan. 1060, cons. 15 Apr. 1061	1088
John de Villula	cons. July 1088	26 × 30 Dec. 1122

(John de Villula transferred his see to Bath, 1090)

---

[1] The letter missive does not always tally in date with the congé, and dates of enrolment sometimes differ from the dates of the original letters. Thus Le Neve-Hardy gives from the Home Office record of the letter missive under the sign-manual the date of George Pretyman's nomination to the see of Lincoln as 19 Feb. 1787; the *London Gazette* announces, as from Whitehall, 20 Feb. 'that the king has been pleased to order a congé d'élire to be passed under the Great Seal . . . and . . . to recommend the Rev. William [*sic*] Pretyman'; the original letter of congé and letter missive preserved at Lincoln (Dj/5/2/1) are both dated 21 Feb.; and the enrolment of the letter of congé on the Patent Roll is dated 25 Feb.

[2] For the last fifteen years the date is usually that of the announcement in the *London Gazette.*

BATH

BISHOPS	ACCESSION	DEATH *unless otherwise stated*
Godfrey	nom. 25 Mar., cons. 26 Aug. 1123	16 Aug. 1135
Robert	cons. *22 Mar.*, temp. *c.* 22 Mar. 1136	31 Aug. 1166
Reginald FitzJocelin	el. late Apr. 1173, cons. 23 June 1174	26 Dec. 1191 (as elect of Canterbury)
Savaric FitzGeldewin	el. *a.* 26 Dec. 1191, cons. 20 Sept. 1192	8 Aug. 1205

(Savaric set up a see in the abbey of Glastonbury, 1197)

Jocelin of Wells	el. *3 Feb.*, temp. 3 May, cons. 28 May 1206	19 Nov. 1242

(Jocelin used the title 'Bath and Glastonbury' from 1213 to 1219)

BATH AND WELLS

('Bath and Wells' became the episcopal title following a papal ruling of 3 Jan. 1245)

Roger of Salisbury	el. *a.* 3 Feb., temp. 10 May, cons. 11 Sept. 1244	21 Dec. 1247
William of Bitton I	el. *a.* 24 Feb., cons 14 June, temp. 20 July 1248	3 Apr. 1264
Walter Giffard	el. 22 May, temp. 1 Sept. 1264, cons. 4 Jan. 1265	trs. York 15 Oct. 1266
William of Bitton II	el. 10 Feb., temp. 4 Mar., cons. *p.* 17 Apr. 1267	4 Dec. 1274
Robert Burnell	el. 23 Jan., temp. 15 Feb., cons. 7 Apr. 1275	25 Oct. 1292
William of March	el. 28 Jan., temp. 19 Mar., cons. 17 May 1293	*a.* 19 June 1302
Walter Haselshaw	el. 7 Aug., temp. 12 Sept., cons. 4 Nov. 1302	11 Dec. 1308
John Droxford	el. 5 Feb., temp. 15 May, cons. 9 Nov. 1309	9 May 1329
Ralph of Shrewsbury	el. 2 June, temp. 22 July, cons. 3 Sept. 1329	14 Aug. 1363
John Barnet	trs. Worcester, prov. 24 Dec. 1363, temp. 6 Apr. 1364	trs. Ely 15 Dec. 1366
John Harewell	prov. 14 Dec. 1366, cons. 7 Mar. 1367, temp. 6 Mar. 1369	29 June × 14 July 1386
Walter Skirlaw	trs. Coventry, prov. 18 Aug., temp. 3 Nov. 1386	trs. Durham 3 Apr. 1388
Ralph Erghum	trs. Salisbury, prov. 3 Apr., temp. 13 Sept. 1388	10 Apr. 1400
[Richard Clifford	prov. 12 May 1400	trs. Worcester 19 Aug. 1401]
Henry Bowet	prov. 19 Aug. 1401, temp. 21 Sept., cons. 20 Nov. 1401	trs. York 7 Oct. 1407
Nicholas Bubwith	trs. Salisbury, prov. 7 Oct., temp. 2 Dec. 1407	27 Oct. 1424
John Stafford	el. 14 Nov. × 19 Dec., prov. 18 Dec. 1424, temp. 12 May, cons. 27 May 1425	trs. Canterbury 13 May 1443
Thomas Beckington	prov. 24 July, temp. 24 Sept., cons. 13 Oct. 1443	14 Jan. 1465
Robert Stillington	prov. 30 Oct. 1465, temp. 29 Jan., cons. 16 Mar. 1466	*a.* 15 May 1491
Richard Fox	trs. Exeter, prov. 8 Feb., temp. 4 May 1492	trs. Durham 30 July 1494
Oliver King	trs. Exeter, prov. 6 Nov. 1495, temp. 6 Jan. 1496	29 Aug. 1503

BISHOPS	ACCESSION	DEATH *unless otherwise stated*
Adriano de Castello	trs. Hereford, prov. 2 Aug., temp. 13 Oct. 1504	depr. 5 July 1518
Thomas Wolsey	abp of York, *in commendam* prov. 27 July 1518	trs. Durham 26 Mar. 1523
John Clerk	prov. 26 Mar., temp. 2 May, cons. 6 Dec. 1523	31 Jan. 1541
William Knight	nom. 9 Apr., cons. 29 May 1541	29 Sept. 1547
William Barlow	trs. St David's, nom. 3 Feb. 1548	res. *a.* 4 Oct. 1553 (bp of Chichester 1559)
Gilbert Bourne	nom. 13 Mar., cons. 1 Apr. 1554	depr. 18 Oct. 1559 × 11 Jan. 1560, d. 10 Sept. 1569
Gilbert Berkeley	nom. 11 Jan., cons. 24 Mar. 1560	2 Nov. 1581
Thomas Godwin	nom. 25 July, cons. 13 Sept. 1584	19 Nov. 1590
John Still	nom. 13 Jan., cons. 11 Feb. 1593	26 Feb. 1608
James Montague	nom. 21 Mar., cons. 17 Apr. 1608	trs. Winchester 4 Oct. 1616
Arthur Lake	el. 17 Oct., cons. 8 Dec. 1616	4 May 1626
William Laud	trs. St David's, nom. 20 June, conf. 18 Sept. 1626	trs. London 15 July 1628
Leonard Mawe	nom. 14 July, cons. 7 Sept. 1628	2 Sept. 1629
Walter Curle	trs. Rochester, el. 29 Oct., conf. 4 Dec. 1629	trs. Winchester 16 Nov. 1632
William Peirs	trs. Peterborough, nom. 19 Nov., conf. 13 Dec. 1632	30 Apr. 1670
Robert Creighton	nom. 2 May, cons. 19 June 1670	20 Nov. 1672
Peter Mews	nom. 23 Nov. 1672, cons. 9 Feb. 1673	trs. Winchester 22 Nov. 1684
Thomas Ken or Kenn	nom. 24 Nov. 1684, cons. 25 Jan. 1685	depr. 1 Feb. 1690, d. 19 Mar. 1711
Richard Kidder	nom. 11 June, cons. 30 Aug. 1691	26 Nov. 1703
George Hooper	trs. St Asaph, nom. 23 Dec. 1703, conf. 14 Mar. 1704	6 Sept. 1727
John Wynne	trs. St Asaph, nom. 19 Sept., conf. 11 Nov. 1727	15 July 1743
Edward Willes	trs. St David's, nom. 13 Sept., conf. 12 Dec. 1743	24 Nov. 1773
Charles Moss	trs. St David's, nom. 23 Apr., conf. 2 June 1774	13 Apr. 1802
Richard Beadon	trs. Gloucester, nom. 27 Apr., conf. 2 June 1802	21 Apr. 1824
George Henry Law	trs. Chester, nom. 8 May, conf. 8 June 1824	22 Sept. 1845
Richard Bagot	trs. Oxford, nom. 15 Oct., conf. 12 Nov. 1845	15 May 1854
Robert John Eden (3rd Baron Auckland 1849)	trs. Sodor and Man, nom. 2 June, conf. 1 July 1854	res. 6 Sept. 1869, d. 25 Apr. 1870
Arthur Charles Hervey	nom. 11 Nov., cons. 21 Dec. 1869	9 June 1894
George Wyndham Kennion	trs. Adelaide, nom. 24 Aug., conf. 17 Oct. 1894	res. 1 Aug. 1921, d. 19 May 1922
St John Basil Wynne Wilson	nom. 6 Oct., cons. 1 Nov. 1921	res. 1 Oct. 1937, d. 15 Oct. 1946
Francis Underhill	nom. 6 Oct., cons. 30 Nov. 1937	24 Jan. 1943
John William Charles Wand	trs. Brisbane, nom. 23 Sept., conf. 27 Oct. 1943	trs. London 22 Aug. 1945
Harold William Bradfield	nom. 5 Mar., cons. 1 May 1946	1 May 1960

229

BISHOPS	ACCESSION	DEATH *unless otherwise stated*
Edward Barry Henderson	trs. Tewkesbury (suff.), nom. 1 July, conf. 19 July 1960	res. 31 May 1975
John Monier Bickersteth	trs. Warrington (suff.), nom. 15 Oct., conf. 12 Dec. 1975	

BIRMINGHAM

Charles Gore	trs. Worcester, nom. 20 Jan., inv. 27 Jan. 1905	trs. Oxford 17 Oct. 1911
Henry Russell Wakefield	nom. 20 Oct., cons. 28 Oct. 1911	res. 1 Aug. 1924, d. 9 Jan. 1933
Ernest William Barnes	nom. 1 Sept., cons. 29 Sept. 1924	29 Nov. 1953
John Leonard Wilson	trs. Manchester (assistant bp), nom. 30 June, conf. 28 Sept. 1953	res. 30 Sept. 1969, d. 18 Aug. 1970
Lawrence Ambrose Brown	trs. Warrington (suff.), nom. 7 Oct., conf. 9 Dec. 1969	res. 1 Nov. 1977
Hugh William Montefiore	trs. Kingston-upon-Thames (suff.), nom. 7 Nov. 1977, conf. 23 Feb. 1978	

BLACKBURN

Percy Mark Herbert	trs. Kingston (suff.), nom. 18 Dec. 1926, conf. 26 Jan. 1927	trs. Norwich 22 July 1942
Wilfred Marcus Askwith	nom. 2 Nov., cons. 30 Nov. 1942	trs. Gloucester 7 July 1954
Walter Hubert Baddeley	trs. Whitby (suff.), nom. 10 Sept., conf. 2 Oct. 1954	11 Feb. 1960
Charles Robert Claxton	trs. Warrington (suff.), nom. 1 July, conf. 18 July 1960	res. 30 Nov. 1971
Robert Arnold Schurhoff Martineau	trs. Huntingdon (suff.), nom. 21 Dec. 1971, conf. 24 Jan. 1972	res. 31 Oct. 1981
David Stewart Cross	trs. Doncaster (suff.), nom. 26 Jan., conf. 26 Feb. 1982	

BRADFORD

Arthur William Thomson Perowne	nom. 8 Jan., cons. 2 Feb. 1920	trs. Worcester 11 Mar. 1931
Alfred Walter Frank Blunt	nom. 15 July, cons. 25 July 1931	res. 31 Oct. 1955, d. 2 June 1957
Frederick Donald Coggan	nom. 6 Dec. 1955, cons. 25 Jan. 1956	trs. York 6 July 1961
Clement George St Michael Parker	trs. Aston (suff.), nom. 19 Sept., conf. 29 Sept. 1961	res. 30 Nov. 1971, d. 5 Mar. 1980
Ross Sydney Hook	trs. Grantham (suff.), nom. 28 Apr., conf. 25 May 1972	res. 30 Sept. 1980
Geoffrey John Paul	trs. Hull (suff.), nom. 9 Feb., conf. 20 Mar. 1981	10 July 1983
Robert Kerr Williamson	nom. 9 Feb., cons. 20 Mar. 1984	

BRISTOL

Paul Bush	nom. 4 June, cons. 25 June 1542	res. June 1554, d. 11 Oct. 1558
John Holyman	nom. 25 Oct., cons. 18 Nov. 1554	20 Dec. 1558
Richard Cheyney	*in commendam* with Gloucester, nom. 29 Apr. 1562	25 Apr. 1579

BISHOPS	ACCESSION	DEATH *unless otherwise stated*
John Bullingham	with Gloucester, cons. 3 Feb. 1581	res. Bristol 1589
Richard Fletcher	nom. 23 Oct., cons. 14 Dec. 1589	trs. Worcester 10 Feb. 1593
John Thornborough	trs. Limerick, nom. 23 May, conf. 12 July 1603	trs. Worcester 17 Feb. 1617
Nicholas Felton	nom. 27 Feb., cons. 14 Dec. 1617	trs. Ely 11 Mar. 1619
Rowland Searchfield	nom. 12 Mar., cons. 9 May 1619	11 Oct. 1622
Robert Wright	el. 28 Jan., cons. 23 Mar. 1623	trs. Lichfield 28 Nov. 1632
George Coke	el. 28 Nov. 1632, cons. 10 Feb. 1633	trs. Hereford 2 July 1636
Robert Skinner	nom. 8 July 1636, cons. 15 Jan. 1637	trs. Oxford 16 Dec. 1641
Thomas Westfield	cons. *26 Apr.* 1642	25 June 1644
Thomas Howell	nom. July, cons. *Aug.* 1644	1646
Gilbert Ironside	nom. 19 Nov. 1660, cons. *6* Jan. 1661	19 Sept. 1671
Guy Carleton	nom. 1 Dec. 1671, cons. 11 Feb. 1672	trs. Chichester 8 Jan. 1679
William Gulston	nom. 3 Jan., cons. 9 Feb. 1679	4 Apr. 1684
John Lake	trs. Sodor and Man, nom. 12 May, conf. 12 Aug. 1684	trs. Chichester 19 Oct. 1685
Jonathan Trelawney (3rd Baronet 1685)	nom. 21 Oct., cons. 8 Nov. 1685	trs. Exeter 13 Apr. 1689
Gilbert Ironside	nom. 28 Mar., cons. 13 Oct. 1689	trs. Hereford 29 July 1691
John Hall	cons. 30 Aug. 1691	4 Feb. 1710
John Robinson	nom. 19 Oct., cons. 19 Nov. 1710	trs. London 13 Mar. 1714
George Smalridge	cons. 4 Apr. 1714	27 Sept. 1719
Hugh Boulter	nom. 15 Oct., cons. 15 Nov. 1719	trs. Armagh 31 Aug. 1724
William Bradshaw	nom. 29 Aug., cons. 18 Oct. 1724	16 Dec. 1732
Charles Cecil	nom. 17 Jan., cons. 25 Feb. 1733	trs. Bangor 1734
Thomas Secker	nom. Dec. 1734, cons. 19 Jan. 1735	trs. Oxford 14 May 1737
Thomas Gooch	nom. 17 May, cons. 12 June 1737	trs. Norwich 17 Oct. 1738
Joseph Butler	nom. 19 Oct., cons. 3 Dec. 1738	trs. Durham 16 Oct. 1750
John Conybeare	nom. 14 Nov., cons. 23 Dec. 1750	13 July 1755
John Hume	nom. 10 May, cons. 4 July 1756	trs. Oxford 3 June 1758
Philip Yonge	nom. 6 June, cons. 29 June 1758	trs. Norwich 25 Nov. 1761
Thomas Newton	nom. 28 Nov., cons. 28 Dec. 1761	14 Feb. 1782
Lewis Bagot	nom. 23 Feb., cons. 7 Apr. 1782	trs. Norwich 14 June 1783
Christopher Wilson	nom. 14 June, cons. 6 July 1783	18 Apr. 1792
Spencer Madan	nom. 2 May, cons. 3 June 1792	trs. Peterborough 7 Mar. 1794
Henry Reginald Courtenay	nom. 31 Mar., cons. 11 May 1794	trs. Exeter 10 Mar. 1797
Ffolliott Herbert Walker Cornewall	nom. 10 Mar., cons. 9 Apr. 1797	trs. Hereford 28 Jan. 1803
George Pelham	nom. 3 Feb., cons. 27 Mar. 1803	trs. Exeter 12 Aug. 1807

BISHOPS	ACCESSION	DEATH _unless otherwise stated_
John Luxmoore	nom. 12 Aug., cons. 4 Oct. 1807	trs. Hereford 23 Aug. 1808
William Lort Mansel	nom. 22 Aug., cons. 30 Oct. 1808	27 June 1820
John Kaye	nom. 1 July, cons. 30 July 1820	trs. Lincoln 1 Mar. 1827
Robert Gray	nom. 2 Mar., cons. 25 Mar. 1827	28 Sept. 1834
Joseph Allen	nom. 13 Oct., cons. 7 Dec. 1834	trs. Ely 17 Aug. 1836
James Henry Monk[1]	bp of Gloucester, nom. Oct. 1836	6 June 1856
Charles Baring	nom. 17 July, cons. 10 Aug. 1856	trs. Durham 6 Nov. 1861
William Thomson	nom. 25 Nov., cons. 15 Dec. 1861	trs. York 23 Jan. 1863
Charles John Ellicott	nom. 6 Feb., cons. 25 Mar. 1863	res. Bristol 1897 (cf. _sub_ Gloucester)
George Forrest Browne	trs. Stepney (suff.), nom. 15 Sept., conf. 23 Oct. 1897	res. 14 May 1914, d. 1 June 1930
George Nickson	trs. Jarrow (suff.), nom. 20 May, conf. 12 June 1914	res. 15 Feb. 1933, d. 23 Feb. 1949
Clifford Salisbury Woodward	nom. 20 Mar., cons. 25 May 1933	trs. Gloucester 25 Feb. 1946
Frederic Arthur Cockin	nom. 14 May, cons. 24 June 1946	res. 31 Oct. 1958, d. 15 Jan. 1969
Oliver Stratford Tomkins	nom. 4 Nov. 1958, cons. 6 Jan. 1959	res. 1 Oct. 1975
Ernest John Tinsley	nom. 12 Nov. 1975, cons. 6 Jan. 1976	res. 30 Apr. 1985
Barry Rogerson	trs. Wolverhampton (suff.), nom. 11 June 1985	

CANTERBURY

ARCHBISHOPS	ACCESSION	DEATH _unless otherwise stated_
Stigand (held Winchester with Canterbury)	_3 Apr._ 1043 1052 trs. from Winchester	dep. _11_ Apr. 1070, d. 21 or 22 Feb. 1072
Lanfranc	nom. 15 Aug., cons. 29 Aug. 1070	28 May 1089
Anselm	nom. 6 Mar., temp. _a._ 25 Sept., cons. 4 Dec. 1093	21 Apr. 1109
Ralph d'Escures	trs. Rochester, el. 26 Apr. 1114	20 Oct. 1122
William of Corbeil	el. 2 or 4 Feb., cons. 18 Feb. 1123	21 Nov. 1136
Theobald of Bec	el. 24 Dec. 1138, cons. 8 Jan. 1139	18 Apr. 1161
Thomas Becket	el. 23 May, cons. 3 June 1162	29 Dec. 1170
Richard of Dover	el. 3 June 1173, cons. 7 Apr. 1174	16 Feb. 1184
Baldwin	trs. Worcester, post. 2 and 16 Dec. 1184	19 or 20 Nov. 1190
[Reginald FitzJocelin	trs. Bath, el. 27 Nov. 1191	26 Dec. 1191]
Hubert Walter	trs. Salisbury, post. 29 May, temp. _a._ 12 Dec. 1193	13 July 1205
[Reginald	el. July × Oct. 1205	qua. 1 Oct. × 20 Dec. 1206]
[John de Gray	bp of Norwich, post. 11 Dec. 1205	qua. _a._ 30 Mar. 1206]

[1] By Order in Council dated 5 Oct. 1836 the see of Bristol was joined to that of Gloucester and thenceforward the bp was styled 'of Gloucester and Bristol' until 1897, when the sees were again divided.

ARCHBISHOPS	ACCESSION	DEATH *unless otherwise stated*
Stephen Langton	cl. 1 Oct. × 20 Dec. 1206, cons. 17 June 1207, temp. 1 June 1213	9 July 1228
[Walter de Eynesham	el. 3 Aug. 1228	qua. 4 or 5 Jan. 1229]
Richard Grant (Wethershed)	prov. 19 Jan., temp. 24 Mar., cons. 10 June 1229	3 Aug. 1231
[Ralph Nevill	bp of Chichester, post. 22 Sept. 1231	qua. 20 Dec. 1231]
[John of Sittingbourne	el. 16 Mar. 1232	qua. 12 June 1232]
[John Blund	el. 26 Aug. 1232	qua. 1 June 1233]
Edmund of Abingdon	el. 20 Sept. 1233, temp. 4 Feb., cons. 2 Apr. 1234	16 Nov. 1240
Boniface of Savoy	el. 1 Feb. 1241, conf. 17 Sept. 1243, temp. *p.* 27 Feb. 1244, cons. 15 Jan. 1245	18 July 1270
[Adam of Chillenden	el. 9 Sept. 1270	qua. summer 1272]
Robert Kilwardby	prov. 11 Oct., temp. 12 Dec. 1272, cons. 26 Feb. 1273	trs. Porto 12 Mar., res. 5 June 1278
[Robert Burnell	bp of Bath, post. 14 June × 10 July 1278	qua. 31 Dec. 1278 × 28 Jan. 1279]
John Pecham	prov. 28 Jan., cons. 19 Feb., temp. 30 May 1279	8 Dec. 1292
Robert Winchelsey	el. 13 Feb. 1293, cons. 12 Sept. 1294, temp. 4 Feb. 1295	11 May 1313
[Thomas Cobham	el. 28 May 1313	qua. 1 Oct. 1313]
Walter Reynolds	trs. Worcester, prov. 1 Oct. 1313, temp. 3 Jan. 1314	16 Nov. 1327
Simon Meopham	el. 11 Dec. 1327, cons. 5 June 1328, temp. 19 Sept. 1328	12 Oct. 1333
John Stratford	trs. Winchester, post. 3 Nov., prov. 26 Nov. 1333, temp. 5 Feb. 1334	23 Aug. 1348
[John Offord	prov. 24 Sept., temp. 14 Dec. 1348	20 May 1349]
Thomas Bradwardine	el. 30 Aug. 1348 and 4 June 1349, prov. 19 June 1349, cons. 19 July, temp. 22 Aug. 1349	25 or 26 Aug. 1349
Simon Islip	el. 29 Sept., prov. 7 Oct., temp. 15 Nov., cons. 20 Dec. 1349	26 Apr. 1366
Simon Langham	trs. Ely, prov. 24 July, temp. 5 Nov. 1366	res. 28 Nov. 1368
William Whittlesey	trs. Worcester, prov. 11 Oct. 1368, temp. 15 Jan. 1369	5 or 6 June 1374
Simon Sudbury	trs. London, prov. 4 May, temp. 5 June 1375	14 June 1381
William Courtenay	trs. London, post. 31 July, prov. 9 Sept., temp. 23 Oct. 1381	31 July 1396
Thomas Arundel	trs. York, prov. 25 Sept. 1396, temp. 11 Jan. 1397	trs. St Andrews 1397
Roger Walden	prov. *a.* 8 Nov. 1397, temp. 21 Jan. 1398	depr. 19 Oct. 1399[1]
Thomas Arundel	restored 19 Oct., temp. 21 Oct. 1399	19 Feb. 1414
Henry Chichele	trs. St Davids, post. 12 Mar., prov. 27 Apr., temp. 30 May 1414	12 Apr. 1443
John Stafford	trs. Bath, prov. 13 May, temp. 25 June 1443	25 May 1452

[1] For the evidence against Walden's acting in spirituals as abp and for Arundel's action as abp before 19 Oct. 1399, *see* I. J. Churchill, *Canterbury administration*, i. 570.

ARCHBISHOPS	ACCESSION	DEATH *unless otherwise stated*
John Kempe	trs. York, prov. 21 July, temp. 6 Sept. 1452	22 Mar. 1454
Thomas Bourgchier	trs. Ely, post. 23 Apr., prov. 21 June, temp. 22 Aug. 1454	30 Mar. 1486
John Morton	trs. Ely, prov. 6 Oct., temp. 6 Dec. 1486	15 or 16 Sept. 1500
[Thomas Langton	trs. Winchester Jan. 1501	27 Jan. 1501]
Henry Deane	trs. Salisbury, post 26 Apr., prov. 26 May, temp. 2 Aug. 1501	15 or 17 Feb. 1503
William Warham	trs. London, prov. 29 Nov. 1503, temp. 24 Jan. 1504	22 Aug. 1532
Thomas Cranmer	el. 1532, prov. 21 Feb., cons. 30 Mar., temp. 19 Apr. 1533	depr. 13 Nov. 1553 d. 21 Mar. 1556
Reginald Pole	prov. 3 Dec. 1555, temp. 21 Mar., cons. 22 Mar. 1556	18 or 19 Nov. 1558
Matthew Parker	nom. 18 July, cons. 17 Dec. 1559	17 May 1575
Edmund Grindal	trs. York, nom. 29 Dec. 1575, conf. 15 Feb. 1576	6 July 1583
John Whitgift	trs. Worcester, nom. 14 Aug., conf. 23 Sept. 1583	29 Feb. 1604
Richard Bancroft	trs. London, nom. 9 Oct., conf. 10 Dec. 1604	2 Nov. 1610
George Abbot	trs. London, nom. 4 Mar., conf. 9 Apr. 1611	4 Aug. 1633
William Laud	trs. London, nom. 6 Aug., conf. 19 Sept. 1633	10 Jan. 1645
William Juxon	trs. London, nom. 2 Sept., conf. 20 Sept. 1660	4 June 1663
Gilbert Sheldon	trs. London, nom. 16 June, conf. 31 Aug. 1663	9 Nov. 1677
William Sancroft	nom. 29 Dec. 1677, cons. 27 Jan. 1678	depr. 1 Feb. 1690 d. 24 Nov. 1693
John Tillotson	nom. 22 Apr., cons. 31 May 1691	22 Nov. 1694
Thomas Tenison	trs. Lincoln, nom. 6 Dec. 1694, conf. 16 Jan. 1695	14 Dec. 1715
William Wake	trs. Lincoln, nom. 17 Dec. 1715, conf. 16 Jan. 1716	24 Jan. 1737
John Potter	trs. Oxford, nom. 9 Feb., conf. 28 Feb. 1737	10 Oct. 1747
Thomas Herring	trs. York, nom. 21 Oct., conf. 24 Nov. 1747	13 Mar. 1757
Matthew Hutton	trs. York, nom. 29 Mar., conf. 29 Apr. 1757	19 Mar. 1758
Thomas Secker	trs. Oxford, nom. 8 Mar., conf. 21 Apr. 1758	3 Aug. 1768
Frederick Cornwallis	trs. Lichfield, nom. 12 Aug., conf. 30 Sept. 1768	19 Mar. 1783
John Moore	trs. Bangor, nom. 31 Mar., conf. 26 Apr. 1783	18 Jan. 1805
Charles Manners Sutton	trs. Norwich, nom. 1 Feb., conf. 21 Feb. 1805	21 July 1828
William Howley	trs. London, nom. 6 Aug., conf. 15 Aug. 1828	11 Feb. 1848
John Bird Sumner	trs. Chester, nom. 17 Feb., conf. 10 Mar. 1848	6 Sept. 1862
Charles Thomas Longley	trs. York, nom. 20 Oct., conf. 26 Nov. 1862	28 Oct. 1868
Archibald Campbell Tait	trs. London, nom. 28 Nov., conf. 30 Dec. 1868	1 Dec. 1882

ARCHBISHOPS	ACCESSION	DEATH *unless otherwise stated*
Edward White Benson	trs. Truro, nom. 13 Jan., conf. 3 Mar. 1883	11 Oct. 1896
Frederick Temple	trs. London, nom. 9 Nov., conf. 22 Dec. 1896	22 Dec. 1902
Randall Thomas Davidson	trs. Winchester, nom. 14 Jan., conf. 6 Feb. 1903	res. 12 Nov. 1928, d. 25 May 1930
Cosmo Gordon Lang (Baron Lang of Lambeth 1942)	trs. York, nom. 13 Nov., conf. 30 Nov. 1928	res. 31 Mar. 1942, d. 5 Dec. 1945
William Temple	trs. York, nom. 1 Apr., conf. 17 Apr. 1942	26 Oct. 1944
Geoffrey Francis Fisher	trs. London, nom. 12 Jan., conf. 2 Feb. 1945	res. 31 May 1961
Arthur Michael Ramsey	trs. York, nom. 1 June, conf. 21 June 1961	res. 15 Nov. 1974
Frederick Donald Coggan	trs. York, nom. 18 Nov., conf. 5 Dec. 1974	res. 25 Jan. 1980
Robert Alexander Kennedy Runcie	trs. St Albans, nom. 1 Feb., conf. 25 Feb. 1980	

CARLISLE

BISHOPS	ACCESSION	DEATH *unless otherwise stated*
Æthelwulf	nom. *a. June*, cons. 6 Aug. 1133	25 May 1156 or 10 May 1157
Bernard	trs. Ragusa, prov. 15 May 1203, temp. 10 Jan. 1204	*a.* 8 July 1214
Hugh of Beaulieu	el. *a.* 1 Aug., temp. 25 Aug. 1218, cons. 24 Feb. 1219	4 June 1223
Walter Mauclerc	el. *a.* 22 Aug., temp. 27 Oct. 1223, cons. 7 Dec. 1223 × 29 Mar. 1224	res. 29 June 1246, d. *c.* 28 Oct. 1248
Silvester Everdon	el. Sept. × 9 Nov., temp. 8 Dec. 1246, cons. 13 Oct. 1247	Feb. or Mar. (*a.* 24) 1254
Thomas Vipont	el. Aug., temp. 24 Dec. 1254, cons. 7 Feb. 1255	Oct. 1256, *a.* 14
Robert de Chaury or Chause	el. *a.* 12 Feb., temp. 29 Sept. 1257, cons. 14 Apr. 1258	Oct. 1278, *a.* 23
Ralph Ireton	el. 14 Dec. 1278, prov. and cons. *a.* 9 Apr., temp. 10 July 1280	1 Mar. 1292
John of Halton	el. 23 Apr., temp. 18 June, cons. 14 Sept. 1292	1 Nov. 1324
[William Ayermine	el. 7 Jan., temp. 19 Feb. 1325	qua. 13 Feb. 1325]
John Ross	prov. 13 Feb., cons. 24 Feb., temp. 20 June 1325	*a.* May 1332
John Kirkby	el. 11 × 18 May, temp. 9 July, cons. 19 July 1332	*a.* 3 Dec. 1353
[John Horncastle	el. 3 × 10 Jan., temp. 22 Feb. 1353	qua. *a.* 26 June 1352]
Gilbert Welton	prov. 13 Feb., cons. 21 Apr., temp. 26 June 1353	Nov.–Dec. 1362
Thomas Appleby	el. *p.* 18 Jan., prov. 12 June, cons. 18 June, temp. 10 Aug. 1363	5 Dec. 1395
Robert Reade	trs. Lismore, prov. 26 Jan., temp. 30 Mar. 1396	trs. Chichester 5 Oct. 1396
Thomas Merks	prov. *4 Jan. 1397*, temp. 18 Mar., cons. *a.* 23 Apr. 1397	trs. Salmas *a.* 6 Dec. 1399, d. 1409
William Strickland	prov. *a.* 6 Dec. 1399, cons. 15 Aug., temp. 15 Nov. 1400	30 Aug. 1419
Roger Whelpdale	prov. 22 Dec. 1419, temp. 17 Mar., cons. *p.* Mar. 1420	4 Feb. 1423

BISHOPS	ACCESSION	DEATH *unless otherwise stated*
William Barrow	trs. Bangor, prov. 19 Apr., temp. 16 June 1423	4 Sept. 1429
Marmaduke Lumley	el. *a.* 5 Dec., prov. 27 Dec. 1429, temp. 15 Apr., cons. 16 Apr. 1430	trs. Lincoln 28 Jan. 1450
Nicholas Close	prov. 30 Jan., temp. 14 Mar., cons. 15 Mar. 1450	trs. Coventry 30 Aug. 1452
William Percy	prov. 30 Aug., temp 24 Oct., cons. 16 Nov. 1452	26 Apr. 1462
John Kingscote	prov. *12 Aug.*, temp. 20 Oct., cons. 24 Oct. 1462	5 Nov. 1463
Richard le Scrope	prov. 1 Feb., temp. 5 June, cons. 24 June 1464	10 May 1468
Edward Story	prov. 18 July, temp. 1 Sept., cons. 2 Oct. 1468	trs. Chichester 11 Feb. 1478
Richard Bell	prov. 11 Feb., temp. 24 Apr., cons. 26 Apr. 1478	res. 4 Sept. 1495, d. 1496
William Sever	prov. 4 Sept., temp. 11 Dec. 1495, cons. 1496	trs. Durham 27 June 1502
Roger Layburne	prov. 21 June 1503, cons. *10 or 17 Sept.*, temp. 12 Nov. 1504	1508
John Penny	trs. Bangor, prov. 22 Sept. 1508	1520
John Kite[1]	trs. Armagh, prov. 12 July, temp. 12 Nov. 1521	19 June 1537
Robert Aldrich	nom. 10 July, cons. 19 Aug. 1537	5 Mar. 1556
Owen Oglethorpe	nom. 21 July, cons. 15 Aug. 1556	depr. 26 June 1559, d. 31 Dec. 1559
John Best	cons. 2 Mar. 1561	22 May 1570
Richard Barnes	trs. Nottingham (suff.), nom. 14 June, conf. *July* 1570	trs. Durham 9 May 1577
John May	nom. *28 May*, cons. 29 Sept. 1577	15 Feb. 1598
Henry Robinson	el. 27 May, cons. 23 July 1598	19 June 1616
Robert Snowden	el. 12 Sept., cons. 24 Nov. 1616	15 May 1621
Richard Milbourne	trs. St Davids, nom. 21 June 1621	May 1624
Richard Senhouse	nom. 13 June, cons. 26 Sept. 1624	6 May 1626
Francis White	cons. 3 Dec. 1626	trs. Norwich 9 Feb. 1629
Barnabas Potter	nom. *Jan.*, cons. 15 Mar. 1629	Jan. 1642
James Ussher	abp of Armagh, to hold *in commendam* 16 Feb. 1642	21 Mar. 1656
Richard Sterne	nom. 7 Oct., cons. 2 Dec. 1660	trs. York 10 June 1664
Edward Rainbowe	nom. Apr., cons. 10 July 1664	26 Mar. 1684
Thomas Smith	nom. 14 Apr., cons. 19 June 1684	12 Apr. 1702
William Nicolson	nom. 8 May, cons. 14 June 1702	trs. Derry *21 Apr.* 1718
Samuel Bradford	nom. 21 Apr., cons. 1 June 1718	trs. Rochester 19 July 1723
John Waugh	nom. 30 May, el. 23 Aug., cons. 13 Oct. 1723	29 Oct. 1734
George Fleming (2nd Baronet 1736)	nom. 30 Oct. 1734, cons. 19 Jan. 1735	2 July 1747
Richard Osbaldeston	nom. 28 July, cons. 4 Oct. 1747	trs. London 18 Feb. 1762
Charles Lyttelton	nom. 20 Feb., cons. 21 Mar. 1762	22 Dec. 1768
Edmund Law	nom. 28 Jan., cons. 24 Feb. 1769	14 Aug. 1787

[1] Also titular abp of Thebes.

BISHOPS	ACCESSION	DEATH *unless otherwise stated*
John Douglas	nom. 26 Sept., cons. 18 Nov. 1787	trs. Salisbury 17 Aug. 1791
Edward Venables Vernon (from 15 Jan. 1831 surnamed Harcourt)	nom. 18 Aug., cons. 6 Nov. 1791	trs. York 19 Jan. 1808
Samuel Goodenough	nom. 20 Jan., cons. 13 Mar. 1808	12 Aug. 1827
Hugh Percy	trs. Rochester, nom. 17 Sept., conf. 10 Nov. 1827	5 Feb. 1856
Henry Montagu Villiers	nom. 3 Mar., cons. 13 Apr. 1856	trs. Durham 24 Aug. 1860
Samuel Waldegrave	nom. 19 Sept., cons. 11 Nov. 1860	1 Oct. 1869
Harvey Goodwin	nom. Oct., cons. 30 Nov. 1869	25 Nov. 1891
John Wareing Bardsley	trs. Sodor and Man, nom. 18 Jan., conf. 26 Feb. 1892	14 Sept. 1904
John William Diggle	nom. 21 Dec. 1904, cons. 2 Feb. 1905	24 Mar. 1920
Henry Herbert Williams	nom. 24 June, cons. 24 Aug. 1920	res. 3 Apr. 1946, d. 29 Sept. 1961
Thomas Bloomer	nom. 23 July, cons. 18 Oct. 1946	res. 31 Oct. 1966, d. 5 Jan. 1984
Sydney Cyril Bulley	trs. Penrith (suff.), nom. 8 Dec. 1966, conf. 10 Jan. 1967	res. 31 Oct. 1972
Henry David Halsey	trs. Tonbridge (suff.), nom. 6 Nov., conf. 30 Nov. 1972	

CHELMSFORD

John Edwin Watts-Ditchfield	nom. 18 Feb., cons. 24 Feb. 1914	14 July 1923
Frederic Sumpter Guy Warman	trs. Truro, nom. 10 Sept., inv. 9 Oct. 1923	trs. Manchester 21 Jan. 1929
Henry Albert Wilson	nom. 24 Jan., cons. 25 Jan. 1929	res. 30 Nov. 1950, d. 16 July 1961
Sherard Falkner Allison	nom. 19 Dec. 1950, cons. 2 Feb. 1951	trs. Winchester 20 Dec. 1961
John Gerhard Tiarks	nom. 30 Jan., cons. 24 Feb. 1962	res. 30 Apr. 1971, d. 2 Jan. 1974
Albert John Trillo	trs. Hertford (suff.), nom. 10 May, conf. 6 July 1971	res. 30 Sept. 1985

CHESTER

John Bird	trs. Bangor, nom. 4 Aug. 1541	depr. 13 Mar. × 31 Mar. 1554, d. 1556
George Cotes	cons. *1 Apr.* 1554	*Dec.* 1555
Cuthbert Scott	nom. *a.* 24 Apr., prov. 6 July 1556	depr. 26 June 1559, d. *9 Oct.* 1564
William Downham	el. *a.* 1 May, cons. 4 May 1561	3 Dec. 1577
William Chaderton	cons. 8 Nov. 1579	trs. Lincoln 24 May 1595
Hugh Bellott	trs. Bangor, nom. 25 June, conf. 25 Sept. 1595	13 June 1596
Richard Vaughan	trs. Bangor, nom. 16 May 1597	trs. London 20 Dec. 1604
George Lloyd	trs. Sodor and Man, nom. *Dec.* 1604	1 Aug. 1615
Thomas Morton	el. 22 May, cons. 7 July 1616	trs. Lichfield 6 Mar. 1619
John Bridgeman	nom. 7 Mar., cons. 9 May 1619	1652
Brian Walton	nom. 5 Oct., cons. 2 Dec. 1660	29 Nov. 1661

BISHOPS	ACCESSION	DEATH
		unless otherwise stated
Henry Ferne	nom. 3 Dec. 1661, cons. 9 Feb. 1662	16 Mar. 1662
George Hall	cons. 11 May 1662	23 Aug. 1668
John Wilkins	nom. 26 Sept., cons. 15 Nov. 1668	19 Nov. 1672
John Pearson	nom. 1 Dec. 1672, cons. 9 Feb. 1673	16 July 1686
Thomas Cartwright	nom. 21 Aug., cons. 17 Oct. 1686	15 Apr. 1689
Nicholas Stratford	nom. 22 June, cons. 15 Sept. 1689	12 Feb. 1707
William Dawes (2nd Baronet)	nom. 13 Jan., cons. 8 Feb. 1708	trs. York 9 Mar. 1714
Francis Gastrell	nom. 12 Mar., cons. 4 Apr. 1714	14 Nov. 1725
Samuel Peploe	nom. 23 Jan., cons. 12 Apr. 1726	21 Feb. 1752
Edmund Keene	nom. 5 Mar., cons. 22 Mar. 1752	trs. Ely 22 Jan. 1771
William Markham	nom. 23 Jan., cons. 17 Feb. 1771	trs. York 20 Jan. 1777
Beilby Porteous	nom. 21 Jan., cons. 9 Feb. 1777	trs. London 7 Dec. 1787
William Cleaver	nom. 7 Dec. 1787, cons. 20 Jan. 1788	trs. Bangor 1800
Henry William Majendie	nom. 23 May, cons. 15 June 1800	trs. Bangor 1809
Bowyer Edward Sparke	nom. 19 Sept. 1809, cons. 21 Jan. 1810	trs. Ely 19 June 1812
George Henry Law	nom. 19 June, cons. 5 July 1812	trs. Bath 8 June 1824
Charles James Blomfield	nom. 8 June, cons. 20 June 1824	trs. London 23 Aug. 1828
John Bird Sumner	nom. 23 Aug., cons. 14 Sept. 1828	trs. Canterbury 10 Mar. 1848
John Graham	nom. 11 Mar., cons. 14 May 1848	15 June 1865
William Jacobson	nom. 12 July, cons. 24 Aug. 1865	res. 1884, d. 13 July 1884
William Stubbs	nom. 4 Mar., cons. 25 Apr. 1884	trs. Oxford 15 Jan. 1889
Francis John Jayne	nom. 21 Jan., cons. 24 Feb. 1889	res. 1 May 1919, d. 23 Aug. 1921
Henry Luke Paget	trs. Stepney (suff.), nom. 27 June, conf. 31 July 1919	res. 15 July 1932, d. 26 Apr. 1937
Geoffrey Francis Fisher	nom. 20 July, cons. 21 Sept. 1932	trs. London 17 Oct. 1939
Douglas Henry Crick	trs. Stafford (suff.), nom. 19 Oct., conf. 18 Nov. 1939	res. 1 Feb. 1955, d. 5 Aug. 1973
Gerald Alexander Ellison	trs. Willesden (suff.), nom. 15 Feb., conf. 5 Apr. 1955	trs. London 16 July 1973
Hubert Victor Whitsey	trs. Hertford (suff.), nom. 7 Dec. 1973, conf. 22 Jan. 1974	res. 31 Dec. 1981
Michael Alfred Baughen	nom. 11 May, cons. 29 June 1982	

CHICHESTER

(Stigand transferred his see from Selsey to Chichester, 1075)

Stigand	nom. 24 May, cons. × *Aug.* 1070	*29 Aug.* 1087
Godfrey[1]	nom. and cons. 1088	25 Sept. 1088
Ralph Luffa	cons. 6 Jan. 1091	14 Dec. 1123
Seffrid I	nom. *c.* Feb., cons. 12 Apr. 1125	depr. 1145, d. 1150/1
Hilary	cons. 3 Aug. 1147	*13* July 1169

[1] Probably mistakenly called 'William' in some sources.

BISHOPS	ACCESSION	DEATH *unless otherwise stated*
John of Greenford	el. late Apr. or 1 May 1173, cons. 6 Oct. 1174	26 Apr. 1180
Seffrid II	cons. 16 Nov. 1180	17 Mar. 1204
Simon of Wells	el. 4 × 9 Apr., cons. 11 July, temp. *a.* 3 Aug. 1204	21 Aug. 1207
[Nicholas de l'Aigle	el. 1209	qua. *a.* 1214]
Richard Poore	temp. 7 Jan., cons. 25 Jan. 1215	trs. Salisbury 9 May × 27 June 1217
Ranulf of Wareham	temp. 17 Dec. 1217, cons. 7 Jan. 1218	14 or 15 Sept. 1222
Ralph Nevill	el. *a.* 1 Nov., temp. 3 Nov. 1222, cons. 21 Apr. 1224	1 × 4 Feb. 1244
[Robert Passelewe	el. *a.* 19 Apr. 1244	qua. 3 June 1244]
Richard Wich	el. 3 June 1244, cons. 5 Mar. 1245, temp. 21 July 1246	2 or 3 Apr. 1253
John Climping	el. 20 May, temp. 27 May 1253, cons. 11 Jan. 1254	18 May 1262
Stephen Bersted	el. 26 May–20 June, temp. 20 June, cons. 24 Sept. 1262	21 Oct. 1287
Gilbert of St. Leofard	el. 30 Jan., temp. 24 June, cons. 5 Sept. 1288	12 Feb. 1305
John Langton	el. 5 Apr., temp. 16 July, cons. 19 Sept. 1305	*a.* 19 July 1337
Robert Stratford	el. 23 July × 18 Aug., temp. 21 Sept., cons. 30 Nov. 1337	9 Apr. 1362
William Lenn	prov. 16 May, cons. *a.* 18 Aug., temp. 12 Oct. 1362	trs. Worcester 11 Oct. 1368
William Reade	prov. 11 Oct. 1368, temp. 9 June, cons. 2 Sept. 1369	18 Aug. 1385
Thomas Rushock	trs. Llandaff, prov. 16 Oct. 1385, temp. 26 Mar. 1386	trs. Kilmore 1389
Richard Mitford	prov. 17 Nov. 1389, temp. 10 Mar., cons. 10 Apr. 1390	trs. Salisbury 25 Oct. 1395
Robert Waldby	trs. Dublin, prov. *3 Nov.* 1395, temp. 4 Feb. 1396	trs. York 5 Oct. 1396
Robert Reade	trs. Carlisle, prov. 5 Oct. 1396, temp. 6 Mar. 1397	*a.* 21 June 1415
[Stephen Patrington	trs. St David's, post. *1415*, prov. 15 Dec. 1417	22 Dec. 1417]
Henry Ware	el. 3 × 28 Feb., prov. 6 Apr., temp. 13 May, cons. *17* July 1418	7 × 26 July 1420
John Kempe	trs. Rochester, post *a.* Feb., prov. 28 Feb., temp. 21 Aug. 1421	trs. London 17 Nov. 1421
Thomas Polton	trs. Hereford 17 Nov. 1421, temp. 28 July 1422	trs. Worcester 27 Feb. 1426
John Rickingale	prov. 27 Feb., temp. 1 May, cons. 30 June 1426	*a.* 3 July 1429
[Thomas Brouns	el. *a.* 3 Aug. 1429	qua. *a.* 14 Oct. 1429]
Simon Sydenham	prov. 14 Oct. 1429, temp. 24 Jan., cons. 11 Feb. 1431	26 Jan. 1438
Richard Praty	prov. 21 Apr., temp. 14 July, cons. 27 July 1438	5 Aug. × 6 Sept. 1445
Adam Moleyns	prov. 24 Sept., temp. 3 Dec. 1445, cons. 6 Feb. 1446	9 Jan. 1450
Reginald Pecock	trs. St Asaph, prov. 23 Mar., temp. 30 May 1450	res. *a.* 8 Jan. 1459 d. 1460 × 1461
John Arundel	prov. 8 Jan., temp. 26 Mar., cons. 3 June 1459	18 Oct. 1477
Edward Story	trs. Carlisle, prov. 11 Feb., temp. 27 Mar. 1478	16 Mar. 1503

BISHOPS	ACCESSION	DEATH *unless otherwise stated*
Richard FitzJames	trs. Rochester, prov. 29 Nov. 1503, temp. 29 Jan. 1504	trs. London 5 June 1506
Robert Sherburne	trs. St David's, prov. 18 Sept., temp. 13 Dec. 1508	res. 25 May × 3 June, d. 21 Aug. 1536
Richard Sampson	el. 3 June, cons. 11 June 1536	trs. Coventry 9 Mar. 1543
George Day	nom. 15 Apr., cons. 6 *May* 1543	depr. 10 Oct. 1551
John Scory	trs. Rochester, nom. 23 May 1552	depr. Aug. 1553 (bp of Hereford 1559)
George Day	restored 8 × 24 Aug. 1553	2 Aug. 1556
John Christopherson	nom. 16 Dec. 1556, prov. 7 May, cons. 21 Nov. 1557	*a.* 28 Dec. 1558
William Barlow	formerly Bath, nom. 22 June, conf. 20 Dec. 1559	13 Aug. 1568
Richard Curtis	nom. 30 Mar., cons. 21 May 1570	30 Aug. 1582
Thomas Bickley	nom. 7 Dec. 1585, cons. 30 Jan. 1586	30 Apr. 1596
Anthony Watson	nom. 1 June, cons. 15 Aug. 1596	6 or 10 Sept. 1605
Lancelot Andrewes	nom. 10 Oct., cons. 3 Nov. 1605	trs. Ely 6 Nov. 1609
Samuel Harsnett	nom. 7 Nov., cons. 3 Dec. 1609	trs. Norwich 28 Aug. 1619
George Carleton	trs. Llandaff, nom. 13 Sept., conf. 20 Sept. 1619	*a.* 12 May 1628
Richard Montague	nom. 5 July, cons. 24 Aug. 1628	trs. Norwich 12 May 1638
Brian Duppa	nom. 14 May, cons. 17 June 1638	trs. Salisbury 14 Dec. 1641
Henry King	el. 5 Jan., cons. 6 Feb. 1642	30 Sept. 1669
Peter Gunning	nom. 3 Feb., cons. 6 Mar. 1670	trs. Ely 4 Mar. 1675
Ralph Brideoake	nom. 27 Feb., cons. 18 Apr. 1675	5 Oct. 1678
Guy Carleton	trs. Bristol, nom. 16 Nov. 1678, conf. 8 Jan. 1679	6 July 1685
John Lake	trs. Bristol, nom. 26 Aug., conf. 19 Oct. 1685	susp. 1 Aug., d. 30 Aug. 1689
Simon Patrick	nom. 17 Sept., cons. 13 Oct. 1689	trs. Ely 2 July 1691
Robert Grove	nom. 30 Apr., cons. 30 Aug. 1691	25 Sept. 1696
John Williams	nom. 23 Oct., cons. 13 Dec. 1696	24 Apr. 1709
Thomas Manningham	nom. 12 Oct., cons. 13 Nov. 1709	24 or 25 Aug. 1722
Thomas Bowers	nom. 26 Aug., cons. 7 Oct. 1722	23 Aug. 1724
Edward Waddington	nom. 25 Aug., cons. 11 or 18 Oct. 1724	7 Sept. 1731
Francis Hare	trs. St Asaph, nom. 8 Oct., conf. 25 Nov. 1731	26 Apr. 1740
Matthias Mawson	trs. Llandaff, nom. 30 Apr., conf. 21 Oct. 1740	trs. Ely 15 Mar. 1754
William Ashburnham (Baronet)	nom. 15 Mar., cons. 31 Mar. 1754	4 Sept. 1797
John Buckner	nom. 2 Oct. 1797, cons. 4 Mar. 1798	1 May 1824
Robert James Carr	nom. 8 May, cons. 6 June 1824	trs. Worcester 10 Sept. 1831
Edward Maltby	nom. 22 Sept., cons. 2 Oct. 1831	trs. Durham 8 June 1836
William Otter	nom. 9 Sept., cons. 2 Oct. 1836	20 Aug. 1840
Philip Nicholas Shuttleworth	nom. 7 Sept., cons. 20 Sept. 1840	7 Jan. 1842

BISHOPS	ACCESSION	DEATH
		unless otherwise stated
Ashurst Turner Gilbert	nom. 22 Jan., cons. 27 Feb. 1842	21 Feb. 1870
Richard Durnford	nom. 28 Mar., cons. 8 May 1870	14 Oct. 1895
Ernest Roland Wilberforce	trs. Newcastle, nom. 12 Dec. 1895, conf. 16 Jan. 1896	9 Sept. 1907
Charles John Ridgeway	nom. 21 Dec. 1907, cons. 25 Jan. 1908	res. 1 May 1919, d. 28 Feb. 1927
Winfrid Oldfield Burrows	trs. Truro, nom. 5 June, conf. 9 July 1919	13 Feb. 1929
George Kennedy Allen Bell	nom. 1 May, cons. 11 June 1929	res. 31 Jan. 1958
Roger Plumpton Wilson	trs. Wakefield, nom. 4 Feb., conf. 16 Apr. 1958	res. 30 Apr. 1974
Eric Waldram Kemp	nom. 25 June, cons. 23 Oct. 1974	

COVENTRY (*see also* LICHFIELD)

Huyshe Wolcott Yeatman-Biggs	trs. Worcester, nom. 17 Oct., inv. 23 Oct. 1918	14 Apr. 1922
Charles Lisle Carr	nom. 15 June, cons. 24 June 1922	trs. Hereford 20 Jan. 1931
Mervyn George Haigh	nom. 12 Feb., cons. 24 Feb. 1931	trs. Winchester 24 Sept. 1942
Neville Vincent Gorton	nom. 26 Nov. 1942, cons. 2 Feb. 1943	30 Nov. 1955
Cuthbert Killick Norman Bardsley	trs. Croydon (suff.), nom. 28 Feb., conf. 14 Mar. 1956	res. 6 May 1976
John Gibbs	trs. Bradwell (suff.), nom. 9 June, conf. 21 July 1976	res. 31 July 1985

DERBY

Edmund Courtenay Pearce	nom. 14 Sept., cons. 18 Oct. 1927	13 Oct. 1935
Alfred Edward John Rawlinson	nom. 16 Jan., cons. 24 Feb. 1936	res. 18 Apr. 1959, d. 17 July 1960
Geoffrey Francis Allen	nom. 30 Apr., conf. 19 May 1959	res. 6 Sept. 1969, d. 8 Nov. 1982
Cyril William Johnston Bowles	nom. 22 Sept., cons. 1 Nov. 1969	

DURHAM

Æthelwine	cons. 1056	depr. 1071, d. winter 1071–2
Walcher	cons. *Mar.* 1071	14 May 1080
William of St Carilef (or Calais)	nom. 9 Nov. 1080, cons. 27 Dec. 1080 or 3 Jan. 1081	2 Jan. 1096
Ranulf Flambard	nom. and temp. 29 May, cons. 5 June 1099	5 Sept. 1128
Geoffrey Rufus	nom. *p.* 14 May, cons. 6 Aug. 1133	6 May 1141
William of Ste Barbe	el. 14 Mar., cons. 20 June 1143	13 Nov. 1152
Hugh du Puiset	el. 22 Jan., cons. 20 Dec. 1153	3 Mar. 1195
Philip of Poitiers	el. Nov. 1195 × Jan. 1196, cons. 20 Apr. 1197	22 Apr. 1208
Richard Marsh	el. *a.* 27 June, temp. 29 June, cons. *2* July 1217	1 May 1226
Richard Poore	trs. Salisbury, el. *a.* 9 May, prov. 14 May, temp. 22 July 1228	15 Apr. 1237
[Thomas Melsonby	el. 1 June 1237	res. 8 Apr. 1240]
Nicholas Farnham	el. 2 Jan., temp. 10 Feb., cons. 26 May or 9 June 1241	res. 2 Feb. 1249, d. 1257

BISHOPS	ACCESSION	DEATH *unless otherwise stated*
Walter Kirkham	el. 21 Apr., temp. 20 Oct., cons. 5 Dec. 1249	9 Aug. 1260
Robert Stichill	el. 30 Sept., temp. 5 Dec. 1260, cons. 13 Feb. 1261	4 Aug. 1274
Robert of Holy Island	el. 24 Sept., temp. 8 Nov., cons. 9 Dec. 1274	7 June 1283
Anthony Bek	el. 9 July, temp. 4 Sept. 1283, cons. 9 Jan. 1284	3 Mar. 1311
Richard Kellaw	el. 31 Mar., temp. 20 May, cons. 30 May 1311	9 Oct. 1316
Lewis de Beaumont	prov. 9 Feb., temp. 4 May 1317, cons. 26 Mar. 1318	24 Sept. 1333
[Robert Graystanes	el. 15 Oct., cons. 14 Nov. 1333	depr. 1333]
Richard of Bury	prov. 14 Oct., temp. 7 Dec., cons. 19 Dec. 1333	14 Apr. 1345
Thomas Hatfield	el. 8 May, cons. 1 June, temp. 7 June 1345	8 May 1381
John Fordham	prov. 9 Sept., temp. 23 Oct. 1381, cons. 5 Jan. 1382	trs. Ely 3 Apr. 1388
Walter Skirlaw	trs. Bath and Wells, prov. 3 Apr., temp. 13 Sept. 1388	24 Mar. 1406
Thomas Langley	prov. 14 May, cons. 8 Aug., temp. 9 Aug. 1406	20 Nov. 1437
Robert Nevill	trs. Salisbury, prov. 27 Jan., temp. 8 Apr. 1438	9 July 1457
Lawrence Booth	prov. 22 Aug., cons. 25 Sept., temp. 18 Oct. 1457	trs. York 1 Sept. 1476
William Dudley	prov. 31 July, cons. 1 Sept. × 12 Oct., temp. 14 Oct. 1476	29 Nov. 1483
John Shirwood	prov. 29 Mar., cons. *26 May 1484*, temp. 16 Aug. 1485	14 Jan. 1494
Richard Fox	trs. Bath and Wells, prov. 30 July, temp. 8 Dec. 1494	trs. Winchester *a. 20 Aug.* 1501
William Sever	trs. Carlisle, prov. 27 June, temp. 15 Oct. 1502	1505
Christopher Bainbridge	prov. 27 Aug., temp. 17 Nov., cons. *12 Dec.* 1507	trs. York 20 Sept. 1508
Thomas Ruthall	prov. *12 June*, cons. 24 June, temp. 3 July 1509	4 Feb. 1523
Thomas Wolsey	abp of York, prov. to hold *in commendam* Feb., temp. 30 Apr. 1523	trs. Winchester 8 Feb. 1529
Cuthbert Tunstall	trs. London, prov. 21 Feb., post. 25 Mar., temp. 25 Mar. 1530	res. 28 Sept. 1559, d. 18 Nov. 1559
James Pilkington	nom. 26 Dec. 1560, cons. 2 Mar. 1561	23 Jan. 1576
Richard Barnes	trs. Carlisle, nom. 27 Mar., conf. 9 May 1577	24 Aug. 1587
Matthew Hutton	el. 9 June, cons. 27 July 1589	trs. York 24 Mar. 1595
Tobias Matthew	nom. 25 Mar., cons. 13 Apr. 1595	trs. York 28 Aug. 1606
William James	cons. 7 Sept. 1606	12 May 1617
Richard Neile	trs. Lincoln, nom. 26 May, conf. 9 Oct. 1617	trs. Winchester 7 Feb. 1628
George Montaigne[1] or Mountain	trs. London, nom. 19 Feb. 1628	trs. York 1 July 1628

[1] It is doubtful whether he was confirmed in this see before nomination to York (5 June 1628).

BISHOPS	ACCESSION	DEATH
		unless otherwise stated
John Howson	trs. Oxford, nom. 4 July, conf. 17 Sept. 1628	6 Feb. 1632
Thomas Morton	trs. Lichfield, nom. June, conf. 2 July 1632	22 Sept. 1659
John Cosin	nom. 5 Oct., cons. 2 Dec. 1660	15 Jan. 1672
Nathaniel Crew (3rd Baron Crew of Stene 1697)	trs. Oxford, nom. 22 Oct., conf. 6 Dec. 1674	18 Sept. 1721
William Talbot	trs. Salisbury, nom. 23 Sept., conf. 7 Nov. 1721	10 Oct. 1730
Edward Chandler	trs. Lichfield, nom. 17 Oct., conf. 21 Nov. 1730	20 July 1750
Joseph Butler	trs. Bristol, nom. 31 July, conf. 16 Oct. 1750	16 June 1752
Richard Trevor	trs. St David's, nom. 18 Oct., conf. 7 Dec. 1752	9 June 1771
John Egerton	trs. Lichfield, nom. 19 June, conf. 20 July 1771	18 Jan. 1787
Thomas Thurlow	trs. Lincoln, nom. 19 Jan., conf. 19 Feb. 1787	27 May 1791
Shute Barrington	trs. Salisbury, nom. 10 June, conf. 7 July 1791	25 Mar. 1826
William Van Mildert	trs. Llandaff, nom. 27 Mar., conf. 24 Apr. 1826	21 Feb. 1836
Edward Maltby	trs. Chichester, nom. 3 Mar., conf. 8 June 1836	res. 1 Oct. 1856, d. 3 July 1859
Charles Thomas Longley	trs. Ripon, nom. 13 Oct. 1856	trs. York 12 July 1860
Henry Montague Villiers	trs. Carlisle, nom. 18 July, conf. 24 Aug. 1860	9 Aug. 1861
Charles Baring	trs. Gloucester, nom. 26 Sept., conf. 6 Nov. 1861	res. Feb. 1879, d. 13 Sept. 1879
Joseph Barber Lightfoot	nom. 4 Mar., cons. 25 Apr. 1879	21 Dec. 1889
Brooke Foss Westcott	nom. 3 Apr., cons. 1 May 1890	27 July 1901
Handley Carr Glyn Moule	nom. 10 Sept., cons. 18 Oct. 1901	8 May 1920
Herbert Hensley Henson	trs. Hereford, nom. 24 June, conf. 27 July 1920	res. 1 Feb. 1939, d. 28 Sept. 1947
Alwyn Terrell Petre Williams	nom. 1 Feb., cons. 25 Mar. 1939	trs. Winchester 8 May 1952
Arthur Michael Ramsey	nom. 8 July, cons. 29 Sept. 1952	trs. York 16 Mar. 1956
Maurice Henry Harland	trs. Lincoln, nom. 20 Apr., conf. 7 July 1956	res. 31 Aug. 1966
Ian Thomas Ramsey	nom. 20 Sept., cons. 1 Nov. 1966	6 Oct. 1972
John Stapylton Habgood	nom. 21 Mar., cons. 1 May 1973	trs. York 18 Oct. 1983
David Edward Jenkins	nom. 14 Mar., cons. 6 July 1984	

ELMHAM

Æthelmaer	cons. 1047	dep. *c.* 11 Apr. 1070
Herfast	cons. 1070	d. 1084

(Herfast set up a see at Thetford *a.* 27 May 1072)

William de Beaufai	nom. 25 Dec. 1085	d. or res. *a.* 27 Jan. 1091
Herbert Losinga	cons. *a.* 27 Jan. 1091	d. 22 July 1119

(Herbert removed from Thetford to Norwich 1094 × 1095)

243

ELY

BISHOPS	ACCESSION	DEATH *unless otherwise stated*
Hervey	trs. Bangor, nom. *a.* 21 Nov. 1108	30 Aug. 1131
Nigel	nom. 28 May, cons. 1 Oct. 1133	30 May 1169
Geoffrey Ridel	el. late Apr., temp. 17 May 1173, cons. 6 Oct. 1174	20 or 21 Aug. 1189
William Longchamp	el. 15 Sept., cons. 31 Dec. 1189	31 Jan. 1197
Eustace	el. 10 Aug. 1197, cons. 8 Mar. 1198	3 Feb. 1215
[Robert of York	el. 16 Mar. × 14 Apr., temp. 25 June 1215	qua. *a.* 11 May 1219]
John of Fountains	el. *a.* 24 Jan., temp. 24 Jan., cons. 8 Mar. 1220	6 May 1225
Geoffrey de Burgo	el. *a.* 2 June, temp. 2 June, cons. 29 June 1225	17 Dec. 1228
Hugh of Northwold	el. *a.* 3 Feb., temp. 26 May, cons. 10 June 1229	6 Aug. 1254
William of Kilkenny	el. Sept. or Oct., temp. 25 Dec. 1254, cons. 15 Aug. 1255	21 Sept. 1256
Hugh Balsham	el. 13 Nov. 1256, cons. 14 Oct. 1257, temp. 15 Jan. 1258	*16* June 1286
John of Kirkby	el. 26 July, temp. 7 Sept., cons. 22 Sept. 1286	26 Mar. 1290
William of Louth	el. 12 May, temp. 30 May, cons. 1 Oct. 1290	25 or 27 Mar. 1298
[John Salmon	el. 19 May 1298	qua. 5 June 1299]
[John Langton	el. 19 May 1298	qua. 5 June 1299]
Ralph Walpole	trs. Norwich, prov. 5 June, temp. 10 Oct. 1299	10 Mar. 1302
Robert Orford	el. 14 Apr., prov. 22 Oct.,[1] cons. 28 Oct. 1302, temp. 4 Feb. 1303	21 Jan. 1310
John Ketton	el. *a.* 2 Mar., temp. 18 July, cons. 6 Sept. 1310	14 May 1316
John Hotham	el. 11 × 14 June, temp. 20 July, cons. 3 Oct. 1316	14 Jan. 1337
Simon Montacute	trs. Worcester, prov. 14 Mar., temp. 11 June 1337	20 June 1345
Thomas de Lisle	prov. 15 July, cons. 24 July, temp. 10 Sept. 1345	23 June 1361
[Reginald Brian	trs. from Worcester 1361, but d. 10 Dec. before translation complete	—]
Simon Langham	prov. 10 Jan., temp. 19 Mar., cons. 20 Mar. 1362	trs. Canterbury 24 July 1366
John Barnet	trs. Bath, prov. 15 Dec. 1366, temp. 28 Apr. 1367	7 June 1373
Thomas Arundel	prov. 13 Aug. 1373, cons. 9 Apr., temp. 5 May 1374	trs. York 3 Apr. 1388
John Fordham	trs. Durham, prov. 3 Apr., temp. 27 Sept. 1388	19 Nov. 1425
Philip Morgan	trs. Worcester, prov. 27 Feb., temp. 22 Apr. 1426	25 Oct. 1435
[Thomas Bourgchier	trs. Worcester, prov. 27 Aug. 1436	prov. annulled 22 June 1437]
Lewis of Luxemburg	(abp of Rouen) prov. *in commendam*, 22 June 1437, temp. 3 Apr. 1438	18 Sept. 1443

[1] William Thomas, *A survey of the cathedral-church of Worcester* (1737), 84–85.

BISHOPS	ACCESSION	DEATH *unless otherwise stated*
Thomas Bourgchier	trs. Worcester, prov. 20 Dec. 1443, temp. 27 Feb. 1444	trs. Canterbury 21 June 1454
William Grey	prov. 21 June, temp. 6 Sept., cons. 8 Sept. 1454	4 Aug. 1478
John Morton	nom. *a.* 7 Aug., el. 8 Aug., prov. 24 Dec. 1478, temp. 4 Jan., cons. 31 Jan. 1479	trs. Canterbury 6 Oct. 1486
John Alcock	trs. Worcester, prov. 6 Oct., temp. 7 Dec. 1486	1 Oct. 1500
Richard Redman	trs. Exeter, prov. 26 May, temp. 26 Sept. 1501	24 or 25 Aug. 1505
James Stanley	prov. 18 July, temp. 5 Nov., cons. 8 Nov. 1506	22 Mar. 1515
Nicholas West	prov. 27 Nov., temp. 6 Sept., cons. 7 Oct. 1515	28 Apr. 1533
Thomas Goodrich	nom. 6 Mar., cons. 19 Apr. 1534	10 May 1554
Thomas Thirlby	trs. Norwich, nom. 10 July 1554, prov. 21 June 1555	depr. 5 July 1559, d. 26 Aug. 1570
Richard Cox	nom. 15 July, cons. 21 Dec. 1559	22 July 1581
Martin Heton	nom. *Dec.* 1599, cons. 3 Feb. 1600	14 July 1609
Lancelot Andrewes	trs. Chichester, el. 22 Sept., conf. 6 Nov. 1609	trs. Winchester 25 Feb. 1619
Nicholas Felton	trs. Bristol, nom. 26 Feb., conf. 11 Mar. 1619	5 or 6 Oct. 1626
John Buckeridge	trs. Rochester, nom. 8 Apr., conf. July 1628	23 May 1631
Francis White	trs. Norwich, el. 15 Nov., conf. 8 Dec. 1631	Feb. 1638
Matthew Wren	trs. Norwich, nom. 19 Mar., conf. 24 Apr. 1638	24 Apr. 1667
Benjamin Laney	trs. Lincoln, el. 24 May, conf. 12 June 1667	24 Jan. 1675
Peter Gunning	trs. Chichester, el. 13 Feb., conf. 4 Mar. 1675	6 July 1684
Francis Turner	trs. Rochester, nom. 21 July, conf. 23 Aug. 1684	depr. 1 Feb. 1690
Simon Patrick	trs. Chichester, nom. 22 Apr., conf. 2 July 1691	31 May 1707
John Moore	trs. Norwich, nom. 5 June, conf. 31 July 1707	31 July 1714
William Fleetwood	trs. St Asaph, el. 19 Nov., conf. 18 Dec. 1714	4 Aug. 1723
Thomas Greene	trs. Norwich, nom. *a.* 27 Aug., conf. 24 Sept. 1723	18 May 1738
Robert Butts	trs. Norwich, nom. 25 May, conf. 27 June 1738	26 Jan. 1748
Thomas Gooch (Baronet)	trs. Norwich, nom. 30 Jan., conf. 11 Mar. 1748	14 Feb. 1754
Matthias Mawson	trs. Chichester, nom. 18 Feb., conf. 15 Mar. 1754	23 Nov. 1770
Edmund Keene	trs. Chester, nom. 24 Dec. 1770, conf. 22 Jan. 1771	6 July 1781
James Yorke	trs. Gloucester, nom. 17 July, conf. 3 Sept. 1781	26 Aug. 1808
Thomas Dampier	trs. Rochester, nom. 10 Sept., conf. 22 Nov. 1808	13 May 1812
Bowyer Edward Sparke	trs. Chester, nom. 22 May, conf. 19 June 1812	4 Apr. 1836
Joseph Allen	trs. Bristol, nom. 18 June, conf. 17 Aug. 1836	20 Mar. 1845

BISHOPS	ACCESSION	DEATH *unless otherwise stated*
Thomas Turton	nom. 28 Mar., cons. 4 May 1845	7 Jan. 1864
Edward Harold Browne	nom. 11 Feb., cons. 29 Mar. 1864	trs. Winchester 23 Oct. 1873
James Russell Woodford	nom. 6 Nov., cons. 14 Dec. 1873	24 Oct. 1885
Alwyne Frederick Compton	nom. 29 Dec. 1885, cons. 2 Feb. 1886	res. 6 July 1905, d. 4 Apr. 1906
Frederick Henry Chase	nom. 8 Aug., cons. 18 Oct. 1905	res. 5 Feb. 1924, d. 23 Sept. 1925
Leonard Jauncey White-Thomson	nom. 6 Feb., cons. 25 Mar. 1924	31 Dec. 1933
Bernard Oliver Francis Heywood	trs. Hull (suff.), nom. 16 Apr., conf. 30 May 1934	res. 16 Dec. 1940, d. 13 Mar. 1960
Harold Edward Wynn	nom. 9 June, cons. 25 July 1941	12 Aug. 1956
Noel Baring Hudson	trs. Newcastle, nom. 23 Nov. 1956, conf. 18 Jan. 1957	res. 31 Dec. 1963, d. 5 Oct. 1970
Edward James Keymer Roberts	trs. Kensington (suff.), nom. 7 Jan., conf. 22 Feb. 1964	res. 31 July 1977
Peter Knight Walker	trs. Dorchester (suff.), nom. 26 Aug., conf. 11 Oct. 1977	

EXETER

Leofric	cons. 19 Apr. 1046	10 or 11 Feb. 1072

(Leofric removed his see from Crediton to Exeter, 1050)

Osbern FitzOsbern	cons. Apr. 1072	1103
William Warelwast	cons. 11 Aug. 1107	*c.* 26 Sept. 1137
Robert Warelwast[1]	nom. 10 Apr., cons. 18 Dec. 1138	*c.* 28 Mar. 1155
Robert II	cons. 5 June 1155	10 Mar. 1160
Bartholomew	el. conf. early 1161, cons. *p.* 18 Apr. 1161	15 Dec. 1184
John the Chanter	cons. 5 Oct. 1186	1 June 1191
Henry Marshal	el. *a.* 10 Feb., cons. *a.* 28 Mar. 1194	*1 Nov.* 1206
Simon of Apulia	el. *a.* 13 Apr., cons. 5 Oct. 1214	9 Sept. 1223
William Briwere	el. *a.* 25 Nov., temp. 25 Nov. 1223, cons. 21 Apr. 1224	24 Nov. 1244
Richard Blund	el. *a.* 30 Jan., temp. 8 Apr., cons 22 Oct. 1245	26 Dec. 1257
Walter Bronescombe	el. 23 Feb., temp. 6 Mar., cons. 10 Mar. 1258	22 July 1280
Peter Quinel or Quivel	el. 7 Aug. × 7 Oct., temp. 11 Oct., cons. 10 Nov. 1280	*1* Oct. 1291
Thomas Bitton	el. 8 Oct. × 30 Nov. 1291, cons. 16 Mar. 1292	21 Sept. 1307
Walter Stapledon	el. 13 Nov., temp. 16 Mar., cons. 13 Oct. 1308	15 Oct. 1326
James Berkeley	el. 5 Dec. 1326, temp. 8 Jan., prov. 10 Mar., cons. 22 Mar. 1327	24 June 1327
[John Godeley	el. 5 July × 22 Aug. 1327	qua. 1327]
John Grandisson	prov. 10 Aug., cons. 18 Oct. 1327, temp. 9 Mar. 1328	16 July 1369
Thomas Brantingham	prov. 4 Mar., cons. 12 May, temp. 16 May 1370	*23* Dec. 1394

[1] For the identification of Robert Warelwast and Robert II, who have usually been confused, *see* C. N. L. Brooke, in *The Letters of John Salisbury*, i (ed. W. J. Millor and H. E. Butler, 1955), 9, note 1.

BISHOPS	ACCESSION	DEATH
		unless otherwise stated
Edmund Stafford	prov. 23 Jan., cons. 20 June, temp. 24 June 1395	3 or 17 Sept. 1419
John Catterick	trs. Lichfield, prov. 20 Nov., post. *a.* Dec. 1419	28 Dec. 1419
Edmund Lacey	trs. Hereford, post. 5 May, prov. 3 July, temp. 31 Oct. 1420	18 Sept. 1455
[John Hales	prov. 20 Oct. 1455	res. *a.* 4 Feb. 1456]
George Nevill	prov. 4 Feb., temp. 21 Mar. 1456, cons. *3 Dec.* 1458	trs. York 15 Mar. 1465
John Booth	prov. 15 Mar., temp. 12 June, cons. 7 July 1465	5 Apr. 1478
Peter Courtenay	el. *a.* 14 June, prov. 9 Sept., temp. 3 Nov., cons. 8 Nov. 1478	trs. Winchester 29 Jan. 1487
Richard Fox	prov. 29 Jan., temp. 2 Apr., cons. 8 Apr. 1487	trs. Bath 8 Feb. 1492
Oliver King	prov. 1 Oct. 1492, cons. *a.* 11 Feb. 1493	trs. Bath 6 Nov. 1495
Richard Redman	trs. St Asaph, prov. 6 Nov. 1495, temp. 7 Jan. 1496	trs. Ely 26 May 1501
John Arundel	trs. Lichfield, prov. 8 Apr., temp. 5 July 1502	14 Mar. 1504
Hugh Oldham	prov. 27 Nov. 1504, temp. 6 Jan., cons. 12 Jan. 1505	25 June 1519
John Veysey	prov. 31 Aug., temp. 4 Nov., cons. 6 Nov. 1519	res. 14 Aug. 1551
Miles Coverdale	nom. 2 Aug., cons. 30 Aug. 1551	depr. Sept. 1553, d. 20 May 1565
John Veysey	restored 28 Sept. 1553	*23* Oct. 1554
James Turberville	nom. 11 Mar., prov. *a.* 8 Sept., cons. 8 Sept. 1555	depr. *10 Aug.* 1559, d. 1 Nov. 1559
William Alley	nom. Mar., cons. 14 July 1560	15 Apr. 1570
William Bradbridge	nom. 20 Jan., cons. 18 Mar. 1571	*28* June 1578
John Woolton	el. 2 July, cons. 2 Aug. 1579	13 Mar. 1594
Gervase Babington	nom. 22 Mar. 1594, conf. 11 Mar. 1595	trs. Worcester 4 Oct. 1597
William Cotton	nom. 18 Aug., cons. 12 Nov. 1598	26 Aug. 1621
Valentine Carey	nom. 13 Sept., cons. 18 Nov. 1621	10 June 1626
Joseph Hall	nom. 5 Oct., cons. 23 Dec. 1627	trs. Norwich 16 Dec. 1641
Ralph Brownrigg	nom. 16 Mar., cons. *15* May[1] 1642	7 Dec. 1659
John Gauden	nom. 17 Oct., cons. 2 Dec. 1660	trs. Worcester 10 June 1662
Seth Ward	nom. 27 June, cons. 20 July 1662	trs. Salisbury 12 Sept. 1667
Anthony Sparrow	el. 14 Oct., cons. 3 Nov. 1667	trs. Norwich 18 Sept. 1676
Thomas Lamplugh	nom. 28 Sept., cons. 12 Nov. 1676	trs. York 8 Dec. 1688
Jonathan Trelawney (3rd Baronet 1685)	trs. Bristol, nom. 16 Nov. 1688,[2] conf. 13 Apr. 1689	trs. Winchester 14 June 1707

[1] 15 May (Sunday) given by Stubbs and by Chanter (transcripts of Sede Vacante material, in Exeter City Library). Episcopal register 23 gives 3 May (Tuesday). *Handbook* (1st edition) gives 25 May (Wednesday).
[2] Le Neve's date from Home Office Church Book. The congé d'élire in Exeter Cathedral muniment 3050 is dated 26 March 1689, and the election only followed the chapter's receipt of this.

BISHOPS	ACCESSION	DEATH *unless otherwise stated*
Offspring Blackall	nom. 13 Jan., cons. 8 Feb. 1708	29 Nov. 1716
Lancelot Blackburn	nom. 28 Jan., cons. 24 Feb. 1717	trs. York 28 Nov. 1724
Stephen Weston	nom. 28 Nov., cons. 27 Dec. 1724	8 Jan. 1742
Nicholas Claget	trs. St Davids, nom. 2 July, conf. 2 Aug. 1742	8 Dec. 1746
George Lavington	nom. 15 Dec. 1746, cons. 8 Feb. 1747	13 Sept. 1762
Frederick Keppel	nom. 14 Oct., cons. 7 Nov. 1762	27 Dec. 1777
John Ross	nom. 7 Jan., cons. 25 Jan. 1778	14 Aug. 1792
William Buller	nom. 8 Sept., cons. 2 Dec. 1792	12 Dec. 1796
Henry Reginald Courtenay	trs. Bristol, nom. 14 Feb., conf. 10 Mar. 1797	9 June 1803
John Fisher	nom. 22 June, cons. 17 June 1803	trs. Salisbury 30 June 1807
George Pelham	trs. Bristol, nom. 4 July, conf. 12 Aug. 1807	trs. Lincoln 16 Oct. 1820
William Carey	nom. 16 Oct., cons. 12 Nov. 1820	trs. St Asaph 7 Apr. 1830
Christopher Bethell	trs. Gloucester, nom. 8 Apr., conf. 11 June 1830	trs. Bangor 28 Oct. 1830
Henry Philpotts	nom. 11 Nov. 1830, cons. 2 Jan. 1831	18 Sept. 1869
Frederick Temple	nom. 2 Nov., cons. 21 Dec. 1869	trs. London 24 Mar. 1885
Edward Henry Bickersteth	nom. 27 Mar., cons. 25 Apr. 1885	res. 26 Nov. 1900, d. 16 May 1906
Herbert Edward Ryle	nom. 15 Dec. 1900, cons. 25 Jan. 1901	trs. Winchester 3 Apr. 1903
Archibald Robertson	nom. 4 Apr., cons. 1 May 1903	res. 1 Nov. 1916, d. 29 Jan. 1931
Rupert Ernest William Gascoyne Cecil	nom. 4 Nov., cons. 28 Dec. 1916	23 June 1936
Charles Edward Curzon	trs. Stepney (suff.), nom. 2 Oct., conf. 6 Nov. 1936	res. 4 Dec. 1948, d. 23 Aug. 1954
Robert Cecil Mortimer	nom. 25 Feb., cons. 25 Apr. 1949	res. 1 Oct. 1973, d. 11 Sept. 1976
Eric Arthur John Mercer	trs. Birkenhead (suff.), nom. 5 Oct., conf. 31 Oct. 1973	res. 31 May 1985
Geoffrey Hewlett Thompson	trs. Willesden (suff.), nom. 7 June 1985	

GLOUCESTER

John Wakeman or Wiche	nom. 3 Sept., cons. 25 Sept. 1541	*a.* 6 Dec. 1549
John Hooper	nom. 3 July 1550, cons. 8 Mar. 1551	res. 26 Apr. 1552, nom. bp of Worcester and Gloucester 20 May 1552, depr. 15 Mar. 1554, d. 9 Feb. 1555
James Brooks	nom. 19 Mar., cons. 1 Apr. 1554	depr. 1559, d. Feb. 1560
Richard Cheyney[1]	nom. 27 Feb., cons. 19 Apr. 1562	25 Apr. 1579
John Bullingham[2]	el. 15 Aug., cons. 3 Sept. 1581	20 May 1598
Godfrey Goldsborough	nom. 2 Aug., cons. 12 Nov. 1598	26 May 1604

[1] Held the bishopric of Bristol *in commendam* from 29 Apr. 1562.
[2] Consecrated to the sees of Gloucester and Bristol; resigned Bristol in 1589.

BISHOPS	ACCESSION	DEATH *unless otherwise stated*
Thomas Ravis	el. 17 Dec. 1604, cons. 17 Mar. 1605	trs. London 18 May 1607
Henry Parry	el. 12 June, cons. 12 July 1607	trs. Worcester 5 Oct. 1610
Giles Thompson	el. 15 Mar., cons. 9 June 1611	14 June 1612
Miles Smith	el. 15 July, cons. 20 Sept. 1612	20 Oct. 1624
Godfrey Goodman	nom. 15 Nov. 1624, cons. 6 Mar. 1625	depr. 1640, d. 19 Jan. 1656
William Nicolson	el. 26 Nov. 1660, cons. 6 Jan. 1661	5 Feb. 1672
John Pritchett	nom. 17 Sept., cons. 3 Nov. 1672	1 Jan. 1681
Robert Frampton	nom. 1 Jan., cons. 27 Mar. 1681	depr. 1 Feb. 1690, d. 25 May 1708
Edward Fowler	nom. 22 Apr., cons. 5 July 1691	26 Aug. 1714
Richard Willis	nom. 19 Nov. 1714, cons. 16 Jan. 1715	trs. Salisbury 21 Nov. 1721
Joseph Wilcocks	nom. 17 Nov., cons. 3 Dec. 1721	trs. Rochester 20 Aug. 1731
Elias Sydall	trs. St David's, nom. 4 Oct., conf. 2 Nov. 1731	24 Dec. 1733
Martin Benson	nom. Dec. 1734, cons. 19 Jan. 1735	30 Aug. 1752
James Johnson	nom. 18 Oct., cons. 10 Dec. 1752	trs. Worcester 9 Nov. 1759
William Warburton	nom. 22 Dec. 1759, cons. 20 Jan. 1760	11 June 1779
James Yorke	trs. St David's, nom. 3 July, conf. 2 Aug. 1779	trs. Ely 3 Sept. 1781
Samuel Hallifax	nom. 1 Sept., cons. 28 Oct. 1781	trs. St Asaph 25 Apr. 1789
Richard Beadon	nom. 6 May, cons. 7 June 1789	trs. Bath 2 June 1802
George Isaac Huntingford	nom. 14 May, cons. 27 June 1802	trs. Hereford 5 July 1815
Henry Ryder	nom. 10 July, cons. 30 July 1815	trs. Lichfield 10 Mar. 1824
Christopher Bethell	nom. 11 Mar., cons. 11 Apr. 1824	trs. Exeter 11 June 1830
James Henry Monk[1]	nom. 11 June, cons. 11 July 1830	6 June 1856
Charles Baring	nom. 17 July, cons. 10 Aug. 1856	trs. Durham 6 Nov. 1861
William Thomson	nom. 25 Nov., cons. 15 Dec. 1861	trs. York 23 Jan. 1863
Charles John Ellicott	nom. 6 Feb., cons. 25 Mar. 1863	res. Gloucester 27 Feb. 1905, d. 15 Oct. 1905
Edgar Charles Sumner Gibson	nom. 10 Mar., cons. 1 June 1905	res. 1 Jan. 1923, d. 9 Mar. 1924
Arthur Cayley Headlam	nom. 2 Jan., cons. 25 Jan. 1923	res. 1 Oct. 1945, d. 17 Jan. 1947
Clifford Salisbury Woodward	trs. Bristol, nom. 22 Jan., conf. 25 Feb. 1946	res. 1 Oct. 1953, d. 14 Apr. 1959
Wilfred Marcus Askwith	trs. Blackburn, nom. 4 May, conf. 7 July 1954	16 July 1962
Basil Tudor Guy	trs. Bedford (suff.), nom. 23 Nov., conf. 18 Dec. 1962	2 Mar. 1975
John Yates	trs. Whitby (suff.), nom. 7 Aug., conf. 30 Oct. 1975	

[1] By Order in Council dated 5 Oct. 1836 the see of Bristol was joined to that of Gloucester and thenceforward the bishop was styled 'of Gloucester and Bristol' until 1897, when the sees were again divided.

GUILDFORD

BISHOPS	ACCESSION	DEATH *unless otherwise stated*
John Harold Greig	trs. Gibraltar, nom. 1 June, cons. 28 June 1927	res. 1934, d. 28 Mar. 1938
John Victor Macmillan	trs. Dover (suff.), nom. 19 Oct., conf. 22 Nov. 1934	res. 15 Oct. 1949, d. 15 Aug. 1956
Henry Colville Montgomery Campbell	trs. Kensington (suff.), nom. 21 Oct., conf. 23 Nov. 1949	trs. London 25 Jan. 1956
Ivor Stanley Watkins	trs. Malmesbury (suff.), nom. 25 May, conf. 11 July 1956	24 Oct. 1960
George Edmund Reindorp	nom. 20 Jan., cons. 25 Mar. 1961	trs. Salisbury 15 Jan. 1973
David Alan Brown	nom. 23 July, cons. 1 Nov. 1973	13 July 1982
Michael Edgar Adie	nom. 5 May, cons. 30 June 1983	

HEREFORD

Walter	cons. 15 Apr. 1061	1079
Robert of Lorraine	cons. 29 Dec. 1079	26 June 1095
Gerard	cons. 15 June 1096	trs. York Apr. 1100
Reinhelm	nom. 29 Sept. 1102, cons. 11 Aug. 1107	27 or 28 Oct. 1115
Geoffrey	cons. 26 Dec., temp. Nov. × Dec. 1115	2 Feb. 1119
Richard de Capella	el. 7 Jan., cons. 16 Jan. 1121	15 Aug. 1127
Robert de Bethune	cons. 28 June 1131	16 Apr. 1148
Gilbert Foliot	cons. 5 Sept. 1148	trs. London 6 Mar. 1163
Robert de Melun	cons. 22 Dec. 1163	27 Feb. 1167
Robert Foliot	el. late Apr. 1173, cons. 6 Oct. 1174	9 May 1186
William de Vere	el. *c.* 25 May, cons. 10 Aug. 1186	24 Dec. 1198
Giles de Braose	el. *a.* 19 Sept., cons. 24 Sept. 1200	*a.* 18 Nov. 1215
Hugh de Mapenore	el. 3 Feb., temp. 9 Dec., cons. 18 Dec. 1216	*16* Apr. 1219
Hugh Foliot	el. June, temp. 2 July, cons. 27 Oct. 1219	7 Aug. 1234
Ralph Maidstone	el. 21 Aug.–30 Sept., cons. 12 Nov. 1234	res. 17 Dec. 1239, d. 27 Jan. 1245
Peter D'Aigueblanche	el. 24 Aug., temp. 6 Sept., cons. 23 Dec. 1240	27 Nov. 1268
John Breton	el. *c.* 6 Jan. 1269, temp. 20 Apr., cons. 2 June 1269	12 May 1275
Thomas Cantilupe	el. *14* June, temp. 26 June, cons. 8 Sept. 1275	25 Aug. 1282
Richard Swinfield	el. 1 Oct. 1282, temp. 8 Jan., cons. 7 Mar. 1283	15 Mar. 1317
Adam Orleton	prov. 15 May, cons. 22 May, temp. 24 July 1317	trs. Worcester 25 Sept. 1327
Thomas Charlton	prov. 25 Sept., cons. 18 Oct., temp. 21 Dec. 1327	11 Jan. 1344
John Trilleck	el. 22 Feb., temp. 29 Mar., cons. 29 Aug. 1344	20 Nov. 1360
Lewis Charlton	prov. 10 Sept., cons. 3 Oct., temp. 14 Nov. 1361	23 May 1369
William Courtenay	prov. 17 Aug. 1369, cons. 17 Mar., temp. 19 Mar. 1370	trs. London 12 Sept. 1375

BISHOPS	ACCESSION	DEATH *unless otherwise stated*
John Gilbert	trs. Bangor, prov. 12 Sept., temp. 4 Dec. 1375	trs. St David's 5 May 1389
John Trefnant	prov. 5 May, cons. 20 June, temp. 16 Oct. 1389	29 Mar. 1404
Robert Mascall	prov. 2 July, cons. 6 July, temp. 25 Sept. 1404	22 Dec. 1416
Edmund Lacy	el. 21 Jan. × 17 Feb., cons. 18 Apr., temp. 1 May 1417	trs. Exeter 15 July 1420
Thomas Polton	prov. 15 July, cons. 21 July, temp. 9 Nov. 1420	trs. Chichester 17 Nov. 1421
Thomas Spofford	prov. 18 Nov. 1421, cons. 24 May, temp. 25 May 1422	res. *a.* 4 Dec. 1448
Richard Beauchamp	prov. 4 Dec. 1448, temp. 31 Jan., cons. 9 Feb. 1449	trs. Salisbury 14 Aug. 1450
Reginald Boulers	prov. 18 Sept., temp. 23 Dec. 1450, cons. 14 Feb. 1451	trs. Coventry 7 Feb. 1453
John Stanbury	trs. Bangor, prov. 7 Feb., temp. 26 Mar. 1453	11 May 1474
Thomas Milling	prov. 22 June, temp. 15 Aug., cons. 21 Aug. 1474	*a.* 12 Jan. 1492
Edmund Audley	trs. Rochester, prov. 22 June, temp. 26 Dec. 1492	trs. Salisbury 10 Jan. 1502
Adriano de Castello	prov. 14 Feb., cons. *a.* May, temp. *a.* 8 Aug. 1502	trs. Bath 4 Aug. 1504
Richard Mayeu	prov. 9 Aug., cons. 27 Oct., temp. 1 Nov. 1504	18 Apr. 1516
Charles Booth	prov. 21 July, cons. 30 Nov. 1516, temp. 19 Feb. 1517	5 May 1535
Edward Fox	nom. 20 Aug., el. 25 Aug., cons. 26 Sept. 1535	8 May 1538
[Edmund Bonner	nom. 5 Oct., el. 26 Oct., conf. 17 Dec. 1538	trs. London 1539]
John Skip or Skyppe	nom. 13 Oct., el. 24 Oct., cons. 23 Nov. 1539	30 Mar. 1552
John Harley	nom. 26 Mar.,[1] cons. 26 May 1553	depr. 15 Mar. 1554
Robert Parfew or Parfoye or Wharton	trs. St Asaph, nom. 17 Mar., conf. 6 July,[2] temp. 24 Apr. 1554	22 Sept. 1557
[Thomas Reynolds	nom. *a.* 7 Nov. 1558	depr. 1559]
John Scory	formerly Chichester, el. 15 July, conf. 20 Dec. 1559	25 June 1585
Herbert Westfaling	nom. 17 Nov. 1585, cons. 30 Jan. 1586	1 Mar. 1602
Robert Bennett	nom. 7 Jan., cons. 20 Feb. 1603	20 Oct. 1617
Francis Godwin	trs. Llandaff, nom. 10 Nov., conf. 28 Nov. 1617	*a.* 29 Apr. 1633
[William Juxon	nom. 23 Sept., el. *a.* 3 Oct. 1633	trs. London 23 Oct. 1633]
Augustine Lindsell	trs. Peterborough, el. 7 Mar., conf. 24 Mar. 1634	6 Nov. 1634
Matthew Wren	nom. 23 Nov. 1634, cons. 8 Mar. 1635	trs. Norwich 5 Dec. 1635
Theophilus Field	trs. St David's, nom. 7 Dec., conf. 23 Dec. 1635	2 June 1636
George Coke	trs. Bristol, nom. 13 June, conf. 2 July 1636	10 Dec. 1646

[1] The date of the warrant for letters patent (*Cal. Pat. Rolls, Edward VI*, v. 3), but his appointment is mentioned as early as 11 Dec. 1552 (*Cal. State Papers, Dom.*, i. 49).

[2] For Parfew's appointment *cf.* W. M. Brady, *Episcopal Succession*, i. 54–59.

BISHOPS	ACCESSION	DEATH *unless otherwise stated*
Nicholas Monk	nom. 29 Nov. 1660, cons. 6 Jan. 1661	17 Dec. 1661
Herbert Croft	el. 21 Jan., cons. 9 Feb. 1662	18 May 1691
Gilbert Ironside	trs. Bristol, nom. 22 Apr., conf. 29 July 1691	27 Aug. 1701
Humphrey Humphries	trs. Bangor, nom. 1 Oct., conf. 2 Dec. 1701	20 Nov. 1712
Philip Bisse	trs. St David's, nom. 26 Jan., conf. 16 Feb. 1713	6 Sept. 1721
Benjamin Hoadly	trs. Bangor, nom. 21 Sept., conf. 7 Nov. 1721	trs. Salisbury 29 Oct. 1723
Henry Egerton	nom. 27 Aug. 1723, cons. 2 Feb. 1724	1 Apr. 1746
James Beauclerk	nom. 8 Apr., cons. 11 May 1746	20 Oct. 1787
John Harley	nom. 29 Oct., cons. 9 Dec. 1787	9 Jan. 1788
John Butler	trs. Oxford, nom. 23 Jan., conf. 28 Feb. 1788	10 Dec. 1802
Ffoliot Herbert Walker Cornewall	trs. Bristol, nom. 18 Dec. 1802, conf. 28 Jan. 1803	trs. Worcester 13 July 1808
John Luxmoore	trs. Bristol, nom. 13 July, conf. 23 Aug. 1808	trs. St Asaph 20 June 1815
George Isaac Huntingford	trs. Gloucester, nom. 21 June, conf. 5 July 1815	29 Apr. 1832
Edward Grey	nom. 4 May, cons. 20 May 1832	24 June 1837
Thomas Musgrave	nom. 5 Aug., cons. 1 Oct. 1837	trs. York 10 Dec. 1847
Renn Dickson Hampden	nom. 11 Dec. 1847, conf. 11 Jan., cons. 26 Mar. 1848	23 Apr. 1868
James Atlay	nom. 21 May, cons. 24 June 1868	24 Dec. 1894
John Percival	nom. 20 Feb., cons. 25 Mar. 1895	res. 31 Oct. 1917, d. 3 Dec. 1918
Herbert Hensley Henson	nom. 20 Dec. 1917, cons. 2 Feb. 1918	trs. Durham 27 July 1920
Martin Linton Smith	trs. Warrington (suff.), nom. 29 July, conf. 5 Oct. 1920	trs. Rochester 5 Nov. 1930
Charles Lisle Carr	trs. Coventry, nom. 17 Nov. 1930, conf. 20 Jan. 1931	res. 30 Sept. 1941, d. 2 Feb. 1942
Richard Godfrey Parsons	trs. Southwark, nom. 1 Oct., conf. 12 Nov. 1941	26 Dec. 1948
Tom Longworth	trs. Pontefract (suff.), nom. 25 Mar., conf. 21 Apr. 1949	res. 15 Nov. 1961, d. 15 Oct. 1977
Mark Allin Hodson	trs. Taunton (suff.), nom. 21 Nov., conf. 20 Dec. 1961	res. 25 Nov. 1973
John Richard Gordon Easthaugh	nom. 5 Dec. 1973, cons. 24 Jan. 1974	

LEICESTER

Cyril Charles Bowman Bardsley	trs. Peterborough, nom. 15 Dec. 1926, conf. 15 Feb. 1927	res. 12 Apr. 1940, d. 20 Dec. 1940
Guy Vernon Smith	trs. Willesden (suff.), nom. 14 May, conf. 19 June 1940	res. 1 Sept. 1953, d. 11 June 1957
Ronald Ralph Williams	nom. 6 Oct., cons. 28 Oct. 1953	res. 31 Dec. 1978, d. 13 Feb. 1979
Cecil Richard Rutt	trs. St Germans (suff.), nom. 22 Jan., conf. 27 Feb. 1979	

LICHFIELD, CHESTER, AND COVENTRY[1]
LICHFIELD

BISHOPS	ACCESSION	DEATH *unless otherwise stated*
Leofwine	cons. 1053	1067
Peter	cons. *p.* 29 Aug. 1072	1085

(Peter transferred his see to Chester, 1075)

CHESTER

Robert de Limesey	nom. 25 Dec. 1085, cons. 1086	1 Sept. 1117

(Robert de Limesey transferred his see to Coventry, 1102)

COVENTRY

Robert Peche	el. *c.* Jan., cons. 13 Mar. 1121	22 Aug. 1126
Roger de Clinton	nom. Oct., cons. 22 Dec. 1129	16 Apr. 1148
Walter Durdent	cons. 2 Oct. 1149	7 Dec. 1159
Richard Peche	cons. *a.* 18 Apr. 1161	res. 1182, d. 6 Oct. 1182
Gerard Pucelle	el. Jan., cons. 25 Sept. 1183	13 Jan. 1184
Hugh de Nonant	el. *Jan.* 1185, cons. 31 Jan. 1188	27 Mar. 1198
Geoffrey Muschamp	cons. 21 June 1198	6 Oct. 1208
William Cornhill	el. *a.* 9 July, temp. 20 Oct. 1214, cons. 25 Jan. 1215	res. *1223*, d. 19–20 Aug. 1223
Alexander Stavensby	prov. *a.* 13 Apr., cons. 14 Apr., temp. 20 May 1224	26 Dec. 1238

(Coventry and Lichfield were both recognized as the bishop's sees in 1228)

COVENTRY AND LICHFIELD

Hugh Pattishall	el. 1239, temp. 1 Jan., cons. 1 July 1240	7 or 8 Dec. 1241
Roger Weseham	prov. and cons. 17 May × 4 July 1245, temp. 25 Mar. 1246	res. Nov. or Dec. 1256, d. *c.* 20 May 1257
Roger Longespee (Meuland)	el. 31 Jan., temp. 17 Feb. 1257, cons. 10 Mar. 1258	16 Dec. 1295
Walter Langton	el. 19 Feb., temp. 16 June, cons. 23 Dec. 1296	9 Nov. 1321
Roger Northburgh	prov. 14 Dec. 1321, temp. 12 Apr., cons. 27 June 1322	22 Nov. 1358
Robert Stretton	el. Dec. 1358, prov. 22 Apr., temp. 19 Sept., cons. 27 Sept. 1360	28 Mar. 1385
Walter Skirlaw	prov. 28 June 1385, temp. 6 Jan., cons. 14 Jan. 1386	trs. Bath 18 Aug. 1386
Richard Le Scrope	prov. 18 Aug., cons. 19 Aug., temp. 15 Nov. 1386	trs. York 27 Feb. × 15 Mar. 1398
John Burghill	trs. Llandaff, prov. 2 July, temp. 16 Sept. 1398	*a.* 27 May 1414

[1] The earliest see was Lichfield (see above pp. 218–19). Chester became the bp's see in 1075, Coventry in 1102. From 1075 the bp styled himself 'bp of Chester' and the title remained in official use during the early twelfth century and unofficially much later. The official title was 'bp of Coventry' from the middle of the twelfth century (despite the continuing claim of Lichfield to be a see) until 1228: from this time 'Coventry and Lichfield' was the usual title until the Reformation. After the Reformation 'Lichfield and Coventry' was the title (although there was no see at Coventry) until 1836 when the title became 'Lichfield'. Meanwhile, Chester became the see of a separate bishopric in 1541; and Coventry became a see of another bishopric in 1918. For the bps of these detached dioceses, *see under* Chester and Coventry.

BISHOPS	ACCESSION	DEATH *unless otherwise stated*
John Catterick	trs. St David's, prov. 1 Feb., temp. 15 May 1415	trs. Exeter 20 Nov. 1419
William Heyworth	prov. 20 Nov. 1419, temp. 15 Apr., cons. 28 July 1420	15 × 24 Mar. 1447
William Booth	prov. 26 Apr., temp. 3 June, cons. 9 July 1447	trs. York 21 July 1452
Nicholas Close	trs. Carlisle, prov. 30 Aug., temp. 6 Sept. 1452	a. 31 Oct. 1452
Reginald Boulers	trs. Hereford, prov. 7 Feb., temp. 26 Mar. 1453	23 Mar. × 10 Apr. 1459
John Hales	prov. 20 Sept., temp. 31 Oct., cons. 25 Nov. 1459	15 × 30 Sept. 1490
William Smith	prov. 1 Oct., el. 24 Nov. 1492, temp. 29 Jan., cons. 3 Feb. 1493	trs. Lincoln 30 Jan. 1496
John Arundel	prov. 3 Aug., cons. 6 Nov., temp. 30 Nov. 1496	trs. Exeter 8 Apr. 1502
Geoffrey Blyth	prov. 5 May, cons. 17 Sept., temp. 26 Sept. 1503	a. 1 Mar. 1531
Rowland Lee	el. 10 Jan., cons. 19 Apr. 1534	25 Jan. 1543
Richard Sampson	trs. Chichester, el. 19 Feb., conf. 9 Mar. 1543	25 Sept. 1554
Ralph Baynes	nom. 25 Oct., cons. 18 Nov. 1554	depr. 26 June 1559, d. 18 Nov. 1559
Thomas Bentham	nom. 27 Dec. 1559, cons. 24 Mar. 1560	21 Feb. 1579
William Overton	nom. 9 Aug., cons. 18 Sept. 1580	9 Apr. 1609
George Abbot	el. 27 May, cons. 3 Dec. 1609	trs. London 1610
Richard Neile	trs. Rochester, el. 12 Oct., conf. 6 Dec. 1610	trs. Lincoln 18 Feb. 1614
John Overall	el. 14 Mar., cons. 3 Apr. 1614	trs. Norwich 30 Sept. 1618
Thomas Morton	trs. Chester, el. a. 16 Feb., conf. 6 Mar. 1619	trs. Durham 2 July 1632
Robert Wright	trs. Bristol, el. 30 Oct., conf. 28 Nov. 1632	Aug. 1643
Accepted Frewen	nom. 17 Aug. 1643, cons. 28 Apr. 1644	trs. York 4 Oct. 1660
John Hacket	nom. 4 Nov., cons. 22 Dec. 1661	28 Oct. 1670
Thomas Wood	el. 9 June, cons. 2 July 1671	18 Apr. 1692
William Lloyd	trs. St Asaph, nom. 19 July, conf. 20 Oct. 1692	trs. Worcester 22 June 1699
John Hough	trs. Oxford, nom. 31 May, conf. 5 Aug. 1699	trs. Worcester 28 Sept. 1717
Edward Chandler	nom. 30 Sept., cons. 17 Nov. 1717	trs. Durham 21 Nov. 1730
Richard Smalbroke	trs. St David's, nom. 28 Dec. 1730, conf. 20 Feb. 1731	22 Dec. 1749
Frederick Cornwallis	nom. 18 Jan., cons. 18 Feb. 1750	trs. Canterbury 30 Sept. 1768
John Egerton	trs. Bangor, nom. 15 Oct., conf. 12 nov. 1768	trs. Durham 20 July 1771
Brownlow North	nom. 3 Aug., cons. 8 Sept. 1771	trs. Worcester 30 Dec. 1774
Richard Hurd	nom. 30 Dec. 1774, cons. 12 Feb. 1775	trs. Worcester 30 June 1781
James Cornwallis (4th Earl Cornwallis 1823)	nom. 11 July, cons. 16 Sept. 1781	20 Jan. 1824
Henry Ryder	trs. Gloucester, nom. 4 Feb., conf. 10 Mar. 1824	31 Mar. 1836

LICHFIELD

BISHOPS	ACCESSION	DEATH *unless otherwise stated*
Samuel Butler[1]	nom. 15 June, cons. 3 July 1836	4 Dec. 1839
James Bowstead	trs. Sodor and Man, nom. 28 Dec. 1839, conf. 23 Jan. 1840	11 Oct. 1843
John Lonsdale	nom. 3 Nov., cons. 3 Dec. 1843	19 Oct. 1867
George Augustus Selwyn	trs. New Zealand, nom. 14 Dec. 1867, conf. 4 Jan. 1868	11 Apr. 1878
William Dalrymple Maclagan	nom. 18 May, cons. 24 June 1878	trs. York 28 July 1891
Augustus Legge	nom. 4 Aug., cons. 29 Sept. 1891	15 Mar. 1913
John Augustine Kempthorne	trs. Hull (suff.), nom. 14 May, conf. 13 June 1913	res. 15 June 1937, d. 24 Feb. 1946
Edward Sydney Woods	trs. Croydon (suff.), nom. 28 June, conf. 29 July 1937	11 Jan. 1953
Arthur Stretton Reeve	nom. 30 June, cons. 29 Sept. 1953	res. 1 Dec. 1974, d. 27 Jan. 1981
Kenneth John Fraser Skelton	nom. 4 Dec. 1974, conf. 2 Jan. 1975	res. 29 Feb. 1984
Keith Norman Sutton	trs. Kingston-upon-Thames (suff.), nom. 20 July, conf. 12 Oct. 1984	

LINCOLN

Remigius	cons. ? 1067	8 May 1092

(Remigius transferred his see from Dorchester to Lincoln, 1072)

Robert Bloet	nom. Mar. 1093, cons. *a.* 22 Feb. 1094	10 Jan. 1123
Alexander	nom. Apr., cons. 22 July 1123	*20* Feb. 1148
Robert de Chesney	el. 13 Dec., cons. 19 Dec. 1148	*27* Dec. 1166
Geoffrey	el. *c.* May 1173, conf. *a.* July 1175	res. 6 Jan. 1182
Walter of Coutances	el. 8 May, cons. 3 July 1183	trs. Rouen summer, conf. 17 Nov. 1184
Hugh of Avallon	el. 25 May, cons. 21 Sept. 1186	16 Nov. 1200
William of Blois	el. *a.* 6 July, temp. ?6 July, cons. 24 Aug. 1203	10 May 1206
Hugh of Wells	el. *a.* 14 Apr., cons. 20 Dec. 1209, temp. 20 July 1213	7 Feb. 1235
Robert Grosseteste	el. 25 Mar., temp. 16 Apr., cons. 17 June 1235	Oct. 1253, *a.* 9
Henry Lexington	el. 21 or 30 Dec. 1253, temp. 1 Apr., cons. 17 May 1254	8 Aug. 1258
Richard Gravesend	el. 21 or 23 Sept., temp. 17 Oct., cons. 3 Nov. 1258	18 Dec. 1279
Oliver Sutton	el. 6 Feb., cons. 19 May 1280	13 Nov. 1299
John Dalderby	el. 15 Jan., temp. 18 Mar., cons. 12 June 1300	12 Jan. 1320
[Anthony Bek	el. 3 Feb. 1320	qua. 1320]
Henry Burghersh	prov. 27 May, cons. 20 July, temp. 5 Aug. 1320	*a.* 27 Dec. 1340
Thomas Bek	el. *a.* 1 Mar. 1341, prov. 26 June, cons. 7 July, temp. 17 Sept. 1342	2 Feb. 1347
John Gynwell	prov. 23 Mar., temp. 2 June, cons. 23 Sept. 1347	5 Aug. 1362

[1] Consecrated as 'Bp of Lichfield and Coventry', he later had the style of 'Bp of Lichfield'.

BISHOPS	ACCESSION	DEATH *unless otherwise stated*
John Buckingham (Bokyngham)	el. 20 Aug. × 4 Oct. 1362, prov. 5 Apr., temp. 23 June, cons. 25 June 1363	res. Mar × July 1398, d. 10 Mar. 1399
Henry Beaufort	prov. 27 Feb., cons. 14 July, temp. 19 July 1398	trs. Winchester 19 Nov. 1404
Philip Repingdon	prov. 19 Nov. 1404, temp. 28 Mar., cons. 29 Mar. 1405	res. 21 Nov. 1419
Richard Fleming	prov. 20 Nov. 1419, cons. 28 Apr., temp. 23 May 1420	25 Jan. 1431
William Gray	trs. London, prov. 30 Apr., temp. 4 Aug. 1431	10 × 18 Feb. 1436
William Alnwick	trs. Norwich, post *a.* 23 May, prov. 19 Sept. 1436, temp. 16 Feb. 1437	5 Dec. 1449
Marmaduke Lumley	trs. Carlisle, prov. 28 Jan., temp. 14 Mar. 1450	*a.* 1 Dec. 1450
John Chedworth	el. *a.* 11 Feb. 1451, prov. 5 May, temp. 2 June, cons. 18 June 1452	23 Nov. 1471
Thomas Rotherham or Scot	trs. Rochester, prov. 8 Jan., temp. 10 Mar. 1472	trs. York 7 July 1480
John Russell	trs. Rochester, prov. 7 July, temp. 9 Sept. 1480	30 Dec. 1494
William Smith	trs. Lichfield, prov. 6 Nov. 1495, temp. 6 Feb. 1496	2 Jan. 1514
Thomas Wolsey	prov. 6 Feb., temp. 4 Mar., cons. 26 Mar. 1514	trs. York 15 Sept. 1514
William Atwater	prov. 15 Sept., temp. 6 Nov., cons. 12 Nov. 1514	4 Feb. 1521
John Longland	prov. 20 Mar., cons. 5 May 1521	7 May 1547
Henry Holbeach or Rands	trs. Rochester, nom. 1 Aug., conf. 20 Aug. 1547	6 Aug. 1551
John Taylor	nom. 18 June, cons. 26 June 1552	depr. 15 Mar. 1554, d. Dec. 1554
John White	nom. *a.* 1 Apr., cons. 1 Apr. 1554	trs. Winchester 6 July 1556[1]
Thomas Watson	nom. 7 Dec. 1556, prov. 24 Mar., cons. 15 Aug. 1557	depr. 26 June 1559, d. Sept. 1584
Nicholas Bullingham	nom. 25 Nov. 1559, cons. 21 Jan. 1560	trs. Worcester 26 Jan. 1571
Thomas Cooper	nom. 15 Jan., cons. 24 Feb. 1571	trs. Winchester 23 Mar. 1584
William Wickham	nom. 24 Oct., cons. 6 Dec. 1584	trs. Winchester 22 Feb. 1595
William Chaderton	trs. Chester, nom. *a.* 28 Mar., conf. 24 May 1595	11 Apr. 1608
William Barlow	trs. Rochester, el. 21 May, conf. 27 June 1608	7 Sept. 1613
Richard Neile	trs. Lichfield, el. 17 Jan., conf. 18 Feb. 1614	trs. Durham 9 Oct. 1617
George Montaigne or Mountain	el. 21 Oct., cons. 14 Dec. 1617	trs. London 20 July 1621
John Williams	el. 3 Aug., cons. 11 Nov. 1621	trs. York Dec. 1641
Thomas Winniffe	nom. 17 Dec. 1641, cons. 6 Feb. 1642	19 Sept. 1654
Robert Sanderson	nom. 3 Oct., cons. 28 Oct. 1660	29 Jan. 1663
Benjamin Laney	trs. Peterborough, nom. 20 Feb., conf. 2 Apr. 1663	trs. Ely 12 June 1667

[1] The date of provision by the pope: but he had been nominated to the see, and may have been elected and confirmed, a few weeks earlier.

BISHOPS	ACCESSION	DEATH
		unless otherwise stated
William Fuller	trs. Limerick, nom. 5 Sept., conf. 27 Sept. 1667	22 Apr. 1675
Thomas Barlow	nom. 1 May, cons. 27 June 1675	8 Oct. 1691
Thomas Tenison	nom. 27 Oct. 1691, cons. 10 Jan. 1692	trs. Canterbury 16 Jan. 1695
James Gardiner	nom. 18 Jan., cons. 10 Mar. 1695	1 Mar. 1705
William Wake	nom. 16 July, cons. 21 Oct. 1705	trs. Canterbury 16 Jan. 1716
Edmund Gibson	nom. 17 Dec. 1715, cons. 12 Feb. 1716	trs. London 4 May 1723
Richard Reynolds	trs. Bangor, nom. 16 May, conf. 10 June 1723	15 Jan. 1744
John Thomas	elect of St Asaph, nom. 20 Jan., cons. 1 Apr. 1744	trs. Salisbury 25 Nov. 1761
John Green	nom. 28 Nov., cons. 28 Dec. 1761	25 Apr. 1779
Thomas Thurlow	nom. 5 May, cons. 30 May 1779	trs. Durham 19 Feb. 1787
George Pretyman (after June 1803, Pretyman-Tomline)	nom. 19 Feb., cons. 11 Mar. 1787	trs. Winchester 18 Aug. 1820
George Pelham	trs. Exeter, nom. 18 Aug., conf. 16 Oct. 1820	7 Feb. 1827
John Kaye	trs. Bristol, nom. 12 Feb., conf. 1 Mar. 1827	19 Feb. 1853
John Jackson	nom. 18 Mar., cons. 5 May 1853	trs. London 1869
Christopher Wordsworth	nom. 9 Feb., cons. 24 Feb. 1869	res. Feb. 1885, d. 20 Mar. 1885
Edward King	nom. 5 Mar., cons. 25 Apr. 1885	8 Mar. 1910
Edward Lee Hicks	nom. 28 Apr., cons. 24 June 1910	14 Aug. 1919
William Shuckburgh Swayne	nom. 26 Nov. 1919, cons. 6 Jan. 1920	res. 14 Nov. 1932 d. 30 June 1941
Frederick Cyril Nugent Hicks	trs. Gibraltar, nom. 12 Dec. 1932, conf. 15 Feb. 1933	10 Feb. 1942
Henry Aylmer Skelton	trs. Bedford (suff.), nom. 27 July, conf. 27 Aug. 1942	res. 1 May 1946, d. 30 Aug. 1959
Leslie Owen	trs. Maidstone (suff.), nom. 12 June, conf. 17 July 1946	2 Mar. 1947
Maurice Henry Harland	trs. Croydon (suff.), nom. 22 May, conf. 11 July 1947	trs. Durham 7 July 1956
Kenneth Riches	trs. Dorchester (suff.), nom. 24 Aug., conf. 26 Sept. 1956	res. 30 Sept. 1974
Simon Wilton Phipps	trs. Horsham (suff.), nom. 7 Oct. 1974, conf. 2 Jan. 1975	

LIVERPOOL

John Charles Ryle	nom. 11 May, cons. 11 June 1880	res. 1 Mar. 1900, d. 10 June 1900
Francis James Chavasse	nom. 24 Mar., cons. 25 Apr. 1900	res. 1 Oct. 1923, d. 11 Mar. 1928
Albert Augustus David	trs. St Edmundsbury, nom. 3 Oct., conf. 18 Oct. 1923	res. 15 Apr. 1944, d. 24 Dec. 1950
Clifford Arthur Martin	nom. 3 July, cons. 25 July 1944	res. 30 Nov. 1965, d. 11 Aug. 1977
Stuart Yarworth Blanch	nom. 22 Dec. 1965, cons. 25 Mar. 1966	trs. York 9 Jan. 1975
David Stuart Sheppard	trs. Woolwich (suff.), nom. 2 May, conf. 3 June 1975	

LONDON

BISHOPS	ACCESSION	DEATH
		unless otherwise stated
William	cons. 1051	1075
Hugh D'Orival	el. *p.* 29 Aug. 1075	12 Jan. 1085
Maurice	nom. 25 Dec. 1085, cons. *5 Apr.* 1086	26 Sept. 1107
Richard de Belmeis I	el. 24 May, temp. 24 May, cons. 26 July 1108	16 Jan. 1127
Gilbert the Universal	el. *Dec.* 1127, cons. 22 Jan. 1128	9 Aug. 1134
[Anselm	el. *22* Mar. 1136	qua. 1138]
Robert de Sigillo	nom. and cons. *July 1141*	29 Sept. 1150
Richard de Belmeis II	cons. 28 Sept. 1152	4 May 1162
Gilbert Foliot	trs. Hereford 6 Mar. 1163	18 Feb. 1187
Richard FitzNeal	nom. 15 Sept., cons. 31 Dec. 1189	10 Sept. 1198
William of Sainte-Mère-Église	el. *p.* 7 Dec. 1198, cons. 23 May 1199	res. 25 or 26 Jan. 1221, d. 27 Mar. 1224
Eustace of Fauconberg	el. 26 Feb., temp. 23 Mar., cons. 25 Apr. 1221	24 × 31 Oct. 1228
Roger Niger	el. 1228, temp. 27 Apr., cons. 10 June 1229	29 Sept. 1241
Fulk Basset	el. *Dec.* 1241, temp. 16 Mar., cons. 9 Oct. 1244	21 May 1259
Henry of Wingham	el. *a.* 29 June, temp. 11 July 1259, cons. 15 Feb. 1260	13 July 1262
[Richard Talbot	el. 18 Aug. 1262	28 Sept. 1262]
Henry of Sandwich	el. 13 Nov. 1262, temp. 15 Jan., cons. 27 May 1263	15 Sept. 1273
John Chishull	el. 7 Dec. 1273, temp. 15 Mar., cons. 29 Apr. 1274	7 Feb. 1280
[Fulk Lovel	el. *p.* 18 Feb. 1280	res. *a.* 8 Apr. 1280]
Richard Gravesend	el. *a.* 7 May, temp. 17 May, cons. 11 Aug. 1280	9 Dec. 1303
Ralph Baldock	el. 24 Feb., temp. 1 June 1304, cons. 30 Jan. 1306	24 July 1313
Gilbert Segrave	el. 17 Aug., temp. 28 Sept., cons. 25 Nov. 1313	18 Dec. 1316
Richard Newport	el. 27 Jan., temp. 31 Mar., cons. 15 May 1317	24 Aug. 1318
Stephen Gravesend	el. 1 Sept., temp. 6 Nov. 1318, cons. 14 Jan. 1319	8 Apr. 1338
Richard Bintworth	el. 4 May, temp. 24 May, cons. 12 July 1338	8 Dec. 1339
Ralph Stratford	el. 26 Jan., temp. 13 Feb., cons. 12 Mar. 1340	17 Apr. 1354
Michael Northburgh	el. 22 Apr., prov. 7 May, temp. 23 June 1354, cons. 12 July 1355	9 Sept. 1361
Simon Sudbury	prov. 22 Oct. 1361, cons. 20 Mar., temp. 15 May 1362	trs. Canterbury 4 May 1375
William Courtenay	trs. Hereford, prov. 12 Sept., temp. 2 Dec. 1375	trs. Canterbury 9 Sept. 1381
Robert Braybrooke	prov. 9 Sept., temp. 27 Dec. 1381, cons. 5 Jan. 1382	28 Aug. 1404
Roger Walden	(abp of Canterbury 1397–99) prov. 10 Dec. 1404, temp. 28 July 1405	6 Jan. 1406
Nicholas Bubwith	prov. 14 May, cons. 26 Sept., temp. 27 Sept. 1406	trs. Salisbury 22 June 1407
Richard Clifford	trs. Worcester, prov. 22 June, temp. 20 Oct. 1407	20 Aug. 1421

BISHOPS	ACCESSION	DEATH *unless otherwise stated*
John Kempe	trs. Chichester, prov. 17 Nov. 1421, temp. 20 June 1422	trs. York 20 July 1425
William Gray	prov. 20 July 1425, el. 8 Apr., temp. 6 May, cons. *26* May 1426	trs. Lincoln 30 Apr. 1431
Robert FitzHugh	prov. 20 Apr., temp. 4 Aug., cons. 16 Sept. 1431	15 Jan. 1436
Robert Gilbert	el. 23 Feb., prov. 21 May, temp. 15 Sept., cons. 28 Oct. 1436	*a.* 27 July 1448
Thomas Kempe	prov. 21 Aug. 1448, temp. 6 Feb., cons. 8 Feb. 1450	28 Mar. 1489
Richard Hill	prov. 21 Aug., temp. 6 Nov., cons. 15 Nov. 1489	20 Feb. 1496
Thomas Savage	trs. Rochester, prov. 3 Aug., temp. 2 Dec. 1496	trs. York *a.* 12 Apr. 1501
William Warham	prov. 20 Oct. 1501, cons. 25 Sept., temp. 1 Oct. 1502	trs. Canterbury 29 Nov. 1503
William Barons	el. *a.* Aug., prov. 2 Aug., temp. 13 Nov., cons. 26 Nov. 1504	10 Oct. 1505
Richard FitzJames	trs. Chichester, nom. 24 Mar., prov. 5 June, temp. 1 Aug. 1506	*a.* 17 Jan. 1522
Cuthbert Tunstall	nom. Jan., prov. 16 May and 10 Sept., temp. 7 Oct., cons. 19 Oct. 1522	trs. Durham 21 Feb. 1530
John Stokesley	prov. 28 Mar., temp. 14 July, cons. 27 Nov. 1530	8 Sept. 1539
Edmund Bonner	elect of Hereford, el. 20 Oct. 1539, cons. 4 Apr. 1540	depr. 1 Oct. 1549
Nicholas Ridley	trs. Rochester, nom. 1 Apr. 1550	depr. July 1553, d. 16 Oct. 1555
Edmund Bonner	restored 5 Sept. 1553	depr. 29 May 1559, d. 5 Sept. 1569
Edmund Grindal	nom. 22 June, cons. 21 Dec. 1559	trs. York 22 May 1570
Edwin Sandes or Sandys	trs. Worcester, nom. 1 June, conf. 13 July 1570	trs. York 8 Mar. 1577
John Aylmer	nom. 23 Feb., cons. 24 Mar. 1577	5 June 1594
Richard Fletcher	trs. Worcester, nom. 26 Dec. 1594, conf. 10 Jan. 1595	15 June 1596
Richard Bancroft	el. 21 Apr., cons. 8 May 1597	trs. Canterbury 10 Dec. 1604
Richard Vaughan	trs. Chester, nom. 8 Dec., conf. 20 Dec. 1604	30 Mar. 1607
Thomas Ravis	trs. Gloucester, nom. *a.* 14 Apr., conf. 18 May 1607	14 Dec. 1609
George Abbot	trs. Lichfield, nom. 24 Dec. 1609, conf. 20 Jan. 1610	trs. Canterbury 9 Apr. 1611
John King	nom. 30 Apr., cons. 8 Sept. 1611	30 Mar. 1621
George Montaigne or Mountain	trs. Lincoln, nom. 26 June, conf. 20 July 1621	trs. Durham *p.* 19 Feb. 1628
William Laud	trs. Bath, nom. 4 July, conf. 15 July 1628	trs. Canterbury 19 Sept. 1633
William Juxon	elect of Hereford, nom. 23 Oct., cons. 27 Oct. 1633	trs. Canterbury 20 Sept. 1660
Gilbert Sheldon	nom. 21 Sept., cons. 28 Oct. 1660	trs. Canterbury 31 Aug. 1663
Humfrey Henchman	trs. Salisbury, nom. 16 June, conf. 15 Sept. 1663	7 Oct. 1675

BISHOPS	ACCESSION	DEATH *unless otherwise stated*
Henry Compton	trs. Oxford, nom. 6 Dec. 1675, conf. 6 Feb. 1676	7 July 1713
John Robinson	trs. Bristol, nom. 8 Aug. 1713, conf. 13 Mar. 1714	11 Apr. 1723
Edmund Gibson	trs. Lincoln, nom. 10 Apr., conf. 4 May 1723	4 Sept. 1748
Thomas Sherlock	trs. Salisbury, nom. 12 Oct., conf. 1 Dec. 1748	18 July 1761
Thomas Hayter	trs. Norwich, nom. 19 Sept., conf. 24 Oct. 1761	9 Jan. 1762
Richard Osbaldeston	trs. Carlisle, nom. 30 Jan., conf. 18 Feb. 1762	13 May 1764
Richard Terrick	trs. Peterborough, nom. 22 May, conf. 6 June 1764	29 Mar. 1777
Robert Lowth	trs. Oxford, nom. 12 Apr. 1777, conf. 1 May 1778	3 Nov. 1787
Beilby Porteus	trs. Chester, nom. 14 Nov., conf. 7 Dec. 1787	14 May 1809
John Randolph	trs. Bangor, nom. 25 May, conf. 9 Aug. 1809	28 July 1813
William Howley	nom. 12 Aug., conf. 1 Oct. 1813	trs. Canterbury 15 Aug. 1828
Charles James Blomfield	trs. Chester, nom. 15 Aug., conf. 23 Aug. 1828	res. 1856, d. 5 Aug. 1857
Archibald Campbell Tait	nom. 11 Oct., cons. 23 Nov. 1856	trs. Canterbury 30 Dec. 1868
John Jackson	trs. Lincoln, nom. 11 Jan., conf. 29 Jan. 1869	6 Jan. 1885
Frederick Temple	trs. Exeter, nom. 26 Feb., conf. 24 Mar. 1885	trs. Canterbury 22 Dec. 1896
Mandell Creighton	trs. Peterborough, nom. 31 Dec. 1896, conf. 15 Jan. 1897	14 Jan. 1901
Arthur Foley Winnington-Ingram	trs. Stepney (suff.), nom. 16 Mar., conf. 17 Apr. 1901	res. 1 Sept. 1939, d. 26 May 1946
Geoffrey Francis Fisher	trs. Chester, nom. 14 Sept., conf. 17 Oct. 1939	trs. Canterbury 2 Feb. 1945
John William Charles Wand	trs. Bath, nom. 10 July, conf. 22 Aug. 1945	res. Nov. 1955, d. 16 Aug. 1977
Henry Colville Montgomery Campbell	trs. Guildford, nom. 10 Jan., conf. 25 Jan. 1956	res. 31 July 1961, d. 26 Dec. 1970
Robert Wright Stopford	trs. Peterborough, nom. 4 Aug., conf. 25 Sept. 1961	res. 11 June 1973, d. 13 Aug. 1976
Gerald Alexander Ellison	trs. Chester, nom. 18 June, conf. 16 July 1973	res. 30 Apr. 1981
Graham Douglas Leonard	trs. Truro, nom. 28 May, conf. 21 July 1981	

MANCHESTER

James Prince Lee	nom. 23 Oct. 1847, cons. 23 Jan. 1848	24 Dec. 1869
James Fraser	nom. 22 Jan., cons. 25 Mar. 1870	22 Oct. 1885
James Moorhouse	trs. Melbourne, nom. 30 Jan., conf. 3 May 1886	res. 3 Nov. 1903, d. 9 Apr. 1915
Edmund Arbuthnott Knox	trs. Coventry, nom. 4 Nov., conf. 26 Nov. 1903	res. 1 Jan. 1921, d. 16 Jan. 1937
William Temple	nom. 1 Jan., cons. 25 Jan. 1921	trs. York 2 Jan. 1929
Frederic Sumpter Guy Warman	trs. Chelmsford, nom. 7 Jan., conf. 21 Jan. 1929	res. 5 June 1947, d. 12 Feb. 1953

BISHOPS	ACCESSION	DEATH *unless otherwise stated*
William Derrick Lindsay Greer	nom. 29 Aug., cons. 29 Sept. 1947	res. 30 Apr. 1970, d. 13 Oct. 1972
Patrick Campbell Rodger	nom. 14 May, cons. 24 June 1970	trs. Oxford 12 Oct. 1978
Stanley Eric Francis Booth-Clibborn	nom. 9 Nov. 1978, cons. 2 Feb. 1979	

NEWCASTLE-UPON-TYNE

Ernest Roland Wilberforce	nom. 4 July, cons. 25 July 1882	trs. Chichester 16 Jan. 1896
Edgar Jacob	nom. 16 Jan., cons. 25 Jan. 1896	trs. St Albans 1903
Arthur Thomas Lloyd	trs. Thetford (suff.), nom. 11 May, inv. 4 June 1903	29 May 1907
Norman Dumenil John Straton	trs. Sodor, nom. 8 July, inv. 2 Sept. 1907	res. 30 Sept. 1915, d. 5 Apr. 1918
Herbert Louis Wild	nom. 16 Oct., cons. 30 Nov. 1915	res. 1 Aug. 1927, d. 28 Mar. 1940
Harold Ernest Bilbrough	trs. Dover (suff.), nom. 14 Sept., inv. 5 Oct. 1927	res. 1 Oct. 1941, d. 15 Nov. 1950
Noel Baring Hudson	trs. St Albans (assistant), nom. 2 Oct., conf. 19 Oct. 1941	trs. Ely 18 Jan. 1957
Hugh Edward Ashdown	nom. 15 Mar., cons. 1 May 1957	res. 2 Oct. 1972, d. 26 Dec. 1977
Ronald Oliver Bowlby	nom. 27 Nov. 1972, cons. 6 Jan. 1973	trs. Southwark 14 Dec. 1980
Andrew Alexander Kenny Graham	trs. Bedford (suff.), nom. 21 May, conf. 29 June 1981	

NORWICH

(Herbert removed his see from Thetford 1094 × 1096)

Herbert Losinga	el. and cons. 1090 × 27 Jan. 1091	22 July 1119
Everard (of Calne?)	*p.* 13 Mar., cons. 12 June 1121	res. 1145, d. 12 Oct. 1146
William Turbe	el. and cons. 1146 or early 1147	16 Jan. 1174
John of Oxford	el. 26 Nov., cons. 14 Dec. 1175	2 June 1200
John de Gray	el. *a.* 3 Sept., cons. 24 Sept. 1200	18 Oct. 1214
Pandulf Masca	el. 18 July × 9 Aug., temp. 9 Aug. 1215, cons. 29 May 1222	16 Sept. 1226
Thomas Blundeville	el. Oct., temp. 21 Nov., cons. 20 Dec. 1226	16 Aug. 1236
[Simon of Elmham	el. *a.* 9 Nov. 1236	qua. 17 Jan. 1239]
William Raleigh	el. 10 Apr., cons. 25 Sept. 1239	trs. Winchester Sept. 1243
Walter Suffield	el. *a.* 9 July, temp. 17 July 1244, cons. 26 Feb. 1245	19 May 1257
Simon Walton	el. 4 June, temp. 11 Aug. 1257, cons. 10 Mar. 1258	*a.* Jan. 1266
Roger Skerning	el. 23 Jan., temp. 17 Mar., cons. 4 Apr. 1266	22 Jan. 1278
William Middleton	el. 24 Feb., temp. 16 Mar., cons. 29 May 1278	31 Aug. or 1 Sept. 1288
Ralph Walpole	el. 11 Nov. 1288, temp. 7 Feb., cons. 20 Mar. 1289	trans. Ely 5 June 1299
John Salmon	prov. 5 × 18 June, temp. 19 Oct. cons. 15 Nov. 1299	6 July 1325
[Robert Baldock	el. 23 July, temp. 12 Aug. 1325	res. 3 Sept. 1325]

BISHOPS	ACCESSION	DEATH
		unless otherwise stated
William Ayermine	prov. 19 July, cons. 15 Sept. 1325, temp. 6 Feb. 1327	27 Mar. 1336
[Thomas Hempnall	el. 6 Apr. 1336	trs. Worcester 14 Mar. 1337]
Anthony Bek	prov. 14 Mar., cons. 30 Mar., temp. 9 July 1337	18 Dec. 1343[1]
William Bateman	prov. 23 or 24 Jan., temp. 2 Mar., cons. 23 May 1344	6 Jan. 1355
Thomas Percy	prov. 4 Feb., temp. 14 Apr. 1355, cons. 3 Jan. 1356	8 Aug. 1369
Henry Dispenser	prov. 3 Apr., cons. 20 Apr., temp. 14 Aug. 1370	23 Aug. 1406
Alexander Tottington	el. 14 Sept. 1406, prov. 19 Jan., cons. 23 Oct., temp. 23 Oct. 1407	*a.* 20 Apr. 1413
Richard Courtenay	el. *a.* June, prov. 28 June, temp. 11 Sept., cons. 17 Sept. 1413	*15* Sept. 1415
John Wakeryng	el. *a.* 24 Nov. 1415, temp. 27 May, cons. 31 May 1416	9 Apr. 1425
William Alnwick	prov. 27 Feb., temp. 4 May, cons. 18 Aug. 1426	trs. Lincoln 19 Sept. 1436
Thomas Brown	trs. Rochester, prov. 19 Sept. 1436, temp. 16 Feb. 1437	6 Dec. 1445
Walter Lyhert	prov. 24 Jan., temp. 26 Feb., cons. 27 Feb. 1446	24 May 1472
James Goldwell	prov. 17 July, cons. 4 Oct. 1472, temp. 25 Feb. 1473	15 Feb. 1499
Thomas Jane	prov. 14 June, temp. 21 July, cons. *20 Oct.* 1499	Sept. 1500
Richard Nykke	prov. 26 Feb., temp. 24 Apr., cons. 6 June 1501	29 Dec. 1535
William Repps or Rugge	el. 31 May, cons. 11 June 1536	res. *a.* 26 Jan. 1550, d. 21 Sept. 1550
Thomas Thirlby	trs. Westminster 1 Apr. 1550	trs. Ely 10 July 1554
John Hopton	nom. 4 Sept., cons. 28 Oct. 1554, prov. 21 June 1555	*p.* 24 Aug. 1558
[Richard Cox	nom. 5 June 1559	trs. Ely 20 Dec. 1559]
John Parkhurst	nom. 27 Mar., cons. 1 Sept. 1560	2 Feb. 1575
Edmund Freke	trs. Rochester, nom. 21 July, conf. 14 Nov. 1575	trs. Worcester 5 Dec. 1584
Edmund Scambler	trs. Peterborough, el. 15 Dec. 1584, conf. 15 Jan. 1585	7 May 1594
William Redman	el. 17 Dec. 1594, cons. 12 Jan. 1595	25 Sept. 1602
John Jegon	nom. 10 Jan., cons. 20 Feb. 1603	13 Mar. 1618
John Overall	trs. Lichfield, nom. 9 May, conf. 30 Sept. 1618	12 May 1619
Samuel Harsnett	trs. Chichester, nom. 1 June, conf. 28 Aug. 1619	trs. York 13 Jan. 1629
Francis White	trs. Carlisle, el. 22 Jan., conf. 9 Feb. 1629	trs. Ely 8 Dec. 1631
Richard Corbet	trs. Oxford, el. 7 Apr., conf. 7 May 1632	28 July 1635
Matthew Wren	trs. Hereford, el. 10 Nov., conf. 5 Dec. 1635	trs. Ely 24 Apr. 1638
Richard Montague	trs. Chichester, nom. 1 May, conf. 12 May 1638	13 Apr. 1641

[1] 'nocte precedente xix diem mensis decembris', Reg. Ep. Norwic. III (Bek, p. 73v).

BISHOPS	ACCESSION	DEATH *unless otherwise stated*
Joseph Hall	trs. Exeter, el. 15 Nov., conf. 16 Dec. 1641	8 Sept. 1656
Edward Reynolds	nom. 30 Sept. 1660, cons. 13 Jan. 1661	28 July 1676
Anthony Sparrow	trs. Exeter, el. 28 Aug., conf. 18 Sept. 1676	18 May 1685
William Lloyd	trs. Peterborough, el. 11 June, conf. 4 July 1685	depr. 1 Feb. 1690, d. 1 Jan. 1710
John Moore	nom. 25 Apr., cons. 5 July 1691	trs. Ely 31 July 1707
Charles Trimnell	nom. 13 Jan., cons. 8 Feb. 1708	trs. Winchester 19 Aug. 1721
Thomas Green	nom. 19 Aug., cons. 8 Oct. 1721	trs. Ely 24 Sept. 1723
John Leng	nom. 27 Aug., cons. 3 Nov. 1723	26 Oct. 1727
William Baker	trs. Bangor, nom. 2 Nov., conf. 19 Dec. 1727	4 Dec. 1732
Robert Butts	nom. 17 Jan., cons. 25 Feb. 1733	trs. Ely 27 June 1738
Thomas Gooch (Baronet)	trs. Bristol, nom. 29 Aug., conf. 17 Oct. 1738	trs. Ely 11 Mar. 1748
Samuel Lisle	trs. St Asaph, nom. 17 Mar., conf. 9 Apr. 1748	3 Oct. 1749
Thomas Hayter	nom. 13 Oct., cons. 3 Dec. 1749	trs. London 24 Oct. 1761
Philip Yonge	trs. Bristol, nom. 27 Oct., conf. 25 Nov. 1761	23 Apr. 1783
Lewis Bagot	trs. Bristol, nom. 15 May, conf. 14 June 1783	trs. St Asaph 24 Apr. 1790
George Horne	nom. 7 May, cons. 6 June 1790	17 Jan. 1792
Charles Manners Sutton	nom. 5 Feb., cons. 8 Apr. 1792	trs. Canterbury 21 Feb. 1805
Henry Bathurst	nom. 5 Mar., cons. 28 Apr. 1805	5 Apr. 1837
Edward Stanley	nom. 14 Apr., cons. 11 June 1837	6 Sept. 1849
Samuel Hinds	nom. 26 Sept., cons. 2 Dec. 1849	res. 1857, d. 7 Feb. 1872
John Thomas Pelham	nom. 5 May, cons. 11 June 1857	res. 16 May 1893, d. 1 May 1894
John Sheepshanks	nom. 26 May, cons. 29 June 1893	res. 19 Feb. 1910, d. 3 June 1912
Bertram Pollock	nom. 19 Feb., cons. 25 Apr. 1910	res. 24 June 1942, d. 17 Oct. 1943
Percy Mark Herbert	trs. Blackburn, nom. 1 July, conf. 22 July 1942	res. 25 July 1959, d. 22 Jan. 1968
William Launcelot Scott Fleming	trs. Portsmouth, nom. 23 Oct., conf. 18 Dec. 1959	res. 30 June 1971
Maurice Arthur Ponsonby Wood	nom. 12 July, cons. 29 Sept. 1971	res. 26 Aug. 1985
Peter John Nott	trs. Taunton (suff.), nom. 1985	

OXFORD[1]

Robert King	bp 'Rheonensis' (*in partibus*), nom. 1 Sept. 1542	4 Dec. 1557
Hugh Curen	trs. Dublin, nom. 1 Sept., conf. 14 Oct. 1567	Oct. 1568
John Underhill	el. 8 Dec., cons. 14 Dec. 1589	12 May 1592
John Bridges	nom. 1 Dec. 1603, cons. 12 Feb. 1604	25 or 26 Mar. 1618

[1] The see, when the diocese was founded on 1 Sept. 1542, was fixed at Osney Abbey (whose last abbot, Robert King, became the first bp). The see was removed to St Frideswide's Priory (Christ Church) at Oxford, 9 June 1545.

BISHOPS	ACCESSION	DEATH *unless otherwise stated*
John Howson	nom. 4 Aug. 1618, cons. 9 May 1619	trs. Durham 17 Sept. 1628
Richard Corbet	nom. 18 Sept., cons. 19 Oct. 1628	trs. Norwich 7 May 1632
John Bancroft	nom. 8 May, cons. 10 June 1632	Feb. 1641
Robert Skinner	trs. Bristol, nom. 11 Nov., conf. 16 Dec. 1641	trs. Worcester 4 Nov. 1663
William Paul	nom. 16 June, cons. 20 Dec. 1663	24 May 1665
Walter Blandford	el. 7 Nov., cons. 3 Dec. 1665	trs. Worcester 14 June 1671
Nathaniel Crew (3rd baron Crew of Stene 1697)	nom. 18 May, cons. 2 July 1671	trs. Durham 6 Dec. 1674
Henry Compton	nom. 24 Aug.,[1] cons. 6 Dec. 1674	trs. London 6 Feb. 1676
John Fell	nom. 14 Dec. 1675, cons. 6 Feb. 1676	10 July 1686
Samuel Parker	nom. 22 Aug., cons. 17 Oct. 1686	20 Mar. 1688
Timothy Hall	el. 18 Aug., cons. 7 Oct. 1688	10 Apr. 1690
John Hough	nom. 14 Apr., cons. 11 May 1690	trs. Lichfield 5 Aug. 1699
William Talbot	nom. 15 Aug., cons. 24 Sept. 1699	trs. Salisbury 23 Apr. 1715
John Potter	nom. 27 Apr., cons. 15 May 1715	trs. Canterbury 28 Feb. 1737
Thomas Secker	trs. Bristol, nom. 24 Mar., conf. 14 May 1737	trs. Canterbury conf. 21 Apr. 1758
John Hume	trs. Bristol, nom. 25 Apr., conf. 3 June 1758	trs. Salisbury 10 Sept. 1766
Robert Lowth	trs. St David's, nom. 11 Sept., conf. 16 Oct. 1766	trs. London 1 May 1778
John Butler	nom. 3 May, cons. 25 May 1777	trs. Hereford 28 Feb. 1788
Edward Smallwell	trs. St David's, nom. 7 Mar., conf. 15 Apr. 1788	26 June 1799
John Randolph	nom. 18 July, cons. 1 Sept. 1799	trs. Bangor 6 Jan. 1807
Charles Moss	nom. 9 Jan., cons. 1 Feb. 1807	16 Dec. 1811
William Jackson	nom. 30 Dec. 1811, cons. 23 Feb. 1812	2 Dec. 1815
Edward Legge	nom. 22 Dec. 1815, cons. 24 Mar. 1816	27 Jan. 1827
Charles Lloyd	nom. 10 Feb., cons. 4 Mar. 1827	31 May 1829
Richard Bagot	el. 13 July, cons. 23 Aug. 1829	trs. Bath 12 Nov. 1845
Samuel Wilberforce	nom. 12 Nov., cons. 30 Nov. 1845	trs. Winchester 11 Dec. 1869
John Fielder Mackarness	nom. 16 Dec. 1869, cons. 25 Jan. 1870	res. 17 Nov. 1888, d. 16 Sept. 1889
William Stubbs	trs. Chester, nom. 5 Dec. 1888, conf. 15 Jan. 1889	22 Apr. 1901
Francis Paget	nom. 29 May, cons. 29 June 1901	2 Aug. 1911
Charles Gore	trs. Birmingham, nom. 6 Sept., conf. 17 Oct. 1911	res. 1 July 1919, d. 17 Jan. 1932
Hubert Murray Burge	trs. Southwark, nom. 7 July, conf. 6 Aug. 1919	11 June 1925
Thomas Banks Strong	trs. Ripon, nom. 10 July, conf. 13 Oct. 1925	res. 30 Sept. 1937, d. 8 June 1944

[1] A second warrant for letters is dated 1 Nov., and Compton was elected 10 Nov.

BISHOPS	ACCESSION	DEATH
		unless otherwise stated
Kenneth Escott Kirk	nom. 6 Oct., cons. 30 Nov. 1937	8 June 1954
Harry James Carpenter	nom. 17 Dec. 1954, cons. 25 Jan. 1955	res. 14 Dec. 1970
Kenneth John Woollcombe	nom. 13 Jan., cons. 16 Mar. 1971	res. 31 Mar. 1978
Patrick Campbell Rodger	trs. Manchester, nom. 5 June, conf. 12 Oct. 1978	

PETERBOROUGH

John Chamber or Chambers	nom. 4 Sept., cons. 23 Oct. 1541	Feb. 1556
David Pole	prov. 24 Mar., cons. 15 Aug. 1557	depr. *Nov.* 1559
Edmund Scambler	nom. 11 Nov. 1560, cons. 16 Feb. 1561	trs. Norwich 15 Jan. 1585
Richard Howland	el. 22 Jan., cons. 7 Feb. 1585	23 June 1600
Thomas Dove	nom. *a.* 3 Feb., cons. 26 Apr. 1601	30 Aug. 1630
William Piers	el. 17 Sept., cons. 24 Oct. 1630	trs. Bath 13 Dec. 1632
Augustine Lindsell	el. 22 Dec. 1632, cons. 10 Feb. 1633	trs. Hereford 24 Mar. 1634
Francis Dee	el. 9 Apr., cons. 18 May 1634	8 Oct. 1638
John Towers	nom. 3 Nov. 1638, cons. 13 Jan. 1639	10 Jan. 1649
Benjamin Laney	nom. 6 Nov., cons. 2 Dec. 1660	trs. Lincoln 2 Apr. 1663
Joseph Henshaw	nom. 9 Apr., cons. 10 May 1663	9 Mar. 1679
William Lloyd	trs. Llandaff, nom. 28 Mar., conf. 16 May 1679	trs. Norwich 4 July 1685
Thomas White	nom. 26 Aug., cons. 25 Oct. 1685	depr. 1 Feb. 1690, d. 30 May 1698
Richard Cumberland	nom. 15 May, cons. 5 July 1691	9 Oct. 1718
White Kennett	nom. 12 Oct., cons. 9 Nov. 1718	19 Dec. 1728
Robert Clavering	trs. Llandaff, nom. 28 Jan., conf. 17 Feb. 1729	21 July 1747
John Thomas	nom. 21 Aug., cons. 4 Oct. 1747	trs. Salisbury 18 June 1757
Richard Terrick	nom. 7 June, cons. 3 July 1757	trs. London 6 June 1764
Robert Lambe	nom. 8 June, cons. 8 July 1764	3 Nov. 1769
John Hinchcliffe	el. 1 Dec., cons. 17 Dec. 1769	11 Jan. 1794
Spencer Madan	trs. Bristol, nom. 3 Feb., conf. 7 Mar. 1794	8 Oct. 1813
John Parsons	nom. 15 Nov., cons. 12 Dec. 1813	12 Mar. 1819
Herbert Marsh	trs. Llandaff, nom. 1 Apr., conf. 28 Apr. 1819	1 May 1839
George Davys	nom. 7 May, cons. 16 June 1839	18 Apr. 1864
Francis Jeune	nom. 8 May, cons. 29 June 1864	21 Aug. 1868
William Connor Magee	nom. 27 Oct., cons. 15 Nov. 1868	trs. York 20 Feb. 1891
Mandell Creighton	nom. 2 Mar., cons. 25 Apr. 1891	trs. London 15 Jan. 1897
Edward Carr Glyn	nom. 1 Feb., cons. 24 Feb. 1897	res. July 1916, d. 14 Nov. 1928
Frank Theodore Woods	nom. 20 July, cons. 21 Sept. 1916	trs. Winchester 28 Dec. 1923

BISHOPS	ACCESSION	DEATH
		unless otherwise stated
Cyril Charles Bowman Bardsley	nom. 31 Dec. 1923, cons. 24 Feb. 1924	trs. Leicester 15 Feb. 1927
Claude Martin Blagden	nom. 19 Jan., cons. 25 Mar. 1927	res. 29 Sept. 1949, d. 7 Sept. 1952
Spencer Stottisbury Gwatkin Leeson	nom. 4 Oct., cons. 1 Nov. 1949	27 Jan. 1956
Robert Wright Stopford	trs. Fulham (suff.), nom. 15 June, conf. 19 July 1956	trs. London 25 Sept. 1961
Cyril Easthaugh	trs. Kensington (suff.), nom. 20 Oct., conf. 20 Dec. 1961	res. 22 July 1972
Douglas Russell Feaver	nom. 13 Sept., cons. 1 Nov. 1972	res. 31 Oct. 1984
William John Westwood	trs. Edmonton (suff.), nom. 7 Nov., conf. 3 Dec. 1984	

PORTSMOUTH

Ernest Neville Lovett	nom. 7 June, cons. 25 July 1927	trs. Salisbury 23 Apr. 1936
Frank Partridge	nom. 12 May, cons. 24 June 1936	1 Oct. 1941
William Louis Anderson	trs. Croydon, nom. 12 Feb., conf. 19 Mar. 1942	trs. Salisbury 14 June 1949
William Launcelot Scott Fleming	nom. 13 Sept., cons. 18 Oct. 1949	trs. Norwich 18 Dec. 1959
John Henry Lawrence Phillips	nom. 29 Jan., cons. 25 Mar. 1960	res. 31 July 1975
Archibald Ronald McDonald Gordon	nom. 5 Aug., cons. 23 Sept. 1975	res. 31 May 1984
Timothy John Bavin	trs. Johannesburg, nom. 2 Nov. 1984, conf. 7 Jan. 1985	

RIPON

Charles Thomas Longley	nom. 15 Oct., cons. 6 Nov. 1836	trs. Durham 1856
Robert Bickersteth	nom. 17 Dec. 1856, cons. 18 Jan. 1857	15 Apr. 1884
William Boyd Carpenter	nom. 11 June, cons. 25 July 1884	res. 8 Nov. 1911, d. 26 Oct. 1918
Thomas Wortley Drury	trs. Sodor, nom. 22 Nov. 1911, conf. 4 Feb. 1912	res. 22 Apr. 1920, d. 12 Feb. 1926
Thomas Banks Strong	nom. 24 June, cons. 24 Aug. 1920	trs. Oxford 13 Oct. 1925
Edward Arthur Burroughs	nom. 29 Oct. 1925, cons. 6 Jan. 1926	23 Aug. 1934
Geoffrey Charles Lester Lunt	nom. 19 Nov. 1934, cons. 25 Jan. 1935	trs. Salisbury 9 Oct. 1946
George Armitage Chase	nom. 11 Oct., cons. 1 Nov. 1946	res. 6 Apr. 1959, d. 30 Nov. 1971
John Richard Humpidge Moorman	nom. 2 May, cons. 11 June 1959	res. 30 Nov. 1975
Stuart Hetley Price	trs. Doncaster (suff.), nom. 10 Feb., conf. 18 Mar. 1976	15 Mar. 1977
David Nigel de Lorentz Young	nom. 11 July, cons. 21 Sept. 1977	

ROCHESTER

Siward	cons. 1058	1075
Arnost	el. and cons. late 1075 or early 1076	*15 July* 1076
Gundulf	cons. 19 Mar. 1077	7 Mar. 1108

BISHOPS	ACCESSION	DEATH *unless otherwise stated*
Ralph d'Escures	nom. 29 June, cons. 9 Aug. 1108	trs. Canterbury 26 Apr. 1114
Ernulf	nom. 28 Sept. 1114, cons. 26 Dec. 1115	*15* Mar. 1124
John I	el. *a.* 12 Apr., cons. 24 May 1125	20 June 1137
John II (of Séez)[1]	cons. *a.* 1139	1142
Ascelin	cons. 1142	24 Jan. 1148
Walter	el. 27 Jan., cons. 14 Mar. 1148	26 July 1182
Waleran	el. 9 or 10 Oct., cons. 19 Dec. 1182	29 Aug. 1184
Gilbert Glanvill	el. 16 July, cons. 29 Sept. 1185	24 June 1214
Benedict of Sawston	el. 13 Dec. 1214, cons. 25 Jan. or 22 Feb. 1215	18 Dec. 1226
Henry Sandford	el. 26 Dec. 1226, cons. 9 May 1227	24 Feb. 1235
Richard Wendene	el. 26 Mar. 1235, cons. 21 Nov. 1238	12 Oct. 1250
Lawrence of St Martin	el. 19 Oct. 1250, cons. 9 Apr. 1251	3 June 1274
Walter of Merton	el. *c.* 20 July, cons. 21 Oct. 1274	27 Oct. 1277
John Bradfield	el. 1278, temp. *p.* 19 Jan., cons. 29 May 1278	23 Apr. 1283
[John Kirkby	el. *a.* 16 June 1283	res. 16 June 1283]
Thomas Ingoldsthorpe	el. *a.* 9 July, cons. 26 Sept. or 3 Oct. 1283	11 May 1291
Thomas Wouldham	el. 6 June, temp. *a.* 11 Dec. 1291, cons. 6 Jan. 1292	28 Feb. 1317
Hamo Hethe	el. 18 Mar. 1317, cons. 26 Aug., temp. from Crown 5 Dec. 1319[2]	res. 1352, d. 4 May 1352
John Sheppey	prov. 22 Oct. 1352, cons. 10 Mar., temp. from Crown 13 Mar. 1353	19 Oct. 1360
William Whittlesey	el. 23 Oct. 1360, prov. 3 July, temp. from Crown 13 Dec. 1361, cons. 6 Feb. 1362	trs. Worcester 6 Mar. 1364
Thomas Trillek	prov. 6 Mar., cons. 26 May 1364, temp. from Crown 6 Feb. 1365	12 × 25 Dec. 1372
Thomas Brinton	prov. 31 Jan., cons. 6 Feb. 1373, temp. from Crown 21 Oct. 1374	4 May 1389
William Bottlesham	trs. Llandaff, prov. 27 Aug. 1389, temp. from Crown 12 Feb. 1390	*a.* 26 Feb. 1400
John Bottlesham	prov. 9 Apr., cons. 4 July 1400	17 Apr. 1404
Richard Young	trs. Bangor, prov. 28 July and 11 Nov. 1404	18 × 25 Oct. 1418
John Kempe	el. Jan., prov. 26 June, cons. *3 Dec.* 1419	trs. Chichester 28 Feb. 1421
John Langdon	prov. 17 Nov. 1421, cons. 7 June 1422	30 Sept. 1434

[1] Cf. A. Saltman, in *EHR*, lxvi (1951), 71–75.

[2] The bps of Rochester held almost all their temporalities from the abp of Canterbury, who was recognized in 1214 to be patron of the see and to have custody of the temporalities during vacancy of the see. But in the fourteenth and fifteenth centuries the bishopric held a few manors from the Crown; these were in royal custody during vacancy and were restored to a new bp often a long time after he received grant of temporalities from the abp.

BISHOPS	ACCESSION	DEATH
		unless otherwise stated
Thomas Brouns	prov. 21 Feb., cons. 1 May, temp. from Crown 12 May 1435	trs. Norwich 19 Sept. 1436
William Wells	prov. 19 Sept. 1436, temp. from Crown 21 Mar., cons. 24 Mar. 1437	8 × 25 Feb. 1444
John Low	trs. St Asaph, prov. 22 Apr. 1444	*a.* 21 Nov. 1467
Thomas Rotherham or Scot	prov. 11 Jan., cons. 3 Apr. 1468	trs. Lincoln 8 Jan. 1472
John Alcock	prov. 8 Jan., cons. 15 Mar. 1472	trs. Worcester 15 July 1476
John Russell	prov. 15 July, cons. 22 Sept. 1476	trs. Lincoln 7 July 1480
Edmund Audley	prov. 7 July, cons. 1 Oct. 1480	trs. Hereford 22 June 1492
Thomas Savage	prov. 3 Dec. 1492, cons. 28 Apr. 1493	trs. London 3 Aug. 1496
Richard FitzJames	el. 2 Jan., prov. 18 Feb., cons. 21 May 1497	trs. Chichester 29 Nov. 1503
John Fisher	prov. 14 Oct., cons. 24 Nov. 1504	depr. 2 Jan. 1535, d. 22 June 1535
John Hilsey	el. 7 Aug., cons. 18 Sept. 1535	4 Aug. 1539
Nicholas Heath	nom. 25 Mar., cons. 4 Apr. 1540	trs. Worcester 20 Feb. 1544
Henry Holbeach or Rands	trs. Bristol,[1] nom. 23 Apr., conf. 9 June 1544	trs. Lincoln 20 Aug. 1547
Nicholas Ridley	nom. 31 Aug., cons. 25 Sept. 1547	trs. London *p.* 1 Apr. 1550
John Ponet	nom. 8 Mar., cons. 29 June 1550	trs. Winchester 23 Mar. 1551
John Scory	nom. 26 Apr., cons. 30 Aug. 1551	trs. Chichester 23 May 1552
Maurice Griffith or Griffin	nom. 19 Mar., cons. 1 Apr. 1554	20 Nov. 1558
[Edmund Allen	nom. 27 July 1559	d. *a.* 27 Aug. 1559]
Edmund Gest	nom. 22 Jan., cons. 24 Mar. 1560	trs. Salisbury 24 Dec. 1571
Edmund Freke	nom. 11 Feb., cons. 9 Mar. 1572	trs. Norwich 14 Nov. 1575
John Piers	nom. 6 Apr., cons. 15 Apr. 1576	trs. Salisbury 2 Dec. 1577
John Young	nom. 31 Jan., cons. 16 Mar. 1578	10 Apr. 1605
William Barlow	nom. 14 May, cons. 30 June 1605	trs. Lincoln 27 June 1608
Richard Neile	nom. 28 June, cons. 9 Oct. 1608	trs. Lichfield 6 Dec. 1610
John Buckeridge	nom. 22 Dec. 1610, cons. 9 June 1611	trs. Ely 15 July 1628
Walter Curle or Curll	nom. 14 July, cons. 7 Sept. 1628	trs. Bath 4 Dec. 1629
John Bowle	nom. 20 Nov. 1629, cons. 7 Feb. 1630	9 Oct. 1637
John Warner	nom. 3 Nov. 1637, cons. 14 Jan. 1638	21 or 22 Oct. 1666
John Dolben	nom. 31 Oct., cons. 25 Nov. 1666	trs. York 16 Aug. 1683
Francis Turner	nom. 31 Aug., cons. 11 Nov. 1683	trs. Ely 23 Aug. 1684

[1] Apparently a suffragan of Bristol, of which see Paul Bush was diocesan.

BISHOPS	ACCESSION	DEATH
		unless otherwise stated
Thomas Sprat	nom. 27 Sept., cons. 2 Nov. 1684	20 May 1713
Francis Atterbury	nom. 14 June, cons. 5 July 1713	depr. by May 1723, d. 22 Feb. 1732
Samuel Bradford	trs. Carlisle, nom. 30 May, conf. 19 July 1723	17 May 1731
Joseph Wilcocks	trs. Gloucester, nom. 21 June, conf. 20 Aug. 1731	28 Feb. 1756
Zachary Pearce	trs. Bangor, nom. 15 Apr., conf. 4 June 1756	29 June 1774
John Thomas	nom. 24 Sept., cons. 13 Nov. 1774	22 Aug. 1793
Samuel Horsley	trs. St David's, nom. 21 Sept., conf. 7 Dec. 1793	trs. St Asaph 1802
Thomas Dampier	nom. 27 July, cons. 22 Aug. 1802	trs. Ely 22 Nov. 1808
Walker King	nom. 2 Dec. 1808, cons. 12 Feb. 1809	22 Feb. 1827
Hugh Percy	nom. 21 June, cons. 15 July 1827	trs. Carlisle 10 Nov. 1827
George Murray	trs. Sodor and Man, nom. 12 Nov., conf. 6 Dec. 1827	16 Feb. 1860
Joseph Cotton Wigram	nom. 16 Apr., cons. 17 May 1860	6 Apr. 1867
Thomas Legh Claughton	nom. 4 May, cons. 11 June 1867	trs. St Albans 12 July 1877
Anthony Wilson Thorold	nom. 29 June, cons. 25 July 1877	trs. Winchester 13 Feb. 1891
Randall Thomas Davidson	nom. 23 Feb., cons. 25 Apr. 1891	trs. Winchester 21 Sept. 1895
Edward Stuart Talbot	nom. 21 Sept., cons. 18 Oct. 1895	trs. Southwark 24 May 1905
John Reginald Harmer	trs. Adelaide, nom. 5 June, conf. 5 July 1905	res. 31 Aug. 1930, d. 9 Mar. 1944
Martin Linton Smith	trs. Hereford, nom. 16 Sept., conf. 5 Nov. 1930	res. 1 Nov. 1939, d. 7 Oct. 1950
Christopher Maude Chavasse	nom. 19 Mar., cons. 25 Apr. 1940	res. 30 Sept. 1960, d. 10 Mar. 1962
Richard David Say	nom. 8 Nov. 1960, cons. 6 Jan. 1961	

ST ALBANS

Thomas Legh Claughton	trs. Rochester, nom. 30 May, inv. 12 July 1877	res. 21 Mar. 1890, d. 25 July 1892
John Wogan Festing	nom. 10 June, cons. 24 June 1890	28 Dec. 1902
Edgar Jacob	trs. Newcastle, nom. 11 May 1903	res. Dec. 1919, d. 25 Mar. 1920
Michael Bolton Furse	trs. Pretoria, nom. 28 Jan., inv. 19 Apr. 1920	res. 1 Sept. 1944
Philip Henry Loyd	trs. Nasik, nom. 13 Oct., conf. 14 Dec. 1944	res. 1 May 1950, d. 11 Jan. 1952
Edward Michael Gresford Jones	trs. Willesden, nom. 23 June, conf. 25 July 1950	res. 16 Dec. 1969, d. 7 Mar. 1982
Robert Alexander Kennedy Runcie	nom. 10 Jan., cons. 24 Feb. 1970	trs. Canterbury 25 Feb. 1980
John Bernard Taylor	nom. 5 Mar., cons. 1 May 1980	

ST EDMUNDSBURY AND IPSWICH

BISHOPS	ACCESSION	DEATH *unless otherwise stated*
Henry Bernard Hodgson	nom. 18 Feb., cons. 24 Feb. 1914	28 Feb. 1921
Albert Augustus David	nom. 21 June, cons. 25 July 1921	trs. Liverpool 18 Oct. 1923
Walter Godfrey Whittingham	nom. 22 Oct., cons. 1 Nov. 1923	res. 31 Aug. 1940, d. 17 June 1941
Richard Brook	nom. 24 Sept., cons. 1 Nov. 1940	res. 1 Oct. 1953, d. 31 Jan. 1969
Arthur Harold Morris	trs. Pontefract (suff.), nom. 4 May, conf. 2 June 1954	res. 31 Dec. 1965, d. 15 Oct. 1977
Leslie Wilfrid Brown	trs. Namirembe, nom. 25 Jan., conf. 25 Mar. 1966	res. 30 Sept. 1978
John Waine	trs. Stafford (suff.), nom. 23 Oct., conf. 21 Nov. 1978	

SALISBURY

Osmund	cons. *a.* 3 June 1078	3–4 Dec. 1099
Roger	nom. 29 Sept. 1102, el. 13 Apr. 1103, cons. 11 Aug. 1107	11 Dec. 1139
[Philip de Harcourt	nom. Mar. 1140	qua. *1141*]
Jocelin de Bohun	cons. 1142	res. 1184, d. 18 Nov. 1184
Hubert Walter	el. 15 Sept., cons. 22 Oct. 1189	trs. Canterbury *p.* 29 May 1193
Herbert Poore	el. *a.* 5 May, temp. *15* May, cons. 5 June 1194	7 Jan. 1217
Richard Poore	trs. Chichester, el. *a.* 9 May, conf. 27 June 1217	trs. Durham 14 May 1228
Robert Bingham	el. 9 Sept. 1228, cons. 27 May 1229	2 or 3 Nov. 1246
William of York	el. 8 or 10 Dec. 1246, temp. 29 Jan., cons. 7 or 14 July 1247	25 or 31 Jan. 1256
Giles of Bridport	el. 13 Feb. × 15 Apr., temp 17 Aug. 1256, cons. 11 Mar. 1257	*13* Dec. 1262
Walter de la Wyle	el. 22 Jan., temp. 10 Apr., cons. 27 May 1263	3 or 4 Jan. 1271
Robert Wickhampton	el. 23 Feb. 1271, cons. 13 May 1274, temp. 15 Aug. 1274	24 Apr. 1284
Walter Scammel	el. 26 June, temp. 10 Aug., cons. 22 Oct. 1284	20 Sept. 1286
Henry Brandeston	el. 2 Jan., temp. 15 Mar., cons. 1 June 1287	11 Feb. 1288
[Laurence Hakeburne	el. 10 May 1288	10 Aug. 1288]
William de la Corner	el. 24 Nov. 1288, temp. 26 Feb., cons. 8 May 1289	*10* Oct. 1291
Nicholas Longespee	el. 8 Nov. × 12 Dec., temp. 16 Dec. 1291, cons. 16 Mar. 1292	18 May 1297
Simon of Ghent	el. 2 June, temp. 7 Aug., cons. 20 Oct. 1297	2 Apr. 1315
Roger Martival	el. *a.* 11 June, temp. 18 July, cons. 28 Sept. 1315	14 Mar. 1330
Robert Wyvil	prov. 16 Apr., temp. 10 June, cons. 15 July 1330	4 Sept. 1375
[John Wormonhale	el. 20 Sept. × 12 Oct. 1375	qua. 12 Oct. 1375]
Ralph Erghum	prov. 12 Oct., cons. 9 Dec., temp. 28 Dec. 1375	trs. Bath 3 Apr. 1388
John Waltham	prov. 3 Apr., temp. 13 Sept., cons. 20 Sept. 1388	18 Sept. 1395

BISHOPS	ACCESSION	DEATH *unless otherwise stated*
Richard Mitford	trs. Chichester, prov. 25 Oct. 1395, temp. 30 Jan. 1396	3 May 1407
[John Chaundler	el. 16 June 1407	qua. 22 June 1407]
Nicholas Bubwith	trs. London, prov. 22 June, temp. 14 Aug. 1407	trs. Bath 7 Oct. 1407
Robert Hallum	prov. 7 Oct., cons. 1407, temp. 1 Dec. 1407	4 Sept. 1417
John Chaundler	el. 15 Nov., cons. 12 Dec. 1417, temp. 8 Jan. 1418	16 July 1426
[Simon Sydenham	el. 16 Sept. 1426	qua. 9 July 1427]
Robert Nevill	prov. 9 July, temp. 10 Oct., cons. 26 Oct. 1427	trs. Durham 27 Jan. 1438
William Aiscough	prov. 12 Feb., temp. 13 July, cons. 20 July 1438	29 June 1450
Richard Beauchamp	trs. Hereford, prov. 14 Aug., temp. 1 Oct. 1450	18 Oct. 1481
Lionel Woodville	prov. 7 Jan., temp. 28 Mar., cons. *p.* 17 Apr. 1482	*a.* 23 June 1484
Thomas Langton	trs. St David's, prov. 9 Feb., temp. 4 May 1485	trs. Winchester 13 Mar. 1493
John Blythe	prov. 13 Nov., temp. 22 Dec. 1493, cons. 23 Feb. 1494	23 Aug. 1499
Henry Deane	trs. Bangor, prov. 8 Jan., temp. 22 Mar. 1500	trs. Canterbury 26 May 1501
Edmund Audley	trs. Hereford, prov. 10 Jan., temp. 2 Apr. 1502	23 Aug. 1524
Lorenzo Campeggio	bp. of Bologna, *in commendam*, prov. 2 Dec. 1524, temp. 11 Jan. 1525	depr. 21 Mar. 1534, d. 1539
Nicholas Shaxton	el. 22 Feb., temp. 1 Apr., cons. 11 Apr. 1535	res. July 1539, d. 5 × 9 Aug. 1556
John Salcot or Capon	trs. Bangor, nom. 7 July, temp. 14 Aug. 1539	6 Oct. 1557
[Gaspar Contarini	prov. 23 July 1539	24 Aug. 1542]
[William Peto	prov. 30 Mar. 1543	? res. 1558]
[Francis Mallett	nom. 14 Oct. 1558	depr. 1558, d. 16 Dec. 1570]
John Jewell	nom. 27 July 1559, cons. 21 Jan. 1560	23 Sept. 1571
Edmund Gest	trs. Rochester, nom. 5 Dec., conf. 24 Dec. 1571	28 Feb. 1577
John Piers	trs. Rochester, nom. 11 Oct., conf. 2 Dec. 1577	trs. York 19 Feb. 1589
John Coldwell	nom. 24 Nov., cons. 26 Dec. 1591	14 Oct. 1596
Henry Cotton	nom. 6 Sept., cons. 12 Nov. 1598	7 May 1615
Robert Abbot	el. 11 Oct., cons. 3 Dec. 1615	2 Mar. 1618
Martin Fotherby	nom. 17 Mar., cons. 19 Apr. 1618	11 Mar. 1620
Robert Townson or Toulson	el. 24 Mar., cons. 9 July 1620	15 May 1621
John Davenant	nom. 29 May, cons. 18 Nov. 1621	20 Apr. 1641
Brian Duppa	trs. Chichester, nom. 26 Nov., conf. 14 Dec. 1641	trs. Winchester 4 Oct. 1660
Humfrey Henchman	nom. 20 Sept., cons. 28 Oct. 1660	trs. London 15 Sept. 1663
John Earle or Earles	trs. Worcester, nom. 16 June, conf. 26 Sept. 1663	17 Nov. 1665
Alexander Hyde	el. 11 Dec., cons. 31 Dec. 1665	22 Aug. 1667

BISHOPS	ACCESSION	DEATH
		unless otherwise stated
Seth Ward	trs. Exeter, nom. 26 Aug., conf. 12 Sept. 1667	6 Jan. 1689
Gilbert Burnet	nom. 9 Mar., cons. 31 Mar. 1689	17 Mar. 1715
William Talbot	trs. Oxford, nom. 19 Mar., conf. 23 Apr. 1715	trs. Durham 7 Nov. 1721
Richard Willis	trs. Gloucester, nom. 8 Nov., conf. 21 Nov. 1721	trs. Winchester 21 Sept. 1723
Benjamin Hoadly	trs. Hereford, nom. 27 Aug., conf. 29 Oct. 1723	trs. Winchester 26 Sept. 1734
Thomas Sherlock	trs. Bangor, nom. 11 Oct., conf. 8 Nov. 1734	trs. London 1 Dec. 1748
John Gilbert	trs. Llandaff, nom. 29 Oct., conf. 29 Dec. 1748	trs. York 24 May 1757
John Thomas	trs. Peterborough, nom. 25 May, conf. 18 June 1757	trs. Winchester 23 May 1761
Robert Hay Drummond	trs. St Asaph, nom. 30 May, conf. 11 June 1761	trs. York 23 Oct. 1761
John Thomas	trs. Lincoln, nom. 27 Oct., conf. 25 Nov. 1761	19 July 1766
John Hume	trs. Oxford, nom. 30 July, conf. 10 Sept. 1766	26 June 1782
Shute Barrington	trs. Llandaff, nom. 29 July, conf. 27 Aug. 1782	trs. Durham 7 July 1791
John Douglas	trs. Carlisle, nom. 12 July, conf. 17 Aug. 1791	18 May 1807
John Fisher	trs. Exeter, nom. 13 May, conf. 30 June 1807	8 May 1825
Thomas Burgess	trs. St David's, nom. 20 May, conf. 17 June 1825	19 Feb. 1837
Edward Denison	nom. 13 Mar., cons. 16 Apr. 1837	6 Mar. 1854
Walter Kerr Hamilton	nom. 27 Mar., cons. 14 May 1854	1 Aug. 1869
George Moberly	nom. 31 Aug., cons. 28 Oct. 1869	6 July 1885
John Wordsworth	nom. 4 Sept., cons. 28 Oct. 1885	16 Aug. 1911
Frederic Edward Ridgeway	trs. Kensington (suff.), nom. 23 Sept., conf. 17 Oct. 1911	4 May 1921
St Clair George Alfred Donaldson	trs. Brisbane, nom. 3 Oct., conf. 16 Dec. 1921	7 Dec. 1935
Ernest Neville Lovett	trs. Portsmouth, nom. 11 Mar., conf. 23 Apr. 1936	res. 1 Apr. 1946, d. 8 Sept. 1951
Geoffrey Charles Lester Lunt	trs. Ripon, nom. 16 July, conf. 9 Oct. 1946	17 Dec. 1948
William Louis Anderson	trs. Portsmouth, nom. 26 Apr., conf. 14 June 1949	res. 31 Dec. 1962, d. 5 Mar. 1972
Joseph Edward Fison	nom. 19 Mar., cons. 25 Apr. 1963	2 July 1972
George Edmund Reindorp	trs. Guildford, nom. 11 Jan., conf. 15 Jan. 1973	res. 30 Sept. 1981
John Austin Baker	nom. 12 Oct. 1981, cons. 2 Feb. 1982	

SELSEY

Æthelric II	cons. 1058	depr. May 1070
Stigand	nom. 23 May 1070	29 Aug. 1087

(Stigand transferred see to Chichester, 1075)

SHEFFIELD

BISHOPS	ACCESSION	DEATH *unless otherwise stated*
Leonard Hedley Burrows	trs. Lewes (suff.), nom. 18 Feb., conf. 21 Mar. 1914	res. 2 Aug. 1939, d. 6 Feb. 1940
Leslie Stannard Hunter	nom. 2 Aug., cons. 29 Sept. 1939	res. 31 Mar. 1962, d. 15 July 1983
Francis John Taylor	nom. 28 May, cons. 25 July 1962	res. 30 Apr. 1971, d. 4 July 1971
William Gordon Fallows	trs. Pontefract (suff.), nom. 1 May, conf. 21 May 1971	17 Aug. 1979
David Ramsay Lunn	nom. 11 Dec. 1979, cons. 25 Jan. 1980	

SODOR AND MAN

The medieval bishopric of the Isles was not originally part of an English province of the Church and the main succession of bishops will be found below among the Scottish lists. During the Great Schism in the Papacy a separate line of English bishops, appointed by the Roman popes, was recognized in the southern part of the diocese. This succession continued until the sixteenth century when, in 1542, the diocese of Sodor and Man was included, by act of the English parliament in 1542 (33 Henr. VIII, c. 31), in the province of York.

John Donegan[1]	*1387*	trs. 'ad Cathadensem ecclesiam' 27 Sept. 1392[2]
John Sproten	prov. 27 Sept. 1392	res. or depr. ?
Conrad	prov. 9 Jan. 1402	?
Theodore Bloc	prov. 16 Apr. 1402	?
John Burgherlin	prov. 20 July 1425	?
Richard Payli or Pulley	*1429*	?
[John Bourgherssh or Burwais	prov. 22 Apr. 1433	?]
John Seyre or Feyre	prov. 10 Oct., cons. 11 Nov. 1435	?
Thomas Burton	prov. 25 Sept. 1455	*p.* 18 Feb. 1458
Thomas Kirkham	prov. 21 June 1458	?
Richard Oldham	prov. 11 Feb. 1478	13 Oct. 1485
Hugh Blackleach	prov. 4 Apr. 1487	?
Hugh Hesketh	prov. 15 Apr. 1513	?
John Howden	prov. 19 June 1523	?
Henry Man	nom. *a.* 22 Jan., cons. 14 Feb. 1546	*19* Oct. 1556
John Salisbury	trs. Thetford (suff.), nom. 27 Mar., conf. 7 Apr. 1570	Sept. 1573
John Meyrick	nom. *a.* 5 Nov. 1575, cons. 15 Apr. 1576	7 Nov. 1599
George Lloyd	nom. 23 Dec. 1599, cons. Feb. 1600	trs. Chester 1605
John Philips	nom. 29 Jan., cons. 10 Feb. 1605	7 Aug. 1633
William Forster	nom. 26 Dec. 1633, cons. 9 Mar. 1634	Feb. 1635
Richard Parr	cons. 10 June 1635	1643
Samuel Rutter	cons. 24 Mar. 1661	*30 May 1663*
Isaac Barrow	nom. *a.* 22 May, cons. 5 July 1663	trs. St Asaph Mar. 1670,[3] d. 24 June 1680

[1] On his deprivation by the anti-pope in 1387 he lost recognition in the Scottish portion of the diocese, but continued in Man. His successors in this list during the continuance of the Schism were appointed by the popes, not by the anti-popes.
[2] Later bp of Down.
[3] He held Sodor and Man *in commendam* until Oct. 1671.

BISHOPS	ACCESSION	DEATH
		unless otherwise stated
Henry Bridgman	cons. 1 Oct. 1671	15 May 1682
John Lake	nom. 4 Sept. 1682, cons. 7 Jan. 1683	trs. Bristol *12 Aug.* 1684
Baptist Levinz	nom. 28 Oct. 1684, cons. 15 Mar. 1685	31 Jan. 1693
Thomas Wilson	nom. *a.* 18 Dec. 1697, cons. 16 Jan. 1698	7 Mar. 1755
Mark Hildesley	nom. 9 Apr., cons. 27 Apr. 1755	7 Dec. 1772
Richard Richmond	nom. 23 Jan., cons. 14 Feb. 1773	4 Feb. 1780
George Mason	nom. 19 Feb., cons. 5 Mar. 1780	8 Dec. 1783
Claudius Crigan	nom. 1 Mar., cons. 4 Apr. 1784	26 Apr. 1813
George Murray	nom. 22 May 1813,[1] cons. 6 Mar. 1814	trs. Rochester 6 Dec. 1827
William Ward[2]	nom. 3 Jan., cons. 9 Mar. 1828	26 Jan. 1838
James Bowstead	nom. 13 July, cons. 22 July 1838	trs. Lichfield 23 Jan. 1840
Henry Pepys	nom. 27 Jan., cons. 1 Mar. 1840	trs. Worcester 18 May 1841
Thomas Vowler Short	nom. 19 May, cons. 30 May 1841	trs. St Asaph 1846
Walter Augustus Shirley	nom. 10 Dec. 1846, cons. 10 Jan. 1847	21 Apr. 1847
Robert John Eden (3rd baron Auckland 1849)	nom. 7 May, cons. 23 May 1847	trs. Bath 1 July 1854
Horace Powys	nom. 11 July, cons. 25 July 1854	31 May 1877
Rowley Hill	nom. 9 Aug., cons. 24 Aug. 1877	27 May 1887
John Wareing Bardsley	nom. 22 July, cons. 24 Aug. 1887	trs. Carlisle 26 Feb. 1892
Norman Dumenil John Straton	nom. 4 Mar., cons. 25 Mar. 1892	trs. Newcastle 2 Sept. 1907
Thomas Wortley Drury	nom. 31 Oct., cons. 30 Nov. 1907	trs. Ripon 4 Feb. 1912
James Denton Thompson	nom. 15 Feb., cons. 25 Mar. 1912	31 Oct. 1924
Charles Leonard Thornton-Duesbury	nom. 5 Jan., cons. 24 Feb. 1925	11 Mar. 1928
William Stanton Jones	nom. 19 Apr., cons. 11 June 1928	res. 30 Oct. 1942, d. 13 Aug. 1951
John Ralph Strickland Taylor	nom. 12 Nov. 1942, cons. 6 Jan. 1943	res. 30 Oct. 1954, d. 13 Dec. 1961
Benjamin Pollard	trs. Lancaster (suff.), nom. 18 Dec. 1954	res. 10 Apr. 1966, d. 11 Apr. 1967
George Eric Gordon	nom. 12 July, cons. 29 Sept. 1966	res. 1 Mar. 1974
Vernon Sampson Nicholls	nom. 28 May, cons. 11 June 1974	res. 31 May 1983
Arthur Henry Attwell	nom. 26 Aug., cons. 14 Sept. 1983	

SOUTHWARK

Edward Stuart Talbot	trs. Rochester, nom. 17 May, inv. 24 May 1905	trs. Winchester 1 May 1911
Hubert Murray Burge	nom. 2 May, cons. 25 May 1911	trs. Oxford 6 Aug 1919
Cyril Forster Garbett	nom. 7 Sept., cons. 18 Oct. 1919	trs. Winchester 13 June 1932

[1] Nominated by the Duke of Atholl on 22 May 1813. The congé d'élire issued from chancery under the date 14 Feb. 1814.

[2] His style in the letters patent of presentation and appointment (28 Jan. 1828) is bp 'of Isle of Man and Sodor and of Sodor or Man'.

BISHOPS	ACCESSION	DEATH *unless otherwise stated*
Richard Godfrey Parsons	trs. Middleton (suff.), nom. 4 July, inv. 20 July 1932	trs. Hereford 12 Nov. 1941
Bertram Fitzgerald Simpson	trs. Kensington (suff.), nom. 15 Dec. 1941, conf. 20 Jan. 1942	res. 30 Nov. 1958, d. 16 July 1971
Arthur Mervyn Stockwood	nom. Jan., cons. 1 May 1959	res. 1 Nov. 1980
Ronald Oliver Bowlby	trs. Newcastle-upon-Tyne, nom. 11 Nov., conf. 14 Dec. 1980	

SOUTHWELL

George Ridding	nom. 12 Mar., cons. 1 May 1884	30 Aug. 1904
Edwyn Hoskyns (12th Baronet)	trs. Burnley (suff.), nom. 10 Oct., conf. 8 Dec. 1904	2 Dec. 1925
Bernard Oliver Francis Heywood	nom. 1 Feb., cons. 25 Mar. 1926	res. 10 May 1928 (trs. Ely 30 May 1934)
Henry Mosley	trs. Stepney (suff.), nom. 10 Sept., conf. *a.* 4 Oct. 1928	res. 1 Oct. 1941, d. 20 Jan. 1948
Frank Russell Barry	nom. 22 Sept., cons. 18 Oct. 1941	res. 18 Oct. 1963, d. 24 Oct. 1976
Gordon David Savage	trs. Buckingham (suff.), nom. 24 Jan., conf. 6 Mar. 1964	res. 1 May 1970
John Denis Wakeling	nom. 24 Aug., cons. 29 Sept., 1970	res. 31 Jan. 1985

TRURO

Edward White Benson	nom. 18 Jan., cons. 25 Apr. 1877	trs. Canterbury 3 Mar. 1883
George Howard Wilkinson	nom. 16 Apr., cons. 25 Apr. 1883	res. 1891, d. 11 Dec. 1907
John Gott	nom. 6 July, cons. 29 Sept. 1891	21 July 1906
Charles William Stubbs	nom. 14 Sept., cons. 30 Nov. 1906	4 May 1912
Winfrid Oldfield Burrows	nom. 30 May, cons. 25 July 1912	trs. Chichester 9 July 1919
Frederic Sumpter Guy Warman	nom. 14 July, cons. 18 Oct. 1919	trs. Chelmsford 9 Oct. 1923
Walter Howard Frere	nom. 10 Oct., cons. 1 Nov. 1923	res. 16 Feb. 1935 d. 2 Apr. 1938
Joseph Wellington Hunkin	nom. 26 Apr., cons. 11 June 1935	28 Oct. 1950
Edmund Robert Morgan	trs. Southampton (suff.), nom. 24 Apr., conf. 30 May 1951	res. 31 Oct. 1959 d. 21 Sept. 1979
John Maurice Key	trs. Sherborne (suff.), nom. 16 Dec. 1959, conf. 19 Feb. 1960	res. 31 Aug. 1973
Graham Douglas Leonard	trs. Willesden (suff.), nom. 5 Sept., conf. 20 Sept. 1973	trs. London 21 July 1981
Peter Mumford	trs. Hertford (suff.), nom. 2 Oct., conf. 19 Nov. 1981	

WAKEFIELD

William Walsham How	trs. Bedford (suff.), nom. 26 May 1888	10 Aug. 1897
George Rodney Eden	trs. Dover (suff.), nom. 29 Oct. 1897	res. 1928, d. 7 Jan. 1940
James Buchanan Seaton	nom. 15 Oct., cons. 1 Nov. 1928	26 May 1938

BISHOPS	ACCESSION	DEATH *unless otherwise stated*
Campbell Richard Hone	trs. Pontefract (suff.), nom. 19 Aug. 1938	res. 15 Sept. 1945, d. 16 May 1967
Henry McGowan	nom. 13 Nov. 1945, cons. 2 Feb. 1946	8 Sept. 1948
Roger Plumpton Wilson	nom. 8 Mar., cons. 25 Apr. 1949	trs. Chichester 16 Apr. 1958
John Alexander Ramsbotham	trs. Jarrow (suff.), nom. 22 Apr. 1958	res. 30 Nov. 1967
Eric Treacy	trs. Pontefract (suff.), nom. 30 Jan., conf. 8 Mar. 1968	res. 30 Sept. 1976, d. 13 May 1978
Colin Clement Walter James	trs. Basingstoke (suff.), nom. 30 Nov. 1976, conf. 7 Jan. 1977	trs. Winchester 1985

WESTMINSTER

Thomas Thirlby	nom. 18 Dec., cons. 19 Dec. 1540	res. 29 Mar. 1550[1]

WINCHESTER

Stigand	cons. *3 Apr.* 1043 to Elmham, nom. to Winchester 29 Aug. 1047	trs. to Canterbury, but retained Winchester; *c.* 11 Apr. 1070
Walkelin	nom. 23 May, cons. 30 May 1070	3 Jan. 1098
William Giffard	nom. 3 or 4 Aug. 1100, temp. *1100*, cons. 11 Aug. 1107	*23 Jan. 1129*
Henry of Blois	nom. 4 Oct., cons. 17 Nov. 1129	8 or 9 Aug. 1171
Richard of Ilchester	el. 1 May, temp. 17 May 1173, cons. 6 Oct. 1174	21 or 22 Dec. 1188
Godfrey de Lucy	nom. 15 Sept., cons. 22 Oct. 1189	11 or 12 Sept. 1204
Peter des Roches	el. *a.* 5 Feb. 1205, cons. 25 Sept. 1205, temp. 24 Mar. 1206	9 June 1238
[Ralph Nevill	post. *a.* 28 Aug. 1238	qua. 17 Feb. 1239]
William Raleigh	trs. Norwich, el. 1240, temp. 10 Sept. 1244	*a.* 1 Sept. 1250
[Andrew London	el. 3 Feb. 1261	qua. 22 June 1262]
[William Taunton	el. 3 Feb. 1261	qua. 22 June 1262]
Aymer de Valence	el. 4 Nov. 1250, cons. 16 May 1260	4 Dec. 1260
John Gervais	prov. 22 June, cons. 10 Sept., temp. 18 Oct. 1262	19 or 20 Jan. 1268
Nicholas of Ely	trs. Worcester, prov. 2 Mar., temp. 2 May 1268	12 Feb. 1280
[Robert Burnell	bp of Bath, el. 21 Mar. 1280	qua. 28 June 1280]
[Richard de la More	el. 6 Nov. 1280	qua. 1282, res. *a.* 9 June 1282]
John of Pontoise	prov. 9 June, cons. *14 June*,[2] temp. 11 Aug. 1282	4 Dec. 1304

---

[1] On Thirlby's resignation the see of Westminster was suppressed, and the diocese merged in that of London. Thirlby was appointed to the see of Norwich on 1 Apr. 1550.

[2] The pope's letter, announcing the provision and stating that John has been consecrated, is dated 15 June (Monday). The bp states that the pope provided him on 9 June (*Reg. J. de Pontissara* (Canterbury and York Soc.), 373).

BISHOPS	ACCESSION	DEATH *unless otherwise stated*
Henry Woodlock	el. 23 × 29 Jan., temp. 12 Mar., cons. 30 May 1305	28–29 June 1316
John Sandale	el. 26 July, temp. 23 Sept., cons. 31 Oct. 1316	2 Nov. 1319
Rigaud of Assier	prov. 26 Nov. 1319, temp. 17 Apr., cons. 16 Nov. 1320	12 Apr. 1323
John Stratford	prov. 20 June, cons. 26 June 1323, temp. 28 June 1324	trs. Canterbury 26 Nov. 1333
Adam Orleton	trs. Worcester, prov. 1 Dec. 1333, temp. 23 Sept. 1334	18 July 1345
William Edendon	prov. 9 Dec. 1345, temp. 15 Feb., cons. 14 May 1346	7 Oct. 1366
William of Wykeham	el. 13 × 24 Oct. 1366, prov. 14 July, cons. 10 Oct., temp. 12 Oct. 1367	27 Sept. 1404
Henry Beaufort	trs. Lincoln, prov. 19 Nov. 1404, temp. 14 Mar. 1405	11 Apr. 1447
William Waynflete	el. 15 × 17 Apr., prov. 10 May, temp. 4 June, cons. 30 July 1447	11 Aug. 1486
Peter Courtenay	trs. Exeter, prov. 29 Jan., temp. 2 Apr. 1487	22 Sept. 1492
Thomas Langton	trs. Salisbury, prov. 13 Mar., temp. 27 June 1493	trs. Canterbury 22 Jan., d. 27 Jan. 1501
Richard Fox	trs. Durham, prov. 20 Aug., temp. 17 Oct. 1501	5 Oct. 1528
Thomas Wolsey	abp of York, *in commendam* prov. 8 Feb., temp. 6 Apr. 1529	29 Nov. 1530
Stephen Gardiner	prov. 20 Oct., cons. 3 Dec., temp. 5 Dec. 1531	depr. 14 Feb. 1551
John Ponet	trs. Rochester, nom. 8 Mar. 1551	depr. 1553 d. 11 Aug. 1556
Stephen Gardiner	restored Aug. 1553	12 Nov. 1555
John White	trs. Lincoln, nom. 16 May, prov. 6 July 1556	depr. 26 June 1559, d. 12 Jan. 1560
Robert Horne	nom. 24 Nov. 1560, cons. 16 Feb. 1561	1 June 1580
John Watson	el. 29 June, cons. 18 Sept. 1580	23 Jan. 1584
Thomas Cooper	trs. Lincoln, nom. 2 Mar., conf. 23 Mar. 1584	29 Apr. 1594
William Wickham	trs. Lincoln, nom. 28 Dec. 1594, conf. 22 Feb. 1595	2 June 1595
William Day	el. 3 Nov. 1595, cons. 25 Jan. 1596	20 Sept. 1596
Thomas Bilson	trs. Worcester, el. 29 Apr., conf. 13 May 1597	18 June 1616
James Montague	trs. Bath, el. 26 June, conf. 4 Oct. 1616	20 July 1618
Lancelot Andrewes	trs. Ely, nom. 20 July 1618, conf. 25 Feb. 1619	25 Sept. 1626
Richard Neile	trs. Durham, nom. 16 Nov. 1627, conf. 7 Feb. 1628	trs. York 19 Mar. 1632
Walter Curle or Curll	trs. Bath, el. 26 Oct., conf. 16 Nov. 1632	5 Apr. 1647
Brian Duppa	trs. Salisbury, nom. 29 Aug., conf. 4 Oct. 1660	26 Mar. 1662
George Morley	trs. Worcester, nom. 11 Apr., conf. 14 May 1662	29 Oct. 1684
Peter Mew or Mews	trs. Bath, nom. 4 Nov., conf. 22 Nov. 1684	9 Nov. 1706

BISHOPS	ACCESSION	DEATH *unless otherwise stated*
Jonathan Trelawney (3rd Baronet 1685)	trs. Exeter, nom. 5 June, conf. 14 June 1707	19 July 1721
Charles Trimnell	trs. Norwich, nom. 1 Aug., conf. 19 Aug. 1721	15 Aug. 1723
Richard Willis	trs. Salisbury, nom. 2 Sept., conf. 21 Sept. 1723	10 Aug. 1734
Benjamin Hoadly	trs. Salisbury, nom. 3 Sept., conf. 26 Sept. 1734	17 Apr. 1761
John Thomas	trs. Salisbury, nom. 2 May, conf. 23 May 1761	1 May 1781
Brownlow North	trs. Worcester, nom. 10 May, conf. 7 June 1781	12 July 1820
George Pretyman- Tomline	trs. Lincoln, nom. 15 July, conf. 18 Aug. 1820	14 Nov. 1827
Charles Richard Sumner	trs. Llandaff, nom. 19 Nov., conf. 12 Dec. 1827	res. 21 Oct. 1869, d. 15 Aug. 1874
Samuel Wilberforce	trs. Oxford, nom. 11 Nov., conf. 11 Dec. 1869	19 July 1873
Edward Harold Browne	trs. Ely, nom. 22 Aug., conf. 23 Oct. 1873	res. Jan. 1891, d. 18 Dec. 1891
Anthony Wilson Thorold	trs. Rochester, nom. 23 Jan., conf. 13 Feb. 1891	25 July 1895
Randall Thomas Davidson	trs. Rochester, nom. 22 Aug., conf. 21 Sept. 1895	trs. Canterbury 6 Feb. 1903
Herbert Edward Ryle	trs. Exeter, nom. 20 Mar., conf. 3 Apr. 1903	res. 17 Apr. 1911, d. 20 Aug. 1925
Edward Stuart Talbot	trs. Southwark, nom. 18 Apr., conf. 1 May 1911	res. 30 Nov. 1923, d. 30 Jan. 1934
Frank Theodore Woods	trs. Peterborough, nom. 3 Dec., conf. 28 Dec. 1923	27 Feb. 1932
Cyril Forster Garbett	trs. Southwark, nom. 18 Apr., conf. 13 June 1932	trs. York 1 June 1942
Mervyn George Haigh	trs. Coventry, nom. 10 July, conf. 24 Sept. 1942	res. 29 Feb. 1952, d. 20 May 1962
Alwyn Terrell Petre Williams	trs. Durham, nom. 21 Mar., conf. 8 May 1952	res. 30 Sept. 1961, d. 18 Feb. 1968
Sherard Falkner Allison	trs. Chelmsford, nom. 13 Oct., conf. 20 Dec. 1961	res. 30 Sept. 1974
John Vernon Taylor	nom. 26 Nov. 1974, cons. 31 Jan. 1975	res. 28 Feb. 1985
Colin Clement Walter James	trs. Wakefield, nom. 1985	

WORCESTER

Wulfstan II	el. 29 Aug., cons. 8 Sept. 1062	*20* Jan. 1095
Samson	el. 1096, cons. 8 June 1096	5 May 1112
Theulf	nom. 28 Dec. 1113, cons. 27 June 1115	20 Oct. 1123
Simon	el. 29 *a.* Mar., cons. 24 May 1125	*20 Mar.* 1150
John of Pagham	cons. 4 Mar. 1151	*Dec.* 1157
Alfred	cons. *a.* 13 Apr. 1158	31 July 1160
Roger of Gloucester	el. Mar. 1163, cons. 23 Aug. 1164	9 Aug. 1179
Baldwin	cons. 10 Aug. 1180	trs. Canterbury Dec. 1184
William of Northolt	el. *c.* 25 May, cons. 21 Sept. 1186	2 or 3 May 1190
Robert FitzRalph	el. 1 July 1190, cons. 5 May 1191	*27* June 1193

BISHOPS	ACCESSION	DEATH *unless otherwise stated*
Henry de Sully	el. 4 Dec., cons. 12 Dec. 1193	24 or 25 Oct. 1195
John of Coutances	el. *Jan.*, cons. 20 Oct. 1196	24 Sept. 1198
Mauger	el. *a.* 8 Aug. 1199, post. Mar.–Apr., cons. 4 June 1200	1 July 1212
[Randulph [? of Evesham]	el. 2 Dec. 1213	qua. *a.* 20 Jan. 1214]
Walter de Gray	el. 20 Jan., temp. 7 July, cons. 5 Oct. 1214	trs. York *p.* Nov. 1215
Sylvester of Evesham	el. 3 Apr., temp. 8 Apr., cons. 3 July 1216	16 July 1218
William de Blois	el. *c.* 25 Aug., temp 10 Sept., cons. 7 Oct. 1218	17 or 18 Aug. 1236
Walter Cantilupe	el. 30 Aug., temp. 27 Sept. 1236, cons. 3 May 1237	12 Feb. 1266
Nicholas of Ely	el. 9 May, temp. 18 June, cons. 19 Sept. 1266	trs. Winchester 2 Mar. 1268
Godfrey Giffard	el. 2 × 24 May, temp. *24 May*, cons. 23 Sept. 1268	26 Jan. 1302
[John St German	el. 25 Mar. 1302	qua. 17 Oct. 1302]
William Gainsborough	prov. 22 Oct., cons. 28 Oct. 1302, temp. 4 Feb. 1303	17 Sept. 1307
Walter Reynolds	el. 13 Nov. 1307, prov. 12 Feb., temp. 5 Apr., cons. 13 Oct. 1308	trs. Canterbury 1 Oct. 1313
Walter Maidstone	prov. 1 Oct., cons. 7 Oct. 1313, temp. 17 Feb. 1314	28 Mar. 1317
Thomas Cobham	prov. 31 Mar., cons. 22 May, temp. 20 Nov. 1317	*27 Aug. 1327*
[Wulstan Bransford	el. 31 Aug. × 8 Sept., temp. 8 Oct. 1327	qua.]
Adam Orleton	trs. Hereford, prov. 28 Sept. 1327, temp. 2 Mar. 1328	trs. Winchester 1 Dec. 1333
Simon Montacute	prov. 11 Dec. 1333, temp. 15 Mar., cons. 8 May 1334	trs. Ely 14 Mar. 1337
Thomas Hempnall	prov. 14 Mar., cons. 30 Mar., temp. 25 July 1337	21 Dec. 1338
Wulstan Bransford	el. *a.* 4 Jan., temp. 17 Feb., cons. 21 Mar. 1339	6 Aug. 1349
John Thoresby	trs. St David's, prov. 4 Sept. 1349, temp. 10 Jan. 1350	trs. York 17 Oct. 1352
Reginald Brian	trs. St David's, prov. 22 Oct. 1352, temp. 31 Mar. 1353	(trs. Ely 1361) d. 10 Dec. 1361
John Barnet	prov. *a.* 16 Dec. 1361, temp. 19 Mar., cons. 20 Mar. 1362	trs. Bath 25 Nov. 1363
William Whittlesey	trs. Rochester, prov. 6 Mar., temp. 28 June 1364	trs. Canterbury 11 Oct. 1368
William Lenn	trs. Chichester 11 Oct. 1368, temp. 4 June 1369	18 Nov. 1373
[Walter Lyghe	el. 7 Dec. 1373	qua. *a.* 12 Sept. 1375]
Henry Wakefield	prov. 12 Sept., temp. 14 Oct., cons. 28 Oct. 1375	11 Mar. 1395
Robert Tideman of Winchcomb	trs. Llandaff, prov. 15 June 1395	13 June 1401
Richard Clifford	el. 27 June, prov. 19 Aug., temp. 21 Sept., cons. 9 Oct. 1401	trs. London 22 June 1407
Thomas Peverel	trs. Llandaff, prov. 4 July, temp. 20 Nov. 1407	1 or 2 Mar. 1419
Philip Morgan	el. 24 Apr., prov. 19 June, temp. 18 Oct., cons. 3 Dec. 1419	trs. Ely 27 Feb. 1426
Thomas Polton	trs. Chichester, prov. 27 Feb., temp. 23 Apr. 1426	23 Aug. 1433
[Thomas Brouns	prov. 24 Sept. 1433	trs. Rochester 21 Feb. 1435]

BISHOPS	ACCESSION	DEATH *unless otherwise stated*
Thomas Bourgchier	el. 9 Dec. 1433, prov. 9 Mar., temp. 15 Apr., cons. 15 May 1435	trs. Ely 20 Dec. 1443
John Carpenter	prov. 20 Dec. 1443, temp. 27 Feb., cons. 22 Mar. 1444	d. *a*. 15 July 1476
John Alcock	trs. Rochester, prov. 15 July, temp. 25 Sept. 1476	trs. Ely 6 Oct. 1486
Robert Morton	prov. 16 Oct. 1486, cons. 28 Jan., temp. 10 Feb. 1487	*a*. 5 May 1497
Giovanni de' Gigli	prov. 30 Aug., cons. 10 Sept., temp. 5 Dec. 1497	25 Aug. 1498
Silvestro de' Gigli	prov. 24 Dec. 1498, temp. 17 Mar., cons. *a*. 6 Apr. 1499	16 Apr. 1521
[Giulio de' Medici	prov. *in commendam* 7 June 1521	res. 26 Sept. 1522]
Geronimo de' Ghinucci	prov. 26 Sept. 1522, temp. 20 Feb. 1523	depr. 21 Mar. 1533
Hugh Latimer	el. *a*. 12 Aug., cons. 26 Sept. 1535	res. 1 July 1539, d. 16 Oct. 1555
John Bell	nom. July, cons. *17 Aug.* 1539	res. 17 Nov. 1543, d. 11 Aug. 1556
Nicholas Heath	trs. Rochester, nom. 14 Dec. 1543, conf. 20 Feb. 1544	depr. 10 Oct. 1551
John Hooper[1]	bp of Gloucester, nom. 20 May 1552	depr. 15 Mar. 1554, d. 9 Feb. 1555
Nicholas Heath	restored 1554	trs. York 21 June 1555
Richard Pates	nom. *a*. 5 Mar. 1555	depr. 26 June 1559, d. 5 Oct. 1565
Edwin Sandes or Sandys	nom. 13 Nov., cons. 21 Dec. 1559	trs. London 13 July 1570
Nicholas Bullingham	trs. Lincoln, el. 18 Jan., conf. 26 Jan. 1571	18 Apr. 1576
John Whitgift	nom. 24 Mar., cons. 21 Apr. 1577	trs. Canterbury 23 Sept. 1583
Edmund Freke	trs. Norwich, nom. 26 Oct., conf. 5 Dec. 1584	21 Mar. 1591
Richard Fletcher	trs. Bristol, nom. *a*. 17 Jan., conf. 10 Feb. 1593	trs. London 10 Jan. 1595
Thomas Bilson	el. 20 Apr., cons. 13 June 1596	trs. Winchester 13 May 1597
Gervase Babington	trs. Exeter, nom. 30 Aug., conf. 4 Oct. 1597	17 May 1610
Henry Parry	trs. Gloucester, el. 13 July 1610, conf. 5 Oct. 1610	12 Dec. 1616
John Thornborough	trs. Bristol, el. 25 Jan., conf. 17 Feb. 1617	9 July 1641
John Prideaux	nom. 11 Nov., cons. 19 Dec. 1641	*29 July 1650*
George Morley	nom. 20 Sept., cons. 28 Oct. 1660	trs. Winchester 14 May 1662
John Gauden	trs. Exeter, nom. 15 May, conf. 10 June 1662	20 Sept. 1662
John Earle or Earles	nom. 13 Oct., cons. 30 Nov. 1662	trs. Salisbury 26 Sept. 1663
Robert Skinner	trs. Oxford, nom. 21 June, conf. 4 Nov. 1663	14 June 1670
Walter Blandford	trs. Oxford, nom. 18 May, conf. 14 June 1671	*9 or 16 July 1675*

[1] John Hooper, bp of Gloucester, resigned that see to the king 26 Apr. 1552. It was then amalgamated with the see of Worcester and Hooper was made 'bp of Worcester and Gloucester'. The sees were divided again after Hooper's deprivation.

YORK

BISHOPS	ACCESSION	DEATH
		unless otherwise stated
James Fleetwood	nom. 13 July, cons. 29 Aug. 1675	17 July 1683
William Thomas	trs. St David's, nom. 23 July, conf. 27 Aug. 1683	25 June 1689
Edward Stillingfleet	nom. 9 Sept., cons. 13 Oct. 1689	27 Mar. 1699
William Lloyd	trs. Lichfield, nom. 23 Apr., conf. 22 June 1699	30 Aug. 1717
John Hough	trs. Lichfield, nom. 7 Sept., conf. 28 Sept. 1717	8 May 1743
Isaac Maddox	trs. St Asaph, nom. May, conf. 12 Nov. 1743	27 Sept. 1759
James Johnson	trs. Gloucester, nom. 5 Oct., conf. 9 Nov. 1759	26 Nov. 1774
Brownlow North	trs. Lichfield, nom. 5 Dec., cons. 30 Dec. 1774	trs. Winchester 7 June 1781
Richard Hurd	trs. Lichfield, nom. 11 June, conf. 30 June 1781	28 May 1808
Ffolliott Herbert Walker Cornewall	trs. Hereford, nom. 11 June, conf. 13 July 1808	5 Sept. 1831
Robert James Carr	trs. Chichester, nom. 10 Sept., conf. 23 Sept. 1831	24 Apr. 1841
Henry Pepys	trs. Sodor and Man, nom. 28 Apr., conf. 18 May 1841	13 Nov. 1860
Henry Philpott	nom. 19 Jan., cons. 25 Mar. 1861	res. 22 Nov. 1890, d. 10 Jan. 1892
John James Stewart Perowne	nom. 16 Dec. 1890, cons. 2 Feb. 1891	res. 10 Dec. 1901, d. 6 Nov. 1904
Charles Gore	nom. 19 Dec. 1901, cons. 23 Feb. 1902	trs. Birmingham 27 Jan. 1905
Huyshe Wolcott Yeatman-Biggs	trs. Southwark (suff.), nom. 28 Jan., conf. 24 Feb. 1905	trs. Coventry 23 Oct. 1918
Ernest Harold Pearce	nom. 6 Jan., cons. 24 Feb. 1919	28 Oct. 1930
Arthur William Thomson Perowne	trs. Bradford, nom. 9 Feb., conf. 11 Mar. 1931	res. 30 Sept. 1941, d. 9 Apr. 1948
William Wilson Cash	nom. 1 Oct., cons. 1 Nov. 1941	18 July 1955
Lewis Mervyn Charles-Edwards	nom. 15 Nov. 1955, cons. 6 Jan. 1956	res. 30 Sept. 1970, d. 20 Oct. 1983
Robert Wilmer Woods	nom. 14 Jan., cons. 20 Feb. 1971	res. 21 Nov. 1981
Philip Harold Ernest Goodrich	trs. Tonbridge (suff.), nom. 24 Feb., conf. 21 Apr. 1982	

YORK

ARCHBISHOPS	ACCESSION	DEATH
		unless otherwise stated
Ealdred (bp of York and Worcester together, 1061–62)	1044 1062 York alone	11 Sept. 1069
Thomas of Bayeux	nom. 23 May, cons. *25 Dec.* 1070	18 Nov. 1100
Gerard	trs. Hereford Apr. 1100	21 May 1108
Thomas II	nom. 27 May 1108, cons. 27 June 1109	21 or 24 Feb. 1114
Thurstan	el. 15 or 16 Aug. 1114, cons. 19 Oct. 1119	res. 25 Jan. 1140 d. 5 Feb. 1140
William FitzHerbert	el. and temp. Jan. 1141, cons. 26 Sept. 1143	depr. 1147
Henry Murdac	el. July 1147, cons. 7 Dec. 1147, temp. *1151*	14 Oct. 1153
William FitzHerbert	restored Oct. 1153	8 June 1154
Roger de Pont L'Evêque	cons. 10 Oct. 1154	26 Nov. 1181
Geoffrey	el. 10 Aug. 1189, cons. 18 Aug. 1191	18 Dec. 1212
[Simon Langton	el. *June* 1215	qua. 20 Aug. 1215]

ARCHBISHOPS	ACCESSION	DEATH *unless otherwise stated*
Walter de Gray	trs. Worcester, post. 10 Nov. 1215, temp. 19 Feb. 1216	1 May 1255
Sewal de Bovill	post. *c.* Oct. 1255, temp. 4 May 1256, cons. 23 July 1256	10 May 1258
Godfrey Ludham	el. *a.* 25 July, cons. 22 Sept., temp. 1 Dec. 1258	12 Jan. 1265
[William Langton	el. 12 Mar. 1265	qua. *a.* 24 Nov. 1265]
[Bonaventura	prov. 24 Nov. 1265	res. *a.* 15 Oct. 1266]
Walter Giffard	trs. Bath, prov. 15 Oct., temp. 26 Dec. 1266	late Apr. 1279
William Wickwane	el. 22 June, prov. *a.* 17 Sept., cons. 17 Sept., temp. 28 Oct. 1279	26–27 Aug. 1285
John le Romeyn	el. 29 Oct. 1285, cons. 10 Feb., temp. 16 Apr. 1286	11 Mar. 1296
Henry Newark	el. 7 May 1296, prov. 4 Mar., temp. 22 June 1297, cons. 15 June 1298	15 Aug. 1299
Thomas Corbridge	el. 12 Nov. 1299, prov. *p.* 29 Jan.,[1] cons. 28 Feb., temp. 30 Apr. 1300	22 Sept. 1304
William Greenfield	el. 4 Dec. 1304, cons. 30 Jan., temp. 31 Mar. 1306	6 Dec. 1315
William Melton	el. 21 Jan. 1316, prov. Sept. 1317, cons. 25 Sept., temp. 8 Oct. 1317	5 Apr. 1340
William Zouche	el. 2 May 1340, prov. 26 June 1342, cons. 7 July, temp. 19 Sept. 1342	10 or 19 July 1352
John Thoresby	trs. Worcester, post. 16 Aug., prov. 17 Oct. 1352, temp. 8 Feb. 1353	6 Nov. 1373
Alexander Neville	el. 23 Nov. × 12 Dec. 1373, prov. 3 or 14 Apr., cons. 4 June, temp. 6 June 1374	trs. St Andrews 30 Apr. 1388, d. May 1392 × 1392
Thomas Arundel	trs. Ely, prov. 3 Apr., temp. 14 Sept. 1388	trs. Canterbury 25 Sept. 1396
Robert Waldby	trs. Chichester, prov. 5 Oct. 1396, temp. 6 Mar. 1397	29 Dec. 1397 × 6 Jan. 1398
Richard le Scrope	trs. Lichfield, prov. 27 Feb. × 15 Mar., temp. 23 June 1398	8 June 1405
[Thomas Langley	el. *a.* 8 Aug. 1405	qua. *a.* 14 May 1406]
[Robert Hallum	prov. 14 May 1406	trs. Salisbury 7 Oct. 1407]
Henry Bowet	trs. Bath, prov. 7 Oct., temp. 1 Dec. 1407	20 Oct. 1423
[Philip Morgan	post. Nov.–Dec. 1423	qua. 14 Feb. 1424]
[Richard Flemyng	trs. Lincoln, prov. 14 Feb. 1424	res. 20 July 1425]
John Kempe	trs. London, prov. 20 July 1425, temp. 22 Apr. 1426	trs. Canterbury 21 July 1452
William Booth	trs. Lichfield, prov. 21 July, temp. 6 Sept. 1452	12 Sept. 1464
George Nevill	trs. Exeter, prov. 15 Mar., temp. 17 June 1465	8 June 1476
Lawrence Booth	trs. Durham, prov. 31 July, temp. 8 Oct. 1476	19 May 1480

[1] The election was quashed and the see reserved 29 Jan. 1300 (*Registres de Boniface VIII*, no. 3876).The papal letters notifying provision are dated 9 Mar. [*Cal. Papal Letters*, i. 586 and P.R.O. Papal bulls 40(6)].

ARCHBISHOPS	ACCESSION	DEATH *unless otherwise stated*
Thomas Rotherham (or Scot)	trs. Lincoln, prov. 7 July, temp. 9 Sept. 1480	29 May 1500
Thomas Savage	trs. London, prov. 18 Jan., temp. 29 Apr. 1501	2 Sept. 1507
Christopher Bainbridge	trs. Durham, prov. 22 Sept., temp. 12 Dec. 1508	14 July 1514
Thomas Wolsey	trs. Lincoln, nom. *a.* 5 Aug., temp. 5 Aug., prov. 15 Sept. 1514	29 Nov. 1530
Edward Lee	prov. 20 Oct., temp. 3 Dec., cons. 10 Dec. 1531	13 Sept. 1544
Robert Holgate	trs. Llandaff, nom. 5 Jan., conf. 16 Jan. 1545	depr. *23* Mar. 1554, d. 15 Nov. 1555
Nicholas Heath	trs. Worcester, nom. 19 Feb., conf. 21 June 1555	depr. 5 July 1559, d. 1579
Thomas Young	trs. St David's, el. 31 Jan., conf. 25 Feb. 1561	26 June 1568
Edmund Grindal	trs. London, nom. 1 Apr., conf. 22 May 1570	trs. Canterbury 10 Jan. 1576
Edwin Sandes or Sandys	trs. London, nom. 19 Jan., conf. 8 Mar. 1577	10 July 1588
John Piers	trs. Salisbury, nom. 18 Jan., conf. 19 Feb. 1589	28 Sept. 1594
Matthew Hutton	trs. Durham, nom. 6 Feb., conf. 24 Mar. 1595	15 Jan. 1606
Tobias Matthew	trs. Durham, nom. 11 July, conf. 28 Aug. 1606	29 Mar. 1628
George Montaigne or Mountain	trs. Durham, nom. 4 June, conf. 1 July 1628	24 Oct. 1628
Samuel Harsnett	trs. Norwich, nom. 3 Nov. 1628, conf. 13 Jan. 1629	25 May 1631
Richard Neile	trs. Winchester, nom. 22 Feb., conf. 19 Mar. 1632	31 Oct. 1640
John Williams	trs. Lincoln, conf. *4 Dec.* 1641	25 Mar. 1650
Accepted Frewen	trs. Lichfield, nom. 2 Sept., conf. 4 Oct. 1660	28 Mar. 1664
Richard Sterne	trs. Carlisle, nom. 7 Apr., conf. *31 May* 1664	18 June 1683
John Dolben	trs. Rochester, nom. 13 July, conf. 16 Aug. 1683	11 Apr. 1686
Thomas Lamplugh	trs. Exeter, nom. 15 Nov., conf. 8 Dec. 1688	5 May 1691
John Sharp	nom. 9 May, cons. 5 July 1691	2 Feb. 1714
William Dawes (2nd baronet)	trs. Chester, el. 20 Feb., conf. 9 Mar. 1714	30 Apr. 1724
Lancelot Blackburn	trs. Exeter, nom. 19 Oct., conf. 28 Nov. 1724	22 or 23 Mar. 1743
Thomas Herring	trs. Bangor, nom. 6 Apr., conf. 21 Apr. 1743	trs. Canterbury 24 Nov. 1747
Matthew Hutton	trs. Bangor, nom. 25 Nov., conf. 10 Dec. 1747	trs. Canterbury 29 Apr. 1757
John Gilbert	trs. Salisbury, nom. 29 Apr., conf. 24 May 1757	9 Aug. 1761
Robert Hay Drummond	trs. Salisbury, nom. 19 Sept., conf. 23 Oct. 1761	10 Dec. 1776
William Markham	trs. Chester, nom. 21 Dec. 1776, conf. 20 Jan. 1777	3 Nov. 1807
Edward Venables Vernon (from 15 Jan. 1831 surnamed Harcourt)	trs. Carlisle, nom. 26 Nov. 1807, conf. 19 Jan. 1808	5 Nov. 1847
Thomas Musgrave	trs. Hereford, nom. 15 Nov., conf. 10 Dec. 1847	4 May 1860

ARCHBISHOPS	ACCESSION	DEATH OR TRS. *unless otherwise stated*
Charles Thomas Longley	trs. Durham, nom. 9 June, conf. 12 July 1860	trs. Canterbury 26 Nov. 1862
William Thomson	trs. Gloucester, nom. 19 Dec. 1862, conf. 23 Jan. 1863	25 Dec. 1890
William Connor Magee	trs. Peterborough, nom. 27 Jan., conf. 20 Feb. 1891	5 May 1891
William Dalrymple Maclagan	trs. Lichfield, nom. 9 July, conf. 28 July 1891	res. 31 Dec. 1908, d. 19 Sept. 1910
Cosmo Gordon Lang	trs. Stepney (suff.), nom. 1 Jan., conf. 20 Jan. 1909	trs. Canterbury 30 Nov. 1928
William Temple	trs. Manchester, nom. 6 Dec. 1928, conf. 2 Jan. 1929	trs. Canterbury 1 Apr. 1942
Cyril Forster Garbett	trs. Winchester, nom. 24 Apr., conf. 1 June 1942	31 Dec. 1955
Arthur Michael Ramsey	trs. Durham, nom. 27 Jan., conf. 16 Mar. 1956	trs. Canterbury 21 June 1961
Frederick Donald Coggan	trs. Bradford, nom. 23 June, conf. 6 July 1961	trs. Canterbury 5 Dec. 1974
Stuart Yarworth Blanch	trs. Liverpool, nom. 30 Dec. 1974, conf. 9 Jan. 1975	res. 31 Aug. 1983
John Stapylton Habgood	trs. Durham, nom. 27 Sept., conf. 18 Oct. 1983	

SUFFRAGAN BISHOPS

The following lists are reprinted from the second edition of the *Handbook*, although it is acknowledged that they stand in need of revision. Dr D. M. Smith, 'Suffragan bishops in the medieval diocese of Lincoln', *Lincolnshire History and Archaeology*, xvii (1982) 17–27, has shown the scale of revision that concentrated work on individual dioceses might achieve. The list of Irish bishops as suffragans in England has been removed from the present edition, the material being found within the lists of bishops of Ireland below (pp. 328–77).

FOREIGN BISHOPS

SAXON AND DANISH BISHOPS

Siegfried, a Norwegian bp of the time of Edgar.
Siward, abbot of Abingdon, coadjutor to Abp Eadsige 1044. Suffragan for Canterbury. d. 23 Oct. 1048.
Ralph, a Norwegian bp, abbot of Abingdon 1050–52.
Osmund, possibly lived at Ely and was buried there between 1066 and 1076.
Christiern, came to England with Sweyn, 1070.

BISHOPS 'IN PARTIBUS' AS SUFFRAGANS IN ENGLAND AND WALES

The titles of these bps are usually given adjectivally, as the papal officials gave them. Only indisputable identifications of sees have been given, and many were probably doubtful even to contemporaries. The dates in brackets denote the period, during which they are recorded in England, and these are followed by the names of the English dioceses in which the suffragans acted, with dates of their recorded activities. For further details see Eubel and Stubbs, also A. H. Thompson in *Yorks. Archaeol. Journal*, xxiv. 248 *sqq.* and David Knowles, *The Religious Orders in England*, ii (1955), 373–75, iii (1959), 493–95.

Other foreign bps, not consecrated to sees *in partibus infidelium*, are sometimes recorded as suffragans in England, being exiles or visitors from their own dioceses: e.g. Ralph, bp of Orkney, in Lincoln diocese *c.* 1147, Bernard, abp of Ragusa, 1199–1203, afterwards bp of Carlisle, Gilbert, bp of Hamar (Norway), in Norwich diocese *c.* 1287, William, bp of Tournai, in London diocese 1399–1406.

Augustine. LAODICEA. Durham 1259.
William or Geoffrey (1266–86). RAGENSIS. Norwich.
Hugh. BYBLOS. Durham *c.* 1300.
David. RECREENSIS.[1] York 1315.
Peter of Bologna, O.F.M. (1300–31). CORBAVIENSIS. London, Canterbury 1326. Winchester 1321–23.
Boniface of Pisa, O.F.M. CORBAVIENSIS. Durham 1338–41.
John Paschal. Norwich 1344.
Benedict (1333–46). SARDICA. Norwich. Winchester.
Hugh (1344–51). abp DAMASCUS. York 1344–51. Lincoln 1347.
Richard, O.F.M. abp NAZARETH. Canterbury 1349. Worcester 1350. Rochester 1362. London. Ely.
Caesarius de Rosis, ? O.F.M. (1349–55). Canterbury. Winchester.
Thomas, O.Cist. (1353 (?)–65). MAGNATIENSIS or MAGNASSIENSIS. Lichfield 1360. Llandaff 1361. Hereford 1361. York 1365.
Thomas Waleys, O.P. (1353–62). LYCOSTOMIUM.
Thomas Salkeld (1349–58). CHRYSOPOLIS. York.
John Ware (1354–86). CUMANAGIENSIS. Exeter 1355–86. Hereford 1371.
Geoffrey (1359). DAMASCENUS. York.
Robert Worksop (1360–75). PRISSINENSIS. Hereford 1360. Chichester 1362. Worcester 1373–75. York.
Geoffrey (1361–64). MILIENSIS. York.
John de Langebrugge, O.F.M. (1362–67). BUDUENSIS. Bath 1362–63. Lincoln 1367.
Thomas de Illeye (1362–66). LAMBERGENSIS. London 1362. Lincoln 1366–68. York. Bangor.
Robert (1366–94). LAMBRENSIS. York 1366. Bangor 1371.
John (1367). LAMBERGENSIS. ? Lincoln.
John (1366–81). AYOBANENSIS. Canterbury 1369.
Richard (1370–99). SERVIENSIS. York.
William Bottlesham, O.P. (1382). NAVATENSIS.
Thomas (1382). SCUTARI. ? Norwich.
Nicholas (1384–1406). CHRISTOPOLITANUS. Bath 1385–1403. Salisbury 1395–1406.
Robert Hyntlesham (1385–89). SEBASTOPOLIS. Norwich. Salisbury 1388–89.
Robert (1371–87). ARCHILIENSIS. Norwich 1371. Hereford 1387.
William Egmund (1390–94). PRISSINENSIS. Lincoln.
William Northbrugge (1385–1408). PHARENSIS. York 1387–1390, 1408. Lichfield 1380–87. Worcester 1395.
William (1394–99). BASILIENSIS. London.
Thomas Botyler, O.F.M. (1395–1420). CHRYSOPOLIS. Lincoln 1395. Salisbury 1395. Winchester 1401. Worcester 1420.
Thomas Edwardston (d. 1396). abp. ? NAZARETH. Norwich.
William Ouneby (1397–99). Lincoln.
John Sewale (1405–26). SURRONENSIS. St David's 1405. Winchester 1417–18. London 1417–23. Salisbury 1420–26.
John Leicester, O. Carm. (1400–24). abp. SMYRNA. Norwich.
Thomas Merks (1404–06). SAMASTRENSIS (1399 formerly Carlisle). Winchester 1404–05. Canterbury 1406.
Thomas (1400 ?). CONSTANTIA.
John Greenlaw, O.F.M. (1401–22). SOLTANIENSIS. Bath 1401–08. Exeter 1402. Salisbury 1409. York 1421. Lincoln 1422.
John Crancroyt, Gilb. (1402–32). ANCORADENSIS. Ely 1402. Lincoln 1420–32. Canterbury 1425.
John Chiveley, O.F.M. (1402). CALLIPOLENSIS. Salisbury 1407–08.
William Yeurde, O.F.M. (1407–17). SALUBRIENSIS. Salisbury 1409–17. Exeter 1414–17. Winchester 1407–17.

[1] For this title, and the possibility of an Irish connection, *see Reg. Wm Greenfield, archbishop of York*, v (Surtees Soc., 1940), 144, n. 3.

Matthew Moore, O.P. (1410). Hebron. Hereford.
William Bellers, O.P. (1411–37). Soltaniensis. Canterbury 1437. Lincoln 1418.
John Greyby, O.F.M. (1423–43). Stephanensis. Lincoln 1423–31. Ely 1424–43.
Robert Ryngman, O.F.M. (1425–52). Gradensis. Norwich.
John Bloxwych (1436–43). Olenensis. Bath 1437–43. Exeter 1442. Canterbury 1443.
John Kegill, O.F.M. Philapolensis. York 1442–58.
Roderic (1454–57). Arlatensis. Exeter.
William Westkarre, O.S.A.[1] (1457–86). Sidon. Winchester 1457–86. Bath 1459. Canterbury 1468. Worcester 1480.
James (1458). Banhorensis. Exeter.
John Valens (1459–79). Tenos (Tinen. in patr. Jerus.). Bath 1459–79. Exeter 1461–62.
Henry Cranebroke, O.S.A. (1469–74). Joppa. Canterbury.
Richard Martin (1474–98). Canterbury.
Richard Wycherly, O.P. (1480–1502). Olensis. Hereford 1480. Worcester 1482–1501.
Thomas Cornish, O.S.J.Jer. (1480–1513). Tenos. Bath 1486–1513. Exeter 1487–1505.
Thomas Wele, O.S.B. (1484–1502, d. 1521). Panadensis. London 1492–1502. Lichfield.
Augustine Church, O.Cist. abbot of Thame (1488–1512). Lydda. Exeter 1493. Salisbury 1494–99. Lincoln 1501–12.
Edward (1503). Gallipoli. London. Worcester.
Ralph Heylesdon (1503–23). Ascalon. Worcester 1503–23. Hereford 1510.
Thomas Carr, O.S.A. prior of Brinkburn (1504). Carensis. Durham.
John Underwood (1505–31). Chalcedon. Norwich.
Thomas Wells, O.S.A. prior of Bicknacre (1505–23, d. 1526). Sidon. Canterbury. London.
John Hatton (1514–16). Nigripontensis. York 1514–16. London.
John ? (1506). Sabastiensis. Exeter.
John Thornden, O.S.B. (1505–14). Cyrene. Canterbury 1508–14.
William Barton (1508–17). Salona. Salisbury.
Thomas Chard, Clun. prior of Kerswell[2] (1508–41). Selymbria. Exeter 1508–34. Bath.
Thomas Fowler (1505–19). Lachorensis. Hereford.
John (Rawlynson ?) (1512–22). Ario. Lincoln 1519–22. York 1516.
John Tinmouth (1510–24). Argos. Salisbury.
Thomas Wolf, O.F.M. (1510–18). Lacedæmon. Bath 1513–17.
John Young (1513–27). Gallipoli. London. Lincoln 1522–27.
Richard (1513). Naturensis (Athyra). Durham.
Roger Smith (1513–18). Lydda. Salisbury 1517–18. Lincoln 1514–c. 1531.
Thomas (1514). Paros (Naxos and Paros). Lincoln 1514.
William Grant, O.S.A. (1515–24). Panadensis. Ely 1516.
Richard Wilson, O.S.A. prior of Drax (1516–23). Nigripontensis. York 1516–23. (Bishop of Meath 1523.)
William Bachelor O.S.J.Jer. (d. 1515). Carvahagonensis in Grecia. Chichester.
Francis Sexello, O.F.M. (1517). Castoria. Bath.
John Pinnock, ? Bonhomme, pr. of Edington (1518–35). Syene. Salisbury 1518–35. Hereford 1525.
Thomas Vivian, O.S.A. prior of Bodmin (1517–33). Megara. Exeter.
Richard Burgh, Prem. abbot of Shap (1519). Suriensis. Carlisle.
William Gilbert, O.S.A. prior and abbot of Bruton (1519–32). Maiorensis. Bath 1519–32.
William Hogeson, O.P. (1520–30). Dara. Winchester 1520–25. York 1530.
William How O.P. (1520–32). Avara (Auriensis). Chichester 1532.
Thomas Bale, O.S.A. (1521–28). Lydda. London.
William Sutton, O.S.B. prior of Avecote (1521–24). Panadensis. Lichfield 1524.
Matthew Mackarell, Prem. abbot of Barlings (1524–37). Chalcedon. York 1524–28. Lincoln 1533–37.

[1] See Reg. Thome Bourgchier (Cant. and York Soc. 1957), xliii.
[2] Not to be confused with Thomas Chard, O.Cist. abbot of Ford, who was not a bp. See A. B. Emden, Biog. register of Univ. of Oxford, i (Oxford, 1957), 389–90.

John Stonywell, O.S.B. prior of Tynemouth, abbot of Pershore (1524–53). POLETENSIS. York.
Andrew Whitney, prior of St Barth. hosp. Gloucester (1525–46). CHRYSOPOLIS. Winchester 1526–41. Hereford 1540. Worcester. Gloucester.
John Smart, O.S.A. abbot of Wigmore (1526–35). PANADENSIS. Hereford 1526–35. Worcester 1526–31.
Alfonso de Villa Sancta (1526). SABULENSIS. St Asaph.
Thomas Chetham, O.S.A. prior of Leeds (1526–35). SIDON. Canterbury. London.
Robert King, O.Cist. abbot of Thame (1527–46). RHEON. Lincoln 1527–35.
John Holt (1530–40). LYDDA.
William Duffield O.F.M. (1531–33). ASCOLENSIS. Canterbury. York. Lincoln 1531.
John 'prior S. Velini' (1532). MAIORENSIS. Winchester.
William Fawell (1532–44. d. 1557). HIPPO. Exeter.
Thomas Swillington, O.S.A. (1532–46). PHILADELPHIA. Lincoln 1533–35. London 1534.
Christopher Lord, Prem. abbot of Newhouse (1533–34). SIDON. Canterbury.
John Draper, O.S.A. prior of Twynham (1534–51). NEAPOLIS. Winchester.

SCOTTISH BISHOPS AS SUFFRAGANS IN ENGLAND

DUNKELD
    Robert Derling. York 1380–84.
    Nicholas. Worcester 1401–19. Hereford 1403–06.
    William Gunwardby. Lincoln 1431. Ely 1448–54.
GLASGOW
    John. London 1393–94. Salisbury 1396.
ROSS
    Reginald. Winchester 1195.
    John. York c. 1480.
WHITHORN (or Galloway)
    Christian. York, Lincoln 1185.
    Walter. Winchester 1214. York 1215.
    Henry. York 1291.
    Thomas Dalton. York 1306–15.
    Oswald. York 1388–98. Durham 1404–13.

ENGLISH SUFFRAGAN TITLES OF THE SIXTEENTH CENTURY

BEDFORD

John Hodgkin	cons. 9 Dec. 1537	d. 1560

BERWICK

Thomas Sparke	cons. a. 1537	d. 1572

COLCHESTER

William More	cons. 22 Oct. 1536	d. 1541
John Sterne	cons. 12 Nov. 1592	d. 1608

DOVER

Richard Yngworth	cons. 9 Dec. 1537	d. 1545
Richard Thornden	cons. 1545	d. 1557
Richard Rogers	cons. 15 May 1569	d. 19 May 1597

HULL

Robert Sylvester or Pursglove	cons. 29 Dec. 1538	d. 2 May 1579

IPSWICH

Thomas Manning   cons. 19 Mar. 1536

MARLBOROUGH

Thomas Morley   cons. 4 Nov. 1537   ? d. 1561

NOTTINGHAM

Richard Barnes   cons. 9 Mar. 1567   trs. Carlisle 1570

PENRITH

John Bird   cons. 24 June 1537   trs. Bangor 1539

SHAFTESBURY

John Bradley   cons. 23 Mar. 1539

SHREWSBURY

Lewis Thomas   cons. 24 June 1537   d. 1561

TAUNTON

William Finch   cons. 7 Apr. 1538   d. 1559

THETFORD

John Salisbury   cons. 19 Mar. 1536   trs. Sodor and Man 1570

Nicholas Shaxton, formerly bp of Salisbury (1535–39), acted as suffragan in the dioceses of Ely and Lincoln in Mary's reign.

BISHOPS OF WALES

INTRODUCTION

There are certain departures in the appended lists from the form adopted in the first edition. In the first place the extensive footnotes introduced into the first edition have been eliminated in order to bring the Welsh lists into line with those for the English dioceses. The essential information of the footnotes has been incorporated in the present text, or, alternatively, omissions are accounted for in the explanatory statement given below of the principles on which the lists have been compiled. Secondly, lists have been added for the new dioceses of Monmouth and of Swansea and Brecon, created respectively in 1921 and 1923. Thirdly, the lists for the four ancient dioceses now begin in each case with the first bishop appointed and consecrated under Norman auspices. Such appointments were made to Bangor in 1092, to Llandaff in 1107, to St David's in 1115, and to St Asaph in 1143.

The exclusion of earlier bishops from the lists calls for a brief explanation. There is still much uncertainty about the details of pre-Norman church organization in Wales and personal data relating to the late 'Celtic' episcopate remain unreliable and obscure. On the eve of the Norman reorganization of the church in Wales, the loose arrangements traditionally associated with a monastic and a tribal church still flourished beneath the emergent authority of bishops whose spheres of jurisdiction were tending to coincide with the *three* major kingdoms situated in North, South-East, and South-West Wales. Episcopal seats were already located at St David's and almost certainly at Bangor. Llandaff and St Asaph were probably chosen to be cathedral centres by the Normans, the former in territory where the tendency towards formal diocesan organization is most discernible in the pre-Norman period, and the latter in a new diocese carved out by the Normans in North-East Wales, possibly from territory formerly subject to the personal jurisdiction of bishops associated with Bangor. But no list can be compiled of the pre-Norman bishops in North Wales, for only a few isolated names are on record. Attempts have been made to draw up lists of bishops in the succession of St David and St Teilo (Llandaff), but although some of the later names are undoubtedly authentic the lists rest on evidence which is suspect and on a chronology which is uncertain. [*See* J. Conway Davies, 'Episcopal Acts Relating to the Welsh Dioceses, *Historical Society of the Church in Wales*, nos. 1, 3, 4, 1946 and 1948 (contains fuller references to the available sources)]; Nora K. Chadwick, ed., *Studies in the Early British Church*, studies nos. I, II, IV (Cambridge, 1958).

Systematic lists can only begin with the appointment of Norman bishops in the fealty of the English crown and professing obedience to Canterbury and with the consequent introduction into Wales of full Roman discipline and administrative practice. The procedure of nomination (or election) and consecration then became sufficiently similar in England and Wales to permit the use of the same types of source material in both countries.

The most striking element in the Norman reorganization was the creation of a rigidly territorial diocesan system based on an existing framework of civil and ecclesiastical administration. The four ancient dioceses with their archdeaconries, rural deaneries, and parochial system are in Wales essentially Norman creations, which gradually emerged in the course of the twelfth century.

Bangor. The diocese was coterminous with the kingdom of Gwynedd and extended from the R. Dyfi to the R. Conway. It also included two rural deaneries detached from the main body of the diocese; (a) Arwystli, in central Wales, which was politically part of the kingdom of Powys, (b) Dyffryn Clwyd, one of the four cantrefs of the Middle Country, lying between the Conway and the Dee and forming an enclave within the diocese of St Asaph. Adjustments of diocesan boundaries effected in 1840 brought Dyffryn Clwyd into St Asaph, in return for the surrender to Bangor of the rural deanery of Cyfeiliog which connected Arwystli to the rest of the diocese. Thus the modern diocese comprises the county of Anglesey, the whole of Caernarvonshire west of the Conway, and the S.W. corners of Merionethshire and Montgomeryshire.

St Asaph. Broadly the diocese covered the kingdom of Powys and the Middle Country. But, as already noted, the deaneries of Arwystli and Dyffryn Clwyd were in Bangor. The Kerry district south of the Severn was in St David's, and several border parishes assigned to Welsh counties in 1536 continued after that date to be included in the Chester diocese. The latter were handed over to St Asaph together with the Kerry district as part of the boundary revision of 1840. On the other hand some border parishes further south, including the Oswestry district which had for centuries constituted the St Asaph deanery of the March, ceased to be part of St Asaph when the Welsh Church was disestablished in 1920. The modern diocese comprises the counties of Denbigh and Flint, the greater part of Montgomeryshire, and a few Caernarvonshire parishes lying east of the Conway.

Llandaff. The diocese was coterminous with the kingdoms of Glamorgan and Gwent, excluding Gower and the Monmouth district, which in the twelfth century controversies over the delimitation of the southern dioceses were lost to St David's and Hereford respectively. The Monmouth district was recovered at the time of the boundary revisions of 1840. As a result of the creation of the new diocese of Monmouth in 1921, Llandaff now includes Glamorgan only, with the continued exclusion of Gower.

St David's. The most extensive of the old Welsh dioceses, St David's formerly covered an area equal to five modern counties. It included the whole of S.W. Wales (Deheubarth), and a group of lordships in the middle march of Wales lying between the Severn and the Black Mountains. The peninsula of Gower and the immediate hinterland were also in St David's. Following the creation of the new diocese of Swansea and Brecon in 1923, St David's is now coterminous with the counties of Cardigan, Carmarthen, and Pembroke. [*See* W. Rees, *An Historical Atlas of Wales*, plate 33 (Cardiff, 1951 and 1958).]

By the Welsh Church Act of 1914, which took effect on 31 March 1920, the four Welsh dioceses (excluding border parishes in England which opted to stay in the established Church) ceased to be part of the province of Canterbury. In the reorganization which followed disestablishment, two new dioceses were created: Monmouth on 29 Sept. 1921, Swansea and Brecon on 4 April 1923. Monmouth diocese is coterminous with Monmouthshire and with the former archdeaconry of that name in the diocese of Llandaff. Swansea and Brecon was carved out of St David's and is made up of the former archdeaconry of Brecon and the rural deaneries of East and West Gower.

These six dioceses now constitute a separate province within the Anglican Communion under an archbishop elected by the diocesan bishops from among their own number. Bishops are elected by an Electoral College composed of clergy and laity representing all the dioceses. Since 1920 there have been eight archbishops.

The sources used are the same as those consulted in preparing the English lists and the reader is referred to the Introduction to the English lists of bishops. Every effort has been made to apply consistently the following rules. The date of translation in the middle ages is the date of the papal provision; after the Reformation it is the date of confirmation. These dates are based on those given in the English and Irish lists, unless there are special reasons to the contrary. Doubtful dates have been italicized.

§ Revisions incorporated in the pre-Reformation lists in the third edition of the *Handbook* (1985) derive from *Fasti Ecclesiae Anglicanae 1300–1541*, xi, *The Welsh Dioceses*, comp. B. Jones (Institute of Historical Research, University of London, 1965) and from D. E. Greenway's unpublished notes in preparation for the Welsh volume of *Fasti Ecclesiae Anglicanae 1066–1300*.

BANGOR

BISHOPS	ACCESSION	DEATH
		unless otherwise stated
Hervey	cons. 1092, trs. to Ely, nom. *a.* 21 Nov. 1108[1]	
David 'the Scot'	cons. 4 Apr. 1120	d. ? *1139*

[1] Driven from Bangor by the Welsh *c.* 1109. Urban, bp of Llandaff was possibly in charge of the diocese during the vacancy that followed.

BISHOPS	ACCESSION	DEATH *unless otherwise stated*
Maurice (Meurig)	el. *a.* Dec. 1139, cons. late Jan. 1140	12 Aug. 1161
Gwion (Guy Rufus)	cons. 22 May 1177	*c.* 1190
Alan (Alban)	cons. 16 Apr. 1195	*May* or *Dec.* 1196
Robert of Shrewsbury	cons. *16* Mar. 1197	1213
Cadwgan (or Martin)	el. *a.* 13 Apr., cons. 21 June 1215	res. 1235/6 (d. 11 Apr. 1241)
Hywel ap. Ednyfed	el. 1236 (not cons.)	
Richard	el. *a.* 3 July 1236, cons. 1237; absent from diocese 1248– *c.* 1258	*a.* 8 Nov. 1267
Anian	el. *a.* 12 Dec. 1267, cons. 1267/8, temp. 5 Jan. 1268	*1305–6*
Gruffydd ab Iorwerth	cons. 26 Mar. 1307	27 Apr. 1309
Anian Sais	el. 2 May × 18 June, temp. 7 Sept., cons. 9 Nov. 1309	26 Jan. 1328
Matthew de Englefield (Madoc ap. Iorwerth)	el. 26 Feb., cons. 12 June 1328	*22 Mar.* × *15 Apr.* 1357
(Ithel ap. Robert,	el. qua. by the pope)	
Thomas de Ringstead	prov. 21 Aug. 1357, cons. *p.* 17 Sept. 1357	8 Jan. 1366
Gervase de Castro	prov. 11 Dec. 1366	24 Sept. 1370
Hywel ap Gronow	prov. 21 Apr. 1371	*a.* 3 Feb. 1372
John Gilbert	prov. 17 Mar., temp. 30 Apr. 1372	trs. Hereford 12 Sept. 1375
John Swaffham	trs. from Cloyne 2 July, temp. 28 Oct. 1376	24 June 1398

(Lewis Aber, el. *a.* 21 Aug. 1398, vacated soon aft.)

Richard Young	prov. 2 Dec. 1398, temp. 20 May 1400, cons. *1400* (absent from the diocese aft. 1401)	trs. Rochester 28 July 1404

(Lewis Byford (Llywelyn Bifort), prov. by Boniface IX and held the diocese *c. 1405–08*)

(Griffin Young,	prov. by Benedict XIII)	
Benedict Nicolls	prov. 18 Apr., cons. 12 Aug. 1408	trs. St David's Dec. 1417
William Barrow	prov. 14 Feb. 1418, cons. *p.* 13 Oct. 1419	trs. Carlisle 19 Apr. 1423
John Cliderow	prov. 19 Apr. 1423, cons. 1425	*a.* 13 Dec. 1435
Thomas Cheriton	prov. 5 Mar., temp. 21 Nov., cons. 25 Nov. 1436	23 Dec. 1447
John Stanbury	prov. 4 Mar., temp. 15 May, cons. 23 June 1448	trs. Hereford 7 Feb. 1453
James Blakedon	trs. from Achonry 7 Feb., temp. 25 Mar. 1453	*a.* 3 Oct. 1464
Richard Edenham (Edenam)	prov. 14 Jan., cons. *p.* 18 Mar. 1465	*a.* 13 Apr. 1494
Henry Dean	prov. 4 July 1494, el. *a.* 13 Sept. 1494, cons. 20 Nov. 1495, second prov. 21 July 1496, temp. 6 Oct. 1496	trs. Salisbury 8 Jan. 1500
Thomas Pigot	prov. 4 May 1500	15 Aug. 1504
Thomas Penny	prov. 30 Aug., cons. *1505*	trs. Carlisle 22 Sept. 1508
Thomas Skevington (Skeffington)	prov. 23 Feb., cons. 17 June 1509	16 Aug. 1533
John Salcot	el. Nov. 1533 × Jan. 1534, cons. 19 Apr. 1534	trs. Salisbury 14 Aug. 1539
John Bird	el. 24 July, temp. 9 Sept. 1539	trs. Chester aft. 4 Aug. 1541

BISHOPS OF WALES

BISHOPS	ACCESSION	DEATH
		unless otherwise stated
Arthur Bulkeley	el. 18 Nov. 1541, cons. 19 Feb. 1542	14 Mar. 1553
William Glynn	cons. 8 Sept. 1555	21 May 1558
[Maurice Clynnog, nom. 1558, withdrew]		
Rowland Meyrick	cons. 21 Dec. 1559	24 Jan. 1566
Nicholas Robinson	cons. 20 Oct. 1566	3 Feb. 1585
Hugh Bellot	cons. 30 Jan. 1586	trs. Chester 25 Sept. 1595
Richard Vaughan	cons. 22 Jan. 1596	trs. Chester 9 July 1597
Henry Rowlands	cons. 12 Nov. 1598	6 July 1616
Lewis Bayly	cons. 8 Dec. 1616	d. 26 Oct. 1631
David Dolben	cons. *c.* 23 Mar. 1632	27 Nov. 1633
Edmund Griffith	cons. 16 Feb. 1634	26 May 1637
William Roberts	cons. 3 Sept. 1637	12 Aug. 1665
[Robert Price		d. bef. election completed]
Robert Morgan	cons. 1 July 1666	1 Sept. 1673
Humphrey Lloyd	cons. 16 Nov. 1673	18 Jan. 1689
Humphrey Humphreys	cons. 30 June 1689	trs. Hereford 2 Dec. 1701
John Evans	cons. 4 Jan. 1702	trs. Meath Jan. 1716
Benjamin Hoadley	cons. 18 Mar. 1716	trs. Hereford 7 Nov. 1721
Richard Reynolds	cons. early 1722	trs. Lincoln 17 June 1723
William Baker	cons. 11 Aug. 1723	trs. Norwich 19 Dec. 1727
Thomas Sherlock	cons. 4 Feb. 1728	trs. Salisbury 8 Nov. 1734
Charles Cecil	trs. from Bristol late 1734	29 May 1737
Thomas Herring	cons. 15 Jan. 1738	trs. York 21 Apr. 1743
Matthew Hutton	cons. 13 Nov. 1743	trs. York 10 Dec. 1747
Zachary Pearce	cons. 21 Feb. 1748	trs. Rochester 4 June 1756
John Egerton	cons. 4 July 1756	trs. Lichfield 12 Nov. 1768
John Ewer	trs. Llandaff 10 Jan. 1769	28 Oct. 1774
John Moore	cons. 12 Feb. 1775	trs. Canterbury 26 Apr. 1783
John Warren	trs. St David's 9 June 1783	27 Jan. 1800
William Cleaver	trs. Chester 24 May 1800	trs. St Asaph 1806 (*p.* 24 Oct.)
John Randolph	trs. Oxford 6 Jan. 1807	trs. London 9 Aug. 1809
Henry William Majendie	trs. Chester 5 Oct. 1809	9 July 1830
Christopher Bethell	trs. Exeter 28 Oct. 1830	19 Apr. 1859
James Colquhoun Campbell	cons. 14 June 1859	res. Apr. 1890 (d. 9 Nov. 1895)
Daniel Lewis Lloyd	cons. 24 June 1890	res. Nov. 1898 (d. 4 Aug. 1899)
Watkin Herbert Williams	cons. 2 Feb. 1899	res. 11 Nov. 1924 (d. 19 Nov. 1944)
Daniel Davies	cons. 24 Feb. 1925	23 Aug. 1928
Charles Alfred Howell Green	trs. Monmouth, el. 25 Sept. 1928, abp of Wales 1934–44	7 May 1944
David Edwardes Davies	cons. 25 July 1944	res. Nov. 1948 (d. 15 May 1950)
John Charles Jones	cons. 6 Jan. 1949	13 Oct. 1956
Gwilym Owen Williams	cons. 1 May 1957; el. abp of Wales, 10 Aug. 1971	res. 30 Sept. 1982
John Cledan Mears	cons. 21 Dec. 1982	

LLANDAFF

BISHOPS	ACCESSION	DEATH *unless otherwise stated*
Urban	cons. 11 Aug. 1107	*a.* 9 Oct. 1134
Uchtryd	cons. late Jan. 1140	? *1148*
Nicholas ap. Gwrgant	cons. 14 Mar. 1148	3 or 4 June 1183
William de Saltmarsh	el. 3 Dec. 1184, cons. 10 Aug. 1186	1191
Henry de Abergavenny	cons. 12 Dec. 1193	12 Nov. 1218
William de Goldcliff	el. *a.* 11 July, temp. 16 July, cons. 27 Oct. 1219	28 Jan. 1229
Elias de Radnor	temp. 30 Aug., cons. 1 Dec. 1230	13 May 1240
William de Christchurch	el. 13 May 1240, apparently not cons.	res. *a.* June 1244
William de Burgh	el. 10 × 17 July, temp. 17 July, cons. 19 Feb. 1245	11 June 1253
John de Ware	el. 13 June × 26 July, temp. 12 Aug. 1253, cons. 11 Jan. 1254	d. *29* or *30* June 1256
William de Radnor	el. *a.* 28 July, temp. 14 Sept. 1256, cons. 7 Jan. 1257	9 Jan. 1266
William de Breuse	el. Feb./Mar., temp. 14 Apr., cons 23 May 1266	19 Mar. 1287
John de Monmouth	prov. 2 Oct. 1294, temp. 4 Apr. 1295, cons. 10 Feb. 1297	8 Apr. 1323
Alexander de Monmouth	el. 25 June 1323	qua. by the pope
John de Eclescliff (Eaglescliffe)	trs. Connor 20 June 1323	d. 2 Jan. 1347
John Coventry	el. qua. by the pope	
John Paschal	cons. *a.* 20 Feb. 1344 in the lifetime of his predecessor;[1] prov. 3 June, temp. 2 × 7 July 1347	11 Oct. 1361
Roger Cradock	trs. Waterford and Lismore 15 Dec. 1361	*a.* 22 June 1382
Thomas Rushook	prov. 14 or 15 Jan., temp. 2 Apr. 1383	trs. Chichester 16 Oct. 1385
William de Bottesham (Bottlesham)	trs. Bethlehem 16 Oct. × 2 Dec. 1385	trs. Rochester 27 Aug. 1389
Edmund Bromfield	temp. 17 Dec. 1389, cons. 20 Jan. 1390	11 June 1393
Tideman de Winchcomb	prov. 13 Oct. 1393, temp. 3 July and 24 Oct. 1394	trs. Worcester *a.* 13 June 1395
Andrew Barret	prov. 2 June, temp. 25 Aug. 1395, cons. *1395*	*a* 12 Apr. 1396
John Burghill	prov. 12 Apr., cons. *p.* 10 July 1396	trs. Lichfield 2 July 1398
Thomas Peverel	trs. Leighlin and Ossory 12 July, temp. 16 Nov. 1398	trs. Worcester 4 July 1407
John de la Zouch	el. *a.* 30 Nov. 1407, temp. 7 June, cons. 12 Aug. 1408	Apr. 1423
John Wells	prov. 9 July 1425, cons. *1425*	*a.* 17 Nov. 1440
Nicholas Ashby	nom. 25 Dec. 1440, prov. 17 Feb., cons. 21 May 1441	*a.* 19 June 1458
John Hunden	prov. 19 June, temp. 25 Aug. 1458	res. *a.* 18 Mar. 1476
John Smith	prov. *c.* 30 Mar., cons. 17 July, temp. 11 Sept. 1476	d. 29 Jan. 1478

[1] *CPL*, i, 43.

BISHOPS	ACCESSION	DEATH *unless otherwise stated*
John Marshall	prov. 18 May, cons. 6 Sept. 1478	Jan. × Feb. 1496
John Ingleby	prov. 27 June, temp. 2 Sept., cons. *p*. 6 Sept. 1496	*a*. 14 Nov. 1499
Miles Salley	cons. 26 Apr. 1500	d. *29 Nov. 1516 × Jan. 1517*
George de Athequa	prov. 11 Feb., cons. 8 Mar. 1517	res. Feb. 1537
Robert Holgate	cons. 25 Mar. 1537	trs. York 16 Jan. 1545
Anthony Kitchin	cons. 3 May 1545	31 Oct. 1566
Hugh Jones	cons. 5 May 1567	*c*. 12 Nov. 1574
William Blethin	cons. 17 Apr. 1575	15 Oct. 1590
Gervase Babington	cons. 29 Aug. 1591	trs. Exeter 11 Mar. 1595
William Morgan	cons. 20 July 1595	trs. St Asaph *17 Sept.* 1601
Francis Godwin	cons. 22 Nov. 1601	trs. Hereford 28 Nov. 1617
George Carleton (Charlton)	cons. 12 July 1618	trs. Chichester 20 Sept. 1619
Theophilus Field	cons. 10 Oct. 1619	trs. St David's 12 July 1627
William Murray	trs. Kilfenora 24 Dec. 1627	Feb. 1640
Morgan Owen	cons. 29 Mar. 1640	4 Mar. 1645
	(Vacancy 1645–60)	
Hugh Lloyd	cons. 2 Dec. 1660	7 June 1667
Francis Davies	conf. 24 Aug. 1667	14 Mar. 1675
William Lloyd	conf. 18 Apr. 1675	trs. Peterborough 16 May 1679
William Beaw	cons. 22 June 1679	10 Feb. 1706
John Tyler	cons. 30 June 1706	6 July 1724
Robert Clavering	nom. 14 Sept. 1724, cons. 2 Jan. 1725	trs. Peterborough 17 Feb. 1729
John Harris	nom. 19 Sept., cons. 19 Oct. 1729	28 Aug. 1738
Matthias Mawson	nom. 17 Jan., cons. 18 Feb. 1739	trs. Chichester 21 Oct. 1740
John Gilbert	nom. 31 Oct., cons. 28 Dec. 1740	trs. Salisbury 29 Dec. 1748
Edward Cressett	nom. 7 Jan., cons. 12 Feb. 1749	13 Feb. 1755
Richard Newcome	nom. 20 Mar., cons. 13 Apr. 1755	trs. St Asaph 9 July 1761
John Ewer	nom. 6 Aug., cons. 28 Dec. 1761	trs. Bangor 10 Jan. 1769
Jonathan Shipley	nom. 19 Jan., cons. 12 Feb. 1769	trs. St Asaph 8 Sept. 1769
Shute Barrington	nom. 13 Sept., cons. 1 Oct. 1769	trs. Salisbury 27 Aug. 1782
Richard Watson	nom. 30 Aug., cons. 20 Oct. 1782	4 July 1816
Herbert Marsh	nom. 5 Aug., cons. 25 Aug. 1816	trs. Peterborough 28 Apr. 1819
William van Mildert	nom. 5 May, cons. 31 May 1819	trs. Durham 24 Apr. 1826
Charles Richard Sumner	nom. 25 Apr., cons. 21 May 1826	trs. Winchester 12 Dec. 1827
Edward Copleston	nom. 18 Dec. 1827, cons. 13 Jan. 1828	14 Oct. 1849
Alfred Ollivant	nom. 9 Nov., cons. 2 Dec. 1849	16 Dec. 1882
Richard Lewis	cons. 25 Apr. 1883	24 Jan. 1905
Joshua Pritchard Hughes	cons. 1 June 1905	res. 24 Feb. 1931 (d. 8 Apr. 1938)

BISHOPS	ACCESSION	DEATH *unless otherwise stated*
Timothy Rees	cons. 25 Apr. 1931	29 Apr. 1939
John Morgan	trs. Swansea and Brecon, el. 22 June, conf. 27 Sept 1939, abp of Wales 1949–57	26 June 1957
William Glyn Hughes Simon	trs. Swansea and Brecon, el. 30 July, conf. 25 Sept. 1957, el. abp of Wales 22 May, conf. 13 June 1968	res. 30 June 1971
Eryl Stephen Thomas	trs. Monmouth, el. 4 Oct., conf. 7 Dec. 1971	res. 9 Nov. 1975
John Richard Worthington Poole-Hughes	trs. from assistant bp of Llandaff, el. 9 Dec. 1975, conf. 23 Jan. 1976	

MONMOUTH

Charles Alfred Howell Green	cons. 21 Dec. 1921	trs. Bangor, el. 25 Sept. 1928
Gilbert Cunningham Joyce	cons. 30 Nov. 1928	res. Apr. 1940 (d. 22 July 1942)
Alfred Edwin Monahan	cons. 24 Aug. 1940	10 Aug. 1945
Alfred Edwin Morris	cons. 1 Nov. 1945, abp of Wales 1957	res. 31 Dec. 1967
Eryl Stephen Thomas	el. 14 Feb., cons. 29 Mar. 1968	trs. Llandaff, 11 Dec. 1971
Derrick Greenslade Childs	el. 25 Jan., cons. 23 May 1972; el. abp of Wales, 8 Feb. 1983	

ST ASAPH

Gilbert	cons. 1143	d. uncertain
Geoffrey [of Monmouth]	cons. 23 Feb. 1152	1154
Richard	el. *1154*	1155
Godfrey	cons. 1160, suspended by the pope 1170	res. 18 May 1175
Adam	cons. 12 Oct. 1175	1180 or 1181
John I	cons. *3 July* 1183	1186
Reiner	cons. *10 Aug.* 1186	1224
Abraham	cons. 29 June 1225	*a.* 4 Feb. 1233
Hugh	cons. 17 June 1235	1240, *p.* Sept.
Hywel ab Ednyfed	cons. *1240–42*	1247
Anian I (Einion)	el. *a.* 2 May, temp. 27 Sept., cons. Nov. 1249	*a.* 29 Sept. 1266
John II	cons. *p.* 17 Apr. 1267	1267 or 1268
Anian II	el. *a.* 24 Sept., cons. 21 Oct. 1268	5 Feb. 1293
Llywelyn de Bromfield	el. 9 Mar., temp. 13 May, cons. 17 May 1293	*a.* 25 Jan. 1314
Dafydd ap Bleddyn	el. 23 June, temp. 1 Nov. 1314, cons. 12 Jan. 1315	*a.* 9 Oct. 1345
John Trevor I	prov. 26 Jan., cons. *c.* 1 Aug., temp. 21 Sept. 1346	3 Feb. 1357
Llywelyn ap Madoc ab Ellis	prov. 19 July 1357	*Oct.* or *Nov.* 1375
William Spridlington	prov. 3 Feb. 1376, cons. 25 May 1377	9 Apr. 1382
Lawrence Child	prov. 18 June 1382, temp. 20 Oct. 1382	20 Dec. 1389
Alexander Bache	prov. 28 Feb., cons. 8 May 1390	*Aug.* or *Sept.* 1394

BISHOPS	ACCESSION	DEATH *unless otherwise stated*
John Trevor II	el. 3, prov. 21 Oct. 1394, cons. *a.* 17 Apr. 1395	24 May × 16 July 1410[1]
Robert Lancaster	prov. 16 July 1410, cons. 28 June 1411	26 Mar. 1433
John Lowe	prov. 17 Aug., temp. 17 Oct., cons. 1 Nov. 1433	trs. Rochester 22 Apr. 1444
Reginald Pecock	prov. 22 Apr., temp. 8 June, cons. 14 June 1444	trs. Chichester 23 Mar. 1450
Thomas Bird (or Knight)	prov. 27 Mar. 1450, cons. *14 Feb.* 1451	d. 1471[2]
Richard Redman	cons. *p.* 13 Oct. 1471, prov. 17 Aug. 1472	trs. Exeter 6 Nov. 1495
Michael Deacon	cons. *p.* 11 Jan. 1496	*a.* 10 Mar. 1500
Dafydd ab Iorwerth	cons. 26 Apr. 1500	*a.* 18 Dec. 1503
Dafydd ab Owain	prov. 18 Dec. 1503, cons. 4 Feb. 1504	12 Feb. 1513
Edmund Birkhead	prov. 15 Apr., cons. 29 May 1513	*a.* 9 Apr. 1518
Henry Standish	cons. 11 July 1518	d. 9 July 1535
William Barlow	el. 16 Jan., conf. 21 Feb. 1536	prob. trs. to St David's bef. consecration, in ? *Apr.* 1536
Robert Warton (or Parfew)	el. 8 June, cons. 2 July 1536	trs. Hereford 6 July 1554
Thomas Goldwell	el. *a.* 12 May, cons. Aug. or Sept. 1555, temp. Jan. 1556	res. June 1559
Richard Davies	cons. 31 Jan. 1560	trs. St David's 21 May 1561
Thomas Davies (Davis)	cons. 26 May 1561	Sept. 1573
William Hughes	cons. 13 Dec. 1573	*18–19* Nov. 1600
William Morgan	trs. Llandaff 17 Sept. 1601	10 Sept. 1604
Richard Parry	cons. 30 Dec. 1604	26 Sept. 1623
John Hanmer	cons. 15 Feb. 1624	23 June 1629
John Owen(s)	cons. 20 Sept. 1629	16 Oct. 1651
(Vacancy 1651–60)		
George Griffith	cons. 28 Oct. 1660	28 Nov. 1666
Henry Glemham	cons. 13 Oct. 1667	17 Jan. 1670
Isaac Barow	trs. Man *21* Mar. 1670	24 June 1680
William Lloyd	cons. 3 Oct 1680	trs. Lichfield 20 Oct. 1692
Edward Jones	trs. Cloyne 13 Dec. 1692	10 May 1703
George Hooper	cons. 31 Oct. 1703	trs. Bath and Wells 14 Mar. 1704
William Beveridge	cons. 16 July 1704	5 Mar. 1708
William Fleetwood	cons. 6 June 1708	trs. Ely 18 Dec. 1714
John Wynne	cons. 6 Feb. 1715	trs. Bath and Wells 11 Nov. 1727
Francis Hare	cons. 17 Dec. 1727	trs. Chichester 25 Nov. 1731
Thomas Tanner	cons. 23 Jan. 1732	14 Dec. 1735
Isaac Maddox	cons. 4 July 1736	trs. Worcester 12 Nov. 1743
John Thomas	el. Dec. 1743	trs. Lincoln (nom. 20 Jan. 1744) before consecration

[1] He adhered to Owen Glyndwr and was declared to be deprived of the diocese by Henry IV in 1404.
[2] He adhered to Henry VI and was compelled to resign in 1460; but was pardoned in 1469 and again on 13 Oct. 1471.

BISHOPS	ACCESSION	DEATH
		unless otherwise stated
Samuel Lisle	cons. 1 Apr. 1744	trs. Norwich 9 Apr. 1748
Robert Hay Drummond	nom. 12 Apr., cons. 24 Apr. 1748	trs. Salisbury 11 June 1761
Richard Newcome	trs. Llandaff 9 July 1761	4 June 1769
Jonathan Shipley	trs. Llandaff 8 Sept. 1769	5 Dec. 1788
Samuel Hallifax	trs. Gloucester 25 Apr. 1789	4 Mar. 1790
Lewis Bagot	trs. Norwich 24 Apr. 1790	4 June 1802
Samuel Horsley	trs. Rochester 1802 (nom. 3 July)	4 Oct. 1806
William Cleaver	trs. Bangor 1806 (*p.* 24 Oct.)	15 May 1815
John Luxmore	trs. Hereford 1815 (nom. 8 June)	21 Jan. 1830
William Carey	trs. Exeter 7 Apr. 1830	13 Sept. 1846
Thomas Vowler Short	trs. Sodor and Man 1846 (nom. 4 Nov.)	res. 22 Feb. 1870 (d. 13 Apr. 1872)
Joshua Hughes	nom. 7 Apr., cons. 8 May 1870	21 Jan. 1889
Alfred George Edwards	cons. 25 Mar. 1889, abp of Wales 1920–34	res. 25 July 1934 (d. 22 July 1937)
William Thomas Havard	cons. 29 Sept. 1934	trs. St David's 1950 (el. 30 Mar.)
David Daniel Bartlett	cons. 21 Sept. 1950	res. 31 Dec. 1970
Harold John Charles	el. 3 Feb., cons. 25 Mar. 1971	res. 31 Mar. 1982
Alwyn Rice Jones	el. 11 May, cons. 29 June 1982	

ST DAVID'S

Bernard	cons. 19 Sept. 1115	? 22 Apr. 1148
David Fitz Gerald	cons. 19 Dec. 1148	8 May 1176
Peter de Leia	cons. 7 Nov. 1176	16 July 1198
Gerald of Wales	el. 29 June 1199, but assent refused by the king	
Geoffrey de Henlaw	nom. July 1199, cons. 7 Dec. 1203	1214
Iorwerth (Gervase)	el. *a.* 18 June, cons. 21 June 1215	*a.* 27 Jan. 1229
Anselm le Gras	el. *a.* 7 Apr. 1229, temp. 20 Nov. 1230, cons. 9 Feb. 1231	*a.* 2 Apr. 1247
Thomas le Waleys	el. 16 Apr. × 16 July, temp. 26 Sept. 1247, cons. 26 July 1248	11 July 1255
Richard de Carew	el. *p.* 4 Aug. 1255, cons. 11 Feb. × 10 Mar. 1256	1 Apr. 1280
Thomas Bek	el. *a.* 17 June, cons. 6 Oct. 1280	14 Apr. 1293
David Martin	el. June, temp. 11 Oct. 1293, cons. 30 Sept. 1296	9 Mar. 1328
Henry Gower	el. 21 Apr., temp. 26 May, cons. 12 June 1328	*a.* 4 May 1347
John Thoresby	prov. 23 May, temp. 14 July, cons. 23 Sept. 1347	trs. Worcester 4 Sept. 1349
Reginald Brian	prov. 11 Sept. 1349, temp. 15 Jan., cons. 26 Sept. 1350	trs. Worcester 22 Oct. 1352
Thomas Fastolf	prov. 22 Oct. 1352, temp. 4 June 1353	June 1361
Adam Houghton	prov. 20 Sept., temp. 8 Dec. 1361, cons. 2 Jan. 1362	13 Feb. 1389
Richard Metford	election qua. 1389	
John Gilbert	trs. Hereford 5 May 1389, temp. 12 July 1389	28 July 1397
Guy Mone	prov. 30 Aug., cons. 11 Nov. 1397	31 Aug. 1407
Henry Chichele	cons. 17 June 1408	trs. Canterbury 27 Apr. 1414

BISHOPS	ACCESSION	DEATH *unless otherwise stated*
John Catterick	prov. 27 Apr., temp. 2 June 1414	trs. Lichfield 1 Feb. 1415
Stephen Patrington	prov. 1 Feb., cons. 9 June, temp. 16 June 1415	trs. Chichester 15 Dec. 1417 (d. 22 Dec. 1417)
Benedict Nichols	trs. Bangor 15 Dec. 1417, temp. 1 June 1418	25 June 1433
Thomas Rodburn (Rudborne)	prov. 5 Oct., temp. 16 Dec. 1433, cons. 31 Jan. 1434	a. 27 June 1442
William Lindwood	prov. 27 June, temp. 14 Aug., cons. 26 Aug. 1442	21 Oct. 1446
John Langton	prov. 23 Jan., temp. 2 Mar., cons. 7 May 1447	22 May 1447
John de la Bere	prov. 15 Sept., temp. 14 Nov., cons. 19 Nov. 1447	res. a. 23 July 1460
Robert Tully	prov. 23 July, cons. p. 28 Aug. 1460	c. 1481
Richard Martin	trs. Waterford and Lismore, prov. 26 Apr., temp. 1 July, cons. 28 July 1482	11 May 1483
Thomas Langton	prov. 4 July, cons. Aug.– Sept. 1483, temp. 25 Mar. 1484	trs. Salisbury 8 Feb. 1485
Hugh Pavy	prov. 6 May, temp. 25 Mar. 1484, cons. 9 Oct. 1485	3 May × 3 Aug. 1496
John Morgan (or Young)	prov. 3 Aug., temp. 23 Nov. 1496	24 Apr. × 19 May 1504
Robert Sherborn	prov. 5 Jan., temp. 12 Apr., cons. 11 May 1505	trs. Chichester 18 Sept. 1508
Edward Vaughan	prov. 13 June, cons. 22 July 1509	a. 27 Jan. 1522
Richard Rawlins	prov. 11 Mar., cons. 26 Apr. 1523	18 Feb. 1536
William Barlow	trs. St Asaph, el. 10 Apr., cons. June 1536	trs. Bath and Wells, nom. 3 Feb. 1548
Robert Ferrar	cons. 9 Sept. 1548	depr. ? 1553 (d. 30 Mar. 1555)
Henry Morgan	cons. 1 Apr. 1554	23 Dec. 1559
Thomas Young	cons. 21 Jan. 1560	trs. York 25 Feb. 1561
Richard Davies	trs. St Asaph 21 May 1561	Oct. or Nov. 1581
Marmaduke Middleton	trs. Waterford and Lismore 30 Nov. 1582	depr. 1590–92 (d. 1593)
Anthony Rudd	cons. 9 June 1594	7 Mar. 1615
Richard Milbourne	cons. 9 July 1615, trs. Carllisle, nom. 21 June 1621	
William Laud	cons. 18 Nov. 1621	trs. Bath and Wells 18 Sept. 1626
Theophilus Field	trs. Llandaff 12 July 1627	trs. Hereford 23 Dec. 1635
Roger Mainwaring	cons. 28 Feb. 1636	1 July 1653
	(Vacancy 1653–60)	
William Lucy	cons. 2 Dec. 1660	4 Oct. 1677
William Thomas	cons. early 1678	trs. Worcester 27 Aug. 1683
Lawrence Womock	cons. 11 Nov. 1683	12 Mar. 1686
John Lloyd	cons. 17 Oct. 1686	13 Feb. 1687
Thomas Watson	cons. 26 June 1687	susp. 21 Aug. 1694, depr. 3 Aug. 1699
	(Vacancy 1699–1705)	
George Bull	cons. 29 Apr. 1705	17 Feb. 1710
Philip Bisse	cons. 19 Nov. 1710	trs. Hereford 16 Feb. 1713

BISHOPS	ACCESSION	DEATH *unless otherwise stated*
Adam Ottley	cons. 15 Mar. 1713	3 Oct. 1723
Richard Smallbrooke	cons. 3 Feb. 1724	trs. Lichfield 20 Feb. 1731
Elias Sydall	cons. 11 Apr. 1731	trs. Gloucester 2 Nov. 1731
Nicholas Claggett	cons. 23 Jan. 1732	trs. Exeter 2 Aug. 1742
Edward Willes	cons. 2 Jan. 1743	trs. Bath and Wells 12 Dec. 1743
Richard Trevor	cons. 1 Apr. 1744	trs. Durham 7 Dec. 1752
Anthony Ellis	cons. 31 Mar. 1753	16 Jan. 1761
Samuel Squire	cons. 24 Mar. 1761	7 May 1766
Robert Lowth	cons. 15 June 1766	trs. Oxford 16 Oct. 1766
Charles Moss	cons. 30 Nov. 1766	trs. Bath and Wells 2 June 1774
James Yorke	cons. 26 June 1774	trs. Gloucester 2 Aug. 1779
John Warren	cons. 19 Sept. 1779	trs. Bangor 9 June 1783
Edward Smallwell	cons. 6 July 1783	trs. Oxford 15 Apr. 1788
Samuel Horsley	cons. 11 May 1788	trs. Rochester 7 Dec. 1793
William Stewart (Stuart)	cons. 12 Jan. 1794	trs. Armagh, nom. 30 Oct. 1800
George Murray	cons. 11 Feb. 1801	3 June 1803
Thomas Burgess	cons. 17 July 1803	trs. Salisbury 17 June 1825
John Banks Jenkinson	cons. 24 July 1825	6 July 1840
Connop Thirlwall	cons. 9 Aug. 1840	res. 16 June 1874 (d. 27 July 1875)
William Basil Tickell Jones	cons. 24 Aug. 1874	14 Jan. 1897
John Owen	cons. 1 May 1897	4 Nov. 1926
David Lewis Prosser	cons. 2 Feb. 1927, abp of Wales 1944–49	28 Feb. 1950
William Thomas Havard	trs. St Asaph, el. 30 Mar. 1950	17 Aug. 1956
John Richards Richards	cons. 30 Nov. 1956	res. 31 Mar. 1971
Eric Matthias Roberts	el. 21 Apr., cons. 1 June 1971	res. 30 Sept. 1981
George Noakes	el. 11 Nov. 1981, cons. 2 Feb. 1982	

SWANSEA AND BRECON

Edward Latham Bevan	cons. (as suffragan bp of Swansea) 29 Sept. 1915, el. as first bp, conf. 11 Aug. 1923	2 Feb. 1934
John Morgan	cons. 22 May 1934	trs. Llandaff, el. 22 June 1939
Edward William Williamson	cons. 30 Nov. 1939	23 Sept. 1953
William Glyn Hughes Simon	cons. 6 Jan. 1954	trs. Llandaff, 30 July 1957
John James Absalom Thomas	el. 28 Nov. 1957, cons. 25 Jan. 1958	res. 15 Feb. 1976
Benjamin Noel Young Vaughan	trs. Mandeville (suff.), el. 17 Mar. 1976	

BISHOPS OF SCOTLAND

The work of revision of the lists below has been based on *Fasti Ecclesiae Scoticanae Medii Aevi ad annum 1638*, second draft, ed. D. E. R. Watt (St Andrews and Scottish Record Society, 1969); D. E. R. Watt, *A Biographical Dictionary of Scottish Graduates to A.D. 1410* (Oxford, 1977); and some unpublished material prepared for the 'New Gams', i.e. *Series Episcoporum Ecclesiae Catholicae Occidentalis ab initio usque ad annum 1198*, ed. O. Engels and S. Weinfurter (Stuttgart, 1978–).

John Dowden, *The Bishops of Scotland* (ed. J. Maitland Thomson, 1912), gives fully documented lists for all the sees from the twelfth century to the Reformation and for Aberdeen and Moray down to the early twentieth century. Supplementary information derives mainly from work published since Dowden wrote, especially the later volumes of the *Calendar of Papal Registers*, the researches at the Vatican of Dr A. I. Dunlop [published in *Scottish Supplications to Rome*, 4 vols (Scot. Hist. Soc.), *The Apostolic Camera and Scottish Benefices* and *James Kennedy*] and Scottish record publications. The older and often unreliable *Catalogue of Scottish Bishops* by Robert Keith (ed. Michael Russel, 1824) gives the succession from early times to the beginning of the nineteenth century. The period between the Reformation and the Revolution of 1689 is dealt with in *Fasti Ecclesiae Scoticanae*, vii. Lists of the post-Revolution bishops of the Scottish Episcopal Church, except in so far as they are included in the works of Dowden and Keith already referred to, are to be found only in that church's *Year Book*.

There are the following studies of particular dioceses: Oluf Kolsrud, 'Den Norske Kirkes Erkebiskoper og Biskoper', in *Diplomatarium Norvegicum*, xvii, sjette hefte (Christiania, 1913), for Orkney and the Isles; John Hunter, *Diocese and Presbytery of Dunkeld, 1660–1689* (1917); and G. Donaldson, 'Bishops and Priors of Whithorn', in *Dumfries and Galloway Nat. Hist. and Antiq. Soc. Transns*, 3rd ser., xxvii (1950).

The obscure history of the Scottish episcopate before the twelfth century is examined in G. Donaldson, 'Scottish Bishops' Sees before the Reign of David I', in *Proc. Soc. Antiq. Scot.*, lxxxvii (1955). In compiling the lists now printed there seemed no point at which to draw the line between excluding all bishops before 1100 (which would have involved the exclusion of the Anglian bishops of Abercorn and Whithorn) and including, either in the text or in footnotes, all bishops whose names are known. The latter course has in general been adopted; but since the status of several of these bishops is indeterminate (especially in the case of early names traditionally associated with St Andrews), it must not be assumed that they represent a diocesan system.

After a prolonged struggle against the claims of York to metropolitan jurisdiction over Scotland, the Scottish church was in 1192 recognized as an independent province, though without an archbishop. Galloway, however, remained subject to York, Orkney and the Isles (being Norwegian dependencies) to Nidaros (Trondheim). Galloway's connexion with York was strained by the war of independence, and showed signs of weakening even before the Schism, which finally brought subjection to York to an end. The Isles (with Man) were ceded to Scotland in 1266, and in Orkney Norwegian sovereignty was already somewhat shadowy before the islands were incorporated in the Scottish kingdom (1468–72). Thus in those dioceses also the Schism contributed to break the allegiance to a foreign archbishop, and in the Isles it led to the division of the diocese into English and Scottish portions, each with its own succession of bishops. On the erection of the archbishopric of St Andrews in 1472, Galloway, Orkney and the Isles were all formally incorporated in its province. When Glasgow became an archbishopric twenty years later, Dunkeld, Dunblane, Galloway and Argyll became its suffragans, but Dunblane was restored to St Andrews on 28 January 1500 and Dunkeld not long afterwards. In the seventeenth century the see of the Isles was a suffragan of Glasgow, and the new see of Edinburgh (1633) naturally fell to St

Andrews. In the following lists, the sees are arranged in alphabetical order, without regard to the brief experiment in archiepiscopal organization.

In almost every period there were complications which sometimes make it difficult to present a straightforward list. In the twelfth and thirteenth centuries, the right to elect was in some dioceses contested between the chapter and the 'clergy and people', while the right of nomination or of 'patronage' was sometimes contested between a local magnate and the king. Later, chapter election from time to time conflicted with royal nomination or with papal provision, and occasionally with both at once.

During the Schism only bishops recognised in some way in what is now Scotland, whichever pope was involved, are included. Normally this means popes of the Avignon line. But since the diocese of Orkney was then part of Norway, it is the bishops appointed by popes of the Roman line who are listed here as in possession, though in this case bishops appointed by the Avignon line are also noted, since they drew some revenues from the Scottish mainland. Square brackets are used throughout to indicate persons who had some claim to a see but did not gain possession.

By the second quarter of the sixteenth century the voice of the crown in episcopal appointments had become all but invariably effective, and the pope's part in the proceedings merely formal. Consequently, at the Reformation there was no change in substance when the crown began to make appointments by simple gift or provision, and, while the ecclesiastical character and significance of its nominees were variable, it was always in the power of the crown to create a bishop *quoad civilia*. The abbreviation 'prov.' is used of papal provisions before 1560 and crown provisions thereafter, except in so far as footnotes indicate otherwise. In 1572 chapters were reformed and were permitted to make a formal election of the royal nominee, who thereafter received the crown's provision.

Between 1560 and 1610 the episcopate, although never extinguished, had a precarious existence, threatened on one side by secularization (through the appointment by the crown of lay administrators) and on the other by presbyterian demands for 'parity' which would exclude the bishops from ecclesiastical functions. When episcopal government in the Church of Scotland was formally abolished (for the first time) in 1638–39, the bishops were 'deposed' by the general assembly and ceased to exercise their episcopal functions. When it was abolished for the second time, in 1689, some of the bishops continued to exercise their functions in relation to the congregations which adhered to them.

It will be noticed that before the Reformation admission to the temporality was sometimes given before consecration and even before papal provision, and is therefore not always conclusive in determining the date of consecration. According to the arrangements made in 1572, the crown confirmation (subsequent to capitular election) was accompanied by a mandate to consecrate, and the stages following consecration were the oath to the sovereign and the restitution of temporality. In only two instances do we have full particulars of 'consecration' according to the *formulae* then in use; but there is every reason to believe that as long as these arrangements operated (1572–*c*. 1586) the mandate to consecrate was normally obeyed and that consecration, forming as it did one stage in a carefully defined procedure designed to secure the bishops in their sees, duly preceded admission to temporality.

ABERCORN

BISHOPS	ACCESSION	DEATH
		unless otherwise stated
Trumwine	681	res. 685[1]

ABERDEEN

Nechtan	*a.* Apr. 1132	prob. *p.* 30 June 1136
Edward	*a.* 1151	1171
Matthew	el. *a.* cons. 2 Apr. 1172	20 Aug. 1199
John	el. *a.* 26 Dec. 1199, cons. *a.* 20 June 1200	13 Oct. 1207
Adam de Kalder	el. Oct. × Dec. 1207, cons. *p.* 29 Jan. 1208	1228

[1] Forced to withdraw aft. the Anglian defeat at Nechtansmere.

BISHOPS	ACCESSION	DEATH
		unless otherwise stated
Gilbert de Strivelyn	el. 1228, cons. *a.* 1230	1239
Radulf de Lamley	el. *a.* conf. 17 June 1239, cons. *a.* 20 Aug. 1240	1247
Peter de Ramsay	el. *a.* conf. 13 May 1247, cons. *a.* 1249	*p.* 18 Apr. 1256, prob. *a.* Dec. 1256
Richard de Pottun	el. *a.* 4 Oct. 1257, cons. *a.* 25 Aug. 1258	1270 or 26 Apr. 1272
Hugh de Bennum	el. *a.* cons. 27 Mar. × 23 July 1272	Dec. 1281 × 17 June 1282
Henry le Chene	el. *a.* prov. 17 June 1282	*p.* 11 Nov. 1328
[Walter Herok	el. and prov. *p.* 15 Mar. 1329, not cons.	*a.* 21 Aug. 1329]
Alexander de Kininmund	prov. and cons. 21 Aug. 1329	10 June × 13 Sept. 1344, prob. 14 Aug. 1344
William de Deyn	el. *a.* prov. 13 Sept. 1344, cons. *a.* 27 Sept. 1344	20 Aug. 1350
John de Rate	el. *a.* prov. 19 Nov. 1350, cons. 26 Jan. × 14 Mar. 1351	12 Nov. 1354 × prob. 6 June 1355
Alexander de Kininmund	el. *a.* prov. 4 Dec. 1355, cons. *a.* 12 July 1356	29 July 1380
[Simon de Ketenis	el. *p.* 31 Aug. 1380, not conf.]	
Adam de Tyningham	prov. 15 Oct. 1380, cons. prob. *a.* 24 Oct. 1380	18 Sept. 1389
Gilbert de Grenlaw	el. *a.* prov. 19 Jan. 1390, cons. prob. *a.* 19 Feb. 1390	*p.* 24 July 1421, prob. 20 Sept. 1421
Henry de Lychton	trs. from Moray 1 Apr. 1422	12 or 14 Dec. 1440
Ingram de Lindsay	el. *p.* 13 Jan. 1441, prov. 28 Apr. 1441	24 Aug. or 17 Nov. 1458
[James Douglas	prov. by anti-pope 30 May 1441, held temporalities for a time]	
Thomas Spens	trs. from Galloway 21 Nov. 1457 abortively, trs. again 15 Dec. 1458, effective 3 × 10 Mar. 1459	15 Apr. 1480
[William Forbes	el. *a.* 27 Feb. 1459, not conf.]	
Robert Blackadder	el. *a.* 12 June 1480, prov. 14 July 1480, not cons.	trs. to Glasgow 19 Mar. 1483
William Elphinstone	trs. uncons. from Ross 19 Mar. 1483, cons. 25 Apr. 1488 × 24 Apr. 1489	25 Oct. 1514
Alexander Gordon	nom. and el. *a.* 20 Jan. 1515, prov. 6 June 1516	30 June 1518
[James Ogilvie	nom. and res. *a.* 24 Sept. 1515]	
[Robert Forman	prov. *a.* 22 Mar. 1515, not cons.	res. *a.* 1515–16]
Gavin Dunbar	nom. *a.* 31 Oct. 1518, prov. 5 Nov. 1518, cons. 20 Feb. 1519	10 Mar. 1532
[George Learmonth	prov. (coadj.) 20 May 1529	18 Mar. 1531]
William Stewart	nom. 22 Mar. 1532, prov. 13 Nov. 1532, cons. 22 Mar. × 10 Apr. 1533	10 Apr. 1545
William Gordon	nom. (coadj.) 21 Jan. 1545 and 15 Mar. 1545, temp. 20 Aug. 1545, prov. 17 May 1546, cons. 23 Dec. 1546 × 26 Jan. 1547	6 Aug. 1577
David Cunningham	prov. 5 Oct. or 5 Nov. 1577, cons. 11 Nov. 1577, temp. 22 Feb. 1578	30 Aug. 1600
Peter Blackburn	prov. 2 Sept. 1600, cons. 21 Oct. 1610 × 3 May 1611	14 June 1616
Alexander Forbes	trs. from Caithness 16 July 1616	24 Nov. 1617

BISHOPS	ACCESSION	DEATH
		unless otherwise stated
Patrick Forbes	el. 24 Mar. 1618, prov. 8 Apr. 1618, cons. 17 May 1618	28 Mar. 1635
Adam Bellenden	trs. from Dunblane 19 May 1635	depr. 13 Dec. 1638, buried 4 Mar. 1648
David Mitchell	prov. 18 Jan. 1662, cons. 3 June 1662	buried 10 Feb. 1663
Alexander Burnet	prov. 4 May 1663, cons. 18 Sept. 1663	trs. to Glasgow 1664
Patrick Scougal	prov. 14 Jan. 1664, cons. 10 or 11 Apr. 1664	16 Feb. 1682
George Haliburton	trs. from Brechin 5 July 1682	29 Sept. 1715

ABERNETHY

There may have been a series of three bishops here in early eighth century. No names have certainly survived, but Fergustus, a Pictish bishop in 721, may have been one of them. Abernethy was later included in Dunblane diocese.

ARGYLL (OR LISMORE)

Harald	? 1192 × 1203	Aug. 1228 × June 1232
William	el. *p.* May 1238, conf. 16 Feb. 1239, cons. *a.* 20 May 1240	1241
Alan	el. 23 Dec. 1248 × 27 Sept. 1250, cons. *a.* 27 Sept. 1253	1262
Laurence de Ergadia	el. *a.* conf. 31 Mar. 1264, cons. *a.* 20 June 1268	*p.* 29 Oct. 1299
Andrew	el. *a.* prov. and cons. 18 Dec. 1300	*p.* 18 Nov. 1327, prob. *p.* 10 Sept. 1334.
[Angus	el. by clergy of city and diocese *a.* 25 Apr. 1342, not cons.	27 May × 20 Dec. 1344]
Martin de Ergaill	el. by chapter *a.* 16 Mar. 1342, prov. and cons. 20 Dec. 1344	*p.* 15 Oct. 1382
John Dugaldi	el. *a.* prov. 26 Apr. 1387, cons. 5 × 8 June 1387	*p.* 7 Nov. 1395
Bean Johannis	el. *a.* prov. 17 Sept. 1397, prob. cons. *a.* 9 Oct. 1397	*p.* 8 July 1411
Finlay de Albany	el. *a.* prov. 31 Jan. 1420, prob. cons. *a.* 11 Mar. 1420	fled to Ireland 3 May × 8 June 1425, prob. died *p.* 13 May 1426
George Lauder	prov. 26 May 1427, cons. 20 Dec. 1427 × 21 Apr. 1428	*p.* 10 May 1467
Robert Colquhoun	prov. 24 Apr. 1475, cons. 3 Dec. 1475 × 2 Dec. 1476	20 June 1493 × 13 Feb. 1496
David Hamilton	prov. 3 Apr. 1497, cons. 3 Jan. 1498 × 13 Mar. 1504	*p.* 4 Dec. 1522, prob. *a.* 5 June 1523
Robert Montgomery	prov. 28 July 1525, cons. *p.* 26 May 1533	*a.* 29 Aug. 1538
William Cunningham	nom. 1 Feb. 1539, prov. 7 May 1539, not cons.	res. 14 July 1553
James Hamilton	prov. 14 July 1553, not cons.	6 Jan. 1580
Neil Campbell	lic. for election 12 Jan. 1580, ? cons.	res. 2 May × 1 June 1608
John Campbell	prov. 1 June 1608, prob. cons. 23 Jan. × 24 Feb. 1611	Jan. 1613
Andrew Boyd	prov. 4 Mar. 1613	22 Dec. 1636
James Fairlie	el. 21 June 1637, conf. 10 July 1637, cons. 8 Aug. 1637	depr. 13 Dec. 1638
David Fletcher	prov. 18 Jan. 1662, cons. June 1662	Mar. 1665
[John Young	prov. 1665, not cons.	June 1665]
William Scroggie	prov. 4 Jan. 1666, cons. 14 Jan. 1666	27 Jan. 1675

BISHOPS	ACCESSION	DEATH *unless otherwise stated*
Arthur Rose	prov. 28 Apr. 1675, cons. May 1675	trs. Galloway 1679
Colin Falconer	el. May 1679, prov. 5 Sept. 1679, cons. 28 Oct. 1679	trs. Moray 1680
Hector MacLean	prov. 31 May 1680	1687
[Alexander Monro	prov. 24 Oct. 1688, not cons.	1698]

BRECHIN

Samson	*a.* 1150	*p.* 1172
Turpin	el. *a.* 1178, prob. cons. Mar. 1179	*p.* 1189
Radulf	el. 1196 × 1199, cons. 1202	*p.* 31 May 1212
Hugh	*a.* 17 Feb. 1215	1218
Gregory	el. *a.* 15 Dec. 1218, cons. *p.* 15 Dec. 1218	*p.* 1242
Albin	el. *a.* 19 July 1246, cons. 19 July 1246 × 13 May 1247	1269
[William de Crachin	el., not cons.	? 1274]
William Comyn	el. *a.* 24 May 1275, cons. 24 May 1275 × 29 Apr. 1276	*p.* June 1291
Nicholas	prov. and cons. 21 Jan. 1297	*a.* 1 June 1298
John de Kininmund	el. *a.* conf. and cons. 1 June 1298	*p.* Mar. 1324
Adam de Moravia	el. 17 Mar. × 28 July 1328, cons. 20 × 31 Oct. 1328	*p.* 30 Apr. 1349
Philip Wilde	el. *a.* prov. 17 Feb. 1350, prob. cons. *a.* 6 Apr. 1350	*p.* 3 May 1351
Patrick de Leuchars	el. *a.* prov. 17 Nov. 1351, cons. *a.* 11 Dec. 1351	res. *a.* 12 June 1383
Stephen de Cellario	el. *a.* prov. 12 June 1383, cons. *p.* 27 June 1383	11 Nov. 1404 × 7 June 1405
Walter Forrester	el. *a.* 11 Apr. 1407, prov. 26 Nov. 1407, prob. cons. *a.* 25 Oct. 1408	*p.* 7 May 1425
John de Crannach	trs. uncons. from Caithness 7 June 1426, cons. 6 Oct. 1426 × 5 Oct. 1427	*p.* 17 Nov. 1453
George Schoriswood	prov. 8 Mar. 1454, cons. *a.* 1 July 1454	*p.* 11 Nov. 1462
Patrick Graham	el. *a.* prov. 28 Mar. 1463, cons. 3 Nov. × 29 Dec. 1464	trs. St Andrews 4 Nov. 1465
John Balfour	prov. 29 Nov. 1465, cons. 8 Dec. 1465	res. 4 June × 4 July 1488
William Meldrum	prov. 4 July 1488, cons. 30 Jan. × 7 July 1489	8 Dec. 1514 × 19 Mar. 1516
John Hepburn	prov. 29 Oct. 1516, cons. June 1522 × 23 Feb. 1523	27 Mar. × 22 May 1557
[Donald Campbell	nom. *a.* 11 Feb. 1558, not cons.	16 Dec. 1562 × 20 Jan. 1563]
John Sinclair	nom. *a.* papal prov. 7 Sept. 1565, prob. not cons.	9 Apr. 1566
Alexander Campbell	crown prov. as minor 6 May 1566, nom. to pope 21 July 1566, ? cons.	res. *a.* 22 Apr. 1607
Andrew Lamb	prov. 22 Apr. 1607, cons. 21 Oct. 1610	trs. Galloway 1619
David Lindsay	el. 10 Apr. 1619, cons. 23 Nov. 1619, prov. 11 Feb. 1620	trs. Edinburgh 1634
Thomas Sydserf	cons. 29 July 1634, prov. 16 Sept. 1634	trs. Galloway 1635
Walter Whitford	prov. 15 Sept. 1635, cons. 7 Dec. 1635	depr. 13 Dec. 1638, d. 1647

BISHOPS	ACCESSION	DEATH *unless otherwise stated*
David Strachan	prov. 3 May 1662, cons. 7 May 1662	9 Oct. 1671
Robert Laurie	prov. 11 July 1672, cons. 14 July 1672	Mar. 1678
George Haliburton	prov. 16 May 1678, cons. 13 June 1678	trs. Aberdeen 1682
Robert Douglas	prov. 21 June 1682, cons. 25 July 1682	trs. Dunblane 1684

CAITHNESS

Andrew	*a.* 1151	29 or 30 Dec. 1184
John	*a.* 27 May 1198	*p.* Sept. 1202
Adam	el. 5 Aug. 1213, cons. 11 May 1214	11 Sept. 1222
Gilbert de Moravia	el. late 1222 or late 1223, cons. *a.* 10 Apr. 1224	1 Apr., prob. 1245
William	cons. 17 Sept. 1246 × 16 Sept. 1247	*p.* 16 Sept. 1255
Walter de Baltrodin	el. *a.* conf. 13 June 1263, cons. *p.* 13 June 1263	1270
[Nicholas	el. but not conf. 27 Mar. 1272] × 4 June 1273	
Archibald Herok	el. *p.* 4 June 1273, conf. 1 Nov. 1274, cons. 10 Jan. × 22 Sept. 1275	*p.* 22 Sept. 1275
[Richard	el. *a.* 9 Dec. 1278, not cons.	ordered to res. 9 Mar. 1279]
[Hervey de Dundee	el. *p.* 9 Mar. 1279, not conf.	1281]
Alan de St Edmund	prov. and cons. 13 Apr. 1282	5 Nov. × 12 Dec. 1291
[John	el. *a.* 29 Apr. 1296, when election quashed]	
Adam de Derlingtun	prov. and cons. 29 Apr. 1296	8 June × 17 Dec. 1296
Andrew (? de Buchan)	prov. 17 Dec. 1296, cons. *p.* 1 Aug. 1297	17 Aug. 1298 × 16 June 1304
Fercard Belegaumbe	el. *a.* 16 June 1304, conf. 22 Jan. 1306, temp. from Edward I 4 Apr. 1306	10 July 1321 × 11 Nov. 1327
David	prov. 26 Jan. 1328	*a.* 16 Jan. 1341
Alan de Moravia	el. *a.* conf. and cons. 16 Jan. 1341	22 May × 29 Nov. 1342
Thomas de Fingask	el. *a.* prov. 29 Nov. 1342, cons. *a.* 1 Dec. 1342	*p.* 21 Jan. 1365
Malcolm de Dumbrek	el. *a.* 11 Jan. 1369, conf. 21 Feb. 1369, cons. 24 Apr. 1369 × 16 Jan. 1370	prob. *p.* Mar. 1379
Alexander Man	el. *p.* 18 Aug. 1381, conf. 21 Oct. 1381, cons. 25 Oct. × 10 Dec. 1381	*p.* May 1412
Alexander Vaus	trs. uncons. from Orkney 4 May 1414, cons. 22 Jan. 1415 × 17 Mar. 1416	trs. to Galloway 4 Dec. 1422
John de Crannach	prov. 4 Dec. 1422, 11 Dec. 1424, 14 May 1425, not cons.	trs. to Brechin 7 June 1426
Robert de Strabrok	el. *a.* prov. 4 June 1427, prob. cons. *a.* 19 Dec. 1427	24 July 1445 × 7 Apr. 1446
[John de Innes	prov. 8 Apr. 1446, prob. not cons.	5 June 1447 × 6 Jan. 1448]
[Andrew Tulloch	el. but not conf.	*a.* 23 Sept. 1448]
William Mudy	prov. 6 Jan. 1448, cons. 15 Mar. × 19 Apr. 1448	*p.* 30 June 1477
Prospero Camogli de' Medici	prov. 25 May 1478, temp. 12 Sept. 1481	res. *a.* 26 May 1484

BISHOPS	ACCESSION	DEATH *unless otherwise stated*
[John Sinclair	prov. 26 May 1484, prob. not cons.	*a.* 21 Jan. 1501]
Andrew Stewart	prov. 26 Nov. 1501, prob. cons. *a.* 26 Mar. 1502	17 June 1517
Robert Stewart	nom. 8 Sept. 1541, prov. as administrator 27 Jan. 1542, not cons.	29 Aug. 1586
[Alexander Gordon	nom. 12 Dec. 1544, prov. by legate 13 Apr. 1546	res. claim 13 Apr. 1548]
[Robert Pont	nom. and el. '1586', but declined *a.* 28 June 1587]	
George Gledstanes	prov. 5 Nov. 1600, not cons.	trs. to St Andrews 12 Oct. 1604
Alexander Forbes	prov. 14 Nov. 1604, cons. *a.* 3 May 1611	trs. to Aberdeen 21 July 1616
John Abernethy	prov. 7 Dec. 1616	res. *a.* 5 Dec. 1638, depr. 13 Dec. 1638
[Robert Hamilton	nom. 5 Dec. 1638, not cons.]	
Patrick Forbes	prov. 11 Mar. 1662, cons. 7 May 1662	1679
Andrew Wood	trs. from The Isles 17 Apr. 1680	1695

DUNBLANE

M	*a.* 27 Feb. 1155	*p.* 27 Feb. 1155
Laurence	*a.* 1161	*p.* 28 Mar. 1165
Simon	el. *a.* late 1178, prob. cons. Mar. 1179	*p.* c. 1193
Jonathan	*a.* Aug. 1198	1210
Abraham	el. 1210 × 1214, cons. *a.* 4 Dec. 1214	*p.* 7 Feb. 1220
[Radulf	el. *a.* 1223 × 1225, not cons.	res. *a.* 12 Jan. 1226]
Osbert	*a.* 11 Apr. 1227	1231
Clement	prov. *a.* cons. 4 Sept. 1233	1258, prob. 19 Mar.
Robert de Prebenda	el. *a.* 2 Jan. 1259, cons. 22 Aug. 1259 × 1 Sept. 1260, prob. late 1259	*p.* 11 Sept. 1283, prob. *p.* 5 Feb. 1284
William	el. *a.* conf. and cons. 18 Dec. 1284	*p.* 31 July 1291
Alpin de Strathern	el. *p.* 4 May 1295, conf. and cons. 16 Oct. 1296	*p.* 1 Oct. 1299
Nicholas	el. *a.* 15 Oct. 1301, prov. and cons. 13 Nov. 1301	*p.* 26 Jan. 1306
Nicholas de Balmyle	el. *a.* conf. and cons. 11 Dec. 1307	8 Feb. 1319 × 30 Jan. 1320
[Richard de Pontefract	nom. by Edward II 30 Jan. and 25 June 1320, not conf.]	
[Roger de Ballinbreich	el. but not conf.	res. *a.* 5 Mar. 1322]
Maurice	el. *a.* prov. 5 Mar. 1322, cons. *a.* 23 Mar. 1322	*a.* 23 Oct. 1347
William (? de Cambuslang)	el. *a.* prov. and cons. 23 Oct. 1347	*p.* 11 Apr. 1358
Walter de Coventre	el. *p.* 4 Sept. 1359, prov. 18 June 1361, prob. cons. by 23 Aug. 1361	*p.* 27 Mar. 1371
Andrew (? Magnus)	el. *a.* prov. 27 Apr. 1372, cons. *a.* 4 Apr. 1373	*p.* 16 Dec. 1377
Dugal de Lorn	el. *a.* prov. 12 Sept. 1380, cons. *a.* 11 Oct. 1380	*p.* Apr. 1398
Finlay Colini	el. *a.* prov. 10 Sept. 1403, cons. *a.* 28 Apr. 1404	*p.* 25 Mar. 1419

DUNKELD

BISHOPS	ACCESSION	DEATH *unless otherwise stated*
William Stephenson	trs. from Orkney 30 Oct. 1419	17 July 1428 × 25 Feb. 1429
Michael Ochiltree	prov. 22 June 1429, cons. 4 July 1430 × 12 Apr. 1431	*p.* 23 Sept. 1446
[Walter Stewart	el. *a.* 27 Oct. 1447, not conf.]	
Robert Lauder	prov. 27 Oct. 1447, cons. *a.* 13 Nov. 1447	res. 12 Sept. 1466
John 'Herspolz'	prov. 12 Sept. 1466, cons. 22 June × 28 Sept. 1467	*p.* 3 Feb. 1485
[John Spalding	nom. *a.* 19 Nov. 1467, not conf.]	
James Chisholm	prov. 31 Jan. 1487, cons. 11 July 1487 × 11 Jan. 1488	res. 6 June 1526, but with rights as administrator, d. 24 Mar. 1534 × 20 Jan. 1546
William Chisholm	prov. 6 June 1526, cons. 14 Apr. 1527	14 or 15 Dec. 1564
William Chisholm	nom. *a.* prov. as coadjutor 2 June 1561, depr. *a.* 25 Aug. 1569, rehabilitated 28 Mar. and 29 July 1587	finally depr. 27 May 1589
Andrew Graham	el. *a.* crown conf. 17 May 1575, temp. 28 July 1575	res. *a.* Feb. 1603
George Graham	prov. Feb. 1603, cons. prob. 23 Jan. × 24 Feb. 1611	trs. to Orkney 26 Aug. 1615
Adam Bellenden	prov. 23 Sept. 1615, cons. *a.* 3 Apr. 1616	trs. Aberdeen 1635
James Wedderburn	prov. 11 Feb. 1636, cons. 1636	depr. 13 Dec. 1638, d. 23 Sept. 1639
Robert Leighton	prov. 12 Dec. 1661, cons. 15 Dec. 1661	trs. Glasgow 1671
James Ramsay	prov. 22 July 1673, cons. 4 Sept. 1673, restored 26 Apr. 1676	trs. The Isles 1674, trs. Ross. 1684
Robert Douglas	trs. from Brechin 23 May 1684	22 Apr. 1716

DUNKELD

Tuathal	abbot of Dunkeld and chief bishop of Fortriu	865
Cormac	bishop without designation *a.* c. 1120, bishop of Dunkeld specifically by 1127 × 1131	*p.* Apr. 1131 × Apr. 1132
Gregory	*a.* 1147	1169
Richard	cons. 9 Aug. 1170	22 Feb. × 8 Apr. 1178
Walter de Bidun	el. 1178, not cons.	1178, prob. after 14 Oct.
John Scot	trs. from St Andrews 1183, *a.* July	1203
Richard de Prebenda	el. 1203	Apr. or May 1210
John de Leicester	el. 22 July 1211, cons. *p.* 13 June 1212	7 Oct. 1214
Hugh de Sigillo	el. 1214, cons. *a.* 29 Sept. 1216	1229
[Matthew Scot	el. 1229, not cons.	1229 or *p.* 30 Apr. 1230]
Gilbert	el. 1229 or 1230	buried 6 Apr. 1236
Geoffrey de Liberatione	el. *a.* conf. 6 Sept. 1236, cons. 3 × 31 Dec. 1236	22 Nov. 1249
Richard de Inverkeithing	el. 1250 *a.* 3 Dec., cons. prob. 3 Aug. × 20 Oct. 1251	16 Apr. 1272
Robert de Stuteville	el. *a.* 7 May 1273, conf. and cons. *a.* 9 Nov. 1273	*p.* 29 Sept. 1277, prob. *p.* 9 Oct. 1282
[Hugh de Strivelyn	el. but not cons.	*a.* 13 Dec. 1283]
William	el. *a.* conf. and cons. 13 Dec. 1283	*p.* 18 May 1285

307

BISHOPS	ACCESSION	DEATH *unless otherwise stated*
Matthew de Crambeth	el. *a.* conf. and cons. 10 Apr. 1288	*p.* 17 Mar. 1309
William de Sinclair	el. *a.* 18 July 1309, nom. by Edward II 8 Feb. 1312, conf. and cons. 8 May 1312	27 June 1337
[John de Leek	el. also *a.* 18 July 1309, had then support of Edward II in litigation with Sinclair	trs. prob. uncons. to Dublin 18 May 1311]
[Malcolm de Innerpeffry	el. with support of Edward III *a.* 3 Jan. 1338, not cons.	*a.* 25 Apr. 1342]
Richard de Pilmor	el. *a.* 3 Jan. 1338, prov. after litigation 5 July 1344, cons. 14 July × 27 Sept. 1344	*p.* 22 Nov. 1345, prob. *p.* 18 July 1346
[Duncan de Strathern	el. *a.* 25 Apr. 1342, recognised as litigant 13 Mar. 1344, not cons.	lost litigation *a.* 5 July 1344]
[Robert de Den	el. but not conf. *a.* 28 Jan. 1348]	
Duncan de Strathern	prov. 15 Oct. 1347, cons. *a.* 9 Nov. 1347	*p.* 1 Apr. 1354, prob. *p.* 14 Dec. 1354
John Luce	el. *a.* prov. 18 May 1355, cons. *a.* 29 June 1355	*p.* 20 July 1369
[John Rede	el. but not conf.	res. right *a.* 13 Nov. 1370]
[John de Carrick	el. prob. *p.* 3 Mar. 1370, but not conf.]	
Michael de Monymusk	prov. 13 Nov. 1370, cons. 5 × 8 Jan. 1371	1 Mar. 1377
Andrew Umfray	el. *a.* prov. 17 June 1377, not cons.	1 July × 7 Sept. 1377
John de Peblis	el. and conf. *a.* 27 Mar. 1378, prob. cons. c. June 1378, cons. again Feb. × July 1379 (earlier ceremony now regarded as schismatic)	*p.* 15 Aug. 1390
Robert de Sinclair	trs. from Orkney 1 Feb. 1391	*p.* 13 Feb. 1395
Robert de Cardeny	el. *a.* prov. 27 Nov. 1398, cons. *a.* 20 Nov. 1399	16 or 17 Jan. 1437
[Donald Macnachtan	perhaps el. Jan. × Feb. 1437, not conf.]	
James Kennedy	el. *a.* 16 Feb. 1437, prov. 1 July 1437, cons. 16 May × 7 July 1438	trs. to St Andrews 22 Apr. and 1 June 1440
Alexander de Lauder	el. 1 × 15 May 1440, prov. 6 June 1440, not cons.	11 Oct. 1440
[Thomas Livingston	prov. by Felix V 29 Nov. 1440, cons., but no possession	9 Apr. × 10 July 1460]
James Brois	el. *a.* prov. 6 Feb. 1441, cons. 4 Feb. 1442	trs. to Glasgow 3 Feb. 1447
William Turnbull	prov. 10 Feb. 1447, not cons.	trs. to Glasgow 27 Oct. 1447
John de Ralston	prov. 27 Oct. 1447, cons. perhaps *a.* 4 Apr., certainly *a.* 20 Apr. 1448	*p.* 5 July 1451
Thomas Lauder	prov. 28 Apr. 1452, temp. 22 June 1452 when prob. not yet cons.	res. on pension 2 Oct. 1475, d. 4 Nov. 1481
James Levington	prov. 2 Oct. 1475, cons. 30 June 1476	28 Aug. 1483
Alexander Inglis	el. on king's nom. *a.* 17 Sept. 1483, still recognised by king 19 Sept. 1485, not cons.	
George Brown	prov. 22 Oct. 1483, cons. 13 June 1484	15 Jan. 1515

308

BISHOPS	ACCESSION	DEATH
		unless otherwise stated
[Andrew Stewart	el. *a.* May 1515 when accepted by duke of Albany, held temp., not cons.	res. temp. 16 × 28 Sept. 1516]
Gavin Douglas	nom. by Queen Margaret 17 Jan. 1515, prov. 25 May 1515, temp. 16 Sept. 1516, cons. 21 Sept. 1516	forfeited 12 Dec. 1521 d. 10 × 19 Sept. 1522
Robert Cockburn	trs. from Ross 27 Apr. 1524, temp. 14 Sept. 1524	12 Apr. 1526
George Crichton	nom. 21 June 1526, prov. 25 June 1526, cons. *p.* 17 July 1526	1 × 20 Jan. 1544
Robert Crichton	nom. and prob. conf. as coadj. *a.* 17 Mar. 1543, lit. with Hamilton and Campbell, no possession 18 Sept. 1553, in office 12 Apr. 1554	forfeited 30 Aug. 1571
John Hamilton	temp. 20 Jan. 1544, nom. 24 Jan. 1544, prov. 17 Dec. 1544, cons. 22 Aug. 1546	trs. to St Andrews 28 Nov. 1547
[Donald Campbell	nom. and rejected by pope *a.* 26 Mar. 1548, temp. 23 June 1549, lit. with Crichton 22 Apr. 1550	res. right 18 Sept. 1553 × 12 Apr. 1554]
James Paton	nom. 8 Sept. 1571, crown conf. after el. 20 July 1572, temp. 27 Apr. 1573	? res. *a.* 22 Aug. 1584
Robert Crichton	restored 22 Aug. 1584	burial arranged 26 Mar. 1585
Peter Rollock	prov. 26 Mar. 1585	res. *a.* 23 Apr. 1607
James Nicolson	prov. 23 Apr. 1607	7 × 27 Aug. 1607
Alexander Lindsay	prov. 28 Dec. 1607, prob. cons. 23 Jan. × 24 Feb. 1611	depr. 13 Dec. 1638
George Haliburton	prov. 18 Jan. 1662, cons. 7 May 1662	5 Apr. 1665
Henry Guthrie	prov. 30 June 1665, cons. 24 Aug. 1665	*a.* 20 Dec. 1676
William Lindsay	prov. 7 May 1677, cons. 26 May 1677	*a.* 15 Apr. 1679
Andrew Bruce	prov. 5 Sept. 1679, cons. 28 Oct. 1679	depr. 3 June 1686, trs. Orkney
John Hamilton	prov. 15 Oct. 1686, cons. 4 Nov. 1686	*a.* 5 Oct. 1689

EDINBURGH[1]

William Forbes	prov. 26 Jan. 1634, cons. 28 Jan. 1634	12 Apr. 1634
David Lindsay	trs. from Brechin 16 Sept. 1634	depr. 13 Dec. 1638, d. Dec. 1641
George Wishart	prov. 18 Jan. 1662, cons. 3 June 1662	buried 29 July 1671
Alexander Young	prov. 11 July 1672, cons. 14 July 1672	trs. Ross 1679
John Paterson	trs. from Galloway 29 Mar. 1679	trs. Glasgow 1687
Alexander Rose	trs. from Moray[2] 31 Dec. 1687	20 Mar. 1720

[1] See erected by Charles I, 29 Sept. 1633.
[2] Nominated to Edinburgh, 25 July 1687, elected 21 Dec. and prov. 31 Dec.

GALLOWAY (OR WHITHORN)[1]

BISHOPS	ACCESSION	DEATH *unless otherwise stated*

For the early bishops of Whithorn, see p. 222 above.

Gilla-Aldan	el. *a.* 9 Dec. 1128, cons. 1128 × 1140	*p.* 16 June 1151
Christian	cons. 19 Dec. 1154	7 Oct. 1186
John	el. *a.* 3 Sept. 1189, cons. 17 Sept. 1189	? res. 1206, d. 1209
Walter	1209, cons. *a.* 2 Nov. 1214	Jan. × Feb. 1235
Gilbert	el. by clergy and people 25 Feb. 1235, royal assent 23 Apr. 1235, cons. 2 Sept. 1235	*p.* 22 June 1253
[Odo Ydonc	el. by prior and convent 11 Mar. 1235, still litigating 19 June 1241, not conf.]	
Henry	el. 1253 or *p.* Oct. 1254, conf. 24 Feb. 1255, cons. uncertain, prob. early 1256	1 Nov. 1293
Thomas de Kirkcudbright	el. *a.* 13 Jan. 1294, royal assent 19 May 1294, conf. 30 May 1294, cons. 10 Oct. 1294	Apr. 1324 × Aug. 1326
Simon de Wedale	prob. el. *a.* 10 Apr. 1323 when see was thought to be vacant, el. again 23 Sept. 1326, conf. 16 Dec. 1326, cons. 1 Feb. 1327	11 Mar. 1355
Michael de Malconhalgh	el. *a.* 4 June 1355, conf. 26 June 1355, cons. 12 July 1355	*p.* 17 Jan. 1358
[Thomas MacDowell	el. but not conf. *a.* 4 Feb. 1360]	
Thomas	prov. and cons. 31 Dec. 1359	*p.* 2 Sept. 1362
Adam de Lanark	el. *a.* prov. 17 Nov. 1363, cons. *a.* 2 Jan. 1364	27 Mar. × 31 Oct. 1378
[Oswald	el. and prov. by Urban VI *p.* 18 Apr. 1378, prob. cons. *a.* 26 Mar. 1379, ousted from possession by Rossy, and lost litigation with him in curia of Clement VII *a.* 29 Oct. 1381, then active only in England	Sept. × Dec. 1417]
[Ingram de Ketenis	prov. by Clement VII 31 Oct. 1378 × 26 Feb. 1379	res. right *p.* 15 July 1379]
Thomas de Rossy	prov. by Clement VII 15 July 1379, cons. 8 Aug. 1379 × 16 July 1380, conf. 29 Oct. 1381	*p.* 6 Sept. 1397
Elisaeus Adougan	el. *a.* prov. 28 May 1406	*p.* ? 1412
[Gilbert Cavan	el. prob. early 1415, not conf.]	
Thomas de Butil	prov. 14 June 1415, cons. *a.* 5 Sept. 1415	*p.* 16 July 1420
Alexander Vaus	trs. from Caithness 4 Dec. 1422	res. 8 Jan. 1450
Thomas Spens	prov. 8 Jan. 1450, cons. 27 May 1450 × 1 Apr. 1451, trs. to Aberdeen 21 Nov. 1457 abortively	trs. to Aberdeen 15 Dec. 1458

[1] The more correct designation was 'Whithorn' (*Candida Casa*), but it was nearly always 'Galloway' in common usage. From 3 July 1504 until the reformation the bps were deans of the chapel royal (of Stirling), and their style was commonly *episcopus Candide Case et capelle regie Strivilingensis.*

BISHOPS	ACCESSION	DEATH *unless otherwise stated*
[Thomas Vaus	prov. 21 Nov. 1457 abortively]	
Ninian Spot	prov. 15 Dec. 1458, cons. 12 Mar. × 16 Apr. 1459, temp. 27 Apr. 1459	*p.* 12 June 1480
George Vaus	prov. 9 Dec. 1482, cons. *a.* 9 Oct. 1483	20 Dec. 1507 × 30 Jan. 1508
James Betoun	nom. 1 Mar. 1508, el. *a.* prov. 12 May 1508, temp. 17 July 1508, not cons.	trs. to Glasgow 19 Jan. 1509
David Arnot	nom. Nov. 1508, prov. 29 Jan. 1509, temp. 27 May 1509	res. on pension 23–24 Jan. 1526, d. 10 July 1536 × 25 Aug. 1537
Henry Wemyss	prov. 23–24 Jan. 1526; cons. *p.* 1 Mar. 1526	14 Mar. × 9 May 1541
Andrew Dury	nom. 3 July 1541, prov. 22 Aug. 1541, cons. 3 Apr. × 9 Dec. 1542	d. prob. Sept. 1558
Alexander Gordon	nom. and trs. from Isles 10 × 28 Feb. 1559, perhaps prov. by pope 1564, res. 4 Jan. 1568 abortively	11 Nov. 1575
[Archibald Crawford		res. some right *a.* 13 June 1564]
John Gordon	prov. 4 Jan. 1568, made good his claim *p.* 11 Nov. 1575	res. right 8 July 1586
[Roger Gordon	el. and nom. *a.* 17 Sept. 1578, prob. no possession	d. *a.* 12 May 1587]
George Gordon	prov. 8 July 1586, prob. not cons.	1 Apr. × 5 Nov. 1588
Gavin Hamilton	prov. 6 Feb. and 3 Mar. 1605, cons. 21 Oct. 1610	Feb. 1612
[John Gordon	renewed his claim 1610	3 Sept. 1619]
William Couper	prov. 31 July 1612, cons. 4 Oct. 1612	15 Feb. 1619
Andrew Lamb	trs. from Brechin 4 Aug. 1619	1634
Thomas Sydserf	trs. from Brechin 30 Aug. 1635	depr. 13 Dec. 1638, trs. to Orkney 1661
James Hamilton	prov. 14 Nov. 1661, cons. 15 Dec. 1661	14 Aug. 1674
John Paterson	prov. 23 Oct. 1674, cons. May 1675	trs. to Edinburgh 1679
Arthur Rose	trs. from Argyll 5 Sept. 1679	trs. to Glasgow 1679
James Aitken	trs. from Moray 1680 [1]	15 Nov. 1687
John Gordon	nom. 3 Dec. 1687, prov. 4 Feb. 1688, cons. 1688	1726

GLASGOW [2]

Michael	nom. by Earl David and cons. 1109 × 1114, appears to have served more in Carlisle area than from a base at Glasgow	
John	nom. by Earl David and cons. c. 1114 × 21 Jan. 1118	*p.* 3 May 1147
Herbert	cons. 24 Aug. 1147	1164
Ingram	el. 13 or 20 Sept. 1164, cons. 28 Oct. 1164	2 Feb. 1174

[1] Nominated to Galloway, 15 Oct. 1679, prov. 6 Feb. 1680.
[2] Magsuea and John, who were cons. at York 1055 × 1060 were thought in early twelfth century to have been bishops of Glasgow, but this is now regarded as improbable.

BISHOPS	ACCESSION	DEATH *unless otherwise stated*
Jocelin	el. 23 May 1174, conf. 16 Dec. 1174, cons. prob. *a.* 10 Apr. 1175	17 Mar. 1199
[Hugh de Roxburgh	el. but not cons.	10 July 1199]
William Malveisin	el. Oct. 1199, cons. 24 Sept. 1200	trs. to St Andrews 18–20 Sept. 1202
[Florence	el. prob. 1202, not cons.	res. 1 Jan. × 15 May 1207]
Walter de St Albans	el. 9 Dec. 1207, cons. 2 Nov. 1208	19 May × 2 Nov. 1232
William de Bondington	el. prob. 11 Apr. × 7 June 1233, cons. 11 Sept. 1233	10 Nov. 1258
[Nicholas de Moffat	el. 2 Jan. × 2 Feb. 1259, not conf.]	
John de Cheam	prov. *a.* 13 June 1259, cons. *a.* 28 Oct. 1259	11 June × 13 Oct. 1268
[Nicholas de Moffat	el. *p.* 13 Oct. 1268, not cons.	1270]
[William Wischard	el. 1270, not cons.	el. to St Andrews 3 June 1271]
Robert Wischard	el. *p.* 3 June 1271, cons. 29 Jan. 1273	*p.* 25 June 1316
[Stephen de Donydouer	el. *a.* 13 June 1317, when conf. delayed	*a.* 18 Aug. 1317]
[John de Lindsay	el. *a.* 17 July 1318, when rejected by pope]	
John de Eglescliffe	prov. and cons. 17 July 1318, not admitted to Scotland	trs. to Connor *a.* 15 Mar. 1323, and to Llandaff 20 June 1323
John de Lindsay	prov. 15 Mar. 1323, cons. 2 July × 10 Oct. 1323	12 Feb. 1334 × 8 Feb. 1336
John Wischard	el. *p.* 8 Feb. 1336, cons. 17 Feb. 1337	15 × 20 Aug. 1337
William Rae	el. *a.* conf. and cons. 22 Feb. 1339	27 Jan. 1367
Walter de Wardlaw	el. *a.* prov. 14 Apr. 1367, cons. prob. *a.* 30 Apr. 1367	22 May × 20 Sept. 1387, prob. 21 or 23 Aug.
Matthew de Glendonwyn	date of prov. unknown, cons. *a.* 18 Dec. 1387, prob. on 8 Dec.	10 May 1408
William de Lauder	perhaps el. *a.* prov. 9 July 1408, prob. cons. 11 July × 24 Oct. 1408	d. prob. 14 Dec. 1425 × 25 Feb. 1426
John Cameron	el. *a.* prov. 22 Apr. 1426, cons. 12 Jan. 1427	24 Dec. 1446
James Brois	trs. from Dunkeld 3 Feb. 1447	19 June × 4 Oct. 1447
William Turnbull	trs. uncons. from Dunkeld 27 Oct. 1447, cons. 1 Dec. 1447 × 7 May 1448	3 Sept. 1454
Andrew de Durisdeer	prov. 7 May 1455, cons. 6 Mar. × 3 May 1456	20 Nov. 1473
John Laing	prov. 28 Jan. 1474, prov. 9 May × 2 Dec. 1474	11 Jan. 1483
[George Carmichael	el. *a.* 18 Feb. 1483, el. annulled by pope 13 Apr. 1483, still recognised by king 28 Feb, 1484]	
Robert Blackadder	trs. uncons. from Aberdeen 19 Mar. 1483, conf. 13 Apr. 1483, cons. 13 × 30 Apr. 1483, made archbishop 9 Jan. 1492	28 July 1508

BISHOPS	ACCESSION	DEATH *unless otherwise stated*
James Betoun	el. 9 Nov. 1508, trs. uncons. from Galloway 19 Jan. 1509, cons. 15 Apr. 1509	trs. to St Andrews 10 Oct. 1522, effective 5 June 1523
Gavin Dunbar	el. *a.* 15 Aug. 1523, prov. 8 July 1524, temp. 27 Sept. 1524, cons. 5 Feb. 1525	30 Apr. 1547
[James Hamilton	nom. 31 July 1547, rejected by pope *a.* 26 Mar. 1548]	
[Donald Campbell	nom. to papal nuncio, but rejected *p.* 9 July 1548]	
Alexander Gordon	prov. 5 Mar. 1550, prob. cons. *p.* 25 Apr. 1550	trs. to Athens 4 Sept. 1551
James Betoun	nom. and el. 27 Feb. 1550, prov. 4 Sept. 1551, cons. 28 Aug. 1552	forfeited 18–19 Sept. 1570
[John Porterfield	nom. and prov. 26 Jan. × 7 Sept. 1571, but not el.]	
James Boyd	el. *p.* 30 Sept. 1573, conf. by crown 3 Nov. 1573, cons. *a.* 9 Nov. 1573 when temp. given	21 June 1581
Robert Montgomery	prov. 3 Oct. 1581, ? not cons., conf. 22 May 1584	depr. *a.* 21 Dec. 1585
William Erskine	prov. 21 Dec. 1585, ? not cons., ? still in office 8 June 1594	
James Betoun	restored to see 29 June 1598	24 Apr. 1603
John Spottiswoode	prov. 20 July 1603 and 24 May 1608, cons. 21 Oct. 1610	trs. St Andrews 1615
James Law	trs. from Orkney 20 July 1615	12 Nov. 1632
Patrick Lindsay	trs. from Ross 16 Aug. 1633	depr. 13 Dec. 1638, d. June 1644
Andrew Fairfoul	prov. 14 Nov. 1661, cons. 15 Dec. 1661	2 Nov. 1663
Alexander Burnet	trs. from Aberdeen 6 Jan. 1664, restored 29 Sept. 1674	res. 24 Dec. 1669, trs. St Andrews 1679
Robert Leighton	trs. from Dunblane[1] 27 Oct. 1671	res. Aug. 1674
Arthur Rose	trs. from Galloway 15 Oct. 1679	trs. St Andrews 1684
Alexander Cairncross	trs. from Brechin 6 Dec. 1684	depr. 13 Jan. 1687, trs. Raphoe 1693, d. 14 May 1701
John Paterson	trs. from Edinburgh[2] 8 Mar. 1687	9 Dec. 1708

IONA[3]

Fergna		623, prob. 2 Mar.
Coeddi	*a.* 697	712, prob. 24 Oct.
? Dorbene	*a.* May 713	28 Oct. 713
? Patrick	bishop in the Hebrides in mid-ninth century	
Fothad	bishop of the isles of Alba	963
Fingin		966
Mugroin		980
Maelciarain		24 Dec. 986

See The Isles

[1] Leighton had held Glasgow *in commendam* from 1669.
[2] Nom. 21 Jan. 1687.
[3] Some of these men are styled bishop only in sources dating from the eleventh century or later. It is not certain that all of them held this office.

THE ISLES[1]

BISHOPS	ACCESSION	DEATH *unless otherwise stated*
Wimund	el. 1134 × c. 1138	res. or depr. *a.* c. 1148
[Nicholas	nom. c. 1148, prob. not cons.]	
John	cons. 1152, may never have had possession	
Gamaliel	prob. el. *a.* cons. *p.* Oct. 1154	prob. res. *a.* 1166
Ragnald	*a.* 1166	c. 1170
Christian	c. 1170	prob. depr. early 1190s
Michael	el. and cons. prob. 1188 × 1194	1203
Nicholas	cons. 1210	1217
Reginald	prob. nom. and cons. and had possession 1217 × 1226	
Nicholas of Meaux	el., conf. and cons. *a.* 9 Nov. 1219, no possession	res. 15 May 1224 × 24 Jan. 1225
John son of Hefare	succeeded Reginald briefly	1217 × 1226
Simon	succeeded John, cons. 1226, prob. Aug. × Sept.	29 Feb. 1248
[Laurence	el. Feb. × Nov. 1248, not conf.]	
Richard (? de Nafferton)	prov. and cons. *a.* 14 Mar. 1253	buried 25 Mar. 1275
[Gilbert	el. 1275, not conf.]	
Mark	nom. *a.* cons. 1275 or 1276 or 3 Jan. 1277 × 2 Jan. 1278	1303
Alan (? de Wigtown)	cons. *a.* 26 Mar. 1305	15 Feb. 1321
Gilbert MacLelan	cons. Jan. × 16 Dec. 1324	20 July 1326 × July 1327
Bernard (? de Linton)	el. 9 Nov. 1327 × 14 Jan. 1328, cons. 26 June × 12 Nov. 1328	*a.* 10 June 1331
[Cormac Cormacii	el. *a.* 6 July 1331, not conf.]	
Thomas de Rossy	prov. and cons. 10 June 1331	20 Sept. 1348
William Russell	el. *a.* prov. 27 Apr. 1349, cons. *a.* 6 May (prob. 4 May) 1349	21 Apr. 1374
John Donkan	el. 31 May–1 June 1374, prov. 6 Nov. 1374, cons. 25–26 Nov. 1374, installed 25 Jan. 1377	depr. by Clement VII 15 July 1387
Michael	trs. from Cashel by Clement VII 15 July 1387	*p.* 1 Nov. 1409
[Richard Pawlie	trs. by John XXIII from Dromore 30 May 1410, recognised within Scottish portion of the diocese at least c. 1421, but not otherwise, still recognised in Man until 1429 × 1433]	
[Michael Ochiltree	prov. 20 Apr. 1422 abortively]	
Angus de Insulis	prov. in succession to Michael 19 June 1426, cons. prob. 11 × 27 Feb. 1428	prob. 4 Feb. 1438 × 5 Aug. 1441
John Hectoris MacGilleon	prov. 2 Oct. 1441, cons. *p.* 6 Nov. 1441	*p.* 11 Mar. 1456
Angus	prov. 3 Aug. 1472, cons. 27 Sept. 1472	3 Sept. 1479 × c. Jan. 1480
John Campbell	prov. 18–19 Jan. 1487, cons. 21 Jan. × 13 Oct. 1487	14 June 1510

[1] Known also as Sudreys or Sodor. See was founded in 1130s by Olaf I king of the Isles for all his dominions. There had previously been more than one bishop in the area. See under Iona, Kingarth, Man and Skye. The diocese was claimed by rival bishops appointed by popes on each side of the Great Schism at end of the fourteenth century. *De facto* it became permanently divided into Scottish and English portions. Only the bishops recognized in Scotland are listed here.

BISHOPS	ACCESSION	DEATH *unless otherwise stated*
George Hepburn	nom. 21 June 1510, prov. 10 Feb. 1511, temp. 11 May 1511, cons. *a.* 4 July 1511	9 Sept. 1513
John Campbell	nom. *a.* 18 Sept. 1514, prov. *a.* 18 June 1515, not cons. but had possession	res. keeping some revenues 17 May 1532, conf. 3–5 Nov. 1534, still alive 1555
[James Stewart	nom. 1 Nov. 1529, not conf.]	
Ferchar MacEachan	prov. in succession to Hepburn 17–21 Feb. 1530, temp. 24 May 1530, prob. cons. by then	crown lic. to res. keeping revenues 18–19 Nov. 1544, d. *a.* 7 Aug. 1547
Roderick MacLean	nom. 19 Nov. 1544, el. *a.* 22 Feb. 1547, prov. 5 Mar. 1550	19 June × 26 Nov. 1553
[Roderick MacAllister	el. *a.* 28 July 1545, sought conf. from Henry VIII, regarded as bishop in English eyes 25 Sept. 1546]	
[Patrick MacLean]	temp. 7 Aug. 1547]	
Alexander Gordon	temp. 26 Nov. 1553 when abp of Athens, el. *a.* 12 Apr. 1554	trs. to Galloway 10 × 28 Feb. 1559
[John Campbell	el. *a.* 13 Aug. 1557 not cons.	? res. 16 Aug. 1560 × 10 Mar. 1562]
[Patrick MacLean	nom. to pope and el.	res. right for pension *a.* 12 Jan. 1565]
John Carswell	temp. 12 Jan. 1565, prov. 24 Mar. 1567	21 June × 4 Sept. 1572
[Lachlan MacLean	? nom.	res. his right 21 May 1567]
John Campbell	el. *p.* 20 Sept. 1572, crown conf. 22 Jan. 1573, prob. cons. *a.* temp. 13 Oct. 1573	15 Oct. 1596 × 15 June 1598
Andrew Knox	prov. 12 Feb. 1605, el. *a.* nom. for trs. to Raphoe 6–7 May 1610, prob. cons. 23 Jan. × 24 Feb. 1611	retained this see *p.* 25 Aug. 1618
Thomas Knox	prov. 24 Feb. 1619	1 Nov. 1627 × 3 Apr. 1628
John Leslie	nom. 3 Apr. 1628, el. *a.* prov. 17 Aug. 1628	trs. to Raphoe 1 June 1633
Neil Campbell	nom. 17 Oct. 1633, el. 17 Dec. 1633, prov. 21 Jan. 1634	depr. 13 Dec. 1638
Robert Wallace	prov. *a.* 19 Mar. 1662, cons. 7 May 1662	16 May 1669
James Ramsay	trs. from Dunblane 28 July 1674	restored Dunblane Apr. 1676
Andrew Wood	prov. 1 Feb. 1677	trs. Caithness 1680
Archibald Graham (or MacIlvernock)	prov. 30 May 1680	28 June 1702

KINGARTH

Dainel	18 Feb. 660
Jolan	689

See The Isles

LISMORE

See Argyll

MAN

BISHOPS	ACCESSION	DEATH
		unless otherwise stated
Roolwer		*a.* 1079
William		*a.* 1079
Hamond	1079 × 1095	

See The Isles

MORAY

Gregory	bishop without designation *a.* c. 1114 or c. 1120, bishop of Moray *a.* 23 Apr. 1124	*p.* 1127
William	*a.* 24 May 1153	24 Jan. 1162
Felix	*a.* 1171	
Simon de Tonei	el. 1171, cons. 23 Jan. 1172	17 Sept. 1184
Richard de Lincoln	el. 1 Mar. 1187, cons. 15 Mar. 1187	1203
Brice de Douglas	1203	1222
Andrew de Moravia	1222, cons. 12 May 1223 × 10 Apr. 1224	18 Sept. × Dec. 1242
Simon (? de Gunby)	el. *a.* 3 Mar. 1244, cons. *p.* 3 Mar. 1244	1251
[Radulf de Leycester	el. c. 1252	? 1253]
Archibald	cons. 1253 *a.* 22 Nov.	9 Dec. 1298
David de Moravia	el. *a.* cons. 28 June 1299, prov. 30 June 1299	9 Jan. 1326
John de Pilmor	cons. 30 Mar. 1326, prov. 31 Mar. 1326	28 Sept. 1362
Alexander Bur	prob. el. *a.* prov. 23 Dec. 1362, cons. 4 Jan. × 7 Feb. 1363	15 May 1397
William de Spyny	el. *a.* prov. 1 Sept. 1397, cons. .16 Sept. 1397, temp. 16 Jan. 1398	2 Aug. 1406
John de Innes	el. *a.* prov. 12 Jan. 1407, cons. prob. 23 Jan. 1407	25 Apr. 1414
Henry de Lychton	el. *p.* 18 May 1414, prov. *a.* 4 Mar. 1415, cons. 8 Mar. 1415	trs. to Aberdeen 1 Apr. 1422
Columba de Dunbar	prov. 3 Apr. 1422, cons. 12 Feb. × 10 Oct. 1423	1435
John Winchester	el. *a.* 7 Nov. 1435, prov. 23 Mar. 1436, cons. 9 May 1437	22 Apr. 1460
James Stewart	prov. 19 May 1460, cons. 25 Oct. × 12 Dec. 1460	res. 21 June 1462
David Stewart	prov. 21 June 1462, cons. 25 June × 10 Dec. 1463	1476 *p.* 5 Sept.
William Tulloch	trs. from Orkney 12 Feb. 1477	*p.* 23 Mar. and 18 Apr. 1482
Andrew Stewart	el. *a.* prov. 12 Aug. 1482, cons. 22 Dec. 1485 × 24 Oct. 1487	29 Sept. 1501
Andrew Forman	el. *a.* 8 Oct. 1501, prov. 26 Nov. 1501, prob. cons. *a.* 24 Jan. 1502	trs. to St Andrews 13 Nov. 1514, effective c. 4 Feb. 1516
James Hepburn	el. *a.* 12 Feb. 1516, prov. 14 May 1516, temp. 28 Aug. 1516	*a.* 11 Nov. 1524
Robert Shaw	nom. 11 Jan. 1525, prov. 17 May 1525, temp. c. Sept. 1525	15 Jan. × Nov. 1527
[Alexander Douglas	nom. *a.* 26 Apr. 1528, not conf.]	
Alexander Stewart	nom. *a.* prov. 13 Sept. 1529, cons. *a.* 16 Apr. 1532	19 Dec. 1537
Patrick Hepburn	nom. 1 Mar. 1538, prov. 14 June 1538, temp. 24 Nov. 1538	*a.* 10 July 1573, prob. 20 June 1573
George Douglas	el. 20–22 Dec. 1573, conf. 5 Feb. 1574, temp. 23 Mar. 1574	28 Dec. 1589

316

BISHOPS	ACCESSION	DEATH *unless otherwise stated*
Alexander Douglas	prov. 30 Nov. 1602, cons. 15 Mar. 1611	9 or 11 May 1623
John Guthrie	nom. 27 June 1623, el. 31 July 1623, prov. 16 Aug. 1623, cons. *a.* 13 Oct. 1623	depr. 13 Dec. 1638
Murdo Mackenzie	prov. 18 Jan. 1662, cons. 7 May 1662	trs. Orkney 1676–77
James Aitken	nom. 9 Sept. 1676, el. 1 Nov. 1676, prov. 7 May 1677	trs. Galloway 1680
Colin Falconer	trs. from Argyll, nom. 7 Feb. 1680, prov. 17 Mar. 1680	11 Nov. 1686
Alexander Rose	nom. 17 Dec. 1686, prov. 8 Mar. 1687, cons. 1 May 1687	trs. Edinburgh 1687
William Hay	nom. 3 Dec. 1687, prov. 4 Feb. 1688, cons. 11 Mar. 1688	19 Mar. 1707

MORTLACH

Beyn	1012 × 1024	
Donericus	? mid eleventh century	
Cormac	? late eleventh century	
Nechtan	? early twelfth century	see moved to Aberdeen *a.* Apr. 1132

ORKNEY

Henry	? *a.* 1035	trs. to Lund 1060 × 1061
Turolf	*p.* 1050	
John	1043 × 1072	
Adalbert	1043 × 1072	
Radulf	cons. 3 Mar., prob. 1073	
Roger	cons. Dec. 1100 × May 1108, rival to William	*p.* 1108 × 1109
William	prob. 1102	1168
Radulf Novell	cons. June 1109 × Feb. 1114, rival to William	prob. expelled from diocese c. 1128, active in England *p.* 16 June 1151
William		1188
Bjarni	*a.* 1192	15 Sept., prob. 1223
Jofreyr	cons. prob. Jan. 1224	1246
Henry	el. *a.* 9 Dec. 1247, cons. late 1248 or early 1249	1269
Peter	cons. 1270, on or *a.* 3 Sept.	1284
Dolgfinn	chosen *a.* 10 July 1286, cons. 1286, ? 14 July	25 Mar. × 12 Sept. 1309
William	el. *a.* 12 Sept. 1309, cons. 1310	*p.* 9 Sept. 1327
William	*a.* 25 May 1369	1382 or 1383
John	el. *a.* prov. 10 Feb. 1384, cons. soon after	trs. to Greenland 9 Mar. 1394
[Robert de Sinclair	el. *a.* 28 Nov. 1383, prov. by Clement VII 27 Jan. 1384, cons. *a.* 31 May 1390, no possession	trs. to Dunkeld 1 Feb. 1391]
Henry	trs. from Greenland 9 Mar. 1394	*p.* 10 Aug. 1394
John Pak	prov. 21 Aug. 1396, cons. *a.* 13 Sept. 1396	*p.* 19 Dec. 1397
[Alexander Vaus	prov. by Benedict XIII 25 July 1398 × 7 Nov. 1407, not cons.	trs. to Caithness by same pope 4 May 1414]

317

BISHOPS	ACCESSION	DEATH *unless otherwise stated*
[William Stephenson	el. *a.* prov. by Benedict XIII 13 Nov. 1415, cons. soon after, litigating at curia of Martin V 6 Sept. 1419	trs. to Dunblane by Martin V 30 Oct. 1419]
Thomas Tulloch	prov. by Martin V 19 Aug. 1418, cons. 20 Dec. 1418 × 10 June 1420	res. 28 June × 11 Dec. 1461
William Tulloch	prov. 11 Dec. 1461, prob. cons. *a.* 23 Dec. 1461	trs. to Moray 12 Feb. 1477
Andrew Painter	prov. 12 Feb. 1477, prob. cons. *a.* 31 Mar. 1477	*p.* 24 Nov. 1503
Edward Stewart	nom. as coadjutor 8 Dec. 1498, prov. as coadjutor 10 July 1500, succeeded *a.* 18 June 1506	*p.* 27 Apr. 1524, *a.* 13 Feb. 1526
John Benston	nom. as coadjutor 13 Dec. 1523, prov. as coadjutor 27 Apr. 1524	*a.* 13 Feb. 1526
Robert Maxwell	nom. *a.* 13 Feb. 1526, prov. 9 Apr. 1526, prob. cons. 25 June × 8 Aug. 1526	20 Feb. 1540 × 26 Mar. 1541
Robert Reid	nom. 5 Apr. 1541, prov. 20 July 1541, cons. 27 Nov. 1541	6 Sept. 1558
Adam Bothwell	nom. *a.* 24 July 1559, prov. 2 Aug. 1559, prob. cons. *a.* temp. 14 Oct. 1559	connection largely ceased 27 × 30 Sept. 1568, d. 23 Aug. 1593
James Law	prov. 28 Feb. 1605, cons. 21 Oct. 1610 × 3 May 1611	trs. to Glasgow 20 July 1615
George Graham	trs. from Dunblane 26 Aug. 1615	depr. 13 Dec. 1638
[Robert Barron	nom. 1639, not cons.	19 Aug. 1639]
Thomas Sydserf	trs. from Galloway 14 Nov. 1661	29 Sept. 1663
Andrew Honeyman	prov. 14 Jan. 1664, cons. 10 or 11 Apr. 1664	21 Feb. 1676
Murdo Mackenzie	trs. from Moray, nom. 12 Aug. 1676, el. 26 Sept. 1676, prov. 13 Feb. 1677	17 Feb. 1688
Andrew Bruce	trs. from Dunkeld, nom. 7 May 1688, prov. 10 Aug. 1688	18 Mar. 1699

ROSS

Curitain	? c. 700	
? Duthac		8 Mar. 1065
Macbeth	*a.* ? 1131	
Simon	*a.* 1151	*p.* 27 Feb. 1155
Gregory	cons. 1161	Jan. × Feb. 1195
Reginald	el. 27 Feb. 1195, cons. 10 Sept. 1195	13 Dec. 1213
[Andrew de Moravia	el., not cons.	res. right 1213 × 1214]
Robert	nom. prob. *a.* 4 Dec. 1214, cons. 17 Feb. × 1 Mar. 1215	prob. 1249
Robert	cons. 21 June 1249 × 20 June 1250	prob. 1271
Matthew	el. *a.* conf. and cons. 28 Dec. 1272	May × July 1274
Robert de Fyvin	el. *a.* 8 Apr. 1275, cons. *a.* 16 Sept. 1278	*p.* 17 Nov. 1292
[Adam de Derlingtun	el., not conf.	res. right *a.* 18 Nov. 1295]
Thomas de Dundee	el. *p.* 24 Apr. 1293, res. right and prov. 18 Nov. 1295, cons. *a.* 2 Jan. 1296, temp. from Edward I 21 July 1297	*p.* 1 Nov. 1321

BISHOPS	ACCESSION	DEATH *unless otherwise stated*
[John de Pilmor	? el. *a.* 17 Apr. 1325, not conf.]	
Roger (? de Ballinbreich)	prov. 17 Apr. 1325, cons. *a.* 19 May 1325	res. *p.* 17 May 1350
Alexander Stewart	prov. 3 Nov. 1350, cons. 26 Jan. × 9 Mar. 1351	*p.* 4 Feb. 1371
Alexander de Kylwos	el. *a.* prov. 9 May 1371, cons. *a.* 6 Mar. 1372	6 July 1398
Alexander de Waghorn	el. *a.* prov. 17 Aug. 1398, swore fealty to pope only *p.* 30 June 1407	*p.* 17 Mar. 1416
[Thomas Lyell	el., not conf. by Benedict XIII	res. right *a.* 9 Mar. 1418]
Griffin Yonge	trs. from Bangor by Martin V 14 Feb. 1418, no possession	trs. to Hippo 1 Feb. 1423
John Bulloch	prov. by Benedict XIII 9 Mar. 1418, cons. 16 July × 16 Aug. 1420, new prov. by Martin V 1 Feb. 1423	*p.* 4 Sept. 1439
[Andrew de Munro	el. *a.* 26 Sept. 1440, but not conf. by Eugenius IV, conf. by Felix V 30 May 1441, no possession]	
Thomas Tulloch	prov. by Eugenius IV 26 Sept. 1440, prob. cons. *a.* 14 Oct. 1440, certainly *a.* 10 Feb. 1441	*p.* 17 June 1455, prob. *p.* 1460
Henry Cockburn	prov. 23 Mar. 1461, cons. 19 Oct. 1463 × 16 Aug. 1464	*p.* 22 July 1476
John Wodman	prov. *a.* 20 Aug. 1476, cons. *p.* 4 May 1478	*a.* 3 Aug. 1481
[James Werk	prov. by Archbishop Patrick Graham as legate *a.* 9 Jan. 1478]	
William Elphinstone	prov. 3 Aug. 1481, not cons.	trs. to Aberdeen 19 Mar. 1483
Thomas Hay	prov. 16 May 1483	11 Jan. 1488 × 26 Feb. 1492
John Guthrie	el. *a.* 26 Feb. 1492, prov. 11 Apr. 1492	*p.* 14 June 1492, per- haps *a.* July 1494
John Fraser	el. *a.* 18 Sept. 1497, prov. 14 Mar. 1498, temp. 3 Jan. 1499	5 Feb. 1507
Robert Cockburn	nom. 10 Mar.–10 May 1507, prov. 9 July 1507, temp. 17 Aug. 1507	trs. to Dunkeld 27 Apr. 1524
James Hay	nom. prob. *a.* 14 Sept. 1523, prov. 27 Apr. 1524, temp. 16 Sept. 1524, cons. *p.* 25 Feb. 1525	Apr. × 3 Oct. 1538
Robert Cairncross	nom. 12 Nov.–15 Dec. 1538, prov. 14 Apr. 1539, temp. 23 June 1539	30 Nov. 1545
David Painter	nom. *a.* 23 Dec. 1545, prov. 28 Nov. 1547, cons. *a.* 14 Feb. 1552	1 Oct. 1558
Henry Sinclair	prob. nom. Nov. 1558, el. *a.* 10 Mar. 1560, papal prov. 2 June 1561	2 Jan. 1565
John Lesley	nom. 26 Mar. × 1 Apr. 1566, papal prov. *a.* 21 Jan. 1567 when inducted, forfeited 19 Aug. 1568, new papal prov. 22 Apr. 1575, rehabilitated in Scotland 13 Mar. 1587	depr. 29 May 1589, trs. by pope to Coutances 16 Dec. 1592
Alexander Hepburn	el. *p.* 14 May 1574, prov. 20 Mar. 1575, temp. 3 Nov. 1575	22 Sept. 1578

BISHOPS	ACCESSION	DEATH *unless otherwise stated*
David Lindsay	prov. 5 Nov. 1600 and 22 Dec. 1604, prob. cons. 24 Feb. 1611	14 Aug. 1613
Patrick Lindsay	prov. 23 Oct. 1613, cons. 1 Dec. 1613, prov. again 6 Nov. 1616	trs. to Glasgow 16 Aug. 1633
John Maxwell	prov. 23 Apr. 1633, prob. cons. *a.* 18 June 1633	depr. 13 Dec. 1638
John Paterson	prov. 18 Jan. 1662, cons. 7 May 1662	Jan. 1679
Alexander Young	trs. from Edinburgh 29 Mar. 1679	Sept. 1683
James Ramsay	trs. from Dunblane 14 Apr. 1684	22 Oct. 1696

ST ANDREWS

Some tenth- and early eleventh-century bishops without territorial designation were in the fifteenth century thought to have been based at St Andrews. The evidence is confused, and since no modern study of it is available, these bishops are omitted here. This list begins with bishops of St Andrews specifically.

Maelduin	? c. 1028	1055
Tuthald	*p.* 1055	
Fothad or Modach	prob. *a.* 1070	1093
[Gregory, Cathre, Godric	one or more persons el. but not cons.]	
Turgot	nom. prob. 1107, cons. 1 Aug. 1109	31 Aug. 1115
[Eadmer	nom. *a.* el. 29 June 1120, not cons.	res. right early 1121]
Robert	nom. and el. 25 Dec. 1123 × 31 Jan. 1124, cons. on or before 17 July 1127	1159
[Waltheof	nom. and el. *a.* May 1159	refused office, d. 3 Aug. 1159]
Arnold	el. 13 Nov. 1160, cons. 20 Nov. 1160	13 Sept. 1162
Richard	el. 1163, prob. early, cons. 28 Mar. 1165	1178, prob. 13 May
John Scot	el. 1178, papal conf. *a.* cons. 15 June 1180, still litigating Jan. 1188	trs. to Dunkeld 1183, *a.* July, finally res. this see Spring 1188
Hugh	nom. 1178 after el. of John, cons. 1178, papal conf. 1183, *a.* July, suspended by pope 1186, *p.* 31 July, absolved before death	4 Aug. 1188
Roger	el. 13 Apr. 1189, cons. 15 Feb. 1198	7 July 1202
William Malveisin	el. for trs. from Glasgow 20 Sept. 1202, prob. conf. by legate on same day	9 July 1238
[Geoffrey de Liberatione	el. for trs. from Dunkeld *a.* conf. refused 12 Feb. 1239]	
David de Bernham	el. 3 June 1239, conf. ordered 1 Oct. 1239, cons. 22 Jan. 1240	26 Apr. 1253
[Robert de Stuteville	el. 28 June 1253, not conf.]	
Abel de Golin	prov. 20 Feb. 1254, cons. 1 Mar. 1254	1254, prob. 31 Aug.
Gamelin	el. 14 Feb. 1255, conf. 1 July 1255, cons. 26 Dec. 1255	29 Apr. 1271

BISHOPS	ACCESSION	DEATH *unless otherwise stated*
William Wischard	el. 3 June 1271, conf. ordered 15 Mar. 1273, cons. 15 Oct. 1273	28 May 1279
William Fraser	el. 4 Aug. 1279, cons. 19 May 1280, conf. ordered 21 May 1280	20 Aug. 1297
William de Lamberton	el. 5 Nov. 1297, cons. 1 June 1298, conf. 17 June 1298	20 May 1328
James Ben	el. 19 June 1328, prob. cons. *a.* 28 July 1328, prov. 1 Aug. 1328	? res. 11 × 19 Aug. 1332, d. 22 Sept. 1332
[Alexander de Kinimund	prob. el. also 19 June 1328, not conf.]	
[William Bell	el. 19 Aug. 1332, not conf.	res. right *a.* 18 Feb. 1342]
William de Laundels	nom. *a.* prov. 18 Feb. 1342, cons. 17 Mar. 1342	23 Sept. 1385
[Stephen Pay	el., d. without conf.	2 Mar. 1386]
Walter Trayl	prov. 29 Nov. 1385, cons. prob. 27 Jan. × 15 Feb. 1386	5 Mar. × 1 July 1401
[Thomas Stewart	el. 1 July 1401, not conf.	res. right c. June 1402]
[Walter de Danielston	el. c. June 1402, not conf.	Christmas 1402]
[Gilbert de Grenlaw	el. for trs. from Aberdeen early 1403, not conf.]	
Henry de Wardlaw	prov. 10 Sept. 1403, cons. prob. 21 Sept. × 4 Oct. 1403	6 Apr. 1440
James Kennedy	el. for trs. from Dunkeld 22 Apr. 1440, prov. 1 June 1440	24 May 1465
[James Ogilvie	prov. by Felix V 26 July 1440, not cons., supported by Felix for pension from see 20 Mar. 1447]	
Patrick Graham	trs. from Brechin 4 Nov. 1465, made archbishop 17 Aug. 1472	depr. 9 Jan. 1478
William Scheves	prov. as coadjutor 13 Sept. 1476, prov. to see 11 Feb. 1478, cons. prob. 28 Mar. 1479	28 Jan. 1497
James Stewart	el. and crown conf. as commendator *a.* 28 May 1497, prov. as administrator 20 Sept. 1497, not cons.	13 Jan. 1504
Alexander Stewart	prov. as administrator 10 May 1504, not cons.	9 Sept. 1513
[Innocenzo Cibo	prov. as administrator 13 Oct. 1513, no possession	res. right when trs. to Bourges 13 Nov. 1514]
[William Elphinstone	el. and nom. for trs. from Aberdeen Oct. 1513, nom. confirmed 22 June–5 Aug. 1514, prob. no possession	25 Oct. 1514]
Andrew Forman	prov. on trs. from Moray and Bourges 13 Nov. 1514, temp. c. 4 Feb. 1516	11 Mar. 1521
[John Hepburn	el. Oct. × Nov. 1514, litigated with Forman and Douglas, not conf.	res. right c. 4 Feb. 1516]
[Gavin Douglas	nom. *a.* 23 Nov. 1514, not conf.	nom. and prov. to Dunkeld 17 Jan.–25 May 1515]
James Betoun	nom. for trs. from Glasgow 1 Dec. 1521, prov. for trs. 10 Oct. 1522, effective 5 June 1523	14 Feb. 1539

BISHOPS	ACCESSION	DEATH *unless otherwise stated*
David Betoun	prov. as coadjutor 1537, *a.* 5 Dec., cons. 26 July × 13 Aug. 1538	29 May 1546
John Hamilton	trs. from Dunkeld 28 Nov. 1547, appointment effective June 1549	7 Apr. 1571
Gavin Hamilton	prov. as coadjutor 4 Sept. 1551	16 June 1571
John Douglas	prov. 6 Aug. 1571, el. 6 Feb. 1572, cons. 10 Feb. 1572	31 July 1574
Patrick Adamson	el. *p.* 10 Mar. 1575, crown conf. 21 Dec. 1576, cons. 23 Dec. 1576, temp. 31 Dec. 1576	19–20 Feb. 1592
George Gledstanes	trs. from Caithness 12 Oct. 1604, cons. Dec. 1610	2 May 1615
John Spottiswoode	trs. from Glasgow 30–31 May 1615	depr. 13 Dec. 1638
James Sharp	prov. 14 Nov. 1661, cons. 15 Dec. 1661	3 May 1679
Alexander Burnet	trs. from Glasgow 13 Aug. 1679	22 or 24 Aug. 1684
Arthur Rose	trs. from Glasgow 31 Oct. 1684	13 June 1704

SKYE

Wimund	1109 × 1114	*a.* 1134

See The Isles

WHITHORN

See Galloway

ARCHBISHOPS AND BISHOPS OF IRELAND TO 1534

INTRODUCTION

The Irish church was not organized on territorial diocesan lines until the first half of the twelfth century. Prior to that date the centres of Irish ecclesiastical life were the great monastic churches, such as Armagh, Derry, Clonard, Clonmacnois, Lismore, Emly and many others. In each of these churches an abbot, commonly known as the successor or heir (*comharba*) of the founder, had jurisdiction over his community (*muintir*). Some of these abbots were also bishops, but more commonly they were not bishops; and in the centuries immediately preceding the reform of the twelfth century they were often laymen. The obits of these abbots and abbot-bishops are recorded in the various Irish annals, and it is probable that contemporary lists were circulated among the monastic churches from the seventh or eighth centuries onwards. In the first edition of this *Handbook* the names of those abbots who are known, from one source or another, to have been bishops were listed as bishops of those churches which became centres of diocesan government in the twelfth century. Other abbots were omitted: and the resulting lists were confusing, even for students familiar with the history of the early Irish church. Moreover the dates of these obits are open to question, particularly in the earlier centuries; and they have little or no interest for students of British history. The second edition of the *Handbook* omitted all these lists of names prior to the period at which Irish dioceses first come into existence. Full lists of abbots of some of the more important monastic churches have been published elsewhere. A critical list of the abbots of Armagh was published by H. J. Lawlor and R. I. Best in *Proceedings of Royal Irish Academy*, xxxv. C (1919), 316–62. A list of the abbots of Derry was published by W. Reeves as an Additional Note to his *Life of St Columba written by Adamnan* (1857), 370–413. A list of the early abbots of Clonmacnois was published by Rev. Professor J. Ryan S.J. in *Essays and Studies presented to Eoin MacNeill* (1940), 490–507. Other lists will be found in the various diocesan histories published in the past century. Lists for twelve representative churches are now printed in *A New History of Ireland*, ed. T. W. Moody, F. X. Martin and F. J. Byrne, ix (Oxford, 1984), 237–63.

The first scheme for an Irish hierarchy was based on two provinces: Armagh and Cashel. Each of the two archbishops was to have twelve suffragan bishops within his jurisdiction; and a list of these 26 dioceses, with the territorial boundaries, has been preserved by Geoffrey Keating, who copied it *c.* 1640 from a lost Book of Clonenagh. The text will be found, with translation and commentary by John Mac Erlean, in *Archivium Hibernicum*, iii (1914), 1–33. The scheme was formally approved at the synod of Rath Breasail which met in the year 1111.[1] Apart from the names of the archbishop of Armagh, the archbishop of Cashel, and Gilbert, bishop of Limerick, who presided as papal legate, this document does not give the names of any of the bishops who were present at the synod or who were appointed to rule the new dioceses. Obits of bishops for almost all the new dioceses can be found in the various Irish annals of the twelfth century. Keating has also preserved, from the same lost Book of Clonenagh, a list of the bishops who were present at the synod which met at Kells in 1152. This list does not include all the bishops of this period, since seven sees were vacant at the opening session of the synod, and some bishops were absent. But three versions of a list of Irish dioceses approved by the synod and by the papal legate Cardinal Paparo have been preserved; in the *Liber Censuum* of Cencius (1192), the *Provinciale* of Albinus (1188–89), and in what seems to be an earlier and contemporary version that has been copied into Montpellier MS. 92. This last text was discovered by E. J. Gwynn, and edited by H. J. Lawlor: 'A fresh authority

---

[1] The date 1118, which is frequently given for this synod, is due to an error in the Annals of the Four Masters.

for the Synod of Kells' in *Proceedings of Royal Irish Academy*, xxxvi. C (1922), 16–22. The four historic provinces of Armagh, Dublin, Cashel and Tuam date from the synod of Kells.

For the names of bishops in the twelfth century the contemporary Irish annals are on the whole a trustworthy source, though a margin of error must be allowed for in the dating. The oldest of these annals are the Annals of Inisfallen, which have been edited with translation and notes by Seán Mac Airt (Dublin, 1951). The text for the twelfth century is here preserved in a series of contemporary hands. The Annals of Ulster are no less important, though they have been preserved in a manuscript that dates from the late fifteenth century. These annals have been edited for the period from 1057 to 1541 by B. MacCarthy (Rolls Series, 1893–95). A Clonmacnois chronicle, which is commonly known as *Chronicon Scotorum*, ends in 1150; it exists in a transcript of the seventeenth century, and was edited for the Rolls Series by W. M. Hennessy (1866). A fragment of annals, perhaps also of Clonmacnois and commonly known as the Fourth Fragment of the Annals of Tigernach, was edited with translation by Whitley Stokes in *Revue Celtique*, vols. 17 and 18 (1896–97). An English version of a lost Clonmacnois chronicle, made by Conell Mageoghegan in 1627, has been edited under the title *The Annals of Clonmacnoise* by Denis Murphy (Dublin, 1896). It is of special value for the thirteenth and fourteenth centuries. Two versions of western annals, which are closely related for the part of the text which covers the thirteenth century, have been edited from two different MSS.: the *Annals of Loch Cé*, edited by W. M. Hennessy for the Rolls Series in 2 vols. (1871; with a modern reprint 1939), and the *Annals of Connacht*, edited by A. M. Freeman (Dublin, 1944). The latter text is of special importance for the fourteenth century. The Irish Cistercian Annals of Boyle, which are followed by a short Premonstratensian set of annals (1228–57), were edited by A. M. Freeman in *Revue Celtique*, vols. 41–44 (1924–27). Robin Flower demonstrated the true character of these annals in an introductory note which was printed *ibid.*, vol. 44 (1927), 339–44. The well-known *Annals of the Four Masters* are a Franciscan compilation of the early seventeenth century, and are as a rule less trustworthy for dating. They were edited with translation and notes by John O'Donovan in 8 volumes (Dublin, 1851).

From these, and a few lesser annals of the medieval period, it is possible to reconstruct the succession of bishops in most of the Irish dioceses prior to the coming of the Normans; and their evidence is also of great value for the succession in those more remote Irish dioceses which did not come under English control until a late date in the thirteenth century. It should be noted, however, that whilst the older annalistic tradition, prior to the ecclesiastical reforms of the twelfth century, aimed at recording obits of abbots and bishops from every church in Ireland, the later medieval annalists are very much more limited in their scope and seldom record obits of bishops or abbots from an area far distant from their immediate neighbourhood. We are thus very much better informed for the succession of Irish bishops in the northern and western dioceses than in the dioceses of Munster. The Annals of Inisfallen, our principal Munster authority, are imperfect for the thirteenth century, and end abruptly in the early fourteenth century. Almost all the other surviving annals come from Ulster or Connacht.

Once the principle of English royal control had been recognized by the Irish bishops assembled in the synod of Cashel (1172) and had been given the full support of the papacy by Alexander III, a new and very much more accurate system of recording comes into existence. Records of licence for election, royal assent, mandates for restitution of temporalities and so forth were normally entered on the English patent rolls in the thirteenth and (to a lesser degree) in the fourteenth century. In the early years of Anglo-Norman government in Ireland, only a small area was subject to sufficiently strong administrative control for the operation of this complicated process of episcopal elections and the control of temporalities. This was extended during the thirteenth century, and by the end of the reign of Edward I it covered almost the whole island. Five northern dioceses of the province of Armagh (Derry, Raphoe, Clogher, Kilmore and Dromore) were then still resisting the claims of the king to temporalities in time of vacancy. In the fourteenth century, the area controlled by the justiciar and his officials declined steadily; the decline began with the shock of Bruce's invasion, and later with an increasing concentration of English resources on the wars in France. None the less, as can be seen from the lists printed below, the system continued to be effective in Leinster, Meath and Louth, and in wide areas of Munster.

From the reign of Richard II onwards, for administrative reasons which have not yet been explained, the custom of enrolling mandates for restitution of temporalities in Ireland as well as licences for episcopal and abbatial elections on the English patent rolls was abandoned; and we are thus left without any official record for this period, so far as royal action is concerned. Even in the thirteenth century it had been customary for the king to delegate his rights to the justiciar in Ireland, with a view to sparing the poorer dioceses unnecessary expense arising from long delays. The official Irish records ought thus to have given us a very much more complete picture of the whole process. But the few surviving rolls which were edited by Edward Tresham in the folio volume *Rotulorum Patentium et Clausorum Cancellariae Hiberniae Calendarium*, i, Pars I: *Hen. II–Hen. VII* (Dublin, 1828) are too fragmentary and scattered to justify detailed conclusions. Another important source, now lost, was the series of Irish pipe rolls—some of which were preserved intact until the destruction of the Irish Record Office in 1922. An inadequate calendar of these rolls, which contained the accounts of several escheators for bishoprics in time of vacancy, was printed by M. J. M'Enery as an appendix to the annual *Reports of the Deputy Keeper of the Public Records, Ireland*: Reports 35–39, 42–45, 47, 53, 54. The calendar of the surviving pipe rolls for Henry III is so brief as to be useless for most purposes: but later instalments of this calendar give more detailed extracts from the pipe rolls of Edward I, Edward II and Edward III. This series (which was destroyed in 1922) was no more than a broken series at that date. A few dates can be determined from the escheator's accounts for temporalities of vacant bishoprics between 1270 and 1350; but no systematic analysis of the evidence is possible. It is plain, however, that delivery of temporalities in Ireland usually followed the royal mandate for restitution after an interval of some weeks. Where the two dates are known from the English patent roll and the Irish pipe roll, they have been entered below with the abbreviations *temp.* and *lib.* As a rule the date given for *temp.* is the date of the royal mandate; but sometimes Walter Harris, who edited and expanded the *De Praesulibus Hiberniae* of Sir James Ware in 1739, has added the date of restitution of temporalities from Irish pipe rolls that are no longer extant. Where the date is known from this source, but without any record of the royal mandate, the abbreviation *temp.* has been used to avoid confusion in these lists. Nor is it easy to determine whether the escheator's account reckons the date of delivery from the date of the royal mandate which had been sent to Ireland, or from the actual date of delivery to the new bishop. There seems to have been some uncertainty in the actual practice, so far as can now be learned from the few surviving specimens.

An obvious cause of weakness in the organization of the medieval Irish church was the large number of dioceses, some of them very small and miserably poor. Since each bishopric was (with a few exceptions such as Dublin, Limerick or Waterford) a recent development from very much older monastic churches, the question of division of property between the new bishop and the older abbot or *comharba* must have always caused some difficulty; and was probably more acute in centres such as Clonmacnois or Glendalough where the older monastic tradition was exceptionally strong. We have no clear information on this point from any record of the twelfth century; but it is plain that many of the later dioceses, such as Dromore, Clonmacnois, Kilfenora, Ross or Emly, were too poor to be efficiently administered. A scheme for a drastic reorganization of the whole diocesan system in Ireland was submitted to John XXII in the name of Edward II in 1325. At the time of the synod of Kells there had been four archbishoprics with thirty-four suffragan bishoprics. Two additional small bishoprics (Ardmore and Mungret) in the province of Cashel were granted a doubtful recognition. The four archbishoprics remained throughout the medieval period. Of the thirty-four bishoprics, Kells was united to Meath *c.* 1211. Duleek had disappeared at an earlier date, and the see of Rathluraigh (Maghera) was transferred to Derry in 1247. Glendalough was united to Dublin in 1216. Roscrea and Scattery Island disappeared in the province of Cashel, together with the two doubtful sees of Ardmore and Mungret; and the small diocese of Mayo was united to Tuam. On the other hand two new dioceses had emerged before the end of the twelfth century: Annadown in the province of Tuam, and Dromore in the province of Armagh. There were thus four archbishoprics and thirty-two suffragan bishoprics in the Irish church during the thirteenth and fourteenth centuries.

The proposal made by Edward II's Irish advisers in 1325 was that this large number should be reduced to ten (including the four archbishoprics), each diocese having a royal city as its administrative centre.[1] So bold a challenge to ancient Irish traditions could end only in failure. In the province of Tuam the archbishop obtained papal sanction for the union of three small dioceses (Annadown, Achonry and Elphin) with the diocese of Tuam; but the union of Achonry and Elphin with Tuam was never carried into effect. The sole result of this ambitious scheme was that Annadown was permanently united to Tuam after 1327. In 1363 Lismore was united with Waterford; and two further unions were effected in the course of the fifteenth century. Cloyne was united with Cork in 1418, and Connor with Down in 1441. At the end of the medieval period there were thus four archbishoprics, with suffragan sees as follows: Armagh, with Meath, Ardagh, Clogher, Clonmacnois, Derry, Down and Connor, Dromore, Kilmore and Raphoe; Dublin, with Ferns, Kildare, Leighlin and Ossory; Cashel, with Ardfert, Cork and Cloyne, Emly, Killaloe, Kilfenora, Limerick, Ross, Waterford and Lismore; Tuam (which included Annadown), with Achonry, Clonfert, Elphin, Killala and Kilmacduagh. How far these dioceses were or were not subject to royal control depended, of course, on the ebb and flow of English power in Ireland; and the tide had definitely turned against English power by the middle of the fourteenth century.

The lists printed below will give a fair general idea of the contrast between the situation in the last years of Edward I, when royal control had made itself felt as far north as Derry, and in the last years of Richard II. Records of restitution of temporalities are by that time confined to a small number of dioceses, mainly in Leinster including Meath. The great majority of the more Irish dioceses had plainly passed from royal control during the fourteenth century. This recession of English power is most obvious in the western dioceses within a few years of Bruce's invasion. Very much the same picture is apparent, from the political point of view, if we judge the situation from the names of bishops and abbots who were summoned to the Irish parliament in the fourteenth century. Indeed, the sharp division between English and Irish areas is sometimes marked by a division within a single diocese. In Armagh, for example, the later division between the clergy *inter Anglos* (co. Louth) and the clergy *inter Hibernos* (co. Armagh) goes back to the fourteenth century. In Kerry the diocese of Ardfert was reorganized in two archdeaconries, the Norman element being ruled from the diocesan centre of Ardfert near Tralee, the Irish element being dominant in the southern territories of the diocese within the archdeaconry of Aghadoe.

There were thus many causes of confusion in the Irish diocesan organization of the fourteenth century. The introduction on a wide scale of the system of papal provisions in a country where the metropolitan authority of the four archbishops had never been very strong, was bound to add a new element of confusion. Papal provisions begin, as might be expected, with the four archbishoprics towards the middle of the thirteenth century, and occur in important dioceses such as Meath soon afterwards. But they are rare outside these limits in the thirteenth century, and do not become the normal process of appointment before the middle of the fourteenth century. Some of the more outlying dioceses, such as Raphoe, Kilmore or Kilfenora, seem to have continued to elect bishops without papal provision until the end of that century. Provision was the invariable method of appointment in the fifteenth century, and the way thus opened for that astonishing development of irresponsible provisions which is characteristic of so many Irish dioceses during the years of the great schism and throughout the first half of the fifteenth century. No adequate check seems to have existed, as in other countries, to prevent abuses which are only too plain in the lists printed below. Provisions were made on false news of the death of a bishop; and rival bishops appear in several of the more remote dioceses.

Under Martin V the confusion that had been allowed to develop when there were two rival popes, was for a time even more marked. English and Irish monks and friars who were ambitious to gain episcopal status made free use of the smaller Irish dioceses to attain their object. Obsolete dioceses like Maghera, Mayo, Annadown, Glendalough or Scattery Island were resurrected as an excuse for a coveted provision. There was no question of securing a grant of the temporalities of the diocese. These absentee bishops were content to earn their living as suffragan bishops in any of the wealthier English dioceses; and they were usually able to obtain a dispensation to hold some English benefice as a compensation for the

[1] This scheme has been described by J. A. Watt in *Irish Historical Studies*, x (1956), 1–20.

326

temporalities which they seldom even attempted to receive.

The most conspicuous example of this abuse is to be found in the diocese of Dromore, where at a given moment (1431–33) no less than four absentee English bishops were using the title 'bishop of Dromore' and were active as suffragans in England. Similar conditions are to be found in Ross about the same period. Stubbs was the first to draw attention to this abuse in *Registrum Sacrum Anglicanum* (2nd edn, 1897), in which he printed a list of Irish suffragans which is occasionally misleading. For Stubbs included a certain number of names of Irish bishops who, for some purely accidental reason, found themselves in England for a short time and made use of their episcopal powers in an English diocese. No regular suffragan, using an Irish title but residing permanently in England, occurs in the English registers before the fourteenth century; and by far the largest number of these absentee bishops are to be found in the fifteenth century. Irish names occur also in this list; but Irish titular bishops usually made some effort to reside in their diocese. The most curious example of absenteeism is to be found in the list of nominal bishops of Mayo in the late fifteenth century. Here an Irish candidate named Odo O Higgins had sought to resurrect the ancient traditions of the former bishopric of Mayo. A Dutch Cistercian, whose name is given on the papal records as Martin Campania, secured a provision to Mayo in 1432. He was succeeded by a German Augustinian friar named Simon. In a petition to Calixtus III (1457) Simon states that his church of Mayo is situated *in partibus infidelium*, and that its fruits are in the possession of infidels and enemies of the Christian name, and that he cannot maintain therewith his estate and himself.

Conditions such as these do not make it easy to construct an intelligible series of bishops for the more remote and poverty-stricken Irish dioceses. Dates of papal provisions can be found as a rule in the published volumes of the *Calendar of Papal Letters*; but no record has survived of several Irish provisions. In his three volumes on *The Episcopal Succession in England, Scotland and Ireland* (1876) W. Maziere Brady has added extracts from the books of *Obbligazioni* which help to fill some of these gaps; and Brady's lists can be supplemented from the lists in Eubel. Further extracts concerning the dioceses of the province of Armagh will be found in *De Annatis Hiberniae I: Ulster* (Dublin, 1912); they were made by an Irish Dominican scholar, M. A. Costello, concerning the payment of annates by Irish bishops elect and bishops in the fifteenth century. Publication of the annates paid by bishops of the three other Irish provinces has been entrusted to various scholars, who are printing their extracts in successive volumes of *Archivium Hibernicum*. The series is not yet (1958) complete.

The absence of Irish entries on the English patent rolls during the fifteenth century deprives us of an obvious source from which the entries on the papal registers could be checked. A graver loss is the absence of any Irish episcopal registers, with the exception of a broken series for Armagh from c.1360 to 1550. From the Armagh registers, combined with the papal records, various contemporary entries in the later section of the Annals of Ulster, and the documents published in the *Letters and Papers of the Reign of Henry VIII*, a more detailed knowledge of the true situation in the province of Armagh can be obtained than for any other section of the Irish church. An attempt to give an over-all picture of this confused scene will be found in *The Medieval Province of Armagh, 1470–1540* by A. Gwynn (Dundalk, 1946). No adequate survey of the Irish church as a whole, in this last phase of its existence before the breach with Rome in the reign of Henry VIII, has yet been attempted.

Henry's breach with Rome inevitably altered the whole system of episcopal appointments, both for those who accepted the new royal policy and for those who remained loyal to the papacy. It has thus been thought best to divide the lists of episcopal succession at this point, and to print separate lists for the two opposing hierarchies.

Owing to the strong Irish tradition in favour of monastic bishops, and later of bishops chosen from the mendicant friars, it has been decided to indicate by abbreviations the religious orders from which many of the diocesan bishops were chosen.

The episcopal lists in the third edition of the *Handbook* (1985) have been extensively revised by the use of *A New Oxford History of Ireland*, ed. T. W. Moody, F. X. Martin and F. J. Byrne, ix (Oxford, 1984), 264–332.

For ease of reference the dioceses are arranged below in a continuous sequence in alphabetical order, instead of by province as in the previous editions of the *Handbook*. The following table shows the arrangement of dioceses by province.

Province of Armagh:	Province of Cashel:	Province of Dublin:
Ardagh	Ardfert	Dublin
Armagh	Ardmore	Ferns
Clogher	Cashel	Glendalough
Clonmacnois	Cloyne	Kildare
Connor	Cork	Leighlin
Derry	Cork and Cloyne	Ossory
Down	Emly	
Down and Connor	Kilfenora	Province of Tuam:
Dromore	Killaloe	Achonry
Duleek	Limerick	Annadown
Kells	Lismore	Clonfert
Kilmore	Roscrea	Elphin
Meath	Ross	Killala
Raphoe	Scattery Island	Kilmacduagh
Rathlurensis (Maghera)	Waterford	Mayo
	Waterford and Lismore	Tuam

ACHONRY (Achadensis)[1]
(TUAM P.)

BISHOPS	ACCESSION	DEATH *unless otherwise stated*
Máel Ruanaid Ua Ruadáin	*a.* Mar. 1152	1170
Gilla na Náem Ua Ruadáin (Gelasius)	*a.* 1179	?res. *a.* 1208; d. 1214
Clemens Ua Sniadaig O.Cist (Carus)	*a.* 1208	1219
Connmach Ó Torpaig,	el. *a.* 10 Mar. 1220	16 Jan. 1227
Gilla Ísu Ó Cléirig (Gelasius)	—	1230
Tomás Ó Ruadáin	—	1237
Áengus Ó Clúmáin	—	res. *a.* 14 Nov. 1248; d. 1264
Tomás Ó Maicín	el. *p.* 14 Feb, cons. *a.* 20 June; temp. *p.* 20 June 1251	*a.* 1 June 1265
Tomás Ó Miadacháin (Dionysius)	el. *a.* 27 Apr., cons. 19 Dec. 1266	*c.* 27 Nov. 1285
Benedictus Ó Brácáin	el. *p.* 29 Apr., temp. 17 Sept. 1286	19 Mar. 1312
David of Kilheny[2]	el. *p.* 1 May, temp. 1 Aug. 1312	1344
Nicol alias Muircheartach Ó hEadhra, O.Cist.	prov. and cons. 22 Oct. 1348, temp. 19 Mar. 1349	1373
William Andrew, O.P.	prov. 17 Oct. 1373, temp. 1 Aug. 1374 (suffr. in Canterbury 1380)	trs. to Meath 1380

[1] This diocese is often called the 'bishopric of Luighne' in the Irish annals. It was not established at the synod of Ráith Bressail; but Ua Ruadáin signs as 'bp of Luighne' at the synod of Kells.
[2] On 31 July 1327 John XXII sanctioned the union of the three dioceses of Enachdun, Kilmacduagh and Achonry with the diocese of Tuam (*CPL*, ii, 263). The union of Achonry with Tuam should have taken effect on the death of Bp David in 1344. In 1346 the chapter of Achonry, with agreement from the abp and chapter of Tuam, petitioned Clement VI for the dissolution of the union, of which no more is heard (*CPL*, iii, 227).

BISHOPS	ACCESSION	DEATH
		unless otherwise stated
Simon, O.Cist.	prov. *a.* 9 July 1385; (suffr. in London 1385, Winchester 1385–95; Canterbury 1386, Lichfield 1387)	—
Donatus Ó hEadhra	—	1396
Johannes	prov. *a.* 13 Sept. 1396	—
Tomás mac Muirgheasa MacDonnchadha	—	1398
Brian mac Seaáin Ó hEadhra	prov. *a.* Sept. 1400; cons. *a.* 26 Jan. 1401	1409
Maghnus Ó hEadhra (Magonius)	prov. 14 Apr. 1410; cons. *a.* 30 June 1410	*p.* Oct. 1434
Richard Belmer, O.P.[1]	prov. 12 Apr.; cons. 14 June 1424; (suffr. Worcester and Hereford 1426–33)	*a.* Sept. 1436
Tadhg Ó Dálaigh, O.P. (Thaddaeus)	prov. 3 Sept. 1436	*a.* 15 Oct. 1442
James Blakedon, O.P.	prov. 15 Oct. 1442; (suffr. Sarum, Wells, Exeter and Worcester 1442–53)	trs. to Bangor 7 Feb. 1453
Cornelius Ó Mocháin, O.Cist.	prov. 15 Oct. 1449; conf. 5 Apr. 1452	*a.* July 1473
Brian Ó hEadhra (Benedictus, Bernardus)	prov. 2 Sept. 1463	*a.* May 1484
Nicholas Forden	prov. 22 Apr. 1470	—
Robert Wellys, O.F.M.[2]	prov. 14 July 1473; cons. 4 June 1475; (did not get possession)	—
Thomas fitzRichard	—	*a.* Oct. 1492
Tomás Ó Conghaláin	prov. 10 May 1484	1508
John Bustamente	prov. 23 Sept. 1489 (did not take effect)	—
Thomas Ford (de Rivis), O.S.A.	prov. 8 Oct. 1492; (suffr. Lichfield 1495, Lincoln 1496–1504)	*p.* 1504
Eugenius Ó Flannagáin, O.P.	prov. 22 Dec. 1508	*a.* June 1522
Cormac Ó Snighe	prov. 15 June 1522; (did not get possession)	*a.* June 1547

ANNADOWN (Enachdun)[3]
(TUAM P.)

Conn Ua Mellaig (Concors)	*a.* 17 Sept. 1189	1202

[1] Titular bp of Scattery Island.

[2] Eubel (ii, 89) inserts Benedict (?), provided on 2 Nov. 1463; and Nicholas Forden, prov. 22 Apr. 1470. But the see is said to be void by the death of Cornelius when Robert Wellys was provided in 1473 (*CPL*, xiii, 331).

[3] Enachdun was not one of the episcopal churches recognized at the synod of Kells, and no bp of Enachdun did fealty to Henry II in 1172. Concors, the first bp, was present at the coronation of Richard I in Westminster Abbey, and it is probable that the diocese was recognized by the synod held in Dublin by the abp of Cashel as papal legate in 1192.

BISHOPS	ACCESSION	DEATH
		unless otherwise stated
Murchad Ua Flaithbertaig	*c.* 1202	1241
Tomás Ó Mellaig, O.Praem.	cons. *c.* 1242 (suffr. in Lincoln 1246)	? depr. 28 May 1247; d. *a.* 27 May 1250
Conchobar (Concors)	el. *a.* 12 Jan.; temp *p.* 8 May 1251	—

In the summer of 1253 the see of Annadown was united to the see of Tuam, and its temporalities asssigned to Tuam. This first union lasted for some 50 years.

Thomas	—	*a.* 12 Sept. 1263
John de Ufford	el. *a.* 14 Mar. 1283 (never cons.)	res. *c.* 1289
Gilbert Ó Tigernaig, O.F.M.	el. *c.* 1306; cons. *a.* 15 July 1308; temp. 15 July 1308 (suffr. in Winchester 1313, Worcester 1313–14, Hereford 1315)	*a.* 16 Dec. 1323
Jacobus Ó Cethernaig	prov. 16 Dec. 1323	trs. to Connor 7 × 15 May 1324
Robert Petit, O.F.M. (former bp of Clonfert)	prov. 8 Nov. 1325; temp. *p.* 22 June 1326 (suffr. in Salisbury 1326)	28 Apr. 1328
Albertus	prov. *a.* Sept.; temp. 23 Sept. 1328	—
Tomás Ó Mellaig	el. *c.* 1328/29 (never cons.)	—

On 31 July 1327 John XXII, on the petition of Abp Máel Mac Áeda, sanctioned the union of the three dioceses of Enachdun, Kilmacduagh and Achonry with the diocese of Tuam (*CPL*, ii, 263). This union of Enachdun with Tuam should have taken effect on the death of Robert Petit in 1328; but John XXII seems to have provided Albertus (of whom nothing else is known) to the see aft. Robert's death, and charged him with a commission to the archdeacon of Canterbury on 23 Sept. 1328 (*CPL*, ii, 486–87). Meanwhile Tomás Ó Mellaig had secured his election on news of Robert's death, but his claim was resisted by Abp Máel. Thomas appealed to Edward III, who supported his case at Avignon. Thomas was still at Avignon in June 1330 (*CPL*, ii, 318). Nothing more is heard of him, and it seems clear that Abp Máel succeeded in establishing his claim to the union of the two dioceses.

In 1350 the chapter of Enachdun petitioned Clement VI for dissolution of the union, and Clement ordered an inquiry on 23 Jan. 1351 (*CPL*, iii, 388). No change was made. In 1359–60 the chapter of Enachdun again petitioned the Holy See, and Innocent VI ordered an inquiry on 23 Mar. 1360 (Theiner, 315; not in *CPL*). The chapter had elected a bp named Dionysius, but there is no proof that he was ever consecrated. English absentee bps were provided to this see by Boniface IX and later popes, but the union was always maintained by the abps of Tuam. Abp John de Burgo obtained a confirmation of the decree of John XXII from Nicholas V on 11 Jan. 1448 (*CPL*, x, 337); and Abp Donatus Ó Muireadhaigh obtained a formal exemplification of the bulls of John XXII and Nicholas V from Pius II on 23 June 1463 (*CPL*, xii, 195–97). None the less, a full chapter of Enachdun, with dean and archdeacon, was maintained by the abps throughout the fifteenth century.

The following list of bps provided to the see of Enachdun is largely a list of absentee bps, with the exception of Seaán Mac Brádaigh and Séamus Ó Lonnhargáin, who seem to have been resident and active in the diocese *c.* 1425–31.

Dionysius	el. *a.* Mar. 1359 (probably never cons.)	—
Johannes	*a.* 6 July 1393	*a.* Oct. 1394
Henry Trillow, O.F.M.	prov. 26 Oct. 1394; (suffr. Exeter, Salisbury and Winchester 1395–1401)	*a.* 25 Jan. 1402

BISHOPS	ACCESSION	DEATH
		unless otherwise stated
John Bryt, O.F.M.	prov. 25 Jan. 1402; (suffr. Winchester 1402; Lincoln 1403–04; York 1417–20)	*p.* 1420
John Wynn	prov. *a.* 17 Dec. 1408	—
Henricus (?Matthaeus)		*a.* June 1421
John Boner (Camere), O.S.A.	prov. 9 June 1421 (suffr. Sarum and Hereford 1421; Exeter 1438)	*a.* 1446
Seeán Mac Brádaigh, O.Carm.	prov. 15 Oct. 1425	—
Seamus Ó Lonnghargáin	prov. 10 Dec. 1428	trs. to Killaloe 9 Dec. 1429
Donatus Ó Madagáin	prov. 19 Nov. 1431	—
Thomas Salscot	prov. 8 July 1446; (suffr. Lincoln 1449, Exeter 1458)	*p.* 1458
Redmund Bermingham	prov. 18 May 1450; cons. May 1450	1451
Thomas Barrett	prov. 17 Apr. 1458 (suffr. Exeter 1458; 1468–75; Wells 1482–5	*p.* 1485
Francis Brunand, O.Carm.	prov. *a.* 4 Dec. 1494 (suffr. in Geneva)	*p.* 1504

ARDAGH[1]
(ARMAGH P.)

Mac Raith Ua Móráin	*a.* Mar. 1152	res. 1166, d. 1168
Gilla Crist Ua hEóthaig	*a.* 1172	1178
Ua hÉislinnén	—	1188
Annud Ua Muiredaig (Adam)	—	1216
Robert, O.Cist.	1217	27 May 1224
M., prior of Inis Mór	*c.* 1224	*c.* 1229
Joseph Mac Teichthecháin alias Mac Eódaig[2] ('Magoday')	el. 1227, cons. *c.* 1228	1230
Mac Raith Mac Serraig[2]	el. and cons. *c.* 1229	1230
Thomas	fl. *c.* 1230	—
Gilla Ísu mac in Scélaige Ó Tormaid (Gelasius)	el. and cons. *c.* 1232	1237
Iocelinus, O.Cist.	el. and cons. *c.* 1232, temp. 1 Mar. 1233	res. *a.* 1237
Brendán Mac Teichthecháin alias Mac Eódaig ('Magoday')	el. *c.* 1238	res. 15 Oct. 1252, d. 1255
Milo of Dunstaple	el. *a.* 20 May 1256, temp. 13 Jan. 1257	23 Oct. 1288
Matha Ó hEóthaig (Matthaeus)	el. Nov. 1289, fealty 28 Jan., temp. 8 Apr. 1290	1322

[1] The diocese of Ardagh is frequently called the diocese of Conmaicne in the Irish annals.
[2] These two bps appear as rival bps; and the rivalry was continued to 1237.

BISHOPS	ACCESSION	DEATH *unless otherwise stated*
Robert Wirsop, O.E.S.A.	prov. 5 Apr. 1323 (did not get possession)	trs. to Connor 20 June 1323
Seoán Mág Eóaigh	el. *a.* Mar., prov. 19 Mar., cons. *a.* 12 May, temp. 20 Oct. 1324	1343
Eóghan alias Maolsheachlainn Ó Fearghail (Audovenus)	el. *c.* 1344, cons. *c.* 1347	1367
Uilliam Mac Carmaic	el. *c.* 1368	*a.* Aug. 1373
Cairbre Ó Fearghail (Carolus)[1]	el. *a.* Sept., conf. *p.* Sept 1373	1378
John Aubrey, O.P.[1]	el. *a.* Sept. 1373, prov. 29 Apr. 1374	—
Henry Nony, O.P.	prov. 29 Apr. 1392 (did not get possession) (suffr. Exeter, 1396–9, Bath 1400)	*p.* 1400
Comedinus Mac Brádaigh (Gilbertus)	prov. 20 Oct. 1395, cons. *p.* 19 Aug. 1396	*a.* Feb. 1400
Adam Leyns, O.P.	prov. 15 Feb. 1400	June 1416
Conchobhar Ó Fearghail (Cornelius)	el. *p.* June 1416, prov. 17 Feb. 1418, cons. 3 Feb. 1419	1423
Risdeárd Ó Fearghail, O.Cist.	el. *a.* Jan., prov. 11 Jan., cons. *p.* 25 May 1425	*c.* June 1444
Mac Muircheartaigh	el. 1444 (never cons.)	res. 1445
Cormac Mág Shamhradháin, O.S.A.	prov. 6 Nov. 1444, cons. *p.* 19 Feb. 1445	res. *c.* 1462
Seaán Ó Fearghail[2]	prov. 30 July, bulls expedited 26 Nov. 1462, prov. (again) 28 July 1469	*a.* Aug. 1479
Donatus Ó Fearghail	prov. 12 Oct. 1467	*a.* 28 Júly 1469
Uilliam Ó Fearghail, O.Cist.	prov. 4 Aug. 1480, cons. 11 June 1482	1516
Ruaidhrí Ó Maoileóin	prov. 14 Dec. 1517	1540

ARDFERT
(CASHEL P.)

Anmchad O h-Anm- chada	—	1117
Máel Brénainn Ua Rónáin	*a.* Mar. 1152	21/2 Sept. 1161
Domnall O Connairche	—	1193
David Ua Duib Díthrib	el. *a.* 1197, conf. 1200/1	1207
Anonymous	—	*c.* 1217
John, O.S.B.	el. *c.* 1217, cons. *a.* 28 Feb. 1218 (suffragan in Canterbury *c.* 1222)	depr. 18 June 1224, d. 14 Oct. 1245
Gilbertus	el. *a.* 28 Feb. 1218, conf. *p.* 16 July 1219, temp. *p.* 7 May 1225	res. *p.* 24 Apr. 1235

[1] There was a disputed election aft. the death of Bp William in 1373. Cairbre Ó Fearghail died at Avignon in 1378, and it is not certain that he ever got possession of the see. John Aubrey O.P., friar of Trim, was one of three rival candidates in 1373.

[2] The date of Bp Cormac's resignation is uncertain; but a 'Joh.', bp elect of Ardagh, was in Rome in 1463 (Rymer, *Foedera*, xi, 503).

BISHOPS	ACCESSION	DEATH *unless otherwise stated*
Brendán	el. *p.* 6 Dec. 1236, conf. 17 Nov. 1237	res. *p.* 1 Aug. 1251, d. *a.* 20 Apr. 1252
Christianus, O.P.	el. *a.* 23 Feb. 1253, cons. *p.* 17 Aug. 1253	*a.* 20 Aug. 1256
Philippus	el. *a.* 25 Mar. 1257, cons. *p.* 25 Mar. 1257, temp. 16 June 1257	*a.* 4 July 1264
Johannes	el. *a.* 3 Mar. 1265, temp. *p.* 3 Mar. 1265	*a.* 6 June 1286
Nicolaus	el. and temp. *p.* 28 June 1286	14 Mar. 1288
Nicol Ó Samradáin, O.Cist.	el. *p.* 26 Apr., temp. *p.* 10 Aug. 1288, lib. 25 Apr. 1289	1335
Edmund of Caermarthen, O.P.[1]	prov. 24 Sept., cons. 24 Sept. 1331, temp. 27 Jan. 1332 (did not get possession)	—
Ailín Ó hEichthighirn	el. *c.* 1335, prov. and cons. 18 Nov. 1336	2 Dec. 1347
John de Valle	el. *a.* Oct., prov. 22 Oct. 1348, temp. 10 Mar. 1349	*a.* Oct. 1372
Cornelius Ó Tigernach, O.F.M.	prov. 22 Oct. 1372, temp. 10 Feb. 1373	*c.* 1379
William Bull	temp. 14 Feb. 1380	*c.* 1404
Nicholas Ball	prov. *a.* Oct. 1404 (did not take effect)	trs. to Emly 2 Dec. 1405
Tomás Ó Ceallaigh, O.P.	prov. *a.* 10 Mar. 1405 (did not take effect)	trs. to Clonfert 11 Mar. 1405
John Attilburgh, O.S.B. (Artilburch)	prov. 10 Mar. 1405, conf. by Alexander V 25 Oct. 1409 (in opposition to Nicholas Fitz-Maurice)	*a.* Jan. 1411
Nicholas FitzMaurice	prov. *a.* 17 Sept. 1408, conf. by John XXIII 27 Jan. 1411	*a.* Apr. 1450
Maurice Stack	prov. 30 Jan., cons. *p.* 29 Apr. 1450	*a.* Jan. 1452
Mauricius Ó Conchobhair	prov. 26 Jan., cons. *p.* 11 Feb. 1452	*a.* Sept. 1458
John Stack[2]	prov. 18 Sept. 1458, cons. *c.* 1461, conf. by Sixtus IV 15 Mar. 1488	*a.* Oct. 1488
John Pigge[2]	prov. 27 Mar. 1461 (rector in London 1462–83)	res. *a.* 22 June 1473, trs. to Beirut *a.* Jan. 1475

[1] On 27 Jan. 1332 Edward III issued a mandate for restitution of temporalities to Edmund, on false news of the death of Alan.

[2] John Stack was provided in 1458 by Pius II, but was not consecrated for more than three years aft. his provision (*CPL*, xii, 164). Meanwhile John Pigge, an English Dominican friar, obtained a provision from Pius II, but resided in London as rector of St Christopher, Threadneedle Street: for details of his career, *see CPL*, xiii, 457 note. Philip Stack was provided to the see in 1473, the see being stated to be void by the resignation of John (*ibid.*, 352). It is probable that this John is John Pigge, who appears as bp of Beirut from 1475 onwards. John Stack seems never to have abandoned his claim. He obtained a confirmation of his letters of provision from Sixtus IV on 15 Mar. 1488 (*CPL*, xiii, 49); and Ware states that he attended Abp Cantwell's provincial synod as bp of Ardfert in July 1480. But he was most prob. dead when Philip Stack obtained his second letters of provision from Sixtus IV on 27 Oct. 1488. Philip complains of opposition from enemies in 1479 (*CPL*, xiii, 250, 654).

BISHOPS	ACCESSION	DEATH *unless otherwise stated*
Philip Stack	prov. 26 June 1473, prov. (again) 27 Oct. 1488	*a.* Nov. 1495
John FitzGerald	prov. 20 Nov. 1495	*a.* May 1536

ARDMORE[1]
(CASHEL P.)

Eugenius	*a.* 1153 (suffr. in Lichfield 1184/5)	—

ARMAGH
(ARMAGH P.)

ARCHBISHOPS	ACCESSION	DEATH *unless otherwise stated*
Cellach mac Áeda meic Máel Ísu, abb. (Celsus)	cons. bp 23 Sept. 1105, abp 1106	1 Apr. 1129
Máel Máedóc Ua Morgair, abb. (Malachias; St Malachy)	el. and cons. 1132, installed 1134	res. 1136, d. 2 Nov. 1148
Gilla Meic Liac mac Diarmata meic Ruaidrí, abb. (Gelasius)	el. and cons. 1137	27 Mar. 1174
Conchobar mac Meic Con Caille, r.c. (St Concors)	el. and cons. *c.* 1174	1175
Gilla in Choimded Ua Caráin (Gillebertus)	el. and cons. *c.* 1175	*c.* Jan. '1180
Tommaltach mac Áeda Ua Conchobair (Thomas)	el. and cons. *a.* Feb. 1180, res. 1184, restored *c.* 1186/7	1201
Máel Ísu Ua Cerbaill (Malachias)	el. 1184	1186/7
Echdonn Mac Gilla Uidir, r.c. (Eugenius)	el. and cons. 1202, temp. 30 Aug. 1206 (suffr. in Exeter and Worcester 1207)	*p.* 11 Aug. 1216
Luke Netterville	el. *a.* Aug. 1217, temp. 16 Sept. 1219	17 Apr. 1227
Donatus Ó Fidabra	trs. from Clogher *c.* Aug., temp. 20 Sept. 1227	*a.* 17 Oct. 1237
Robert Archer, O.P.	el. *a.* 4 Apr. 1238 (never cons.)	—
Albert Suerbeer of Cologne (Albertus)	prov. *a.* 4 Mar. 1239, temp. *c.* 30 Sept., cons. 30 Sept. 1240	trs. to Prussia-Livonia 10 Jan. 1246
Reginald, O.P.	prov. and cons. *a.* 28 Oct., temp. 28 Oct. 1247	*p.* July 1256
Abraham Ó Conalláin	el. *p.* 20 Feb. 1257, cons. *a.* 16 Mar., temp. 16 Mar. 1258	21 Dec. 1260

[1] Ardmore was not included in the list of Irish dioceses approved at the synod of Kells; but is named as a church which claimed the right to a bishopric. A bp of Ardmore took the oath of fealty to Henry II in 1172; and Eugenius appears as a witness to a charter some years later. Ua Selbaig, who died at Cork in 1205, may have been bp of Ardmore or of Ross.

ARCHBISHOPS	ACCESSION	DEATH
		unless otherwise stated
Máel Pátraic Ó Scannail, O.P. (Patricius)	el. *c.* Mar., conf. *a.* 13 Aug., trs. from Raphoe 5 Nov. 1261, temp. 20 Apr. 1262	16 Mar. 1270
Nicol Mac Máel Ísu	el. *p.* 9 May, conf. 14 July 1270, temp. 23 Sept., lib. 27 Oct. 1272	10 May 1303
Michael Mac Lochlainn, O.F.M.	el. *a.* 31 Aug. 1303 (never cons.)	el. bp Derry 1319
Dionysius	prov. 1303/4 (never cons.)	res. *c.* 1304
John Taaffe	prov. 27 Aug., cons. *p.* 27 Aug. 1306	*a.* 6 Aug. 1307
Walter Jorz, O.P.	prov. 6 Aug., cons. 6 Aug., temp. 30 Sept. 1307	res. *a.* 13 Nov. 1311
Roland Jorz, O.P.	prov. and cons. 13 Nov. 1311, temp. 15 Sept. 1312, lib. 20 Dec. 1312	res. *a.* 22 Aug. 1322 (suffr. in Canterbury 1323, York 1332)
Stephen Segrave	prov. 16 Mar., temp. 31 July 1323, cons. Apr. 1324	27 Oct. 1333
David Mág Oireachtaigh	el. *a.* July, prov. 4 July, cons. *a.* 26 July 1334, temp. 16 Mar. 1335	16 May 1346
Richard FitzRalph	el. *a.* July, prov. 31 July 1346, fealty 15 Feb., temp. 15 Apr., cons. 8 July 1347	16 Nov. 1360
Milo Sweetman	prov. 29 Oct., cons. 17×21 Nov. 1361, temp. 5 Feb. 1362	11 Aug. 1380
Thomas Ó Calmáin, O.F.M.	prov. by Clement VII 14 Jan. 1381	—
John Colton	prov. *p.* Jan. 1381, cons. 1381, temp. 9 Mar. 1383	res. *a.* Apr. 1404, d. 27 Apr. 1404
Nicholas Fleming	prov. 18 Apr., cons. 1 May, prov. (again) 11 Nov. 1404	*p.* 22 June 1416
John Swayne[1]	prov. 10 Jan., cons. *c.* 2 Feb. 1418	res. 27 Mar. 1439, d. *a.* Oct. 1442
John Prene	prov. 27 Mar., cons. Nov. 1439	June 1443
John Mey	prov. 26 Aug. 1443, cons. 20 June 1444	1456
John Bole (Bull), O.S.A.	prov. 2 May, cons. *a.* 13 June 1457	18 Feb. 1471
John Foxhalls (Foxholes), O.F.M.	prov. 16 Dec., cons. *p.* Dec. 1471	*a.* 23 Nov. 1474
Edmund Connesburgh[2]	prov. 5 June, cons. *c.* 1475 (did not get possession) (suffr. Ely 1477, Norwich 1502)	res. Nov. 1477

[1] Soon aft. the death of Fleming the chapter of Armagh elected Richard Talbot, but the election could not be confirmed owing to the prolonged vacancy in the Roman see. Meanwhile Abp Cranley died in Dublin, and Talbot was elected to the vacant see in the summer of 1417. Talbot withdrew his consent to the Armagh election. The chapter then elected Robert FitzHugh, chancellor, St Patrick's Dublin; but this election was annulled by Martin V, who provided John Swayne.

[2] According to Stubbs, Connesburgh became bp of Chalcedon in 1478. In Mar. 1483 he is styled 'abp in the universal church' (*CPL*, xiii, 133).

ARCHBISHOPS	ACCESSION	DEATH *unless otherwise stated*
Ottaviano Spinelli (de Palatio)[1]	prov. 3 July 1478, cons. *a.* Jan 1480	June 1513
John Kite	prov. 24 Oct., cons. *p.* Oct. 1513	trs. to Carlisle 12 July 1521
George Cromer	prov. 2 Oct., cons. *c.* Dec. 1521, suspended by Paul III 23 July 1539	16 Mar. 1543

CASHEL[2]
(CASHEL P.)

Máel Ísu Ua hAinmere, O.S.B. (Malchus)	*c.* 1111	—
Máel Ísu Ua Fogluda (Mauricius)	—	1131
Domnall Ua Conaing	trs. from Killaloe, 1131	1137
Domnall Ua Lonngargáin	trs. from Killaloe, 1137/8	1158
Domnall Ua hUallacháin (Donatus)	*a.* 1172	1182
Muirges Ua hÉnna, O.Cist. (Matthaeus; Mauricius)	*a.* 1186	1206
Donnchad Ua Lonngargáin I (Donatus; Dionysius)	*c.* 1208	*a.* July 1216
Donnchad Ó Lonngargáin II, O.Cist. (Donatus)	cons. *a.* July 1216	res. *a.* Aug. 1223, d. 1232
[Michael Scottus	prov. 1223 (never cons.)	res. 1223]
Mairín O Briain, O.S.A. (Marianus)	el. *p.* 19 Aug. 1223; trs. from Cork 20 June, temp. 25 Aug. 1224, (again) 20 Jan. 1225	*a.* 6 June 1237, d. 1238
David mac Cellaig, O.P. (O'Kelly)	el. *a.* Dec. 1238, conf. 1239	4 Apr. 1253
David Mac Cerbaill (Mac Carwill), O.Cist. after 1269	el. *a.* 17 Aug., prov. 17 Aug. 1254, temp. 19 Feb. 1255	*a.* 4 Sept. 1289
Stiamna Ó Brácáin	el. *a.* 31 Jan. 1290, prov. 21 Aug. 1290; temp. 27 Mar. 1291	25 July 1302
Mauricius Mac Cerbaill	el. *a.* 17 May 1303, fealty 24 May 1303, prov. 17 Nov. 1303, temp. 28 July 1304	*c.* 25 Mar. 1316
William FitzJohn	trs. from Ossory 26 Mar. 1317, temp. *p.* 3 Mar. 1318	15 Sept. 1326
Seoán Mac Cerbaill	trs. from Meath 19 Jan., temp. 18 May, fealty 26 Sept. 1327	*c.* 27 July 1329

[1] The exact date of Spinelli's provision is not known. He had been governing the diocese by special commission of Sixtus IV (19 Apr. 1477), but Edward IV was opposed to his rule and confirmed Connesburgh in his rights on 20 May 1478. Spinelli was still nuncio and governor of Armagh on 31 Aug. 1479, but had probably been consecrated before 29 Oct. 1479, when he held a convocation of his clergy at Dundalk.

[2] Cashel was not an ancient monastic church, but became a metropolitan see in the twelfth century.

ARCHBISHOPS	ACCESSION	DEATH *unless otherwise stated*
Walter le Rede	trs. from Cork 20 Oct. 1329, temp. 20 July, lib. 19 Aug. 1330	17 June 1331
Eóin Ó Gráda[1]	prov. 27 Mar., temp. 12 June, lib. 9 July 1332	8 July 1345
Radulphus Ó Ceallaigh (? Ó Caollaidhe), O.Carm.	trs. from Leighlin 9 Jan., temp. 9 Mar., lib. 4 Apr. 1346 (suffr. in Winchester 1346)	20 Nov. 1361
George Roche (de Rupe)	(no date of provision) *a.* 12 Sept. 1362	*c.* 1362
Tomás Mac Cearbhaill	trs. from Tuam *a.* 8 Mar. 1365	8 Feb. 1372
Philip of Torrington, O.F.M.	prov. 5 Sept. 1373, temp. 19 Dec. 1373, lib. 19 Sept. 1374	1380
Michael, O.F.M.	prov. (by Clement VII) 22 Oct. 1382	trs. to Sodor 15 July 1387
Peter Hackett	prov. (by Urban VI) (no date of provision), temp. 28 Oct. 1385	*c.* 1405
Richard O Hedian	prov. *a.* 6 Apr., cons. *a.* 17 June 1406, temp. 14 Sept. 1408	21 July 1440
John Cantwell I	el. *a.* Nov., prov. 21 Nov. 1440, cons. *a.* 28 Mar. 1442	14 Feb. 1451/2
John Cantwell II	prov. 2 May, cons. *p.* 2 May 1452	*a.* May 1484
David Creagh	prov. 10 May 1484, cons. 14 June 1484	5 Sept. 1503
Maurice FitzGerald	(no date of provision) *c.* 1504	*a.* Oct. 1524
Edmund Butler, O.Trin.	prov. 21 Oct. 1524, cons. *p.* 3 Jan. 1525	5 Mar. 1551

CLOGHER[2]
(ARMAGH P.)

BISHOPS	ACCESSION	DEATH *unless otherwise stated*
Cináeth Ua Baígill	—	1135
Gilla Críst Ua Morgair (Christianus)	1135	1138
Áed Ua Cáellaide, r.c. (Edanus)	1138	res. *a.* May 1178, d. 29 Mar. 1182
Mael Ísu Ua Cerbaill (Malachias)	el. *a.* 18 May 1178	1186/7
Gilla Críst Ua Mucaráin, r.c. (Christinus)	*c.* 1187	1193
Máel Ísu Ua Máel Chiaráin, O.Cist.	*a.* Sept. 1194	1197

[1] In *CPL*, ii, 325, the date of provision is given as 6 kal. Apr. 15 John XXII (27 Mar. 1331). But there is a very detailed statement in the calendar of a lost Irish pipe roll of 6 Edw. III, that the temporalities of Cashel were in the king's hand from 17 June *a.r.* V to 9 July *a.r.* VI (17 June 1331 to 9 July 1332) for the space of 1 year, three weeks and 1 day; and the see was not vacant until aft. the death of Walter le Rede in June 1331.

[2] From *c.* 1140 to *c.* 1190 the territory which now corresponds with the county of Louth was transferred from the diocese of Armagh to the diocese of Clogher (frequently called Oirghialla in the Irish annals). During this period the bps of Oirghialla used the style 'bps of Louth'. The title 'bp of Clogher' was resumed aft. 1193, when this territory was restored to the diocese of Armagh, and Clogher became once more the seat of the bps of Oirghialla.

BISHOPS	ACCESSION	DEATH
		unless otherwise stated
Gilla Tigernaig Mac Gilla Rónáin, r.c. (Thomas)	*c.* 1197	1218
Donatus Ó Fidabra, r.c.	*c.* 1218	trs. to Armagh *c.* Aug. 1227
Nehemias Ó Brácáin, O.Cist.	el. Sept. 1227, cons. *c.* 1228	*a.* 15 Nov. 1240
David Ó Brácáin, O.Cist.[1]	el. *c.* 1245	1267
Michael Mac in tSaír	el. *a.* Sept., cons. 9 Sept. 1268	res. *a.* 1287, d. 1288
Matthaeus Mac Cathasaig I	el. *a.* 29 June, cons. 29 June 1287	*c.* 1316
Henricus	*fl.* 1310	*c.* 1316
Gelasius alias Cornelius Ó Bánáin,[2] r.c.	el. and cons. *c.* 1316	1319
Nicolaus Mac Cathasaigh	el. 23 Feb., cons. 1320	1356
Brian Mac Cathmhaoil (Bernardus)	el. *p.* Sept. 1356, prov. *c.* 1357	1358
Matthaeus Mac Cathasaigh II	el. *c.* 1361, cons. *p.* Feb. 1362	—
Aodh Ó hEóthaigh (alias Ó Néill) (Odo)	—	27 July 1369
Johannes Ó Corcráin, OSB (Würzburg)	prov. 6 Apr. 1373	? *c.* 1389
Art Mac Cathmhaoil	prov. 15 Feb., cons. *a.* 28 Apr. 1390	10 Aug. 1432
Piaras Mág Uidhir (Petrus)	prov. 31 Aug. 1433	res. *a.* July 1447, d. 5 Dec. 1450
Rossa mac Tomáis Óig Mág Uidhir (Rogerius)	prov. 21 July 1447, cons. *a.* 6 Jan. 1450	1483
Florence Woolley, O.S.B.[3]	prov. 20 Nov. 1475 (did not get possession), (suffr. Norwich 1478–1500)	1500
Niall mac Séamuis Mac Mathghamhna	prov. *a.* 14 June 1484 (bulls not expedited)	1488
John Edmund de Courci, O.F.M.	prov. 14 June, bulls expedited 12 Sept. 1484	prov. to Ross 26 Sept. 1492
Séamus mac Pilip Mac Mathghamhna	prov. 5 Nov. 1494 (did not take effect)	trs. to Derry 26 Nov. 1503
Andreas[4]	prov. 10 June 1500	—
Nehemias Ó Cluainín, O.E.S.A.	prov. 24 Jan. 1502	res. 1503
Giolla Pádraig Ó Condálaigh (Patricius)	prov. 6 Mar. 1504	*a.* Dec. 1504

[1] The long interregnum aft. the death of Nehemias is prob. due to the action of the abp (Donatus) of Armagh, who was seeking at this time to unite the two dioceses of Armagh and Clogher.

[2] No accurate records for this period have survived.

[3] Provided on apparently false news of Bp Ross's resignation.

[4] Edmund de Courci did not renounce his claim to Clogher when he was provided to Ross in Sept. 1492, and Andreas was provided as his coadjutor with right of succession to Clogher in 1500. But the see was declared void by resignation of Edmund when Nehemias Ó Cluainín was provided in Jan. 1502.

BISHOPS	ACCESSION	DEATH *unless otherwise stated*
Eoghan Mac Cathmhaoil (Eugenius)	prov. 4 Apr. 1505	1515
Pádraig Ó Cuilín, O.E.S.A.	prov. 11 Feb. 1517	*a.* 26 Mar. 1534

CLONARD: *see* MEATH

CLONFERT
(TUAM P.)

Muiredach Ua hÉnlainge	—	1117
Gilla Pátraic Ua hAilchinned	—	1149
Petrus Ua Mórda, O.Cist.	*c.* 1150	27 Dec. 1171
Máel Ísu Mac in Baird	1172	1173
Celechair Ua hAirmedaig	*a.* 1179	1186
Muirchertach Ua Máel Uidir, bp of Clonmacnois	1186	1187
Domnall Ua Finn	—	1195
Muirchertach Ua Carmacáin	—	1203
Máel Brigte Ua hEruráin	el. 1205	—
Cormac Ó Luimlín (Carus)	*a.* 1224	*c.* 19 June 1259
Tomás mac Domnaill Móir Ó Cellaig	el. *a.* 7 Nov., temp. *p.* 7 Nov. 1259	6 Jan. 1263
Johannes de Alatre	prov. *a.* Sept., temp. 29 Sept, cons. 19 Dec. 1266	trs. to Benevento 2 Oct. 1295
Robert, O.S.B.	prov. 2 Jan., cons. *a.* 21 Apr., temp. 24 Sept. 1296 (suffr. in Canterbury 1296–1307)	*a.* Dec. 1307
Gregorius Ó Brócaig	el. *a.* 22 Mar, temp. *p.* 22 Mar. 1308	1319
Robert Le Petit, O.F.M.	el. 10 Feb. 1320, cons. *c.* 1320 (suffr. in Worcester 1322, Exeter 1324)	depr. *c.* 1323, prov. to Annadown 27 Oct. 1325
Seoán Ó Leaáin	el. 10 Nov. 1319, prov. 6 Aug, cons. 20 Sept., temp. 29 Dec. 1322	7 Apr. 1336
Tomás mac Gilbert Ó Ceallaigh	*a.* 14 Oct. 1347	1378
Muircheartach mac Pilib Ó Ceallaigh (Mauricius)	prov. *a.* 6 Mar., cons. 1378	trs. to Tuam 26 Jan. 1393
Uilliam Ó Cormacáin	trs. from Tuam 27 Jan 1393	depr. 1398
David Corre, O.F.M.	prov. 20 Mar. 1398 (did not take effect)	—
Énrí Ó Connmaigh	prov. *c.* July 1398	trs. to Kilmacduagh 11 Mar. 1405

BISHOPS	ACCESSION	DEATH *unless otherwise stated*
Tomás mac Muircheartaigh Ó Ceallaigh, O.P.	trs. from Ardfert 11 Mar. 1405	trs. to Tuam 15 July 1438
Cobhthach Ó Madagáin	el. 1410 (never cons.)	1410
Seaán Ó hEidhin, O.F.M.	prov. 18 July 1438, (again) 25 Oct. 1441, (suffr. in London, Exeter, Worcester 1443–59)	1459
John White, O.F.M.	prov. 25 Oct. 1441 (did not get possession)	res. July 1448
Conchobhar Ó Maolalaidh, O.F.M. (Cornelius)	prov. 22 May 1447, (again) 18 July 1448	trs. to Emly 30 Aug. 1448
Cornelius Ó Cuinnlis, O.F.M.	trs. from Emly 30 Aug. 1448	res. 1463, d. *p.* 1469
Matthaeus Mág Raith, O.S.A.	prov. 22 June 1463	1507
David de Burgo	prov. 5 July 1508	1509
Dionysius Ó Mórdha, O.P.	prov. 7 Nov. 1509	1534

CLONMACNOIS[1]
(ARMAGH P.)

?Domnall mac Flannacáin Ua Dubthaig	?1111	17 Mar. 1136
Muirchertach Ua Máel Uidir II	*a.* 1152	1187
Cathal Ua Máel Eóin	—	6 Feb. 1207
Muiredach Ua Muirecén	el. *c.* 1207	1214
Áed Ó Máel Eóin I	el. 1214	1220
Máel Ruanaid Ó Modáin	el. 1220	?res. *a.* 1227, d. 1230
Áed Ó Máel Eóin II, O.Cist. (Elias)	el. *a.* 1227	res. 27 Apr. 1236
Thomas Fitz Patrick	el. *a.* Apr. 1236, temp. *p.* 18 Apr. 1236	*c.* 1252
Tomás Ó Cuinn, O.F.M.	el. *a.* Nov., conf. 26 Nov. 1252, temp. *p.* 20 Feb. 1253	18 Nov. 1278
Anonymous, O.F.M.	el. *a.* 20 July 1280	res. 13 Sept. 1289
Gilbertus	el. *a.* Feb., temp 18 Feb. 1282 (blinded: never cons.)	

[1] Cluan Mac Nois was an ancient monastic church, founded by Saint Ciaran in the sixth century, and one of the main centres of Old Irish tradition and culture. It was not chosen as one of the diocesan churches established by the synod of Ráith Bressail (1111); but in the same year it was recognized as the diocesan centre of West Meath at the synod of Uisnech. No name of any bp of Clonmacnois is recorded bef. the synod of Kells (1152); and it seems probable that the former jurisdiction of the abbot was maintained for some time at the expense of the bp's jurisdiction. The diocese lost much of its territory to the diocese of Meath in the late twelfth and early thirteenth centuries, and was thereafter permanently impoverished.

BISHOPS	ACCESSION	DEATH
		unless otherwise stated
Uilliam Ó Dubthaig, O.F.M.	el. *a.* 18 July, temp. 6 Oct. 1290	*a.* Aug. 1297
Uilliam Ó Finnéin, O.Cist.	el. 1298	*a.* 28 Aug. 1302
Domnall Ó Bráein, O.F.M., guardian of Killeigh	el. *a.* 26 Oct. 1302, temp. *p.* 14 Apr. 1303	—
Lughaidh Ó Dálaigh	—	1337
Henricus, O.P.	el. *c.* 1337	*a.* 1368
[Simon, O.P.[1]	prov. 11 May 1349 (did not take effect)	trs. to Derry 18 Dec. 1349]
Richard (Braybroke)	cons. *a.* 28 Aug. 1369	*a.* Sept. 1371
Hugo	cons. *a.* 25 Sept. 1371	*p.* 1380
Philippus Ó Maoil	—	res. *a.* 30 Jan. 1388, d. 1420
Milo Corr, O.F.M.	prov. 30 Jan. 1338, (again) 9 Nov. 1389	*a.* Sept. 1397
Philip Nangle, O.Cist.	prov. *a.* 24 Nov., cons. *a.* 26 Nov. 1397	*a.* Sept. 1423
David Prendergast, O.Cist.	prov. 24 Sept. 1423 (did not take effect)	—
Cormac Mac Cochláin (Cornelius)	prov. 10 Jan. 1425, (again) 8 July, cons. *p.* 2 Aug. 1426	22 June 1444
Seaán Ó Dálaigh, O.F.M.[2]	prov. 18 Sept. 1444	*a.* 26 Mar. 1487
Thomas	*a.* 27 Oct. 1449	—
Robertus	—	—
William, O.S.A.[3]	prov. 14 July 1458 (suffr. in Durham)	*p.* 1484
Jacobus	1480	1486
Walter Blake[4]	prov. 26 Mar. 1487	1508
Tomás Ó Maolalaidh, O.F.M.	*c.* 1509	trs. to Tuam 19 June 1514
Quintinus Ó hUiginn, O.F.M.[5]	prov. 10 Nov. 1516	*a.* 16 June 1539

[1] Simon obtained his provision to Clonmacnois on false news of the death of Bp Henry.

[2] On 27 Oct. 1449 (*CPL*, x, 53) Nicholas V dispensed a Bp Thomas of Clonmacnois to hold a benefice *in commendam* owing to the poverty of his diocese, and the lack of a suitable episcopal residence. Nothing further is known of this Thomas.

[3] William obtained his provision on false news of the death of an otherwise unknown Bp Robert of Clonmacnois (*CPL*, xi, 359).

[4] Walter Blake had been provided to the see of Tuam by Innocent VIII on 8 Aug. 1483 during the lifetime of Abp Donatus Ó Muireadhaigh, and had then secured consecration. He was a canon of Tuam and bp in the universal church until his provision to the see of Clonmacnois in 1487.

[5] Quintinus was unable to reside in his diocese, and was for a time administrator of the diocese of Down and Connor in place of the absentee Robert Blyth. Meanwhile the diocese of Clonmacnois was being administered by Ruaidhri Ó Maoileóin, who had been a canon of Clonmacnois bef. his provision to the see of Ardagh in 1517.

CLOYNE¹
(CASHEL P.)

BISHOPS	ACCESSION	DEATH
		unless otherwise stated
Gilla na Náem Ua Muirchertaig (Nehemias)	*a.* 1148	1149
Ua Dubchróin, abbot of Cloyne	—	1159
Ua Flannacáin	—	1167
Matthaeus Ua Mongaig	*fl.* 1173 × 1177	1192
Laurentius Ua Súillebáin	*a.* 1201	1205
C.	*c.* 1205	—
Luke	*a.* 1218	1223
Daniel²	el. *p.* 31 Aug. 1226	*p.* Oct. 1234
David mac Cellaig, O.P.	el. *a.* Sept. 1237	trs. to Cashel *a.* Dec. 1238
Ailinn Ó Súillebáin, O.P.	*c.* 1240, conf. 1240	trs. to Lismore *p.* 26 Oct. 1246
Daniel, O.F.M.	el. *a.* 12 Oct., cons. *p.* 12 Oct. 1247, temp. 2 July 1248	*a.* 2 June 1264
Reginaldus	trs. from Down 13 Apr. 1265	7 Feb. 1274
Alanus Ó Longáin, O.F.M.	el. *a.* 18 Feb., temp. 21 Feb., lib. 21 Apr. 1275	*c.* 5 Jan. 1284
Nicholas of Effingham	el. *p.* 18 Mar., temp. 2 Sept. 1284	June 1321
Mauricius Ó Solcháin	prov. 8 Oct. 1321, temp. 1 Aug. 1322, cons. *p.* 25 Aug. 1323	31 Mar. 1333
John Brid, O.Cist.	prov. 10 Aug., cons. *a.* 9 Oct. 1333, temp. 16 Sept. 1335	*c.* 1351
John Whitekot	el. *a.* June, prov. 8 June, cons. *a.* 27 June, temp. 18 Sept. 1351	7 Feb.ʼ1362
John Swaffham, O.Carm.	prov. 1 Mar. 1363, temp. 14 July 1363	trs. to Bangor 2 July 1376
Richard Wye, O.Carm.	prov. 2 July, temp. 9 Nov. 1376	depr. *a.* 16 Mar. 1394
Gerard Caneton, O.E.S.A.	prov. 16 Mar. 1394, temp. 9 Nov. 1394	trs. to Elphin *c.* 1405
Adam Payn, O.E.S.A.³	prov. 26 July 1413	res. *a.* 15 June 1429, d. *a.* Jan. 1432

(Cloyne united to Cork, 1429)

¹ Cloyne was not one of the churches chosen as a diocesan centre at the synod of Ráith Bressail; but a bp of Cloyne was ruling the diocese bef. the death of St Malachy in 1148, and the see was recognised at the synod of Kells.
² There was a disputed election aft. the death of Luke. Two candidates, Florentius (el. *a.* 24 Aug. 1224) and William, O.Cist. (el. *a.* 20 July 1226), were never consecrated.
³ Adam Payn obtained a confirmation of the union of the two dioceses of Cork and Cloyne, as decreed by John XXII in 1326, from Martin V, 21 Sept. 1418 (*CPL*, vii, 65). But this union did not take effect owing to opposition from the bp of Cork, Milo FitzJohn. Milo died in 1423; and Adam resigned in 1429, thus leaving the way open for the provision of Jordan Purcell, then chancellor of Limerick, to the united dioceses of Cork and Cloyne (*CPL*, viii, 109). In 1490 Thomas Hartepyry, bp of Cloyne, otherwise unknown, appears as a suffragan in Hereford (Stubbs).

CONNOR[1]
(ARMAGH P.)

BISHOPS	ACCESSION	DEATH unless otherwise stated
Flann Ua Sculu	—	1117
Máel Máedóc Ua Morgair (Malachias; St Malachy)	1124	res. 1136, d. 2 Nov. 1148
Máel Pátraic Ua Bánáin	a. Mar. 1152	res. a. 1172, d. 1174
Nehemias	a. 1172	a. 1178
Reginaldus	c. 1178	p. 19 Apr. 1225
Eustacius	el. a. 5 May, temp. 5 May 1226	a. Oct. 1241
Adam, O.Cist.	el. a. 27 Jan., temp. 27 Jan., cons. Sept. 1242	7 Nov. 1244
Isaac of Newcastle	el. a. 4 Apr., temp. 8 May 1245	c. 6 Oct. 1256
William of Portroyal, O.S.B.	prov. 27 Oct. 1257, temp 7 Jan. 1258	a. 16 July 1260
William de la Hay	el. 10 Oct. 1260, cons. and temp. p. 21 Mar. 1261 (suffr. in Lincoln 1262)	a. 25 Dec. 1262
Robert of Flanders	el. 3 Feb. 1263, temp. p. Feb. 1263	25 Nov. 1274
Petrus de Dunach'	el. a. 2 Mar. 1275	a. Jan. 1292
Johannes	el. a. 23 Jan. 1292, temp. 27 Apr. 1293	c. 1319
Richard	el. c. 1320	—
James of Couplith[2]	el. a. 26 July 1321 (did not get possession)	—
John of Eglecliff, O.P.	trs. from Glasgow a. 5 Mar. 1323 (did not get possession)	trs. to Llandaff 20 June 1323
Robert Wirsop, O.E.S.A.	trs. from Ardagh 20 June 1323	a. May 1324
Jacobus Ó Cethernaig (O'Kearney)	trs. from Annaghdown 7 × 15 May, temp. 22 Dec. 1324	1351
William Mercier	prov. 8 July, cons. p. 12 Aug., temp. 2 Nov. 1353	1374
Paulus	prov. 11 Dec. 1374, temp. 10 May 1376, lib. 4 July 1377	1389
Johannes	el. a. 29 Mar. 1389, temp. 23 July 1389, prov. 9 Nov. 1389	c. 1416
Seaán Ó Luachráin	prov. 22 May 1420	a. Feb. 1421
Eóghan Ó Domhnaill ('Machivenan') (Eugenius)	prov. 5 May 1421, cons. p. June 1422	trs. to Derry 9 Dec. 1429
Domhnall Ó Mearaich	trs. from Derry 9 Dec. 1429	a. 28 Jan. 1431

[1] The diocese of Connor was established as a separate diocese at the synod of Ráith Bressail; but it seems to have been vacant c. 1117–24. From c. 1124–37 it was united with Down under St Malachy (Máel Máedóc). Máel Pátraic Ua Bánáin may have succeeded immediately aft. St Malachy's resignation as bp of Connor in 1137.
[2] The diocese had been recently disturbed by Edward Bruce's invasion.

BISHOPS	ACCESSION	DEATH *unless otherwise stated*
John Fossade[1] (Festade)	prov. 28 Jan., cons. *p.* 2 June 1431	—
Patricius	prov. *a.* 1459	*a.* 1459
Simon Elvington, O.P.	prov. 12 Feb. 1459 (suffr. in Salisbury and Exeter 1459–81)	1481

(For bps of united sees of Down and Connor, see below)

CORK
(CASHEL P.)

?Ua Menngoráin	—	1147
Gilla Áeda Ua Maigín, r.c. (Gregorius)	*a.* 1148	1172
Gregorius Ua h-Aeda	*fl.* 1173 × 1177	1182
Reginaldus I	*c.* 1182	1187
Aicher	*c.* 1187	1188
Murchad Ua h-Áeda	*a.* 1192	1206
Mairín Ua Briain, O.S.A. (Marianus)	*a.* 1208	trs. to Cashel 20 June 1224
Gilbertus	el. *a.* 5 June 1225	*p.* 1237
Laurentius	el. *a.* 5 May 1248	*a.* 27 Mar. 1265
William of Jerpoint, O.Cist.	el. *p.* 27 Mar. 1265, temp. 28 Nov. 1266	*a.* 8 July 1267
Reginaldus II	el. *a.* 5 Aug. 1267	16 Dec. 1276
Robert Mac Donnchada, O.Cist.	el. *a.* 8 May, temp. 11 June, lib. 13 Oct. 1277	6 Mar. 1302
Seoán Mac Cerbaill (John Mac Carwill)	el. 30 Apr., temp. 12 June, lib. 20 July 1302	trs. to Meath 20 Feb. 1321,
Philip of Slane, O.P.[2]	prov. 20 Feb., temp. 16 July 1321	*a.* Mar. 1327
Walter le Rede	prov. 20 Mar., cons. *a.* 12 July 1327, temp. 18 Oct. 1327	trs. to Cashel 20 Oct. 1329
John of Ballyconingham	trs. from Down *a.* Jan 1329, temp. 30 May 1330	29 May 1347
John Roche	el. *a.* Dec., cons. Dec. 1347	4 July 1358

[1] Plans for the permanent union of the two dioceses of Down and Connor were submitted to Henry VI for his sanction, which was given on 29 July 1438. Twelve months later (29 July 1439) Eugenius IV issued his bull uniting the two dioceses, the union to take effect on the resignation or death of either bp. Bp John Sely of Down was deprived of his bishopric by Eugenius IV at some date bef. Nov. 1442, most probably on the petition of Primate Prene, who wrote to that effect on 29 May 1441. John Fossade thus became bp of the united dioceses of Down and Connor in 1442. He died in 1450.

On 12 Feb. 1459 Pius II provided Simon Elvington, an English Dominican friar, to the see of Connor; and mention is made in his bull of provision (*CPL*, xii, 12) of an earlier provision to Patrick, who is said to have died bef. his letters of provision were drawn up. Nothing further is known of Patrick. Simon Elvington went to England, where he was vicar of Gillingham (1463–75), and suffragan of Sarum (1459–81).

[2] On 30 July 1326 John XXII, on the petition of Edward II, issued a bull for the union of the two dioceses of Cork and Cloyne, the union to take effect on the death of the bp of either see. The union should have taken effect on the death of Philip in 1327, but nothing was done. The bull of John XXII was exemplified, on the petition of Richard Wye, bp of Cloyne, on 10 Sept. 1376 (Theiner, 257–58); but the union of the dioceses was not effected until 1429; *see under* Cloyne.

BISHOPS	ACCESSION	DEATH *unless otherwise stated*
Gerald de Barri	prov. *a.* 14 Feb. 1359, cons. irregularly soon after, temp. 2 Feb 1360, prov. (again) 8 Nov. 1362, conf. 1 Feb. 1365	4 Jan. 1393
Roger Ellesmere	prov. 3 Dec. 1395, temp. 31 Mar. 1396	*a.* 14 Feb. 1406
Richard Kynmoure	prov. *a.* 6 Oct. 1406	*a.* June 1409
Milo fitzJohn	prov. (by Gregory XII) July 1409, prov. (by Martin V) 11 Jan. 1418	mid-June 1431
Patrick Fox	prov. by Alexander V 14 Oct. 1409, conf. by John XXIII 25 May 1410	trs. to Ossory 15 Dec. 1417
John Paston, O.S.B., prior of Brownholm	prov. 23 May 1425 (did not get possession)	*p.* 1459 (in Utrecht)

CORK AND CLOYNE
(CASHEL P.)

Jordan Purcell	prov. 15 June 1429, conf. 6 Jan., temp. 25 Sept. 1432	res. *p.* 18 Apr. 1469
Gerald FitzGerald[1]	prov. *a.* 3 Feb. 1462	d. *c.* 1477
William Roche	prov. 26 Oct. 1472	res. *a.* Apr. 1490
Tadhg Mac Carthaigh (Thaddaeus)[2]	prov. 21 Apr. 1490	24 Oct. 1492
Patrick Cant, O.Cist., abbot of Fermoy	prov. 15 Feb. 1499 (annulled 26 June 1499)	—
John fitzEdmund FitzGerald	prov. 26 June 1499	*a.* 27 Aug. 1520
John Benet	prov. 28 Jan. 1523	1536

DERRY[3]
(ARMAGH P.)

?Máel Coluim Ua Brolcháin[4]	cons. 13 Sept. 1107	1122
?Máel Brigte Ua Brolcháin[4]	—	29 Jan. 1139
?Ua Gormgaile	—	1149
Muiredach Ua Cobthaig (Mauricius)	*a.* Mar. 1152	10 Feb. 1173
Amlaím Ua Muirethaig[4]	—	1185

[1] The provision of Gerald FitzGerald in opposition to the claim of William Roche, who had been granted right of succession in 1461, seems to have been followed by a period of 35 years during which there were two rival bps of the united dioceses. The rivalry was ended in 1499 by the resignation of Gerald FitzGerald in favour of John fitzEdmund FitzGerald, who seems to have been accepted as bp of both dioceses; *see* the documents printed by Brady, ii, 80–84.

[2] He had been provided in error to the see of Ross in 1482. (*See under* Ross.)

[3] Derry was not chosen at the synod of Ráith Bressail as the seat of the diocese which later became the diocese of Derry, but which is commonly called the diocese of Cinél nEógain by the Irish annalists of the twelfth century. The seat was fixed first at Ardstraw, then at Ráith Lúraig (Maghera); it was finally transferred from Ráith Lúraig to Derry in 1254.

[4] These three bps are called bps of Armagh (*Ard Macha*) in the Annals of Ulster, but they were almost certainly bps of Ardstraw (*Ard Sratha*). Amlaím Ua Muirethaig was certainly bp of Cinél nEógain.

BISHOPS	ACCESSION	DEATH *unless otherwise stated*	
Fogartach Ua Cerballáin I (Florentius)	1185	1230	
Gilla in Choimded Ó Cerballáin, O.P. (Germanus)	el. *c.* 1230	1279	
Fogartach Ó Cerballáin II (Florentius)	el. *c.* 1280	*a.* 24 July 1293	
[Michael	el. *a.* 10 Oct. 1293, temp. 8 Feb. 1294 (never cons.)	—	]
Énrí Mac Airechtaig ('O'Reghly'), O.Cist. (Henry of Ardagh)[1]	el. *a.* 12 Aug. 1294, (again) *a.* Mar., temp. 16 June 1295	1297	
Gofraid Mac Lochlainn	el. *a.* 26 June, temp. *p.* 26 June 1297	*c.* 1315	
Áed Ó Néill (Odo)	el. 1316	June 1319	
Michael Mac Lochlainn, O.F.M. (Mauricius)	el. *p.* 19 Aug. 1319	*a.* 18 Dec. 1349	
Simon, O.P.	prov. 18 Dec. 1349	*p.* 1380	
Johannes	—	*a.* July 1391	
John Dongan, O.S.B.	prov. *a.* 11 July 1391 (suffr. in London 1392)	trs. to Down 16 Sept. 1394	
Seoán Ó Mocháin[2]	prov. 16 Sept. 1394 (did not take effect)	—	
Aodh (Hugo)	prov. *a.* 25 Feb. 1398	? res. *a.* Aug. 1401	
Seoán Ó Flannabhra, O.Cist.	prov. 19 Aug. 1401	*a.* Feb. 1415	
Domhnall Mac Cathmhaoil	prov. 20 Feb. 1415 (never cons.)	*a.* Oct. 1419	
Domhnall Ó Mearaich	prov. 16 Oct. 1419	trs. to Connor 9 Dec. 1429	
Eoghan Ó Domhnaill (Eugenius)	trs. from Connor 9 Dec. 1429	*a.* Sept. 1433	
Johannes 'Oguguin' alias 'Ogubun'	prov. 18 Sept., cons. *p.* 17 Oct. 1433	*a.* May 1458	
Bartholomaeus Ó Flannagáin, O.Cist.	prov. 27 May 1458	res. 1463	
Johannes	*c.* 1464	*a.* Apr. 1466	
Nicholas Weston	prov. 21 Feb. 1467	Dec. 1484	
Domhnall Ó Fallamhain, O.F.M.	prov. 16 May 1485, cons. *p.* July 1487	5 July 1501	
Séamus mac Pilip Mac Mathghamhna	trs. from Clogher 26 Nov. 1503	1519	
Ruaidhri Ó Domhnaill	prov. 11 Jan. 1520	8 Oct. 1550 or 1551	

[1] On the death of Florentius the chapter of Derry elected their treasurer, who secured the royal assent; but was passed over by the Primate *in casu negligentie*, and Henry was appointed in 1294.

[2] He is said to have been a priest of Achonry, and nothing is known of him apart from this provision. Hugo undertook in 1398 to pay his own and his predecessor's debts, but he had either died or resigned bef. Aug. 1401.

DOWN[1]
(ARMAGH P.)

BISHOPS	ACCESSION	DEATH *unless otherwise stated*
Máel Muire	—	1117
Óengus Ua Gormáin, abb.	—	1123
Máel Máedóc Ua Morgair,[2] abb. (Malachias I; St Malachy)	1124	2 Nov. 1148
Máel Ísu mac in Chléirig Chuirr (Malachias II)	*a.* Mar. 1152	1175
Gilla Domangairt Mac Cormaic (Gilla Domnaig Mac Carmaic), r.c.	1175	1175
Amláin, abb.	1175	1175
Echmílid (?mac Máel Martain) (Malachias III)	*c.* 1176	res. *a.* 1202, d. 1204
Radulfus, O.Cist.	*c.* 1202	—
Thomas	*a.* 1224	1242
Randulphus	*a.* May 1251	*a.* Nov. 1257
Reginaldus[3]	el. *a.* Apr., temp. and cons. *p.* Oct. 1258	trs. to Cloyne 13 Apr. 1265
Thomas Lydel[3]	el. *a.* Apr. 1258, (again) 1265, cons. *p.* 5 July 1265, temp. 5 Nov. 1266 (suffr. in Lincoln 1270)	*a.* Feb. 1277
Nicholas le Blund, O.S.B.	el. *a.* 19 Mar., temp. *p.* 29 Mar. 1277	*a.* 28 Mar. 1305
Thomas Ketel	el. *a.* 18 Aug., temp. *p.* 18 Aug. 1305	*c.* 20 Mar. 1314
Thomas Bright, O.S.B.	el. *p.* 20 Mar. 1314	1327
John of Baliconingham[4]	el. *a.* Aug., temp. 4 Aug. 1328	trs. to Cork *a.* Jan. 1329
Ralph of Kilmessan, O.F.M.[4]	prov. 12 Dec. 1328, temp. 1 Apr. 1329	Aug. 1353
Richard Calf I, O.S.B.[5]	prov. 4 Dec., cons. *a.* 23 Dec. 1353, temp. 6 Mar. 1354	16 Oct. 1365
Robert of Aketon, O.E.S.A.	el. 18 Nov. 1365 (did not get possession)	res. *a.* Feb. 1366, prov. to Kildare 2 May 1366

[1] The diocese of Down is often called the diocese of Uladh in the Irish annals. From *c.* 1224–37 it was united with the diocese of Connor under St Malachy.

[2] St Malachy was abp of Armagh 1132–37, but may have retained the adm. of Down and Connor during those years. In 1137 he resigned from Armagh and became bp of Down (without Connor).

[3] This disputed election was ended by Clement IV on 19 May 1265.

[4] On 5 Jan. 1330 John XXII granted faculties for these two bps once more to exchange their sees, Ralph going to Cork and John to Down; but nothing came of this proposal (Theiner, 250; not in *CPL*).

[5] On 29 Jan. 1353, within the lifetime of Bp Ralph, Gregory, provost of Killala, secured a provision to the see of Down and was consecrated at Avignon; but this provision was annulled on 31 May 1354, and Gregory was restored to his provostship (*CPL*, iii, 482, 540).

BISHOPS	ACCESSION	DEATH
		unless otherwise stated
William White, O.S.A.	prov. *a.* Dec., temp. 30 June 1367	*c.* 10 Aug. 1368
Richard Calf II, O.S.B.	prov. 19 Feb., temp. 28 Apr. 1369	16 May 1386
John Ross, O.S.B.	prov. *a.* 8 Nov. 1386, temp. 14 Mar. 1388	*a.* Sept. 1394
John Dongan, O.S.B.	trs. from Derry 16 Sept. 1394, temp. 26 July 1395	res. *a.* 28 July 1413
John Sely, O.S.B.[1]	prov. 28 July 1413	depr. *a.* Nov. 1442, d. *a.* 26 Apr. 1445
Ralph Alderle, O.S.A.	prov. 26 Apr. 1445 (did not get possession)	—
Thomas Pollard, O.Carth.	prov. 21 June, cons. 27 Aug. 1447	*a.* June 1451
Richard Wolsey, O.P.	prov. 21 June 1451 (suffr. in Lichfield 1452; Worcester 1465–79, Hereford 1479)	res. *a.* Aug. 1453, d. *p.* 1479

DOWN AND CONNOR
(ARMAGH P.)

Thomas Knight, O.S.B.	prov. 24 Aug. 1453, cons. 31 May 1456 (suffr in London 1459–63)	*a.* July 1469
Tadhg Ó Muirgheasa, O.S.A. (Thaddaeus)	prov. 10 July, cons. 10 Sept. 1469	*p.* July 1480
Tiberio Ugolino	prov. 14 Feb. 1483, (again) 12 Sept. 1484, (again) 1 Sept. 1485, cons. 12 Mar. 1489	*a.* Apr. 1519
Robert Blyth, O.S.B.[2]	prov. 16 Apr. 1520	(depr. by Paul III in 1539) (suffr. in Ely 1539–41), d. *p.* 19 Oct. 1547

DROMORE[3]
(ARMAGH P.)

Ua Ruanada	*a.* 1197	—
Geraldus, O.Cist.	*a.* 15 Apr. 1227	—
Andreas	el. *a.* Oct. 1245	—
Tigernach I	el. *c.* 1284	1309

[1] On 29 July 1439 Eugenius IV issued his bull providing for the union of Down and Connor on the death or resignation of either bp. The deprivation of John Sely, which had taken effect bef. Nov. 1442, ought thus to have been the occasion of a permanent union; but there was strong local opposition, and Primate Prene's register shows that he also was for a time opposed to the union. Thomas Knight seems to have been the first bp who had effective control of the two dioceses; but he was dispensed to hold an English benefice *in commendam* owing to the poverty of the two dioceses (*CPL*, xii, 192–3).

[2] Blyth was almost continuously an absentee bp, and retained his position as abbot of Thorney until he surrendered it in 1540.

[3] The diocese of Dromore was not established until the last years of the twelfth century. No bp of Dromore took the oath of fealty to Henry II in 1172. The diocese corresponds with the territory of Iveagh (Ui Echach) in Co. Down. The obit of Riagan, bp of Dromore (*epscop Dromamoir*), occurs in the Annals of Ulster, *a.* 1101; but Riagan was probably a monastic bp, and had died bef. the establishment of an Irish diocesan hierarchy.

BISHOPS	ACCESSION	DEATH *unless otherwise stated*
Gervasius	1290	—
Tigernach II	—	1309
Florentius Mac Donnocáin	el. *c.* 1309, temp. *c.* 1309	—
Anonymous	5 Feb. 1351 (papal mandate to bp of Dromore)	—
Milo	20 Oct. 1366 (mandate of primate to Milo)	—
Christophorus	28 Aug. 1369 (mandate of primate)	—
Cornelius	(no date of provision)	*a.* Nov. 1382
John, O.F.M.	prov. 14 June × 15 July, temp. 10 Nov. 1382	—
Thomas Orwell, O.F.M.	trs. from Killala *a.* Nov. 1398 (suffr. in Ely and Norwich 1389–1406)	*p.* 1406
John Waltham, O.S.A.	trs. from Ossory 14 May 1400	trs. (again) to Ossory 11 Oct. 1402
Roger Appleby, O.S.A.[1]	trs. from Ossory 11 Oct. 1402	trs. to Waterford *a.* Oct. 1407
Richard Payl, O.P.	prov. 30 Dec. 1407, cons. *a.* 11 Nov. 1408	trs. to Sodor 30 May 1410
John Chourles, O.S.B.	prov. 16 July 1410, cons. *a.* 4 Jan. 1411 (suffr. in Canter- bury 1420–33, London 1419– 26, Rochester 1423)	12 June 1433
Marcus[2]	prov. (?) *p.* 1410	*a.* Jan. 1429
Seaán Ó Ruanadha	*fl.* 1414	—
Nicholas Wartre, O.F.M.[3]	prov. 17 Mar. 1419 (suffr. in York 1420–45)	*p.* 1445
Thomas Rackelf, O.E.S.A.[3]	prov. 31 Jan. 1429, cons. 21 Dec. 1433 (suffr. in Durham 1441–46)	1453
William	—	*a.* June 1431
David Chirbury, O.Carm.[3]	prov. 22 June 1431 (suffr. in St David's 1437)	*p.* 1451
Thomas Scrope, O.Carm. (Bradley)	prov. ?1434 (suffr. in Norwich 1450–77, Canterbury 1469)	res. *a.* 1440, d. 15 Jan. 1492
Thomas Radcliff	cons. 1 Feb. 1450	res. 1454/5 (suffr. in Durham until 1487)
Donatus Ó h-Anluain[4] (Ohendua)	prov. *c.* 1454/5, cons. *p.* 17 Apr. 1456	—

[1] From Primate Fleming's register it is plain that Roger Appleby was an absentee bp, 1402–07.

[2] There is an entry in Fleming's register, f.34, according to which the primate gave authority to Marcus, 'a bp sojourning in the diocese of Dromore', to correct certain offenders. On 31 Jan. 1429 Martin V provided Thomas Radcliff to the see of Dromore, void by the death of Marcus: *see* Costello, *De Annatis Hiberniae*, p. 299.

[3] From 1420 to 1450 Dromore was nominally ruled by absentee bps, of whom in the years 1431–33 no less than four were simultaneously using the title of bp of Dromore whilst acting as suffragans in various English dioceses.

[4] Donatus is mentioned in the bull of provision for Yvo Guillen in Apr. 1480; but it is not known when he died.

BISHOPS	ACCESSION	DEATH *unless otherwise stated*
Richard Messing, O.Carm.	prov. 29 July 1457 (suffr. in York 1458–62)	*a.* June 1463
William Egremond, O.E.S.A.	prov. 15 June 1463 (suffr. in York 1463–1501)	*p.* 1501
Aonghus (Aeneas)[1]	(no date of provision)	*a.* Aug. 1476
Robert Kirke,[1] O.Cist.	prov. 28 Aug. 1476	*a.* Apr. 1480
Yvo Guillen	prov. 14 Apr. 1480	*a.* Apr. 1483
George Braua[2]	prov. 18 Apr., cons. 3 May 1483 (suffr. in St Andrews 1484–5, Worcester and London 1497)	trs. to Elphin 15 Apr. 1499
Tadhg Ó Raghallaigh, O.E.S.A. (Thaddaeus)[3]	prov. 30 Apr. 1511 (suffr. in London 1511)	*a.* June 1526

DUBLIN[4]
(DUBLIN P.)

	ACCESSION	DEATH
Dúnán (Donatus)	*c.* 1028	6 May 1074
Gilla Pátraic, O.S.B. (Patricius)	cons. 1074	10 Oct. 1084
Donngus, O.S.B. (Donatus)	cons. *p.* Aug. 1085	22 Nov. 1095
Samuel Ua hAingliu, ?O.S.B.	cons. 27 Apr. 1096	*a.* Sept. 1121

ARCHBISHOPS	ACCESSION	DEATH *unless otherwise stated*
Gréne (Gregorius)	cons. 2. Oct. 1121, abp. Mar. 1152	8 Oct. 1161
Lorcán Ua Tuathail (Laurentius), abb.	cons. 1162	14 Nov. 1180
John Cumin	el. 6 Sept., temp. 6 Sept. 1181, cons. 21 Mar. 1182	*c.* Nov. 1212
Henry of London	el. *a.* Mar., temp. *a.* Mar, cons. *c.* Aug. 1213	*a.* Nov. 1228
Luke	el. *a.* 13 Dec. 1228, temp. 22 Jan, prov. *a.* 11 Oct. 1229, cons. *p.* May 1230	12 Dec. 1255
Fulk de Sanford	prov. 26 July, temp. *c.* Oct. 1256, cons. *a.* 25 Mar. 1257	4 May 1271
John de Derlington, O.P.	prov. 28 Jan., temp. 27 Apr., cons. 27 Aug. 1279	29 Mar. 1284
John de Sanford	el. *a.* 20 July 1284, conf. 30 May, temp. 6 Aug. 1285, cons. 7 Apr. 1286	2 Oct. 1294

[1] These two names occur in the bull of Apr. 1480, and *Robertus Herlic* is cited by Eubel from the *Obligationes: CPL*, xiii, 83.

[2] George Braua was a Greek by birth, but he seems to have been normally resident in Ireland after his provision to Dromore.

[3] On 23 Dec. 1519, Leo X provided Thaddaeus to the see of Ross in the province of Cashel, to be held simultaneously with the diocese of Dromore owing to the poverty of the two sees.

[4] Dublin was organized as a suffragan diocese of Canterbury in the early eleventh century. The establishment of the diocese of Glendalough at the synod of Ráith Bressail in 1111 evidently envisaged the eventual incorporation of Dublin under the primacy of Armagh. Bp Gregorius of Dublin received the pall as one of the four abps of Ireland at the final session of the synod of Kells (Mar. 1152).

ARCHBISHOPS	ACCESSION	DEATH *unless otherwise stated*
Thomas de Chadworth	el. *a.* 28 Apr. 1295 (never cons.), el. (again) 14 Feb. 1299	—
William Hotham, O.P.	prov. 24 Apr., temp. 23 Nov. 1296, lib. 2 Feb. 1297, cons. *c.* Nov. 1297	27 Aug. 1298
Richard de Ferings	prov. *c.* June, cons. *a.* 1 July 1299, temp. 1 June 1300	17 Oct. 1306
Richard de Haverings	el. *a.* 30 Mar., prov. 10 July, temp. 13 Sept. 1307 (never cons.)	res. 21 Nov. 1310
John de Leche	prov. 16 May, cons. *a.* 18 May, temp. 20 July 1311	10 Aug. 1313
Alexander de Bicknor	prov. 20 Aug., cons. 25 Aug., temp. 9 Sept. 1317	14 July 1349
John of St Paul	prov. 4 Sept. 1349, temp. 16 Dec. 1349, cons. 14 Feb. 1350	9 Sept. 1362
Thomas Minot	prov. 20 Mar., cons. 16 Apr., temp. 21 Sept. 1363	10 July 1375
Robert Wikeford	prov. 12 Oct. 1375, temp. 30 Jan. 1376	29 Aug. 1390
Robert Waldeby, O.E.S.A.	trs. from Aire (Gascony) 14 Nov. 1390, temp. 27 July 1391	trs. to Chichester 25 Oct. 1395, to York 5 Oct. 1396
Richard Northalis, O.Carm.	trs. from Ossory 1395, temp. 4 Feb. 1396	20 July 1397
Thomas Cranley	prov. *a.* 26 Sept., cons. *p.* 26 Sept., temp. 21 Dec. 1397	25 May 1417
Richard Talbot, abp-el. of Armagh	el. *p.* May, prov. 20 Dec. 1417, cons. *a.* Aug. 1418	15 Aug. 1449
Michael Tregury	prov. *a.* 24 Oct. 1449, temp. 10 Feb. 1450	21 Dec. 1471
John Walton, O.S.A.	prov. 4 May, cons. *a.* 27 Aug. 1472, temp. 15 Aug. 1474, temp. (again) 20 May 1477	res. 14 June 1484
Walter FitzSimons	prov. 14 June, cons. 26 Sept. 1484	14 May 1511
William Rokeby	trs. from Meath 28 Jan., temp. 22 June 1512	29 Nov. 1521
Hugh Inge, O.P.	trs. from Meath 27 Feb. 1523	3 Aug. 1528
John Alan	prov. 3 Sept. 1529, cons. 13 Mar. 1530	28 July 1534

DULEEK[1]
(ARMAGH P.)

BISHOPS	ACCESSION	DEATH *unless otherwise stated*
Gilla Mo Chua mac Camchuarta	—	1117
[Áed[2]	—	1160]

[1] Duleek was one of the two dioceses into which Meath was divided at the synod of Ráith Bressail; but this division was altered within the same year (1111) at the synod of Uisneach. Duleek was still recognized as a separate diocese at the synod of Kells; but it disappears from view aft. that date.

[2] Áed, whose death is recorded by the Four Masters in 1160, is not specifically styled bp in his obit.

ELPHIN[1]
(TUAM P.)

BISHOPS	ACCESSION	DEATH *unless otherwise stated*
Domnall mac Flannacáin Ua Dubthaig, bp of Clonmacnois	?1111	17 Mar. 1136
Flannacán Ua Dubthaig	—	res. *a.* 1152, d. 1168
Máel Ísu Ua Connachtáin	*a.* Mar. 1152	1174
Tommaltach mac Áeda Ua Conchobair (Thomas)	—	trs. to Armagh *a.* Feb. 1180
Floirint Ua Riacáin Uí Máelruanaid, O.Cist.	*c.* 1180	1195
Ardgar Ua Conchobair	*a.* 14 Feb. 1206	1215
Dionysius Ó Mórda	*fl.* 1217 × 1221	res. 1229, d. 15 Dec. 1231
Alanus	*c.* 1230 (probably did not get possession)	—
Donnchad mac Fíngein Ó Conchobhair (Dionysius Donatus)	cons. 1231	24 Apr. 1244
Eóin Ó Mugróin	el. *p.* 12 June 1244, prov. 2 July, temp. *p.* 4 Sept., cons. 1245	1246
Tomaltach mac Toirrdelbaig Ó Conchobhair (Thomas)	el. *a.* 21 Aug. 1246, cons. 21 Jan. 1247	trs. to Tuam 23 Mar. 1259
	(A disputed election followed)	
Máel Sechlainn mac Taidg Ó Conchobair (Milo)	el. *a.* 30 Jan., temp. 8 Nov., cons. *c.* Nov. 1260	9 Jan. 1262
Tomás mac Fergail Mac Diarmata, O.Cist.	el. *a.* 26 Jan. 1260, temp. 10 May 1262	1265
Muiris mac Néill Ó Conchobhair, O.P. (Mauricius)	el. *p.* 27 Feb., temp. *p.* 23 Apr. 1266	*c.* 5 Dec. 1284
Amlaím Ó Tommaltaig	el. and conf. 1285 (never cons.)	1285
Gilla Ísu mac in Liathánaig Ó Conchobair, O.Praem. (Gelasius)	el. 10 Aug., temp. *p.* 5 Mar. 1285	*a.* Sept. 1296
Máel Sechlainn Mac Briain, O.Cist. (Malachias)	el. *a.* 2 Nov. 1296, temp. 7 Sept. 1297	*a.* Mar. 1303
Marianus Ó Donnabair, O.P.	el. Sept./Oct. 1296	1297
Donnchad Ó Flannacáin, O.Cist. (Donatus)	el. *a.* 28 June, temp. *p.* 28 June 1303	22 June 1307

[1] For the dioceses of Elphin and Tuam bef. the synod of Kells, *see* note under Tuam.

BISHOPS	ACCESSION	DEATH
		unless otherwise stated
Cathal Ó Conchobair, O.Praem. (Carolus)	el. *p.* 2 Sept., cons. *c.* Oct. 1307, temp. 12 Mar. 1309	res. 1310, d. 1343
Máel Sechlainn Mac Áeda (Malachias)	el. *p.* 2 Sept. 1307, prov. 22 June, cons. 22 June, temp. 7 Dec. 1310	trs. to Tuam 19 Dec. 1312
Lúirint Ó Lachtnáin, canon of Elphin (Laurentius)	prov. 21 Jan., cons. *p.* 19 Feb. 1313, temp. 22 Sept. 1314	1326
Seoán Ó Fínnachta	el. and cons. 1326, temp. *p.* 31 Dec. 1326	1354
Carolus	el. *c.* 1355	depr. 1357
Gregorius Ó Mocháin	prov. 27 Feb. 1357, temp. 26 June 1357	trs. to Tuam 1372
Thomas Barrett	prov. 16 June, temp. 24 Nov. 1372, depr. by Clement VII 17 Jan. 1383 (without effect)	1404
Seoán Ó Mocháin	prov. by Clement VII 17 Jan. × 19 Feb. 1383	?trs. to Derry 16 Sept. 1394
Seaán Ó Gráda	prov. *a.* 12 Oct. 1407	1417
Gerald Caneton	trs. from Cloyne *c.* 1405 (did not take effect)	—
Thomas Colby, O.Carm.	prov. by John XXIII 18 Mar. 1412 (did not take effect)	trs. to Waterford and Lismore Feb. 1414
Robert Fosten, O.F.M.	prov. 18 Feb. 1418 (suffr. Durham 1426)	*p.* 1430
Edmund Barrett	prov. 1421	1421
Johannes	—	depr. *a.* 26 Jan. 1429, d. *a.* Mar. 1434
Laurentius Ó Beólláin	prov. 26 Jan. 1429	*a.* Dec. 1429
Uilliam Ó hÉidigheáin	prov. 2 Dec. 1429	trs. to Emly 20 Oct. 1449
Conchobhar Ó Maolalaidh, O.F.M. (Cornelius)	trs. from Emly 20 Oct. 1449	1468
Nicol Ó Flannagáin, O.P.	prov. 7 June 1458, (again) 10 July 1469	res. Sept. 1494
'Hugo Arward' (?Aodh Mac an Bhaird)	prov. 24 Jan. 1487	?1495
Riocard Mac Briain Ó gCuanach, O.P.	prov. 22 June 1492	*p.* 1501
Cornelius Ó Flannagáin	*a.* 1501	—
Georgius de Brana, bp of Dromore	trs. from Dromore 15 Apr. 1499	18 Aug. × 27 Dec. 1529
Christopher Fisher	prov. 12 Dec. 1508	—
John Maxey, O.Praem.	prov. 7 Apr. 1525 (suffr. in York 1525)	15 Aug. 1536

EMLY
(CASHEL P.)

Diarmait Ua Flainn Chua	—	1114
Gilla in Choimded Ua hArdmaíl (Deicola)	*a.* Mar. 1152	—

BISHOPS	ACCESSION	DEATH *unless otherwise stated*
Máel Ísu Ua Laigenáin, O.Cist.	—	1163
Ua Meic Stia	*a.* 1172	1173
Ragnall Ua Flainn Chua	—	1197
M.[1]	*a.* 1205	*a.* 1209
William	el. *c.* 1209 (never cons.)	depr. Jan. 1210
Henry, O.Cist.	el. 1212	*a.* 13 July 1227
John Collingham	el. *a.* 13 July, conf. (by Gregory IX) 1228, cons. *a.* 25 June 1228, temp. *p.* 25 June 1230	*a.* 14 June 1236
Daniel	el. *a.* Apr., temp. *p.* 8 Apr. 1238 (did not get possession)	—
Christianus	el. *a.* 18 Oct. 1238	*a.* 12 Dec. 1249
Gilbertus	el. *a.* Oct, temp. 12 Oct. 1251	9 Oct. 1265
[Laurentius 'of Dunlak'	el. *a.* 30 Mar. 1266 (never cons.)	—]
Florentius Ó hAirt	el. and conf. *a.* 17 Apr., temp. *p.* 17 Apr. 1266	18 Jan. 1272
Matthew MacGormáin	el. *p.* 3 Apr., temp. 18 June, lib. 2 Aug. 1272	24 Mar. 1275
David Ó Cossaig, O.Cist.	el. *a.* 24 June, temp. 2 Aug., lib. 14 Sept. 1275	11 June 1281
William de Clifford	prov. 1 Oct. 1286	*a.* 10 Aug. 1306
Thomas Cantock (Quantok)	el. *a.* 3 Sept., temp. 3 Sept. 1306	4 Feb. 1309
William Roughead	el. *a.* May, temp. 14 May 1309	15 June 1335
Richard le Walleys	el. *a.* 16 Aug., temp. 16 Aug. 1335	*a.* 15 Mar. 1356
John Esmond[2]	prov. 28 Feb., temp. 27 Apr. 1356	4 Apr. 1362
David Penlyn (Foynlyn)	prov. 4 July 1362, cons. *a.* June 1363	—
William	prov. 7 June 1363, temp. 11 Oct. 1363	*a.* Dec. 1405
Nicholas Ball	trs. from Ardfert 2 Dec. 1405	*a.* Apr. 1421
John Rishberry, O.E.S.A.	prov. 21 Apr. 1421 (bull not expedited)	—
Robert Windell, O.F.M.	prov. 14 Jan. 1423 (suffragan in Norwich 1424, Worcester 1433, Sarum 1435–41)	depr. 1425
Thomas de Burgo, O.S.A.	prov. 19 Dec. 1425, cons. *p.* 23 Feb. 1428	*a.* Sept. 1444
Robert Portland, O.F.M.	prov. 5 Mar. 1429 (did not take effect)	trs. to Tiberias 1444, suffr. in Winchester 1456
Cornelius Ó Cuinnlis, O.F.M.	prov. 11 Sept. 1444, cons. *a.* 16 Jan. 1445	trs. to Clonfert 30 Aug. 1448
Cornelius Ó Maolalaidh, O.F.M.	trs. from Clonfert 30 Aug. 1448	trs. to Elphin 20 Oct. 1449
William Ó hEidigheáin	trs. from Elphin 20 Oct. 1449	*p.* Feb. 1475

[1] 'Isaac O Hanmy' is mentioned in 1302 as an early 13th-century bp of Emly; he may be identical with M. if that initial stands for Máel Ísu.

[2] Esmond had been elected bp of Ferns and consecrated by the abp of Tuam in 1349; but did not get possession of Ferns owing to a prior papal reservation (*CPL*, iii, 462, 475).

BISHOPS	ACCESSION	DEATH *unless otherwise stated*
Pilib Ó Cathail	prov. 1 Dec. 1475, cons. *p.* 9 Jan. 1476	*a.* Nov. 1494
Donatus Mac Briain[1]	prov. 10 Nov. 1494	res. *a.* Apr. 1498, suffr. in Worcester 1500
Cinnéidigh Mac Briain (Carolus)	prov. 30 Apr. 1498	*a.* Oct. 1505
Tomás Ó hUrthaile	prov. 6 Oct. 1505, cons. *c.* 1507	1542

ENACHDUN *see* ANNADOWN

FERNS
(DUBLIN P.)

Ceallach Ua Colmáin	—	1117
?Máel Eoin Ua Dúnacaín[2]	—	1125
Ua Cattaín	—	1135
Ioseph Ua h-Áeda	*fl.* 1160 × 1161	1183
Ailbe Ua Máel Muaid (Albinus), O.Cist.	*c.* 1186 (suffr. in Winchester 1201, 1214)	1223
John of St John	el. *a.* 6 July 1223, cons. *a.* 2 Apr. 1224	*a.* Oct. 1253
Geoffrey of St John	el. *a.* Mar., temp. *p.* 16 Mar. 1254	*a.* May 1258
Hugh of Lamport	el. *a.* 11 July, temp. 27 Sept. 1258	15 May 1282
Richard of Northampton	el. 28 July, temp. 13 Oct. 1282, cons. 1283	13 Jan. 1304
Simon of Evesham	el. *p.* 12 Mar., cons. 22 June 1304	1 Sept. 1304
Robert Walrand	el. *p.* 14 Feb., cons. *p.* 13 Apr. 1305	17 Nov. 1311
Adam of Northampton	el. *a.* 14 Mar., temp. 14 Mar., cons. 18 June 1312	29 Oct. 1346
Hugh de Saltu (of Leixlip)	el. *a.* 10 Mar. 1347, cons. 8 Apr. 1347	depr. 1347
Geoffrey Grandfeld, O.E.S.A.	prov. 5 Mar., cons. June, temp. 15 Nov. 1347	22 Oct. 1348
John Esmond	el. and cons. 1349 (did not get possession)	depr. 1349, trs. to Emly 11 Jan. 1353
William Charnells, O.P.	prov. 19 Apr., cons. 19 Apr., temp. 15 Oct. 1350	July 1362
Thomas Dene	prov. *a.* 15 Apr., cons. 18 June, temp. 26 May 1363	27 Aug. 1400
Patrick Barret, O.S.A.	prov. 10 Dec., cons. Dec. 1400, temp. 11 Apr. 1401	10 Nov. 1415
Robert Whittey	prov. 16 Feb. 1418	res. 5 Oct. 1457, d. 1458
Tadhg O Beirn, O.S.B. (Thaddaeus)	prov. 8 Oct. 1451 (did not take effect)	—
John Purcell I	prov. 4 Oct. 1457	*a.* Oct. 1479
Laurence Nevill	prov. 26 Oct. 1479, temp. 20 May 1480	1503

[1]Lynch, ii, 64, inserts at this point three bps who are otherwise unknown, but cites no authentic record for any of them: Cathaldus O Murchu, from Leinster; Dermicius O Cahill; Edmund Pillin.

[2] He died at Leighlin and may have been bp of that see, but is called 'bp of Uí Chennselaig' in the Annals of the Four Masters.

BISHOPS	ACCESSION	DEATH
		unless otherwise stated
Edmund Comerford	cons. 1505	15 Apr. 1509
	cons. 20 Jan. 1510	trs. to Waterford and
Nicholas Comyn		Lismore Apr. 1519
John Purcell II, O.S.A.	prov. 13 Apr. 1519, cons. 6 May	20 July 1539
	1519	

GLENDALOUGH[1]
(DUBLIN P.)

Áed Ua Modáin	—	1126
Anonymous	*a.* 1140	—
Gilla na Náem	*a.* Mar. 1152	res. *c.* 1157, d. 7 Apr.
Laignech		1160/1
Cináed Ua Rónáin	*c.* 1157	1173
(Celestinus;		
Clemens)		
Máel Callann Ua	*a.* 1176	1186
Cléirchén (Malchus)		
Macrobius	—	*c.* 1192
William Piro	1192	*a.* 30 July 1212
Robert de Bedford[2]	el. *c.* 1213/14 (did not get possession)	el. bp of Lismore *a.* 13 Dec. 1218

The following provisions of titular bps were made in the late fifteenth and early sixteenth centuries. None of these 'bps of Glendalough' had effective possession of the see: but the formal record of Bp Denis White's resignation, of which there is a copy in Abp Alen's register, fo. 71v, states that he had obtained possession to some extent, though unjustly, and that he now resigns his claim to the bishopric 'for the relief of his conscience, the peace of the church of Dublin and the true dignity of the church of Glendalough'.

Michael	—	*a.* 22 Oct. 1481
Denis White, O.P.	prov. 22 Oct. 1481 (did not get possession)	res. 30 May 1497
John	—	*a.* 10 Nov. 1494
Ivo Ruffi, O.F.M.	prov. 10 Nov. 1494	*a.* 21 Aug. 1495
Francis FitzJohn of	prov. 21 Aug. 1500	—
Corduba, O.F.M.		

[1] Glendalough was one of the dioceses established at the synod of Ráith Bressail (1111). It was absorbed into the diocese of Dublin soon aft. William Piro's death; and the union of the two dioceses was confirmed by Innocent III 25 Feb. 1216, and again by Honorius III 6 Oct. 1216.

[2] There is no record of Robert's election, but on 25 Feb. 1216 Innocent III confirmed the sentence of Abp Felix of Tuam *contra magistrum Robertum de Bedeford*. It is thus probable that Robert made an effort to secure the bishopric of Glendalough aft. the death of William Piro in 1212. The presence of Brictius (Brycheus) in the list of bps of Glendalough *c.* 1214 seems to be due to an error in the Great Register of St Thomas, Dublin, fo. 10v, where a charter granted by Bp *Matheus* has been copied as a charter of *Brycheus*.

KELLS

KELLS *see under* Kilmore

KILDARE (Darensis)
(DUBLIN P.)

BISHOPS	ACCESSION	DEATH
		unless otherwise stated
Cormac Ua Cathassaig	—	1146
Ua Duibín	—	1148
Finn mac Máel Muire Mac Cianáin	*a.* Mar. 1152	—
Finn mac Gussáin Ua Gormáin, O.Cist.	—	1160
Malachias Ua Brain	*a.* 1161	1 Jan. 1175
Nehemias	*a.* Mar. 1177, *fl.* 1180 × 1190	—
Cornelius Mac Fáeláin (Mac Gelain)	1206	*a.* Mar. 1223
Ralph of Bristol	el. *a.* 12 Mar., temp. *p.* 12 Mar. 1223	24 Aug. 1232
John of Taunton	el. *a.* 6 Aug., temp. 11 Nov. 1233	*c.* 22 June 1258
Simon of Kilkenny	el. *a.* 21 Oct., temp. *p.* 21 Oct. 1258, lib. 5 Feb. 1259	20 Apr. 1272
Nicholas Cusack, O.F.M.	prov. 27 Nov. 1279, cons. 15 May × 7 Sept., temp. 24 Dec. 1280, lib. 19 Feb. 1281	5 Sept. 1299
Walter Calf (de Veel)	el. *a.* Jan, temp. 5 Jan. 1300	*c.* 29 Nov. 1332
Richard Houlot	el. *a.* May, prov. 24 May, cons. 18 Oct. 1333, temp. 5 Feb. 1334, lib. 26 Apr. 1334	24 June 1352
Thomas Giffard	el. *p.* June, prov. 21 Nov., cons. *a.* 31 Dec. 1352	25 Sept. 1365
Robert of Aketon (Acton), O.E.S.A.	el. 18 Nov. 1365, prov. 2 May 1366, temp. 23 Mar. 1367	res. *a.* Apr. 1404
John Madock	prov. 9 Apr. 1404	*a.* July 1431
William fitzEdward	prov. 20 July, prov. (again) 8 Aug. 1431	Apr. 1446
Geoffrey Hereford, O.P.[2]	prov. 23 Aug. 1447, cons. 20 Apr. 1449 (suffr. in Hereford 1449)	*a.* 1464
John Bole (Bull), O.S.A.	el. *c.* 1456/7 (never cons.)	prov. to Armagh 2 May 1457
Richard Lang	prov. (by Pius II) *a.* Aug. 1464 (letters never expedited), cons. *c.* 1464	depr. 28 July 1474 (suffr. in Chichester 1480, Winchester 1488)

[1] No diocese of Kells was established at the synod of Ráith Bressail (1111). The diocese is named on a list of Irish dioceses approved by Cardinal Paparo in 1152, although no bp of Kells signs the acts of the synod of Kells in Feb. 1152. It is likely that Kells was ruled together with Kilmore in the second half of the twelfth century. The diocese was incorporated into the diocese of Meath soon aft. 1211. Kells is one of five rural deaneries organized by Simon Rochfort in 1216; later Kells became one of the two archdeaconries of the diocese of Meath.

[2] Bp Geoffrey abandoned his diocese in 1452 (*CPL*, x, 245).

357

BISHOPS	ACCESSION	DEATH *unless otherwise stated*
David Conel	prov. 28 July 1474, cons. *p.* 6 Sept. 1474	*a.* 5 Apr. 1475
James Wall, O.F.M. (?Edmund)	prov. 5 Apr. 1475 (suffr. in London 1485–91)	28 Apr. 1494
William Barret (Barnett)	(suffr. in Winchester 1502–25, York 1530)	res. *a.* 1492
Edward Lane	—	*c.* 1513
Thomas Dillon, O.S.A.	prov. 24 Aug. 1526	*a.* July 1529
Walter Wellesley, O.S.A.	prov. 1 July 1529, temp. 23 Sept. 1531	*a.* 18 Oct. 1539

KILFENORA[1]
(CASHEL P.)

Anonymous	1172	—
F.	*a.* 1205	—
Johannes	*a..* 1224	—
Christianus	*fl.* 1251 × 1254	*a.* Dec. 1255
Anonymous	—	*a.* 28 Feb. 1264
Mauricius	el. *p.* 3 Mar. 1265, cons. *a.* 12 Feb., temp. 12 Feb. 1266	*a.* 14 July 1273
Florentius Ó Tigernaig, O.S.A.	el. *a.* 18 Sept., temp. 30 Nov. 1273	*a.* 12 July 1281
Congalach Ó Lochlainn (Carolus)	el. *a.* Sept., temp. 6 Sept. 1281	*a.* 21 Dec. 1298
Simon Ó Cuirrín	el. 16 May, conf. 22 July 1300	*a.* 26 Dec. 1302
Mauricius Ó Briain	el. 16 Mar. × 10 June, temp. 8 Oct. 1303	1319
Risdeárd Ó Lochlainn	cons. 17 Apr. 1323	3 Feb. 1359
Dionysius	—	*a.* Oct. 1372
Henricus	prov. 6 Oct. 1372	—
Cornelius	—	*c.* 1389
Patricius	el. *a.* Feb., prov. 28 Feb., cons. *p.* 19 Mar. 1390	*a.* Jan 1421
Feidhlimidh mac Mathghamhna Ó Lochlainn (Florentius)	prov. 15 Jan. 1421, cons. *p.* 6 Feb. 1421	*a.* Aug. 1433
Fearghal	prov. 7 Aug. 1433	*a.* Nov. 1434
Dionysius Ó Connmhaigh	prov. 17 Nov., cons. 26 Dec. 1434	res. 12 Dec. 1491
Muircheartach mac Murchadha Ó Briain (Mauricius)	prov. 12 Dec. 1491 (bulls expedited 26 Aug. 1492)	*a.* 21 Nov. 1541

[1] Kilfenora was not one of the churches chosen as a diocesan centre at the synod of Ráith Bressail; but it appears on the list of episcopal churches recognized by Cardinal Paparo at the synod of Kells. An unnamed bp took the oath of fealty to Henry II in 1172, but apart from bp 'A.' who occurs in a forged charter of the 15th century, the name of no bp is recorded bef. *c.* 1205. The diocese was always one of the smallest in the medieval Irish church.

KILLALA[1] (Aladensis)
(TUAM P.)

BISHOPS	ACCESSION	DEATH *unless otherwise stated*
Ua Máel Fogmair I	—	1137
Ua Máel Fogmair II	—	1151
Ua Máel Fogmair III	*a.* 1179	—
Domnall Ua Bécda (Donatus)	*a.* 29 Mar. 1199	1206
?Muiredach Ua Dubthaig	*fl.* 1208	—
Aengus Ó Máel Fogmair (Elias)	*a.* 1224	1234
Donatus	1235, *fl.* 7 Sept. 1244	—
Seoán Ó Laidig, O.P.	el. *p.* 22 June, cons. 7 Dec. 1253	res. *p.* 21 Feb. 1264, d. 1275
Seoán Ó Máel Fogmair	—	25 Oct. 1280
Donnchad Ó Flaithbertaig (Donatus)	el. *a.* 16 Apr., temp. 29 Sept. 1281	*c.* Feb. 1306
John Tankard	el. 13 June, temp. *p.* 13 June 1306, cons. *c.* 1307	1343
James Bermingham	el. and cons. 1344	*c.* 1346
Uilliam Ó Dubhda	el. 1344, prov. 26 June 1346, temp. 25 Mar. 1348	1350
Robert Elyot	prov. 8 June 1351	depr. by Clement VII *a.* 17 Jan. 1383, d. *a.* Jan. 1390
Thomas Lodowys, O.P.	prov. 9 Aug. 1381 (did not take effect)	—
Conchobhar Ó Coineóil (Cornelius)	prov. by Clement VII *a.* 19 Feb. 1383	1422/3
Thomas Horwell (Orwell), O.F.M.	prov. 31 Jan. 1390 (suffr. in Ely 1389–1406)	trs. to Dromore *a.* Nov. 1398
Thomas Barrett	prov. *a.* 14 Apr. 1400, temp. 12 Mar. 1401	25 Jan. 1425
Muircheartach Cléireach mac Donnchadha Ó Dubhda	el. *c.* 1403 (never cons.)	1403
Fearghal Ó Martain, O.E.S.A.	prov. 26 Sept. 1425, cons. 11 Nov. 1427	30 Jan. 1431/2
Thaddaeus 'Mac Creagh'	prov. *a.* Sept. 1431	—
Brian Ó Coineóil (Bernardus)	prov. 30 Jan. 1432, deposed 1436,[2] rest. 1439	31 May 1461
Robert Barrett	prov. 3 July 1447 (did not take effect)	1447
Ruaidhrí Bairéad (Barrett), O.E.S.A.	prov. 3 Mar. 1452 (did not take effect)	*p.* May 1458
Thomas	prov. *a.* 7 Jan. 1453 (did not take effect)	—

[1] This diocese is often called the diocese of Uí Fiachrach Muaide in the Irish annals.
[2] Maghnus Ó Dubhda was elected but died 22 Feb. 1436.

BISHOPS	ACCESSION	DEATH
		unless otherwise stated
Richard Viel, O.Carth.	prov. 17 Oct. 1459 (did not take effect)	—
Donatus Ó Conchobhair, O.P.	prov. 2 Dec. 1461	*p.* Oct. 1467
Tomás Bairéad (Thomas Barrett), O.S.A.	prov. 9 Feb. 1470 (suffr. in Ely 1497)	*p.* 1497
Seaán Ó Caissín (John de Tuderto), O.F.M.	prov. 18 Jan. 1487	res. 1490
Thomas Clerke	prov. 4 May 1500	res. 1505, d. 1508
Malachias Ó Clúmháin	prov. 12 Feb. 1506, cons. 3 Sept. 1508	*a.* 1513
Risdéard Bairéad (Richard Barrett)	prov. 7 Jan. 1513	*a.* Nov. 1545

KILLALOE
(CASHEL P.)

Domnall Ua hÉnna I[1]	—	1 Dec. 1098
Gilla Pátraic Ua hÉnna, abb.	—	—
Domnall Ua Conaing[2]	—	trs. to Cashel 1131
Domnall Ua Lonngargáin[2]	*c.* 1131	trs. to Cashel 1137/8
Tadg Ua Lonngargáin	*c.* 1138	1161
Donnchad mac Diarmata Ua Briain	*c.* 1161	1164
Constantín mac Toirrdelbaig Ua Briain	*a.* 1179	1194
Diarmait Ua Conaing	1194	1195
Conchobar Ua hÉnna (Cornelius)	*a.* 1201	1216
Domnall Ó hÉnna II (Donatus)	el. 1216, conf. by Honorius III 1219, cons. 1221	—
Robert Travers	el. *a.* 14 Jan., cons. *p.* 14 Jan. 1217	depr. 1221, (again) May 1226
Domnall Ó Cennéitig (Donatus)	el. *a.* 1231, temp. *p.* 20 Aug. 1231	*a.* 22 Nov. 1252
Ísóc Ó Cormacáin (Isaac)	el. *a.* 5 Apr., prov. and cons. 23 June, temp. 1 Oct. 1253	res. *a.* 10 Nov. 1267
Mathgamain Ó hÓcáin (Matthaeus)	el. *a.* 20 Mar., temp. *p.* 26 Mar. 1268	12 Aug. 1281
Mauricius Ó hÓcáin	el. 23 Nov. 1281, temp. 15 Feb., lib. 6 July 1282	*a.* Oct. 1298
David Mac Mathgamna	el. 7 Jan., temp. *p.* 22 Apr., cons. May 1299	9 Feb. 1317
Tomás Ó Cormacáin I	el. *a.* 2 July, temp. 2 July 1317	31 July 1322

[1] The name of Mael Muire O Dunain appears on a manuscript list of the bps of Killaloe in the library of the Royal Irish Academy (MS. 3.A.11). He seems to have taken the place of Domnall O h-Enni, who died as bp of Dal Cais and chief bp of Munster in 1098; but the diocese of Killaloe had not been formally erected at that date.

[2] There is some doubt as to whether these two bps were bps of Killaloe as well as Cashel at the time of their death.

BISHOPS	ACCESSION	DEATH
		unless otherwise stated
Brian Ó Coscraig (Benedictus)	el. *a.* 1 Aug. 1323	*c.* 1325
David Mac Briain ('David of Emly')	el. *a.* May, prov. 25 May, temp. 26 Sept. 1326	12 Dec. 1342
'Unatus O Heime' (?Uaithne Ó hÉnna)	?el. 1326	1334
Tomás Ó hÓgáin	—	30 Oct. 1354
Tomás Ó Cormacáin II	el. *a.* May, prov. 27 May, temp. 12 Aug. 1355	1382
Mathghamhain Mág Raith (Matthaeus)	prov. *a.* Aug. 1389, temp. 1 Sept. 1391	*a.* Feb. 1400
Donatus Mág Raith, O.S.A.	prov. *a.* 8 Feb., cons. *a.* 9 Apr. 1400	*p.* Aug. 1421
Robert Mulfield, O.Cist.[1]	prov. 9 Sept. 1409 (did not get possession)	(suffragan in Lichfield *c.* 1418–40)
Eugenius Ó Faoláin[1]	trs. from Kilmacduagh 6 July 1418	*a.* 24 July 1431
Thaddaeus Mág Raith I[2]	prov. 25 Oct., cons. *p.* 5 Nov. 1423, temp. 1 Sept. 1431	*a.* July 1443
Séamus Ó Lonnghargáin[2]	trs. from Annaghdown 9 Dec., cons. *c.* Dec. 1429, prov. (again) 24 July 1431	res. *c.* July 1443
Donnchadh mac Toirdhealbhaigh Ó Briain (Donatus)	prov. 26 July, cons. *p.* 12 Aug. 1443	*a.* Aug. 1460
Thaddaeus Mág Raith II	prov. 18 Aug., cons. 2 Sept. 1460	*a.* May 1463
Matthaeus Ó Gríobhtha	prov. 23 May, cons. *p.* 7 July 1463	*c.* Sept. 1483
Toirdhealbhach mac Mathghamhna Ó Briain (Theodoricus; Thaddaeus)	prov. 19 Sept. 1483	*a.* Aug. 1526
Séamus Ó Cuirrín	prov. 24 Aug. 1526	res. 5 May 1542, d. *a.* June 1554

KILMACDUAGH[3]
(TUAM P.)

?Ua Cléirig	—	1137
Ímar Ua Ruaidín	—	1176
Mac Gilla Cellaig Ua Ruaidín	*a.* 1179	1204
I. Ua Cellaig	*a.* Feb. 1206	1215
Máel Muire Ó Connmaig	—	1224

[1] Robert and Eugenius were provided within the lifetime of Donatus Mág Raith. Eugenius was resident for some years in a portion of the diocese, but Robert was unable to get possession.
[2] During the years 1429–43 these bps were rival bps within the same diocese.
[3] The diocese of Kilmacduagh was recognized at the synod of Kells. This diocese is sometimes called the diocese of Uí Fiachrach Aidne in the Irish annals.

BISHOPS	ACCESSION	DEATH
		unless otherwise stated
Áed, precentor of Kilmacduagh (Odo)	el. *a.* 12 May, temp. *p.* 12 May 1227	—
Conchobar Ó Muiredaig	—	1247
Gilla Cellaig Ó Ruaidín (Gillebertus)	el. *a.* 5 May, temp. *p.* 5 May 1248	*a.* 10 Nov. 1253
Mauricius Ó Leaáin	el. *a.* 15 May, temp. *p.* 15 May 1254	*a.* 16 Jan. 1284
David Ó Sétacháin	el. *p.* 27 Mar., temp. *p.* 27 Mar. 1284	*a.* 13 June 1290
Lúirint Ó Lachtnáin, O.Cist. (Laurentius), abbot of Knockmoy	el. *a.* 10 Aug., temp. *p.* 10 Aug. 1290	*a.* 1 Mar. 1307
Lucas	el. *c.* 1307	1325
Johannes[1]	el. *a.* May, temp. 14 May 1326	*c.* 1357
Nicol Ó Leaáin	prov. 16 Nov. 1358, cons. 1360	*a.* Oct. 1393
Gregorius Ó Leaáin	prov. 14 Oct. 1393, cons. *c.* 1394, conf. 30 Aug. 1396	1397
Énri Ó Connmhaigh	trs. from Clonfert 11 Mar. 1405	—
Dionysius	—	*a.* May 1410
Eugenius Ó Faoláin	prov. 23 Sept. 1409 (bulls expedited 25 May 1410)	trs. to Killaloe 6 July 1418
Diarmaid Ó Donnchadha	prov. and cons. *c.* July 1418	*a.* Oct. 1419
Nicol Ó Duibhghiolla	el. *a.* Oct. 1419 (did not take effect)	—
Seaán Ó Connmhaigh, O.Cist.	prov. 23 Oct. 1419	*a.* May 1441
Dionysius Ó Donnchadha	prov. 10 May 1441	*a.* Dec. 1478
Cornelius 'O'Mullony' (?Ó Maoldomhnaigh)	prov. 8 Jan. 1479	res. 8 Mar. 1503
Matthaeus Ó Briain	prov. 8 Mar. 1503	*a.* Aug. 1533
Malachias 'O Mullony'	prov. 8 Aug. 1533 (did not take effect)	—
Christopher Bodkin	prov. 3 Sept., cons. 4 Nov. 1533	1572

KILMORE[2]
(ARMAGH P.)

Áed Ua Finn	—	1136
Muirchertach Ua Máel Mochéirge	—	1149

[1] On 31 July 1327, John XXII sanctioned the union of the three dioceses of Annadown, Kilmacduagh and Achonry with the diocese of Tuam (*CPL*, ii, 262). The union of Kilmacduagh with Tuam should have taken effect on the death of Bp John in 1357. But the chapter of Kilmacduagh, with agreement from the abp and chapter of Tuam, petitioned Innocent VI for the dissolution of the union, of which no more is heard (*CPL*, iii, 591).

[2] No diocese of Kilmore or Bréifne was established at the synod of Ráith Bressail; but bps of Bréifne are recorded from 1136. Kilmore, the later seat of the diocese, is not recorded bef. 1231. The diocese is known officially as *Tirbrunensis* (from Tír mBriúin).

BISHOPS	ACCESSION	DEATH *unless otherwise stated*
Tuathal Ua Connachtaig (Thaddaeus)[1]	*a.* Mar. 1152	1179
Anonymous, O.Cist.[2]	el. and cons. *a.* 1185	expelled *c.* 1185
M. Ua Dobailén[2]	*a.* Aug. 1202	1211
Flann Ó Connachtaig (Florentius)	—	1231
Congalach Mac Idneóil	*a. c.* 1233	res. *a.* May 1250, d. 1250
Simon Ó Ruairc	el. *a.* 20 June 1251	1285
Mauricius, O.S.A.	el. *a.* Oct. 1286	1307
Matha Mac Duibne	—	1314
Pátraic Ó Cridecáin	el. *a.* 1320	1328
Conchobhar Mac Conshnámha (Ford)	—	1355
Riocard Ó Raghallaigh	el. *c.* 1356	1369
Johannes	el. *a.* 1373	*c.* 1389
Thomas Rushook, O.P.	trs. from Chichester *c.* 1388	?res. 1390, d. *c.* 1393
Seoán Ó Raghallaigh I	*p.* 2 Nov. 1389	1393
Nicol (alias Ruaidhrí) Mac Brádaigh	prov. *a.* 27 Aug. 1395; cons. *a.* July 1398	1421
John Stokes	(no date of provision) (suffr. in Lichfield 1407, Worcester 1416)	—
David Ó Faircheallaigh	prov. by Gregory XII and cons. *c.* 1408–09	—
Domhnall O Gabhann (Donatus)	prov. 13 Aug. 1421, cons. *p.* 30 June 1422	res. *c.* 1445
Aindrias Mac Brádaigh	prov. 9 Mar. 1445	1455
Fear Síthe Mág Dhuibhne, O.S.A.	prov. 11 July 1455	27 Nov. 1464
Seaán Ó Raghallaigh II, O.S.A.	prov. 17 May 1465	*a.* Nov. 1476
Cormac Mág Shamhradháin, O.S.A.[3]	prov. 4 Nov. 1476	Dec. 1512
Tomás mac Aindriais Mac Brádaigh[3]	prov. 20 Oct. 1480	1511
Diarmaid Ó Raghallaigh	prov. 28 Jan. 1512	*a.* June 1530
Edmund Nugent, O.S.A.[4]	prov. 22 June 1530	depr. 5 Nov. 1540, d. *c.* 1550

[1] Thaddaeus takes the oath of fealty to Henry II in 1172 as bp of Kells.

[2] These two are possibly identical.

[3] For more than thirty years there were two rival bps of Kilmore, who were probably supported by rival septs within the diocese. The two bps were present at provincial councils held by Primate Ottaviano in 1492 and 1495, and were both then recognized as bps of Kilmore (Ottaviano's register, fos. 397, 404). But Diarmaid was provided to the see in 1512 bef. Cormac's death, though Cormac was still maintaining his rights at that date (Costello, *De Annatis Hiberniae*, 258).

[4] Edmund Nugent surrendered his bulls to Henry VIII, and Paul III provided John MacBrady to the see against him in 1540.

LEIGHLIN
(DUBLIN P.)

BISHOPS	ACCESSION	DEATH *unless otherwise stated*
?Máel Eóin Ua Dúnacáin	—	1125
Sluaigedach Ua Catháin	—	1145
Dúngal Ua Cáellaide	*a.* Mar. 1152	1181
Johannes	*fl.* 1192	—
Johannes, O.Cist.	cons. 18 Sept. 1198	*c.* 1201
Herlewin, O.Cist.	*a.* 1202	*a.* Apr. 1217
Richard (Fleming)	*c.* 1217	*a.* Nov. 1228
William	el. *a.* Nov. 1228	*a.* 21 Apr. 1252
Thomas, O.S.A.	el. *a.* 4 Sept. 1252, prov. 7 Jan., temp. *p.* 9 Mar. 1253	25 Apr. 1275
Nicholas Chever	el. *a.* Nov. 1275, temp. 7 Mar, conf. 28 Sept. 1276	20 July 1309
Maurice de Blanchville	el. *a.* Nov., temp. *p.* 13 Nov. 1309	*a.* Nov. 1320
Meiler le Poer	el. 5 Nov. 1320, cons. 12 Apr. 1321	*a.* Nov. 1348
Radulphus Ó Ceallaigh, O.Carm.	prov. 6 Feb., cons. Feb. 1344 (did not take effect, suffr. in York 1344)	trs. to Cashel 9 Jan. 1346
William St Leger	el. *a.* 3 Nov. 1348 (did not take effect)	—
Thomas of Brakenberg, O.F.M.	prov. 20 Mar., cons. 30 Mar., temp. 15 Aug. 1349	July 1360
Johannes	prov. 1360	1361
William	prov. 14 Jan. 1362 (never cons.)	1362
John Young	prov. 20 Feb., temp. 21 Sept. 1363	*c.* 12 Feb. 1385
John Griffin[1]	temp. 2 Aug. 1385	trs. to Ossory 2 July 1399
Richard Bocomb, O.P.	prov. 1 Oct. 1400 (suffr. in Exeter and Salisbury)	res. *a.* July 1419
Seaán Ó Maolagáin	prov. 5 July 1419, temp. 1 Sept. 1422	1431
Thomas Fleming, O.F.M.	prov. 29 Apr. 1432	—
Diarmaid	—	*a.* Feb. 1464
Milo Roche, O.Cist.	prov. 3 Feb. 1464	*a.* Apr. 1490
Nicholas 'Magwyr'[2]	prov. 21 Apr. 1490	*c.* 1512
Thomas Halsey	prov. 20 May 1513 (suffr. in York 1519)	*c.* 1523
Mauricius Ó Deóradháin, O.P.	prov. 19 Jan. 1524	1525
Matthew Sanders	prov. 10 Apr. 1527	23/24 Dec. 1549

[1] In *CPL*, v, 88, it is stated that Thomas Peverel, O.Carm., has been translated from Leighlin to Llandaff on 2 July 1398. *See also Cal. Pat. Rolls 1396–99*, 446–47. But there is no record that Peverel was translated from Ossory to Leighlin.

[2] Eubel (ii, 193) gives two additional provisions: John Caroys, O.S.A., of All Hallows, Dublin, prov. 10 Oct. 1483; and Galebrandus de Andree, O.F.M., prov. 15 Nov. 1484. These two names are ignored in the provision of Nicholas Maguire, the see being then void by death of Milo.

LIMERICK
(CASHEL P.)

BISHOPS	ACCESSION	DEATH *unless otherwise stated*
Gilli alias Gilla Espaic	cons. *c.* 1106	res. 1140, d. 1145
Patricius[1]	cons. 1140	*p.* Dec. 1148
Erolb[1]	—	1151
Torgesius	*a.* Mar. 1152	1167
Brictius	*a. fl.* 1167 × 1178	*c.* 1186 × 1189
Donnchad Ua Briain (Donatus)	*a.* 1190	*a.* 5 Dec. 1207
Edmund[2]	*a.* July 1215	1222
Hubert de Burgo, O.S.A.[3]	custodian 11 Mar. 1223, el. *a.* 7 May 1224, temp. *c.* 21 Apr. 1225	14 Sept. 1250
Robert of Emly	el. *a.* 11 Apr. 1251, temp. 6 Jan. 1252	8 Sept. 1272
Gerald le Mareshall	el. *a.* 11 Jan, temp. 17 Jan. 1273	10 Feb. 1302
Robert of Dundonald	el. *a.* 2 May, temp. 30 July, lib. 23 Sept. 1302	3 May 1311
Eustace de l'Eau (de Aqua)	el. *c.* 20 Nov., temp. *p.* 1 Dec. 1312	3 May 1336
Maurice Rochfort (de Rupe)	el. *a.* Nov., temp. 7 Nov. 1336, cons. 6 Apr. 1337	9 June 1353
Stephen Lawless	prov. 19 Feb., cons. *a.* 7 Apr., temp. 29 Apr., lib. 13 May 1354	28 Dec. 1359
Stephen Wall (de Valle)	el. *a.* Nov., prov. 6 Nov. 1360, temp. 2 Mar. 1361	trs. to Meath 19 Feb. 1369
Peter Curragh	prov. 19 Feb., fealty 4 Aug. 1369, temp. 10 Feb. 1370	trs. to Ross *c.* 1399
Bernardus Ó Conchobhair	trs. from Ross *c.* 1399 (did not take effect)	—
Conchobhar Ó Deadhaidh, O.F.M. (Cornelius O Dea)	prov. 26 May 1400	res. *a.* Oct. 1425, d. 27 July 1434
John Mothel, O.S.A.	prov. 7 Oct. 1426, temp. 23 Jan. 1427	res. *a.* Apr. 1458, d. 1468
Thomas Leger, O.S.A.[4]	prov. 10 May 1456	depr. 23 Nov. 1456
William Creagh (Russell)	prov. 19 Apr. 1458	*a.* July 1469
Thomas Arthur	prov. 14 July, cons. 10 Sept. 1469	19 July 1486

[1] Patrick was consecrated at Canterbury, and took an oath of fealty there; but his name does not occur in any Irish record. Erolb was prob. his successful rival, and ruled the see *c.* 1140–51.

[2] Geoffrey, parson of Dungervan, was nominated by John to the vacant see on 5 Dec. 1207, but there is no evidence that he was ever validly elected or consecrated. Edmund probably ruled the see *c.* 1208–23.

[3] There is no record of restitution of temporalities for Hubert; but Henry III made several grants in his favour on 21 Apr. 1225, and it is probable that he did fealty at this time.

[4] This provision was within the lifetime of John Mothel, who did not resign until 1458.

BISHOPS	ACCESSION	DEATH *unless otherwise stated*
Richard Stackpoll[1]	prov. 18 Sept. 1486	*a.* 20 Nov. 1486
John Dunowe	prov. 13 Nov. 1486 (suffragan in Exeter 1489)	*a.* Apr. 1489
John Folan	prov. 24 Apr. 1489	30 Jan. 1522
Seaán Ó Cuinn, O.P.	prov. 21 Oct. 1524, cons. *a.* 3 Jan. 1525	res. 9 Apr. 1551, d. 1554/5

LISMORE[2]
(CASHEL P.)

Niall mac Meic Áedacáin	—	1113
Ua Daigthig	—	1119
Máel Ísu Ua hAinmere, O.S.B. (Malchus)[3]	—	1135
Máel Muire Ua Loingsig[4]	—	?res. *c.* 1151, d. 1159
Gilla Críst Ua Connairche, O.Cist. (Christianus)	cons. 1151	res. *c.* 1179, d. 1186
Felix	el. *c.* 1179	res. 1202
Malachias, O.Cist.	el. *c.* 1202, cons. *a.* 5 Nov. 1203	*a.* 1216
Thomas	el. and cons. *a.* June 1216	*a.* Dec. 1218
Robert of Bedford[5]	el. *a.* 13 Dec., temp. 13 Dec. 1218, cons. *a.* 17 Apr. 1219	*a.* Nov. 1223
Griffin Christopher	el. *a.* 6 Nov., temp. 6 Nov. 1223, (again) 8 July 1225, (again) 11 July 1227, cons. *a.* 25 Apr. 1228	res. 17 July × 8 Aug. 1246, d. *p.* 22 Aug. 1252
Ailinn Ó Súillebáin, O.P.	trs. from Cloyne *p.* 26 Oct. 1246, temp. 25 May 1248	*a.* 27 Apr. 1253
Thomas	el. *a.* 25 July, temp. *p.* 27 July, cons. *p.* 15 Oct. 1253	*a.* 2 July 1270
John Roche	el. *a.* 20 Aug., temp. *p.* 20 Aug. 1270	11 June 1279
Richard Corre	el. 19 July, cons. *p.* 24 Oct., temp. 18 Nov. 1279	Oct. 1308
William Fleming	el. *p.* 24 Nov. 1308	Nov. 1321

[1] Richard was only 24 years old at the date of this provision. He was provided as adm. with right of succession as bp when he reached the age of 27. But the see was held to be void when John Dunowe was provided 13 Nov. 1486: Reg. Lat Innocent VIII, 854, fo. 142v; 912, fo. 40.

[2] At the synod of Ráith Bressail a choice was left between Lismore and Waterford as the centre of a diocese that was later divided into the two separate dioceses of Lismore and Waterford.

[3] He died at Lismore in 1135. It is probable that he was bp of Lismore-Waterford during the last years of his life.

[4] The death of Máel Muire as bp of Lismore is recorded in the Annals of Ulster 1159. It seems probable that he was bp *c.* 1135–51, and that his resignation created a vacancy for Christianus who was also papal legate 1152–79.

[5] Robert did not get full possession until aft. a mandate of Henry III (8 May 1221). His successor Griffin Christopher had similar difficulties in the first years of his rule.

BISHOPS	ACCESSION	DEATH *unless otherwise stated*
John Leynagh	el. *p.* 13 Dec. 1321, cons. 17 Apr. 1323	Dec. 1354
Thomas le Reve[1]	prov. *a.* 18 May, temp. 24 Aug. 1358	*a.* Sept. 1394 (as bp of Waterford and Lismore)

(Waterford and Lismore united 1363)

MAYO[2]
(TUAM P.)

Gilla Ísu Ua Maílín	*a.* 1172	1184
Céle Ua Dubthaig	—	1210
?Patricius	el. *c.* 1210, not cons.	res. 1216, d. ?1216

The following bps were provided in the fifteenth century:

William Prendergast, O.F.M.	prov. 16 July 1428 (did not take effect)	—
Nicholas 'Wogmay', O.F.M.	prov. 17 July 1430	*p.* Oct. 1436
Martinus Campania, O.Cist.	prov. 29 Apr. 1432 (suffr. in Münster and Utrecht)	res. *a.* 31 Aug. 1439
Aodh Ó hUiginn, O.S.A.	prov. 31 Aug. 1439	depr. *a.* Jan. 1448, d. 1478
Simon de Düren, O.E.S.A.[3]	prov. 12 Aug. 1457 (suffr. in Münster and Worms 1461)	28 Aug. 1470
John Bell, O.F.M.	prov. 4 Nov. 1493 (suffr. in England 1499–*c.* 1530)	*c.* 1541

MEATH (CLONARD)[4]
(ARMAGH P.)

Máel Muire Ua Dúnáin	*a.* 1096	24 Dec. 1117
Eochaid Ua Cellaig	*a.* 11 Nov. 1133	1140

[1] On 18 Nov. 1356, Edward III ordered the temporalities of Lismore, then vacant, to be delivered to Roger Cradock, bp of Waterford, in accordance with the terms of the bull of John XXII (31 July 1327). This was not done, and Urban VI provided Thomas le Reve to the see of Lismore in 1358. Five years later, when Roger Cradock had meanwhile been translated from Waterford to Llandaff, Urban VI united the two dioceses 11 June 1363. Bp Thomas became bp of Lismore and Waterford from that date.

[2] The diocese of Mayo was not established at the synod of Ráith Bressail, but was recognized at the synod of Kells. A bp of Mayo took the oath of fealty to Henry II in 1172, prob. Gille Iosa O Mailin. In 1202 the papal legate, Cardinal John, united Mayo to Tuam. In 1216 Innocent III heard the case in Rome, and gave sentence in favour of Tuam. His sentence was maintained by the legate James in 1221, and was finally confirmed by Gregory IX on 3 July 1240.

[3] Simon is described as a Carmelite friar in the provision of 12 Aug. 1457 (*CPL*, xi, 309); but in his petition of 2 Sept. 1461 it is stated that he had made his profession in the order of Augustinian friars (*ibid.*, xii, 126). He was active as a suffragan in Worms, 1461.

[4] During the twelfth century the bps of Clonard acquired most of Meath as their territory, and frequently used the title 'bp of Meath' or 'bp of the men of Meath'. Cf. above under Clonmacnois. The title 'bp of Meath' became normal aft. 1202, when Simon Rochfort transferred his seat from Clonard to Trim.

BISHOPS	ACCESSION	DEATH
		unless otherwise stated
Étrú Ua Miadacháin (Eleuzerius)	*a.* Mar. 1152	1173
Echthigern Mac Máel Chiaráin (Eugenius)	*a.* Mar. 1177	1191
Simon Rochfort	el. 1192	*a.* Aug. 1224
Dónán Dé (Deodatus)	el. Aug. 1224 (not cons.)	*p.* 21 Oct. 1226
Ralph Petit	el. *a.* 30 Mar., temp. 30 Mar. 1227	*c.* 28 Sept. 1230
Richard de la Corner	el. and cons. 1231	*a.* 29 June 1252
Geoffrey Cusack, O.F.M.	el. and cons. *a.* July 1253	res. July 1253, d. *a.* Oct. 1254
Hugo of Taghmon	temp. 23 Dec. 1252, conf. (by pope) 31 Oct. 1254, cons. *p.* June 1255	*c.* 30 Jan. 1282
Walter de Fulburn[1]	el. and cons. *a.* Jan. 1283 (did not get possession)	trs. to Waterford 12 July 1286
Thomas St Leger	el. *a.* 5 Nov. 1282, prov. 12 July 1286, cons. 3 Nov. 1287	Dec. 1320
Seoán Mac Cerbaill (John MacCarwill)	trs. from Cork 20 Feb. 1321, temp. 23 June 1322	trs. to Cashel 19 Jan. 1327
William of St Paul, O.Carm.	prov. 16 Feb., cons. *c.* Feb., temp. 24 July 1327	July 1349
William St Leger	prov. 5 Oct. 1349, temp. 24 Feb. 1350, cons. 2 May 1350	24 Aug. 1352
Nicholas Allen, O.S.A.	el. *a.* Jan., prov. 9 Jan., cons. 31 Jan., temp. 15 Mar. 1353	15 Jan. 1367
Stephen de Valle (Wall)	trs. from Limerick 19 Feb. 1369, temp. 15 Feb. 1370, (again) 6 Sept. 1373	10 Nov. 1379
William Andrew, O.P.	trs. from Achonry 1380 (suffr. in Canterbury 1380), temp. 12 Nov. 1380	28 Sept. 1385
Alexander Petit (de Balscot)	trs. from Ossory 10 Mar. 1386	10 Nov. 1400
Robert Montayne	prov. 7 Feb., cons. *a.* 13 Sept. 1401	24 May 1412
Edward Dantsey	prov. 31 Aug. 1412, temp. 11 Apr. 1413	4 Jan. 1430
William Hadsor	prov. 29 May 1430	28 May 1433
William Silk[2]	el. *a.* 30 Aug. 1433, prov. 22 Sept., cons. *p.* 14 Oct. 1434	9 May 1450
Edmund Ouldhall, O.Carm.	prov. 7 Aug. 1450	9 (?29) Aug. 1459

[1] Walter de Fulburn was appd by Abp Nicol of Armagh, who claimed that the appointment was his by devolution. St Leger carried his cause to Rome, but was not successful until 1286.

[2] Ware gives Ascension Thursday (3 June) 1434 for the death of William Hadsor; but an entry in Abp Swayne's register for 30 Aug. 1433 makes it plain that William Silk had been elected as Hadsor's successor bef. that date. The Council of Basle confirmed Silk's election in Aug. 1433, but he was not consecrated until he had obtained a provision from Eugenius IV in Sept. 1434.

BISHOPS	ACCESSION	DEATH
		unless otherwise stated
William Shirwood	prov. 26 Mar. 1460	3 Dec. 1482
John Payne, O.P.	prov. 17 Mar., temp. 16 July, cons. *a.* 4 Aug. 1483	6 May 1507
William Rokeby	prov. 28 May 1507	trs. to Dublin 28 Jan. 1512
Hugh Inge, O.P.	prov. 28 Jan. 1512	trs. to Dublin 27 Feb. 1523
Richard Wilson, O.S.A.	prov. 27 Feb. 1523	res. *a.* Sept. 1529
Edward Staples	prov. 3 Sept. 1529	depr. 29 June 1554, d. *c.* 1560

OSSORY[1]
(DUBLIN P.)

Domnall Ua Fogartaig	*a.* Mar. 1152	1178
Felix Ua Duib Sláine, O.Cist.	*a.* 1180	24 Jan. 1202
Hugo de Rous, O.S.A. (Hugo Rufus)	*c.* 1202	*a.* Dec. 1218
Peter Mauveisin, O.S.A.	el. *a.* 8 Dec. 1218; cons. *p.* 31 Aug. 1220, temp. *p.* 8 Mar. 1221	*a.* Mar. 1231
William of Kilkenny	el. *p.* 16 Mar., temp. *p.* 25 June 1231	res. *a.* May 1232
Walter de Brackley	el. *a.* 13 June 1232, temp. *p.* 25 Mar., cons. *a.* 15 July 1233	*a.* 12 Oct. 1243
Geoffrey de Turville	el. *p.* 5 Feb., temp. *p.* 13 June 1244, cons. *a.* 28 Oct. 1245	*a.* 18 Oct. 1250
Hugh de Mapilton	el. *a.* 17 Apr., temp. 18 May, cons. *p.* 20 Aug. 1251	*a.* 4 June 1260
Geoffrey St Leger	el. *a.* 29 June, temp. 30 Aug. 1260	10 Jan. 1287
Roger of Wexford	el. *a.* 22 June, temp. 24 July, cons. 3 Nov. 1287	28 June 1289
Michael d'Exeter	el. 28 Sept., temp. 2 Nov. 1289, lib. 6 Feb. 1290	12 July 1302
William FitzJohn	el. 10 Sept., temp. 24 Oct. 1302, lib. 9 May, cons. *p.* 6 Jan. 1303	trs. to Cashel 26 Mar. 1317
Richard Ledred, O.F.M.	prov. 24 Apr., cons. *c.* May, temp. 24 July 1317, lib. 3 Mar. 1318	*c.* 1361
John de Tatenhale, O.P.	prov. 8 Nov., cons. *a.* 14 Dec. 1361, temp. 12 Feb. 1362	*p.* Mar. 1364

---

[1] Kilkenny was chosen as the seat of the diocese commonly known as the diocese of Ossory at the synod of Ráith Bressail. No bp is recorded bef. Domnall O Fogartaig, who attended the synod of Kells as vicar general of an absent bp.

BISHOPS	ACCESSION	DEATH
		unless otherwise stated
William	*a.* Feb. 1366	—
John of Oxford, O.E.S.A.	—	*c.* 1370
Alexander Petit (de Balscot)	el. *c.* 1370, prov. 9 Feb., temp. 12 May 1371	trs. to Meath *c.* 10 Mar. 1386
Richard Northalis, O.Carm.	el. 1386, prov. *a.* 17 Feb., cons. *a.* 4 Dec. 1387	trs. to Dublin 25 Oct. 1395
Thomas Peverell, O.Carm.	prov. 25 Oct. 1395, temp. 4 Feb. 1396	trs. to Llandaff 2 July 1398
John Waltham, O.S.A.	prov. 1 Feb. 1398, temp. 20 Mar. 1399	trs. to Dromore 14 May 1400
John Griffin	trs. from Leighlin 2 July 1399, temp. 7 Feb. 1400	*c.* Mar. 1400
John	prov. *a.* 14 May 1400	*p.* 8 June 1400
Roger Appleby, O.S.A.	prov. 26 Sept. 1400, temp. 3 Jan. 1401, lib. 6 Apr. 1401	res. Oct. 1402
John Waltham, O.S.A. (again)	trs. from Dromore 9/11 Oct. 1402	5 Nov. 1405
Thomas Snell	trs. from Waterford and Lismore 11 Mar. 1407	16 Oct. 1417
Patrick Foxe	trs. from Cork 15 Dec. 1417	20 Apr. 1421
Dionysius Ó Deadhaidh	prov. 4 July 1421	*a.* 12 Dec. 1426
Thomas Barry	prov. 19 Feb. 1427	3 Mar. 1460
David Hacket	prov. 4 July 1460	24 Oct. 1478
Seaán Ó hÉidigheáin	prov. 15 Jan., cons. 21 Feb. 1479	6 Jan. 1487
Oliver Cantwell, O.P.	prov. 26 Mar. 1487, temp. 28 Feb. 1496	9 Jan. 1527
Milo Baron, O.S.A. (Fitzgerald)	prov. 8 June 1528	1 July × 27 Sept. 1550

RAPHOE[1]
(ARMAGH P.)

Sean O Gairedain[2]	—	—
Donell O Garvan[2]	—	—
Felemy O Syda[2]	—	—
Gilla in Choimded Ua Caráin (Gillebertus)	*a.* 1156	trs. to Armagh *c.* 1175
Anonymous	—	res. *a.* 18 May 1198
Máel Ísu Ua Doirig	*a.* 1204	res. *a.* 7 Mar. 1252
Máel Pátraic Ó Scannail, O.P. (Patricius)	el. *c.* Nov., cons. 30 Nov. 1253	trs. to Armagh 5 Nov. 1261
Johannes de Alneto, O.F.M.	prov. 3 Dec. 1263	res. 28 Apr. 1265

[1] This diocese is often called the diocese of Tír Conaill in the Irish annals. Raphoe or Derry are named as alternative seats of this diocese at the synod of Ráith Bressail; but Raphoe was from the first the seat of the diocese of Tír Conaill.

[2] These three bps are named as the first known bps of Raphoe in a seventeenth-century 'Catalogue of the bps of Raphoe'; but no dates are given for them in this catalogue. The early history of this diocese is unrecorded.

BISHOPS	ACCESSION	DEATH
		unless otherwise stated
Cairpre Ó Scuapa, O.P.	prov. *p.* 28 Apr. 1265 (suffr. in Canterbury 1273)	9 May 1274
Fergal Ó Firgil (Florentius)	*c.* 1275	1299
Tomás Ó Naán	el. *a.* 1306 (never cons.)	1306
Énrí Mac in Chrossáin (Henricus)	*c.* 1306	1319
Tomás Mac Carmaic Uí Domnaill, O.Cist., abbot of Assaroe	el. 1319	1337
Pádraig Mac Maonghail	—	*a.* Oct. 1367
Conchobhar Mac Carmaic Uí Dhomhnaill, O.Cist. (Cornelius)	prov. 23 Dec. 1367	res. 21 Feb. 1397, d. 1399
Seoán Mac Meanmain, O.Cist.	prov. 21 Feb. 1397	—
Eóin Mac Carmaic (Johannes)	prov. *a.* 8 Dec. 1400	1419
Lochlainn Ó Gallchobhair I (Laurentius)	el. *a.* 27 Feb. prov. 28 Feb. 1420	1438
Cornelius Mac Giolla Bhrighde	prov. 20 July, cons. *p.* 30 July 1440	*a.* June 1442
Lochlainn Ó Gallchobhair II (Laurentius)	prov. 18 June 1442, cons. *p.* 23 July 1443	*a.* Nov. 1479
Johannes de Rogeriis	prov. 12 Nov. 1479	*a.* Nov. 1482
Meanma Mac Carmaic (Menelaus Mac Carmacáin)	prov. 4 Nov. 1482	res. 6 Feb. 1514, d. 9 May 1515
Conn Ó Catháin (Cornelius)[1]	prov. 13 Feb. 1514	depr. (?) 1534, d. *p.* 1550
Éamonn Ó Gallchobhair[1]	prov. 11 May 1534	26 Feb. 1543

RATHLURENSIS (Maghera)
(ARMAGH P.)

In the list of Irish bishoprics approved by Cardinal Paparo at the synod of Kells a bishop *de Rathlurig* appears in the list of suffragan bishops in the province of Armagh. The Irish name of Maghera is Machaire Ratha Luraigh (the plain of Lurach's fort): see the note in *CPL*, xiii, 398. The Irish annalists commonly style the bishops of this area 'bishops of Cenel Eoghan' (Tyrone); and they are listed above, under Derry. Henry III issued a mandate to the bishop *Radlurensi* 1 Oct. 1245; and the title *epscop Ratha Luraigh* occurs in an additional entry to the Annals of Ulster for the year 1246, when Germanus, bishop of Ráith Lúraig, was elected as

---

[1] In the record of the provision of Éamonn Ó Gallchobhair by Paul III (1534) it is stated that the diocese of Raphoe had been vacant for the past 17 years since the death of Menelaus *extra Romanam curiam*: Brady, i, 307. This statement implies a rejection of the provision of Cornelius in Feb. 1514. Cornelius accepted royal supremacy, but no record of his deprivation survives.

primate by the Irish bishops, but was passed over in favour of the German primate Albert Suerbeer. In May 1247 Bishop Germanus obtained sanction from Innocent IV for the transfer of his see from Ráith Lúraig to Derry: *CPL*, i, 233–34; Theiner, 48.

Ráith Lúraig is mentioned as a rectory in 1411 and 1412 (*CPL*, vi, 258, 267); and again in 1459 and 1469 (*ibid.*, xii, 35, 692). On 3 Apr. 1471 Thomas Ingleby obtained a provision to the see of Rathlure from Paul II: Brady, i, 323. On 1 Feb. 1475 Thomas, 'bishop of Rathlure, residing in the diocese of Lincoln,' appears as a mandatary with the bishops of Winchester and Bangor (*CPL*, xii, 398). On 25 Apr. 1491 Innocent VIII addressed a mandate to the bishop of London and 'the present (*moderno*) bishop of Rathlure residing in the city of London': Register Lat. 908, fo. 84. The identity of this bishop is uncertain; but he was probably Thomas Ingleby, who had successfully revived a defunct Irish see in his own favour in 1471.

ROSCREA[1]
(CASHEL P.)

BISHOPS	ACCESSION	DEATH *unless otherwise stated*
Ísác O Cuanáin	—	1161
?Ua Cerbaill	—	1168

ROSS[2]
(CASHEL P.)

Nechtan Mac Nechtain	—	1160
Benedictus[3]	*fl.* 1173 × 1177	—
Mauricius	*fl.* 1192 × 1195	*c.* 1195
Daniel[4]	e. *c.* 1196, cons. *a.* Jan. 1198	1223
Fingen Ó Clothna (Florentius)	el. *p.* 7 May 1224	res. *a.* Jan. 1253
Mauricius	el. *a.* 16 July 1253, cons. *p.* 2 Mar. 1254, temp. *p.* 18 July 1254	res. *c.* 25 Apr. 1265
Ualter Ó Mithigéin, O.F.M.	el. *a.* 23 Sept., temp. *p.* 23 Sept. 1269	*a.* 13 Dec. 1274
Matthaeus	el. *c.* 1269, conf. by Gregory X 28 Dec. 1272 (did not get possession)	—

[1] Roscrea was not chosen as one of the episcopal sees of Ireland at the synod of Ráith Bressail; but it appears as one of the episcopal churches recognized at the synod of Kells. Ua Cerbaill, who died in 1168, is given as 'bp of Ross' (*Ruis Ailithir*) in the Annals of the Four Masters; but the family name suggests the bishopric of Roscrea. The Four Masters may have found the title *epscop Ruis* in their original, and have expanded this to *Ruis Ailithir*, not *Ruis Cré*. The see disappears before the end of the twelfth century.

[2] Ros Ailithir was not one of the churches chosen to be a diocesan centre at the synod of Ráith Bressail; but it is included in the list of churches recognized by Cardinal Paparo at the synod of Kells.

[3] For Ua Cerbaill, bp of either Ross or Roscrea, who died in 1168, *see under* Roscrea.

[4] There was a disputed election *c.* 1195–98, on which Innocent III was called to adjudicate. Florence, the rival candidate to Daniel, was at first confirmed by Innocent III, 17 Sept. 1198; but nothing is heard of him aft. this. Daniel was bp in 1205, attended the Lateran Council in 1215 and died in 1223. Bp Ua Selbaig, who died at Cork in 1205 according to the Annals of Inisfallen, may have been Florence, the rejected candidate of 1198, or a bp of Ardmore (*see under* Ardmore, note).

BISHOPS	ACCESSION	DEATH *unless otherwise stated*
Peter Ó h-Uallacháin, O.Cist. (? Patricius)	el. *a.* 25 Mar., temp 25 Mar., lib. 14 Apr. 1275	21 Sept. 1290
Laurentius	el. *a.* 12 Jan., temp. 12 Jan., lib. 10 Apr. 1291	*a.* 8 Mar. 1310
Matthaeus Ó Finn	el. *p.* 8 Mar., temp. *p.* 8 Mar. 1310	16 Oct. 1320
Laurentius Ó h-Uallacháin	el. 30 Apr., temp. 14 Aug. 1331	1335
Dionysius	el. 1336	1377
Bernard Ó Conchobhair, O.F.M.	temp. 3 Feb. 1379	trs. to Limerick *c.* 1399
Peter Curragh	trs. from Limerick *c.* 1399 (did not take effect)	—
Thaddaeus Ó Ceallaigh, O.Cist.	prov. *c.* 1399 (did not take effect)	—
Mac Raith Ó hEidirsgeóil (Macrobius; Matthaeus)	prov. *a.* 4 Aug. 1401 (provision annulled 25 June 1403)	1418
Stephen Brown, O.Carm.	prov. *p.* 1420, temp. 6 May 1402, prov. (again) 25 June 1403 (suffr. of St Davids 1408, Wells 1410, Hereford 1418, Worcester 1420)	*p.* 1420
Walter Formay, O.F.M.	prov. 14 Nov. 1418	*a.* Sept. 1423
John Bloxworth, O.Carm.	prov. 24 Sept. 1424 (did not take effect)	—
Conchobhar Mac Fhaolchadha, O.F.M. (Cornelius)	prov. 19 Aug. 1426	*a.* Dec. 1448
Maurice Broun	—	*a.* July 1431
Walter of Leicester, O.P.	prov. 13 July 1431	—
Richard Clerk	prov. 10 Mar. 1434 (suffr. in London 1434–41, Canterbury 1439–65, Salisbury 1454)	*p.* 1465
Domhnall Ó Donnobháin	prov. 4 Nov. 1448	res. *a.* 1474, d. *a.* 1474
Johannes	(suffr. in Bath 1450–60)	*a.* Mar. 1460
Robert Colynson	prov. 19 Mar. 1460	—
John Hornse	(suffr. in Norwich 1466–9, Bath 1479–81)	*p.* 1481
Aodh Ó hEidirsgeóil (Odo)	prov. 24 Mar., cons. 11 Apr. 1473	*a.* Sept. 1494
Tadhg MacCarthaigh (Thaddaeus)	prov. 29 Mar., cons. 3 May 1482	depr. 3 Aug. 1483, prov. to Cork and Cloyne 21 Apr. 1490
John Edmund Courci, O.F.M.[1]	prov. 26 Sept. 1494	res. 4 Nov. 1517
Seaán Ó Muirthile, O.Cist.	prov. 4 Nov. 1517	9 Jan. 1519

[1] He held the two sees of Ross and Clogher, 1492–1502 (*see under* Clogher).

BISHOPS	ACCESSION	DEATH *unless otherwise stated*
Tadhg Ó Raghallaigh, O.E.S.A.[1] (Thaddaeus)	prov. 23 Dec. 1519	*a.* June 1526
Bonaventura	*fl.* 27 Mar. 1523	—
Diarmaid Mac Carthaigh, O.E.S.A.	prov. 6 June 1526	1552

SCATTERY ISLAND (Inis Cathaigh)[2]
(CASHEL P.)

Áed Ua Bécháin (Edanus)	—	1188
Cerball Ua hÉnna (Carous)	—	*c.* 1193
Tomás Mac Mathghamhna, O.F.M.	prov. 11 May 1360, cons. *p.* 11 May 1360	depr. 20 Dec. 1366
Richard Belmer, O.P.	prov. 1414 (suffr. in Bath 1414–18, Exeter 1418–33)	trs. to Achonry 12 Apr. 1424
Dionysius		res. *a.* 1447
John Grene, O.S.A.	prov. 30 Mar. 1447 (vicar in Lincoln dioc. 1458, suffr. in York 1452–62, Canterbury 1465–7)	*p.* 1467

TUAM[3]
(TUAM P.)

Cathussach Ua Conaill	—	1117
Muiredach Ua Dubthaig	*a.* 1134	15/16 May 1150

ARCHBISHOPS	ACCESSION	DEATH *unless otherwise stated*
Áed Ua h-Oissín (Edanus)	abp Mar. 1152	1161
Cadla Ua Dubthaig (Catholicus)	*a.* 1167	1201
Felix Ua Ruanada, O.S.A.	1202	res. 23 Mar. 1235, d. 1238
Máel Muire Ó Lachtáin (Marianus)	el. *a.* 6 Apr., temp. *p.* 6 Apr. 1236, cons. 1236	*a.* 25 Dec. 1249

[1] He held the two sees of Ross and Dromore, 1519–26.

[2] There was an ancient monastic church on Inis Cathaigh, founded by St Senan in the sixth century. The diocese was not included in the hierarchy established at Ráith Bressail. Two bps of Inis Cathaigh are recorded in the annals of the twelfth century; and Inis Cathaigh (*Insula Cathai*) was one of the suffragan sees of Cashel as recognized by Cardinal Paparo in 1152. After the twelfth century, its church became a collegiate church, with traditional rights over certain churches on both banks of the Shannon.

[3] At the synod of Ráith Bressail, Tuam is named as the seat of a diocese corresponding roughly with the diocese of Elphin, whilst Cong was chosen as the seat of a diocese corresponding with the later archdiocese of Tuam in West Connacht. No bp of Cong is recorded; and no bp is given the title 'bp of Tuam' in the Irish annals bef. 1152.

ARCHBISHOPS	ACCESSION	DEATH *unless otherwise stated*
Flann Mac Flainn (Florentius)	el. *a.* 27 May, temp. 25 July, cons. 25 Dec. 1250	*a.* 29 June 1256
Walter de Salerno	prov. 29 May, cons. 6 Sept 1257, temp. 6 Nov. 1257	*a.* 22 Apr. 1258
Tommaltach Ó Conchobair (Thomas)	trs. from Elphin, el. *p.* 17 July 1258, trs. 23 Mar., temp. 20 July 1259	16 June 1279
[Nicol Mac Flainn	el *a.* 20 Oct. 1283 (never cons.)	—]
Stephen de Fulbourn	trs. from Waterford, prov. 12 July, temp. 15 Sept. 1286	3 July 1288
William de Bermingham	el. *c.* autumn 1288, prov. 2 May, temp. 29 Sept. 1289	Jan. 1312
Máel Sechlainn Mac Áeda (Malachias)	trs. from Elphin, el. *c.* Mar. 1312, trs. 19 Dec. 1312, temp. 1 Apr. 1313	10 Aug. 1348
Tomás MacCearbhaill (MacCarwill)	prov. 26 Nov. 1348, temp. 6 Oct. 1349	trs. to Cashel *a.* 8 Mar. 1365
Eóin Ó Gráda	prov. *p.* 20 Nov. 1364, temp. 19 July 1365	19 Sept. 1371
Gregorius Ó Mocháin I	trs. from Elphin 7 May 1372, temp. 24 Nov. 1372	1383
Gregorius Ó Mocháin II	prov. *c.* 1384 (by Clement VII)	depr. by Urban VI 5 May 1386, d. 1392
Uilliam Ó Cormacáin	prov. by Urban VI 5 May 1386, temp. 15 Mar. 1387	trs. to Clonfert 27 Jan. 1393
Muircheartach mac Pilib Ó Ceallaigh	trs. from Clonfert, el. summer 1392, trs. 26 Jan. 1393	29 Sept. 1407
John Babingle, O.P. (Baterley)	prov. *a.* 25 Oct. 1408 by Gregory XII, prov. 2 Sept. 1409 by Alexander V, conf. 25 May 1410 by John XXIII	prov. to Achonry 1410
Cornelius, O.F.M.	prov. 7 Oct. 1411 (did not take effect)	—
John Bermingham (Winfield)	prov. 7 June, cons. *p.* 5 Dec. 1430	1437
Tomás mac-Muirchearthaigh Ó Ceallaigh, O.P.	trs. from Clonfert 1438 (did not get possession)	1441
John de Burgo, O.S.A.	prov. 9 Oct. 1441, cons. *c.* Nov./ Dec. 1441	*a.* Dec. 1450
Donatus Ó Muireadhaigh, O.S.A.	prov. 2 Dec., cons. *p.* Dec. 1450	17 Jan. 1485
[Walter Blake	prov. 8 Aug. 1483 (did not take effect)	prov. to Clonmacnois 26 Mar. 1487]
Uilliam Seóighe (Joyce)	prov. 16 May 1485	20 Dec. 1501
Philip Pinson, O.F.M.	prov. 2 Dec. 1503 (did not take effect)	5 Dec. 1503
Muiris Ó Fithcheallaigh, O.F.M. (de Portu)	prov. 26 June 1506	25 May 1513
Tomás Ó Maolalaidh, O.F.M.	trs. from Clonmacnois 19 June 1514	28 Apr. 1536

375

WATERFORD[1]
(CASHEL P.)

BISHOPS	ACCESSION	DEATH *unless otherwise stated*
Máel Ísu Ua hAinmere, O.S.B. (Malchus)[2]	cons. 27 Dec. 1096	1135
Toistius	*a.* Mar. 1152	—
Augustinus Ua Selbaig	el. 6 Oct. 1175	1182
Robert I	*fl.* 1195 × 1198	*a.* Oct. 1204
David the Welshman	el. *a.* 19 Oct. 1204	1209
Robert II	el. *p.* June 1210	*a.* Apr. 1223
William Wace	el. *a.* 5 Apr., temp. 6 Apr. 1223	*a.* 19 Apr. 1225
Walter, O.S.B.	el. *c.* 20 Aug., temp. *p.* 20 Aug. 1227	1 Aug. 1232
Stephen, O.S.B.	el. *a.* 19 Dec., temp. *p.* 19 Dec. 1232	*a.* Mar. 1250
Henry	el. *a.* 11 Mar., temp. *p.* 11 Mar. 1250	*a.* 20 July 1251
Philip	el. *a.* 26 Mar. 1252, temp. 14 June 1252	*a.* 15 Apr. 1254
Walter de Southwell	el. *a.* Apr., conf. by Alexander IV 2 Apr. 1255	*c.* 24 Mar. 1271
Stephen de Fulbourn	el. *a.* 10 June, temp. 28 Oct. 1274, lib. *p.* 6 Jan. 1275	trs. to Tuam 12 July 1286
Walter de Fulbourn	trs. from Meath 12 July 1286	*a.* 14 Dec. 1307
Matthew	el. 7 Feb. 1308	18 Dec. 1322
Nicholas Welifed[3]	cons. 17 Apr., temp. 28 July 1323	27 June 1337
Richard Francis	el. *a.* Apr., temp. 6 Apr. 1338 (suffr. in Exeter 1338)	*c.* 1349
Robert Elyot	el. *c.* 1349, cons. *c.* June 1349	depr. *a.* Mar. 1350, prov. to Killala 8 June 1351
Roger Cradock, O.F.M.	prov. 2 Mar., temp. 17 Aug. 1350, (again) 10 May 1352	trs. to Llandaff Dec. 1361, d. *a.* 22 June 1382

WATERFORD AND LISMORE
(CASHEL P.)

Thomas le Reve, bp of Lismore	prov. 16 June, temp. 7 Oct. 1363	*a.* Sept. 1394
Robert Read, O.P.	prov. 9 Sept. 1394	trs. to Carlisle 26 Jan. 1396, to Chichester 5 Oct. 1396
Thomas Sparkford	prov. 27 Jan. 1396	*a.* 11 July 1397
John Deping, O.P.	prov. 11 July, temp. 14 Oct. 1397	4 Feb. 1400

[1] Waterford became the centre of a diocese in 1096 when St Anselm consecrated Malchus first bp of the city.
[2] Abp of Cashel from *c.* 1111.
[3] On 31 July 1327 John XXII decreed the union of the two dioceses of Waterford and Lismore, the union to take effect on the death or resignation of either bp Nothing was done to implement this decree on the death of Welifed in 1337.

BISHOPS	ACCESSION	DEATH *unless otherwise stated*
Thomas Snell	prov. 26 May, temp. 16 Nov. 1400	trs. to Ossory 11 Mar. 1407
Roger of Appleby, O.S.A.	trs. from Dromore *a.* Oct. 1407	*a.* Aug. 1409
John Geese, O.Carm.	prov. 23 Aug. 1409 (depr. by John XXIII Feb. 1414), prov. (again) 4 Dec. 1422 (suffr. in London 1424)	22 Dec. 1425
Thomas Colby, O.Carm.	trs. from Elphin Feb. 1414 (by John XXIII)	*a.* Dec. 1422
Richard Cantwell	prov. 27 Feb. 1426	7 May 1446
Robert Poer	prov. 2 Sept. 1446, cons. *a.* 23 Aug. 1447	*c.* 1472
Richard Martin, O.F.M.	prov. 9 Mar. 1473	—
John Bulcomb (de Cutwart)	prov. 17 Mar. 1475	res. *a.* 17 Oct. 1483
Nicol Ó hAonghusa, O.Cist.	prov. 20 May 1480	—
Thomas Purcell	prov. 17 Oct., cons. *p.* 6 Nov. 1483	res. 13 Apr. 1519
Nicholas Comin	trs. from Ferns 13 Apr. 1519	depr. 21 July 1550

ARCHBISHOPS AND BISHOPS OF THE CHURCH OF IRELAND FROM 1534

1534 has been taken as the year in which the Reformation was extended to Ireland. By May of that year Henry VIII had issued instructions to the Dublin government to ignore papal provisions and jurisdiction. The bishops then in office continued to be recognized by the crown. Their successors, except for some papal provisions in Mary's reign and for some confirmations of papal nominees by Henry VIII and Edward VI, were appointed by the crown until disestablishment came into force on 1 January 1871. The congé d'élire was abolished in 1560 by statute (2 Eliz. I, c. 4). Bishops who were not recognized by the crown have not been included in the lists.

Up to the time of disestablishment the dates given for the accession of new bishops are ordinarily those of nomination (*i.e.* the first letter from the crown relating to the appointment) and of consecration. If either of these is not available and the date of the letters patent is known, that date has been given. For translations the dates of nomination and of the patent of translation have been given whenever possible. For dates up to 1752 old style has been used, except that the year has been treated as beginning on January 1.

The lists for 1534–1870 are primarily based on the unpublished succession lists compiled by the late H. J. Lawlor, sometime Dean of St Patrick's and Professor of Ecclesiastical History in the University of Dublin. Lawlor's sources were chiefly the patent rolls and diocesan registers, nearly all of which perished as a result of the destruction of the Public Record Office of Ireland in 1922. The principal additional sources used by him were Sir James Ware's lists (in *Works*, revised by Walter Harris, vol. i, Dublin, 1739) and Cotton, *Fasti Ecclesiae Hibernicae*, 6 vols. (Dublin, 1847–78). In addition to Lawlor's lists, which are for all dioceses, reference has been made to the lists compiled for individual dioceses by W. M. Brady, J. B. Leslie, G. R. Rennison, H. B. Swanzy and C. A. Webster.

From 1871 onwards archbishops and bishops have been elected. The election of the archbishop of Armagh is made by the house of bishops. The archbishop of Dublin and the bishops are elected either by the diocesan synods or, if a two-thirds majority is not gained in the synod election, by the house of bishops.[1] Elections by diocesan synods require confirmation by the house of bishops. For the accession of new bishops since 1871 the dates of election and consecration have been given. For translations the dates are those of election and, for those elected by diocesan synods, of confirmation. Dates of resignation relate, as far as can be ascertained, to the last day on which the bishop held office. The lists from 1871 have in the main been compiled from the annual *Irish Church Directory*.

Amalgamations of dioceses have been recorded at appropriate places in the lists. In particular, the Church Temporalities Act, 1833, provided for a number of such amalgamations, which were to take effect as vacancies occurred. That act also reduced the provinces to two, Cashel and Tuam ceasing to be archbishoprics.

The following lists had been revised for the third edition of the *Handbook* (1986) by reference to *A New Oxford History of Ireland*, ed. T. W. Moody, F. X. Martin and F. J. Byrne, ix (Oxford, 1984), 392–438.

The dioceses are arranged below in a continuous alphabetical sequence. For a table of dioceses arranged by province, see above p. 328.

ACHONRY
(TUAM P.)

BISHOPS	ACCESSION	DEATH
		unless otherwise stated
Cormac O'Quin [O'Coyn]	prov. 31 Aug. 1522	—
Thomas O'Fihely	prov. 15 June 1547	trs. to Leighlin 30 Aug. 1555
Eugene O'Hart[2]	prov. 28 Jan. 1562	1603

[See granted *in commendam* to Miler Magrath, abp of Cashel, 1613; united to Killala 1622]

ANNADOWN (Enachdun)
(TUAM P.)

Francis	prov. 8 Feb. 1496	—
John O'More[3]	prov. *c.* 1539 ?	*p.* 1553

[See united to Tuam *c.* 1555]

ARDAGH
(ARMAGH P.)

Rory O'Malone	prov. 2 Dec. 1517	1540
[Roger O'Melline]		1553
Richard O'Ferrall	nom. 2 May 1541	*c.* 1572
Patrick MacMahon[4]	1553	
[John Garvey[5]	nom. 6 Nov. 1572]	
Lysach O'Ferrall	nom. 4 Nov. 1583	*a.* 26 Apr. 1601

[Held with Kilmore 1604–33]

[1] For vacancies occurring on or after 1 Dec. 1959 the primary election is no longer made by the diocesan synod but by an electoral college containing representatives of the house of bps and of the clergy and laity of each diocese of the province concerned.
[2] Papal nominee; appears to have been recognized by crown *c.* 1585.
[3] No papal record of provision. He was imprisoned on the ground that he had accepted the bishopric from Rome; he was released in 1540 and then appears to have been recognized by the crown. In 1551 and 1553 he was officially referred to as the bp of the see. The diocese is stated to have been held with Tuam in 1555.
[4] Prov. by pope 24 Nov. 1541, but did not get possession until 1553.
[5] Nominated by crown to Ardagh, but not cons. bp of that see; later bp of Kilmore and abp of Armagh.

BISHOPS	ACCESSION	DEATH *unless otherwise stated*
John Richardson	nom. 8 Apr., cons. Sept. 1633	11 Aug. 1654
	[Held with Kilmore 1661–92]	
Ulysses Burgh	nom. 7 Apr., cons. 11 Sept. 1692	1692

[Held with Kilmore 1693–1742; held with Tuam 1742–1839; since 1839 united to Kilmore]

ARDFERT
(CASHEL P.)

[See vacant in 1534]

James Fitzmaurice[1] [Fitzrichard Pierce]	prov. 15 May 1536	1583
Nicholas Kenan	nom. 26 June, l.p. 22 Oct. 1588	*c.* 1599
John Crosbie	nom. 2 Oct., l.p. 15 Dec. 1600	Sept. 1621
John Steere	trs. from Kilfenora, nom. 8 Dec. 1621, l.p. 20 July 1622	May 1628
William Steere	nom. 21 July, cons. Oct. 1628	21 Jan. 1638
Thomas Fulwar	nom. 27 June 1641, cons. 1641	trs. to Cashel 1 Feb. 1661

[See then united to Limerick]

ARMAGH
(ARMAGH P.)

ARCHBISHOPS	ACCESSION	DEATH *unless otherwise stated*
George Cromer	prov. 2 Oct. 1521, cons. Apr. 1522	16 Mar. 1543
George Dowdall	nom. 19 Apr. 1543, cons. Dec. 1543	deemed to have deserted see *a.* 28 July 1551
Hugh Goodacre	nom. 28 Oct. 1552, cons. 2 Feb. 1553	1 May 1553
George Dowdall (reinstated)	rest. 23 Oct. 1553	15 Aug. 1558
Adam Loftus	nom. 30 Oct. 1562,[2] cons. 2 Mar. 1563	trs. to Dublin 9 Aug. 1567
Thomas Lancaster	nom. 12 Mar., cons. 13 June 1568	1584
John Long	nom. 7 July, cons. 13 July 1584	*a.* 16 Jan. 1589
John Garvey	trs. from Kilmore, nom. 24 Mar., l.p. 10 May 1589	2 Mar. 1595
Henry Ussher	nom. 24 May, cons. Aug. 1595	2 Apr. 1613
Christopher Hampton	nom. 16 Apr., cons. 8 May 1613	3 Jan. 1625
James Ussher[3]	trs. from Meath, nom. 29 Jan., l.p. 21 Mar. 1625	21 Mar. 1656
John Bramhall	trs. from Derry, nom. 1 Aug. 1660, l.p. 18 Jan. 1661	25 June 1663

[1] Papal nominee, recognized by crown.
[2] Congé d'élire, in spite of the act 2 Eliz. I, c. 4; the chapter refused to elect and the crown proceeded to appoint directly.
[3] *See also* Carlisle.

ARCHBISHOPS	ACCESSION	DEATH *unless otherwise stated*
James Margetson	trs. from Dublin, nom. 25 July, l.p. 20 Aug. 1663	28 Aug. 1678
Michael Boyle	trs. from Dublin, nom. 21 Jan, l.p. 27 Feb. 1679	10 Dec. 1702
Narcissus Marsh	trs. from Dublin, nom. 26 Jan., l.p. 18 Feb. 1703	2 Nov. 1713
Thomas Lindsay	trs. from Raphoe, nom. 22 Dec. 1713, l.p. 4 Jan. 1714	13 July 1724
Hugh Boulter	trs. from Bristol, nom. 12 Aug., l.p. 31 Aug. 1724	27 Sept. 1742
John Hoadly	trs. from Dublin, nom. 6 Oct., l.p. 21 Oct. 1742	16 July 1746
George Stone	trs. from Derry, nom. 28 Feb., l.p. 13 Mar. 1747	19 Dec. 1764
Richard Robinson (Baron Rokeby 1777)	trs. from Kildare, nom. 8 Jan., l.p. 8 Feb. 1765	10 Oct. 1794
William Newcome	trs. from Waterford, nom. 16 Jan, l.p. 27 Jan. 1795	11 Jan. 1800
Hon. William Stuart	trs. from St David's, nom. 30 Oct, l.p. 22 Nov. 1800	6 May 1822
Lord John George Beresford	trs. from Dublin, nom and l.p. 17 June 1822	18 July 1862

[Clogher united to Armagh 1850–86)

Marcus Gervais Beresford	trs. from Kilmore, l.p. 15 Oct. 1862	26 Dec. 1885
Robert Bent Knox	trs. from Down, el. 11 May 1886	23 Oct. 1893
Robert Samuel Gregg	trs. from Cork, el. 14 Dec. 1893	10 Jan. 1896
William Alexander	trs. from Derry, el. 25 Feb. 1896	res. 1 Feb. 1911, d. 12 Sept. 1911
John Baptist Crozier	trs. from Down, el. 2 Feb. 1911	11 Apr. 1920
Charles Frederick D'Arcy	trs. from Dublin, el. 17 June 1920	1 Feb. 1938
John Godfrey Fitzmaurice Day	trs. from Ossory, el. 27 Apr. 1938	26 Sept. 1938
John Allen Fitzgerald Gregg	trs. from Dublin, el. 15 Dec. 1938, accepted 1 Jan. 1939	res. 18 Feb. 1959
James McCann	trs. from Meath, el. 19 Feb. 1959	res. 16 July 1969
George Otto Simms	trs. from Dublin, el. 17 July 1969	res. 11 Feb. 1980
John Ward Armstrong	trs. from Cashel, el. 25 Feb. 1980	

CASHEL
(CASHEL P., from 1838 DUBLIN P.)

Edmund Butler	prov. 21 Oct. 1524, cons. *p.* 3 Jan. 1525	5 Mar. 1551
Roland Baron [Fitzgerald]	nom. 14 Oct., cons. Dec. 1553	28 Oct. 1561
James MacCawell	nom. 12 Feb., l.p. 2 Oct. 1567	1570

[Emly united to Cashel 1569]

ARCHBISHOPS	ACCESSION	DEATH *unless otherwise stated*
Miler Magrath[1]	trs. from Clogher, app. 3 Feb. 1571	14 Nov. 1622
Malcolm Hamilton	nom. 8 Mar., cons. 29 June 1623	25 Apr. 1629
Archibald Hamilton	trs. from Killala, nom. 14 Nov. 1629, l.p. 20 Apr. 1630	1659
Thomas Fulwar	trs. from Ardfert, nom. 2 Aug. 1660, l.p. 1 Feb. 1661	31 Mar. 1667
Thomas Price	trs. from Kildare, nom. 20 Apr., l.p. 30 Mar. 1667	4 Aug. 1685
Narcissus Marsh	trs. from Ferns, nom. 25 Dec. 1690, l.p. 26 Feb. 1691	trs. to Dublin 24 May 1694
William Palliser	trs. from Cloyne, nom. 10 Apr., l.p. 26 June 1694	1 Jan. 1727
William Nicolson	trs. from Derry, nom. 10 Jan., l.p. 28 Jan. 1727	14 Feb. 1727
Timothy Godwin	trs. from Kilmore, nom. 20 June, l.p. 3 July 1727	13 Dec. 1729
Theophilus Bolton	trs. from Elphin, nom. 26 Dec. 1729, l.p. 6 Jan. 1730	31 Jan. 1744
Arthur Price	trs. from Meath, nom. 20 Apr., l.p. 7 May 1744	17 July 1752
John Whitcombe	trs. from Down, nom. 12 Aug., l.p. 1 Sept. 1752	22 Sept. 1753
Michael Cox	trs. from Ossory, nom. 3 Jan., l.p. 22 Jan. 1754	28 May 1779
Charles Agar[2]	trs. from Cloyne, nom. 26 July, l.p. 6 Aug. 1779	trs. to Dublin 7 Dec. 1801
Hon. Charles Brodrick	trs. from Kilmore, nom. 21 Nov., l.p. 9 Dec. 1801	6 May 1822
Richard Laurence	nom. 28 June, cons. 21 July 1822	28 Dec. 1838

[Waterford and Lismore united to Cashel from 14 Aug. 1833; on death of Abp Laurence province united to Dublin and see ceased to be archbishopric]

BISHOPS	ACCESSION	DEATH *unless otherwise stated*
Stephen Creagh Sandes	trs. from Killaloe, nom. 23 Jan., l.p. Feb. 1839	13 Nov. 1842
Robert Daly	nom. 28 Dec. 1842, cons. 29 Jan. 1843	16 Feb. 1872
Maurice Fitzgerald Day	el. 19 Mar., cons. 14 Apr. 1872	res. 30 Sept. 1899, d. 13 Dec. 1904
Henry Stewart O'Hara	el. 6 Feb., cons. 24 Feb. 1900	res. 31 Mar. 1919, d. 11 Dec. 1923
Robert Miller	el. 12 May, cons. 11 June 1919	13 Mar. 1931
John Frederick McNeice	el. 29 Apr., cons. 24 June 1931	trs. to Down 12 Dec. 1934
Thomas Arnold Harvey	el. 25 Jan., cons. 25 Mar. 1935	res. 15 May 1958
William Cecil de Pauley	el. 18 June, cons. 29 Sept. 1958	30 Mar. 1968

[1] Also held Waterford and Lismore 1582–89 and 1592–1607; held Killala and Achonry 1607–22.
[2] Created Baron Somerton, 1795; Viscount Somerton, 1800; earl of Normanton, 1806.

BISHOPS	ACCESSION	DEATH *unless otherwise stated*
John Ward Armstrong	el. 22 May, cons. 21 Sept. 1968[1]	trs. to Armagh 25 Feb. 1980
Noel Vincent Willoughby	el. 28 Mar., cons. 25 Apr. 1980	

CLOGHER
(ARMAGH P.)

Patrick O'Cullen	prov. 11 Feb. 1517	1534
Hugh O'Carolan[2]	prov. 6 Aug. 1535, cons. Jan. 1537.	1569
Miler Magrath[3]	l.p. 18 Sept. 1570	trs. to Cashel 3 Feb. 1571
	[See unfilled by crown 1571–1604]	
George Montgomery[4]	nom. 15 Feb., l.p. 13 June 1605	15 Jan. 1621
James Spottiswood	nom. 20 Jan., mandate for cons. 22 Oct. 1621	Mar. 1645
Henry Jones	nom. 29 Sept, cons. 9 Nov. 1645	trs. to Meath 25 May 1661
John Leslie	trs. from Raphoe, nom. 29 Apr., l.p. 17 June 1661	8 Sept. 1671
Robert Leslie	trs. from Raphoe, l.p. 26 Oct. 1671	10 Aug. 1672
Roger Boyle	trs. from Down, nom. 29 Aug, l.p. 19 Sept. 1672	26 Nov. 1687
Richard Tennison	trs. from Killala, nom. 4 Dec. 1690, l.p. 28 Feb. 1691	trs. to Meath 25 June 1697
St George Ashe	trs. from Cloyne, nom. 1 June, l.p. 25 June 1697	trs. to Derry 25 Feb. 1717
John Stearne	trs. from Dromore, nom. 28 Feb., l.p. 30 Mar. 1717	6 June 1745
Robert Clayton	trs. from Cork, nom. 3 Aug., l.p. 26 Aug. 1745	26 Feb. 1758
John Garnett	trs. from Ferns, nom. 14 Mar., l.p. 4 Apr. 1758	1 Mar. 1782
John Hotham (bt. 1794)	trs. from Ossory, nom. 11 Apr., l.p. 17 May 1782	3 Nov. 1795
William Foster	trs. from Kilmore, nom. 26 Dec. 1795, l.p. 21 Jan. 1796	*a.* 4 Nov. 1797
John Porter	trs. from Killala, nom. 18 Dec., l.p. 30 Dec. 1797	27 July 1819
Lord John George Beresford	trs. from Raphoe, nom. 29 Aug., l.p. 25 Sept. 1819	trs. to Dublin 21 Apr. 1820
Hon. Percy Jocelyn	trs. from Ferns, nom. and l.p. 3 Apr. 1820	depr. 21 Oct. 1822, d. 2 Dec. 1843
Lord Robert Ponsonby Tottenham Loftus	trs. from Ferns, nom. 26 Nov., l.p. 21 Dec. 1822	26 Apr. 1850
	[See united to Armagh 1850–86]	

---

[1] In 1977 the dioceses of Cashel and Emly, Waterford and Lismore and Ossory, Ferns and Leighlin were united and John Ward Armstrong was confirmed as bishop of the united dioceses.

[2] Renounced prov. 1 Oct. 1542; conf. by crown 8 Oct. 1542.

[3] Papal bp of Down; accepted royal supremacy.

[4] Held with Derry and Raphoe to 1610; from 1612 held with Meath.

BISHOPS	ACCESSION	DEATH *unless otherwise stated*
Charles Maurice Stack	el. 4 June, cons. 29 June 1886	res. 31 Dec. 1902, d. 9 Jan. 1914
Charles Frederick D'Arcy	el. 21 Jan., cons. 24 Feb. 1903	trs. to Ossory 6 Nov. 1907
Maurice Day	el. 19 Dec. 1907, cons. 25 Jan. 1908	27 May 1923
James MacManaway	el. 9 July, cons. 6 Aug. 1923	res. 30 Sept. 1943, d. 29 Nov. 1947
Richard Tyner	el. 9 Nov. 1943, cons. 6 Jan. 1944	6 Apr. 1958
Alan Alexander Buchanan	el. 17 June, cons. 29 Sept. 1958	trs. to Dublin 22 Nov. 1969
Richard Patrick Crosland Hanson	el. 9 Dec. 1969, cons. 17 Mar. 1970	res. 31 Mar. 1973
Robert William Heavener	el. 4 May, cons. 29 June 1973	res. 31 May 1980
George McMullan	el. 13 June, cons. 7 Sept. 1980	

CLONFERT
(TUAM P.)

Denis O'More	prov. 7 Nov. 1509	1534
Richard Nangle	cons. 1536	expelled[1] *a.* 19 July 1538
Roland de Burgo [Burke]	prov. 18 May 1534, cons. *p.* 8 June 1537	20 June 1580
Stephen Kirwan	trs. from Kilmacduagh, nom. 30 Mar., l.p. 24 May 1582	*a.* 4 Nov. 1601

[See granted *in commendam* to Roland Lynch, bp of Kilmacduagh, 1602; after his death in 1625 Kilmacduagh was held by the bp of Clonfert until 1834, when both sees were united to Killaloe]

Robert Dawson	nom. 29 Aug. 1626, cons. 4 May 1627	13 Apr. 1643
William Baily	nom. 22 Dec. 1643, cons. 2 May 1644	11 Aug. 1664
Edward Wolley	nom. 5 Nov. 1664, cons. 16 Apr. 1665	1684
William Fitzgerald	nom. 9 Dec. 1690, cons. 26 July 1691	1722
Theophilus Bolton	nom. 17 Aug., cons. 30 Sept. 1722	trs. to Elphin 16 Apr. 1724
Arthur Price	nom. 19 Mar., cons. 3 May 1724	trs. to Ferns 26 May 1730
Edward Synge	nom. 14 May, cons. 7 June 1730	trs. to Cloyne 22 Mar. 1732
Mordecai Cary	nom. 18 Feb., cons. 26 Mar. 1732	trs. to Killala 20 Dec. 1735
John Whitcombe	nom. 22 Nov. 1735, cons. 4 Jan. 1736	trs. to Down 21 Mar. 1752
Arthur Smyth	nom. 24 Feb., cons. 5 Apr. 1752	trs. to Down 24 Jan. 1753
Hon. William Carmichael	nom. 28 Dec. 1752, cons. 1 Apr. 1753	trs. to Ferns 5 Apr. 1758

[1] Expelled by papal nominee, de Burgo, who was conf. by crown 24 Oct. 1541.

383

BISHOPS	ACCESSION	DEATH
		unless otherwise stated
William Gore	nom. 17 Mar., cons. 16 Apr. 1758	trs. to Elphin 3 May 1762
John Oswald	nom. 1 Apr., cons. 4 July 1762	trs. to Dromore 7 May 1763
Denison Cumberland	nom. 19 Apr., cons. 19 June 1763	trs. to Kilmore 6 Mar. 1772
Walter Cope	nom. 27 Jan, cons. 15 Mar. 1772	trs. to Ferns 9 Aug. 1782
John Law	nom. 26 July, cons. 21 Sept. 1782	trs. to Killala 10 Nov. 1787
Richard Marlay	nom. 10 Sept., cons. 30 Dec. 1787	trs. to Waterford 21 Mar. 1795
Hon. Charles Brodrick	nom. 11 Mar., cons. 22 Mar. 1795	trs. to Kilmore 19 Jan. 1796
Hugh Hamilton	nom. 31 Dec. 1795, cons. 31 Jan. 1796	trs. to Ossory 24 Jan. 1799
Matthew Young	nom. 15 Jan., cons. 3 Feb. 1799	28 Nov. 1800
George de la Poer Beresford	nom. 23 Dec. 1800, cons. 1 Feb. 1801	trs. to Kilmore 1 Mar. 1802
Nathaniel Alexander	nom. 13 Jan, cons. 21 Mar. 1802	trs. to Killaloe 22 May 1804
Christopher Butson[1]	nom. 5 May, cons. 29 July 1804	22 Mar. 1836

CLONMACNOIS
(ARMAGH P.)

Quintin O'Higgin	prov. 10 Nov. 1516	1538
Florence Kirwan[2]	prov. 5 Dec. 1539	1554
Peter Wall [Wale]	prov. 4 May 1556	1568

[See united to Meath 1569]

CLOYNE
(CASHEL P.)

[See united to Cork 1418–1638]

George Synge	nom. 21 June, cons. 11 Nov. 1638	3 Aug. 1652

[See held with Cork 1661–78]

Patrick Sheridan	nom. 11 Feb., cons. 27 Apr. 1679	22 Nov. 1682
Edward Jones	nom. 22 Dec. 1682, cons. 11 Mar. 1683	trs. to St Asaph 13 Dec. 1692
William Palliser	nom. 20 Jan., cons. 5 Mar. 1693	trs. to Cashel 26 June 1694
Tobias Pullein	nom. 29 Sept., cons. Nov. 1694	trs. to Dromore 7 May 1695
St George Ashe	nom. 17 Mar., cons. 18 July 1695	trs. to Clogher 25 June 1697
John Pooley	nom. 1 June, cons. 5 Dec. 1697	trs. to Raphoe 12 Sept. 1702

---

[1] Became bp of the united diocese of Killaloe, Kilfenora, Clonfert and Kilmacduagh, 29 Jan. 1834.
[2] Papal nominee conf. by crown 23 Sept. 1541.

BISHOPS	ACCESSION	DEATH *unless otherwise stated*
Charles Crow	nom. 18 May, cons. 18 Oct. 1702	26 June 1726
Henry Maule	nom. 28 July, cons. 11 Sept. 1726	trs. to Dromore 20 Mar. 1732
Edward Synge	trs. from Clonfert, nom. 18 Feb., l.p. 22 Mar. 1732	trs. to Ferns 8 Feb. 1734
George Berkeley	nom. 18 Jan., cons. 19 May 1734	14 Jan. 1753
James Stopford	nom. 19 Jan., cons. 11 Mar. 1753	24 Aug. 1759
Robert Johnson	nom. 19 Sept., cons. 21 Oct. 1759	16 Jan. 1767
Hon. Frederick Augustus Hervey	nom. 2 Feb., cons. 31 May 1767	trs. to Derry 18 Feb. 1768
Charles Agar	nom. 12 Feb., cons. 20 Mar. 1768	trs. to Cashel 6 Aug. 1779
George Chinnery	trs. from Killaloe, nom. 29 Jan., l.p. 15 Feb. 1780	13 Aug. 1780
Richard Woodward	nom. 17 Jan., cons. 4 Feb. 1781	12 May 1794
William Bennet	trs. from Cork, nom. 20 May, l.p. 27 June 1794	16 July 1820
Charles Mongan Warburton	trs. from Limerick, nom. 26 Aug., l.p. 18 Sept. 1820	9 Aug. 1826
John Brinkley	nom. 13 Sept., cons. 8 Oct. 1826	14 Sept. 1835

[See then united to Cork]

CONNOR
(ARMAGH P.)

[See united to Down 1441 to 31 Dec. 1944]

Charles King Irwin [1]	1 Jan. 1945	res. 31 May 1956
Robert Cyril Hamilton Glover Elliott	el. 28 June, cons. 21 Sept. 1956	res. 31 Aug. 1969
Arthur Hamilton Butler	trs. from Tuam, el. 16 Sept., conf. 14 Oct. 1969	res. 30 Sept. 1981
William John McCappin	el. 28 Oct., cons. 30 Nov. 1981	

CORK
(CASHEL P., from 1833 DUBLIN P.)

John Bennet	prov. 28 Jan. 1523	1536
Dominic Tirrey	nom. 11 June, l.p. 25 Sept. 1536	1556
Roger Skiddy	temp. [2] 2 Nov. 1557, cons. 30 Oct. 1562	res. 18 Mar. 1567
Richard Dixon	nom. 17 May, l.p. 6 June 1570	depr. 8 Nov. 1571
Matthew Sheyn	nom. 2 Jan., l.p. 29 May 1572	1582 or 1583
William Lyon [3]	nom. Nov. 1583	4 Oct. 1617

[1] Bp of united diocese of Down, Connor and Dromore; retained Connor on the separation of the see.
[2] The grant of temp. in 1557 was confirmed by l.p. of 1562.
[3] Bp of Ross; granted Cork *in commendam.*, Cork and Ross have since been held by the same bp.

BISHOPS	ACCESSION	DEATH
		unless otherwise stated
John Boyle	nom. 22 Apr., l.p. 25 Aug. 1618	10 July 1620
Richard Boyle	nom. 23 Aug., cons. Nov. 1620	trs. to Tuam 30 May 1638
William Chappell	nom. 30 Aug., cons. 11 Nov. 1638	13 May 1649
Michael Boyle	nom. 6 Aug. 1660, cons. 27 Jan. 1661	trs. to Dublin 27 Nov. 1663
Edward Synge	trs. from Limerick, nom. 24 Aug., l.p. 21 Dec. 1663	22 Dec. 1678
Edward Wetenhall	nom. 3 Feb., cons. 23 Mar. 1679	trs. to Kilmore 18 Apr. 1699
Dive Downes	nom. 9 Mar., cons. 4 June 1699	13 Nov. 1709
Peter Browne	nom. 26 Dec. 1709, cons. 8 Apr. 1710	25 Aug. 1735
Robert Clayton	trs. from Killala, nom. 22 Nov., l.p. 19 Dec. 1735	trs. to Clogher 26 Aug. 1745
Jemmett Browne	trs. from Dromore, nom. 3 Aug., l.p. 27 Aug. 1745	trs. to Elphin 6 Mar. 1772
Isaac Mann	nom. 27 Jan., cons. 15 Mar. 1772	10 Dec. 1788
Euseby Cleaver	nom. 21 Mar., cons. 28 Mar. 1789	trs. to Ferns 13 June 1789
William Foster	nom. 5 June, cons. 14 June 1789	trs. to Kilmore 11 June 1790
William Bennet	nom. 7 May, cons. 13 June 1790	trs. to Cloyne 27 June 1794
Hon. Thomas Stopford	nom. 20 May, cons. 29 June 1794	24 Jan. 1805
Lord John George Beresford	nom. 13 Feb., cons. 24 Mar. 1805	trs. to Raphoe 10 Aug. 1807
Hon. Thomas St Lawrence	nom. 3 Sept., cons. 27 Sept. 1807	10 Feb. 1831
Samuel Kyle	nom. 2 Mar., cons. 27 Mar. 1831	18 May 1848

[Cloyne united to Cork from 14 Sept. 1835]

James Wilson	nom. 24 June, cons. 30 July 1848	5 Jan. 1857
William Fitzgerald	nom. 27 Jan., cons. 8 Mar. 1857	trs. to Killaloe 3 Feb. 1862
John Gregg	nom. 15 Jan., cons. 16 Feb. 1862	26 May 1878
Robert Samuel Gregg	trs. from Ossory, el. 27 June, conf. 4 July 1878	trs. to Armagh 14 Dec. 1893
William Edward Meade	el. 5 Dec. 1893, cons. 6 Jan. 1894	12 Oct. 1912
Charles Benjamin Dowse	trs. from Killaloe, el. 22 Nov., conf. 23 Dec. 1912	res. 15 Sept. 1933, d. 13 Jan. 1934
William Edward Flewett	el. 6 Oct., cons. 30 Nov. 1933	5 Aug. 1938
Robert Thomas Hearn	el. 19 Oct., cons. 13 Nov. 1938	14 July 1952
George Otto Simms	el. 2 Oct., cons. 28 Oct. 1952	trs. to Dublin 11 Dec. 1956
Richard Gordon Perdue	trs. from Killaloe, el. 31 Jan., conf. 19 Feb. 1957	res. 20 May 1978
Samuel Greenfield Poyntz	el. 20 June, cons. 17 Sept. 1978	

DERRY
(ARMAGH P.)

BISHOPS	ACCESSION	DEATH *unless otherwise stated*
Rory O'Donnell	prov. 11 Jan. 1520	8 Oct. 1551 [1]
Eugene O'Doherty	prov. 25 June 1554	c. 1569
	[See not filled by crown until 1605]	
George Montgomery [2]	nom. 15 Feb., l.p. 13 June 1605	trs. to Meath 8 July 1609
Brutus Babington	nom. 11 Aug. 1610, cons. 1610	10 Sept. 1611
John Tanner	nom. 16 Apr., cons. May 1613	14 Oct. 1615
George Downham	nom. 28 Oct. 1616, cons. Jan. 1617	17 Apr. 1634
John Bramhall	nom. 9 May, cons. 26 May 1634	trs. to Armagh 18 Jan. 1661
George Wild	nom. 6 Aug. 1660, cons. 27 Jan. 1661	29 Dec. 1665
Robert Mossom	nom. 11 Jan, cons. 1 Apr. 1666	21 Dec. 1679
Michael Ward	trs. from Ossory, nom. 6 Jan, l.p. 22 Jan. 1680	3 Oct. 1681
Ezekiel Hopkins	trs. from Raphoe, nom. 21 Oct., l.p. 11 Nov. 1681	22 June 1690
William King	nom. 7 Dec. 1690, cons. 25 Jan. 1691	trs. to Dublin 11 Mar. 1703
Charles Hickman	nom. 17 Feb., cons. 11 June 1703	28 Nov. 1713
John Hartstonge	trs. from Ossory, nom. 7 Feb., l.p. 3 Mar. 1714	30 Jan. 1717
St George Ashe	trs. from Clogher, nom. 16 Feb., l.p. 25 Feb. 1717	27 Feb. 1718
William Nicolson	trs. from Carlisle, l.p. 2 May 1718	trs. to Cashel 28 Jan. 1727
Henry Downes	trs. from Meath, nom. 11 Jan, l.p. 8 Feb. 1727	14 Jan. 1735
Thomas Rundle	nom. 20 Feb., cons. 3 Aug. 1735	15 Apr. 1743
Carew Reynell	trs. from Down, nom. 25 Apr., l.p. 6 May 1743	1 Jan. 1745
George Stone	trs. from Kildare, nom. 26 Apr., l.p. 11 May 1745	trs. to Armagh 13 Mar. 1747
William Barnard	trs. from Raphoe, nom. 28 Feb., l.p. 19 Mar. 1747	10 Jan. 1768
Hon. Frederick Augustus Hervey (earl of Bristol 1779)	trs. from Cloyne, nom. 28 Jan., l.p. 18 Feb. 1768	8 July 1803
Hon. William Knox	trs. from Killaloe, nom. 27 Aug., l.p. 9 Sept. 1803	10 July 1831
Hon. Richard Ponsonby	trs. from Killaloe, nom. 14 Sept., l.p. 21 Sept. 1831	27 Oct. 1853
	[Raphoe united to Derry from 5 Sept. 1834]	
William Higgin	trs. from Limerick, nom. 18 Nov., l.p. 7 Dec. 1853	12 July 1867
William Alexander	nom. 27 July, cons. 6 Oct. 1867	trs. to Armagh 25 Feb. 1896

[1] Ware's date; 1550 in Annals of the Four Masters.
[2] Also held Clogher and Raphoe; resigned on promise of trs. to Meath.

BISHOPS	ACCESSION	DEATH *unless otherwise stated*
George Alexander Chadwick	el. 18 Feb, cons. 25 Mar. 1896	res. 31 Jan. 1916, d. 27 Dec. 1923
Joseph Irvine Peacocke	el. 15 Mar., cons. 25 Apr. 1916	res. 31 Dec. 1944
Robert M'Neil Boyd	trs. from Killaloe, el. 18 Mar., conf. 20 Mar. 1945	1 July 1958
Charles John Tyndall	trs. from Kilmore, el. and conf. 14 Oct. 1958	res. 30 Sept. 1969
Cuthbert Irvine Peacocke	el. 16 Oct. 1969, cons. 6 Jan. 1970	res. 31 Mar. 1975
Robert Henry Alexander Eames	el. 9 May, cons. 9 June 1975	trs. to Down 20 May 1980
James Mehaffey	el. 27 June, cons. 7 Sept. 1980	

DOWN[1]
(ARMAGH P.)

Robert Blyth	prov. 16 Apr. 1520	res. *c.* 1541, d. 1547
Eugene Magennis[2]	prov. 16 June 1539, l.p. 8 May 1542	*c.* 1563
[James MacCawell[3]	nom. 6 June 1565]	
John Merriman	temp. 20 Dec. 1568, cons. 19 Jan. 1569	*a.* 6 July 1571
Hugh Allen	l.p. 21 Nov. 1572	trs. to Ferns 24 May 1582
Edward Edgeworth	nom. 31 July 1593, cons. 1593	1595
John Charden	cons. 4 May 1596	1601
Robert Humpston	nom. 17 July 1601, cons. 5 Apr. 1602	*a.* 14 Jan. 1607
John Todd[4]	nom. 24 Jan., l.p. 16 May 1607	res. 20 Jan. 1612
James Dundas	nom. 23 Feb., cons. July 1612	1612
Robert Echlin	nom. 29 Nov. 1612, l.p. 4 Mar. 1613	17 July 1635
Henry Leslie	nom. 8 Aug., cons. 4 Oct. 1635	trs. to Meath 19 Jan. 1661
Jeremy Taylor	nom. 6 Aug. 1660, cons. 27 Jan. 1661	13 Aug. 1667
Roger Boyle	nom. 26 Aug., cons. 18 Oct. 1667	trs. to Clogher 19 Sept. 1672
Thomas Hacket	nom. 29 Aug., cons. 28 Sept. 1672	depr. 21 Mar. 1694, d. Aug. 1697
Samuel Foley	nom. 17 Aug., cons. 2 Sept. 1694	22 May 1695
Edward Walkington	nom. 10 July, cons. 4 Aug. 1695	Jan. 1699
Edward Smyth	nom. 21 Jan., cons. 2 Apr. 1699	16 Oct. 1720
Francis Hutchinson	nom. 30 Nov. 1720, cons. 22 Jan. 1721	23 June 1739
Carew Reynell	nom. 4 Sept., cons. 18 Nov. 1739	trs. to Derry 6 May 1743

[1] Connor was united to Down from 1441 to 31 Dec. 1944.
[2] Papal nominee subsequently conf. by crown.
[3] Did not get possession; later abp of Cashel.
[4] Also held Dromore. Ware says he was deprived and did not resign. *Cal. S.P. Ire., 1611–14*, 248, shows that he resigned.

BISHOPS	ACCESSION	DEATH *unless otherwise stated*
John Ryder	trs. from Killaloe, nom. 25 Apr., l.p. 1 Aug. 1743	trs. to Tuam 19 Mar. 1752
John Whitcombe	trs. from Clonfert, nom. 24 Feb., l.p. 21 Mar. 1752	trs. to Cashel 1 Sept. 1752
Robert Downes	trs. from Ferns, nom. 12 Aug., l.p. 13 Oct. 1752	trs. to Raphoe 16 Jan. 1753
Arthur Smyth	trs. from Clonfert, nom. 28 Dec. 1752, l.p. 24 Jan. 1753	trs. to Meath 28 Oct. 1765
James Traill	nom. 27 Sept., cons. 3 Nov. 1765	12 Nov. 1783
William Dickson	nom. 19 Nov. 1783, cons. 1 Feb. 1784	19 Sept. 1804
Nathaniel Alexander	trs. from Killaloe, nom 2 Nov., l.p. 21 Nov. 1804	trs. to Meath 21 Mar. 1823
Richard Mant	trs. from Killaloe, nom. 13 Mar., l.p. 23 Mar. 1823	2 Nov. 1848

[Dromore united to Down from 9 Apr. 1842]

Robert Bent Knox	nom. 2 Apr., cons. 1 May 1849	trs. to Armagh 11 May 1886
William Reeves	el. 18 Mar., cons. 29 June 1886	12 Jan. 1892
Thomas James Welland	el. 19 Feb., cons. 25 Mar. 1892	29 July 1907
John Baptist Crozier	trs. from Ossory, el. 3 Sept., conf. 26 Sept. 1907	trs. to Armagh 2 Feb. 1911
Charles Frederick D'Arcy	trs. from Ossory, el. 27 Mar., conf. 29 Mar. 1911	trs. to Dublin 6 Aug. 1919
Charles Thornton Primrose Grierson	el. 9 Oct., cons. 28 Oct. 1919	res. Nov. 1934, d. 9 July 1935
John Frederick McNeice	trs. from Cashel, el. 11 Dec., conf. 12 Dec. 1934	14 Apr. 1942
Charles King Irwin[1]	trs. from Limerick, el. 6 Aug., conf. 17 Nov. 1942	relinquished see 1 Jan. 1945
William Shaw Kerr[2]	el. 9 Dec. 1944, cons. 25 Jan. 1945	res. 31 July 1955
Frederick Julian Mitchell	trs. from Kilmore, el. and conf. 18 Oct. 1955	res. 7 Nov. 1969
George Alderson Quin	el. 26 Nov. 1969, cons. 6 Jan. 1970	res. 31 Mar. 1980
Robert Henry Alexander Eames	trs. from Derry, el. 23 Apr., conf. 20 May 1980	

DROMORE
(ARMAGH P.)

[See was vacant in 1534 and remained unfilled by crown until 1550]

Arthur Magennis[3]	prov. 16 Apr. 1540	*c.* 1575

[See not filled by crown until 1607]

---

[1] Retained Connor on the division of the united diocese.
[2] Bp of Down and Dromore.
[3] Papal nominee subsequently conf. by crown; fiant of 10 May 1550 pardons him and states that he had renounced Pope's authority.

BISHOPS	ACCESSION	DEATH
		unless otherwise stated
John Todd[1]	nom. 24 Jan., l.p. 16 May 1607	res. 20 Jan. 1612
[John Tanner[2]	nom. 9 Feb. 1612, l.p. 7 Jan. 1613]	
Theophilus Buckworth	nom. 16 Apr., cons. May 1613	*c.* 8 Sept. 1652[3]
Robert Leslie	nom. 6 Aug. 1660, cons. 27 Jan. 1661	trs. to Raphoe 20 June 1661

[Diocese administered by Jeremy Taylor, bp of Down 1661–67]

George Rust	nom. 27 Sept., cons. 15 Dec. 1667	Dec. 1670
Essex Digby	nom. 6 Jan., cons. 27 Feb. 1671	12 May 1683
Capel Wiseman	nom. 23 June, cons. 23 Sept. 1683	Sept. 1694
Tobias Pullein	trs. from Cloyne, nom. 17 Mar., l.p. 7 May 1695	22 Jan. 1713
John Stearne	nom. 23 Apr., cons. 10 May 1713	trs. to Clogher 30 Mar. 1717
Ralph Lambert	nom. 14 Mar., cons. 23 Apr. 1717	trs. to Meath 10 Feb. 1727
Charles Cobbe	trs. from Killala, nom. 13 Jan., l.p. 16 Feb. 1727	trs. to Kildare 16 Mar. 1732
Henry Maule	trs. from Cloyne, nom. 18 Feb., l.p. 20 Mar. 1732	trs. to Meath 24 May 1744
Thomas Fletcher	nom. 10 May, cons. 10 June 1744	trs. to Kildare 14 May 1745
Jemmett Browne	trs. from Killaloe, nom. 26 Apr., l.p. 16 May 1745	trs. to Cork 27 Aug. 1745
George Marlay	nom. 3 Aug., cons. 15 Sept. 1745	12 Apr. 1763
John Oswald	trs. from Clonfert, nom. 19 Apr., l.p. 7 May 1763	trs. to Raphoe 25 Aug. 1763
Edward Young	nom. 19 July, cons. 16 Oct. 1763	trs. to Ferns 4 Mar. 1765
Hon. Henry Maxwell	nom. 8 Feb., cons. 10 Mar. 1765	trs. to Meath 15 Apr. 1766
William Newcome	nom. 28 Feb., cons. 27 Apr. 1766	trs. to Ossory 13 Apr. 1775
James Hawkins	nom. 23 Mar., cons. 29 Apr. 1775	trs. to Raphoe 1 Apr. 1780
Hon. William Beresford	nom. 20 Mar., cons. 8 Apr. 1780	trs. to Ossory 21 May 1782
Thomas Percy	nom. 17 Apr., cons. 26 May 1782	30 Sept. 1811
George Hall	nom. 10 Oct., cons. 17 Nov. 1811	23 Nov. 1811
John Leslie	nom. 5 Dec. 1811, cons. 26 Jan. 1812	trs. to Elphin 16 Nov. 1819
James Saurin	nom. 2 Nov., cons. 19 Dec. 1819	9 Apr. 1842

[See then united to Down]

[1] Held with Down.
[2] Not cons. bp of Dromore; appd to Derry instead.
[3] Date of burial.

DUBLIN
(DUBLIN P.)

ARCHBISHOPS	ACCESSION	DEATH *unless otherwise stated*
John Alen	prov. 3 Sept. 1529, cons. 13 Mar. 1530	28 July 1534
George Browne	nom. 11 Jan., cons. 19 Mar. 1536	depr. 1554, d. 1556
Hugh Curwin	prov. 21 June, cons. 8 Sept. 1555	trs. to Oxford 1 Sept. 1567
Adam Loftus	trs. from Armagh, nom. 5 June, l.p. 9 Aug. 1567	5 Apr. 1605
Thomas Jones	trs. from Meath, nom. 8 Oct., l.p. 8 Nov. 1605	10 Apr. 1619
Lancelot Bulkeley	nom. 30 Apr., cons. 3 Oct. 1619	8 Sept. 1650
James Margetson	nom. 3 Aug. 1660, cons. 27 Jan. 1661	trs. to Armagh 20 Aug. 1663
Michael Boyle	trs. from Cork, nom. 24 Aug., l.p. 27 Nov. 1663	trs. to Armagh 27 Feb. 1679
John Parker	trs. from Tuam, nom. 22 Jan., l.p. 28 Feb. 1679	28 Dec. 1681
Francis Marsh	trs. from Kilmore, nom. 10 Jan., l.p. 14 Feb. 1682	16 Nov. 1693
Narcissus Marsh	trs. from Cashel, nom. 9 Apr., l.p. 24 May 1694	trs. to Armagh 18 Feb. 1703
William King	trs. from Derry, nom. 16 Feb., l.p. 11 Mar. 1703	8 May 1729
John Hoadly	trs. from Ferns, nom. 26 Dec. 1729, l.p. 13 Jan. 1730	trs. to Armagh 21 Oct. 1742
Charles Cobbe	trs. from Kildare, l.p. 4 Mar. 1743	14 Apr. 1765
Hon. William Carmichael	trs. from Meath, nom. 29 May, l.p. 12 June 1765	15 Dec. 1765
Arthur Smyth	trs. from Meath, nom. 28 Feb., l.p. 14 Apr. 1766	14 Dec. 1771
John Cradock	trs. from Kilmore, nom. 27 Jan., l.p. 5 Mar. 1772	10 Dec. 1778
Robert Fowler	trs. from Killaloe, nom. 21 Dec. 1778, l.p. 8 Jan. 1779	10 Oct. 1801
Charles Agar, viscount Somerton (earl of Normanton 1806)	trs. from Cashel, nom. 7 Nov., l.p. 7 Dec. 1801	14 July 1809
Euseby Cleaver[1]	trs. from Ferns, nom. 29 July, l.p. 25 Aug. 1809	Dec. 1819
Lord John George Beresford	trs. from Clogher, nom. 21 Mar., l.p. 21 Apr. 1820	trs. to Armagh 17 June 1822
William Magee	trs. from Raphoe, nom. 17 June, l.p. 24 June 1822	18 Aug. 1831
Richard Whately	nom. 20 Oct., cons. 23 Oct. 1831	8 Oct. 1863

[Kildare united to Dublin 8 Aug. 1846]

Richard Chenevix Trench	nom. 18 Dec. 1863, cons. 1 Jan. 1864	res. 28 Nov. 1884, d. 28 Mar. 1886

---

[1] Found to be of unsound mind; apb of Cashel appd coadjutor 27 Aug. 1811.

ARCHBISHOPS	ACCESSION	DEATH *unless otherwise stated*
William Conyngham, Baron Plunket	trs. from Meath, el. 18 Dec., conf. 23 Dec. 1884	1 Apr. 1897
Joseph Ferguson Peacocke	trs. from Meath, el. 19 May 1897	res. 3 Sept. 1915, d. 26 May 1916
John Henry Bernard	trs. from Ossory, el. 7 Oct. 1915	res. 30 June 1919, d. 29 Aug. 1927
Charles Frederick D'Arcy	trs. from Down, el. 6 Aug., conf. 15 Oct. 1919	trs. to Armagh 17 June 1920
John Allen Fitzgerald Gregg	trs. from Ossory, el. 10 Sept. 1920	trs. to Armagh 1 Jan. 1939
Arthur William Barton	trs. from Kilmore, el. 7 Feb., conf. 15 Feb. 1939	res. 15 Nov. 1956
George Otto Simms	trs. from Cork, el. 4 Dec., conf. 11 Dec. 1956	trs. to Armagh 17 July 1969
Alan Alexander Buchanan	trs. from Clogher, el. 10 Sept., conf. 14 Oct. 1969	res. 10 Apr. 1977
Henry Robert McAdoo	trs. from Ossory, el. 15 Apr., conf. 19 Apr. 1977	

ELPHIN
(TUAM P.)

BISHOPS	ACCESSION	DEATH *unless otherwise stated*
John (Max)	prov. 7 Apr. 1525	15 Aug. 1536
Conach O'Shiel [O'-Shyagall, O'Negall]	nom. 23 Sept. 1541	*a.* 28 July 1551
Roland de Burgo[1]	nom. 23 Nov. 1551, l.p. 10 Apr. 1552	20 June 1580
Thomas Chester	nom. 25 May 1582	1583
John Lynch	nom. 4 Nov. 1583	res. 19 Aug. 1611
Edward King	nom. 6 July, cons. Dec. 1611	8 Mar. 1639
Henry Tilson	nom. 7 Aug., cons. 23 Sept. 1639	31 Mar. 1655
John Parker	nom. 6 Aug. 1660, cons. 27 Jan. 1661	trs. to Tuam 9 Aug. 1667
John Hodson	nom. 17 July, cons. 8 Sept. 1667	18 Feb. 1686
Simon Digby	trs. from Limerick, nom. 4 Dec. 1690, l.p. 12 Jan. 1691	7 Apr. 1720
Henry Downes	trs. from Killala, nom. 1 May, l.p. 12 May 1720	trs. to Meath 9 Apr. 1724
Theophilus Bolton	trs. from Clonfert, nom. 18 Mar., l.p. 16 Apr. 1724	trs. to Cashel 6 Jan. 1730
Robert Howard	trs. from Killala, nom. 26 Dec. 1729, l.p. 13 Jan. 1730	3 Apr. 1740
Edward Synge	trs. from Ferns, nom. 30 Apr., l.p. 15 May 1740	27 Jan. 1762
William Gore	trs. from Clonfert, nom. 21 Apr., l.p. 3 May 1762	trs. to Limerick 5 Mar. 1772
Jemmett Browne	trs. from Cork, nom. 27 Jan., l.p. 6 Mar. 1772	trs. to Tuam 11 Apr. 1775

[1] Bp of Clonfert; granted Elphin in addition.

BISHOPS	ACCESSION	DEATH _unless otherwise stated_
Charles Dodgson	trs. from Ossory, nom. 23 Mar., l.p. 12 Apr. 1775	7 Mar. 1795
John Law	trs. from Killala, nom. 11 Mar., l.p. 27 Mar. 1795	19 Mar. 1810
Hon. Power Le Poer Trench	trs. from Waterford, nom. 12 Apr., l.p. 30 Apr. 1810	trs. to Tuam 10 Nov. 1819
John Leslie[1]	trs. from Dromore, nom. 16 Nov. 1819	22 July 1854

EMLY
(CASHEL P.)

Thomas O'Hurley	prov. 6 Oct. 1505	1542
Angus [Aeneas] O'Hernan	nom. 8 Oct. 1542, l.p. 6 Apr. 1543	1553
Raymond de Burgo[2]	prov. 20 Oct. 1550	29 July 1562

[See united to Cashel 1569]

ENACHDUN _see_ ANNADOWN

FERNS
(DUBLIN P.)

John Purcell	prov. 13 Apr., cons. 6 May 1519	20 July 1539
Alexander Devereux	cons. 14 Dec. 1539	_a._ 19 Aug. 1566
John Devereux	nom. 10 Oct., l.p. 19 Oct. 1566	1578
Hugh Allen	trs. from Down, l.p. 24 May 1582	1599

[Leighlin united to Ferns 1597]

Robert Grave	nom. 30 Apr., cons. Aug. 1600	1 Oct. 1600
Nicholas Stafford	nom. 16 Jan., cons. 18 Mar. 1601	15 Nov. 1604
Thomas Ram	nom. 6 Feb., cons. 2 May 1605	24 Nov. 1634
George Andrews	nom. 11 Jan., cons. 14 May 1635	Oct. 1648
Robert Price	nom. 6 Aug. 1660, cons. 27 Jan. 1661	26 Mar. 1666[1]
Richard Boyle	nom. 2 May, cons. 10 June 1666[3]	_c._ Jan. 1683
Narcissus Marsh	nom. 9 Feb., cons. 6 May 1683	trs. to Cashel 26 Feb. 1691
Bartholomew Vigors	nom. 25 Dec. 1690, cons. 8 Mar. 1691	3 Jan. 1722
Josiah Hort	nom. 17 Jan., cons. 25 Feb. 1722	trs. to Kilmore 27 July 1727
John Hoadly	nom. 22 June, cons. 3 Sept. 1727	trs. to Dublin 13 Jan. 1730
Arthur Price	trs. from Clonfert, nom. and l.p. 26 May 1730	trs. to Meath 2 Feb. 1734
Edward Synge	trs. from Cloyne, nom. 18 Jan., l.p. 8 Feb. 1734	trs. to Elphin 15 May 1740
George Stone	nom. 12 May, cons. 3 Aug. 1740	trs. to Kildare 19 Mar. 1743

[1] Became bp of the united diocese of Kilmore, Elphin and Ardagh, 15 Oct. 1841.
[2] Papal nominee, presumably recognized by crown in Mary's reign.
[3] Harris has 26 May 1666 and 10 Jan. 1667. Ware gives the correct dates in his diary for this year (B.M., Add. MS. 4784, fo. 254).

BISHOPS	ACCESSION	DEATH *unless otherwise stated*
William Cottrell	nom. 15 Feb., cons. 19 June 1743	21 June 1744
Robert Downes	nom. 14 July, cons. 19 Aug. 1744	trs. to Down 13 Oct. 1752
John Garnet	nom. 12 Aug., cons. 12 Nov. 1752	trs. to Clogher 4 Apr. 1758
Hon. William Carmichael	trs. from Clonfert, nom. 17 Mar., l.p. 5 Apr. 1758	trs. to Meath 8 June 1758
Thomas Salmon	nom. 30 May, cons. 11 June 1758	19 Mar. 1759
Richard Robinson	trs. from Killala, nom. 27 Mar., l.p. 19 Apr. 1759	trs. to Kildare 13 Apr. 1761
Charles Jackson	nom. 20 Mar., cons. 19 Apr. 1761	trs. to Kildare 25 Feb. 1765
Edward Young	trs. from Dromore, nom. 8 Feb., l.p. 4 Mar. 1765	29 Aug. 1772
Joseph Dean Bourke[1]	nom. 7 Sept., cons. 11 Oct. 1772	trs. to Tuam 8 Aug. 1782
Walter Cope	trs. from Clonfert, nom. 26 July, l.p. 9 Aug. 1782	31 July 1787
William Preston	trs. from Killala, nom. 10 Sept., l.p. 9 Nov. 1787	19 Apr. 1789
Euseby Cleaver	trs. from Cork, nom. 5 June, l.p. 13 June 1789	trs. to Dublin 25 Aug. 1809
Hon. Percy Jocelyn	nom. 31 July, cons. 13 Sept. 1809	trs. to Clogher 3 Apr. 1820
Lord Robert Ponsonby Tottenham Loftus	trs. from Killaloe, nom. 3 Apr., l.p. 5 May 1820	trs. to Clogher 21 Dec. 1822
Thomas Elrington	trs. from Limerick, nom. 26 Nov., l.p. 21 Dec. 1822	12 July 1835

[See then united to Ossory]

KILDARE
(DUBLIN P.)

Walter Wellesley	prov. 1 July 1529	15 May × 18 Oct. 1539
William Miagh	app. 1540	15 Dec. 1548
Thomas Lancaster	nom. 20 Apr., cons. July 1550	depr. 1554[2]
Thomas Leverous	prov. 30 Aug. 1555	depr. 1560, d. *c.* 1577
Alexander Craik	nom. 17 May, cons. Aug. 1560	*a.* 3 Mar. 1564
Robert Daly	nom. 16 Apr., cons. May 1564	23 Feb. × 3 July 1583
Daniel Neylan	nom. 3 July, cons. Nov. 1583	18 May 1603
William Pilsworth	nom. 23 July, cons. 11 Sept. 1604	9 May 1635
Robert Ussher	nom. 19 Oct. 1635, cons. 25 Feb. 1636	7 Sept. 1642
William Golborne	nom. 17 May, cons. 1 Dec. 1644	1650
Thomas Price	nom. 8 Oct. 1660, cons. 10 Mar. 1661	trs. to Cashel 30 May 1667
Ambrose Jones	nom. 20 Apr., cons. 29 June 1667	15 Dec. 1678
Anthony Dopping	nom. 3 Jan., cons. 2 Feb. 1679	trs. to Meath 11 Feb. 1682

[1] Styled hon. 1781; later 3rd earl of Mayo.   [2] Later abp of Armagh.

BISHOPS	ACCESSION	DEATH
		unless otherwise stated
William Moreton	nom. 14 Jan., cons. 19 Feb. 1682	trs. to Meath 18 Sept. 1705
Welbore Ellis	nom. 28 Aug., cons. 11 Nov. 1705	trs. to Meath 13 Mar. 1732
Charles Cobbe	trs. from Dromore, nom. 18 Feb., l.p. 16 Mar. 1732	trs. to Dublin 4 Mar. 1743
George Stone	trs. from Ferns, nom. 15 Feb., l.p. 10 Mar. 1743	trs. to Derry 11 May 1745
Thomas Fletcher	trs. from Dromore, nom. 26 Apr., l.p. 14 May 1745	18 Mar. 1761
Richard Robinson	trs. from Ferns, nom. 26 Mar., l.p. 13 Apr. 1761	trs. to Armagh 8 Feb. 1765
Charles Jackson	trs. from Ferns, nom. 8 Feb., l.p. 25 Feb. 1765	29 Mar. 1790
George Lewis Jones	trs. from Kilmore, nom. 7 May, l.p. 5 June 1790	9 Mar. 1804
Hon. Charles Lindsay	trs. from Killaloe, nom. 9 May, l.p. 14 May 1804	8 Aug. 1846

[See then united to Dublin, in 1976 separated from Dublin and united to Meath]

KILFENORA
(CASHEL P.)

Maurice O'Kelly	prov. 6 Nov. 1514	*c.* 1541
John O'Nialain [O'Neylan][1]	prov. 21 Nov. 1541	1572

[See apparently not filled by crown until 1606;[2] held with Limerick 1606–17]

John Steere	nom. 9 July 1617	trs. to Ardfert 20 July 1622
William Murray	nom. 15 Mar., cons. 18 Dec. 1622	trs. to Llandaff 24 Dec. 1627
James Heygate	nom. 28 Feb., cons. 9 May 1630	30 Apr. 1638
Robert Sibthorp	nom. 19 June, cons. 11 Nov. 1638	trs. to Limerick 1643

[See held with Tuam 1661–1741; with Clonfert 1742–52; since 1752 united to Killaloe]

KILLALA
(TUAM P.)

Richard Barrett	prov. 7 Jan. 1513	*a.* 6 Nov. 1545
Redmond O'Gallagher[3]	prov. 6 Nov. 1545	trs. to Derry 22 June 1569
Owen O'Connor	nom. 18 Oct. 1591, cons. *a.* 25 Mar. 1592	14 Jan. 1607[4]
Archibald Hamilton	nom. 8 Mar., cons. 29 May 1623	trs. to Cashel 20 Apr. 1630
Archibald Adair[5]	nom. 23 Nov. 1629, cons. 9 May 1630	trs. to Waterford 13 July 1641

[1] Papal nominee; fiant of 1552 shows that he was recognized by crown.
[2] Ware refers to 'one Daniel' as bp elect in 1585.
[3] Papal nominee, presumably recognized by crown in Mary's reign. There is no record of his recognition by Elizabeth.
[4] See held *in commendam* by Miler Magrath, abp of Cashel, 1613–22.
[5] Depr. 18 May 1640; deprivation subsequently set aside and trs. to Waterford.

BISHOPS	ACCESSION	DEATH *unless otherwise stated*
John Maxwell	trs. from Ross (Scot.), nom. 13 Jan., l.p. 26 Feb. 1641	trs. to Tuam 30 Aug. 1645
Henry Hall	nom. 7 Aug. 1660, cons. 27 Jan. 1661	19 July 1663
Thomas Bayly	nom. 17 Dec. 1663, cons. 5 June 1664	20 July 1670
Thomas Otway	nom. 19 Oct. 1670, cons. 29 Jan. 1671	trs. to Ossory 7 Feb. 1680
John Smith	nom. 6 Jan., l.p. 13 Feb. 1680	2 Mar. 1681
William Smyth	nom. 15 Apr., cons. June 1681	trs. to Raphoe 17 Feb. 1682
Richard Tennison	nom. 16 Jan., cons. 19 Feb. 1682	trs. to Clogher 28 Feb. 1691
William Lloyd	nom. 7 Dec. 1690, cons. 23 Aug. 1691	11 Dec. 1716
Henry Downes	nom. 24 Jan., cons. 12 May 1717	trs. to Elphin 12 May 1720
Charles Cobbe	nom. 20 May, cons. 14 Aug. 1720	trs. to Dromore 16 Feb. 1727
Robert Howard	nom. 14 Jan., cons. 19 Mar. 1727	trs. to Elphin 13 Jan. 1730
Robert Clayton	nom. 26 Dec. 1729, cons. 10 May 1730	trs. to Cork 19 Dec. 1735
Mordecai Cary	trs. from Clonfert, l.p. 20 Dec. 1735	2 Oct. 1751
Richard Robinson	nom. 31 Oct. 1751, cons. 19 Jan. 1752	trs. to Ferns 19 Apr. 1759
Samuel Hutchinson	nom. 27 Mar., cons. 22 Apr. 1759	27 Oct. 1780
William Cecil Pery	nom. 7 Jan., cons. 18 Feb. 1781	trs. to Limerick 13 May 1784 '
William Preston	nom. 13 Oct., cons. 11 Nov. 1784	trs. to Ferns 9 Nov. 1787
John Law	trs. from Clonfert, nom. 10 Sept., l.p. 10 Nov. 1787	trs. to Elphin 27 Mar. 1795
John Porter	nom. 6 May, cons. 7 June 1795	trs. to Clogher 30 Dec. 1797
Joseph Stock	nom. 1 Jan., cons. 28 Jan. 1798	trs. to Waterford 1 May 1810
James Verschoyle	nom. 12 Apr., cons. 6 May 1810	13 Apr. 1834

[See then united to Tuam]

KILLALOE
(CASHEL P., from 1833 DUBLIN P.)

James O'Currin	prov. 24 Aug. 1526	res. 5 May 1542
Con [Cornelius] O'Dea	nom. 30 May, cons. 12 July 1546	1568 × 1576
Turlough [Terence] O'Brien	prov.¹ 25 June 1554	1569
Murtagh [Maurice] O'Brien-Arra²	nom. 17 May 1570, cons. 1576	res. 1612, d. 30 Apr. 1613
John Rider	nom. 5 July 1612, cons. 12 Jan. 1613	12 Nov. 1632

¹ In succession to O'Currin.
² The queen ordered the revenues of the see to be allowed to him until he should be old enough to be cons. In 1575 she considered that he was still too young.

BISHOPS	ACCESSION	DEATH unless otherwise stated
Lewis Jones	nom. 14 Dec. 1632, cons. 12 Apr. 1633	2 Nov. 1646
Edward Parry	nom. 29 Dec. 1646, cons. 28 Mar. 1647	20 July 1650
Edward Worth	nom. 7 Aug. 1660, cons. 27 Jan. 1661	2 Aug. 1669
Daniel Wytter	nom. 4 Aug., cons. Sept. 1669	16 Mar. 1675
John Roan	nom. 28 Mar., cons. June 1675	5 Sept. 1692
Henry Ryder	nom. 13 May, cons. 11 June 1693	30 Jan. 1696
Thomas Lindsay	nom. 12 Feb., cons. 22 Mar. 1696	trs. to Raphoe 6 June 1713
Sir Thomas Vesey, bt	nom. 11 May, cons. 12 July 1713	trs. to Ossory 28 Apr. 1714
Nicholas Forster	nom. 7 Oct., cons. 7 Nov. 1714	trs. to Raphoe 8 June 1716
Charles Carr	nom. 26 May, cons. June 1716	26 Dec. 1739
Joseph Story	nom. 16 Jan., cons. 10 Feb. 1740	trs. to Kilmore 29 Jan. 1742
John Ryder	nom. 18 Jan., cons. 21 Feb. 1742	trs. to Down 1 Aug. 1743
Jemmett Browne	nom. 29 Aug., cons. 9 Oct. 1743	trs. to Dromore 16 May 1745
Richard Chenevix	nom. 26 Apr., cons. 28 July 1745	trs. to Waterford 15 Jan. 1746
Nicholas Synge	nom. 23 Dec. 1745, cons. 26 Jan. 1746	19 Jan. 1771

[Kilfenora united to Killaloe 1752]

Robert Fowler	nom. 13 June, cons. 28 July 1771	trs. to Dublin 8 Jan. 1779
George Chinnery	nom. 21 Dec. 1778, cons. 7 Mar. 1779	trs. to Cloyne 15 Feb. 1780
Thomas Barnard	nom. 29 Jan., cons. 20 Feb. 1780	trs. to Limerick 12 Sept. 1794
Hon. William Knox	nom. 14 Aug., cons. 21 Sept. 1794	trs. to Derry 9 Sept. 1803
Hon. Charles Dalrymple Lindsay	nom. 27 Aug., cons. 13 Nov. 1803	trs. to Kildare 14 May 1804
Nathaniel Alexander	trs. from Clonfert, nom. 15 May, l.p. 22 May 1804	trs. to Down 21 Nov. 1804
Lord Robert Ponsonby Tottenham Loftus	nom. 3 Nov., cons. 16 Dec. 1804	trs. to Ferns 5 May 1820
Richard Mant	nom. 10 Apr., cons. 7 May 1820	trs. to Down 23 Mar. 1823
Alexander Arbuthnot	nom. 13 Mar., cons. 11 May 1823	9 Jan. 1828
Hon. Richard Ponsonby	nom. 22 Feb., cons. 16 Mar. 1828	trs. to Derry 21 Sept. 1831
Hon. Edmund Knox	nom. 23 Sept., cons. 9 Oct. 1831	trs. to Limerick 29 Jan. 1834
Christopher Butson[1]	29 Jan. 1834	23 Mar. 1836

[1] Bp of Clonfert; became bp of the united diocese of Killaloe, Kilfenora, Clonfert and Kilmacduagh.

BISHOPS	ACCESSION	DEATH
		unless otherwise stated
Stephen Creagh Sandes	nom. 27 Apr., cons. 12 June 1836	trs. to Cashel Feb. 1839
Hon. Ludlow Tonson (Baron Riversdale, 1848)	nom. 23 Jan., cons. 17 Feb. 1839	13 Dec. 1861
William Fitzgerald	trs. from Cork, nom. 15 Jan., l.p. 3 Feb. 1862	24 Nov. 1883
William Bennett Chester	el. 16 Jan., cons. 24 Feb. 1884	27 Aug. 1893
Frederick Richards Wynne	el. 15 Nov., cons. 10 Dec. 1893	3 Nov. 1896
Mervyn Archdall	el. 8 Jan., cons. 2 Feb. 1897	res. 31 Mar. 1912, d. 18 May 1913
Charles Benjamin Dowse	el. 17 May, cons. 11 June 1912	trs. to Cork 23 Dec. 1912
Thomas Sterling Berry	el. 18 Feb., cons. 25 Mar. 1913	res. 6 Mar. 1924, d. 25 Feb. 1931
Henry Edmund Patton	el. 4 Apr., cons. 1 May 1924	28 Apr. 1943
Robert M'Neil Boyd	el. 23 June, cons. 21 Sept. 1943	trs. to Derry 20 Mar. 1945
Hedley Webster	el. 19 June, cons. 25 July 1945	res. 30 Sept. 1953
Richard Gordon Perdue	el. 11 Nov. 1953, cons. 2 Feb. 1954	trs. to Cork 19 Feb. 1957
Henry Arthur Stanistreet	el. 5 Apr., cons. 11 June 1957	res. 1 Nov. 1971
Edwin Owen	el. 1 Dec. 1971, cons. 25 Jan. 1972	

[The see was united to Limerick in 1976]

KILMACDUAGH
(TUAM P.)

Christopher Bodkin[1]	prov. 3 Sept., cons. 4 Nov. 1533	1572
Stephen Kirwan	nom. 6 Nov. 1572, l.p. 13 Apr. 1573	trs. to Clonfert 24 May 1582
[Thomas Burke[2]]		
Roland Lynch[3]	nom. 9 Jan., cons. Aug. 1587	Dec. 1625

KILMORE
(ARMAGH P.)

Edmund Nugent	prov. 22 June 1530	*c.* 1550
John MacBrady[4]	prov. 5 Nov. 1540	1559

[See not filled by crown until 1585]

John Garvey	nom. 20 Jan., l.p. 27 Jan. 1585	trs. to Armagh 10 May 1589

[See unfilled by crown 1589–1603]

[1] Became abp of Tuam in 1537, but continued to hold Kilmacduagh in addition.
[2] Referred to as bp elect in 1585; not cons.
[3] Held Clonfert *in commendam* 1602–25; thereafter see of Kilmacduagh was held by bps of Clonfert.
[4] Papal nominee, presumably recognized by crown in Mary's reign.

BISHOPS	ACCESSION	DEATH *unless otherwise stated*
Robert Draper[1]	nom. 9 Dec. 1603, l.p. 2 Mar. 1604	Aug. 1612
Thomas Moigne	nom. 6 Dec. 1612, cons. 12 Jan. 1613	1 Jan. 1629
William Bedell	nom. 16 Apr., cons. 13 Sept. 1629	7 Feb. 1642
Robert Maxwell	nom. 17 Nov. 1642, cons. 24 Mar. 1643	1 Nov. 1672
Francis Marsh	trs. from Limerick, nom. 4 Dec. 1672, l.p. 10 Jan. 1673	trs. to Dublin 14 Feb. 1682
William Sheridan	nom. 14 Jan., cons. 19 Feb. 1682	depr. 1691, d. 1 Oct. 1711
William Smyth	trs. from Raphoe, l.p. 5 Apr. 1693	24 Feb. 1699
Edward Wetenhall	trs. from Cork, nom. 19 Mar., l.p. 18 Apr. 1699	12 Nov. 1713
Timothy Godwin	nom. 7 Oct. 1714, cons. 16 Jan. 1715	trs. to Cashel 3 July 1727
Josiah Hort	trs. from Ferns, l.p. 27 July 1727	trs. to Tuam 27 Jan. 1742
Joseph Story	trs. from Killaloe, nom. 7 Jan., l.p. 29 Jan. 1742	22 Sept. 1757
John Cradock	nom. 14 Oct., cons. 4 Dec. 1757	trs. to Dublin 5 Mar. 1772
Denison Cumberland	trs. from Clonfert, nom. 27 Jan., l.p. 6 Mar. 1772	*a.* 22 Nov. 1774[2]
George Lewis Jones	nom. 21 Nov. 1774, cons. 22 Jan. 1775	trs. to Kildare 5 June 1790
William Foster	trs. from Cork, nom. 7 May, l.p. 11 June 1790	trs. to Clogher 21 Jan. 1796
Hon. Charles Broderick	trs. from Clonfert, nom. 28 Dec. 1795, l.p. 19 Jan. 1796	trs. to Cashel 9 Dec. 1801
George de la Poer Beresford	trs. from Clonfert, nom. 12 Jan., l.p. 1 Mar. 1802	15 Oct. 1841
John Leslie[3]	15 Oct. 1841	22 July 1854
Marcus Gervais Beresford	nom. 14 Aug., cons. 24 Sept. 1854	trs. to Armagh 15 Oct. 1862
Hamilton Verschoyle	l.p. 24 Oct., cons. 26 Oct. 1862	28 Jan. 1870
Charles Leslie	nom. 8 Apr., cons. 24 Apr. 1870	8 July 1870
Thomas Carson	nom. 9 Sept., cons. 2 Oct. 1870	7 July 1874
John Richard Darley	el. 23 Sept., cons. 25 Oct. 1874	20 Jan. 1884
Samuel Shone	el. 26 Mar., cons. 25 Apr. 1884	res. *c.* 1 Sept. 1897, d. 5 Oct. 1901
Alfred George Elliott	el. 2 Sept., cons. 17 Oct. 1897	28 Sept. 1915
William Richard Moore	el. 10 Nov., cons. 30 Nov. 1915	23 Feb. 1930
Arthur William Barton	el. 4 Apr., cons. 1 May 1930	trs. to Dublin 15 Feb. 1939

[1] The bps of Kilmore held Ardagh in addition 1604–33, 1661–92 and 1693–1742.
[2] Date of burial.
[3] Bp of Elphin; on the death of Bp Beresford succeeded to the united dioceses of Kilmore, Elphin and Ardagh.

BISHOPS	ACCESSION	DEATH *unless otherwise stated*
Albert Edward Hughes	el. 14 Dec. 1938, cons. 25 Apr. 1939	res. 12 May 1950, d. 12 May 1954
Frederick Julian Mitchell	el. 28 July, cons. 21 Sept. 1950	trs. to Down 18 Oct. 1955
Charles John Tyndall	el. 16 Dec. 1955, cons. 2 Feb. 1956	trs. to Derry 14 Oct. 1958
Edward Francis Butler Moore	el. 28 Nov. 1958, cons. 6 Jan. 1959	res. 31 May 1981
William Gilbert Wilson	el. 11 June, cons. 21 Sept. 1981	

LEIGHLIN
(DUBLIN P.)

Matthew Sanders	prov. 10 Apr. 1527	23 Dec. 1549
Robert Travers	nom. 5 Aug. 1550	depr. 1554
Thomas O'Fihely	trs. from Achonry, prov. 30 Aug. 1555	1566[1]
Daniel Cavanagh	nom. 10 Apr., l.p. 7 May 1567	4 Apr. 1587
Richard Meredith	nom. 11 Jan., cons. Apr. 1589	3 Aug. 1597

[See then united to Ferns]

LIMERICK
(CASHEL P., from 1833 DUBLIN P.)

John Quin [Coyn]	prov. 21 Oct. 1524	res. 9 Apr. 1551
William Casey	nom. 6 July 1551	depr. 1556
Hugh Lacy	prov. 24 Nov. 1556	depr. 8 May 1571, d. 1580
William Casey (again)	rest. 8 May 1571	7 Feb. 1591
John Thornburgh	nom. 20 Sept. 1593, l.p. 9 Jan. 1594	trs. to Bristol 4 July 1603
Bernard Adams[2]	nom. 5 Aug. 1603, cons. Apr. 1604	22 Mar. 1626
Francis Gough	nom. 18 Apr., cons. 17 Sept. 1626	29 Aug. 1634
George Webb	nom. 6 Oct., cons. 18 Dec. 1634	22 June 1642
Robert Sibthorp	trs. from Kilfenora, nom. 7 Apr. 1643	Apr. 1649
Edward Synge	nom. 6 Aug. 1660, cons. 27 Jan. 1661	trs. to Cork 21 Dec. 1663

[Ardfert united to Limerick 1661]

William Fuller	nom. 4 Mar., cons. 20 Mar. 1664	trs. to Lincoln Sept. 1667
Francis Marsh	nom. 27 Sept., cons. 22 Dec. 1667	trs. to Kilmore 10 Jan. 1673
John Vesey	l.p. 11 Jan., cons. 22 Dec. 1673	trs. to Tuam 18 Mar. 1679
Simon Digby	nom. 24 Jan., cons. 23 Mar. 1679	trs. to Elphin 12 Jan. 1692
Nathaniel Wilson	nom. 7 Dec. 1690, cons. 8 May 1692	3 Nov. 1695

[1] Ware has 'Friday before Palm Sunday 1567' (Mar. 21); the correspondence about his successor began in 1566.

[2] Held Kilfenora in addition 1606–17.

BISHOPS	ACCESSION	DEATH *unless otherwise stated*
Thomas Smyth	nom. 15 Nov., cons. 8 Dec. 1695	4 May 1725
William Burscough	nom. 29 May, cons. 20 June 1725	*c.* 3 Apr. 1755[1]
James Leslie	nom. 30 Sept., cons. 16 Nov. 1755	24 Nov. 1770
John Averill	nom. 14 Dec. 1770, cons. 6 Jan. 1771	14 Sept. 1771
William Gore	trs. from Elphin, nom. 27 Jan., l.p. 5 Mar. 1772	25 Feb. 1784
William Cecil Pery (Baron Glentworth 1790)	trs. from Killala, nom. 29 Apr., l.p. 13 May 1784	4 July 1794
Thomas Barnard	trs. from Killaloe, nom. 14 Aug., l.p. 12 Sept. 1794	7 June 1806
Charles Mongan Warburton	nom. 28 June., cons. 12 July 1806	trs. to Cloyne 18 Sept. 1820
Thomas Elrington	nom. 1 Sept., cons. 8 Oct. 1820	trs. to Ferns 21 Dec. 1822
John Jebb	nom. 26 Nov. 1822, cons. 12 Jan. 1823	9 Dec. 1833
Hon. Edmund Knox	trs. from Killaloe, nom. 18 Dec. 1833, l.p. 29 Jan. 1834	3 May 1849
William Higgin	nom. 21 May, cons. 15 July 1849	trs. to Derry 7 Dec. 1853
Henry Griffin	nom. 18 Nov. 1853, cons. 1 Jan. 1854	5 Apr. 1866
Charles Graves	nom. 14 Apr., cons. 29 June 1866	17 July 1899
Thomas Bunbury	el. 6 Oct., cons. 1 Nov. 1899	19 Jan. 1907
Raymond D'Audemar Orpen	el. 28 Feb., cons. 2 Apr. 1907	res. 31 Dec. 1920, d. 9 Jan. 1930
Harry Vere White	el. 20 Sept., cons. 18 Oct. 1921	res. 31 Oct. 1933, d. 20 Jan. 1941
Charles King Irwin	el. 12 Dec. 1933, cons. 2 Feb. 1934	trs. to Down 6 Aug. 1942
Evelyn Charles Hodges	el. 17 Nov., cons. 2 Feb. 1942	res. 30 Sept. 1960
Robert Wyse Jackson	el. 2 Nov. 1960, cons. 6 Jan. 1961	res. 12 July 1970
Donald Arthur Richard Caird	el. 31 July, cons. 29 Sept. 1970	trs. to Meath and Kildare 9 Sept. 1976

[The see was then united with Killaloe]

Edwin Owen	el. 21 Sept., enthroned 5 Dec. 1976	res. 6 Jan. 1981
Walton Newcombe Francis Empey	el. 14 Jan., cons. 25 Mar. 1981	

MAYO
(TUAM P.)

John Bell	prov. 4 Nov. 1493	1541
Eugene MacBrehon[2]	prov. 21 Nov. 1541	*c.* 1559

[See then united to Tuam]

---

[1] Date of burial.
[2] Papal nominee, presumably recognized by crown in Mary's reign.

MEATH
(ARMAGH P., from 1976 DUBLIN P.)

BISHOPS	ACCESSION	DEATH *unless otherwise stated*
Edward Staples	prov. 3 Sept. 1529	depr. 29 June 1554, d. *c.* 1560
William Walsh	l.p. 22 Nov. 1554	depr. 1560, d. 4 Jan. 1577
Hugh Brady	nom. 21 Oct., cons. 19 Dec. 1563	14 Feb. 1584
[Clonmacnois united to Meath 1569]		
Thomas Jones	nom. 18 Apr., cons. 12 May 1584	trs. to Dublin 8 Nov. 1605
Roger Dod	l.p. 13 Nov. 1605	27 July 1608
George Montgomery[1]	trs. from Derry, nom. 8 July 1609, l.p. 24 Jan. 1612	15 Jan. 1621
James Ussher	nom. 16 Jan., cons. 2 Dec. 1621	trs. to Armagh 21 Mar. 1625
Anthony Martin	nom. 22 Feb., cons. 25 July 1625	July 1650
Henry Leslie	trs. from Down, nom. 3 Aug. 1660, l.p. 19 Jan. 1661	7 Apr. 1661
Henry Jones	trs. from Clogher, nom. 9 Apr., l.p. 25 May 1661	5 Jan. 1682
Anthony Dopping	trs. from Kildare, nom. 14 Jan., l.p. 11 Feb. 1682	25 Apr. 1697
Richard Tennison	trs. from Clogher, nom. 1 June, l.p. 25 June 1697	29 July 1705
William Moreton	trs. from Kildare, nom. 27 Aug., l.p. 18 Sept. 1705	21 Nov. 1715
John Evans	trs. from Bangor, nom. 19 Jan., l.p. 10 Feb. 1716	2 Mar. 1724
Henry Downes	trs. from Elphin, nom. 17 Mar., l.p. 9 Apr. 1724	trs. to Derry 8 Feb. 1727
Ralph Lambert	trs. from Dromore, nom. 12 Jan., l.p. 10 Feb. 1727	6 Feb. 1732
Welbore Ellis	trs. from Kildare, nom. 18 Feb., l.p. 13 Mar. 1732	1 Jan. 1734
Arthur Price	trs. from Ferns, nom. 18 Jan., l.p. 2 Feb. 1734	trs. to Cashel 7 May 1744
Henry Maule	trs. from Dromore, nom. 10 May, l.p. 24 May 1744	13 Apr. 1758
Hon. William Carmichael	trs. from Ferns, nom. 30 May, l.p. 8 June 1758	trs. to Dublin 12 June 1765
Richard Pococke	trs. from Ossory, nom. 22 June, l.p. 16 July 1765	15 Sept. 1765
Arthur Smyth	trs. from Down, nom. 27 Sept., l.p. 28 Oct. 1765	trs. to Dublin 14 Apr. 1766
Hon. Henry Maxwell	trs. from Dromore, nom. 28 Feb., l.p. 15 Apr. 1766	7 Oct. 1798
Thomas Lewis O'Beirne	trs. from Ossory, nom. 1 Dec., l.p. 18 Dec. 1798	17 Feb. 1823
Nathaniel Alexander	trs. from Down, nom. 12 Mar., l.p. 21 Mar. 1823	21 Oct. 1840

[1] Bp of Clogher, which he continued to hold in addition.

BISHOPS	ACCESSION	DEATH *unless otherwise stated*
Charles Dickinson	nom. 21 Dec., cons. 27 Dec. 1840	12 July 1842
Edward Stopford	nom. 20 Oct., cons. 6 Nov. 1842	17 Sept. 1850
Thomas Stewart Townsend	nom. 9 Oct., cons. 1 Nov. 1850	1 Sept. 1852
Joseph Henderson Singer	nom. 2 Nov., cons. 28 Nov. 1852	16 July 1866
Samuel Butcher	l.p. 21 Aug., cons. 14 Oct. 1866	29 July 1876
William Conyngham, Baron Plunket	el. 18 Oct., cons. 10 Dec. 1876	trs. to Dublin 23 Dec. 1884
Charles Parsons Reichel	el. 19 Aug., cons. 29 Sept. 1885	29 Mar. 1894
Joseph Ferguson Peacocke	el. 15 May, cons. 11 June 1894	trs. to Dublin 19 May 1897
James Bennett Keene	el. 10 Sept., cons. 17 Oct. 1897	5 Aug. 1919
Hon. Benjamin John Plunket	trs. from Tuam, el. 3 Oct., conf. 15 Oct. 1919	res. 31 Mar. 1925, d. 26 Jan. 1947
Thomas Gibson George Collins	el. 4 Feb., cons. 17 Mar. 1926	3 July 1927
John Orr	trs. from Tuam, el. 22 Sept., conf. 15 Nov. 1927	21 July 1938
William Hardy Holmes	trs. from Tuam, el. 14 Oct., conf. 19 Oct. 1938	res. 31 May 1945, d. 26 May 1951
James McCann	el. 4 July, cons. 24 Aug. 1945	trs. to Armagh 19 Feb. 1959
Robert Bonsall Pike	el. 14 Apr., cons. 19 May 1959	27 Dec. 1973
Donald Arthur Richard Caird	trs. from Limerick, el. 9 Sept., conf. 14 Sept. 1976	

OSSORY
(DUBLIN P.)

Milo Baron [Fitzgerald]	prov. 8 June 1528	*a.* 27 Sept. 1550
John Bale	nom. 22 Oct. 1552, cons. 2 Feb. 1553	left diocese Sept. 1553, d. Nov. 1563
John Tonory[1]	nom. 14 Oct. 1553, cons. Jan. 1554	*c.* 1565
Christopher Gaffney	nom. 4 Dec. 1566, cons. May 1567	3 Aug. 1576
Nicholas Walsh	l.p. 23 Jan., cons. Feb. 1578	14 Dec. 1585
John Horsfall	nom. 1 Aug., l.p. 15 Sept. 1586	13 Feb. 1610
Richard Deane	nom. 7 Mar., l.p. 18 Apr. 1610	20 Feb. 1613
Jonas Wheeler	nom. 14 Mar., cons. 8 May 1613	19 Apr. 1640
Griffith Williams	nom. 19 July, cons. 26 Sept. 1641	29 Mar. 1672
John Parry	nom. 5 Apr., cons. 28 Apr. 1672	21 Dec. 1677
Benjamin Parry	nom. 29 Dec. 1677, cons. 27 Jan. 1678	4 Oct. 1678

[1]His position under Elizabeth is uncertain. See referred to as vacant *c.* 1561.

BISHOPS	ACCESSION	DEATH *unless otherwise stated*
Michael Ward	nom. 25 Oct., cons. 24 Nov. 1678	trs. to Derry 22 Jan. 1680
Thomas Otway	trs. from Killala, nom. 6 Jan., l.p. 7 Feb. 1680	6 Mar. 1693
John Hartstonge	nom. 16 Mar., cons. 2 July 1693	trs. to Derry 3 Mar. 1714
Sir Thomas Vesey, bt.	trs. from Killaloe, nom. 18 Feb., l.p. 28 Apr. 1714	6 Aug. 1730
Edward Tennison	nom. 11 Sept. 1730, cons. 4 July 1731	29 Nov. 1735
Charles Este	nom. 17 Dec. 1735, cons. 1 Feb. 1736	trs. to Waterford 4 Oct. 1740
Anthony Dopping	nom. 19 June, cons. 19 July 1741	1 Feb. 1743
Michael Cox	nom. 15 Feb., cons. 29 May 1743	trs. to Cashel 22 Jan. 1754
Edward Maurice	nom. 3 Jan., cons. 27 Jan. 1754	10 Feb. 1756
Richard Pococke	nom. 5 Mar., cons. 21 Mar. 1756	trs. to Meath 16 July 1765
Charles Dodgson	nom. 22 June, cons. 11 Aug. 1765	trs. to Elphin 12 Apr. 1775
William Newcome	trs. from Dromore, nom. 23 Mar., l.p. 13 Apr. 1775	trs. to Waterford 5 Nov. 1779
John Hotham	nom. 22 Oct., cons. 14 Nov. 1779	trs. to Clogher 17 May 1782
Hon. William Beresford	trs. from Dromore, nom. 11 Apr., l.p. 21 May 1782	trs. to Tuam 10 Oct. 1794
Thomas Lewis O'Beirne	nom. 17 Jan., cons. 1 Feb. 1795	trs. to Meath 18 Dec. 1798
Hugh Hamilton	trs. from Clonfert, nom. 15 Jan., l.p. 24 Jan. 1799	1 Dec. 1805
John Kearney	nom. 4 Jan., cons. 2 Feb. 1806	22 May 1813
Robert Fowler	nom. 7 June, cons. 20 June 1813	31 Dec. 1841

[Ferns united to Ossory 12 July 1835]

James Thomas O'Brien	nom. 24 Feb., cons. 20 Mar. 1842	12 Dec. 1874
Robert Samuel Gregg	el. 4 Mar., cons. 30 Mar. 1875	trs. to Cork 4 July 1878
William Pakenham Walsh	el. 30 Aug., cons. 29 Sept. 1878	res. 30 Sept. 1897, d. 30 July 1902
John Baptist Crozier	el. 20 Oct., cons. 30 Nov. 1897	trs. to Down 26 Sept. 1907
Charles Frederick D'Arcy	trs. from Clogher, el. 5 Nov. 1907	trs. to Down 29 Mar. 1911
John Henry Bernard	el. 14 June, cons. 25 July 1911	trs. to Dublin 7 Oct. 1915
John Allen Fitzgerald Gregg	el. 20 Nov., cons. 28 Dec. 1915	trs. to Dublin 10 Sept. 1920
John Godfrey Fitzmaurice Day	el. 15 June, cons. 1 Nov. 1920	trs. to Armagh 27 Apr. 1938
Forde Tichborne	el. 1 Mar., cons. 24 June 1938	18 Feb. 1940
John Percy Phair	el. 13 Mar., cons. 11 June 1940	res. 31 Dec. 1961
Henry Robert McAdoo	el. 31 Jan., cons. 11 Mar. 1962	trs. to Dublin 19 Apr. 1977

[The see was then united to Cashel]

RAPHOE
(ARMAGH P.)

BISHOPS	ACCESSION	DEATH *unless otherwise stated*
Con [Cornelius] O'Cahan	prov. 6 Feb. 1514	*p.* 1550
Art [Arthur] O'Gallagher[1]	prov. 28 Nov. 1547	13 Aug. 1561
	[See unfilled by crown 1561–1604]	
George Montgomery[2]	nom. 15 Feb., l.p. 13 June 1605	trs. to Meath 8 July 1609
Andrew Knox	trs. from the Isles, nom. 7 May 1610, l.p. 26 June 1611	17 Mar. 1633
John Leslie	trs. from the Isles, nom. 8 Apr., l.p. 1 June 1633	trs. to Clogher 17 June 1661
Robert Leslie	trs. from Dromore, nom. 29 Apr., l.p. 20 June 1661	trs. to Clogher 26 Oct. 1671
Ezekiel Hopkins	nom. 6 Sept., cons. 29 Oct. 1671	trs. to Derry 11 Nov. 1681
William Smyth	trs. from Killala, nom. 16 Jan., l.p. 17 Feb. 1682	trs. to Kilmore 5 Apr. 1693
Alexander Cairncross	former abp of Glasgow, nom. 22 Mar., l.p. 16 May 1693	14 May 1701
Robert Huntington	nom. 7 June, cons. 20 July 1701	2 Sept. 1701
John Pooley	trs. from Cloyne, nom. 14 May, l.p. 12 Sept. 1702	16 Oct. 1712
Thomas Lindsay	trs. from Killaloe, nom. 23 Apr., l.p. 6 June 1713	trs. to Armagh 4 Jan. 1714
Edward Synge	nom. 7 Oct., cons. 7 Nov. 1714	trs. to Tuam 8 June 1716
Nicholas Forster	trs. from Killaloe, nom. 22 May, l.p. 8 June 1716	5 June 1743
William Barnard	nom. 20 Apr., cons. 19 Aug. 1744	trs. to Derry 19 Mar. 1747
Philip Twysden	nom. 28 Feb., cons. 29 Mar. 1747	2 Nov. 1752
Robert Downes	trs. from Down, nom. 28 Dec. 1752, l.p. 16 Jan. 1753	30 June 1763
John Oswald	trs. from Dromore, nom. 18 July, l.p. 25 Aug. 1763	4 Mar. 1780
James Hawkins	trs. from Dromore, nom. 20 Mar., l.p. 1 Apr. 1780	23 June 1807
Lord John George Beresford	trs. from Cork, nom. 23 July, l.p. 10 Aug. 1807	trs. to Clogher 25 Sept. 1819
William Magee	l.p. 22 Sept., cons. 24 Oct. 1819	trs. to Dublin 24 June 1822
William Bissett	nom. 17 June, cons. 21 July 1822	5 Sept. 1834

[See then united to Derry]

---

[1] Papal nominee, presumably recognized by crown in Mary's reign.
[2] Also bp of Clogher and Derry; resigned on promise of trs. to Meath.

ROSS
(CASHEL P.)

BISHOPS	ACCESSION	DEATH
		unless otherwise stated
Dermot MacCarthy[1]	prov. 6 June 1526	1552
Maurice O'Fihely[2]	prov. 12 Jan. 1554	*a.* 27 Jan. 1559
	[See not filled by crown until 1582]	
William Lyon[3]	nom. 30 Mar. 1582, l.p. 12 May 1582	4 Oct. 1617

TUAM
(TUAM P., from 1839 ARMAGH P.)

ARCHBISHOPS	ACCESSION	DEATH
		unless otherwise stated
Thomas O'Mullally	prov. 19 June 1514	28 Apr. 1536
Christopher Bodkin[4]	l.p. 15 Feb. 1537	1572
William O'Mullaly	nom. 11 Nov. 1572, cons. Apr. 1573	1595
Nehemiah Donnellan	nom. 24 May, l.p. 17 Aug. 1595	res. 1609
William Daniel [O'Donnell]	nom. 28 June, cons. Aug. 1609	11 July 1628
Randolph Barlow	nom. 6 Feb., cons. Apr. 1629	22 Feb. 1638
Richard Boyle	trs. from Cork, nom. 2 Apr., l.p. 30 May 1638	19 Mar. 1645
John Maxwell	trs. from Killala, l.p. 30 Aug. 1645	14 Feb. 1647
Samuel Pullen	nom. 3 Aug. 1660, cons. 27 Jan. 1661	24 Jan. 1667
John Parker	trs. from Elphin, nom. 26 Feb., l.p. 9 Aug. 1667	trs. to Dublin 28 Feb. 1679 ,
John Vesey	trs. from Limerick, nom. 23 Jan., l.p. 18 Mar. 1679	28 Mar. 1716
Edward Synge	trs. from Raphoe, nom. 19 May, l.p. 8 June 1716	23 July 1741
Josiah Hort[5]	trs. from Kilmore, nom. 5 Jan., l.p. 27 Jan. 1742	14 Dec. 1751
John Ryder	trs. from Down, nom. 24 Feb., l.p. 19 Mar. 1752	4 Feb. 1775
Jemmett Browne	trs. from Elphin, l.p. 11 Apr. 1775	15 June 1782
Hon. Joseph Deane Bourke (earl of Mayo 1792)	trs. from Ferns, l.p. 8 Aug. 1782	17 Aug. 1794

[1] Appears to be the bp referred to by Ware as Dermod MacDomnuil. Ware suggests that he may have resigned, as he found a reference to a John as bp in 1551.
[2] In succession to MacCarthy.
[3] Granted Cork *in commendam* 1583; since then Cork and Ross have been held by the same bp.
[4] Bp of Kilmacduagh, which he continued to hold in addition to Tuam.
[5] Ardagh, which had been held by bp of Kilmore, was held by abp of Tuam 1742–1839.

ARCHBISHOPS	ACCESSION	DEATH
		unless otherwise stated
Hon. William Beresford (Baron Decies 1812)	trs. from Ossory, l.p. 10 Oct. 1794	8 Sept. 1819
Hon. Power Le Poer Trench	trs. from Elphin, l.p. 10 Nov. 1819	25 Mar. 1839

[Killala united to Tuam from 13 Apr. 1834. On death of Abp Trench province united to Armagh and see ceased to be archbishopric]

BISHOPS	ACCESSION	DEATH
		unless otherwise stated
Hon. Thomas Plunket (Baron Plunket 1854)	nom. 5 Apr., cons. 14 Apr. 1839	19 Oct. 1866
Hon. Charles Brodrick Bernard	l.p. 30 Nov. 1866, cons. 30 Jan. 1867	31 Jan. 1890
James O'Sullivan	el. 14 Apr., cons. 15 May 1890	res. Feb. 1913, d. 10 Jan. 1915
Hon. Benjamin John Plunket	el. 13 Apr., cons. 10 May 1913	trs. to Meath 15 Oct. 1919
Arthur Edwin Ross	el. 15 Jan., cons. 24 Feb. 1920	24 May 1923
John Orr	el. 18 July, cons. 6 Aug. 1923	trs. to Meath 15 Nov. 1927
John Mason Harden	el. 15 Nov. 1927, cons. 6 Jan. 1928	2 Oct. 1931
William Hardy Holmes	el. 15 Dec. 1931, cons. 2 Feb. 1932	trs. to Meath 19 Oct 1938
John Winthrop Crozier	el. 23 Nov. 1938, cons. 2 Feb. 1939	res. 31 Dec. 1957
Arthur Hamilton Butler	el. 9 Apr., cons. 27 May 1958	trs. to Connor 14 Oct. 1969
John Coote Duggan	el. 27 Nov., cons. 2 Feb. 1970	

WATERFORD AND LISMORE
(CASHEL P.)

Nicholas Comyn	trs. from Ferns, prov. 13 Apr. 1519	res. July 1551
Patrick Walsh	nom. 9 June, cons. 23 Oct. 1551	1578
Marmaduke Middleton	nom. 11 Apr., l.p. 31 May 1579	trs. to St David's[1] 30 Nov. 1582
Thomas Weatherhead [Walley]	nom. 21 Mar., l.p. 20 July 1589	*a.* 15 Mar. 1592
John Lancaster	nom. 5 Jan., l.p. 26 Feb. 1608	1619
Michael Boyle	nom. 7 Aug. 1619	29 Dec. 1635
John Atherton	nom. 5 Apr., l.p. 4 May 1636	executed 5 Dec. 1640
Archibald Adair	trs. from Killala, nom. 7 June, l.p. 13 July 1641	*c.* 1647
George Baker	nom. 6 Aug. 1660, cons. 27 Jan. 1661	13 Nov. 1665
Hugh Gore	nom. 8 Feb., cons. 25 Mar. 1666	*c.* 27 Mar. 1691[2]
Nathaniel Foy	nom. 16 Apr., cons. 9 Aug. 1691	31 Dec. 1707

[1] See then granted *in commendam* to Miler Magrath, abp of Cashel, until 1589 and again from 1592 to 1608.
[2] Date of burial.

BISHOPS	ACCESSION	DEATH *unless otherwise stated*
Thomas Mills	nom. 17 Jan., cons. 18 Apr. 1708	13 May 1740
Charles Este	trs. from Ossory, nom. 10 July, l.p. 4 Oct. 1740	29 Nov. 1745
Richard Chenevix	trs. from Killaloe, nom. 23 Dec. 1745, l.p. 15 Jan. 1746	11 Sept. 1779
William Newcome	trs. from Ossory, nom. 22 Oct., l.p. 5 Nov. 1779	trs. to Armagh 27 Jan. 1795
Richard Marlay	trs. from Clonfert, nom. 11 Mar., l.p. 21 Mar. 1795	1 July 1802
Hon. Power Le Poer Trench	nom. 18 Aug., cons. 21 Nov. 1802	trs. to Elphin 30 Apr. 1810
Joseph Stock	trs. from Killala, nom. 12 Apr., l.p. 1 May 1810	14 Aug. 1813
Hon. Richard Bourke	nom. 25 Aug., cons. 10 Oct. 1813	15 Nov. 1832

[See united to Cashel under Church Temporalities Act 1833]

ROMAN CATHOLIC ARCHBISHOPS AND BISHOPS
OF IRELAND FROM 1534

INTRODUCTION

˙Once the breach between the Crown and the papacy had become final, it was inevitable that the appointment of bishops in Ireland by the Holy See should be made according to new forms. The change was not at first thought likely to be a final departure from long-established custom. The last years of Henry VIII's reign and the short reign of Edward VI left the future development of English policy uncertain; and hopes of a return to older traditions were for a short time confirmed by the restoration under Mary. During these years of uncertainty it is often a matter of great difficulty to define the relation between each individual bishop and the Holy See. Bishops were summoned to surrender their bulls of provision, and in many cases complied with the order. This formal act of surrender was designed by the framers of government policy to mark a formal breach with Rome; but it is plain from the surviving records that many bishops who had surrendered their bulls under Henry were quick to re-affirm their loyalty to the Holy See when opportunity occurred. For the purpose of these lists those bishops have been included who were in the first instance provided to their sees by the pope, and whose names are mentioned in the provision of their immediate successor. In one or two cases bishops have been included who were appointed by Mary without any formal Roman provision, but who are known to have been recognized by Rome and whose names are mentioned in the provision of their successors.

Once it had been made plain by public acts that Elizabeth was not prepared to follow the religious policy of her sister, the Roman authorities had to face a new situation. Was it possible to maintain an Irish hierarchy in the face of a total loss of all the temporalities in every Irish diocese, and of all the Irish cathedrals and churches? That the attempt was made, and made successfully, is perhaps unique in the history of modern Europe. But the process by which the ancient hierarchy of four provinces was maintained in the face of active persecution was far from regular. In some of those dioceses in which English influence was strongest the Roman authorities seem for a time to have abandoned all hope of maintaining an episcopal succession. Dublin, where the succession breaks down for more than thirty years (1568–1600), is a notable example; but there is a gap (so far as our records go) of more than forty years in Meath (1577–1621), and of twenty years in Waterford (1578–1600). In the more remote Irish dioceses the succession was better maintained in Elizabeth's reign, though there is often great uncertainty as to the situation in any given year. A full list of the Irish bishops for this period, with references to the extant contemporary sources of information, has been printed by Professor R. D. Edwards in *Irish Ecclesiastical Record*, fifth series, vol. 43 (1935). Neither from Roman nor from English sources have we any satisfactory archival evidence for this period.

The overwhelming disaster of the Armada may perhaps be the reason why the Roman authorities began to introduce a new system of vicars apostolic or vicars general in the last decade of the sixteenth century. Clement VIII (1592–1605) and his advisers seem to have made up their minds that the prospect of maintaining a full Irish hierarchy, with its four provinces and its numerous small bishoprics, was too slight to justify a rigidly conservative policy. The first break with tradition was made in the single year of Gregory XIV's short pontificate (Dec. 1590–Oct. 1591). On 15 May 1591 Gregory appointed an Irish priest, Cornelius Stanley, to be vicar general of the two great dioceses of Meath and Dublin, both of which had been without a resident bishop for many years; and on the same day Myler Cantwell was appointed vicar general of the small diocese of Killala in the province of Tuam. This new policy of appointing vicars to act in place of bishops was followed in many Irish dioceses during the next forty years. The titles *vicarius generalis* and *vicarius apostolicus* seem to have been used more or less indifferently for these vicars, who were simple priests to whom the Holy See gave special faculties for quasi-episcopal government. In a recent study of this problem Rev. F. M. Jones, C.SS.R., has printed the text of the brief, dated 30 May 1597, by which Clement VIII granted faculties of this kind to Owen MacEgan for the diocese of Ross.[1] To avoid confusion, the title 'vicar apostolic' had been reserved in these lists for vicars who were appointed by the Holy See, whilst the title 'vicar general' is used for priests who were appointed by their own bishop, often an absentee from Ireland, to act in his place during his absence. A good example of the faculties granted in this latter type of appointment will be found in the faculties which Peter Lombard, the absentee archbishop of Armagh and primate of all Ireland, granted to David Rothe, the future bishop of Ossory, on 13 June 1609. The text has been printed from a contemporary copy, now preserved among Ussher's papers in T.C.D., M.S. E.3.15, fo. 60, by W. Carrigan in his *History and Antiquities of the Diocese of Ossory*, i (1905), 87–88. By virtue of this commission Rothe was able to hold a provincial synod of the clergy of the province of Armagh at Drogheda in February 1614. Its acts have been preserved, and we can see how Rothe was striving to restore ecclesiastical discipline in an area in which episcopal government can have been little more than a distant memory for most of the clergy and people.

From the lists printed below it will be seen that bishops were still being provided to some Irish sees at this time when the appointment of vicars apostolic was becoming more and more common. Presumably local reasons, as to which we have now insufficient information, were the deciding factor in each provision. With the reign of Charles I normal episcopal government becomes once more the rule, though vicars were still occasionally appointed. The year 1647 is notable for the number of provisions to Irish sees. Not all of the bishops so provided were resident in Ireland, but the Irish hierarchy was very nearly restored to its former traditional state when the crisis of the Cromwellian invasion caused fresh confusion.

In the former edition of this *Handbook* the periods during which no evidence could be found for episcopal provisions were covered for each diocese by the simple statement: 'Under vicars'. This formula was often deceptive, for there remain periods in the history of almost every Irish diocese in which no record survives of either bishop or vicar apostolic. In this revised edition it has been thought better to print the names of all known vicars apostolic, but not of vicars general. These names are distinguished from the names of bishops by the use of brackets, and the date of appointment is the date (when known) of the papal brief. Footnotes have been added to call attention to those periods for which no record of vicars survives today, though we must always bear in mind the exceedingly scanty and inadequate nature of our surviving records. In this way it is hoped that students will have a more trustworthy guide as to the gradual development of this whole complicated process.

The erection of a new Congregation *De Propaganda Fide* in 1622 gave the Holy See a new organ of directive policy as well as an administrative centre to which trustworthy information and advice could be sent from Ireland as well as from other missionary countries. The new congregation soon began to play an important part in the appointment of Irish bishops, supplying the Holy See with valuable information as to the qualifications and personal character of possible candidates for the various episcopal sees. The working of this system can now be studied in a long series of extracts from the contemporary *Processus Datariae* for the years 1623–97, which Rev. Cathaldus Giblin, O.F.M., has printed in *Luke Wadding: a Commemorative Volume* (Dublin, 1957), 508–616.

The storm of the Cromwellian war and subsequent persecution made normal episcopal government in Ireland once more impossible. The Roman reaction to this new crisis is apparent in the large number of briefs issued on 17 Apr. 1657, by which vicars apostolic were appointed for dioceses where episcopal government had broken down. It was no more than a passing phase, and the accession of Charles II altered the whole situation in Ireland. Vicars apostolic were still appointed, especially in 1665 and 1671; and it is plain that the Irish church owes an immense debt to those simple priests who acted as vicars apostolic in so many dioceses at an hour of great hardship and danger. Without their services these dioceses would have been almost destitute of pastoral care. One service, it is true, these vicars could not render to their people. Their faculties did not include the power of ordaining priests. That simple fact throws light on the very real service performed by Patrick Plunkett, bishop of Ardagh (1647–69) and of Meath (1669–79), who had been forced into exile during the period of Cromwellian persecution, but who returned to Ireland soon after the restoration. For some years he seems to have

---

[1] *Irish Theological Quarterly*, vol. 20 (1953), 155.

been almost the only resident bishop in Ireland, and tradition attributes to him the ordination of some 250 priests soon after the restoration. His nephew, Oliver Plunkett, archbishop of Armagh (1669–81), ordained an even greater number of priests during the nine years of his active pontificate.

On the accession of James II it became customary for the Holy See to fill vacancies in Irish bishoprics on royal nomination, after due consultation with the appropriate authorities in Rome and in Ireland. This practice was continued after the flight of James from Ireland, and throughout the lifetime of his son whom the Holy See always recognized as James III. Documents which illustrate the formal nature of this right to nominate Irish bishops by an exiled king have been printed by L. Renehan in his *Collections of Irish Church History* (Dublin, 1861), 297–98. The bulls of provision issued from Rome for each new Irish bishop include a clause which makes it plain that the appointment has been made on royal nomination, and this practice was maintained until shortly before the death of the Old Pretender in 1766. After his death the Holy See did not recognize Charles Edward as king of England, and the right of nomination lapsed by disuse, though Stuart influence was still strong in Rome as long as the Cardinal of York was alive. An example of an appointment, which was felt in Ireland to be a Stuart nomination against the declared wishes of the local diocesan chapter and of the bishops of the province of Dublin, can be found in documents concerning the appointment of the Dominican John Troy to be bishop of Ossory in December 1776. They have been printed by Carrigan in his *History and Antiquities of the Diocese of Ossory*, 1, 180–82.

The election of candidates by the diocesan chapter and by the suffragan bishops of the province becomes increasingly important after 1766, though the Holy See frequently appointed bishops who had not been chosen in this way. The influence of the Roman officials of Propaganda was always very great; and, partly for this reason, it is not easy to determine which date in a long and slow process of provision should be given as the formal date of appointment. Candidates were recommended to the Holy See by Propaganda after careful selection on information received from Ireland; the recommendation was approved or confirmed by the Holy See; there was an act of provision; and finally the issue of a brief or bull of provision, by which the appointment was made known to those concerned. In the lists printed below, the latest known date in this long process is normally given; and it is very often (from the eighteenth century onwards) the date of the brief or bull. Since there was seldom more than a short interval between the formal decision of the Holy See and the issue of the brief, this latter date can safely be given without the necessity of complicating these lists by an additional series of entries or footnotes.

The date of consecration is often unknown. During the seventeenth and eighteenth centuries Irish bishops were commonly consecrated abroad, and the record of consecration has been lost or is not easily accessible. Even when the bishop was consecrated in his own cathedral at home, the absence of episcopal registers, due very largely to the breakdown of curial routine in periods of open persecution, means that so elementary a date as the *dies consecrationis* is not known.

During the nineteenth century the rights of the diocesan chapter in the election of a new bishop were more clearly acknowledged at Rome, and it became traditional that at each vacancy the chapter should send a *terna* of names to Rome in order of preference (*dignissimus, dignior, dignus*). The Holy See almost always appointed one of the three candidates so named, but not necessarily in the order of the chapter's declared preference. This system of selection by *terna*, coupled with the recommendations of the suffragan bishops of the province, was continued throughout the nineteenth century and down to more recent times.

The emergence of the Irish Free State in 1922 caused the Holy See to adjust its method of appointment to a new and more favourable situation. Within a few years of the establishment of a native and Catholic government a new system of appointment was introduced which had already obtained in other countries where similar conditions prevailed. Every three years the bishops of each province are required to submit a list of worthy candidates to the metropolitan of the province, who has power to add names to the list of his own choice. After due consultation in Ireland this list of candidates is submitted to the Consistorial Congregation in Rome, with recommendations as to the special needs of each diocese in the province. The provision is made by the Holy See, and the date of appointment is determined by the date of the papal bull of provision. The dates of provision (election) and consecration for every bishop throughout the world will be found in the annual volumes of the *Annuario Pontificio*, published in Rome. The dates of death of each Irish bishop and the consecration of his successor will be found in the annual volumes of the *Irish Catholic Directory*, which has been published in Dublin since 1837.

As compared with the structure of the medieval Irish church, the division of the hierarchy into four provinces has been maintained, though the number of suffragan bishoprics in each province has been somewhat modified. In the province of Armagh the union of Down and Connor has been maintained; and Clonmacnois has been united to Ardagh since 1756. In the province of Dublin, Leighlin has been united to Kildare since 1694. In the province of Cashel, Emly has been united to Cashel since 1718. The union of Cork and Cloyne was maintained to 1747, when the two dioceses were once more separated. Ross was united to Cloyne in that year, but this union was terminated in 1850 when three separate dioceses of Cork, Cloyne and Ross were once more recognized. Ross has been administered by the bishop of Cork since 1952. In the province of Tuam, Annaghdown was once more united to Tuam in 1555, and Mayo was united to Tuam after 1631. Galway was erected as a new diocese in 1831. Kilmacduagh, which had been united to Kilfenora in the province of Cashel since 1750, was united to Galway in 1883. The bishop of Galway and Kilmacduagh is today also the apostolic administrator of Kilfenora.

The preparation of these lists is mainly due to Mrs T. Wall of University College, Dublin, who undertook the laborious task of compiling lists from sources which could often be reached only by private correspondence. To those who have co-operated in this work by supplying information from diocesan archives the thanks of the editorial committee are hereby extended. Rev. Professor P. J. Corish of St Patrick's College, Maynooth, and Rev. John Brady of the diocese of Meath have been especially helpful in compiling the lists for the seventeenth and eighteenth centuries. The following lists have been revised for the third edition of the *Handbook* (1986) by reference to *A New Oxford History of Ireland*, ed. T. W. Moody, F. X. Martin and F. J. Burne, ix (Oxford, 1984), 333–91.

ACHONRY
(TUAM P.)

BISHOPS	ACCESSION	DATE OF DEATH *unless otherwise stated*
Thomas O'Fihely[1]	prov. 15 June 1547	trs. to Leighlin 30 Aug. 1555
Cormac O'Coyn, O.P.[2]	nom. 1556	*a.* 12 Oct. 1561
Eugene O'Harte, O.P.	prov. 28 Jan. 1562	1603
(Andrew Lynch, vic. ap.)	brief 28 Nov. 1629	—
(James Fallon, vic. ap.[3])	brief 13 Jan. 1631	*ob.* 1662
(Maurice Durcan, vic. ap.[4])	brief 8 July 1677	—

[1] In his provision mention is made of Eugene O'Flanagan as the last bp O'Flanagan was dead bef. 31 Aug. 1522 when Cormac paid his annates as bp of Achonry. But this Cormac is ignored in the provision of 1547, and there is no record for the years 1522–47.

[2] There is no record of Cormac O'Coyn's provision. He was perhaps appd by Mary, but he is mentioned in the provision of Eugene O'Harte, who was his nephew.

[3] Fallon was active as vicar ap. 1631–52, when he was imprisoned. He was released aft. 1660, but was in broken health. There is no record of a vicar 1662–77. Brady includes the name of Louis Dillon, O.F.M., who was recommended for provision 14 May 1641, but was not in fact provided. The diocese of Achonry was thus under vicars 1603–1707.

[4] Durcan's brief was repeated 14 Mar. 1678.

BISHOPS	ACCESSION	DEATH
		unless otherwise stated
Hugh MacDermot	(vic. ap.) brief 21 Dec. 1684, prov. 30 Apr. 1707	*c.* 1725
Dominic O'Daly, O.P.	prov. 20 Sept., cons. 30 Nov. 1725	1735
John O'Hart	prov. 30 Sept. 1735	May 1739
Walter Blake	prov. 13 Aug. 1739	1758
Patrick Robert Kirwan	prov. 21 Aug. 1758	Mar.–Apr. 1776
Philip Phillips	trs. from Killala 22 June 1776	trs. to Tuam 22 Nov. 1785
Boetius Egan	prov. 22 Nov. 1785	trs. to Tuam 15 Dec. 1787
Thomas O'Connor	prov. 4 Jan., cons. Apr. 1788	18 Feb. 1803
Charles Lynagh	prov. 29 Apr. 1803	Apr.–May 1808
John O'Flynn	prov. 9 June, cons. 12 Nov. 1809	17 July 1817
Patrick MacNicholas	prov. 1 Mar., cons. 17 May 1818	11 Feb. 1852
Patrick Durcan	prov. 4 Oct., cons. 30 Nov. 1852	1 May 1875
Francis MacCormack	prov. coadj. with succ. 21 Nov. 1871, cons. 4 Feb. 1872, succ. 1 May 1875	trs. to Galway 26 Apr. 1887
John Lyster	prov. 25 Feb., cons. 8 Apr. 1888	17 Jan. 1911
Patrick Morrisroe	prov. 13 May, cons. 3 Sept. 1911	27 May 1946
James Fergus	prov. 15 Feb., cons. 4 May 1947	res. 17 Mar. 1976
Thomas Flynn	prov. 30 Dec. 1976, cons. 20 Feb. 1977	

ANNAGHDOWN (Enachdun)
(TUAM P.)

Henry de Burgo	prov. 16 Apr. 1540	—

Aft. 1555 Abp Bodkin held this see along with Tuam. The union of Tuam and Annaghdown was finally decreed 17 Oct. 1580, when Nicholas Skerrett was provided to Tuam.

ARDAGH
(ARMAGH P.)

Rory O'Malone	prov. 2 Dec. 1517	1540
Patrick MacMahon, O.F.M.	prov. 14 Nov. 1541	*c.* 1572
Richard Brady, O.F.M.	prov. 23 Jan. 1576	trs. to Kilmore 9 Mar. 1580
Edmund Magauran	prov. 11 Sept. 1581	trs. to Armagh 1 July 1587
(John Gaffney, vic. ap.[1])	brief 14 Jan. 1622	*c.* 1637
Patrick Plunkett, O. Cist.[2]	prov. 11 Mar. 1647, cons. 19 Mar. 1648	trs. to Meath 11 Jan. 1669

[1] John Gaffney was vicar gen. of Ardagh in 1597, and was prob. still vicar gen. in 1622. There is no record of a vicar appd 1587–1622.

[2] During the years 1637–47 Cornelius Gaffney is named as vicar gen. of Ardagh, though there is no record of a brief appointing him vicar ap. He remained as vicar gen. of the diocese during the episcopate of Patrick Plunkett, who left Ireland *c.* 1652 and did not return until 1664.

BISHOPS	ACCESSION	DEATH *unless otherwise stated*
(Gerard Farrell, vic. ap.)	brief 31 July 1669	June 1683
(Gregory Fallon, adm.)[1]	proposed 17 May 1688, brief 1 July 1697	c. 1698
(Charles Tiernan, vic. ap.[2])	brief 6 July 1696	—
(Bernard Donogher, vic. ap.)	brief 20 Aug. 1699	—
(Ambrose O'Conor, O.P.[3])	proposed 16 June 1709 (never cons.)	20 Feb. 1711
Thomas Flynn	prov. 18 May, cons. p. 15 July 1718	29 Jan. 1730
Peter Mulligan, O.E.S.A.	prov. Sept. 1730, brief 9 May 1732	23 July 1739
Thomas O'Beirne	prov. 19 Sept. 1739	Feb. 1747
Thomas MacDermot Roe	prov. 8 May 1747	Feb. 1751
Augustine Cheevers, O.S.A.	prov. 17 July 1751	trs. to Meath 7 Aug. 1756

ARDAGH AND CLONMACNOIS
(ARMAGH P.)

Anthony Blake[4]	prov. 11 Aug. 1756	trs. to Armagh 21 Aug. 1758
James Brady	prov. 21 Aug. 1758	11 Jan. 1788
John Cruise	prov. 10 June, cons. 17 Aug. 1788	28 June 1812
James Magauran	prov. 12 Mar. 1815	3 June 1829
William O'Higgins	prov. 2 Oct., cons. 30 Nov. 1829	3 Jan. 1853
John Kilduff	prov. 29 Apr., cons. 29 June 1853	21 June 1867
Neale MacCabe, C.M.	prov. 29 Nov. 1867, cons. 2 Feb. 1868	22 July 1870
George Michael Conroy	prov. 19 Feb., cons. 11 Apr. 1871	4 Aug. 1878
Bartholomew Woodlock[5]	prov. 4 Apr., cons. 1 June 1879	res. 1894, *ob.* 13 Dec. 1902

[1] For Gregory Fallon *see under* Clonmacnois.

[2] Tiernan was vicar gen. at the time of his appointment, which suggests that Gregory Fallon was not in fact administering the see of Ardagh 1688–96.

[3] On 16 June 1709 James II petitioned that Ambrose O'Conor, then prior provincial of the Irish Dominicans, should be provided to the united dioceses of Ardagh and Clonmacnois. But the provision had not taken effect when O'Conor died in London 20 Feb. 1711. On his death Thomas Moran, O.F.M., was proposed, but no provision was made.

[4] On 30 May 1756 Stephen MacEgan, bp of Meath, who had been administering the see of Clonmacnois, died. On his death the union of Ardagh and Clonmacnois, which had been proposed in 1709, was carried into effect, and Anthony Blake was appointed as the first bp of the united dioceses.

[5] On his resignation in 1894 Bp Woodlock was given the title *in partibus* of bp of Trapezopolis. He returned to All Hallows College, Dublin, where he died in 1902.

BISHOPS	ACCESSION	DEATH
		unless otherwise stated
Joseph Hoare	prov. 8 Feb., cons. 19 Mar. 1895	14 Apr. 1927
James Joseph MacNamee	prov. 20 June, cons. 31 July 1927	24 Apr. 1966
Cahal Brendan Daly	prov. 26 May, cons. 16 July 1967	trs. to Down and Connor 24 Aug. 1982
Colm O'Reilly	prov. 24 Feb., cons. 10 Apr. 1983	

ARMAGH
(ARMAGH P.)

ARCHBISHOPS	ACCESSION	DEATH
		unless otherwise stated
George Cromer[1]	prov. 2 Oct. 1521, cons. Apr. 1522	depr. 23 July 1539, *ob.* 16 Mar. 1543
Robert Wauchop[2]	appd adm. Armagh 23 July 1539, cons. 17 Mar. 1545	10 Nov. 1551
George Dowdall[3]	prov. 1 Mar., temp. 23 Oct. 1553	15 Aug. 1558
Donat O'Teige	prov. 7 Feb. 1560, cons. Feb. 1560	1562
Richard Creagh[4]	prov. 22 Mar., cons. Easter 1564	14 Oct. 1585
Edmund Magauran	trs. from Ardagh, prov. 1 July 1587	23 June 1593
Peter Lombard[5]	prov. 9 July 1601	1625
Hugh MacCaghwell, O.F.M.	prov. 27 Apr., cons. 7 June 1626	22 Sept. 1626
Hugh O'Reilly[6]	trs. from Kilmore, prov. 21 Aug. 1628	*c.* 1652
Edmund O'Reilly	prov. 16 Apr. 1657, cons. 26 May 1658	8 Mar. 1669
Oliver Plunkett	prov. 9 July, brief 3 Aug., cons. 1 Dec. 1669	1 July 1681
Dominic Maguire, O.P.	prov. 14 Dec. 1683, brief 12 Jan. 1684	21 Sept. 1707
Hugh MacMahon[7]	trs. from Clogher, prov. 6 Aug. 1714, brief 9 July 1715	2 Aug. 1737
Bernard MacMahon[8]	trs. from Clogher, prov. 8 Nov. 1737, brief (again) Dec. 1738	27 May 1747

[1] Cromer was suspended by Paul III in 1539 on a charge of heresy.

[2] Wauchop was appd to administer the see on the suspension of Cromer, and was cons. aft. Cromer's death.

[3] Dowdall had been appd by Henry VIII 28 Nov. 1543, and was cons. soon aft. that date. He abandoned his see in 1551.

[4] Richard Creagh was committed to the Tower in 1567, and died there as a prisoner.

[5] Peter Lombard never came to Ireland, but remained in Rome. David Rothe, who became bp of Ossory in 1618, administered the see of Armagh as vicar general 1609–25.

[6] Hugh O'Reilly was proposed for the vacant see of Armagh 21 Aug. 1628, but the exact date of his provision is not known.

[7] Hugh MacMahon was also adm. of Dromore 1731–37.

[8] Bernard MacMahon obtained a second brief of provision since the first brief did not mention his title as Primate of All Ireland. He was adm. of Dromore 1737–47.

ARCHBISHOPS	ACCESSION	DEATH *unless otherwise stated*
Ross MacMahon	trs. from Clogher, prov. 3 Aug. 1747	29 Oct. 1748
Michael O'Reilly	trs. from Derry, prov. 23 Jan. 1749	1758
Anthony Blake	trs. from Ardagh, prov. 21 Aug. 1758	11 Nov. 1787
Richard O'Reilly[1]	prov. coadj. with succ. 1782, succ. 11 Nov. 1787	31 Jan. 1818
Patrick Curtis	prov. 8 Aug., cons. 28 Oct. 1819	26 July 1832
Thomas Kelly[2]	trs. from Dromore, coadj. with succ., prov. 1 Dec. 1828, succ. 26 July 1832	13 Jan. 1835
William Crolly	trs. from Down and Connor, prov. 12 Apr. 1835	6 Apr. 1849
Paul Cullen	prov. 19 Dec. 1849, cons. 24 Feb. 1850	trs. to Dublin 1 May 1852
Joseph Dixon	prov. 4 Oct., cons. 21 Nov. 1852	29 Apr. 1866
Michael Kieran	prov. 6 Nov. 1866, cons. 3 Feb. 1867	15 Sept. 1869
Daniel MacGettigan	trs. from Raphoe, prov. 11 Mar. 1870	3 Dec. 1887
Michael Logue	trs. from Raphoe, coadj. with succ., prov. 30 Apr. 1887, succ. 3 Dec. 1887, cardinal 19 Jan. 1893	19 Nov. 1924
Patrick O'Donnell	trs. from Raphoe, coadj. with succ., prov. 14 Feb. 1922, succ. 19 Nov. 1924, cardinal 14 Dec. 1925	22 Oct. 1927
Joseph McRory	trs. from Down and Connor, prov. 22 June 1928, cardinal 16 Dec. 1929	13 Oct. 1945
John D'Alton	trs. from Meath, prov. 25 Apr. 1946, cardinal 12 Jan. 1953	1 Feb. 1963
William Conway	trs. from Neve, prov. 10 Sept. 1963, cardinal 22 Feb. 1965	17 Apr. 1977
Tomás Séamus O'Fiaich	prov. 22 Aug., cons. 2 Oct. 1977, cardinal 30 June 1979	

CASHEL
(CASHEL P.)

Edmund Butler[3]	prov. 21 Oct. 1524	5 Mar. 1551
(Roland Baron Fitzgerald)[4]	nom. 14 Oct., cons. Dec. 1553	28 Oct. 1561

[1] Richard O'Reilly had been appd coadj. in Kildare by brief of 20 June 1781.
[2] Archbishop Kelly retained Dromore in adm. until the provision of Michael Blake to Dromore in Jan. 1833.
[3] Butler accepted royal supremacy, and is not mentioned in the provision of Maurice MacGibbon.
[4] Fitzgerald was appd by Mary and cons. in 1553, but he does not seem to have been confirmed by Julius III. He is not mentioned in the provision of MacGibbon.

CASHEL

ARCHBISHOPS	ACCESSION	DEATH *unless otherwise stated*
Maurice MacGibbon O. Cist.[1]	prov. 4 June 1567	1578
Dermot O'Hurley	prov. 11 Sept. 1581	19 June 1584
David Kearney[2]	prov. 21 May, cons. 31 Aug. 1603	14 Aug. 1624
Thomas Walsh	prov. 27 Apr., cons. 8 July 1626	5 May 1654
(John de Burgo, vic. ap.)[3]	brief 17 Apr. 1657	—
(Gerald Fitzgerald, vic. ap.)	brief 24 Nov. 1665	—
William Burgat	prov. 11 Jan., cons. 12 Oct. 1669	1674
John Brenan[4]	trs. from Waterford and Lis- more, prov. 8 Mar. 1677	1693
Edward Comerford[5]	prov. 14 Nov. 1695	21 Feb. 1710
Christopher Butler[6]	prov. 1 Sept. 1711, cons. 18 Oct. 1712	4 Sept. 1757
James Butler I	prov. coadj. with succ. 16 Jan., cons. May 1750, succ. 4 Sept. 1757	17 May 1774
James Butler II	prov. coadj. with succ. 15 Mar., cons. 4 July 1773, succ. 17 May 1774	29 July 1791
Thomas Bray	prov. 20 July, cons. 14 Oct. 1792	15 Dec. 1820
Patrick Everard	prov. coadj. with succ. 29 Sept. 1814, succ. 15 Dec. 1820	1822
Robert Laffan	prov. 18 Mar. 1823	1833
Michael Slattery	prov. 22 Dec. 1833, cons. 24 Feb. 1834	4 Feb. 1857
Patrick Leahy	prov. 5 May, cons. 29 June 1857	26 Jan. 1875
Thomas William Croke[7]	trs. from Auckland, N.Z., prov. 24 June 1875	22 July 1902
Thomas Fennelly	prov. coadj. with succ. 9 June 1901, succ. 27 July 1902	res. 7 Mar. 1913, d. 24 Dec. 1927
John Harty	prov. 4 Dec. 1913, cons. 18 Jan. 1914	11 Sept. 1946
Jeremiah Kinane	trs. from Waterford and Lis- more, prov. coadj. with succ. 4 Feb. 1942, succ. 11 Sept. 1946	18 Feb. 1959
Thomas Morris	prov. 24 Dec. 1959, cons. 28 Feb. 1960	

[1] Bishop Landes of Cork was given faculties as adm. of Cashel in the absence of the abp 10 Apr. 1575.
[2] There is no record of vicars 1584–1603.
[3] John de Burgo was vicar ap. of Killaloe *c.* 1666–69.
[4] Brenan continued to hold Waterford and Lismore in adm. 1677–93.
[5] Comerford was adm. of Emly and of Kilfenora 1705–10.
[6] Butler was adm. of Ross 1711–30; and Emly was united to Cashel May 1718.
[7] Croke had been cons. bp of Auckland in New Zealand 10 July 1870.

417

CLOGHER
(ARMAGH P.)

BISHOPS	ACCESSION	DEATH *unless otherwise stated*
Patrick O'Cullen, O.E.S.A.	prov. 11 Feb. 1517	*a.* 26 Mar. 1534
Hugh O'Carolan[1]	prov. 6 Aug. 1535	1 Oct. 1542
Raymund MacMahon	prov. 27 Aug. 1546	*c.* 1560
Cornelius MacArdel	prov. 29 May 1560	*c.* 1592
Eugene Matthews[2]	prov. 31 Aug. 1609	trs. to Dublin 2 May 1611
(Patrick Quinn, vic. ap.)	brief 30 July 1622	—
(Heber MacMahon, vic. ap.)	brief 17 Nov. 1627	bishop of Down and Connor 10 Mar. 1642
Heber MacMahon	trs. from Down and Connor 27 June 1643	17 Sept. 1650
(Philip Crolly, vic. ap.)[3]	brief 15 Nov. 1651	—
Patrick Duffy, O.F.M.	prov. 26 May 1671	1675
Patrick Tyrell, O.F.M.[4]	prov. 13 May 1676	trs. to Meath 24 Jan. 1689
Hugh MacMahon[5]	prov. 15 Mar. 1707	trs. to Armagh 5 July 1715
Bernard MacMahon	prov. 7 Apr. 1727	trs. to Armagh 8 Nov. 1737
Ross MacMahon	prov. 17 May, cons. 27 Aug. 1738	trs. to Armagh 3 Aug. 1747
Daniel O'Reilly	prov. 11 Sept. 1747	24 Mar. 1778
Hugh O'Reilly	prov. coadj. with succ. 16 May 1777, succ. 24 Mar. 1778	3 Nov. 1801
James Murphy	prov. coadj. with succ. May 1798, succ. 3 Nov. 1801	19 Nov. 1824
Edward Kernan	prov. coadj. with succ. 18 Aug. 1816, cons. 11 (or 12) Apr. 1818, succ. 19 Nov. 1824	20 Feb. 1844
Charles MacNally	prov. coadj. with succ. 21 July, cons. 5 Nov. 1843, succ. 20 Feb. 1844	20 Nov. 1864
James Donnelly[6]	prov. coadj. with succ. 11 Dec. 1864, cons. 26 Feb. 1865	29 Dec. 1893
Richard Owens	prov. 6 July, cons. 26 Aug. 1894	3 Mar. 1909
Patrick MacKenna	prov. 12 June, cons. 10 Oct. 1909	7 Feb. 1942
Eugene O'Callaghan	prov. 17 Feb, cons. 4 Apr. 1943	res. 3 Dec. 1969
Patrick Mulligan	prov. 3 Dec. 1969, cons. 18 Jan. 1970	res. 3 Sept. 1979
Joseph Duffy	prov. 7 July, cons. 2 Sept. 1979	

[1] Hugh O'Carolan accepted the royal supremacy, and is not mentioned in the provision of his successor.

[2] There is no record of a vicar 1592–1609 or 1611–22.

[3] Philip Crolly was re-appd vic. ap. 17 Apr. 1657.

[4] Tyrell was also adm. of Kilmore from 21 Mar. 1678.

[5] There is no record of a vicar 1689–1707 or 1715–27.

[6] Bishop MacNally had died bef. the date of Donnelly's provision as coadjutor with right of succession.

CLONFERT
(TUAM P.)

BISHOPS	ACCESSION	DEATH *unless otherwise stated*
Roland de Burgo[1]	prov. 18 May 1534	20 June 1580
Thady Farrell, O.P.	prov. 8 June 1587	1602
(Dermot Nolan, vic. ap.)	brief 4 Feb. 1609	—
(Thady Egan, vic. ap.)	brief 13 July 1622	—
John de Burgo	(vic. ap.) brief 13 Oct. 1629, prov. 16 Sept. 1641, cons. 29 May 1642	trs. to Tuam 11 Mar. 1647
Walter Lynch[2]	prov. 11 Mar. 1647, cons. 9 Apr. 1648	14 July 1663
Thady Keogh, O.P. (Mac Eogha)	prov. 13 July, cons. Oct. 1671	1687
Maurice Donnellan[3]	prov. 14 Nov. 1695	2 July 1706
Ambrose Madden[4]	prov. 15 Sept. 1713, cons. 15 Apr. 1714	July 1715
Edmund Kelly	prov. Feb., cons. *a.* 14 May 1718	1733
Peter O'Donnellan	prov. 11 Aug. 1733	7 May 1778
Andrew Donnellan	prov. coadj. with succ. 1 Dec. 1776, succ. 7 May 1778	*a.* 6 July 1786
Thomas Costello	prov. coadj. with succ. 30 June 1786	8 Oct. 1831
Thomas Coen	prov. coadj. with succ. 26 Jan., cons. 5 May 1816, succ. 8 Oct. 1831	25 Apr. 1847
John Derry	prov. 9 July, cons. 21 Sept. 1847	28 June 1870
(Hugh O'Rorke)	prov. 13 Feb. 1871 (provision not accepted)	—
Patrick Duggan	prov. 2 Oct. 1871, cons. 14 Jan. 1872	15 Aug. 1896
John Healy	prov. coadj. with succ. 26 June, cons. 31 Aug. 1884, succ. 15 Aug. 1896	trs. to Tuam 13 Feb. 1903
Thomas O'Dea	prov. 12 June, cons. 30 Aug. 1903	trs. to Galway 29 Apr. 1909
Thomas Gilmartin	prov. 3 July 1909, cons. 13 Feb. 1910	trs. to Tuam 10 July 1918
Thomas O'Doherty	prov. 3 July, cons. 14 Sept. 1919	trs. to Galway 13 July 1923
John Dignan	prov. 24 Mar., cons. 1 June 1924	12 Apr. 1953
William Philbin	prov. 22 Dec. 1953, cons. 14 Mar. 1954	trs. to Down and Connor 5 June 1962
Thomas Ryan	prov. 9 May, cons. 16 June 1963	

[1] Roland de Burgo accepted royal supremacy and received the temporalities 24 Oct. 1541. In Mary's reign he was pardoned, but again accepted royal supremacy under Elizabeth. He is mentioned in the provision of his successor.
[2] Lynch came to Ireland in 1647, but left *c.* 1648 and spent the rest of his life in Hungary. There is no record of vicars 1648–71.
[3] Donnellan was vicar gen. of Clonfert at the time of his provision.
[4] Madden had been provided to Killala in 1695, and to Kilmacduagh in 1703, but had never been consecrated.

CLONMACNOIS
(ARMAGH P.)

BISHOPS	ACCESSION	DEATH *unless otherwise stated*
Quintin O Higgins, O.F.M.	prov. 10 Nov. 1516	1538
Richard Hogan, O.F.M.[1]	prov. 16 June 1539	1539
Florence Kirwan, O.F.M.[1]	prov. 5 Dec. 1539	*c.* 1555
Peter Wall, O.P.	prov. 4 May 1556	1568
Alan Sullivan[2]	prov. 29 July 1585	—
(Terence Coghlan, vic. ap.)	brief 3 July 1630	—
Anthony MacGeoghegan, O.F.M.	prov. 11 Mar. 1647, cons. 2 Apr. 1648	trs. to Meath 16 Apr. 1657
(William O Shiel, vic. ap.)	brief 10 July 1657	—
(Moriarty Kearney, vic. ap.)	brief 14 Dec. 1683	—
Gregory Fallon[3]	prov. 17 May 1688, (again) 1 July 1697	*c.* 1698
Stephen MacEgan, O.P.[4]	prov. 20 Sept., cons. 29 Sept. 1725	trs. to Meath 26 Sept. 1729

CLOYNE
(CASHEL P.)

William Keane[5]	trs. from Ross, prov. 5 May 1857	15 Jan. 1874
James MacCarthy	prov. 22 Aug., cons. 28 Oct. 1874	9 Dec. 1893
Robert Browne	prov. 26 June, cons. 19 Aug. 1894	23 Mar. 1935
James Roche	trs. from Ross, prov. as coadj. with succ. 26 June 1931, succ. 23 Mar. 1935	31 Aug. 1956
John Ahern	prov. 30 Mar., cons. 9 June 1957	

[1] Both these provisions carried with them the adm. of Killaloe. During the lifetime of Florence Kirwan (20 Aug. 1549) Roderick Maclene, a priest of the diocese of Ross in Scotland, obtained a provision to Clonmacnois, and was trs. to Sodor 5 Mar. 1550.

[2] There is no record of a vicar 1568–85; and the date of Alan Sullivan's death is unknown. The situation bef. 1630 is thus quite uncertain.

[3] Gregory Fallon obtained a provision to Clonmacnois with adm. of Ardagh 17 May 1688; but this provision does not seem to have had effect. Fallon was still dean of Elphin and more than 80 years old, when he obtained his second provision 1 July 1697.

[4] From 1688 to 1725 the see of Clonmacnois was adm. by the bps of Ardagh. John O Daly was elected vicar gen. by the chapter 28 Sept. 1723 in succession to Thadeus Coghlan. In 1729 Stephen MacEgan was trs. from Clonmacnois to Meath, but he continued to adm. the see of Clonmacnois to his death in 1756. The see of Clonmacnois was then united to Ardagh.

[5] Bishop Murphy was bp of Cloyne aft. the separation of Ross from Cloyne to his death 4 Dec. 1856. William Keane, who had been the first bp of Ross aft. the separation, was translated to Cloyne 5 May 1857.

CLOYNE AND ROSS[1]
(CASHEL P.)

BISHOPS	ACCESSION	DEATH *unless otherwise stated*
John O'Brien[2]	prov. 10 Jan. 1748	13 Mar. 1769
Matthew McKenna[3]	prov. 7 Aug. 1769	4 June 1791
William Coppinger	prov. coadj. with succ. 15 Jan 1788, succ. 4 June 1791	1830
Michael Collins	prov. coadj. with succ. 7 Apr. 1827, succ. 1830	1832
Bartholomew Crotty	prov. 22 Mar., cons. 11 June 1833	3 Oct. 1846
David Walsh	prov. 6 Feb., cons. 2 May 1847	19 Jan. 1849
Timothy Murphy[4]	prov. 19 Apr., cons. 16 Sept. 1849	4 Dec. 1856

CORK
(CASHEL P.)

Richard Walsh[5]	prov. 10 Jan. 1748	7 Jan. 1763
John Butler	prov. 16 Apr., cons. June 1763	res. 13 Dec. 1786, d. 8 May 1800
Francis Moylan	trs. from Ardfert 19 June 1787	10 Feb. 1815
John Murphy	prov. coadj. with succ. 25 Jan., cons. 23 Apr. 1815	1 Apr. 1847
William Delany	prov. 9 July, cons. 15 Aug. 1847	14 Nov. 1886
Thomas Alphonsus O'Callaghan, O.P.	prov. coadj. with succ. 13 June cons. 29 June 1884, succ. 13 Nov. 1886	14 June 1916
Daniel Cohalan[6]	prov. 25 May, cons. 7 June 1914, succ. 29 Aug. 1916	24 Aug. 1952
Cornelius Lucey	prov. coadj. with succ. 18 Nov. 1950, cons. 14 Jan. 1951, succ. 24 Aug. 1952	res. 23 Aug. 1980
Michael Murphy	prov. coadj. with succ. 1 Apr., cons. 23 May 1976, succ. 23 Aug. 1980	

[1] The union of Ross with Cloyne was decreed on the same day (10 Dec. 1747) as the separation of Cloyne from Cork.

[2] Bishop O'Brien was provided to the two dioceses of Cloyne and Ross on 10 Dec. 1747, but the brief of his provision is dated 10 Jan. 1748. The date of his death is given in T.C.D. MS. H.1.18, f. 3. This MS. contains Irish texts gathered together by Bp O'Brien.

[3] Brady erroneously gives the date of provision as 1767.

[4] Bishop Murphy was provided to Cloyne and Ross, and recommended the separation of the two dioceses at the synod of Thurles in 1850. Ross was separated from Cloyne 24 Nov. 1850.

[5] The separation of Cork from Cloyne was decreed 10 Dec. 1747, and Walsh was then provided to the see of Cork. The brief of his provision is dated 10 Jan. 1748.

[6] Bishop Cohalan was consecrated as auxiliary bp without right of succession. He was provided to the see 29 Aug. 1916.

CORK AND CLOYNE[1]
(CASHEL P.)

BISHOPS	ACCESSION	DEATH *unless otherwise stated*
John Bennet	prov. 28 Jan. 1523	1536
(Lewis Macnamara, O.F.M.)	prov. 24 Sept. 1540, (not cons.)	Sept. 1540
John O'Heyne[2]	prov. 5 Nov. 1540	*a.* 1556
Dominic Tirrey[3]	nom. 27 Nov. 1556	*c.* Aug. 1557
Nicholas Landes[4]	prov. 27 Feb. 1568	*c.* 1574
Edmund Tanner	prov. 5 Nov. 1574	4 June 1579
Dermot McCraghe[5]	prov. 12 Oct. 1580	*p.* 1603
(James Miagh, vic. ap.)	brief 3 Sept. 1614	—
(Robert Miagh, vic. ap.)	brief 13 July 1621	—
William Tirry	prov. 24 Jan. 1622, cons. 4 Apr. 1623	Mar. 1646
Robert Barry	prov. 8 Apr. 1647, cons. 25 Mar. 1648	6 July 1662
Peter Creagh[6]	prov. 13 May 1676	trs. to Dublin 9 Mar. 1693
John Baptist Sleyne,[7] O.S.A.	prov. 13 Apr. 1693	res. 22 Jan. 1712, d. 16 Feb. 1712
Donogh MacCarthy	prov. 16 July 1712, cons. 16 Aug. 1713	Mar. 1726
Thadeus MacCarthy[8]	prov. 7 Apr. 1727	14 Aug. 1747

(The separation of Cork from Cloyne was approved by Benedict XIV 10 Dec. 1747.)

DERRY
(ARMAGH P.)

Rory O'Donnell	prov. 11 Jan. 1520	8 Oct. 1550 (or 1551)
Eugene O'Doherty	prov. 25 June 1554	*c.* 1569
Redmond O'Gallagher	trs. from Killala 22 June 1569	15 Mar. 1601
(Luke Rochford, vic. ap.)[9]	brief 13 Mar. 1622	—
(Eugene Sweeney, vic. ap.)	brief 10 Sept. 1623	prov. to Kilmore 18 Sept. 1628
(Terence Kelly, vic. ap.)	brief 10 Jan. 1629	depr. 1668
(Eugene Conwell, vic. ap.)	brief 30 June 1671	—
(Bernard O'Cahan, vic. ap.)	brief Jan. 1684	*c.* 1711

[1] The two sees of Cork and Cloyne had been united since 1418.

[2] John O'Heyne was provided to Elphin as well as Cork and Cloyne 1545.

[3] Tirrey was appd by Henry VIII in 1536, and was cons. He was absolved from heresy, etc., by Cardinal Pole 27 Nov. 1556, and continued as bp until his death in Aug. 1557.

[4] Aft. the death of Tirrey in 1557 Mary ordered the temporalities of Cork and Cloyne to be granted to Roger Skiddy 18 Sept. 1557. Skiddy was cons. *papali ritu* 30 Oct. 1562, but was not recognized in Rome as a catholic bp. He is not mentioned in the provision of Nicholas Landes. Skiddy resigned his bishopric 1567.

[5] The date of McCraghe's death is not known.

[6] There is no record of a vicar 1662–76.

[7] Sleyne was adm. of Ross from 6 Oct. 1693.

[8] Thadeus MacCarthy was adm. of Ross from 20 June 1733.

[9] There is no record of a vicar 1601–22.

BISHOPS	ACCESSION	DEATH *unless otherwise stated*
Fergus Laurence Lea[1]	prov. 8 Feb. 1694	c. 1696
Terence Donnelly	prov. 5 Jan., cons. 27 Mar. 1720	—
Neil Conway	prov. 7 Apr. 1727	6 Jan. 1738
Michael O'Reilly	prov. 24 Apr. 1739	trs. to Armagh 23 Jan. 1749
John Brullaghaun (O Brolchain)	prov. 7 May 1749	1750
Patrick Bradley, O.P.[2] (O Brolchain)	prov. 29 Jan., cons. 3 Mar. 1751	res. 1752
John MacColgan	prov. 19 Mar., brief 4 May 1752	1765
Philip MacDevitt	prov. 4 Jan. 1766	24 Nov. 1797
Charles O'Donnell	prov. coadj. with succ. 11 (or 14) Jan., succ. 24 Nov. 1797	19 July 1824
Peter MacLaughlin[3]	prov. 4 Apr., brief 11 May 1824	18 Aug. 1840
John MacLaughlin	prov. coadj. with succ. 21 Feb., cons. 16 July 1837, succ. 18 Aug. 1840	res. 1864, d. 18 June 1864
Francis Kelly	prov. coadj. with succ. 19 Apr. cons. 21 Oct. 1849, succ. 1864	1 Sept. 1889
John Keys O'Doherty	prov. 28 Dec. 1889, cons. 2 Mar. 1890	25 Feb. 1907
Charles MacHugh	prov. 14 June, cons. 29 Sept. 1907	12 Feb. 1926
Bernard O'Kane	prov. 21 June, cons. 26 Sept. 1926	5 Jan. 1939
Neil Farren	prov. 5 Aug., cons. 1 Oct. 1939	res. 14 Apr. 1973
Edward Daly	prov. 31 Jan., cons. 31 Mar. 1974	

DOWN AND CONNOR (ARMAGH P.)

Robert Blyth, O.S.B.[4]	prov. 16 Apr. 1520	depr. 1539, d. 1547
Eugene Magennis[5]	prov. 16 June 1539	p. 1559
Miler Magrath, O.F.M.[6]	prov. 12 Oct. 1565	depr. 14 Mar. 1580
Donat O'Gallagher, O.F.M.	trs. from Killala, prov. 23 Mar. 1580	c. 1581
Cornelius O'Devany, O.F.M.	prov. 27 Apr. 1582, cons. 2 Feb. 1583	1 Feb. 1612

[1] Bp Lea was appd adm. of Raphoe 18 Feb. 1695; but it seems probable that he never took possession of his see. Bernard O Cahan remained as vicar ap. of Derry until his death c. 1711.

[2] Bradley did not accept this provision, being chaplain to the Sardinian ambassador in London.

[3] Peter MacLaughlin had been bp of Raphoe since 1802, but resigned this see 12 Jan. 1819 when he was appd adm. of Derry. His provision as bp was made within the lifetime of Bp O Donnell, who was incapacitated by age and infirmity.

[4] Blyth accepted royal supremacy, and is not mentioned in the provision of his successor.

[5] Magennis accepted royal supremacy in 1541, but remained in possession during Mary's reign. He is mentioned in the provision of his successor.

[6] Magrath accepted royal supremacy in 1567, and was finally deprived by Gregory XIII. Elizabeth appd him abp of Cashel in 1571.

BISHOPS	ACCESSION	DEATH *unless otherwise stated*
(Patrick Hanratty, vic. ap.)	brief 7 Mar. 1614	trs. to Dromore *c.* 1625
Edmund Dungan	prov. 9 June 1625, cons. July 1626	1629
Hugh Magennis, O.F.M.(Bonaventura)	prov. 22 Apr. 1630, (again) 28 June 1630	24 Apr. 1640
Heber MacMahon	prov. 10 Mar. 1642	trs. to Clogher 27 June 1643
Arthur Magennis, O.Cist.	prov. 11 Mar. 1647, cons. 1 May 1648	24 Mar. 1653
(Michael O'Beirn, vic. ap.[1])	brief 17 Apr. 1657	—
Daniel Mackey[1]	prov. 4 May 1671	24 Dec. 1673
(Terence O'Donnelly, vic. ap.)	brief 22 Aug. 1711	—
James O'Shiel, O.F.M.	prov. 2 Oct., cons. Nov. 1717	13 Aug. 1724
John Armstrong	prov. 7 Apr. 1727	Dec. 1739
Francis Stuart, O.F.M.	prov. 19 Sept., cons. 24 Nov. 1740	May 1749
Edmund O'Doran	prov. 30 Jan. 1751	18 June 1760
Theophilus MacCartan	prov. 10 Sept. 1760	16 Dec. 1778
Hugh MacMullan	prov. 11 Aug. 1779	8 Oct. 1794
Patrick MacMullan	prov. coadj. with succ. 29 July, cons. 21 Sept. 1793, succ. 8 Oct. 1794	25 Oct. 1824
William Crolly	prov. 6 Feb., cons. 1 May 1825	trs. to Armagh Apr. or May 1835
Cornelius Denvir	prov. 6 Sept., cons. 22 Nov. 1835	res. May 1865, d. 10 July 1866
Patrick Dorrian	prov. coadj. with succ. 13 June, cons. 19 Aug. 1860, succ. May 1865	3 Nov. 1885
Patrick MacAlister	cons. 28 Mar. 1886	26 Mar. 1895
Henry Henry	prov. 16 Aug., cons. 22 Sept. 1895	8 Mar. 1908
John Tohill	prov. 5 Aug., cons. 20 Sept. 1908	4 July 1914
Joseph MacRory	prov. 18 Aug., cons. 14 Nov. 1915	trs. to Armagh 22 June 1928
Daniel Mageean	prov. 31 May, cons. 25 Aug. 1929	18 Jan. 1962
William Philbin	trs. from Clonfert, prov. 5 June 1962	res. 24 Aug. 1982
Cahal Brendan Daly	trs. from Ardagh and Clonmacnois, prov. 24 Aug., cons. 17 Oct. 1982	

[1] During the years 1673–1711 the two dioceses of Down and Connor seem to have been ruled by separate vicars general. Aft. the death of Michael O'Beirn, probably *c.* 1670, Patrick Beirn was vicar gen. of Down 1683 whilst Patrick O'Mulderig was vicar gen. of Connor 1670 and 1683. Quilan, who died in 1692, was vicar gen. of Connor, and was succeeded by Cormac Shiel, 1692–1708. Lea was vicar gen. of Down 1704–08, and vic. gen of both dioceses 1708–10. James Shiel was vicar gen. of both dioceses in 1711. Terence O'Donnelly was appd vicar ap. of Down in August 1711, and vicar ap. of both dioceses in Feb. 1714.

DROMORE
(ARMAGH P.)

BISHOPS	ACCESSION	DEATH *unless otherwise stated*
Quintin Cogly, O.P.	prov. 29 May 1536	c. 1539
Roger MacCiadh[1]	prov. 16 June 1539	—
Arthur Magennis[2]	prov. 16 Apr. 1540	c. 1575
Patrick MacCual	prov. 23 (or 26) Jan. 1576	a. Feb. 1589
(Eugene MacGibbon, vic. ap.)	brief 20 Feb. 1598	—
(Patrick Hanratty, vic. ap.)[3]	brief 13 Aug. 1625	—
Oliver Darcy, O.P.	prov. 11 Mar. 1647, cons. 7 May 1648	1662
(Ronan Maginn, vic. ap.)	brief 30 June 1671	—
Patrick Donnelly[4]	prov. 22 July 1697	1716
Anthony O'Garvey[5]	prov. 1 Sept. 1747	24 Aug. 1766
Denis Maguire, O.F.M.	prov. 10 Feb. 1767	trs. to Kilmore 20 Mar. 1770
Patrick Brady, O.F.M.	prov. 10 Apr. 1770	4 July 1780
Matthew Lennan	prov. 20 Dec. 1780	22 Jan. 1801
Edmund Derry	prov. 19 July 1801	29 Oct. 1819
Hugh O'Kelly	prov. 30 Jan., cons. 16 Apr. 1820	14 Aug. 1825
Thomas Kelly[6]	prov. 4 June, cons. 27 Aug. 1826	trs. to Armagh as coadj. 1 Dec. 1828
Michael Blake	prov. 13 Jan., cons. 17 Mar. 1833	res. 27 Feb. 1860, d. 6 Mar. 1860
John Pius Leahy, O.P.	prov. coadj. with succ. 7 July cons. 1 Oct. 1854, succ. 27 Feb. 1860	6 Sept. 1890
Thomas MacGivern	prov. coadj. with succ. 9 Mar. cons. 6 May 1887, succ. 6 Sept. 1890	24 Nov. 1900
Henry O'Neill	prov. 10 May, cons. 7 July 1901	9 Oct. 1915
Edward Mulhern	prov. 19 Jan., cons. 30 Apr. 1916	12 Aug. 1943
Eugene O'Doherty	prov. 18 Mar., cons. 28 May 1944	res. 22 Nov. 1975
Francis Gerard Brooks	prov. 22 Nov. 1975, cons. 25 Jan. 1976	

[1] Roger MacCiadh is not mentioned in the provision of his successor.

[2] Arthur Magennis had renounced papal authority bef. 10 May 1550, but he must have been absolved and recognized by Mary, for he continued to hold the see throughout her reign and is mentioned in the provision of his successor.

[3] Hanratty had been vicar ap. of Down and Connor 1614–25.

[4] In the provision of Patrick Donnelly his predecessor is named as Daniel Mackey, who was bp of Down and Connor 1671–73. There is no record of his provision to the see of Dromore, and he is described as a priest in his provision to Down and Connor in May 1671. He may perhaps have administered the see of Dromore for some time before 1671. Patrick Donnelly had been vicar gen. of Armagh for some time bef. his provision in 1697. The position in Dromore at this time is obscure.

[5] No record exists of a vicar aft. Bp Donnelly's death in 1716. During the years 1731–47 Dromore was adm. by the abps of Armagh.

[6] After his translation to Armagh Bp Kelly retained the adm. of Dromore until the appointment of Michael Blake in Jan. 1833.

DUBLIN
(DUBLIN P.)

ARCHBISHOPS	ACCESSION	DEATH
		unless otherwise stated
John Allen	prov. 3 Sept. 1528, cons. 13 Mar. 1529	28 July 1534
Hugh Curwin[1]	prov. 21 June, cons. 8 Sept. 1555	trs. to Oxford 14 Oct. 1567, d. 1568
(Donald)[2]	(no date of provision)	—
Matthew de Oviedo, O.F.M.	prov. 5 May, cons. *a.* 5 July 1600	10 Jan. 1610
Eugene Matthews	trs. from Clogher 2 May 1611	1 Sept. 1623
Thomas Fleming, O.F.M.	prov. 23 Oct. 1623	2 Aug. 1651
(James Dempsey, vic. ap.[3])	brief 17 Apr. 1657	trs. to Kildare
(Richard Butler, vic. ap.)	brief 24 Nov. 1665	—
Peter Talbot	prov. 11 Jan., cons. 9 May 1669	15 Nov. 1680
Patrick Russell	prov. 13 July 1683	14 July 1692
Piers Creagh	trs. from Cork and Cloyne 6 Mar. 1693	20 July 1705
Edmund Byrne	prov. 15 Mar. 1707	*c.* June 1724
Edward Murphy[4]	trs. from Kildare Sept. 1724	*c.* Jan. 1729
Luke Fagan	trs. from Meath Sept. 1729	11 Nov. 1733
John Linegar[5]	prov. 20 Mar. 1734	21 June 1757
Richard Lincoln	prov. coadj. with succ. 21 Nov. 1755, succ. 21 June 1757	21 June 1763
Patrick Fitzsimons	prov. 20 Sept. 1763	24 Nov. 1769
John Carpenter	prov. 10 Apr., cons. 3 June 1770	29 Oct. 1786
John Thomas Troy, O.P.	trs. from Ossory 3 Dec. 1786	11 May 1823
Daniel Murray	prov. coadj. with succ. 3 June, cons. 30 Nov. 1809, succ. 11 May 1823	26 Feb. 1852
Paul Cullen	trs. from Armagh 3 May 1852, cardinal 22 June 1866	24 Oct. 1878
Edward M'Cabe	prov. 4 Apr., cons. 25 July 1879, cardinal 12 Mar. 1882	11 Feb. 1885
William Walsh	prov. 23 June, cons. 2 Aug. 1885	9 Apr. 1921

[1] No effort was made by the Holy See to fill the see of Dublin 1534–55. Curwin was provided at Mary's request, but accepted royal supremacy under Elizabeth and was translated to Oxford in 1567 at his own request.

[2] There is no record of vicars in Dublin 1567–91. On 15 May 1591 Cornelius Stanley was appd vicar gen. of Dublin and Meath, the two sees being then vacant. Nothing is known of Donald, who is mentioned as the last abp in the provision of Matthew de Oviedo.

[3] James Dempsey was dean of Kildare before Apr. 1657, and vicar ap. of Kildare 1665–71.

[4] Murphy petitioned the Holy See for a coadj. 25 Nov. 1728. His death was announced at Rome 13 Feb. 1729.

[5] Linegar was appd bp of Glendalough 31 July 1734, an unusual departure from tradition.

ARCHBISHOPS	ACCESSION	DEATH *unless otherwise stated*
Edward Byrne	prov. coadj. with succ. 19 Aug., cons. 27 Oct. 1920, succ. 9 Apr. 1921	9 Feb. 1940
John Charles McQuaid, C.S.Sp.	prov. 6 Nov., cons. 27 Dec. 1940	res. 4 Jan. 1972
Dermot Ryan	prov. 29 Dec. 1971, cons. 13 Feb. 1972	

ELPHIN
(TUAM P.)

BISHOPS	ACCESSION	DATE OF DEATH *unless otherwise stated*
William Magennis[1] (Maginn)	prov. 16 June 1539	—
Gabriel de S. Serio, O.S.B.	prov. 27 Aug. 1539	trs. to Ferns 3 June 1541
Bernard O'Donnell, O.F.M.	trs. from Ferns 3 June 1541	*a.* 5 July 1542
Bernard O'Higgin, O.E.S.A.[2]	prov. 5 May, cons. 7 Sept. 1542	res. 1561, *ob.* 1564
Andrew O'Crean, O.P.	prov. 28 Jan. 1562	1594
(Nicholas a S. Patritio, O.E.S.A., vic. ap.[3])	brief 29 Aug. 1620	—
Raymund Galvin	prov. 9 June 1625	—
Boetius Egan, O.F.M.[4]	prov. 9 June 1625, cons. 1626	19 Apr. 1650
Dominic de Burgo, O.P.	prov. 13 July, cons. 22 Nov. 1671	1 Jan. 1701
Ambrose MacDermott, O.P.	prov. 15 Mar. 1707	Sept. 1717
Gabriel O'Kelly (Carbry)	prov. 20 Mar., cons. 8 June 1718	4 Aug. 1731
Patrick French, O.F.M.	prov. Nov. 1731	1748
John Brett, O.P.	trs. from Killala 28 Aug. 1748	12 June 1756
James O'Fallon	prov. 4 Aug. 1756	2 Dec. 1786
Edward French	prov. 13 Feb. 1787	29 Apr. 1810
George Thomas Plunket	prov. 4 Oct. 1814, cons. 24 Feb. 1815	8 May 1827
Patrick Burke	prov. coadj. with succ. 12 Jan., cons. 27 June 1819, succ. 8 May 1827	16 Sept. 1843
George Joseph Plunket Browne	trs. from Galway 26 Mar. 1844	1 Dec. 1858
Laurence Gillooly, C.M.	prov. coadj. with succ. 18 Feb. cons. 7 Sept. 1856, succ. 1 Dec. 1858	15 Jan. 1895

[1] Eugene Magennis was provided to Down and Connor on the same day (16 June 1539), and it is possible that there is some confusion here. Nothing further is known of William Magennis (Maginn).

[2] Bernard O'Higgin left Ireland during the last years of the reign of Henry VIII, but returned under Mary. During his absence the diocese was adm. by John O'Heyne, bp of Cork; but O'Heyne was never bp of Elphin.

[3] There is no record of vicars 1594–1620.

[4] After the death of Boetius Egan there is no record of vicars 1650–71.

BISHOPS	ACCESSION	DEATH
		unless otherwise stated
John Clancy	prov. coadj. with succ. 12 Jan., succ. 8 Feb. 1895, cons. 24 Mar. 1895	19 Oct. 1912
Bernard Coyne	prov. 18 Jan., cons. 30 Mar. 1913	17 July 1926
Edward Doorly	prov. coadj. with succ. 5 Apr., cons. 24 June 1923, succ. 17 July 1926	4 Apr. 1950
Vincent Hanly	prov. 19 July, cons. 24 Sept. 1950	9 Nov. 1970
Dominic Joseph Conway	prov. as aux. 16 Oct., cons. 8 Nov. 1970, succ. 1 May 1971	

EMLY
(CASHEL P.)

Thomas O'Hurley	prov. 6 Oct. 1505	1542
Raymund de Burgo, O.F.M.	prov. 19 Jan. 1551	23 July 1562
Maurice O'Brien[1]	prov. 24 Jan. 1567	*c.* 1586
Maurice O'Hurley[2]	prov. 1 June 1620, cons. 7 Sept. 1623	Sept. 1646
Terence Albert O'Brien, O.P.[3]	prov. coadj. with succ. 11 Mar. 1647, cons. 2 Apr. 1648	26 Nov. 1651
(William Burghat, vic. ap.)	brief 17 Apr. 1657[4]	prov. to Cashel 11 Jan. 1669
James Stritch[5]	prov. 3 Aug. 1695	—

(Emly was united to Cashel 10 May 1718)

FERNS
(DUBLIN P.)

John Purcell, O.S.A.	prov. 13 Apr., cons. 6 May 1519	20 July 1539
Bernard O'Donnell, O.F.M.	prov. 30 Mar. 1541	trs. to Elphin 3 June 1541
Gabriel de S. Serio, O.S.B.	trs. from Elphin 3 June 1541	5 May 1542
Alexander Devereux, O. Cist.[6]	(nom. 1539)	*a.* 19 Aug. 1566
Peter Power[7]	prov. 27 Apr. 1582	1587

[1] The date of Maurice O'Brien's death is not known, and there is no record of vicars 1586–1620. Emly was perhaps administered by abps of Cashel for part of this time.

[2] Maurice O'Hurley's bulls, dated 25 July 1620, were lost; they were re-expedited in 1622.

[3] Maurice O'Hurley died towards the end of Sept. 1646: *Commentarius Rinuccinianus* II, 491. News of his death cannot have reached Rome before 11 Mar. 1647, when Terence O'Brien was appd his coadjutor with right of succession.

[4] William Burghat was re-appd vic. ap. 24 Nov. 1665, and was provided to the see of Cashel 11 Jan. 1669.

[5] Emly was adm. by abps of Cashel 1669–1718. Nothing is known of Stritch apart from the record of his provision: he may never have had possession. The union of Cashel and Emly was finally decreed by Clement XI 10 May 1718.

[6] Devereux was appd by Henry VIII in 1539, but was not depr. in Mary's reign. He is mentioned in the provision of his successor.

[7] There is no record of vicars 1566–82.

BISHOPS	ACCESSION	DEATH *unless otherwise stated*
(Daniel Drihin, vic. ap.[1])	brief 17 Nov. 1607	—
John Roche[2]	prov. 29 Apr. 1624	9 Apr. 1636
Nicholas French[2]	prov. 6 Feb., cons. 23 Nov. 1645	23 Aug. 1678
Luke Wadding[3]	prov. coadj. with succ. 26 Aug. 1671	1691 (or 1692)
Michael Rossiter	prov. 1 July 1697	1709 (?)
John Verdon	prov. 14 Sept. 1709	*c.* 1728
Ambrose O'Callaghan, O.F.M.	prov. 26 Sept. 1729	8 Aug. 1744
Nicholas Sweetman	prov. 25 Jan. 1745	19 Oct. 1786
James Caulfield	prov. coadj. with succ. 26 Feb., cons. 7 July 1782, succ. 19 Oct. 1786	14 Jan. 1814
Patrick Ryan	prov. coadj. with succ. 2 Oct. 1804, cons. 2 Feb. 1805, succ. 14 Jan. 1814	9 Mar. 1819
James Keatinge	prov. coadj. with succ. 6 Dec. 1818, cons. 21 Mar. 1819	7 Sept. 1849
Myles Murphy	prov. 19 Nov. 1849, cons. 10 Mar. 1850	13 Aug. 1856
Thomas Furlong	prov. 9 Jan., cons. 22 Mar. 1857	12 Nov. 1875
Michael Warren	prov. 13 Feb., cons. 7 May 1876	22 Apr. 1884
James Browne	prov. 8 July, cons. 14 Sept. 1884	21 June 1917
William Codd	prov. 7 Dec. 1917, cons. 25 Feb. 1918	12 Mar. 1938
James Staunton	prov. 10 Dec. 1938, cons. 5 Feb. 1939	26 June 1963
Donal Herlihy	prov. 30 Oct., cons. 15 Nov. 1964	2 Apr. 1983
Brendan Comiskey	prov. titular bp of Tibili 3 Dec. 1979, cons. 20 Jan. 1980, trs. 11 Apr. 1984	

GALWAY
(TUAM P.)

(Nicholas Foran)[4]	prov. 16 Apr. 1831 (was not cons.)	—
George Joseph Plunket Browne	prov. 6 Aug., cons. 23 Oct. 1831	trs. to Elphin 26 Mar. 1844

[1] There is no record of vicars 1587–1607.

[2] The name of John Roche II is given by Brady and others as the immediate predecessor of Nicholas French. This name seems to be due to a scribal error, the name John Roche having been written in the brief of provision for French. No brief of provision for Nicholas French has ever been traced, though witnesses were examined as to his suitability for the episcopate on 21 Jan. 1645: see the report in *Father Luke Wadding: a commemorative volume* (1957), 568. No provision was made 1636–45.

[3] Wadding was appd coadj. to French in 1671, with the title of bp of Zenopolis *in partibus*. But he declined the provision as coadj. in that year. Aft. French's death there was a vacancy for five or six years, and Wadding was finally cons. bp of Ferns in 1683 or 1684.

[4] Foran fell ill and did not accept the provision. He became bp of Waterford and Lismore 1837.

BISHOPS	ACCESSION	DEATH
		unless otherwise stated
Laurence O'Donnell	prov. 26 Sept. 1844, cons. 28 Oct. 1844	29 June 1855
John MacEvilly[1]	prov. 24 Dec. 1856, cons. 22 Mar. 1857	trs. to Tuam as coadj. 2 Feb. 1878

GALWAY, KILMACDUAGH AND KILFENORA
(TUAM P.)

Thomas Carr[2]	prov. 5 June, cons. 26 Aug. 1883	trs. to Melbourne Sept. 1886
Francis MacCormack	trs. from Achonry 26 Apr. 1887	res. 21 Oct. 1908, *ob.* 14 Nov. 1909
Thomas O'Dea	trs. from Clonfert 29 Apr. 1909	9 Apr. 1923
Thomas O'Doherty	trs. from Clonfert 13 July 1923	15 Dec. 1936
Michael Browne	prov. 6 Aug., cons. 10 Oct. 1937	res. 21 July 1976
Eamonn Casey	trs. from Kerry, prov. 21 July 1976	

KERRY
(CASHEL P.)

James Fitzmaurice, O. Cist. (Fitz-Richard)	prov. 15 May 1536	1583
Michael FitzWalter	prov. 9 Aug. 1591	*c.* 1600
(Eugene Egan, vic. ap.)	brief 1 Dec. 1601	—
Richard O'Connell	(vic. ap. *c.* 1611), prov. 16 Sept. 1641, cons. 10 June 1643	*c.* 1650
(Moriarty O'Brien, vic. ap.)	brief 17 Apr. 1657	—
(Aeneas O'Leyne, vic. ap.)	brief 12 Mar. 1700	—
Denis Moriarty	prov. 7 Mar. 1720	Feb. 1739
Eugene O'Sullivan	prov. 24 Apr. 1739	1743
William O'Meara	prov. Nov. 1743	trs. to Killaloe 23 Feb. 1753
Nicholas Madgett	trs. from Killaloe, prov. 23 Feb. 1753	Aug. 1774
Francis Moylan	prov. 8 May 1775	trs. to Cork 3 June 1787
Gerard Teehan	prov. 19 June 1787	4 (5) July 1797
Charles Sughrue	prov. 6 Feb., cons. 11 June 1798	29 Sept. 1824
Cornelius Egan	prov. coadj. with succ. 4 Apr., cons. 25 July 1824, succ. 29 Sept. 1824	22 July 1856

[1] Bp MacEvilly was adm. of Kilmacduagh and Kilfenora from Sept. 1866 to 1883. When he was translated to Tuam as coadj. 1878, he retained Galway, but vacated it when he succeeded to Tuam in 1881. He did not vacate the adm. of Kilmacduagh and Kilfenora until 1883, when Carr was provided to the united sees of Galway, Kilmacduagh and Kilfenora.

[2] Galway and Kilmacduagh were united 5 June 1883, and the bp of the two united dioceses was also appd apostolic adm. of Kilfenora, which is in the province of Cashel.

BISHOPS	ACCESSION	DEATH
		unless otherwise stated
David Moriarty	prov. coadj. with succ. 18 Feb. cons. 25 Apr. 1854, succ. 22 July 1856	1 Oct. 1877
Daniel M'Carthy	prov. 7 June, cons. 25 Aug. 1878	23 July 1881
Andrew Higgins	prov. 18 Dec. 1881, cons. 5 Feb. 1882	1 May 1889
John Coffey	prov. 27 Aug., cons. 10 Nov. 1889	14 Apr. 1904
John Mangan	prov. 8 July, cons. 18 Sept. 1904	1 July 1917
Charles O'Sullivan	prov. 10 Nov. 1917, cons. 27 Jan. 1918	29 Jan. 1927
Michael O'Brien	prov. 9 May, cons. 24 July 1927	4 Oct. 1952
Denis Moynihan	trs. from Ross 10 Feb. 1953	res. 17 July 1969
Eamonn Casey	prov. 17 July, cons. 9 Nov. 1969	trs. to Galway 21 July 1976
Kevin McNamara	prov. 22 Aug., cons. 7 Nov. 1976	

KILDARE
(DUBLIN P.)

Walter Wellesley, O.S.A.	prov. 1 July 1529	May–Oct. 1539
(Donald O Beachan, O.F.M.[1])	prov. 16 July 1540	July 1540
Thady Reynolds[2]	prov. 15 Nov. 1540	—
Thomas Leverous[3]	prov. 30 Aug. 1555	*c.* 1577
(James Talbot, vic. ap.)	brief 14 Sept. 1619	—
(Donatus Doolin, vic. ap.)	brief 14 Jan. 1622	—
Roche MacGeoghegan, O.P.	prov. 5 May 1628, (again) 12 Feb. 1629	*c.* 1641–44
(James Dempsey, vic. ap.[4])	brief 24 Nov. 1665	—
(Patrick Dempsey, vic. ap.)	brief 30 June 1671	—
Mark Forestal, O.S.A.[5]	prov. 8 Oct. 1676	7 Feb. 1683
Edward Wesley	prov. 2 Aug. 1683	1693
John Dempsey	prov. 8 Feb. 1694	

[1] Died a few days aft. this provision. He is not mentioned in the provision of Reynolds

[2] Reynolds accepted royal supremacy. He was recognized by Henry VIII as a suffragan of Abp Browne in Dublin, but not as bp of Kildare. He is not mentioned in the provision of Leverous.

[3] Leverous had been provided to Leighlin Nov. 1541, on false news of the death of Sanders. In his provision to Kildare he is given the title 'bp of Leighlin' though he never held that see. In 1560 he refused to take the oath of supremacy, and lost the temporalities of Kildare.

[4] James Dempsey had been vicar ap. in Dublin 1657–65. There is no record of vicars in Kildare 1644–65.

[5] Forestal was appd adm. of Leighlin 5 Sept. 1678.

KILDARE AND LEIGHLIN
(DUBLIN P.)

(Leighlin was united to Kildare 29 Nov. 1694)

BISHOPS	ACCESSION	DEATH
		unless otherwise stated
John Dempsey	prov. 29 Nov. 1694	*c.* 1707
Edward Murphy[1]	prov. 11 Sept., cons. 18 Dec. 1715	trs. to Dublin Sept. 1724
Bernard Dunne	prov. 16 Dec. 1724	*a.* 4 Sept. 1733
Stephen Dowdall	prov. 22 Dec. 1733	*a.* May 1737
James Gallagher	trs. from Raphoe 18 May 1737	May 1751
James O'Keeffe	prov. 19 Jan. 1752	18 Sept. 1787
Daniel Delany	prov. coadj. with succ. 13 May, cons. 31 Aug. 1783, succ. 18 Sept. 1787	9 July 1814
(Arthur Murphy)	prov. 29 Sept. 1814 (provision not accepted)	—
Michael Corcoran	prov. 12 Mar., cons. 21 Sept. 1815	22 Feb. 1819
James Doyle, O.E.S.A.	prov. 8 Aug., cons. 14 Nov. 1819	15 June 1834
Edward Nolan	prov. 31 Aug., cons. 28 Oct. 1834	14 Oct. 1837
Francis Haly	prov. 10 Feb., cons. 25 Mar. 1838	19 Aug. 1855
James Walshe	prov. 14 Feb., cons. 30 Mar. 1856	5 Mar. 1888
James Lynch, C.M.[2]	prov. coadj. with succ. 15 Apr. 1869, succ. 5 Mar. 1888	19 Dec. 1896
Patrick Foley	prov. *a.* May, cons. 31 May 1896, succ. 19 Dec. 1896	24 July 1926
Matthew Cullen	prov. 25 Mar., cons. 5 June 1927	2 Jan. 1936
Thomas Keogh	prov. 8 Aug., cons. 18 Oct. 1936	res. 25 Sept. 1967
Patrick Lennon	prov. titular bp of Vina 14 May, cons. 3 July 1966, trs. 25 Sept. 1967	

KILFENORA
(CASHEL P.)

Maurice O'Kelly	prov. 6 Nov. 1514	—
John O'Neylan[3] (O Nialain)	prov. 21 Nov. 1541	1572
(Daniel Gryphaeus, vic. ap.[4])	brief 1 Apr. 1631	—

[1] Murphy was provided to Kildare 11 Sept. 1715, and received a second brief for Kildare and Leighlin 20 Mar. 1716.

[2] Lynch was elected coadj. to the vicar ap. of the western district in Scotland 26 Aug. 1866, and was cons. 4 Nov. 1866. He was translated to Kildare and Leighlin in Apr. 1869.

[3] John O'Neylan was provided by Paul III, but seems to have accepted royal supremacy since he was recognized by Henry VIII. His death is recorded by the Four Masters 1572.

[4] There is no record of vicars 1572–1629. In 1629 Gryphaeus (prob. O'Grioffa, Griffith), who was appd vicar ap. 1634, was vicar general.

BISHOPS	ACCESSION	DEATH *unless otherwise stated*
Andrew Lynch	prov. 11 Mar., cons. 21 Apr. 1647	c. 1673
William O'Daly[1]	prov. 7 Aug. 1722	—
James Augustine O'Daly, O.S.A.[2]	prov. 27 July 1726	20 Aug. 1749

(Kilfenora was united to Kilmacduagh Sept. 1750)

KILLALA
(TUAM P.)

Richard Barrett[3]	prov. 7 Jan. 1523 (? 1513)	a. Nov. 1545
Redmond O'Gallagher, O.S.A.[4]	prov. 6 Nov. 1545	trs. to Derry 22 June 1569
Donat O'Gallagher, O.F.M.	prov. 4 Sept. 1570	trs. to Down and Connor 23 Mar. 1580
John O'Cahasy, O.F.M.	prov. 27 July 1580	1583
(Miler Cawell, vic. ap.)	brief 15 May 1591	—
(Andrew Lynch, vic. ap.)	brief 28 Nov. 1629	—
(John de Burgo, vic. ap.)	brief 30 June 1671	—
(Ambrose Madden)[5]	prov. 30 Aug. 1695 (did not take effect)	—
Thadeus Francis O'Rourke, O.F.M.[6]	prov. 15 Nov. 1703, (again) 15 Mar., cons. 24 Aug. 1707	c. 1735
Peter Archdekin, O.F.M.	prov. 30 Sept. 1735, cons. 5 Feb. 1736	a. 1739
Bernard O'Rourke	prov. 24 Apr. 1739	c. 1743
John Brett, O.P.	prov. 27 July, cons. 8 Sept. 1743	trs. to Elphin 28 Aug. 1748
Mark Skerrett	prov. 23 Jan. 1749	trs. to Tuam 5 May 1749
Bonaventura Mac- Donnell, O.F.M.	prov. 7 May 1749	a. 16 Sept. 1760
Philip Philips	prov. 24 Nov. 1760	trs. to Achonry 22 June 1776
Alexander Irwin	prov. 1 July 1776	a. 25 Sept. 1779
Dominic Bellew	prov. 18 Dec. 1779, cons. 1780	c. 1812
Peter Waldron	prov. 4 Oct. 1814, cons. 24 Feb. 1815	20 May 1834

[1] William O'Daly was vicar gen. of Kilfenora bef. his provision in 1722. But there is no other record of a vicar 1673–1722.

[2] Aft. the death of James O'Daly the union of Kilfenora and Kilmacduagh was decreed by Benedict XIV. The bp of the united dioceses was to be alternately bp of one diocese and adm. of the other, since the two dioceses were in different provinces. The first bp under this new arrangement was Peter Kilkelly, who had been provided to the see of Kilmacduagh 22 Jan. 1744.

[3] Gams and Eubel give 1523 for the provision of Barrett; Brady gives 1513.

[4] Gams and Eubel give 1549 for the provision of O'Gallagher; Brady gives 1545.

[5] For Ambrose Madden, *see under* Clonfert.

[6] Thadeus O'Rourke was bp of Killala 1707–35. The situation bef. 1703, the date of his first provision, is not clear. Madden's provision in 1695 did not take effect, and the diocese was prob. ruled by a vicar.

BISHOPS	ACCESSION	DEATH
		unless otherwise stated
John MacHale	prov. coadj. with succ. 12 Feb., cons. 5 June 1825, succ. 20 May 1834	trs. to Tuam 26 Aug. 1834
Francis Joseph O'Finan, O.P.	prov. 13 Feb., cons. Mar. 1835	Dec. 1847
Thomas Feeny[1]	prov. 11 Jan. 1848	9 June 1873
Hugh Conway	prov. coadj. with succ. 21 Nov. 1871, cons. 4 Feb. 1872, succ. 9 June 1873	23 Apr. 1893
John Conmy	prov. coadj. with succ. *a.* Aug. 1892, cons. 23 Apr. 1893	26 Aug. 1911
James Naughton	prov. 27 Nov. 1911, cons. 7 Jan. 1912	16 Feb. 1950
Patrick O'Boyle	prov. 12 Dec. 1950, cons. 25 Feb. 1951	res. 12 Oct. 1970
Thomas McDonnell	prov. 12 Oct., cons. 13 Dec. 1970	

KILLALOE
(CASHEL P.)

James O'Currin[2]	prov. 24 Aug. 1526	depr. *c.* 1539
(Under administrators)[3]	1539–54	
Turlough O'Brien	prov. 25 June 1554	1569
Malachy O'Molony	prov. 10 Jan. 1571	trs. to Kilmacduagh 22 Aug. 1576
Cornelius O'Mulrian, O.F.M.	prov. 22 Aug. 1576	1616
(Malachy O'Queely, vic. ap.)	brief 30 Aug. 1619	prov. to Tuam 22 Apr. 1630
John O'Molony I	prov. 12 Aug., cons. Nov. 1630	Oct. 1651
(John O'Molony II, vic. ap.)	brief 17 Oct. 1652	—
(Denis Harty, vic. ap.)	brief 17 Apr. 1657	—
John O'Molony II[4]	prov. 26 May 1671, cons. 6 Mar. 1672	trs. to Limerick 24 Jan. 1689
Eustace Browne[5]	prov. 30 June, cons. 16 Aug. 1713	*c.* 1729
Sylvester Lloyd, O.F.M.	prov. 25 Sept. 1729	trs. to Waterford 29 May 1739
Patrick MacDonogh	prov. 14 Aug. 1739	25 Feb. 1752

[1] In July 1839 Feeny was appd adm. of Killala, and was cons. as bp of Ptolemais 13 Oct. 1839.

[2] O'Currin accepted royal supremacy, and Paul III appd an adm. for Killaloe in 1539.

[3] In 1539 Paul III provided Richard Hogan, O.F.M. (16 June 1539), and aft. his death Florence Kirwan, O.F.M. (5 Dec. 1539) as bps of Clonmacnois and adm. of Killaloe. Dermot O'Brien was appd adm. of Killaloe 5 May 1542, being then aged 22 years. It is possible that Florence Kirwan continued to act as adm. until his death in 1555.

[4] He is prob. to be identified as John O'Molony who was appd vic. ap. 1652. When he was translated from Killaloe to Limerick in Jan 1689, John O'Molony continued to act as adm. of Killaloe until his death in 1702. There is no record of vicars 1702–13.

[5] Bishop Browne was suspended for a time from 4 Oct. 1723, when the abp of Cashel acted as adm.

BISHOPS	ACCESSION	DEATH *unless otherwise stated*
(Patrick O'Nachten)	prov. 12 May 1752 (provision not accepted)	—
Nicholas Madgett	prov. 11 Dec. 1752, cons. 23 Feb. 1753	trs. to Ardfert 23 Feb. 1753
William O'Meara	trs. from Ardfert 23 Feb. 1753	*p.* 1763
Michael Peter Mac-Mahon, O.P.	prov. 5 June, cons. 4 Aug. 1765	20 Feb. 1807
James O'Shaughnessy	prov. coadj. with succ. 23 Sept. 1798, cons. 13 Jan. 1799, succ. 20 Feb. 1807	5 Aug. 1829
Patrick MacMahon	prov. coadj. with succ. 8 Aug. cons. 18 Nov. 1819, succ. 5 Aug. 1829	7 June 1836
Patrick Kennedy	prov. coadj. with succ. 31 May 1835, cons. 17 Jan. 1836, succ. 7 June 1836	19 Nov. 1850
Daniel Vaughan	prov. 30 Mar., cons. 8 June 1851	29 July 1859
Michael Flannery	prov. coadj. with succ. 6 July, cons. 5 Sept. 1858, succ. 29 July 1859	19 June 1891
Thomas MacRedmond	prov. coadj. with succ. Sept. 1889, cons. 12 Jan. 1890, succ. 19 June 1891	5 Apr. 1904
Michael Fogarty	prov. 8 July, cons. 4 Sept. 1904	25 Oct. 1955
Joseph Rodgers	prov. coadj. with succ. 10 Jan., cons. 7 Mar. 1948, succ. 25 Oct. 1955	10 July 1966
Michael Harty	prov. 28 Sept., cons. 19 Nov. 1967	

KILMACDUAGH
(TUAM P.)

Christopher Bodkin[1]	prov. 3 Sept. 1533	depr. 5 May 1542
Cornelius O'Dea[2]	prov. 5 May 1542	—
Christopher Bodkin	prov. (again) 7 Oct. 1555	1572
Malachy O'Moloney	trs. from Killaloe 22 Aug. 1576	1610
(Oliver Burke, O.P., vic. ap.)	brief 28 Nov. 1629	—
Hugh Burke, O.F.M.	prov. 11 Mar. 1647	*c.* 1656
(Michael Lynch, vic. ap.)	brief 30 June 1671	—
(Ambrose Madden)[3]	prov. 15 Nov. 1703 (again) 15 Mar. 1707	trs. to Clonfert 6 Aug. 1713
Francis de Burgo	prov. 5 June, cons. 1 May 1720	—
Bernard O'Hara, O.F.M.	prov. Dec. 1723	*a.* Nov. 1732
Martin (Milo) Burke	prov. 22 Nov. 1732, cons. 8 Mar. 1733	—
Peter Killikelly, O.P.	prov. 22 June, cons. 14 Oct. 1744	

[1] Bodkin accepted royal supremacy in 1537 (*see under* Tuam).
[2] O'Dea was opposed successfully by Bodkin, and prob. resigned.
[3] For Ambrose Madden, *see under* Clonfert. It is probable that he acted as adm. of Kilmacduagh 1695–1714.

KILMACDUAGH AND KILFENORA
(TUAM P.)

BISHOPS	ACCESSION	DEATH *unless otherwise stated*
Peter Killikelly, O.P.[1]	prov. Sept. 1750	29 May 1783
Laurence Nihill	prov. 23 Dec. 1783	29 June 1795
Edward Dillon	prov. coadj. with succ. 21 Jan. 1794, succ. 29 June 1795	trs. to Tuam 19 Nov. 1798
(Richard Luke Concannon, O.P.)	prov. 19 Nov. 1798, (was not cons.)	res. *a.* 11 Dec. 1799
Nicholas Joseph Archdeacon	prov. 12 Oct. 1800	27 Nov. 1823
Edmund French, O.P.	prov. 24 Aug. 1824, cons. 13 Mar. 1825	20 July 1852
Patrick Fallon[2]	prov. 26 Jan. 1853	res. 31 Aug. 1866, d. 13 May 1879

KILMORE
(ARMAGH P.)

Edmund Nugent, O.S.A., prior of Tristernagh[3]	prov. 22 Jan. 1530	depr. 1540, d. *c.* 1550
John MacBrady	prov. 5 Nov. 1540	1559
Hugh O'Sheridan	prov. 7 Feb. 1560	1579
Richard Brady, O.F.M.	trs. from Ardagh 9 Mar. 1580	Sept. 1607
Hugh O'Reilly[4]	prov. 9 June, cons. July 1625	trs. to Armagh 5 May 1628
Eugene Sweeney[5]	prov. 18 Sept. 1628, cons. 1630	18 Oct. 1669
Michael MacDonagh, O.P.	cons. 12 Dec. 1728	26 Nov. 1746
Laurence Richardson, O.P.	prov. 6 Feb., cons. 1 May 1747	29 Jan. 1753
Andrew Campbell	prov. 3 Apr. 1753	1 Dec. 1769
Denis Maguire, O.F.M.	trs. from Dromore 25 Mar. 1770	23 Dec. 1798
Charles O'Reilly	prov. coadj. with succ. 17 May 1793, succ. 23 Dec. 1798	6 Mar. 1800
James Dillon	trs. from Raphoe 10 Aug. 1800	1806
Farrell O'Reilly	prov. 16 Jan., cons. 24 Aug. 1807	30 Apr. 1829
James Browne	prov. coadj. with succ. 20 Mar., cons. 10 June 1827, succ. 30 Apr. 1829	11 Apr. 1865

[1] Killikelly was provided as first bp of the united dioceses of Kilmacduagh and Kilfenora in Sept. 1850.

[2] Fallon resigned his bishopric in 1866 and entered the Passionist order; he died at Mount Argus, Dublin, 13 May 1879. For the dates of John MacEvilly as adm. of the two dioceses, *see under* Tuam.

[3] Nugent accepted royal supremacy and was deprived by Paul III in 1540.

[4] There is no record of a vicar 1607–25.

[5] In 1666, three years bef. Sweeney's death, Thomas Fitzsymons was appd vicar gen. of Kilmore by Primate Edmund O'Reilly, but was depr. 1677. From 1678 to 1689 the diocese was adm. by Patrick Tyrell, bp of Clogher (and later of Meath). No vicar ap. was appd 1689–1711, and the diocese was ruled by vicars general. Kilmore was adm. by Hugh MacMahon as bp of Clogher (and later abp of Armagh) 1711–28.

BISHOPS	ACCESSION	DEATH *unless otherwise stated*
Nicholas Conaty	prov. coadj. with succ. 7 Mar., cons. 24 May 1863, succ. 11 Apr. 1865	17 Jan. 1886
Bernard Finegan	prov. 10 May, cons. 13 June 1886	11 Nov. 1887
Edward MacGennis	prov. 3 Feb., cons. 15 Apr. 1888	15 May 1906
Andrew Boylan, C.SS.R.	prov. 1 Mar., cons. 19 May 1907	25 Mar. 1910
Patrick Finegan	prov. 4 July, cons. 11 Sept. 1910	25 Jan. 1937
Patrick Lyons	prov. 6 Aug., cons. 3 Oct. 1937	27 Apr. 1949
Austin Quinn	prov. 19 July, cons. 10 Sept. 1950	res. 10 Oct. 1972
Francis McKiernan	prov. 11 Oct., cons. 10 Dec. 1972	

LEIGHLIN
(DUBLIN P.)

Matthew Sanders	prov. 10 Apr. 1527	23 Dec. 1549
(Thomas Leverous[1])	prov. 14 Nov. 1541	—
Thomas O'Fihely[2]	trs. from Achonry 30 Aug. 1555	1567
Francis de Ribera[3]	prov. 14 Sept. 1587	10 Sept. 1604
(Luke Archer, O. Cist., vic. ap.)	brief 19 Jan. 1609	—
(Matthew Roche, vic. ap.)	brief 15 Jan. 1622	—
Edmund Dempsey, O.P.	prov. 10 Mar. 1642	*c.* 1661

On 5 Sept. 1678 Mark Forestal, bp of Kildare, was appd adm. of Leighlin, and the see was adm. by bps of Kildare 1678–94. The formal decree of union is dated 29 Nov. 1694.

LIMERICK
(CASHEL P.)

John Quin (Coyn), O.P.[4]	prov. 21 Oct. 1524	1554 (or 1555)
Hugh Lacy[5]	prov. 24 Nov. 1556	1580
Cornelius O'Boyle	prov. 20 Aug. 1582	*p.* 1591
(Richard Cadan, vic. ap.)	brief 22 Feb. 1602	—

[1] Leverous was provided on false news of the death of Sanders. The provision of Leverous to Kildare bears the same date as the provision of Thomas O'Fihely to Leighlin. Leverous is not mentioned in the provision of O'Fihely, though he is styled bp of Leighlin in his own provision to Kildare.
[2] O'Fihely submitted to the queen 23 July 1559, but no effort was made to deprive him bef. his death in 1567.
[3] There is no record of a provision to Leighlin 1567–87. In the provision of Francis de Ribera (who never came to Ireland) there is mention of William Ophily as his predecessor. This is most prob. an error for Thomas O'Fihely.
[4] Quin was forced to resign by Edward VI 9 Apr. 1551, but was restored by Mary in 1553.
[5] Hugh Lacy received special faculties 3 May 1575 for the whole province of Cashel in the absence of the abp.

BISHOPS	ACCESSION	DEATH
		unless otherwise stated
Richard Arthur[1]	prov. 18 May 1620, cons. 7 Sept. 1623	23 May 1646
Edmund O'Dwyer	prov. coadj. with succ. 6 Feb., cons. 7 May 1645, succ. 23 May 1646	5 Apr. 1654
(James Dowley, vic. ap.)[2]	brief 17 Apr. 1657	—
James Dowley	prov. 4 May 1676, brief 8 Mar. 1677	*c.* Jan. 1685
John O'Molony[3]	trs. from Killaloe 24 Jan. 1689	3 Sept. 1702
Cornelius O'Keeffe[4]	prov. 7 Mar. 1720	4 May 1737
Robert Lacy	prov. 30 Aug. 1737, cons. 23 Feb. 1738	4 Aug. 1759
Daniel O'Kearney	prov. 27 Nov. 1759, cons. 27 Jan. 1760	24 Jan. 1778
(John Butler S.J.)	prov. 10 Apr. 1778 (provision not accepted)	—
Denis Conway	prov. 25 Feb., cons. 20 June 1779	19 June 1796
John Young	prov. coadj. with succ. 4 Jan., cons. 20 May 1793, succ. 19 June 1796	22 Sept. 1813
Charles Tuohy	prov. 1 Oct. 1814, cons. 23 Apr. 1815	17 Mar. 1828
John Ryan	prov. coadj. with succ. 31 Sept., cons. 11 Dec. 1825, succ. 17 Mar. 1828	6 June 1864
George Butler	prov. coadj. with succ. 10 June, cons. 25 July 1861, succ. 6 June 1864	3 Feb. 1886
Edward Thomas O'Dwyer	prov. 10 May, cons. 29 June 1886	19 Aug. 1917
Denis Hallinan	prov. 10 Jan., cons. 10 Mar. 1918	2 July 1923
David Keane	prov. 24 Dec. 1923, cons. 2 Mar. 1924	12 Mar. 1945
Patrick O'Neill	prov. 15 Dec. 1945, cons. 24 Feb. 1946	26 Mar. 1958
Henry Murphy	prov. 1 July, cons. 31 Aug. 1958	8 Oct. 1973
Jeremiah Newman	prov. 17 May, cons. 14 July 1974	

MAYO
(TUAM P.)

John Bell	prov. 4 Nov. 1493	*c.* 1541
Eugene MacBrehon, O. Carm.[5]	prov. 21 Nov. 1541	—

[1] Richard Arthur is named as vicar gen. of Limerick in a report to the government 1613; and he is reported as 'bp elect and resident in the diocese' in a later report 1617.

[2] Dowley was again appd vicar ap. 31 July 1669. He was provided to the see 4 May 1676.

[3] Retained adm. of Killaloe 1689–1702.

[4] There is no record of vicars 1702–20.

[5] MacBrehon cannot have got possession, since the diocese was held by Abp Bodkin 1537–72.

BISHOPS	ACCESSION	DEATH
		unless otherwise stated

Dermot O'Dwyer, O.F.M. (Odiera)	prov. 12 Feb. 1574	—
Patrick O'Hely, O.F.M.	prov. 4 July 1576	*p.* June 1579
Adam Magauran[1]	prov. 28 July 1585	—

(Mayo was united to Tuam after 1631)

MEATH
(ARMAGH P.)

Edward Staples[2]	prov. 3 Sept. 1529	depr. 29 June 1554, d. *c.* 1560
William Walsh[3]	prov. 22 Nov. 1554	4 Jan. 1577
Thomas Dease[4]	prov. 5 May 1621, cons. 22 May 1622	1652
Anthony MacGeoghegan, O.F.M.	trs. from Clonmacnois 16 Apr. 1657	res. 1661, d. 1664
(Edmund Mac Teige, vic. ap.)	brief 24 Nov. 1665	—
Patrick Plunkett, O. Cist.	trs. from Ardagh 11 Jan. 1669	18 Nov. 1679
James Cusack	prov. coadj. with succ. 5 Oct. 1678, succ. 18 Nov. 1679	1688
Patrick Tyrell, O.F.M.	trs. from Clogher 24 Jan. 1689	1692
(James Fagan)[5]	prov. 30 Apr. 1707 (did not accept provision)	—
Luke Fagan	prov. 15 Sept. 1713, cons. 7 Feb. 1714	trs. to Dublin Sept. 1729
Stephen MacEgan, O.P.	trs. from Clonmacnois 26 Sept. 1729	30 May 1756
Augustine Cheevers, O.E.S.A.	trs. from Ardagh 7 Aug. 1756	18 Aug. 1778
Patrick Joseph Plunkett	prov. 19 Dec. 1778, cons. 28 Feb. 1779	11 Jan. 1827
Robert Logan	prov. coadj. with succ. 26 July cons. 29 Oct. 1824, succ. 11 Jan. 1827	22 Apr. 1830
John Cantwell	prov. 4 July, cons. 21 Sept. 1830	11 Dec. 1866

[3] There is no record of any bp of Mayo aft. 1585. The diocese may have been adm. by bps of Achonry. On 12 Mar. 1631 the earl of Tyrconnell wrote, recommending the appointment of Nicholas Lynch to the see of Mayo and Achonry in Connacht, which is stated to have been long vacant. On 20 May 1631 Abp O'Queely wrote to Cardinal Ludovisi, petitioning for the union of Tuam and Mayo. Brady (ii, 156) says that 'Mayo was subsequently united to Achonry'; and this statement was repeated in the former edition of this *Handbook*. But Mayo was united to Tuam, prob. in response to the petition of Abp O'Queely, though the exact date of the union is not known.

[2] Staples accepted royal supremacy, but no action was taken against him by Paul III. He was deprived in 1554.

[3] Walsh was appd by Cardinal Pole as papal legate in 1554. He was deprived of the temporalities of his see in 1560. His appointment by Cardinal Pole was confirmed in consistory 6 Sept. 1564.

[4] There is no record of any vicar 1577–91. Cornelius Stanley was appd vicar gen. of Meath and Dublin 15 May 1591. No record survives 1591–1621.

[5] There is no record of a vicar 1692–1711.

BISHOPS	ACCESSION	DEATH *unless otherwise stated*
Thomas Nulty	prov. coadj. with succ. 29 Aug., cons. 23 Oct. 1864, succ. 11 Dec. 1866	24 Dec. 1898
Matthew Gaffney	prov. 22 June, cons. 25 June 1899	res. 1906, d. 15 Dec. 1909
Laurence Gaughran	prov. 19 May, cons. 24 June 1906	14 June 1928
Thomas Mulvany	prov. 12 Apr., cons. 30 June 1929	16 June 1943
John D'Alton	prov. coadj. with succ. 7 Apr. cons. 29 June 1942, succ. 16 June 1943	trs. to Armagh 25 Apr. 1946
John Kyne	prov. 17 May, cons. 29 June 1947	23 Dec. 1966
John McCormack	prov. 29 Jan., cons. 10 Mar. 1968	

OSSORY
(DUBLIN P.)

Milo Baron (Fitzgerald), O.S.A.[1]	prov. 8 June 1528	June–Sept. 1550
John Tonory, O.S.A.[1]	nom. Dec. 1553, cons. Jan. 1554	1565
Thomas Strong[2]	prov. 28 Mar., cons. 5 Apr. 1582	20 Jan. 1602
(William Brenan, vic. ap.[3])	brief 13 Nov. 1603	*c.* 1609
David Rothe[4]	prov. 1 Oct. 1618, cons. 1620	20 Apr. 1650
(Terence Fitzpatrick, vic. ap.)	brief 17 Apr. 1657	*c.* 1668
James Phelan	prov. 11 Jan., cons. 1 Aug. 1669	Jan. 1695
William Daton (? Dalton)	prov. 20 Feb. 1696	26 Jan. 1712
Malachy Dulany	prov. 20 Sept. 1713, cons. 17 Feb. 1714	May 1731
Patrick Shee	prov. 28 July 1731	June 1736
Colman O'Shaughnessy, O.P.	prov. 5 Oct. 1736	2 Sept. 1748
James Bernard Dunne	prov. 17 Dec. 1748	30 Apr. 1758
Thomas de Burgo, O.P.	prov. 9 Jan., cons. 22 Apr. 1759	25 Sept. 1776
John Thomas Troy, O.P.	prov. 16 Dec. 1776, cons. 8 June 1777	trs. to Dublin 3 Dec. 1786

[1] John Tonory was nominated by Mary, whose mandate for cons. is dated 31 Dec. 1553. The cons. was valid, and Tonory was confirmed by Cardinal Pole as bp of Ossory.

[2] The see was vacant 1565–82. Strong came to Ireland 1583–84, but spent the rest of his life in Spain. George Power, his vicar gen., died in prison in 1599.

[3] William Brenan was active as vicar ap. 1603–09. In 1609 he entered the Franciscan order, and died in Flanders *c.* 1610. Laurence Reneghan was vicar gen. 1609–13. His place was taken by Luke Archer, titular abbot of Holy Cross, who was also vicar ap. of Leighlin.

[4] David Rothe came to Ireland as vicar gen. of Armagh in 1609. He is styled 'titular bp of Ossory' in some government reports on the state of that diocese 1610–15, but he was most prob. vicar gen. at that time. For the evidence, see Carrigan, *History of the Diocese of Ossory*, i, 86–93.

BISHOPS	ACCESSION	DEATH
		unless otherwise stated
John Dunne	prov. 13 July, cons. 16 Sept. 1787	15 Mar. 1789
James Lanigan	prov. 10 July, cons. 21 Sept. 1789	11 Feb. 1812
Kyran Marum	prov. 4 Oct. 1814, cons. 5 Mar. 1815	22 Dec. 1827
(Miles Murphy)	prov. 8 June 1828, brief 5 Mar. 1829, (provision not accepted)	—
William Kinsella	prov. 15 May, cons. 26 July 1829	12 Dec. 1845
Edward Walsh	prov. 24 Apr., cons. 26 July 1846	11 Aug. 1872
Patrick Francis Moran	prov. coadj. with succ. 28 Dec. 1871, cons. 5 Mar. 1872, succ. 11 Aug. 1872	trs. to Sydney Mar. 1884, d. 16 Aug. 1911
Abraham Brownrigg	prov. 28 Oct., cons. 14 Dec. 1884	1 Oct. 1928
Patrick Collier	prov. coadj. with succ. 18 May, cons. 5 Aug. 1928, succ. 1 Oct. 1928	10 Jan. 1964
Peter Birch	prov. coadj. with succ. 24 July, cons. 23 Sept. 1962, succ. 10 Jan. 1964	7 Mar. 1981
Laurence Forristal	prov. titular bp of Rotdon, cons. 20 Jan. 1980, trs. 10 June 1981	

RAPHOE
(ARMAGH P.)

Cornelius O'Cahan[1]	prov. 6 Feb. 1514	depr. 1534, d. *p.* 1550
Edmund O'Gallagher	prov. 11 May 1534	26 Feb. 1543
Art O'Gallagher	prov. 5 Dec. 1547	13 Aug. 1561
Donald MacGongail	prov. 28 Jan. 1562	29 Sept. 1589
Niall O'Boyle	prov. 9 Aug. 1591	6 Feb. 1611
John O'Cullenan[2]	brief as vicar ap. 1 Dec. 1621, prov. 9 June 1625	24 Mar. 1661
(Hugh O'Gallagher, vic. ap.)	brief 10 July 1657	—
James O'Gallagher[3]	prov. 21 July, cons. 14 Nov. 1725	trs. to Kildare 18 May 1737
Daniel O'Gallagher, O.F.M.	prov. 10 Dec., cons. 29 Dec. 1737	1749
Anthony O'Donnell, O.F.M.	prov. 19 Jan. 1750	26 Apr. 1755
Nathaniel O'Donnell	prov. 18 July 1755	1758
Philip O'Reilly	prov. 9 Jan., cons. 22 Apr. 1759	1782

[1] O'Cahan accepted royal supremacy, and is not mentioned in the provision of his successor.

[2] There is no record of a vicar 1611–21. Bp O'Cullenan left the country in Mar. 1653, and Hugh O'Gallagher was appd vicar ap. of Raphoe within his lifetime.

[3] No record survives 1657–95. On 18 Feb. 1695 Fergus Lea, bp of Derry, was appd adm. of Raphoe; but he died in the following year. There is no record of a vicar 1696–1725.

BISHOPS	ACCESSION	DEATH
		unless otherwise stated
Anthony Coyle	prov. coadj. with succ. 27 Apr., cons. 14 Sept. 1777, succ. 1782	21 Jan. 1801
Peter MacLaughlin[1]	prov. 25 Apr., cons. 24 Aug. 1802	res. 12 Jan. 1819
Patrick MacGettigan	prov. 25 June, cons. 17 Sept. 1820	1 May 1861
Daniel MacGettigan	prov. coadj. with succ. 13 Feb., cons. 18 May 1856, succ. 1 May 1861	trs. to Armagh 7 Mar. 1870
James MacDevitt	prov. 13 Feb., cons. 30 Apr. 1871	5 Jan. 1879
Michael Logue	prov. 13 May, cons. 20 July 1879	trs. to Armagh as coadj. 30 Apr. 1887
Patrick O'Donnell	prov. 26 Feb., cons. 3 Apr. 1888	trs. to Armagh as coadj. 14 Feb. 1922
William MacNeely	prov. 21 Apr., cons. 22 July 1923	11 Dec. 1963
Anthony McFeely	prov. 14 May, cons. 27 June 1965	res. 16 Feb. 1982
Séamus Hegarty	prov. 16 Feb., cons. 28 Mar. 1982	

ROSS
(CASHEL P.)

Dermot MacCarthy, O.E.S.A.	prov. 6 June 1526	1552
Maurice O'Fihely, O.F.M.	prov. 12 Jan. 1554	*a.* 27 Jan. 1559
Maurice O'Hea	prov. 7 Apr. 1559	*c.* 1561
Thomas O'Herlihy	prov. 17 Dec. 1561	11 Mar. 1580
Bonaventura Naughton, O.F.M.	prov. 20 Aug. 1582	14 Feb. 1587
(Eugene Egan, vic. ap.)	brief 30 May 1597	—
(Florence MacCarthy, vic. ap.)	brief 15 July 1619	—
(Robert Barry, vic. ap.)	brief 27 May 1620	—
Boetius MacEgan, O.F.M.	prov. 11 Mar. 1647, cons. 25 Mar. 1648	6 May 1650
(Eugene Egan, vic. ap.)	brief 17 Apr. 1657	—

From 1693 to 1747 Ross was normally adm. by the bps of Cork and Cloyne. Benedict XIV decreed the union of Ross and Cloyne 10 Dec. 1747. Ross was separated from Cloyne 24 Nov. 1850.

William Keane	prov. 24 Nov. 1850, cons. 2 Feb. 1851	trs. to Cloyne 5 May 1857
Michael O'Hea	prov. 11 Dec. 1857, cons. 7 Feb. 1858	18 Dec. 1876
William Fitzgerald	prov. 7 Sept., cons. 11 Nov. 1877	24 Nov. 1877
Denis Kelly	prov. 19 Apr., cons. 9 May 1897	18 Apr. 1924

[1] Bp MacLaughlin was appd adm. of Derry when he resigned from Raphoe in 1819. He was provided to Derry in Apr. 1824.

BISHOPS	ACCESSION	DEATH *unless otherwise stated*
James Roche	prov. 31 Mar., cons. 30 May 1926	trs. to Cloyne as coadj. 26 June 1931
Patrick Casey	prov. 22 June, cons. 15 Sept. 1935	19 Sept. 1940
Denis Moynihan	prov. 5 July, cons. 21 Sept. 1941	trs. to Kerry 10 Feb. 1953

Aft. the translation of Bp Moynihan from Ross to Kerry, Bp Lucey of Cork was appd apostolic adm. of Ross 20 Feb. 1954.

TUAM
(TUAM P.)

ARCHBISHOPS	ACCESSION	DEATH *unless otherwise stated*
Thomas O'Mullally	trs. from Clonmacnois 19 June 1514	28 Apr. 1536
Arthur O'Friel[1]	prov. 7 Oct. 1538	*c.* 1573
Christopher Bodkin[2]	prov. 7 Oct. 1555	1572
Nicholas Skerrett	prov. 17 Oct. 1580	Feb. 1583
Miler O'Higgin	prov. 24 Mar. 1586	*c.* 1590
James O'Hely	prov. 20 Mar. 1591	1595
Florence Conry, O.F.M.[3]	prov. 30 Mar., cons. 3 May 1609	Nov. 1629
Malachy O'Queely	prov. 28 June, cons. 10 Oct. 1630	25 Oct. 1645
John de Burgo	trs. from Clonfert 11 Mar. 1647	4 Apr. 1667
James Lynch[4]	prov. 11 Jan., cons. 16 May 1669	31 Oct. 1713
Francis de Burgo	prov. coadj. with succ. 22 Aug. 1713, cons. 4 Apr. 1714	*a.* 23 Sept. 1723
Bernard O'Gara	prov. 23 Dec. 1723, cons. 24 May 1724	*c.* June 1740
Michael O'Gara	prov. 19 Sept. 1740	1748
Michael Skerrett	trs. from Killala 5 May 1749	19 Aug. 1785
Philip Phillips	trs. from Achonry 22 Nov. 1785	Sept. 1787
Boetius Egan	trs. from Achonry 15 Dec. 1787, brief 4 June 1788	25 Jan. 1798
Edward Dillon[5]	trs. from Kilmacduagh 19 Nov. 1798	13 Aug. 1809
Oliver O'Kelly	prov. 4 Oct. 1814, cons. 12 Mar. 1815	18 Apr. 1834

[1] O'Friel was unable to get possession as against Bodkin, and it is probable that he resigned when Bodkin was absolved in 1555. He made no effort to get possession of the see when Bodkin died in 1572, and he is not mentioned in the provision of Skerrett.

[2] Bodkin was appd by Henry VIII 15 Feb. 1537. In 1555 he was absolved from schism by Cardinal Pole, and was appd adm. of Tuam. He is mentioned in the provision of Skerrett as the last abp.

[3] Florence Conry spent the years 1609–29 in Flanders and Spain. John Lynch, who was archdeacon of Tuam 1630–52, says that he appd suitable vicars general, but their names have not been recorded.

[4] Brady gives the date of Lynch's death as Oct. 1714; but the correct date is in Gams and Oliver J. Burke.

[5] Brady gives the date of Dillon's death as 30 Aug. 1809.

CATHOLIC BISHOPS OF IRELAND

ARCHBISHOPS	ACCESSION	DEATH *unless otherwise stated*
John MacHale	trs. from Killala 26 Aug. 1834	7 Nov. 1881
John MacEvilly[1]	trs. from Galway as coadj. 2 Feb. 1878, succ. 7 Nov. 1881	26 Nov. 1902
John Healy	trs. from Clonfert 13 Feb. 1903	16 Mar. 1918
Thomas Gilmartin	trs. from Clonfert 10 July 1918	14 Oct. 1939
Joseph Walsh	prov. auxiliary bp 16 Dec. 1937, cons. 2 Jan. 1938, prov. as abp 16 Jan. 1940	res. 31 Jan. 1969
Joseph Cunnane	prov. 31 Jan., cons. 17 Mar. 1969	

WATERFORD AND LISMORE
(CASHEL P.)

BISHOPS	ACCESSION	DEATH *unless otherwise stated*
Nicholas Comyn[2]	trs. from Ferns 13 Apr. 1519	depr. 1550, *ob.* 12 July 1557
John Magrath, O.F.M.	prov. 21 July 1550	*c.* 1551
Patrick Walsh[3]	nom. 9 June, cons. 23 Oct. 1551	1578
(James White, vic. ap.[4])	brief 24 July 1600	—
Patrick Comerford, O.E.S.A.[5]	prov. 12 Feb., cons. 18 Mar. 1629	10 Mar. 1652
(Patrick Hacket, vic. ap.)	brief 17 Apr. 1657	—
John Brenan[6]	prov. 26 May, cons. 6 Sept. 1671	trs. to Cashel 8 Mar. 1677
Richard Piers	prov. 21 May 1696	4 June 1739
Sylvester Lloyd, O.F.M.	trs. from Killaloe 29 May 1739	1747
Peter Creagh	prov. coadj. with succ. 12 Apr. 1745, succ. 1747	12 Feb. 1775
William Egan	prov. coadj. with succ. 3 Feb. 1771, succ. 12 Feb. 1775	22 July 1796
Thomas Hussey	prov. Jan., cons. 26 Feb. 1797	11 July 1803
John Power	prov. 7 Jan., cons. 25 Apr. 1804	27 Jan. 1816
Robert Walsh	prov. 4 July 1817	1 Oct. 1821
Patrick Kelly[7]	prov. 9 Feb. 1822	8 Oct. 1829
William Abraham	prov. 12 Jan. 1830	23 Jan. 1837

[1] MacEvilly had been bp of Galway since 1857, and adm. of Kilmacduagh and Kilfenora since 1866. He retained the see of Galway until he succeeded to Tuam in 1881; and he retained the adm. of Kilmacduagh and Kilfenora until 1883. *See under Galway.*

[2] Comyn accepted royal supremacy, and is not mentioned in the provision of his successor.

[3] Walsh was appd by Edward VI and cons. by royal mandate; but he was recognized as bp in Mary's reign and is mentioned in the provision of his successor.

[4] There is no record of a vicar 1578–1600. James White was active as vicar ap. from July 1600 to some date aft. 22 Apr. 1610. In 1617 the clergy elected Nicholas Fagan, O.Cist., as bp of Waterford and petitioned the Holy See for his provision. But Fagan died in Waterford bef. the bulls of his provision came.

[5] On 22 Apr. 1623 Peter Lombard, abp of Armagh and a native of the city of Waterford, was appd adm.; but he died in Rome 1625 without coming to Ireland.

[6] Brenan retained the adm. of Waterford and Lismore aft. his translation to Cashel 1677–93.

[7] Bp Kelly had been cons. bp of Richmond, Virginia, in 1820.

BISHOPS	ACCESSION	DEATH *unless otherwise stated*
Nicholas Foran	prov. 6 June, cons. 24 Aug. 1837	11 May 1855
Dominic O'Brien	prov. 29 July, cons. 30 Sept. 1855	12 June 1873
John Egan	prov. 19 Nov. 1889, cons. 19 Jan. 1890	10 June 1891
Richard Alphonsus Sheehan	prov. 15 Jan., cons. 31 Jan. 1892	14 Oct. 1915
Bernard Hackett, C.SS.R.	prov. 29 Jan., cons. 19 Mar. 1916	1 June 1932
Jeremiah Kinane	prov. 21 Apr., cons. 29 June 1933	trs. to Cashel as coadj. 4 Feb. 1942
Daniel Cohalan	prov. 3 Feb., cons. 4 Apr. 1943	27 Jan. 1965
Michael Russell	prov. 8 Nov., cons. 19 Dec. 1965	

DUKES, MARQUESSES AND EARLS (ENGLAND), 1066–1714

The chief sources from which this compilation is taken are the *Complete Peerage* (1st and 2nd editions), the *Dictionary of National Biography* and the Close, Patent and Fine Rolls. The use of specialized publications and of unpublished sources has been indicated in the text or notes whenever special circumstances warranted this.

An attempt has been made to supply the following information, when available: the date of birth, the date of creation or succession to the title, the date of resignation, forfeiture (with note of any subsequent reinstatement) and death.

In the absence of the date of birth, the date of baptism is sometimes given. About the dates of death nothing need be said except that the days and months, being often taken in the earlier times from lists of obits, monastic annals and the like, deserve only so much confidence as attaches to this kind of evidence, even though the words *probably* and *possibly* have not always been added.

In dealing with the succession to dignities, an attempt is made to take into account various possible complications: when no special mention regarding creation or succession is made, it indicates only that no significant fact can be brought forward and that so far as we know succession took place on the death of the previous holder. The practice in the succession to earldoms during the period covered by the list changed once certainly and probably, though more obscurely, twice. In the thirteenth century and, doubtless, in the twelfth, the heir to an earldom did not succeed to the dignity of earl until he had been ceremoniously girt with the sword of the county. While no doubt, in general, this took place without much delay after he had received possession of his lands, there are cases where the interval was considerable; nor does the investiture ever seem to have preceded the livery. When, as is generally the case, the date of investiture is unknown, it has been thought useful to give, if possible, the date at which the heir obtained his lands. The chief exceptions to the rule that investiture should precede succession to the dignity are the two earls of Pembroke and Essex in Richard I's reign, who were officially known as earls before being girded with the sword of the county; but whatever the reason for this, the words of Hoveden clearly show that their case was exceptional, and that the irregularity did not pass unnoticed: 'Eodem die coronationis suae Johannes res accinxit Willelmum Marescallum gladio comitatus de Striguil, et Gaufredum Filium Petri gladio comitatus de Exsex; qui licet antea vocati essent comites, et administrationem suorum comitatuum habuissent, tamen non erant accincti gladio comitatus' (iv, 90; *see also* under these titles). The last known case when the heir to an earldom was girded with the sword of the county was in 1272, when Edward I invested Edmund of Almaine with the earldom of Cornwall, though of course the ceremony continued to be performed when new creations were made until the time of James I. After this practice with regard to succession fell into disuse, it is more difficult to determine the exact date at which an heir succeeded to his earldom: in the fourteenth century it seems that the title descended with the lands. Several indications of this could be given, but it is enough to say that in general an heir was not officially styled earl until he was in possession of his inheritance. It is for this reason that it has been thought useful to give the dates at which homage was done, and livery obtained. Nevertheless, it would be possible to point out exceptions to this rule, especially when the heir was closely related to the royal house or in some other position of influence. By the fifteenth century it seems impossible to draw any general conclusion about the date at which the title was assumed, although the idea that the dignity and the lands were inseparable was not yet extinct. In the sixteenth century, this last link with the old conception of an earldom had gone, and the dignity descended to the heir without the interposition either of a ceremony of investiture or of a previous succession to the lands of the earldom.

Attention is drawn to the following rules which are observed in these lists:

1. NUMBERING

All holders of a dignity under each title are numbered consecutively regardless of successive creations.

New creations are indicated by printing in bold type the serial number of the first new holder.

When a dignity descended to a female heiress she alone (to the exclusion of husbands) is allotted the serial number, while the husbands are listed after her, as part of the same entry.

2. LAWFUL HOLDERS, CLAIMANTS, HEIRESSES

(i) Names of all male persons known to have been fully invested with their dignity or otherwise legally recognized as its holders are printed in bold type.
(ii) Names of claimants or heirs never invested with their family dignity are printed in ordinary type and enclosed within square brackets.
(iii) Names of female heiresses are printed in ordinary type and only those of their husbands who are known to have been fully recognized as earls are indicated by bold type.

3. CROSS-REFERENCES

When more than one of the titles listed in the present compilation was held by the same person this is indicated according to the following rules:

All the dignities to which cross-reference is necessary are listed only under the first of the holder's dignities to occur in the alphabetical list. The recurrence of his name in any subsequent list is followed merely by a cross-reference to that initial full list of his dignities.

ABINGDON, *earldom*
1. **James Bertie**, Lord Norreys of Rycote; bapt. 16 June 1653; cr. Nov. 1682; d. 22 May 1699
2. **Montagu Venables-Bertie**, s. & h.; b. aft. 1672; d.s.p.s. 16 June 1743

AILESBURY, *earldom*
1. **Robert Bruce** (*see* Elgin); b. bef. 1638; cr. 18 Mar. 1664; d. 26 Oct. 1685
2. **Thomas Bruce** (*see* Elgin), 1st surv. s. & h.; b. 1656; d. 16 Dec. 1741

ALBEMARLE, *dukedom*
1. **George Monck** (*see* Torrington); b. 6 Dec. 1608; cr. 7 July 1660; d. 3 Jan. 1670
2. **Christopher Monck** (*see* Torrington), only surv. s. & h.; b. 1653 ?; d.s.p.s. 6 Oct. 1688

Earldom
3. **Arnold Joost van Keppel**; b. 1670; cr. 10 Feb. 1697; d. 19 May 1718

ALTON, *marquessate*
[Cr. 1694 with the dukedom of Shrewsbury; extinct 1718]

ANGLESEY, *earldom*
1. **Christopher Villiers**; b. aft. 1592; cr. 18 Apr. 1623; d. 3 Apr. 1630
2. **Charles Villiers**, only s. & h.; b. *c.* 1627; d.s.p. 4 Feb. 1661
3. **Arthur Annesley**, Viscount Valentia; b. 10 July 1614; cr. 20 Apr. 1661; d. 6 Apr. 1686
4. **James Annesley**, s. & h.; b. *c.* 1645; d. 1 Apr. 1690
5. **James Annesley**, s. & h.; bapt. 13 July 1674; d.s.p.m. 21 Jan. 1702
6. **John Annesley**, br. & h. male; bapt. 18 Jan. 1676; d.s.p.s. 18 Sept. 1710
7. **Arthur Annesley**, br. & h. male; d.s.p. 1 Apr. 1737

ARLINGTON, *earldom*
1. **Henry Bennet**, Lord Arlington; b. *c.* 1620: cr. 22 Apr. 1672; d.s.p.m. 28 July 1685
2. Isabella Bennet, only da. & h.; b. *c.* 1668; d. 7 Feb. 1723
   m. 1. 1 Aug. 1672 Henry Fitzroy, duke of Grafton; d. 9 Oct. 1690
   2. shortly aft. 14 Oct. 1698 Sir Thomas Hanmer, Bt.; d.s.p. 5 May 1746

ARUNDEL, *earldom*
[The history of this earldom is somewhat complicated by the decision in 1433 that the possession of the castle of Arundel carried with it the right to the earldom of Arundel. There is, however, no evidence that it was considered to have done so before this date.
Robert of Torigni (William of Jumièges, *Gesta Normannorum ducum*, ed. Marx, 322) gives the title of earl to Arundel to Roger de Montgomery.[1] L. C. Loyd has, however, pointed out that there is no contemporary evidence to justify this assertion. Ordericus Vitalis (ed. Le Prévost, ii, 220) knows of no such title, and on a strict reading seems even to exclude it. Five subsequent holders of the castle of Arundel are not known to have been styled earls of Arundel.[2]]
1. **William d'Aubigny** (*see* Lincoln), s. & h. of William d'Aubigny, *pincerna regis*; cr. prob. 1139–41; d. 12 Oct. 1176
2. **William d'Aubigny**, s. & h.; b. ? bef. 1150; st. by Christmas 1186, but he was not granted the castle and honour of Arundel until 27 June 1190; d. 24 or 25 Dec. 1193[3]
3. **William d'Aubigny**, s. & h.; b. aft. 1173; d. 1 Feb. 1221[4]
4. **William d'Aubigny**, s. & h.; b. *c.* 1200; liv. hom. Apr. 1221; d.s.p. 5 Aug. 1224[5]
5. **Hugh d'Aubigny**, br. & h.; b. *c.* 1214; liv. 10 May 1235[6]; d.s.p. 6–7 May 1243[7]
6. **Richard fitz Alan**, gt-gt-gds. of 3 & s. of John fitz Alan; b. 3 Feb. 1267; st. 12 Feb. 1291; d. shortly bef. 15 Jan. 1302
7. **Edmund fitz Alan**, s. & h.; b. 1 May 1285; st. 9 Nov. 1306; exec. 17 Nov. 1326 & forf.

---

[1] If he was right, Roger de Montgomery (possibly cr. Dec. 1067) and his two sons, Hugh de Montgomery and Robert de Bellême, should be added to the list of earls (for their dates, *see under* Shrewsbury).
[2] The following is a list of them: the dates are those at which they held the castle.
(*a*) John fitz Alan, 27 Nov. 1243—d. 1267 (bef. 10 Nov.).
(*b*) John fitz Alan, s. & h., 1267—d. 18 Mar. 1272.
(*c*) Edmund of Woodstock, earl of Kent, 26 Feb. 1327—exec. 19 Mar. 1330.
(*d*) John de Holand, duke of Exeter, 7 Aug. 1397—exec. 9–10 Jan. 1400.
(*e*) John d'Arundel 1415—d. 21 Apr. 1421.
[3] *E.H.R.*, lxx, 71.
[4] B. M. Cotton MS. Julius D VII, fo. 87 (Liber fratris Johannis de Wallingford).
[5] *Ibid.*, fo. 88v, and *E.H.R.*, lxx, 71.
[6] He had already had seizin of some of his br.'s lands on 8 Nov. 1233.
[7] His lands were divided between his four sisters or their heirs. The castle of Arundel was assigned to John fitz Alan, who was the son of Isabel, the 2nd sister. She had d. bef. 1240.

8. **Richard fitz Alan** (*see* Surrey), s. & h.; b. *c.* 1313; rest. 12 Dec. 1330; d. 24 Jan. 1376
9. **Richard fitz Alan** (*see* Surrey), s. & h.; b. 1346; exec. 21 Sept. 1397 and forf.
10. **Thomas fitz Alan** (*see* Surrey), only surv. s. & h.; b. 13 Oct. 1381; rest. Oct. 1400; d.s.p. 13 Oct. 1415
    [John d'Arundel, cous. & h. male, may have been summ. to parlt. as earl of Arundel 3 Sept. 1416, but never aft.; d. 21 Apr. 1421. His wid., m. to Walter, Lord Hungerford, was styled countess of Arundel]
11. **John d'Arundel**, s. & h. of John d'Arundel above (cr. duke of Touraine 1434); b. 14 Feb. 1408; recog. Nov. 1433; d. 12 June 1435
12. **Humphrey fitz Alan**, s. & h.; b. 30 Jan. 1429; d. 24 Apr. 1438
13. **William fitz Alan** (or Mautravers), uncle & h.; b. 23 Nov. 1417; liv. Nov. 1438; d. late in 1487
14. **Thomas fitz Alan** (or Arundel or Mautravers), s. & h.; b. 1450; d. 25 Oct. 1524
15. **William fitz Alan**, s. & h.; b. *c.* 1476; d. 23 Jan. 1544
16. **Henry fitz Alan**, s. & h.; b. 23 Apr. 1512; d.s.p.m.s. 24 Feb. 1580
17. **Philip Howard** (*see* Surrey), gds. & h.; b. 28 June 1557; forf. 14 Apr. 1589; d. 19 Oct. 1595
18. **Thomas Howard** (*see* Norfolk, Surrey), only s. & h.; b. 7 July 1585; rest. 18 Apr. 1604; d. 4 Oct. 1646
19. **Henry Frederick Howard** (*see* Norfolk, Surrey), 1st surv. s. & h.; b. 15 Aug. 1608; d. 17 Apr. 1652
20. **Thomas Howard** (*see* Norfolk, Surrey), s. & h.; b. 9 Mar. 1628; d. unm. 13 Dec. 1677

[This earldom henceforth descends with the dukedom of Norfolk]

AUMALE, *counts of*
1. **Adelaide or Adeliz**, sist. of Wm. I; st. 1082; d. bef. 1090
    m. 1. **Enguerrand II**, count of Ponthieu; d.s.p.m. 1053
    2. **Lambert**, count of Lens; d.s.p.m. 1054
    3. **Eudes** (disinherited count of Champagne); forf. 1096
2. **Stephen**, s. & h. by 3rd husband; b. bef. 1070; st. 14 July 1096; d. 1121–30
3. **William le Gros** (*see* York (note)), s. & h.; cr.[1] 1138 (prob. Sept.); d.s.p.m. 20 Aug. 1179
4. **Hawise**, da. & h.; d. 11 Mar. 1214
    m. 1. 14 Jan. 1180 **William de Mandeville**, earl of Essex; d.s.p. leg. 12 Dec. 1189
    2. Aft. 3 July 1190 **William de Forz**; d. 1195
    3. Bef. 29 Sept. 1195 **Baldwin de Béthune**; d. 13 or 14 Oct. 1212
5. **William de Forz**, s. & h. by 2nd husband; liv. *c.* Sept. 1214; d. 29 Mar. 1241
6. **William de Forz**, s. & h.; liv. hom. 18 Sept. 1241; d. 23 May 1260
7. **Thomas de Forz**, s. & h.; b. 9 Sept. 1253; d.s.p. bef. 6 Apr. 1269
8. **Aveline de Forz**, sist. & h.; b. 20 Jan. 1259; d.s.p. 10 Nov. 1274.
    m. 8 or 9 Apr. 1269 **Edmund, earl of Lancaster**; b. 16 Jan. 1245; d. 5 June 1296

Dukedom
9. **Edward 'of York'** or 'of Norwich' (*see* Cambridge, Cork, Rutland, York); b. *c.* 1373; cr. 29 Sept. 1397; depr. 3 Nov. 1399; d.s.p. 25 Oct. 1415

Earldom
10. **Thomas of Lancaster** (*see* Clarence), 2nd s. of K. Henry IV; b. 1388;[2] cr. 9 July 1412; d.s.p. leg. 22 Mar. 1421

BANBURY, *earldom*
1. **William Knollys**, Viscount Wallingford, b. *c.* 1547; cr. 18 Aug. 1626; d. 25 May 1632
2. **Edward Knollys**, eldest s. and h. b. 10 Apr. 1627; d. unm. *c.* June 1645
3. **Nicholas Knollys**, br. and h., b. 3 Jan. 1631, d. 14 Mar. 1674
4. **Charles Knollys**, s. and h.; bapt. 3 June 1662; his right to the earldom denied by the House of Lords on 17 Jan. 1693 on the ground of alleged illegitimacy of his father. He was henceforth denied writs of summons and this never reversed either for him or his descendants; d. 26 Aug. 1710.

[1] The creation was, according to John of Hexham, to the earldom of Yorkshire, but aft. this date, and only aft. this date, he calls himself sometimes *comes Albemarlie* and sometimes *comes Eboraci*.
[2] *Cf.* Wylie, *Henry IV*, iii, 324, for discussion of possible dates.

BATH, *earldom*
1. **Philibert de Chandée**; cr. 6 Jan. 1486. Nothing is known of him aft. this date
2. **John Bourchier,** Lord Fitz Warine; b. 20 July 1470; cr. 9 July, 1536; d. 30 Apr., 1539
3. **John Bourchier,** s. & h.; b. *c.* 1499; d. 10 Feb. 1561
4. **William Bourchier,** gds. & h.; b. bef. 1557 (his father is said to have d. 28 Feb. 1556); d. 12 July 1623
5. **Edward Bourchier,** 1st surv. s. & h.; bapt. 1 Mar. 1590; d.s.p.m. 2 Mar. 1637
6. **Henry Bourchier,** cous. & h. male; b. *c.* 1587; d.s.p. 16 Aug. 1654
7. **Sir John Granville**; b. 29 Aug. 1628; cr. 20 Apr. 1661; d. 22 Aug. 1701
8. **Charles Granville,** s. & h.; bapt. 31 Aug. 1661; d. 4 Sept. 1701
9. **William Henry Granville,** only s. & h.; b. 30 Jan. 1692; d. unm. 17 May 1711

BEAUFORT, *dukedom*
1. **Henry Somerset,** marquess of Worcester (*see* Worcester); b. *c.* 1629; cr. 2 Dec. 1682; d. 21 Jan. 1700
2. **Henry Somerset,** gds. & h.; b. 2 Apr. 1684; d. 24 May 1714
3. **Henry Somerset,** s. & h.; b. 26 Mar. 1707; d.s.p. 24 Mar. 1745

BEDFORD, *earldom*
   [Stephen apparently made an attempt to create an earldom of Bedford for Hugh de Beaumont ('Hugo Pauper'), 3rd s. of Robert, count of Meulan, in 1138, but it does not appear to have been made effective][1]
1. **Ingelram** or **Enguerrand de Coucy**; b. 1340; cr. 11 May 1366; res. 26 Aug. 1377; d.s.p.m. 18 Feb. 1397

   Dukedom
2. **John of Lancaster** (*see* Kendal, Richmond), 3rd s. of K. Henry IV; b. 20 June 1389; cr. 16 May 1414; d.s.p. leg. s. 15 Sept. 1435
3. **George Neville** (*see* Montagu); b. *c.* 1457; cr. 5 Jan. 1470; depr. Jan. 1478; d. 4 May 1483
4. **Jasper Tudor** (*see* Pembroke); b. 1431; cr. 27 Oct. 1485; d.s.p. leg. 21 Dec. 1495

   Earldom
5. **John Russell,** Lord Russell; b. *c.* 1485; cr. 19 Jan. 1550; d. 14 Mar. 1555
6. **Francis Russell,** s. & h.; b. 1527; d. 28 July 1585
7. **Edward Russell,** gds. & h. male; b. 20 Dec. 1572; d.s.p.s. 3 May 1627
8. **Francis Russell,** cous. & h. male; b. 1593; d. 9 May 1641
9. **William Russell** (*see* Tavistock, and *below*, *Dukedom*), s. & h.; b. 6 Aug. 1616

   Dukedom
9. *Idem*; cr. 11 May 1694; d. 7 Sept. 1700
10. **Wriothesley Russell** (*see* Tavistock), gds. & h.; b. 1 Nov. 1680; d. 26 May 1711
11. **Wriothesley Russell** (*see* Tavistock), 1st surv. s. & h.; b. 25 May 1708; d.s.p. 23 Oct. 1732

BERKELEY, *marquessate*
1. **William de Berkeley** (*see* Nottingham); b. 1426; cr. 28 Jan. 1489; d.s.p.s. 14 Feb. 1492

   Earldom
2. **George Berkeley,** descendant of neph. & h. male of **1**; b. *c.* 1627; cr. 11 Sept. 1679; d. 14 Oct. 1698
3. **Charles Berkeley,** s. & h.; b. 8 Apr. 1649; d. 24 Sept. 1710
4. **James Berkeley,** 1st surv. s. & h.; b. aft. 1679; d. 17 Aug. 1736

BERKSHIRE, *earldom*
1. **Francis Norris,** Lord Norris of Rycote; b. 6 July 1579; cr. 28 Jan. 1621; d.s.p.m. leg. 29 Jan. 1622
2. **Thomas Howard,** Viscount Andover; b. *c.* 1590; cr. 5 Feb. 1626; d. 16 July 1669
3. **Charles Howard,** s. & h.; b. *c.* 1615; d.s.p.m. Apr. 1679
4. **Thomas Howard,** br. & h. male; bapt. 14 Nov. 1619; d. 12 Apr. 1706

[1] Hugh appears to have fallen into poverty (on the loss of his wife's inheritance) some three or four years later. (*See* G. H. White, *TRHS*, 4th ser., xiii, 77–82. *See also* R. H. C. Davis, *King Stephen* (1967), 135.)

5. **Henry Bowes Howard** (later (1745) earl of Suffolk), cous. & h. male; b. 4 Nov. 1687; d. 21 Mar. 1757

BERWICK-UPON-TWEED, *dukedom*
1. **James Fitz James** (*see* Tinmouth), illeg. s. of James II; b. 21 Aug. 1670; cr. 19 Mar. 1687; forf. 1695; d. 12 June 1734

BEVERLEY, *marquessate*
[Cr. 1708 with dukedom of Dover]

BINDON, *earldom*
1. **Henry Howard** (*see* Suffolk); b. 1670; cr. 30 Dec. 1706; d. 19 Sept. 1718

BLANDFORD, *marquessate*
[Cr. 1702 with dukedom of Marlborough]

BOLINGBROKE, *earldom*
1. **Oliver St. John,** Lord St. John of Bletso; b. *c.* 1584; cr. 28 Dec. 1624; d. June 1646
2. **Oliver St. John,** gds. & h.; b. 1634; d.s.p. 18 Mar. 1688
3. **Paulet St. John,** br. & h.; d. unm. 5 Oct. 1711

BOLTON, *dukedom*
1. **Charles Paulet** (*see* Winchester); b. *c.* 1630; cr. 9 Apr. 1689; d. 27 Feb. 1699
2. **Charles Paulet** (*see* Winchester), 1st surv. s. & h.; b. 1661; d. 21 Jan. 1722

BRADFORD, *earldom*
1. **Francis Newport,** Viscount Newport of Bradford; b. 23 Feb. 1620; cr. 11 May 1694; d. 19 Sept. 1708
2. **Richard Newport,** s. & h.; b. 3 Sept. 1644; d. 14 June 1723

BRANDON, *dukedom*
1. **James Hamilton** (*see* Arran); b. 11 Apr. 1658; cr. 10 Sept. 1711; d. 15 Nov. 1712
[This dukedom henceforth descends with Hamilton]

BRECKNOCK, *earldom* (*see* ORMOND)

BRENTFORD, *earldom*
1. **Patrick Ruthven** (*see* Forth); b. *c.* 1573; cr. 27 May 1644; d.s.p.m. 2 Feb. 1651
[Again cr. with dukedom of Schomberg 1689]

BRIDGWATER, *earldom*
1. **Henry Daubeney,** Lord Daubeney; b. Dec. 1493; cr. 19 July 1538; d.s.p. 12 Apr. 1548
2. **John Egerton,** Viscount Brackley; b. *c.* 1579; cr. 27 May 1617; d. 4 Dec. 1649
3. **John Egerton,** 1st surv. s. & h.; b. June 1623; d. 26 Oct. 1686
4. **John Egerton,** s. & h.; b. 9 Nov. 1646; d. 19 Mar. 1701
5. **Scroop Egerton,** later (1720) duke of Bridgwater, 1st surv. s. & h.; b. 11 Aug. 1681; d. 11 Jan. 1745

BRISTOL, *earldom*
1. **John Digby,** Lord Digby of Sherborne; b. Feb. 1586; cr. 15 Sept. 1622; d. 21 Jan. 1653
2. **George Digby,** s. & h.; b. Oct. 1612; d. 20 Mar. 1677
3. **John Digby,** 1st s. & h.; b. *c.* 1635; d.s.p. 18 Sept. 1698

BUCKINGHAM, *earldom*
1. **Walter Giffard;** cr. prob. 1100;[1] d. 15 July 1102

---

[1] According to Ordericus Vitalis (ii, 221) K. William I was responsible for this creation, but his statement is not supported by documentary evidence. Several copies of the coronation charter of Henry I give Walter Giffard the title of earl and a place immediately aft. the earls of Northampton and Warwick. It is probable that the creation was one of the first acts of Henry I, but even under this king the evidence is ambiguous.

2. **Walter Giffard,** s. & h.;[1] st. 1107–09;[2] d.s.p. 1164
3. **Thomas of Woodstock** (*see* Essex, Gloucester, Hereford, Northampton (note)), yst. s. of Edw. III; b. 7 Jan. 1355; cr. 16 July 1377; d. prob. 8 or 9 Sept. 1397 and forf.[3]

Dukedom (and earldom)
4. **Humphrey Stafford** (*see* Hereford, Northampton (note), Stafford), gds. of 3; b. 15 Aug. 1402; cr. 14 Sept. 1444;[4] d. 10 July 1460
5. **Henry Stafford** (*see* Stafford), gds. & h.; b. uncertain; exec. 2 Nov. 1483 and forf.
6. **Edward Stafford** (*see* Stafford), s. & h.; b. 3 Feb. 1477 or 1478; st. 29 Oct. 1485 (formally rest. Nov. 1485); exec. 17 May 1521 and forf.

Earldom
7. Mary, Lady Compton; cr. 1 July 1618; d. 19 Apr. 1632

Earldom, marquessate and dukedom
8. **George Villiers** (*see* Coventry), s. of 7; b. 28 Aug. 1592; d. 23 Aug. 1628
   Earldom, cr. 5 Jan. 1617; *marquessate*, cr. 1 Jan. 1618; *dukedom*, cr. 18 May 1623
9. **George Villiers,** s. & h.; b. 30 Jan. 1628; d.s.p. leg. 16 Apr. 1687

BUCKINGHAM and NORMANBY, *dukedom*
1. **John Sheffield** (*see* Mulgrave); b. 8 Sept. 1647; cr. 23 Mar. 1703; d. 24 Feb. 1721

BURFORD, *earldom*
1. **Charles Beauclerk** (*see* St. Albans); b. 8 May 1670; cr. 27 Dec, 1676; d. 10 May 1726

BURLINGTON, *earldom*
1. **Richard Boyle** (*see* Cork); b. 20 Oct. 1612; cr. 20 Mar. 1664; d. 15 Jan. 1689

[This earldom henceforth descends with that of Cork]

CAMBRIDGE, *earldom*
[In the twelfth and thirteenth centuries, this earldom seems (though contemporaries were not always clear on the point) to have been included in the earldom of Huntingdon (there being one sheriff for both counties). This appears by implication in the creation of Aubrey de Vere as earl of Oxford in 1142 (*see* note to that creation) and in a writ of 23 May 1205 enquiring into the manner in which Earl David received the third penny from the counties of Cambridge and Huntingdon (*Rot. Litt. Claus.*, i. 33*b*).]
1. **William de Roumare** (*see* Lincoln); b. *c.* 1096; st. 1139;[5] d. bef. 1161
2. **William of Juliers,** count (later duke) of Juliers; b. *c.* 1299; cr. 7 May 1340; d. Feb. 1361[6]
3. **Edmund of Langley** (*see* York), 5th s. of K. Edward III; b. prob. 5 June 1342; cr. 13 Nov. 1362; d. 1 Aug. 1402
4. **Edward 'of York'** or 'of Norwich' (*see* Aumale), s. & h.; b. *c.* 1373; d.s.p. 25 Oct. 1415
5. **Richard 'of Conisburgh'** or 'of York', 2nd s. of 3; b. *c.* 1375; recog. 1 May 1414; exec. 5 Aug. 1415 and forf.
6. **Richard Plantagenet** (*see* March, Ulster, York), only s. & h.; b. 1411; recog. as h. to the titles and lands of 4; liv. 12 May 1432; att. 20 Nov. 1459; att. nullified Oct. 1460; d. 30 Dec. 1460

---

[1] He was a minor at his father's death.
[2] *Regesta Regum Anglo-Normannorum*, ii, no. 911.
[3] Humphrey, his only s. and h., was styled earl of Buckingham during his father's lifetime, but owing to the attainder he never succeeded to the earldom. He d. unm. 1399.
[4] Before this he appears to have been considered earl of Buckingham in the right of his mother (who d. 16–24 Oct. 1438).
[5] He is never known again by this title, and in ?1140 he became earl of Lincoln.
[6] His s. William formally res. the earldom 15 June 1366.

7. **Edward Plantagenet,** 1st surv. s. & h.; later K. Edward IV; b. 28 Apr. 1442. Became K. 4 Mar. 1461
8. **James Hamilton** (*see* Hamilton); cr. 16 June 1619; d. 3 Mar. 1625
9. **James Hamilton** (*see* Hamilton),[1] s. & h.; b. 19 June 1606; exec. 9 Mar. 1649
10. **William Hamilton** (*see* Hamilton); br. & h. male; b. 14 Dec. 1616; d.s.p.m. 11 Dec. 1651
11. **Henry Stewart** (*see* Gloucester), 3rd s. of Charles I; b. 8 July 1640; cr. 13 May 1659 ?; d. unm. 13 Sept. 1660

Earldom and dukedom[2]
12. **James Stewart;** b. 11 July 1663; cr. 23 Aug. 1664; d. 20 June 1667
13. **Edgar Stewart,** br. of **12**; b. 14 Sept. 1667; cr. 7 Oct. 1667; d. 8 June 1671

Marquessate and dukedom
14. **George Augustus,** electoral prince of Brunswick and Lüneburg, aft. K. George II (*see* Milford Haven); b. 30 Oct. 1683; cr. 9 Nov. 1706. Became K. 11 June 1727

CARDIGAN, *earldom*
1. **Thomas Brudenell,** Lord Brudenell of Stonton; b. in or bef. 1583; cr. 20 Apr. 1661; d. 16 Sept. 1663
2. **Robert Brudenell,** s. & h.; b. 5 Mar. 1607; d. 16 July 1703
3. **George Brudenell,** gds. & h.; b. aft. 1668; d. 5 July 1732

CARLISLE, *earldom*
1. **Andrew de Harcla;** cr. 25 Mar. 1322; exec. and forf. 3 Mar. 1323
2. **James Hay,** Viscount Doncaster; b. *c.* 1580; cr. 13 Sept. 1622; d. 25 Apr. 1636
3. **James Hay,** only surv. s. & h.; b. *c.* 1612; d.s.p. 30 Oct. 1660
4. **Charles Howard;** b. 1629 ?; cr. 30 Apr. 1661; d. 24 Feb. 1685
5. **Edward Howard,** s. & h.; b. *c.* 1646; d. 23 Apr. 1692
6. **Charles Howard,** s. & h.; b. 1669; d. 1 May 1738

CARMARTHEN, *marquessate*
1. **Thomas Osborne** (*see* Danby, Leeds), b. 20 Feb. 1632; cr. 9 Apr. 1689; d. 26 July 1712
2. **Peregrine Osborne** (*see* Danby, Leeds); only surv. s. & h.; b. 1659; d. 25 June 1729

CARNARVON, *earldom*
1. **Robert Dormer,** Lord Dormer of Wing; b. *c.* 1610; cr. 2 Aug. 1628; d. 20 Sept. 1643
2. **Charles Dormer,** only s. & h.; b. 25 Oct. 1632; d.s.p.m.s. 29 Nov. 1709

CHESTER, *earldom*
1. **Gherbod,** cr. early in 1070[3]
2. **Hugh d'Avranches,** 'Vras' or 'le Gros'; cr. 1071–77[4]; res. 23 July 1101; d. 27 July 1101
3. **Richard,** only s. & h.; b. 1094; d.s.p. leg. 25 Nov. 1120
4. **Ranulph le Meschin,** 1st cous. & h.; cr. 1120–21; d. *c.* 1129
5. **Ranulph 'de Gernon',** s. & h.; b. bef. 1100; d. 16 Dec. 1153
6. **Hugh 'of Cyveiliog',** s. & h.; b. 1147; liv. *c.* 29 Sept. 1162; depr. 1174; rest. Jan. 1177; d. 30 June 1181
7. **Ranulph 'de Blundeville'** (*i.e.* of Oswestry) (*see* Richmond, Lincoln), only s. & h.; b. *c.* 1172; liv. prob. Jan. 1188; d.s.p. 26 Oct. 1232[5]

[1] He was cr. earl of Arran and Cambridge 12 Apr. 1643. This earldom has continued ever since with the dukedom of Hamilton.
[2] Two other brs of **12** and **13** were designated dukes of Cambridge, but died bef. the patent could pass; they were: Charles Stewart, b. 22 Oct. 1660; d. 5 May 1661;—Charles Stewart, b. 7 Nov. 1677; d. 12 Dec. 1677.
[3] He left England permanently soon aft., at a date that remains uncertain (Ordericus Vitalis, ii, 219; iii, 3–4).
[4] We have no attestation of Hugh as earl to a clearly genuine charter before 1077 (J. Tait in *Essays presented to R. L. Poole*, 161).
[5] *Annals of Tewkesbury*, 87 and *Annals of Chester*. On his death his estates were divided between his four sisters and the earldom lapsed.

8. **John 'de Scocia'**[1] (or 'le Scot') (*see* Cambridge, Huntingdon), neph. of 7; b. *c.* 1207; cr. 21 Nov. 1232; d.s.p. shortly bef. 6 June 1237

9. **Edward**, 1st s. of K. Henry III; b. 17 June 1239; cr. 14 Feb. 1254; res. 24 Dec. 1264; rest. aft. battle of Evesham (4 Aug. 1265). Became K. Edw. I 20 Nov. 1272

10. [Simon de Montfort (*see* Leicester); b. prob. 1208; given the custody of the earldom 24 Dec. 1264, but was never e.; d. 4 Aug. 1265]

11. **Alphonso**, 1st surv. s. & h. of 9; b. 24 Nov. 1273; ?cr. 1284; d. 19 Aug. 1284

12.[2] **Edward**, next surv. s. & h. of 9; b. 25 Apr. 1284; cr. 7 Feb. 1301. Became K. Edw. II 8 July 1307

13. **Edward**, 1st s. & h.; b. 13 Nov. 1312; cr. 24 Nov. 1312.[3] Became K. Edw. III 25 Jan. 1327

14. **Edward 'of Woodstock'**, the Black Prince (*see* Cornwall), 1st s. & h.; b. 15 June 1330; cr. 18 Mar. 1333; d. 8 June 1376

15. **Richard 'of Bordeaux'** (*see* Cornwall), 1st surv. s. & h.; b. *c.* 6 Jan. 1367; cr. 20 Nov. 1376. Became K. Richard II 22 June 1377

16. **Henry 'of Monmouth'** (*see* Cornwall, Lancaster), 1st s. & h. of K. Henry IV (later K. Henry V); b. 16 Sept. 1387; cr. 15 Oct. 1399. Became K. 21 Mar. 1413

17. **Edward** (*see* Cornwall), only s. & h. of K. Henry VI; b. 13 Oct. 1453; cr. 15 Mar. 1454; d.s.p. 4 May 1471

18. **Edward Plantagenet** (*see* Cornwall, March, Pembroke), 1st s. & h. of K. Edward IV; later K. Edw. V; b. 2 or 3 Nov. 1470; cr. 26 June 1471. Became K. 9 Apr. 1483

19. **Edward Plantagenet** (*see* Cornwall, Salisbury), s. & h. of K. Richard III; b. 1473; cr. 24 Aug. 1483; d. unm. 9 Apr. 1484

20. **Arthur Tudor** (*see* Cornwall), s. & h. of K. Henry VII; b. 19 Sept. 1486; cr. 29 Nov. 1489; d.s.p. 2 Apr. 1502

21. **Henry Tudor** (*see* Cornwall, York), next surv. s. & h. of K. Henry VII, later K. Henry VIII; b. 28 June 1491; cr. 18 Feb. 1504. Became K. 22 Apr. 1509

22. **Henry Frederick Stewart** (*see* Cornwall, Rothesay), 1st s. & h. of James I; b. 19 Feb. 1594; cr. 4 June 1610; d. unm. 6 Nov. 1612

23. **Charles Stewart**, next surv. s. & h. of James I; b. 19 Nov. 1600; cr. 4 Nov. 1616. Became K. Charles I 27 Mar. 1625

[Charles Stewart (aft. Charles II), 1st surv. s. & h. of **23**, was styled earl of Chester, but never formally cr. such. He was b. 29 May 1630; succ. *de jure* 30 Jan. 1649 et *de facto* 29 May 1660]

[James Francis Edward Stewart, 1st surv. s. & h. of James II, was styled prince of Wales and earl of Chester, but never formally cr. such. He was b. 10 June 1688; forf. Mar. 1702 and d. 1 Jan. 1766]

CHESTERFIELD, *earldom*

1. **Philip Stanhope**, Lord Stanhope of Shelford; b. 1584; cr. 4 Aug. 1628; d. 12 Sept. 1656

2. Katherine Wotton; cr. 29 May 1660; d. 9 Apr. 1667
   m. 1. 4 Dec. 1628 Henry, Lord Stanhope, s. & h. of **1**; d. 29 Nov. 1634
      2. Jan van den Kerchhove or Polyander, Lord of Henvliet; d. 7 Mar. 1660
      3. Daniel O'Neale; d. 24 Oct. 1664

3. **Philip Stanhope**, gds. of **1** & h.; b. 1634; d. 28 Jan. 1714

4. **Philip Stanhope**, 1st surv. s. & h.; b. 3 Feb. 1673; d. 9 Feb. 1726

CHICHESTER

Until 1243 the earls of Arundel are often known as earls of Chichester; for these *see under* Arundel.

CHICHESTER, *earldom*

1. **Francis Leigh**, Lord Dunsmore; cr. 3 June 1644; d.s.p.m. 21 Dec. 1653

2. **Thomas Wriothesley** (*see* Southampton), son-in-law & h. to earldom; b. 10 Mar. 1608; d.s.p.m.s. 16 May 1667

3. **Charles Fitzroy** (*see* Southampton, Cleveland); bapt. 18 June 1662; cr. 10 Sept. 1675; d. 9 Sept. 1730

[1] He invariably styles himself thus in his own *acta*.
[2] For nos 12, 14–21, *see* also Wales. A statute of 1398 inseparably linked the earldom of Chester with the principality of Wales.
[3] Granted the county of Chester on that date to hold as his father had held it (*Cal. Charter Rolls, 1300–26*, 202).

CHOLMONDELEY, *earldom*
1. **Hugh Cholmondeley,** Viscount Cholmondeley of Kells; b. *c.* 1662; cr. 29 Dec. 1706; d. unm. 18 Jan. 1725

CLARE
The earls of Hertford are often known as earls of Clare; for these *see under* Hertford

CLARE, *earldom*
1. **John Holles,** Baron Houghton; b. May 1564; cr. 2 Nov. 1624; d. 4 Oct. 1637
2. **John Holles,** s. & h.; b. 13 June 1595; d. 2 Jan. 1666
3. **Gilbert Holles,** only surv. s. & h.; b. 24 Apr. 1633; d. 16 Jan. 1689

Earldom and marquessate
4. **John Holles** (*see* Newcastle upon Tyne), 1st s. & h.; b. 9 Jan. 1662; *marquessate,* cr. 14 May 1694; d.s.p.m. leg. 15 July 1711

CLARENCE, *dukedom*
1. **Lionel 'of Antwerp'** (*see* Ulster), 3rd s. of K. Edw. III; b. 29 Nov. 1338; cr. 13 Nov. 1362; d.s.p.m. 17 Oct. 1368
2. **Thomas 'of Lancaster'** (*see* Aumale), 2nd s. of K. Henry IV; b. 1388; cr. 9 July 1412; d.s.p. leg. 22 Mar. 1421
3. **George Plantagenet** (*see* Salisbury, Warwick) 6th s. of Richard, duke of York; b. 21 Oct. 1449; cr. 28 June 1461;[1] forf. 8 Feb. 1478; exec. 18 Feb. 1478

CLARENDON, *earldom*
1. **Edward Hyde,** Lord Hyde of Hindon; b. 18 Feb. 1609; cr. 20 Apr. 1661; d. 19 Dec. 1674
2. **Henry Hyde,** 1st s. & h.; b. 2 June 1638; d. 31 Oct. 1709
3. **Edward Hyde,** only s. & h.; b. 28 Nov. 1661; d.s.p.s. 31 Mar. 1723

CLEVELAND, *earldom*
1. **Thomas Wentworth,** Lord Wentworth, cr. 5 Feb. 1626; d.s.p.m.s. 25 Mar. 1667

Dukedom
2. Barbara Villiers (*see* Southampton); b. *c.* 1641; cr. 3 Aug. 1670; d. 9 Oct. 1709
   m. 1. 14 Apr. 1659 Roger Palmer, aft. earl of Castlemaine.
      2. 25 Nov. 1705 Robert Feilding (marriage null 23 May 1707)
3. **Charles Fitz-Roy** (formerly Palmer), (*see* Chichester), 1st s. & h. to peerage; bapt. 18 June 1662; d. 9 Sept. 1730

CONWAY, *earldom*
1. **Edward Conway,** Viscount Conway; b. *c.* 1623; Cr. 3 Dec. 1679; d. s.p. 11 Aug. 1683

CORNWALL, *earldom*
1. **Alan,** Count of Brittany (*see* Richmond); b. bef. 1100; st. 1140;[2] depr. 1140; d. 15 Sept. 1146
2. **Reginald,** illeg. s. of K. Henry I; cr. 1140; d.s.p.m. leg. 1 July 1175[3]
3. **Richard,** later k. of the Romans, 2nd s. of K. John; b. 5 Jan. 1209; cr. 30 May 1227;[4] d. 2 Apr. 1272
4. **Edmund 'of Almaine',** 1st. surv. s. & h.; b. 26 Dec. 1249; inv. 13 Oct. 1272; d.s.p. 24–25 Sept. 1300
5. **Peter Gaveston;** b. *c* 1284; cr. 6 Aug. 1307; d.s.p.m. 19 June 1312
6. **John 'of Eltham',** 2nd s. of K. Edward II; b. *c.* 15 Aug. 1316; cr. 16–31 Oct. 1328; d.s.p. 13 Sept. 1336

Dukedom
7. **Edward 'of Woodstock'** (*see* Chester), 1st s. of K. Edw. III; b. 15 June 1330; cr. 16 Mar. 1337,[5] d. 8 June 1376

---

[1] In 1469 he joined Richard Nevill, earl of Warwick, was exiled and returned to England in his company in 1470 (*see under* Warwick).
[2] He obtained the county of Cornwall from K. Stephen. There is later, but no contemporary, evidence that his uncle, Count Brian of Brittany (d. bef. 1086) had also been earl of Cornwall [C. T. Clay, ed., *Early Yorkshire Charters,* iv. (1935), 15–16].
[3] His illegitimate son, Henry Fitz Count, was granted in 1215 the custody of the county of Cornwall but was never recognized as earl.
[4] N. Denholm-Young, *Richard of Cornwall* (Oxford, 1947), 9.
[5] BL MS Cotton. Nero C. VIII, fo. 284v.

8. **Richard** (*see* Chester), 1st surv. s. & h.; b. *c.* 6 Jan. 1367; cr. 20 Nov. 1376. Became K. Richard II 22 June 1377
9. **Henry 'of Monmouth'** (*see* Chester), 1st s. & h. of K. Henry IV, later K. Henry V; b. 16 Sept. 1387; cr. 15 Oct. 1399. Became K. 21 Mar. 1413
10. **Henry,** s. & h., later K. Henry VI; b. 6 Dec. 1421; prob. succ. at birth. Became K. 1 Sept. 1422
11. **Edward** (*see* Chester), s. & h.; b. 13 Oct. 1453; succ. at birth; d.s.p. 4 May 1471
12. **Edward Plantagenet** (*see* Chester); 1st s. & h. of K. Edw. IV, later K. Edw. V; b. 2–3 Nov. 1470; cr.[1] 17 July 1471. Became K. 9 Apr. 1483
13. **Edward Plantagenet** (*see* Chester), only s. & h. of K. Richard III; b. 1473; succ. ? 26 June 1483;[2] d. 9 Apr. 1484
14. **Arthur Tudor** (*see* Chester), 1st s. of K. Henry VII; b. 19 Sept. 1486; succ. at birth; d. 2 Apr. 1502
15. **Henry Tudor** (*see* Chester), next br. of 14, later K. Henry VIII; b. 28 June 1491; succ. 2 Apr. 1502. Became K. 22 Apr. 1509
16. **Henry Tudor,** 1st s. & h.; b. 1 Jan. 1511; succ. at birth; d. 22 Feb. 1511[3]
17. **Edward Tudor,** 1st surv. s. & h. of 15, later K. Edw. VI; b. 12 Oct. 1537; succ. at birth. Became K. 28 Jan. 1547
18. **Henry Frederick Stewart** (*see* Chester), 1st s. of K. James I; b. 19 Feb. 1594; succ. 24 Mar. 1603; d. unm. 6 Nov. 1612
19. **Charles Stewart** (*see* Albany), next br., later K. Charles I; b. 19 Nov. 1600; succ. 6 Nov. 1612. Became K. 27 Mar. 1625
20. **Charles James Stewart,** 1st s. and h.; b. and d. 13 May 1629 (succ. at birth)
21. **Charles Stewart** (*see* Chester), 1st surv. s. & h., later K. Charles II; b. 29 May 1630; succ. at birth. Became K. 29 May 1660
22. **James Francis Edward Stewart** (*see* Chester), 1st surv. s. & h. of James II; b. 10 June 1688; succ. at birth; forf. 2 Mar. 1702;[4] d. 1 Jan. 1766

COVENTRY, *earldom*
1. **George Villiers** (*see* Buckingham); cr. 18 May 1623; d. 23 Aug. 1628
2. **George Villiers,** s. & h.; d.s.p. leg. 16 Apr. 1687
3. **Thomas Coventry,** Lord Coventry of Aylesborough; b. *c.* 1629; cr. 26 Apr. 1697; d. 15 July 1699
4. **Thomas Coventry,** s. of h.; b. *c.* 1662; d. Aug. 1710
5. **Thomas Coventry,** only surv. s. & h.; b. 7 Apr. 1702; d. unm. 28 Jan. 1712
6. **Gilbert Coventry,** uncle & h.; b. *c.* 1668; d.s.p.m. 27 Oct. 1719

CRAVEN, *earldom*
1. **William Craven,** Lord Craven of Hampstead Marshall; bapt. 26 June 1608; cr. 16 Mar. 1665; d. unm. 9 April 1697

CUMBERLAND, *earldom*
1. **Henry Clifford,** Lord Clifford; b. 1493; cr. 18 June 1525; d. 22 Apr. 1542
2. **Henry Clifford,** s. & h.; b. *c.* 1517; d. 2 Jan. 1570
3. **George Clifford,** s. & h.; b. 8 Aug. 1558; d.s.p.m.s. 29 Oct. 1605
4. **Francis Clifford,** br. & h. male; b. 1559; d. 21 Jan. 1641
5. **Henry Clifford,** only s. & h.; b. 28 Feb. 1592; d.s.p.m.s. 11 Dec. 1643

   Dukedom
6. **Rupert,** count palatine of the Rhine (*see* Holderness); b. 27 Dec. 1619; cr. 24 Jan. 1644; d. unm. 29 Nov. 1682
7. **George,** prince of Denmark (*see* Kendal); b. 2 Apr. 1653; cr. 6 Apr. 1689; d.s.p.s. 28 Oct. 1708

---

[1] Although, by the creation of 1337, the dukedom of Cornwall had been conferred on the eldest s. of the reigning K., and although no. 10 had succ. to the dukedom at birth under the terms of this creation, yet a new creation was apparently thought necessary to avoid confusion, no. 11 having been born during his father's exile and in the lifetime of the last holder. The case may be paralleled by the new creation of 1399 (*see* no. 9), which is accounted for by the change of dynasty.

[2] He appears to have been considered duke of Cornwall aft. the accession of his father to the throne at this date.

[3] Another s. of K. Henry VIII, b. and d. on the same day in Nov. 1514, succ. at birth.

[4] But he was presumably not recognized aft. his father was declared to have abdicated, Feb. 1689 (with retrospective effect to 11 Dec. 1688).

DANBY, *earldom*
1. **Henry Danvers,** Lord Danvers of Dantsey; b. 28 June 1573; cr. 5 Feb. 1626; d. unm. 29 Jan. 1644
2. **Thomas Osborne,** Viscount Latimer (*see* Carmarthen); b. 20 Feb. 1632; cr. 27 June 1674; d. 26 July 1712
3. **Peregrine Osborne** (*see* Carmarthen), only surv. s. & h.; b. 1659; d. 25 June 1729

DARTMOUTH, *earldom*
1. **William Legge,** Lord Dartmouth; b. 14 Oct. 1672; cr. 5 Sept. 1711; d. 15 Dec. 1750

DENBIGH, *earldom*
1. **William Feilding,** Viscount Feilding; b. *c.* 1582; cr. 14 Sept. 1622; d. 8 Apr. 1643
2. **Basil Feilding,** 1st s. & h.; b. *c.* 1608; d.s.p. 28 Nov. 1675
3. **William Feilding** (*see* Desmond), neph. & h.; b. 29 Dec. 1640; d. 23 Aug. 1685
4. **Basil Feilding** (*see* Desmond), s. & h.; b. 1668; d. 18 Mar. 1717

DERBY, *earldom*
1. **Robert de Ferrières,** 3rd s. & h. to the English possessions of Henry de Ferrières; cr. shortly aft. Aug. 1138; d. 1139
2. **Robert de Ferrières** (*see* Nottingham (note)), s. & h.; d. bef. Mich. 1159
3. **William de Ferrières,** s. & h.; liv. 1161–62; d. 1190 (bef. 21 Oct.)
4. **William de Ferrières,** s. & h.; liv. 1190–91; st. 16 Apr. 1194; g. 7 June 1199; d. 22 Sept. 1247
5. **William de Ferrières,** s. & h.; b. aft. 1192; inv. 2 Feb. 1248; d. 24 or 28 Mar. 1254
6. **Robert de Ferrières,** s. & h.; b. *c.* 1239; liv. hom. 1260; forf. May 1266;[1] d. 1279
7. **Henry 'of Grosmont'** (*see* Lancaster, Leicester, Lincoln, Moray); b. *c.* 1300; cr. 16 Mar. 1337; d.s.p.m. 23 Mar. 1361
8. **John of Gaunt** (*see* Lancaster, Leicester, Lincoln, Richmond), 4th s. of K. Edw. III; b. Mar. 1340
   m. 19 May 1359 Blanche, yr. d. & coh. of 7 (she d. 12 Sept. 1369); st. himself e. 21 July 1361; succ. 10 Apr. 1362 on the death of Maud, elder sis. of his wife;[2] d. 3–4 Feb. 1399
9. **Henry 'of Bolingbroke'** (*see* Hereford, Lancaster, Leicester, Lincoln, Northampton), s. & h., later K. Henry IV; b. prob. Apr. 1366; st. 16 July 1377.[3] Became K. 30 Sept. 1399
10. **Thomas Stanley,** Lord Stanley; b. *c.* 1435; cr. 27 Oct. 1485; d. 29 July 1504
11. **Thomas Stanley,** gds. & h.; b. bef. 1485; d. 23 May 1521
12. **Edward Stanley,** 1st surv. s. & h.; b. 10 May 1509; d. 24 Oct. 1572
13. **Henry Stanley,** s. & h.; b. Sept. 1531; d. 25 Sept. 1593
14. **Ferdinando Stanley,** 1st surv. s. & h.; b. *c.* 1559; d.s.p.m. 16 Apr. 1594
15. **William Stanley,** br. & h. to earldom; b. *c.* 1561; d. 29 Sept. 1642
16. **James Stanley,** s. & h.; b. 31 Jan. 1607; exec. 15 Oct. 1651
17. **Charles Stanley,** s. & h.; b. 19 Jan. 1628; d. 21 Dec. 1672
18. **William George Richard Stanley,** s. & h.; b. *c.* 1655; d.s.p.m.s. 5 Nov. 1702
19. **James Stanley,** br. & h. male; b. 3 July 1664; d.s.p.s. 1 Feb. 1736

DERWENTWATER, *earldom*
1. **Sir Francis Radclyffe,** bt.; b. 1625; cr. 7 Mar. 1688; d. Apr. 1696 (aft. 20)
2. **Edward Radclyffe,** s. & h.; b. 9 Dec. 1655; d. 29 Apr. 1705
3. **James Radclyffe,** s. & h.; b. 28 June 1689; exec. 24 Feb. 1716 and forf.

---

[1] Edmund, the king's son (*see* Lancaster) was granted his lands; he does not seem to have used the title of earl of Derby. His son Thomas, however, had a first seal in which he was called earl of Ferrers (1301). The br. and h. of Thomas was Henry, earl of Lancaster, whose s. was cr. earl of Derby, in 1337 (no. 7).

[2] Writs to escheators ordering the livery of Maud's lands to him and his wife dated 6 May 1362. *See Complete Peerage*, x, Appendix K, 123 for the view that the creation of 1337 was limited to heirs male.

[3] *Anonimalle Chronicle,* ed. V. H. Galbraith, 114 (*cf.* also *Lords' Report*, II, 132–33). He continued to be so styled during his father's lifetime.

DEVON, *earldom*

1. **Baldwin de Reviers** (or Redvers); cr. prob. 1141 (by June); d. 4 June 1155
2. **Richard de Reviers**, s. & h.; d. 21 or 27 Apr. 1162
3. **Baldwin de Reviers**, s. & h.; a minor at his father's death; inv. 1185–86; d.s.p. 10 or 28 May 1188
4. **Richard de Reviers**, next br. & h.; d.s.p. 19 Aug. in or bef. 1193
5. **William de Reviers** (called de Vernon), uncle & h.; st. 17 Apr. 1194; d. 8 or 10 Sept. 1217
6. **Baldwin de Reviers**, gds. & h.; b. ? 1218; inv. 25 Dec. 1239; d. 15 Feb. 1245
7. **Baldwin de Reviers**, s. & h.; b. 1 Jan. 1236; liv. hom. 29 Jan. 1257; d.s.p.s. 1262 (bef. 13 Sept.)
8. **Isabella, Countess of Aumale**, sis. & h. (widow of William de Forz, who d. 1260); b. July 1237; liv. 17 Aug. 1263; d.s.p.s. 10 Nov. 1293
9. **Hugh de Courtenay**, cousin & h.; b. 1275–76; st. from 22 Feb. 1335;[1] d. 23 Dec. 1340
10. **Hugh de Courtenay**, s. & h.; b. 12 July 1303; liv. 11 Jan. 1341; d. 2 May 1377
11. **Edward de Courtenay**, gds. & h.; b. *c.* 1357; d. 5 Dec. 1419
12. **Hugh de Courtenay**, 1st surv. s. & h.; b. 1389; d. 16 June 1422
13. **Thomas de Courtenay**, s. & h.; b. 1414; liv. 20 Feb. 1423; d. 3 Feb. 1458
14. **Thomas Courtenay**, s. & h.; b. 1432; exec. 3 Apr. 1461 and forf.
15. **Humphrey Stafford**, Lord Stafford of Southwick; b. *c.* 1439; cr. 17 May 1469; exec. 17 Aug. 1469 (d.s.p.s.)
16. **John Courtenay**, only surv. br. & h. of 14; b. *c.* 1435–40; rest. 9 Oct. 1470; d. unm. 4 May 1471 and forf.
17. **Edward Courtenay**, gt-gt-gds. of 10 & h. male; cr. 26 Oct. 1485; d. 28 May 1509
18. **William Courtenay**, s. & h.; b. *c.* 1475; cr.[2] 10 May 1511; d. 9 June 1511
19. **Henry Courtenay** (*see* Exeter), only surv. s. & h.; b. *c.* 1498; forf. 3 Dec. 1538, exec. 9 Jan. 1539
20. **Edward Courtenay**, only surv. s. & h.; b. 1526–27; cr. 3 Sept. 1553; d. unm. 18 Sept. 1556

DEVONSHIRE, *earldom*

1. **Charles Blount**, Lord Mountjoy; cr. 21 July 1603; d.s.p. leg. 3 Apr. 1606
2. **William Cavendish**, Lord Cavendish of Hardwick; b. 27 Dec. 1552; cr. 7 Aug. 1618; d. 3 Mar. 1626
3. **William Cavendish**, 1st surv. s. & h.; b. 1590; d. 20 June 1628
4. **William Cavendish**, 1st s. & h.; b. 10 Oct. 1617; d. 23 Nov. 1684

Earldom and *dukedom*
5. **William Cavendish** (*see* Hartington), 1st s. & h.; b. 25 Jan. 1641

Dukedom
Idem; cr. 12 May 1694; d. 18 Aug. 1707
6. **William Cavendish** (*see* Hartington), 1st surv. s. & h.; b. *c.* 1673; d. 4 June 1729

DONCASTER, *earldom*

1. **Sir James Scott** (*see* Buccleuch); cr. 14 Feb. 1663; exec. 15 July 1685 and forf.

DORCHESTER, *marquessate*

1. **Henry Pierrepont** (*see* Kingston-on-Hull); b. Mar. 1607; cr. 25 Mar. 1645; d.s.p.m.s. 8 Dec. 1680

Earldom
2. **Catherine Sedley**; b. 21 Dec. 1657; cr. 20 Jan. 1686; d. 26 Oct. 1717. m. in or shortly aft. Aug. 1696 Sir David Colyear, bt. aft. lord and earl of Portmore

Marquessate
3. **Evelyn Pierrepont** (*see* Kingston-on-Hull), gt-neph. of **1**; b. *c.* 1665; cr. 23 Dec. 1706; d. 5 Mar. 1726

DORSET, *earldom*
William de Mohun, cr. 1141, dismissed 1141 (*see under* Somerset)

---

[1] Bef. that date he had been summ. to parl. among the barons.
[2] He was under attainder at his father's death, having been att. Feb. 1504.

DORSET, *marquessate*
1. **John Beaufort** (*see* Somerset), s. of John of Gaunt; b. *c.* 1371; cr. 29 Sept. 1397;[1] depr. 3 Nov. 1399; d. 16 Mar. 1410

Earldom
2. **Thomas Beaufort** (*see* Exeter), yst. br. of 1; cr. 5 July 1411; d.s.p.s. 31 Dec. 1426

Earldom and marquessate
3. **Edmund Beaufort** (*see* Somerset), yr. s. of 1; b. *c.* 1406
earldom; cr. 18 or 28 Aug. 1441
marquessate; cr. 24 June 1443; d. 22 May 1455
4. **Henry Beaufort** (*see* Somerset), s. & h.; b. *c.* Apr. 1436; st. marquis of Dorset during his father's lifetime 1448–55; att. 4 Nov. 1461; rest. 1463; rest. nullified 29 Apr. 1464; exec. 15 May 1464

Marquessate
5. **Thomas Grey** (*see* Huntingdon), Lord Ferrers of Groby, stepson of K. Edw. IV; date of birth uncertain; cr. 18 Apr. 1475; forf. bef. 23 Oct. 1483; rest. Nov. 1485; d. 30 Sept. 1501
6. **Thomas Grey,** s. & h.; b. 22 June 1477; st. 1511;[2] d. 10 Oct. 1530
7. **Henry Grey** (*see* Suffolk), s. & h.; b. 17 Jan. 1517; forf. 17 Feb. and exec. 23 Feb. 1554

Earldom
8. **Thomas Sackville,** Lord Buckhurst; b. 1527–36; cr. 13 Mar. 1604; d. 19 Apr. 1608
9. **Robert Sackville,** s. & h.; b. 1561; d. 27 Feb. 1609
10. **Richard Sackville,** s. & h.; b. 28 Mar. 1589; d.s.p.m.s. 28 Mar. 1624
11. **Edward Sackville,** br. & h. male; b. 1590; d. 18 July 1652
12. **Richard Sackville,** s. & h.; b. 16 Sept. 1622; d. 27 Aug. 1677
13. **Charles Sackville** (*see* Middlesex), s. & h.; b. 24 Jan. 1638; d. 29 Jan. 1706

Earldom and dukedom
14. **Lionel Cranfield Sackville** (*see* Middlesex), only s. & h.; b. 18 Jan. 1688; *dukedom*; cr. 17 June 1720; d. 10 Oct. 1765

DOVER, *earldom*
1. **Henry Carey,** Viscount Rochford; b. *c.* 1580; cr. 8 Mar. 1628; d. shortly bef. 13 Apr. 1666
2. **John Carey,** s. & h.; b. *c* 1608; d.s.p.m. 26 May 1677

Dukedom
3. **James Douglas** (*see* Queensberry); b. 18 Dec. 1662; cr. 26 May 1708; d. 6 July 1711
4. **Charles Douglas** (*see* Queensberry), 1st surv. s. & h.; b. 24 Nov. 1698; d.s.p.s. 22 Oct. 1778

DUDLEY, *dukedom*
1. Lady **Alice Dudley,** b. *c.* 1579; cr. 23 May 1644; d.s.p.m. 22 or 23 Jan. 1669

EAST ANGLIA, *earldom*
1. **Ralph the Staller;** st. bef. Mar. 1068; d. prob. 1069 (bef. Apr. 1070)
2. **Ralph de Gael,** s. and h.; b. prob. bef. 1040; st. bef. Apr. 1070; forf. 1075; d. *c.* 1100

[Twelfth-century earls of Norfolk are often known as earls of East Anglia (for these earls *see under* Norfolk)]

ESSEX, *earldom*
1. **Geoffrey de Mandeville,** cr. 1140; d. 14 or 16 Sept. 1144
2. **Geoffrey de Mandeville,** 2nd s. but h.; cr.[3] *c.* Jan. 1156; d.s.p. 21 Oct. 1166
3. **William de Mandeville** (*see* Aumale), br. & h.; d.s.p. leg. 14 Nov. 1189

---

[1] The entry on Charter Roll is erased, with note *Vacat, quia nihil inde actum est* and this is followed on the roll by the creation of the marquessate of Somerset. He was however later summ. to parlt. as marquis of Dorset.
[2] 17 Oct. 1509 he had been summ. to parlt. by writ directed to Thomas Grey, *dominus Ferrers de Groby*, but in 1511 he was summ. as marquis of Dorset.
[3] His father had died when in revolt; hence the necessity for a new creation.

4. **Geoffrey fitz Peter;**[1] liv. 1190 (bef. Easter); g. 27 May 1199; d. 14 Oct. 1213
5. [Geoffrey de Mandeville (*see* Gloucester), s. & h.; hom. & liv. 4 Nov. 1213;[2] d.s.p. 23 Feb. 1216]
6. **William de Mandeville,** next br. & h.; liv. 4 Oct. 1217; st. 4 Nov. 1217; d.s.p. 8 Jan. 1227
7. Maud de Mandeville, sis. & h.; liv. 29 Oct. 1227; d. 27 Aug. 1236
   m. 1. **Henry de Bohun,** earl of Hereford; b. aft. 1171; d. 1 June 1220.
      2. bef. 1227 Roger de Dauntsey (divorced 1233; divorce rescinded 1236); d. aft. Aug. 1238
8. **Humphrey de Bohun** (*see* Hereford), s. & h. by 1st husb.; liv. 9 Sept. 1236; st. 21 Oct. 1236; d. 24 Sept. 1275
9–13. [From this point until 16 Jan. 1373, the earldom, descended with that of Hereford. Humphrey de Bohun then dying without male issue, the earldoms were divided between two co-heiresses, and the earldom of Essex descended as under]:
14. **Thomas 'of Woodstock'** (*see* Buckingham); b. 7 Jan. 1355; m. ? 1374 (possibly 1376) Eleanor, elder da. & coh. of Humphrey de Bohun (no. 11 in the list of earls of Hereford); grant of fee 13 Apr. 1374; liv. 22 June 1380; d. prob. 8–9 Sept. 1397 and forf.
   [Anne, eldest da. & h. of 14. She does not seem ever to have called herself countess, but on 20 June 1400 she had a grant of £40.10s as her fee of the earldom of Essex; d. 16–24 Oct. 1438.
   m. 1. 1398 Edmund, earl of Stafford; b. 2 Mar. 1378; d. 21 July 1403.
      2. Before 20 Nov. 1405 Sir William Bourchier, later count of Eu; d. 28 May 1420]
15. **Henry Bourchier,** count of Eu, s. of Anne and her 2nd husband; cr. 30 June 1461; d. 4 Apr. 1483
16. **Henry Bourchier,** gds. & h.; b. *c.* 1472; lic. of entry 27 Sept. 1493; d.s.p.m. 13 Mar. 1540
17. **Thomas Cromwell,** Lord Cromwell, b. *c.* 1485; cr. 17 Apr. 1540; forf. 29 June 1540; exec. 28 July 1540
18. **William Parr,** Lord Parr (*see* Northampton), m. Anne, da. of no. **16** (whom, however, he repudiated Apr. 1543); b. Aug.–Sept. 1513; cr. 23 Dec. 1543; forf. Aug. 1553; not restored to the earldom of Essex when cr. again marquess of Northampton in Jan. 1559; d.s.p. 28 Oct. 1571
19. **Walter Devereux,** Viscount Hereford, gt-gt-gds. of no. **15**; b. 16 Sept. 1539; cr. 4 May 1572; d. 22 Sept. 1576
20. **Robert Devereux,** s. & h.; b. 19 Nov. 1566; forf. 19 Feb. and exec. 25 Feb. 1601
21. **Robert Devereux,** 1st s. & h.; bapt. 22 Jan. 1591; rest. 18 Apr. 1604; d.s.p.s. 14 Sept. 1646
22. **Arthur Capell,** Lord Capell of Hadham; bapt. 28 Jan. 1632; cr. 20 Apr. 1661; d. 13 July 1683
23. **Algernon Capell,** only surv. s. & h.; b. 28 Dec. 1670; d. 10 Jan. 1710
24. **William Capell,** only s. & h.; b. 1697; d. 8 Jan. 1743

EU, *counts of*

   [The counts of Eu are here included from the Conquest until the loss of Normandy, which separated them from their English allegiance]

1. **Robert,** s. & h. of William, count of Eu; st. 1059; d. 1089–93 (8 Sept.)
2. **William,** 1st surv. s & h.[3]
3. **Henry,** s. & h.; st. 1101; d. 12 July 1140
4. **John,** s. & h.; d. 26 June 1170

[1] On the death of **3**, the heiress to the earldom was Beatrice de Mandeville (d. in or bef. 1197), sis. of no. **1**. Geoffrey Fitz Peter had married one of her gd-das and about Easter 1190 he fined 3000 marks for the lands of the last earl. Thereafter he received the third penny of the county, but was not styled earl till aft. he was girt by K. John in 1199.
[2] In 1214 it was pleaded that Geoffrey was not yet an earl. Except in the writs of 26 and 28 Jan. 1214 concerning his marriage, he is never styled earl of Essex in the chancery rolls. He is, however, styled earl of Gloucester *iure uxoris* in June 1215.
[3] L. C. Loyd writes that there is no reliable evidence for the date of William's death; the date (Jan. 1096) given in the *Complete Peerage* is due to a confusion.

5. **Henry,** s. & h.; b. prob. *c.* 1155; st. 1173; d. prob. 1190–91[1] [Ralph d'Eu, s. & h.; d.s.p. 1186]
6. Alice, only da. & h. of 5; d. 13–15 May 1246
   m. in or bef. 1191 **Ralph de Lusignan** (or d'Exoudun); st. 1191; d. 1 May 1219

EUSTON, *earldom*
1. **Henry FitzRoy** (*see* Grafton); b. 2 Sept. 1663; cr. 16 Aug. 1672; d. 9 Oct. 1690
2. **Charles FitzRoy** (*see* Grafton), only s. & h.; b. 25 Oct. 1683; d. 6 May 1757

EXETER, *earldom*
   [The earls of Devon are sometimes called earls of Exeter; for these *see under* Devon]

   Dukedom
1. **John de Holand** (*see* Huntingdon, Arundel (note)), yr. s. of Thomas, earl of Kent, & half br. of K. Richard II; b. aft. 1350; cr. 29 Sept. 1397; depr. 3 Nov. 1399; d. 9 or 10 Jan. 1400
2. **Thomas Beaufort** (*see* Dorset); cr. 18 Nov. 1416; d.s.p.s. 31 Dec. 1426
3. **John Holand** (*see* Huntingdon), 1st surv. s. of 1; b. 29 Mar. 1395; cr. 6 Jan. 1444; d. 5 Aug. 1447
4. **Henry Holand** (*see* Huntingdon), only s. & h.; b. 27 June 1430; liv. 23 July 1450;[2] forf. Nov. 1461;[3] d.s.p.s. Sept. 1475

   Marquessate
5. **Henry Courtenay** (*see* Devon); b. *c.* 1498; cr. 18 June 1525; forf. 3 Dec. 1538; exec. 9 Jan. 1539

   Earldom
6. **Thomas Cecil,** Lord Burghley; b. 5 May 1542; cr. 4 May 1605; d. 8 Feb. 1623
7. **William Cecil,** 1st s. & h.; b. Jan. 1566; d.s.p.m.s. 6 July 1640
8. **David Cecil,** neph. & h. male; b. *c.* 1604; d. 18 Apr. 1643
9. **John Cecil,** s. & h.; bapt. 26 Oct. 1628; d. 1 Feb. 1678
10. **John Cecil,** s. & h.; b. *c.* 1648; d. 29 Aug. 1700
11. **John Cecil,** s. & h.; b. 15 May 1674; d. 31 Dec. 1721

FALMOUTH, *earldom*
1. **Charles Berkeley,** Viscount FitzHardinge; bapt. 11 Jan. 1630; cr. 17 Mar. 1664; d.s.p.m. 3 June 1665

FAREHAM, *earldom*
1. **Louise Renée de Penancoët de Kérouaille** (*see* Portsmouth); b. Sept. 1649; cr. 19 Aug. 1673; d. 14 Nov. 1734

FAUCONBERG, *earldom*
1. **Thomas Belasyse,** Viscount Fauconberg of Henknowle; bapt. 16 Mar. 1628; cr. 9 Apr. 1689; d.s.p. 31 Dec. 1706

FERRERS
   [The twelfth- and thirteenth-century earls of Derby were often styled earls of Ferrers; for these *see under* Derby]

   Earldom
1. **Robert Shirley,** Lord Ferrers; bapt. 20 Oct. 1650; cr. 3 Sept. 1711; d. 25 Dec. 1717

FEVERSHAM, *earldom*
1. **Sir George Sandes;** b. Nov. 1599; cr. 8 Apr. 1676; d.s.p.m.s. 16 Apr. 1677
2. **Louis de Duras,** s.-in-law & h. to earldom; b. 1641; d.s.p. 19 Apr. 1709

GAINSBOROUGH, *earldom*
1. **Edward Noel,** Viscount Campden; bapt. 27 Jan. 1641; cr. 1 Dec. 1682; d. Jan. 1689

---

[1] *See* C. T. Clay, *Early Yorkshire Charters*, viii (1949), **22**, n. 9.
[2] Special livery of his father's lands, without proof of age.
[3] The forfeiture was to take effect from the preceding 4 Mar.

2. **Wriothesley Baptist Noel,** only s. & h.; b. bef. 1665; d.s.p.m. 21 Sept. 1690
3. **Baptist Noel,** cous. & h. male; b. 1684; d. 17 Apr. 1714
4. **Baptist Noel,** 1st s. & h.; b. 1708; d. 21 Mar. 1754

GIFFARD

[The Giffards, earls of Buckingham, are generally known as earls Giffard. For these *see under* Buckingham]

GLAMORGAN, *earldom*
1. **Edward Somerset,** 1st s. and h. of Henry, 1st marquess of Worcester; b. perhaps shortly bef. 9 Mar. 1603; possibly cr. earl of Glamorgan 1644[1]; (succ. to marquessate of Worcester 18 Dec. 1646). The earldom is supposed to have become extinct on his d., 3 Apr. 1667

GLOUCESTER, *earldom*
1. **Robert,** illeg. s. of Henry I; b. *c.* 1090; cr. June–Sept. 1122; d. 31 Oct. 1147
2. **William,** 1st s. & h.; st. 1153; d.s.p.m.s. 23 Nov. 1183
3. **Isabel,** yst. da. & coh.[2]; b. bef. 1176; d. 14 Oct. 1217
   m. 1. 29 Aug. 1189 **John,** yst. s. of Henry II (*see* Mortain); b. 24 Dec. 1167; st. 3 Sept. 1189; became K. 27 May 1199; divorced bef. 30 Aug. 1199
   2. 16–26 Jan. 1214 **Geoffrey de Mandeville** (*see* Essex); st. 23 June 1215; d.s.p. 23 Feb. 1216
   3. Sept.–Oct. 1217 Hubert de Burgh (*see* Kent); d. 12 May 1243
4. **Amauri de Montfort,** s. of Mabel, eldest da. of 2; recog. [1–3 June] 1200;[3] d.s.p. bef. Nov. 1213

   [Aft. the death of 3, her sis. Amice, 2nd da. of 2, was apparently recog. as countess of Gloucester till her death, *c.* 1 Jan. 1225, for it is then that the third penny was ordered to be paid to her s., *as under:*]

5. **Gilbert de Clare** (*see* Hertford), s. & h. of Amice, 2nd da. of 2; b. prob. *c.* 1180; st. 18 Nov. 1217; d. 25 Oct. 1230
6. **Richard de Clare** (*see* Hertford), 1st s. & h.; b. 4 Aug. 1222; liv. hom. 28 Sept. 1243; d. prob. 15 July 1262
7. **Gilbert de Clare** (*see* Hertford), s. & h.; b. 2 Sept. 1243; liv. 3 Aug. 1263 and 24 Sept. 1264; d. 7 Dec. 1295
8. **Ralph de Monthermer** (*see* Atholl); st. 12 Nov. 1297;[4] d. 5 Apr. 1325. m. 1297 (bef. July) Joan of Acre, wid. of 7; d. 23 Apr. 1307
9. **Gilbert de Clare** (*see* Hertford), s. & h. of 7 and his w. Joan of Acre; b. 10 or 11 May 1291; liv. 18 Aug. and 26 Nov. 1307; d.s.p.s. 24 June 1314
10. **Hugh de Audley,** m. 28 Apr. 1317 Margaret, 2nd da. of 7; b. *c.* 1289; cr. 16 Mar. 1337; d.s.p.m. 10 Nov. 1347

    Dukedom
11. **Thomas 'of Woodstock'** (*see* Buckingham); b. 7 Jan. 1355; cr. 6 Aug. 1385; d. prob. 8 or 9 Sept. 1397 and forf.

    Earldom
12. **Thomas le Despenser,** Lord le Despenser, gt-gt-gds. of 7; b. 22 Sept. 1373; cr. 29 Sept. 1397; forf. 3 Nov. 1399; exec. 13 Jan. 1400

---

[1] This title is included in the inscription on his tomb.

[2] A Tynemouth chronicle says Isabel's two sisters resigned their claims to the earldom on her marriage to John (H. H. E. Craster, *History of Northumberland*, vii, 120, note).

[3] The royal writ granting Amauri the third penny is in *Pipe Roll Soc.*, NS xxi, 89–90, and can be dated by the king's itinerary. Only aft. Amauri's death was Isabel's claim to the title revived, when her marriage was sold for 20,000 marks to Geoffrey de Mandeville.

[4] He was styled earl only during the lifetime of his wife. In 1290, Earl Gilbert, having recently m. Joan of Acre as his 2nd wife, surr. his estates to the K. and received them back in a joint grant to himself and his wife. This accounts for the exclusion of no. 9 until the death of his mother, and for the assumption of the title by her second husband.

Dukedom

13. **Humphrey of Lancaster** (*see* Pembroke), yst. s. of K. Henry IV; b. prob.
    Aug.–Sept. 1390; cr. 16 May 1414; d.s.p. leg. 23 Feb. 1447
14. **Richard Plantagenet**, later K. Richard III; b. 2 Oct. 1452; cr. 1 Nov. 1461; in
    exile in the Netherlands Oct. 1470–Mar. 1471. Became K. 26 June 1483
15. **Henry Stewart** (*see* Cambridge), 3rd surv. s. of Charles I; b. 8 July 1640; ? cr.
    13 May 1659;[1] d. unm. 13 Sept. 1660

GODOLPHIN, *earldom*

1. **Sidney Godolphin,** Lord Godolphin of Rialton; bapt. 15 June 1645; cr. 26 Dec.
   1706; d. 15 Sept. 1712
2. **Francis Godolphin,** only s. & h.; b. 3 Sept. 1678; d.s.p.m.s. 17 Jan. 1766

GRAFTON, *dukedom*

1. **Henry FitzRoy** (*see* Euston), illeg. s. of Charles II; b. 2 Sept. 1663; cr. 11 Sept.
   1675; d. 9 Oct. 1690
2. **Charles FitzRoy** (*see* Euston), only s. & h.; b. 25 Oct. 1683; d. 6 May 1757

GRANBY, *marquessate*

[Cr. 29 Mar. 1703 with the dukedom of Rutland; *see under* that title]

GRANTHAM, *earldom*

1. **Henry d'Auverquerque**; b. *c.* 1672; cr. 24 Dec. 1698; d.s.p.m.s. 5 Dec. 1754

GREENWICH, *earldom and dukedom*

1. **John Campbell** (*see* Argyll); b. 10 Oct. 1680
   earldom; cr. 26 Nov. 1705
   dukedom; cr. 27 Apr. 1719; d.s.p.m. 4 Oct. 1743

GUILDFORD of GUILDFORD, *earldom*

1. **Elizabeth**, Viscountess Boyle of Kinalmeaky; cr. 14 July 1660; d.s.p. *c.* 3 Sept.
   1667
2. **John Maitland** (*see* Lauderdale); b. 24 May 1616; cr. 25 June 1674; d.s.p.m.
   24 Aug. 1682

HALIFAX, *earldom and marquessate*

1. **George Saville,** Viscount Halifax; b. 11 Nov. 1633
   earldom; cr. 16 July 1679
   marquessate; cr. 22 Aug. 1682; d. 5 Apr. 1695
2. **William Saville,** 1st surv. s. & h.; b. 1665; d.s.p.m.s. 31 Aug. 1700

HAROLD, *earldom*

1. **Henry Grey** (*see* Kent); bapt. 28 Sept. 1671; cr. 14 Nov. 1706; d.s.p.m. ? 5 June
   1740

HARTINGTON, *marquessate*

1. **William Cavendish** (*see* Devonshire); b. 25 Jan. 1641; cr. 12 May 1694; d.
   18 Aug. 1707

   [This marquessate descends with the dukedom of Devonshire; *see under* that
   title]

HARWICH, *marquessate*

[Cr. 1689 with the dukedom of Schomberg; *see under* that title]

HEREFORD, *earldom*

1. **William fitz Osbern**; cr. 1067;[2] d. 20 Feb. 1071
2. **Roger,** 2nd s. & h. to English estates; depr. 1075; d. aft. 1087
3. **Miles of Gloucester**; cr. 25 July 1141;[3] d. 24 Dec. 1143

[1] He was known by this title several years earlier. William, 1st s. & h. of the
future Queen Anne, was styled duke of Gloucester, but never created so in form.
He was b. 24 July 1689, d. unm. 30 July 1700.
[2] Florence of Worcester, ii, 1.
[3] Cr. by Empress Matilda. K. Stephen had granted Robert, earl of Leicester
(prob. in 1140), the county of Hereford. *See* R. H. C. Davis, *King Stephen* (1967),
140.

4. **Roger** (of Gloucester or fitz Miles), s. & h.; b. aft. 1121; dismissed Dec. 1154, and became monk; d. 1155
5. **Henry de Bohun** (*see* Essex), gt-gds. of **3**; b. aft. 1171; cr. 28 Apr. 1200; d. 1 June 1220
6. **Humphrey de Bohun** (*see* Essex), s. & h.; b. prob. *c.* 1200; liv. hom. 27 June 1221; d. 24 Sept. 1275
7. **Humphrey de Bohun** (*see* Essex), gds. & h.; b. *c.* 1249; liv. 26 Oct. 1275; d. 31 Dec. 1298
8. **Humphrey de Bohun** (*see* Essex), s. & h.; b. *c.* 1276; liv. 16 Feb. 1299; surr. Oct. 1302; rest. 26 Nov. 1302; d. 16 Mar. 1322 and forf.
9. **John de Bohun** (*see* Essex), s. & h.; b. 23 Nov. 1306; rest. and liv. 1 Nov. 1326; d.s.p. 20 Jan. 1336
10. **Humphrey de Bohun** (*see* Essex), br. & h.; b. *c.* 1309. liv. hom. 18 Feb. 1336; d. unm. 15 Oct. 1361
11. **Humphrey de Bohun** (*see* Essex), neph. & h.; b. 25 Mar. 1342; liv. hom. 5 May 1363; d.s.p.m. 16 Jan. 1373
12. **Henry 'of Bolingbroke'** (*see* Derby), later K. Henry IV; b. prob. Apr. 1366. m. July 1380–Mar. 1381, Mary yr. da. and coh. of 11.

> Received the third penny of Herefordshire 22 Dec. 1384 and should possibly from this date be considered earl of Hereford (given this title in the record of his coronation)
> *dukedom*: cr. 29 Sept. 1397. Became K. 30 Sept. 1399

[Thomas of Woodstock (*see* Buckingham), m. ? 1374 (possibly 1376) Eleanor, elder da. and coh. of 11. He received the third penny of the county of Hereford from 1380–84, although not st. earl. His da. Anne st. herself Countess of Hereford, but neither she, nor her descendants, the Stafford dukes of Buckingham, received official recognition in this dignity]

HERTFORD, *earldom*
1. **Gilbert de Clare**; cr. ? *c.* 1138; st. Dec. 1141; d.s.p. 1152
2. **Roger de Clare**, br. & h.; st. bef. Jan. 1156; d. 1173
3. **Richard de Clare**, s. & h.; d. 30 Oct.–28 Nov. 1217
4. **Gilbert de Clare** (*see* Gloucester), s. & h.; b. prob. *c.* 1180; succ. Nov. 1217; d. 25 Oct. 1230
5. **Richard de Clare** (*see* Gloucester), s. & h.; b. 4 Aug. 1222; liv. hom. 28 Sept. 1243; d. prob. 15 July 1262
6. **Gilbert de Clare** (*see* Gloucester), s. & h.; b. 2 Sept. 1243; liv. 3 Aug. 1263 and 24 Sept. 1264; d. 7 Dec. 1295
7. **Ralph de Monthermer** (*see* Atholl); st. 12 Nov. 1297;[1] d. 5 Apr. 1325. m. 1297 (bef. July) Joan of Acre, wid. of 6; d. 23 Apr. 1307
8. **Gilbert de Clare** (*see* Gloucester), s. & h. of 6; b. 10 or 11 May 1291; st. Apr. 1307; liv. 26 Nov. 1307; d.s.p.s. 24 June 1314
9. **Edward Seymour**, Viscount Beauchamp (*see* Somerset); b. *c.* 1506; cr. 18 Oct. 1537; exec. 22 Jan. 1552 and forf. (att. 12 Apr. 1552)
10. **Edward Seymour**, 1st surv. s. by 2nd w.; b. 25 May 1539; cr. 13 Jan. 1559; d. 6 Apr. 1621

Earldom and marquessate
11. **William Seymour** (*see* Somerset), gds. & h.; b. 1 Sept. 1587 *marquessate*; cr. 3 June 1641; d. 24 Oct. 1660
12. **William Seymour** (*see* Somerset), gds. & h.; b. *c.* 1651; d. unm. 12 Dec. 1671
13. **John Seymour** (*see* Somerset), uncle & h. male; d.s.p. 29 Apr. 1675

Earldom only
14. **Francis Seymour** (*see* Somerset), cous. & h. male; b. 17 Jan. 1658; d. unm. 20 Apr. 1678
15. **Charles Seymour** (*see* Somerset), br. & h.; b. 13 Aug. 1662; d. 2 Dec. 1748

HOLDERNESS, *earldom*
1. **John Ramsay**, Viscount Haddington; b. *c.* 1580; cr. 22 Jan. 1621; d.s.p.s. shortly bef. 28 Feb. 1626
2. **Rupert**, count palatine of the Rhine (*see* Cumberland); b. 27 Dec. 1619; cr. 24 Jan. 1644; d. unm. 29 Nov. 1682

[1] He was styled earl only during his wife's lifetime (*see* Gloucester).

3. **Conyers Darcy,** Lord Darcy and Conyers; bapt. 24 Jan. 1599; cr. 5 Dec. 1682; d. 14 June 1689
4. **Conyers Darcy,** 1st surv. s. & h.; bapt. 3 Mar. 1622; d. 13 Dec. 1692
5. **Robert Darcy,** gds. & h.; b. 24 Nov. 1681; d. 20 Jan. 1722

HOLLAND, *earldom*
1. **Henry Rich,** Lord Kensington; bapt. 19 Aug. 1590; cr. 24 Sept. 1624; exec. 9 Mar. 1649
2. **Robert Rich** (*see* Warwick), s. & h.; b. *c.* 1620; d. shortly bef. 16 Apr. 1675
3. **Edward Rich** (*see* Warwick), 1st surv. s. & h.; b. *c.* 1673; d. 31 July 1701
4. **Edward Henry Rich** (*see* Warwick), only s. & h.; b. 20 Jan. 1698; d. unm. 16 Aug. 1721

HUNTINGDON, *earldom*
[Huntingdon and Northampton originally formed a single earldom until the reign of K. Stephen. The two earldoms were perhaps united again in 1155–57 under Simon of St Liz III and were combined by him for the last time from 1174 to 1184 (*see also* note to Cambridge). The lists for these two earldoms start in 1065 because the creation of that year determined the later succession to both of them]
1. **Waltheof** (*see* Northampton, Northumberland); cr. 1065; forf. 1075; exec. 31 May 1076
2. Maud (*see* Northampton), da. of **1.**
    m. 1. Simon of St Liz; st. 1091;[1] d. *c.* 1111.
       2. **David I,** K. of Scotland; b. *c.* 1080; st. 1113–14;[2] res. Feb. 1136; d. 24 May 1153
3. **Henry of Scotland** (*see* Northumberland), s. of K. David I; b. *c.* 1114; succ. Feb. 1136; prob. lost earldom in 1141; d. 12 June 1152
4. **Simon of St Liz II** (*see* Northampton), s. of Maud by 1st marriage; recog. as earl of Huntingdon by K. Stephen 1138–9 and from 1141; b. prob. aft. 1103; d. Aug. 1153
5. **Malcolm IV,** K. of Scotland, s. & h. of 3; b. prob. 1141; recog. *c.* July 1157; d. unm. 9 Dec. 1165
6. **William I 'the Lion',** K. of Scotland, br. & h.; b. *c.* 1143; depr. soon aft. 12 July 1174; rest. 1185 and res. 1185; d. 4 Dec. 1214
7. **Simon of St Liz III** (*see* Northampton), s. of 4; b. *c.* 1138; poss. succ. to his father's lands 1155; rec. as earl 1174; d. June 1184
8. **David of Scotland,** yr. br. of 5 and 6; succ. 1185; depr. 1215 or 1216; rest. 13 Mar. 1218; d. 17 June 1219
9. **John 'de Scocia'** (*see* Chester), only surv. s. & h.; b. *c.* 1207; liv. 25 Apr. 1227; d.s.p. shortly bef. 6 June 1237
10. **William de Clinton,** b. *c.* 1304; cr. 16 Mar. 1337; d.s.p. 25 Aug. 1354
11. **Guichard d'Angle;** cr. 16 July 1377; d. 25 Mar.–4 Apr. 1380
12. **John de Holand** (*see* Exeter); b. aft. 1350; cr. 2 June 1388; exec. 9 or 10 Jan. 1400 & forf.
13. **John Holand** (*see* Exeter), 1st surv. s. & h.; b. 29 Mar. 1395 or 1396; rest. 1417 (but st. on Parlt. Roll 8 Feb. 1416); d. 5 Aug. 1447
14. **Henry Holand** (*see* Exeter), s. & h.; b. 27 June 1430; liv. 23 July 1450; forf. Nov. 1461; d.s.p.s. Sept. 1475
15. **Thomas Grey,** Lord Ferrers of Groby (*see* Dorset); b. uncertain; cr. 14 Aug. 1471; res. bef. 18 Apr. 1475; d. 30 Sept. 1501
16. **William Herbert** (*see* Pembroke); b. *c.* 1455; cr. 4 July 1479; d.s.p.m. 16 July 1491
17. **George Hastings,** Lord Hastings; b. 1488; cr. 8 Dec. 1529; d. 24 Mar. 1544
18. **Francis Hastings,** s. & h.; b. *c.* 1514; d. 23 June 1560
19. **Henry Hastings,** s. & h.; b. *c.* 1536; d.s.p. 14 Dec. 1595
20. **George Hastings,** br. & h.; b. *c.* 1540; d. 30 Dec. 1604
21. **Henry Hastings,** gds. & h.; b. 24 Apr. 1586; d. 14 Nov. 1643
22. **Ferdinando Hastings,** 1st s. & h.; b. 18 Jan. 1609; d. 13 Feb. 1656

[1] In a charter of this date he is simply styled earl without designation of place (*Regesta Regum Anglo-Normannorum*, i, no. 315). The charter of 1090 in *Registrum Antiquissimum of the Church of Lincoln*, i. 4–11, cannot be accepted as genuine.
[2] See *TRHS*, 1953, 85.

23. **Theophilus Hastings,** only surv. s. & h.; b. 10 Dec. 1650; d. 30 May 1701
24. **George Hastings,** 1st surv. s. & h.; b. 22 Mar. 1677; d. unm. 22 Feb. 1705
25. **Theophilus Hastings,** br. & h.; b. 12 Nov. 1696; d. 13 Oct. 1746

JERSEY, *earldom*
1. **Edward Villiers,** Viscount Villiers of Dartford; b. *c.* 1656; cr. 13 Oct. 1697; d. 25 Aug. 1711
2. **William Villiers,** s. & h.; b. *c.* 1682; d. 13 July 1721

KENDAL, *earldom*
1. **John of Lancaster** (*see* Bedford), 3rd s. of K. Henry IV; b. 20 June 1389; cr. 16 May 1414; d.s.p.leg. s. 15 Sept. 1435
2. **John Beaufort** (*see* Somerset); b. *c.* Apr. 1404; cr. 28 Aug. 1443; d.s.p.m. 27 May 1444
3. **Jean de Foix,** Vicomte de Castillon; cr. *c.* 12 May 1446; prob. res. 1462; d. shortly aft. 5 Dec. 1485

Dukedom
[4. **Charles Stuart;**[1] b. 4 July 1666; d. 22 May 1667]

Earldom
5. **George,** prince of Denmark (*see* Cumberland); b. 2 Apr. 1653; cr. 6 Apr. 1689; d.s.p.s. 28 Oct. 1708

KENT, *earldom*
1. **Odo,** bishop of Bayeux, half-br. of William the Conqueror; b. *c.* 1030; cr. 1066–67; depr. 1082; rest. 1087; depr. 1088; d. Feb. 1097
2. **Hubert de Burgh;** cr. 14 Feb. 1227;[2] depr. 11–13 Nov. 1232; rest. 28 May 1234; d. 12 May 1243 (leaving no children by his 3rd w., Margaret, sis. of Alexander, K. of Scotland, on whose issue the earldom had been entailed)
3. **Edmund of Woodstock,** yst. s. of Edward I (*see* note to Arundel); b. 5 Aug. 1301; cr. 28 July 1321; exec. and forf. 19 Mar. 1330
4. **Edmund,** 1st s. & h.; b. 1326; rest. 7 Dec. 1330; d. bef. 5 Oct. 1331
5. **John,** next br. & h.; b. 7 Apr. 1330; liv. hom. 10 Apr. 1351; d.s.p. 26–27 Dec. 1352
6. Joan, sist. & h.; b. *c.* 1328; liv. 22 Feb. 1353; d. prob. 8 Aug. 1385
    m. 1. *c.* 1339 **Sir Thomas de Holand**; st. 20 Nov. 1360; d. 26 or 28 Dec. 1360
    2. *c.* 1340 William de Montacute, earl of Salisbury; d. 3 June 1397; marriage annulled in 1349 and the validity of marriage to Sir Thomas de Holand confirmed.
    3. 10 Oct. 1361 **Edward**, prince of Wales; b. 15 June 1330; d. 8 June 1376
7. **Thomas de Holand,** s. & h.; b. *c.* 1350; st. 5 June 1380; d. 25 Apr. 1397
8. **Thomas de Holand** (*see* Surrey), s. & h.; b. in or bef. 1371; st. 28 May 1397; liv. hom. 16 July 1397; d.s.p. 7–8 Jan. 1400
9. **Edmund de Holand,** br. & h.; b. 6 Jan. 1383;[3] st. 29 Sept. 1401; d.s.p. leg. 15 Sept. 1408
10. **William Nevill,** Lord Fauconberg; cr. 1 Nov. 1461; d.s.p.m. leg. 9 Jan. 1463
11. **Edmund Grey,** Lord Grey of Ruthin; b. 26 Oct. 1416; cr. 30 May 1465; d. 22 May 1490
12. **George Grey,** 1st surv. s. & h.; liv. 26 May 1490; d. 16 Dec. 1503
13. **Richard Grey,** s. & h.; b. uncertain; lic. of entry 7 Sept. 1504; d.s.p. 3 May 1523. [Sir Henry Grey, br. & h.; b. aft. 1489, never assumed title by reason of his poverty; d. 24 Sept. 1562]
14. **Reynold Grey,** gds. & h. of Sir Henry Grey; rec. 1571; d.s.p. 17 Mar. 1573
15. **Henry Grey,** br. & h.; b. 1541; d.s.p. 31 Jan. 1615
16. **Charles Grey,** br. & h.; b. *c.* 1545; d. 28 Sept. 1623
17. **Henry Grey,** only s. & h.; b. *c.* 1583; d.s.p. 28 Nov. 1639
18. **Anthony Grey,** cous. & h. male; b. 1557; d. 9 Nov. 1643
19. **Henry Grey,** s. & h.; b. 24 Nov. 1594; d. 28 May 1651
20. **Anthony Grey,** 1st surv. s. & h.; b. 11 June 1645; d. 19 Aug. 1702

[1] He was known as duke of Kendal, but there is no evidence of a formal creation.
[2] MS. Cotton. Julius D. V, fo., 25d. (chronicle of St Martin, Dover).
[3] This is the date given in one inquest, but elsewhere he is still called a minor on 10 Jan. 1405.

Earldom, marquessate and dukedom

21. **Henry Grey** (*see* Harold), only s. & h.; bapt. 28 Sept. 1671;
    marquessate; cr. 14 Nov. 1706
    dukedom; cr. 28 Apr. 1710; d.s.p.m.s. 5 June 1740

KINGSTON-UPON-HULL, *earldom*

1. **Robert Pierrepont,** Viscount Newark; b. 6 Aug. 1584; cr. 25 July 1628; d.
   25 July 1643
2. **Henry Pierrepont** (*see* Dorchester), s. & h.; b. Mar. 1607; d.s.p.m.s. 8 Dec.
   1680
3. **Robert Pierrepont,** gt-neph. & h. male; b. *c.* 1660; d. unm. June 1682
4. **William Pierrepont,** br. & h.; b. *c.* 1662; d.s.p. 17 Sept. 1690
5. **Evelyn Pierrepont** (*see* Dorchester), br. & h.; later (1715) duke of Kingston-
   upon-Hull; b. *c.* 1665; d. 5 Mar. 1726

LANCASTER, *earldom*

1. **Edmund 'Crouchback'** [*see* Leicester and Derby (note)], yst s. of K. Henry III;
   b. 16 Jan. 1245; cr. 30 June 1267; d. 5 June 1296
2. **Thomas 'of Lancaster'** [*see* Leicester, Lincoln and Derby (note)], s. & h.; b. *c.*
   1278; liv. hom. 8 Sept. 1298; exec. 22 Mar. 1322 and forf.
3. **Henry 'of Lancaster'** (*see* Leicester), br. & h.; b. *c.* 1281; st. 26 Oct. 1326;[1] d.
   22 Sept. 1345
4. **Henry 'of Grosmont'** (*see* Derby), only s. & h.; b. *c.* 1300; succ. 22 Sept. 1345

   dukedom; cr. 6 Mar. 1351; d.s.p.m. 23 Mar. 1361[2]

   Earldom

5. **John of Gaunt** (*see* Derby), 4th s. of K. Edward III; b. Mar. 1340; st.[3] 14 Aug.
   1361

   m. 19 May 1359 Blanche, yr da. and coh. of 4 (she d. 12 Sept. 1369)
   dukedom; cr. 13 Nov. 1362; d. 3–4 Feb. 1399
6. **Henry 'of Bolingbroke'** (*see* Derby), s. & h., later K. Henry IV; b. prob. Apr.
   1366. Became K. 30 Sept. 1399
7. **Henry** (*see* Chester), s. & h., later K. Henry V; b. 16 Sept. 1387;[4] cr. 10 Nov.
   1399.[5] Became K. 21 Mar. 1413

LEEDS, *dukedom*

1. **Thomas Osborne** (*see* Carmarthen); b. 20 Feb. 1632; cr. 4 May 1694; d. 26 July
   1712
2. **Peregrine Osborne,** only surv. s. & h.; b. 1659; d. 25 June 1729

LEICESTER, *earldom*

1. **Robert de Beaumont,** count of Meulan; b. *c.* 1046; st. *c.* 1107;[6] d. 5 June 1118
2. **Robert,** 2nd s. & h. to English possessions; b. 1104; st. 1118; d. 5 Apr. 1168
3. **Robert ès Blanchemains,** s. & h.; b. *c.* 1130; d. 1190 (31 Aug. ?) [*C.P.*, x, App.,
   106, n.b]

---

[1] His title is undisputed from this time forward, but he was formally restored on
3 Feb. 1327.
[2] *BIHR*, xx (1944) 143, citing M. Bateson, *Records of the Borough of Leicester*,
ii, 124.
[3] Summ. to Parliament under this title on that date. His share of the estates of his
father-in-law included the castle and honour of Lancaster.
[4] This date has been favoured by most modern writers on the authority of
Henry's biographer, Elmham. *Cf.* Wylie, *Henry IV*, iii. (1896), 323–24, for
arguments that he was born in Aug. 1386; according to *C.P.*, vii, 419, he was born
on 9 Aug. 1387. Other writers have suggested Aug. or Sept. 1388, but this seems
unlikely.
[5] The duchy of Lancaster, as distinct from the dukedom, remained vested in the
king, and 'the Lancastrian kings were considered as dukes of Lancaster although
not so styled' (R. Somerville, *Hist. of the Duchy of Lancaster* (1953) i, 153). A
number of official documents in the fifteenth century, however, refer to the kings as
dukes of Lancaster.
[6] *Regesta Regum Anglo-Normannorum*, ii, no. 844.

4. **Robert 'Fitz Pernel'**, 1st surv. s. & h.; inv. 1 Feb. 1191; d.s.p. 20 or 21 Oct. 1204

   [Aft. the death of 4, his eldest sis. & coh., Amice, is st. countess of Leicester. She m. Simon de Montfort and their s. obtained recognition of his claim to the earldom as below. She d. 3 Sept. 1215]
5. **Simon de Montfort**, s. & h. of Amice de Montfort; b. *c.* 1170; recog. 1205 or 1206[1]; d. 25 June 1218

   [Amauri de Montfort, s. & h., st. himself earl of Leicester, but was never recog. Surrendered his claims in favour of yr br. Simon, prob. in 1229]
6. **Simon de Montfort** (*see* Chester), yst s. of 5; b. prob. 1208; liv. hom. 13 Aug. 1231; inv. prob. 11 Apr. 1239[2]; d. and forf. 4 Aug. 1265
7. **Edmund 'Crouchback'** (*see* Lancaster), yst s. of K. Henry III; b. 16 Jan. 1245; cr. 26 Oct. 1265; d. 5 June 1296
8. **Thomas 'of Lancaster'** (*see* Lancaster), s. & h.; b. *c.* 1278; liv. hom. 8 Sept. 1298; exec. 22 Mar. 1322 and forf.
9. **Henry 'of Lancaster'** (*see* Lancaster), br. & h.; b. *c.* 1281; rest. 29 Mar. 1324; d. 22 Sept. 1345
10. **Henry 'of Grosmont'** (*see* Derby), only s. & h.; b. *c.* 1300; d.s.p.m. 23 Mar. 1361
11. **William**, count of Hainault, *etc.*; b. *c.* 1327; succ. 23 Mar. 1361; d. Apr. 1389
    m. 1352 Maud, 1st da. & coh. of 10 (she d.s.p. 10 Apr. 1362)
12. **John of Gaunt** (*see* Derby), 4th s. of K. Edward III; b. Mar. 1340; m. 19 May 1359 Blanche, yr da. and coh. of 10 (she d. 12 Sept. 1369); succ. 10 Apr. 1362 (*see* Derby, note); d. 3–4 Feb. 1399
13. **Henry 'of Bolingbroke'** (*see* Derby), s. and h., later K.; b. prob. Apr. 1366. Became K. 30 Sept. 1399
14. **Robert Dudley**; b. 24 June 1532 or 1533; cr. 29 Sept. 1564; d.s.p.s. leg. 4 Sept. 1588
15. **Robert Sydney**, Viscount L'Isle, neph. of **14**; b. 19 Nov. 1563; cr. 2 Aug. 1618; d. 13 July 1626
16. **Robert Sydney**, 1st surv. s. & h.; b. 1 Dec. 1595; d. 2 Nov. 1677
17. **Philip Sydney**, s. & h.; b. 10 Jan. 1619; d. 6 Mar. 1698
18. **Robert Sydney**, s. & h.; b. 1649; d. 11 Nov. 1702
19. **Philip Sydney**, s. & h.; b. 8 July 1676; d.s.p.s. 24 July 1705
20. **John Sydney**, br. & h.; b. 14 Feb. 1680; d. unm. 27 Sept. 1737

LICHFIELD, *earldom*

   [Lord Bernard Stuart, who was b. 28 Dec. 1622, is referred to in various sources as earl of Lichfield, evidently in anticipation of a formal creation. He d. 26 Sept. 1645]
1. **Charles Stuart** (*see* Darnley etc.), neph. of Lord Bernard; b. 7 Mar. 1639 or 1640; cr. 10 Dec. 1645; d.s.p.s. 12 Dec. 1672
2. **Sir Edward Henry Lee**, bt; b. 4 Feb. 1663; cr. 5 June 1674; d. 14 July 1716

LINCOLN, *earldom*
1. **William d'Aubigny** (*see* Arundel); cr. ? 1139 (bef. Sept.); res. in or bef. 1141
2. **William de Roumare** (*see* Cambridge); b. *c.* 1096; cr. ? 1140; d. bef. 31 May 1161
3. **William de Roumare**, gds. & h.; b. *c.* 1145;[3] d.s.p. *c.* 1198
4. **Gilbert de Gant** or Gaunt; b. *c.* 1120; cr. ? 1149;[4] d.s.p.m. 1156
5. **Ranulph de Blundeville** (*see* Chester); b. *c.* 1172; cr. 23 May 1217; res. shortly bef. he d.s.p. 26 Oct. 1232

---

[1] He was deprived of his lands 13 Feb. 1207, until he paid his debts to the crown, but he continued to be st. earl.

[2] At this date his br. Amauri publicly res. to him all his English lands and titles. According to Matthew Paris, however, Simon was inv. earlier, on 2 Feb. 1239. He styled himself e. Oct. 1236.

[3] He is st. earl William de Romara, never earl of Lincoln.

[4] This grant was made despite the previous grant to William de Roumare. The neph. of no. **4**, Gilbert de Gant, was given the sword of the county by Louis of France in 1216 and he was called earl of Lincoln, but he failed to capture the castle of Lincoln and nothing more is heard of his earldom.

6. Hawise de Quincy, sis. & designated h.; recog. 27 Oct. 1232; res. 22 Nov. 1232; d. shortly bef. 3 Mar. 1243
7. Margaret, da. & h.; d. Mar. 1266
   m. I. shortly bef. 21 June 1221 **John de Lacy**; b. *c.* 1192; recog. 22 Nov. 1232; d. 22 July 1240
     2. *c.* Jan. 1242 Walter Marshal (*see* Pembroke); d.s.p. 24 Nov. 1245.
     3. bef. 7 June 1252 Richard de Wiltshire
8. Edmund de Lacy, only s. & h.; b. ? 1230; liv. May 1248; d. 2 June 1258[1]
9. **Henry de Lacy**, s. & h.; b. 6 or 13 Jan. 1251; liv. 13 Oct. 1272; d.s.p.m.s. 5 Feb. 1311
10. Alice de Lacy, da. & h.; b. 25 Dec. 1281; d.s.p. 2 Oct. 1348.
   m. 1. on or bef. 28 Oct. 1294 **Thomas**, later earl of Lancaster; exec. 22 Mar. 1322.
     2. bef. 10 Nov. 1324 Sir Ebles Lestraunge; d.s.p. 8 Sept. 1335.
     3. bef. 23 Mar. 1336 Sir Hugh de Frene, Lord Frene; d. Dec. 1336 or Jan. 1337
11. **Henry 'of Grosmont'** (*see* Derby); b. *c.* 1300; cr. 20 Aug. 1349; d.s.p.m. 23 Mar. 1361
12. **John of Gaunt** (*see* Derby), 4th s. of K. Edw. III; b. Mar. 1340; m. 19 May 1359 Blanche, yr da. and coh. of **11** (she d. 12 Sept. 1369); succ. 10 Apr. 1362;[2] d. 3–4 Feb. 1399
13. **Henry 'of Bolingbroke'** (*see* Derby), s. & h., later K.; b. prob. Apr. 1366. Became K. 30 Sept. 1399
14. **John de la Pole**, neph. of K. Edw. IV; b. *c.* 1462; cr. 13 Mar. 1467; d. & forf. 16 June 1487
15. **Henry Brandon**, neph. of K. Henry VIII; b. 11 Mar. 1516; cr. 18 June 1525; d. unm. 1 Mar. 1534
16. **Edward Clinton** or Fiennes, Lord Clinton; b. 1512; cr. 4 May 1572; d. 16 Jan. 1585
17. **Henry Clinton** or Fiennes, s. & h.; b. aft. 1539; d. 29 Sept. 1616
18. **Thomas Clinton** or Fiennes, s. & h.; b. *c.* 1568; d. 15 Jan. 1619
19. **Theophilus Clinton** or Fiennes, 1st surv. s. & h.; b. *c.* 1600; d. 21 May 1667
20. **Edward Clinton** or Fiennes, gds. & h.; d.s.p. 25 Nov. 1692
21. **Francis Clinton**, cous. & h. male; b. *c.* 1635; d. 25 Aug.–3 Sept. 1693
22. **Henry Clinton**, 1st surv. s. & h.; b. 1684; d. 7 Sept. 1728

LINDSEY, *earldom*
1. **Robert Bertie**, Lord Willoughby of Eresby; b. prob. 16 Dec. 1582; cr. 22 Nov. 1626; d. *c.* 24 Oct. 1642
2. **Montagu Bertie**, s. & h.; b. shortly before 1608; d. 25 July 1666
3. **Robert Bertie**, s. & h.; b. *c.* 1630; d. 8 May 1701

   Earldom and marquessate
4. **Robert Bertie**, s. & h.; b. 30 Oct. 1660
   marquessate; cr. 21 Dec. 1706; d. 26 July 1723[3]

MACCLESFIELD, *earldom*
1. **Charles Gerard**, Lord Gerard of Brandon; b. *c.* 1618; cr. 21 July 1679; d. 7 Jan. 1694
2. **Charles Gerard**, s. & h.; b. *c.* 1659; d.s.p. leg. 5 Nov. 1701
3. **Fitten Gerard**, br. & h.; b. *c.* 1665; d. unm. 26 Dec. 1702

MANCHESTER, *earldom*
1. **Henry Montagu**, Viscount Mandeville; b. *c.* 1563; cr. 5 Feb. 1626; d. 7 Nov. 1642
2. **Edward Montagu**, s. & h.; b. 1602; d. 7 May 1671

---

[1] He was not formally invested with the earldom, probably because he died in his mother's lifetime, but he received the 3rd penny of the pleas of the county and was called earl in royal documents.

[2] Blanche may be held to have succ. to the earldom on the death of her elder and only sister at this date. *See*, however, *Complete Peerage*, x, Appendix K, 123, for the view that the creation of 1349 was limited to heirs male. John of Gaunt had already (21 July 1361) st. himself, among his other titles, earl of Lincoln.

[3] Cr. duke of Ancaster and Kesteven in 1715.

3. **Robert Montagu,** s. & h.; bapt. 25 Apr. 1634; d. 14 Mar. 1683
4. **Charles Montagu,** 1st surv. s. & h., aft. (1719) duke of Manchester; b. *c.* 1662; d. 20 Jan. 1722

MARCH, *earldom*
 1. **Roger de Mortimer,** b. 1287–88; cr. 16–31 Oct. 1328; forf. 26 Nov. and exec. 29 Nov. 1330
 2. **Roger de Mortimer,** gds. & h.; b. 11 Nov. 1328; rest. 28 Apr.–2 June 1354; d. 26 Feb. 1360
 3. **Edmund de Mortimer** (*see* Ulster), s. & h.; b. 1 Feb. 1352; d. 27 Dec. 1381
 4. **Roger de Mortimer** (*see* Ulster), s. & h.; b. 11 Apr. 1374; liv. 25 Feb. 1394; d. 20 July 1398
 5. **Edmund de Mortimer** (*see* Ulster), s. & h.; b. 6 Nov. 1391; liv. 9 June 1413; d.s.p. 18 Jan. 1425
 6. **Richard Plantagenet** (*see* Cambridge), neph. & h.; b. 1411; liv. 12 May 1432; att. 20 Nov. 1459; att. nullified Oct. 1460; d. 30 Dec. 1460
 7. **Edward Plantagenet** (*see* Cambridge), s. & h., later K. Edw. IV; b. 28 Apr. 1442; st. in the lifetime of his father. Became K. 4 Mar. 1461
 8. **Edward Plantagenet** (*see* Chester), 1st s. & h., later K. Edw. V; b. 2 or 3 Nov. 1470; cr. 8 July 1479. Became K. 9 Apr. 1483
 9. **Lord Esmé Stewart** (*see* Lennox); b. 1579; cr. 7 June 1619; d. 30 July 1624
10. **James Stewart** (*see* Lennox), s. & h.; b. 6 Apr. 1612; d. 30 Mar. 1655
11. **Esmé Stewart** (*see* Lennox), only s. & h.; b. 2 Nov. 1649; d. unm. 10 Aug. 1660
12. **Charles Stewart** (*see* Lennox), cous. & h. male; b. 7 Mar. 1639 or 1640; d.s.p.s. 12 Dec. 1672
13. **Charles Lennox** (*see* Richmond, Lennox), illeg. s. of Charles II; b. 29 July 1672; cr. 9 Aug. 1675; d. 27 May 1723

MARLBOROUGH, *earldom*
 1. **James Ley,** Lord Ley; b. *c.* 1552; cr. 5 Feb. 1626; d. 14 Mar. 1629
 2. **Henry Ley,** s. & h.; bapt. 3 Dec. 1595; d. 1 Apr. 1638
 3. **James Ley,** only s. & h.; b. 28 Jan. 1618; d. unm. 2 June 1665
 4. **William Ley,** uncle & h. male; bapt. 10 or 12 Mar. 1612; d.s.p. 1679

 Earldom and dukedom
 5. **John Churchill,** Lord Churchill (*see* Blandford); b. 24 June 1650
 earldom; cr. 9 Apr. 1689
 dukedom; cr. 14 Dec. 1702; d.s.p.m.s. 16 June 1722

MIDDLESEX, *earldom*
 1. **Lionel Cranfield,** Lord Cranfield, bapt. 13 Mar. 1575; cr. 16 Sept. 1622; d. 5 Aug. 1645
 2. **James Cranfield,** s. & h.; b. on or shortly bef. 10 Nov. 1621; d.s.p.m. 7–13 Sept. 1651
 3. **Lionel Cranfield,** br. & h. male; b. *c.* 1625; d.s.p. 26 Oct. 1674
 4. **Charles Sackville** (*see* Dorset), neph. of 3; b. 24 Jan. 1638; cr. 4 Apr. 1675; d. 29 Jan. 1706
 5. **Lionel Cranfield Sackville** (*see* Dorset), only s. & h.; b. 18 Jan. 1688; d. 10 Oct. 1765

MILFORD HAVEN, *earldom*
 1. **George Augustus** (*see* Cambridge); b. 30 Oct. 1683; cr. 9 Nov. 1706; succ. 11 June 1727

MOHUN. *See* SOMERSET (no. 1)

MONMOUTH, *earldom*
 1. **Robert Carey,** Lord Carey of Lepington; b. 1560; cr. 5 Feb. 1626; d. 12 Apr. 1639
 2. Henry Carey, s. & h.; b. 27 Jan. 1596; d.s.p.m.s. 13 June 1661
 Dukedom
 3. **James Scott** (formerly Crofts) (*see* Doncaster, Buccleuch, Dalkeith), illeg. s. of Charles II; b. 9 Apr. 1649; cr. 14 Feb. 1663; forf. 16 June 1685; exec. 15 July 1685
 Earldom
 4. **Charles Mordaunt** (*see* Peterborough); b. *c.* 1658; cr. 9 Apr. 1689; d. 25 Oct. 1735

MONTAGU, *marquessate*
1. **John Nevill** (*see* Northumberland); b. *c.* 1431; cr. 25 Mar. 1470; d. 14 Apr. 1471
2. **George Nevill** (*see* Bedford), s. & h.; birth uncertain (still a minor on 9 Mar. 1480); depr. Jan. or Mar. 1478; d.s.p. 4 May 1483

MONTAGU, *earldom and dukedom*
3. **Ralph Montagu** (*see* Monthermer), Lord Montagu of Boughton; bapt. 24 Dec. 1638
   earldom; cr. 9 Apr. 1689
   dukedom; cr. 14 Apr. 1705; d. 9 Mar. 1709
4. **John Montagu,** only surv. s. & h.; b. 29 Mar. 1690; d.s.p.m.s. 6 July 1749

MONTGOMERY, *earldom*
1. **Philip Herbert** (*see* Pembroke); b. 10 Oct. 1584; cr. 4 May 1605; d. 23 Jan. 1650
   [This earldom henceforth descends with that of Pembroke. *See* Pembroke]

MONTHERMER, *marquessate*
[Cr. 1705 with the dukedom of Montagu]

MORTAIN, *counts of*
[The counts of Mortain in Normandy are here included until the end of the twelfth century owing to their intimate connection with English history]
1. **Robert,** half-br. of K. William the Conqueror; b. *c.* 1031; cr. *c.* 1056; d. 8 Dec. 1090
2. **William,** s. & h.; b. prob. bef. 1084; forf. Apr. 1106; d. in or aft. 1140
3. **Stephen,** later count of Boulogne (1125) and K.; cr. prob. bef. 1115. Became K. 22 Dec. 1135
4. **William** (*see* Surrey), only surv. s. & h.; succ. 25 Oct. 1154;[1] d.s.p. Oct. 1159[2]
5. **John** (*see* Gloucester), yst s. of K. Henry II, later K; cr. 1189. Became K. 27 May 1199

MULGRAVE, *earldom*
1. **Edmund Sheffield,** Lord Sheffield; b. 7 Dec. 1565; cr. 5 Feb. 1626; d. Oct. 1646
2. **Edmund Sheffield,** gods. & h.; b. *c.* Dec. 1611; d. 24 Aug. 1658
3. **John Sheffield** (*see* Buckingham, Normanby), only s. & h.; b. 8 Sept. 1647; d. 24 Feb. 1721

NEWCASTLE-UPON-TYNE, *earldom*
1. **Ludovic Stuart** (*see* Lennox); b. 29 Sept. 1574; cr. 17 May 1623; d.s.p. leg. 16 Feb. 1624

   Earldom, marquessate and dukedom
2. **William Cavendish,** Viscount Mansfield (*see* Ogle); bapt. 16 Dec. 1593;
   earldom; cr. 7 Mar. 1628
   marquessate; cr. 27 Oct. 1643
   dukedom; cr. 16 Mar. 1665; d. 25 Dec. 1676
3. **Henry Cavendish,** only surv. s. & h.; b. 24 June 1630; d.s.p.m.s. 26 July 1691
   Dukedom only
4. **John Holles** (*see* Clare); b. 9 Jan. 1662; cr. 14 May 1694; d.s.p.m. leg. 15 July 1711

NEWPORT, *earldom*
1. **Mountjoy Blount,** Lord Mountjoy of Thurveston; b. *c.* 1597; cr. 3 Aug. 1628; d. 12 Feb. 1666
2. **Mountjoy Blount,** s. & h.; b. *c.* 1630; d. unm. shortly bef. 20 Mar. 1675
3. **Thomas Blount,** br. & h.; d. unm. shortly bef. 4 May 1675
4. **Henry Blount,** br. & h.; d.s.p. shortly bef. 25 Sept. 1679

---

[1] He succ. on the death of his father, K. Stephen.
[2] J. H. Round, *Studies in Peerage and Family History*, 171.

NORFOLK, *earldom*
 1. **Hugh Bigod**; b. *c.* 1095 ?; cr. by empress, prob. 1141; recog. by King 1153;[1] d. shortly bef. 9 Mar. 1177
 2. **Roger le Bigod,** s. & h.; cr. 25 Nov. 1189;[2] d. 1221 (bef. 2 Aug.)
 3. **Hugh le Bigod,** s. & h.; liv. hom. 2 Aug. 1221; d. 11–18 Feb. 1225
 4. **Roger le Bigod,** s. & h.; b. 1212–13; g. 22 May 1233; d.s.p. 3 or 4 July 1270
 5. **Roger Bigod,** neph. & h.; b. *c.* 1245; hom. 25 July 1270; surr. 12 Apr. 1302; rest. 11 July 1302; d.s.p. shortly bef. 6 Dec. 1306
 6. **Thomas 'of Brotherton',** 5th s. of Edward I; b. 1 June 1300; cr. 16 Dec. 1312; d.s.p.m.s. 1338 (bef. 10 Sept.)[3]

 Earldom and dukedom
 7. Margaret, elder da. & h. to earldom; succ. 1338[4]
 dukedom; cr. 29 Sept. 1397;[5] d.s.p.m. 24 Mar. 1399

 Dukedom and earldom
 8. **Thomas de Mowbray** (*see* Nottingham), gds. & h.; b. 1366;
 dukedom; cr. 29 Sept. 1397
 earldom; succ. 24 Mar. 1399; d. 22 Sept. 1399

 Earldom
 9. **Thomas de Mowbray** (*see* Nottingham), s. & h.; b. 17 Sept. 1385; exec. 8 June 1405 (d.s.p. but not forf.)

 Earldom and dukedom
 10. **John de Mowbray** (*see* Nottingham), br. & h.; b. 1392; liv. 24 Nov. 1413
 dukedom; rest. 30 Apr. 1425;[6] d. 19 Oct. 1432
 11. **John de Mowbray** (*see* Nottingham), s. & h.; b. 12 Sept. 1415; d. 6 Nov. 1461
 12. **John de Mowbray** (*see* Nottingham, Surrey, Warenne), s. & h.; b. 18 Oct. 1444; liv. 23 Mar. 1465; d.s.p.m. 16–17 Jan. 1476
 13. **Richard Plantagenet** (*see* Nottingham, Surrey, Warenne, York), yr s. of K. Edward IV; b. prob. 17 Aug. 1473; cr. duke of Norfolk 7 Feb. 1477; d. prob. July–Sept. 1483.
 m. 15 Jan. 1478 Anne, only da. & h. of 12 (st. countess of Norfolk). She was b. 10 Dec. 1472; d. 25 Jan.–10 Nov. 1481
 14. **John Howard,** Lord Howard, gds. of 8 (through his mother); cr. 28 June 1483; d. 22 Aug. 1485 and forf.
 15. **Thomas Howard** (*see* Surrey), s. & h.; b. 1443; cr. 1 Feb. 1514; d. 21 May 1524
 16. **Thomas Howard** (*see* Surrey), s. & h.; b. 1473; forf. 27 Jan. 1547; rest. 3 Aug. 1553; d. 25 Aug. 1554
 17. **Thomas Howard** (*see* Surrey), gds. & h.; b. 10 Mar. 1538; forf. 16 Jan. 1572; exec. 2 June 1572

 Earldom
 18. **Thomas Howard** (*see* Arundel, Surrey, gds. of 17); b. 7 July 1585; cr. 6 June 1644; d. 14–24 Sept. 1646
 19. **Henry Frederick Howard** (*see* Arundel, Surrey), s. & h.; b. 15 Aug. 1608; d. 17 Apr. 1652
 Earldom and dukedom
 20. **Thomas Howard** (*see* Arundel, Surrey), s. & h.; b. 9 Mar. 1627; succ. 17 Apr. 1652
 dukedom; rest. 29 Dec. 1660; d. unm. Dec. 1677
 21. **Henry Howard** (*see* Arundel, Surrey), br. & h.; b. 12 July 1628; d. 13 Jan. 1684

---

[1] He was earl of both Norfolk and Suffolk. *See* R. H. C. Davis, *King Stephen* (1967), 141–3, where it is suggested that Stephen's son William held the county of Norfolk, 1149–53, in addition to the earldom of Surrey.
[2] Henry II had not allowed him to inherit the earldom.
[3] P.R.O., E 143/11/1, no. 24
[4] Although she succ. to the earldom at this date under the terms of the creation, no case of her being st. countess is known until July 1377, nor are either of her husbands, John, Lord Segrave (m. 1337 or 1338; d. 1353) and Walter, Lord Mauny (m. shortly bef. 30 May 1354; d. Jan. 1372), known as earls.
[5] She was cr. duchess on same day as no. 8 was cr. a duke.
[6] The grant of the dukedom was annulled by the Parliament which met 6 Oct. 1399 and was not revived until 30 Apr. 1425.

22. **Henry Howard** (*see* Arundel, Surrey), s. & h.; b. 11 Jan. 1655; d.s.p. 2 Apr. 1701
23. **Thomas Howard** (*see* Arundel, Surrey), neph. & h.; b. 11 Dec. 1683; d.s.p. 23 Dec. 1732

NORMANBY, *marquessate*
1. **John Sheffield** (*see* Buckingham, Mulgrave); b. 8 Sept. 1647; cr. 10 May 1694; d. 24 Feb. 1721

NORTHAMPTON, *earldom* (*see* note to Huntingdon)
1. **Waltheof** (*see* Huntingdon); cr. 1065; forf. 1075; exec. 31 May 1076
2. **Maud** (*see* Huntingdon), da. of 1.
   m. 1. **Simon of St Liz**; st. 1091; d. *c.* 1111
   2. **David I**, K. of Scotland; b. *c.* 1080; st. 1113–14[1]; res. Feb. 1136; d. 24 May 1153
3. **Simon of St Liz II** (*see* Huntingdon), s. of Maud by 1st marriage. May have been recog. as earl of Northampton by K. Stephen during the later years of his reign (possibly by 1141); b. prob. aft. 1103; d. Aug. 1153
4. **Simon of St Liz III** (*see* Huntingdon), s. & h.; b. *c.* 1138; prob. recog. from 1155 to 1157; st. *comes* in exchequer records 1155 and aft. 1165; certainly recog. 1174; d.s.p.s. June 1184
5. **William de Bohun**; b. *c.* 1312; cr. 16 Mar. 1337; d. *c.* 10–17 Sept. 1360
6. **Humphrey de Bohun** (*see* Essex, Hereford), s. & h.; b. 25 Mar. 1342; d.s.p.m. 16 Jan. 1373[2]
7. **Henry 'of Bolingbroke'** (*see* Derby), later K.; b. prob. Apr. 1366
   m. July 1380–Mar. 1381 Mary, 2nd da. and coh. of 6, received 3rd penny of the county 22 Dec. 1384 and st. earl of Northampton in the official record of his coronation. Became K. 30 Sept. 1399

Marquessate
8. **William Parr** (*see* Essex); b. Aug.–Sept. 1513; cr. 16 Feb. 1547; forf. Aug. 1553; cr. again 13 Jan. 1559; d.s.p. 28 Oct. 1571

Earldom
9. **Henry Howard**; b. 24 Feb. 1540; cr. 13 Mar. 1604; d. unm. 16 June 1614
10. **William Compton**, Lord Compton; b. *c.* 1568; cr. 2 Aug. 1618; d. 24 June 1630
11. **Spencer Compton**, only s. & h.; b. May 1601; d. 19 Mar. 1643
12. **James Compton**, 1st s. & h.; b. 19 Aug. 1622; d. 15 Dec. 1681
13. **George Compton**, 1st surv. s. & h.; b. 18 Oct. 1664; d. 13 Apr. 1727

NORTHUMBERLAND, *earldom*
[Until 1095 Northumberland was in the hands either of descendants of its ancient earls or of administrators appd. by the K. Both these classes are given the title of earl by the chroniclers and in later lists, but only in the case of no. 5 is there charter evidence for the use of the title. The dates at which they received charge of the government are given below]
   i. **Siward,** in or bef. 1041—d. 1055
   ii. **Tostig,** 1055—Oct. 1065

1. **Morcar;** ? cr. 3 Oct. 1065; surr. 1067[3]
2. **Waltheof** (*see* Huntingdon), only surv. s. of Siward (*above*); cr. 1072; forf. 1075; exec. 31 May 1076
3. **Walcher**, bp of Durham; cr. 1076; d. 14 May 1080
4. **Aubrey** (a Norman knight); cr. ? 1080; res. shortly before 1086.

---

[1] *TRHS*, 1953, 85.
[2] On 3 Apr. 1374 Thomas of Woodstock, intending to marry Eleanor, elder da. and coh. of 6, received the 3rd penny of the county of Northampton, but he does not appear, during the 11 years when he held this, to have been recog. as earl of Northampton (*see also* Hereford). His gds: Humphrey Stafford (*see* Buckingham and Hereford) is styled earl of Northampton in an indenture of 13 Feb. 1444, but he is not otherwise known by this title.
[3] In the confused few years which followed Morcar's withdrawal to Normandy at this date, the administration was in the hands successively of Copsi (d. 1068), Robert de Comines (d. 28 Jan. 1069) and Gospatric (depr. 1072).

5. **Robert de Mowbray**; cr. *c.* 1086; depr. 1095
6. **Henry of Scotland** (*see* Huntingdon); b. *c.* 1114; cr. 1139; d. 12 June 1152
7. **William,** 2nd s., aft. K. of Scotland; b. 1143; succ. 1152; surr. 1157[1]
8. **Hugh du Puiset,** bp of Durham; cr. 25 Nov. 1189;[2] surr. 19 Apr. 1194; d. 3 Mar. 1195
9. **Henry de Percy,** Lord Percy; b. 10 Nov. 1341; cr. 16 July 1377; regarded as having forfeited his title and estates since his flight abroad in Apr. 1405; attainted 4 Dec. 1406; d. 19 Feb. 1408
10. **Henry de Percy,** gds. & h.; b. 3 Feb. 1394; cr. 16 Mar. 1416; d. 22 May 1455
11. **Henry Percy,** s. & h.; b. 25 July 1421; d. 29 Mar. 1461 and forf.
12. **John Nevill** (*see* Montagu); b. *c.* 1431; cr. 27 May 1464; surr. 25 Mar. 1470; d. 14 Apr. 1471
13. **Henry Percy,** only s. & h. of 11; b. *c.* 1449; rest. 25 Mar. 1470; d. 28 Apr. 1489
14. **Henry Algernon Percy,** s. & h.; b. 14 Jan. 1478; d. 19 May 1527
15. **Henry Percy,** s. & h.; b. *c.* 1502; d.s.p. 30 June 1537

Dukedom
16. **John Dudley** (*see* Warwick); b. 1502; cr. 11 Oct. 1551; forf. 18 Aug. and exec. 22 Aug. 1553

Earldom
17. **Thomas Percy,** neph. & h. of 15; b. 1528; cr. 1 May 1557;[3] forf. 1571; exec. 22 Aug. 1572
18. **Henry Percy,** br. & h. male; b. *c.* 1532; succ. 22 Aug. 1572;[4] d. 20–21 June 1585
19. **Henry Percy,** 1st s. & h.; b. Apr. 1564; d. 5 Nov. 1632
20. **Algernon Percy,** 1st surv. s. & h.; b. 29 Sept. 1602; d. 13 Oct. 1668
21. **Joceline Percy,** only s. & h.; b. 4 July 1644; d.s.p.m.s. 21/31 May 1670

Earldom and dukedom
22. **George FitzRoy,** formerly Palmer, illeg. s. of Charles II; b. 28 Dec. 1665
earldom; cr. 1. Oct. 1674
dukedom; cr. 6 Apr. 1683; d.s.p. leg. 28 June 1716

NORWICH, *earldom*
1. **Edward Denny,** Lord Denny; b. 15 Aug. 1569; cr. 24 Oct. 1626; d.s.p.m. 24 Oct. 1637
2. **George Goring,** Lord Goring of Hurstpierpoint; b. 28 Apr. 1585; cr. 28 Nov. 1644; d. 6 Jan. 1663
3. **Charles Goring,** only surv. s. & h.; b. *c.* 1615; d.s.p. 3 Mar. 1671
4. **Henry Howard** (*see* Arundel etc.); b. 12 July 1628; cr. 19 Oct. 1672; d. 13 Jan. 1684
5. **Henry Howard** (*see* Arundel, etc.), s. & h.; b. 11 Jan. 1655; d.s.p. 2 Apr. 1701
6. **Thomas Howard** (*see* Arundel, etc.), neph. & h.; b. 11 Dec. 1683; d.s.p. 23 Dec. 1732

NOTTINGHAM, *earldom*

[In the twelfth century Nottingham and Derby, which had one sheriff, were possibly considered as forming one earldom. There is some evidence that Robert de Ferrers, 2nd earl of Derby, styled himself earl of Nottingham (though this interpretation is disputed in the *Complete Peerage*)]

1. **John de Mowbray,** Lord Mowbray; b. *c.* 1363–65; cr. 16 July 1377; d. unm. shortly bef. 12 Feb. 1383
2. **Thomas de Mowbray** (*see* Norfolk), br. & h.; b. 1366; cr. 12 Feb. 1383; d. 22 Sept. 1399
3–7. [From this date until 16–17 Jan. 1476 this earldom descended with the earldom of Norfolk. John de Mowbray then dying without male issue, Richard, duke of York, was, in contemplation of his marriage with Anne, only da. of this earl, created earl of Nottingham 12 June 1476 and a few months later, duke of Norfolk. *See under* Norfolk]

[1] Malcolm IV, K. of Scotland, surrendered the earldom to Henry II at this date.
[2] At this date he purchased the earldom.
[3] He did not succeed his uncle in 1537 because of the attainder of his father barring succession; hence the necessity for new creation.
[4] By the terms of the creation he succ. to the earldom despite his br.'s attainder.

 8. **William de Berkeley** (*see* Berkeley), gds. of 2 through his mother; b. 1426; cr. June 1483; d.s.p.s. 14 Feb. 1492
 9. **Henry Fitz Roy** (*see* Richmond, Somerset), illeg. s. of Henry VIII; b. 1519 ?; cr. 18 June 1525; d.s.p. 22 July 1536
10. **Charles Howard,** Lord Howard of Effingham; b. 1536; cr. 22 Oct. 1597; d. 14 Dec. 1624
11. **Charles Howard,** 1st surv. s. & h.; b. 17 Sept. 1579; d.s.p. 3 Oct. 1642
12. **Charles Howard,** half br. & h. male; b. 25 Dec. 1610; d.s.p. 26 Apr. 1681
13. **Heneage Finch,** Lord Finch of Daventry; b. 23 Dec. 1621; cr. 12 May 1681; d. 18 Dec. 1682
14. **Daniel Finch,** s. & h., later (1729), earl of Winchilsea; b. 1647; d. 1 Jan. 1730

OGLE, *earldom*
 1. **William Cavendish** (*see* Newcastle); bapt. 16 Dec. 1593; cr. 16 Mar. 1665; d. 25 Dec. 1676
 2. **Henry Cavendish** (*see* Newcastle), only surv. s. & h.; b. 24 June 1630; d.s.p.m.s. 26 July 1691

ORFORD, *earldom*
 1. **Edward Russell**; b. 1652; cr. 7 May 1697; d.s.p. 26 Nov. 1727

ORMOND, *dukedom* (E)
 1. **James Butler,** duke of Ormond (Irish) and earl of Brecknock (cr. 20 July 1660); b. 19 Oct. 1610; cr. 9 Nov. 1682; d. 21 July 1688
 2. **James Butler,** gds. & h.; b. 29 Apr. 1665; forf. in England 20 Aug. 1715; d.s.p.m.s. 5–16 Nov. 1745

OXFORD, *earldom*
 1. **Aubrey de Vere** (or Ver), count of Guisnes; b. prob. *c.* 1110; cr. July 1141;[1] d. 26 Dec. 1194
 2. **Aubrey de Vere,** s. & h.; b. *c.* ? 1172; g. 26 Jan.–5 May 1204; d.s.p. leg. shortly bef. 1 Sept. 1214
 3. **Robert de Vere,** br. & h.; liv. 23 Oct. 1214; d. 19–25 Oct. 1221
 4. **Hugh de Vere,** s. & h.; b. *c.* 1210; hom. 23 Oct. 1231; inv. 22 May 1233; d. bef. 23 Dec. 1263
 5. **Robert de Vere,** s. & h.; b. *c.* 1240; hom. 5 Mar. 1264; forf. Aug.–Sept. 1265; rest. soon aft.; d. bef. 7 Sept. 1296
 6. **Robert de Vere,** 1st s. & h.; b. prob. *c.* 24 June 1257; hom. 5 Dec. 1296; d.s.p.s. 17 Apr. 1331
 7. **John de Vere,** neph. & h.; b. *c.* 12 Mar. 1312; liv. hom. 17 May 1331; d. 23–24 Jan. 1360
 8. **Thomas de Vere,** 1st surv. s. & h.; b. prob. 1336–37; hom. June 1360; d. 12–18 Sept. 1371
 9. **Robert de Vere** (*see* Dublin), only s. & h.; b. 16 Jan. 1362; st. 10 July 1381;[2] forf. 3 Feb. 1388; d.s.p. 22 Nov. 1392
10. **Aubrey de Vere,** uncle & h.; b. *c.* 1338–40; rest. Jan.–Feb. 1393; d. 23 Apr. 1400
11. **Richard de Vere,** 1st s. & h.; b. prob. 1385; liv. 21 Dec. 1406; d. 15 Feb. 1417
12. **John de Vere,** 1st s. & h.; b. 23 Apr. 1408; liv. 4 July 1429;[3] exec. 26 Feb. 1462
13. **John de Vere,** 1st surv. s. & h.; b. 8 Sept. 1442; lic. of entry 18 Jan. 1464; forf. early in 1475; rest. Oct. 1485; d.s.p.s. 10 Mar. 1513
14. **John de Vere,** neph. & h.; b. 14 Aug. 1499; d.s.p. 14 July 1526
15. **John de Vere,** 2nd cous. & h. male; b. ? *c.* 1482; d. 21 Mar. 1540

---

[1] In July 1141, the Empress Matilda cr. him earl of Cambridge, unless it should be found that the K. of Scotland held this earldom together with the earldom of Huntingdon, in which case he was to have the choice of Oxfordshire, Berkshire, Wiltshire or Dorset. We next know of him in a charter of 1142–47, as earl of Oxford. He was probably recog. by Stephen 1152–53 and by Henry II in 2–10 Jan. 1156.

[2] In a royal commission (*Cal. Patent Rolls, 1381–85*, 73). He was said to be 'almost of full age' on 4 July 1380 (*Cal. Close Rolls, 1377–81*, 402).

[3] 5 Feb. 1427, he is called 'John, earl of Oxford, a minor in ward of the king' (*Cal. Close Rolls, 1422–29*, 293).

16. **John de Vere,** 1st s. & h.; b. *c.* 1516; d. 3 Aug. 1562
17. **Edward de Vere,** only s. & h.; b. 12 Apr. 1550; d. 24 June 1604
18. **Henry de Vere,** only surv. s. & h.; b. 24 Feb. 1593; d.s.p. 2–9 June 1625
19. **Robert de Vere,** cous. & h. male; b. aft. 23 Aug. 1575; recog. 5 Apr. 1626; d. 7 Aug. 1632
20. **Aubrey de Vere,** 1st s. & h.; b. 28 Feb. 1627; d.s.p.m.s. 12 Mar. 1703

OXFORD and MORTIMER, *earldom*
 1. **Robert Harley;** b. 5 Dec. 1661; cr. 23 May 1711; d. 21 May 1724

PEMBROKE, *earldom*
 1. **Gilbert Fitz Gilbert** or de Clare; b. prob. *c.* 1100; cr. 1138; d. prob. 6 Jan. 1148 (or 1149)
 2. **Richard Fitz Gilbert,** s. & h.; b. prob. *c.* 1130; st. 7 Nov. 1153; d. prob. 20 Apr. 1176
 3. [Gilbert de Strigoil, only s. & h.; b. 1173; d.s.p. in or soon aft. 1185; being a minor at his death was never st. earl]
 4. Isabel, da. & h.; b. 1171–76; d. 1220
    m. Aug. 1189 **William Marshal,** b. prob. 1146; g. 27 May 1199;[1] d. 14 May 1219
 5. **William Marshal,** 1st s. & h.; b. *c.* 1190; succ. prob. May 1219; st. 21 Oct. 1219; d.s.p. 6 Apr. 1231
 6. **Richard Marshal,** br. & h.; b. aft. 1190; liv. hom. on or bef. 8 Aug. 1231; st. 11 Aug. 1231; d.s.p. 16 Apr. 1234
 7. **Gilbert Marshal,** br. & h.; inv. 11 June 1234; d.s.p. leg. 27 June 1241
 8. **Walter Marshal,** br. & h.; b. aft. 1198; inv. 27 Oct. 1241; d.s.p. 24 Nov. 1245
 9. [Anselm Marshal, br. & h.; d.s.p. 22–24 Dec. 1245; (never inv. with the earldom)]
10. Joan, niece of 5–9; d. bef. 20 Sept. 1307 (usually st. countess of Pembroke)
    m. on or bef. 13 Aug. 1247 **William of Valence,** half-br. of Henry III; b. aft. 1225; d. bef. 18 May 1296
11. **Aymer of Valence,** only surv. s. & h.; b. prob. *c.* 1270; st. 6 Nov. 1307; d.s.p. 23 June 1324
12. **Laurence Hastings,** only neph. of 11; b. 20 Mar. 1320; recog. 13 Oct. 1339; d. 28–31 Aug. 1348
13. **John Hastings,** only s. & h.; b. 29 Aug. 1347; liv. and hom. 12 Sept. 1368; d. 16 Apr. 1375
14. **John Hastings,** only s. & h.; b. 11 Nov. 1372; d.s.p. 30 or 31 Dec. 1389
15. **Humphrey** (*see* Gloucester), yst. s. of K. Henry IV; b. prob. Aug.–Sept. 1390; cr. 16 May 1414; d.s.p. leg. 23 Feb. 1447
16. **William de la Pole** (*see* Suffolk); b. 16 Oct. 1396; succ. 23 Feb. 1447 (under the terms of a reversionary grant of 27 Feb. 1443 in favour of him and his w.); d. 2 May 1450 and the earldom seems to have lapsed
17. **Jasper Tudor** (*see* Bedford), half-br. of K. Henry VI; b. *c.* 1431; cr. prob. 23 Nov. 1452 (bef. 30 Jan. 1453); forf. Nov. 1461; st. again during the Lancastrian restoration Oct. 1470–May 1471; in exile in France May 1471–Aug. 1485; formally rest. 12 Dec. 1485; d.s.p. leg. 21 Dec. 1495
18. **William Herbert,** Lord Herbert; b. *c.* 1423; cr. 8 Sept. 1468; exec. 27 July 1469
19. **William Herbert** (*see* Huntingdon), only leg. s. & h.; b. *c.* 1455; res. on or bef. 4 July 1479; d.s.p.m. 16 July 1491
20. **Edward Plantagenet;** b. 2–3 Nov. 1470; cr. 8 July 1479. Became K. 9 Apr. 1483

    Marquessate
21. **Anne Boleyn;** b. prob. *c.* 1501; cr. 1 Sept. 1532; m. K. Henry VIII ? 25 Jan. 1533; exec. 19 May 1536 and forf.

    Earldom
22. **William Herbert,** gds. of 18; b. *c.* 1506; cr. 11 Oct. 1551; d. 17 Mar. 1570
23. **Henry Herbert,** s. & h.; b. prob. aft. 1538; d. 19 Jan. 1601
24. **William Herbert,** s. & h.; b. 8 Apr. 1580; d.s.p.s. 10 Apr. 1630
25. **Philip Herbert** (*see* Montgomery), only br. & h.; b. 10 Oct. 1584; d. 23 Jan. 1650

[1] Styled earl in 5 royal charters of Sept. and Oct. 1197, but otherwise not till aft. he was girt.

26. **Philip Herbert** (*see* Montgomery), 1st surv. s. & h.; bapt. 21 Feb. 1621; d. 11 Dec. 1669
27. **William Herbert** (*see* Montgomery), 1st s. & h.; b. 1640; d. unm. 8 July 1674
28. **Philip Herbert** (*see* Montgomery), half-br. & h.; bapt. 5 Jan. 1653; d.s.p.m. 29 Aug. 1683
29. **Thomas Herbert** (*see* Montgomery), br. & h. male; b. *c.* 1656; d. 22 Jan. 1733

PETERBOROUGH, *earldom*
1. **John Mordaunt,** Lord Mordaunt; bapt. 18 Jan. 1599; cr. 9 Mar. 1628; d. 19 June 1643
2. **Henry Mordaunt,** 1st s. & h.; bapt. 18 Oct. 1623; d.s.p.m. 19 June 1697
3. **Charles Mordaunt** (*see* Monmouth), neph. & h. male; b. *c.* 1658; d. 25 Oct. 1735

PLYMOUTH, *earldom*
1. **Charles FitzCharles,** illeg. s. of Charles II; b. 1657; cr. 29 July 1675; d.s.p. 17 Oct. 1680
2. **Thomas Windsor Windsor,** Lord Windsor; b. *c.* 1627; cr. 6 Dec. 1682; d. 3 Nov. 1687
3. **Other Windsor,** gds. & h.; b. 27 Aug. 1679; d. 26 Dec. 1725

PORTLAND, *earldom*
1. **Richard Weston,** Lord Weston of Neyland; bapt. 1 Mar. 1577; cr. 17 Feb. 1633; d. 13 Mar. 1635
2. **Jerome Weston,** 1st surv. s. & h.; b. 16 Dec. 1605; d. 17 Mar. 1663
3. **Charles Weston,** only s. & h.; bapt. 19 May 1639; d. unm. 3 June 1665
4. **Thomas Weston,** uncle & h. male; bapt. 9 Oct. 1609; d.s.p. May 1688
5. **Hans Willem Bentinck,** lord of Drummelin; b. 20 July 1649; cr. 9 Apr. 1689; d. 23 Nov. 1709
6. **William Henry Bentinck,** later (1716) duke of Portland, 1st surv. s. & h.; b. 1682; d. 4 July 1726

PORTSMOUTH, *dukedom*
1. Louise Renée de Penancoët de Kérouaille (*see* Fareham); b. Sept. 1649; cr. 19 Aug. 1673; d. 14 Nov. 1734

POULETT, *earldom*
1. **John Poulett,** Lord Poulett of Hinton St. George; b. *c.* 1668; cr. 24 Dec. 1706; d. 28 May 1743

POWIS, *earldom and marquessate*
1. **William Herbert,** Lord Powis; b. *c.* 1626
   earldom; cr. 4 Apr. 1674
   marquessate; cr. 24 Mar. 1687; d. 2 July 1696
2. **William Herbert,** 1st s. & h.; b. *c.* 1665; d. 22 Oct. 1745

RADNOR, *earldom*
1. **John Robartes,** Lord Robartes of Truro; b. 1606; cr. 23 July 1679; d. 17 July 1685
2. **Charles Bodvile Robartes,** gds. & h.; b. 26 July 1660; d.s.p. 3 Aug. 1723

RICHMOND, *earldom*
1. **Alan,** count of Brittany (*see* Cornwall); b. bef. 1100; st. 1136; d. 15 Sept. 1146
2. **Conan,** later (1156) duke of Brittany, s. & h.; b. prob. aft. 1134–35; st. prob. 1155; d.s.p.m. 20 Feb. 1171
3. **Constance,** duchess of Brittany, da. & h.; b. aft. 1160; d. 3–4 Sept. 1201
   m. 1. 1181 **Geoffrey,** 3rd s. of K. Henry II; b. 23 Sept. 1158; st. soon aft. 6 Sept. 1181; d. 19 Aug. 1186
   2. 1187 **Ranulf,** earl of Chester (*q.v.*). Marriage ended in 1199 when Constance deserted him and married her 3rd husband.
   3. 1199 Guy de Thouars (never st. earl of Richmond); d. in or aft. 1213
4. **Arthur,** s. & h. by 1st husband; b. 29 Mar. 1187; st. 18 Apr. 1199; d. unm. prob. *c.* 3 Apr. 1203
[Eleanor, sis. & h.; st. 27 May 1208 (*Rot. Pat.*, 91 b.); d. unm. 1241]

478

5. Alice, elder da. of 3 by 3rd husband; b. *c.* 1200; d. 1221
   m. **Peter** [Mauclerc] de Braine (or Dreux); b. 1187–90; st. 1215, gr. seisin 16 Jan. 1219; depr. Nov. 1224 but soon restored; depr. again Apr. 1227 and rest. Oct. 1229; forf. Jan. 1235; res. Nov. 1237 on abdicating Brittany to his son (no. 6 below); d. May or June 1250
   [Peter of Savoy, count of Savoy 1263–68; b. ? 1203. Granted the honour of Richmond (greater part) 20 Apr. 1240 or 6 May 1241; never cr. earl; d.s.p.m. prob. 14–15 May 1268]
6. **John de Bretagne,** duke of Brittany, s. & h. of 5; b. 1217; succ. to Brittany 16 Nov. 1237; recog. 15 July 1268; res. immediately in favour of 7; d. 8 Oct. 1286
7. **John de Bretagne,** duke of Brittany, 1st s. & h.; b. 3 Jan. 1239; st. 28 Jan. 1269; d. 16–17 Nov. 1305. On his death Edw. I claimed that the earldom had come into his hands.
8. **John de Bretagne,** 2nd s.; b. ? 1266; cr. 15 Oct. 1306; d. unm. 17 Jan. 1334
9. **John de Bretagne,** duke of Brittany, neph. & h.; b. 7 Mar. 1286; hom. 8 May 1334; d.s.p. leg. 30 Apr. 1341
10. **John de Montfort,** duke of Brittany, half-br. & h. male; b. 1293; granted the honour of Richmond but no evidence that cr. earl; liv. 24 Sept. 1341; d. 26 Sept. 1345
11. **John of Gaunt** (*see* Derby), 4th s. of Edw. III; b. Mar. 1340; cr. 20 Sept. 1342; surr. 25 June 1372; d. 3–4 Feb. 1399
12. **John de Montfort,** duke of Brittany, only s. & h. of 10; b. prob. Nov.–Dec. 1339; rest. to earldom 20 July 1372; forf. Nov. 1384; rest. May 1398;[1] d. 1 or 2 Nov. 1399. At his death the earldom was apparently seized by the crown
   [Between 1399 and 1425 the castle, honour and lordship of Richmond was held by Ralph Nevill, earl of Westmorland, but he was never granted the title of earl]
13. **John** (*see* Bedford), 3rd s. of K. Henry IV; b. 20 June 1389; cr. 24 Nov. 1414; d.s.p.s. leg. 14 Sept. 1435
14. **Edmund Tudor,** half-br. of K. Henry VI; b. *c.* 1430; cr. 23 Nov. 1452; d. 3 Nov. 1456
15. **Henry Tudor,** only s. & h., later K.; b. 28 Jan. 1457; depr. bef. 12 Aug. 1462; att. 25 Jan. 1484. Became K. 22 Aug. 1485

Dukedom
16. **Henry fitz Roy** (*see* Nottingham), illeg. s. of K. Henry VIII; b. ? 1519; cr. 18 June 1525; d.s.p. 22 July 1536

Earldom and dukedom
17. **Ludovic Stuart** (*see* Lennox, etc.); b. 29 Sept. 1574
   earldom; cr. 6 Oct. 1613;
   dukedom; cr. 17 May 1623; d. s.p.s. leg. 16 Feb. 1624

Dukedom only
18. **James Stuart** (*see* Lennox, etc.); b. 6 Apr. 1612; cr. 8 Aug. 1641; d. 30 Mar. 1655
19. **Esmé Stuart** (*see* Lennox), 1st surv. s. & h.; b. 2 Nov. 1649; d. unm. 10 Aug. 1660
20. **Charles Stuart** (*see* Lennox, etc., Lichfield), cous. & h. male; b. ? 7 Mar. 1639; d.s.p.s. 12 Dec. 1672
21. **Charles Lennox** (*see* Darnley, Lennox, March), illeg. s. of Charles II; b. 29 July 1672; cr. 9 Sept. 1675; d. 27 May 1723

RIVERS, *earldom*
1. **Richard Woodville,** lord de Ryvers (de Ripariis); cr. 24 May 1466; exec. 12 Aug. 1469
2. **Anthony Woodville,** Lord Scales, s. & h.; b. *c.* 1440; exec. 23 June 1483 (d.s.p.)
3. **Richard Woodville,** br. & h.; forf. 1483; rest. 1485; d.s.p. 6 Mar. 1491
4. **Thomas Darcy,** Viscount Colchester; cr. 4 Nov. 1626; d.s.p.m.s. 25 Feb. 1640
5. Elizabeth, Viscountess Savage, 1st da. & coh.; b. 1581; cr. 21 Apr. 1641; d. 9 Mar. 1651

[1] Among the numerous references to him in the Close Rolls (1384–98), where he is called duke of Brittany, there is one (23 June 1393) where he is styled earl of Richmond; this may point to a second restoration and a second forfeiture.

6. **John Savage,** s. & h. of **5** & h. to earldom; b. *c.* 1603; succ. 25 Feb. 1640; d. 10 Oct. 1654
7. **Thomas Savage,** s. & h.; b. *c.* 1628; d. 14 Feb. 1694
8. **Richard Savage,** only surv. s. & h.; b. *c.* 1654; d.s.p.m.s. 18 Aug. 1712
9. **John Savage,** cous. & h. male; b. 29 Apr. 1665; d. unm. shortly bef. 9 May 1737

ROCHESTER, *earldom*
1. **Henry Wilmot,** Viscount Wilmot; bapt. 26 Oct. 1613; cr. 13 Dec. 1652; d. 19 Feb. 1658
2. **John Wilmot,** 1st surv. s. & h.; b. 10 Apr. 1647; d. 26 July 1680
3. **Charles Wilmot,** only s. & h.; bapt. 2 Jan. 1671; d. 12 Nov. 1681
4. **Laurence Hyde,** Viscount Hyde; bapt. 15 Mar. 1642; cr. 29 Nov. 1682; d. 2 May 1711
5. **Henry Hyde,** s. & h.; b. 1672; d.s.p.m.s. 10 Dec. 1753

ROCHFORD, *earldom*
1. **William Henry van Nassau van Zuylestein**; bapt. 7 Oct. 1649; cr. 10 May 1695; d. 2 July 1708
2. **William Nassau de Zuylestein,** s. & h.; b. 1681; d. unm. 27 July 1710
3. **Frederick Nassau de Zuylestein,** br. & h.; b. 1683; d. 14 June 1738

ROMNEY, *earldom*
1. **Henry Sydney** or **Sidney,** Viscount Sydney; b. spring 1641; cr. 14 May 1694; d. unm. 8 Apr. 1704

RUTLAND, *earldom*
1. **Edward 'of York'** or 'of Norwich' (*see* Aumale); b. *c.* 1373; cr. 25 Feb. 1390; d.s.p. 25 Oct. 1415
   [**Edmund Plantagenet,** 2nd s. of Richard, duke of York; b. 17 May 1443; st. 29 Jan. 1446[1] without a regular creation; att. Nov. 1459; att. nullified Oct. 1460; d. unm. 30 Dec. 1460]
2. **Thomas Manners,** Lord Ros; b. bef. 1492; cr. 18 June 1525; d. 20 Sept. 1543
3. **Henry Manners,** s. & h.; b. 23 Sept. 1526; d. 17 Sept. 1563
4. **Edward Manners,** s. & h.; b. 12 July 1549; d.s.p.m. 14 Apr. 1587
5. **John Manners,** br. & h. male; b. bef. 1552; d. 24 Feb. 1588
6. **Roger Manners,** s. & h.; b. 6 Oct. 1576; d.s.p. 26 June 1612
7. **Francis Manners,** br. & h.; b. 1578; d.s.p.m. 17 Dec. 1632
8. **George Manners,** br. & h. male; b. *c.* 1580; d.s.p. 29 Mar. 1641
9. **John Manners,** 2nd cous. & h. male; b. 10 June 1604; d. 29 Sept. 1679

   Earldom and dukedom
10. **John Manners** (*see* Granby), only surv. s. & h.; b. 29 May 1638
    dukedom; cr. 29 Mar. 1703; d. 10 Jan. 1711
11. **John Manners** (*see* Granby), 1st surv. s. & h.; b. 18 Sept. 1676; d. 22 Feb. 1721

SAINT ALBANS, *earldom*
1. **Richard Bourke** or **De Burgh** (*see* Clanricarde); b. *c.* 1572; cr. 23 Aug. 1628; d. 12 Nov. 1635
2. **Ulick Bourke** or **De Burgh** (*see* Clanricarde), only s. & h.; b. bef. 8 Dec. 1604; d.s.p.m. July 1657
3. **Henry Jermyn,** Baron Jermyn of St. Edmundsbury; b. *c.* 1604; cr. 27 Apr. 1660; d. unm. 2 Jan. 1684

   Dukedom
4. **Charles Beauclerk** (*see* Burford), illeg. s. of Charles II; b. 8 May 1670; cr. 10 Jan. 1684; d. 10 May 1726

SALISBURY,[2] *earldom*
[Hervey Brito, st. 1140]
1. **Patrick de Salisbury,** cr. June 1142–47 (prob. aft. July 1143); d. *c.* 7 Apr. 1168
2. **William fitz Patrick,** s. & h.; d. 1196

---

[1] Bibl. Nat., MS. Fr. nouv. acq. 3624 (367).
[2] Until the creation of a separate earldom of Wiltshire (1397) the earls of Salisbury are sometimes known as earls of Wiltshire.

3. Ela or Isabel, only da. & h.; b. Jan.–July 1188; res. 25 Dec. 1238; d. 24 Aug. 1261
   m. ? 1196 **William Longespée,** illeg. s. of K. Henry II; received 3rd penny of
   Wiltshire 1196–97; st. 8 Sept. 1197; d. 7 Mar. 1226
   [Sir William Longespée, s. & h. of 3, was sometimes called earl between 1238
   and 1242, when his claim was finally disallowed in court. He d. 7 Feb. 1250.
   None of his descendants are known to have assumed the title in their lifetime]
4. **William de Montague;** b. shortly bef. 21 Feb. 1302; cr. 16 Mar. 1337; d. 30 Jan.
   1344
5. **William de Montague,** s. & h.; b. 19 June 1328; liv. & hom. 11 July 1349;
   d.s.p.s. 3 June 1397
6. **John de Montague,** neph. & h.; b. c. 1350; st. 18 July 1397; exec. 7–8 Jan. 1400
   & forf.
7. **Thomas Montague,** 1st s. & h.; b. bef. 14 June 1388; st. 26 Oct. 1409 (summ. to
   Parliament at this date as earl of Salisbury though not restored to his father's
   other dignities until May 1421. There is evidence that he was using the title
   as early as 1401); d.s.p.m. 3 Nov. 1428
8. Alice, only da. & h.; b. c. 1406; d. 3 Apr.–9 Dec. 1462. m. in or bef. Feb. 1421
   Sir Richard Nevill; b. 1400 ?; recog. 1429; forf. 20 Nov. 1459; rest. 10 Oct.
   1460; d. 30 Dec. 1460
9. **Richard Nevill** (see Warwick), 1st s. & h.; b. 22 Nov. 1428; procl. traitor
   31 Mar. 1470; returned from exile 13 Sept. 1470; d.s.p.m. 14 Apr. 1471
10. **George Plantagenet** (see Clarence); b. 21 Oct. 1449; cr. 25 Mar. 1472; forf.
    8 Feb. 1478; exec. 18 Feb. 1478.
    m. 11 July 1469, Isabel, 1st da. & coh. of 9
    [Edward Plantagenet, only surv. s. & h. never called earl of Salisbury in his
    lifetime]
11. **Edward Plantagenet,** s. of Richard, duke of Gloucester, and Anne, 2nd da. &
    coh. of 9 (see Chester); b. 1473; cr. 15 Feb. 1478; d. 9 Apr. 1484
12. Lady Margaret Pole, only surv. d. & h. of **10;** b. Aug. 1473; rest. 1513–14; forf.
    12 May 1539; exec. 28 May 1541
13. **Robert Cecil,** Viscount Cranborne; b. 1 June 1563; cr. 4 May 1605; d. 24 May
    1612
14. **William Cecil,** only s. & h.; b. 28 Mar. 1591; d. 3 Dec. 1668
15. **James Cecil,** gds. & h.; bef. 27 Mar. 1646; d. May 1683
16. **James Cecil,** s. & h.; bapt. 25 Sept. 1666; d. 24 Oct. 1694
17. **James Cecil,** only s. & h.; b. 8 June 1691; d. 9 Oct. 1728

SANDWICH, *earldom*
1. **Sir Edward Montagu** or **Mountagu;** b. 27 July 1625; cr. 12 July 1660; d. 28 May
   1672
2. **Edward Montagu,** 1st s. & h.; b. 3 Jan. 1648; d. shortly bef. 29 Nov. 1688
3. **Edward Montagu,** 1st s. & h.; b. 10 Apr. 1670; d. 20 Oct. 1729

SCARBOROUGH, *earldom*
1. **Richard Lumley,** Viscount Lumley; b. c. 1650; cr. 15 Apr. 1690; d. 17 Dec.
   1721

SCARSDALE, *earldom*
1. **Francis Leke** or **Leake,** Lord Deincourt of Sutton; b. bef. 1581; cr. 11 Nov.
   1645; d. 9 Apr. 1655
2. **Nicholas Leke,** 1st surv. s. & h.; bapt. 1 Oct. 1612; d. 27 Jan. 1681
3. **Robert Leke,** 1st s. & h.; b. 9 Mar. 1654; d.s.p.s. 27 Dec. 1707
4. **Nicholas Leke,** neph. & h.; b. c. 1682; d. unm. 17 July 1736

SCHOMBERG, *dukedom*
1. **Frederick Herman von Schönberg** or **de Schomberg,** count of Mertola (*see*
   Brentford, Harwich); b. 6 Dec. 1615; cr. 9 May 1689; d. 1 July 1690
2. **Charles Schomberg** (*see* Brentford, Harwich), 3rd surv. s. & h. to dukedom; b.
   5 Aug. 1645; d. unm. 16 Oct. 1693
3. **Meinhard Schomberg** (*see* Bangor, Brentford, Harwich, Leinster), next elder
   surv. br.; b. 30 June 1641; d.s.p.m.s. 5 July 1719

SHAFTESBURY, *earldom*
1. **Anthony Ashley Cooper,** Lord Ashley of Wimborne St Giles; b. 22 July 1621;
   cr. 23 Apr. 1672; d. 21 Jan. 1683
2. **Anthony Ashley Cooper,** s. and h.; b. 16 Jan. 1652; d. 2 Nov. 1699
3. **Anthony Ashley Cooper,** s. and h.; b. 26 Feb. 1671; d. 4–15 Feb. 1713
4. **Anthony Ashley Cooper,** s. and h.; b. 9 Feb. 1711; d. 27 May 1771

SHEPPEY, *earldom*
1. Elizabeth Walter, Lady Dacre; b. *c.* 1625; cr. 6 Sept. 1680; d. 7–19 July 1686

SHREWSBURY, *earldom*
1. **Roger de Montgomery** (*see* Arundel); cr. 1–4 Dec. 1074; d. 27 July 1094[1]
2. **Hugh de Montgomery** (*see* Arundel), 2nd surv. s. & h. to English possessions; b. prob. 1053–59; st. 1094; d. unm. *c.* 31 July 1098
3. **Robert de Bellême** (*see* Arundel), elder br. & h.; b. prob. 1052–56; depr. 1102; d. 8 May 1113 or later
4. **John Talbot,**[2] Lord Furnival and Talbot; b. *c.* 1384; cr. 20 May 1442; d. 17 July 1453
5. **John Talbot,** s. & h.; b. *c.* 1413; d. 10 July 1460
6. **John Talbot,** s. & h.; b. 12 Dec. 1448; d. 28 June 1473
7. **George Talbot,** s. & h. b. 1468; d. 26 July 1538
8. **Francis Talbot,** 1st surv. s. & h.; b. 1500; d. 28 Sept. 1560
9. **George Talbot,** s. & h.; b. *c.* 1552; d. 18 Nov. 1590
10. **Gilbert Talbot,** 1st surv. s. & h.; b. 20 Nov. 1552; d.s.p.m.s. 8 May 1616
11. **Edward Talbot,** br. & h. male; bapt. 25 Feb. 1561; d.s.p.s. 8 Feb. 1618
12. **George Talbot,** cous. & h. male; b. 19 Dec. 1566; d. unm. 2 Apr. 1630
13. **John Talbot,** neph. & h.; b. before 1601; d. 8 Feb. 1654
14. **Francis Talbot,** 1st surv. s. & h.; b. *c.* 1623; d. 16 Mar. 1668

Earldom and dukedom
15. **Charles Talbot** (*see* Alton), 1st surv. s. & h.; b. 24 July 1660
dukedom; cr. 30 Apr. 1694; d.s.p. 1 Feb. 1718

SOMERSET, *earldom*
1. **William de Mohun;** cr.[3] 8 Apr.–24 June, 1141; d. prob. in or bef. 1155

Earldom and marquessate
2. **John Beaufort** (*see* Dorset), s. of John of Gaunt; b. *c.* 1371
earldom; cr. 10 Feb. 1397;
marquessate; cr. 29 Sept. 1397; depr. 3 Nov. 1399;[4] d. 16 Mar. 1410

Earldom
3. **Henry Beaufort,** 1st s. & h.; bapt. 26 Nov. 1401; d. unm. 25 Nov. 1418

Earldom and dukedom
4. **John Beaufort** (*see* Kendal), next br. & h.; b. *c.* Apr. 1404; liv. 24 Sept. 1425
dukedom; cr. 28 Aug. 1443; d.s.p.m. 27 May 1444

Earldom and dukedom
5. **Edmund Beaufort** (*see* Dorset), br. & h. male; b. *c.* 1406
earldom; succ. 27 May 1444
dukedom; cr. 31 Mar. 1448; d. 22 May 1455
6. **Henry Beaufort** (*see* Dorset), 1st s. & h.; b. *c.* Apr. 1436; att. 4 Nov. 1461; rest. 1463; rest. nullified 29 Apr. 1464; exec. 15 May 1464
[Edmund Beaufort, next br. & h.; b. *c.* 1439; appears to have st. himself duke after his br.'s death; d. 6 May 1471]

Dukedom
7. **Edmund Tudor,** 3rd s. of K. Henry VII; b. 21 or 22 Feb. 1499; d. 19 June 1500
[He may have been st. duke, but prob. d. bef. formal creation]
8. **Henry Fitzroy** (*see* Nottingham); illeg. s. of K. Henry VIII; b. 1519?; cr. 18 June 1525; d.s.p. 22 July 1536
9. **Edward Seymour** (*see* Hertford); b. *c.* 1506; cr. 16 Feb. 1547; exec. 22 Jan. 1552 and att. 12 Apr. 1552

Earldom
10. **Robert Ker** or Carr, Viscount Rochester; b. *c.* 1587; cr. 3 Nov. 1613; d.s.p.m. shortly bef. 17 July 1645

[1] He had become a monk, a few days bef. his death.
[2] 17 July 1446, he war cr. earl of Waterford (I). This earldom descended with that of Shrewsbury until it was considered to have been forfeited by the 'act of absentees' of 1536–37.
[3] This earldom, which was cr. by Matilda, does not appear to have been recog. by Stephen or Henry II, and none of the earl's descendants bore the title.
[4] Having been degraded from the marquessate, he continued to be considered as earl of Somerset.

Dukedom
11. **William Seymour** (*see* Hertford), gt.-gds. of 9; b. 1 Sept. 1587; rest. 13 Sept. 1660; d. 24 Oct. 1660
12. **William Seymour**, gds. & h.; b. 17 Apr. 1652; d. unm. 12 Dec. 1671
13. **John Seymour**, uncle & h. male; d.s.p. 29 Apr. 1675
14. **Francis Seymour**, cous. & h. male; b. 17 Jan. 1658; d. unm. 20 Apr. 1678
15. **Charles Seymour**, only surv. br. & h.; b. 13 Aug. 1662; d. 2 Dec. 1748

SOUTHAMPTON, *earldom*
1. **Sir William Fitzwilliam**; b. *c.* 1490; cr. 18 Oct. 1537; d.s.p. leg. 15 Oct. 1542
2. **Thomas Wriothesley**, Lord Wriothesley; b. 21 Dec. 1505; cr. 16 Feb. 1547; d. 30 July 1550
3. **Henry Wriothesley**, only surv. s. & h.; bapt. 24 Apr. 1545; d. 4 Oct. 1581
4. **Henry Wriothesley**, only s. & h.; b. 6 Oct. 1573; forf. 19 Feb. 1601; cr. again 21 July 1603; d. 10 Nov. 1624
5. **Thomas Wriothesley**, only surv. s. & h.; b. 10 Mar. 1608; d.s.p.m.s. 16 May 1667
6. Barbara Palmer (*see* Cleveland); cr. 3 Aug. 1670; d. 9 Oct. 1709

Dukedom and earldom
7. **Charles Palmer**, aft. Fitzroy (*see* Chichester, Cleveland); bapt. 18 June 1662
dukedom; cr. 10 Sept. 1675
earldom; succ. 9 Oct. 1709; d. 9 Sept. 1730

STAFFORD, *earldom*
1. **Ralph de Stafford**; b. 24 Sept. 1301; cr. 5 Mar. 1351; d. 31 Aug. 1372
2. **Hugh de Stafford**, 1st surv. s. & h.; b. in or bef. 1342; st. 6 Oct. 1372; d. 16 Oct. 1386
3. **Thomas de Stafford**, 1st surv. s. & h.; b. in or bef. 1368; liv. hom. 20 Oct. 1390; d.s.p. 4 July 1392
4. William de Stafford, br. & h.; b. 21 Sept. 1375. [never st. earl]; d. unm. 6 Apr. 1395
5. **Edmund de Stafford** (*see* Essex), br. & h. b. 2 Mar. 1378; d. 21 July 1403
6. **Humphrey Stafford** (*see* Buckingham), only s. & h.; b. 15 Aug. 1402; d. 10 July 1460
[Humphrey Stafford, s. & h.; st. in the lifetime of his father; d.v.p. in or aft. Dec. 1457, prob. between 29 Sept. and Nov. 1458]
7. **Henry Stafford** (*see* Buckingham), gds. & h.; b. uncertain; exec. 2 Nov. 1483 and forf.
8. **Edward Stafford** (*see* Buckingham), 1st s. & h.; b. 3 Feb. 1477; formally rest. Nov. 1485; exec. 17 May 1521 and forf.
[Henry Stafford, s. & h. b. 18 Sept. 1501; st. until his father's exec.]
9. Mary Howard, Lady Stafford; b. *c.* 1619; cr. 5 Oct. 1688; d. 13 Jan. 1694
10. **Henry Stafford-Howard**, 1st s. & h.; b. *c.* 1648; cr. 5 Oct. 1688; d.s.p. 27 Apr. 1719

STAMFORD, *earldom*
1. **Henry Grey**, Lord Grey of Groby; b. *c.* 1600; cr. 26 Mar. 1628; d. 21 Aug. 1673
2. **Thomas Grey**, gds. & h.; b. *c.* 1653; d.s.p.s. 31 Jan. 1720

STRAFFORD, *earldom*
1. **Thomas Wentworth**, Viscount Wentworth; b. 13 Apr. 1593; cr. 12 Jan. 1640; exec. 12 May 1641 & forf.
2. **William Wentworth**, only s. & h.; b. 8 June 1626; cr. 1 Dec. 1641; d.s.p. 16 Oct. 1695
3. **Thomas Wentworth**, Lord Raby, cous. of 2; bapt. 17 Sept. 1672; cr. 29 June 1711; d. 19 Sept. 1754

SUFFOLK, *earldom*
[Until the creation of a separate earldom of Suffolk, the earls of Norfolk are sometimes known as earls of Norfolk and Suffolk (*see under* Norfolk)]
1. **Robert de Ufford**; b. 9 Aug. 1298; cr. 16 Mar. 1337; d. 4 Nov. 1369
2. **William de Ufford**, s. & h.; b. *c.* 1330; d.s.p.s. 5 Feb. 1382
3. **Michael de la Pole**; b. *c.* 1330; cr. 6 Aug. 1385; forf. 13 Feb. 1388; d. 5 Sept. 1389

4. **Michael de la Pole**, s. & h.; b. in or bef. 1367; rest. 28 Jan. 1398; forf. 1399; rest. 15 Nov. 1399; d. 18 Sept. 1415
5. **Michael de la Pole**, s. & h.; b. 1394–95; d.s.p.m. 25 Oct. 1415

Earldom, marquessate and dukedom
6. **William de la Pole** (*see* Pembroke), br. & h. male; b. 16 Oct. 1396; liv. 9 May 1418
marquessate; cr. 14 Sept. 1444
dukedom; cr. 2 June 1448; d. 2 May 1450 and forf.

Dukedom
7. **John de la Pole**, s. & h.; b. 27 Sept. 1442; recog. 23 Mar. 1463; d. 29 Oct. 1491–27 Oct. 1492

Dukedom and earldom
8. **Edmund de la Pole**, 1st surv. s. & h.; b. 1471–72; surr. dukedom 26 Feb. 1493 and was known thereafter only as earl of Suffolk; forf. Jan. 1504; exec. 4 May 1513
[Richard de la Pole, yst. br. living in exile, st. himself duke of Suffolk, being so called as early as 1510, in his br.'s lifetime, though without official recognition. He d. unm. 24 Feb. 1525]

Dukedom
9. **Charles Brandon**, Viscount L'Isle; b. *c.* 1484; cr. 1 Feb. 1514; d. 22 Aug. 1545
10. **Henry Brandon**, 1st surv. s. & h.; b. 18 Sept. 1535; d. unm. 14 July 1551
11. **Charles Brandon**, only surv. br. & h.; b. 1537 or 1538; d. unm. same day as his brother
12. **Henry Grey** (*see* Dorset); b. 17 Jan. 1517; cr. 11 Oct. 1551; forf. 17 Feb. 1554; exec. 23 Feb. 1554

Earldom
13. **Thomas Howard**, Lord Howard of Walden; b. 24 (?) Aug. 1561; cr. 21 July 1603; d. 8 May 1626
14. **Theophilus Howard**, 1st s. & h.; bapt. 13 Aug. 1584; d. 3 June 1640
15. **James Howard**, 1st s. & h.; bapt. 10 Feb. 1620; d.s.p.m.s. 7 Jan. 1689
16. **George Howard**, next surv. br. & h. male; b. *c.* 1624; d.s.p.m. 21 Apr. 1691
17. **Henry Howard**, next br. & h. male; bapt. 18 July 1627; d. 10 Dec. 1709
18. **Henry Howard** (*see* Bindon), 1st s. & h.; b. 1670; d. 19 Sept. 1718

SUNDERLAND, *earldom*
1. **Emanuel Scrope**, Lord Scrope of Bolton; b. 1 Aug. 1584; cr. 19 June 1627; d.s.p. leg. 30 May 1630
2. **Henry Spencer**, Lord Spencer of Wormleighton; bapt. 23 Nov. 1620; cr. 6 June 1643; d. 20 Sept. 1643
3. **Robert Spencer**, s. & h.; b. 1641; d. 28 Sept. 1702
4. **Charles Spencer**, only surv. s. & h.; b. *c.* 1674; d. 19 Apr. 1722

SURREY, *earldom*
1. **William de Warenne**; cr. shortly aft. 16 Apr. 1088; d. 24 June 1088
2. **William de Warenne**, 1st s. & h.; depr. aft. 3 Sept. 1101; rest. 1103; d. prob. 11 May 1138
3. **William de Warenne**, 1st s. & h.; b. prob. 1119; d.s.p.m. 19 Jan. 1148
4. Isabel de Warenne, only da. & h.; d. ? 13 July 1203.
    m. 1. 1148 **William**, count of Boulogne and Mortain, yr. s. of K. Stephen; b. 1132–37; d.s.p. Oct. 1159
       2. prob. Apr. 1164, **Hamelin**, illeg. br. of K. Henry II; d. 7 May 1202
5. **William de Warenne**, s. & h. by 2nd husband; liv. 12 May 1202; d. 27 May 1240
6. **John de Warenne**, only s. & h.; b. in or aft. Aug. 1231; d. *c.* 29 Sept. 1304
7. **John de Warenne** (*see* Stratherne), gds. & h.; b. 30 June 1286; liv. 7 Apr. 1306; hom. aft. July 1307; d.s.p. leg. 29 June 1347
8. **Richard Fitz Alan** (*see* Arundel), neph. & h.; b. *c.* 1313; st. 31 Aug. 1361;[1] d. 24 Jan. 1376
9. **Richard Fitz Alan** (*see* Arundel), s. & h.; b. 1346; exec. 21 Sept. 1397 and forf.

---

[1] He assumed the title of earl on the death of his aunt, Joan, the dowager countess, at this date.

Dukedom
10. **Thomas de Holand** (*see* Kent); b. in or bef. 1371; cr. 29 Sept. 1397; forf. 3 Nov. 1399; d.s.p.m. 7 or 8 Jan. 1400

Earldom
11. **Thomas Fitz Alan** (*see* Arundel); only surv. s. & h. of 9; b. 13 Oct. 1381; rest. Oct. 1400; d.s.p. 13 Oct. 1415
12. **John de Mowbray** (*see* Norfolk); b. 18 Oct. 1444; cr. earl of Surrey and Warenne 24 Mar. 1451; d.s.p.m. 16–17 Jan. 1476
13. **Richard Plantagenet** (*see* Norfolk), yr. s. of K. Edward IV; b. prob. 17 Aug. 1473; cr. earl of Surrey and Warenne 7 Feb. 1477; d. prob. July–Sept. 1483
14. **Thomas Howard** (*see* Norfolk); b. 1443; cr. 28 June 1483; depr. 22 Aug. and formally forf. 7 Nov. 1485; rest. 1489; res. 1 Feb. 1514; d. 21 May 1524
15. **Thomas Howard** (*see* Norfolk), s. & h.; b. 1473; succ. 1 Feb. 1514; forf. 27 Jan. 1547; rest. 3 Aug. 1553; d. 25 Aug. 1554
    [Henry Howard, s. & h.; b. 1516–18; st. since 1524 earl of Surrey; att. 13 Jan. and exec. 21 Jan. 1547]
16. **Thomas Howard** (*see* Norfolk), gds. & h. of 15; b. 10 Mar. 1538; st. since the restoration of his gd.-father in 1553; succ. 25 Aug. 1554; forf. 16 Jan. and exec. 2 June 1572
    [Philip Howard (*see* Arundel), s. & h.; b. 28 June 1557; st. earl of Surrey until his father's attainder on 16 Jan. 1572; d. 19 Oct. 1595]
17. **Thomas Howard** (*see* Arundel, Norfolk), s. & h. of Philip above; b. 7 July 1585; rest. 18 Apr. 1604; d. 14/24 Sept. 1646
    [This earldom henceforth descends with that of Arundel]

SUSSEX, *earldom*
    [Until 1243 the titles of the earl of Arundel, Chichester and Sussex were used indifferently; for these earls *see under* Arundel.
    Aft. 1282 John de Warenne, earl of Surrey, is st. in several writs, earl of Surrey and Sussex, but he did not have the third penny of Sussex. His gds. & h., John de Warenne (d. 1347), is the last to be officially so styled]

1. **Robert Radcliffe,** Viscount Fitz Walter; b. *c.* 1483; cr. 8 Dec. 1529; d. 27 Nov. 1542
2. **Henry Radcliffe,** s. & h.; b. *c.* 1507; d. 17 Feb. 1557
3. **Thomas Radcliffe,** 1st s. & h.; b. *c.* 1525; d.s.p.s. 9 June 1583
4. **Henry Radcliffe,** br. & h.; b. *c.* 1532; d. 14 Dec. 1593
5. **Robert Radcliffe,** only s. & h.; b. 12 June 1573; d.s.p. leg. s. 22 Sept. 1629
6. **Edward Radcliffe,** cous. & h. male; b. bef. 10 Nov. 1559; d.s.p. July 1643
7. **Thomas Savile,** Viscount Savile; bapt. 14 Sept. 1590; cr. 25 May 1644; d. 8 Nov. 1657–8 Oct. 1659
8. **James Savile,** only s. & h.; b. 1647; d.s.p.s. 11 Oct. 1671
9. **Thomas Lennard,** Lord Dacre; b. 13 May 1654; cr. 5 Oct. 1674; d.s.p.m.s. 30 Oct. 1715

TANKERVILLE, *earldom*
1. **Ford Grey,** Lord Grey of Warke; bapt. 20 July 1655; cr. 11 July 1695; d.s.p.m. 24 June 1701

TAVISTOCK, *marquessate*; cr. 1694 with the dukedom of Bedford

THANET, *earldom*
1. **Nicholas Tufton,** Lord Tufton; bapt. 19 Jan. 1578; cr. 5 Aug. 1628; d. 1 July 1631
2. **John Tufton,** 1st surv. s. & h.; b. 15 Dec. 1608; d. 7 May 1664
3. **Nicholas Tufton,** 1st s. & h.; b. 7 Aug. 1631; d.s.p. 24 Nov. 1679
4. **John Tufton,** next br. & h.; b. 7 Aug. 1638; d. unm. 27 Apr. 1680
5. **Richard Tufton,** next br. & h.; b. 30 May 1640; d. unm. 8 Mar. 1684
6. **Thomas Tufton,** next br. & h.; b. 30 Aug. 1644; d.s.p.m.s. 30 July 1729

TINMOUTH, *earldom*; cr. 1687 with the dukedom of Berwick; forf. 1695

TORRINGTON, *earldom*
1. **George Monck** (*see* Albemarle); cr. 7 July 1660; d. 3 Jan. 1670
2. **Christopher Monck** (*see* Albemarle), s. & h.; d.s.p. 6 Oct. 1688
3. **Arthur Herbert**; b. 1647–49; cr. 29 May 1689; d.s.p. 14 Apr. 1716

TOTNESS, *earldom*
1. **George Carew,** Lord Carew of Clopton; b. 29 May 1555; cr. 5 Feb. 1626; d.s.p. (leg. ?) 27 Mar. 1629

WALES
The title 'prince of Wales' was conferred on Edward (eldest surv. s. of Edward I) together with the earldom of Chester, 7 Feb. 1301. The title lapsed when he succ. to the throne, 8 July 1307. It was again conferred, 12 May 1343, on Edward, the Black Prince, and since then has been regularly conferred with the earldom of Chester. A statute of 1398 inseparably linked the principality of Wales with the earldom of Chester.

WARENNE
The title 'earl Warenne' is used interchangeably with that of earl of Surrey. For these earls, *see under* the latter title (but *see* earls of Surrey, nos. 12 and 13)

WARRINGTON, *earldom*
1. **Henry Booth,** Lord Delamer of Dunham Massey; b. 13 Jan. 1652; cr. 17 Apr. 1690; d. 2 Jan. 1694
2. **George Booth,** s. & h.; b. 2 May 1675; d.s.p.m. 2 Aug. 1758

WARWICK, *earldom*
1. **Henry de Beaumont**; b. *c.* 1048; cr. prob. 1089; d. prob. 20 June 1119
2. **Roger,** 1st s. & h.; b. bef. 1102; st. 1123; d. 12 June 1153
3. **William,** 1st s. & h.; b. *c.* 1137; d.s.p. 15 Nov. 1184
4. **Waleran,** br. & h.; b. bef. 1153; d. poss. 24 Dec. 1203 and certainly bef. 13 Oct. 1204
5. **Henry,** 1st s. & h.; b. 1192; st. 1 June 1213 (granted 3rd penny); d. 10 Oct. 1229
6. **Thomas,** only s. & h.; b. 1213; liv. hom. 17 Oct. 1229; g. 22 May 1233; d.s.p. 26 June 1242
7. **Margaret,** sis. & h.; b. *c.* 1215; d.s.p. 3 June 1253
   m. 1. John Marshal; liv. 22 Aug. 1242;[1] d. Oct. 1242
   2. Bef. 14 Sept. 1243 **John du Plessis**; granted 3rd penny 26 Apr. 1245; st. 11 Aug. 1247;[2] d. 25 Feb. 1263
8. **William Mauduit,** 1st cous. & h. to Margaret (7); b. 1220; liv. hom. 4 Apr. 1263; d.s.p. 8 Jan. 1268
9. **William Beauchamp,** neph. & h.; b. *c.* 1240; hom. 9 Feb. 1268; d. 5 or 9 June 1298
10. **Guy Beauchamp,** 1st s. & h.; b. 1271–75; liv. hom. 5 Sept. 1298; d. 12 Aug. 1315
11. **Thomas Beauchamp,** 1st s. & h.; b. prob. 14 Feb. 1314; liv. hom. 20 Feb. 1329; d. 13 Nov. 1369
12. **Thomas Beauchamp,** 1st surv. s. & h.; b. bef. 16 Mar. 1339; liv. hom. 7 Feb. 1370; forf. 28 Sept. 1397; rest. 19 Nov. 1399; d. 8 Apr. 1401
13. **Richard Beauchamp** (*see* Aumale), only s. & h.; b. 25 or 28 Jan. 1382; liv. 13 Feb. 1403; d. 30 Apr. 1439

Earldom and dukedom
14. **Henry Beauchamp,** only s. & h.; b. 22 Mar. 1425 *dukedom*; cr. 5 Apr. 1445; d,s.p.m. 11 June 1446

Earldom
15. **Anne,** da. & h.; b. Feb. 1443; d. 3 Jan. 1449
16. **Richard Nevill** (*see* Salisbury); b. 22 Nov. 1428; recog. 23 July 1449; forf. Nov. 1459; rest. Oct. 1460; procl. traitor 31 Mar. 1470; returned from exile 13 Sept. 1470; d.s.p.m. 14 Apr. 1471.
    m. Anne, only sis. & h. of 14. She d. shortly bef. 8 Feb. 1493
17. **George Plantagenet** (*see* Clarence); b. 21 Oct. 1449; cr. 25 Mar. 1472; forf. 8 Feb. and exec. 18 Feb. 1478.
    m. Isabel, 1st da. & coh. of 16

[1] He was evidently never inv. with the earldom, for aft. his death he is called simply John Marshal and the k. was not sure if he had ever had seizin of Warwick castle (*Close Rolls, 1242–47*, 9, 9 Jan. 1243).
[2] Until 21 July 1247 he appears in the *Close Rolls* several times without the title of earl.

18. **Edward Plantagenet** (*see* Salisbury), 1st s. & h.; b. 21 or 25 Feb. 1475; st. since birth, exec. 24 Nov. 1499 and forf.
19. **John Dudley** (*see* Northumberland), gt.-gt.-gt.-gds. of 13; b. 1502; cr. 16 Feb. 1547; forf. 18 Aug. 1553; exec. 22 Aug. 1553
20. **John Dudley,** 1st surv. s. & h.; b. bef. 1528; st. earl of Warwick since Oct. 1551, in the lifetime of his father and summ. to parlt. under this title 5 Jan. 1553; d.s.p. 21 Oct. 1554
21. **Ambrose Dudley,** br. & h.; b. *c.* 1528; cr. 26 Dec. 1561; d.s.p.s. 21 Feb. 1590
22. **Robert Rich,** Lord Rich; b. Dec. 1559; cr. 6 Aug. 1618; d. 24 Mar. 1619
23. **Robert Rich,** s. & h.; b. May–June 1587; d. 19 Apr. 1658
24. **Robert Rich,** s. & h.; b. 28 June 1611; d.s.p.m.s. 30 May 1659
25. **Charles Rich,** br. & h. male; b. 1616; d.s.p.m.s. 24 Aug. 1673
26. **Robert Rich** (*see* Holland), cous. & h. male; b. *c.* 1620; d. shortly bef. 16 Apr. 1675
27. **Edward Rich,** s. & h.; b. 1673; d. 31 July 1701
28. **Edward Rich,** s. & h.; b. 20 Jan. 1698; d. unm. 16 Aug. 1721

WESTMORLAND, *earldom*
  1. **Ralph de Nevill**; b. *c.* 1354; cr. 29 Sept. 1397; d. 21 Oct. 1425
  2. **Ralph Nevill,** gds. & h.; b. *c.* Feb. 1408; liv. hom. 24 Feb. 1429; d.s.p.s. 3 Nov. 1484
  3. **Ralph Nevill,** neph. & h.; b. 1456; d. 6 Feb. 1499
  4. **Ralph Nevill,** gds. & h.; b. *c.* 1495; d. 24 Apr. 1549
  5. **Henry Nevill,** 1st s. & h.; b. 1524–25; d. 10 Feb. 1564
  6. **Charles Nevill,** only surv. s. & h.; b. 1542–43; forf. 1571; d.s.p.m. 16 Nov. 1601
  7. **Francis Fane**; b. Feb. 1580; cr. 29 Dec. 1624; d. 23 Mar. 1629
  8. **Mildmay Fane,** s. & h.; b. 24 Jan. 1602; d. 12 Feb. 1666
  9. **Charles Fane,** s. & h.; b. 6 Jan. 1635; d.s.p. 18 Sept. 1691
 10. **Vere Fane,** br. & h.; b. 13 Feb. 1645; d. 29 Dec. 1693
 11. **Vere Fane,** s. & h.; b. 25 May 1678; d. unm. 19 May 1699
 12. **Thomas Fane,** br. & h.; b. 3 Oct. 1683; d.s.p. 4 July 1736

WHARTON, *earldom*
  1. **Thomas Wharton,** 5th Lord Wharton; b. Aug. 1648; cr. 23 Dec. 1706 (later, 1715, cr. marquess of Wharton); d. 12 Apr. 1715

WILTSHIRE, *earldom*
   [Until the creation of the earldom of Wiltshire the earls of Salisbury are sometimes known by this title (*see under* Salisbury)]

  1. **William le Scrope**; b. *c.* 1350; cr. 29 Sept. 1397; exec. 30 July 1399 and forf.
  2. **James Butler** (*see* Ormond (I. and E.)); b. 24 Nov. 1420; cr. 8 July 1449; exec. *c.* 1 May 1461 and forf.
  3. **John Stafford**; b. bef. 1440; cr. 5 Jan. 1470; d. 8 May 1473
  4. **Edward Stafford,** only s. & h.; b. 7 Apr. 1469; d.s.p. 24 Mar. 1499
  5. **Henry Stafford,** gt.-neph. of 3; b. *c.* 1479; cr. 27 Jan. 1510; d.s.p. 6 Apr. 1523
  6. **Thomas Boleyn,** Viscount Rochford (*see* Ormond (I. and E.)); b. 1477; cr. 8 Dec. 1529; d.s.p.m.s. 13 Mar. 1539
  7. **William Paulet,** Lord St John (*see* Winchester);[1] b. *c.* 1483; cr. 19 Jan. 1550; d. 10 Mar. 1572
   [From this date, the succession is the same as that to the marquessate of Winchester. *See under* this title]

WINCHESTER, *earldom*
  1. **Saher de Quincy**; cr. 13 Mar. 1207;[2] d. 3 Nov. 1219
  2. **Roger de Quincy,** 2nd s. & h.; succ.[3] Feb. 1235; d.s.p.m. 25 Apr. 1264

---

[1] After 1551, when he was cr. marquis of Winchester, the heirs to this earldom possibly had the courtesy title, earls of Wiltshire, during their fathers' lifetime.
[2] Date of writ granting him the third penny of Hampshire, but the *Pipe Roll* for 9 John (138) shows that this was retroactive to about Easter 1206.
[3] He succeeded to the title only aft. his mother's death (shortly bef. 19 Feb. 1235), for it was through his mother that he inherited the Beaumont and Grantemesnil estates, in virtue of which acquisition Saher de Quincy, his father, had been cr. earl of Winchester.

3. **Hugh le Despenser**; b. 1 Mar. 1261; cr. 10 May 1322; exec. 27 Oct. 1326 and forf.
4. **Lewis de Bruges**; cr. 13 Oct. 1472; d. 26 Nov. 1492
5. **John de Bruges**; s. & h.; b. *c.* 1457; res. 8 May–16 June 1500; d. 1512, bef. 6 Sept.

Marquessate
6. **William Paulet** (*see* Wiltshire); b. *c.* 1483; cr. 11 Oct. 1551; d. 10 Mar. 1572
7. **John Paulet** (*see* Wiltshire), s. & h.; b. *c.* 1510; d. 4 Nov. 1576
8. **William Paulet** (*see* Wiltshire), s. & h.; b. 1532–33; d. 24 Nov. 1598
9. **William Paulet** (*see* Wiltshire), only s. & h.; b. bef. 1560; d. 4 Feb. 1629
10. **John Paulet**, s. & h.; b. *c.* 1598; d. 5 Mar. 1675
11. **Charles Paulet** (*see* Bolton); s. & h.; b. *c.* 1630; d. 27 Feb. 1699
12. **Charles Paulet** (*see* Bolton); s. & h.; b. 1661; d. 21 Jan. 1722

WINCHILSEA, *earldom*
1. **Elizabeth Heneage**; b. 9 July 1556; cr. 12 July 1628; d. 23 Mar. 1634 m. 4 Nov. 1572 Sir Moyle Finch, 1st bt.
2. **Thomas Finch**, s. & h.; b. 13 June 1578; d. 4 Nov. 1639
3. **Heneage Finch**, s. & h.; b. 1627–28; d. 28 Aug. 1689
4. **Charles Finch**, gds. & h.; b. 26 Sept. 1672; d.s.p.s. 5–16 Aug. 1712
5. **Heneage Finch**, uncle & h. male; b. 3 Jan. 1657; d.s.p. 30 Sept. 1726

WORCESTER, *earldom*
1. **Waleran**, count of Meulan; b. 1104; cr. ? autumn 1138; st. 1139; depr. 1153;[1] d. 9 or 10 Apr. 1166
2. **Thomas Percy**; b. *c.* 1343; cr. 29 Sept. 1397; exec. 23 July 1403 & forf.
3. **Richard Beauchamp**, Lord Abergavenny; b. 1397; cr. Feb. 1421; d.s.p.m. 16 Apr. 1422
4. **John Tiptoft** (or Tibetot); b. *c.* 1427; cr. July 1449; exec. 18 Oct. 1470
5. **Edward Tiptoft** (or Tibetot); only surv. s. & h.; b. *c.* 1469;[2] d. unm. 12 Aug. 1485
6. **Charles Somerset**, Baron Herbert; b. *c.* 1460; cr. 1 Feb. 1514; d. 15 Apr. 1526
7. **Henry Somerset**, 1st s. & h.; b. *c.* 1499; d. 26 Nov. 1549
8. **William Somerset**, 1st s. & h.; b. *c.* 1527; d. 21 Feb. 1589
9. **Edward Somerset**, only s. & h.; b. *c.* 1550; d. 3 Mar. 1628

Earldom and marquessate
10. **Henry Somerset**, s. & h.; b. 1576–77; cr. marquess 2 Mar. 1643; d. 18 Dec. 1646
11. **Edward Somerset** (*see* Glamorgan), s. & h.; b. perhaps shortly bef. 9 Mar. 1603; d. 3 Apr. 1667
12. **Henry Somerset** (*see* Beaufort), s. & h.; b. *c.* 1629; d. 21 Jan. 1700

[Thereafter the marquessate descended with the dukedom of Beaufort]

YARMOUTH, *earldom*
1. **Robert Paston**, 1st Viscount Yarmouth; b. 29 May 1631; cr. 30 July 1679; d. 8 Mar. 1683
2. **William Paston**, s. & h.; b. 1653–54; d.s.p.m.s. 25 Dec. 1732

YORK, *earldom*

[William of Aumale, cr. earl after Aug. 1138, took the title sometimes of earl of York and sometimes of Aumale. The latter title soon ousted the former, which is not heard of in this family aft. Stephen's reign. For these earls, *see under* Aumale. In 1190, Roger of Hoveden (*Chron.*, III, 86) says that Richard I gave his neph., Otto of Saxony, the county of York, but exchanged it, owing to the opposition he met with, for that of Poitou.]

[1] The evidence for the existence of this earldom under Stephen is scanty, and there is none for its existence under Henry II. After 1143 Waleran seems to have severed his connection with England (*see* G. H. White, *TRHS* 4th ser., xiii, 56 ff.; xvii, 19 ff.).
[2] It seems that his father was never att., and, in any case, he would succ. to the title aft. the re-accession of Edward IV in 1471.

Dukedom

1. **Edmund 'of Langley'** (*see* Cambridge); b. prob. 5 June 1342; cr. 6 Aug. 1385; d. 1 Aug. 1402
2. **Edward 'of York'** or 'of Norwich' (*see* Aumale), 1st s. & h.; b. *c.* 1373; liv. 5 Nov. 1402; d.s.p. 25 Oct. 1415
3. **Richard Plantagenet** (*see* Cambridge), neph. & h.; b. 1411; st. 24 Feb. 1425;[1] liv. 12 May 1432; att. 20 Nov. 1459; att. nullified Oct. 1460; d. 30 Dec. 1460
4. **Edward Plantagenet** (*see* Cambridge), 1st surv. s. & h., later K.; b. 28 Apr. 1442. Became K. 4 Mar. 1461
5. **Richard Plantagenet** (*see* Norfolk), 2nd s.; b. prob. 17 Aug. 1473; cr. 28 May 1474; d. prob. July–Sept. 1483
6. **Henry Tudor** (*see* Chester), later K.; b. 28 June 1491; cr. 31 Oct. 1494. Became K. 22 Apr. 1509
7. **Charles Stewart** (*see* Albany), later K.; b. 19 Nov. 1600; cr. 6 Jan. 1605. Became K. 27 Mar. 1625
8. **James Stewart**; b. 14 Oct. 1633 and designated at birth; cr. 27 Jan. 1644. Became K. 6 Feb. 1685

---

[1] *Cal. Patent Rolls, 1422–29*, 266.

DUKES, MARQUESSES AND EARLS (IRELAND)

The Irish peerage presents certain peculiarities, of which the chief is, perhaps, that in the first century and a half after the Norman conquest of Ireland none of the really great feudatories, with the exception of the earl of Ulster, had an Irish title. The great lordship of Leinster, held by the earls of Pembroke and earls Marshal, with liberties very little below those of a palatine earl, never gave rise to an Irish title, and when in 1247 it was divided among the Marshal heiresses the lordships which resulted were again held by men with English titles: Carlow by the earls of Norfolk and earls Marshal (it passed to Thomas of Brotherton under Edward II); Wexford by the earls of Pembroke and Kilkenny by the earls of Gloucester (extinct in 1314), till the partition of the Gloucester inheritance in 1317.[1] The lordship of Meath again gave its holders no Irish title: half of it eventually passed by marriage to the earls of March and descended with that title.

In the fourteenth century several new earldoms, with extensive liberties attached, were created for feudatories previously of the second rank, whose descendants were to be the leading figures of the later middle ages. After this, with the exception of the short-lived titles conferred on Robert de Vere by Richard II, the equally short-lived earldom of Cork, and the earldom of Waterford created in 1446, the position remained unchanged till the sixteenth century, when six or seven earldoms (the number depends on whether the uncompleted grant of the earldom of Clanconnell is included) were created. All but one, the earldom of Ossory, were conferred on the heads of great Gaelic families as part of the Tudor policy of uniting Ireland under the crown, Donald Maccarty being created earl of Clancare; Donough Maccarty, earl of Clancarty; Ulick Bourke (a Gaelicized Norman), earl of Clanricarde; Turlough O'Neill, earl of Clanconnell; Con O'Neill, earl of Tyrone and Murrough O'Brien, earl of Thomond. In the seventeenth century creations and promotions in the Irish peerage rapidly increased, some of the recipients having very little connection with Ireland.

The chief source for this section is the *Complete Peerage*, with some revisions taken from *A New History of Ireland*, ed. T. W. Moody, F. X. Martin and F. J. Byrne, ix (Oxford, 1984).

ANTRIM, *earldom*
1. **Randal MacSorley MacDonnell,** Viscount Dunluce; cr. 12 Dec. 1620; d. 10 Dec. 1636

---

[1] The modern dukedom of Leinster has of course no connection with the Norman lordship, while the earldom of Kildare was created for a family unrelated to the Marshals in the fourteenth century, after the surrender of the original lordship to Edward I. For the partition of 1247, *see* Orpen, *The Normans in Ireland*, iii, chapter 26. There were in all five shares, but the fourth and fifth, consisting mainly of Kildare, were greatly divided among co-heiresses.

Earldom and marquessate
2. **Randal MacDonnell,** s. & h.; b. 1609
   marquessate; cr. 26 Jan. 1645; d.s.p. 3 Feb. 1682

Earldom only
3. **Alexander MacDonnell,** only br. & h.; b. 1615; forf. aft. 1689; rest. 1697; d. shortly bef. 11 June 1699
4. **Randal MacDonnell,** only s. & h.; b. 1680; d. 19 Oct. 1721

ARDGLASS, *earldom*
1. **Thomas Cromwell,** Viscount Lecale; b. 11 June 1594; cr. 15 Apr. 1645; d. 1653
2. **Wingfield Cromwell,** only s. & h.; b. 12 Sept. 1624; d. 3 Oct. 1668
3. **Thomas Cromwell,** only s. & h.; b. 29 Nov. 1653; d.s.p. 11 Apr. 1682
4. **Vere Essex Cromwell,** uncle & h.; b. 2 Oct. 1625; d.s.p.m. 26 Nov. 1687

ARRAN, *earldom*
1. **Lord Richard Butler**; b. 15 June 1639; cr. 13 May 1662; d.s.p.m.s. 25 Jan. 1686
2. **Charles Butler,** neph. of 1; b. 4 Sept. 1671; cr. 8 Mar. 1693; d.s.p. 17 Dec. 1758

ATHLONE, *earldom*
1. **Godard van Reede** or Ginkel; b. 4 June 1644; cr. 4 Mar. 1692; d. 11 Feb. 1703
2. **Frederik Christiaan van Reede,** s. & h.; b. 20 Oct. 1668; d. 15 Aug. 1719

BANGOR, *earldom*
   [Cr. 1691 with the dukedom of Leinster; extinct 1719]

BARRYMORE, *earldom*
1. **David Barry,** Viscount Barry, Barrymore or Buttevant; b. *c.* 10 Mar. 1605; cr. 28 Feb. 1628; d. 29 Sept. 1642
2. **Richard Barry,** s. & h.; bapt. 4 Nov. 1630; d. Nov. 1694
3. **Laurence Barry,** s. & h.; b. 1656–64; forf. 1689; rest. soon aft.; d.s.p. 17 Apr. 1699
4. **James Barry,** br. & h.; b. 1667; d. 5 Jan. 1748

BELLOMONT, *earldom*
1. **Charles Henry Kirkhoven,** or Van des Kerchove, Lord Wotton; cr. 9 Dec. 1680; d.s.p. 5 Jan. 1683
2. **Richard Coote,** Lord Coote of Coloony; cr. 2 Nov. 1689; d. 5 Mar. 1701
3. **Nanfan Coote,** s. & h.; b. *c.* 1681; d.s.p.m. 14 June 1708
4. **Richard Coote,** only br. & h. male; d.s.p.m.s. 10 Feb. 1766

CARLINGFORD, *earldom*
1. **Theobald Taaffe,** Viscount Taaffe; cr. 26 June 1661; d. 31 Dec. 1677
2. **Nicholas Taaffe,** s. & h.; d.s.p. 2 July 1690
3. **Francis Taaffe,** br. & h.; b. 1639; d.s.p.s. Aug. 1704
4. **Theobald Taaffe,** neph. & h.; d.s.p. 24 Nov. 1738

CARLOW, *earldom*

William Brabazon

   [Lord Brabazon of Ardee, was about to be cr. earl of Carlow 1627, but the K.'s letters (8 Feb. 1627), were superseded by others of 10 Mar. 1627, creating him earl of Meath (*see under* Meath, *earldom*)]

CARBERY, *earldom*
1. **John Vaughan,** Lord Vaughan of Mullenger; b. *c.* 1575; cr. 5 Aug. 1628; d. 6 May 1634
2. **Richard Vaughan,** only s. & h.; d. 3 Dec. 1686
3. **John Vaughan,** 1st surv. s. & h.; bapt. 18 July 1639; d.s.p.m.s. 16 Jan. 1713

CARRICK, *earldom*
   [Edmund Butler (father of James, later 1st earl of Ormond) received a grant of the earldom of Carrick, 1 Sept. 1315, but was never cr. earl, prob. because he was unable to visit England for the creation. Between 1315 and 1317 he is occasionally st. earl of Carrick in official documents. He d. 13 Sept. 1321]

CASTELHAVEN, *earldom*
1. **George Tuchet,** Lord Audley; b. *c.* 1551; cr. 6 Sept. 1616; d. 20 Feb. 1617
2. **Mervyn Tuchet** or Audley, s. & h.; b. *c.* 1585; exec. 14 May 1631[1]
3. **James Tuchet,** s. & h.; b. *c.* 1617; d.s.p. 11 Oct. 1684
4. **Mervin Tuchet,** br. & h.; d. 2 Nov. 1686
5. **James Tuchet,** s. & h.; d. 9 Aug. 1700
6. **James Tuchet,** s. & h.; d. 12 Oct. 1740

CASTLEMAINE, *earldom*
1. **Roger Palmer**; bapt. 4 Sept. 1634; cr. 11 Dec. 1661; d.s.p.m. 28 July 1705

CAVAN, *earldom*
1. **Charles Lambart,** Lord Lambart of Cavan; b. *c.* Apr. 1600; cr. 1 Apr. 1647; d. 25 June 1660
2. **Richard Lambart,** s. & h.; d. shortly bef. May 1691
3. **Charles Lambart,** s. & h.; b. 7 Sept. 1649; d. 5 Dec. 1702
4. **Richard Lambart,** 1st surv. s. & h.; d. 8 Mar. 1742

CLANBRASSILL, *earldom*
1. **James Hamilton,** Viscount Claneboye; cr. 7 June 1647; d. 20 June 1659
2. **Henry Hamilton,** 1st surv. s. & h.; b. *c.* 1647; d.s.p. 12 Jan. 1675

CLANCARE [Glencar], *earldom*
1. **Donald Maccarty More;** cr. 24 June 1565; res. 1597; d.s.p.m.s. bef. 12 Feb. 1597

CLANCARTY, *earldom*
1. **Donough Maccarty,** Viscount Muskerry; b. 1594; cr. 27 Nov. 1658; d. 4 Aug. 1665
2. **Charles James Maccarty,** gds. & h.; b. aft. 1660; d. 22 Sept. 1666
3. **Callaghan or Kelme Maccarty,** uncle & h.; d. 21 Nov. 1676
4. **Donough Maccarty,** s. & h.; b. aft. May 1668; forf. 11 May 1691; d. 1 Oct. 1734

CLANCONNELL or CLANCONNEIL, *earldom*
1. **Furlough Lynach O'Neil;** cr. 18 May 1578 (date of letters patent creating him earl, which were, however, never delivered to him); d. 9 Sept. 1596

CLANRICARDE, *earldom*
1. **Ulick Bourke** or de Burgh; cr. 1 July 1543; d. 19 Oct. 1544
2. **Richard Bourke** or de Burgh, s. & h.; b. aft. 16 Sept. 1527; d. 24 July 1582
3. **Ulick Bourke** or de Burgh, s. & h.; st. 1585; d. 20 May 1601
4. **Richard Bourke** or de Burgh (*see* St. Albans (E.)), 1st surv. s. & h.; b. 1572; d. 12 Nov. 1635
5. **Ulick Bourke** or de Burgh (*see* St. Albans (E.)), s. & h.; b. bef. 8 Dec. 1604 *marquessate;* cr. 21 Feb. 1646; d.s.p.m. July 1657

   Earldom only
6. **Richard Bourke,** cous. & h. male; d.s.p.m. Aug. 1666
7. **William Bourke,** br. & h. male; d. Oct. 1687
8. **Richard Bourke,** s. & h.; d.s.p.m.s. 1709
9. **John Bourke,** br. & h. male; b. 1642; d. 17 Oct. 1722

CORK, *earldom*
1. **Edward 'of York'** or 'of Norwich' (*see* Aumale (E.)); b. *c.* 1373; cr. 25 Feb. 1390–15 Jan. 1395;[2] d.s.p. 25 Oct. 1415
2. **Richard Boyle;** b. 13 Oct. 1566; cr. 16 Oct. 1620; d. 15 Sept. 1643
3. **Richard Boyle** (*see* Burlington), 1st surv. s. & h.; b. 20 Oct. 1612; d. 13 Jan. 1698
4. **Charles Boyle** (*see* Burlington), gds. & h.; b. bef. 1674; d. 9 Feb. 1704
5. **Richard Boyle** (*see* Burlington), only s. & h.; b. 24 Apr. 1694; d.s.p.m. 3 Dec. 1753

---

[1] He was convicted of felony, not treason, and the earldom appears to have descended to his heir without forfeiture.
[2] E. Curtis, *Richard II in Ireland*, 27, 147.

DESMOND, *earldom*
1. **Maurice Fitz Thomas;** b. 1293; cr. on or bef. 27 Aug. 1329; d. 25 Jan. 1356
2. **Maurice Fitz Maurice,** s. & h.; b. 31 July 1336; liv. 16 Oct. 1357; d.s.p. 20 Apr.–5 June 1358
3. **Gerald or Garrett Fitz Maurice,** br. & h.;[1] liv. 20 July 1359; st. 30 May 1363; d. 1398
4. **John Fitz Gerald,** s. & h.;[2] d. 11 Oct. 1399
   Maurice Fitz Gerald, *de facto* 1399–1401
5. **Thomas Fitz John,** s. & h.; b. *c.* 1386; st. 12 Mar. 1406; deposed 1411; d. Aug. (bef. 10th) 1420
6. **James Fitz Gerald,** uncle & h.;[3] b. bef. Dec. 1388; st. 1 Apr. 1421; d. 1463
7. **Thomas Fitz James Fitz Gerald,** s. & h.; exec. 15 Feb. 1468
8. **James Fitz Thomas Fitz Gerald,** s. & h.; b. *c.* 1459; d.s.p.m. 7 Dec. 1487
9. **Maurice Fitz Thomas Fitz Gerald,** br. & h. male; lic. of entry 7 Apr. 1488; d. 1520
10. **James Fitz Maurice Fitz Gerald,** only surv. s. & h.; d.s.p.m. 18 June 1529
11. **Thomas Fitz Thomas Fitz Gerald,** uncle & h. male; d. 1534[4]
12. **James Fitz Maurice Fitz Gerald,** gds. & h.; d.s.p.m. 1541[5]
13. **James Fitz John Fitz Gerald,** cous. & h. male;[6] d. 14 Oct. 1558
14. **Gerald Fitz James Fitz Gerald,** s.;[7] b. *c.* 1533; recog. 12 Jan. 1560; forf. 15 Nov. 1582; d. 11 Nov. 1583
15. **James Fitz Gerald,** s. & h.; b. 1570–71; cr. 1 Oct. 1600; d. unm. about Nov. 1601[8]
16. **Richard Preston,** Lord Dingwall; cr. 11 July 1619; d.s.p.m. 28 Oct. 1628
17. **George Feilding,** h. to earldom;[9] b. *c.* 1615; d. 31 Jan. 1666
18. **William Feilding** (*see* Denbigh), s. & h.; b. 29 Dec. 1640; d. 23 Aug. 1685
19. **Basil Feilding** (*see* Denbigh), s. & h.; b. 1688; d. 18 Mar. 1717

DONEGALL, *earldom*
1. **Arthur Chichester;** b. 16 June 1606; cr. 30 Mar. 1647; d.s.p.m.s. 18 Mar. 1675
2. **Arthur Chichester,** neph. & h. male; d. 26 Oct. 1678
3. **Arthur Chichester,** s. & h.; b. 1666; d. 10 Apr. 1706
4. **Arthur Chichester,** s. & h.; b. 28 Mar. 1695; d.s.p. 30 Sept. 1757

DOWNE, *earldom*
1. **Sir William Pope,** bt.; bapt. 15 Oct. 1573; cr. 16 Oct. 1628; d. 2 June 1631
2. **Thomas Pope,** gds. & h.; bapt. 16 Dec. 1622; d.s.p.m. 28 Dec. 1660
3. **Thomas Pope,** uncle & h. male; b. 1598; d. 11 Jan. 1668
4. **Thomas Pope,** s. & h.; bapt. 29 Sept. 1640; d. unm. 18 May 1668

---

[1] The true heir in 1358 was Nicolas Fitz Maurice, 2nd s. of **1**, b. *c.* 1338, who was an idiot. On 20 July 1359 his father's lands, in the king's hands because of his idiocy, were granted to 3 on condition of maintaining him.

[2] He was knighted before Apr. 1395.

[3] It is probable that 5 left no legitimate children. He is said to have resigned the earldom to 6 in 1418 (*see C.P.*).

[4] He is said to have been 80 at his death, but must have been born aft. 8.

[5] He was a child in 1532. His gt.-uncle, Sir John Desmond, father of 13, who d. June 1536, disputed his right and assumed the title of earl.

[6] He proclaimed himself earl in the lifetime of 12, but was not recog. by the English government until later (precise date unknown).

[7] By 2nd w.; & h. if children of 1st w. were bastards. The descendants of the 1st w., however, assumed the title of earl as follows:
1. Sir Thomas Fitz James Fitz Gerald s. of 13 by 1st w. Summoned to parliament in 1556 as earl in the lifetime of his father; d. 18 Jan. 1595
2. James Fitz Thomas Fitz Gerald, s. & h.; att. 10 Mar. 1601; d.s.p. leg. Apr. 1607
3. John Fitz Thomas Fitz Gerald, br. & h.; d. in or aft. 1615
4. Gerald Fitz John Fitz Gerald, only s. & h.; d. unm. 1632

[8] Cr. earl to neutralise claim of his cous. James Fitz Thomas ('The Súgán earl'), st. 10 Oct. 1598, deposed 1601, d. *a.* 28 Apr. 1607. John Fitz Thomas, br. of James, was rival earl 1607–*p.* 1615, and was succeeded in the claim by his son, Gerald Fitz John, *p.* 1615–1632.

[9] He was granted the earldom in reversion 22 Nov. 1622.

DROGHEDA, *earldom*
1. **Henry Moore,** Viscount Moore of Drogheda; cr. 14 June 1661; d. 12 Jan. 1676
2. **Charles Moore,** s. & h.; d.s.p.s. 18 June 1679
3. **Henry Hamilton Moore,** br. & h.; d. 7 June 1714
4. **Henry Moore,** gds. & h.; b. 7 Oct. 1700; d.s.p.s. 29 May 1727

DUBLIN, *marquessate*
1. **Robert de Vere** (*see* Oxford, Ireland); b. 16 Jan. 1362; cr. 1 Dec. 1385; res. bef. 13 Oct. 1386; forf. 3 Feb. 1388; d.s.p. ? 22 Nov. 1392

FINGALL, *earldom*
1. **Luke Plunkett,** Lord Killeen; cr. 26 Sept. 1628; d. 29 Mar. 1637
2. **Christopher Plunkett,** s. & h.; b. aft. 1611; d. shortly bef. 18 Aug. 1649
3. **Luke Plunkett,** s. & h.; b. 1639; d. *c.* 1684
4. **Peter Plunkett,** s. & h.; b. 1678; d. 24 Jan. 1718

GALWAY, *earldom*
1. **Henry de Massue,** marquis de Ruvigny; b. 9 Apr. 1648; cr. 12 May 1697; d. unm. 3 Sept. 1720

GOWRAN, *earldom*
1. **Lord John Butler;** b. 1643; cr. 13 Apr. 1676; d.s.p. Aug. 1676

GRANARD, *earldom*
1. **Arthur Forbes,** Viscount Granard; b. *c.* 1623; cr. 30 Dec. 1684; d. 1695
2. **Arthur Forbes,** 1st s. & h.; b. *c.* 1656; d. 24 Aug. 1734

INCHIQUIN, *earldom*
1. **Murough O'Brien,** Lord Inchiquin; b. *c.* 1614; cr. 21 Oct. 1654; d. 9 Sept. 1674
2. **William O'Brien,** s. & h.; b. *c.* 1640; d. Jan. 1692
3. **William O'Brien,** s. & h.; b. *c.* 1666; d. 24 Dec. 1719

IRELAND, *dukedom*
1. **Robert de Vere** (*see* Dublin); b. 16 Jan. 1362; cr. 13 Oct. 1386; forf. 3 Feb. 1388; d.s.p. ? 22 Nov. 1392

KILDARE, *earldom*
1. **John Fitz Thomas Fitz Gerald;** cr. 14 May 1316; d. 12 Sept. 1316
2. **Thomas Fitz John Fitz Gerald;** 1st surv. s. & h.; st. 10 Sept. 1317; d. 5 Apr. 1328
3. **Richard Fitz Thomas Fitz Gerald,** yr. s. & h.; b. 1318–19; liv. 8 June 1328; d. unm. 7 July 1331
4. **Maurice Fitz Thomas Fitz Gerald,** br. & h.; liv. 9 Aug. 1342; st. 20 Apr. 1344; d. 15 Aug. 1390[1]
5. **Gerald Fitz Maurice Fitz Gerald,** s. & h.; b. aft. 1347; d.s.p.m. leg. 11 Dec. 1432

   [The succession becomes here doubtful. Perhaps it passed to (6) **John,** br. of 5. This John was either father or gdfather of 7. *See C.P.*]

7. **Thomas Fitz Maurice Fitz Gerald;** forf. Feb. 1468, rest. shortly aft. Feb. 1468; d. 25 Mar. 1478[2]
8. **Gerald Fitz Maurice Fitz Gerald,** s. & h.; b. prob. aft. Jan. 1456; forf. Dec. 1494; rest. Oct. 1495; d. 3 Sept. 1513
9. **Gerald Fitz Gerald,** s. & h.; b. 1487; d. 13 Dec. 1534
10. **Thomas Fitz Gerald,** s. & h.; b. 1513; forf. 1 May 1536; d. 3 Feb. 1537
11. **Gerald Fitz Gerald,** half-br. & h.; b. 28 Feb. 1525; cr. 13 May 1554; d. 16 Nov. 1585
12. **Henry Fitz Gerald,** 1st surv. s. & h. male; b. 1562; d.s.p.m. 1 Aug. 1597
13. **William Fitz Gerald,** br. & h. male; d. unm. early in Apr. 1599
14. **Gerald Fitz Gerald,** cous. & h. male; d. 11 Feb. 1612
15. **Gerald Fitz Gerald,** only s. & h.; b. 26 Dec. 1611; d. 11 Nov. 1620
16. **George Fitz Gerald,** cous. & h. male; bapt. 23 Jan. 1612; d. early in 1660 (bef. May 29)

---

[1] His obit was celebrated on this date.
[2] This date, given by the *Annals of Connacht*, seems to be clearly correct.

17. **Wentworth Fitz Gerald,** 1st surv. s. & h.; b. 1634; d. 5 Mar. 1664
18. **John Fitz Gerald,** only s. & h.; b. 1661; d.s.p.s. 9 Nov. 1707
19. **Robert Fitz Gerald,** cous. & h. male; b. 4 May 1675; d. 20 Feb. 1744

LEINSTER, *earldom*
  1. **Robert Cholmondeley,** Viscount Cholmondeley of Kells; b. 26 June 1584; cr. 5 Mar. 1646; d.s.p. leg. 2 Oct. 1659

    Dukedom
  2. **Lord Meinhard Schomberg** (*see* Schomberg (E.)); b. 30 June 1641; cr. 3 Mar. 1691; d.s.p.m. 5 July 1719

LIFFORD, *earldom*
  [**Frederic William de Roye de la Rochefoucauld,** count de Marthon; b. 1666, was apparently cr. Jan. 1699 earl of Lifford, though no patent was enrolled. He d. unm. 24 Feb. 1749]

LIMERICK, *earldom*
  1. **William Dungan,** Viscount Dungan of Clane; b. 1630; cr. 2 Jan. 1686; forf. 1691; d.s.p.m.s. Dec. 1698
  2. **Thomas Dungan,** br. & h. to earldom;[1] b. 1634; d.s.p. 14 Dec. 1715

LONDONDERRY, *earldom*
  1. **Thomas Ridgeway,** Lord Gallen-Ridgeway; b. *c.* 1565; cr. 23 Aug. 1622; d. 24 Jan. 1632
  2. **Robert Ridgeway,** s. & h.; d. 19 Mar. 1641
  3. **Weston Ridgeway,** s. & h.; b. 25 Mar. 1620; d. bef. 7 Nov. 1672
  4. **Robert Ridgeway,** s. & h.; b. aft. 1650; d.s.p.m.s. 7 Mar. 1714

LONGFORD, *earldom*
  1. **Francis Aungier,** Viscount Longford; cr. 18 Dec. 1677; d.s.p. 22 Dec. 1700
  2. **Ambrose Aungier,** br. & h.; d.s.p. 23 Jan. 1704

LORNE. *See* KINTYRE AND LORNE (S.)

LOUTH, *earldom*
  1. **John de Bermingham;** cr. 12 May 1319; d.s.p.m.s. 10 June 1329

MEATH, *earldom*
  1. **William Brabazon,** Lord Brabazon of Ardee; b. *c.* 1580; cr. 16 Apr. 1627; d. 18 Dec. 1651
  2. **Edward Brabazon,** s. & h.; b. *c.* 1610; d. 25 Mar. 1675
  3. **William Brabazon,** s. & h.; b. *c.* 1635; d.s.p.m.s. shortly bef. 1 Mar. 1685
  4. **Edward Brabazon,** next br. & h. male; b. *c.* 1638; d.s.p. 22 Feb. 1708
  5. **Chambre Brabazon,** br. & h.; b. *c.* 1645; d. 1 Apr. 1715

MOUNT-ALEXANDER, *earldom*
  1. **Hugh Montgomery,** Viscount Montgomery of the Great Ardes; b. *c.* 1625; cr. 28 July 1661; d. 15 Sept. 1663
  2. **Hugh Montgomery,** s. & h.; b. 24 Feb. 1651; d.s.p.s. 12 Feb. 1717

MOUNTRATH, *earldom*
  1. **Sir Charles Coote,** bt.; b. *c.* 1610; cr. 6 Sept. 1660; d. 18 Dec. 1661
  2. **Charles Coote,** s. & h.; b. *c.* 1630; d. 30 Aug. 1672
  3. **Charles Coote,** s. & h.; b. *c.* 1655; d. 29 May 1709
  4. **Charles Coote,** s. & h.; b. *c.* 1680; d. unm. 14 Sept. 1715

ORMOND, *earldom*
  1. **James Butler** or Le Botiller; b. *c.* 1305; cr. 16–31 Oct. 1328; d. Jan. or Feb. 1338 (bef. 18 Feb.)
  2. **James Butler,** only surv. s. & h.; b. on or shortly bef. 1 Nov. 1330 or 4 Oct. 1331;[2] liv. 16 or 24 Feb. 1347; d. 18 Oct. or 6 Nov. 1382

[1] He appears to have succeeded as if there had been no forfeiture.
[2] His father's inquisitions *post mortem* give these variant dates, the one taken in Ireland giving his age as 7 on the feast of All Saints 1337.

3. **James Butler,** s. & h.; b. *c.* 1360; liv. 10 Mar. 1385; d. 6 or 7 Sept. 1405
4. **James Butler,** s. & h.; b. prob. 1390; liv. 8 Aug. 1411; d. 23 Aug. 1452
5. **James Butler** or Ormond (*see* Wiltshire), s. & h.; b. 24 Nov. 1420; liv. 3 May 1452; exec. *c.* 1 May 1461 and forf. (att. in Ireland Oct. 1462)
6. **John Butler** or Ormond, br. & h.; recog. during the Lancastrian restoration Oct. 1470–May 1471; pardoned by Edw. IV bef. 23 Nov. 1474; formally rest. 21 July 1475; d. bef. 15 June 1477 (poss. 14 Oct. 1476)
7. **Thomas Butler** or Ormond, br. & h.; b. *c.* 1424; lic. entry 15 June 1477; d.s.p.m. 3 Aug. 1515
8. **Thomas Boleyn,** Viscount Rochford (*see* Wiltshire), gds. of 7; b. 1477; cr. 8 Dec. 1529; d.s.p.m.s. 12 Mar. 1539
9. **Piers Butler** (*see* Ossory), cous. & h. male of 7; b. *c.* 1467; [for the view that he was the rightful heir to the original earldom cr. in 1328 and that he succeeded in 1515, *see Complete Peerage*]; res. 18 Feb. 1528; st. 23 Oct. 1537; rest. 22 Feb. 1538; d. 26 Aug. 1539
10. **James Butler** (*see* Ossory), s. & h.; b. bef. 20 July 1504; d. 28 Oct. 1546
11. **Thomas Butler** (*see* Ossory), s. & h.; b. 1531; d.s.p.m. leg. s. 22 Nov. 1614
12. **Walter Butler** (*see* Ossory), neph. & h. male; b. 1569; d. 24 Feb. 1633
13. **James Butler** (*see* Ossory), gds. & h.; b. 19 Oct. 1610
    marquessate; cr. 30 Aug. 1642
    dukedom; cr. 30 Mar. 1661 (*see also* in the English section *under* Ormond); d. 21 July 1688
14. **James Butler,** gds. & h.; b. 29 Apr. 1665; forf. the English and Scottish titles 20 Aug. 1715; [it was assumed at the time that the Irish act of 20 June 1716, forfeiting his estates, deprived him of his Irish titles also, but this assumption was corrected in 1791]; d.s.p.m.s. 5–16 Nov. 1745

ORRERY, *earldom*
1. **Roger Boyle,** Lord Broghill; b. 25 Apr. 1621; cr. 5 Sept. 1660; d. 16 Oct. 1679
2. **Roger Boyle,** s. & h.; bapt. 24 Oct. 1646; d. 29 Mar. 1682
3. **Lionel Boyle,** s. & h.; b. 1670; d.s.p. 30 Aug. 1703
4. **Charles Boyle,** br. & h.; b. 28 July 1674; d. 28 Aug. 1731

OSSORY, *earldom. See* ORMOND
1. **Piers Butler,** b. *c.* 1467; cr. 23 Feb. 1528; d. 26 Aug. 1539

[The earldom of Ossory descended with that of Ormond. *See under* this title]

RANELAGH, *earldom*
1. **Richard Jones,** Viscount Ranelagh; b. 8 Feb. 1641; cr. 11 Dec. 1677; d.s.p.m.s. 5 Jan. 1712

ROSCOMMON, *earldom*
1. **James Dillon,** Lord Dillon of Kilkenny-West; cr. 5 Aug. 1622; d. Mar. 1642
2. **Robert Dillon,** s. & h.; d. 27 Aug. 1642
3. **James Dillon,** s. & h.; b. *c.* 1605; d. 8 Nov. 1649
4. **Wentworth Dillon,** s. & h.; b. *c.* 1637; d.s.p. 17 Jan. 1685
5. **Carey or Cary Dillon,** uncle & h.; bapt. 1 July 1627; d. 24 or 25 Nov. 1689
6. **Robert Dillon,** s. & h.; d. 14 May 1715

THOMOND, *earldom*
1. **Murrough O'Brien;** cr. 1 July 1543; d. 7 Nov. 1551
2. **Donough O'Brien,** neph. & h. to earldom; res. bef. or on 7 Jan. 1552 and cr. again 7 Jan. 1552; d. 1 Apr. 1553
3. **Connor O'Brien,** s. & h.; b. *c.* 1535; d. Jan. 1581
4. **Donough O'Brien,** s. & h.; b. aft. 1560; d. 5 Sept. 1624
5. **Henry O'Brien,** s. & h.; b. *c.* 1588; d.s.p.m. shortly bef. 22 Apr. 1639
6. **Barnabus O'Brien,** br. & h. male; b. *c.* 1590; d. shortly bef. 15 Nov. 1657
7. **Henry O'Brien,** only s. & h.; b. *c.* 1620; d. 2 May 1691
8. **Henry O'Brien,** gds. & h.; b. 14 Aug. 1688; d.s.p. 20 Apr. 1741

TYRCONNELL or TYRCONNEL, *earldom*
1. **Roderick** (or Rory) **O'Donnell;** b. 1575; cr.[1] 27 Sept. 1603; d. 28 July 1608

---

[1] His honours were forfeited by his attainders in 1614.

2. **Oliver Fitzwilliam,** Viscount Fitzwilliam of Meryon; cr. 20 Apr. 1661; d.s.p.
   10 Apr. 1667
3. **Richard Talbot;** b. 1630; cr. 20 June 1685;[1] d.s.p.m. 14 Aug. 1691

TYRONE, *earldom*
1. **Con Bacagh O'Neill;** b. *c.* 1484; cr. 1 Oct. 1542; d. bef. 16 July 1559
2. **Brien O'Neill,** gds. & h. to earldom;[2] b. *c.* 1535; d. unm. 12 Apr. 1562
3. **Hugh O'Neill,** next br. & h.; b. *c.* 1550;[3] st. 1585; forf. 28 Oct. 1614; d. 20 July
   1616

ULSTER, *earldom*
1. **Hugh de Lacy;** cr. 29 May 1205; forf. 1210; rest. 20 Apr. 1227; d. prob. s.p.m.
   leg. bef. 26 Dec. 1242
2. **Walter de Burgh,** lord of Ulster from 15 July 1263;[4] st. 1265; d. 28 July 1271
3. **Richard de Burgh,** 1st. s. & h.; b. *c.* 1259; liv. 6 Jan. 1280; st. 27 June 1280; d.
   1326 (shortly bef. 25 June)
4. **William de Burgh,** gds. & h.; b. 13 Sept. 1312; st. 19 June 1330; d. 6 June 1333
5. **Elizabeth,** only da. & h.; b. 1332; d. 1363
   m. 9 Sept. 1342 **Lionel,** 3rd s. of K. Edw. III (*see* Clarence); b. 29 Nov. 1338; st.
   26 Jan. 1347; d.s.p.m. 17 Oct. 1368
6. **Phillippa,** only da. & h.; b. 16 Aug. 1355; d. bef. 9 Feb. 1381
   m. 1368 **Edmund Mortimer,** earl of March; b. 1 Feb. 1352; liv. 24 Aug. 1369; d.
   27 Dec. 1381
7. **Roger Mortimer** (*see* March); s. & h.; b. 11 Apr. 1374; liv. hom. 18 June 1393;
   d. 20 July 1398
8. **Edmund Mortimer** (*see* March), s. & h.; b. 6 Nov. 1391; liv. 9 June 1413; d.s.p.
   18 Jan. 1425
9. **Richard Plantagenet** (*see* Cambridge), neph. & h.; b. 1412; liv. 12 May 1432;
   forf. 20 Nov. 1459; rest. Oct. 1460; d. 30 Dec. 1460
10. **Edward Plantagenet** (*see* Cambridge), s. & h., later K.; b. 28 Apr. 1442.
    Became K. 4 Mar. 1461

WATERFORD, *earldom*
1. **John Talbot** (*see* Shrewsbury); b. 1390; cr. 17 July 1446; d. 17 July 1453

   [The earldom of Waterford descended with that of Shrewsbury, though it
   seems to have been thought at one time that it was forfeited with the Irish
   estates by the 'act of absentees' of 1536–37]

WESTMEATH, *earldom*
1. **Richard Nugent,** Lord Delvin; b. 1583; cr. 4 Sept. 1621; d. 1641
2. **Richard Nugent,** gds. & h.; b. *c.* 1620; d. bef. Feb. 1684
3. **Richard Nugent,** gds. & h.;[5] d. unm. Apr. 1714
4. **Thomas Nugent,** br. & h.; b. 1669; d.s.p.m.s. 30 June 1752

WEXFORD, *earldom*
   [The title of earl of Wexford was assumed by some of the Talbot earls of
   Shrewsbury, and was occasionally recog. in official documents]

[1] Richard Talbot was created marquess and duke of Tyrconnell on 20 Mar. 1689
by James II, then still *de facto* K. of Ireland. All his honours were forfeited in 1691
as a result of his attainder.
[2] He seems never to have been recog. as earl. The succession was disturbed by
Shane O'Neill, the eldest legitimate s. of **1**, who had been excluded from the
succession by the patent of 1542, and who asserted his right to the earldom.
[3] For the date of Hugh O'Neill's birth, *see* 'The birth-date of Hugh O'Neill, 2nd
earl of Tyrone' by J. K. Graham in *Irish Historical Studies*, i, 58–59.
[4] Br. Mus. MSS. Add. 4790, fo. 104v and Add. 6041, fo. 100v. This was a grant
by Edw. I as lord of Ireland of the land of Ulster, in exchange for lands in
Tipperary, to hold as **1** had held it. The order for livery is dated 3 Sept. 1263 (MS.
Lansdowne 229, fo. 98d). There must have been a new creation of the earldom, but
no evidence of this seems to have survived. De Burgh was the son of the niece of **1**,
but in no sense his heir.
[5] As he was a member of the Capuchin order he apparently was considered as
disabled from holding the peerage and his yr. br. and heir sat as earl of Westmeath
in the parliament held by James II in Ireland.

DUKES, MARQUESSES AND EARLS
(SCOTLAND)

The following list is based on the *Scots Peerage* and the *Complete Peerage* (2nd edn.) but for the medieval period where exact dates of birth, accession and death are very rare an attempt has been made to check the sources and to work out dates more closely than was done in the *Peerages*.

No attempt has been made to compile a list of mormaers for the Celtic period, nor to show any relationship between mormaer and province on the one hand and earldom on the other. For the early earls the evidence of hereditary succession is scanty. In this list the evidence of the charter of Alexander I to Scone priory (*c.* 1120) with its several subscribing earls (whose earldoms are not specified) is ignored, since the authenticity of the charter (and still more of its witnesses) is open to question. In the fourteenth century it becomes clear that the grant of the lands and barony of an earldom did not confer the title, for many of those who married 'countesses suo jure' were not (or not immediately) styled earl. An attempt has been made to indicate such cases but since the whole subject requires investigation, it is certain that much fuller information could be obtained from the sources.

ABERCORN, *earldom*
1. James Hamilton, Lord Abercorn, b. aft. 1574; cr. 10 July 1606; d. 23 Mar. or 2 Apr. 1618
2. James Hamilton, s. & h.; b. *c.* 1604; d. *c.* 1670
3. George Hamilton, 1st surv. s. & h.; b. *c.* 1636; d. unm. bef. 1683
4. Claud Hamilton, gt.-gds. of 1; bapt. 13 Sept. 1659; d. unm. aft. 13 July 1691
5. Charles Hamilton, br. & h.; d.s.p.s. June 1701
6. James Hamilton, gt.-gds. of 1; b. *c.* 1661; d. 28 Nov. 1734

ABERDEEN, *earldom*
1. Sir George Gordon, Lord Haddo; b. 3 Oct. 1637; cr. 30 Nov. 1682; d. 20 Apr. 1720

ABERNETHY, *earldom*
Cr. with the dukedom of Douglas (10 Aug. 1703) and descended with it

ABOYNE, *earldom*
1. Charles Gordon, 4th s. of Huntly 7; cr. 10 Sept. 1660; d. Mar. 1681
2. Charles Gordon, s. & h.; d. Apr. 1702
3. John Gordon, s. & h.; serv. 7 Oct. 1702; d. 11 Apr. 1732

AIRLIE, *earldom*
1. James Ogilvy, Lord Airlie; b. 1586; cr. 2 Apr. 1639; d. 1664
2. James Ogilvy, s. & h.; b. *c.* 1610–15; d. 1703
3. David Ogilvy, 1st surv. s. & h.; serv. h. 1704; d. 1717

AIRTH, *earldom*
1. William Graham (*see* Menteith, Strathearn); b. aft. July 1589; cr. 21 Jan. 1633; d. aft. 13 Apr. 1661

[*Thereafter descended with the earldom of Menteith*]

ALBANY, *dukedom*
1. Robert Stewart (*see* Atholl, Buchan, Fife, Menteith), 3rd s. of K. Robert II of Scotland; b. *c.* 1340; cr. 28 Apr. 1398; d. 3 Sept. 1420
2. Murdoch Stewart (*see* Fife, Menteith), s. & h.; b. prob. 1362; forf. & exec. 25 May 1425
3. Alexander Stewart (*see* Mar, March), 2nd s. of K. James II of Scotland; b. *c.* 1454; cr. 4 July 1457–3 July 1458; forf. 4 Oct. 1479; rest. June–Dec. 1482; forf. 27 June 1483; d. ? 1485
4. John Stewart, only leg. s. & h.; b. 1484–85; st. from June 1505; rest. 8 Apr. 1514–? May 1515; d.s.p. leg. 2 June 1536
5. Arthur Stewart, 2nd s. of K. James V of Scotland; b. Apr. 1541; cr. at birth; d. 8 days aft. birth
6. Henry Stewart (*see* Ross), 1st s. of Lennox 14, later K. of Scots; b. 7 Dec. 1545; cr. 20 July 1565; became K. 29 July 1565; d. 10 Feb. 1567
7. James Stewart, only s. & h. later K. James VI of Scotland; b. 19 June 1566; succ. to dukedom 10 Feb. 1567; became K. 24 July 1567
8. Charles Stewart, 2nd but (from 6 Nov. 1612) 1st surv. s. & h., later K. Charles I of Great Britain; b. 19 Nov. 1600; cr. 23 Dec. 1600; became K. 27 Mar. 1625
9. James Stewart, 2nd s. later K. James II of Great Britain; b. 14 Oct. 1633; cr. 31 Dec. 1660; became K. 6 Feb. 1685

ANCRAM, *earldom*
1. Sir Robert Kerr of Ancram; b. 1578; cr. 24 June 1633; d. Dec. 1654
2. Charles Kerr, 2nd s. & h. to this earldom; d.s.p.s. 1–11 Sept. 1690
3. Robert Kerr (*see* Lothian), neph. & h.; b. 8 Mar. 1636; d. 15 Feb. 1701

[*This earldom afterwards descended with the marquessate of Lothian*]

ANGUS, *earldom, marquessate*

Earldom
1. Gillebrigte, or Gilbert; st. *c.* 1150–24 May 1153; d. 15 Mar. 1187–1 Aug. 1189
2. Adam, s. & h.; b. bef. May 1164; d. bef. 17 Mar. 1199
3. Gilchrist, br. & h.; d. bef. 11 Apr. 1206
4. Duncan, s. & h.; st. 1204–11 Apr. 1206; d. prob. bef. 4 Dec. 1214, certainly by 21 Mar. 1225
5. Malcolm (*see* Caithness), s. & h.; st. 21 Mar. 1225; last st. 26 July 1236; d. bef. 1242
6. Matilda, da. & h.; d. aft. 2 Dec. 1247
   m. 1. bef. 1242 John Comyn; d.s.p.s. (as earl of Angus) 1242
      2. 1243 Gilbert de Umfraville; d. shortly bef. 13 Mar. 1245
      3. bef. 2 Dec. 1247 Richard of Chilham or Dover; d. aft. 22 Nov. 1265
7. Gilbert Umfraville, s. & h.; b. *c.* 1244; succ. Apr.–June 1267; d. shortly bef. 13 Oct. 1307
8. Robert de Umfraville, 1st surv. s. & h.; b. *c.* 1277; liv. hom. 6 Nov. 1307; forf. by K. Robert I of Scotland ? 6 Nov. 1314, certainly by 1321; recog. by Edw. II until d.; d. Mar. 1325
9. Gilbert de Umfraville, s. & h.; b. *c.* 1310; liv. hom. 6 July 1331; recog. only in England; d.s.p.s. 6 Jan. 1381
10. John Stewart of Bunkle, co. Berwick; b. ? *c.* 1310; cr. 24 Oct. 1328 (? 7 June 1329)–15 June 1329; d. 9 Dec. 1331
11. Thomas Stewart, only s. & h.; st. 22 Aug. 1344; d. 14 Aug. 1362–10 Dec. 1364
12. Margaret Stewart, elder da. & coh.; succ. or rest. (on res. of her yr. sist.'s rights) Feb. 1379; res. in favour of 13 on 9 Apr. 1389, reserving life rent to herself; d.s.p. leg. 1417–23 Mar. 1418.
    m. bef. 21 June 1374 Thomas, earl of Mar; b. *c.* 1330; not found st. earl of Angus; d.s.p. 22 Oct. 1373–21 June 1374
13. George Douglas, illeg. s. of 12 and of Douglas 1; st. lord of Angus from 9 Apr. 1389 until 24 May 1397 when st. earl; d. 14 Sept. 1402–05
14. William Douglas, s. & h.; b. *c.* 1398; d. Oct. 1437
15. James Douglas, s. & h.; serv. 27 Feb. 1438; forf. 1 July 1445; rest. prob. soon aft.; d.s.p. bef. 9 Sept. 1446
16. George Douglas, br. & h.; d. 12 Mar. 1463
17. Archibald Douglas, s. & h.; b. *c.* 1453; d. 29 Nov. 1513–31 Jan. 1514

499

18. Archibald Douglas, gds. & h.; b. *c.* 1490; forf. 5 Sept. 1528; rest. Mar. 1543; d.s.p. m.s. bef. 22 Jan. 1557
19. David Douglas, neph. & h.; b. *c.*1515; d. June 1557
20. Archibald Douglas (*see* Morton), only s. & h.; b. 1554–55; forf. Oct. 1581; rest. Dec. 1585; d.s.p.m. 5 Aug. 1588
21. William Douglas, cous. & h. male; b. *c.* 1532; recog. 7 Mar. 1589; d. 1 July 1591
22. William Douglas, s. & h.; b. *c.* 1552; serv. Nov. 1591; forf. June 1594; rest. Dec. 1597; d. 3 Mar. 1611
23. William Douglas, s. & h.; b. *c.* 1589; d. 19 Feb. 1660; cr. marquess of Douglas June 1633 with which marquessate the earldom of Angus descended except for the following special creation
24. Archibald Douglas, s. & h.; b. *c.* 1609; cr. 3 Apr. 1651, but the creation was not completed; d. *c.* 15 Jan. 1655

Marquessate, and earldom of Angus and Abernethy
Cr. with the dukedom of Douglas (10 Aug. 1703), and descended with it

ANNANDALE, *earldom and marquessate*

Earldom
1. John Murray, Viscount Annand; cr. 13 Mar. 1624; d. Sept. 1640
2. James Murray, only s. & h.; serv. h. 30 Mar.; d.s.p. 28 Dec. 1658
3. James Johnston (*see* Hartfell); b. 1625; cr. 13 Feb. 1661; d. 17 July 1672
4. William Johnston (*see* Hartfell), 1st surv. s. & h.
marquessate; cr. 24 June 1701; d. 14 Jan. 1721

ARGYLL, *earldom, marquessate, dukedom*

Earldom
1. Colin Campbell, Lord Campbell; b. ? aft. 1431; cr. 1457–24 Oct. 1458; d. May 1493
2. Archibald Campbell, s. & h.; d. 9 Sept. 1513
3. Colin Campbell, s. & h.; d. 9 Oct. 1529
4. Archibald Campbell, s. & h.; d. 21 Aug.–2 Dec. 1558
5. Archibald Campbell, s. & h.; d.s.p. 12 Sept. 1573
6. Colin Campbell, half br. & h.; b. bef. 1546; d. 10 Sept. 1584
7. Archibald Campbell, s. & h.; b. 1575; forf. 16 Feb. 1619; rest. 22 Nov. 1621; d. 9 Oct.–29 Nov. 1638
8. Archibald Campbell, s. & h.; b. 1607
marquessate; cr. 15 Nov. 1641; forf. 25 May 1661; exec. 27 May 1661
9. Archibald Campbell, s. & h.; b. 26 Feb. 1629
earldom; rest. 16 Oct. 1663; forf. 19 Dec. 1681; exec. 30 June 1685
10. Archibald Campbell (*see* Kintyre & Lorne, Campbell & Cowall), s. & h.; b. prob. July 1658
earldom; rest. 1 Aug. 1689
dukedom; cr. 23 June 1701; d. 23 Sept. 1703
11. John Campbell (*see* Greenwich); b. 10 Oct. 1680; d.s.p.m. 4 Oct. 1743

ARRAN, *earldom*
1. Thomas Boyd; cr. 26 Apr. 1467; forf. 22 Nov. 1469; d. ? 1473–74
2. James Hamilton, Lord Hamilton, s. of w. of 1 by her 2nd m.; b. *c.* 1475; cr. 8 & 11 Aug. 1503; d. 26 Mar.–21 July 1529
3. James Hamilton, s. & h.; d. 22 Jan. 1575
4. James Hamilton, s. & h.; b. 1537–38; declared insane and forf. 1579; res. 1581; forf. reversed and rest. 10 Dec. 1585; res. annulled 1586; d.s.p. Mar. 1609
5. James Stewart, gt.-gds. of 2; cr. on res. of 4, 28 Oct. 1581; forf. Nov. 1585; d. 5 Dec. 1595
6. John Hamilton (*see* Hamilton), next surv. br. of 4; cr. 17 Apr. 1599; st. in lifetime of 4; d. 6 Apr. 1604

[*From 17 Apr. 1599, or Mar. 1609, descended with marquessate and dukedom of Hamilton*]

ATHOLL, *earldom, marquessate, dukedom*
Earldom
1. Matad; succ. or cr. in or bef. 1136; d. 1139–59

2. Malcolm, s. & h.; st. 1153–59; d. 15 Mar. 1187–15 Feb. 1198
3. Henry, s. & h.; st. bef. 15 Feb. 1198; d.s.p.m. bef. Jan. 1211
4. Isabel, 1st da. & h.; d. ? 23 Feb. 1235–7 July 1235
   m. 1. bef. Jan. 1211 Thomas of Galloway; st. Jan. 1211; d. 1231 aft. 19 Mar.
   ? 2. Alan Durward whose right to be earl is not clear; married or cr. 11 June–25 Dec. 1234; res. 23 Feb.–7 July 1235; d. 1275
5. Patrick, only s. & h. by 1; st. 25 Sept. 1237; d. unm. 1242
6. Forueleth or Fofwht, 2nd da. of 3 & h.; d. aft. 3 July 1247
   m. bef. 1242 David de Hastings; st. Aug. 1244; d. bef. 3 July 1247
7. Ada, da. & h.
   m. John de Strathbogie.
   [The existence of these two and their relationship to 6 and 8 rest on the evidence of a supposed charter unreliably cited in the seventeenth century]
8. David de Strathbogie, s. & h.; st. Dec. 1264; d. 6 Aug. 1270
9. John de Strathbogie, s. & h.; st. 5 Feb. 1284; forf. and exec. 7 Nov. 1306
10. Ralph de Monthermer (see Gloucester, Hertford); cr. by K. Edw. I of England 12 Oct. 1306; res. 24 June 1307; d. 5 Apr. 1325
11. David de Strathbogie, s. & h. of 9; rest. by K. Edw. II 21 Aug. 1307, 20 May 1308; forf. by K. Robert I Nov. 1314 but recog. by the English K.; d. 28 Dec. 1326
12. David de Strathbogie, s. & h.; b. 1 Feb. 1309; not recog. by Robert I and David II except 27 Sept. 1334–July 1335 but recog. by Edw. II, Edw. III, and Edw. Balliol; d. 30 Nov. 1335
13. David de Strathbogie, only s. & h.; b. c. 1332; not recog. by David II; d.s.p.m. 10 Oct. 1369
14. Sir John Campbell; b. c. 1313–14; cr. bef. 7 June 1329; d.s.p. 19 July 1333
15. Sir William Douglas; cr. ? 1335, 18 July 1341; res. 16 Feb. 1342
16. Robert Stewart (see Strathearn), later K. Robert II of Scotland; b. 2 Mar. 1316; cr. 16 Feb. 1342, but st. only (and infrequently) lord of Atholl; res. 31 May 1367
17. John Stewart (see Carrick), later K. Robert III of Scotland, s. & h.; b. c. 1337; st. earl of Atholl only once (17 Oct. 1379). Became K. 19 Apr. 1390
18. David Stewart (see Carrick, Rothesay), s. & h.; b. 1378; cr. 6 Sept. 1398; d.s.p. 26 Mar. 1402
19. Robert Stewart (see Albany, Fife, Menteith), next surv. br. of 17; b. c. 1340; granted earldom for lifetime of K. Robert III (d. 4 Apr. 1406) 2 Sept. 1403 but nowhere st. earl of Atholl; ? res. almost immediately; d. 3 Sept. 1420
20. Walter Stewart (see Caithness, Strathearn), next surv. br. of 17 and 19; b. ? c. 1360; cr. on or very shortly bef. 28 Apr. 1404; forf. and exec. 26 Mar. 1437
21. Sir John Stewart, s. of Queen Joan (Beaufort); b. c. 1440; cr. on or bef. 17 June 1455; d. 15 Sept. 1512
22. John Stewart, s. & h.; d. 1520–Jan. 1522
23. John Stewart, only s. & h.; b. 6 Oct. 1507; serv. 3 May 1522; d. c. Nov. 1542
24. John Stewart, s. & h.; d. 24 Apr. 1579
25. John Stewart, only s. & h.; b. 22 May 1563; serv. 5 May 1579; d.s.p.m. 25 Aug. 1595
26. John Stewart, Lord Innermeath; b. c. 1566; cr. 6 Mar. 1596; d. 26 Aug.–8 Oct. 1603
27. James Stewart, only s. & h.; b. 1583; serv. 29 July 1609; d.s.p. 1626
28. John Murray, s. of da. & h. of 25, 1st s. of Tullibardine 2; b. aft. 1604; cr. 17 Feb. 1629; d. June 1642
29. John Murray (see Tullibardine), s. & h.; b. 2 May 1631
    marquessate; cr. 7 Feb. 1676; d. 6 May 1703
30. John Murray (see Strathtay and Strathardle), s. & h.; b. 24 Feb. 1660
    dukedom; cr. 30 June 1703; d. 14 Nov. 1724

AVANDALE, earldom
 1. James Douglas (see Douglas); cr. prob. aft. 20 Feb. 1437; st. 28 Nov. 1437; d. 24 or 25 Mar. 1443
    [Thereafter descended with the earldom of Douglas until the forfeiture of 1455]

BALCARRES, *earldom*
1. Alexander Lindsay, Lord Lindsay of Balcarres; b. 6 July 1618; cr. 9 Jan. 1651; d. 30 Aug. 1659
2. Charles Lindsay, s. & h.; bapt. 7 Feb. 1651; d. unm. 15 Oct. 1662
3. Colin Lindsay, br. & h.; bapt. 23 Aug. 1652; d. 1722–23

BAMBREICH, *marquessate*
Cr. 29 May 1680 with the dukedom of Rothes; extinct with it, 26 July 1681

BOTHWELL, *earldom*
1. Patrick Hepburn, Lord Hailes; cr. 17 Oct. 1488; d. 18 Oct. 1508
2. Adam Hepburn, s. & h.; b. *c.* 1492; serv. 7 Nov. 1508; d. 9 Sept. 1513
3. Patrick Hepburn, s. & h.; b. 1511–12; d. Sept. 1556
4. James Hepburn (*see* Orkney), only s. & h.; b. *c.* 1535; serv. 9 Nov. 1556; forf. 20 Dec. 1567; d.s.p. leg. 14 Apr. 1578
5. Francis Stewart, Lord Darnley, neph. of 4; b. prob. 1563; cr. 16 June 1581; forf. 21 July 1593; d. 7 Sept. 1611–30 July 1614
6. Francis Stewart, s. & h.; b. 1584; rest. 30 July 1614; d. 1639
7. Charles Stewart, s. & h.; bapt. 7 Feb. 1618; d. unm. *c.* 1652

BOWMONT and CESSFORD, *marquessate*
Cr. 25 Apr. 1707 with the dukedom of Roxburghe and descended with it

BREADALBANE and HOLLAND, *earldom*
1. John Campbell of Glenorchy (*see* Caithness); b. *c.* 1635; cr. 13 Aug. 1681; d. 19 Mar. 1717

BUCCLEUCH, *earldom and dukedom*

Earldom
1. Walter Scott, Lord Scott of Buccleugh; cr. 16 Mar. 1619; d. 20 Nov. 1633
2. Francis Scott, only surv. s. and h.; b. 21 Dec. 1626; d.s.p.m.s. 25 Nov. 1651
3. Mary Scott, elder da. and coh.; b. 31 Aug. 1647; d.s.p. 11 Mar. 1661
   m. 9 Feb. 1659 Walter Scott (*see* Tarras); b. 23 Dec. 1644; d. 9 Apr. 1693
4. Anne Scott (*see* Dalkeith), only surv. sis. & h.; b. 11 Feb. 1651; d. 6 Feb. 1732
   m. 1. 20 Apr. 1663 James Scott, illeg. s. of K. Charles II (see Monmouth)
   dukedom; cr. duke on the same day. Creation repeated both conjointly and
        separately 16 Jan. 1666 and therefore the dukedom not affected by his
        forf. He was b. 9 Apr. 1649; forf. and exec. 15 July 1685.
   2. 6 May 1688 Charles Cornwallis, lord Cornwallis; bapt. 28 Dec. 1655; d.
        29 Apr. 1693

BUCHAN, *earldom*
1. Gartnach; st. *c.* 1150
2. Eve, da.; m. Colban; st. 1173; d. aft. 1178
3. Roger, gds. of 1, perhaps s. of 2; known only from a cartulary copy of one undatable charter, where his name may be an error for 'Fergus'
4. Fergus, perhaps s. or br. of 3; st. 1187–99; d. bef. 25 Feb. 1214
5. Margaret, da. & h.; d. 8 Apr. 1242–19 Nov. 1244
   m. bef. 17 Aug. 1214, as 2nd w. William Comyn; st. 9 Oct. 1211–17 Aug. 1214; d. 1233
6. Alexander Comyn, s. & h.; st. 19 Nov. 1244; d. shortly bef. 14 Mar. 1290
7. John Comyn, s. & h.; b. bef. 1260; st. 14 Mar. 1290; d.s.p.m. 11 Aug.–3 Dec. 1308; forf. by K. Robert I, perhaps posthumously
8. Alice, niece & h.
   m. bef. 14 July 1310 Henry Beaumont (*see* Moray). He had liv. hom. when his
        w. came of age, 12 Dec. 1312; forf. by Robert I Nov. 1314, but recog.
        by English ks. and Edw. Balliol; d. shortly bef. 10 Mar. 1340
   [Margaret, sis. & coh.
   m. 1. Sir John Ross
        2. Sir William Lindsay who alone styles his w. countess of Buchan and that aft. her death]
9. Sir Alexander Stewart, 4th s. of K. Robert II of Scotland; cr. or recog. 22–25 July 1382; d.s.p. leg. 1 Aug. 1405–25 Mar. 1406
   m. on or shortly bef. 22 July 1382 Euphemia, lady (countess) of Ross, gt.-niece of Sir John Ross above.

10. Robert Stewart (*see* Albany, Atholl, Fife, Menteith), 3rd s. of K. Robert II of Scotland; b. *c.* 1340; st. 20 Sept. 1406; res. 20 Sept. 1406; d. 3 Sept. 1420
11. John Stewart, 2nd s.; b. *c.* 1380; granted earldom 20 Sept. 1406, but st. lord of Buchan until 3 Aug. 1411; st. earl officially in a very few earlier documents and always from 10 Aug. 1412; d.s.p.m. 17 Aug. 1424

   [George Dunbar (*see* Dunbar); b. *c.* 1370. Said to have been cr. earl of Buchan when deprived of the earldom of Dunbar (1435) but nowhere st. earl of Buchan; d. 1455–57]

12. Lady Mary Stewart, da. of K. James I of Scotland; d.s.p.s. 20 Mar. 1465
   m. 1444 Wolfart van Borssele; d. 29 Apr. 1487
13. Sir James Stewart, half br. of James II; cr. 17 Apr.–17 Sept. 1470; d. 12 Feb. 1498–12 July 1499
14. Alexander Stewart, only s. & h.; serv. 23 Jan. 1500; d. 1505 bef. 20 Oct.
15. John Stewart, s. & h.; b. *c.* 1498; st. Master until serv. 29 Aug. 1519; d. 1561, aft. 13 Feb.
16. Christian, gd.-da. & h.; d. 20 Sept. 1580
   m. Robert Douglas; st. 7 Apr. 1574; d. 18 Aug. 1580
17. James Douglas, s. & h.; serv. 24 May 1588; d. 26 Aug. 1601
18. Mary, only da. & h.; d. 20 Aug. 1628
   m. bef. 1617 James Erskine; d. Jan. 1640
19. James Erskine, s. & h.; succ. Jan. 1640; d. Oct. 1664
20. William Erskine, s. & h.; d.s.p. 1695
21. David Erskine, Lord Cardross, gt.-gd. neph. & h. of James Erskine, husband of 18; recog. 18 Aug. 1698; d. 14 Oct. 1745

BUTE, *earldom*
1. James Stewart; cr. 14 Apr. 1703; d. 4 June 1710
2. James Stewart, s. & h.; b. *c.* 1690; d. 28 Jan. 1723

CAITHNESS, *earldom*
   [Until *c.* 1350 this earldom was held jointly with the Norwegian one of Orkney sometimes by a single earl, sometimes by two, and in Norse sources the earldom is usually st. simply 'of Orkney'. Aft. 1379 a distinct earldom of Orkney existed (*see under* Orkney). For the complicated history of these earldoms from the ninth century until *c.* 1350, *see* the *Complete Peerage*, 2nd edn, X, Appendix A]

1. Harald Maddadson, s. of Atholl 1; united earldoms 1198; d. 1206
2. David, s.; succ. (with 3) 1206; d. 1214
3. John, br.; succ. (with 2) 1206; succ. to united earldom 1214; d.s.p.m. 1231, autumn
4. Malcolm (*see* Angus); st. 7 Oct. 1232; both bef. and aft. this date he is st. simply earl of Angus; d. 26 July 1236–42
5. Magnus, ? uncle; st. perhaps 7 July 1235, certainly 26 July 1236; d. 1239
6. Gilbert ? s.; st. Aug. 1244; d. 1256
7. Magnus, s.; st. 1263; d. 1273
8. Magnus, s.; st. and ? succ. 29 July 1276; d.s.p. 1284
9. John, br.; st. 14 Mar. 1290, d. 1299–28 Oct. 1312
10. Magnus, s. & h.; st. 28 Oct. 1312; d. 6 Apr. 1320–? 4 Aug. 1321, certainly by 1329
11. Malise (*see* Strathearn), gt.-gt.-gds. of 5; b. *c.* 1275–80; succ. ? bef. 1330; ? depriv. 10 June 1344 when he was depriv. of the earldom of Strathearn; st. earl of Caithness only once, 28 May 1344, when he st. his 4th da. heiress to his earldom—she m. Sir William Sinclair, and for their s. *see* Orkney; d.s.p.m. 10 June 1344–Apr. 1359
12. David Stewart (*see* Strathearn), 5th s. of K. Robert II of Scotland; b. aft. 1355; cr. 21 Nov. 1375–28 Dec. 1377; d.s.p.m. Feb. 1382–89
13. Euphemia Stewart (*see* Strathearn), only da. & h.; b. *c.* 1375; res. Caithness bef. 29 Apr. 1401; d. Oct. 1415
   m. bef. 24 Aug. 1406 Patrick Graham; d. 10 Aug. 1413
14. Walter Stewart (*see* Atholl, Strathearn), uncle, yst. s. of King Robert II of Scotland; b. ? *c.* 1360; st. 29 Apr. 1401; res. 13 Dec. 1429–15 May 1430; *see* 14 *bis*
15. Alan Stewart, yr. s.; st. 15 May 1430; d. unm. late summer 1431

14. *bis.* Walter Stewart above named; succ. late summer 1431; forf. & exec. 26 Mar. 1437
16. George Crichton; cr. 12 June–8 July 1452; d. Aug. 1454
17. William Sinclair (*see* Orkney); cr. 28 Aug. 1455; res. 29 July 1478–30 July 1479; d. 30 July 1479–3 Aug. 1480
18. William Sinclair, yr. s.; d. 9 Sept. 1513
19. John Sinclair, s. & h.; serv. 24 Nov. 1513; d. 18 May 1529
20. George Sinclair, 1st surv. s. & h.; b. bef. 14 July 1527; st. 6 Sept. 1540 when still a minor; succ. to lands 1546; d. 9 Sept. 1582
21. George Sinclair, gds. & h.; b. 1566; d. Feb. 1643
22. George Sinclair, gt.-gds. & h.; sought to convey earldom to 23 ultimately without success; d.s.p. May 1676
23. John Campbell of Glenorchy (*see* Breadalbane); b. *c.* 1635; cr. 28 June 1677; res. claim Aug. 1681; d. 19 Mar. 1717
24. George Sinclair, gds. of 21, h. of 22; recog. 15 July 1681; d. unm. 1698
25. John Sinclair, gt.-gt.-gds. of 19, h. of 24; d. 1705
26. Alexander Sinclair, s. & h.; b. *c.* 1684; d.s.p.m. 9 Dec. 1765

CALLANDER, *earldom*
1. James Livingstone, Lord Livingstone of Almond, 3rd s. of Linlithgow 1 ?; cr. 6 Oct. 1641; d.s.p. shortly bef. 25 Mar. 1674
2. Alexander Livingstone, neph. & h. by entail, 2nd s. of Linlithgow 2; d.s.p. leg. Aug. 1685
3. Alexander Livingstone, neph. & h. by entail, 2nd s. of Linlithgow 3; serv. 16 May 1688; d. Dec. 1692
4. James Livingstone (*see* Linlithgow), only s. & h.; forf. 17 Feb. 1716; d.s.p.m.s. 25 Apr. 1723

CAMPBELL and COWALL, *earldom*
Cr. with the dukedom of Argyll (23 June 1701) and descended with it

CARNWATH, *earldom*
1. Robert Dalzell, lord Dalzell; cr. 21 Apr. 1639; forf. 25 Feb. 1645 (but estates and title excepted from forf.); rest. (uncompleted) 1651; d. bef. 21 June 1654
2. Gavin Dalzell, s. & h.; st. 31 July 1646 (because of forf. of 1); d. June 1674
3. James Dalzell, s. & h.; b. bef. 4 July 1648; serv. 30 May 1676; d.s.p.m. 1683
4. John Dalzell, br. & h.; serv. 13 Nov. 1688; d. unm. 7 June 1702
5. Robert Dalzell, gt.-gd. neph. & h. of 1; b. *c.* 1687; serv. Nov. 1702; forf. 9 Feb. 1716; d. 4 Aug. 1737

CARRICK, *earldom*
1. Duncan; b. bef. 1176; st. earl 1189–96 but frequently thereaft. st. only Duncan of Carrick; d. 13 June 1250
2. Nigel, s. & h.; d. 1256
3. Margaret, da. & h.; d. bef. 9 Nov. 1292
    m. 1. bef. 4 Oct. 1266 Adam de Kilconquhar; d.s.p. 1270
        2. 1271 Robert de Bruce; b. 1243; res. 9 Nov. 1292; d. shortly bef. 4 Apr. 1304
4. Robert Bruce, s. & h., later K. Robert I of Scotland; b. 11 July 1274; succ. 9 Nov. 1292; became K. 25 Mar. 1306
5. Henry Percy; granted earldom by K. Edw. I of England, 1306; not st. e.; d. 23 Feb. 1352
6. Edward Bruce, 2nd s. of 3; cr. 1 Mar.–21 Oct. 1313; succ. as K. of Ireland 2 May 1316 but still occasionally st. earl of Carrick; d.s.p. leg. 14 Oct. 1318
7. David Bruce, s. & h. of 4, later K. David II of Scotland; b. 5 Mar. 1324; cr. 17 Mar.–17 July 1328; became K. 7 June 1329
8. Alexander Bruce, illeg. s. of 5; cr. aft. 7 June 1329; d.s.p.m. 19 July 1333
9. William Cunningham; b. *c.* 1320; cr. prob. 1362, *c.* 12 Sept.; found st. only lord of Carrick; res. or depr. bef. 22 June 1368 (? depr. 27 Sept. 1367); d. Dec. 1396–8 July 1399
10. John Stewart, later K. Robert III of Scotland; b. *c.* 1337; cr. 22 June 1368; became K. 19 Apr. 1390
11. David Stewart (*see* Atholl, Rothesay), s. & h.; b. 1378; cr. 19 Apr. 1390–2 Jan. 1391; d.s.p. 26 Mar. 1402

12. James Stewart, br. & h., later K. James I of Scotland; b. 1394, ? 25 July; cr. 10 July 1404, not however st. earl; became K. 4 Apr. 1406

[*By Act of Parliament, 22 Nov. 1469, the earldom of Carrick and in effect the dukedom of Rothesay were annexed to the oldest s. of the reigning K. of Scotland. There were the following exceptions:*]

13. Robert Stewart (*see* Kintyre, Wigtown), 3rd s. of K. James VI of Scotland; b. 18 Jan. or 18 Feb. 1602; cr. bef. 27 May 1602; d. 27 May 1602
14. John Stewart, 2nd surv. s. of Orkney 6; cr. 22 July 1628; d. 22 June 1643–3 Mar. 1646

CASSILIS, *earldom*
1. David Kennedy, Lord Kennedy; cr. 22–24 Oct. 1509; d. 9 Sept. 1513
2. Gilbert Kennedy, s. & h.; d. 24–31 Aug. 1527
3. Gilbert Kennedy, s. & h.; b. 1515; d. 28 Nov. 1558
4. Gilbert Kennedy, s. & h.; b. *c.* 1541; d. 12 Dec. 1576
5. John Kennedy, s. & h.; b. Nov. 1574–Apr. 1575; d.s.p. Oct.–14 Nov. 1615
6. John Kennedy, neph. & h.; d. Apr. 1668
7. John Kennedy, 1st surv. s. & h.; b. aft. 1644; d. 23 July 1701
8. John Kennedy, gds. & h.; b. Apr. 1700; d.s.p. 7 Mar. 1759

CLYDESDALE, *marquessate*
Cr. with the dukedom of Hamilton (12 Apr. 1643), and descended with it

CRAWFORD, *earldom*
1. David Lindsay; b. *c.* 1360; cr. 21 Apr.–2 May 1398; d. Feb. 1407
2. Alexander Lindsay, s. & h.; b. *c.* 1387; d. 1438, aft. 31 Mar.
3. David Lindsay, s. & h.; d. 17 or 27 Jan. 1446
4. Alexander Lindsay, s. & h.; forf. June 1452; rest. *c.* Apr. 1453; d. Sept. 1453
5. David Lindsay (*see* Montrose), s. & h.; b. 1440; d. Christmas 1495
6. John Lindsay, 1st surv. s. & h.; d.s.p. leg. 9 Sept. 1513
7. Alexander Lindsay, uncle & h. male; b. *c.* 1443; d. May 1517
8. David Lindsay, s. & h.; d. 27 Nov. 1542, his son having been excluded from the succession for wickedness
9. David Lindsay, gt.-gt.-gds. of 3; d. 20 Sept. 1558
10. David Lindsay, gds. of 8; b. 1526–27; d. Feb. 1572 according to inquis. of 1611—perhaps Feb. 1573 N.S.
11. David Lindsay, s. & h.; b. *c.* 1552; d. 22 Nov. 1607
12. David Lindsay, s. & h.; bapt. 8 Mar. 1576; d.s.p.m. June 1620
13. Henry Lindsay, uncle & h.; d. bef. 16 Jan. 1623
14. George Lindsay, s. & h.; d.s.p.m. 1633
15. Alexander Lindsay, br. & h.; d. unm. bef. 28 Aug. 1639
16. Ludovic Lindsay, br. & h.; st. 28 Aug. 1639; forf. 26 July 1644; d.s.p. leg. Nov. 1652
17. John Lindsay (*see* Lindsay); b. 1611. Having a fourteenth-century ancestor in common with the preceding earls, he succ. to the exclusion of right heirs in terms of an entail by 16; d. 1678
18. William Lindsay, 1st surv. s. & h.; b. Apr. 1644; d. 6 Mar. 1698
19. John Lindsay, s. & h.; b. 1671–72; d. 4 Jan. 1714
20. John Lindsay, s. & h.; b. 4 Oct. 1702; d.s.p. 24 Dec. 1749

CROMARTY, *earldom*
1. George Mackenzie, Viscount Tarbat; b. 1630; cr. 1 Jan. 1703; d. 17 or 27 Aug. 1714
2. John Mackenzie, 1st s. & h.; b. 1656; d. 20 Feb. 1731

DALHOUSIE, *earldom*
1. William Ramsay, Lord Ramsay of Dalhousie; b. aft. 1593; cr. 29 June 1633; d. Nov. 1672
2. George Ramsay, s. & h.; b. 1618–22; d. 11 Feb. 1674
3. William Ramsay, s. & h.; d. Nov. 1682
4. George Ramsay, s. & h.; b. aft. 1661; d. unm. 1696
5. William Ramsay, br. & h.; d. unm. Oct. 1710
6. William Ramsay, gds. of 2 & h.; b. *c.* 1660; serv. 9 Feb. 1711; d. 8 Dec. 1739

DALKEITH, *earldom*
Cr. with the dukedom of Buccleuch (20 Apr. 1663), and descended with it

DARNLEY, *earldom*
Cr. with the dukedom of Lennox (5 Aug. 1581), and descended with it

DELORAIN, *earldom*
1. Henry Scott, 3rd s. of Buccleuch 4; b. 1676; cr. 29 Mar. 1706; d. 25 Dec. 1730

DIRLETOUN, *earldom*
1. James Maxwell; cr. 1646; d.s.p.m.s. 19 Apr. 1650

DOUGLAS, *earldom, marquessate, dukedom*

Earldom
1. Sir William Douglas (*see* Mar); b. *c.* 1327; cr. 20–28 Jan. 1358; d. *c.* May 1384
2. James Douglas, only s. & h.; b. *c.* 1358; d.s.p.s. leg. Aug. 1388, bef. 18th
3. Archibald Douglas, illeg. s. of uncle of **1**; b. *c.* 1325; d. prob. 24 Dec. 1400
4. Archibald Douglas, duke of Touraine (1424), s. & h.; b. *c.* 1372; d. 17 Aug. 1424
5. Archibald Douglas, count of Longueville (see Wigtown), only surv. s. & h.; b. *c.* 1390; d. 26 June 1439
6. William Douglas, duke of Touraine and count of Longueville, s. & h.; b. *c.* 1424; exec. 24 Nov. 1440
7. James Douglas (*see* Avandale), 2nd s. of 3 & h. male; d. 24 or 25 Mar. 1443
8. William Douglas, s. & h.; b. *c.* 1425; d.s.p. 22 Feb. 1452
9. James Douglas, br. & h.; forf. 10 June 1455; d.s.p. soon aft. 22 May 1491

Marquessate
10. William Douglas (*see* Angus); b. *c.* 1589; cr. June 1633; d. 19 Feb. 1660
11. James Douglas, gds. & h.; b. *c.* 1646; d. 25 Feb. 1700
12. Archibald Douglas (*see* Abernethy), 1st surv. s. & h.; b. 1694 *dukedom;* cr. 10 Aug. 1703; d.s.p. 21 July 1761

DRUMLANRIG and SANQUHAR, *earldom*
Cr. with the marquessate of Queensberry (11 Feb. 1682) and descended with it and the dukedom of Queensberry except in the case of James Douglas, 1st surv. s. & h. of Queensberry 4 (an idiot barred from the succession to the dukedom of Queensberry but styled, by courtesy, earl of Drumlanrig). He was b. 2 Nov. 1697, d. unm. 17 Feb. 1715

DUMFRIES, *earldom*
1. William Crichton, Viscount Ayr; b. bef. 1598; cr. 12 June 1633; d. 15 Aug. 1642–24 Mar. 1643
2. William Crichton, 1st s. & h.; b. in or aft. 1605; d. 1691
3. William Crichton, gds. & h.; b. in or aft. 1683; d. unm. 28 Feb. 1694
4. Penelope, eldest sis. & coh.; m. 26 Feb. 1698 William Dalrymple of Glenmure; d. 3 Dec. 1744

DUMFRIESSHIRE, *marquessate*
Cr. with the dukedom of Queensberry (3 Nov. 1684), and descended with it

DUNBAR, *earldom*

[These earls are sometimes in the twelfth century st. earls of Lothian and aft. Mar. 1290 are generally st. earls of March]
1. Gospatrick, br. of Dolfin; usually st. himself so, he once st. himself earl; d. prob. 22 Aug. 1138
2. Gospatrick, s. & h.; st. 1 Nov. 1140; d. 1166, bef. 8 Dec.
3. Waltheof, s. & h.; st. 1166, bef. 8 Dec.; d. 1182
4. Patrick, s. & h.; b. 1152; entered religion Christmas 1232; d. 31 Dec. 1232
5. Patrick, s. & h.; liv. (of English lands) 22 Feb. 1233; d. May–Nov. (prob. Sept.) 1248
6. Patrick, s. & h.; b. 1212–13; serv. (to English lands) 13 Dec. 1248; d. 24 Aug. 1289
7. Patrick de Dunbar, s. & h.; b. 1241–42; liv. (of English lands) 14 May 1290; d. 10 Oct. 1308

8. Patrick de Dunbar (*see* Moray), s. & h.; b. *c.* 1283; liv. (of English lands) 10 Nov. 1308; res. 25 July 1368; d.s.p.s. 11 Nov. 1368
9. George Dunbar, gt.-neph. & h. male; b. *c.* 1336; d. 8 Sept. 1422–17 Feb. 1423
10. George Dunbar (*see* Buchan), s. & h.; b. *c.* 1370; forf. 11 Jan. 1435; d. aft. 4 Aug. 1455
11. George Home; cr. 3 July 1605; d.s.p.m. 20 Jan. 1611

DUNBARTON, *earldom*
1. George Douglas, 5th s. of Douglas 10; b. *c.* 1635–36; cr. 9 Mar. 1675; d. 20 Mar. 1692
2. George Douglas, s. & h.; b. *c.* Apr. 1687; d.s.p. aft. 7 Jan. 1749

DUNDEE, *earldom*
1. John Scrimgeour, Viscount Dudhope; cr. 8 Sept. 1660; d.s.p. 23 June 1668

DUNDONALD, *earldom*
1. William Cochrane, Lord Cochrane; b. 1605; cr. 12 May 1669; d. 1685–86
2. John Cochrane, gds. & h.; b. in or aft. 1653; d. 16 May 1690
3. William Cochrane, s. & h.; b. 1686; d. unm. 22 Nov. 1705
4. John Cochrane, br. & h.; b. 4 July 1687; d. 5 June 1720

DUNFERMLINE, *earldom*
1. Alexander Seton, Lord Fyvie; b. 1555; cr. 4 Mar. 1605; d. 16 June 1622
2. Charles Seton, only surv. s. & h.; b. Nov. 1615; d. *c.* 11 May 1672
3. Alexander Seton, 1st surv. s. & h.; b. 12 June 1642; d.s.p. 23 Aug.–27 Oct. 1677
4. James Seton, next br. & h.; forf. 1690; d.s.p. 26 Dec. 1694

DUNMORE, *earldom*
1. Charles Murray, 2nd s. of Atholl 29; b. 28 Feb. 1661; cr. 16 Aug. 1686; d. 19 Apr. 1710
2. John Murray, 1st surv. s. & h.; b. 31 Oct. 1685; d. unm. 18 Apr. 1752

DYSART, *earldom*
1. William Murray; b. bef. 1605; cr. 3 Aug. 1643; d.s.p.m. aft. 11 Sept. 1653
2. Elizabeth, 1st da. & coh.; d. 5 June 1698
   m. 1. Sir Lionel Tollemache, bt.; d. shortly bef. 25 Mar. 1669
   2. John Maitland, duke of Lauderdale; b. 24 May 1616; d.s.p.m. 24 Aug. 1682
3. Lionel Tollemache, 1st surv. s. & h.; b. 30 Jan. 1649; d. 23 Feb. 1727

EDIRDALE *or* ARDMANACH, *earldom*
1. James Stewart (*see* Ross, Ormond (S), abps. of St. Andrews); b. prob. 1479; cr. 29 Jan. 1488; d. unm. 12–17 Jan. 1504

EGLINTON, *earldom*
1. Hugh Montgomery, Lord Montgomery; b. 1459–60; cr. 3–20 Jan. 1507; d. 23 Sept.–3 Oct. 1545
2. Hugh Montgomery, gds. & h.; b. prob. *c.* 1510; d. 3 Sept. 1546
3. Hugh Montgomery, s. & h.; b. aft. 1533; d. 3 June 1585
4. Hugh Montgomery, s. & h.; b. 1563; d. 18 or 20 Apr. 1586
5. Hugh Montgomery, only s. & h.; b. *c.* 1584; d.s.p. 4 Sept. 1612
6. Alexander Seton or Montgomery, gds. of 3, 3rd s. of Winton 1; b. 1588; d. 14 Jan. 1661
7. Hugh Montgomery, s. & h.; b. 30 Mar. 1613; d. Feb. 1669
8. Alexander Montgomery, s. & h.; b. in or aft. 1636; d. 1701
9. Alexander Montgomery, s. & h.; b. *c.* 1660; d. 18 Feb. 1729

ELGIN, *earldom*
1. Thomas Bruce, Lord Kinloss; b. 2 Dec. 1599; cr. 21 June 1633; d. 21 Dec. 1663
2. Robert Bruce (*see* Ailesbury), only s. & h.; b. 1622–27; d. 20 Oct. 1685
3. Thomas Bruce (*see* Ailesbury), 1st surv. s. & h.; b. 1656; d. 16 Dec. 1741

ENZIE, *earldom*
Cr. with the marquessate of Huntly (17 Apr. 1599) and descended with it

ERROLL, *earldom*
1. William Hay; cr. 12 June–12 Aug. 1452, perhaps 31 July or 11–12 Aug. 1452; d. aft. 15 Nov. 1461, prob. Oct. 1462
2. Nicholas Hay, s. & h.; b. aft. 1441; d.s.p. 12 Aug. 1467–1470, ? 24 Aug. 1467
3. William Hay, br. & h.; d. 14 Jan. 1507
4. William Hay, s. & h.; serv. 21 Sept. 1507; d. 9 Sept. 1513
5. William Hay, only s. & h.; serv. 20 Oct. 1513; d. 28 July 1522
6. William Hay, only s. & h.; b. 1521–22; d.s.p.m. 11 Apr. 1541
7. George Hay, gds. of 3; serv. 10 Dec. 1541; d. 30 Jan. 1574
8. Andrew Hay, s. & h.; d. 8 Oct. 1585
9. Francis Hay, s. & h.; b. 1564 bef. 30 Apr.; succ. to exclusion of elder brs. who suffered physical defects, were debarred from succeeding and in 1596 found insane; forf. 8 June 1594; rest. 16 Dec. 1597; d. 16 July 1631
10. William Hay, s. & h.; b. *c.* 1591; d. 7 Dec. 1636
11. Gilbert Hay, only s. & h.; b. 13 June 1631; serv. 30 Aug. 1638; d.s.p. 21 Feb.–4 Mar. 1674
12. John Hay, gt.-gds. of 8 & h.; d. 30 Dec. 1704
13. Charles Hay, s. & h.; serv. 24 Apr. 1705; d. unm. 16 Oct. 1717

ETHIE, *earldom*
1. John Carnegie, Lord Lour (*see* Northesk), yr. br. of Southesk 1; b. *c.* 1579; st. altered to earldom of Northesk 25 Oct. 1666; d. 8 Jan. 1667

FIFE, *earldom*
1. Ethelred, s. of Malcolm III, K. of Scotland; st. at uncertain date, but prob. bef. 1107 rather than aft.
2. Constantine, 's. of Macduff'; st. prob. bef. 1124; d. 1128–36
3. Gillemichael Macduff; st. 1128–39; d. bef. 16 Aug. 1139 and prob. bef. 11 July 1136
4. Duncan, st. 16 Aug. 1139 and prob. 11 July 1136; d. 1154
5. Duncan, s. & h.; st. 1159; d. 1204
6. Malcolm, s. & h.; d.s.p. 1230
7. Malcolm, neph. & h.; d. 1266
8. Colban, s. & h.; b. *c.* 1245; d. 1270–72
9. Duncan, s. & h.; b. *c.* 1262; d. 25 Sept. 1288
10. Duncan, only s. & h.; b. *c.* 1285; d. 17 Mar. 1351–16 Apr. 1355, ? 1353
11. Isabella; b. bef. 1332; st. 1359; res. ? 1359–60, and again 30 Mar. 1371–6 Mar. 1372; d. aft. 12 Aug. 1389
    m. 1. Sir William Ramsay of Colluthie; cr. 6 Mar.–12 Apr. 1358; d. 3 Apr. 1359–22 July 1360
    2. aft. 22 July 1360 Walter Stewart, 2nd s. of Strathearn 11 (K. Robert II of Scotland). He is st. only lord of Fife and d.s.p. 14 Aug. 1362–10 January 1363
    3. 10 Jan.–8 June 1363 Sir Thomas Bisset of Upsetlington. He was granted the earldom 8 June 1363, but is st. only lord of Fife; d. 17 Apr. 1366–11 Jan. 1369
    4. John Dunbar. He was granted the earldom Apr.–May 1370; d. ? bef. 30 Mar. 1371
12. Robert Stewart (*see* Albany, Menteith), 3rd s. of Robert II, K. of Scotland; b. *c.* 1340; cr. 4 Dec. 1371–6 Mar. 1372; d. 3 Sept. 1420
13. Murdoch Stewart (*see* Albany, Menteith), s. & h.; b. prob. 1362; forf. and exec. 25 May 1425

FINDLATER, *earldom*
1. James Ogilvy, Lord Ogilvy; cr. 20 Feb. 1638; d.s.p.m. 1652
2. Patrick Ogilvy, s.-in-law & h. to earldom; d. May 1659
3. James Ogilvy, s. & h.; serv. 15 Apr. 1662; d. 1711
4. James Ogilvy (*see* Seafield), 1st surv. s. & h.; b. 11 July 1663; d. 15 Aug. 1730

FORFAR, *earldom*
1. Archibald Douglas, yr. s. of Ormond 4; b. 3 May 1653; cr. 2 Oct. 1661; d. 11 Dec. 1712
2. Archibald Douglas, only s. & h.; b. 25 May 1692; d. unm. 8 Dec. 1715

FORTH, *earldom*
1. Patrick Ruthven (*see* Brentford); b. *c.* 1573; cr. 27 March 1642; d.s.p.m. 2 Feb. 1651

GALLOWAY, *earldom*
1. Alexander Stewart, Lord of Garlies; b. *c.* 1580; cr. 19 Sept. 1623; d. 1649
2. James Stewart, 1st surv. s. & h.; b. *c.* 1610; d. June 1671
3. Alexander Stewart, s. & h.; serv. 15 Feb. 1681; d. in or shortly bef. 1690
4. Alexander Stewart, s. & h.; b. 8 Jan. 1670; d.s.p. 26 Sept. 1690
5. James Stewart, br. & h.; d. 16 Feb. 1746

GARIOCH, ? *earldom*
[The separate existence of this earldom is doubtful; as a lordship it was held by the earls of Mar in the fourteenth century and they assumed the style 'earl of Mar and Garioch', and so an earldom was reputed to exist (*see under* Mar). In consequence K. James II of Scotland granted to his queen, Mary of Gueldres, 'the earldom of Garioch' (26 Aug. 1452), but otherwise, if it existed, it descended with the earldom of Mar.]

GIFFORD, *earldom*
Cr. with the marquessate of Tweeddale (17 Dec. 1694), and descended with it

GLASGOW, *earldom*
1. David Boyle, Lord Boyle; b. 1666; cr. 12 Apr. 1703; d. 31 Oct. 1733

GLENCAIRN, *earldom*
1. Alexander Cunningham, Lord Kilmaurs; b. 1426–30; cr. 28 May 1488; d. 11 June 1488
2. Robert Cunningham, s. & h.; depr. 17 Oct. 1488; d. bef. 25 June 1492
3. Cuthbert Cunningham, s. & h.; rest. 13 Aug. 1503; d. May 1540–May 1541
4. William Cunningham, s. & h.; b. *c.* 1493; d. Mar. 1548
5. Alexander Cunningham, s. & h.; d. 23 Nov. 1574
6. William Cunningham, s. & h.; d. 31 July 1579–24 Feb. 1580
7. James Cunningham, s. & h.; b. *c.* 1552; d. 30 June 1630–2 Apr. 1631
8. William Cunningham, s. & h.; st. 2 Apr. 1631; d. bef. 3 Mar. 1635
9. William Cunningham, s. & h.; b. *c.* 1610; d. 30 May 1664
10. Alexander Cunningham, 1st surv. s. & h.; d.s.p.m. 26 May 1670
11. John Cunningham, br. & h.; d. 14 Dec. 1703
12. William Cunningham, s. & h.; d. 14 Mar. 1734

GORDON, *dukedom* (*see* Huntly, Enzie)
1. George Gordon; b. *c.* 1649; cr. 1 Nov. 1684; d. 7 Dec. 1716

GOWRIE, *earldom*
1. William Ruthven, Lord Ruthven; cr. 23 Aug. 1581; forf. & exec. 4 May 1584
2. James Ruthven, s. & h.; bapt. 25 Sept. 1575; rest. 1586; d. 1588
3. John Ruthven, br. & h.; b. *c.* 1577; d. 5 Aug. 1600 & forf.

GRAHAM and BUCHANAN, *marquessate*
Cr. with the dukedom of Montrose (24 Apr. 1707) and descended with it

HADDINGTON, *earldom*
1. Thomas Hamilton (*see* Melrose); b. 1563; cr. by change of st. 17 Aug. 1627; d. 29 May 1637
2. Thomas Hamilton, s. & h.; b. 25 May 1600; d. 30 Aug. 1640
3. Thomas Hamilton, s. & h.; b. *c.* 1625; d.s.p. 8 Feb. 1645
4. John Hamilton, br. & h.; b. 1626; d. 31 Aug. 1669
5. Charles Hamilton, only s. & h.; b. 1 July 1650; d. May 1685
6. Thomas Hamilton, 2nd s. & h. to earldom; b. 29 Aug. 1680; d. 28 Nov. 1735

HAMILTON, *marquessate and dukedom* (*see* Arran)
Marquessate
1. John Hamilton (*see* Arran); b. *c.* 1537–38; cr. 17 Apr. 1599; d. 6 Apr. 1604
2. James Hamilton (*see* Cambridge), s. & h.; b. *c.* 1589; d. 2 Mar. 1625
3. James Hamilton (*see* Clydesdale), s. & h.; b. 19 June 1606
dukedom; cr. 12 Apr. 1643; exec. s.p.m.s. 9 Mar. 1649

4. William Hamilton (*see* Lanark), br. & h.; b. 14 Dec. 1616; d.s.p.m.s. 12 Sept. 1651
5. Ann Hamilton, eldest da. & h. of 3; b. *c.* 1636; res. 9 July 1698; d. Oct. 1716
   m. 29 Apr. 1656 William Douglas, earl of Selkirk; cr. 20 Sept. 1660; d. 18 Apr. 1694
6. James Douglas (*see* Brandon), s. & h.; b. 11 Apr. 1658; cr. 10 Aug. 1698; d. 15 Nov. 1712
7. James Douglas, s. & h.; b. 5 Jan. 1703; d. 9 Mar. 1743

HARTFELL, *earldom*
1. James Johnston, Lord Johnston of Lochwood; b. 1602; cr. 18 Mar. 1643; d. Apr. 1653
2. James Johnston (*see* Annandale), 1st s. & h.; b. 1625; d. 17 July 1672
   [*Thereafter descended with the earldom and marquessate of Annandale, which see*]

HOME, *earldom*
1. Alexander Home, Lord Home; b. *c.* 1566; cr. 4 Mar. 1605; d. 5 Apr. 1619
2. James Home, 1st s. & h.; b. *c.* 1607, serv. 28 Sept. 1620; d.s.p. 13 Feb. 1633
3. James Home, had a common fifteenth-century ancestor with 2; serv. 22 Mar. 1633; d. Dec. 1666
4. Alexander Home, s. & h.; d.s.p. 1674
5. James Home, br. & h.; d.s.p. 1687
6. Charles Home, next br. & h.; d. 22 July 1706
7. Alexander Home, s. & h.; d. 1720

HOPETOUN, *earldom*
1. Charles Hope; b. 1681; cr. 15 Apr. 1703; d. 26 Feb. 1742

HUNTLY, *earldom and marquessate*

Earldom
1. Sir Alexander Seton of Gordon; cr. 30 Oct. 1444–3 July 1445; d. 15 July 1470
2. George Gordon, 2nd s. (1st s. by 2nd w. whose children had their name changed from Seton to Gordon 1457–58); d. *c.* 8 June 1501
3. Alexander Gordon, s. & h.; serv. 11 Aug. 1501; d. 16 Jan. 1524
4. George Gordon (*see* Moray), gds. & h.; b. *c.* 1510; serv. 7 Nov. 1530; d. 22 Oct. 1562 and forf.
5. George Gordon, 1st surv. s. & h.; rest. Apr. 1567; forf. Aug. 1571; rest. 26 Jan.–20 Feb. 1573; d. 19 Oct. 1576
6. George Gordon (*see* Enzie), s. & h.
   marquessate; cr. 17 Apr. 1599; d. 13 June 1636
7. George Gordon, s. & h.; forf. & exec. 22 Mar. 1649
8. Lewis Gordon, 1st surv. s. & h.; b. *c.* 1626; rest. 25 Mar. 1651; d. Dec. 1653
9. George Gordon (*see* Gordon), s. & h.; b. *c.* 1649; d. 7 Dec. 1716

HYNDFORD, *earldom*
1. John Carmichael, Lord Carmichael; b. 28 Feb. 1638; cr. 25 June 1701; d. 20 Sept. 1710
2. James Carmichael, s. & h.; d. 16 Aug. 1737

IRVINE, *earldom*
1. James Campbell, Lord Kintyre, 2nd s. of Argyll 7; bapt. 25 Sept. 1611; cr. 28 Mar. 1642; d.s.p. shortly bef. 13 Sept. 1645

ISLAY, *earldom*
1. Archibald Campbell, br. and h. of Argyll 11; b. June 1682; cr. 19 Oct. 1706; succ. to dukedom of Argyll 1743; d.s.p. leg. 15 Apr. 1761

KELLIE, *earldom*
1. Thomas Erskine, Viscount Fentoun; b. 1566; cr. 12 Mar. 1619; d. 12 June 1639
2. Thomas Erskine, gds. & h.; bapt. 4 May 1615; d. unm. 3 Feb. 1643
3. Alexander Erskine, br. & h.; serv. 18 Apr. 1643; d. May 1677
4. Alexander Erskine, only surv. s. & h.; bapt. 14 Sept. 1677; serv. 26 Oct. 1699; d. 8 Mar. 1710
5. Alexander Erskine, only s. & h.; d. 3 Apr. 1756

KELSO, *earldom*
 Cr. with the dukedom of Roxburghe (25 Apr. 1707) and descended with it

KILMARNOCK, *earldom*
1. William Boyd, Lord Boyd; cr. 17 Aug. 1661; d. Mar. 1692
2. William Boyd, s. & h.; b. *c.* 1663–64; d. 20 May 1692
3. William Boyd, s. & h.; b. 1683–84; serv. 20 July 1699; d. Sept. 1717

KINCARDINE,[1] *earldom*
 Cr. with the marquessate of Montrose (6 May 1644) and descended with it

KINCARDINE,[2] *earldom*
1. Sir Edward Bruce of Carnock; cr. 26 Dec. 1647; d. unm. 1662
2. Alexander Bruce, br. & h.; b. *c.* 1629; d. 9 July 1680
3. Alexander Bruce, only surv. s. & h.; bapt. 5 June 1666; d. unm. 10 Nov. 1705
4. Alexander Bruce, cous. of 1; recog. Oct. 1706; d. 3 Oct. 1715

KINGHORN, *earldom*
1. Patrick Lyon, Lord Glamis; b. 1575; cr. 10 July 1606; d. 19 Dec. 1615
2. John Lyon, s. & h.; b. 13 Aug. 1596; d. 12 May 1646
3. Patrick Lyon, only s. & h.; b. 29 May 1643; d. 15 May 1695
 [On 1 July 1677 the title of the earldom was changed to Strathmore and Kinghorn *q.v.*]

KINNOULL, *earldom*
1. George Hay, Viscount Dupplin; bapt. 4 Dec. 1570; cr. 25 May 1633; d. 16 Dec. 1634
2. George Hay, only surv. s. & h.; d. 5 Oct. 1644
3. George Hay, 1st s. & h.; d. 20 Nov. 1649–Mar. 1650
4. William Hay, br. & h.; d. 28 Mar. 1677
5. George Hay, 1st s. & h.; d. unm. 1687
6. William Hay, only br. & h.; b. aft. 1666; d. unm. 10 May 1709
7. Thomas Hay, gt.-gds. of br. of 1 & h.; b. *c.* 1660; d. 5 Jan. 1719

KINTORE, *earldom*
1. Sir John Keith, 4th s. of Marischal 5; cr. 26 June 1677; d. 12 Apr. 1715

KINTYRE and LORNE, *dukedom and marquessate*

 Dukedom
1. Robert Stewart (*see* Carrick, Wigtown), 3rd s. of K. James VI of Scotland; b. 18 Jan. or 18 Feb. 1602; cr. bef. he d. 27 May 1602

 Marquessate
 Cr. with the dukedom of Argyll (23 June 1701) and descended with it

LANARK, *earldom*
1. William Hamilton (*see* Arran, Hamilton, Clydesdale); b. 14 Dec. 1616; cr. 31 Mar. 1639; d.s.p.m.s. 12 Sept. 1651
 [*Thereafter descended with the dukedom of Hamilton, which see*]

LAUDERDALE, *earldom, dukedom*

 Earldom
1. John Maitland, Viscount Lauderdale; cr. 14 Mar. 1624; d. 18 Jan. 1645
2. John Maitland (*see* March, Guildford), 1st surv. s. & h.; b. 24 May 1616; serv. 5 Sept. 1649
 dukedom; cr. 26 May 1672; d.s.p.m. 24 Aug. 1682

 Earldom only
3. Charles Maitland, br. & h. male; b. *c.* 1620; d. 9 June 1691
4. Richard Maitland, s. & h.; b. 20 June 1653; d.s.p.s. 1695
5. John Maitland, br. & h.; b. *c.* 1655; d. 13 Aug. 1710
6. Charles Maitland, 1st surv. s. & h.; b. *c.* 1688; serv. 8 Jan. 1711; d. 15 July 1744

---

[1] Prob. Kincardine in the Mearns.
[2] Prob. Kincardine-on-Forth.

LENNOX, *earldom and dukedom*

Earldom
1. Alwin; st. earl of Lennox by 3 but not mentioned in his own lifetime; d. prob. by 1178
2. David (*see* Huntingdon), yr. br. of K. Malcolm IV and K. William I of Scotland; b. 1142–52; granted earldom of Lennox 1178–82, and prob. 1178; apparently in consequence of this st. earl 1178; res. bef. 17 Mar. 1199; d. 17 June 1219
3. Alwin, s. & h. of **1**; st. bef. 17 Mar. 1199; d. 1208–4 Dec. 1214
4. Maldoven, s. & h.; st. 1208–4 Dec. 1214; d. aft. 12 Mar. 1251
5. Malcolm, gds. & h.; st. bef. 18 Oct. 1270; d. 1290–1305, prob. 1303–05
6. Malcolm, s. & h.; st. 1305; d. 19 July 1333
7. Donald, s. & h.; st. 1 Nov. 1351; d. 2 May 1361–20 Nov. 1364
8. Margaret, da. & h.; d. 19 Aug. 1388–? 17 Feb. 1392
   m. ? 1344 Walter of Faslane, h. male of yr. br. of 4; st. earl 20 Nov. 1364 and 30 Mar. 1372 but otherwise always lord of (the earldom of) Lennox; d. aft. 17 Feb. 1392. They res. in favour of 9 on 8 May 1385 and again 19 Aug. 1388
9. Duncan, s. & h.; b. *c.* 1345; st. 17 Feb. 1392; exec. 25 May 1425
10. Isabel, da. & h.; b. prob. *c.* 1370; st. 12 May 1437 and subsequently but apparently never completed her title to the earldom; d.s.p.m.s. 7 Oct. 1456–4 May 1458
    m. 17 Feb. 1392–? 8 Nov. 1392 Murdach Stewart (*see* Albany, Fife, Menteith); forf. & exec. 25 May 1425
11. Sir John Stewart of Darnley, gds. & h. of yr. sis. of 10; serv. 23–27 July 1473; st. 6 Aug. 1473; revoked 12 Jan. 1476, and not st. earl of Lennox—except in a few places—until 6 Oct. 1488, from which date he is once more so st.; forf. June 1489; rest. 5 Feb. 1490; d. 31 Aug.–? 11 Sept. 1495
12. Matthew Stewart, s. & h.; d. 9 Sept. 1513
13. John Stewart, s. & h.; d. 4 Sept. 1526
14. Matthew Stewart, s. & h.; b. 21 Sept. 1516; forf. 1 Oct. 1545; rest. 4 Oct. and 9 Dec. 1564; d. 4 Sept. 1571. His heir was K. James VI of Scotland his gds.
15. Charles Stewart, yr. s.; b. *c.* 1555; cr. 18 Apr. 1572; d.s.p.m. 1576
16. Robert Stewart (*see also* March, bps. of Caithness), yr. s. of 13; b. *c.* 1517; cr. 16 June 1578; res. shortly bef. 5 Mar. 1580; d.s.p. leg. 29 Aug. 1586
17. Esme Stuart (*see* Darnley), neph. of 14 and 16; b. *c.* 1542; cr. 5 Mar. 1580 *dukedom*; cr. 5 Aug. 1581; d. 26 May 1583
18. Ludovic Stuart (*see* Richmond, Newcastle), s. & h.; b. 29 Sept. 1574; d.s.p.s. leg. 16 Feb. 1624
19. Esme Stuart (*see* Darnley, March), br. & h.; b. 1579; d. 30 July 1624
20. James Stuart (*see* Richmond), s. & h.; b. 6 Apr. 1612; d. 30 Mar. 1655
21. Esme Stuart, only s. & h.; b. 2 Nov. 1649; d. unm. 10 Aug. 1660
22. Charles Stuart (*see* Lichfield), gds. of 19; b. 7 Mar. 1639; d.s.p.s. 12 Dec. 1672. His heir male was K. Charles II
23. Charles Lennox (*see* Richmond, Darnley, March), illeg. s. of K. Charles II; b. 29 July 1672; cr. 9 Sept. 1675; d. 27 Mar. 1723

LESLIE, *earldom*
Cr. with the dukedom of Rothes (29 May 1680); extinct with it, 26 July 1681

LEVEN, *earldom*
1. Alexander Leslie; b. *c.* 1580; cr. 11 Oct. 1641; d. 4 Apr. 1661
2. Alexander Leslie, gds. & h.; b. *c.* 1637; d.s.p.m. 15 July 1664
3. Margaret, 1st da. & coh.; b. aft. 1656; d.s.p. 6 Nov. 1674
   m. early 1674 Francis Montgomery, d. Jan. 1729
4. Catherine, only surv. sis. & h.; b. 1663–64; serv. 22 May 1675; d. unm. 21 Jan. 1676
5. David Leslie (formerly Melville) (*see* Melville), h. by entail; b. 5 May 1660; st. 21 Jan. 1676; recog. 27 July 1681; d. 2 Sept. 1754

LINDSAY, *earldom*
1. John Lindsay (*see* Crawford), Lord Lindsay of the Byres; b. *c.* 1611; cr. 8 May 1633; d. 1678
   This earldom descends with that of Crawford until 1808

LINLITHGOW, *earldom*
1. Alexander Livingstone, Lord Livingstone; cr. *c.* 25 Dec. 1600; st. 13 Jan. 1601; d. 24 Dec. 1621
2. Alexander Livingstone, 1st surv. s. & h.; d. 11 June–20 Dec. 1648
3. George Livingstone, s. & h.; d. 1 Feb. 1690
4. George Livingstone, s. & h.; d.s.p. 7 Aug. 1695
5. James Livingstone (*see* Callendar), neph. & h.; forf. 17 Feb. 1716; d.s.p.m.s. 25 Apr. 1723

LOTHIAN, *earldom and marquessate*

Earldom
1. Mark Kerr, Lord Newbattle; b. *c.* 1553; cr. 10 July 1606; d. 8 Apr. 1609
2. Robert Kerr, s. & h.; serv. 24 May 1609; d.s.p.m.s. 6 Mar. 1624
3. Sir William Kerr of Ancram, s. & h. of Ancram 1; b. *c.* 1605
   m. 9 Dec. 1630 Anne eldest da. of 2, but she seems not to have been recog. as countess in her own right; cr. 31 Oct. 1631; d. Oct. 1675
4. Robert Kerr (*see* Ancram), s. & h.; b. 8 Mar. 1636
   marquessate; cr. 23 June 1701; d. 15 Feb. 1703
5. William Kerr (*see* Ancram), s. & h.; b. 1661; d. 22 Feb. 1722

LOUDOUN, *earldom*
1. Sir John Campbell, Lord Loudoun; b. 1598; cr. 12 May 1633; but suspended until 1641; d. 15 Mar. 1662
2. James Campbell, s. & h.; d. Nov.–Dec. 1684
3. Hugh Campbell, s. & h.; d. 20 Nov. 1731

MAR, *earldom*
   [Although the Garioch was not an earldom, nos. 11, 13, 14, and 15 in the following list st. themselves earl (or countess) of Mar and Garioch]
1. Ruadri; st. earl 1138–36; st. mormaer Apr. 1131–Apr. 1132
2. Morgund, st. 1150; d. 1182–30 Mar. 1183
3. Gilchrist; st. 1187–99; d. aft. 28 Sept. 1203 with male issue
4. Duncan, s. & ? h. of 2; succ. or recog. 15 May 1222–29 Aug. 1228; d. 8 Apr. 1242–7 Feb. 1244
5. William, s. & h.; st. 7 Feb. 1244; d. 20 Nov. 1276–25 July 1281
6. Donald, s. & h.; st. 25 July 1281; d. 25 July (? 20 Nov.) 1297–Sept. 1305
7. Gartnait, s. & h.; d. bef. Sept. 1305
8. Donald, s. & h.; st. Donald of Mar until his return from England to Scotland, 1327; d. 12 Aug. 1332
9. Thomas (*see* Menteith), only s. & h.; b. *c.* 1330; d. 22 Oct. 1373–21 June 1374
10. Margaret, only sis. & h.; d. 5 Dec. 1389–19 Oct. 1393 and perhaps 1391
    m. 1. bef. 13 Nov. 1357 Sir William Douglas (*see* Douglas); b. *c.* 1327; st. 21 June 1374; d. *c.* May 1384
       Their s. James Douglas (d.s.p. 5 Aug. 1388) is st. earl of Douglas aft. the d. of his father except in a charter given by him 27 July 1388 where he st. himself earl of Douglas and of Mar
    2. May 1384–27 July 1388 Sir John Swinton; st. lord of Mar, never earl; d. 14 Sept. 1402
11. Isabel, da. & h. by 1; b. *c.* 1360; succ. 5 Dec. 1389–19 Oct. 1393 and perhaps 1391; res. 9 Dec. 1404 (royal confirmation 21 Jan. 1405) in favour of her 2nd husband and their heirs; d.s.p. 28 July–26 Oct. 1408
    m. 1. bef. 27 July 1388 Sir Malcolm Drummond, st. lord of Mar; d.s.p. 1402 bef. 8 Nov.
    2. 5 Dec. 1404–2 Jan. 1405 Sir Alexander Stewart, illeg. s. of Buchan 9; st. lord of Mar 2 Jan. 1405; st. earl of Mar from 21 Jan. 1405, aft. his w.'s death in virtue of her resignation, until granted earldom 28 May 1426; d.s.p. leg. 25–26 July 1435
12. Sir Robert Erskine, gt.-gt.-gds. of 7; self-st. earl of Mar aft. 21 Nov. 1438 but never secured royal recognition; d. 7 Sept. 1451–6 Nov. 1452
13. John Stewart, yst. s. of K. James II of Scotland; b. 1456–57; cr. 21 June 1458–25 June 1459; d. 9 July 1479 or more prob. 1480, having been previously forfeited

14. Alexander Stewart (*see* Albany, March), 2nd s. of K. James II of Scotland; b. *c.* 1454; st. 10 Oct. 1482; granted earldom in charter dated *c.* 18–20 Jan. 1483 but prob. cr. 29 Sept.–10 Oct. 1482; forf. 27 June 1483; d. ? 1485

15. John Stewart, yst. s. of K. James III of Scotland; b. July 1479–July 1480; cr. 2 Mar. 1486; d. unm. 11 Mar. 1503

16. James Stewart (*see* Moray), illeg. s. of K. James V of Scotland; b. *c.* 1531; cr. 7 Feb. 1562; res. 10 Sept.–15 Oct. 1562; d.s.p.m.s. 21 Jan. 1570

17. John Erskine, gt.-gt.-gds. & h. of 12; recog. 23 June 1565; d. 28 Oct. 1572

18. John Erskine, only s. & h.; b. *c.* 1562; serv. 3 Mar. 1573; forf. 22 Aug. 1584; rest. 10 Dec. 1585; d. 14 Dec. 1634

19. John Erskine, s. & h.; b. bef. 1592; serv. 25 Mar. 1635; d. Jan.–Oct. 1653

20. John Erskine, s. & h.; d. 1–11 Sept. 1668

21. Charles Erskine, s. & h.; b. 19 Oct. 1650; d. 23 May 1689

22. John Erskine, s. & h.; b. Feb. 1675; forf. 19 Jan. 1716; d. May 1732

MARCH, *earldom and marquessate*

[For earls of March (1290–1435) of the family of Dunbar *see under* Dunbar]

Earldom

1. Alexander Stewart (*see* Albany, Mar), 2nd s. of K. James II of Scotland; b. *c.* 1454; st. 4 Aug. 1455; forf. 27 June 1483; d. ? 1485

2. Robert Stewart (*see* Lennox, bps. of Caithness); b. *c.* 1517; cr. 5 Mar. 1580; d.s.p. leg. 29 Aug. 1586

Marquessate

3. John Maitland (*see* Lauderdale, Guildford); b. 24 May 1616; cr. 26 May 1672; d.s.p.m. 24 Aug. 1682

Earldom

4. William Douglas, 2nd s. of Queensberry 3; b. *c.* 1665; cr. 20 Apr. 1697; d. 9 Sept. 1705

5. William Douglas, s. & h.; b. *c.* 1696; d. 7 Mar. 1731

MARCHMONT, *earldom*

1. Patrick Hume, Lord Polwarth; b. 13 Jan. 1631; cr. 23 Apr. 1697; d. 2 Aug. 1724

MARISCHAL, *earldom*

1. William Keith, Lord Keith; b. aft. 1425; cr. 20 Mar.–4 July 1458; d. 10 Dec. 1482–1483

2. William Keith, s. & h.; d. 24 Nov. 1526–2 May 1527

3. William Keith, gds. & h.; d. 7 Oct. 1581

4. George Keith, gds. & h.; b. 1550–1553; d. 2 Apr. 1623

5. William Keith, s. & h.; b. *c.* 1585; d. 28 Oct. 1635

6. William Keith, s. & h.; b. 1614; d.s.p.m.s. Mar. 1671

7. George Keith, br. & h.; d. Mar. 1694

8. William Keith, only s. & h.; b. *c.* 1664–66; d. 27 May 1712

9. George Keith, s. & h.; b. 1693–28 Nov. 1694; forf. 30 June 1716; d. unm. 28 May 1778

MELFORT, *earldom*

1. John Drummond, Viscount Melfort, 2nd s. of Perth 3; b. *c.* 1650; cr. 12 Aug. 1686; forf. 2 July 1695; d. 25 Jan. 1715

MELROSE, *earldom*

1. Thomas Hamilton (*see* Haddington), Lord Binning; b. 1563; cr. 20 Mar. 1619; style altered to earl of Haddington 17 Aug. 1627; d. 29 May 1637

MELVILLE, *earldom*

1. George Melville, Lord Melville; b. 1636; cr. 8 Apr. 1690; d. 20 May 1707

2. David Melville (*see* Leven), 1st surv. s. & h.; b. 5 May 1660; d. 2 Sept. 1754

MENTEITH, *earldom*

1. Gilchrist; st. 24 May 1163–23 May 1164; d. aft. 1189

2. Maurice or Murethach; st. 1189–1202; res. in favour of 3 on 6 Dec. 1213 (royal confirmation 7 Dec. 1213)

3. Maurice, yr. br.; succ. ? 7 Dec. 1213; st. 6 Dec. 1214; d. 22 Oct. 1231 (? 30 June 1233)–9 Jan. 1234

4. Isabel, ? elder da. & h.; res. Nov. 1258–17 Apr. 1261; d. 1264–73.
   m. 1. bef. 9 Jan. 1234 Walter Cumyn, yr. br. of Buchan 6. He was not st. earl
   30 June 1233 and married, or succ. by the d. of 3, thereaft.;
   d.s.p.s. Oct.–Nov. 1258
   2. Nov. 1258–59 Sir John Russell who was not st. earl; res. bef. 17 Apr.
   1261; d. with issue bef. 1291
5. Mary, yr. sis. of 4; d. bef. 28 Apr. 1296
   m. bef. 17 Apr. 1261 Walter Stewart; d. 1294–28 Apr. 1296
6. Alexander Menteith, s. & h.; st. 28 Apr. 1296; d. 26 Sept. 1297–1306
7. Alan Menteith, s. & h.; st. bef. Mar. 1306; forf. by K. Edw. I Mar.–22 May
   1306; d. bef. 16 Mar. 1309
8. Murdoch Menteith, next surv. br.; succ. or recog. 19 Jan. 1317–5 Dec. 1318; d.
   prob. 12 Aug. 1332
9. Mary Menteith, da. & h. of 7; d. c. 1350–29 Apr. 1360
   m. bef. 1 May 1334 Sir John Graham; exec. 28 Feb.–6 Mar. 1347
10. Margaret Graham, da. & h.; st. 29 Apr. 1360; d. 20 July 1372–4 May 1380
    m. 1. (dispensation 21 Nov. 1348) Sir John Murray; d.s.p. 20 Apr. 1351–15
    Aug. 1352
    2. 15 Aug. 1352–29 May 1354 Thomas earl of Mar (*see* Mar. 9); b. c. 1330;
    divorced c. 1359; d. 22 Oct. 1373–21 June 1374.
    3. c. 1359 Sir John Drummond of Concraig; not found st. earl; d. 17 May
    1360–9 Sept. 1361
    4. (dispensation 9 Sept. 1361) Robert Stewart, 3rd s. of K. Robert II of
    Scotland (*see* Albany, Fife, Buchan, Atholl); b. c. 1340; st. Lord of
    Menteith until 27 Mar. 1371, when st. earl and so st. aft. the d. of this
    w.; d. 3 Sept. 1420
11. Murdoch Stewart (*see* Albany, Fife), s. & h. by 4; b. prob. 1362; forf. and exec.
    25 May 1425
12. Malise Graham (*see* Strathearn); b. c. 1407 or later; granted earldom of
    Menteith 6 Sept. 1427 when he is st. earl of Menteith; d. 11 June 1488–19
    May 1490, and prob. in 1490
13. Alexander Graham, gds. & h.; b. prob. c. 1472; serv. 6 May 1493; d. 27
    Feb.–16 May 1537
14. William Graham, s. & h.; serv. 16 May 1537; d. Sept. 1543–23 Jan. 1544
15. John Graham, s. & h.; b. c. 1523–25; enfeoffed 4 Jan. 1547; d. Jan. 1565
16. William Graham, s. & h.; b. c. 1551; enfeoffed 20 Nov. 1571; d. Sept. 1578
17. John Graham, s. & h.; b. c. 1573; enfeoffed soon aft. 7 Oct. 1587; d. Dec. 1578
18. William Graham (*see* Strathearn, Airth), s. & h.; b. c. 1590; serv. 7 Aug. 1610;
    d. 1661 aft. 13 Apr.
19. William Graham, gds. & h.; b. c. 1634; d.s.p. 12 Sept. 1694

MIDDLETON, *earldom*
1. John Middleton; b. c. 1608; cr. 1 Oct. 1660; d. 1673 (aft. June)
2. Charles Middleton, s. & h.; b. c. 1650; forf. 2 July 1695; d. 8 Aug. 1719

MONTROSE, *earldom, marquessate and dukedom*

Dukedom
1. David Lindsay (*see* Crawford); b. 1440; cr. 18 May 1488; depr. 17 Oct. 1488;
   rest. for life 18 Sept. 1489; d. Christmas 1495

Earldom
2. William Graham, Lord Graham; b. 1463–64; cr. 7 July–20 Nov. 1503; d. 9
   Sept. 1513
3. William Graham, s. & h.; b. aft. 9 Sept. 1492; serv. 24 Oct. 1513; d. 24 May
   1571
4. John Graham, gds. & h.; b. 1548; d. 9 Nov. 1608
5. John Graham, s. & h.; b. 1573, d. 14 Nov. 1626
6. James Graham (*see* Kincardine), only s. & h.; b. 1612; serv. 28 Mar. 1627
   marquessate; cr. 6 May 1644; forf. by the Scottish Parliament 11 Feb. 1645;
   exec. 21 May 1650
7. James Graham, 1st surv. s. & h.; b. 1633; d. Feb. 1669
8. James Graham, s. & h.; b. 20 Oct. 1657; d. 25 Apr. 1684
9. James Graham (*see* Graham, Buchanan), only s. & h.; b. c. Apr. 1682; serv.
   18 Feb. 1685
   dukedom; cr. 24 Apr. 1707; d. 7 Jan. 1742

MORAY, *earldom*

[For the early rulers of Moray, sometime st. earls, of whom the last, Angus, was killed in 1130, *see* O. A. Anderson, *Early Sources of Scottish History*, esp. i, 580. The province was reputed in a document forged *c.* 1257 to have been an earldom in the twelfth century; it was the first earldom cr. since the early thirteenth century]

1. Sir Thomas Randolph; b. prob. bef. 1280; cr. 12 Apr.–29 Oct. 1312; d. 20 July 1332
2. Thomas Randolph, s. & h.; d.s.p. 12 Aug. 1332
3. John Randolph, br. & h.; d.s.p. 17 Oct. 1346
4. Henry Beaumont (*see* Buchan); self-st. 16 June 1334, but this may have been an error for 'Atholl'. He was father-in-law of Atholl 12; d. shortly bef. 10 Mar. 1340
5. Agnes Randolph, elder da. of **1**; d.s.p. aft. 24 May 1367 and perhaps aft. 1 Sept. 1367

   m. Patrick Dunbar, earl of March (*see* Dunbar); b. *c.* 1283; last st. earl of Moray 1 Sept. 1357; d.s.p.s. 11 Nov. 1368

   They were officially recog. as earl and countess of Moray (although the earldom was granted to **1** and his heirs *male*) Oct. 1357–31 Aug. 1358 (in spite of which the earldom was granted by K. David II of Scotland to **6**). They may have lost the earldom under the general act of revocation 27 Sept. 1367

6. Henry of Grosmont (*see* Derby, Lancaster); b. *c.* 1300; cr. 5 Apr. 1359; d.s.p.m.s. 23 Mar. 1361; not st. earl of Moray
7. John Dunbar, yr. br. of Dunbar 9 and 2nd s. of yr. da. of **1** above; cr. 9 Mar. 1372; d. 13 June 1391–15 Feb. 1392
8. Thomas Dunbar, s. & h.; d. 3 June 1415–9 Aug. 1422
9. Thomas Dunbar, s. & h.; d.s.p. leg. aft. 16 July 1425
10. James Dunbar, cousin or br.; d.s.p.m. 10 Aug. 1429
11. Elizabeth Dunbar, yr. da.; d. shortly bef. 17 Feb. 1486

    m. 1. Aug. 1434–26 Apr. 1442 Archibald Douglas, 3rd s. of Douglas 7; cr. shortly bef. 3 July 1445; d. 1 May 1455; forf. 12 June 1455
    The earldom was apparently forf. and subsequent husbands of Elizabeth were not st. earl, though she was sometimes st. countess
12. Janet Dunbar, elder da. of 10; d. 18 Mar. 1494–1506

    m. 1. 1442–1446 James Crichton; cr. 12 June–18 July 1452 (when Archibald Douglas was in rebellion though not forf.); d. Aug. 1454
    This creation or recognition seems to have been ineffective aft. the reconciliation of Archibald Douglas to K. James II of Scotland. James Crichton is sometimes then st. earl; his w. is occasionally st. countess aft. his d. but her 2nd husband was not st. earl
13. David Stewart, 3rd s. of K. James II of Scotland; b. 1454–56; cr. 12 Feb. 1456; d. bef. 18 July 1457
14. James Stewart, illeg. s. of K. James IV of Scotland; b. *c.* 1499; cr. 12 June 1501; d.s.p. leg. 2 Dec. 1544–14 Mar. 1545
15. George Gordon (*see* Huntly); b. *c.* 1510; cr. 13 Feb. 1549; res. Mar. 1555; d. 22 Oct. 1562
16. James Stewart (*see* Mar), illeg. s. of K. James V of Scotland; b. *c.* 1531; cr. 30 Jan. 1562; creation made public Sept. 1562; belted earl of Moray 10 Feb. 1563; d.s.p.m.s. 21 Jan. 1570
17. Elizabeth Stewart, 1st da. & coh.; b. *c.* Aug. 1565; d. 18 Nov. 1591

    m. 23 Jan. 1581 James Stewart; d. 7 Feb. 1592
18. James Stewart, s. & h.; b. 1581–83; d. 6 Aug. 1638
19. James Stewart, s. & h.; b. aft. 1607; serv. 15 Nov. 1638; d. 4 Mar. 1653
20. Alexander Stewart, 1st surv. s. & h.; bapt. 8 May 1634; serv. 23 June 1653; d. 1 Nov. 1701
21. Charles Stewart, 1st surv. s. & h.; b. *c.* 1660; d.s.p. 7 Oct. 1735

MORTON, *earldom*

1. James Douglas, Lord of Dalkeith; cr. 14 Mar. 1458; d. 22 June–22 Oct. 1493
2. John Douglas, only s. & h.; b. *c.* 1458; st. 22 Oct. 1493; d. 8 Nov. 1511–26 Nov. 1513
3. James Douglas, s. & h.; d.s.p.m. Dec. 1548

4. James Douglas, yr. br. of Angus 20; succ. by entail made by 3 to exclusion of
   right heirs
   m. yst. da. & coh. of 3; forf. 1 June 1581; exec. 2 June 1581
5. John Maxwell, 1st surv. s. of 2nd da. & coh. of 3; cr. 5 June 1581; depr. (? of
   lands only) 9 Apr. 1585; on rest. of 6 he was st. indifferently lord Maxwell or
   earl of Morton; d. 6 or 7 Dec. 1593
6. Archibald Douglas (*see* Angus), neph. & h. of 4; b. 1554–55; rest. 29 Jan. 1586;
   d.s.p.m. 4 Aug. 1588
7. William Douglas, right h. & h. by entail to 3, they having a common ancestor in
   the fourteenth century; b. 1539–40; d. 22–27 Sept. 1606
8. William Douglas, gds. & h.; b. 1583–85; serv. 4 Nov. 1606; d. 7 Aug. 1648
9. Robert Douglas, s. & h.; b. bef. 1619; serv. 29 Mar. 1649; d. 12 Nov. 1649
10. William Douglas, s. & h.; d.s.p.s. shortly bef. 1 Nov. 1681
11. James Douglas, uncle & h.; d. 25 Aug. 1686
12. James Douglas, 1st surv. s. & h.; b. *c.* 1652; d. unm. 7 Dec. 1715

NEWBURGH, *earldom*
1. James Livingstone, Viscount Newburgh; b. *c.* 1622; cr. 31 Dec. 1660; d. 4 Dec.
   1670
2. Charles Livingstone, 1st s. & h.; b. *c.* 1662–66; serv. h. 25 Jan. 1684; d.s.p.m.
   6 Apr. 1694
3. Charlotte Maria, dau. & h.; b. 1694; d. 4 Aug. 1755
   m. 1. 1713–14, Thomas Ciifford; b. 12 Dec. 1687; d.s.p.m. 21 Feb. 1719.
      2. 24 June 1724, Charles Radcliffe, st. earl of Derwentwater; b. 3 Sept.
      1693; exec. 8 Dec. 1746

NITHSDALE, *earldom*
1. Robert Maxwell, Lord Maxwell, s. of Morton 5; b. aft. 1586; cr. 29 Aug. 1620;
   d. May 1646
2. Robert Maxwell, only s. & h.; b. 1 Sept. 1620; d. unm. 5 Oct. 1667
3. John Maxwell, s. & h. of sis. of 1; d. 16 Feb.–29 June 1677
4. Robert Maxwell, s. & h.; b. *c.* Jan. 1628; d. shortly bef. 23 Mar. 1683
5. William Maxwell, only s. & h.; b. 1676; serv. 26 May 1696; forf. 1716; d.
   20 Mar. 1744

NORTHESK, *earldom*
1. John Carnegie (*see* Ethie), yr. br. of Southesk 1, Lord Lour; b. *c.* 1579;
   assumed style of earl of Northesk 25 Oct. 1666; d. 8 Jan. 1667
2. David Carnegie, s. & h.; serv. 16 Apr. 1667; d. 12 Dec. 1679
3. David Carnegie, s. & h.; b. Nov. 1643; serv. 5 May 1681; d. 3 Oct. 1688
4. David Carnegie, s. & h.; serv. 26 Oct. 1693; d. 14 Jan. 1729

ORKNEY, *earldom* (Norway & S.), *dukedom* (S.)

Earldom
Held jointly with Caithness until *c.* 1350, which *see*
1. Erngisl Sunesson
   m. 3rd da. & coh. of Caithness 10; inv. 10 Apr.–6 May 1353; depr. ? 1357 or ?
   1375; still self-st. earl 4 Mar. 1388; d. 1392
2. Henry Sinclair, s. of 4th da. & coh. of Caithness 10 (which *see*); cr. 2 Aug.
   1379; d. 13 May 1396–14 Sept. 1402 (? *c.* 1400)
3. Henry Sinclair, s. & h.; b. *c.* 1375; d. 1 Feb. 1420
4. William Sinclair (*see* Caithness), s. & h.; inv. 9 Aug. 1434; Norwegian royal
   rights pledged to K. James III of Scotland 8 Sept. 1468 when the islands
   became Scottish; res. in favour of K. James III of Scotland 1470, bef. 16
   Sept.; d. 30 July 1479–3 Aug. 1480

Dukedom
5. James Hepburn (*see* Bothwell); b. *c.* 1535; cr. 12 May 1567; forf. 20 Dec. 1567;
   d.s.p. leg. 14 Apr. 1578

Earldom
6. Robert Stewart, illeg. s. of K. James V of Scotland; b. *c.* 1533; cr. 28 Oct. 1581;
   d. 4 Feb. 1593
7. Patrick Stewart, 1st surv. s. & h.; b. 18 Sept. 1568–25 June 1569; forf. 1 Feb.
   1615; exec. 6 Feb. 1615
8. George Hamilton, 5th s. of Hamilton 5; bapt. 9 Feb. 1666; cr. 3 Jan. 1696;
   d.s.p.m. 29 Jan. 1737

ORMOND, *earldom and marquessate*

Earldom
1. Hugh Douglas, 4th s. of Douglas 7; cr. 1445 bef. 3 July; forf. and exec. May–June 1455

Marquessate
2. James Stewart (*see* Edirdale, Ross, abps. of St. Andrews); b. prob. 1479; cr. 29 Jan. 1488; d. unm. 12–17 Jan. 1504
3. Charles Stewart (*see* Albany), later K. Charles I of Great Britain; b. 19 Nov. 1600; cr. 23 Dec. 1600; became K. 27 Mar. 1625

Earldom
4. Archibald Douglas, s. & h. of Douglas 10; b. *c.* 1609; cr. 3 Apr. 1651 but ineffective and never st. earl of Ormond; d. 16 Jan. 1655

PANMURE, *earldom*
1. Patrick Maule; b. 29 May 1585; cr. 3 Aug. 1646; d. 22 Dec. 1661
2. George Maule, s. & h.; b. 1619; d. 24 Mar. 1671
3. George Maule, 1st surv. s. & h.; b. *c.* 1650; serv. 16 May 1671; d.s.p.s. 1 Feb. 1686
4. James Maule, br. & h.; b. *c.* 1658; forf. 30 June 1716; d.s.p. 22 Apr. 1723

PERTH, *earldom*
1. James Drummond, Lord Drummond; b. *c.* 1580; cr. 4 Mar. 1605; d.s.p.m. 18 Dec. 1611
2. John Drummond, br. & h. male; b. *c.* 1584; serv. 11 Mar. 1612; d. 11 June 1662
3. James Drummond, 1st surv. s. & h.; b. *c.* 1615; serv. 27 Sept. 1662; d. 2 June 1675
4. James Drummond, 1st surv. s. & h.; b. 7 July 1648; serv. 1 Oct. 1675; d. 11 May 1716

PORTMORE, *earldom*
1. David Colyear, Lord Portmore and Blackness; b. *c.* 1656; cr. 13 Apr. 1703; d. 2 Jan. 1730

QUEENSBERRY, *earldom, marquessate and dukedom*

Earldom
1. William Douglas, Viscount Drumlanrig; cr. 13 June 1633; d. 8 Mar. 1640
2. James Douglas, s. & h.; b. bef. Jan. 1622; serv. 20 May 1640; d. 1671
3. William Douglas (*see* Drumlanrig and Sanquhar, Dumfriesshire), s. & h.; b. 1637
   marquessate; cr. 11 Feb. 1682
   dukedom; cr. 3 Nov. 1684; d. 28 Mar. 1695
4. James Douglas (*see* Beverley, Dover), s. & h.; b. 18 Dec. 1662; d. 6 July 1711 (for his 1st. s. & h., *see* Drumlanrig and Sanquhar)
5. Charles Douglas (*see* Solway), 2nd surv. s. & h.; b. 24 Nov. 1698; d. 22 Oct. 1778

ROSEBERY, *earldom*
1. Archibald Primrose, Viscount Rosebery; b. 18 Dec. 1664; cr. 10 Apr. 1703; d. 20 Oct. 1723

ROSS, *earldom and dukedom*

Earldom
1. Florence, Count of Holland; cr. 1162; but apparently without effect; d. 1 Aug. 1190. (The evidence that he was given the earldom comes from the end of the thirteenth century and is unreliable, especially in view of 2 below)
2. Malcolm Macheth, ? illeg. s. of K. Alexander I of Scotland; b. *c.* 1105–15; cr. aft. 1157; st. Nov. 1160–Sept. 1162; d. 23 Oct. 1168
3. Ferquhard; cr. 1225–35; d. Jan. 1251
4. William, s. & h.; b. bef. Sept. 1232; d. May (bef. 20) 1274
5. William, s. & h.; st. 5 Feb. 1284; d. 28 Jan. 1323
6. Hugh, s. & h.; st. 28 Mar. 1324; d. 19 July 1333
7. William, s. & h.; inv. 17 May 1336; d.s.p.m.s. 9 Feb. 1372

8. Euphemia (*see* Buchan), 1st da. & coh.; b. aft. 1342; st. lady of Ross during her 1st m., countess of Ross during her 2nd; d. 5 Sept. 1394–? 20 Feb. 1395
   m. 1. 1357–13 Sept. 1366 Sir Walter Leslie, self-st. lord of Ross but by others earl of Ross; d. 27 Feb. 1382.
   2. on or shortly bef. 22 July 1382 Alexander Stewart, 4th s. of K. Robert II of Scotland (*see* Buchan); d.s.p. leg. 1 Aug. 1405–25 Mar. 1406
9. Alexander Leslie, only s. & h. by **1**; d.s.p.m. 8 May 1402
10. Euphemia Leslie, da. & h.; b. ? 1392–94; st. neither countess nor lady of Ross, ? because of nonage; res. with regrant to her whom failing 11 below, 15 June 1415; ? entered religion immediately thereafter
11. John Stewart (*see* Buchan), 2nd s. of Robert, Duke of Albany, Governor of Scotland; b. *c.* 1380; self.-st. earl of Ross 24 May 1417; d.s.p. 17 Aug. 1424
12. Margaret Leslie, only sister of 9; st. lady of the Isles and of (the earldom of) Ross; d. 2 July 1435–Jan. 1436.
   m. bef. June 1411 Donald Lord of the Isles ('and of Ross'); b. bef. 1369; d. *c.* 1423
13. Alexander MacDonald, s. & h.; st. Jan. 1436; d. 8 May 1449
   Although 11 left an heir to the earldom, he did not claim it, and it was found on the death of K. James I of Scotland to have been in the hands of the crown (which recog. 12 and 13 as Lords of the Isles only) since 17 Aug. 1424, although 11 was never *officially* st. earl of Ross; 13 is st. earl of Ross officially 14 July 1438 and was presumably rest. aft. 21 Feb. 1437
14. John MacDonald, s. & h.; b. *c.* 1435; forf. 1 Dec. 1475; d.s.p.s. leg. *c.* 1498
15. James Stewart (*see* Ormond (S), Edirdale, Abps. of St. Andrews), 2nd s. of K. James III of Scotland; b. prob. 1479; cr. 23 Jan. 1481 *dukedom*; cr. 29 Jan. 1488; d. unm. 12–17 Jan. 1504
16. Alexander Stewart, 4th but 2nd surv. s. of K. James IV of Scotland; b. 30 Apr. 1514; ? cr. at birth; st. duke, perhaps of Ross; d. 18 Dec. 1515

Earldom
17. Henry Stewart (*see* Albany), 1st s. of Lennox 14, later K. of Scots; b. 7 Dec. 1545; cr. 15 May 1565; became K. 29 July 1565; d. 10 Feb. 1567
   In 1566–67, 1600–25 the earldom of Ross was held by the dukes of Albany, which *see*

ROTHES, *earldom, dukedom*
1. George Leslie, Lord Leslie; b. *c.* 1417; cr. 5 Nov. 1457–20 Mar. 1458; d. 31 Aug. 1489–24 May 1490
2. George Leslie, gds. & h.; d.s.p.m.s. 24 Feb.–31 Mar. 1513
3. William Leslie, br. & h.; not st. earl because not enfeoffed.; d. 9 Sept. 1513
4. George Leslie, s. & h.; d. 9 Nov. 1558
5. Andrew Leslie, 4th s.; b. *c.* 1528; assumed title because assignee (and therefore h.) to his father's lands; serv. 1560; finally recog. 15 Jan. 1565; d. 1611
6. John Leslie, gds. & h.; b. *c.* 1600; d. 23 Aug. 1641
7. John Leslie (*see* Bambreich, Leslie), only s. & h.; b. *c.* 1630; serv. 27 Apr. 1642 *dukedom*; cr. 29 May 1680; d.s.p.m. 26 July 1681

Earldom
8. Margaret Leslie, elder da. & coh.; d. 20 Aug. 1700
   m. 8 Oct. 1674 Charles Hamilton (*see* Haddington 5); b. *c.* 1650; d. May 1685
9. John Hamilton or Leslie, 1st s. & h.; bapt. 21 Aug. 1679; d. 9 May 1722

ROTHESAY, *dukedom*
1. David Stewart (*see* Atholl, Carrick), 1st s. & h. of K. Robert III of Scotland; b. 1378; cr. 28 Apr. 1398; d.s.p. 26 Mar. 1402
2. James Stewart, 1st surv. s. & h. of K. James I of Scotland; b. 16 Oct. 1430; cr. ? at death of older twin br.; st. 22 Apr. 1431; succ. 21 Feb. 1437; d. 3 Aug. 1460
   On 27 Nov. 1469 the earldom of Carrick, lordship of Bute and castle of Rothesay, were perpetually united to the oldest s. of the K. of Scots, and thereafter the dukedom of Rothesay is found so to descend. (According to chronicle evidence this was its destination when cr. in 1398, but it was held neither by James I nor James III when heirs to the throne.) For 3 *see* James IV, for 6 *see* James V, for 8 *see* James VI, Ks. of Scotland. For dukes of Rothesay subsequent to 6 Nov. 1612 *see* Cornwall

4. James Stewart, 1st s. & h. of K. James IV of Scotland; b. 21 Feb. 1507; succ. at birth; d. 27 Feb. 1508
5. Arthur Stewart, 1st surv. s. & h. of K. James IV of Scotland; b. 20 Oct. 1509; succ. at birth; d. 14 July 1510
7. James Stewart, 1st s. & h. of K. James V of Scotland; b. 22 May 1540; succ. at birth; d. 1541
9. Henry Frederick Stewart, 1st s. & h. of K. James VI of Scotland; b. 19 Feb. 1594; succ. at birth; d.s.p. 6 Nov. 1612

ROXBURGHE, *earldom, dukedom*
1. Robert Ker, Lord Roxburghe; b. *c.* 1570; cr. 18 Sept. 1616; d. 18 Jan. 1650
2. William Drummond, aft. Ker, gds. & h.; serv. 2 May 1650; d. 2 July 1675
3. Robert Ker, 1st s. & h.; b. *c.* 1658; serv. 7 Oct. 1675; d. 6 May 1682
4. Robert Ker, 1st s. & h.; b. *c.* 1677; serv. 5 June 1684; d. unm. 13 July 1696
5. John Ker (*see* Bowmont and Cessford, Kelso), next br. & h.; b. *c.* 1680; serv. 22 Oct. 1696
    dukedom; cr. 25 Apr. 1707; d. 27 Feb. 1741

RUGLEN, *earldom*
1. John Hamilton, 4th s. of Hamilton 5; bapt. 26 Jan. 1665; cr. 15 Apr. 1697; d.s.p.m.s. 3 Dec. 1744

SEAFIELD, *earldom*
1. James Ogilvy (*see* Findlater), Viscount Seafield; b. 11 July 1663; cr. 24 June 1701; d. 15 Aug. 1730

SEAFORTH, *earldom*
1. Colin Mackenzie, Lord Mackenzie; b. *c.* 1593; cr. 3 Dec. 1623; d.s.p.m. 15 Apr. 1633
2. George Mackenzie, half br. & h.; b. 1605–11; d. Aug. 1651
3. Kenneth Mackenzie, 1st s. & h.; d. 16 Dec. 1678
4. Kenneth Mackenzie, 1st s. & h.; bapt. 8 Dec. 1661; d. Jan. 1701
5. William Mackenzie, 1st s. & h.; forf. 30 June 1716; d. 8 Jan. 1740

SELKIRK, *earldom*
1. Lord William Douglas (*see* Hamilton), 4th s. of Douglas 10; b. 24 Dec. 1634; cr. 4 Aug. 1646; res. 6 Oct. 1688; d. 18 Apr. 1694
2. Charles Hamilton Douglas, 2nd surv. s. & h. to this earldom; b. 3 Feb. 1662; succ. by res. of 1 and regrant to him 6 Oct. 1688; d. unm. 13 Mar. 1739

SOLWAY, *earldom*
1. Charles Douglas (*see* Queensberry); b. 27 Nov. 1698; cr. 17 June 1706; d. 22 Oct. 1778

SOUTHESK, *earldom*
1. David Carnegie, Lord Carnegie of Kinnaird; b. 1575; cr. 22 June 1633; d. Feb. 1658
2. James Carnegie, 1st surv. s. & h.; d. Jan. 1669
3. Robert Carnegie, only s. & h.; d. 19 Feb. 1688
4. Charles Carnegie, only surv. s. & h.; b. 7 Apr. 1661; d. 9 Aug. 1699
5. James Carnegie, only s. & h.; b. 4 Apr. 1692; forf. 30 June 1716; d.s.p.m.s. 10 Feb. 1730

STAIR, *earldom*
1. John Dalrymple, Viscount Stair; b. 1648; cr. 8 Apr. 1703; d. 8 Jan. 1707
2. John Dalrymple, 1st surv. s. & h.; b. 20 July 1673; d.s.p. 9 May 1747

STIRLING, *earldom*
1. William Alexander, Viscount of Stirling; b. *c.* 1576; cr. 14 June 1633; d. 12 Feb. 1640
2. William Alexander, gds. & h.; b. *c.* 1632; d. May 1640
3. Henry Alexander, uncle & h.; b. *c.* 1610; d. bef. 11 June 1649
4. Henry Alexander, only s. & h.; b. *c.* 1639; d. 5 Feb. 1691
5. Henry Alexander, 1st s. & h.; b. 7 Nov. 1664; d.s.p. 4 Dec. 1739

STRATHEARN, *earldom*

1. Malise; st. Dec. 1123–Apr. 1124 in a writ of doubtful authenticity; st. certainly 1128–36; d. aft. 14 June 1141
2. Ferteth, ? s.; st. 1160; d. 1171
3. Gilbert, s. & h.; b. bef. 1164, ? *c.* 1150; d. 1223
4. Robert, 1st surv. s. & h.; d. 25 Sept. 1237–Aug. 1244
5. Malise, s. & h.; st. Aug. 1244; d. 1271 bef. 23 Nov.
6. Malise, s. & h.; b. 1257 or later; d. 28 Jan.–25 Mar. 1313
7. Malise, s. & h.; b. *c.* 1275–80; d. 1323–29
8. Malise (*see* Caithness), s. & h.; res. to Edward Balliol 24 Sept. 1332–27 Feb. 1333 and by this res. held (10 June 1344) to have depr. himself of this earldom in favour of K. David II of Scotland; self-st. earl of Strathearn so late as 28 May 1344; d.s.p.m. 10 June 1344–11 Nov. 1357
9. John Warenne (*see* Surrey); b. 30 June 1286; cr. by Edward Balliol 24 Sept. 1332–27 Feb. 1333; d.s.p. leg. 29 June 1347
10. Sir Maurice Moray; cr. 9 Feb. 1344; d.s.p.m. 17 Oct. 1346
11. Robert Stewart (*see* Atholl), later K. Robert II of Scotland; b. 2 Mar. 1316; cr. 6–13 Nov. 1357; st. earl of Strathearn until 18 Apr. 1369; not so st. (? because depr.) 16 Sept. 1369 until 4 Apr. 1370; rest. 4–7 Apr. 1370; became K. 22 Feb. 1371
12. David Stewart (*see* Caithness), 5th s.; b. aft. 1355; cr. 26–27 Mar. 1371; d.s.p.m. Feb. 1382–89
13. Euphemia Stewart (*see* Caithness), only da. & h.; b. *c.* 1375; d. Oct. 1415 m. bef. 24 Aug. 1406 Patrick Graham; d. 10 Aug. 1413
14. Malise Graham (*see* Menteith), only s. & h.; b. *c.* 1407 or later; depr. 24 May 1425–22 July 1427; d. 11 June 1488–19 May 1490, and prob. in 1490
15. Walter Stewart (*see* Atholl, Caithness), yst. s. of **11** above; b. ? *c.* 1360; cr. 22 July 1427; forf. and exec. 26 Mar. 1437
16. William Graham (*see* Menteith, Airth); b. *c.* 1590; recog. (as heir to 12 above) 31 July 1631; reduced 22 Mar. 1633; d. 1661 aft. 13 Apr.

STRATHMORE and KINGHORN, *earldom*

1. Patrick Lyon (*see* Kinghorn); b. 29 May 1643; cr. 1 July 1677; d. 15 May 1695
2. John Lyon, 1st s. & h.; b. 8 May 1663; serv. 29 Oct. 1695; d. 10 May 1712
3. John Lyon, 1st surv. s. & h.; bapt. 27 Apr. 1690; serv. 11 Sept. 1712; d. unm. 13 Nov. 1715

STRATHTAY and STRATHARDLE, *earldom*

Cr. with the dukedom of Atholl (30 June 1703) and descended with it

SUTHERLAND, *earldom*

1. William, Lord of Sutherland; succ. aft. 1214; st. 1223–45; d. ? *c.* 1250–60
2. William, s. & h.; st. 1263; d. Apr. 1306–Sept. 1307
3. William, s. & h.; b. *c.* 1286; st. 16 Mar. 1309; d. 5 Aug. 1321–7 Dec. 1330
4. Kenneth, br. & h.; st. 7 Dec. 1330; d. 19 July 1333
5. William, s. & h.; d. 27 Feb. 1370–19 June 1371
6. Robert Sutherland, 1st surv. s. & h.; d. 1408–prob. 1427
7. John Sutherland, s. & h.; b. bef. 1408; st. prob. 1427, certainly 12 July 1444; d. aft. 22 Feb. 1456, ? 1460
8. John Sutherland, 1st surv. s. & h.; b. bef. 1436; d. 15 Nov. 1501–24 July 1509, ? 1508
9. John Sutherland, only surv. s. & h.; serv. 24 July 1509 (uncompleted) and 14 Dec. 1512; d. unm. July 1514
10. Elizabeth Sutherland, only sis. & h.; serv. 3 Oct. 1514; d. Sept. 1535 m. about 1500 Adam Gordon; d. 17 Mar. 1538
11. John Gordon, gds. & h.; b. 1525; serv. 4 May 1546; forf. 28 May 1563; rest. 12 Dec. 1565 and 19 Apr. 1567; d. 23 June 1567
12. Alexander Gordon, only surv. s. & h.; b. *c.* June 1552; serv. 8 July 1573; d. 6 Dec. 1594
13. John Gordon, s. & h.; b. 20 July 1576; d. 11 Sept. 1615
14. John Gordon, 1st surv. s. & h.; b. 9 Mar. 1609; serv. 4 June 1616; d. 14 Oct. 1679
15. George Gordon, only surv. s. & h.; b. 2 Nov. 1633; d. 4 Mar. 1703
16. John Gordon or Sutherland, only s. & h.; bapt. 2 Mar. 1661; d. 27 June 1733

TARRAS, *earldom*
1. Walter Scott (*seep* Buccleuch); b. 23 Dec. 1644; cr. for life only 4 Sept. 1660; forf. 6 Jan. 1685; rest. 28 June 1687 and 22 July 1690; d. 9 Apr. 1693

TEVIOT, *earldom*
1. Andrew Rutherford, Lord Rutherford; cr. 2 Feb. 1663; d.s.p. 3 May 1664

TRAQUAIR, *earldom*
1. John Stewart, b. *c.* 1600; cr. 23 June 1633; d. 27 Mar. 1659
2. John Stewart, only s. & h.; b. 1622; d. Apr. 1666
3. William Stewart, s. & h.; b. 18 June 1657; d. unm. bef. 1685
4. Charles Stewart, br. & h.; d. 13 June 1741

TULLIBARDINE, *earldom and marquessate*

Earldom
1. Sir John Murray; cr. 10 July 1606; d. 23 June–5 July 1613
2. William Murray, s. & h.; b. 1574; res. in favour of 3, 1 Apr. 1626, but res. not completed; d. bef. 30 July 1627
3. Patrick Murray, br.; cr. 24 July 1628; d. 7 Sept. 1644
4. James Murray, s. & h.; b. *c.* Sept. 1617; d. Jan. 1670
5. John Murray (*see* Atholl), gds. of 2; b. 2 May 1631; cr. 7 Feb. 1676; d. 6 May 1703
   [*Thereafter this earldom descended with the marquessate of Atholl, and the marquessate of Tullibardine, cr. June 1703, with the dukedom of Atholl*]

TWEEDDALE, *earldom and marquessate*

Earldom
1. John Hay, Lord Hay of Yester; b. *c.* 1593; cr. 1 Dec. 1646; d. 25 May 1653
2. John Hay (*see* Gifford), s. & h.; b. 1626
   marquessate; cr. 17 Dec. 1694; d. 11 Aug. 1697
3. John Hay, s. & h.; b. 1645; d. 20 Apr. 1713
4. Charles Hay, s. & h.; b. bef. 1670; d. 17 Dec. 1715

WEMYSS, *earldom*
1. John Wemyss, lord Wemyss of Elcho; b. bef. 1604; cr. 25 June 1633; d. 22 Nov. 1649
2. David Wemyss, s. & h.; b. 6 Sept. 1610; d.s.p.m.s. July 1679
3. Margaret Wemyss, yr. da. & h.; b. 1 Jan. 1659; d. 11 Mar. 1705
   m. 1. 28 Mar. 1672 Sir James Wemyss; d. Dec. 1682
      2. 29 Apr. 1700 George Mackenzie, earl of Cromarty; d. 27 Aug. 1714
4. David Wemyss, s. & h.; bapt. 29 Apr. 1678; d. 15 Mar. 1720

WIGTOWN, *earldom and marquessate*
1. Malcolm Fleming; b. *c.* 1300 or earlier; cr. 9 Nov. 1341; d. 3 Oct. 1357–13 Oct. 1362
2. Thomas Fleming, gds. & h.; b. *c.* 1345 or earlier; succ. 26 Jan. 1367; res. 8 or 15 Feb. 1372; d.s.p. ? 1382 or later
   [Archibald Douglas and James Douglas (Douglas 5 and 9) were each st. on one occasion (Archibald by the French chancery, James by the English chancery) 'earl of Wigtown'. The ascription of this title was unwarranted]

Marquessate
3. Robert Stewart (*see* Carrick, Kintyre), 3rd s. of K. James VI of Scotland; b. 18 Jan. or 18 Feb. 1602; cr. bef. 27 May 1602; d. 27 May 1602

Earldom
4. John Fleming, Lord Fleming, descendant & h. of cous. of 2; b. 1567; cr. 19 Mar. 1606; d. Apr. 1619
5. John Fleming, s. & h.; bapt. ? *c.* 9 Dec. 1589; d. 7 May 1650
6. John Fleming, s. & h.; b. *c.* 1612; d. Feb. 1665
7. John Fleming, s. & h.; d. Apr. 1668
8. William Fleming, br. & h.; d. 8 Apr. 1681
9. John Fleming, s. & h.; d. 10 Feb. 1744

WINTON, *earldom*
1. Robert Seton, Lord Seton; cr. 16 Nov. 1600; d. 22 Mar. 1603
2. Robert Seton, s. & h.; b. 1583; rest. 26 June 1606; d. aft. 28 Dec. 1636
3. George Seton, br. & h.; b. Dec. 1584; granted earldom 12 May 1607; d. 17 Dec. 1650
4. George Seton, gds. & h.; b. 4 May 1642; d. 6 Mar. 1704
5. George Seton, s. & h.; b. *c.* 1678; serv. 4 July 1710; forf. 19 Mar. 1716; d. unm. 19 Dec. 1749

ENGLISH AND BRITISH PARLIAMENTS AND RELATED ASSEMBLIES TO 1832

THE compiling of lists of parliaments has been repeatedly attempted. The most important previous publications containing such lists are the following:

Reports from the Lords Committees touching the Dignity of a Peer of the Realm (5 vols, 1829). Vol. I contains a table of writs issued for election of knights and burgesses, 1264–1483 (pp. 489–99); enrolled writs of summons to parliaments and other assemblies down to 1483 printed in vols III–IV.

C. H. Parry, *The Parliaments and Councils of England chronologically arranged from the reign of William I to the Revolution of 1688* (1839).

Return of the Name of every Member of the Lower House of Parliament, 1213–1874, H.C. Parliamentary Papers, 69, 69–I, 69–II, 69–III of 1878 (2 parts, 1878 and 1888).

Lists published by H. G. Richardson and G. O. Sayles: H. G. Richardson in *TRHS*, 4th ser., XI (1928), pp. 172–75 (for 1258–72). H. G. Richardson and G. O. Sayles in *BIHR*, V (1928), pp. 151–54 (for 1272–1307); *ibid.*, VI (1928), pp. 85–88 (for 1307–27); *ibid.*, VIII (1930), pp. 78–82 (for 1327–77).

The Interim Report of the Committee on House of Commons Personnel and Politics, 1264–1832, Cmd 4130 (1932): list of parliaments 1258–1832, pp. 60–107; list of other assemblies to which representatives of the Commons were summoned, 1268–1371, p. 108; assemblies of merchants, 1316–56, pp. 109–10—quoted thereafter as *The Interim Report* [the lists to 1399 based on the work of H. G. Richardson and G. O. Sayles].

Handbook of British Chronology, 1st edn (1939), list 1258–1547 [by H. G. Richardson], pp. 342–50.

All these various attempts to provide a list of parliaments have been characterized by a certain one-sidedness, tending in either of two directions: they have placed their main emphasis either upon the representative character of parliament, or upon what has been called the 'judicial' character of parliament. Both tendencies, in turn, have rightly deserved and have duly received subsequent criticism. Since the publication of the second edition of the *Handbook* H. G. Richardson and G. O. Sayles have reiterated their criticisms of any list of parliaments in the thirteenth century that attempts to go beyond including the periodic 'judicial' assemblies [*EHR*, LXXXII (1967), p. 748]. Their views on the *importance* of this aspect of parliament during its formative period command, of course, fairly general acceptance. Their insistence that nothing else is of comparable significance, does, however, represent an unjustifiably one-sided approach to parliamentary origins.

The main difficulties of compiling a list arise in the first century of the English parliament's history, the period, broadly, from the middle of the reign of Henry III to the middle of the reign of Edward III. Since about the middle of the fourteenth century the term 'parliament' has, in England, connoted a political body composed in a particular way and summoned by writs of a stereotyped form, so that thereafter a precise list of English parliaments can be compiled without difficulty. By 1350, however, the term 'parliament' had already been current in England, both in chronicles and in official, royal records, for fully a hundred years. During this initial period the writs of summons to parliaments were by no means stereotyped in form, and neither parliament's composition nor its functions can be defined with any exactness.

Very few *writs of summons* to parliaments survive previous to 1290 and systematic use of this type of evidence for the study of the nature and purpose of parliamentary assemblies can only begin at that date. Two main patterns in the wording of the writs of summons can be clearly discerned, though variations of detail persisted for at least another fifty years. All the writs of summons refer in general terms to the intended *function* of the assembly: the king expresses his intention of having conference, discussion, deliberation or consultation with the persons summoned ('habere colloquium', 'tractatum', 'deliberacionem', 'consilium'). One or more of these, or other equivalent words, descriptive of function, appear in all the writs. The second pattern is rarer at first, but it becomes virtually the norm in the course of the reign of Edward III. It prefaced the description of function by a sentence stating the king's intention of holding a parliament (after 1295 invariably 'parliamentum tenere'), using the word 'parliament' clearly as a description of an assembly. The list below includes meetings summoned by both types of writs (with or without mention of 'parliamentum'), but only the terms descriptive of an assembly have been noted under the heading 'designation of assembly in official records'. This includes all the cases where 'parliamentum' occurs and those mentions of 'consilium' where it is used to describe the meeting itself. Where 'consilium' merely connotes the function of counselling, usually in combination with words such as 'colloquium', 'tractatus', etc., it has been omitted together with those other terms.

In its *composition*, parliament was basically a session of the king's continual council afforced by the presence of such other persons as the king deemed it necessary or desirable to summon on each particular occasion. During its first hundred years, however, parliament was in process of evolving into an assembly which always included representatives as well as the individually summoned lay and ecclesiastical magnates. In that formative period, representatives were also summoned, not only to parliaments in association with lay and ecclesiastical magnates, but at times by themselves to separate assemblies unconnected in time or place with any other gathering. As these separate assemblies of representatives are part of the background of the increasing recourse to representation in parliament, they have been noted in the table below: down to 1327 they are distinguished by smaller type, and in Edward III's reign are mentioned in the notes to the main table.

The *function* of English parliaments was described on separate occasions in the thirteenth century as being 'to treat the common business of the kingdom and the king' and 'to deal with the great business of his realm and of his foreign lands'. The essence of parliament's function was therefore not specifically judicial, or specifically legislative, or specifically taxative, or even specifically deliberative: it consisted in being unspecific, in being omnicompetent, in ranging over the whole field of government. A satisfactory list of the assemblies fulfilling this purpose cannot avoid including, during the first century of parliament's history, a variety of gatherings differing considerably in composition and in the type of business transacted. The exact make-up of each assembly is indicated down to 1377 by the notes on its composition and designation in official records, together, in some cases, with further information on the purpose of the meeting and any other special features. (*See also* below for the discussion of certain categories of assemblies omitted from our list.)

No further discussion of the nature and development of parliament can be attempted here; for further study reference may be made to the bibliographical note below.

Bibliographical Note

The principal published lists of parliaments have been already mentioned above. Other works, containing information about the membership of the two houses and about parliamentary officials, are mentioned in the special bibliographical section of the Handbook (*supra*, pp. xxix–xxxiii).

The development of the medieval parliament was the central theme of W. Stubbs's *Constitutional History of England* (3 vols, Oxford, 1874–78; last edns, 1895–97). Stubbs acquired an unrivalled mastery of the evidence contained in the printed parliamentary records and his work remains invaluable. [For recent appreciations, *see* H. M. Cam, 'Stubbs seventy years after', *Cambridge Historical Journal*, IX (1948) and J. G. Edwards, *William Stubbs* (Historical Association, 1952).] While Stubbs's interests centred in the development of representative institutions, the importance of parliament as a court was brought out in a striking fashion by F. W. Maitland's introduction to his *Memoranda de Parliamento* (R.S., 1893). Most of the subsequent publications have been greatly influenced by those two works. References to later contributions to the history of the medieval English parliament will be found in G. T. Lapsley, 'Some recent advances in English constitutional history', *Cambridge Historical Journal*, V (1936), pp. 122–35 [republished with further additions (until 1948) in G. T. Lapsley, *Crown Community and Parliament* (ed. H. M. Cam and G. Barraclough, Oxford, 1951)]; and in J. G. Edwards, *Historians and the Medieval English Parliament* (Glasgow, 1960). More recent general surveys include E. B. Fryde and E. Miller (eds), *Historical Studies of the English Parliament, Origins to 1603*, 2 vols (Cambridge, 1970) and R. G. Davies and J. H. Denton (eds), *The English Parliament in the Middle Ages* (Manchester, 1981). The various studies of H. G. Richardson and G. O. Sayles, listed below have been republished, with some additions, in *The English Parliament in the Middle Ages* (1981).

For the developments in Henry III's reign, see especially H. G. Richardson, 'The origins of parliament', *TRHS*, 4th ser., XI (1928); J. E. A. Jolliffe, 'Some factors in the beginning of parliament', *ibid.*, XXII (1940), and, most recently, F. M. Powicke, *Henry III and Lord Edward*

(2 vols, Oxford, 1947) and *The Thirteenth Century, 1216–1377* (Oxford, 1953); R. F. Treharne, 'The nature of parliament in the reign of Henry III', *EHR* LXXIV (1959) and P. Spufford (ed.), *Origins of the English Parliament* (1967).

For the period 1272–1377, see H. G. Richardson and G. O. Sayles 'The early records of the English parliaments', *BIHR*, V and VI (1928), 'The parliaments of Edward III', *ibid.*, VIII (1930), and 'The king's ministers in parliament' [1272–1377], *EHR*, XLVI–XLVII (1931–32) (these and other articles, some revised, on the Parliamentary history of the thirteenth and fourteenth centuries, are collected in H. G. Richardson and G. O. Sayles, *The English Parliament in the Middle Ages* (1981)); J. G. Edwards, 'The Plena Potestas of English parliamentary representatives', *Oxford Essays in Medieval History presented to H. E. Salter* (Oxford, 1934); M. V. Clarke, *Medieval Representation and Consent* (London, 1936); T. F. T. Plucknett, 'Parliament' in *English Government at Work, 1327–36*, vol. I (Cambridge, Mass., 1940); D. Rayner, 'The forms and machinery of the "Commune Petition" in the fourteenth century', *EHR*, LVI (1941); H. M. Cam, 'The legislators of medieval England', *Proceedings of British Academy*, 1945; F. M. Powicke, *Thirteenth Century* (*cit. supra*, 1953); J. S. Roskell, 'The problem of the attendance of the Lords in medieval parliaments', *BIHR*, XXIX (1956); J. G. Edwards, *The Commons in Medieval English Parliaments* (1958); G. Holmes, *The Good Parliament* (Oxford, 1975); J. S. Roskell, *Parliament and Politics in Late Medieval England*, 3 vols (1981–83).

For the period 1377–1485, see H. L. Gray, *The Influence of the Commons on Early Legislation* (Cambridge, Mass., 1932); K. B. McFarlane, 'Parliament and "Bastard Feudalism"', *TRHS*, 4th ser., XXVI (1944); H. G. Richardson 'The commons and medieval politics', *ibid.*, XXVIII (1946); H. M. Cam's two articles cited above (*Proc. British Acad.*, 1945, and *Cambridge Historical Journal*, 1948) and J. S. Roskell, *The Commons in the Parliament of 1422* (Manchester, 1954); S. B. Chrimes, *English Constitutional Ideas in the XV Century* (Cambridge, 1936); Sir Goronwy Edwards, *The Second Century of English Parliament* (Oxford, 1979).

For the period 1485–1603, see M. A. R. Graves, *Tudor Parliaments: Crown, Lords and Commons, 1485–1603* (1985), a recent introductory survey; G. R. Elton, *Studies in Tudor and Stuart Politics and Government*, II, *Parliament and Political Thought* (1974); S. E. Lehmberg, *The Reformation Parliament, 1529–1536* (Cambridge, 1970) and *The Later Parliaments of Henry VIII, 1536–1547* (Cambridge, 1977); J. G. Edwards, 'The emergence of majority rule in the procedure of the House of Commons', *TRHS*, 5th ser., XV (1965); J. E. Neale, *The Elizabethan House of Commons* (1949) and *Elizabeth I and her Parliaments* (2 vols, 1953–57); P. W. Hasler, *The History of Parliament: The House of Commons, 1558–1603*, I (HMSO, 1981).

For later periods, see the relevant sections of the Bibliographical Guide.

ARRANGEMENT OF THE LIST

The present list starts at the beginning of the reign of Henry III.[1] The bulk of the evidence about assemblies during his reign has had to be derived from chronicles and other unofficial sources. For the period 1216–42 (listed for the first time in this edition), a smaller number of headings has been used than in the remainder of the list. Because of the very heterogeneous nature of the evidence for this initial period fuller explanatory notes are necessary. From 1273 onwards an attempt has been made to compile a list based almost exclusively on royal records. Down to 1327 a wide variety of official sources had to be used, and a still more prolonged search among various classes of unpublished records in the Public Record Office would probably result in a fuller and better list. The problem of deciding which assemblies ought to be listed arose chiefly in this part of our table. In a list that was intended to be as all-inclusive as possible, some doubt arose only over certain assemblies of townsmen and merchants. The only ones left out are those known to have been held for a very limited purpose [e.g. to help in the planning of a new town or to elect a mayor of the wool staple]. From 1327 to 1509 the list consists, with one exception noted below, of only those assemblies for which the writs of summons under the great seal have been enrolled on the Close Rolls.[2] The numerous separate merchant assemblies of the reign of Edward III have been mentioned in the notes to the main table. From 1509 to 1832 the list is derived entirely from the *Interim Report*, pp. 88–107.

The following categories of assemblies have been omitted from our list: military musters; ecclesiastical assemblies included in the list of the English church councils, elsewhere in this Handbook; Scottish parliaments held by the English kings (with the sole exception of the joint meetings of English and Scottish prelates and magnates held by Edward I in 1291–92).

The list below is arranged as follows:

Main features

Normal entries (in ordinary type) are based on official writs of summons or, in their absence, on other official records.

All uncertain information (including everything derived from chronicles) has been italicized.

Mere intention to hold an assembly has been indicated by the insertion of square brackets round all such items and round the sources from which this information is derived. Adjournments of legal cases to future assemblies are dealt with in this way.

When it is certain that an intended assembly never took place, all mention of its having been summoned is omitted.

The purpose and arrangement of different columns are in most cases self-explanatory. The notes below deal only with certain special features.

[1] H. G. Richardson and G. O. Sayles had discovered another official record mentioning a parliament expected on 20 Jan. 1237 [*EHR*, LXXII (1967), pp. 747–50].
[2] A few merchant assemblies of the reign of Edward III for which only the original returns survive (but no enrolments of writs of summons) have been added from the *Interim Report (cit. supra)*, pp. 109–10.

Designation of assembly (column 3, to 1377)

Down to 1327 designation in every kind of official record emanating from the central government is noted: the terms requiring mention have been already discussed above. For the reign of Edward III designation in the sources used for this portion of the list is alone noted, and the terms used in the writs of summons are distinguished from those mentioned in the marginal summaries on the close rolls. This particular column has been discontinued after 1377, as the list consists henceforth solely of parliaments uniformly designated as such.

Persons summoned

Special assemblies of elected representatives of counties and boroughs, and of nominated knights or burgesses or merchants, are indicated by an asterisk (*) in front of the assembly. If they were held apart from a meeting of magnates this is indicated by the use of smaller type (down to 1327). The special assemblies of burgesses or merchants held under Edward III are mentioned in the notes to the main table.

Down to 1327 the categories of persons known to have been present are enumerated for each assembly in a special column of this table (column 4).

This particular column has been discontinued after 1327 and henceforth the presence of prelates, lay magnates, knights and burgesses is presumed unless otherwise indicated; after 1327 the absence of elected knights and burgesses is indicated by the sign † in front of the assembly. Other variations in composition of assemblies are mentioned under 'Sources and remarks'.

No attempt has been made after 1327 to indicate the presence or absence of the representatives of the diocesan clergy. This is a matter demanding further research.

Terminating dates (penultimate column)

In the thirteenth and fourteenth centuries (and even later) the date at which a parliament ended can seldom be determined with absolute certainty, because a session of the king's council might continue after some or most of the persons summoned 'to afforce' it had been allowed to depart. It is only occasionally, sometimes through an accidental survival of special records, that such prolongation of the session of the council can be clearly observed [see for example under 1315]. Much of the information recorded in this column refers, therefore, only to the approximate date of the departure of the Commons. Financial grants were made, as a general rule, on the last day of the session of the Commons. The writs 'de expensis' were usually issued on the same or the following day, or very shortly afterwards (the enrolment of these writs, though not their issue, ceased after 1414).

Sources

No attempt has been made to give exhaustive references to sources: we have merely tried to give the minimum necessary to cover all the information recorded under each assembly.

The following abbreviations have been used:

I. *List of ordinary abbreviations (other than references to sources)*

Bps	= bishops	Magn.	= magnates
Burg.	= burgesses	Parl.	= parliament
Cons.	= 'consilium'	Prel.	= prelates
Dioc. clergy	= diocesan clergy	summ.	= summoned
Kts	= knights		

II. *References to documentary series in the Public Record Office*

C.47	=	Chancery Miscellanea
C.49	=	Chancery, Parliamentary and Council Proceedings
C.202	=	Chancery Files, Tower Series
C.219	=	Parliament, Writs and Returns of Members
D.L.10	=	Duchy of Lancaster, Ancient Deeds
E.101	=	Exchequer, K.R., Accounts Various
E.159	=	Exchequer, K.R., Memoranda Rolls
E.175	=	Exchequer, Parliamentary and Council Proceedings
E.368	=	Exchequer, L.T.R., Memoranda Rolls
K.B.27	=	Coram Rege Plea Rolls
S.C.8	=	Ancient Petitions
S.C.10	=	Parliamentary Proxies

III. *List of abbreviations used in references to published sources*

Annales Londonienses = *Annales Londonienses and Annales Paulini* (RS, ed. W. Stubbs, 1882)

Annales Monastici = *Annales Monastici* (RS, ed. H. R. Luard, 3 vols, 1864–69)

Anonimalle Chronicle = *The Anonimalle Chronicle, 1333 to 1381,* ed. V. H. Galbraith (Manchester, 1927)

B.J.R.L. = *Bulletin of the John Rylands Library*

C.C.R. = *Calendar of Close Rolls*

C.F.R. = *Calendar of Fine Rolls*

Cole, *Documents* = H. Cole, ed., *Documents illustrative of English history in the 13th and 14th centuries from the records of the Queen's remembrancer in the exchequer* (RC, 1844)

Cotton, *Historia Anglicana* = *Bartholomei de Cotton Historia Anglicana, A.D. 449–1298* (RS, ed. H. R. Luard, 1859)

C.P.R. = *Calendar of Patent Rolls*

C.R. = *Close Rolls*

English Parliament (1981) = R. G. Davies and J. H. Denton (eds), *The English Parliament in the Middle Ages* (Manchester, 1981).

Essays to R. L. Poole = *Essays in History presented to Reginald Lane Poole* (Oxford, 1927)

Flores Historiarum = *Flores Historiarum per Matthaeum Westmonasteriensem collecti* (RS, ed. H. R. Luard, 3 vols, 1890)

Foedera = Th. Rymer's *Foedera, 1066–1383* (RC, 4 vols, 1816–69)

H. of C. Interim Report = *The Interim Report of the Committee on House of Commons Personnel and Politics 1264–1832. Cmd 4130* (1932)

Liber de Antiquis Legibus = *De Antiquis legibus liber. Cronica maiorum et vice-comitum Londoniarum 1178–1274,* ed. T. Stapleton (Camden O.S., 34, 1846)

M. Paris, *Chron. Maj.* = *Matthaei Parisiensis Chronica Majora* (RS, ed. H. R. Luard, 7 vols, 1872–83)

Meyer = P. Meyer, ed., *L'Histoire de Guillaume le Marechal (Société de l'Histoire de France,* II–III, 1894–1901)

Mitchell = S. K. Mitchell, *Studies in Taxation under John and Henry III* (Yale U.P., New Haven, 1914).

Official Return = *Return of the Name of every member of the Lower House of Parliament, 1213–1874* (HMSO 1878 and 1888)

Oxenedes, *Chronica* = *Chronica Johannis de Oxenedes* (RS, ed. Sir H. Ellis, 1859)

Pat. R. = *Patent Rolls*

Powicke = F. M. Powicke, *King Henry III and the Lord Edward* (2 vols, Oxford, 1947)

P.W. = *Parliamentary writs and writs of military summons,* ed. Sir F. Palgrave (RC, 1827–34)

R.D.P. = *Reports from the Lords Committees touching the Dignity of a Peer of the Realm,* vols III and IV (1829)

Richardson and Sayles, *Procedure without Writ* = *Select cases of procedure without writ under Henry III,* ed. H. G. Richardson and G. O. Sayles (Selden Soc., vol. 60, 1941)

R. Litt. Cl. = *Rotuli Litterarum Clausarum . . . 1204–27,* ed. T. D. Hardy, *RC,* 2 vols (1833–44)

Rôles Gascons = *Rôles Gascons,* ed. Ch. Bémont, vol. III (1906)

R.P. = *Rotuli Parliamentorum,* 6 vols (1783)

R.P.In. = *Rotuli Parliamentorum Anglie hactenus inediti,* ed. H. G. Richardson and G. O. Sayles (Camden 3rd ser., 51, 1935)

R.S. = Rolls Series

Sayles, *King's Bench* = *Select Cases in the Court of King's Bench* (Edward I and Edward II), ed. G. O. Sayles, 4 vols [Selden Society, vols 55 (1936), 57 (1938), 59 (1939), 74 (1955)]

Shirley, *Royal Letters* = *Royal Letters, Henry III,* ed. W. W. Shirley (RS, 2 vols, 1862–66)

Stat. = *Statutes of the Realm,* vol. I (RC, 1810)

Tout, *Chapters* = T. F. Tout, *Chapters in the administrative history of medieval England,* 6 vols (Manchester, 1920–33)

Treaty R. = *Treaty Rolls, I, 1234–1325* (HMSO, 1956)

Treharne, *Plan of Reform* = R. F. Treharne, *The baronial plan of reform, 1258–63* (Manchester, 1932)

Trivet, *Annales* = Nicholas Trivet, *Annales sex regum Angliae, 1135–1307* (ed. T. Hog, 1845)

Vincent, *Lancashire Lay Subsidies* = J. A. C. Vincent, *Lancashire Lay Subsidies* (Record Society for Lancashire and Cheshire, 1893)

Wedgwood = *History of Parliament, Register of the Ministers and of the Members of both Houses, 1439–1509,* ed. by J. Wedgwood and others (HMSO, 1938)

Date and place of assembly	Date of summons	Designation of assembly in official records	Persons summoned	Sources and remarks
1216, 27–28 Oct. Gloucester				Council of prelates and magnates supporting the king presided by the papal legate Guala; King Henry III crowned on 28 Oct. Roger Wendover in M. Paris, *Chron. Maj.*, III, p. 1; Meyer, III (1901), p. 213
1216, c. 11–12 Nov. Bristol				Council of prelates and magnates supporting Henry III who swore fealty to him. Presided by the papal legate, Guala. The Great Charter reissued on 12 Nov. *Stat.* (Charters), pp. 14–16; Annales Monastici, II (Waverley), p. 286
? March 1217				Council of magnates supporting Henry III granted a carucage and hidage. *R. Litt. Cl.*, I, p. 348; Mitchell, p. 122
1217, 12 Sept. Kingston on Thames; 1217, 20 Oct.–6 Nov. Merton and later at St Paul's, London			Prel., Magn.	Meeting to conclude peace with Prince Louis of France Powicke, I, pp. 16–17; *Liber de Antiquis Legibus*, p. 203. Great Council of prelates and magnates presided by the papal legate Guala. Aid of 2 marks per knight's fee granted. Writs ordering collection dated 30 Oct. The Great Charter reissued under the seals of Guala and of William, earl of Pembroke. Charter of the Forest issued on 6 Nov. under their seals at St Paul's, London. *Pat. R*, I (1216–25), p. 125; *R. Litt. Cl.*, p. 371; *Stat.* (Charters), pp. 17–21; *Liber de Antiquis Legibus*, p. 203; *Annales Monastici*, II (Waverley), p. 290; Mitchell, pp. 125–26
1218, March Worcester				Assembly of prelates, magnates and sheriffs to witness the rendering of homage by Llywelyn ap Iorwerth of Gwynedd. Meyer, II, p. 279
1218, after 29 Sept. London				Council held by William Marshal, earl of Pembroke Meyer, III, p. 252, n. 2
1219, before May Reading			Prel., Magn.	Council of prelates and magnates presided by the papal legate Pandulf. William Marshal, earl of Pembroke laid down his office of regent (*rector noster et regni nostri*) Meyer, II, pp. 284–85; III, pp. 253–55
1220, 17 May Westminster				Second coronation of Henry III. Roger Wendover in M. Paris, *Chron. Maj.*, III, p. 58

Date and place of assembly	Date of summons	Designation of assembly in official records	Persons summoned	Sources and remarks
1220, May Shrewsbury				Meeting of Henry III, archbishop Stephen Langton, Justiciar Hubert de Burgh and other notables with Llywelyn ap Iorwerth of Gwynedd to recognise the right of succession of his son David Powicke, II, p. 630
1220, before 9 Aug.				Council of magnates granted a carucage. Writs ordering collection dated 9 Aug. R. Litt. Cl., pp. 437, 442; Mitchell, p. 130
1221, 19 July Westminster			Prel.	Surrender by the papal legate, Pandulf, of his office as well as of his special position as the guardian, on the pope's behalf, of King Henry III Flores Historiarum, II, p. 173
1222, before 25 June			Prel. Magn.	Grant by a council of an aid for the defence of the Holy Land (a poll tax). Writs ordering collection dated 25 June. R. Litt. Cl., pp. 516, 567; Mitchell, p. 141
1223, 13 Jan. London			Prel. Magn.	Council of prelates and magnates. Roger Wendover in M. Paris, Chron. Maj., III, pp. 75–76
1224, 3 Feb.			Prel. Magn.	Meeting of Henry III with some prelates and magnates Pipe Roll Soc., n. ser., 44 (1982), p. 37
1224, June Northampton				A council of notables to consider the affairs of Gascony Mitchell, p. 159
1225, 2–11 Feb. Westminster			Prel. Magn.	A Great Council of bishops, heads of religious houses and magnates. The Great Charter and the Charter of the Forests reissued on 11 Feb. A fifteenth of movables granted to Henry III. Writs ordering collection dated 15 Feb. Pat. R., I (1216–25), p. 160; Stat. (Charters), pp. 22–7; Annales Monastici, III (Dunstable), p. 93; Mitchell, pp. 160–62; BIHR, 34 (1961), p. 67
1225, March Westminster			Magn.	Council of magnates. Decision to exile Faukes de Breauté Roger Wendover in M. Paris, Chron. Maj., III, p. 94
1226, 13 Jan. Westminster			Prel. Magn.	Council of prelates and magnates to hear the demands of the papal legate Otho. Because of illness the king may have failed to attend Roger Wendover in M. Paris, Chron. Maj., III, pp. 102–3

Date / Place		Type	Business and references
1227, Feb. Oxford		Prel. Magn.	Declaration that Henry III has come of age. Roger Wendover in M. Paris, Chron. Maj., III, p. 122
1227, 19 Sept. Westminster	13 Aug.		Thirty-five counties ordered to send four knights each to appear before the king to discuss contentions between the sheriffs and the county communities. R. Litt. Cl., II, pp. 212–13; J. C. Holt in English Parliament (1981), pp. 16, 23
1229, 29 April Westminster		Prel. Magn.	Prel. Magn., Templars and Hospitallers, priors, tenants-in-chief asked to grant a tenth in aid of Pope Gregory IX. The clergy granted a tenth Mitchell, pp. 176–77; Powicke, I, p. 350; Roger Wendover in M. Paris, Chron. Maj., III, pp. 186–89
1229, 22 July Northampton		Lay tenants-in-chief	Council of lay tenants-in-chief to discuss the proposed invasion of France. Agreement to levy a scutage. Mitchell, pp. 181, 184, 186
1231, 26 Jan. Westminster		Prel. Magn.	'Colloquium' with prelates and magnates. Scutage conceded to the king by the magnates Roger Wendover in M. Paris, Chron. Maj., III, p. 200
1232, 7 March Westminster		Prel. Magn.	'Colloquium' with prelates and magnates. A grant of an aid refused Roger Wendover in M. Paris, Chron. Maj., III, pp. 211–12
1232, 3 May London 1232, 14 Sept. Lambeth		Lay Magn.	'Colloquium' with lay magnates. Pat. R., II (1225–32), p. 473
1233, c. 22 May Gloucester 1233, 24 June Oxford		Prel. Magn.	Great Council of prelates and magnates. Grant of a fortieth on movables. Writs ordering its assessment dated 28 Sept. C.R. 1231–34, pp. 155–56; Roger Wendover in M. Paris, Chron. Maj., III, pp. 155–56; Mitchell, p. 200 Council Ordinance for the keeping of the peace C.R. 1231–34, pp. 309–10; Powicke, I, p. 127 'Colloquium'. Many of the magnates summoned to it refused to attend. A second assembly summoned to meet at Westminster on 1 August possibly not held because of a similar refusal Roger Wendover and Matthew Paris in M. Paris, Chron. Maj., III, pp. 244–45; Powicke, I, pp. 129, 133.

535

Date and place of assembly	Date of summons	Designation of assembly in official records	Persons summoned	Sources and remarks
1233, 9 Oct. Westminster			Prel. Magn.	'Colloquium' Roger Wendover in M. Paris, Chron. Maj., III, pp. 251–52
1234, 2–4 Feb. Westminster			Prel. Magn.	Council of prelates and magnates Roger Wendover in M. Paris, III, Chron. Maj., p. 268; Powicke, I, p. 135
1234, 9–10 April Westminster			Prel. Magn.	Council. Dismissal of the king's Poitevin councillors Roger Wendover in M. Paris, Chron. Maj., III, pp. 272–73; Powicke, I, pp. 135–36
1234, 29 May Gloucester				Council of prelates and magnates. Reconciliation of Henry III with his baronial opponents Roger Wendover in M. Paris, Chron. Maj., III, pp. 290–91
1235, before 10 July				Council of prelates and magnates who were tenants-in-chief. An aid of 2 marks per knight's fee conceded for the marriage of Isabella, the king's sister, to Emperor Frederick II (called aid and scutage in royal writs) C.R. 1234–37, pp. 186, 189. Writs ordering its levy dated 10 July and 17 July.
1236, 23 Jan. Merton			Prel. Magn.	The 'nova constitucio' ordained at this council sent to sheriffs for proclamation on 30 January (Close. R. 1234–37, p. 337–39), Annales Monastici (Burton), I, pp. 249–53; Powicke, II, pp. 769–71; Stat., I, pp. 1–4
1236, 28 Apr. London			Magn.	'Colloquium' M. Paris, Chron. Maj., III, pp. 362–63.
1236, 8 June Winchester			Magn.	Council M. Paris, Chron. Maj., III, p. 368
1237, 20–28 Jan. Westminster		Parl.	Prel. Magn.	Great Council. Grant of a thirtieth of movables in return for a confirmation of the charters (charter of confirmation 28 Jan.) Mitchell, pp. 214–15; H. G. Richardson and G. O. Sayles, in EHR, LXXXII (1967), pp. 747–50; Stat., I (charters), p. 28; Close, R. 1234–47, pp. 543–45, 555.
1237, 14–28 Sept. York			Magn.	Council to witness the treaty with Alexander II, king of Scotland (conclusion announced on 28 Sept.) M. Paris, Chron. Maj., III, pp. 413–14; Powicke, II, p. 751

1238, 22 Feb.
Westminster — Prel. Magn. — Council. Settlement reached between Henry III and Richard, earl of Cornwall and his supporters. N. Denholm-Young, *Collected Papers on Mediaeval Subjects* (Oxford, 1946), p. 147. The 'paper constitution' which he ascribed to this political crisis, should most probably be attributed to 1244 (*infra* under 3 Nov. 1244)

1241, 2 Aug.
Shrewsbury — Council. Decision to attack David ap Llywelyn of Gwynedd M. Paris, *Chron. Maj.*, IV, p. 149

Date and place of assembly	Date of summons with note of initial prorogations	Designation of assembly in official records	Persons summoned	Terminating dates		Sources and remarks
				Writs 'de expensis'	Other evidence	
1242, 27 Jan. London [*1242, 22 July*] [*London*]	14 Dec. 1241	[Parl.]	Prel., Magn.			*R.D.P.*, III, 7; M. Paris, *Chron. Maj.*, IV, 181–87 [*C.R. 1237–42*, p. 447]
1244, c. 15 Aug. Newcastle on Tyne			*Magn.*			M. Paris, *Chron. Maj.*, IV, 380
1244, 9 Sept. Windsor						*Annales Monastici*, III, 164–65 (Dunstable)
1244, c. 3 Nov. Westminster			*Prel., Magn.*			M. Paris, *Chron Maj.*, IV 362 ff. 395; *E.H.R.*, LXV, 213–21; Powicke, *Henry III and Lord Edward*, I, p. 298, n. 2.
1245, 23 Feb. London			*Prel., Magn.*			M. Paris, *Chron. Maj.*, IV, 372–74
1245, c. 4 June Westminster			*Magn.*			*R.D.P.*, III, 11
1246, 18 Mar. London			*Prel., Magn.*			M. Paris, *Chron. Maj.*, IV, 518, 526
1246, 7 July Winchester			*Magn.*			M. Paris, *Chron. Maj.*, IV, 560,

Date and place of assembly	Date of summons with note of initial prorogations	Designation of assembly in official records	Persons summoned	Terminating dates		Sources and remarks
				Writs 'de expensis'	Other evidence	
1247, 3 Feb. London			Magn., Prel., Archdeacons			M. Paris, Chron. Maj., IV, 590, 594. Bps said to have absented themselves
1247, Apr. Oxford			Prel., Magn.			M. Paris, Chron. Maj., IV, 622; Annales Monastici, IV, 96 (J. Wykes)
1248, 9 Feb. London		Parl.	Prel., Magn.			[C.R. 1247–51, p. 104]; L.T.R. Mem. R., E. 368/20, mm. 4, 13; M. Paris, Chron. Maj., V, 5–8; letters of proxy of two abbots may refer to this assembly (Parl. Proxies, S.C. 10/1, nos. 1 and 3). In session 16 Feb. 1248 (C.R. 1247–51, p. 106–7)
1248, 8 July London			Magn.			M. Paris,, Chron. Maj., V, 20–21
1249, 5 Jan. Westminster			Prel., Magn.			M. Paris, Chron. Maj., V, 47 ff.
1249, 11 Apr. London			Magn.			M. Paris, Chron. Maj., V, 73
1251, 17 Feb. London			Magn.			M. Paris, Chron. Maj., V, 223–24
1252, May–June Westminster			Prel., Magn.			C. Bémont, Simon de Montfort, Earl of Leicester (1930), 103 ff. (proceedings concerning Montfort's rule in Gascony)
1252, 13 Oct. London			Prel.			M. Paris, Chron. Maj., V, 324 ff.
1253, 4 May Westminster			Prel., Magn.			M. Paris, Chron. Maj., V, 373 ff. Excommunication of violators of Magna Carta on 13 May [Foedera, I (I), 289–90]
1254, 27 Jan. Westminster	27 Dec. 1253	Cons.	Prel., Magn.			R.D.P., III, 12; Foedera, I (I), 296. Held in the king's absence by the queen and

Date / Place	Type	Attendance	References and notes
1254, 26 Apr.	Parl.	Prel., Magn.	Richard, earl of Cornwall, keepers of the realm. Discussions between the keepers of the realm and prelates continued on or after 5 Feb. (Shirley, *Royal Letters*, II, p. 101–2) Shirley, *Royal Letters*, II, pp. 101–2
26 Apr.	Cons.	Kts	*R.D.P.*, III, 13 [copy of an original writ in M. Paris, *Additamenta* (*Chron. Maj.*, VI, 286–87) dated 14 Feb.]. Held in the king's absence by the queen and Richard, earl of Cornwall. [The initial date of 26 Apr. is that for which the assembly summoned; a memorandum on Patent R. speaks of a parliament held on 3 May, *C.P.R., 1247–58*, p. 370]
1254, 19 July Oxford	Cons.	Prel., Magn.	*R.D.P.*, III, 13 Held in the king's absence by Richard, earl of Cornwall
1255, Jan. Merton	Cons.		*C.R., 1254–56*, pp. 157–58, 159–60. Decision to levy a tallage
7 Feb. Westminster	Cons.	Councillors including Magn. and Prel.	*C.R., 1254–56*, pp. 159–60. decision on the liability of the city of London to tallage
[1255, 18 Apr.] [Westminster]	[Parl.]	*Prel., Magn.*	[*C.R., 1254–56*, p. 162; *C.P.R. 1247–58*, p. 399]; *Annales Monastici*, I, 336 (Burton) mention an assembly on 11 Apr. and M. Paris, *Chron. Maj.*, V, 493, on 6 Apr.

Date and place of assembly	Date of summons with note of initial prorogations	Designation of assembly in official records	Persons summoned	Terminating dates		Sources and remarks
				Writs 'de expensis'	Other evidence	
1255, 13 Oct. Westminster			Prel., Magn.			[C.R., 1254–56, pp. 223–24]; M. Paris, Chron. Maj., V, 524–27; C.R. 1254–56, p. 406. Cp. Lunt, Financial Relations of the Papacy with England to 1327 (1939), 269
1256, 30 Apr. London			Prel., ? Magn.			M. Paris,, Chron. Maj., V, 553
1257, 16 Mar. London	12 Feb.		Prel., Magn.			Annales Monastici, I, 384 (Burton, copy of original royal writ). Cp. Lunt, Financial Relations of the Papacy with England, to 1327, 277
1258, 24 Feb. Westminster	24 Jan.		Prel., Magn.			M. Paris, Chron. Maj., VI (Additamenta), 392
1258, c. 7 Apr. London			Prel., Magn.		5 May	Foedera, I (I), 370–71; M. Paris, Chron. Maj., V, 676 ff. The clergy withdrew at an unknown date in Apr. [Annales Monastici, I, 163–64 (Tewkesbury)]
1258, [9] June Oxford		Parl.	Prel., Magn.		? 28 July	[Foedera, I (I), 371; C.P.R., 1247–58, p. 632] 11 June is given as the initial date in M. Paris, Chron. Maj., V, 695, ff. and Liber de Antiquis Legibus, 37. Letters under the great seal began apparently to be attested at Oxford on 12 June (C.R., 1256–59, p. 232) See also B.J.R.L., XVII, pp. 291–321 and R. F. Treharne 'The nature of parliament in the reign of Henry III', E.H.R., LXXIV, 599 (for descriptions of

Date, Place	Type	Composition		Notes and references
1258, 3 July Winchester	Parl.	Prel., Magn.	11 July	Adjournment of the Oxford assembly. *Annales Monastici*, II, 97 (Winchester); Treharne, *Plan of Reform*, 79–81, 383
1258, 13 Oct. Westminster	Parl.	Prel., Magn.		*Annales Monastici*, II, 97 (Winchester) and III, 210 (Dunstable); *Foedera*, I (I), 377–78
1258, 27 Oct. Westminster		Kts	4 Nov.	Four knights from each county summoned to come before the council at the parliament at Westminster with a record of inquests (*E.H.R.*, XLVI, 630–32)
1259, 9 Feb. London	[Parl.]	Prel., Magn.		[*C.R.*, 1256–59, p. 345]; M. Paris, *Chron. Maj.*, V, 73 and VI, 496; *Foedera*, I (I), 381; [Richardson and Sayles, *Procedure without Writ*, 91]
1259, 27 Apr. London		Magn.		*Annales Monastici*, I, 167 (Tewkesbury) and II, 98 (Winchester)
1259, c. 24 June London		Magn.		*Flores Historiarum*, II, 428–29. (Possibly identical with the previous assembly)
1259, 13 Oct. Westminster 1260, 23 Feb. London	Parl.	Prel., Magn. Magn.		*Annales Monastici*, I, 471–79 (Burton); *Stat.*, I, 8–11; Bémont, *Simon de Montfort* (1884), 351
1260, post 30 Apr. London	[Parl.]			Held in the King's absence [*C.R.*, 1259–61, pp. 251, 287]; *Liber de Antiquis Legibus*, 44–45 Henry III reached London on 30 Apr. (Treharne, *Plan of Reform*, 385)
1260, 8 July London	Parl.	Magn.		*C.P.R.*, 1258–66, p. 85

this assembly as parliament in official records

Date and place of assembly	Date of summons with note of initial prorogations	Designation of assembly in official records	Persons summoned	Terminating dates		Sources and remarks
				Writs 'de expensis'	Other evidence	
1260, 13 Oct. London		[Parl.]	Magn.			[C.P.R., 1258–66, p. 90]; Liber de Antiquis Legibus, 45
1261, [23 Feb.] London		[Parl.]				[C.P.R., 1258–66, p. 141]; probably assembled early in March (Treharne, Plan of Reform, 250–53)
[1261, 21 Sept. Windsor]	11 Sept.		Kts			R.D.P., III, 23 Sheriffs ordered to send from each county to the king the same three knights as had been returned to attend an assembly summoned for the same day to St Albans by the bishop of Worcester and the earls of Leicester and Gloucester. Probably no assembly of knights took place at either Windsor or St Albans
1262, c. 2 Feb. London			Magn.			Annales Monastici, IV, 130 (Wykes)
1262, 23 Apr. London			Magn.			Ibid.
1262, c. 28 May London			Magn.			Annales Monastici, IV, 130 (Osney) and 131 (Wykes)
1263, [9 Sept.] London		[Parl.]	Prel., Magn.		? ante 18 Sept.	[Excerpta e Rotulis Finium, II, 402; Parl. Proxies, S.C. 10/1/ no. 5]; Annales Monastici, I, 176 (Tewkesbury) C.P.R., 1258–66, p. 321
1263, 13 Oct. London		[Parl.]	Magn.		16 Oct.	Annales Monastici, III, 225 (Dunstable); Flores Historiarum, II, 484; [Foedera, I (I), 433]
1264, c. 24 June London		Parl.	Prel., Magn.			Foedera, I (I), 442–43

Date & place	Date	Classification	Estates summoned	Date	Date	References
London	22 June / 4 June		Kts			Four knights summoned from each county. *Annales Monastici*, IV, 154 (Osney) and III, 235 (Dunstable)
1264, 30 Nov. Oxford			*Magn.*			Very brief assembly
1265, 20 Jan. London	14 Dec. 1264		Prel., Magn., Kts, Burg.	15 Feb.	? 14 Mar.	*R.D.P.*, III, 33–35; *Stat.* I, 32–33; *Foedera*, I (I), 451–53. Two knights summoned from each county and two burgesses from York, Lincoln, the Cinque Ports and other boroughs
1265, *14 Sept.* Winchester		Parl.	Magn.		22 Sept.	*Annales Monastici*, II, 102 (Winchester) and 366 (Waverley); *Foedera*, I (I), 462; *C.P.R., 1266–72*, p. 265
1266, c. 1 May Northampton						*Liber de Antiquis Legibus*, 84–86
1266, 22 Aug. Kenilworth			Prel., Magn.			*C.P.R., 1258–66*, pp. 671–72 (cp. Powicke, *Henry III and Lord Edward*, II, p. 532, n. 1); *Annales Monastici*, II, 371 (Waverley). Dictum de Kenilworth dated 31 Oct. (*Stat.*, I, 12–17)
1267, 9 Feb. Bury St Edmunds		Parl.	*Prel., Magn.*			*Annales Monastici*, IV, 196 (Wykes); *C.P.R., 1266–72*, p. 133
1267, post 16 June London						*C.R., 1264–68*, p. 379. This assembly presumably held between 16 June (*Foedera*, I (I), 472) and 13 July
1267, Sept. Shrewsbury						Shirley, *Royal Letters*, II, 314. Peace with Llywelyn ap Gruffydd concluded 25 Sept. (*Foedera*, I (I), 474)
1267, c. 18 Nov. Marlborough						Trivet, *Annales*, p. 274. Statute of Marlborough dated 18 Nov. (*Stat.* I, 19ff.)

Date and place of assembly	Date of summons with note of initial prorogations	Designation of assembly in official records	Persons summoned	Terminating dates		Sources and remarks
				Writs 'de expensis'	Other evidence	
1268, 18 Apr. Westminster			Councillors, some Magn.			E.H.R., XL, 583–85. Assembly of councillors coinciding with a legatine council at St Paul's, London
22 Apr. Westminster			Burg.			Representatives of 27 towns summoned before the king's council
1268, June–July Northampton						Annales Monastici, II, 106–7 (Waverley); Oxenedes, Chronica, 235. This assembly usually ascribed to June (cf. Powicke, Henry III and Lord Edward, II, 562), but letters under the great seal were attested at Northampton only between 19 and 25 July (C.R., 1264–68, pp. 472–73; C.P.R., 1266–72, pp. 247–49)
1268, 13 Oct. London		Parl.	Magn.			C.R., 1264–68, p. 552
1269, 7 Apr. London			Magn.			Annales Monastici, IV, 221 (Wykes)
1269, 24 June London		Parl.	Prel., Magn.			C.P.R., 1266–72, p. 384. This parliament began at some later date because of the king's illness
1269, 13 Oct. Westminster			Prel., Magn.			Annales Monastici, IV, 226 ff. (Wykes)
1270, 11 Feb. Westminster			Prel. and Magn. of king's council			Foedera, I (1), 483. Exchequer ordinance of 12 Feb. discussed and approved
1270, 27 Apr. London			Prel., Magn. (Presence of Kts and other free tenants also			Cotton, Historia Anglicana, 143–44; Liber de Antiquis Legibus, 122–23; annales Monastici, II, 108 (Winchester)

Date & place	Summons and session	Designation	Attendance	Sources
			(... mentioned) Prel., Magn.	
1270, July Winchester				Liber de Antiquis Legibus, 125 Writs under the great seal attested at Winchester from 30 July (C.R., 1268–72, pp. 215–16)
[1270, 13 Oct.] [Westminster]		[Parl.]		[C.R., 1268–72, pp. 290–91]; Liber de Antiquis Legibus, 127
1271, 13 Oct. Westminster				Liber de Antiquis Legibus, 142
1272, 27 Jan. London				Ibid.
[1272, post 29 Sept.] [Westminster]		[Parl.]		[C.R., 1268–72, p. 524]
1273, post 13 Jan. Westminster			Prel., Magn., Kts, Burg.	Annales Monastici, II, 113 (Winchester) Held in the king's absence Sayles, King's Bench, II, pp. CXXX–XXXI; Parl. and Council Proc., C. 49/53/19; Chancery Files, C. 202/H/2, no. 6.
1274, 26 Mar. London	summ. 13 Mar. for 28 Mar.; date of meeting advanced by writs of 17 Mar.	Cons.	Councillors, Magn.	Held in the king's absence P.W., I, 1; E.H.R., XXV, 236–42; Stat., I, 26–39
1275, 25 Apr. London	summ. for 16 Feb. 1275; prorogued 26–27 Dec. 1274	'generale parliamentum'	Prel., Magn., Kts, Burg.	'Nova custuma' granted by 10 May (Chancery Files, C. 202/H/2, no. 8; C. 202/C/1, no. 67) P.W., I, 3; Parl. Writs. C. 219/1/1, no. 11. Fifteenth granted by 24 Oct.
1275, 13 Oct. Westminster	1 Sept.	Parl.	Prel., Magn., Kts	[C.F.R., 1272–1307, p. 65]; C.C.R., 1272–79, p. 338. In session 7 May
1276, [3] May Westminster		Parl.		
1276, post 29 Sept. Westminster		Parl.	Prel., Magn.	Stat., I, 42–43; R.P., I, 348; P.W., I, 6

Date and place of assembly	Date of summons with note of initial prorogations	Designation of assembly in official records	Persons summoned	Terminating dates		Sources and remarks
				Writs 'de expensis'	Other evidence	
1276, Nov. Westminster			Magn. and some Prel.			P.W., I, 5 Decision to start war with Llywelyn ap Gruffydd taken on 12 Nov.
1278, *1 May* Westminster		Parl.				C.P.R. 1272–81, p. 275; B.I.H.R., V, p. 137, n. 7
1278, *8 July* Gloucester		Parl., Cons.	Prel., Magn.			Stat., I, 45–50, 71; B.I.H.R., V, 138–39 Statute of Gloucester dated 7 Aug. P.W., I, 7
1278, 29 Sept. Westminster		Parl.	Some Prel. and Magn.			
1279, [16 Apr.] Westminster		Parl.				[C.F.R., 1272–1307, p. 120]; R.P. In., 1–7. In session, 27 Apr.
1279, [20 Oct.] Westminster		Parl.	*Prel., Magn.*			C.F.R. 1272–1307, p. 120, C.C.R., 1272–79, p. 582; Stat., I, 51
1280, [12 May] Westminster		Parl.				[B.I.H.R., V, 134]; R.P. In., 8–11
1280, [*post* 29 Sept.] Westminster		Parl.				[Sayles, King's Bench, I, 92] Possibly postponed until 3 Nov. 1280 (E.H.R., XLIII, p. 13 and n. 3)
1281, [11 May] Westminster		Parl.				Some clerical proctors present (E.H.R., XLVIII, p. 448) [Sayles, King's Bench, I, 79]; Ancient Petitions 6881; Treaty R., I, no. 183
1281, [*post* 29 Sept.] Westminster		Parl.				Some clerical proctors present (E.H.R., XLVIII, p. 448) [Coram Rege R., K.B. 27/64, m. 51]; C.P.R. 1272–81, p. 476
*1283, 20 Jan. Northampton and York	24 Nov. 1282		Kts, Burg.			P.W., I, 10 Two assemblies of kts and burg., coinciding with the assemblies

Date and place		Parl./Cons.	Attendance	Reference
1283, 30 Sept. Shrewsbury (continued at Acton Burnell)	28 June		Magn., Kts, Burg.	of the clergy of each province P.W., I, 15–16; R.P. In., 12–25. Statute of Merchants (of Acton Burnell) dated 12 Oct. (Stat., I, 53–54)
1284, post 25 Dec. Bristol		Cons.	Some Magn.	Annales Monastici, IV, 300 (Osney): B.I.H.R., V, 150, n. 4
1285, 4 May Westminster		Parl.	Prel., Magn.	Stat., I, 71; C.C.R., 1279–88, pp. 331–32; Cotton, Historia Anglicana, 166. Cp. E.H.R., LII, p. 221
1285, Oct. Winchester				Stat., I, 98 Statute of Winchester dated 8 Oct.
1286, 9 Feb. Westminster			Prel., Magn.	B.I.H.R., V, p. 150, n. 5
[1286, post 14 Apr.] [Westminster]		[Parl.]		[C.C.R., 1279–88, p. 388; L.T.R. Memoranda R., E. 368/59 m.4 d.]; Annales Monastici, IV, 306 (Osney)
				Assemblies between Michaelmas 1286 and June 1289 held in the king's absence by Edmund, earl of Cornwall
[1286, 13 Oct.] [Westminster]		[Cons.]		[C.C.R., 1279–88, p. 399]
[1287, 3 Feb.] [Westminster]		[Cons.]		[C.C.R., 1279–88, p. 441]
[1287, 4 May] [Westminster]		[Cons.]		[C.C.R., 1279–88, p. 446; Chancery Miscellanea, C. 47/34/4, no. 58]
[1287, 27 Oct.] [Westminster]		[Cons.]		[C.C.R., 1279–88, p. 458]
[1288, 27 Jan.] [Westminster]		[Cons.]		[C.C.R., 1279–88, p. 497]
[1288, 18 Apr.] [Westminster]		[Cons.]		[C.F.R., 1272–1307, p. 245]

Date and place of assembly	Date of summons with note of initial prorogations	Designation of assembly in official records	Persons summoned	Terminating dates		Sources and remarks
				Writs 'de expensis'	Other evidence	
1288, 13 Oct. Westminster	22 Aug.	Cons.	Some Magn.			P.W., I, 18; [C.C.R., 1279–88, p. 517]
1289, [24 Apr.] Westminster		[Cons.], Parl.				[C.C.R., 1288–96, p. 6]; B.I.H.R., V, 142; Sayles, King's Bench, I, 179
[1289, c. 19 June] Westminster		[Cons.]				[C.C.R., 1288–96, p. 12]
1289, post 25 Dec. Westminster		Parl.				R.P., I, 32, 35; Sayles, King's Bench, I, 181; Cole, Documents, 55
1290, post 13 Jan. Westminster		Parl.				R.P., I, 15 ff., Cole; Documents, 65. Possibly a continuation of the previous parliament
1290, [23 Apr.] Westminster		Parl.	Magn.			[R.P., I, 17]; ibid. 23 ff.; P.W., I, 20. Feudal aid granted 29 May
15 July Westminster	13–14 June	Parl.	Kts			P.W., I, 21–24; Parl. Writs, C.219/1/3. Fifteenth granted with concurrence of kts
1290, 27 Oct. Clipstone		Parl.				R.P., I, 45 ff.
1291, 7 Jan. Ashridge		Parl.				R.P., I, 66–69
1291, 10 May Norham	adjourned 11 May until 2 June		English and Scottish Prel. and Magn.		13 June	Foedera, I, (II), 762 ff.
1291, 2 Aug. Berwick			English and Scottish Prel. and Magn.			Foedera, I (II), 774 ff.
1291, 20 Oct. Abergavenny		Cons.	Magn.			R.P., I, 72 ff.
1292, 7 Jan. London		Parl.				R.P., I, 70 ff.

Date and place	Summons / session	Type	Attendance	References
1292, 2 June Berwick		Parl.	English and Scottish Prel. and Magn.	*Foedera*, I (II), 777
1292, 13 Oct. Berwick	17 Nov.	Parl.	English and Scottish Prel. and Magn.	*Foedera*, I (II), 761, 777 ff.
1293, *post* 29 Mar. London (continued at Canterbury)		Parl.		*R.P.*, I, 91 ff.; *R.P. In.*, 26–29 In session at Canterbury in July
1293, 13 Oct. Westminster		Parl.		*R.P.*, I, 112 ff.; *C.P.R., 1292–1301*, p. 108
1293, *post* 25 Dec. London		Parl.		L.T.R. Mem. R., E. 368/65, m. 32 (partly printed in *E.H.R.*, XLVI, 539, n. 1; the comments there, denying the existence of this assembly, do not seem sufficient to disprove this exchequer record)
294, June Westminster	8 June		Magn.	*P.W.*, I, 25; *R.P.*, I, 127 (cp. *B.I.H.R.*, VI, 148); Cotton, *Historia Anglicana*, 233–34 In session prob. c. 18–20 June (*Rôles Gascons*, III, no. 2676 and *C.P.R., 1292–1301*, p. 102, confirming the presence of John Balliol, King of Scots, in London)
1294, 12 Nov. Westminster	8–9 Oct.	Cons.	Magn., Kts	*P.W.*, I, 26–27; *B.I.H.R.*, III, 110–12. Two pairs of knights summoned from each county on 8 and 9 Oct. respectively. Tenth granted on 12 Nov.
1295, *1–4* Aug. Westminster	24 June	Parl.	Prel., Magn.	*P.W.*, I, 28–29; *R.P.*, I, 132 ff.
1295, 27 Nov. Westminster	summ. 30 Sept., 1 and 3 Oct. for 13 Nov.; prorogued 2 Nov.	Parl.	Prel., Magn., Kts, Burg., Dioc. Clergy	*P.W.*, I, 32–33, 45 Eleventh and Seventh granted on 4 Dec.

Date and place of assembly	Date of summons with note of initial prorogations	Designation of assembly in official records	Persons summoned	Terminating dates		Sources and remarks
				Writs 'de expensis'	Other evidence	
1296, 3 Nov. Bury St Edmunds	26 Aug.	Parl.	Prel., Magn., Kts, Burg., Dioc. Clergy			P.W., I, 47–48. Twelfth and Eighth granted on 29 Nov. (Vincent, Lancashire lay subsidies, 195)
1297, 24 Feb. Salisbury	26 Jan.	Parl.	Magn.			P.W., I, 51–52
1297, 8 July Westminster		Parl.				L.T.R. Memoranda R., E. 368/69, m. 14d. An assembly of prelates and magnates swore fealty to Edward, king's son, at Westminster on 14 July (Vincent, Lancashire Lay Subsidies, 200–1)
1297, 30 Sept. 6 Oct. London	9 Sept. 15 Sept.	Parl.	Prel., some Magn. Kts			P.W., I, 56–64 Held in the king's absence by Edward, king's son. Ninth granted 14 Oct.
1298, 30 Mar. Westminster	15 Mar.	Parl.				R.P., I, 143 P.W., I, 65
1298, 25 May York	10, 11 and 13 Apr.	Cons.	Magn., Kts, Burg.			P.W., I, 65–77
1299, 8 Mar. London	6 Feb.	Parl.	Prel., Magn.			P.W., I, 78–79
1299, 3 May Westminster (continued at Stepney)	10 Apr.	Parl.	Prel., Magn.			P.W., I, 80–81; R.D.P., III, 105–6; B.I.H.R., V, p. 147 and n. 1 Statute about false coinage dated at Stepney, 15 May (Stat., I, 131–33)
1299, 18 Oct. London	21 Sept.	Parl.	Some Prel. and Magn.			P.W., I, 81
1300, 6 Mar. London	29 Dec. 1299	Parl.	Prel., Magn., Kts, Burg., Dioc. Clergy	20 Mar.		P.W., I, 82–86
1300, 20 May York	27 and 30 Mar.		Kts			P.W., I, 87; Parl. Writs, C. 219/1/10. A special assembly arising

Date & Place	Summons	Type	Attendance	Days	Notes / References
1301, 20 Jan. Lincoln	26 Sept. 1300	Parl.	Prel., Magn., Kts, Burg.	27 and 30 Jan.	out of the confirmation of the charters in the parliament of Mar. 1300 *P.W.*, I, 89–102; Parl. Writs, C. 219/1/12 Possibly summoned originally for 13 Oct. 1300 (Parl. and Council Proceedings, E. 175/Roll 10) The same representatives of shires and boroughs ordered to be returned to the January parliament as came 'ad parliamentum . . . ultimo preteritum' *P.W.*, I, 112–13
1302, 1 July Westminster	2 June	Parl.	Prel., Magn.		*P.W.*, I, 114–31; Parl. Proxies, S.C. 10/1/no. 11B
1302, 14 Oct. Westminster	summ. 14, 20 and 24 July for 29 Sept.; prorogued 13 Sept.	Parl.	Prel., Magn., Kts, Burg.	21 Oct.	Parl. and Council Proceedings, E. 175/file 1/12 (cp. also *P.W.*, I, 134, no. 3)
1303, *post* 7 Apr. York			Councillors		*P.W.*, I., 134–35 Assembly of burgesses (merchants), to discuss new duties on exports and imports
*1303, 25 June York	7 May	Parl.	Burg.		*P.W.*, I, 136–58; Maitland, *Memoranda de Parliamento* (R.S., 1893)
1305, 28 Feb. Westminster	summ. 12 Nov. 1304 for 16 Feb. 1305; prorogued 22 Jan. 1305	Parl.	Prel., Magn., Kts, Burg., Dioc. Clergy	20 Mar.	*P.W.*, I, 136–58; Maitland, *Memoranda de Parliamento* (R.S., 1893)
1305, 15 Sept. Westminster	summ. for 15 July; prorogued to 15 Aug. and finally prorogued on 30 July to 15 Sept.	Parl.	Some Prel. and Magn.	In session on 29 Mar. and on 5–6 Apr.	*P.W.*, I, 158–60 Opened in the king's absence (Parl. and Council Proceedings, E. 175/file 1/20)

551

Date and place of assembly	Date of summons with note of initial prorogations	Designation of assembly in official records	Persons summoned	Terminating dates		Sources and remarks
				Writs 'de expensis'	Other evidence	
1306, 30 May Westminster	5 Apr.	Parl.	Prel., Magn., Kts, Burg.	30 May		P.W., I, 164–78
1307, 20 Jan. Carlisle	3 Nov. 1306	Parl.	Prel., Magn., Kts, Burg., Dioc. Clergy	20 Jan. (Burg) 19 Mar. (Kts)		P.W., I, 181–91; B.I.H.R. III, 111–12
1307, 13 Oct. Northampton	26 Aug.	Parl.	Prel., Magn., Kts, Burg., Dioc. Clergy	16 Oct.		P.W., II (II), 1–14 Parl. Writs, C. 219/2/2
1308, 3 Mar. Westminster	19 Jan.	Parl.	Prel., Magn., Kts			P.W., II (II), 18–19 Kts were probably summoned (C.C.R., 1307–13, p. 51; P.W., II (II), 56, 116)
1308, 28 Apr. Westminster	10 Mar.	Parl.	Prel., Magn.			P.W., II (II), 20–21
1308, 20 Oct. Westminster	16 Aug.	Parl.	Prel., Magn.			P.W., II (II), 22–23
1309, 23 Feb. Westminster	8 Jan.	Parl.	Prel., Magn.			P.W., II (II), 23–24
1309, 27 Apr. Westminster	4 Mar.	Parl.	Prel., Magn., Kts, Burg., Dioc. Clergy	13 May		P.W., II (II), 24–36, 38–39
1309, 27 July Stamford	11 June	Parl.	Prel., Magn.			P.W., II (II), 37–38 R.P., I, 444
1310, 8 Feb. Westminster	summ. 26 Oct. 1309 to York; changed to Westminster 12 Dec.	Parl.	Prel., Magn.		12 Apr.	P.W., II (II), 40–42 Annales Londonienses (R.S., 1882), p. 168
1311, 8 Aug. London	16 June		Prel. Magn., Dioc. Clergy, Kts, Burg.	9 Oct.		P.W., II (II), 44–56 and app. 37–39, 41
5 Nov. 12 Nov. 18 Nov. Westminster	8 Oct. 11 Oct. 8 Oct.		Prel., Magn.., Kts, Burg., Dioc. Clergy	18 Dec.		1st session ended 8–9 Oct. 2nd session of same Plt. The same representatives of shires and boroughs ordered to be returned, if possible (P.W., II (II), 57–68)

1312, 20 and 27 Feb. York	28 Jan. and 15 Feb.		Some councillors, judges and Magn.		P.W., II (II), 70
1312, 20 Aug. Westminster	summ. 3 June for 23 July to Lincoln; prorogued 8 July to Westminster	Parl.	Prel., Magn., Kts, Burg., Dioc. Clergy	16 Dec.	P.W., II (II), 72–80 and app., 53; Parl. Writs, C. 219/2/9 Representatives of shires and boroughs dismissed 28 Aug. and resummoned for 30 Sept.
1313, 18 Mar. Westminster	8 Jan.	Parl.	Prel., Magn., Kts, Burg., Dioc. Clergy	9 May	P.W., II (II), 80–91 Adjourned 7 Apr. and reassembled 6 May
1313, 8 July Westminster	23 May	Parl.	Prel., Magn., Kts, Burg., Dioc. Clergy	27 July	P.W., II (II), 94–100
1313, 23 Sept. Westminster	26 July	Parl.	Prel., Magn., Kts, Burg., Dioc. Clergy	15 Nov.	P.W., II (II), 100–19
1314, 9 Sept. York	29 July	Parl.	Prel., Magn., Kts, Burg., Dioc. Clergy	27–28 Sept.	P.W., II (II); 126–35; Parl. Writs, C. 219/3/4
1315, 20 Jan. Westminster	24 Oct. 1314 / 14 Mar. 1315	Parl. / Parl.	Prel., Magn. Kts, Burg., Dioc. Clergy	9 Mar.	P.W., II (II), 136–51 Councillors reconvened for 13 Apr. to conclude unfinished business of parl. (Duchy of Lancaster Ancient Deeds, D.L. 10/217). Parl. was in session on 30 Apr. (Sayles, King's Bench, IV, 64)
1316, 27 Jan. Lincoln	16 Oct. 1315	Parl.	Prel., Magn., Kts, Burg., Dioc. Clergy	20 Feb.	P.W., II (II), 152–58; Parl. Writs, C. 219/3/5A
*27 Jan. Lincoln	16 Dec. 1315		Representatives from London, Shrewsbury and other towns		P.W., II (II), 154 Merchant assembly to discuss the wool staple

Date and place of assembly	Date of summons with note of initial prorogations	Designation of assembly in official records	Persons summoned	Terminating dates Writs 'de expensis'	Terminating dates Other evidence	Sources and remarks
*1316, Apr.–May Westminster	20 Feb.		Kts of twenty-three counties	29 May (1st group) 27 June (2nd group)		*P.W.*, II (II), 158–59, 161–62; Parl. Writs, C. 219/3/5B Knights summoned before the King's council for different dates to discuss perambulations of the forest
*1316, 29 July Lincoln	25 June		Kts	8 Aug.		*P.W.*, II (II), 166–67; Parl. Writs, C. 219/3/6 (writs and returns for 27 counties). Assembly of knights before the King's council. Two sheriff's returns refer to it as parliament
1317, 15 Apr. Westminster	14 Mar.		Selected Prel., Magn. and other councillors			*P.W.*, II (II), 170
1317, 18 July Nottingham	1 July		Selected Prel., Magn. and other councillors			*P.W.*, II (II), 171
1318, July Northampton			Prel., Magn., councillors			Assembled for negotiations with Thomas, earl of Lancaster (*Essays presented to R. L. Poole*, 360 ff.)
1318, 20 Oct.	24–25 Aug.	Parl.	Prel., Magn., Kts, Burg., Dioc. Clergy	9 Dec.		*P.W.*, II (II), 182–95; Parl. Writs, C. 219/3/8
*1319, 20 Jan. London	22 Nov. 1318		Representatives from towns			Merchant assembly to discuss the wool staple. *P.W.*, II (II), 196
*1319, 24 Apr. Westminster	8–9 Mar.		Representatives from towns			Merchant assembly before the King's council to discuss the wool staple *E.H.R.*, XXIX, 94–97; *Calendar of Letter Books of London, Letter Book E.*, 105

Date and place	Summons	Type	Composition	Met	References
1319, 6 May York	20 Mar.	Parl.	Prel., Magn., Kts, Burg., Dioc. Clergy	25 May	*P.W.*, II (II), 197–214
1320, 20 Jan. York	6 Nov. 1319	Parl.	Prel., Magn.		*P.W.*, II (II), 215–16
1320, 6 Oct. Westminster	5 Aug.	Parl.	Prel., Magn., Kts, Burg.	25–26 Oct.	*P.W.*, II (II), 219–30
1321, 15 July Westminster	15 May	Parl.	Prel., Magn., Kts, Burg., Dioc. Clergy	22 Aug.	*P.W.*, II (II), 234–43
1322, 2 May York	14 Mar.	Parl.	Prel., Magn., Kts, Burg., Dioc. Clergy	19 May	*P.W.*, II (II), 245–60
*1322, 13 June York	18 May		'Omnes maiores mercatores lanarum'		Assembly of wool merchants before the king's council to discuss the wool staple *E.H.R.*, XXXI, 596–606
1322, 14 Nov. York	summ. 18 Sept. to Ripon; changed to York 30 Oct.	Parl.	Prel., Magn., Kts, Burg.	29 Nov.	*P.W.*, II (II), 261–80
1323, 30 May Bishopsthorp (near York)		Cons.	Prel., Magn., Councillors, mayors of York and Newcastle		J. Conway-Davies, *Baronial Opposition to Edward II* (1918), 291–92, 584–85; *P.W.*, II (II), 284–85; *Foedera*, II (I), 521 (truce with Scotland)
1324, 23 Feb. Westminster	summ. 20 Nov. 1323 for 20 Jan. 1324; prorogued 26 Dec. 1323	Parl.	Prel., Magn., Kts, Burg., Dioc. Clergy	18 Mar.	*R.D.P.*, III, 342–44; *P.W.*, II (II), 289–315
1324, 27 May Westminster			Prel., Magn., judges		*P.W.*, II (II), 316
1324, 20 Oct. London	summ. 13 and 20 Sept. to Salisbury; changed to London 24 Sept.		Prel., Magn., Kts	10 Nov.	*P.W.*, II (II), 317–25
1325, 25 June Westminster	6 May	Parl.	Prel., Magn., representatives from Cinque Ports		*P.W.*, II (II), 328–33
1325, 18 Nov. Westminster	10 Oct.	Parl.	Prel., Magn., Kts, Burg., Dioc. Clergy	5 Dec.	*P.W.*, II (II), 334–47

Date and place of assembly	Date of summons with initial prorogations	Designation of assembly in writs of summons	Terminating dates Writs 'de expensis'[1]	Terminating dates Other evidence	Sources and remarks
1327, 7 Jan. Westminster	summ. 28 Oct. for 14 Dec. 1326; prorogued 3 Dec. 1326	Parl.	9 Mar. 1327		*P.W.*, II (II), 350–66; *C.C.R., 1327–30*, p. 107 Reassembled without a resummons 3 Feb. 1327 after the coronation of Edward III
1327, 15 Sept. Lincoln	7 Aug.	Parl. in the margin of enrolment	23 Sept.		*R.D.P.*, IV, 376–78; *C.C.R., 1327–30*, pp. 225–26
1328, 7 Feb. York	10 Dec. 1327	Parl.	5 Mar.		*R.D.P.*, IV, 378–80; *C.C.R., 1327–30*, p. 374
1328, 24 Apr. Northampton	5 Mar.	Parl.	14 May		*R.D.P.*, IV, 381–84; *C.C.R., 1327–30*, p. 388
1328, 31 July York	15 June	Parl.	6 Aug.		*R.D.P.*, IV, 384–86; *C.C.R., 1327–30*, p. 411
1328, 16 Oct. Salisbury	28 Aug.	Parl.	31 Oct.		*R.D.P.*, IV, 386–89; *C.C.R., 1327–30*, pp. 419–20
1329, 9 Feb. Westminster		Parl.	22 Feb.		Adjourned session of the previous parl. *R.D.P.*, IV, 389; *C.C.R., 1327–30*, pp. 527–28
†1329, 23 July Windsor	14 June				*R.D.P.*, IV, 390–91
1330, 11 Mar. Winchester	25 Jan.	Parl.	21 Mar.		*R.D.P.*, IV, 391–93; *C.C.R., 1330–33*, pp. 137–38
†1330, 9 July Osney	5 June				*R.D.P.*, IV, 394–95
†1330, 15 Oct. Nottingham	6 Sept.			? 20 Oct.	*R.D.P.*, IV, 395–97 Edward III seized Roger Mortimer on 19 Oct. and was at Leicester from 21 Oct.
1330, 26 Nov. Westminster	23 Oct.	Parl.	9 Dec.		*R.D.P.*, IV, 397–99; *C.C.R., 1330–33*, p. 177
1331, 30 Sept. Westminster	16 July	Parl.	9 Oct.		*R.D.P.*, IV, 403–5; *C.C.R., 1330–33*, pp. 412–13

[1] Wool merchants from 28 towns were summoned on 2 Dec. 1327 to appear before the king at York on 20 Jan. 1328 (*Official Return*, I, 80, note).

20 Nov. 1331	†1332, 20 Jan. Westminster				R.D.P., IV, 406-7
27 Jan.	1332, 16 Mar. Westminster	21 Mar.	Parl.		R.D.P., IV, 408-11; C.C.R., 1330-33, pp. 551-52
20 July	1332, 9 Sept. Westminster	12 Sept.	Parl.		R.D.P., IV, 411-13; C.C.R., 1330-33, p. 608
20 Oct.	1332, 4 Dec. York	26 Jan. 1333	Parl.	Dissolved 27 Jan. 1333	R.D.P., IV, 416-18. Because of absence of some Prel. and Magn. prorogued 11 Dec. to 20 Jan. 1333. R.P., II, 69; R.D.P., IV, 418-19; C.C.R., 1333-37, p. 95
2 Jan.	1334, 21 Feb. York	2 Mar.	Parl.		R.D.P., IV, 422-25; C.C.R., 1333-37, p. 304
24 July	1334, 19 Sept. Westminster	23 Sept.	Parl.		R.D.P., IV, 427-30; C.C.R., 1333-37, pp. 349-50
22 Feb.	†1335, 26 Mar. Nottingham		Cons. in the margin of enrolment		R.D.P., IV, 441
1 Apr.	1335, 26 May York	3 June	Parl.	Some secular Prel. and lay Magn. summ.	R.D.P., IV, 443-46; C.C.R., 1333-37, p. 500
7 Aug.	†1335, 25 Aug. London		Cons. in the margin of enrolment		R.D.P., IV, 452-53
22 Jan.	1336, 11 Mar. Westminster[1]	20 Mar.	Parl.	Some Prel. and lay Magn. summ.	R.D.P., IV, 454-56; C.C.R., 1333-37, p. 662
24 Aug.	1336, 23 Sept. Nottingham	27 Sept.	Cons. in the margin of enrolment		R.D.P., IV, 460-63; C.C.R., 1333-37, p. 707
1 Sept.	†23 Sept. Nottingham			37 nominated merchants from 23 towns and 4 wool merchants from London (R.D.P., IV, 464). Subsidy on exported wool granted by the merchants (C.C.R., 1337-39, p. 97)	

557

[1] 106 nominated merchants from 19 towns were summoned on 1 June 1336 to appear before the king's council at Northampton on 28 June (R.D.P., IV, 458-60).

Date and place of assembly	Date of summons with initial prorogations	Designation of assembly in writs of summons	Terminating dates		Sources and remarks
			Writs 'de expensis'	Other evidence	
[1] 1337, 3 Mar. Westminster	summ. 29 Nov. 1336 for 13 Jan. 1337 to York; prorogued 10 Dec. 1336 for 9 Feb. 1337 to York; prorogued 14 Jan. 1337 to Westminster	Parl.	20 Mar.	possibly ended 16 Mar.	*R.D.P.*, IV, 464–73; *C.C.R.*, *1337–39*, pp. 113–114; Tout, *Chapters*, III, 62, n. 1
†1337, 30 May Stamford	23 Apr.	Cons. in the margin of enrolment			*R.D.P.*, IV, 473–74 Some bishops and lay Magn. summ.
†[2] 1337, 21 July Westminster	21 June	Cons. in the margin of enrolment			*R.D.P.*, IV, 475–79 Prel. and Magn. summ.
[3] 1337, 26 Sept. Westminster	18 Aug.	Cons. in the margin of enrolment	4 Oct.		*R.D.P.*, IV, 479-82; *C.C.R.*, *1337–39*, p. 244 Referred to as Parl. in writs 'de expensis'
[4] 1338, 3 Feb. Westminster	20 Dec. 1337	Parl.	14 Feb.		*R.D.P.*, IV, 488–91; *C.C.R.*, *1337–39*, pp. 388–89

[1] Two assemblies of representatives from towns were summoned on 13 Dec. 1336 for 3 Jan. 1337: those from 43 towns towards the west from the mouth of the Thames were to assemble at London and the rest (from 25 towns north of the Thames) at Norwich (*R.D.P.*, IV, 469–70).

[2] 20 nominated merchants were summoned on 1 June 1337 to appear before the king's council at Stamford on 16 June (*R.D.P.*, IV, 474). Agreement concluded at this meeting for the foundation of a company with a monopoly of English wool trade [H. Wharton, ed., *Anglia Sacra*, I (1691), p. 30].

[3] 35 nominated merchants and 2 wool merchants from each of six southern counties were summoned on 24 June 1337 to appear before the king's council at Westminster on 9 July.

81 nominated merchants and representatives of additional towns were likewise summoned on 13 July for 25 July (*R.D.P.*, IV, 477–79).

A company with a monopoly of English wool trade formally created on 26 July (*C.C.R.*, *1337–39*, pp. 148–50).

[4] 120 notables were individually summoned to Westminster for 26 Sept. 1337 in addition to the elected representatives of shires (*R.D.P.*, iv, 482–84).

90 towns separately ordered on 2 Sept. to send 3 or 4 townsmen each (*R.D.P.*, iv, 486–87).

1338, 26 July Northampton[1]	15 June	'magnum consilium'	2 Aug.	tax grant 1 Aug.	R.D.P., IV, 492–95; C.C.R., 1337–39, p. 526; K.R. Memoranda R., E. 159/115, m. 18d.
†1338, 5 Nov. Westminster[2]	18 Oct.	Cons.			R.D.P., IV, 496–97
1339, 3 Feb. Westminster	summ. 15 Nov. 1338 for 14 Jan. 1339; prorogued 26 Dec. 1338	Parl.	17 Feb.		R.D.P., IV, 497–503; C.C.R., 1339–41, p. 97
1339, 13 Oct. Westminster	25 Aug.	Parl.	28 Oct.	? ended c. 3 Nov.	R.D.P., IV, 503–05; C.C.R., 1339–41, p. 275 Richard de Bury, bp of Durham, left this parliament on 3 Nov. (K.R. Exch. Acc. Various, E. 101/311/36)
1340, 20 Jan. Westminster[3]	16 Nov. 1339	Parl.	19 Feb.	tax grant 19 Feb.	R.D.P., IV, 507–09; C.C.R., 1339–41, pp. 446–47; R.P., II, 107
1340, 29 Mar. Westminster[4]	21 Feb.	Parl.	10 May		R.D.P., IV, 515–18; C.C.R., 1339–41, p. 468
1340, 12 July Westminster[5]	30 May	Parl.	26 July	tax grant 24 July	R.D.P., IV, 521–24; C.C.R., 1339–41, p. 493; R.P., II, 122
†1340, 2 Oct. Westminster	14 Sept.	Cons. in the margin of enrolment			R.D.P., IV, 528 Some Prel. and Magn. summ.

[1] 107 nominated merchants were summoned on 24 Feb. 1338 to appear before the king's council at London on 16 Mar. (R.D.P., IV, 491–92).

[2] An assembly of merchants was summoned on 16 July 1338 to Northampton for 3 Aug. (Official Return, I, 121, note (a) and H. of C. Interim Report, 109).

[3] 44 nominated merchants were summoned on 13 Dec. 1339 to appear before the king's council at Westminster on 20 Jan. 1340 (R.D.P., IV, 510–11).

[4] 154 nominated merchants were summoned on 20 Feb. 1340 to appear before the king's council at Westminster on 27 Mar. (R.D.P., IV, 512–15). The same merchants were again summoned on 15 Apr. to appear before the council on 26 May at London or Westminster (R.D.P., IV, 518–21).

[5] 109 merchants from certain named towns and 163 other persons were ordered on 27 July 1340 to be sent by the sheriffs to appear before the king's council at London or Westminster on 21 Aug. (R.D.P., IV, 524–25).

Date and place of assembly	Date of summons with initial prorogations	Designation of assembly in writs of summons	Terminating dates Writs 'de expensis'	Terminating dates Other evidence	Sources and remarks
[1] 1341, 23 Apr. Westminster	3 Mar.	Parl.	27–28 May		R.D.P., IV, 529–31; C.C.R., 1341–43, p. 144
†1341, 11 July London	12 June				R.D.P., IV, 532–33 Some bps and Magn. summ.
[2] †1342, 29 Apr. Westminster	summ. 25 Feb. for 8 Apr.; prorogued 15 Mar.	Cons. in the margin of enrolment			R.D.P., IV, 537–39 Some bps and 106 lay Magn. summ.
[3] 1342, 16 Oct. Westminster	12 Sept.	Cons.			R.D.P., IV, 542–43 Prel. of the province of Canterbury, some lay Magn. knights from the shires south of Trent summ.
†1342, 14 Dec. Westminster	20 Nov.	Cons. in the margin of enrolment			R.D.P., IV, 545 Some bps and Magn. summ.
1343, 28 Apr. Westminster	24 Feb.	Parl.	20 May		R.D.P., IV, 546–48; C.C.R., 1343–46, pp. 136–37
[4] †1344, 18 Apr. Westminster	7 Mar.	Cons. in the margin of enrolment			R.D.P., IV, 550–51 Bps and some other Prel. summ.
1344, 7 June Westminster	20 Apr.	Parl.	28 June	tax grant 26 June	R.D.P., IV, 551–53; C.C.R., 1343–46, p. 446; R.P., II, 148

1 16 nominated merchants and representatives from 15 coast towns were summoned on 15 Sept. 1340 to appear before the king's council at Westminster on 2 Oct. (R.D.P., IV, 527).
2 31 priors and other religious from the alien priories summoned on 15 June 1341 to appear before the king's council at London on 8 July (R.D.P., IV, 533).
3 142 merchants were individually summoned on 20 June 1342 to come to Westminster on 8 July 1342 to treat with the king's council (R.D.P., IV, 540–41).
4 138 merchants were individually summoned on 8 Apr. 1343 to appear before the king's council at Westminster on 25 Apr. 1343 (R.D.P., IV, 548–50).
40 merchants (mainly members of the English company collecting the royal customs since 24 June 1343) were summoned on 22 July 1343 to treat with the king's council at Westminster on 18 Aug., 1343 (R.D.P., IV, 550).

†1346, 3 Feb. Westminster	26 Nov. 1345	Cons. in the margin of enrolment		*R.D.P.*, IV, 556–57 Bps of the province of Canterbury to meet with Magn. Another meeting of northern Prel. with Magn. was due to be held at York on 20 Mar. (*R.D.P.*, IV, 557)
1346, 11 Sept. Westminster	30 July	Parl.	20 Sept.	*R.D.P.*, IV, 558–61; *C.C.R., 1346–49*, pp. 161–62.
†1347, 3 Mar.² Westminster	18 Feb.	Cons. in the margin of enrolment		*R.D.P.*, IV, 562–63 Prel. and Magn. summ.
1348, 14 Jan. Westminster	13 Nov. 1347	Parl.	12 Feb.	*R.D.P.*, IV, 572–75; *C.C.R., 1346–49*, p. 495
1348, 31 Mar. Westminster	14 Feb.	Parl.	13 Apr.	*R.D.P.*, IV, 575–77; *C.C.R., 1346–49*, pp. 511–12
1351, 9 Feb. Westminster	25 Nov. 1350	Parl.	1 Mar.	*R.D.P.*, IV, 587–90; *C.C.R., 1349–54*, p. 358
1352, 13 Jan. Westminster	15 Nov. 1351	Parl.	11 Feb.	*R.D.P.*, IV, 590–93; *C.C.R., 1349–54*, pp. 468–69
1352, 16 Aug. Westminster	20 July	Cons. in the margin of enrolment	25 Aug.	*R.D.P.*, IV, 593–95; *C.C.R., 1349–54*, p. 506

¹ 68 merchants were individually summoned to appear before the king's council at Westminster at various dates between 18 July and 11 Aug. 1345 (*R.D.P.*, IV, 555–56).
These meetings were connected with the reorganization of the English company farming the royal customs (*T.R.H.S.*, 1959, pp. 3, 10–11).
² An assembly of merchants was summoned to Westminster for 7 Mar. 1347 (*H. of C. Interim Report*, 110).
This assembly followed the grant to the king on 3 Mar. 1347 by 'the community of the realm' of 20,000 sacks of wool (*C.C.R., 1346–49*, pp. 290–91).
³ 79 merchants from 13 counties were individually summoned on 20 Mar. 1347 to appear before the king's council at Westminster on 27 Apr. 1347 at the latest. The sheriff of each of these counties was ordered to send 4 or 6 other merchants as well (*R.D.P.*, IV, 562–65).
70 merchants from 18 counties were individually summoned on 28 May 1347 to appear before the king's council at Westminster on 20 June 1347 for a 'colloquium personale' (*R.D.P.*, IV, 565–67).
186 persons (mainly merchants) of 18 counties were summoned individually on 30 June 1347 to appear before the council at London at various dates between 8 July and 2 Aug. 1347 (*R.D.P.*, IV, 567–71).
21 persons (11 from Sussex) were summoned individually on 15 Sept. 1347 to appear before the council at London on 6 Oct. 1347 (*R.D.P.*, IV, 572).
⁴ 76 merchants were summoned on 26 Mar. 1349 to appear before the king's council at Westminster on 20 Apr. 1349 for a 'colloquium personale' (*R.D.P.*, IV, 586).
This assembly connected with the impending liquidation of the company farming the royal customs (*T.R.H.S.*, 1959, pp. 15–16).

Date and place of assembly	Date of summons with initial prorogations	Designation of assembly in writs of summons	Terminating dates		Sources and remarks
			Writs 'de expensis'	Other evidence	
1					
1353, 23 Sept. Westminster	15 July	Cons. in the margin of enrolment	12 Oct.		Bps and 2 other Prel., lay Magn., 1 Kt from each shire, Burg. from London, Cinque Ports and 10 other towns summ. *R.D.P.*, IV, 598–601; *C.C.R., 1349–54*, p. 620
1354, 28 Apr. Westminster	15 Mar.	Parl.	20 May		Prel., Magn., 1 Kt from each shire, Burg. from London, Cinque Ports and 37 other towns summ. *R.D.P.*, IV, 601–03; *C.C.R., 1354–60*, p. 72
1355, 23 Nov. Westminster	summ. 20 Sept. for 12 Nov.; prorogued 22 Oct.	Parl.	30 Nov.		*R.D.P.*, IV, 603–8; *C.C.R., 1354–60*, pp. 241–42
2					
1357, 17 Apr. Westminster	15 Feb.	Parl.	8 May (Burg.) 16 May (Kts)		*R.D.P.*, IV, 611–13; *C.C.R., 1354–60*, p. 401
1358, 5 Feb. Westminster	15 Dec. 1357	Parl.	27 Feb.		*R.D.P.*, IV, 614–16; *C.C.R., 1354–60*, pp. 501–2
†1358, 22 July Westminster	20 June	Cons. in the margin of enrolment			*R.D.P.*, IV, 616–18 Prel. and 108 other named persons (Magn. and other notable persons from the shires) summ.
†1359, 10 Nov. Westminster	10 Oct.	Cons.			*R.D.P.*, IV, 618–19 Some Prel. and Magn. summ.
1360, 9 Mar. Westminster	10 Feb.	Cons. in the margin of enrolment			*R.D.P.*, IV, 619–20 Kts and Burg. of 15 counties and London summ. to meet with Magn. at Westminster. Kts and Burg. of other counties summ. to 'tractatus' on 18

[1] 71 English merchants from 23 towns (mainly ports) and 12 foreign merchants were individually summoned on 10 June 1353 to appear before the king's council at Westminster on 1 July 1353 (*R.D.P.*, IV, 596–98).

[2] 170 merchants (including many Londoners) were individually summoned on 8 June 1356 to appear before the king's council at Westminster on 26 June 1356 (*R.D.P.*, IV, 609–10).

Date, place	Summons / prorogation	Type	Assembly	Note	Reference
1360, 15 May Westminster	3 Apr.	Parl.			Mar. to be held for different regions at Taunton, Worcester, Leicester and Lincoln (R.D.P., IV, 620–21)
1361, 24 Jan. Westminster	20 Nov. 1360	Parl.	18 Feb.		R.D.P., IV, 624–27; C.C.R., 1360–64, pp. 251–53
1362, 13 Oct. Westminster	14 Aug.	Parl.	17 Nov.		R.D.P., IV, 631–33; C.C.R., 1360–64, pp. 439–41
1363, 6 Oct. Westminster	1 June	Parl.	30 Oct.		R.D.P., IV, 634–36; C.C.R., 1360–64, pp. 556–58
1365, 20 Jan. Westminster	4 Dec. 1364	Parl.	27 Feb.	dissolved 17 Feb.	R.D.P., IV, 636–38; R.P., II, 288; C.C.R., 1364–68, pp. 168–69
1366, 4 May Westminster	20 Jan.	Parl.	12 May	dissolved 11 May	R.D.P., IV, 639–41; R.P., II, 290–91; C.C.R., 1364–68, pp. 272–74
1368, 1 May Westminster	24 Feb.	Parl.	21 May	dissolved 21 May	R.D.P., IV, 641–44; R.P., II, 295; C.C.R., 1364–68, pp. 479–81
1369, 3 June Westminster	6 Apr.	Parl.	11 June	Common petitions answered on 11 June	R.D.P., IV, 644–46; C.C.R., 1369–74, pp. 100–1; R.P., II, pp. 300–2
1371, 24 Feb. Westminster	8 Jan.	Parl.	29 Mar.	tax grant 28 Mar.	R.D.P., IV, 646–49; R.P., II, 300; C.C.R., 1369–74, pp. 288–90
1371, 8 June Winchester		Cons.	17 June		R.D.P., IV, 650–53; C.C.R., 1369–74, p. 316. Some Prel. and Magn.; one knight from each shire and one burgess from each borough out of those returned to the previous parliament
1372, 3 Nov. Westminster	summ. 1 Sept. for 13 Oct.; prorogued 6 Oct.	Parl.	24 Nov.	tax grant 23 Nov.	R.D.P., IV, 653–59; R.P., II, 310; C.C.R., 1369–74, pp. 475–77 After the grant of the subsidy the burgesses were told to remain
1373, 21 Nov. Westminster	4 Oct.	Parl.	10 Dec.		R.D.P., IV, 659–62; C.C.R., 1369–74, pp. 611–13

¹ Magnates and others holding land in Ireland were individually summoned on 15 Mar. 1361 to appear before the king's council at Westminster on 11 Apr. 1361 and others, including clergy holding land or benefices in Ireland, were summoned to appear on 18 Apr. (R.D.P., IV, 627–29). Many of the same persons were also summoned on 10 Feb. 1362 to appear likewise on 18 Mar. 1362 (R.D.P., IV, 629–31).

Date and place of assembly	Date of summons with initial prorogations	Designation of assembly in writs of summons	Terminating dates		Sources and remarks
			Writs 'de expensis'	Other evidence	
1376, 28 Apr. Westminster	summ. 28 Dec. 1375 for 12 Feb. 1376; prorogued 20 Jan.	Parl.	10 July	probably dissolved 10 July	R.D.P., IV, 662–67; C.C.R., 1374–77, pp. 428–30; R.P. II, 360; Tout, Chapters, III, p. 304, n. 5
1377, 27 Jan. Westminster	1 Dec. 1376	Parl.	2 Mar.		R.D.P., IV, 669–71; C.C.R., 1374–77, pp. 535–37

Date and place of assembly	Date of summons with initial prorogations	Sessional prorogations	Terminating dates		Sources and remarks
			Writs 'de expensis'	Other evidence	
1377, 13 Oct. Westminster	4 Aug.		5 Dec.	? dissolved 28 Nov.	R.D.P., IV, 673–75; R.P., III, 29; C.C.R., 1377–81, pp. 105–7 Anonimalle Chronicle, 116, says that this parliament sat until 6 Dec.
1378, 20 Oct. Gloucester	3 Sept.		16 Nov.		R.D.P., IV, 676–78; C.C.R., 1377–81, pp. 220–22
1379, 24 Apr. Westminster	16 Feb.		27 May	tax grant 27 May	R.D.P. IV, 679–81; R.P., III, 58; C.C.R., 1377–81, pp. 252–54
1380, 16 Jan. Westminster	20 Oct. 1379		3 Mar.		R.D.P., IV, 682–84; C.C.R., 1377–81, pp. 355–57
1380, 5 Nov. Northampton	26 Aug.		6 Dec.	tax grant 6 Dec.	R.D.P., IV, 686–88; R.P., III, 90; C.C.R., 1377–81, pp. 496–98
1381, 3 Nov. Westminster	summ. 16 July for 16 Sept.; prorogued 22 Aug.	prorogued from 13 Dec. 1381 to 24 Jan. 1382	25 Feb.	tax grant 25 Feb.	R.D.P., IV, 688–94; R.P., III, 113, 114; C.C.R., 1381–85, pp. 106–8
1382, 7 May Westminster	24 Mar.		22 May		R.D.P., IV, 694–97; C.C.R., 1381–85, pp. 133–34
1382, 6 Oct. Westminster	9 Aug.		24 Oct.		R.D.P., IV, 698–700; C.C.R., 1381–85, pp. 227–28

Date & place of assembly	Date of writs	Date dissolved	Notes	References
1383, 23 Feb. Westminster	7 Jan.	10 Mar.		*R.D.P.*, IV, 700–3; *C.C.R.*, *1381–85*, pp. 290–91
1383, 26 Oct. Westminster	20 Aug.	26 Nov.		*R.D.P.*, IV, 703–6; *C.C.R.*, *1381–85*, pp. 414–16
1384, 29 Apr. Salisbury	3 Mar.	27 May		*R.D.P.*, IV, 707–10; *C.C.R.*, *1381–85*, pp. 452–54
1384, 12 Nov. Westminster	28 Sept.	14 Dec.		*R.D.P.*, IV, 711–13; *C.C.R.*, *1381–85*, pp. 599–600
1385, 20 Oct. Westminster	3 Sept.	6 Dec.		*R.D.P.*, IV, 717–20; *C.C.R.*, *1385–89*, 118–20
1386, 1 Oct. Westminster	8 Aug.	28 Nov.	dissolved 28 Nov.	*R.D.P.*, IV, 721–24; *R.P.*, III, 224; *C.C.R.*, *1385–89*, pp. 298–300
1388, 3 Feb. Westminster	17 Dec. 1387	4 June	prorogued from 20 Mar. to 13 Apr.; tax grant 2 June; dissolved 4 June	*R.D.P.*, IV, 724–26; amended writs to sheriffs regarding the election of knights of the shire issued 1 Jan. 1388 (*ibid*, 726–27). *R.P.*, III, 245; prelates and magnates were individually resummoned by writs dated 20 Mar., *R.D.P.*, IV, 727–29. *R.P.*, III, 245, 252; *C.C.R.*, *1385–89*, pp. 494–96
1388, 9 Sept. Cambridge	28 July	17 Oct.		*R.D.P.*, IV, 728–32; *C.C.R.*, *1385–89*, pp. 656–58
1390, 17 Jan. Westminster	6 Dec. 1389	2 Mar.	tax grant 2 Mar.; session ended 2 Mar.	*R.D.P.*, IV, 732–35; *R.P.*, III, 262, 273; *C.C.R.*, *1389–92*, pp. 177–80
1390, 12 Nov. Westminster	12 Sept.	3 Dec.	tax grant and dissolved 3 Dec.	*R.D.P.*, IV, 735–38; *R.P.*, III, 279–83; *C.C.R.*, *1389–92*, pp. 305–7
1391, 3 Nov. Westminster	7 Sept.	2 Dec.	dissolved 2 Dec.	*R.D.P.*, IV, 738–41; *R.P.*, III, 296; *C.C.R.*, *1389–92*, pp. 511–13
1393, 20 Jan. Winchester	23 Nov. 1392	10 Feb.	dissolved 10 Feb.	*R.D.P.*, IV, 746–48; *R.P.*, III, 308; *C.C.R.*, *1392–96*, pp. 114–16

Date and place of assembly	Date of summons with initial prorogations	Sessional prorogations	Terminating dates Writs 'de expensis'	Terminating dates Other evidence	Sources and remarks
1394, 27 Jan. Westminster	13 Nov. 1393		6 Mar.	dissolved 6 Mar.	R.D.P., IV, 749-52; R.P., III, 323; C.C.R., 1392-96, pp. 277-79
1395, 27 Jan. Westminster	20 Nov. 1394		15 Feb.		R.D.P., IV, 752-55; C.C.R., 1392-96, pp. 417-19
1397, 22 Jan. Westminster	30 Nov. 1396		12 Feb.		R.D.P., IV, 755-58; C.C.R., 1396-99, pp. 134-35
1397, 17 Sept. Westminster	18 July	prorogued from 29 Sept. to meet on 27 Jan. 1398 at Shrewsbury	31 Jan.	tax grant and dissolved 31 Jan.	R.D.P., IV, 758-61; R.P., III, 355, 369; C.C.R., 1396-99, pp. 302-4
1399, 30 Sept. Westminster	19 Aug. (writs dated at Chester)			30 Sept.	R.D.P., IV, 765-67 The writs of summons were regarded as invalidated by the abdication of Richard II on 29 Sept. and the assembly ended on the day of meeting
1399, 6 Oct. Westminster	30 Sept.		19 Nov.		R.D.P., IV, 768-70; C.C.R., 1399-1402, pp. 107-9
1401, 20 Jan. Westminster	summ. 9 Sept. 1400 for 27 Oct. 1400 to York; prorogued 3 Oct. to Westminster		10 Mar.	dissolved 10 Mar.	R.D.P., IV, 770-75; R.P., III, 465-66; C.C.R., 1399-1402, pp. 329-31
1402, 30 Sept. Westminster	summ. 19 June for 15 Sept.; prorogued 14 Aug.		25 Nov.	tax grant and dissolved 25 Nov.	R.D.P., IV, 778-83; R.P., III, 493; C.C.R., 1402-5, pp. 124-27
1404, 14 Jan. Westminster	summ. 20 Oct. 1403 for 3 Dec. 1403 to Coventry; prorogued 24 Nov. to Westminster		20 Mar.		R.D.P., IV, 785-90; C.C.R., 1402-5, pp. 366-68
1404, 6 Oct. Coventry	25 Aug.		13 Nov.	tax grant 12 Nov.	R.D.P., IV, 790-92; R.P., III, 546; C.C.R., 1402-5, pp. 519-21
1406, 1 Mar. Westminster	summ. 21 Dec. 1405 for 15 Feb. to Coventry; 1 Jan. prorogued to Gloucester; 9 Feb. prorogued to Westminster	prorogued 3 Apr. to 25 Apr.; prorogued 19 June to 13 Oct.	22 Dec.	tax grant and dissolved 22 Dec.	R.D.P., IV, 793-99; R.P., III, 568, 580, 603; C.C.R., 1405-9, 281-83

Date and place of assembly	Date of summons with initial prorogations	Sessional prorogations	Date of financial grant	Date of dissolution	Sources and remarks
1407, 20 Oct. Gloucester	26 Aug.		2 Dec.	tax grant and dissolved 2 Dec.	*R.D.P.*, IV, 801–3; *R.P.*, III, 611–12; *C.C.R., 1405–9*, pp. 397–99
1410, 27 Jan. Westminster	summ. 26 Oct. 1409 to Bristol; resummoned 18 Dec. 1409 to Westminster	prorogued from 15 Mar. to 6 Apr.		tax grant 8 May dissolved 9 May	*R.D.P.*, IV, 804–9; *R.P.*, III, 623, 634–35
1411, 3 Nov. Westminster	21 Sept.			dissolved 19 Dec.	*R.D.P.*, IV, 809–12; *R.P.*, III, 658
1413, 3 Feb. Westminster	1 Dec. 1412				*R.P.*, IV, 813–15 This parliament was dissolved by the death of Henry IV on 20 Mar. 1413 and its proceedings were nullified
1413, 14 May Westminster	22 Mar.		9 June	tax grant 9 June	*R.D.P.*, IV, 816–18; *R.P.*, IV, 6; *C.C.R., 1413–19*, pp. 102–4
1414, 30 Apr. Leicester	summ. 1 Dec. 1413 for 29 Jan. 1414; prorogued on 24 Dec.		29 May	tax grant 28 May; dissolved probably 29 May	*R.D.P.*, IV, 818–23; *R.P.*, IV, 16–17; *C.C.R., 1413–19*, pp. 183–85

Date and place of assembly	Date of summons with initial prorogations	Sessional prorogations	Terminating dates		Sources and remarks
			Date of financial grant	Date of dissolution	
1414, 19 Nov. Westminster	26 Sept.				*R.D.P.*, IV, 823–26
1415, 4 Nov. Westminster	summ. 12 Aug. for 21 Oct.; prorogued 29 Sept.		12 Nov.		*R.D.P.*, IV, 827–32; *R.P.*, IV, 71
1416, 16 Mar. Westminster	21 Jan.	prorogued from 8 Apr. to 4 May			*R.D.P.*, IV, 832–35; *R.P.*, IV, 71
1416, 19 Oct. Westminster	3 Sept.			18 Nov.	*R.D.P.*, IV, 835–38; *R.P.*, IV, 96
1417, 16 Nov. Westminster	5 Oct.		17 Dec.		*R.D.P.*, IV, 838–41; *R.P.*, IV, 107
1419, 16 Oct. Westminster	24 Aug.		13 Nov.		*R.D.P.*, IV, 842–44; *R.P.*, IV, 117

Date and place of assembly	Date of summons with initial prorogations	Sessional prorogations	Terminating dates		Sources and remarks
			Date of financial grant	Date of dissolution	
1420, 2 Dec. Westminster	21 Oct.				R.D.P., IV, 845–48
1421, 2 May Westminster	26 Feb.				R.D.P., IV, 848–51
1421, 1 Dec. Westminster	20 Oct.				R.D.P., IV, 851–54
1422, 9 Nov. Westminster	29 Sept.			18 Dec.	R.D.P., IV, 855–57; R.P., IV, 173
1423, 20 Oct. Westminster	1 Sept.	prorogued from 17 Dec. 1423 to 17 Jan. 1424		28 Feb. 1424	R.D.P., IV, 857–59; R.P., IV, 200
1425, 30 Apr. Westminster	24 Feb.	prorogued from 25 to 31 May		14 July	R.D.P., IV, 860–63; R.P., IV, 275
1426, 18 Feb. Leicester	7 Jan.	prorogued from 20 Mar. to 29 Apr.		1 June	R.D.P., IV, 863–66; R.P., IV, 301–2
1427, 13 Oct. Westminster	15 July	prorogued from 8 Dec. 1427 to 27 Jan. 1428		25 Mar. 1428	R.D.P., IV, 866–68; R.P., IV, 317–18
1429, 22 Sept. Westminster	summ. 12 July for 13 Oct.; date advanced by writs of 3 Aug.	prorogued from 20 Dec. 1429 to 16 Jan. 1430		23 Feb. 1430	R.D.P., IV, 869–75; R.P., IV, 338, 341
1431, 12 Jan. Westminster	27 Nov. 1430		20 Mar. 1431		R.D.P., IV, 875–79; R.P., IV, 368
1432, 12 May Westminster	25 Feb.			17 July	R.D.P., IV, 879–83; R.P., IV, 389
1433, 8 July Westminster	24 May	prorogued from 13 Aug. to 13 Oct.			R.D.P., IV, 883–86; R.P., IV, 420. This parliament was still in session on 18 Dec. (R.P., IV, 423)
1435, 10 Oct. Westminster	5 July		23 Dec.		R.D.P., IV, 888–91; R.P., IV, 486
1437, 21 Jan. Westminster	summ. 29 Oct. 1436 to Cambridge; re-summoned 10 Dec. 1436 to Westminster			27 Mar.	R.D.P., IV, 891–97; R.P., IV, 503

Summoned	Notes	Prorogations/adjournments	Met	References
1439, 12 Nov. Westminster	originally summ. to Oxford; changed to Westminster in writs of 26 Sept.	prorogued from 21 Dec. 1439 to 14 Jan. 1440 to reassemble at Reading	15–24 Feb. 1440	R.D.P., IV, 898–902; R.P., V, 4; Wedgwood, CXLVII and 1
1442, 25 Jan. Westminster	3 Dec. 1441		27 Mar.	R.D.P., IV, 902–06; R.P., V, 37; Wedgwood, CXLVII and 20
1445, 25 Feb. Westminster	13 Jan.	prorogued from 15 Mar. to 29 Apr.; from 5 June to 20 Oct.; from 15 Dec. 1445 to 24 Jan. 1446	9 Apr. 1446	R.D.P., IV, 907–11; R.P., V, 67, 69; Wedgwood, CXLVII and 44
1447, 10 Feb. Bury St Edmunds	summ. 14 Dec. 1446 to Cambridge; re-summoned 20 Jan. 1447 to Bury St Edmunds		3 Mar.	R.D.P., IV, 911–17; R.P., V, 135; Wedgwood, CXLVII and 65
1449, 12 Feb. Westminster	2 Jan.	prorogued from 4 Apr. to 7 May; from 30 May to 16 June to meet at Winchester	16 July	R.D.P., IV, 918–22; R.P., V, 143; Wedgwood, CXLVII and 88
1449, 6 Nov. Westminster	23 Sept.	adjourned to the Dominican Friary by Ludgate in London on 6 Nov. and adjourned back to Westminster on 4 Dec.; prorogued from 17 Dec. 1449 to 22 Jan. 1450; prorogued from 30 Mar. to 29 Apr. 1450 to reassemble at Leicester	5–8 June 1450	R.D.P., IV, 922–26; R.P., V, 172; Wedgwood, CXLVII and 115
1450, 6 Nov. Westminster	5 Sept.	prorogued from 18 Dec. 1450 to 20 Jan. 1451; prorogued from 29 Mar. to 5 May 1451	24–31 May 1451	R.D.P., IV, 927–31; R.P., V, 213–14; Wedgwood, CXLVII and 145

Date and place of assembly	Date of summons with initial prorogations	Sessional prorogations	Terminating dates		Sources and remarks
			Date of financial grant	Date of dissolution	
1453, 6 Mar. Reading	20 Jan.	prorogued from 28 Mar. to 25 Apr. to reassemble at Westminster; from 2 July to 12 Nov. to reassemble at Reading; from 12 Nov. 1453 to 14 Feb. 1454 to reassemble at Westminster			*R.D.P.*, IV, 931–35; *R.P.*, V, 231, 236, 238, 245; Wedgwood, CXLVII and 174 This parliament was still in session on 16 Apr. 1454 and was probably dissolved shortly before Easter (21 Apr. 1454)
1455, 9 July Westminster	26 May	prorogued 31 July to 12 Nov.; from 13 Dec. 1455 to 14 Jan. 1456		12 Mar. 1456	*R.D.P.*, IV, 935–39; *R.P.*, V, 283, 321; Wedgwood, CXLVII and 211
1459, 20 Nov. Coventry	9 Oct.			20 Dec.	*R.D.P.*, IV, 940–44; Wedgwood, CXLVII and 243
1460, 7 Oct. Westminster	30 July	prorogued probably from 1 Dec. 1460 to 28 Jan. 1461			*R.D.P.*, IV, 945–49; Wedgwood, CXLVII and 266. This parliament was still sitting on 3 Feb. 1461 and continued to sit perhaps until the beginning of the reign of Edward IV on 4 Mar. 1461
1461, 4 Nov. Westminster	summ. 23 May for 6 July; prorogued 13 June	prorogued from 21 Dec. 1461 to 6 May 1462		6 May 1462	*R.D.P.*, IV, 950–56; *R.P.*, V, 487; Wedgwood, CXLVII and 289
1463, 29 Apr. Westminster	summ. 22 Dec. 1462 for 5 Feb. 1463 to York, then to Leicester for 7 Mar.; prorogued 28 Feb. to Westminster	prorogued from 17 June to 4 Nov., from 4 Nov. 1463 to 20 Feb. 1464 to reassemble at York; from 20 Feb. 1464 to 5 May; from 5 May 1464 to 26 Nov.; from		28 Mar. 1465	*R.D.P.*, IV, 956–65; *R.P.*, V, 498–99, 500; Wedgwood, CXLVII and 313

Parliament summoned			Prorogations / sittings	Dissolved	References
1467, 3 June Westminster	28 Feb.		26 Nov. 1464 to 21 Jan. 1465 to reassemble at Westminster; prorogued 1 July to 6 Nov. to reassemble at Reading; from 6 Nov. 1467 to 5 May 1468; from 5 May to 12 May to reassemble at Westminster	7 June 1468	*R.D.P.*, IV, 965–69; *R.P.*, V, 618–19; Wedgwood, CXLIX and 334
1470, 26 Nov. Westminster	15 Oct.				*R.D.P.*, IV, 976–79; Wedgwood, CXLIX and 374. This parliament of the Readeption of Henry VI was probably prorogued for Christmas and may have sat until the restoration of Edward IV in Apr. 1471
1472, 6 Oct. Westminster	19 Aug.		prorogued from 30 Nov. 1472 to 8 Feb. 1473; from 8 Apr. 1473 to 6 Oct.; from 13 Dec. 1473 to 20 Jan. 1474; from 1 Feb. 1474 to 9 May; from 28 May 1474 to 6 June; from 18 July 1474 to 23 Jan. 1475	14 Mar. 1475	*R.D.P.*, IV, 980–84; *R.P.*, VI, 9, 41–42, 98–99, 104, 120; Wedgwood, CXLIX and 393
1478, 16 Jan. Westminster	26 Feb.	20 Nov. 1477			4 Wedgwood, CXLIX and 423
1483, 20 Jan. Westminster	18 Feb.	15 Nov. 1482			*R.D.P.*, IV, 984–88; Wedgwood, CXLIX and 447
1484, 23 Jan. Westminster	20 Feb.	9 Dec. 1483			Wedgwood, CXLIX and 475

Date and place of assembly	Date of summons with initial prorogations	Sessional prorogations	Terminating dates		Sources and remarks
			Date of financial grant	Date of dissolution	
1485, 7 Nov. Westminster	15 Sept.	prorogued from 10 Dec. 1485 to 23 Jan. 1486		c. 4 Mar. 1486	Wedgwood, CXLIX and 494
1487, 9 Nov. Westminster				c. 18 Dec.	Wedgwood, CXLIX and 511
1489, 13 Jan. Westminster		prorogued from 23 Feb. to 14 Oct.; from 4 Dec. 1489 to 25 Jan. 1490		27 Feb. 1490	R.P., VI, 424, 426; Wedgwood, CXLIX and 527
1491, 17 Oct. Westminster	12 Aug.	prorogued from 4 Nov. 1491 to 26 Jan. 1492		5 Mar. 1492	R.P.; VI, 444; Wedgwood, CXLIX and 542
1495, 14 Oct. Westminster	15 Sept.			21–22 Dec.	Wedgwood, CXLIX and 564
1497, 16 Jan. Westminster	20 Nov. 1496			13 Mar.	Wedgwood, CXLIX and 583
1504, 25 Jan. Westminster				c. 1 Apr.	Wedgwood, CXLIX and 597

Date of assembly	Date of summons with initial prorogations	Dates of sessions of Commons	Date of dismissal of Commons	Remarks
				Henceforth all Parliaments met at Westminster except where otherwise stated
1510, 21 Jan.	17 Oct. 1509	21 Jan. to 23 Feb.	23 Feb. 1510	
1512, 4 Feb.	28 Nov. 1511	1st, 4 Feb. to 30 Mar. 1512; 2nd, 4 Nov. to 20 Dec. 1512; 3rd, 23 Jan. to 4 Mar. 1514	4 Mar. 1514	
1515, 5 Feb.	23 Nov. 1514	1st, 5 Feb. to 5 Apr.; 2nd, 12 Nov. to 22 Dec.	22 Dec. 1515	

1523, 15 Apr.		1st, 15 Apr. to 21 May 2nd, 10 June to 29 July 3rd, 31 July to 13 Aug.	13 Aug. 1523	summ. to Blackfriars, London
1529, 3 Nov.	summ. 9 Aug. to Blackfriars (London); prorogued to Westminster for 4 Nov.	1st, 4 Nov. to 17 Dec. 1529 2nd, 16 Jan. to 31 Mar. 1531 3rd, 15 Jan. to 28 Mar. 1532 4th, 10 Apr. to 14 May 1532 5th, 4 Feb. to 7 Apr. 1533 6th, 15 Jan. to 30 Mar. 1534 7th, 3 Nov. to 18 Dec. 1534 8th, 4 Feb. to 14 Apr. 1536	14 Apr. 1536	
1536, 8 June	27 Apr.	8 June to 18 July 1536	18 July 1536	
1539, 28 Apr.	1 Mar.	1st, 28 Apr. to 23 May 1539 2nd, 30 May to 28 June 3rd, 12 Apr. to 11 May, 25 May to 24 July 1540	24 July 1540	
1542, 16 Jan.	23 Nov. 1541	1st, 16 Jan. to 1 Apr. 1542 2nd, 22 Jan. to 12 May 1543 3rd, 14 Jan. to 28 Mar. 1544	28 Mar. 1544	
1545, 23 Nov.	summ. 1 Dec. 1544 for 30 Jan. 1545; prorogued 20 Dec. 1544 to 15 Oct. 1545 (both to Westminster); prorogued 21 Sept. 1545 to Windsor	1st, 23 Nov. to 24 Dec. 1545 2nd, 14 to 31 Jan. 1547, at Westminster	31 Jan. 1547	Dissolved by the King's death
1547, 4 Nov.	2 Aug.	4 Nov. to 24 Dec. 1547 24 Nov. 1548 to 14 Mar. 1549 4 Nov. 1549 to 1 Feb. 1550 23 Jan. to 15 Apr. 1552	15 Apr. 1552	
1553, 1 Mar. 1553, 5 Oct.	5 Jan. 14 Aug.	1 Mar. to 31 Mar. 1553 5 Oct. to 21 Oct. 1553	31 Mar. 1553 5 Dec. 1553	
1554, 2 Apr.	summ. 17 Feb. to Oxford; prorogued 15 Mar. to Westminster	2 Apr. to 5 May 1554	5 May 1554	
1554, 12 Nov. 1555, 21 Oct. 1558, 20 Jan.	3 Oct. 3 Sept. 6 Dec. 1557	12 Nov. 1554 to 16 Jan. 1555 21 Oct. to 9 Dec. 1555 20 Jan. to 7 Mar. 1558 5 Nov. to 17 Nov. 1558	16 Jan. 1555 9 Dec. 1555 17 Nov. 1558	Automatically ended with the queen's death
1559, 23 Jan.	5 Dec. 1558	23 Jan. to 8 May 1559	8 May 1559	

Date of assembly	Date of summons with initial prorogations	Dates of sessions of Commons	Date of dismissal of Commons	Remarks
1563, 11 Jan.	10 Nov. 1562	11 Jan. to 10 Apr. 1563 30 Sept. 1566 to 2 Jan. 1567	2 Jan. 1567	
1571, 2 Apr. 1572, 8 May	28 Mar.	2 Apr. to 29 May 1571 8 May to 30 June 1572 8 Feb. to 15 Mar. 1576 16 Jan. to 18 Mar. 1581	29 May 1571 19 Apr. 1583	
1584, 23 Nov.	12 Oct.	23 Nov. to 21 Dec. 1584 4 Feb. to 29 Mar. 1585	14 Sept. 1585	
1586, 15 Oct.	15 Sept.	29 Oct. to 2 Dec. 1586 15 Feb. to 23 Mar. 1587	23 Mar. 1587	
1589, 4 Feb.	summ. 18 Sept. 1588 for 12 Nov. 1588; prorogued 14 Oct. 1588	4 Feb. to 29 Mar. 1589	29 Mar. 1589	
1593, 19 Feb. 1597, 24 Oct.	4 Jan. 23 Aug.	19 Feb. to 10 Apr. 1593 24 Oct. to 20 Dec. 1597 11 Jan. to 9 Feb. 1598	10 Apr. 1593 9 Feb. 1598	
1601, 27 Oct. 1604, 19 Mar.	11 Sept. 31 Jan.	27 Oct. to 19 Dec. 1601 19 Mar. to 7 July 1604 5 Nov. 1605 to 27 May 1606 18 Nov. 1606 to 4 July 1607 9 Feb. to 23 July 1610 16 Oct. to 6 Dec. 1610	19 Dec. 1601 9 Feb. 1611	
1614, 5 Apr. 1621, 16 Jan.	13 Nov. 1620	5 Apr. to 7 June 1614 30 Jan. to 4 June 1621 20 Nov. to 18 Dec. 1621	7 June 1614 8 Feb. 1622	
1624, 12 Feb.	20 Dec. 1623	12 Feb. to 29 May 1624	27 Mar. 1625	Automatically ended with the king's death
1625, 17 May	2 Apr.	18 June to 11 July 1625 1 Aug. to 12 Aug. 1625	12 Aug. 1625	Adjourned to Oxford on 1 Aug.
1626, 6 Feb. 1628, 17 Mar.	20 Dec. 1625 31 Jan.	6 Feb. to 15 June 1626 17 Mar. to 26 June 1628 20 Jan. to 10 Mar. 1629	15 June, 1626 10 Mar. 1629	
1640, 13 Apr.	20 Feb.	13 Apr. to 5 May	5 May 1640	The Short Parliament

1640, 3 Nov.	24 Sept.	3 Nov. 1640 to 20 Apr. 1653	20 Apr. 1653	The Long Parliament. In one long session of 12½ years. On 6 Dec. 1648, 143 members were excluded and secluded by the army 'with sundry others driven away.' May also be held to have been dissolved by its own Act on 16 Mar. 1660
1644, 22 Jan.	22 Dec. 1643	22 Jan. to 16 Apr. 1644. Adjourned to 8 Oct. 1644		King's anti-Parliament at Oxford. Consisted of those members of the Long Parliament who adhered to the king, summ. on 22 Dec. 1643 (at least 174 members of the Commons known)
1653, 4 July		4 July to 12 Dec.	12 Dec. 1653	Little Parliament. Nominated 20 June 1653 by Cromwell and the Council of Officers; summ. to meet 4 July by letters under the hand of the Lord General; declared itself a Parliament on 6 July; resigned its powers into the hands of the Lord General 12 Dec. 1653
1654, 3 Sept.	1 June	3 Sept. 1654 to 22 Jan. 1655	22 Jan. 1655	Included representatives from Scotland and Ireland as did the next two assemblies
1656, 17 Sept.	10 July	17 Sept. 1656 to 26 June 1657 20 Jan. to 4 Feb. 1658	4 Feb. 1658	
1659, 27 Jan.	9 Dec. 1658	27 Jan. to 22 Apr. 1659	22 Apr. 1659	From 22 Apr. 1659 Richard Cromwell was no longer considered Protector and the Republican Government was restored

Date of assembly	Date of summons with initial prorogations	Dates of sessions of Commons	Date of dismissal of Commons	Remarks
1659, 7 May		7 May to 13 Oct. 1659		Rump Parliament. Reconvened by the Declaration of the Officers of the Army on 6 May 1659 inviting the members of the Long Parliament who continued sitting until 20 Apr. 1653 'to return to the Exercise and Discharge of their Trust' (about 100 members were eligible to sit) This assembly was prevented by the army from sitting after 13 Oct. 1659, but became re-established on 26 Dec. 1659
		26 Dec. 1659 to 16 Mar. 1660	16 Mar. 1660	On 21 Feb. 1660 the surviving members secluded at Pride's Purge re-entered the House. Dissolved by its own Act 16 Mar. 1660
1660, 25 Apr.	16 Mar.	25 Apr. to 13 Sept. 6 Nov. to 29 Dec.	29 Dec. 1660	Convention
1661, 8 May	18 Feb.	1st, 8 May 1661 to 19 May 1662 2nd, 18 Feb. 1663 to 27 July 1663 3rd, 16 Mar. 1664 to 17 May 1664 4th, 24 Nov. 1664 to 2 Mar. 1665 5th, 9 Oct. to 31 Oct. 1665 6th, 18 Sept. 1666 to 8 Feb. 1667 7th, 10 Oct. 1667 to 9 May 1668 8th, 19 Oct. 1669 to 11 Dec. 1669 9th, 14 Feb. 1670 to 22 Apr. 1671 10th, 4 Feb. 1673 to 29 Mar. 11th, 27 Oct. 1673 to 4 Nov. 1673 12th, 7 Jan. 1674 to 24 Feb. 13th, 13 Apr. 1675 to 9 June 1675 14th, 13 Oct. 1675 to 22 Nov. 1675 15th, 15 Feb. 1677 to 15 July 1678	24 Jan. 1679	The Long or Pensionary Parliament. 5th session held at Oxford (9–31 Oct. 1665), other sessions at Westminster

1679, 6 Mar.	25 Jan. 1679	16th, 21 Oct. 1678 to 30 Dec. 1678 / 1st, 6 Mar. to 13 Mar. 1679 / 2nd, 15 Mar. to 27 May 1679	12 July 1679	
1680, 21 Oct.	summ. 24 July 1670 for 17 Oct. 1679; prorogued 7 times to 21 Oct. 1680	21 Oct. 1680 to 10 Jan. 1681	18 Jan. 1681	
1681, 21 Mar.	20 Jan.	21–28 Mar. 1681	28 Mar. 1681	Held at Oxford
1685, 19 May	14 Feb.	1st, 19 May to 2 July 1685 / 2nd, 9 Nov. to 20 Nov. 1685	2 July 1687	
1689, 22 Jan.	29 Dec. 1688	1st, 22 Jan. to 20 Aug. 1689 / 2nd, 19 Oct. to 27 Jan. 1690	6 Feb. 1690	Convention. This assembly declared itself a Parliament on 20 Feb. 1689. The declaration received the Royal Assent on 23 Feb. 1689
1690, 20 Mar.	6 Feb.	1st, 20 Mar. to 23 May 1690 / 2nd, 2 Oct. to 5 Jan. 1691 / 3rd, 22 Oct. to 24 Feb. 1692 / 4th, 4 Nov. to 14 Mar. 1693 / 5th, 7 Nov. to 25 Apr. 1694 / 6th, 12 Nov. to 3 May 1695	11 Oct. 1695	
1695, 22 Nov.	12 Oct.	1st, 22 Nov. to 27 Apr. 1696 / 2nd, 20 Oct. to 16 Apr. 1697 / 3rd, 3 Dec. to 5 July 1698	7 July 1698	
1698, 24 Aug.	summ. 13 July; prorogued 24 Aug. and three more times to 4 May 1699	1st, 6 Dec. to 4 May 1699 / 2nd, 16 Nov. to 11 Apr. 1700	19 Dec. 1700	
1701, 6 Feb.	26 Dec. 1700	6 Feb. to 24 June 1701	11 Nov. 1701	
1701, 30 Dec.	3 Nov.	30 Dec. to 23 May 1702	2 July 1702	
1702, 20 Aug.	summ. 2 July; prorogued 6 Aug. and once more to 20 Oct.	1st, 20 Oct. to 27 Feb. 1703 / 2nd, 9 Nov. to 3 Apr. 1704 / 3rd, 24 Oct. to 14 Mar. 1705	5 Apr. 1705	
1705, 14 June	summ. 2 May; prorogued 31 May and once more to 25 Oct.	1st, 25 Oct. to 21 May 1706 / 2nd, 3 Dec. to 24 Apr. 1707 / 3rd, 23 Oct. to 1 Apr. 1708	3 Apr. 1708	By proclamation dated 29 Apr. 1707 declared to be the first Parliament of Great Britain
1708, 8 July	summ. 26 Apr.; prorogued 8 July and twice more to 16 Nov. 1708	1st, 16 Nov. 1708 to 21 Apr. 1709 / 2nd, 15 Nov. to 5 Apr. 1710	21 Sept. 1710	
1710, 25 Nov.	27 Sept.	1st, 25 Nov. to 12 June 1711 / 2nd, 7 Dec. to 8 July 1712 / 3rd, 9 Apr. 1713 to 16 July	8 Aug. 1713	

Date of assembly	Date of summons with initial prorogations	Dates of sessions of Commons	Date of dismissal of Commons	Remarks
1713, 12 Nov.	summ. on 18 Aug.; prorogued 12 Nov. and twice more to 16 Feb. 1714	1st, 16 Feb. 1714 to 9 July 1714 2nd, 1 Aug. to 25 Aug. 1714	15 Jan. 1715	
1715, 17 Mar.	17 Jan.	1st, 17 Mar. 1715 to 26 June 1716 2nd, 20 Feb. to 15 July 1717 3rd, 21 Nov. to 21 Mar. 1718 4th, 11 Nov. to 18 Apr. 1719 5th, 23 Nov. to 11 June 1720 6th, 8 Dec. to 29 July 1721 7th, 31 July to 7 Aug. 1721 8th, 19 Oct. to 7 Mar. 1722	10 Mar. 1722	
1722, 10 May	summ. 14 Mar.; prorogued 10 May and three more times to 9 Oct. 1722	1st, 9 Oct. 1722 to 27 May 1723 2nd, 9 Jan. 1724 to 24 Apr. 1724 3rd, 12 Nov. 1724 to 31 May 1725 4th, 20 Jan. 1726 to 24 May 1726 5th, 17 Jan. 1727 to 15 May 1727 6th, 27 June 1727 to 17 July 1727	5 Aug. 1727	
1727, 28 Nov.	summ. 10 Aug.; prorogued 28 Nov. to 11 Jan.	1st, 23 Jan. 1728 to 28 May 2nd, 21 Jan. 1729 to 14 May 3rd, 13 Jan. 1730 to 15 May 4th, 21 Jan. 1731 to 7 May 5th, 13 Jan. 1732 to 1 June 6th, 16 Jan. 1733 to 13 June 7th, 17 Jan. 1734 to 16 Apr.	17 Apr. 1734	
1734, 13 June	summ. 18 Apr.; prorogued 13 June and four more times to 14 Jan. 1735	1st, 14 Jan. 1735 to 15 May 2nd, 15 Jan. 1736 to 20 May 3rd, 1 Feb. 1737 to 21 June 4th, 24 Jan. 1738 to 20 May 5th, 1 Feb. 1739 to 14 June 6th, 15 Nov. 1739 to 29 Apr. 1740 7th, 18 Nov. 1740 to 25 Apr. 1741	27 Apr. 1741	
1741, 25 June	summ. 28 Apr., prorogued 25 June and twice more to 1 Dec. 1741	1st, 1 Dec. 1741 to 15 July 1742 2nd, 16 Nov. 1742 to 21 Apr. 1743 3rd, 1 Dec. 1743 to 12 May 1744	18 June 1747	

		Sessions	
1747, 13 Aug.	summ. 22 June; prorogued 13 Aug. and once more to 10 Nov. 1747	4th, 27 Nov. 1744 to 2 May 1745 5th, 17 Oct. 1745 to 12 Aug. 1746 6th, 18 Nov. 1746 to 17 June 1747 1st, 10 Nov. 1747 to 13 May 1748 2nd, 29 Nov. 1748 to 13 June 1749 3rd, 16 Nov. 1749 to 12 Apr. 1750 4th, 17 Jan. 1751 to 25 June 1751 5th, 14 Nov. 1751 to 26 Mar. 1752 6th, 11 Jan. 1753 to 7 June 1753 7th, 15 Nov. 1753 to 6 Apr. 1754	8 Apr. 1754
1754, 31 May	9 Apr.	1st, 31 May 1754 to 5 June 1754 2nd, 14 Nov. 1754 to 25 Apr. 1755 3rd, 13 Nov. 1755 to 27 May 1756 4th, 2 Dec. 1756 to 4 July 1757 5th, 1 Dec. 1757 to 20 June 1758 6th, 23 Nov. 1758 to 2 June 1759 7th, 13 Nov. 1759 to 22 May 1760 8th, 26 Oct. 1760 to 29 Oct. 1760 9th, 18 Nov. 1760 to 19 Mar. 1761	20 Mar. 1761
1761, 19 May	summ. 21 Mar., prorogued 19 May and twice more to 3 Nov. 1761	1st, 3 Nov. 1761 to 2 June 1762 2nd, 25 Nov. 1762 to 19 Apr. 1763 3rd, 15 Nov. 1763 to 19 Apr. 1764 4th, 10 Jan. 1765 to 25 May 1765 5th, 17 Dec. 1765 to 6 June 1766 6th, 11 Nov. 1766 to 2 July 1767 7th, 24 Nov. 1767 to 10 Mar. 1768	11 Mar. 1768
1768, 10 May	12 Mar.	1st, 10 May 1768 to 21 June 1768 2nd, 8 Nov. 1768 to 9 May 1769 3rd, 9 Jan. 1770 to 19 May 1770 4th, 13 Nov. 1770 to 8 May 1771 5th, 21 Jan. 1772 to 9 June 1772 6th, 26 Nov. 1772 to 1 July 1773 7th, 13 Jan. 1774 to 22 June 1774	30 Sept. 1774
1774, 29 Nov.	1 Oct.	1st, 29 Nov. 1774 to 26 May 1775 2nd, 26 Oct. 1775 to 23 May 1776 3rd, 31 Oct. 1776 to 6 June 1777 4th, 20 Nov. 1777 to 3 June 1778 5th, 26 Nov. 1778 to 3 July 1779 6th, 25 Nov. 1779 to 8 July 1780	1 Sept. 1780

Date of assembly	Date of summons with initial prorogations	Dates of sessions of Commons	Date of dismissal of Commons	Remarks
1780, 31 Oct.	2 Sept.	1st, 31 Oct. 1780 to 18 July 1781 2nd, 27 Nov. 1781 to 11 July 1782 3rd, 5 Dec. 1782 to 16 July 1783 4th, 11 Nov. 1783 to 24 Mar. 1784	25 Mar. 1784	
1784, 18 May	26 Mar.	1st, 18 May 1784 to 20 Aug. 1784 2nd, 25 Jan. 1785 to 2 Aug.; adjourned to 27 Oct. when prorogued 3rd, 24 Jan. 1786 to 11 July 4th, 23 Jan. 1787 to 30 May 5th, 15 Nov. 1787 to 11 July 1788 6th, 20 Nov. 1788 to 11 Aug. 1789 7th, 21 Jan. 1790 to 10 June	11 June 1790	

1790, 10 Aug.	summ. 12 June; prorogued
	  10 Aug. and once more to
	  25 Nov. 1790
		1st, 25 Nov. 1790 to 10 June 1791
		2nd, 31 Jan. 1792 to 15 June 1792
		3rd, 13 Dec. 1792 to 21 June 1793
		4th, 21 Jan. 1794 to 11 July
		5th, 30 Dec. 1794 to 27 June 1795
		6th, 29 Oct. 1795 to 19 May 1796
			20 May 1796	

1796, 12 July	summ. 21 May; prorogued
	  12 July and once more to
	  27 Sept. 1796
		1st, 27 Sept. 1796 to 20 July 1797
		2nd, 2 Nov. 1797 to 29 June 1798
		3rd, 20 Nov. 1798 to 12 July 1799
		4th, 24 Sept. 1799 to 29 July 1800
		5th, 11 Nov. to 31 Dec. 1800
		6th, 22 Jan. 1801 to 2 July 1801
		7th, 29 Oct. 1801 to 28 June 1802
			29 June 1802	By proclamation dated 5 Nov. 1800 the Members of Parliament then sitting on the part of England were declared to be Members of the Parliament of the United Kingdom of Great Britain and Ireland to meet on 22 Jan. 1801 (the 6th session of the Parliament of 1796) Henceforth the dates of summons here listed are for Great Britain only; the dates for Ireland were usually a few days later

1802, 31 Aug.	summ. 30 June; prorogued
	  31 Aug. and once more to
	  16 Nov. 1802
		1st, 16 Nov. 1802 to 12 Aug. 1803
		2nd, 22 Nov. 1803 to 31 July 1804
		3rd, 15 Jan. 1805 to 12 July 1805
		4th, 21 Jan. 1806 to 23 July 1806
			24 Oct. 1806	

580

1806, 13 Dec.	24 Oct.	15 Dec. 1806 to 27 Apr. 1807	29 Apr. 1807	Owing to the king's illness it was impossible to prorogue the 5th session of this parliament from the 1st to 15 Nov. 1810, so it met and adjourned itself
1807, 22 June	30 Apr.	1st, 22 June 1807 to 14 Aug. 1807	29 Sept. 1812	
		2nd, 21 Jan. 1808 to 4 July 1808		
		3rd, 19 Jan. 1809 to 21 June 1809		
		4th, 23 Jan. 1810 to 21 June 1810		
		5th, 1 Nov. 1810 to 24 July 1811		
		6th, 7 Jan. 1812 to 30 July 1812		
1812, 24 Nov.	30 Sept.	1st, 24 Nov. 1812 to 22 July 1813	10 June 1818	
		2nd, 4 Nov. 1813 to 30 July 1814		
		3rd, 8 Nov. 1814 to 12 July 1815		
		4th, 1 Feb. 1816 to 2 July 1816		
		5th, 28 Jan. 1817 to 12 July 1817		
		6th, 27 Jan. 1818 to 10 June 1818		
1818, 4 Aug.	summ. 11 June; prorogued 4 Aug. and twice more to 14 Jan. 1819	1st, 14 Jan. 1819 to 13 July	29 Feb. 1820	
		2nd, 23 Nov. 1819 to 28 Feb. 1820		
1820, 21 Apr.	1 Mar.	1st, 21 Apr. 1820 to 23 Nov. 1820	2 June 1826	
		2nd, 23 Jan. 1821 to 11 July 1821		
		3rd, 5 Feb. 1822 to 6 Aug.		
		4th, 4 Feb. 1823 to 19 July 1823		
		5th, 3 Feb. 1824 to 25 June 1824		
		6th, 3 Feb. 1825 to 6 July 1825		
		7th, 2 Feb. 1826 to 31 May 1826		
1826, 25 July	summ. 3 June; prorogued 25 July and twice more to 14 Nov. 1826	1st, 14 Nov. 1826 to 2 July 1827	24 July 1830	
		2nd, 29 Jan. 1828 to 28 July, 1828		
		3rd, 5 Feb. 1829 to 24 June 1829		
		4th, 4 Feb. 1830 to 23 July 1830		
1830, 14 Sept.	summ. 24 July; prorogued 14 Sept. to 26 Oct.	26 Oct. 1830 to 22 Apr. 1831	23 Apr. 1831	
1831, 14 June	23 Apr.	1st, 14 June 1831 to 22 Nov. 1831	3 Dec. 1832	
		2nd, 6 Dec. 1831 to 16 Aug. 1832		

PROVINCIAL AND NATIONAL COUNCILS OF THE CHURCH IN ENGLAND, *c.* 600 TO 1536

ANGLO-SAXON CHURCH COUNCILS

THE list of Anglo-Saxon church councils presented in the second edition of this *Handbook* was based largely on the information assembled by A. W. Haddan and W. Stubbs in *Councils and Ecclesiastical Documents relating to Great Britain and Ireland* III (Oxford, 1871), covering the period up to the accession of King Alfred the Great in 871. The same work naturally underlies the revised (and augmented) list which follows, but rather than perpetuate the earlier practice in the *Handbook* of giving references to 'Haddan and Stubbs', it seemed preferable to cite the actual source or sources on which our knowledge of the council in question depends.

It should be emphasized that the evidence relating to church councils in the Anglo-Saxon period is of decidedly uneven quality. It sometimes amounts to no more than a literary account of a meeting in a source such as Bede's *Ecclesiastical History* or Stephanus's *Life of St Wilfrid*, or to a passing reference in a set of annals, such as the *Anglo-Saxon Chronicle* or the material underlying the *Historia Regum*. In other cases, we are dependent on documents which emanate from a council, and if there is not some doubt about the authenticity of the received text there may well be uncertainty about its status as an authoritative and impartial record of proceedings; several councils are known from more than one document apiece (notably those held at *Clofesho* in 803, 824 and 825), affording a fairly detailed impression of the range of business conducted on these occasions, but others are known from only a single text (which might be a document recording the settlement of a dispute of some ecclesiastical import, or which might be a charter recording a transaction of purely secular interest). A few councils, however, are known from formal accounts of their deliberations and decisions on matters concerning the organization of the church: these are the Council of Hertford (672 or 673), the Council of Hatfield (679), the Council of *Clofesho* (747), a Northumbrian council (786), the Council of *Clofesho* (803), and the Council of Chelsea (816). Needless to say, there must have been many councils of which no record has been preserved, and many councils of which the surviving accounts afford a very incomplete record of the business conducted; it is also to be expected that research in progress may reveal evidence of councils not included in the list, and that it may sharpen our judgement of the evidence already known.

The nature of the councils listed below is as varied as the evidence on which our knowledge of them depends. It has to be admitted, for example, that rather few of them could be characterized as gatherings of bishops and other clergy (whether general or provincial) convened exclusively for the discussion of matters pertaining to the church. The problem arises from the fact that a majority of the gatherings here described as 'church councils' exhibit a degree of royal or lay participation which might properly exclude them from consideration as such. The problem is, however, unavoidable. The ecclesiastics themselves stood to gain some advantage from the presence of the powers of state at their deliberations, while the kings, for their part, seem to have found it convenient (particularly in the late eighth and early ninth centuries) to treat church councils held within their territory as useful forums for the settlement of disputes and for the conduct of their own affairs. Many of the councils, therefore, were attended by kings and other laymen, and dealt with matters of secular as well as ecclesiastical concern, or with disputes involving both church and state; but one could hardly exclude them from the list simply for that reason. By the same token, it is difficult to maintain a clear distinction between a council held under the auspices of the church (and attended by the king) and a council convened by the king (and attended by the bishops), so the list also includes some 'royal' councils at which a full (or nearly full) complement of the bishops of the southern province are known to have been present. The act of reducing the information to a simple list inevitably involves lending an impression of uniformity and even formality to the councils as a group, so it has to be stressed that this impression is liable to be misleading. Again, research in progress should refine our understanding of the distinctions in nature between the different councils of the seventh, eighth and ninth centuries, but for the time being one should err, perhaps, on the side of aiming to cover all the options.

There are, however, certain obvious common denominators between at least some of the councils: the meeting-places to which they regularly returned. *Clofesho* was designated the site of what were intended to be annual councils of the church, by a decision of the Council of Hertford in 672 or 673. One can only imagine that meetings were held there on a regular basis in the later seventh and early eighth centuries, and indeed thereafter; but the first reliably attested gathering at *Clofesho* is that which took place in 747, and the evidence otherwise suggests that the site enjoyed its heyday during the period from *c.* 790 to *c.* 825. Unfortunately, *Clofesho* remains unidentified; it was probably in Mercia, and possibly somewhere in the eastern midlands. A second place regularly used for 'church' councils, at least in the years between 785 and 816, was Chelsea in Middlesex (then, of course, a place quite separate from London), and a third was *Aclea* (also unidentified, but probably somewhere in the south east). Of these three places, *Clofesho* was undoubtedly an ecclesiastical meeting-place, and any gathering held there has a *prima facie* claim to inclusion in a list of church councils; a similar claim could be entertained on behalf of Chelsea and *Aclea*, and accordingly all recorded meetings at these places are included in the list.

The significance of these councils extends far beyond the domain of ecclesiastical history. The accounts of the settlements of disputes, which were apparently drawn up at or in the wake of these meetings, are of the utmost importance for our understanding of legal procedure in Anglo-Saxon England, even if they normally represent partisan versions of the particular case at issue. It is also of interest that gatherings of all the bishops of the southern province, held in the late eighth and early ninth centuries, were attended by the Mercian king, for this could be interpreted as evidence that the authority of the king was recognized throughout the area south of the Humber, including Wessex; and this would, of course, be of considerable political importance. The presence of the Mercian king at such meetings certainly reflects his interest in the activities of ecclesiastics, and allowed him to exert an influence on proceedings; but perhaps the political significance of his presence should not be pressed too far. The Mercian king was present because the meeting was being held in his territory, and the bishops were present because the meeting was conceived as a council of the church; so what the councils show is the remarkable cohesion of the church in a period of political turmoil and change.

There do not appear to have been any gatherings which might be regarded as church councils in the second half of the ninth century. This could be explained in terms of political developments, for it coincides with the eclipse of Mercia as the dominant power and (perhaps more relevantly) the assumption by the West Saxon kings of control of the former kingdom of Kent; but it is not clear why the archbishops of Canterbury should have been less inclined to convene general councils of the southern province under West Saxon authority than they had been under Mercian authority. Alternatively, the phenomenon might be understood as the result of a change in practice at the councils themselves, whereby they were no longer exploited as forums for the settlement of disputes or for the ratification of the king's grants of land, and so they no longer generated the kind of document from which so many earlier councils are known. The simplest explanation would be to attribute the phenomenon to disruption caused by the Viking invasions; but while this external factor must have had some such effect on the organization of the Anglo-Saxon church, the principal cause was, perhaps, an internal development much remarked on by contemporaries, namely negligence and carelessness on the part of the churchmen themselves.

The councils of the seventh, eighth and ninth centuries were until recently a neglected aspect of the early Anglo-Saxon church. Reference should now be made, however, to: N. Brooks, *The Early History of the Church of Canterbury: Christ Church from 597 to 1066* (Leicester, 1984), H. Vollrath, *Die Synoden Englands bis 1066* (Paderborn, 1985); and see also C. R. E. Coutts, 'Synodal Councils of the Early Anglo-Saxon Church', Ph.D. thesis, University of Cambridge (in preparation). The list given below was compiled before the appearance of the studies by Vollrath and Coutts, and will doubtless require further revision in the light of their research.

So far as one can judge, meetings of church officials alone, convened exclusively for the discussion of ecclesiastical affairs, seem to have occurred rather infrequently in the tenth and eleventh centuries (up to 1066); but that is not to say, of course, that the Anglo-Saxon bishops did not assemble as a body from time to time. For during this later period such gatherings took place within the context of the meetings of the king and his councillors, convened for general purposes of government perhaps three or four times a year. In some cases, the actual meeting-place is identified (see S. D. Keynes, *The Diplomas of King Æthelred 'the Unready' 978–1016*

(Cambridge, 1980), pp. 269–73); but it is noticeable that whereas the 'church councils' of the earlier period had returned time and again to one or other of a relatively small group of sites (specifically *Clofesho*, *Aclea* and Chelsea), the later meetings tend to occur on a variety of royal estates and other important secular centres, reflecting their nature as fundamentally royal councils. There can be no doubt that matters of general ecclesiastical concern were dealt with on some of these occasions, but it would be impossible to select particular meetings from the whole series in an attempt to produce a list of later councils to complement that for the earlier period. For the tenth and eleventh centuries, therefore, it is best to refer generally to the material assembled in *Councils & Synods with other Documents relating to the English Church, I, A.D. 871–1204, pt 1: 871–1066*, ed. D. Whitelock, M. Brett and C. N. L. Brooke (Oxford, 1981), and to Professor Whitelock's discussion, *ibid.*, pp. vi–vii; see also F. Barlow, *The English Church 1000–1066*, 2nd ed. (London, 1979), esp. pp. 137–8, 237–8, 245–6, and 273. There is some evidence here for meetings which could be characterized as church councils (most notably the Council of Winchester in the early 970s, at which the *Regularis Concordia* was drawn up), but even to fasten on these meetings would be to misrepresent the more complex situation overall.

ABBREVIATIONS USED IN THE PROVISIONAL LIST

ASC . . . *Anglo-Saxon Chronicle*

BCS . . . W. de G. Birch, *Cartularium Saxonicum*, 3 vols (London, 1885–93)

Dümmler . . *Epistolae Karolini Aevi, II*, ed. E. Dümmler, MGH Epist. 4 (Berlin, 1895)

Ehwald . . *Aldhelmi Opera*, ed. R. Ehwald, MGH Auct. Ant. 15 (Berlin, 1919)

HA . . . . Bede's *Historia Abbatum*, in *Venerabilis Baedae Opera Historica*, ed. C. Plummer, 2 vols (Oxford, 1896), I, pp. 364–404

HE . . . . *Bede's Ecclesiastical History of the English People*, ed. B. Colgrave and R. A. B. Mynors (Oxford, 1969)

HR . . . . *Historia Regum*, in *Symeonis Monachi Opera Omnia* II, ed. T. Arnold (London, 1885)

H&S . . . A. W. Haddan and W. Stubbs, *Councils and Ecclesiastical Documents relating to Great Britain and Ireland* III (Oxford, 1871)

S . . . . P. H. Sawyer, *Anglo-Saxon Charters: an Annotated List and Bibliography* (London, 1968)

Tangl . . . *Die Briefe des heiligen Bonifatius und Lullus*, ed. M. Tangl (Berlin, 1916)

VSBoniface . Willibald's *Life of St Boniface*, in *Vitae Sancti Bonifatii Archiepiscopi Moguntini*, ed. W. Levison (Hanover, 1905)

VSCuthbert . Anonymous *Life of St Cuthbert*, in B. Colgrave, *Two Lives of Saint Cuthbert* (Cambridge, 1940)

VSEcgwine . Byrhtferth's *Life of St Ecgwine*, in *Byrhtferth: The Lives of Oswald and Ecgwine*, ed. M. Lapidge (Oxford, forthcoming)

VSWilfrid . . Stephanus's *Life of St Wilfrid*, in B. Colgrave, *The Life of Bishop Wilfrid by Eddius Stephanus* (Cambridge, 1927)

PROVISIONAL LIST OF CHURCH COUNCILS, *c.* 600–*c.* 850

(An asterisk against an entry signifies that the evidence for the meeting is of uncertain or dubious authority.)

602 or 603	Meeting between Augustine, archbishop of Canterbury, and the British bishops, at '**Augustine's Oak**'; second meeting held sometime thereafter [HE ii.2]
c. 605	Council of **London** [letter of Boniface to Pope Zacharias (Tangl no. 50); see also letter of Pope Zacharias to Boniface (Tangl no. 80)]
664, bef. July	Council of **Whitby** (Northumbrian) [VSWilfrid, ch. 10; HE iii.25]
672 or 673, 24 Sept.	Council of **Hertford** [acts of the council, in HE iv.5; ch. 7 records decision to hold yearly councils on 1 August, at *Clofesho*]
678	Council of — ? — [VSWilfrid, ch. 30; see also ch. 24]
679, 17 Sept.	Council of **Hatfield** [extracts from acts of the council, in HE iv.17–18]
680	Council of — ? — (Northumbrian) [VSWilfrid, ch. 34]
c. 680	Council of — ? — (Northumbrian) [HA, ch. 15; see also ch. 6, and HE iv.18]
684, beg. of winter	Council of **Adtuifyrdi** [VSCuthbert, bk IV, ch. 1; HE iv.28; see also S 66]
*685, July	Council of **Burford** [S 1169 (charter of King Berhtwald)]
c. 701	Council of — ? — (Northumbrian) [HA, ch. 15]
c. 703	Council of **Ouestraefelda** [VSWilfrid, chs 46–7; see also chs 53 and 60]
675 × 705	Council of — ? — [letter of Aldhelm to Geraint (Ehwald, pp. 480–6)]
704 × 705	Council of — ? — [letter of Wealdhere, bishop of London, to Brihtwold, archbishop of Canterbury (BCS 115)]
*705	Council on the **river Nadder, Wilts**. [BCS 114 (charter of Aldhelm, bishop of Sherborne)]
c. 705	Council of — ? — [HE v.18]
706	Council on the **river Nidd** (Northumbrian) [VSWilfrid, ch. 60]
*709	Council of **Alne** [VSEcgwine, III.4]
c. 675 × 709	Council of — ? — [Aldhelm, *De uirginitate*, ch. 1 (Ehwald, p. 229)]
*696 × 716	Council of **Bapchild** [S 22 (charter of King Wihtred)]
710 × 716	Council of — ? — (West Saxon) [VSBoniface, ch. 4]
*716, July	Council of **Clofesho** [S 22 (confirmation of a charter of King Wihtred)]
736 × 737	Council of — ? — [S 1429 (decree of a council held by Nothhelm, archbishop of Canterbury)]
*742	Council of **Clofesho** [S 90 (charter of King Æthelbald)]
747, Sept.	Council of **Clofesho** [acts of the council, ptd H&S, pp. 360–76, from Spelman (and ultimately from London, BL Cotton Otho A.i)]
749	Council of **Gumley** [S 92 (charter of King Æthelbald)]
c. 754	Council of — ? — [letter of Cuthbert, archbishop of Canterbury, to Lul (Tangl, no. 111)]
761–764	councils [see S 1258 for reference to councils of Bregowine, archbishop of Canterbury]
765, Nov.	? Council of **Pincanheale** (Northumbrian) [HR, s.a. 765]
765 × 774	Council of — ? — (Northumbrian) [Anskar's *Life of St Willehad*, ch. 1, in H&S, p. 433]
781	Council of **Brentford** [S 1257 (record of settlement of a dispute between King Offa and Heathored, bishop of Worcester)]
782	Council of **Aclea** [ASC (northern recension) s.a. 782]
785	Council of **Chelsea** [S 123 (charter of King Offa)]
*786	Council of **Chelsea** [S 125 (charter of King Offa)]

786	Council of — ? — (Northumbrian) [acts of the council incorporated in report of legates to Pope Hadrian, ptd Dümmler, pp. 19–29]
786	Council of — ? — [council held in southern England, mentioned in report of legates to Pope Hadrian, ptd Dümmler, pp. 19–29; see also letter of Pope Leo III to King Cenwulf (Dümmler, pp. 187–9)]
*787	Council of **Aclea** [S 127 (charter of King Offa)]
787	Council of **Chelsea** [ASC s.a. 787]
787, Sept.	Council of **Pincanheale** (Northumbrian) [HR, s.a. 787; ASC (northern recension), s.a. 788]
788	Council of **Aclea** [ASC (northern recension) s.a. 789; Richard of Hexham supplies date 29 Sept.]
788	Council of **Chelsea** [S 128 (charter of King Offa)]
789	Council of **Chelsea** [S 1430 (record of settlement of a dispute involving Heathored, bishop of Worcester); S 130 and 131 (charters of King Offa) may refer to this council]
792	Council of **Clofesho** [S 134 (charter of King Offa)]
765–792	councils [see S 1258 for references to councils of Jænberht, archbishop of Canterbury]
*793	Council of **Chelsea** [S 136 (charter of King Offa)]
794	Council of **Clofesho** [S 137 (charter of King Offa); S 139 (charter of King Offa) may refer to this council]
*? 795	Council of **London** [S 132 (charter of King Offa)]
*796	Council of **Chelsea** [S 150, 151 (charters of King Ecgfrith)]
*798	Council of **Bapchild** [BCS 290; ASC MS. F, s.a. 798]
798	Council of **Clofesho** [S 1258 (record of settlement of a dispute between Æthelheard, archbishop of Canterbury, and Cynethryth, abbess); S 153 (charter of King Cenwulf) and S 1187 (private charter) may refer to this council]
798	Council of **Pincanheale** (Northumbrian) [HR, s.a. 798]
799	Council of **Tamworth** [S 155 (charter of King Cenwulf)]
799	Council of **Chelsea** [see S 1435]
801	Council of **Chelsea** [S 158 (charter of King Cenwulf); S 106 (charter of King Offa, endorsement) may refer to this council]
*? 802	Council of **Coleshill** [S 154 (charter of King Cenwulf)]
803, Oct.	Council of **Clofesho** [S 1260 (charter of Deneberht, bishop of Worcester); BCS 310 (document abolishing archbishopric of Lichfield); S 1431 (record of agreement between Deneberht, bishop of Worcester, and Wulfheard, bishop of Hereford); BCS 312 (document in name of Æthelheard, archbishop of Canterbury)]
804	Council of **Aclea** [S 1187 (private charter)]
805	Council of — ? — [S 1259 (charter of Æthelheard, archbishop of Canterbury)]
805, July	Council of **Aclea** [S 40 (charter of King Cuthred) and S 161 (charter of King Cenwulf); S 41 (charter of King Cuthred) may refer to this council]
810	Council of **Aclea** [see S 1439 (record of a Kentish dispute); see also S 1188 (private charter)]
*? 811	Council of **Chelsea** [S 166 (charter of King Cenwulf)]
811, Aug.	Council of **London** [S 168 (charter of King Cenwulf); S 165 (charter of King Cenwulf) may refer to this council]
*811, Nov.	Council of — ? — [S 167 (charter of King Cenwulf)]
814	Council of — ? — [S 173 (charter of King Cenwulf)]
816, July	Council of **Chelsea** [acts of the council, ptd H&S, pp. 579–84 (from London, BL Cotton Vespasian A. xiv); S 180 (charter of King Cenwulf) may refer to this council]
*? 824	Council of **Aclea** [S 283 (charter of King Egbert)]
824, Oct.	Council of **Clofesho** [ASC s.a. 824; S 1433 (record of settlement of a dispute between Heahberht, bishop of

	Worcester, and the community at Berkeley, Gloucs.); S 1434 (record of a recovery of land by Wulfred, archbishop of Canterbury, from Cwenthryth, abbess of Minster in Thanet)]
825	Council of **Clofesho** [see S 1436 (record of a dispute between Wulfred, archbishop of Canterbury, and Cenwulf, king of Mercia, and of its settlement); S 1437 (record of settlement of a dispute concerning swine-pasture at Sinton in Leigh, Worcs.); S 1435 (record of settlement of a dispute concerning land at Denton, Sussex)]
836	Council of **Croft** [S 190 (charter of King Wiglaf)]
838	Council of **Kingston** [S 1438 (record of agreement between Ceolnoth, archbishop of Canterbury, and Kings Egbert and Æthelwulf); see also S 281 (charter of King Egbert)]
839	Council **aet Astran** [S 1438, MSS. 1 and 3 (confirmation of the agreement reached at Kingston in 838); see also S 281]
845, Nov.	Council of **London** [S 1194 (private charter)]

CHURCH COUNCILS 1066–1536

With the Norman Conquest it becomes less difficult to define and list meetings of ecclesiastical councils. The following list of councils to 1313 has been drawn up from the two volumes of *Councils and Synods* covering the period. From 1314 onwards, however, the list is an unrevised reprint of that which appeared in the second edition of this *Handbook*. This is largely based on authorities cited in Wilkins, *Concilia*, to which references are given; where Wilkins is inaccurate or insufficient, references are to bishops' registers and other sources.

Church councils after 1066 may usually be classified as 'English', or 'Canterbury', or 'York'. When councils were held by legatine authority, the fact has been noted in the final column of the list. In cases in which the ecclesiastical character of the assembly is uncertain, doubt is indicated by an *asterisk* in the final column. Some councils are only attested by possibly spurious documents, while others are inferred doubtfully from records open to a variety of interpretations; all these councils are marked ? in the final column. Councils of which only the summons are known appear in the list within *parentheses*. In some of these cases, the certainty that a second council was summoned immediately afterwards offers a strong presumption against the meeting of the first; but a search of the unprinted bishops' registers and other sources would doubtless prove the session of some councils recorded here only by the writs of summons.

It has not generally been possible to give the date of every session of a council, when it was continued or prorogued; the extreme dates for which we have a record of sessions are given thus: 8 *Feb.*–7 *Mar.* In some cases, when a council was prorogued beyond the end of a year, sessions in subsequent years are marked with the letter P in the final column. Doubtful dates and places of meeting are marked ? in the appropriate column. Dates given thus: 8 *Feb.* × 7 *Mar.* signify the period within which a council of uncertain date is known to have been held.

The year 1536 has been chosen as the final date of this list, not because it marks the end of formal meetings of the clergy, but because it marks a turning-point in their constitutional history, after which their freedom to assemble, to deliberate, and to legislate is far more narrowly restricted than before. This change was effected by the parliamentary 'Act for the submission of the Clergie to the Kynges Majestie' of 25 Henry VIII, c. 19 (1534), consequent upon the remarkable resolution of the convocation of Canterbury on 15 May 1532. With that statement of royal authority the Church lost the partial independence which it had possessed before this time: never before had the king claimed the exclusive right to summon assemblies of the clergy, although he had often summoned them, nor had royal ratification of ecclesiastical canons been deemed necessary.[1]

Lists of meetings of the convocations after the year 1536 will be found in the works of Wake (to 1678) and Wilkins and Joyce (to 1717). For the later period, readers are referred to the sources named by Makower (*Constit. Hist.*, 352 n.), and to subsequent issues of *The Chronicle of Convocation . . . of Canterbury* (London, S.P.C.K.) and of *The York Journal of Convocation* (York, W. H. Smith; London, Simpkin, Marshall).

Abbreviations used in the following List

C. & S. . . .	*Councils and Synods, with other Documents relating to the English Church.* I, *A.D. 871–1204*, ed. D. Whitelocke, C. N. L. Brooke and M. Brett (Oxford, 1981); II, *A.D. 1205–1313*, ed. F. M. Powicke and C. R. Cheney (Oxford, 1964)
CCR . . .	*Calendar of Close Rolls* for the year cited
CFR . . .	*Calendar of Fine Rolls* for the year cited
HMCR . .	*Historical Manuscripts Commission Reports*
RDP . . .	*Report on the Dignity of a Peer*
RNC . . .	*The Records of the Northern Convocation* (Surtees Society, vol. cxiii)
RS	*Rolls Series* (*Chronicles & Memorials of Great Britain & Ireland*)
W.	*Concilia Magnae Britanniae et Hiberniae*, ed. D. Wilkins, 4 vols (1737)
Wake . . .	Wm Wake, *The State of the Church* (1703)
Weske, *Convocation* .	D. B. Weske, *Convocation of the Clergy* (1937)

Date of Meeting	Place of Meeting	Reference	Nature of Assembly
1070, 7 or 11 Apr.	Winchester	*C. & S.*, i. 563–76	English legatine
1070, 24 May	Windsor	*C. & S.*, i. 577–81	English legatine
1072, c. 8 Apr.	Winchester	*C. & S.*, i. 591–607	*English legatine
1074, 25 Dec. × 1075, 28 Aug.	London	*C. & S.*, i. 607–16	English
1076, 1 Apr.	Winchester	*C. & S.*, i. 616–20	English primatial
1077, 29 Aug. × 1078, 28 Aug.	London	*C. & S.*, i. 624–5	*English
1080, Christmas	Gloucester	*C. & S.*, i. 629–32	English

[1] Cf. Felix Makower, *Constitutional History and Constitution of the Church of England* (London, 1895), 51 *sqq.*, 365 *sqq.*; and Sir Lewis Dibdin, in the *Report* of the Archbishops' Committee on Church and State (London, 1917), 281 *sqq.*

Date of Meeting	Place of Meeting	Reference	Nature of Assembly
1085, Christmas	Gloucester	*C. & S.*, i. 632–4	English
1100, 23 Sept. × 11 Nov.	Lambeth	*C. & S.*, i. 661–7	*English
1102, *c.* 29 Sept.	Westminster	*C. & S.*, i. 668–88	English
1107, 1–*c.* 4 Aug.	London	*C. & S.*, i. 689–94	English
1108, *c.* 28 May	London	*C. & S.*, i. 694–704	English primatial
1114, 26 Apr.	Windsor	*C. & S.*, i. 707–8	*Canterbury
1125, 8 Sept.	Westminster	*C. & S.*, i. 733–41	English legatine
1127, 13–16 May	Westminster	*C. & S.*, i. 743–9	English legatine
1129, 30 Sept.–4 Oct.	London	*C. & S.*, i. 750–4	English legatine
1132, 24 Apr.	London	*C. & S.*, i. 757–61	English
1138, Dec.	Westminster	*C. & S.*, i. 768–79	English legatine
1139, 29 Aug.–1 Sept.	Winchester	*C. & S.*, i. 781–7	English legatine[1]
1141, 7–10 Apr.	Winchester	*C. & S.*, i. 788–92	English legatine
1141, 7 Dec.	Westminster	*C. & S.*, i. 792–4	English legatine
1143, *c.* 14 Mar.	London	*C. & S.*, i. 794–804	English legatine
1143, *c.* Sept.	Winchester	*C. & S.*, i. 804–10	English legatine
1143, *c.* 18 × 30 Nov.	London	*C. & S.*, i. 804–10	English legatine
1151, *c.* 18 Mar.	London	*C. & S.*, i. 821–6	English legatine
1152, 7 Dec.	London	*C. & S.*, i. 826–8	Canterbury?
1156	London	*C. & S.*, i. 829–35	*English
1160, June–July	London	*C. & S.*, i. 835–41	English
1161, Jan. × 18 Apr.	Canterbury	*C. & S.*, i. 841–2	English
1162, May	Westminster	*C. & S.*, i. 843–5	*Canterbury
1166, *c.* Jan.	Oxford	*C. & S.*, i. 920–6	*English
1173, late Apr. and June	London	*C. & S.*, i. 956–65	Canterbury
1175, May	Westminster	*C. & S.*, i. 965–93	Canterbury
1176, Jan. × Feb.	Northampton	*C. & S.*, i. 996–8	*English and Scottish
1176, 14–19 Mar.	Westminster	*C. & S.*, i. 998–1000	English legatine
1190, 15 Oct.	Westminster	*C. & S.*, i. 1029–31	Canterbury legatine
1193, 29–30 May	London	*C. & S.*, i. 1037–41	Canterbury
1195, 14–15 June	York, St Peter's	*C. & S.*, i. 1042–52	York legatine
1197, 7 Dec.	Oxford	*C. & S.*, i. 1052–3	English or Canterbury?
1199, May	Westminster	*C. & S.*, i. 1053–5	English or Canterbury?

[1] This council and the next three were apparently summoned by the legate and composed of ecclesiastics, but were concerned with political business.

Date of Meeting	Place of Meeting	Reference	Nature of Assembly
1200, 19–?23 Sept.	Westminster	C. & S., i. 1055–74	Canterbury
1206, 18 × 20 Oct.	Reading	C. & S., ii. 4–5	English legatine
1213, 25 Aug.	London, St Paul's or Westminster	C. & S., ii. 19–20	English or Canterbury
1214, Jan	Dunstable	C. & S., ii. 21–3	Canterbury
1214, 1–2 July	London, St Paul's	C. & S., ii. 36–8	English legatine
1216, 29 May	Winchester	C. & S., ii. 50	English legatine
1218, 24 July × 10 Sept	Winchester	C. & S., ii. 51	*English legatine
1222, 17 Apr.	Oxford, Osney abbey	C. & S., ii. 100–25	Canterbury
1226, 7 Jan and 3 May	London, St Paul's	C. & S., ii. 155–8	English
1226, 13 Oct.	London	C. & S., ii. 158–64	English
1229, 29 Apr.	Westminster	C. & S., ii. 167–9	*English
1237, Nov.	London, St Paul's	C. & S., ii. 238–59	English legatine
1238, 17 May	London	C. & S., ii. 260–1	English legatine
1239, 6 Mar	London	C. & S., ii. 278–9	English legatine
1239, 31 July	London	C. & S., ii. 279–84	English legatine
1240, May–Nov.	Reading, London, London	C. & S., ii. 285–93	English legatine
1241, 30 Nov.	Oxford	C. & S., ii. 338–40	English
1242, May	London	C. & S., ii. 340–2	Canterbury?
1250, aft. 20 Apr.	Oxford	C. & S., ii. 445–7	Canterbury
1251, 12 Mar.	Reading	C. & S., ii. 448–9	English or Canterbury?
1252, May–Sept.	Blyth	C. & S., ii. 450	York
1253, 13 Jan.	London	C. & S., ii. 467–72	Canterbury
1255, 13 Oct.	London	C. & S., ii. 501–3	English
1255, Dec.	London	C. & S., ii. 503	English?
1256, 18 Jan.	London, New Temple	C. & S., ii. 504–9	English
1256, 30 Apr.	London	C. & S., ii. 509–10	English?
1257, Mar.–May	London	C. & S., ii. 524–30	English
1257, 22 Aug.	London	C. & S., ii. 530–48	Canterbury
1258, June	? Merton and Westminster	C. & S., ii. 568–85	English
1259, 16 July	Lambeth	C. & S., ii. 659–60	English
1261, 8–13 May	Lambeth	C. & S., ii. 660–92	Canterbury
1261, 23 (?) May	Beverley	C. & S., ii. 692	York
1263, June	Westminster	C. & S., ii. 692–3	English
1264, Aug and Oct.	London, St Paul's, Westminster, Reading	C. & S., ii. 694–700	English
1265, 1 Dec.	London or Westminster	C. & S., ii. 725–8	English legatine
1267, 9 × 22 Feb.	Bury St Edmunds	C. & S., ii. 732–5	English legatine
1267, 25 June	London	C. & S., ii. 735–8	English legatine
1268, Apr.	London, St Paul's	C. & S., ii. 738–92	English legatine
1269, 14 Oct.	London, New Temple	C. & S., ii. 797–800	English
1271, 16 Mar.	Reading	C. & S., ii. 801–2	Canterbury
1272, 18 Oct.	London	C. & S., ii. 802	English?
1273, 13 × 19 Jan.	Westminster	C. & S., ii. 804–7	Canterbury
1273, 11 Oct.	London, New Temple	C. & S., ii. 807–9	Canterbury
1275, Mar.	?London	C. & S., ii. 816–17	English?

Date of Meeting	Place of Meeting	Reference	Nature of Assembly
1276, Nov. and 1277, Feb.	uncertain	*C. & S.*, ii. 820–2	Canterbury
1277 ? *c.* 3 May	Northampton	*C. & S.*, ii. 822–3	Canterbury
1278, 14 Jan.	London	*C. & S.*, ii. 824–6	Canterbury
1278, July–Oct.?	London	*C. & S.*, ii. 827–8	Canterbury
1279, 29 July–1 Aug.?	Reading	*C. & S.*, ii. 828–57	Canterbury
1279, late Oct.	London	*C. & S.*, ii. 858–64	Canterbury
1280, 20 Jan.	London	*C. & S.*, ii. 865–8	Canterbury
1280, 9 Feb.	Pontefract	*C. & S.*, ii. 868–70	York
1280, 12 May	London	*C. & S.*, ii. 870–1	Canterbury
1280, *c.* 6 Oct.	Lincoln	*C. & S.*, ii. 871	Canterbury
1281, 6 × 18 May	London	*C. & S.*, ii. 886	Canterbury?
1281, 7–10 Oct.	Lambeth	*C. & S.*, ii. 886–918	Canterbury
1282, 5 Feb.	London, New Temple	*C. & S.*, ii. 918–20	Canterbury
1282, 19–25 Apr.	London	*C. & S.*, ii. 921–39	Canterbury
1283, 20 Jan.	Northampton	*C. & S.*, ii. 939–44	Canterbury
1283, 20 Jan.?	York	*C. & S.*, ii. 944–5	York
1283, 9 May	London	*C. & S.*, ii. 945–51	Canterbury
1283, 20 Oct.	London, New Temple	*C. & S.*, ii. 951–4	Canterbury
1285, aft. 25 Mar.	London	*C. & S.*, ii. 955	Canterbury
1285, *c.* 1 Nov.	London	*C. & S.*, ii. 972–3	Canterbury
1286, mid-Feb.	London	*C. & S.*, ii. 973–4	Canterbury?
1286, 13 Oct.	London, New Temple	*C. & S.*, ii. 975–8	Canterbury
1286, 13 Nov.	York	*C. & S.*, ii. 978–82	York
1287, 2 May	London, New Temple	*C. & S.*, ii. 1077–8	Canterbury?
1287, 13 Oct.	London, New Temple	*C. & S.*, ii. 1080	Canterbury?
1288, 4–7 May	Lambeth, Westminster and Northfleet	*C. & S.*, ii. 1080	Canterbury
1288, 14 Oct.	London, New Temple	*C. & S.*, ii. 1081	Canterbury?
1290, Jan.	London	*C. & S.*, ii. 1090	English or Canterbury
1290, Oct.	Ely	*C. & S.*, ii. 1091–3	Canterbury
1290, 7 Dec.	York, St Peter's	*C. & S.*, ii. 1093–6	York
1292, 13–16 Feb.	London, New Temple and Lambeth	*C. & S.*, ii. 1097–1113	Canterbury
1292, bef. 3 Mar.	uncertain	*C. & S.*, ii. 1113–15	York
1294, 21–24 Sept.	Westminster	*C. & S.*, ii. 1125–34	English
1295, 15 July	London, New Temple	*C. & S.*, ii. 1134–47	Canterbury
1297, 13–?20 Jan.	London, St Paul's	*C. & S.*, ii. 1150–62	English
1297, 24–?30 Mar.	London, St Paul's	*C. & S.*, ii. 1162–8	Canterbury
1297, 10–13 Aug.	London, New Temple	*C. & S.*, ii. 1168–77	Canterbury
1297, 20 Nov.	London, New Temple	*C. & S.*, ii. 1177–85	Canterbury
1297, 29 Nov.	York, St Peter's	*C. & S.*, ii. 1185–6	York
1298, 25–28 June	London, New Temple	*C. & S.*, ii. 1187–99	Canterbury
1299, 4 Nov.	London, New Temple	*C. & S.*, ii. 1199–1204	Canterbury

Date of Meeting	Place of Meeting	Reference	Nature of Assembly
1300, 13 June	Canterbury, Ch. Ch.	*C. & S.*, ii. 1204–5	Canterbury
1302, 1–8? June	London, New Temple	*C. & S.*, ii. 1218–22	Canterbury
1302, 10 Dec.	London, St Paul's	*C. & S.*, ii. 1222–6	Canterbury
1305, Feb.	Lambeth	*C. & S.*, ii. 1227–9	Canterbury?
1309, 24 Nov. –17 Dec.	London, St Paul's	*C. & S.*, ii. 1240–77	Canterbury
1310, 20–21 May	York	*C. & S.*, ii. 1277–84	York
1310, 23 Sept. –14 Nov.	London, St Paul's	*C. & S.*, ii. 1285–90	Canterbury P
1310, 9 Dec.	London, St Paul's	*C. & S.*, ii. 1290–8	Canterbury
1311, 23 Apr. –14 Sept.	London, St Paul's	*C. & S.*, ii. 1298–1318	Canterbury P
1311, 24 May –30 July	York, St Peter's	*C. & S.*, ii. 1319–48	York
1312, 18 Apr. –14 May	London, St Paul's	*C. & S.*, ii. 1356–76	Canterbury
1312, 28 Sept., 9 Oct.	London	*C. & S.*, ii. 1377	English or Canterbury, legatine
1313, 27 Mar. –May?	London, St Paul's	*C. & S.*, ii. 1378–81	Canterbury
1314, 17–22 May	Westminster	W. ii. 442–45	Canterbury
1314, 3–26 June	York, St Peter's	*Reg. Palat. Dunelm.* (RS), i. 574, 577, *Reg. Greenfield, York*, ii 190, and Durham Priory Reg. Mag. ii. fo. 27v.	York
(1314, 8 July	London, St Paul's	W. ii. 444, 447–48	Canterbury)
(1316, 28 Apr.	London, St Paul's	W. ii. 456	Canterbury)
(1316, ?9 May	York, St Peter's	W. ii. 462	York)
(1316, 7 June	York, St Peter's	W. ii. 462	York)
1316, 11 Oct.	London, St Paul's	W. ii. 458	Canterbury
1316, 26 Oct. (?)–23 Nov.	York	W. ii. 462	York
(1318, 23 Feb.	London, St Paul's	*HMCR, Wells*, i. 179	Canterbury)
1319, 20 Jan.	York	W. ii. 485–86	York
(1319, 3 Feb.	London	W. ii. 485	Canterbury)
1319, 19 Mar.	York	W. ii. 485–86, & *Reg. Gravesend, London*, 209	York
1319, 20 Apr.	London, St Paul's & Carmelites'	*Reg. Gravesend*, 203, 207 & *Chron. Edw. I & II*, (RS), i. 286	Canterbury
1321, 1 Dec.	London, St Paul's	W. ii. 507–09 & *Chron. Murimuth* (RS), 35	Canterbury
1322, 10 May	York	W. ii. 519	York
(1322, 9 June	London, St Paul's	W. ii. 515–16	Canterbury)
1322, 17 Dec.	York, St Peter's	Reg. Melton, York, fo. 462v	York
1323, 14 Jan.	Lincoln	W. ii. 516–19	Canterbury
1323, 26 Jan.	York, St Peter's	W. ii. 519	York
(1324, 20 Jan.	London, St Paul's	W. ii. 519	Canterbury)[1]
(1324, 7 Feb.	York	W. ii. 520	York)[1]
(1326, 13 Oct.	London, St Paul's	W. ii. 532–33	Canterbury)

[1] Summons revoked.

Date of Meeting	Place of Meeting	Reference	Nature of Assembly
(1326, 3 Nov.	London, St Paul's	W. ii. 532	Canterbury P)
1327, 16 Jan.	London, St Paul's	W. ii. 534, & *Chron.*	Canterbury P
		Edward I & II, i. 324	
1327, 12 Oct.	York?	W. ii. 546–47	York
1327, 4 Nov.	Leicester abbey	W. ii. 538–39, & *Chron.*	Canterbury
		Edward I & II, i. 338	
1329, 27 Jan. –10 Feb.	London, St Paul's	W. ii. 548, 552, & *Chron. Edward I & II*, i. 344–45	Canterbury
1330, 11 Mar.	Winchester	W. ii. 557	Canterbury
1330, 16 Apr.	Lambeth	W. ii. 558–59, & Bodleian MS. Kent rolls 6 ii. & *Chron. Edward I & II*, i. 348	Canterbury
(1330, 25 Apr.	?York	*CCR*, 130	York)
(1331, 14 Apr.	York	W. ii. 559	York)
1332, 4 Sept.	London, St Paul's	W. ii., 561 & *Chron. Edward I & II*, i. 357	Canterbury
(1333, 22 Nov.	London	W. ii. 562–63	Canterbury)
(1333, 29 Nov.	York	W. ii. 570	York[1]
(1334, 10 Jan.	Northampton	W. ii. 562–3, & *RDP*, iv. 422	Canterbury)
(1334, 17 Jan.	York	W. ii. 570	York)
(1334, 28 July	York	*RDV*, iv. 426–27	York)
1334, 19 & 26 Sept.	London, St Paul's	W. ii. 575–76, & *Chron. Edward I & II*, i. 362	Canterbury
1334, 19 Oct.	York	W. ii. 578	York
1336, 11 Mar.	London, St Paul's	W. ii. 581, & *CFR*, 16	Canterbury
1336, 6 May	York	W. ii. 583–84	York
1336, 30 Sept.	Leicester	W. ii. 582, & *CFR*, 16	Canterbury
1336, 21 Oct.	York, St Peter's	*CCR* (1337–39), 81	York
1337, 30 Sept. –1 Oct.	London, St Paul's, & St Bride's	*Reg. Salop., Wells*, i. 336–37, & *CFR*, 57, 79, 98	Canterbury
1337, 12 Nov.	York	*CCR*, 242, & Wake, 287	York
1338, 1 Oct.	London, St. Paul's	*Reg. Salop., Wells*, i. 325, & *RDP*, iv. 495–96, & *Chron. Murimuth*, 85	Canterbury
(1338, 1 Oct.	York, St Peter's	*Reg. Palat. Dunelm.*, iii. 220–22, & *RDP*, iv. 496	York
1339, aft. 8 Feb.	York, St Peter's	W. ii. 653	York
(1339, aft. 10 Oct.	York, St Peter's	*RDP*, iv. 506	York (?diocesan))
1340, 27 Jan. –17 Feb.	London, St Paul's & Friars preachers'	W. ii. 653, & *CFR*, 174	Canterbury
1340, 9 Feb.	York, St Peter's	*RDP*, iv. 510, & *CFR*, 173	York
1340, 11 Dec.	York	W. ii. 673	York
1341, 19 Oct.	London, St Paul's	W. ii. 680, & *Chron. Murimuth*, 122, 223	Canterbury
1342, 9 Oct.	London, St Paul's	W. ii. 696 n., & *Reg. Salop., Wells*, ii. 452	Canterbury

[1] Summons revoked.

Date of Meeting	Place of Meeting	Reference	Nature of Assembly
1342, 14–21 Oct.	London, St Paul's	W. ii. 710	Canterbury
(1342, 2 Dec.	Pontefract	W. ii. 711	York)
1342, 11 Dec.	York, St Peter's	W. ii. 712, & *Reg. Palat. Dunelm.* (RS), iii. 509	York
1344, 31 May	London, St Paul's	*Reg. Trillek, Hereford,* 6, 254	Canterbury
1344, 25 (?) June	York, St Peter's	W. ii. 727, & *CFR*, 384	York
1346, 4 May	London, St Paul's	*Reg. Trillek*, 15 271, 277	Canterbury
1346, 16 Oct.	London, St Paul's	W. ii. 728, & *CFR*, 79	Canterbury
(1346, 18 Dec.	York, St Peter's	W. ii. 735	York)
(1347, 29 Jan.	York, St Peter's	W. ii. 735	York)
(1347, 1 Oct.	London, St Paul's	W. ii. 735	Canterbury)
1348, 13 June	York	W. ii. 746 and Reg. Zouche, York, fo. 247v.	York
(1351, 2 May	London, St Paul's	W. ii. 16–17, 18	Canterbury)
1351, 18 May	York, St Peter's	W. iii. 17, & *RNC*, 86	York
(1355, 16 Nov.	London, St Paul's	W. iii. 33	Canterbury)
(1355, 7 Dec.	York, St Peter's	W. iii. 36	York)
1356, 16–24 May	London, St Paul's	W. iii. 38	Canterbury
1356, 3 June	York	W. iii. 39	York
1357, 26 Apr.	London, St Bride's	W. iii. 39, 41	Canterbury
1357, 19 May	York	W. iii. 41	York
1360, 3–9 Feb.	London, St Paul's	W. iii. 44–45, & *Reg. L. de Charltone, Hereford*, 38	Canterbury
1360, 12 Feb.	York, St Peter's	*RNC*, 90–4, 100	York
(1361, 7 May	Southwark, St Mary Overy	W. iii. 47–48	Canterbury)[1]
(1361, 31 May	Southwark, St Mary Overy	*Reg. Grandisson, Exeter,* iii, 1222–25	Canterbury)
(1361, 7 Oct.	London, St Paul's	*Reg. Grandisson,* iii. 1228	Canterbury)
(1361, 15 Dec.	York	York Chapter Acts, iv. fo. 40v	York)
1362 or 1363, 2 Dec.	London	W. iii. 59, & Wake, 300	Canterbury?
1370, 21 Jan. –1 Feb.	London, St Paul's	W. iii. 82–84	Canterbury
(1370, 4 Feb.	York, St Peter's	W. iii. 85	York)
1371, 24 Apr. –3 May	London, St Paul's & the Savoy	W. iii. 91	Canterbury
(1371, 8 May	York, St Peter's	Reg. Appleby, Carlisle, fo. 227	York)
(1371, 10 July	York?	W. iii. 91	York
(1373, 30 May	London, St Paul's	W. iii. 93	Canterbury)
(1373, 11 June	York	York Chapter Acts, iv. fo. 107	York)
(1373, 6 Oct.	London, St Paul's	W. iii. 94	Canterbury)
1373, 1–7 Dec.	London, St Paul's	W. iii. 96 and Reg. Whittlesey, fos. 64–65	Canterbury

[1] This summons, for bps only, was possibly cancelled by a summons issued on the same day for bps and clergy to meet on the 31 May.

Date of Meeting	Place of Meeting	Reference	Nature of Assembly
(1374, 6 Feb.	York, St Peter's	W. iii. 96	York)
(1374, 17 Aug.	York, St Peter's	York Chapter Acts, iv, fo. 117	York)
1376, 2 or 9 June–23 23 June	London, St Paul's	W. iii. 104, & *Reg. Wykeham, Winchester*, ii. 252	Canterbury
(1376, 28 July	York, St Peter's	W. iii. 114	York)
1377, 3 Feb. –2 Mar.	London, St Paul's	W. iii. 104–05	Canterbury
(1377, 15 Apr.	York, St Peter's	*RDP*, iv. 672, & *RNC*, 103	York)
1377, 9 Nov.– 5 Dec.	London, St Paul's	W. iii. 122, & *CFR*, 42	Canterbury
1377, 1 Dec.– 1378, 4 Jan.	York, St Peter's	W. iii. 125	York
1378, 22 Mar.	York, St Peter's	W. iii. 125, & *CFR*, 97–98	York
1378, 16 Nov.	Gloucester	W. iii. 135	Canterbury
1379, 29 Apr.	York	W. iii. 145	York
1379, 9–25 May	London, St Paul's	W. iii. 141, & *HMCR, Wells*, i. 285	Canterbury
1380, 4–29 Feb.	London, St Paul's	W. iii. 142, & *CFR*, 190	Canterbury
1380, 4 Apr.	York, St Peter's	W. iii. 150	York
1380, 1–6 Dec.	Northampton, All Saints' church	W. iii. 150, & *CFR*, 223	Canterbury
1381, 10 Jan.	York, St Peter's	W. iii. 150 and York Chapter Acts, iv, fo. 143	York
(1382, aft. 14 Jan.	London, St Paul's?	*RDP*, iv. 694	Canterbury)
(1382, aft. 14 Jan.	York, St Peter's?	*RDP*, iv. 694	York)
1382, 18–26 Nov.	Oxford, St Frideswide's	W. iii. 172, & *CFR*, 346	Canterbury
1383, 13–21 Jan.	London, Friars preachers'	W. iii. 172, & *Reg. Brantyngham, Exeter*, i. 207	Canterbury P
1383, aft. 28 Jan.	York, St Peter's	W. iii. 176	York
(1383, *c.* 12 Nov.	York	*RDP*, iv. 707	York)
1383, 2–4 Dec.	London, St Paul's	W. iii. 179	Canterbury
1384, 21–23 Jan.	York, St Peter's	*RNC*, 113, & Weske, *Convocation*, 290	York[1]?
1384, 20–27 May	Salisbury cathedral	W. iii. 185	Canterbury
(1384, 8 July	York, St Peter's	W. iii. 193	York)
1384, 1–19 Dec.	London, St Paul's	W. iii. 185	Canterbury
1385, 11 Jan.	York, St Peter's	*RDP*, iv. 711, & Weske, *Convocation*, 290	York
(1385, 17 Apr.	York, St Peter's	*RDP*, iv. 715	York)
1385, 4 May– 2 June	London, St Paul's	W. iii. 185 & Wake, 317	Canterbury

[1] *RNC* records without reference a mandate of the abp for this date; it may be for the assembly summoned for November 1383 by royal writ.

597

Date of Meeting	Place of Meeting	Reference	Nature of Assembly
1385, 6–18 Nov.	London, St Paul's	W. iii. 193–4, & *Reg. Wykeham, Winchester*, ii. 376	Canterbury
(1386, 14 Jan.	York, St Peter's	W. iii. 195, & *RDP*, iv. 720	York)
1386, 5 Nov.–3 Dec.	London, St Paul's	W. iii. 200	Canterbury
(1386, 1 Dec.	York, St Peter's	*CCR*, 258	York)
(1388, 10 Feb.	York, St Peter's	*RDP*, iv. 727	York)
1388, 26 Feb. –23 Mar.	London, St Paul's	W. iii. 204, & *RDP*, iv. 727	Canterbury
1388, 14 Sept.	Cambridge, St Mary's	W. iii. 205	Canterbury
(1388, 14 Sept.	York?	W. iii. 205	York)
1388, 12 Oct., 20–21 Oct.	London, St Paul's	W. iii. 205, & *Reg. Wykeham*, ii. 413, 599, & *Reg. Brantyngham*, ii. 675	Canterbury P
(1389, 24 Jan.	York	Wake, 320	York)
1391, 17–21 Apr.	London, St Paul's	W. iii. 212	Canterbury
1391, 4 Dec.	York	W. iii. 218	York
1391, 9 Dec.	London, St Paul's	*CFR*, 33	Canterbury
1392, 6 Mar.	York, St Peter's	*CFR*, 43	York
1393, 17 Feb. –17 Mar.	York, St Peter's	W. iii. 219, & *CFR*, 80	York
1393, 24 Feb. –? 3 Mar.	London, St Paul's	W. iii. 219, & *CFR*, 79, & Wake, 323	Canterbury
(1394, 1 Mar.	York, St Peter's	W. iii. 220	York)
1394, 14–21 May	London, St Paul's	*RDP*, iv. 752, & *Reg. Wykeham*, ii. 454, 602	Canterbury
1394, 1 June	York, St Peter's	W. iii. 224, Durham Priory Reg. Mag. ii, fo. 315, Reg. Arundel, York, fo. 48	York
1394, 20 or 27 July	York, St Peter's	Ibid.	York
1394, 1 Oct.	York, St Peter's	Ibid.	York
1394, 3 Dec.	York, St Peter's	*CFR*, 143	York
1395, 4 Feb.–7 Mar.	York, St Peter's	W. iii. 224, & *RDP*, iv. 775, & *CFR*, 150	York
1395, 5–18 Feb.	London, St Paul's	W. iii. 223	Canterbury
1397, 19–27 Feb.	London, St Paul's	W. iii. 227, & *RDP*, iv. 758	Canterbury
(1397, 15 Mar.	York, St Peter's	*RDP*, iv. 758, & *RNC*, 119	York)
1397, 6 Apr.	London	*CCR*, 184	Canterbury
(1397, 19 June	York, St Peter's	*RDP*, iv. 758 and Reg. Waldby, York, fo. 7v.	York)
1397, 5, 10 Oct.	York, St Peter's	W. iii. 234, & *RDP*, iv. 761	York
(1397, 8 Oct.	London, St Paul's	W. iii. 234, & *RDP*, iv. 761	Canterbury)[1]
(1398, 13 Feb.	uncertain	W. iii. 234	York P)

[1] This council, summoned originally by the king's writ for 1 Oct. and by the abp's mandate for the 8th, did not sit.

Date of Meeting	Place of Meeting	Reference	Nature of Assembly
1398, 28 Feb.–2 Mar.	London, St Paul's	W. iii. 234–6, 238	Canterbury
(1398, 17 May	London	W. iii. 236	Canterbury)
(1398, 20 June	York, St Peter's	W. iii. 237–8	York)
(1398, 1 Sept.	York, St Peter's	W. iii. 237–8	York)
(1399, 27 Jan.	Oxford	W. iii. 236	Canterbury)
1399, 11 Mar.	York, St Peter's	W. iii. 238, & *CFR*, 160	York
1399, 6–16 Oct.	London, St Paul's	W. iii. 238	Canterbury
1401, 26 Jan.–11 Mar.	London, St Paul's	W. iii. 254	Canterbury
1401, 3 June–26 July	York, St Peter's	W. iii. 267, & *CFR*, 135	York
(1402, 13 Feb.	London, St Paul's	*RDP*, iv. 778	Canterbury)
(1402, 13 Feb.	uncertain	*RDP*, iv. 778	York)
(1402, 6 or 13 Apr.	York, St Peter's	W. iii. 273, & *RDP*, iv. 776	York)
(1402, 5 Sept.	York, St Peter's	W. iii. 273, & *RDP*, iv. 781	York)
1402, 21 Oct.–29 Nov.	London, St Paul's	W. iii. 270	Canterbury
(1403, 15 Jan.	York, St Peter's	W. iii. 273, & *RDP*, iv. 784	York)
1403, 6 Oct.	London, St Paul's	W. iii. 274, & *Reg. Wykeham, Winchester*, ii. 550, & *CFR*, 225	Canterbury
1404, 21 Apr.–6 May	London, St Paul's	W. iii. 279, 305, & *CFR*, 246	Canterbury
1404, 2 June	York, St Peter's	W. iii. 281, & *RDP*, iv. 790	York
1404, 24–28 Nov.	London, St Paul's	W. iii. 280, & *CFR*, 292	Canterbury
1404, 11–17 Dec., 1405, 14 Jan.	York, St Peter's	W. iii. 281	York
1406, 26 Apr., 10 May–16 June	London, St Paul's	W. iii. 284, & *CCR*, 117	Canterbury
1406, 12 July	York, St Peter's	W. iii. 303	York
1407, 28 Nov.–10 Dec.	Oxford, St Frideswide's	W. iii. 306, & *Reg. Mascall, Hereford*, 105, 107	Canterbury
(1408, bef. 25 Mar.	York, St Peter's	W. iii. 306	York)
(1408, 4 May	York	Durham Priory Reg. Mag. iii, fo. 26v.	York)
1408, 28 June–10 Dec.	York	W. iii. 319	York
1408, 23–28 July	London, St Paul's	W. iii. 306	Canterbury
1409, 14–30 Jan.	London, St Paul's	W. iii. 311, 314	Canterbury
1410, 15 Feb.–17 Mar.	Beverley	W. iii. 333, & *Reg. Bowet York*, i, 284, 297	York

Date of Meeting	Place of Meeting	Reference	Nature of Assembly
1410, 17 Feb. –10 Mar.	London, St Paul's	W. iii. 324, & *RDP*, iv. 807	Canterbury
1410, 11 Apr. –23 May	Clementhorp nunnery	*Reg. Langley, Durham*, i. 133	York P
1410, 3 Oct.	York, Holy Trinity	*Reg. Langley, Durham*, i. 130	York
1411, 17 Mar.	London, St Paul's	*Snappe's Formulary* (Oxf. Hist. Soc.), 156	Canterbury
(1411, 17 Nov.	York	W. iii. 338	York)
1411, 1–21 Dec.	London, St Paul's	W. iii. 334, & *CFR*, 243	Canterbury
1412, 18–20 Jan.	York, St Peter's	W. iii. 338	York
(1413, bef. 9 Feb.	York, St Peter's	W. iii. 351, & *RDP*, iv. 815	York)
1413, 6 Mar. –? 6 June	London, St Paul's, & Lambeth	W. iii. 338, 351, & *CFR*, 31	Canterbury
1413, 27–28 July	York, St Peter's	W. iii. 358	York
1413, 20 Nov.	London, St Paul's	*Reg. Stafford, Exeter*, 67, Reg. Repyngdon Linc., fo. 98v. & *Chron. Adae de Usk*, 122	Canterbury
1414, 1–20 Oct.	London, St Paul's	W. iii. 358, & *CFR*, 90	Canterbury
1414, 5 Nov.	York, St Peter's	W. iii. 370	York
1415, 9–11 Jan.	York, St Peter's	W. iii. 371, & *CFR*, 98	York
1415, 18 Nov. –2 Dec.	London, St Paul's	W. iii. 375, & *CFR*, 158	Canterbury
1415, 16 Dec. –1416, 16 Jan.	York, St Peter's	W. iii. 377	York
1416, 1 Apr.– 6 June	London, St Paul's	W. iii. 377, & Church- ill, ii. 169	Canterbury
1416, 30 Apr.	York	W. iii. 380	York
1416, 9–23 Nov.	London, St Paul's	W. iii. 377, & *CFR*, 185, 211	Canterbury
1417, 5–12 Jan.	York, St Peter's	W. iii. 380	York
1417, 26 Nov. –20 Dec.	London, St Paul's	W. iii. 381, & *CFR*, 218	Canterbury
1418, 20–26 Jan.	York	W. iii. 389	York
1419, 30 Oct. –21 Nov.	London, St Paul's	W. iii. 393, & *CFR*, 309	Canterbury
1420, 13–18 Jan.	York, St Peter's	W. iii. 396	York
1421 5–27 May	London, St Paul's	W. iii. 399	Canterbury
1421, 22 Sept. –1422, 14 Jan.	York, St Peter's	W. iii. 403	York
1422, 6–11 July	London, St Paul's	W. iii. 404	Canterbury
1422, 23 Sept. –20 Nov.	York, St Peter's	W. iii. 419, & *RNC*, 142–5	York
1424, 6 Oct., 1 Dec.	York, St Peter's	W. iii. 432	York
1424, 12–26 Oct.	London, St Paul's	W. iii. 428	Canterbury

Date of Meeting	Place of Meeting	Reference	Nature of Assembly
1425, 27 Jan. –17 Feb.	London, St Paul's	W. iii. 429, & *Reg. Spofford, Hereford*, 60	Canterbury P
1425, 23 Apr. –18 July	London, St Paul's	W. iii. 433	Canterbury
1426, 15–27 Apr.	London, St Paul's	W. iii. 459	Canterbury
1426, 12 Aug. –1427, 25 Feb.	York, St Peter's	W. iii. 487–91	York
1428, 5–21 July, 12 Nov.– 7 Dec.	London, St Paul's	W. iii. 493–503	Canterbury
1428, 2–7 Aug.	York, St Peter's	W. iii. 514, & *RNC*, 172	York
1429, 28 July –1430, 3 Feb.	York	*RNC*, 172	York P
1429, 19 Oct. –20 Dec.	London, St Paul's	W. iii. 514, & *CFR*, 306	Canterbury P
1430, 8 Aug.	York, St Peter's	W. iii. 518 & Durham Priory Reg. Mag. iii, fo. 135v	York
1431, 19 Feb. –21 Mar.	London, St Paul's	W. iii. 515, & *Reg. Spofford*, 128, & *CFR*, 62	Canterbury
1432, 15–24 Sept.	London, St Paul's	W. iii. 520, & *CFR*, 159	Canterbury
1432, 3 Oct.–?	York	W. iii. 521, & *CFR*, 180	York
1433, 7 Nov.– 21 Dec.	London, St Paul's	W. iii. 521, & *CFR*, 227	Canterbury
1434, 7–23 Oct.	London, St Paul's	W. iii. 523	Canterbury
1435, 12 Nov. –23 Dec.	London, St Paul's	W. iii. 525, & *CFR*, 269	Canterbury
1436, 11 June	York	W. iii. 525	York
1437, 29 Apr. –8 May	London, St Paul's	W. iii. 525, & *Reg. Stafford, Wells*, ii. 204, 213	Canterbury
1437, ? Apr.	York	W. iii. 525	York
(1438, 21 Apr.	York	W. iii. 533	York)
1438, 28 Apr. –14 May, 6–18 Oct.	London, St Paul's	W. iii. 525, & Wake 368	Canterbury
1439, 28 Feb.	London, St Paul's	*Reg. Lacy, Exeter*, ii. 765	Canterbury
1439, 21 Nov. –22 Dec.	London, St Paul's	W. iii. 533–6	Canterbury
1440, 17 Aug.	York	W. iii. 536	York
1442, 16–26 Apr.	London, St Paul's	W. iii. 536, & *CFR*, 244	Canterbury
1442, 4 Oct.	York	W. iii. 536–7 & *RDP*, 906	York
1444, 19–26 Oct.	London, St Paul's	W. iii. 539–41, & *Reg. Bekynton*, i. 14, 27	Canterbury
1445, 30 Sept.	York, St Peter's	W. iii. 544 & *RDP*, 911	York

Date of Meeting	Place of Meeting	Reference	Nature of Assembly
1446, 22 June –8 July	London, St Paul's	W. iii. 554, & *Reg. Spofford*, 280, & *Reg. Bekynton*, i. 63, 75	Canterbury
1446, Oct.	Lambeth	W. iii. 549	English?
1449, 1–28 July	London, St Paul's	W. iii. 556–7	Canterbury
1449, 14 Nov.	London, St Paul's	W. iii. 557	Canterbury
(1451, aft. 6 Mar.	uncertain	W. iii. 559	York)
1452, 12 June, 6 Oct.– 1453, 29 Jan.	York, St Peter's	W. iii. 563	York
1453, 7 Feb.– 15 Mar.	London, St Paul's	W. iii. 562	Canterbury
1460, 30 Apr. –1462, 23 Mar.	York	W. iii. 580	York
1460, 6 May– 1461, 15 July	London, St Paul's	W. iii. 577 & *Reg. Bourgchier, Cant.*, 77	Canterbury
1462, 21 July –2 Aug., 8–25 Nov.	London, St Paul's	W. iii. 580, & *Reg. Bekynton*, i. 380–1	Canterbury
1462, 1 Sept.	York	W. iii. 580	York
1463, 6–23 July	London, St Paul's	W. iii. 580, 585	Canterbury
1463, 8 Aug.	York	W. iii. 587	York
1466, 26 Apr.	York, St Peter's	W. iii. 599, Wake, 377, & Durham Priory Reg. Mag. iv, fo. 165v	York
1468, 12 May –3 June	London, St Paul's	W. iii. 606, & *Reg. Stanbury, Hereford*, 117	Canterbury
1468, 14 June	York, St Peter's	Durham Priory Reg. Mag. iv, fo. 198v	York
(1470, aft. 11 June	York, St Peter's	W. iii. 606	York)
1470, 27 July	London, St Paul's	W. iii. 606	Canterbury
1472, 23 Jan. –25 Feb.	London, St Paul's	W. iii. 607–8, & *HMCR*, IX. i. 107a	Canterbury
(1472	York, St Peter's	*RDP*, iv. 980	York)
1473, 3 Feb.– 9 Apr., 11 Oct.– 15 Dec.	London, St Paul's	W. iii. 607 & P.R.O., K.R., Mem. R. Communia M.T. 14 Ed. IV, r.16	Canterbury
(1473	York, St Peter's	W. iii. 607, & *RDP*, iv. 984	York)
1474, 24 Jan. –21 Feb.	London, St Paul's	Wake, 379	Canterbury P
1475, 6 Feb.	York, St Peter's	W. iii. 608 & Reg. G. Neville, York, fo. 2	York
1475, 9 or 10 Feb.–? 16 Mar.	London, St Paul's	W. iii. 607, & *Reg. Myllyng, Hereford*, 5, 13, 55	Canterbury
1477, 21 Oct.	York, St Peter's	W. iii. 612 & Durham Priory Reg. Mag. iv, fo. 181	York
1478, 10 Apr. –26 June	London, St Paul's	W. iii. 612, & *Reg. Myllyng*, 37, 54, 55–56	Canterbury

Date of Meeting	Place of Meeting	Reference	Nature of Assembly
1478, 27 Oct.	York, St Peter's	W. iii. 612 & Durham Priory Reg. Mag. iv, fo. 184	York
1479, 17 Feb.	York, St Peter's	W. iii. 612 & Reg. L. Booth, York, fo. 307	York
1481, 21 Mar. –7 Nov.	London, St Paul's	W. iii. 612	Canterbury
1481, 29 Oct.	York	W. iii. 614 & Reg. Rotherham, York, fo. 290	York
1482, 6 May– 12 Nov.	London, St Paul's	W. iii. 613	Canterbury P
1483, 18 Apr.	London, St Paul's	W. iii. 614	Canterbury
1484, 3–24 Feb.	London, St Paul's	W. iii. 614, Wake, 382, & Reg. Goldwell, Norwich, fo. 244	Canterbury
1485, 10 Feb. –11 Mar.	London, St Paul's	W. iii. 616, & Reg. *Myllyng*, 97	Canterbury
1487, 13 Feb. –? 6 Mar.	London, St Paul's	W. iii. 618–19	Canterbury
1487, 19 Feb.	York, St Peter's	W. iii. 621 & Durham Priory Reg. Mag. v, fo. lv	York
1489, 14 Jan. –27 Feb., 23 Oct.	London, St Paul's	W. iii. 625	Canterbury
1489, 27 Jan. –27 Feb.	York, St Peter's	W. iii. 630	York
1491, 21 June –8 Nov.	London, St Paul's	W. iii. 634 & Reg. Alcock, Ely, fo. 199	Canterbury
1492, 1 Mar.	York, St Peter's	W. iii. 635	York
1495, 19 Oct. –21 Dec.	London, St Paul's	W. iii. 644, & Wake, 387, *HMCR Wells*, ii. 142, & Reg. Blyth, Salisbury, fo. 46	Canterbury
1496, 16 May	York, St Peter's	W. iii. 644	York
1497, 23 Jan. –11 Mar.	London, St Paul's	W. iii. 645, & Wake, 387, & *HMCR Wells*, ii. 146	Canterbury
1497, 26 Apr.	York, St Peter's	W. iii. 646	York
1501, 12 May	York, St Peter's	*Reg. Fox, Durham*, 154–64	York
1502, 14 Feb. 11 Oct.	London, St Paul's	W. iii. 464, & *HMCR Wells*, ii. 166, 168	Canterbury
1502, 21 Feb. –15 Oct.	York	W. iii. 647	York
1504, 16 Feb. –18 May	London, St Paul's	W. iii. 647, & *Reg. Mayhew, Hereford*, 54, 60	Canterbury
1504, 5–14 Aug.	York, St Peter's	W. iii. 649	York
1509, 7 Feb.	York, St Peter's	W. iii. 651	York
1510, 26 Jan. –15 Feb.	London, St Paul's	W. iii. 651, & *Reg. Mayhew*, 94, 106, & *H. of Lords Journals*, i. 5–7	Canterbury
1512, 6 Feb.– 17 Dec.	London, St Paul's	W. iii. 652, & *Reg. Mayhew*, 148, 168, & *Ep. Reg. St David's*, ii. 789	Canterbury
1512, 26 Apr. –1513, 4 Feb.	York, St Peter's	W. iii. 657, York Chapter Acts, viii, fo. 52	York

Date of Meeting	Place of Meeting	Reference	Nature of Assembly
1514, 22 June –1 July, 6 Nov.–20 or 23 Dec.	London, St Paul's	W. iii. 658, & *Reg. Booth, Hereford*, 26, & *Ep. Reg. St David's*, ii. 817, & *Letters & Papers, Henry VIII* (1862), i. 5209	Canterbury
1515, 22–25 Jan.	York, St Peter's	W. iii. 658 & Durham Priory Reg. Mag., v, fo. 156v	York
1515, 9 Feb.– 26 Mar.	London, St Paul's	*H. of Lords Journals*, i. 21, 23, 29, 32, 38	Canterbury ? P
1515, 13 Nov. –20 Dec.	London, St Paul's	W. iii. 658, & Wake, 390, & *Reg. Mayhew*, 213–17	Canterbury P
1516, 9 Apr.	York, St Peter's	W. iii. 659 & Durham Priory Reg. Mag. v, fo. 168	York
(1518	Lambeth	W. iii. 660	Canterbury)
c. 1518	uncertain	W. iii. 662	York
1519, 14 Mar.	Westminster	W. iii. 661, & *Reg. Booth*, 65	English legatine?
(1519, 9 Sept.	Westminster	W. iii. 66	English legatine)[1]
1520, 26 Feb.	Westminster	W. iii. 661, & *Reg. Booth*, 74	English legatine
1523, 22 Mar.	York	W. iii. 698	York
1523, 20 Apr. –14 Aug.	London, St Paul's	W. iii. 699–700, & A. F. Pollard, *Wolsey*, 189–90	Canterbury
1523, 22 Apr. –18 Aug.	Westminster	W. iii. 698	York P
(1523, 22 Apr., 2 June, 8 June	Westminster	W. iii. 700, & *Letters and Papers, Henry VIII*, III. ii. no. 3013, & Pollard, *Wolsey*, 189–91	English legatine)
1529, 5 Nov. –24 Dec.	London, St Paul's	W. iii. 717, & Wake, 473, & *Letters and Papers, Henry VIII*, IV. iii., no. 6047	Canterbury
(1529, 7 Nov.	York, St Peter's	Wake, 473, & Pollard, *Wolsey*, 292	York)[1]
1530, 29 Apr.–?	London, St Paul's	W. iii. 724–6	Canterbury P
1531, 12 Jan. –4 May	York, St Peter's	W. iii. 744	York
1531, 21 Jan. –16 Oct.	Westminster	W. iii. 726, 746	Canterbury P
1532, 16 Jan. –15 May	Westminster	W. iii. 746–9, & Wake, 475	Canterbury P
1532, 7 Feb.– ?	York, St Peter's	W. iii. 748, 767	York
(1532, 5 Nov.	Westminster	W. iii. 749	Canterbury P)[2]
1533, 5–11 Feb.	Westminster	W. iii. 749	Canterbury P
1533, 17 Mar. –7 June, 4 Nov.	London, St Paul's	W. iii. 749, 756	Canterbury P
1533, 13 May	York, St Peter's	W. iii. 767	York P

[1] This council did not meet.
[2] This session did not take place, owing to the death of Warham in Aug.

Date of Meeting	Place of Meeting	Reference	Nature of Assembly
1534, 16 Jan. –19 Dec.	London, St Paul's	W. iii. 757, 769–70, 776, & *H. of Lords Journals*, i. 59	Canterbury P
1534, 5 May– 1535, 3 Feb.	York, St Peter's	W. iii. 782–83, & Wake, App. 221	York
(1535, 4 Feb.	York, St Peter's	W. iii. 783, & *Letters and Papers, Henry VIII* (1885), nos. 2, 32, 104	York P)[1]
(1535, 4 Nov.	London, St Paul's	W. iii. 770, 802	Canterbury P)
1536, 5 Feb.– 24 Apr.	uncertain	W. iii. 802–3	Canterbury P

[1] Before this session, the convocation was postponed indefinitely (Wake, 489, App. 221).